ISBN 978-0-260-27966-8
PIBN 11010060

FB &c Ltd, Dalton House, 60 Windsor Avenue, London, SW19 2RR.
Company number 08720141. Registered in England and Wales.

For support please visit www.forgottenbooks.com

THE NEW
ANNUAL ARMY LIST

FOR

1849.

(BEING THE TENTH ANNUAL VOLUME,)

CONTAINING

THE DATES OF COMMISSIONS, AND A STATEMENT OF THE WAR SERVICES AND WOUNDS OF NEARLY EVERY OFFICER IN THE ARMY, ORDNANCE, AND MARINES.

CORRECTED TO 28TH DECEMBER, 1848.

WITH AN INDEX.

BY

MAJOR H. G. HART, 49TH REGT.

LONDON:
JOHN MURRAY, ALBEMARLE STREET.
1849.

EXPLANATIONS.

K. . night of the Order of the Garter.

K.T. Knight of the Order of the Thistle.

K.P. Knight of the Order of St. Patrick.

G.C.B. Knight *Grand Cross* of the Order of the Bath.

K.C.B. Knight *Commander* of the Order of the Bath.

C.B. *Companion* of the Order of the Bath.

G.C.M.G. Knight *Grand Cross* of the Order of St. Michael and St. George.

K.C.M.G. Knight *Commander* of ditto ditto

C.M.G. *Companion* of ditto ditto

G.C.H. Knight *Grand Cross* of the Royal Hanoverian Guelphic Order.

K.C.H. Knight *Commander* of ditto ditto

K.H. Knight of ditto ditto

K.C. Knight of the Crescent.

Before the Name, denotes that the Officer was at the Battle of *Trafalgar*.

Before the Name, denotes that the Officer served in the *Peninsula*, or the *South of France*.

Waterloo Medal. { Officers actually present in either of the actions of the 16th, 17th, or 18th June, 1815. Such Officers are allowed two years' additional service.

N. B. In the List of General and Field Officers, the Names printed in Italic are those of Officers retired from the Army, who have been specially allowed to retain their Rank, but without receiving Pay or progressive Promotion.

The Figures prefixed to the Names denote the Battalions to which the Officers are *actually attached;* the Letters *s.* and *r. after* the name distinguish Officers employed on the *Staff*, or on the *Recruiting Service;* the letter *r.* before the name denotes that the Officer belongs to the Reserve Battalion. The Letters *R. M.* in the Cavalry Regiments, allude to the Riding Masters; the Letters *d. pm.* and *d. adj.* denote the Depôt Paymaster and Depôt Adjutant respectively.—The * *before* the Name or Date of Commission, denotes Temporary Rank only. The Letter P *before* the Date indicates that the Commission was *purchased*.

The words subscribed to the titles of Regiments, as "Peninsula," "Waterloo," &c. denote the Honorary Distinctions permitted to be borne by such Regiments on their Colours and appointments, in commemoration of their Services.

*** *All communications to be addressed to* Major HART, 60, Albemarle Street, London.

LONDON: PRINTED BY STEWART AND MURRAY, OLD BAILEY.

CONTENTS.

OFFICERS RECEIVING REWARDS FOR DISTINGUISHED SERVICES.

General John M'Kenzie
——— Pinson Bonham
——— William Eden
——— *Sir* Alexander Halkett, *KCH*
Lieut.-Gen. Samuel Huskisson
——— Henry Monckton
——— Dennis Herbert
——— Heiter Tonsel.
Major-Gen. Edward Darley.
——— James Hay, *CB.*
——— William Wood, *CB. KH.*
——— George Burrell, *CB.*
——— Henry James Riddell, *KH.*
——— *Sir* Dudley St. Leger Hill, *KCB.*
——— Alexander Thomson, *CB.*
——— John Duffy, *CB.*
——— Jacob Tonson, *CB.*
——— Wm. Alex. Gordon, *CB.*
——— James Fergusson, *CB.*
——— Thomas William Brotherton, *CB.*
——— *Sir* James Henry Reynett, *KCH.*
——— William Smelt, *CB.*
——— John Bell, *C.B.*
——— Samuel Benjamin Auchmuty, *CB.*
——— Thomas Lighfoot, *CB.*
——— Alured Dodsworth Faunce, *CB.*
——— Roger Parke.
——— R. B. Macpherson, *CB., KH.*
——— James Allan, *CB.*
——— John Fred. Ewart, *CB.*
——— Thomas Hunter Blair, *CB.*
——— Richard Lluellyn, *CB.*
——— Richard Egerton, *CB.*
——— *Sir* William Chalmers, *CB., KCH.*
——— William Campbell, *CB.*
——— *Sir* De Lacy Evans, *KCB.*
——— *Sir* Thomas Willshire, *Bt. KCB.*

Major-Gen. Edward Fleming, *CB.*
——— *Sir* John Rolt, *KCB.*
——— William Henry Sewell, *CB.*
——— John M'Donald, *CB.*
——— George William Paty, *CB. KH.*
——— Thomas James Wemyss, *CB.*
——— Henry Thomas, *CB.*
——— William Rowan, *CB.*
——— James Shaw Kennedy, *CB.*
——— *Sir* Thomas Henry Browne, *KCH.*
——— R. B. Fearon, *CB.*
——— Henry Balneavis, *CMG. KH.*
——— George Leigh Goldie, *CB.*
——— Thomas Bunbury, *KH.*
——— Henry Godwin, *CB.*
——— Roderick Macneil.
——— William Sutherland.
Quarter-Master James Murray, h. p. 94 F.
——— T. W. Edwards, h. p. 84 F..

ROYAL ARTILLERY.

Lieut.-Gen. *Sir* C. W. Thornton, *KCH.*
Major-Gen. J. W. Smith, *CB.*
——— *Sir* Hew D. Ross, *KCB.*
——— *Sir* R. Gardiner, *KCB., KCH.*
——— J. Boteler Parker, *CB.*
Colonel Robert Douglas, *CB.*
Lieut.-Col. *Sir* J. Hartmann, *KCB., KCH.*
Lieut. J. G. Barslem.
Surgeon N. Fitzpatrick.
Quartermaster S. Barnes.

ROYAL ENGINEERS.

Lieut.-Gen. *Sir* S. R. Chapman, *CB., KCH.*
Major-Gen. *Sir* John F. Burgoyne, *KCB.*

ROYAL MARINES.

Major-Gen. W. Tremenheere, *KH.*
Colonel John M'Callum.
——— Charles Menzies, *KH.*

THE

NEW ANNUAL ARMY LIST.

1849.

FIELD-MARSHALS.

P W *His Grace* ARTHUR, *Duke of* WELLINGTON, KG. GCB. GCH., *Ensign*, 7 March, 1787; *Lieut.* 25 Dec. 87; *Captain*, 30 June, 91; *Major*, 30 April, 93; *Lieut.-Colonel*, 30 Sept. 93; *Colonel*, 3 May, 96; *Major-General*, 29 April, 02; *Lieut.-General*, 25 April, 08; *General* (in Spain and Portugal), 31 July, 11; *Field Marshal*, 21 June, 13. Colonel of the Grenadier Regiment of Foot Guards, 22 Jan. 1827; Colonel-in-Chief of the Rifle Brigade, 19 Feb. 1820; Constable of the Tower of London, 29 Dec. 1826; Lord Warden of the Cinque Ports, 27 Dec. 1828; Commander-in-Chief, 15 Aug. 1842.

His Majesty the KING *of* HANOVER, KG. KP. GCB., *Lieut.-General*, 18 May, 1798; *General*, 25 Sept. 1803; *Field Marshal*, 26 Nov. 1813.

His Royal Highness ADOLPHUS FREDERICK, *Duke of* CAMBRIDGE, KG. GCB. GCMG. GCH., *Lieut.-General*, 24 Aug. 1798; *General*, 25 Sept. 1803; *Field Marshal*, 26 Nov. 1813. Colonel of the Coldstream Regiment of Foot Guards, 5 Sept. 1805; and Colonel-in-Chief of the 60th (or the King's Royal Rifle Corps), 22 Jan. 1827.

His Majesty the KING *of the* BELGIANS, KG. GCB. GCH., *General*, 2 May, 1816; *Field Marshal*, 24 May, 1816.

His Royal Highness FRANCIS ALBERT AUGUSTUS CHARLES EMANUEL, *Duke of* SAXONY, *Prince of* SAXE COBURG AND GOTHA, KG. KT. KP. GCB. GCMG., 8 Feb. 1840. Colonel of the Scots Fusilier Guards, 25 April, 1842; Governor and Constable of Windsor Castle, 18 May, 1843.

P W *His Majesty the* KING *of the* NETHERLANDS,[1] GCB., *Lieutenant-Colonel*, 11 June, 11; *Colonel*, 17 Oct. 11; *Major-General*, 13 Dec. 13; *Lieutenant-General*, 8 July, 14; *General*, 25 July, 14; *Field Marshal*, 28 July, 45.

Sir GEORGE NUGENT, *Bart.*, GCB., *Ensign*, 5 July 1773; *Lieut.* 23 Nov. 75; *Captain*, 28 April 78; *Major*, 3 May 82; *Lieut.-Colonel*, 8 Sept. 83; *Colonel*, 1 Mar. 94; *Major-General*, 3 May 96; *Lieut.-General*, 25 Sept. 03; *General*, 4 June 13; *Field Marshal*, 9 Nov. 46; Colonel of the 6th Foot, 26 May 06; Captain of St. Mawes, 2 Nov. 96.

THOMAS GROSVENOR, *Ensign*, 1 Oct. 79; *Lieut. and Captain*, 20 Oct. 84; *Captain and Lieut.-Colonel*, 25 April 93; *Colonel*, 3 May 96; *Major General*, 29 April 02; *Lieut. General*, 25 April 08; *General*, 12 Aug. 19; *Field Marshal*, 9 Nov. 46; Colonel of the 65th Foot, 8 Feb. 14.

P W HENRY WILLIAM, *Marquis of* ANGLESEY, KG. GCB. GCH., *Lieut.-Colonel*,* 12 Sept. 93; *Colonel*, 3 May 96; *Major General*, 29 April 02; *Lieut.-General*, 25 April 08; *General*, 12 Aug. 19; *Field Marshal*, 9 Nov. 46; Colonel of the Royal Regiment of Horse Guards, 20 Dec. 42; Captain of Cowes Castle, 25 Mar. 26; *Master General of the Ordnance.*

---

1 His Majesty the King of the Netherlands served in the Peninsula from 1811 to the end of that war in 1814, the principal part of which period as extra Aide-de-Camp to the Duke of Wellington, and was present at the sieges of Ciudad Rodrigo and Badajoz, and battles of Salamanca, Vittoria, Pyrenees, and Nivelle, for which his Majesty has received a cross and two clasps. Commanded the Dutch troops in the campaign of 1815; and the first corps d'armée of the Duke of Wellington's forces at the battle of Waterloo, and was shot through the left shoulder at the close of that action, having, also, been present in the preceding engagements.

	CORNET, 2d LIEUT. or ENSIGN.	LIEUT.	CAPTAIN.	MAJOR.	LIEUT.-COLONEL.	COLONEL.	MAJOR-GENERAL.	LIEUT.-GENERAL.	GENERAL.
Sir Alexander Mackenzie, *Bt.* GCH.[1] from 36 Foot	30 June 87	23 Feb. 91	22 Feb. 93	25 July 93	10 Feb. 94	26 Jan. 97	25 Sept. 03	25 July 10	19 July 21
Sir Gordon Drummond, GCB., 8 Foot	21 Sept. 89	31 Mar. 91	31 Jan. 92	28 Feb. 94	1 Mar. 94	22 July 95	do	do	do
Edmund, *Earl of* Cork, KP.[2]	13 April 85	7 Dec. 85	24 Jan. 91	18 Sept. 93	29 Mar. 94	1 Jan. 98	1 Jan. 05	4 June 11	27 May 25
Hon. Sir Edward Paget, GCB., 28 Foot, *Governor of Chelsea Hospital*	23 Mar. 92	never	7 Dec. 92	14 Nov. 93	30 April 94	do	do	do	do
Stapleton, *Visc.* Combermere, GCB. GCH., 1 Life Guards, *Governor of Sheerness*	26 Feb. 90	16 Mar. 91	28 Feb. 93	Mar. 94	9 Mar. 94	1 Jan. 00	30 Oct. 05	1 Jan. 12	do
Wm. Carr, *Visc.* Beresford, GCB. GCH., 16 Foot, *Governor of Jersey*	27 Aug. 85	25 June 89	24 Jan. 91	1 Mar. 94	11 Aug. 94	do	25 April 08	do	do
Thomas Baker	23 July 74	never	3 April 79	do	22 Aug. 94	do	do	4 June 13	22 July 30
Francis Moore	30 Sept. 87	31 Aug. 91	22 June 93	20 July 94	20 Dec. 94	1 Jan. 01	do	do	do
Robert Edward, *Viscount* Lorton[3], *Colonel of Roscommon Militia*	30 June 92	28 Feb. 93	3 Dec. 93	7 Mar. 94	do	do	do	do	do
Francis Thomas Hammond, GCH., *Lieut.-Governor of Edinburgh Castle*	24 Aug. 80	2 Jan. 82	23 Feb. 93	10 Mar. 94	3 Feb. 95	29 April 02	25 Oct. 09	4 June 14	10 Jan. 37
Robert Dudley Blake	8 Mar. 93	20 June 93	21 May 94	18 Sept. 94	28 Feb. 95	do	do	do	do
Hon. Robert Meade, 12 Foot	7 Nov. 87	15 May 93	23 Sept. 93	30 Oct. 94	10 Mar. 95	do	do	do	do
Sir John Slade, *Bart.*, GCH., 5 Dragoon Guards	11 May 80	28 April 83	24 Oct. 87	1 Mar. 94	29 April 95	do	do	do	do
Hon. Sir Wm. Lumley, GCB., 1 Dragoon Guards, *Extra Groom in Waiting to the Queen*	24 Oct. 87	19 May 90	4 Dec. 93	10 Mar. 95	25 May 95	do	do	do	do
John M'Kenzie[4]	never	1 Jan. 78	13 Feb. 82	1 Mar. 94	15 July 95	do	do	do	do
Alexander Graham Stirling[5]	18 Mar. 82	11 Feb. 83	30 June 90	28 Feb. 95	12 Aug. 95	do	do	do	do
Sir Henry Fred. Campbell, KCB. GCH., 25 Foot	20 Sept. 86	never	25 April 93	never	6 April 96	25 Sept. 03	25 July 10	do	do
C. W., *Marq. of* Londonderry, GCB. GCH., 2 Life Gds.	11 Oct. 94	30 Oct. 94	12 Nov. 94	31 July 95	1 Jan. 97	do	do	do	do
John Sullivan Wood,[6] from 8 Hussars, *Lieutenant of the Tower of London*	30 May 87	20 April 91	3 May 93	10 Feb. 94	3 May 96	1 Jan. 05	do	12 Aug. 19	10 Jan. 37
Frederick Charles White,[7] from Grenadier Guards	19 Feb. 81	30 Dec. 82	6 May 83	1 Jan. 94	5 Sept. 96	do	do	do	do
Sir George Anson, GCB., 4 Dragoon Guards, *Lieutenant Governor of Chelsea Hospital*	3 May 86	16 Mar. 91	9 Sept. 92	25 Dec. 94	21 Dec. 97	do	do	do	do
Thomas R. Charleton, from Royal Artillery	17 June 72	7 July 79	1 Dec. 82	1 Mar. 94	1 Jan. 98	28 June 05	4 June 11	do	do
Pinson Bonham,[8] from 60 Foot	24 April 89	26 Jan. 91	9 June 93	4 Nov. 95	9 Sept. 97	30 Oct. 05	do	do	do
Sir Warren Marmaduke Peacocke, KCH. KC., 19 Foot	12 Dec. 80	22 May 82	14 April 83	1 Mar. 94	1 Jan. 98	25 April 08	do	19 July 21	28 June 38
Sir John Ormsby Vandeleur, GCB., 16 Lancers	29 Dec. 81	21 July 83	7 Mar. 92	do	do	do	do	do	do
Sir Roger Hale Sheaffe, *Bart.*, 36 Foot	1 May 78	27 Dec. 80	6 May 95	13 Dec. 97	22 Mar. 98	do	do	do	do
Hon. Sir Alexander Duff, GCH., 37 Foot	23 May 93	15 Jan. 94	16 Jan. 94	28 Mar. 94	14 April 98	do	do	do	do

	CORNET, 2d LIEUT. or ENSIGN.	LIEUT.	CAPTAIN.	MAJOR.	LIEUT.-COLONEL.	COLONEL.	MAJOR-GENERAL.	LIEUT.-GENERAL.	GENERAL.
William Eden,[10] from 84 Foot	26 Aug. 86	31 May 90	3 June 95	16 Dec. 95	15 Aug. 98	25 April 08	4 June 11	19 July 21	28 June 38
John, *Earl of* Stair, KT., 46 Foot	28 Feb. 90	30 April 92	26 April 93	never	6 Dec. 98	do	do	do	do
P W *Right Hon. Sir* Jas. Kempt, GCB. GCH., 1 Foot, *Lieut.-Governor of Fort William*	31 Mar. 83	18 Aug. 84	30 May 94	18 Sept. 94	28 Aug. 99	9 Mar. 09	1 Jan. 12	27 May 25	23 Nov. 41
P Richard Blunt, 66 Foot	31 Jan. 87	23 Feb. 91	12 July 93	17 May 96	23 Aug. 99	25 Oct. 09	do	do	do
Gerard Gosselin[11]	29 Nov. 80	26 Jan. 91	6 June 94	15 June 94	1 Jan. 00	25 July 10	4 June 13	do	do
P *Sir* Frederick Philipse Robinson, GCB., 39 Foot	11 Sept. 78	1 Sept. 79	3 July 94	1 Sept. 94	do	do	do	do	do
Sir Phineas Riall, KCH., 15 Foot	31 Jan. 92	28 Feb. 94	31 May 94	8 Dec. 94	do	do	do	do	do
P W John, *Earl of* Strafford, GCB. GCH., 29 Foot, *Governor of Londonderry and Culmore*	30 Sept. 93	1 Dec. 93	24 May 94	Dec. 99	14 Mar. 00	do	do	do	do
P *Sir* T. Makdougall Brisbane, *Bt.*, GCB. GCH., 34 Foot	10 Jan. 82	30 July 91	12 April 93	5 Aug. 95	4 April 00	do	do	do	do
Sir Alexander Halkett, KCH.,[13] from late 104 Foot	31 Mar. 90	31 Mar. 93	25 Mar. 94	27 Nov. 99	25 Aug. 00	do	do	do	do
Sir William Keir Grant, KCB. GCH., 2 Dragoons	30 May 92	18 Feb. 93	6 July 94	6 Jan. 96	3 Dec. 00	do	do	do	do
Hon. Arthur Annesley	7 Aug. 94	24 Sept. 94	30 Oct. 94	10 July 95	1 Jan. 01	do	do	do	do
Boyle Travers, from 56 Foot	31 July 90	28 Feb. 93	19 July 94	19 Aug. 95	do	do	do	do	do
P *Sir* Thomas Bradford, GCB. GCH., 4 Foot	20 Oct. 93	9 Dec. 93	15 April 94	9 Sept. 95	do	do	do	do	do
Gage John Hall, 70 Foot	29 May 83	13 Dec. 83	16 Dec. 94	23 Dec. 95	do	do	do	do	do
William, *Lord* de Blaquiere	31 Aug. 91	12 April 93	1 Aug. 93	1 Feb. 98	22 Jan. 01	do	do	do	do
P *Sir* J. W. Gordon, *Bt.* GCB. GCH., 23 Foot, *Qr.-Mast.-Gen.*	17 Oct. 83	5 Mar. 89	2 Sept. 95	9 Nov. 97	21 May 01	do	do	do	do
Sir Thomas Gage Montresor, KCH., 2 Dragoon Guards	12 Mar. 83	4 April 83	17 June 94	12 April 99	27 June 01	do	do	do	do
Sir Ralph Darling, GCH., 69 Foot	15 May 93	2 Sept. 95	6 Sept. 96	2 Feb. 00	17 July 01	do	do	do	do
P *Sir* Rob. Tho. Wilson, 15 Hussars	April 94	31 Oct. 94	21 Sept. 96	28 June 00	27 Feb. 02	do	do	do	do
P Matthew, *Lord* Aylmer, GCB., 18 Foot	19 Oct. 87	26 Oct. 91	8 Aug. 94	9 Oct. 00	25 Mar. 02	do	do	do	do
Sir Charles Imhoff	24 June 83	29 Mar. 90	4 April 99	20 Nov. 01	25 Feb. 02	4 June 11	4 June 14	22 July 30	9 Nov. 46
Gabriel Gordon, 91 Foot	6 Jan. 81	26 Nov. 94	10 July 94	16 May 00	9 Mar. 02	do	do	do	do
Charles Craven	31 Jan. 90	30 Nov. 92	30 May 94	17 May 96	29 April 02	do	do	do	do
James Orde, from late 99 Foot	28 Sept. 94	Jan. 95	6 Feb. 95	June 02	13 Aug. 02	do	do	do	do
P *Sir* Charles Bulkeley Egerton, GCMG. KCH., 89 Foot	16 Nov. 91	21 Mar. 93	22 April 95	1 June 98	14 Nov. 02	do	do	do	do
P *Sir* Henry John Cumming, KCH., 12 Lancers	12 May 90	9 Feb. 93	21 Feb. 94	25 Oct. 98	17 Feb. 03	1 Jan. 12	do	do	do
P John, *Earl of* Carysfort,[14] from Grenadier Guards	3 June 95	3 Sept. 95	28 Feb. 98	25 Mar. 02	27 April 03	do	do	do	do
P W *Sir* Peregrine Maitland, KCB., 17 Foot	25 June 92	never	30 April 94	never	25 June 03	do	do	do	do
P *Hon.* Thomas Edward Capel,[15] from Grenadier Guards	10 April 93	never	4 Oct. 94	never	25 June 03	do	do	do	do
P W *Sir* Colin Halkett, GCB. GCH., 45 Foot	never	never	never	never	17 Nov. 03	do	do	do	do
P W *Rt. Hon. Sir* Fred. Adam, GCB. GCMG., 21 Foot	4 Nov. 95	2 Feb. 96	30 Aug. 99	9 July 03	28 Aug. 04	20 Feb. 12	do	do	do

	CORNET, 2d LIEUT. or ENSIGN.	LIEUT.	CAPTAIN.	MAJOR.	LIEUT.-COLONEL.	COLONEL.	MAJOR-GENERAL.	LIEUT.-GENERAL.
George Meyrick	21 April 84	30 June 87	8 April 93	14 June 94	19 Mar. 96	1 Jan. 05	25 July 10	12 Aug. 19
Frederick William Buller,[18] late of Coldstream Guards	20 Jan. 90	14 Dec. 91	30 Mar. 93	1 Sept. 95	1 Jan. 01	25 July 10	4 June 13	27 May 25
Sir Henry Edw. Bunbury, *Bt.*, KCB.,[19] late of R. Newf. Fenc.	14 Jan. 95	never	16 Aug. 97	11 Mar. 02	31 Dec. 03	1 Jan. 12	4 June 14	22 July 30
Sir Lewis Grant, KCH., 96 Foot	14 Feb. 94	15 Feb. 94	11 June 96	8 Sept. 02	16 April 04	4 June 13	12 Aug. 19	10 Jan. 37
Peter Carey, from 84 Foot	9 Dec. 95	21 June 97	14 Aug. 01	9 July 03	29 June 04	do	do	do
Sir John Alexander Wallace, *Bt.*, KCB., 88 Foot	28 Dec. 87	6 April 90	8 June 96	do	28 Aug. 04	do	do	do
Hastings Fraser, CB., 61 Foot	9 April 88	3 Nov. 90	7 Dec. 97	28 July 02	7 Sept. 04	do	do	do
Sebright Mawby,[20] from 53 Foot	20 June 87	18 May 91	2 Sept. 95	1 June 99	5 Oct. 04	do	do	do
Hon. John Meade, CB.,[21] from 45 Foot	30 Oct. 94	12 Nov. 94	29 Aug. 00	4 June 01	1 Dec. 04	do	do	do
Sir George Pownoll Adams, KCH., 6 Dragoons	5 Oct. 95	12 Mar. 96	11 Oct. 97	5 Feb. 02	8 Dec. 04	do	do	do
Sir John Macleod, CB. KCH., 77 Foot	9 Mar. 93	2 May 94	24 June 95	9 June 99	1 Jan. 05	do	do	do
Sir Benjamin D'Urban, GCB. KCH., 51 Foot, *Commander of the Forces in North America*	April 94	1 July 94	2 July 94	21 Nov. 99	do	do	do	do
Sir Loftus William Ottway, CB., 84 Foot	17 May 96	2 Sept. 96	27 Oct. 98	24 Feb. 03	28 Mar. 05	do	do	do
Sir E. Kerrison, *Bart.*, KCB. GCH., 14 Lt. Dragoons	23 June 96	1 Feb. 98	18 Oct. 98	12 May 03	4 April 05	do	do	do
Sir Robert Barton, KCH.[22]	April 94	14 May 94	5 April 96	17 Feb. 03	14 June 05	do	do	do
Sir Wm. Paterson, KCH.,[23] from 7 F., *Captain of Carisbrook Castle*	27 Jan. 86	24 Jan. 91	2 Sept. 95	17 Dec. 02	20 June 05	do	do	do
Sir John Wright Guise, *Bt.*, KCB., 85 Foot	4 Nov. 94	never	25 Oct. 98	never	25 July 05	do	do	do
Sir James Bathurst, KCB.,[24] from late 1 Argyll Fencibles, *Governor of Berwick*	10 May 94	16 Nov. 94	25 Dec. 99	1 Oct. 03	10 Oct. 05	do	do	do
Paul Anderson, CB., 78 Foot	31 Mar. 88	13 Mar. 91	1 July 95	25 June 01	17 Oct. 05	do	do	do
Sir Andrew F. Barnard, GCB. GCH., Rifle Brigade	26 Aug. 94	Sept. 94	13 Nov. 94	1 Jan. 05	28 Jan. 08	do	do	do
Richard Pigot,[25] from 21 Dragoons	4 Sept. 93	16 Sept. 94	21 Dec. 93	29 April 02	1 May 06	4 June 14	19 July 21	do
Sir James Watson, KCB., 14 Foot	24 June 83	18 April 92	11 Mar. 95	3 Dec. 02	15 May 06	do	do	do
Sir Augustus De Butts, KCH., Royal Engineers	22 Aug. 87	21 Nov. 92	3 Mar. 97	never	1 July 06	do	do	do
Sir Richard Bourke, KCB., 64 Foot	22 Nov. 98	never	25 Nov. 99	27 Aug. 05	16 Sept. 06	do	do	do
Hon. Sir Patrick Stuart, GCMG., 44 Foot	26 Sept. 93	6 June 94	12 April 96	1 Feb. 03	25 Sept. 06	do	do	do
Hon. Henry Otway Trevor, CB., 31 Foot	27 April 93	never	23 June 95	never	25 Oct. 06	do	do	do
Sir James Stevenson Barns, KCB., 20 Foot	11 July 92	2 Jan. 94	27 Feb. 96	17 Sept. 02	6 Nov. 06	do	do	do
Sir Howard Douglas, *Bt.*, GCB. GCMG., 99 Foot	1 Jan. 94	30 May 94	2 Oct. 99	12 Oct. 04	31 Dec. 06	do	do	do
Hon. Arthur Percy Upton, CB.,[26] from Grenadier Guards, *Equerry to H. R. H. the Duchess of Kent*	28 April 93	never	2 Dec. 95	7 May 07	14 May 07	do	do	do
Samuel Huskisson,[27] from 67 Foot	17 May 99	27 Jan. 01	24 Feb. 03	4 July 05	28 May 07	do	do	do
Henry Monckton,[28] from 72 Foot	5 Mar. 95	29 April 95	20 April 96	24 July 02	18 June 07	do	do	do
John Maister, 86 Foot	13 Nov. 93	14 Jan. 94	30 Mar. 95	20 June 01	20 Aug. 07	do	do	do

	CORNET, 2d LIEUT. or ENSIGN.	LIEUT.	CAPTAIN.	MAJOR.	LIEUT.-COLONEL.	COLONEL.	MAJOR-GENERAL.	LIEUT.-GENERAL.
Sir Jasper Nicolls, KCB., 5 Foot	24 May 93	25 Nov. 94	12 Sept. 99	6 July 04	29 Oct. 07	4 June 14	19 July 21	10 Jan. 37
Samuel Brown,[30] from late York Lt. Infantry Volunteers	15 Mar. 98	18 April 00	2 May 00	10 Nov. 04	16 Jan. 08	do	27 May 25	28 June 38
Dennis Herbert[31]	Jan. 94	4 Sept. 94	21 Feb. 99	30 Jan. 00	28 Jan. 08	do	do	do
Sir John Macdonald, GCB., 42 Foot, *Adjutant General*	15 April 95	2 Feb. 96	22 Oct. 02	28 Feb. 05	17 Mar. 08	do	do	do
John Bruce Richard, *Visc.* O'Neill, from Coldstream Guards	10 Oct. 99	never	8 May 00	30 July 07	21 April 08	do	do	do
Alex. Armstrong,[32] *Major* on ret. full pay, late R. Irish Art.	7 July 83	31 Oct. 92	16 Dec. 93	24 July 00	25 April 08	do	do	do
Rt. Hon. Sir Edward Blakeney, KCB., GCH., 7 Foot, *Commanding the Troops in Ireland*	28 Feb. 94	24 Sept. 94	24 Dec. 94	17 Sept. 01	25 April 08	do	do	do
John Home, late of Royal Marines	21 Nov. 76	18 Aug. 78	30 April 93	29 April 02	27 July 08	do	do	do
Sir Thomas Hawker, KCH., 6 Dragoon Guards	12 May 95	5 April 96	10 July 99	23 Nov. 04	2 Sept. 08	do	do	do
Sir George A. Quentin, CB. KCH.[33]	25 Feb. 93	1 Oct. 94	17 May 96	14 Feb. 05	13 Oct. 08	do	do	do
Sir John Wilson, KCB., 11 Foot	26 Mar. 94	12 Aug. 95	18 Jan. 99	27 May 02	22 Dec. 08	do	do	do
John, *Lord* Seaton, GCB. GCMG. GCH., 26 Foot, *Lord High Commissioner of the Ionian Islands*	10 July 94	4 Sept. 95	12 Jan. 00	21 Jan. 08	2 Feb. 09	do	do	do
Sir Thomas M'Mahon, *Bt.*, KCB., 10 Foot	2 Feb. 97	24 Oct. 99	8 Oct. 03	6 Nov. 06	4 May 09	do	do	do
Sir Alexander Woodford, KCB. GCMG., 40 Foot	6 Dec. 94	15 July 95	11 Dec. 99	never	8 Mar. 10	do	do	do
Sir Thomas Arbuthnot, KCB., 71 Foot	23 Nov. 95	1 May 96	25 June 98	7 April 08	24 May 10	do	do	do
Sir Henry Fred. Bouverie, KCB. GCMG., 97 Foot	5 Aug. 99	never	19 Nov. 00	never	28 June 10	do	do	do
John, *Earl of* Westmorland, GCB. GCH., 56 Foot	17 Dec. 03	5 Jan. 04	3 May 05	20 Dec. 10	12 Dec. 11	do	do	do
Lord FitzRoy J. H. Somerset, GCB., 53 Foot, *Military Secretary to his Grace the Commander-in-Chief*	9 June 04	30 May 05	5 May 08	9 June 11	27 April 12	28 Aug. 15	do	do
Henry Evatt, Royal Engineers	11 July 88	16 Jan. 93	29 Aug. 98	never	24 June 09	16 Nov. 16	do	do
Lord Charles Somerset Manners, KCB., 3 Lt. Dragoons	7 Feb. 98	1 June 99	21 Aug. 00	13 Oct. 08	1 Aug. 11	6 Nov. 17	do	do
Robert Ellice, 24 Foot, *Commanding the Forces at Malta*	8 Nov. 98	5 Jan. 99	4 May 01	12 May 08	16 Mar. 09	12 Aug. 19	22 July 30	23 Nov. 41
Sir John Buchan, KCB., 32 Foot	29 July 95	21 Oct. 95	15 Mar. 02	30 June 04	30 Mar. 09	do	do	do
Cosmo Gordon[34]	6 Dec. 92	28 Oct. 94	23 Oct. 00	12 Feb. 07	20 July 09	do	do	do
Hugh, *Lord* Gough, GCB., 87 Foot, *General and Commander-in-Chief in the East Indies*	7 Aug. 94	11 Oct. 94	25 June 03	8 Aug. 05	29 July 09	do	do	do
Sir James Macdonell, KCB. KCH., 79 Foot	25 Jan. 96	2 Feb. 96	10 Sept. 03	17 April 04	7 Sept. 09	do	do	do
Sir Andrew Pilkington, KCB., 82 Foot	7 Mar. 83	24 Jan. 91	2 Mar. 95	31 Mar. 04	5 Oct. 09	do	do	do
Sir John Gardiner, KCB., 50 Foot	23 Nov. 91	12 July 93	17 May 96	18 Dec. 06	29 Oct. 09	do	do	do
George Middlemore, CB., 48 Foot	Jan. 93	5 April 93	15 Oct. 94	14 Sept. 04	2 Nov. 09	do	do	do
James Wallace Sleigh, CB., 9 Lancers	Feb. 95	29 April 95	25 Oct. 98	14 June 05	14 Dec. 09	do	do	do

	CORNET, 2d LIEUT. or ENSIGN.	LIEUT.	CAPTAIN.	MAJOR.	LIEUT.-COLONEL.	COLONEL.	MAJOR-GENERAL.	LIEUT.-GENERAL.
Alexander Nesbitt	4 Dec. 94	28 Feb. 96	1 Dec. 99	25 Mar. 05	21 Dec. 09	12 Aug. 19	22 July 30	23 Nov. 41
Sir William Gabriel Davy, CB. KCH., 60 Foot	Mar. 97	22 May 97	1 Jan. 02	5 Feb. 07	28 Dec. 09	do	do	do
William Augustus Johnson	18 Sept. 93	2 Jan. 94	23 April 94	2 April 03	17 May 10	do	do	do
Jonathan Yates[26]	14 Feb. 99	21 Feb. 99	11 Dec. 01	18 Dec. 06	19 July 10	do	do	do
Sir John Forster Fitzgerald, KCB., 62 Foot	29 Oct. 93	31 Jan. 94	9 May 94	25 Sept. 03	25 July 10	do	do	do
Robert Crawford,[27] *Capt.* on ret. full pay, late R. Irish Artillery, and h. p. 73 Foot	never	7 Aug. 93	17 June 94	do	do	do	do	do
Sir Arthur Benj. Clifton, KCB. KCH., 1 Dragoons	6 June 94	7 Aug. 94	27 Feb. 99	17 Dec. 03	do	do	do	do
Sir Wm. Cornwallis Eustace, CB. KCH., 60 Foot	never	27 Sept. 83	24 Dec. 02	17 Mar. 08	23 Aug. 10	do	do	do
C. M. *Earl* Cathcart, KCB., 3 Dragoon Guards	May 99	10 Aug. 99	3 Feb. 03	14 May 07	30 Aug. 10	do	do	do
Sir Alexander Leith, KCB., 90 Foot	8 Aug. 93	Oct. 94	27 Nov. 94	1 Aug. 04	7 Feb. 11	19 July 21	do	do
Sir Francis *Count* Rivarola, KCMG. KCH., Royal Malta Fencible Regiment	4 April 95	21 Feb. 98	18 Mar. 04	6 Feb. 07	7 Mar. 11	do	do	do
Sir John Browne, KCH., 8 Hussars	27 May 95	17 May 96	1 June 97	16 Feb. 09	14 Mar. 11	do	do	do
Hon. Hugh Arbuthnott, CB., 38 Foot	18 May 96	15 Sept. 96	20 Mar. 99	23 Nov. 04	9 May 11	do	do	do
Sir Robert Arbuthnot, KCB., 76 Foot	1 Jan. 97	1 June 97	20 Aug. 02	13 April 09	22 May 11	do	do	do
Sir James Douglas, KCB., 93 Foot	10 July 99	19 June 00	16 Sept. 02	16 Feb. 09	30 May 11	do	do	do
Sir William Macbean, KCB., 92 Foot	20 Feb. 96	1 Oct. 96	25 Oct. 04	do	do	do	do	do
Henry, *Visc.* Hardinge, GCB., 57 Foot	8 Oct. 98	25 Mar. 02	7 April 04	13 April 09	do	do	do	do
Sir Willoughby Cotton, GCB. KCH., 98 Foot, *Commander-in-Chief at Bombay*	31 Oct. 98	never	25 Nov. 99	never	12 June 11	25 July 21	do	do
John Clitherow, 67 Foot	19 Dec. 99	never	24 Feb. 03	never	8 Oct. 12	do	do	do
Sir John Hanbury, KCH., from Grenadier Guards	20 July 99	26 Sept. 99	3 June 02	never	20 Dec. 12	do	do	do
Hon. Henry Beauchamp Lygon, 10 Hussars	9 July 03	24 May 04	15 Jan. 07	14 May 12	18 June 15	24 Mar. 22	10 Jan. 37	do
Hon. Edward Pyndar Lygon, CB., 13 Lt. Dragoons	1 June 03	7 Nov. 05	15 Feb. 08	never	27 April 15	27 April 22	do	9 Nov 46
Elias Walker Durnford, Royal Engineers	24 April 93	5 Feb. 96	11 Feb. 01	4 June 13	21 July 13	23 Mar. 25	do	do
Sir George Whitmore, KCH., Royal Engineers	18 Sept. 93	5 Feb. 96	28 Feb. 01	do	do	do	do	do
Henry Shadforth	23 May 97	26 Aug. 99	21 Mar. 00	25 Feb. 04	4 June 11	27 May	do	do
Arthur Lloyd		8 July 94	31 Aug. 95	22 May	do	do	do	do
John Millet Hamerton, CB.[28]	31 Oct. 92	31 Jan. 94	28 Oct. 96	15 June	do	do	do	do
Sir Love Parry Jones Parry, KH.[29]	April 94	15 Oct. 94	30 Oct. 94	28 Aug. 04	4 June 11	do	do	do
Charles Nicol, CB., 68 Foot	June 95	31 Aug. 95	30 Nov. 95	3 April 06	13 June	do	do	do
Sir William Tuyll, KCH., 7 Hussars	22 Oct. 99	18 July 01	7 April 04	20 Nov. 06	do	do	do	do

	CORNET, 2d LIEUT. or ENSIGN.	LIEUT.	CAPTAIN.	MAJOR.	LIEUT.-COLONEL.	COLONEL.	MAJOR-GENERAL.	LIEUT.-GENERAL.
P WM *Sir* George Henry Fred. Berkeley, KCB., 35 Foot, *Commander-in-Chief at Madras*	21 Jan. 02	27 Aug. 03	1 May 05	28 Jan. 08	13 June 11	27 May 25	10 Jan. 37	9 Nov. 46
Sackville Hamilton Berkeley, 75 Foot, *Commanding the Troops in the Windward and Leeward Islands*	1 May 00	5 Nov. 00	25 Dec. 04	18 Feb. 08	20 June	do	do	do
P *Sir* Charles James Napier, GCB., 22 Foot	31 Jan. 94	8 May 94	22 Dec. 03	29 May 06	27 June 11	do	do	do
Helier Touzel	20 Feb. 95	9 Dec. 95	4 Aug. 04	14 July 08	11 July 11	do	do	do
Sir Charles Wade Thornton, KCH.,[42] *Lt.-Governor of Hull*	9 July 79	8 May 82	1 Nov. 93	23 Feb. 97	4 Nov.	do	do	do
P *Sir* Henry King, CB. KCH., 3 Foot	25 Mar. 94	12 Aug. 95	3 May 00	5 Feb. 07	31 Dec.	do	do	do
P *Sir* George Thomas Napier, KCB., 1 West India Regt.	25 Jan. 00	18 June 00	5 Jan. 04	30 May 11	6 Feb. 12	do	do	do
P *Hon. Sir* Hercules Robert Pakenham, KCB., 43 Foot	23 July 03	3 Mar. 04	2 Aug. 05	30 Aug. 10	27 April 12	do	do	do
Sir John Harvey, KCB. KCH., 59 F., *Lt.-Gov. of Nova Scotia*	18 Sept. 94	15 July 95	8 Jan. 04	28 Jan. 08	25 June 12	do	do	do
P WM *Sir* Geo. Scovell, KCB., 4 Lt. Gds. *Gov. of R. Mil. Coll.*	5 April 98	4 May 00	10 Mar. 04	30 May 11	17 Aug.	do	do	do
P Ulysses, *Lord* Downes, KCB., 54 Foot	31 Mar. 04	12 Nov. 04	4 Sept. 06	31 Mar. 11	5 Sept.	do	do	do
P WM *Sir* Neil Douglas, KCB. KCH., 72 Foot	28 Jan. 01	16 July 02	19 April 04	31 Jan. 11	3 Dec.	do	do	do
P *Sir* Thomas Downman, CB. KCH., Royal Artillery	24 April 93	11 Sept. 93	1 Nov. 97	22 Jan. 10	17 Dec.	do	do	do
P George, *Marquis* of Tweeddale, KT. CB., 30 Foot	June 04	12 Oct. 04	14 May 07	14 May 12	21 June 13	do	do	do
Sir Frederick William Trench, KCH.[43]	12 Nov. 03	never	12 Nov. 07	1 Aug. 11	25 Nov.	do	do	do
P WM Alex. Geo. *Lord* Saltoun, KCB. GCH., 2 Foot	28 April 02	2 Sept. 02	7 Sept. 04	never	25 Dec.	do	do	do
P WM Henry Wyndham, 11 Hussars	27 Mar. 06	never	8 June 09	9 Aug. 13	20 Jan. 14	do	do	do
P Frederick Rennell Thackeray, CB., Royal Engineers	18 Sept. 93	18 June 96	18 April 01	19 May 10	21 July 13	2 June	do	do
P *Sir* Stephen Remnant Chapman, CB. KCH., from do.	do	20 Nov. 96	do	30 Sept. 10	26 April 12	29 July	do	do
P John Francis Birch, CB., Royal Engineers	do	do	do	6 Mar. 11	21 July 13	do	do	do
Gustavus Nicolls, from do.	6 Nov. 94	3 Mar. 97	30 Mar. 02	4 June 13	1 Sept.	do	do	do
Alexander Watson, do.	19 June 92	17 Jan. 93	9 Jan. 97	20 June 09	1 May 14	do	do	do
Edward Vaughan Worsley, do.	23 Jan. 93	15 Aug. 93	1 April 97	4 Sept. 09	4 June	do	do	do
P Henry Evelegh, Royal Artillery	24 April 93	1 Jan. 94	3 Nov. 97	25 July 10	20 Dec.	do	do	do
Hon. William Henry Gardner, do.	18 Sept. 93	do	16 July 99	4 June 11	do	do	do	do
George Wright, from Royal Engineers	15 Aug. 96	29 Aug. 98	3 April 04	4 June 14	do	do	do	do
Frederick Walker, Royal Artillery	18 Sept. 93	1 Jan. 94	16 July 99	4 June 11	3 July 15	do	do	do
P WM *Sir* Edward Bowater, KCH., 49 Foot, *Groom in Waiting to the Queen*	31 Mar. 04	never	23 Aug. 09	never	25 July 14	12 Oct. 26	do	do
Joseph Webbe Tobin, Royal Artillery	1 Jan. 94	14 Aug. 94	4 Feb. 00	1 Jan. 12	19 July 21	31 Dec. 27	do	do
P WM *Sir* Wm. Maynard Gomm, KCB., 13 Foot, *Governor and Commander-in-Chief of the Mauritius*	24 May 94	16 Nov. 94	25 June 03	10 Oct. 11	17 Aug. 12	16 May 29	do	do

	CORNET, 2d LIEUT. or ENSIGN.	LIEUT.	CAPTAIN.	MAJOR.	LIEUT.-COLONEL.	COLONEL.	MAJOR-GENERAL.
Lawrence Bradshaw, KC.,[46] late of 1 Life Guards	25 Sept. 80	3 Sept. 81	30 April 90	11 Sept. 94	1 Sept. 95	25 Sept. 03	25 July 10
Louis Wm. Viscount *de Chabot*, KCH.,[47] late of 50 Foot	30 April 93	19 Dec. 93	23 July 99	24 Oct. 02	12 Feb. 07	4 June 14	19 July 21
Sir Patrick Ross, GCMG. KCH.,[48] late of 75 Foot, *Governor of St. Helena*	10 May 94	12 Mar. 94	14 May 94	25 Sept. 03	9 April 07	do	do
Charles Palmer[49]	17 May 96	29 Mar. 97	17 May 99	22 Aug. 05	3 May 10	do	27 May 25
Edward James O'Brien	31 Jan. 88	13 Nov. 93	28 Oct. 95	3 June 02	25 July 10	12 Aug. 19	22 July 30
William Stewart,[50] late of 3 Foot	10 Mar. 94	1 Sept. 95	25 Jan. 99	14 Mar. 05	16 Aug. 10	do	do
Sir Henry Willoughby Rooke, CB. KCH.[51]	26 Dec. 98	never	14 Mar. 00	1 Jan. 12	28 Feb. 12	25 July 21	do
Sir John Geo. Woodford, KCB. KCH.,[52] late of Gr. Gds.	23 May 00	never	13 Nov. 04	never	1 July 13	20 Nov. 23	10 Jan. 37
John Pringle, late Unattached	17 Mar. 94	2 Sept. 95	29 June 97	1 Aug. 04	4 June 11	27 May 25	do
Henry D'Oyly, 33 Foot	2 Aug. 97	never	25 Nov. 99	4 June 11	27 May 18	12 Feb. 30	28 June 38
Richard Unlacke, *Captain* on ret. full pay, late R. Irish Art.		16 Dec. 93	1 July 94	1 Jan. 05	1 Jan. 12	22 July	do
George Irving, do. do.	16 Dec. 93		25 July	do	do	do	do
Edward Darley,[53] from 61 Foot	21 Nov. 92	30 April 94	3 Dec. 94	do	do	do	do
Matthew Mahon[54]	31 Dec. 89	11 May 91	9 Sept. 95	28 Nov. 05	do	do	do
Hon. Henry Murray, CB., 7th Dr. Gds.	16 May 00	11 June 01	24 Aug. 02	26 Mar. 07	2 Jan.	do	do
Sir John Grey, KCB., 73 Foot	18 July 98	8 May 99	31 Oct. 03	27 Nov. 06	6 Feb.	do	do
Sir Alexander Cameron, KCB., 74 Foot	22 Oct. 99	6 Sept. 00	6 May 05	30 May 11	27 April	do	do
Sir John Fox Burgoyne, KCB., from Royal Engineers, *Inspector General of Fortifications*	29 Aug. 98	1 July 00	1 Mar. 05	6 Feb. 12	do	do	do
Thomas Dalmer, CB., 47 Foot	22 May 97	12 June 99	23 Oct. 04	10 Dec. 07	17 Aug.	do	do
Sir Henry Watson, CB., 63 Foot	6 May 95	10 Feb. 96	25 June 03	18 Jan. 10	do	do	do
Thomas Evans, CB., 81 Foot	3 Dec. 94	1 Oct. 95	19 Nov. 03	6 Feb. 12	13 Oct.	do	do
Sir Archibald Maclaine, CB., 52 Foot	16 April 94	29 April 95	22 Dec. 04	4 Oct. 10	25 Jan. 13	do	23 Nov. 41
James Hay, CB.[56]	10 June 95	26 April 98	28 Feb. 05	2 Jan. 12	18 Feb.	do	do
William Wood, CB. KH.[57]	27 Jan. 97	27 Dec. 97	3 Dec. 02	14 May 07	8 April	do	do
Sir William Warre, CB., 94 Foot	5 Nov. 03	2 June 04	25 April 06	30 May 11	13 May	do	do
Charles Ashe A'Court, CB. KH., 41 Foot	17 Dec. 01	2 Sept. 02	25 July 04	26 Feb. 11	19 May	do	do
George Charles D'Aguilar, CB., 58 Foot	24 Sept. 99	1 Dec. 02	30 Mar. 08	1 April 13	20 May	do	do
Sir Charles William Pasley, KCB., from Royal Engineers	1 Dec. 97	28 Aug. 99	1 Mar. 05	5 Feb. 12	27 May	do	do
Jacob Glyn Cuyler	26 Oct. 99	11 June 01	9 July 03	26 Jan. 06	4 June	do	do
Charles Turner[60]	29 April 95	5 Mar. 96	22 Nov. 98	9 April 07	do	do	do
William Francis Bentinck Loftus[61]	30 Aug. 99	16 July 00	20 April 04	do	do	do	do
George Burrell, CB.,[62] from 18 Foot	4 Feb. 97	3 May 97	15 Aug. 05	30 April 07	do	do	do
James Farrer	17 Mar. 94	29 July 95	5 April 96	2 July	do	do	do
Thomas Brabazon Aylmer[63]	9 Aug. 97	15 Aug. 98	31 May 00	2 Sept.	do	do	do
Henry James Riddell, KH.,[64] *Governor of Edinburgh Castle*	Mar. 98	19 April 98	24 Dec. 02	10 Dec.	do	do	do
Henry Charles Edward Vernon, CB.[65]	8 Nov. 98	26 Sept. 99	17 July 01	13 June 11	do	do	do

	Cornet, 2d Lieut. or Ensign.	Lieut.	Captain.	Major.	Lieut.-Colonel.	Colonel.	Major-General.
Sir James Archibald Hope, KCB., 9 Foot	12 Jan. 00	3 June 01	18 Feb. 06	6 Mar. 11	21 June 13	22 July 30	23 Nov. 41
Sir Robert John Harvey, CB., 2 West India Regt.	8 Oct. 03	24 Mar. 04	2 Jan. 06	25 July 11	do	do	do
Sir Hew Dalrymple Ross, KCB., Royal Artillery, *Deputy Adjutant General*	6 Mar. 95	10 May 96	1 Sept. 03	31 Dec. 11	do	do	do
Sir Dudley St. Leger Hill, KCB.[68]	27 Aug. 04	10 Oct. 05	16 Aug. 10	27 April 12	do	do	do
Sir Edmund Keynton Williams, KCB., 80 Foot	30 Aug. 99	18 April 00	25 Sept. 07	8 Oct. 12	do	do	do
Sir Richard Armstrong, CB., 95 Foot	23 June 96	5 Nov. 99	9 July 03	30 May 11	26 Aug.	do	do
Sir Frederick Stovin, KCB. KCMG., 83 Foot, *Groom in Waiting to the Queen*	22 Mar. 00	7 Jan. 01	24 June 02	27 April 12	do	do	do
Sir Guy Campbell, *Bart.* CB., 3 West India Regiment	9 Dec. 94	4 April 96	14 Sept. 04	1 April 13	do	do	do
Richard Goddard Hare-Clarges, CB.[74]	6 July 96	1 Nov. 96	9 July 03	1 July 13	16 Sept.	do	do
Sir Charles Felix Smith, KCB., from Royal Engineers	1 Oct. 02	9 Oct. 02	18 Nov. 07	31 Dec. 11	21 Sept.	do	do
Alexander Thomson, CB.[75]	23 Sept. 03	29 Feb. 04	14 May 07	9 April 12	do	do	do
Charles Grene Ellicombe, CB., from Royal Engineers	never	1 July 01	1 July 06	27 April 12	21 Sept.	do	do
Henry Goldfinch, CB., from Royal Engineers	1 Mar. 98	11 June 00	1 Mar. 05	17 Dec. 12	do	do	do
James Webber Smith, CB., *R. Artillery*, Director Gen.	6 Mar. 95	3 Oct. 95	25 Nov. 02	4 June 13	do	do	do
Sir William Fra. Pat. Napier, KCB., 27 Foot	14 June 00	18 April 01	2 June 04	30 May 11	22 Nov.	do	do
John Duffy, CB.[77]	21 Oct. 95	6 Jan. 96	12 Aug. 04	6 Feb. 12	do	do	do
Henry Daubeney, KH.[78]	8 July 95	21 Oct. 95	7 Sept. 96	25 May 08	11 Dec.	do	do
Douglas Mercer, CB.[79]	24 Mar. 03	never	20 Mar. 06	never	20 Dec.	do	do
Francis Miles Milman[80]	3 Dec. 00	never	28 April 04	never	25 Dec.	do	do
John Reeve[81]	23 Oct. 00	never	11 April 05	never	do	do	do
Jacob Tonson, CB.,[82]	9 Feb. 91	19 Mar. 93	13 Sept. 95	26 May 08	26 Dec.	do	do
William Alexander Gordon, CB.,[83]	2 Oct. 94	29 Dec. 94	2 Oct. 01	4 June 13	do	do	do
Thomas Kenah, CB.[84]	14 Aug. 99	9 May 00	3 Mar. 04	5 Nov. 12	27 Dec.	do	do
Sir Robert Wm. Gardiner, KCB. KCH., from R. Artillery, *Governor and Commander-in-Chief at Gibraltar*	7 April 97	16 July 99	12 Oct. 04	27 April 12	3 Mar. 14	do	do
Edward Buckley Wynyard, CB.[86]	17 Dec. 03	never	7 Jan. 08	25 Mar. 13	28 April	do	do
James Fergusson, CB.[87]	20 Aug. 01	9 Feb. 04	1 Dec. 06	3 Dec. 12	16 May	do	do
Thomas William Brotherton, CB.,[88] from 16 Dragoons	24 Jan. 00	never	27 July 01	28 Nov. 11	19 May	do	do
Sir Adolphus John Dalrymple,[89] *Bart.*	25 Oct. 99	12 June 00	7 Jan. 03	15 Sept. 08	1 June	do	do
Sir James Henry Reynett, KCH.,[89] *Lieut.-Gov. of Jersey*	25 Nov. 99	14 Mar. 00	24 Mar. 04	8 April 13	do	do	do
William Smelt, CB.[90]	16 Mar. 98	11 Dec. 99	21 Mar. 05	28 Jan. 08	4 June	do	do
James Robertson Arnold, KH., from Royal Engineers	1 Mar. 98	11 June 00	1 Mar. 05	never	20 Dec.	do	do
William Wemyss, *Equerry to the Queen*	3 July 03	12 Sept. 05	18 Aug. 08	27 May 13	16 Mar. 15	do	do
Walter Tremenheere, KH., late of Royal Marines	2 Jan. 79	12 Jan. 82	28 Jan. 96	25 April 08	4 June 14	28 Dec.	do
John Bell, CB.[91], *Lieut.-Governor of Guernsey*	15 Aug. 05	1 Oct. 07	12 Mar. 12	21 June 13	12 April 14	6 May 31	do
Samuel Benjamin Auchmuty, CB.[92]	15 Oct. 97	13 Mar. 00	14 Nov. 05	26 Aug. 13	do	do	do
Thomas Lightfoot, CB.[93]	Aug. 99	14 Mar. 00	15 Dec. 04	21 June 13	19 May	do	do

	Cornet, 2d Lieut. or Ensign.	Lieut.	Captain.	Major.	Lieut.-Colonel.	Colonel.	Major-General.
Alured Dodsworth Faunce, CB.,[94] from Insp. Field Officer ..	2 Dec. 95	13 Oct. 96	6 Aug. 03	14 Feb. 11	29 Sept. 14	6 May 31	23 Nov. 41
George Brown, CB. KH.,[95] from Rifle Brigade, *Deputy Adjutant General*	23 Jan. 06	18 Sept. 06	20 June 11	26 May 14	do	do	do
Lord Frederick Fitz Clarence, GCH., *Lieutenant Governor of Portsmouth*	never	12 May 14	23 Feb. 20	10 Jan. 22	1 April 24	do	do
George Prescott Wingrove,[96] late of Royal Marines	3 May 93	17 Dec. 94	1 Nov. 01	4 June 13	26 Aug. 26	do	do
Richard Secker Brough, Royal Artillery..........	never	2 Sept. 94	1 Jan. 98	25 July 10	12 Aug. 19	21 Nov. 33	do
James Power, Royal Artillery	never	30 Sept. 94	22 Feb. 09	4 June 11	do	5 June 35	do
John Aitchison,[97] from Scots Fusilier Guards	25 Oct. 05	never	22 Nov. 10	never	15 Dec. 14	20 May 36	do
His Royal Highness Prince George W. F. C. of Cambridge, KG. Colonel 17 Lancers	never	never	never	never	never	3 Nov. 37	7 May 45
Charles Edward Conyers, CB.[98]	13 Sept. 94	2 Sept. 95	25 June 02	16 Feb. 09	3 Mar. 14	10 Jan. 37	9 Nov. 46
George Augustus Henderson, KH.[99]	1 Sept. 93	1 Mar. 95	20 Aug. 01	4 June 13	12 April	do	do
Roger Parke[100]	30 June 95	1 Oct. 95	9 Oct. 00	25 Feb. 08	4 June	do	do
Robert Barclay Macpherson, CB. KH.[101]	3 June 95	22 July 95	3 Dec. 00	17 Mar.	do	do	do
Philip Hay[102]	31 Dec. 94	16 Feb. 95	22 July 95	25 April	do	do	do
John Slessor,[112]	1794	14 June 94	25 July 95	do	do	do	do
James Irving, *Captain*, on retired full pay, late R. Irish Art. ..	never	3 Aug. 94	do	do	do	do	do
James Allan, CB.,[103] from 57 Foot..........	1 Jan. 95	18 Mar. 95	10 Sept. 99	20 July 09	do	do	do
Archibald Money, CB.[104]	April 94	13 May 94	3 May 00	14 Dec.	do	do	do
David Forbes, CB.[105]	13 Mar. 93	3 May 94	25 June 03	29 Aug. 11	28 July 14	do	do
John Fred. Ewart, CB.,[106] from Insp. Field Officer	1 Nov. 03	10 Mar. 04	17 April 06	29 Oct. 12	15 Sept.	do	do
Henry Adolphus Proctor, CB.[107]	14 Jan. 01	25 Mar. 02	16 May 05	30 April	17 Sept.	do	do
William Jervois, KH.,[108] *Captain*, h. p. 53 Foot	7 April 04	8 Aug. 04	14 July 08	19 Dec. 13	22 Sept.	do	do
William Riddall, KH.[109]	6 Dec. 98	27 Nov. 99	23 July 03	4 June 14	13 Oct.	do	do
Thomas Fenn Addison,[110] *Captain*, h. p. 99 Foot	4 May 00	17 Dec. 02	24 Dec. 03	do	do	do	do
Sir Francis Cockburn,[111] from 2 West India Regt.	16 Oct. 00	6 April 03	3 Mar. 04	27 June 11	27 Oct.	do	do
Thomas Charretie[114]	9 June 04	6 Feb. 05	25 Dec. 07	27 April 15	21 May 15	do	do
Sir George Arthur, *Bart.*, KCH.	25 Aug. 04	24 June 05	5 May 08	5 Nov. 12	1 June	do	do
Patrick Campbell,[115] *Lt.-Col.*, R. Artillery, on retired full pay	6 Mar. 95	3 Oct. 95	20 Mar. 03	14 Oct. 13	do	do	do
Edward Parkinson, CB.[116]	27 Feb. 96	12 Jan. 00	7 Mar. 05	27 Oct. 10	18 June	do	do
Thomas Hunter Blair, CB.[117]	24 July 02	14 Sept. 04	28 Mar. 05	30 May 11	do	do	do
Richard Lluellyn, CB.[118]	24 July 03	7 April 04	28 Feb. 05	23 April 12	do	do	do
Peter Aug. Lautour, CB. KH.[119]	31 Mar. 04	4 July 05	8 May 06	20 May 13	do	do	do
Richard Egerton, CB.[120]	1 Dec. 98	29 Mar. 00	28 Sept. 04	26 Aug.	do	do	do
Sir William Chalmers, CB. KCH.[121]	9 July 03	25 Oct. 03	27 Aug. 07	do	do	do	do
John Boteler Parker, CB.,[122] *Lt.-Col.*, R.Art., on ret. full pay	1 April 02	1 Sept. 03	5 June 08	21 Sept.	do	do	do
Charles Beckwith, CB.[123]	2 June 03	20 Aug. 04	28 July 08	3 Mar. 14	do	do	do
William Campbell, CB.	4 May 04	18 April 05	23 June 08	12 April	do	do	do

	CORNET, 2d LIEUT. or ENSIGN.	LIEUT.	CAPTAIN.	MAJOR.	LIEUT.-COLONEL.	COLONEL.	MAJOR-GENERAL.
James Claud. Bourchier,[124]	28 Sept. 97	6 Aug. 99	20 Jan. 03	4 June 14	16 June 15	10 Jan. 37	9 Nov. 46
James Grant, CB.,[125] *Governor of Scarborough Castle*	22 Mar. 97	22 Jan. 01	9 July 03	do	do	do	do
Thomas Wm. Taylor, CB.,[126] *Lt. Governor R. Military College*	14 July 04	12 June 05	22 Jan. 07	7 July	do	do	do
Lawrence Arguimbau, CB.[127] *Captain*, h. p. 1 Foot	9 Oct. 01	26 Oct. 03	9 Mar. 09	11 Aug.	do	do	do
Sir Henry George Wakelyn Smith, *Bart.* GCB., Rifle Brigade, *Gov. and Comm.-in-Chief at the Cape of Good Hope*	8 May 05	15 Aug. 05	28 Feb. 12	29 Sept.	do	do	do
Felix Calvert, CB.[128]	1 Oct. 07	15 Sept. 08	27 June 11	27 Oct.	do	do	do
William Staveley, CB.[129]	14 July 04	21 April 08	6 May 13	15 Dec.	do	do	do
Sir De Lacy Evans, KCB.[130]	1 Feb. 07	1 Dec. 08	12 Jan. 15	11 May 15	do	do	do
William Henry Scott,[131]	27 Oct. 05	never	28 Mar. 11	never	5 July	do	do
Hugh Percy Davison	25 Oct. 05	11 Nov. 06	26 Nov. 07	19 Mar. 14	24 Aug.	do	do
Sir Thomas Willshire, *Bart.*, KCB.[132]	June 95	5 Sept. 95	28 Aug. 04	21 Sept. 13	4 Dec.	do	do
Hon. Henry Edward Butler.[133]	15 Feb. 00	21 June 00	22 May 04	30 May 11	4 July 16	do	do
Edward Fleming, CB.,[134] from Inspecting Field Officer	24 June 02	6 July 04	30 May 07	1 April 13	18 July	do	do
Sir John Rolt, KCB.[135]	7 Mar. 00	1 June 01	5 Sept. 05	25 Nov. 13	2 Nov.	do	do
George Cardew, from Royal Engineers	20 Dec. 98	18 April 01	1 Mar. 05	never	26 Nov.	do	do
Philip Bainbrigge, CB.[136]	30 June 00	13 Oct. 00	17 Oct. 05	15 Oct. 12	21 June 17	do	do
Wm. Greenshields Power, CB. KH., from Royal Artillery	31 May 00	11 Feb. 02	13 June 07	21 Sept. 13	do	do	do
Thomas Erskine Napier, CB.[137]	3 July 05	1 May 06	27 Oct. 08	26 Dec. 13	do	do	do
Nathaniel Thorn, CB. KH.[138]	15 Oct. 02	25 June 03	4 Jan. 10	3 Mar. 14	do	do	do
William Henry Sewell, CB., from 94 Foot	27 Mar. 06	26 Feb. 07	12 Mar. 12	do	do	do	do
William Lindsay Darling[140]	13 Dec. 01	23 June 02	13 June 08	14 April	do	do	do
Sir Joseph Thackwell, KCB. KH.,[141] from 3 Dragoons	23 April 00	13 June 01	9 April 07	18 June 15	do	do	do
Alexander Macdonald, CB., from Royal Artillery	3 Dec. 03	1 May 04	1 Oct. 12	do	do	do	do
Sir Wm. Lewis Herries, CB. KCH.[142]	23 Jan. 01	17 Mar. 03	9 Oct. 09	2 June 14	31 July	do	do
John M'Donald, CB.,[143] from 92 Foot	17 Dec. 03	21 Mar. 05	7 Sept. 09	26 Aug. 13	4 Sept.	do	do
George William Paty, CB. KH.[144]	28 April 04	7 May 05	28 April 08	2 June 14	do	do	do
Lord James Hay	23 Jan. 06	6 Aug. 07	8 Feb. 10	never	26 Mar. 18	do	do
Thomas James Wemyss,[139] CB.	Oct. 00	1 Mar. 04	30 Nov. 06	21 June 13	21 Jan. 19	do	do
Robert Burd Gabriel, CB. KH.,[145] *Capt.*, h. p. 22 Dragoons	28 Sept. 97	3 May 00	9 May 05	26 Aug.	do	do	do
Henry Thomas, CB.[146]	1 April 98	29 Dec. 98	10 Sept. 05	do	do	do	do
[illegible], CB.[147]	4 Nov. 03	15 June 04	19 Oct. 08	3 Mar. 14	do	do	do
James Shaw Kennedy, CB.[148]	18 April 05	23 Jan. 06	16 July 12	18 June 15	do	do	do
Arthur W. M. *Lord* Sandys[149]	27 July 09	19 July 10	25 Aug. 13	27 July 15	do	do	do
Sir Thomas Henry Browne, KCH.[150]	28 Oct. 05	18 Sept. 06	15 April 13	21 June 17	do	do	do
Richard W. Howard Howard Vyse	5 May 00	17 June 01	24 June 02	4 June 13	13 May	do	do
Archibald Maclachlan[151]	6 May 95	7 July 96	1 Dec. 97	25 July 10	12 Aug.	do	do
Robert William Mills, *Capt.*, h. p. 9 Foot	June 95	12 Aug. 95	19 July 98	do	do	do	do
Edward Nicolls,[152] *Major*, Royal Marines, on retired full pay	24 [illegible] 95	27 [illegible] 96	25 July 05	8 Aug.	do	do	do

	CORNET, 2d LIEUT. or ENSIGN.	LIEUT.	CAPTAIN.	MAJOR.	LIEUT.-COLONEL.	COLONEL.	MAJOR-GENERAL.
P Frederick Ashworth	6 July 99	23 April 00	18 Oct. 02	22 Nov. 10	12 Aug. 19	10 Jan. 37	9 Nov. 46
Robert Bryce [illegible]in, CB.,[163] from 40 Foot	June 95	4 Sept. 95	21 April 14	20 Dec.	do	do	do
P Henry [illegible]ellis, [illegible]G. KH.,[164]	3 Jan. 97	5 Nov. 99	11 Sept. 05	30 May 11	do	do	do
Vincent Edw. Eyre, *Lt. & Capt.*, ate Horse Gr. Gds. on ret. full pay	21 May 94	27 May 95	15 Mar. 99	4 June	do	do	do
John Wi[illegible]im[155]		6 Dec. 94	23 July 03	13 June	do	do	do
P George Leigh Goldie, [illegible][156]	3 Sept. 03	14 Mar. 05	4 Dec. 06	20 June	do	do	do
P George Powell Higginson[157]	6 Nov. 05	never	3 April 11	never	26 Oct. 20	do	do
P [illegible] George Bowles,[158] *M[illegible]ster of The Queen's Household*	20 Dec. 04	never	1 Feb. 10	18 June 15	14 June 21	do	do
Thomas Bunbury, KH.,[159] from 67 Foot	25 Mar. 04	22 Dec. 04	3 Nov. 08	14 April 14	5 July	do	do
P *Hon.* Henry Fred. Compton [illegible]dish,[160] from 1 Life Guards	never	26 May 08	6 June 11	2 April 18	12 July	do	do
John [illegible]ins Aldred		17 Aug. 97	19 Nov. 00	1 Jan. 12	19 July	do	do
P Henry Godwin, CB.[161]	30 Oct. 99	19 Aug. 03	28 Mar. 08	26 May 14	26 July 21	do	do
P [illegible] Thomas Wm. Robbins [162]	26 Sept. 05	5 May 08	25 May 09	24 Dec. 18	24 Oct.	do	do
P [illegible] Roderick Macneil,[163] [illegible]m 78 Foot	17 Mar. 08	9 May 09	1 [illegible]. 14	9 Aug. 21	25 Jan. 22	do	do
P George Dean [illegible], KH.,[164] [illegible]m Inspecting Field Officer	4 June 05	5 Dec. 05	10 Aug. 09	13 Jan. 14	18 April	do	do
William Sutherland,[165] from 5 Foot	15 Dec. 04	1 July 06	18 Aug. 14	25 Sept. 17	16 May	do	do
P Henry [illegible]Raly, CB. KH.[166]	24 Aug. 04	1 Nov. 04	13 April 09	21 June 17	15 Aug.	do	do
P [illegible] *Hon.* Charles Gore, CB. KH.[167]	21 Oct. 08	4 Jan. 10	13 Mar. 15	21 Jan. 19	19 Sept.	do	do
P [illegible] Wm. Lovelace Walton[168]	8 May 06	never	7 Mar. 11	never	20 Feb. 23	do	do
P Edward Fanshawe, CB., from Royal Engineers, *Assistant Inspector General of Fortifications*	never	1 July 01	1 July 06	12 Aug. 19	23 Mar. 25	do	do
Thomas John Forbes, Royal Artillery	6 Mar. 95	13 April 95	9 [illegible]pt. 02	4 June 13	29 July	do	do
Alexander Munro, KH., do.	do	27 Jan. 96	2 May 03	4 June 14	do	do	do
Thomas Colby, from Royal Engineers	2 July 01	6 Aug. 02	1 July 07	19 July 21	do	do	do
P Robert Henry Birch, from Royal Artillery	9 Mar. 95	25 July 96	12 Sept. 03	4 June 14	12 Dec. 26	do	do
Charles Richard Fox, *Surveyor-General of the Ordnance*	29 June 15	5 Nov. 18	9 Aug. 20	6 Nov. 24	14 Aug. 27	do	do
James Armstrong, from Royal Artillery	9 Mar. 95	31 July 96	12 Sept. 03	4 June 14	13 Oct.	do	do
Thomas Paterson, do.	1 Dec. 95	3 June 97	6 Dec. 03	do	6 Nov.	do	do
Nathaniel Wilmot Oliver, do.	2 June 96	13 Feb. 98	2 Mar. 04	do	do	do	do
P Richard John J[illegible]mes [illegible]y, from Royal Artillery	8 Aug. 96	17 Mar. 98	20 July 04	do	31 Dec. 27	23 June	do
George Lewis, CB.,[169] *Col. Comm.*, R. Marines, on retired full pay	25 April 93	6 Oct. 94	1 Oct. 01	4 June 13	28 Sept. 26	10 July	do
C P Elias Lawrence, CB.,[170] *do.* do. do.	8 May 93	14 Feb. 95	3 Dec. 01	do	15 Nov. 26	do	do
George Jones,[171] from Royal Marines	19 June 93	24 April 95	16 July 03	4 June 14	22 July 30	do	do
P Thomas Benj. Adair, CB.,[172] *Col. Com.*, R. Mar., on ret. full pay	1 Dec. 93	do	20 Sept. 03	do	do	do	do
William Hallett Connolly,[173] *do.* do. do.	8 May 95	7 April 96	15 Aug. 05	12 Aug. 19	10 April 32	do	do
P Charles Augu[illegible]tus [illegible]ie,[174] from Coldstream Guards	26 May 08	never	23 April 12	never	28 April 25	8 Aug.	do
George Beatty,[175] from Royal Marines	16 May 95	20 Nov. 96	15 Aug. 05	12 Aug. 19	16 April 32	27 Dec.	do

War Services of the General Officers who are not Colonels of Regiments.

1 Sir Alexander Mackenzie served with Lord Moira's army on the expedition for the relief of Ostend, in 1794; as second in command at the capture of the Cape of Good Hope, in 1795; in command of a division on the expedition against Naples, in 1808; and afterwards in command of the army in the two Calabrias.

2 Lord Cork served in Flanders, in 1793, and was present at the sieges of Valenciennes and Dunkirk, at the former of which he was one of the storming party. In 1794 he accompanied the expedition under Lord Moira; was present at the battle of Alost, and made prisoner at the capitulation of Bergen-op-Zoom. Served with the Guards in Holland, in 1799. Commanded the first battalion of the Coldstream Guards in Egypt, in 1801, and was present at the taking of Alexandria, and in the different engagements with the army under Sir Eyre Coote, to the westward of Alexandria.

3 Lord Lorton served with the 58th as a marine on board the *Vengeance* 74. Went out with Sir Charles Grey's expedition to the West Indies, in 1793, and served in the 1st battalion of Grenadiers, under the command of the late Duke of Kent, at the captures of Martinique, St. Lucia, and Guadaloupe; on the conclusion of the campaign rejoined the 58th at Martinique. In about six weeks following, in consequence of a French force having re-taken Grande Terre, he was ordered with the Grenadiers again to Guadaloupe, and was engaged in the several actions of that second campaign; in covering the retreat of the troops from Point-à-Pitre, was struck by a spent ball, which was the occasion of a handsome compliment from Sir Charles Grey in front of the Grenadiers, while inspecting the remains of the army on the afternoon of that fatal day, as in fact he was a volunteer on this second expedition, having previously received permission from Sir Charles to return to Europe in consequence of promotion. During the night the troops were re-embarked, he commanded an advanced position close to the French lines while the operation was in progress. Served also during the rebellion in Ireland, in 1798, at Vinegar Hill, &c., and subsequently as a Brigadier-General in the Western District.

4 General M'Kenzie served the campaign of 1794 on the Continent, including the several actions between the Waal and Rhine, forcing the enemy from St. André, sortie from Nimeguen, and the actions at Thuyl and Geldermalsen. Served also on the eastern coast of Spain under Sir Wm. Henry Clinton.

5 General Stirling, in command of the Light Company of the 50th, at the storming of the Convention Redoubts, the taking of St. Fiorenza and Bastia, the storming the Moselle Fort, the siege of Calvi, and the capture of Corsica, in 1794. He afterwards commanded a District in Ireland and in Great Britain.

6 General Wood served as a Major-General on the staff in the East Indies, and was actively employed in the Nepaul war.

7 General White was appointed, in 1793, Brigade-Major to the Guards employed in the campaigns in Flanders, and was present at the sieges of Valenciennes and Dunkirk, and at the action and storming of Lincelles.

8 General Bonham served upwards of 22 years in the West Indies, and acted as chief of the Quarter-Master-General's department on the two expeditions against St. Lucia and Tobago, and Demerara and Berbice; on the latter he was second in command. He was also present at the storming of Morne Fortunée, St. Lucia, on the night of the 2d of June, 1803.

10 General Eden served as Assistant-Quarter-Master-General in Flanders in 1794, and in Holland in 1795; also at the capture of Java in 1811, for which he has received a medal.

11 General Gosselin served on the expedition against Genoa, under Lord Wm. Bentinck; and subsequently in the American War.

13 Sir Alexander Halkett served at the captures of Martinique, St. Lucia, and Guadaloupe, in 1794; at Ostend, under Sir Eyre Coote, where he was taken prisoner; with the expedition to the Helder, in 1799, where he was twice wounded; and at the capture of the Cape of Good Hope, in 1806.

14 Lord Carysfort served as Secretary to the mission of Colonel Crawfurd, at the head-quarters of the Archduke Charles, and was present at all the battles of the campaign of 1796 in Germany, at the siege of Kehl, and the affair at the beginning of 1797, on the Rhine. Served as Aide-de-camp to Lord Cornwallis in Ireland during the Rebellion; after which he was employed in Germany, and was present at all the actions of that year in Switzerland, under General Hotze, and with the Russian army at the battle of Zurich. Campaign in Egypt as Aide-de-camp to Sir Ralph Abercromby, and afterwards to Lord Hutchinson. On the Quarter-Master-General's staff on the expedition to Sweden, and afterwards to Spain, under Sir John Moore, including the battle of Corunna. Embarked with the Guards for Walcheren in July 1809, and served in the reserve in South Beveland. Accompanied the Guards to Spain in 1811, and was appointed to the command of the garrison of Cadiz. At the defence of Tarifa, he was second in command. Marched from thence with the detachment of the Guards that joined Lord Hill, and subsequently formed a junction with the Duke of Wellington on his retreat from Burgos. In 1813 he returned to England, and shortly afterwards he again embarked with a detachment of Guards for Flanders, a brigade of which he commanded in the attack on Bergen-op-Zoom. Medal for services in Egypt.

15 General the Honourable T. E. Capel served the campaigns in Flanders under the Duke of York. Employed as Assistant-Adjutant-General at Cadiz in 1811.

18 Lieut.-General Buller served the campaigns of 1793 and 94 in Flanders; and subsequently in the West Indies, including the siege of St. Lucia, and reduction of Grenada.

19 Sir Henry Edw. Bunbury served in Holland in 1799, including the battles of the 19th Sept., 2nd and 7th October. Served also on the expedition to Naples and Calabria in 1805 and 6, and was present at the battle of Maida, for which he has received a medal.

20 Lieut.-General Mawby embarked with the 18th for Toulon, in October 1793; and, after serving with it there, he was appointed Assistant-engineer, and sent to the out-post of Cape Brun, where he remained until that place was evacuated, 17th December following. Embarked for Corsica 12th May 1794; proceeded with the Grenadiers from Bastia for Calvi, in June, and was present during the whole of the siege of that place, as also at the storming of the Mozelle fort. Embarked for India 20th April 1805, in command of the 53rd. In November 1809, he accompanied the regiment into the province of Bundelcund, and was appointed to command the first brigade of Infantry, and which command he held until the army was ordered into cantonments, 29th March 1812. At the storming of Callinger, 2nd February 1812, he commanded the British troops.

21 Lieut.-General the Honourable John Meade served in Holland under the Duke of York. Accompanied the expeditions to the Ferrol and to Portugal in 1800. Served also in the Peninsula, and commanded the 45th at the battle of Busaco, for which he has received a medal.

22 Sir Robert Barton served the campaign of 1799 in Holland, and was present in the actions of the 8th, 10th, and 19th September. Accompanied the Life Guards to the Peninsula, where he served for a short period.

23 Sir Wm. Paterson served at the taking of the French West India Islands in 1794. Served also in the American war, and was present at several operations in the Chesapeak, and with the expedition against New Orleans, where he was severely wounded.

24 Sir James Bathurst served at the capture of Surinam, as Aide-de-camp to Sir Thomas Trigge. He was attached as Captain to the 1st battalion of the 54th during the whole of the Egyptian campaign of 1801 (medal), and was present in the action at the landing, and in the various actions during the campaign to the east and west of Alexandria, and also at the siege of Marabout. He served on the staff in the expedition to Hanover in 1805. He was with the Russian Army in 1807 in the actions fought for the relief of Dantzig, and in those of Lomitten, Deppen, Gutstadt, Heilsberg, and Freedland. He next served on the Quarter-Master-General's Staff at Rugen, and at the siege of Copenhagen. He accompanied Sir Brent Spencer's secret expedition in 1808; and in 1809 and 10 he served with the Army in Portugal as Assistant-Quarter-Master-General, and afterwards as Military Secretary to the Duke of Wellington; he was present at the battles of Roleia, Vimiera, and Corunna, passage of the Douro, and battles of Talavera and Busaco. Sir James has received a cross.

25 Lieut.-General Pigot was actively employed in the West Indies in 1794; in the Mediterranean and capture of Minorca in 1798; at the capture of the Cape of Good Hope in 1806; and in the East Indies in 1818.

26 Lieut.-General the Honourable A. P. Upton joined the Duke of York's army in Holland, in Nov. 1794, with which he served the ensuing winter campaign, and returned to England with the army in May 1795. In 1799 he was appointed Aide-de-camp to Sir Ralph Abercromby, and was present at the battle of the 27th Aug. on the landing near the Helder, as also at those of the 10th Sept., 2nd and 6th Oct. Appointed Assistant-Quarter-Master General to the army under Lord Chatham in 1809: landed at Walcheren 27th July with the troops, and was present at the actions in which the enemy were driven into Flushing, and also at the siege of that place. Served at Cadiz from Apr. 1811 to Aug. 1812, and with the Duke of Wellington's army on the Quarter-Master-General's staff, from Sept. 1812 to the end of the war in 1814, including the retreat into Portugal, actions of San Munos and Osma, battle of Vittoria, action at Tolosa, passage of the Bidassoa, battle of the Nivelle, battles of the Nive on the 9th, 10th, 11th, and 12th Dec., passage of the Adour, action of St. Etienne, investment of Bayonne, and repulse of the sortie. Employed as military correspondent with the Bavarian army in 1815, and was present with it in its various operations. He has received a medal and one clasp for the battles of Vittoria and the Nive.

27 Lieut.-General Huskisson served in the field, in India, under Lord Lake, and subsequently at the siege of Ryghur, and at the capture of several towns and forts. In October 1818, commanded at Candeish, at the taking of Behauderpore and Amulneir.

28 Lieut.-General Monckton served in Ireland during the Rebellion in 1798.

30 Lieut.-General S. Brown served in Egypt in 1801, as an Assistant-Quarter-Master-General. In January 1808, he was sent on a secret service under the orders of the Secretary of State, and appointed Deputy-Quarter-Master-General to the forces under General Spencer. In June 1808, he was employed on a secret service in Portugal, and was present as a volunteer at the battle of Roleia.

31 Lieut.-General Herbert served on the Continent with the army under Lord Moira and the Duke of York. Engaged during the Carib war in St. Vincent's; at Port-au-Prince, in St. Domingo; and at Fort Irois during the three months' siege. Served also at the siege of Copenhagen, 1807.

32 Lieut.-General Armstrong went out to Flanders with Lord Moira, in 1794; joined the Duke of York at Antwerp, and was in that disastrous retreat through Holland in the winter of 1794-95, and embarked at Bremen. Served in Ireland during the Rebellion in 1798, and was Assistant-Adjutant-General of the Centre District under General R. Dundas, until the peace of 1802.

33 Sir George Quentin served in the Peninsula in command of the 10th Hussars, and has received a medal and one clasp for the battles of Orthes and Toulouse. Served also the campaign of 1815, and was severely wounded at Waterloo.

34 Lieut.-General Gordon served at the siege of Pondicherry, battle of Argaum, sieges of Asseerghur, Gawilghur, and various other hill forts. Served also at Walcheren in 1809.

36 Lieut.-General Yates served in Egypt in 1801, and has received the Egyptian medal.

37 Lieut.-General Crawford served in Holland in 1794 and 95, and was present at Tiel when bombarded by the French; at Nimeguen during the siege and at the sortie; at the attack of Fort St. André, the attack on the enemy's works at Thuyl, the several engagements in and near Geldermansel; and on the retreat, his guns, which were in rear of the Army, were constantly engaged. In 1798 he was actively employed in Ireland during the rebellion.

38 Lieut.-General Hamerton served on the Continent under the Duke of York, in 1794. Embarked for the West Indies in 1795, and was at the capture of St Lucia the following year. Served in Egypt in 1801. Commanded the 1st battalion of the 44th regt. in Spain; and the 2nd battalion in the campaign of 1815, and was wounded at the battle of Waterloo.

39 Sir Love Jones Parry served in the last American war; commanded a frontier brigade in Upper Canada, and was wounded and had a horse shot under him at the battle of Lundy's Lane.

42 Sir Charles Thornton accompanied the Guards to Holland, in March 1793, under the Duke of York, and was present at the battle of Famars (wounded), siege of Valenciennes, retreat from Dunkirk, taking of Lannoy, where he lost his right arm by a cannon-shot.

43 Sir Frederick Trench served in Sicily in 1806 and 7; at Walcheren, in 1809; in the Peninsula, in 1811; and in Holland, in 1814.

46 Major-General Bradshaw was actively employed in St. Domingo in 1793, 94, and 95, and commanded at St. Maries and Tiburon, when those posts were attacked by the enemy. Served in Ireland during the rebellion, in 1798; with the expedition to the Ferrol, in 1800; and the Egyptian campaign of 1801, including the actions of the 8th, 13th, and 21st March. Medal for services in Egypt.

47 Viscount de Chabot served in Holland, in 1799; in Spain, under Sir John Moore; with the expedition to Walcheren, 1809; and subsequently in the Peninsula, until 1810.

48 Sir Patrick Ross served nine years in India as Captain of the 25th, afterwards the 22nd Light Dragoons, in the Mysore campaign under Lord Harris, in 1799, including the battle of Mallavelly, and siege of Seringapatam; with the division under Sir Arthur Wellesley, in the campaign of 1801, against the Mahratta Chief Dhoondiah; and from 1802 to 1804, in the Mahratta country, and at the reduction of the ceded provinces. He returned from India in 1805, soon after which he was appointed Major; and, in 1807, Lieut.-Colonel of the 23rd Light Dragoons. Having exchanged to Infantry, he joined the 2nd battalion of the 48th regt. in Portugal, in 1810, and as the senior officer held the command of General (the late Lord) Hill's brigade until compelled by severe illness to return to England. On his recovery, he was placed as Assistant-Adjutant-General on the Home Staff, on which he continued till the Peace of 1814. In 1816, he was appointed to the 75th regt., joined it in the Ionian Islands, and remained in command of that corps, and of the Island of Santa Maura and Zante until 1821, when he was promoted to the rank of Major-General. In 1824 he was appointed to the Staff of the Ionian Islands, from which he was advanced to the Government of Antigua, Montserrat, and Barbuda, in the following year.

49 Major-General Palmer served in the Peninsula with the 10th Hussars.

50 Major-General Wm. Stewart served in the Peninsula, and has received a medal for the battle of Albuhera.

51 Sir Henry W. Rooke embarked with the 3rd Guards for Holland, in Aug. 1799, and was present in the actions of the 27th Aug., 10th and 19th Sept., 2nd and 6th October. Embarked again for Holland, Nov. 1813, in command of the 2nd battalion of that regt., and was present at the advance to Antwerp, bombardment of the French fleet at Antwerp, and attack on Bergen-op-Zoom. Also the campaign of 1815, including the battles of Quatre Bras and Waterloo.

52 Sir John Geo. Woodford served as Deputy-Assistant-Adjutant-General on the Expedition to Stralsund, and afterwards to Copenhagen, in 1807; and as Deputy-Assistant-Quarter-Master-General on the Expedition under Sir David Baird, which joined Sir John Moore's army in Galicia, and was present at the battle of Corunna. Served afterwards in the Peninsula as an Assistant-Quarter-Master-General, and has received a cross for the battles of Nivelle, Nive, Orthes, and Toulouse. Also the campaign of 1815, including the battle of Waterloo, and the taking of Cambray.

53 Major-General Darley served at the siege of Port-au-Prince, in St. Domingo, in 1794; subsequently at the siege of Morne-Fortunée, in St. Lucia; in Egypt, in 1807. Commanded 300 men on an expedition in a joint attack with H. M. frigates the *Imperieuse* and *Thames*, and

in co-operation with a party of seamen, ascending the heights of Palinura in Calabria, against a strongly-posted enemy three times the strength of the assailants: drove them off the ground, and maintained the post for three days. Served afterwards in the Peninsula from August 1813 to the end of that war in 1814, including the battle of the Nivelle, and the actions before Bayonne, on the 9th, 10th, and 11th Dec. 1813.

54 Major-General Mahon served in Ireland in the rebellion of 1798. He served also twenty years in the West Indies, and was present at the capture of Surinam, and also of Guadaloupe in 1810.

56 Major-General James Hay served in the Peninsula, France, and Flanders, with the 16th Light Dragoons, and was severely wounded at Waterloo. Medal and a clasp for the battles of Vittoria and the Nive.

57 Major-General Wood, after serving six years in the West Indies, accompanied the expedition to Hanover in 1805. He next served the campaign of 1808-9, including the battle of Corunna. Subsequently at the siege of Flushing, he volunteered to storm the enemy's entrenchments, which he carried; and in November he was again sent to Walcheren to cover the embarkation of the troops when the island was evacuated. In 1810 he proceeded to the Mediterranean, where he served three years, and on being promoted, in 1813, to the Lieut.-Colonelcy of the 85th, he joined the army in Spain. In 1814 he accompanied the 85th to America, and commanded it at the battle of Bladensburg, where he received four severe wounds, had a horse shot under him, and was obliged to surrender himself as a prisoner of war.

60 Major-General Charles Turner, served in Portugal as Captain of the 26th Light Dragoons from December 1799 to December 1800. Embarked from Lisbon to join the expedition under Sir Ralph Abercromby; proceeded to Malta and Marmorice Bay, was appointed Brigade-Major of the Cavalry; landed with the Cavalry on the 8th March in Egypt; was in the advance with the army on the 11th, 12th, and general action of the 13th; was made prisoner in a skirmish with the French cavalry near Lake Mareotis, on the 18th March; confined in Fort Pharos, Alexandria, till released by the capitulation of that city in September 1801. In October 1803 appointed Aide-de-camp to Lieut.-General Floyd, second in command in Ireland. In March 1806 appointed Assistant Adjutant-General. In January 1808, having exchanged as Major 23rd Light Dragoons to the 13th regiment, accompanied that corps to Bermuda, thence in December embarked for Barbadoes, and sailed with the expedition against Martinique, was present at the landing actions and capture of that island in 1809. Medal for services in Egypt. In March 1812 was re-appointed Assistant Adjutant-General in Ireland, which appointment he held till he was promoted to the rank of Major-General; and in March 1844 was appointed to the command of the Cork District.

61 Major-General Loftus served with the 2nd battalion of the 38th during the time it was employed in the Peninsula, and was present at the battle of Busaco, retreat to the lines of Torres Vedras, advance in pursuit of Massena, storming of Badajoz—commanded the detachment of the 5th division which took possession of the Tête-de-Pont, St. Christonal, and the other Forts on the right bank of the Guadiana, and to which General Phillipon surrendered;—battle of Salamanca, capture of Madrid,—commanded the light troops of the 5th division upon the advance to Burgos, retreat from thence, action at Villa Muriel, and other minor affairs.

62 Major-General Burrell served at the capture of Guadaloupe in 1810; and the campaign of 1814 in Upper Canada. Served also in China, and commanded the land force at the first capture of Chusan, and a brigade at the attack upon Canton.

63 Major-General Aylmer served at the Helder in 1799, including the action of the 18th Sept.; Egyptian campaign of 1801; campaign of 1808-9 in Spain and Portugal, including the battles of Roleia, Vimiera, and Corunna. Subsequently with the expedition to Walcheren.

64 Major-General Riddell served as Deputy-Assistant-Quarter-Master-General at the capture of Copenhagen in 1807; and as Assistant-Quarter-Master-General on the eastern coast of Spain and at Genoa, with the army under Lord William Bentinck.

65 Major-General Vernon served the campaign of 1808-9 in the Peninsula, as a Deputy-Assistant-Adjutant-General. Subsequently in the same capacity with the Duke of Wellington's army until June 1811, and was present at the battle of Talavera. Served with the 2nd battalion 66th, at the surprise of a French division at Arroyo de Molino, and other operations, until the capture of Badajoz. With the Queen's at the reduction of the Forts and battle of Salamanca—slightly wounded early in the day, and very severely at the close of the action, a ball having entered his breast and lodged near the heart, after tearing along two ribs. Followed the army again at the expiration of three weeks, and resumed the command of his regiment, with which he served in the various operations preceding, during, and subsequent to the siege of Burgos. Medal for Salamanca.

68 Sir Dudley Hill accompanied the 95th (Rifle Brigade) to South America, in 1806; volunteered the Forlorn Hope at Monte Video, and led the storming party that scaled the walls of the batteries at the south end of the fortress; present also at the battle of Colonia, and at the attack on Buenos Ayres, where he was wounded in the thigh and taken prisoner. Served afterwards the campaign of 1808-9, including the battle of Roleia (wounded in the leg), action at Benevente, and retreat to Corunna. Returned to Portugal in the Rifle Brigade in 1809,

and was present at the battle of Talavera, action of the Coa, and all the different actions the Rifles were engaged in, until appointed major in the Lusitanian Legion previous to the battle of Busaco, at which he commanded a wing of the regiment and was wounded. Commanded half the regiment and the British Light Companies at the battle of Fuentes d'Onor; the 8th Caçadores at the storming of Badajoz, and, unassisted, took the strong fort of Pardaleras early on the night of the assault. Commanded the same battalion at the battle of Salamanca, and was twice severely wounded — in the breast and through the left arm. Assisted with his battalion at the siege of Burgos, and during the retreat defended the passage over the Carrion, where more than half of the battalion were killed, and was himself wounded and taken prisoner, but was afterwards retaken. Commanded the battalion at the battle of Vittoria, and during the entire siege of San Sebastian: at the storming of this fortress he headed the attack of the 5th Division, and was twice wounded. Also commanded the regiment at the investment of Bayonne and repulse of the sortie. Sir Dudley has received a cross and one clasp.

74 Major-General Hare-Clarges served the following campaigns: in Egypt under Sir Ralph Abercromby in Hanover under Lord Cathcart; and in Spain under Sir John Moore, including the retreat to Corunna. Was on the Staff of Sir T. Graham in the Walcheren expedition, and Assistant-Adjutant-General of a Division in the Duke of Wellington's army in the Peninsula. Major-General Clarges has received a medal and one clasp for the battles of Nivelle and Nive.

75 Major-General Thomson served as an Assistant-engineer at San Sebastian, and has received a medal.

77 Major-General Duffy served in the campaign of 1796 in the West Indies under Sir Ralph Abercromby; on an expedition to the coast of Holland in the winter of 1796; in the East Indies in 1799; and with the force under Sir David Baird from thence to Egypt in 1801 (medal); at the siege and capture of Copenhagen and battle of Kioge, in 1807; the campaign of 1808-9 in Spain under Sir John Moore, in the Light Brigade; in the Peninsula with the 43rd Light Infantry, from 1809 to the end of 1813, including the actions of Condeixa, Pombal, Redinha, and Sabugal; battle of Fuentes d'Onor, siege of Ciudad Rodrigo—commanded the assaulting party at the capture of Fort Reynard, an outwork of Ciudad Rodrigo. Siege and assault of Badajoz (medal), battle of Vittoria (wounded in the head), several skirmishes in the Pyrenees and on the Bidassoa, action of the heights of Vera, battles of the Nivelle and Nive.

78 Major-General Daubeney served at the taking of the Cape of Good Hope and capture of the Dutch fleet at Saldanha Bay, in 1796; subsequently for upwards of fourteen years in the East Indies, including the campaign of 1801-2 against the Mahratta chieftains, and commanded the Grenadiers of his regt. (the 84th), at the assault and capture of Kurree; also in the Guzerate in 1802, 3, and 4, at the reduction of other forts by Sir John Murray's army. Proceeded to Walcheren in 1809, and was present at the siege and surrender of Flushing.

79 Major-General Mercer accompanied the 3rd Guards on the expedition to Hanover in 1805; and on that to Walcheren in 1809. Served in the Peninsula from March 1810 to May 1811, and again from July 1811 to March 1814, including the affair at Sobral—wounded whilst acting as Aide-de-camp to Sir Brent Spencer; battle of Barrosa—wounded when Aide-de-camp to Br.-General Dilkes; siege of Ciudad Rodrigo, battle of Salamanca, capture of Madrid, siege of Burgos, passage of the Bidassoa, and battle of the Nive. Served also the campaign of 1815, including the battles of Quatre Bras and Waterloo, and capture of Paris.

80 Major-General Milman was appointed Aide-de-camp to Major-General Catlin Cranfurd, in 1808, and was present at the battles of Roleia and Vimiera; on the same General's Staff in the retreat of Sir John Moore, and was engaged on the heights of Lugo, and at the battle of Corunna. He subsequently joined his regiment, the Coldstream Guards, at Lisbon, and was with them at the passage of the Douro and capture of Oporto, as also at the battle of Talavera, where he was most severely wounded, and saved from being burnt on the field of battle by a private soldier of the Guards. He was made prisoner in the Hospital of Talavera, and detained in France until 1814. Major-General Milman was latterly in command of the Coldstream Gds.

81 Major-General Reeve served with the Grenadier Guards in Sicily in 1806-7; Sir John Moore's campaign in 1808-9, and was present at the battle of Corunna. With the expedition to Walcheren in 1809. Went to Cadiz in 1811, and remained in the Peninsula until the beginning of 1814; present at the passage of the Bidassoa, battles of the Nivelle and Nive. Served also the campaign of 1815, including the battles of Quatre Bras and Waterloo, storming of Peronne and capture of Paris. Remained with the Army of Occupation until its return to England in 1818.

82 Major-General Tonson served at the capture of Martinique in 1794; and was wounded and taken prisoner at St. Vincent's the following year. Actively employed in Ireland during the Rebellion in 1798; in Holland in 1799; and at Walcheren in 1809. Served in the Peninsula from July 1813, including the battle of the Nive, for which he has received a medal.

83 Major-General Gordon served in Holland in 1799; at Walcheren in 1809; and in the Peninsula from 1810 to the end of that war in 1814, including the battle of Fuentes d'Onor, action at Arroyo de Molino, battle of Vittoria—severely wounded in the left arm. Commanded a light battalion in the actions of the Pyrenees, battles of the Nive and St. Pierre (wounded and horse killed under him), actions of Hasparen and Hellette—wounded in the right foot in forcing the enemy's lines at Hasparen, 14th Feb. 1814. Medal for the Nive.

84 Major-General Kenah served in Holland in 1799, and was present in the action of the

19th of Sept. as well as in several other minor affairs. In Egypt, under Sir Ralph Abercromby in 1801; in Sicily from 1808 to 1812; subsequently on the eastern coast of Spain, as Assistant, and afterwards as Deputy-Adjutant-General at the Head of the Department, and was present at the battle of Castalla, as also several other affairs. Served also at the siege and capture of Genoa, in April 1814.

85 Sir Adolphus John Dalrymple served as Aide-de-camp to Sir James Craig in the Eastern District, Malta, Naples, and Sicily, from July 1803 to May 1806, and as Military Secretary to Sir Hew Dalrymple in Portugal in 1808.

86 Major-General Wynyard served with the army in Sicily from 1808 to March 1810, when he was severely wounded at the attack on Santa Maura, for which he subsequently obtained the Brevet rank of Major; he was also present and on the staff with the force that occupied Ischia and Procida.

87 Major-General Fergusson served the campaign of 1808-9, including the battles of Vimiera and Corunna. Expedition to Walcheren in 1809. Peninsular campaigns from March 1810 to the end of that war in 1814, including the passage of the Coa, near Almeida, battle of Busaco, actions at Pombal, Redinha, Miranda de Corvo, Foz d'Arouce, and Sabugal; battle of Fuentes d'Onor, sieges and assaults of Ciudad Rodrigo and Badajoz, battle of Salamanca, action of San Munos, passage of the Bidassoa, battle of the Nivelle, battles of the Nive on the 9th, 10th, 11th, 12th, and 13th Dec. 1813; and investment of Bayonne. Major-General Fergusson has received five wounds, viz., at Vimiera, slightly; at the storming of Ciudad Rodrigo, severely in the body and slightly in the foot; at Badajoz, slightly in the side by a splinter of a shell in the trenches, and in the head at the assault. Medal for Badajoz.

88 Major-General Brotherton served in the Peninsula, and was wounded at the battle of Salamanca.

89 Sir James Reynett served with the 52nd on the expedition against Ferrol in 1800, and was present at the action before that place. Appointed to the Quarter-Master-General's staff upon the army entering Spain in Nov. 1808; present at Lugo, the affairs upon the retreat to Corunna, and also at the battle of Corunna. Re-appointed to the Quarter-Master-General's staff in Portugal, in April 1809; present at the affairs previous to and at the passage of the Douro, and capture of Oporto; affair of Salamonde, battles of Talavera and Busaco, affairs upon the retreat to the lines before Lisbon, and subsequently in 1811 at those upon the advance from thence, at Pombal, Redinha, Sabugal, and Foz d'Arouce; also at the battle of Fuentes d'Onor.

90 Major-General Smelt served in the American war, and was present at the taking of Plattsburg, storm and capture of Oswego, action of Lundy's Lane, storming of Fort Erie, 13th August 1814, where he was severely and dangerously wounded. Served also during the Burmese war, in 1824, 25, and part of 1826, and was present at the capture of Rangoon, and other actions in Ava.

91 Major-General Bell served in Sicily, in 1806 and 7; in the Peninsula and France, from July 1808 to Feb. 1809, and again from May 1809 to July 1814, including the battle of Vimiera, action at the bridge of Almeida, battle of Busaco, all the actions during the retreat of the French from Portugal, siege and storming of Ciudad Rodrigo, siege and storming of Badajoz, action at the heights of Castrillos, battle of Salamanca, action of Sabijana de Morillos, battles of Vittoria, the Pyrenees, Nivelle, Orthes, and Toulouse. Served afterwards with the army employed against Louisiana, from Dec. 1814 to June 1815. He has received a cross for the battles of the Pyrenees, Nivelle, Orthes, and Toulouse.

92 Major-General Auchmuty served several years in the West Indies, and was present at the storming of Morne Fortuné, St. Lucia. In 1809 he accompanied the second battalion Royal Fusiliers to Portugal, and was present at Oporto and Talavera as Major of Brigade to Sir Alex. Campbell; and at the battle of Busaco, the retreat of the Army to and subsequent advance from the lines of Torres Vedras, and battle of Fuentes d'Onor, as Deputy Assistant Adjutant General to the Sixth Division. On return to the Peninsula from sick leave he was appointed extra Aide-de-camp to Sir Lowry Cole, and was in action with the Fourth Division at Vittoria and the Pyrenees,—at the latter was promoted to the Brevet rank of Major. Succeeding soon afterwards to the Regimental Majority, he commanded the light companies of Major General Ross's brigade, and served with them at Orthes and Toulouse,—at the latter, was promoted Brevet Lt.-Colonel. He has received a medal and a clasp for the battles of Orthes and Toulouse.

93 Major-General Lightfoot served in Holland in 1799. Accompanied the 45th to the Peninsula in 1808, and was present at the battles of Roleia, Vimiera, Talavera, and Busaco; [illegible]ions of Pombal, Redinha, Condeixa, and Sabugal; battle of Fuentes d'Onor, siege of Badajoz, in 1811; siege and assault of Ciudad Rodrigo, siege and assault of Badajoz (slightly wounded); storming of Fort Picurina (slightly wounded), battles of Salamanca, Vittoria, and the Pyrenees; attack on the lines at St. Jean de Luz, affair at Bastide, and the battles of Orthes and Toulouse (severely wounded). Medal and two clasps for Vittoria, Pyrenees, and Toulouse.

94 Major-General Faunce served in Holland, in 1799, including the actions of the 2nd and 6th October. With the army in Hanover, in 1805-6; siege and capture of Copenhagen, in 1807; with the army under Sir John Moore, first at Gottenburgh, and afterwards throughout the operations in Portugal and Spain, in 1808-9; with the army in the Scheldt, in 1809; in the

Peninsula from Nov. 1810 to Feb. 1813, including the storm and capture of Badajoz (wounded in the thigh), and battle of Salamanca; also at the investment of Bayonne, in 1814. Served also in the American war, including the battle of Bladensburg and capture of Washington, action near Baltimore, and operations before New Orleans in 1814 and 15; severely wounded 8th Jan. 1815. Medal for Salamanca.

95 Major-General Brown served at the siege and capture of Copenhagen, in 1807; in the Peninsula from Aug. 1808 to July 1811; and again from July 1813 to May 1814, including the battle of Vimiera, passage of the Douro and capture of Oporto, with the previous and subsequent actions; battle of Talavera (severely wounded through both thighs), action of the Light Division at the bridge of Almeida, battle of Busaco, the different actions during the retreat of the French army from Portugal, action at Sabugal, battle of Fuentes d'Onor, siege of San Sebastian, battles of the Nivelle and Nive, and the investment of Bayonne. Served afterwards in the American war, and was present at the battle of Bladensburg and capture of Washington. Slightly wounded in the head and very severely in the groin at Bladensburg.

96 Major-General Wingrove served at the taking of the Cape of Good Hope, in 1795; at the battle of Trafalgar; the taking of Genoa, in 1814; on board the *Boyne*, when that ship singly engaged three French ships of the line and three frigates off Toulon, in 1814; and on board the *Hercules* in a single action off Cape Nichola Mole.

97 Major-General Aitchison served in 1807 at the siege and capture of Copenhagen. Embarked in 1808 for the Peninsula, and in 1809 was present at the passage of the Douro, capture of Oporto, and subsequent pursuit of Soult's army to Salamonde. He was wounded in the arm at the battle of Talavera, while carrying the King's colour, which was also shot through. He served the campaigns of 1810, 12, 13, and 14, and was present at the battle of Busaco, and retreat to the lines of Torres Vedras; battle of Salamanca, capture of Madrid, siege of Burgos, and retreat from thence into Portugal; affair at Osma, battle of Vittoria, affair at Tolosa, siege of San Sebastian, battles of the Nivelle and the Nive, passage of the Adour, investment of Bayonne, siege of the citadel, and repulse of the sortie. He was Lieut.-Colonel of the Scots Fusilier Guards when promoted to Major-General, and had commanded that regiment upwards of four years.

98 Major-General Conyers served three years and a half in the West Indies, and was engaged on several occasions, particularly in the Mirebalois, at L'Ance à Veau, and at the siege of Irois in St. Domingo in 1798, where he was wounded while on the staff: during this siege, of three months' duration, the garrison lost more men than composed its original strength: commanded the remains of the 82nd at the evacuation of this island. Served in an expedition to the coast of France in 1800, and subsequently in the Mediterranean until 1802. From 1805 to 1809 he served throughout the Mediterranean, and in Egypt on the staff, and received a severe contusion there, having been at the attack on Alexandria, at the storming of Rosetta, and at the subsequent siege of that place. Served in the Peninsula and France in 1813 and 14, and in command of the 82nd during the operations on the Gave d'Oleron, at Hastingues and Oyer le Gave, and was severely wounded at the head of the regiment at Orthes, for which battle he has received a medal.

99 Major-General Henderson served in Ireland during the Rebellion, in 1798; at the Helder, in 1799; and was present at the first landing, and battles of the 19th Sept., 2nd and 6th Oct. Expedition to Egypt under Sir Ralph Abercromby, in 1801. Landed in Portugal in 1808, and was present at the battle of Vimiera, retreat to, and battle of Corunna. Expedition to the Scheldt and siege of Flushing in 1809. Served afterwards in the Peninsula from 1811 to the end of that war in 1814, and commanded the Queen's at the battle of Toulouse.

100 Major-General Parke was present with the 39th at the original capture of Demerara, Essequibo, and Berbice, in the spring of 1796, when the expedition commanded by General White captured those colonies. He was in Sir James Kempt's Light Infantry Battalion during the campaign in Naples in 1805-6. Served afterwards in the Peninsula with the 39th from May 1809 to Feb. 1812, and was present at the battles of Albuhera and Busaco, at the raising the siege of Campo Mayor when the French sustained a considerable defeat; commanded the four light companies of the brigade at the action of Arroyo de Molino, where the guns, baggage, and fourteen hundred men with their officers were captured; he was also employed in the trenches at the first siege of Badajoz.

101 Major-General Macpherson accompanied part of the 88th to the West Indies, the latter part of 1795, and was present at the taking of St. Lucia, in 1796; also at the reduction of the Brigands in Grenada, at the storm of Port Royal, and several other places in that island. Embarked with the regiment for the East Indies, in June 1799, and during a period of six years he was actively employed in the three Presidencies. In 1806 embarked with the expedition to South America; was present in several skirmishes on the march to and in front of Buenos Ayres, and at the storming of it, when he was wounded. In June 1809, he accompanied the 2nd battalion to the Peninsula, and was present at the defence of Cadiz. In March 1813 he succeeded to the command of the 1st battalion; commanded it at the battle of Vittoria, and at those in the Pyrenees. Present also at the battle of the Nivelle; succeeded to the command of the regt. at the battle of Orthes, and again at the battle of Toulouse, besides being in several minor affairs. Proceeded in command of the first battalion to Canada in July 1814; embarked from thence for the Netherlands in June 1815. Medal and one clasp for Vittoria and Orthes.

102 Major-General Hay embarked for the West Indies early in 1796, and served the campaign of that and the following year. In 1797 he was actively employed in the Island of St. Vincent. He served the campaign of 1808-9 in Portugal and Spain under Sir John Moore, in the 18th Hussars, and was present in the cavalry actions of Mayorga and Benevente; and was with the detachment that surprised and captured the enemy's outlying piquet at Rueda—commanded the rear-guard from Astorga—and Batanzas on the retreat terminating with the battle of Corunna. He served also with the Army of Occupation in France until its return to England in 1818.

103 Major-General Allan was present at the capture of the Cape of Good Hope in 1795, and subsequently in 1806, including the battle of Blueberg. Served the whole of the Mysore campaign of 1799, including the battle of Mallavelly, siege and storm of Seringapatam, for which he has received a medal. Engaged in the pursuit and dispersion of the Rebel Dundeah, and all his forces; the reduction and occupation of Tranquebar; and the whole of the southern Polygar war in 1800. Served in the Peninsula from 1810 to the end of the war, and was present at the defence of Cadiz, where he commanded a light battalion and was stationed on the heights of Isla de Leon to observe Marshal Soult's force: he was afterwards present in the actions of Vic Bigorre and Tarbes, and at the battle of Toulouse, for which he has received a Medal.

104 Major-General Money served twenty-five years in the 11th Dragoons:—in Flanders and Holland in 1794 and 95, and in Germany the latter year, including the attack on the French lines, 17th April; their defeat on the heights of Cateau, 26th April, and near Tournay; 3rd May; battles of Roubaix and Lannoy, defeat of the French near Tournay, 22nd May 1794; and affair at Bommel, 2nd Jan. 1795. Campaign of 1799 in Holland, including the actions of the 10th and 19th Sept., 2nd and 6th October. Commanded a detachment of the regt. under Sir Ralph Abercromby, at Leghorn, Minorca, and the expedition to Cadiz, in 1800; in Egypt, in 1801, including the actions of the 8th, 13th, and 21st March, together with the capture of Grand Cairo and Alexandria. Peninsular campaigns of 1811 and 12; present at the siege of Badajos, battle of Salamanca, and affair of cavalry near the Tormes on the following day, when three French battalions were taken; cavalry affairs of Callada Camino and Venta de Poso. Served also the campaign of 1815, including the battles of Quatre Bras and Waterloo, towards the close of which last the command of the 11th Dragoons devolved on him. Present also at the capture of Paris. Medal for services in Egypt.

105 Major-General Forbes served in Holland in 1794 and 95, including the sortie from Nimeguen against the French lines, action in driving the French across the Waal at Bommel, and at Geldermansel. Accompanied the 78th to Quiberon Bay, and was at the taking of Isle Dieu, in 1795; to the Cape of Good Hope, in 1796, and capture of the Dutch fleet in Saldanha Bay. Proceeded with the regiment to India in November following, and served with it during the campaign in Oude, in 1798 and 99; also in part of the Mahratta campaign in 1803, including the storming of the Petah of Ahmednughur, and during the siege of the Fort. Present in every action in which his regiment was engaged in Java during 1811, 12, and 13, including the forcing of the enemy's position at Weltevreden, storm of the lines of Cornelis, the heights of Serandole, and Djocjocarta. Quelled an insurrection which broke out in the east-end of Java in May 1813, when Lieut.-Colonel Fraser and Captain Macpherson of the 78th were murdered by the insurgents. Medal for services in Java, and five times thanked in general orders.

106 Major-General Ewart, as captain in the 52nd Light Infantry, accompanied the Expedition to Copenhagen in 1807, and was present at the action near Keog. Served in the Peninsula in 1808 and 9 under Sir John Moore, and was wounded at Vimiera. Accompanied Expedition to the Scheldt. Served with the Light Division in the Peninsula from March 1811 to December 1812, including the battles of Fuentes d'Onor and Salamanca; the sieges of Ciudad Rodrigo and Badajoz (wounded when in command of a detachment carrying ladders for the storming of Fort Picurina); and the actions of Sabugal and San Munos. Served in the West Indies with the Royal York Rangers and the York Chasseurs from 1813 to 1816 inclusive, and was at the capture of Guadaloupe. Served in the East Indies in command of the 67th regt., from March 1819 to Feb. 1823, and was employed as a Brigadier at the siege of Asseerghur.

107 Major-General Proctor served with the 82nd on the expedition to Walcheren, in 1809, and was present at the siege of Flushing. Served also at Gibraltar, Tarifa, and in the Peninsula, from 1810 to Dec. 1812, and subsequently in the Peninsula and south of France, from April to July 1814, including the affair of Posts near Malaga, battle of Barrosa (contusion on the body), and retreat from Madrid. Embarked from Bourdeaux for Canada in July 1814, and commanded the 82nd before Fort Erie from 2nd Sept., and throughout the successive operations of the campaign on the Niagara frontier. Received the Brevet promotion of Lieut.-Colonel for his conduct in the repelling of the attack made by the Americans on our batteries and position before Fort Erie on the 17th Sept. 1814.

108 Major-General Jervois accompanied the 89th on the expedition to Hanover in 1805. In 1810 he was appointed to the staff of Lord Blayney; accompanied him on the expedition to Malaga, and was slightly wounded in the attack on the Fortress of Frangerola. In 1813 he was appointed to the staff of Sir Gordon Drummond, and embarked with him for Canada, where during the operations of that and the following year, he was present in almost every action fought with the American Army either in that Province or on the Frontier, including the storming of Fort Niagara, Lewistown, the attacks on Black Rock and Buffalo, operations against

the forts and batteries of Oswego, and action of Lundy's Lane. He received the brevet rank of Major for Buffalo, and that of Lieut.-Colonel for Lundy's Lane.

109 Major-General Riddall was actively employed with the 62nd, in Sicily, Egypt, Calabria, Italy, Spain, and North America, from 1806 to the end of the war. Detached with his Grenadier company to retard the advance of the French on their march to invest Scylla Castle in Calabria, and invade Sicily. Served in the Grenadier battalion at the Faro, in Sicily, for several weeks, under the fire of the French batteries erected in Calabria. Second in command to General Blommart in a Grenadier Battalion sent from Sicily to Spain. He was advanced with his Grenadier Company and two field-pieces, in the attack on, and expulsion of, the French from the heights before Genoa. Second in command to Lieut.-Col. John with the flank company detachments up the Penobscot river in North America, and commanded the advance in forming a position at Hampden defended by treble our numbers.

110 Major-General Addison served in the American war, on the staff of Sir John Sherbrooke.

111 Sir Francis Cockburn served in South America in 1807; in the Peninsula in 1809 and 1810; and in Canada from 1811 to 1814.

112 Major-General Slessor served in Ireland during the Rebellion of 1798, and was engaged at Antrim, and subsequently against the French force under General Humbert (wounded in the head). In 1806 he accompanied the 35th to Sicily; and was on several expeditions in Calabria, at the battle of Scylla, and with gun-boats. In 1807 he served the campaign in Egypt, and was wounded in the leg on the retreat from Rosetta to Alexandria. His next service was with Sir John Oswald's expedition against the Greek Islands; subsequently to which he was employed in constant desultory service in the Mediterranean, and was also with the English corps attached to the Austrian Army under Count Nugent,—for the latter service he received a gold Medal from the Emperor of Austria. He served also the campaign of 1815 under the Duke of Wellington.

114 Major-General Charretie served three years in the East Indies, and was present at the mutiny at Vellore in 1806, when nearly the whole of the 69th were massacred in their barracks. In the Peninsula with the 2nd Life Guards, from 1812 to the end of that war in 1814, including the battles of Vittoria, Pampeluna, and Toulouse.

115 Major-General Patrick Campbell (R. Artillery) was at the capture of St. Lucia in 1796, and subsequently in the Carib war in St. Vincent. Served also in the Peninsula from Jan. 1809 to the end of that war in 1814, including the battles of Talavera and Castalla.

116 Major-General Parkinson served at the capture of the Island of Bourbon in 1810, as Deputy-Adjutant-General. Proceeded with the 33rd to Stralsund in Pomerania in 1813; and from thence to Holland in 1814; was present at the attack on Merxem and bombardment of Antwerp, and commanded the regt. at the storming of Bergen-op-Zoom, where he received a severe contusion. Served also the campaign of 1815, and was severely wounded at Quatre Bras.

117 Major-General Hunter Blair accompanied the Duke of Wellington's expedition to Portugal in July 1808 as a Major of Brigade, and was present with Catlin Craufurd's brigade at the affair of Obidos, and the battles of Roleia and Vimiera. He was appointed Aide-de-Camp to Sir Hew Dalrymple on that General assuming the command in Portugal; but on the army advancing into Spain, he became Aide-de-camp to the Earl of Hopetoun, and was present at the affair of Lugo and battle of Corunna. In April 1809, he re-embarked for Portugal, as a Major of Brigade, with the corps under Lord Hill; and was present with Sir Alan Cameron's brigade at the capture of Oporto, affair of Salamonde, and battle of Talavera, where he was severely wounded; and being taken prisoner in hospital, he was not liberated until the end of that war in 1814, when he obtained the rank of Major, antedated to the 30th May 1811. In December 1814 he sailed, as Major of Brigade, with the force destined for New Orleans; but, this corps being recalled, he was transferred to the staff in Flanders, and appointed to the Light Brigade under Sir Frederick Adam, and was severely wounded at Waterloo; for which battle he received the rank of Lieut.-Colonel, and was also appointed Assistant-Adjutant-General to Sir Thomas Brisbane's division. On the formation of the Army of Occupation, however, he was nominated Major-de-Place, with duty of commandant of Valenciennes. In May 1819 he accompanied Sir Charles Colville to Bombay as Military Secretary; but his regiment (the 87th) being ordered on service in Sept. 1825, he resigned the staff, and joined it in Ava, where he was appointed a Brigadier; and he commanded a brigade at the capture of Melloon.

118 Major-General Lluellyn served in the 52nd at Ferrol, Cadiz, and in the Mediterranean, in 1800 and 1801. Having obtained a company by purchase in the 28th regt., he accompanied it to the Peninsula in 1809, and, with the exception of one year's absence in England, occasioned by ill-health, he was actively employed with it in the various duties that fell to its share in the campaigns in which it bore such a conspicuous part. Besides many services of minor importance, he was present with his regiment at the battle of Busaco, defence of the Lines of Lisbon, advance on Campo Mayor, siege of Badajoz, battle of Albuhera, capture of a French corps at Arroyo de Molino, attack and capture of the Forts and Bridge of Almaraz, advance on Aranjuez and Madrid, occupation of Bourdeaux. In 1815 he embarked with his regiment for the Netherlands, where he was personally engaged with it in the battles of Quatre Bras and Waterloo, in the latter of which he was severely wounded, and received for his conduct in the field the brevet rank of Lt.-Colonel and the Companionship of the Bath.

119 Major-General Lautour served in the Peninsula with the 11th Dragoons in 1811 and 12;

he attacked, with a squadron, on the 26th Sept. 1811, near El Bodon, a French Cavalry Regt. which had captured part of the baggage of the Light Division, and covered the retreat of the 74th, and five companies of the 60th, from Ciudad Rodrigo. Present also at the siege of Badajoz and battle of Salamanca. Whilst in command of a squadron he attacked, and took prisoners, a company of French Artillery posted in a vineyard, near Valladolid, supporting the enemy's cavalry on 7th Sept. 1812, during the time the Army was crossing the Douro; he also repulsed an attack of the enemy's piquets, making one officer and many men prisoners, at Monasterio and in front of Burgos on 2nd Oct. 1812; and he was continually on outpost duty, and almost daily engaged with the enemy's skirmishers, and was slightly wounded in the retreat from Burgos by the bursting of a shell. Served the campaign of 1815, with the 23rd Light Dragoons, and was present in the actions of the 16th and 17th June, and at the battle of Waterloo, where he succeeded to the command of the regiment and of the brigade.

120 Major General Egerton, after serving as a subaltern with the 29th in North America, and proceeding as a Captain with the 89th to South America, accompanied the 2nd battalion of the 34th to the Peninsula in 1809. In the following year he was appointed to the staff as Deputy-Assistant-Adjutant-General, and attached to the second division, in which capacity he served at the battle of Busaco, and on the retreat to, and during the subsequent occupation of, the Lines before Lisbon. He was then removed as senior of the Adjutant-General's department to the fourth division; was present at the siege and capture of Olivença, the first siege of Badajoz, battle of Albuhera (wounded), and action of Aldea de Ponte. Relinquished his staff appointment and rejoined his regiment in the winter of 1811, and continued to serve with it until appointed Aide-de-camp to Sir Rowland Hill in 1812, on whose personal staff he remained until the termination of the war, and was present at the battles of Vittoria, Pyrenees,—for which he obtained the brevet rank of Major,—Nivelle, Nive, Orthes, and Toulouse. On Lord Hill's appointment to a command with the army in Flanders in the spring of 1815, he selected Colonel Egerton as his first Aide-de-camp, who served as such at the battle of Waterloo,—where he obtained the brevet of Lieut.-Colonel,—and continued in the same capacity until the return of the Army of Occupation from France in 1818. When Lord Hill assumed the command of the army in chief in 1828, he was pleased to name Colonel Egerton for the confidential appointment of first Aide-de-camp and private Secretary, which he held during the whole period of his Lordship's continuance at the head of the army.

121 Sir William Chalmers served in Sicily in 1806 and 7; campaigns of 1808-9 in Portugal and Spain; expedition to Walcheren, including bombardment of Flushing; at Cadiz in 1810 and 11; and all the succeeding Peninsular campaigns, including the battle of Barrosa, attack of the enemy on the heights near Moresco, affair of Senhora de la Pena, battle of Salamanca, action of San Munos, battle of Vittoria, attack at Maya, battles of the Pyrenees on the 30th and 31st July, repulse of the enemy in his attack of the heights of St. Antonio, 31st August, attack of the enemy's forts near Sarre, 9th Oct. 1813, battle of Nivelle, besides a great many minor affairs and skirmishes on the advance to Madrid and capture of the Retiro. He was present with the army in the Peninsula during almost all the sieges, and was engaged in the following affairs during the retreat from Burgos, viz, Olmos, Monasterio, bridge of Valladolid, and passage of the Huebra. Served also in the Netherlands in 1814 and 15, including the battle of Waterloo, capture of Paris, and posterior operations in France, to Aug. 1817. He was severely wounded in assault of the entrenchments at Sarre, and has had nine horses killed or wounded under him in action, three of them at Waterloo. During the above campaigns he was on the staff, except at Waterloo. Subsequently to his services in Sir John Moore's campaign and Lord Chatham's expedition, he was, in the course of about four years (from 5th March 1811 to 18th June 1815), in seventeen engagements, six of them general actions—exclusive of sieges; and for his conduct in the field he was twice promoted, viz., to the brevet rank of Major at the battles of the Pyrenees, and of Lieut.-Colonel at the battle of Waterloo, on which occasion he commanded the left wing of the 52nd regt.

122 Major-General Parker served at Walcheren in 1809, and was employed in the operations previous to, and at the siege of, Flushing. Embarked for Lisbon in Feb. 1812, and remained with the Duke of Wellington's army till the conclusion of the war in 1814; was present at the battle of Vittoria, both the sieges of San Sebastian, battle of Orthes, action at Tarbes, and battle of Toulouse. Served also the campaign of 1815, and lost his left leg at the battle of Waterloo. Medal for the battle of Vittoria, where he commanded a brigade of artillery.

123 Major-General Beckwith served in Hanover in 1805-6; at Copenhagen in 1807, including the action at Kioge. On the expedition to Sweden in 1808; and that to Portugal in 1808-9, including the action at Calcavellas on the retreat, and battle of Corunna. Proceeded to Walcheren in 1809; subsequently to the Peninsula, and was present in the actions of Pombal, Redinha, Condeixa, Foz d'Arouce, and Sabugal, battle of Fuentes d'Onor, sieges of Ciudad Rodrigo and Badajos, battle of Salamanca, siege of Burgos, action at San Milan, battles of Vittoria, the Pyrenees, Vera, Nivelle, near Bayonne, Orthes, and Toulouse. Served also the campaign of 1815, including the battles of Quatre Bras and Waterloo. During the great portion of the above service he was employed on the Staff. Medal for Toulouse, and lost left leg at Waterloo.

124 Major-General Bourchier served under Sir Ralph Abercromby in the expedition against Cadiz in 1800, and also in the campaign in Egypt in 1801, and was present at the battles of the

13th and 21st March, and at Rhamania on the 9th May. He served afterwards the campaigns of 1811, 12, and 15, including the siege of Badajoz, battle of Salamanca, cavalry affairs at Callada de Camino and Venta de Poso, battles of Quatre Bras and Waterloo, and capture of Paris.

125 Major-General Grant served five years in India with the 25th—afterwards the 22nd—Dragoons, and was present at the battle of Mallavelly, siege of Seringapatam, action with Doondia, storming the fort of Turnioul, where he volunteered and led the assault with 50 dismounted Dragoons; engaged also in the reduction of various fortresses. Served with the 21st Fusiliers in Sicily in 1806; with the 17th Light Dragoons in India from 1807 to 1811: and with the 18th Hussars in the campaigns of 1813, 14, and 15, including the action at the bridge of Croix d'Orade, battle of Toulouse, covering the retiring army on the 17th of June 1815, and battle of Waterloo.

126 Major-General Taylor served as Assistant-Adjutant-General to the force under Sir James Craig, in the Mediterranean, during 1805 and 6. Employed on the staff at the attack and capture of Java in 1811, including the attack of the outpost near Weltevreden, and the storming of the lines of Cornelis. Served also the campaign of 1815, with the 10th Hussars, and was present at the battle of Waterloo.

127 Major-General Arguimbau served in the Peninsula with the 3rd battalion of the Royals, and lost an arm at San Sebastian. Served also the campaign of 1815, and was slightly wounded at Quatre Bras, and also at Waterloo.

128 Major-General Calvert served with the 52nd on the expedition to Sweden in 1808; in the Peninsula in 1808-9, including the retreat to Corunna; and on the Walcheren expedition. Appointed Aide-de-camp to Lord Lynedoch in April 1810, and joined him at Cadiz, then besieged by the French; present at the battles of Barrosa and Vittoria; also at both the attacks and capture of San Sebastian. Accompanied the 29th to America in 1814, and was present at the taking of Castine, and the different American settlements in the Bay of Fundy. Served also the campaign of 1815 with the 32nd, including the battles of Quatre Bras and Waterloo, and capture of Paris.

129 Major-General Staveley joined the army under the Duke of Wellington at Oporto in May 1809, and was present at the battle of Talavera, actions at Pombal, Redinha, Foz d'Arouce, and Sierra de Moita; battle of Fuentes d'Onor, storming and capture of Ciudad Rodrigo and Badajoz. Deputy-Assistant-Quarter-Master-General at the actions of Osma and Morillas, battle of Vittoria, passage of the Bidassoa, storming the Heights of Vera, action at Sarre, battle of the Nivelle, battles of the 9th, 10th, 11th, and 12th Dec. 1813 near Bayonne, passage of the Adour, storming St. Etienne and investment of the citadel of Bayonne, actions at Vic Bigorre and Tarbes, and battle of Toulouse. Served also the campaign of 1815, including the battle of Waterloo and capture of Paris.

130 Sir De Lacy Evans served in India, in 1807, 8, 9, and 10. Portugal, Spain, and France, in 1812, 13, and 14. America part of 1814-15. Belgium and France in 1815, 16, 17, and 18. In Spain in 1835, 36, and 37. Present during the operations against Ameer Khan and the Pindarries, capture of the Mauritius, part of the retreat from Burgos, action on the Hormaza (wounded), battle of Vittoria, investment of Pampeluna, battle of the Pyrenees, investment of Bayonne (horse shot), actions of Vic Bigorre and Tarbes, battle of Toulouse (horse shot), battle of Bladensburg (two horses shot), capture of Washington, attack on Baltimore, operations before New Orleans (boarding and capture of American Flotilla—action 25th Dec. wounded severely—unsuccessful assault Jan. wounded severely), battle of Quatre Bras, retreat of 17th of June, Waterloo (horse shot and one sabred), investment and capitulation of Paris. Continued on Staff of allied Army of Occupation in France. Accepted under an allied power (1835) command of an auxiliary British and Spanish corps of army by sanction and desire of the English Government, and by order of the King in council. Acted, while so employed, in conjunction with the British forces (under Lord J. Hay), and through mediation of British authorities:—raising investments of San Sebastian and Bilboa, action of Arlaban, capture of port and castle of Passages. Defeated the enemy in general actions on the 5th of May, 6th of June, 1st of Oct. (wounded) 1836; also 10th and 15th of March 1837. Attacked near Hernani, 16th March, by the *elite* of the Carlist army, 16,000 strong (about double the allied force), and obliged to retreat about one mile, but with a less loss in killed and wounded (600) than that of the enemy. Resumed the offensive the following month—capture of Hernani by escalade, 14th May—of Oyarzun 16th May—of Yrun by storm 17th May—of Fontarabia by capitulation 18th May. These and other minor affairs were for the most part severely contested, and cost (including those of the enemy) above ten thousand killed and wounded. Excepting occasionally two or three stragglers, generally without arms, the Legion never lost (under his command) prisoners, artillery, or equipage, though utterly contrary statements repeatedly appeared at the time,—while he took from the enemy 100 officers, 1000 men, thirty pieces of cannon, several entrenched positions, fortified towns and posts, with an extensive and most important strategical tract of the insurgent territory, including their main line of retreat, communication and supply. Thenceforth "The frontier was effectually closed against the entrance of resources to the Carlists, except by the small mountain passes, which are only accessible to foot passengers or mules lightly laden" (British Commissioners' Despatch, Parliamentary Paper)—and thus did this auxiliary corps decisively contribute to the successful termination of the war. He holds the rank of Lieut.-General in the national army of Spain, by license of a British royal warrant,—also,

honoured by her Majesty for these services with the Cross of Commander of the Bath, and by the government of Spain with the grand crosses of St. Ferdinand and Charles III. Received his Company, Majority, and Lt.-Coloneley in the British service for conduct against the enemy.

131 Major-General Scott proceeded to the Peninsula in 1808, and was present with the Scots Fusilier Guards at the Passage of the Douro, capture of Oporto, subsequent retreat of Soult's army, and battle of Talavera, where he was wounded through the body, and being left there in hospital he was made prisoner. He commanded the Scots Fusilier Guards for upwards of three years.

132 Sir Thomas Willshire served with the 38th in the West Indies from August 1797 to August 1800; the campaign of 1808-9, including the battles of Roleia and Vimiera, retreat to, and battle of, Corunna. Accompanied the expedition to Walcheren in 1809. Served afterwards in the Peninsula, from June 1812 to the end of that war in 1814; commanded the light company at the battle of Salamanca (twice wounded), on the retreat from Burgos and action at Villa Muriel, the action of Osma, battle of Vittoria, first assault of San Sebastian, also second assault and capture, when he received the brevet rank of Major. Commanded a brigade of light companies at the passage of Bidassoa, battle of Nivelle, and battles of the Nive on the 9th, 10th, and 11th Dec. 1813, for which services he was in 1815 appointed Brevet Lieut.-Colonel. Repulsed with three hundred men the attack of ten thousand Caffres upon the open village of Graham's Town, on the frontiers of the Cape of Good Hope, on the 22nd April 1819, and commanded during the subsequent operations against the Caffres in the same year. Served afterwards in the East Indies from May 1822 to 1840. Commanded a wing of the 46th at the capture of Kittoor in the Dooab, in Dec. 1824. Served also throughout the whole of the campaign in Affghanistan under Lord Keane; present at the capture of the fortress of Ghuznée, 23rd July 1839, upon which occasion he was appointed *K.C.B.*; and while in command of the Bombay column of the army of the Indus he captured the fortress of Khelat on the 13th Nov. following, for which service he was created a baronet.

133 Major-General the Honourable H. E. Butler served the Egyptian campaign of 1801, with the 2nd battalion of the 27th, including the battles of the 13th and 21st March, and has received the medal. Served also with the Portuguese army in 1810 and 1811, and was wounded at the battle of Busaco.

134 Major-General Fleming served in Calabria in 1806; at the capture of Alexandria, and attack on Rosetta in Egypt in 1807; in the Peninsula during the campaigns of 1808, 9, 10, and 11, and was present, with the advance brigade, at the passage of the Alberche, at the battles of Talavera (27th and 28th July 1809), and Albuhera, at which last he was severely wounded. Served in the West Indies, and with the expedition to the Southern States of America, in 1815. He served afterwards in the East Indies, from 1820 to 1823, and in Canada, from 1829 to 1833.

135 Sir John Rolt served with the 58th in Egypt in 1801, and was shot through the body in the action on the landing. Accompanied the expedition to Naples in 1805, and remained with that army until its arrival in Sicily, Served with the 2nd battalion in the Peninsula the latter part of 1809 and until Feb. 1810, when he was appointed to the Portuguese service; present at the battle of Busaco, covering the operations against Ciudad Rodrigo, and capture of Badajoz. Commanded the 17th Portuguese regiment from April 1812 to the conclusion of the war, including the actions of Berlanza and near Las Casas, battle of Vittoria, actions in the Pyrenees at Santa Barbara, 2nd Aug., and attack of Vera heights 7th Oct., battle of the Nivelle, battle and operations of the Nive on the 9th, 10th, 11th, 12th, and 13th Dec. 1813, battles of Orthes and Toulouse. From the period of landing in the Peninsula in 1809, until the conclusion of hostilities in April 1814, he was never one day absent from his duty. Medal for services in Egypt; and a cross and one clasp for Vittoria, Nivelle, Nive, Orthes, and Toulouse.

136 Major-General Bainbrigge served in the Peninsula in the Quarter-Master-General's department from 1810 to the end of that war in 1814, and was present at the Lines of Torres Vedras, part of the siege of Olivença, siege of Ciudad Rodrigo, last siege of Badajoz, affair of the Guarena, battle of Salamanca, part of the siege of Burgos, affair of Villa Muriel, retreat from Burgos to Ciudad Rodrigo, battles of Vittoria and the Pyrenees, part of the last siege of San Sebastian, battle of the Nive, and actions near Bidart, Bussussary, and Villa Franque; actions of Garris, Tarbes, and Vic Bigorre, and battle of Toulouse.

137 Major-General Napier served with the 52nd at the siege of Copenhagen and battle of Kioge in 1807. Aide-de-camp to Sir John Hope on the expedition to Sweden in 1808; and subsequently in Sir John Moore's campaign in Spain, including the retreat to, and battle of, Corunna. In Sicily with the regiment until the autumn of 1810. Served afterwards in the Peninsula on the staff, including the defence of Cadiz, battle of Fuentes d'Onor, 2nd siege of Badajoz, battles of Salamanca, Vittoria, Nivelle, and the Nive—including the various engagements near the Mayor's house—slightly wounded on the 10th Dec., and severely on the 11th—lost an arm.

138 Major-General Thorn accompanied the Buffs to the Peninsula in Aug. 1808, where he served until Jan. 1809. Returned to the Peninsula in June following, and commanded the Light Company of the Buffs at the battle of Talavera Employed as an officer of observation in Spanish Estremadura from 29th Jan. to 3rd March 1810, from which period until the termination of that war in 1814, he served as Deputy-Assistant-Quarter-Master-General with the 2nd Division, and was present at the battle of Busaco, 1st siege of Badajoz, battle of Albuhera, actions at Arroyo de Molino and Almaraz, battles of Vittoria, the Pyrenees, and Nivelle, battles of the Nive on the 9th and 12th Dec. (wounded); action of Garris, battle of Orthes, action of

Aire, and battle of Toulouse. Embarked with the troops from Bourdeaux to Canada in July 1814, as an Assistant-Quarter-Master-General, and was present at the affair of Plattsburg. Horse killed under him at Albuhera; another in the action at the Pass of Maya; and a third in the action of the 12th Dec. 1813, near Bayonne.

139 Major-General Wemyss served with the Walcheren expedition in 1809, and subsequently in the Peninsula as Major of Brigade to the 50th, 71st, and 92nd, from the formation of that Brigade under Lord Howard in 1810, to its final embarkation at Bourdeaux in 1814; and was present in the different affairs during the retreat to the Lines near Lisbon, actions of Pombal, Redinha, Foz d'Arouce, battle of Fuentes d'Onor, surprise of Gerard at Arroyo de Molinos, storm of Fort Napoleon, and the bridge of Almaraz, action of Alba de Tormes, defence of Bejar, battle of Vittoria (received the Brevet rank of Major), and the Pyrenees, at Maya, Lesacca, and Donna Maria (severely wounded), battles of the Nivelle, Cambo, Nive, St. Pierre (wounded), Hellette, Garris, St. Palais, Tarbes, Arriveriette, Orthes, Aire, and Toulouse, besides numerous minor affairs. He served also against the Kandians in Ceylon.

140 Major-General Darling served at the reduction of Guadaloupe in 1810, and was severely wounded in the left knee by a musket-shot in storming the heights of Matauba. Proceeded to the Peninsula, and joined the 51st Light Infantry at Castello Branco, in May 1812; engaged on the heights of San Christoval, the battle of Salamanca, and surrender of the Retiro at Madrid; employed with his regiment before Burgos; and after the retreat from thence he was attacked by typhus fever, and sent to England for recovery, in May 1813. Rejoined the army on the heights of Echallar in September following, and was present at the battle of Nivelle, and the subsequent attack of the heights of St. Pé. Appointed Major of Brigade in Dec. 1813, and attached to Major-General Hay's brigade in the 5th division, and was employed throughout the blockade and operations before Bayonne. Appointed Assistant-Adjutant-General to the 5th division in April 1814, and remained in charge of that department until the embarkation of the division in Aug. 1814. On the renewal of the war in 1815, he was re-appointed to the staff as Assistant-Adjutant-General, and attached to the 4th division, under Sir Charles Colville; employed with his division in the operations connected with the battle of Waterloo, the storming of Cambray, and capitulation of Paris.

141 Sir Joseph Thackwell served the campaign in Galicia and Leon under Sir John Moore, and was engaged in several skirmishes, and present at the battle of Corunna. Served the campaigns of 1813 and 14 in the Peninsula, including the battles of Vittoria, the Pyrenees in front of Pampeluna, 27th, 28th, 29th, and 30th July; blockade of Pampeluna, from 18th to the 31st Oct., when it surrendered; battle of Orthes, affair at Tarbes, and battle of Toulouse; besides many affairs of advanced guards, out-posts, &c. Served also the campaign of 1815, including the action at Quatre Bras, the retreat on the following day, and battle of Waterloo. Commanded the cavalry division of the army of the Indus during the Affghanistan campaign; was present at the storm and capture of Ghuznee; and commanded the 2nd column of the army on its march from Cabool to Bengal. Commanded the cavalry division in the action at Maharajpore on the 29th Dec. 1843. Contused on the right shoulder at Vittoria, and severely wounded at Waterloo (left arm amputated close to the shoulder) in charging a square of infantry; had also two horses shot under him. He commanded the cavalry in the battle of Sobraon.

142 Sir Wm. Lewis Herries accompanied the 9th Dragoons to South America in Sept. 1806, and served as a Brigade-Major in the expedition against Buenos Ayres. Aide-de-camp to Sir Eyre Coote on the Walcheren expedition in 1809, and was actively employed at the siege and taking of Flushing. Accompanied Sir Edward Paget to Spain as his Aide-de-camp, in June 1812; and when Sir Edward was taken prisoner on the retreat from Burgos, Lord Wellington appointed him a Deputy-Quarter-Master-General, in which capacity he served until the end of that war in 1814, and was present at the battle of Vittoria, siege of San Sebastian, passage of the Bidassoa, the three successive days' actions at the Mayor's House, in front of Bidart, where he had a horse shot under him. On the 14th of April 1814, whilst endeavouring with Lieut. Moore (now Colonel W. G. Moore) to extricate Sir John Hope from his horse, which in the sortie from Bayonne was killed and had fallen upon him, he received a musket-shot in the left knee, was taken prisoner with Sir John Hope and Lieut. Moore (both being wounded), and his left leg was amputated the next morning.

143 Major-General M'Donald's services:—Expedition to South America, and assault of Buenos Ayres; Peninsula, from Nov. 1808 to 1813, and in the South of France from March 1814, including the battle of Busaco, Lines of Torres Vedras, affairs at Red nha, Pombal, and Campo Mayor; first siege of Badajoz, battle of Albuhera, third siege and assault of Badajoz, affairs at Alva de Tormes, battles of Vittoria, the Pyrenees, 25th (had two horses shot under him), 30th, and 31st July, and Toulouse. Wounded in the head and right thigh at the assault of Buenos Ayres, 5th July 1807; in the left leg and right groin in the Pyrenees 30th July; and in the right shoulder and lungs at the assault of the fortified rock on the mountain Arolla, and surprising the enemy's posts in the valley of Banca, Pyrenees, 2nd Oct. 1813. Medal and one clasp for Vittoria and the Pyrenees.

144 Major-General Paty served on the expedition to Copenhagen in 1807. Served afterwards in the Peninsula from June 1811 to the end of that war in 1814, including the siege and capture of Badajoz, battle of Salamanca, retreat from Madrid to Burgos, battles of Vittoria, the Pyrenees and Nivelle, battles of the Nive on the 9th, 10th, 11th, 12th, and 13th Dec. 1813, besides various minor affairs.

145 Major-General Gabriel was employed on the Walcheren expedition in 1809. Served afterwards on the staff in the Peninsula until the end of that war in 1814. Received the brevet rank of Major for the battle of the Pyrenees; and that of Lieut.-Colonel for former services in the field.

146 Major-General Thomas served in Sicily from 1805 to 1812. Joined the 3rd battalion of the 27th in Portugal in April 1813, and was present with it at the battles of Vittoria and the Pyrenees. Commanded the Light Companies of the right brigade of the 4th division at the battles of Nivelle, Orthes, and Toulouse, for which he has received a medal and two clasps. Served afterwards in the American war; also at the capture of Paris.

147 Major-General Rowan served with the 52nd in Sicily, in 1806 and 7; on the expedition to Sweden, in 1808; in the Peninsula under Sir John Moore in 1808-9; at Walcheren in 1809, including the bombardment and surrender of Flushing. In Portugal from 26th Jan. to 1st June 1811, including the action at Sabugal. Subsequently in the Peninsula and South of France from 10th Jan. 1813, to the end of that war in 1814, including the battle of Vittoria, passage of the Bidassoa, battles of the Nivelle, Nive, Orthes, and Toulouse, together with the intermediate affairs. Served also the campaign of 1815, and was present at the battle of Waterloo. Received the brevet rank of Major for the battle of Orthes, and that of Lieut.-Colonel for former services in the field.

148 Major-General Shaw Kennedy served with the 43rd at the siege of Copenhagen and battle of Kioge in 1807. In the Peninsula from 1808 to 1812 inclusive, and was present at the action of the Coa, siege and capture of Ciudad Rodrigo and Badajoz, and battle of Salamanca. Served also the campaign of 1815, including the battles of Quatre Bras and Waterloo.

149 Lord Sandys accompanied the 10th Hussars to the Peninsula in 1812, and was present in the action at Morales, and battles of Vittoria and Pampeluna. Served also the campaign of 1815, as an Aide-de-camp to the Duke of Wellington, and was present at the battle of Waterloo.

150 Sir Thomas Henry Browne carried the King's Colour of the 23rd at the siege of Copenhagen in 1807. Accompanied his regiment to America; thence to the West Indies, and was wounded at the capture of Martinique. Proceeded again to America, and thence to Portugal in 1811. He was appointed to the Staff of the Adjutant-General in 1812, and was in the field at the battles of Salamanca, capture of Madrid and the Retiro, siege of Burgos, Vittoria (where he was wounded in the head), the Pyrenees, Nivelle, the actions of the 11th, 12th, and 13th Dec. 1813, before Bayonne, Nive, Tarbes, Orthes, and Toulouse. On the escape of Napoleon from Elba, he was appointed Aide-de-camp to Lord Stewart (the present Marquis of Londonderry), and served the campaign of 1815 with him, at the head-quarters of the Austrian and Russian armies.

151 Major-General Maclachlan was honourably mentioned in Colonel Gillespie's despatch, for his conduct at the suppression of the mutiny at Vellore in 1806, on which occasion he was the senior officer present, and severely wounded.

152 Major-General Nicolls with thirteen volunteers in a boat of the *Blanche* frigate, boarded and captured, on the 3rd Nov. 1803, the French armed cutter *Albion* from under the guns of Monte Christie, St. Domingo,—in this action he was severely wounded by a musket-ball, which entering the abdomen, and coming out at his right side, lodged in the arm. On board the *Standard* at the passage of the Dardanelles on the 19th Feb. 1807. On the 26th June 1808, with a boat's crew, he boarded and captured the Italian gun-boat *Volpe* near Corfu. Present at the reduction of the Island of Anholt in May 1809. Severely wounded at the attack on Fort Bowyer 15th Sept. 1814.

153 Major-General Fearon's services:—Campaign of 1796 and 7 in the West Indies, including the storming of the Vigie (wounded in the knee by a bayonet); attack on Morne Fortunee; and surrender of St. Lucia. Campaign of 1799 in Holland, including the battles of the 19th Sept., 2nd and 6th Oct. Campaign of 1800 on the coast of France and Spain. Expedition to Quiberon Bay. Attack on Ferrol. Expedition to Vigo and Cadiz. Egyptian campaign of 1807, including the surrender of Alexandria; attack and storming of Rosetta Campaign of 1814 and 15 in Italy, including the surrender of Naples and Genoa. Major-General Fearon commanded the troops on board the unfortunate ship *Kent*, when she was burned in the Bay of Biscay 1st March 1825.

154 Major-General Balneavis proceeded under Sir David Baird to Corunna in 1808; from thence to Lisbon, and was appointed Major of Brigade to Major-General R. M'Kenzie's Brigade; served throughout the whole of the war in Spain, and was present at the battles of Talavera and Busaco, retreat to the Lines of Torres Vedras, occupation of them and subsequent advance, battle of Fuentes d'Onor—for which he received the brevet rank of Major; siege of Ciudad Rodrigo, covering the siege of Badajos, storming of Fort St. Michael, siege of Burgos, battle of Salamanca, capture of Madrid, and battle of Toulouse, at which battle he succeeded to the command of the 3rd battalion of the 27th regt. Embarked at Bourdeaux for North America: on arriving there he was appointed Assistant-Quarter-Master-General, and was present at the battle of Plattsburg. Gave up his staff situation and proceeded to New Orleans. Present at the capture of Paris as Aide-de-camp to Sir Manley Power, and served afterwards with the Army of Occupation.

155 Major-General Whetham served with the 40th in Holland, in 1799. Also on the expedition to South America, and was severely wounded at the assault of Monte Video,—right leg amputated.

156 Major-General Goldie served in the Peninsula from March 1809 to Nov. 1813, including the passage of the Douro, battles of Talavera, Busaco, Albuhera, Vittoria, and the Pyrenees, besides many other minor actions and skirmishes. Severely wounded in the Pyrenees on the 30th July 1813, by a musket-ball which is still lodged in the lungs—this wound was long considered mortal. Medal for Albuhera.

157 Major-General Higginson served with the Grenadier Guards in Sicily in 1807, in the campaign in the North of Spain with Sir John Moore in 1808-9, and was present at the battle of Corunna. Went with the expedition to Walcheren in 1809. Joined his regiment in Portugal in 1812, and advanced with the army into Spain in 1813; commanded a detachment of the Grenadier Guards at the storming and capture of San Sebastian, 31st August in the same year, entered France by the Pyrenees, was present at the passages of the Nive, the Nivelle, and the Adour, also during the investment of Bayonne. Embarked with his regiment at Bourdeaux when the army left France in 1814. Went with re-enforcements to the Netherlands in June 1815, arrived at Paris shortly after its capture, and remained in France during the three years of its occupation by the allied army. In 1830 he was appointed Aide-de-camp to Lord Hill, then Commander-in-chief, and continued on his staff upwards of twelve years, until his lordship's resignation of office from ill health.

158 Major-General Bowles served in the north of Germany in 1805 and 6, under Lord Cathcart. Present at the siege and capture of Copenhagen in 1807. In the Peninsula from 1809 to 1814 (excepting the winters of 1810 and 11), and was present at the passage of the Douro; battles of Talavera, Salamanca, and Vittoria; sieges of Ciudad Rodrigo, Badajoz, Burgos, and San Sebastian; capture of Madrid; passages of the Bidassoa, Nivelle, Nive, and Adour; and the investment of Bayonne. Present at the battles of Quatre Bras and Waterloo, and at the capture of Paris.

159 Major-General Bunbury led the storming party at Forts Frederick and Zelandia, as a volunteer, at the capture of Surinam in 1804. Served the campaign of 1814 in Holland, including the attacks on Merxem, and the bombardment of the French fleet at Antwerp. Served also in the American war.

160 Major-General the Hon. Henry Cavendish served in the Peninsula from July 1808 to January 1809, and was wounded through the wrist at the battle of Corunna, where he served as aide-de-camp to Lord William Bentinck.

161 Major-General Godwin served with the 9th on the expedition to the Ferrol in 1800; on that to Hanover in 1805; and in Portugal from Sept. 1808 to July 1809, including the passage of the Douro. In 1810 marched with the light company in a flank battalion from Gibraltar to the first defence of Tarifa. He was a volunteer with Lord Blayney from Gibraltar on the expedition to Malaga, and present at the attack on the fortress of Fuengarola. In 1811 he proceeded again to Tarifa, in command of the two flank companies, to join the force under Lord Lynedoch, and was present at the battle of Barrosa, and severely wounded. In 1822 he embarked in command of the 41st for Madras. In 1824 he joined Sir Archibald Campbell with that regiment in the invasion of the Burmese empire, and served throughout that war, from the landing and capture of Rangoon to the Peace in Feb. 1826. During this period he was employed in six separate commands against the enemy. In October 1824 he embarked with a force from Rangoon to capture the province of Martaban: he stormed its strongly fortified town, taking 32 pieces of heavy ordnance and other arms. On the 8th Feb. 1825, he captured the fortified position of Tantabain, taking 36 pieces of Artillery, and other arms. He was also present at every action with the enemy (except those in Dec. 1824, when he was still employed at Martaban), particularly at Sembike on 1st Dec. 1825, when in command of the advanced guard he carried the front face of the enemy's position. He commanded the 1st Brigade of the Madras division, and was twice thanked by the Governor-General in Council.

162 Major-General Robbins served in Sicily in 1806-7 with the 1st Regt. of Guards; also in the Peninsula, France, and Flanders, with the 7th Hussars, and was severely wounded at Waterloo.

163 Major-General Macneil served in Sir John Moore's retreat, and subsequently at Walcheren in 1809; in Swedish Pomerania in 1813, in Holland in 1814, including the attack on Bergen-op-Zoom. Served also the campaign of 1815, including battle of Waterloo.

164 Major-General Pitt served at the capture of the Danish West India Islands in 1807; and of Martinique in 1809. Served also in the Peninsula from Jan. 1811 to Jan. 1814, including the battle of Albuhera; actions at Usagre and Almaraz; siege of Badajoz; battles of Vittoria, Pampeluna, and the Pyrenees.

165 Major-General Sutherland commanded the few troops on the Gold Coast in the successful operations and actions against the Ashantees, whom he defeated and dispersed (about 20,000 strong) in June and July 1824.

166 Major-General Rainey served with the 82nd at the siege and capture of Copenhagen in 1807; with Sir Brent Spencer's expedition off the coast of Spain, and at Cadiz on surrender of the French fleet; from thence joined Sir Arthur Wellesley's army at Mondego Bay, and was afterwards present at the battles of Roleia, Vimiera, and Corunna, also the retreat under Sir John Moore. Accompanied the regiment to Walcheren in 1809, and was present at the surrender of Middleburgh, siege and capture of Flushing. Joined the army in the Peninsula in May 1812, and served as Aide-de-camp to Sir Thomas Bradford during the siege of the Forts of

Salamanca, battle of Salamanca, capture of Madrid, siege of Burgos, and retreat therefrom. Served afterwards in the Portuguese service in advance through the Tras-os-Montes in 1813, at the battle of Vittoria, actions of Villa Franca and Toloso, storm of the fortified convent in front of San Sebastian, at both the sieges and storm of San Sebastian, passage of the Bidassoa, battle of the Nivelle, battles of the Nive on the 9th and 10th Dec.—severely wounded: wounded also at the siege of San Sebastian. Served in France with the Army of Occupation from the capitulation of Paris in 1815 to the end of 1818.

167 Major-General the Honorable Charles Gore joined the 43rd in the Peninsula in July 1811, and was present and one of the storming party of Fort San Francisco at the investment of Ciudad Rodrigo; also at the siege and storming of that fortress and of Badajoz, battle of Salamanca, as Aide-de-camp to Sir Andrew Barnard; and in a similar capacity to Sir James Kempt in the battles of Vittoria, the Nivelle, the Nive (9th, 10th, and 11th Dec.), Orthes, and Toulouse. He was also in the action of San Milan, capture of Madrid, storming of the heights of Vera, bridge of Yanzi, and all the skirmishes of the Light Division from 1812 to the close of the war in 1814; after which he accompanied Sir James Kempt with the troops sent to Canada under his command; returned to Europe in time for the campaign of 1815, and was first and principal Aide-de-camp to Sir James Kempt, and present at the battles of Quatre Bras (horse shot), and Waterloo (three horses shot), and capture of Paris.

168 Major-General Walton served with the Coldstream Guards at the siege and capture of Copenhagen in 1807. He embarked for the Peninsula in 1808, and served the campaigns of 1809, 1810, and the first part of 1811; and was present at the passage of the Douro and capture of Oporto, the battles of Talavera and Busaco, the retreat to the Lines of Torres Vedras, and the subsequent advance to the Spanish frontier. He served also in Holland, Belgium, and France, from Nov. 1813 to Nov. 1818; and was present at the bombardment of Antwerp, the attack on Bergen-op-Zoom, the battles of Quatre Bras and Waterloo, and the capture of Paris. He served 40 years in the Coldstream Guards, and commanded the regiment upwards of six years.

169 Major-General Lewis served in Sir Richard Strachan's action, 4th Nov. 1805. Commanded a battalion of Marines in the American war, including the action at Bladensburg, attack on Baltimore, and various skirmishes in the Chesapeak.

170 Major-General Lawrence, prior to entering the Royal Marines, served four years and a half as Midshipman in the Royal Navy. In 1793 he served at Toulon; landed at Fort La Malgue and Fort Mulgrave during the siege. In 1798, at the capture of a French squadron of three frigates and two brigs off Toulon. In 1805, battle of Trafalgar; the ship in which he served, the *Colossus*, lost 200 in killed and wounded. In 1810, at Cadiz during the blockade, was the senior captain of the expedition against Malaga. In 1814 and 15, served off New York on the American coast, until hostilities finally ceased.

171 Major-General Jones was at the defeat of the French fleet by Lord Howe, 1st June 1794; and by Lord Bridport, 23 June 1795. On board *La Revolutionaire* when she captured the *Unite*, 12th April 1798. Wrecked off Brest in 1804, and detained a prisoner of war until 1814.

172 Major-General Adair's services:—Battle of the Nile; siege and capitulation of the Castle of St. Elmo, Naples, and the town of Capua, in 1798; blockade of Malta, and surrender of La Valetta; blockade of Cadiz, and present at an attack made by Spanish gun-vessels when becalmed under the batteries of that town; on board H. M. S. *Genereux*, at the capture of *La Diane*, French frigate. Served also at New Orleans.

173 Major-General Connolly served in Lord Bridport's action, 23d June 1795. In 1796 served in the Mediterranean, including the evacuation of Bastia, capture of Porto Ferrajo, and destruction of Martello Tower in St. Fiorenzo Bay. On board H. M. S. *Excellent* in the battle off Cape St. Vincent, 14th Feb. 1797. Capture of Admiral Perrie's squadron off Toulon in 1798, consisting of three frigates and two brigs. On board the *Hannibal*, in the battle of Algesiras, 6th July 1801, wounded and taken prisoner. On board H. M. S. *Penelope*, in the action off Flushing and Ostend, under Sir Sydney Smith, 16th May 1804. Present at the siege of Copenhagen, and capture of Danish fleet in 1807, and at Nyebourgh in 1808. In 1812, on board H.M.S. *Hamadryad*, when attacked by French privateers; debarked with detachments at Scheveling, and took possession of the Hague in 1814. During the above periods he has been very frequently engaged with the enemy in affairs of gun-boats and batteries, &c. &c. He has received a reward from the Patriotic Fund.

174 Major-General Shawe served the campaigns of 1810, 1811, and part of 1812, in the Peninsula, including the battle of Busaco. Served also in Holland and Belgium from Nov. 1813 to Sept. 1814, and was severely wounded at Bergen-op-Zoom.

175 Major-General Beatty's services: landed at the attack of Santa Cruz, Teneriffe, when Lord Nelson lost his arm; battle of the Nile; siege of St. Jean d'Acre (wounded); was favourably mentioned in Sir Sidney Smith's despatch, and is the only officer now serving who participated in that celebrated defence. In 1803 he was at the capture of the *Harmonie* privateer, and the surprise and destruction of Fort Dunkirk, Martinique. The publication of the despatches connected with these events, in which he was most favourably mentioned, procured him a patriotic sword of the value of 50*l*. Captain of Marines in the *Courageux*, at the capture of the *Marengo* and *Belle Poule* in March 1805; and in the *Donegal*, Capt. P. Malcolm, when the small squadron under his command attacked two French frigates under the batteries of La Hogue, near Cape Barfleur, 10th November 1810. He has been engaged in other affairs of minor importance, and was selected for the duty of accompanying Sir G. Cockburn with Napoleon in the *Northumberland* to St. Helena.

	CORNET, 2d LIEUT. or ENSIGN.	LIEUT.	CAPTAIN.	MAJOR.	LIEUT.-COLONEL.	COLONEL.	WHEN PLACED ON HALF PAY.
Sir *David Cunynghame*, Bart.,[1] late of 82 Foot	14 Nov. 81	5 Sept. 83	20 Mar. 83	never	15 Jan. 94	26 Jan. 97	
Henry Mordaunt Clavering, late of 98 Foot	7 Feb. 94	12 Feb. 94	13 Feb. 94	30 July 94	19 Aug. 95	29 April 02	
Francis, Wm., Earl of *Seafield*, late of 2 Argyll Fencibles, *Colonel of Inverness Militia*	July 93	31 July 93	14 Feb. 94	29 Nov. 94	23 Jan. 99	25 Oct. 09	
Hugh Baillie, late of Surrey Rangers	12 April 93	27 Nov. 93	13 Feb. 94	29 Dec. 94	1 Jan. 00	25 July 10	
John Richard Broadhead, late of 121 Foot	24 Oct. 89	Nov. 93	9 Dec. 93	9 Sept. 95	1 Jan. 01	do	
John Dick Burnaby, late of Grenadier Guards	1 Feb. 92	never	5 Mar. 94	never	25 June 03	1 Jan. 12	
Edward Drummond, late of 86 Foot		4 Feb. 95	8 Nov. 98	11 June 01	29 Dec. 04	4 June 13	
Launcelot Holland, late of 134 Foot	27 Oct. 98	never	25 Nov. 99	1 Nov. 04	16 Sept. 06	4 June 14	
Charles, *Earl of* Harrington, *Lieut.-Col.*, h. p. 3 West India Regt.	2 Dec. 95	never	21 Nov. 99	24 Jan. 03	25 June 07	do	13 Aug. 12
P W Hon. *Alex. Abercromby*, CB.,[3] late of Coldstream Guards	16 Aug. 99	19 Mar. 00	21 May 01	17 July 06	28 Jan. 08	do	
Augustus Rottiger, of late German Legion	never	never	never	24 Dec. 05	25 Nov. 08	do	
P W Sir *Robert Chambre Hill*, CB.,[6] late of R. Horse Guards	May 93	15 Oct. 93	11 April 00	14 Nov. 05	1 Jan. 12	1 Jan. 19	
P Sir *William Cox*,[7] late of Portuguese Service	1 Oct. 94	3 Sept. 95	7 Aug. 00	19 June 06	16 Feb. 09	12 Aug. 19	
Thomas Francklin, late of Royal Artillery	1 July 82	24 Mar. 91	6 Mar. 95	27 June 07	1 May	do	
P *John Potter Hamilton*, KH.,[8] late of Scots Fusilier Guards	April 94	13 Aug. 94	16 Aug. 99	27 Feb. 02	25 Oct.	do	
Francis Dunne, late of 7 Dragoon Guards	31 Jan. 92	never	26 Aug. 93	29 April 02	do	do	
Nathaniel Burslem, KH.,[9] late of 67 Foot	2 Dec. 89	16 Aug. 93	4 April 95	7 Mar. 05	1 Mar. 11	19 July 21	
William Gravatt, late of R. Invalid Engineers	18 June 92	27 Nov. 93	1 July 99	never	1 May	do	
George Gauntlett,[11] late of 62 Foot	2 Mar. 91	12 Feb. 94	9 Feb. 97	1 Aug. 04	2 May	do	
P *William Woodgate*, CB.,[12] late of 60 Foot	21 Mar. 00	19 Nov. 00	6 April 03	13 Aug. 07	30 May	do	
P *Christopher C. Patrickson*, CB.,[13] late of 43 Foot	31 Aug. 93	25 Mar. 94	25 Mar. 00	28 Sept. 09	do	do	
P *James Johnstone Cochrane*, late of Scots Fusilier Guards	26 Dec. 99	never	5 Jan. 04	never	10 Dec. 12	25 July 21	
P *Henry Thornton*, CB.,[14] late of 82 Foot	8 Oct. 94	24 June 95	23 Nov. 96	1 Aug. 04	4 June 11	27 May 25	
Sir *Frederick Hankey*, GCMG., late of 15 Foot	Sept. 00	2 Oct. 00	3 Dec. 02	22 Sept. 08	15 Aug. 11	do	
P Sir *John Milley Doyle*, KCB.,[16] late of 12 Garrison Battalion	31 May 94	21 June 94	9 July 03	16 Feb. 09	26 Sept. 11	do	
P *John Hamilton*,[17] late of Coldstream Guards	21 Nov. 99	never	13 May 01	never	30 Jan. 12	do	
P *William Henry Raikes*,[18] late of Coldstream Guards	9 May 00	10 May 00	26 April 02	never	3 June 13	do	
P *Wm. Augustus Keate*,[19] late of Scots Fusilier Guards	28 Aug. 00	never	24 May 04	never	9 Aug. 13	15 Sept. 25	
P *John Richard Ward*, CB.,[20] late of 2 Dragoons			8 Dec. 94	1 Jan. 05	1 Jan. 12	22 July 30	
P *William Williams Blake*, CB.,[21] late of 11 Dragoons	26 April 97	31 Oct. 99	18 Feb. 02	21 Mar. 05	do	do	
John Matthias Everard, late of Grenadier Guards	5 Dec. 96	28 Dec. 96	18 Dec. 99	10 July 06	23 Jan.	do	
P *George Wyndham*, late of 27 Foot	31 Mar. 03	April 05	19 Sept. 05	31 Jan. 11	13 Mar.	do	

	CORNET, ETC.	LIEUT.	CAPTAIN.	MAJOR.	LIEUT.-COLONEL.	COLONEL.	WHEN PLACED ON HALF PAY.
David Williams, late of 17 Foot	19 May 94	14 Jan. 95	25 May 98	25 April 08	4 June 14	10 Jan. 37	
P *Henry Edmund Jodrell*,[26] late of Grenadier Guards	29 Dec. 03	never	7 April 08	never	25 July 14	do	
P W *Henry Dawkins*,[27] late of Coldstream Guards	10 Mar. 04	never	25 Aug. 08	never	do	do	
P Peter Brown, *Lieut.-Col.*,[29] Unattached, *Commandant of Royal Military Asylum at Chelsea*	7 Dec. 99	18 Dec. 02	21 Mar. 05	21 June 13	18 June 15	do	5 Sept. 16
P W Francis Dalmer, *Lieut.-Col.*, Unattached	10 Mar. 04	18 April 05	10 Dec. 07	26 Aug. 13	do	do	20 July 26
P W *Fielding Browne*, CB.,[31] late of 66 F., *Barrack-Master at Malta*	7 Mar. 00	1 Oct. 02	22 Dec. 04	4 June 14	do	do	
P W *Michael Childers*, CB.,[32] late of 6 Dragoons	25 Feb. 99	25 Aug. 01	14 June 05	25 Aug.	do	do	
Hon. Leicester Stanhope, CB.,[33] *Lieut.-Col.*, Unattached	25 Sept. 99	20 Oct. 02	31 Mar. 03	4 June 14	29 June 15	do	26 June 23
P *Alexander Higginson*,[34] late of Grenadier Guards	26 Jan. 04	never	14 Sept. 09	never	1 July	do	
P W *Charles Allix*, late of Grenadier Guards	28 April 04	never	13 Dec. 10	never	4 July	do	
P *Thomas Brooke*, late of Grenadier Guards	7 Mar. 05	never	14 Feb. 11	never	5 July	do	
P *Sir* Thomas Reade, CB.,[35] *Captain*, h. p. 24 Foot	6 Aug. 99	18 May 00	8 Sept. 05	3 Jan. 11	19 Oct. 15	do	27 May 24
P *Sir* John Morillyon Wilson, CB. KH.,[36] *Maj.*, Unattached, *Adjt. of Chelsea Hospital, Gentleman Usher to the Queen Dowager*	1 Sept. 04	28 Feb. 05	1 Jan. 07	5 July 14	27 Nov.	do	25 July 22
Matthew Stewart, *Lieut.-Col.*, h. p. Portuguese Service	1 Mar. 04	1 Mar. 05	4 May 09	8 Dec. 14	1 Feb. 16	do	8 Jan. 24
P *Arthur Helsham Gordon*, late of Grenadier Guards	25 Apr. 96	6 July 98	8 Apr. 99	4 June 11	8 Feb. 16	do	
P W *William Drummond*,[37] late of Scots Fusilier Guards	20 Mar. 06	never	24 Oct. 11	18 June 15	4 July	do	
P *Kenneth Snodgrass*, CB.,[38] late Unattached	22 Oct. 03	9 Aug. 04	20 Oct. 08	21 Sept. 13	21 June 17	do	
P *William Balvaird*, CB.,[39] late of 37 Foot	24 Mar. 03	17 April 04	16 May 05	22 Nov.	do	do	
P *Harry Bulteel Harris*, KH.,[40] late of 93 Foot	17 Mar. 04	29 Dec. 04	15 Jan. 07	27 Oct. 14	17 Dec. 18	do	
P W *Thomas Wildman*,[41] late of 5 Dragoon Guards	5 Mar. 07	29 Sept. 08	18 Feb. 13	18 July 16	23 Dec. 19	do	
Hon. Frederick Macadam Cathcart,[42] *Capt.*, h. p. 92 Foot	12 Jan. 05	1 May 06	17 Sept. 07	28 July 14	24 Feb. 20	do	18 May 20
William Henry Meyrick, late of Grenadier Guards	28 Feb. 05	30 May 05	11 Aug. 08	24 Feb. 17	29 June	do	
Thomas Younghusband, *Capt.*, h. p. 4 Dragoon Guards	31 May 93	19 Dec. 93	3 May 00	1 Jan. 12	19 July 21	do	18 Dec. 23
P Henry Standish, *Major*, h. p. 39 Foot	21 Oct. 95	20 Jan. 96	24 July 00	do	do	do	25 Feb. 16
P Sir *George Couper*,[44] Bart., CB. KH., late of 10 Foot, *Principal Equerry to H. R. H. the Duchess of Kent*	2 Nov. 97	2 Nov. 99	14 April 08	21 June 13	23 July 21	do	
P *William Richardson*,[45] late of Royal Horse Guards	27 Feb. 06	20 Aug. 07	26 Dec. 11	never	24 July 23	do	
George Greenwood, late of 2 Life Guards	23 June 17	26 Jan. 19	1 Jan. 24	26 Nov. 30	2 Jan. 31	12 Jan. 38	
P Thomas Adams Parke, CB., *Colonel Commandant*, R. Marines at Woolwich, *Aide-de-Camp to the Queen*	19 May 95	23 Nov. 96	15 Aug. 05	12 Aug. 19	31 Dec. 32	26 April 38	
Frederick Campbell, *Colonel*, Royal Artillery	12 Jan. 97	16 July 99	29 July 04	4 June 14	23 Nov. 28	11 June 38	
P W Mildmay Fane, *Lt.-Col.*, 54 Foot	11 June 12	25 Sept. 13	28 July 14	2 Mar. 20	12 June	28 June	
P W John Martin,[47] *do.* Unattached	30 July 07	16 May 09	8 Feb. 13	10 Jan. 22	do	do	12 June 23

	2D LIEUT. ETC.	LIEUT.	CAPTAIN.	MAJOR.	LIEUT.-COLONEL.	COLONEL.	WHEN PLACED ON HALF PAY.
Sir George Henry Hewett, *Bart.*, *Lt.-Col.*, Unattached	12 June 06	18 Dec. 06	12 April 10	18 June 12	26 June 23	28 June 38	28 June 27
Charles Wyndham, late of 76 Foot	17 Oct. 11	5 Nov. 12	24 Feb. 17	20 Dec. 21	do	do	
P *James Payler*,[49] late of 17 Foot	2 Nov. 03	24 Mar. 04	30 Nov. 06	13 Jan. 14	31 July	do	
Henry, Earl of *Uxbridge*, late of 42 Foot	14 July 14	21 July 14	27 Feb. 17	never	5 Aug.	do	
W Hon. *Henry Hely Hutchinson*, late of 6 Dragoons	28 July 08	21 Mar. 11	22 July 13	5 July 21	4 Sept.	do	
W *Sir* Jas. Maxwell Wallace, KH.,[50] *Lieut.-Col.*, h. p. 9 Dragoons	14 Aug. 05	5 June 06	22 Oct. 07	1 Jan. 17	25 Sept.	do	3 July 40
P *Hon.* John Finch, CB.,[51] *Lt.-Col.*, Unattached	5 Oct. 09	20 Dec. 10	17 Feb. 14	5 Mar. 18	25 Oct.	do	12 Dec. 26
P James Lindsay,[52] *do.* do.	16 Dec. 07	never	10 Dec. 12	never	20 Nov.	do	19 Nov. 30
George Edward Pratt Barlow,[53] late of 22 Foot	24 April 03	25 Dec. 03	14 Oct. 05	26 Mar. 12	4 Dec.	do	
P W Wm. George Moore,[54] *Lt.-Col.*, Unattached	18 April 11	10 Sept. 12	14 April 14	21 Jan. 19	12 Feb. 24	do	16 Sept. 26
P W *Sir* Henry Floyd,[55] *Bart.*, *Lt.-Col.*, Unattached	7 July 08	15 Mar. 10	2 Dec. 13	16 Nov. 20	6 May	do	6 May 24
Sir Augustus F. d'Este, KCH.,[56] late of 69 Foot	never	26 Sept. 11	14 Mar. 15	11 July 22	1 July	do	
James Campbell, KH., *Lt.-Col.*, 95 Foot	17 Sept. 03	25 Aug. 04	31 Mar. 08	3 June 19	10 July	do	
P Wm. Cochrane,[57] *Lt.-Col.*, Unatt., *Deputy Adj.-Gen. in Ireland*	13 Feb. 05	29 May 06	11 Aug. 12	17 Mar. 14	15 July	do	10 July 37
P W Henry Somerset, CB. KH., *Lt.-Col.*, Cape Mounted Riflemen	5 Dec. 11	30 Dec. 12	6 Oct. 15	25 Mar. 23	17 July	do	
P Nicholas Wodehouse,[57*] *do.* h. p. 50 Foot	3 June 07	31 Aug. 07	26 Sept. 11	18 Oct. 21	2 Sept.	do	12 Aug. 48
Henry, *Duke of* Cleveland, KG., *Lt.-Col.*, Unattached, *Colonel of Durham Militia*	6 July 15	22 May 17	22 Oct. 18	3 July 23	23 Sept.	do	6 July 26
Geo. Aug. Wetherall,[58] CB. KH., *do.* do., *Deputy Adjutant General in Canada, Aide-de-Camp to the Queen*	never	29 July 05	13 May 05	12 Aug. 19	11 Dec.	do	14 July 43
William Douglas, *Lieut.-Col.*, h. p. Royal Engineers	1 July 01	12 Oct. 01	1 July 06	12 Aug.	23 Mar. 25	do	27 Jan. 29
P W James Simpson, *do.*,[59] Unattached, *Commandant at Chatham*	3 April 11	never	25 Dec. 13	never	28 April	do	8 Dec. 46
P W James Fred. Love,[60] CB. KH., *Lt.-Col.*, Unattached	26 Oct. 04	5 June 05	11 July 11	16 Mar. 15	5 May	do	23 Sept. 45
W *Hon.* George Anson,[61] *Lt.-Col.*, Unattached, *Aide-de-Camp to his Grace the Commander-in-Chief, Clerk of the Ordnance*	8 Jan. 14	never	20 Jan. 20	1 April 24	19 May	do	19 May 25
P Duncan M'Gregor,[62] *Lt.-Col.*, Unattached	12 July 00	31 Aug. 01	17 April 04	25 Nov. 13	26 May	do	27 July 38
Edward Warner, *Major*, h. p. 26 Foot	22 Nov. 98	5 Aug. 99	14 Sept. 03	30 Jan. 12	27 May	do	25 Dec. 14
P Nicholas Hamilton, KH., Insp. Field Officer of a Recruiting District	15 June 96	9 Dec. 96	25 June 03	18 June 12	27 May	do	
Sir James Dennis, KCB., *Lieut.-Col.*, 3 Foot	2 Sept. 96	12 April 97	6 Aug. 03	13 Oct.	do	do	
Matthew Gregory Blake, late of R. Canadian Rifle Regt.	20 Feb. 96	4 May 00	13 Feb. 04	12 Nov. 12	27 May 25	do	
Thomas Kennedy, *Captain*, h. p. 96 Foot	never	4 Dec. 05	18 Feb. 08	3 Dec.	do	do	1811
P W Charles Anth. Ferdinand Bentinck,[62*] *Lt.-Col.*, Unattached	16 Nov. 08	never	24 Sept. 12	18 June 15	do	do	25 April 48
P W *Henry Lane*,[63] late of Grenadier Guards	4 Dec. 11	3 Sept. 12	25 Dec. 18	5 Aug. 24	9 June	do	
John Gregory Baumgardt, CB., *Lt.-Col.*, *Inspecting Field Officer*	1 Aug. 98	20 Mar. 01	10 Jan. 10	21 Oct. 24	do	do	
P *Sir* Robert Nickle,[64] KH., *do.*, Unattached	22 Jan. 01	26 Jan. 02	1 June 09	21 Jan. 19	30 June	do	29 Aug. 43

	ENSIGN, ETC.	LIEUT.	CAPTAIN.	MAJOR.	LIEUT.-COLONEL.	COLONEL.	WHEN PLACED ON HALF PAY.
Daniel Falls, *Lt.-Col.* Unattached	8 Mar. 98	26 April 98	1 Dec. 04	4 June 14	25 July 25	28 June 38	25 July 22
P Griffith George Lewis, CB., *Colonel*, Royal Engineers	15 Mar. 03	2 July 03	18 Nov. 07	21 Sept. 13	29 July	do	
P George Judd Harding, CB., *do.* do.	1 Oct. 02	1 Dec. 02	do	19 July 21	do	do	
John Ross Wright, *do.* do.	1 Mar. 03	1 April 03	do	do	do	do	
P W Sampson Stawell,[65] *Lieut.-Col.*, Unattached	15 Jan. 01	9 July 02	28 Feb. 05	18 June 15	1 Oct.	do	30 Mar. 47
Charles George James Arbuthnot, *Lieut.-Col.*, Unattached	never	26 Dec. 16	16 Mar. 20	3 July 23	do	do	
Chesborough Grant Falconar, KH., *Insp. F. Officer Recr. Distr.*	1 Sept. 95	1 Nov. 99	26 Dec. 05	12 Aug. 19	22 Oct.	do	
Sir Richard England,[66] KCB., KH., *Lieut.-Col.*, Unattached	25 Feb. 08	1 June 09	11 June 11	4 Sept. 23	29 Oct.	do	22 July 45
Charles Middleton, *Lt.-Col.*, 3 Lt. Drs., *Commandant of the Cavalry Depôt at Maidstone*	19 Sept. 04	28 April 06	18 July 15	8 Feb. 19	19 Nov.	do	
P Alexander Fisher Macintosh,[67] KH., *Lt.-Col.*, Unattached	31 Oct. 11	11 June 12	6 June 16	18 Sept. 23	15 Dec.	do	18 Jan. 39
P W Beaumont, *Lord* Hotham,[68] *do.* do.	27 June 10	never	25 Dec. 13	21 Jan. 19	24 Dec.	do	24 Dec. 25
P Joseph Paterson, *Lt.-Col.*, Unattached	17 May 99	7 Feb. 01	23 Oct. 06	29 Sept. 14	31 Dec.	do	6 Feb. 30
P W *Henry Madox*,[69] KH. late of 12 Lancers	14 Mar. 00	23 July 03	19 Dec. 05	18 June 15	31 Dec. 25	do	
P George Turner, CB., *Colonel*, Royal Artillery	14 Jan. 97	16 July 99	29 July 04	4 June 14	25 Nov. 28	do	
Richard Francis Cleaveland, *do.* do	24 Feb. 97	do	9 Oct. 04	do	9 Dec.	10 Aug. 39	
C John Owen, CB. KH., *Colonel-Commandant and Deputy-Adj.-General to the R. Marines, Aide-de-Camp to the Queen*	1 Mar. 96	22 Oct. 98	4 May 07	19 July 21	10 Jan. 37	26 Aug.	
John Wright, KH., *Col. Commandant*, Royal Marines at Chatham	21 April 96	10 June 99	27 July 08	16 Sept. 16	do	do	
Thompson Aslett,[69*] *Col. Commandant*, R. Marines, on retired full pay	1 June 96	2 May 00	do	27 May 25	do	do	
George Alexander Reid, *Lt.-Col.*, Unattached	7 Mar. 18	20 Mar. 21	11 Nov. 24	23 July 31	17 Feb. 32	10 April 40	30 Dec. 45
John Home, *Lt.-Col.*, Grenadier Guards	19 Jan. 13	never	30 June 15	never	10 May 27	11 Sept.	
P Mathias Everard,[69*] CB. KH., *Lieut.-Col.*, h. p. 3 Foot	28 Sept. 04	21 Mar. 05	23 April 07	19 July 21	19 Jan. 26	23 Nov. 41	25 Dec. 47
P Cecil Bisshopp, CB.,[70] *Lt.-Col.*, Unattached	10 Dec. 99	14 Oct. 00	23 June 08	27 May 25	do	do	17 May 44
P W Charles Parker Ellis,[71] *Lieut.-Col.*, h. p. Roll's Regt.	28 Jan. 11	never	25 Dec. 13	never	16 Feb.	do	10 May 31
Warner Westenra Higgins, KH.,[72] late of 79 Foot	4 Mar. 98	4 May 00	28 Feb. 05	16 June 14	25 Feb. 26	23 Nov. 41	
P W *Sir* Wm. Robert Clayton, *Bart.*,[73] *Lieut.-Col.*, Unattached	28 Sept. 04	14 Nov. 05	27 April 09	21 Dec. 15	8 April	do	8 April 26
P *William Macadam*, KH.,[75] late of 8 Foot	14 Jan. 08	10 Aug. 08	17 Nov. 14	23 Sept. 24	22 April	do	
W *Hon.* George Cathcart,[76] *Lieut.-Col.*, Unattached, *Deputy Lieutenant of the Tower of London*	10 May 10	1 July 11	24 Dec. 18	8 April 26	13 May 26	do	19 Jan. 44
John Spink, KH.,[77] *Lt.-Col.*, Unatt., *Asst. Qr.-Mast. Gen. at Cork*	2 Sept. 06	9 Mar. 07	13 Oct. 12	13 May 24	20 May	do	20 May 26
P W James Jackson, KH., *Lt.-Col.*, 6 Dragoon Guards	9 Oct. 06	25 Jan. 08	25 June 13	18 June 15	25 May	do	
P Robt. Chr. Mansel, KH.,[78] *do.*, Unatt., *Dep. Qr.-Mast. Gen. in Ireland*	29 Jan. 07	27 Jan. 08	4 Feb. 13	5 July 21	10 June	do	10 June 26
P George Paris Bradshaw,[78*] KH., *Lt.-Col.*, Unattached	2 Oct. 06	16 June 08	23 May 16	26 Dec. 22	do	do	5 Aug. 48

	CORNET, ETC.	LIEUT.	CAPTAIN.	MAJOR.	LIEUT.-COLONEL.	COLONEL.	WHEN PLACED ON HALF PAY.
Thomas Dobbin,[79] late of 3 Dragoon Guards	April 06	7 Aug. 07	10 April 13	3 Nov. 25	10 June 26	23 Nov. 41	
𝔓 John Drummond,[80] *Lt.-Col.*, Unattached	22 Nov. 10	never	26 May 14	never	22 June	do	13 April 39
𝔓 *Robert Francis Melville Browne,*[81] late of Scots Fus. Guards	22 Oct. 99	24 June 02	27 Aug. 04	13 Jan. 14	11 July	do	
𝔓 James Freeth, KH.,[82] *Lt.-Col.*, Unatt., *Assist.-Quar.-Mas.-Gen.*	25 Dec. 06	30 May 09	21 April 14	21 Jan. 19	do	do	25 June 30
𝔓 𝔚 *Francis Le Blanc*, late of 46 Foot	30 May 07	16 Mar. 09	28 Sept. 13	31 Dec. 22	do	do	
𝔓 𝔚 *George Wm. Horton*, late of 7 Dragoon Guards	22 Feb. 10	25 July 11	5 Oct. 20	17 Aug. 21	1 Aug.	do	
𝔓 𝔚 John Buck Riddlesden, *Lieut.-Col.*, Unattached	19 Jan. 09	4 April 11	20 July 15	never	do	do	1 Aug. 26
Sir Charles Routledge O'Donnell, *do.* do.	9 Sept. 13	7 Sept. 15	11 July 22	14 Jan. 26	15 Aug.	do	15 Aug. 26
𝔓 Thomas Chaplin, *Lieut.-Col.*, Coldstream Guards	18 April 11	never	6 Oct. 14	never	do	do	
John Leslie, KH., *Lieut.-Col.* h.p. 4 Foot	7 Aug. 06	2 June 08	30 Nov. 09	1 Jan. 19	29 Aug.	do	29 Nov. 48
𝔓 Robert Bartlett Coles, *do.* Unattached	20 Aug. 03	1 May 05	8 Sept. 08	24 Oct. 21	19 Sept.	do	19 Sept. 26
James Fleming,[83] late of 55 Foot	4 Aug. 00	25 June 03	10 Feb. 14	26 June 23	do	do	
𝔓 𝔚 Edward Pery Buckley,[84] *Lt.-Col.*, Unatt., *Equerry to the Queen*	24 June 12	never	23 Mar.	19 July 21	26 Sept.	do	9 Nov. 30
Sir Richard Doherty, *Lieut.-Col.*, *Inspecting Field Officer*	10 Sept. 03	22 Nov. 04	21 May 12	16 Sept. 24	26 Sept.	do	
𝔓 𝔚 Edward Byam,[86] *Lt.-Col.*, Unattached	14 Nov. 11	29 April 13	26 Aug. 19	16 June 25	do	do	26 Sept. 26
William Rogers, *Lt.-Col.*, do	24 June 02	20 Feb. 06	4 Mar. 13	23 June 25	do	do	do
𝔓 Charles O'Neil Prendergast,[88] *Lt.-Col.*, do.	26 Aug. 09	never	25 Dec. 13	never	26 Oct.	do	5 July 39
George Charles, *Earl of* Lucan, *do.* do.	29 Aug. 16	24 Dec. 18	16 May 22	23 June 25	29 Nov.	do	14 April 37
𝔓 *Thomas Drake,*[89] CMG., late of Grenadier Guards	23 May 05	15 May 06	28 May 07	22 April 13	16 Nov.	do	
𝔓 𝔚 Charles Yorke, *Major*, Unatt., *Assist.-Quar.-Mas.-Gen. at Manchester*	22 Jan. 07	18 Feb. 08	24 Dec. 13	9 June 25	30 Nov.	do	9 June 25
𝔓 *John Hogge*, KH., late of 11 Foot	3 Sept. 03	1 Aug. 05	9 Mar. 09	17 Dec. 18	12 Dec.	do	
𝔓 Holman Custance,[90*] *Lieut.-Col.*, Unattached	20 Oct. 08	22 Feb. 10	26 May 14	2 Sept. 24	do	do	
John Henry Richardson, *do.*, Unattached	16 Aug. 09	5 Sept. 11	4 Dec. 17	14 July 25	do	do	12 Dec. 26
Sir John Rowland Eustace,[91] KH., *Lt.-Col.*, Unattached	June 08	3 Nov. 08	17 Mar. 14	9 Nov. 21	19 Dec.	do	24 April 40
𝔓 *Henry Stisted,*[92] late of Coldstream Guards	8 Dec. 03	24 Jan. 05	5 Jan. 09	25 Sept. 23	do	do	
𝔚 Berkeley Drummond, *Lt.-Col.*, Sco. Fus. Gds., *Equerry to the Queen*	5 Mar. 12	never	4 July 15	never	21 Dec.	do	
𝔓 *Hon. Sir* Edward Cust, KCH.,[93] *Lieut.-Col.*, Unattached, *Master of Ceremonies to the Queen*	15 Mar. 10	27 Dec. 10	9 Dec. 13	24 Oct. 21	26 Dec.	do	26 Dec. 26
Dennis Daly,[94] *Lieut.-Col.*, Unatt.	28 Aug. 00	15 Jan. 01	13 May 07	19 July 21	30 Dec. 26	do	30 Dec. 26
Lieut.-Col., Unattached	19 Aug. 06	18 Dec. 06	9 May 11	1 July 24	do	do	do
of 2 Dragoons	13 June 11	never	20 July 15	never	do	do	
H Unattached	11 Feb. 13	10 Nov. 14	13 June 19	10 Sept. 25	10 Jan. 27	do	10 Sept. 25
𝔓 *Sir Henry Robartes Wyatt,*[97] late of 29 Foot	22 Sept. 12	22 Nov. 13	11 Nov. 19	never	21 May	do	
𝔓 John Fraser,[98] *Maj.*, h.p. 1 R. Vet. Bn., *Dep.-Qr.-Mas.-Gen. Ceylon*	19 April 09	12 Sept. 11	28 Jan. 13	31 Oct. 18	24 May	do	16 Aug. 27

	2D LIEUT. ETC.	LIEUT.	CAPTAIN.	MAJOR.	LIEUT.-COLONEL.	COLONEL.	WHEN PLACED ON HALF PAY.
Jonathan Peel, *Lt.-Col.*, Unattached	15 June 15	3 Dec. 18	13 Dec. 21	19 May 25	7 June 27	23 Nov. 41	9 Aug. 27
William Roberts,[99] *Lt.-Col.*, R. Art., on retired full pay	1 Dec. 96	23 April 97	24 Oct. 03	4 June 14	6 Nov.	do	
Sir *Henry Fairfax*,[100] Bart., late of 2 Life Guards	21 April 08	23 Nov. 09	22 July 13	17 July 23	do	do	
Marcus Beresford, *Lt.-Col.*, Unatt., *Assist.-Adjt.-Gen. at Cork*	4 Sept. 17	1 Feb. 21	16 Sept. 24	26 Sept. 26	do	do	13 May 42
James Chas. Chatterton, KH.,[100*] *Lieut.-Col.*, Unattached, *Gentleman of the Privy Chamber*	23 Nov. 09	6 June 11	26 Mar. 18	22 July 24	18 Dec.	do	3 Oct. 48
John Vandeleur,[101] late of 4 Dragoons	6 July 09	30 May 11	28 Feb. 22	1 Oct. 25	do	do	
John Hobart, *Lord Howden*,[102] KH., *Major*, Unattached, *Equerry to H. R. H. the Duchess of Kent*	never	13 July 15	22 Oct. 18	9 June 25	25 Dec.	do	9 June 25
Robert Douglas,[103] CB., *Lieut.-Col.*, R. Art., on retired full pay	1 Nov. 96	1 Sept. 98	20 July 04	4 June 14	31 Dec.	do	
James M'Alpine, late of 6 Dragoons	4 May 15	16 Nov. 15	31 Oct. 22	15 Aug. 26	do	do	
James Alex. *Earl of Rosslyn*, *Lt.-Col.*, Unattached	25 Feb. 19	9 July 20	25 Mar. 23	12 Dec. 26	do	do	28 Jan. 42
Wm. Thomas Knollys, *Major*, Scots Fusilier Guards	9 Dec. 13	never	25 Sept. 17	never	do	do	
Charles F. R. Lascelles, *Major*, Grenadier Guards	10 Sept. 12	never	9 June 14	never	21 Feb. 28	do	
Wm. Cuth. Elph. Holloway, CB., *Colonel*, Royal Engineers	1 Jan. 04	1 Mar. 05	24 June 09	21 June 17	26 Feb.	do	
Edward Studd, *Lt.-Col.*, Unattached	22 Feb. 16	17 July 17	7 Aug. 23	26 Sept. 26	do	do	31 Aug. 38
Charles Stuart Campbell, CB.,[104] *Lt.-Col.*, h. p. 1 Foot	7 Dec. 96	14 Dec. 97	14 May 04	21 Sept. 13	25 April	do	27 Oct. 38
Sir Henry Robert Ferguson Davie, *Bart. Lt.-Col.* Unatt.	18 Mar. 18	25 Feb. 19	26 Sept. 22	19 Dec. 26	8 May	do	6 Aug. 47
Ernest Fred. Gascoigne, *Capt. & Lt.-Col.*, Grenadier Guards	2 May 11	13 May 13	6 July 15	19 May 25	3 June	do	
Dugald Campbell,[105] *Lt.-Col.*, R. Art., on retired full pay	6 Dec. 96	16 July 99	29 July 04	4 June 14	17 June	do	
Richard Beauchamp, late of 49 Foot	14 Mar. 11	19 Feb. 12	6 July 20	13 Aug. 25	5 Aug.	do	
Lovel Benjamin Lovell, KH., *Lt.-Col.*, 15 Hussars	18 Dec. 05	19 May 08	12 Dec. 11	21 Jan. 19	21 Nov.	do	
Geo. Ralph, Lord *Abercromby*, late of Coldstream Guards	never	26 June 17	14 Mar. 22	8 April 26	do	do	
Henry Armytage,[108] late of Grenadier Guards	27 Nov. 12	never	5 Mar. 18	never	21 Nov.	do	
Peter Margetson Wallace, *Colonel*, Royal Artillery	10 May 97	16 July 99	15 Nov. 04	4 June 14	30 Dec.	do	
St. John Augustus Clerke, KH.,[109] *Lt.-Col.*, Unattached	13 Oct. 08	6 June 11	11 Mar. 19	26 May 25	do	do	30 Dec. 28
Richard Jones, *Colonel*, Royal Artillery	12 May 97	16 July 99	5 Dec. 04	4 June 14	31 Dec.	do	
John Edward Jones, *do.* do., *Assistant-Adjutant-General*	14 July 97	do	20 Dec. 04	do	do	do	
Robert Wallace,[110] KH., late of 3 Foot	4 Dec. 06	25 Mar. 08	20 Oct. 14	5 Nov. 25	do	do	
Sir James Holmes Schoedde, KCB.,[111] *Lt.-Col.*, Unattached, *Aide-de-Camp to the Queen*	May 00	8 Oct. 01	19 Sept. 05	21 June 13	20 Mar. 29	do	26 Nov. 45
Henry John Wm. Bentinck, *Major*, Coldstream Guards, *do.*	25 Mar. 13	never	18 Jan. 20	never	16 May	do	
Thomas Reed, CB., *Lt.-Col.*, 62 Foot, *Aide-de-Camp to the Queen*	26 Aug. 13	2 May 15	19 Feb. 24	15 June 26	11 Aug.	do	
Thomas Alston Brandreth, CB., *Colonel*, Royal Artillery	12 July 97	16 July 99	20 Dec. 04	4 June 14	27 Oct.	do	
Hon. Henry Dundas, CB., *Lieut.-Col.*, 60 Foot	never	18 Nov. 19	1 April 24	11 July 26	3 Dec.	do	

	ENSIGN, ETC.	LIEUT.	CAPTAIN.	MAJOR.	LIEUT.-COLONEL.	COLONEL.	WHEN PLACED ON HALF PAY.
P W Alexander Kennedy Clarke Kennedy,[112] CB. KH., *Lt.-Col.*, Unattached, *Aide-de-Camp to the Queen*	8 Sept. 02	15 Dec. 04	13 Dec. 10	26 May 25	11 June 30	23 Nov. 41	22 Dec. 45
P Horatio George Broke, *Major*, Unattached, *do.*	29 May 06	15 Feb. 08	18 Mar. 13	28 July 14	20 July	do	20 July 30
P Thomas Weare, KH., *Lt.-Col.*, Provisional Battalion at Chatham, *Aide-de-Camp to the Queen*	14 Sept. 04	25 June 05	19 April 10	21 June 13	22 July	do	
P John Michell, CB., *Colonel*, Royal Artillery	1 Mar. 98	2 Oct. 99	20 Sept. 05	29 Sept. 14	do	do	
P W Edw. Chas. Whinyates, CB. KH., *do.* do.	do	do	8 July 05	18 June 15	do	do	
P W Thomas Hutcheson, *do.* do.	1 Dec. 97	do	10 April 05	12 Aug. 19	do	do	
P Arthur Hunt, *do.* do.	11 Nov. 98	18 April 01	1 June 06	do	26 Oct. 31	do	
W John Oldfield, K.H., *Colonel*, R. Eng., *Aide-de-Camp to the Queen*	2 April 06	1 July 06	1 May 11	22 July 30	12 Nov.	do	
P W Thomas Dyneley, CB., *Colonel*, Royal Artillery, *do.*	1 Dec. 01	1 July 03	28 May 08	18 June 15	10 Jan. 37	do	
C John M'Callum, *Colonel Commandant*, R. Marines at Plymouth	29 Jan. 98	18 Oct. 03	12 May 12	22 July 30	10 July 37	12 Feb. 42	
P Colin Campbell, CB., *Lt.-Col.*, 98 F., *do.*, *Aide-de-camp to the Queen*	26 May 08	28 June 09	9 Nov. 13	26 Nov. 25	26 Oct. 32	23 Dec.	
Peter Edmondstone Craigie, CB.,[114] *Lt.-Col.*, h. p. 55 Foot, *do.*	3 June 13	29 Sept. 14	24 Oct. 21	10 Aug. 26	21 Nov. 34	do	11 Aug. 44
Edmund Morris, CB.,[115] *Lt.-Col.*, Unatt., *do.*	21 June 10	21 April 13	1 Dec. 25	13 Sept. 33	22 Nov. 36	do	17 Nov. 43
P Charles Menzies, KH., *Col. Commandant*, R. Marines at Portsmouth	17 Feb. 98	21 Dec. 06	13 April 13	10 Jan. 37	10 July 37	10 July 44	
Henry Colvile, *Major*, Scots Fusilier Guards	never	29 Dec. 13	6 Dec. 17	never	6 July 36	31 Dec.	
P W *Lonsdale Boldero*,[116] late of Grenadier Guards	15 Dec. 09	never	20 Oct. 13	never	22 July 36	15 April 45	
P Henry William Vavasour, *Colonel*, Royal Engineers	1 Feb. 04	1 Mar. 05	24 June 09	never	28 Jan. 29	22 April	
P W Everard Wm. Bouverie, *Lieut.-Col.*, Royal Horse Guards, *Equerry to H. R. H. Prince Albert*	2 April 12	15 Oct. 12	9 Sept. 19	6 May 31	4 Dec. 33	16 Sept.	
George Graydon, *Colonel*, Royal Engineers	1 June 04	1 Mar. 05	2 Dec. 09	never	22 May 29	1 April 46	
P Robert Thomson, *do.* do.	1 Nov. 04	1 Mar. 05	10 July 10	never	26 Dec. 29	do	
George Cobbe, *Colonel*, Royal Artillery	9 Oct. 99	7 Sept. 01	2 June 06	12 Aug. 19	20 Nov. 34	do	
W Alexander Cavalie Mercer, *Colonel*, Royal Artillery	20 Dec. 99	1 Dec. 01	3 Dec. 06	12 Aug. 19	5 June 35	1 April 46	
Hon. Thomas Ashburnham, CB.,[117] *Lt.-Col.*, h. p. 62 Foot, *Aide-de-Camp to the Queen*, *Military Sec. to the Governor of Bombay*	never	30 Jan. 23	22 June 26	never	27 Mar. 35	3 April 46	21 Sept. 47
P Charles Robert Cureton, CB.,[118] *Lt.-Col.*, h. p. 16 Lancers, *Aide-de-Camp to the Queen*, *Adjutant-General East Indies*	24 Feb. 14	27 June 16	12 Nov. 25	6 Dec. 33	23 July 39	do	13 Aug. 46
Michael White, CB., *Lt.-Col.*, 3 Drs., *Aide-de-Camp to the Queen*	15 Aug. 04	14 May 05	7 Nov. 15	10 Jan. 37	13 Dec. 39	do	
John Scott, CB., *Lt.-Col.*, 9 Lancers, *do.*	4 May 15	26 Oct. 15	28 June 21	9 Nov. 26	31 Aug. 39	19 June	
John Lysaght Pennefather, CB.,[119] *Lt.-Col.*, h. p. 28 Foot, *do.*	14 Jan. 18	20 Feb. 23	5 Nov. 25	22 Mar. 31	18 Oct. 39	do	
Armine Simcoe Henry Mountain, CB., *Lt.-Col.*, 29 F., *do.*, *Military Secretary to the Governor-General of India*	20 July 15	3 Dec. 18	26 May 25	30 Dec. 26	23 June 40	do	
Sir Ord Honyman, *Bart.*, *Major*, Grenadier Guards	12 Dec. 11	never	4 July 15	never	28 Sept. 30	2 Oct.	

	CORNET, ETC.	LIEUT.	CAPTAIN.	MAJOR.	LIEUT.-COLONEL.	COLONEL.	WHEN PLACED ON HALF PAY.
Alex. Findlay, KH., *Lt.-Col.*, h.p. R. Afr. Corps, *Fort-Maj. at Inverness*	27 July 14	1 Feb. 16	34 Oct. 21	28 Dec. 26	19 Mar. 29	9 Nov. 46	19 Mar. 29
William Bush, KH., *Lt.-Col.*, Inspecting Field Officer	7 Jan. 08	29 June 09	22 July 13	8 April 26	22 May	do	
Frederick Thomas Buller, *Lt.-Col.*, Unattached	never	30 Dec. 13	6 Sept. 21	never	4 June	do	3 Feb. 32
Henry Despard, CB., *do.* 99 Foot	25 Oct. 99	25 June 03	19 Nov. 06	12 Aug. 19	13 Aug.	do	
Benjamin Chapman Browne, late of 85 Foot	17 June 13	2 Jan. 17	18 July 22	29 Aug. 26	16 Mar. 30	do	
Sir John Mark Fred. Smith, KH., *Colonel*, R. Engineers, *Gentleman Usher of the Privy Chamber*	1 Dec. 05	1 Mar. 06	1 May 11	never	do	do	
P Rice Jones, KH., *Colonel*, Royal Engineers	1 Feb. 06	1 July 06	1 May 11	never	8 June	do	
P Saumarez Brock, KH.,[130] *Lt.-Col.* h. p. 48 Foot	1803	14 April 04	28 Mar. 05	12 Oct. 15	12 June	do	13 May 35
P Edward Wells Bell, *do.* Unattached	never	16 May 11	20 June 22	19 Dec. 26	29 June	do	29 June 30
Alexander Campbell, CB. KH., *Lt.-Col.*, 9 Lancers	24 Aug. 06	4 Sept. 06	13 Aug. 12	9 Aug. 21	16 July	do	
P John Reed,[121] *Lt.-Col.*, h. p. 54 Foot	26 Mar. 99	21 Mar. 00	12 May 08	27 May 25	20 July	do	28 Oct. 40
P James Jones,[122] KH., *Major*, Unattached	6 Nov. 01	23 Nov. 04	17 Aug. 08	14 April 13	22 July	do	31 Aug. 15
William Fawcett, late of 34 Foot	8 June 96	1 Nov. 96	7 Sept. 04	22 April 13	do	do	
P Henry Bristow, *Major*, h. p. 38 Foot	14 Feb. 05	30 Sept. 05	1 Sept. 08	20 Jan. 14	do	do	
Sir William M. George Colebrooke, CB. KH., *Colonel*, R. Artillery, *Governor and Commander-in-Chief of Barbadoes*	17 Aug. 03	12 Sept. 03	27 Sept. 10	1 June	do	do	
Tho. Tisdall, 1*st Lt.* late R. Irish Art. on retired full pay	never	10 Oct. 94	18 April 01	4 June	do	do	
Maxwell Close, late of 79 Foot	6 Dec. 98	8 Aug. 99	24 April 01	4 June 14	do	do	
William Henry Taynton,[123] late of 44 Foot	27 Feb. 94	1 April 95	4 July 01	do	do	do	
Wm. Mansfield Morrison, *Captain*, h. p. 23 Dragoons	10 July 99	14 Aug. 01	24 Aug. 02	do	do	do	8 Aug. 22
Edward Carlyon,[124] *Major*, h. p. 66 Foot	24 Mar. 03	9 Feb. 04	25 July 05	do	do	do	25 Nov. 17
P Thomas Burke, *Major*, h. p. 4 Foot	1 Oct. 94	25 Oct. 99	12 Aug. 04	22 July	do	do	25 Feb. 16
Joseph Creighton, *Major*, h. p. 59 Foot	1 Jan. 01	17 Mar. 03	6 Nov. 06	23 Sept. 13	do	do	20 Sept. 19
P Thomas Samuel Trafford,[125] *Major*, h. p. 24 Foot	Nov. 03	7 Sept. 04	20 Mar. 06	22 Nov. 13	do	do	27 May 24
P William Cator, *Colonel*, Royal Artillery	7 May 03	12 Sept. 03	1 May 09	12 April 14	do	do	
P *George Torey*,[126] late of 60 Foot	8 Nov. 04	21 Nov. 05	9 Nov. 09	12 Apr. 14	do	do	
P *Edward Anthony Angelo*,[127] KH., late of 30 Foot	9 July 03	28 Aug. 04	1 Dec. 06	2 June 14	do	do	
P George Saunders Thwaites,[128] *Captain*, h. p. 57 Foot	12 Sept. 95	23 Dec. 95	2 July 03	4 June 14	do	do	6 Feb. 17
Joseph Jerrard, *Captain*, h. p. 6 Garrison Battalion	13 May 95	1 June 97	8 Oct.	do	do	do	4 Feb. 15
P Arthur Morris, *Captain*, h. p. 14 Foot	29 Nov. 98	23 Feb. 00	3 Dec.	do	do	do	8 Mar. 21
W *John Linton*,[129] late of Coldstream Guards	8 Sept. 08	25 Jan. 09	15 May 17	21 July 25	31 Aug.	do	
William Graham, *Lt.-Col.*, Unattached	29 May 17	13 Dec. 21	30 Jan. 23	18 Dec. 27	do	do	31 Aug. 30
Thomas Moody, *Colonel*, Royal Engineers	1 April 06	1 July 06	1 May 11	23 May 16	2 Dec.	do	
James Thomas, *Earl of* Cardigan, *Lt.-Col.*, 11 Hussars	6 May 24	13 Jan. 25	9 June 26	3 Aug. 30	3 Dec.	do	

	2D LIEUT. ETC.	LIEUT.	CAPTAIN.	MAJOR.	LIEUT.-COLONEL.	COLONEL.	WHEN PLACED ON HALF PAY.
Godfrey Thornton, *Major*, Grenadier Guards	20 Jan. 14	never	11 Oct. 21	never	3 Dec. 30	9 Nov. 46	
P Wm Cowper Coles,[130] *Lieut.-Col.*, Unattached	31 Oct. 05	8 Feb. 07	19 Nov. 12	9 June 25	10 Dec.	do	20 Jan. 32
Sir Michael Creagh,[131] KH., *do.* Unattached	9 May 02	28 Feb. 04	25 Nov. 09	24 Oct. 21	31 Dec.	do	27 June 45
John Eden,[132] CB., *Lt.-Col.*, Unatt. *Asst. Adj.-Gen. in N. Britain*	14 Feb. 07	14 Aug. 07	26 Dec. 18	9 June 25	do	do	31 Dec. 30
P Richd Richard Story,[133] *Lt.-Col.*, Unattached	15 Oct. 03	11 Mar. 06	21 Dec. 09	15 Aug. 22	8 Feb. 31	do	14 Sept. 38
W *William Fraser*,[134] late of Grenadier Guards	10 June 13	19 July 15	23 Sept. 24	13 July 26	do	do	
Sir Robert Burdett, Bart., late of 68 Foot	22 Oct. 18	7 June 19	4 Oct. 21	7 Nov. 26	8 Mar.	do	
P Jas Shee,[135] *Lt.-Col.*, Unattached	never	3 Sept. 07	18 Nov. 13	20 May 26	5 April	do	5 April 31
George Teulon, late of 16 Foot	17 Aug. 09	14 July 11	13 Mar. 17	17 Oct. 26	12 April	do	
P Humphrey Robert Hartley,[136] *Lt.-Col.*, Unattached	8 Oct. 12	2 Sept. 13	29 Nov. 21	8 Nov. 27	do	do	4 Sept. 35
Henry William Barnard, *Capt. & Lt.-Col.*, Gren. Guards, *Assistant Adjutant-General at Manchester*	9 June 14	never	15 Aug. 22	never	17 May	do	
P W Jas Campbell, KH., *Lt.-Col.*, Inspecting Field Officer	12 June 99	25 Dec. 00	1 Aug. 05	12 Aug. 19	12 July	do	
Hon. Charles Grey, *Lt.-Col.*, Unattached, *Equerry to the Queen*	16 Nov. 20	10 April 23	16 June 25	19 Feb. 28	do	do	8 April 42
P John Chester,[137] *Lt.-Col.*, h. p. Royal Artillery	28 April 98	6 Oct. 99	29 Dec. 05	12 Aug. 19	3 Sept.	do	26 Oct. 31
Wm. *Lord* de Ros, *Maj.* Unatt., *Brig.-Maj. to Inspec. Gen. of Cav.*	29 Mar. 19	24 Aug. 21	23 Oct. 24	5 June 27	8 Sept.	do	5 June 27
P John Geddes,[138] KH., *Lt.-Col.*, Unattached	Aug. 04	25 Oct. 05	1 Dec. 08	24 Feb. 25	11 Nov.	do	11 Nov. 31
Wm. Hen. Cornwall, *Lt.-Col.*, h. p. 83 Foot, *Equerry to the Queen Dowager*	never	10 Aug. 15	6 Nov. 24	never	10 Feb. 32	do	26 May 48
Sir Charles Fitzroy Maclean, Bart., late of 13 Dragoons	never	10 Oct. 16	18 Oct. 21	1 Aug. 26	16 Mar.	do	
Philip Spencer Stanhope, *Capt. & Lt.-Col.*, Grenadier Guards	30 Mar. 15	never	17 July 23	never	do	do	
Charles Collins Blane, *Lt.-Col.*, Unattached	never	4 July 15	31 July 23	19 Sept. 26	20 April	do	20 April 32
Brinckman Brinckman, late of Coldstream Guards	never	11 Sept. 17	28 April 25	never	do	do	
Philip Dundas, late of 6 Foot	24 July 23	17 Sept. 25	11 July 26	3 Dec. 30	27 April	do	
P Alexander Maclachlan, *Lt.-Col.*, Royal Artillery	3 Dec. 03	6 Dec. 03	17 June 12	22 July 30	1 June 32	do	
P Edward French Boys, *Lt.-Col.*, 45 Foot	17 Nov. 08	3 April 10	8 June 15	3 Feb. 39	21 June	do	
Charles Murray Hay, *Major*, Colds. Guards	20 April 20	1 Nov. 21	24 Dec. 25	never	22 June	do	
Frederick Farquharson, *Lt.-Col.*, 7 Foot	17 Sept. 13	25 May 14	23 Sept. 19	29 June 30	7 Sept.	do	
W Henry *Lord* Rokeby, *Capt. & Lt.-Col.*, Scots Fus. Gds.	21 April 14	never	12 June 23	never	21 Sept.	do	
P Charles Gilmour,[139] *Lt.-Col.*, R. Art. on retired full pay	20 Dec. 98	3 Dec. 00	1 June 06	12 Aug. 19	27 Sept.	do	
P *Charles Leslie*,[140] KH., late of Grenadier Guards	18 Dec. 06	10 Feb. 08	5 Nov. 13	18 Dec. 28	28 Dec.	do	
Henry Edward Porter, *Lt.-Col.*, Unattached	3 July 17	23 Dec. 19	14 July 25	4 Oct. 31	1 Feb. 33	do	1 Feb. 33
Lord *Thomas Cecil*, late of Coldstream Guards	24 Oct. 16	30 Mar. 20	24 Oct. 22	28 June 27	5 April	do	
John Wolrige,[141] *Lt.-Col.*, Royal Marines, on retired full pay	29 Oct. 95	30 Aug. 97	26 Nov. 05	12 Aug. 19	5 Aug.	do	
George E. Jones,[142] KH., *Lt.-Col.*, h. p. 31 Foot	16 June 06	16 April 07	8 Oct. 12	22 July 30	8 Nov.	do	6 Aug. 47

	ENSIGN, ETC.	LIEUT.	CAPTAIN.	MAJOR.	LIEUT.-COLONEL.	COLONEL.	WHEN PLACED ON HALF PAY.
John Dawson Rawdon, *Lieut-Col.*, Unattached	18 Dec. 22	30 Jan. 22	10 June 26	never	15 Nov. 33	9 Nov. 46	13 May 42
William Persse, CB.,[143] *Lt.-Col.*, late of 16 Lancers	10 Jan. 06	27 Nov. 06	23 Jan. 12	25 May 22	6 Dec.	do	
William Beckwith,[144] KH., *Lt.-Col.*, Unattached	7 Jan. 13	12 Dec. 15	9 May 22	14 Feb. 28	do	do	6 Dec. 33
James Macdonald Robertson,[145] late of 4 Dr. Gds.	13 Aug. 04	7 Nov. 05	2 Mar. 20	14 Nov. 26	31 Dec.	do	
Henry Edward Robinson,[146] *Lt.-Col.*, Unattached	28 May 06	9 Feb. 08	26 July 22	20 Sept. 27	1 Jan. 34	do	10 Feb. 43
George Todd, late of Coldstream Guards	3 May 21	24 July 23	17 Sept. 25	22 Mar. 33	31 Jan.	do	
Hon. Edw. Gordon Douglas Pennant, late of Scots Fusilier Guards	never	31 Aug. 15	13 May 24	never	18 April	do	
Francis Venables Harcourt, late of Coldstream Guards	11 July 16	26 Mar. 17	8 July 24	never	2 May	do	
Hon. Henry Sutton Fane, *Lt.-Col.*, Unattached	18 July 22	27 Nov. 23	22 Oct. 25	18 Dec. 28	9 May	do	9 Feb. 38
Henry William Breton, *Lt.-Col.*, 53 Foot	16 Mar. 15	27 July 20	21 July 25	31 Dec. 28	11 July	do	
Allen Thomas Maclean,[147] *do.* h. p. 13 Dragoons	4 Jan. 10	11 July 11	23 Dec. 18	29 Oct. 30	do	do	
Stephen Kirby, *Lt.-Col.*, Royal Artillery, on retired full pay	1 Aug. 09	31 Dec. 09	1 June 06	12 Aug. 19	20 July	do	
Arthur, *Marquis of* Douro, *Lt.-Col.*, Unatt., *Aide-de-Camp to His Grace the Commander-in-Chief*	20 Mar. 23	1 July 27	8 May 28	2 Nov. 30	12 Aug.	do	12 Aug. 34
George Gawler,[148] KH., *Lt.-Col.*, Unattached	4 Oct. 10	12 May 12	9 June 25	6 Feb. 31	do	do	do
John Julius Wm. Angerstein, *Capt. & Lt.-Col.*, Gr. Gds.	never	9 April 18	2 April 25	never	12 Sept.	do	
John Wilson Kettlewell,[149] *Lt.-Col.*, R. Artillery, on retired full pay	13 Dec. 99	14 Oct. 01	24 Oct. 06	12 Aug. 19	6 May 35	do	
Thomas Marten, KH., *Lt.-Col.*, 1 Dragoons	22 Nov. 13	23 June 17	4 May 22	13 Dec. 26	29 May	do	
Sir John Montagu Burgoyne, Bart., late of Grenadier Guards	17 Oct. 16	1 Oct. 18	28 April 25	never	5 June	do	
Matthew Charles Dixon, *Colonel*, Royal Engineers	2 April 06	1 July 06	1 May 11	22 July 30	25 June	do	
Patrick Doul Calder, *Lt.-Col.*, do	1 Aug. 06	1 Dec. 06	13 May 11	do	do	do	
Philip James Yorke, late of Scots Fus. Gds.	5 May 14	never	24 Feb. 25	never	7 Aug. 35	do	
Thomas Gerrard Ball,[150] *Lt.-Col.*, Unattached	17 Sept. 07	1 Dec. 08	27 April 14	24 June 24	2 Oct.	do	25 Oct. 42
Eaton Monins,[150a] *Lt.-Col.*, Unattached	1 Dec. 14	9 Sept. 19	23 June 25	19 Nov. 30	do	do	10 Nov. 46
Guy Carleton Coffin, *do.* Royal Artillery, on retired full pay	1 July 00	11 Feb. 02	18 June 07	19 July 21	4 Feb. 36	do	
William Cox,[151] KH., *do.* Unattached	6 June 05	19 Nov. 07	16 Sept. 13	1 Aug. 26	5 Feb.	do	
William Croker,[152] CB., late of 17 Foot	27 Mar. 03	2 June 04	30 Nov. 06	12 Aug. 19	1 April	do	
James Stokes Bastard, *Colonel*, Royal Artillery	15 Nov. 00	12 May 02	1 Feb. 08	27 May 25	27 April	do	
George Morton Eden, *Capt. & Lt.-Col.*, Scots Fus. Gds.	18 July 22	10 Sept. 25	12 Dec. 26	11 Oct. 31	20 May	do	
George Dixon, *do.* do.	never	20 Jan. 20	8 April 28	never	do	do	
Frederick Maunsell, *Lt.-Col.*, *Insp. Field Officer of Rec. Dist.*	16 Mar. 12	28 Jan. 13	24 June 19	14 Aug. 27	23 May	do	
George Baker, late of 16 Lancers	6 July 09	15 Aug. 11	19 Oct. 20	18 July 26	3 June	do	
Thomas Gore Browne, *Colonel*, Royal Artillery	28 Feb. 01	12 Nov. 02	1 Feb. 08	27 May 25	1 July	do	
William John Codrington, *Capt. & Lt.-Col.*, Coldstream Guards	22 Feb. 21	24 April 23	20 July 26	never	8 July	do	

	CORNET, ETC.	LIEUT.	CAPTAIN.	MAJOR.	LIEUT.-COLONEL.	COLONEL.	WHEN PLACED ON HALF PAY.
Duncan Grant, *Colonel*, Royal Artillery	23 Feb. 01	23 Nov. 02	1 Feb. 08	27 May 25	12 July 36	9 Nov. 46	
Henry Alexander Scott, *Colonel*, Royal Artillery	28 April 01	20 April 03	1 Feb. 08	27 May 25	10 Aug.	do	
William Wylde, CB., *Lieut.-Col.*, do. *Groom of the Bed-chamber to H. R. H. Prince Albert*	8 Sept. 08	6 Dec. 03	16 Mar. 12	16 July 30	19 Aug.	do	
William Turnor,[153] *do.*, Unattached	15 Aug. 04	23 May 05	15 Aug. 11	19 Dec. 26	22 Nov.	do	22 Nov. 36
William Fludyer, *Capt. & Lt.-Col.*, Grenadier Guards	30 Dec. 19	25 Oct. 21	7 July 25	never	2 Dec.	do	
John Ross, *Lieut.-Col.*, St. Helena Regiment	1 July 03	1 Nov. 05	15 April 13	5 Nov. 25	9 Dec.	do	
John Wharton Frith, *do. Insp. F. O. of a Rec. Dist.*	17 July 04	27 Feb. 05	29 Jan. 12	22 July 30	16 Dec.	do	
Thomas Falls,[154] *do.* Unattached	21 Mar. 05	4 Dec. 06	23 Sept. 13	29 Sept. 14	23 Dec.	do	23 Dec. 36
Henry Charles Russel, *Colonel*, Royal Artillery	1 Apr. 02	12 Sept. 03	15 July 08	27 May 25	10 Jan. 37	do	
Charles Cornwallis Dansey, CB., *do.* do.	19 July 03	12 Sept. 03	1 Oct. 09	22 July 30	do	do	
Wm. Fergusson, *Col. 2nd Comm.*, Royal Marines	10 Sept. 98	29 April 04	23 Feb. 14	10 Jan. 37	10 July	do	
John Hall, *Lt.-Col. & Colonel*, 1 Life Guards	12 June 17	24 July 17	2 Aug. 22	8 Sept. 31	27 Dec.	do	
James M'Douall, *Lt.-Col. & Col.* 2 Life Guards	19 Feb. 18	2 Oct. 23	19 Oct. 25	28 June 38	10 April 40	10 April 47	
Adam Fife Crawford, *Colonel*, Royal Artillery	17 Aug. 03	12 Sept. 03	3 Aug. 10	22 July 30	10 Jan. 37	20 July	
Walter Powell, *Col. 2nd Commandant*, R. Marines at Portsmouth	31 Jan. 00	21 Sept. 04	14 Nov. 23	18 Mar. 37	7 Nov. 38	27 Dec. 47	
Abraham Henry Gordon, *do. do.* do. at Woolwich	5 Jan. 01	16 July 05	16 Dec. 24	28 June 38	26 Aug. 39	4 Jan. 48	
John Montresor Pilcher, *do. do.* do. at Chatham	15 Jan. 01	15 Aug. 05	11 Feb. 26	never	11 May 41	17 Aug. 48	
William Bolden Dundas, CB. *do.* do.	8 Sept. 03	12 Sept. 03	11 July 11	21 Aug. 19	10 Jan. 37	1 Nov.	
Henry William Gordon, *Colonel*, Royal Artillery	17 Aug. 03	do	3 Aug. 10	22 July 30	do	do	
William Daniel Jones, *do.* do.	8 Sept. 03	do	8 May 11	do	do	do	
Courtenay Cruttenden, *do.* do.	do	24 Oct. 03	11 Aug. 11	do	28 June 38	do	
Jeremiah Taylor, *Lt.-Col.* Depot Battalion, Isle of Wight	28 Feb. 05	1 Oct. 07	2 Oct. 17	1 April 24	23 Mar. 27	21 Dec. 48	

War Services of the Colonels.

1 Sir David Cunynghame served the campaign of 1793, including the actions at Famars, St. Amand, and Lincelles (severely wounded); also the siege of Valenciennes. Taken prisoner in the action at Ostend in May 1798.

3 Colonel the Honourable Alexander Abercromby served the campaign of 1799 in Holland, as a volunteer with the 92nd; with the 52nd on the expedition to the Ferrol in 1800; in Sicily in 1806 and 1807, as Aide-de-camp to Sir John Moore. Proceeded to the Peninsula in 1809, and commanded the 28th at the battle of Busaco, and in the Lines before Lisbon; a brigade at the battle of Albuhera; the 28th at Arroyo de Molino and Almaraz; and was Assistant-Quarter-Master-General at the battles of Vittoria, the Pyrenees, and Orthes. He served also the campaign of 1815, in the same capacity, and was present at the battles of Quatre Bras and Waterloo, storming of Peronne, and capture of Paris. He has received a cross for Albuhera, Vittoria, Pyrenees, and Orthes.

6 Sir Robert Chambre Hill served on the Continent in 1794 and 95. Embarked with the Blues for the Peninsula in Oct. 1812. Soon after his arrival in Lisbon, was ordered to take command of the Household Brigade of Cavalry, which he commanded at and for some time after the battle of Vittoria, for which he has received a medal. Present also at the actions in the Pyrenees; and subsequently with Lord Hill's Division until after the battle of the 13th Dec. 1813 near Bayonne. Served also the campaign of 1815, in command of the regiment, including the action on the 17th June, and battle of Waterloo, where he was severely wounded.

7 Sir William Cox served at the re-taking of Grenada in 1796; in Egypt in 1801; employed on a particular service in Spain in 1808-9, and was present in the action at Lugo, and battle of Corunna. Commanded the fortress of Almeida, from April 1809 to the 27th August 1810, when, by the unfortunate explosion of its magazines, he was obliged to surrender it to the army under Marshal Massena.

8 Colonel J. P. Hamilton served two years in Spain during the Peninsular war, and commanded a battalion at the battle of Castalla.

9 Colonel Burslem served at Toulon in 1793, and was present in the various actions there, and afterwards at Corsica. Employed as Assistant-Quarter-Master-General at the taking of the Isle of France in 1810; and as Deputy-Quarter-Master-General at the conquest of Java, including the attack of Cornelis. Medal for Java.

11 Colonel Gauntlett was actively employed against the Maroons in the West Indies. Served also the campaign in Egypt.

12 Colonel Woodgate embarked with the 5th battalion of the 60th on the expedition to Portugal in 1808 under Sir Arthur Wellesley, and was present at the battles of Roleia, Vimiera, Talavera, and Busaco; action at Sabugal, battle of Fuentes d'Onor (wounded), siege of Badajoz in 1811; action at El Bodon, siege and capture of Ciudad Rodrigo. Medal for Fuentes d'Onor.

13 Colonel Patrickson served in Ireland with the 9th Dragoons during the Rebellion in 1798; in 1807 he served with the 43rd at the siege of Copenhagen and at the battle of Kioge; in 1808-9 in Spain, under Sir John Moore. Served afterwards in the Peninsula (a great part of the time in command of the regiment) from Sept. 1809 to the end of that war in 1814 (except during two short intervals when he was ordered to England to command the 2nd battalion), including the action of the Coa, battle of Busaco, Lines of Torres Vedras, actions of Redinha, Foz d'Arouce, Condeixa, and Sabugal; battles of Fuentes d'Onor, Vittoria, and Toulouse, for which last he has received a medal. Embarked for America in Oct. 1814, and commanded the 43rd at the attack on New Orleans. Joined the Army in Flanders on the 16th of June 1815, and was present at the capture of Paris.

14 Colonel Thornton served in the Peninsula, and commanded the 40th regiment at the battles of Talavera, Nivelle (severely wounded), Orthes, and Toulouse, for which he has received a cross.

16 Sir John Milley Doyle served the Egyptian campaign of 1801, including the actions of the 8th, 13th, and 21st of March, captures of Grand Cairo and Alexandria, together with the other operations of that campaign. Served afterwards in the Peninsula from Feb. 1809 to the end of that war in 1814—either in command of a regiment of Portuguese or a brigade—and was present at the action of Grijon, passage of the Douro, battle of Fuentes d'Onor, first siege of Badajoz, siege and assault of Ciudad Rodrigo, battles of Vittoria, the Pyrenees, Nivelle, and Orthes. Sir John has received a medal for services in Egypt; and a cross and one clasp for Fuentes d'Onor, Ciudad Rodrigo, Vittoria, the Pyrenees, and Orthes.

17 Colonel John Hamilton served the Egyptian Campaign of 1801 with the Coldstream Guards. Accompanied a detachment of that regiment to the Peninsula in March 1810; and in

April was appointed Deputy-Assistant-Quarter-Master-General at Isla de Leon. Went to England in March 1812; rejoined the regiment in the Peninsula in July 1813, and served there until the end of that war in 1814.

18 Colonel Raikes served with the Coldstream Guards on the expedition to Hanover in 1805-6; and at Copenhagen in 1807. Embarked with the regiment for the Peninsula, 31st of Dec. 1808, and served there until 26th of January 1812; and again from August 1812 to 16th May 1813.

19 Colonel Keate served in the Peninsula from Dec. 1808 to Jan. 1813, including the passage of the Douro, affair near Salamanca, battle of Busaco, siege of Ciudad Rodrigo, covering the siege of Badajoz, battle of Salamanca, capture of Madrid, and siege of Burgos.

20 Colonel Ward served in the Peninsula, and has received a medal and two clasps for Salamanca, Badajoz (severely wounded at the assault), and the Pyrenees.

21 Colonel Blake served with the 20th Dragoons at the capture of the Cape of Good Hope in 1806; proceeded from thence to South America, and was in the action at Maldonado and siege of Monte Video. Served in Portugal in 1808 and 9, including the battles of Roleia and Vimiera (medal); also at the passage of the Douro. In Sicily in 1810 and 11; subsequently on the eastern coast of Spain, including the battle of Castalla, and action at Villa Franca.

26 Colonel Jodrell served in Sicily in 1806 and 1807. He went to Cadiz in March 1810, and remained there till April 1811, having been present at the battle of Barrosa. In Sept. 1812 he joined the Duke of Wellington's army in the Peninsula, and served there until the end of that war in 1814.

27 Colonel Henry Dawkins served in the Peninsula with the Guards, from Feb. 1810 to the end of that war in 1814: Major of Brigade from June 1810, including the battle of Fuentes d'Onor, siege of Ciudad Rodrigo, battle of Salamanca, siege of Burgos, battles of Vittoria, Nivelle, and Nive; passage of the Adour, blockade of Bayonne and repulse of the sortie, on which last occasion he was severely wounded. Served also the campaign of 1815, including the battle of Waterloo.

29 Colonel Peter Brown served with the 82nd on an expedition to the coast of France early in 1800, and subsequently in the Mediterranean. He served with the 23rd at the siege and capture of Copenhagen in 1807; afterwards in North America; also at the siege and capture of Martinique in 1809; and in the Peninsula from 1810 to the end of that war in 1814. As Commandant of detachments at Belem he established a school upon the model of the Royal Military Asylum at Chelsea, for the numerous children of the soldiers' families left at that station. He also served on the Staff in the Netherlands, as Commandant of Ghent, and subsequently with the Army of Occupation in France.

31 Colonel Fielding Browne accompanied the 40th to the Peninsula in July 1808, and was present at the battles of Roleia, Vimiera, Talavera, and Busaco; on the retreat to, and at the occupation of, the Lines of Torres Vedras, siege of Badajoz, in May 1811, and repulse of the sortie from Fort San Christoval; actions of El Bodon and Aldea de Ponte, siege and storming of Ciudad Rodrigo, siege and storming of Badajoz, action at Canizal, battle of Salamanca, capture of Madrid, and subsequent retreat therefrom. Served also on the expedition against New Orleans. Commanded the regiment at the battle of Waterloo. Medal for Badajoz, having commanded the regiment at the assault.

32 Colonel Childers served with the 11th Dragoons at the Helder in 1799; the Peninsular campaigns from May 1811 to the end of that war in 1814. Also the campaign of 1815, as Major of Brigade to Sir John Vandeleur, including the battle of Waterloo. Commanded a brigade of Cavalry at the siege and capture of Bhurtpore, under Lord Combermere.

33 Colonel the Honourable Leicester Stanhope was employed in South America in 1807, and was present at the attack on Buenos Ayres. Served also in the Mahratta war of 1817 and 18, including the battle of Maheidpore, and storming of Talneir.

34 Colonel Alexander Higginson served the campaign of 1808-9, including the battle of Corunna; the expedition to Walcheren in 1809; and the Peninsular campaigns of 1812, 13, and 14.

35 Sir Thomas Reade served the campaign of 1799 in Holland with the 27th, including the actions of the 19th Sept., 2nd and 6th October. Present at the operations before Ferrol in 1800; in the Egyptian campaign of 1801; and on the expedition to Naples under Sir James Craig. In May 1808 appointed to command a Flotilla in the Mediterranean for the defence of Sicily; employed at the capture of the islands of Ischia and Procida; and at the same time took and destroyed in company with H.M.S. *Cyane*, a flotilla of thirty-four gun-boats. On the 10th June 1810, captured a flotilla of twenty-six gun-boats in the bay of Ragusa. He was afterwards constantly employed against Murat's armament on the coast of Calabria during his projected invasion of Sicily, in which service fifty of the enemy's vessels with a considerable portion of field artillery and other military stores, and many prisoners, were captured by the flotilla under his command. Served on the Eastern Coast of Spain with the forces under Lord Wm. Bentinck and Sir Wm. Clinton. At the conclusion of that war in 1814, he embarked with his regiment for America, where he served until the termination of hostilities with that country.

36 Sir John Morillyon Wilson served as midshipman in the navy for nearly six years. He was employed on the coast of Ireland during the rebellion in 1798; in the expedition to the Helder in 1799, and Egypt in 1801, where he received a medal from the Capitan Pasha for

having saved the lives of a boat's crew belonging to a Turkish man-of-war. He received three wounds while a midshipman; and the last was a severe wound on the head, which produced total deafness, in consequence of which he was invalided, and quitted the navy in 1803. His health being restored, he entered the army in 1804; and served in the third battalion Royals at Walcheren in 1809, where he was twice wounded during the siege of Flushing. He afterwards served in the Peninsula, and was in the battles of Busaco, the retreat to the lines of Torres Vedras, and in the actions of the Coa, Pumbal, Redinha, Condeixa, Casal Nova, Fos d'Arouce, the blockade of Almeida, and battle of Fuentes d'Onor. In 1812 he joined the 2nd battalion Royals in Canada, and was in the attack made on Sackett's Harbour, and Great Sodus (where he received a severe bayonet wound). He was also in the actions at Black Rock, Buffalo, and the battle of Chippewa, in which he received seven wounds, and being left on the field of battle, he fell into the hands of the enemy. During his career in the two professions he received thirteen wounds, and has two balls still lodged. The brevet rank of Major, and that of Lieutenant-Colonel was conferred upon him for his conduct at Buffalo and Chippewa.

37 Colonel William Drummond's services:—Peninsular campaigns, from 1809 to 1812, including the battles of Busaco and Fuentes d'Onor, the retreat to the lines of Torres Vedras, and subsequent advance from thence. Campaign of 1814 in Holland, including the bombardment of Antwerp and storming of Bergen-op-Zoom. Campaign of 1815, including the battles of Quatre Bras and Waterloo. Received the rank of Brevet Major for his conduct at Waterloo.

38 Colonel Snodgrass accompanied the 52nd to Sicily in 1806; to Sweden in 1808; from thence to the Peninsula, and was present during Sir John Moore's advance and retreat, and at the battle of Corunna. Served afterwards in the Peninsula, and was present at the pursuit of Massena from Santarem, action of Sabugal, battle of Fuentes d'Onor, action near Guinaldo, siege and capture of Ciudad Rodrigo, and action of San Munos. Appointed Major in the Portuguese service, 24th Nov. 1812; commanded a corps of 400 Grenadiers at the battle of Vittoria, and in the actions of Villa Franca and Tolosa. Volunteered and commanded the storming party that assaulted and carried the Convent, Redoubt, and other outworks at San Sebastian (wounded). Volunteered and commanded the detachment of the 10th Portuguese Brigade that stormed the small breach of the same place on the 31st Aug. 1813—having previously, by entering the river at night, discovered a ford under the walls, through which he led the detachment. Present when the army crossed the Bidassoa. Commanded the 1st Caçadores at the battle of Nivelle, battle of the Nive on the 9th, 10th, and 11th Dec. (wounded on the 11th), and battle of Orthes, where he was severely wounded in the head. He has received a cross for San Sebastian, Nivelle, Nive, and Orthes.

39 Colonel Balvaird served in the Peninsula with the Rifle Brigade, and has received a medal and a clasp for the battles of the Nivelle and Nive.

40 Colonel Harris served the campaign of 1808-9 as a Deputy-Assistant-Quarter-Master-General to Sir David Baird's Division, and was present at the principal operations of the army, and at the battle of Corunna.

41 Colonel Thomas Wildman served with the 7th Hussars in the campaign of 1808-9 under Sir John Moore, and was present in the cavalry engagements at Mayorga, Benevente, and throughout the retreat to Corunna. Subsequently in the Peninsular campaigns of 1813 and 14, including the investment and surrender of Pampeluna, the battle of Orthes and intermediate affairs. Served also the campaign of 1815 as Aide-de-camp to the Earl of Uxbridge, including the action at Quatre Bras, retreat on the 17th, and battle of Waterloo, at which last he was slightly wounded.

42 Colonel the Honourable Frederick M. Cathcart served as Aide-de-camp to the Commander of the Forces in the expedition sent to the North of Germany in 1805-6 under General Lord Cathcart; and on the expedition sent to the Island of Rugen in the Baltic, to co-operate with the King of Sweden in 1807; and subsequently in the same year at the siege and capture of Copenhagen, on which occasion, being sent home with the despatches, he was promoted to a Troop in the 25th Light Dragoons. He continued to serve as Aide-de-camp to Lord Cathcart during the campaigns of 1813 and 1814 in Germany and France, and was present at the battles of Lutzen 3rd May, Bautzen 20th and 21st May, Dresden 28th Aug., Leipsic 16th, 18th, and 19th Oct. 1813, Brienne 1st Feb., Ferè Champenoise 25th March, and capture of Paris 31st March 1814. In 1815 he was also employed in the same capacity at the head-quarters of the Allied Army under Marshal Prince Schwartzenberg.

44 Sir George Couper was Assistant-engineer at Copenhagen; Captain in the 92nd with Sir John Moore's army in Sweden and Portugal; Aide-de-camp to Lord Dalhousie in Walcheren; 1st Aide-de-camp to Sir H. Clinton in the Peninsula in 1811 and 12, to Lord Dalhousie from 1812 to the end of the war, and was present in all the actions in which they commanded Divisions during those periods. He was Assistant-Quarter-Master-General with the army in the Gulf of Mexico in 1814-15.

45 Colonel Richardson served with the Royal Horse Guards in Spain and France from Dec. 1813 to the end of the war in 1814.

47 Colonel Martin served in the 23rd Light Dragoons at the battles of Talavera, on the 22nd, 27th, and 28th July 1809; also the campaign of 1815, including the battle of Quatre Bras, retreat on the following day, and battle of Waterloo.

49 Colonel Payler served in Sicily in 1806 and 7; the campaign of 1808-9, under Sir John

Moore; and subsequently in the Peninsula under the Duke of Wellington, including the battle of Fuentes d'Onor, siege of Ciudad Rodrigo, and battles of the Nivelle and Nive.

50 Sir Maxwell Wallace served the campaign of 1815, and was present in the action at Quatre Bras, the retreat on the 17th June, and battle of Waterloo. On the 16th June 1815, he was appointed, by Major-General Baron Dornberg, Orderly Officer, to assist his Brigade-Major, Captain Robais; the General's Aide-de camp, Captain Krachenburg, being taken prisoner the following day, he took Robais as Aide-de-camp, and named Captain Wallace, Acting-Brigade-Major; and, Robais being killed on the 18th, the Duke of Wellington confirmed Captain Wallace on the Major-General's recommendation.

51 Colonel the Honourable John Finch served the campaigns of 1813 and 14 with the 15th Hussars, and was engaged at the battle of Vittoria (sabre wound), Orthes, and Toulouse. He was also present, although not personally engaged, at the battles of the Pyrenees and the Nive. Accompanied Lord Combermere to India as his Military Secretary, and was present at the siege and capture of Bhurtpore.

52 Colonel James Lindsay served on the expedition to Walcheren in 1809; at the defence of Cadiz in 1811; the Peninsular campaigns of 1812 and 1813; the subsequent campaign in Holland, under Lord Lynedoch, including the assault of Bergen-op-Zoom, at which he was severely wounded.

53 Colonel Barlow served in India under Lord Lake, during the campaigns of 1803, 4, and 5, and was present at the siege of Deig, battle of Futtyghur, siege of Bhurtpore, and battle of Afzalghur. Served also at the captures of Bourbon and the Isle of France in 1810.

54 Colonel Moore served in the Peninsula, France, and Flanders, and was severely wounded and taken prisoner at the repulse of the sortie from Bayonne.

55 Sir Henry Floyd accompanied General Sir William H. Clinton to Sicily in 1811, and to Spain in 1813, as his Aide-de-camp, and was present at the battles of Biar and Castalla, siege and blockade of Tarragona, in conveying orders to Ordal, and subsequent blockade of Barcelona. Served also the campaign of 1815, with the 10th Hussars, and was present at the battles of Quatre Bras and Waterloo, and at the capture of Paris.

56 Sir Augustus d'Este served at New Orleans on the Staff of Sir John Lambert, and behaved with great gallantry.

57 Colonel Cochrane landed with the first army in Portugal on the 3rd Aug. 1808, and served in the Peninsula during the campaigns of 1808, 9, 10, 11, and part of 1812, including the battles of Roleia, Vimiera, Talavera, and Busaco, action of Redinha, siege of Olivença, first siege of Badajoz, siege of Ciudad Rodrigo. Served nearly two years in Canada during the American war, as Aide-de-camp to the Governor-General and Commander of the forces, Lieutenant-General Sir George Prevost.

57* Colonel Wodehouse served in Portugal from May 1808 to Dec. 1811, including the battle of Vimiera, campaign from Lisbon to Oporto, and battles of Busaco and Fuentes d'Onor; served the campaign of 1814 in the South of France, including the affair at Tarbes and battle of Toulouse.

58 Colonel Wetherall was in action with a squadron of French frigates in the Mozambique Channel in June 1810; in the attack of a squadron of French frigates in port S.E. of the Isle of France in July 1810. At the attack and conquest of Java in 1811, as Aide-de-camp to Major-General Wetherall. He was appointed a *C.B.* for his distinguished services in the suppression of the insurrection in Canada.

59 Colonel Simpson served in the Peninsula from May 1812 to May 1813, including the latter part of the defence of Cadiz, and the attack on Seville. Served also the campaign of 1815, and was severely wounded at Quatre Bras. He served as second in command to Sir Charles Napier during the campaign against the Mountain and Desert Tribes situated on the right bank of the Indus, early in 1815.

60 Colonel Love served with the 52nd regiment in the expedition to Sweden under Sir John Moore, and afterwards in Portugal and Spain, including the advance into Spain, retreat to, and battle of, Corunna, besides the different affairs on the retreat. Served afterwards in the Peninsula with the Light Division, including the storming of Ciudad Rodrigo, and all the affairs and battles in which the Light Division took a part up to 1812. During the campaign in Holland under Lord Lynedoch, he was present at the attack on the fortified village of Merxem, and the bombardment of Antwerp. Present in the several affairs before New Orleans, and in the attack on that place, on which occasion he had two horses shot under him, and was slightly wounded in the arm by a rifle-ball. Served also the campaign of 1815, and received four severe wounds at the battle of Waterloo, when the 52nd regiment charged the French Imperial Guards.

61 Colonel the Honourable George Anson served the campaign of 1815 with the Scots Fusilier Guards, and was present at the battle of Waterloo.

62 Colonel M'Gregor was actively employed in Sicily and Italy in 1806, including the skirmishes at St. Euphemie, battle of Maida, attack on Scylla Castle, and capture of Catrone. Campaign of 1807 in Egypt, including the attacks in the Desert, and siege of Rosetta. Campaign in Holland in 1809, including the attacks and captures of Ter Vere and Flushing. Campaigns in the Peninsula during part of 1813 and 14. Capture of Corsica in May 1814. Wounded through the right shoulder by a musket-shot at the battle of Maida.

62* Colonel Bentinck served in the Peninsula with the Coldstream Guards, and was wounded at the battle of Barrosa. He served also the campaign of 1815, and was present at Waterloo.

63 Colonel Lane served with the 15th Hussars during the campaigns of 1813, 14, and 15, in the Peninsula, France, and Flanders, and was present at the battle of Waterloo.

64 Sir Robert Nickle served with the 88th in the action of the 2nd July 1807, before Buenos Ayres; volunteered and led the Forlorn Hope on the 5th July, and was very severely wounded, and his party all either killed or wounded. Served, with the exception of about five months, during the whole of the Peninsular war from 1809 to the embarkation of his regiment, the 88th, in 1814, at Bourdeaux for North America, including the passage of the Douro, battles of Talavera and Busaco, second siege of Badajoz, the retreat and advance of the army to and from the Lines at Torres Vedras, battle of Vittoria, sortie from Pampeluna, battles of the Pyrenees, Nivelle, Nive, and Orthes, actions of Vic Bigorre and Tarbes, and battle of Toulouse (very severely wounded), independent of a great many skirmishes of advanced and outposts. Served afterwards in the American war in the affair of Plattsburg, where he led the advance across the Sarinac River, and was wounded. Upon the breaking out of the insurrection in British North America in the winter of 1837, Sir Robert Nickle volunteered his services there. Medal for the battle of Nivelle.

65 Colonel Stawell served with the Walcheren expedition, and subsequently in the Peninsula from 1811 to 1814, including the sieges of Ciudad Rodrigo and Badajos, the cavalry affair of La Rena, destruction of the bridge of Almaraz, battle of Vittoria, siege and capture of San Sebastian. Served also at Waterloo.

66 Sir Richard England served at the siege and capture of Flushing in 1809; and subsequently on the Staff of the Adjutant-General with the army in Sicily in 1810. He was employed in all the operations of the Caffre war on the eastern frontier of the Cape of Good Hope in 1835 and 36; and he commanded a division of the army in Scinde and in Affghanistan in 1841 and 42, and was engaged in several affairs with the enemy in the advance by the Bombay column, and in its retreat from Candahar.

67 Colonel Macintosh served in the Peninsula with the 3rd Dragoon Guards from August 1812 to the end of that war in 1814, including the retreat from Madrid to Salamanca, and action at Alba de Tormes, retreat to Ciudad Rodrigo, and action at San Munos, passage of the Tormes above Salamanca, and attack on the French rear-guard under General Villate, action at Hormasa before Burgos, battle of Vittoria, investment of Pampeluna, action at Tarbes, attack on the French cavalry rear-guard at St. Gaudens, and battle of Toulouse.

68 Lord Hotham served in the Peninsula with the Coldstream Guards from April 1812 to Feb. 1814, with the exception of a short absence in consequence of a wound received at the battle of Salamanca. Served also the campaign of 1815, and was present at the battle of Waterloo.

68* Colonel Aslett was present in the battle off Camperdown 11th Oct. 1797. Has been repeatedly in action with the Flotilla off Boulogne, Havre-de-Grace, but was employed principally blockading Cadiz, Brest, Rochfort, Carthagena, and Toulon.

69 Colonel Madox served the campaign of 1815 with the 6th Dragoons, and was present at the battle of Waterloo.

69* Colonel Everard's services:—Expedition to South America, including taking of Maldonado; actions previous to, and assault of Monte Video, where he commanded the Forlorn Hope. Campaign and battle of Corunna. Expedition to Walcheren, and siege of Flushing. Commanded 14th regt. at the siege of Hattras, 1817. Commanded Flank Battalion in the campaigns of 1817 and 18, under Lord Hastings. Commanded 14th Regt. at the siege and assault of Bhurtpore, 1826.

70 Colonel Bisshopp's services:—Campaign and battle of Corunna; expedition to Walcheren; campaign in the south of France; capture of Bhurtpore in 1826.

71 Colonel Ellis served the campaigns of 1812, 13, 14, and 15, with the Grenadier Guards, and was present at the defence of Cadiz, action of San Munos, passage of the Bidassoa, battles of the Nivelle, Nive, before Bayonne, Quatre Bras, and Waterloo. Severely contused at Quatre Bras, and severely wounded at Waterloo.

72 Colonel Higgins served in Ireland during the Rebellion in 1798. In 1806 he was at the landing and taking of Maldonado, in South America; at the affair of San Carlos, in which he was slightly wounded, and had his horse shot; also at the siege and taking of Monte Video.

73 Sir Wm. Robert Clayton accompanied his regiment, the Royal Horse Guards, to the Peninsula in Oct. 1812, and commanded a squadron at the battles of Vittoria, the Pyrenees, and at the period when Marshal Soult attempted to relieve Pampeluna. In 1815 again accompanied his regiment to the Netherlands, and was at the battles of Quatre Bras, Genappe, and Waterloo.

75 Colonel Macadam landed in Portugal 1st Aug. 1808 with the 9th, and served throughout the whole of the Peninsular war, including the battles of Roleia and Vimiera, passage of the Douro, defence of Tarifa, affairs on the retreat from Burgos in 1812, siege and storming of San Sebastian (twice wounded, and commanded the false attack on the breach on the night of the 29th of Aug.), passages of the Bidassoa (shot through the body) and Adour, several affairs connected with the investment of Bayonne, and also the repulse of the sortie, besides a variety of minor affairs, and other desultory services during the Peninsular war. Proceeded to Canada with his regiment, and served the campaign of 1814.

76 Colonel Hon. G. Cathcart served the campaigns of 1813 and 14 in Germany, as Aide-de-

camp to Lord Cathcart, and was engaged at Lutzen 3rd May, Bautzen 20th and 21st May, Dresden 28th August, Leipsic 16th, 18th, and 19th October 1813, Brienne 1st February, Bar-sur-Aube, Arcis 21st March, and Fere Champenoise 25th March 1814. Served also the campaign of 1815, as Aide-de-camp to the Duke of Wellington, and was present at the battles of Quatre Bras and Waterloo.

77 Colonel Spink served with the Light Company of the 12th in several actions in the Travancore war, East Indies. Severely wounded through the leg when leading a night attack against the enemy's position at St. Mary, in the island of Bourbon. Present also at the capture of the Isle of France, his company forming the advance on landing, and repeatedly engaged previous to its capture.

78 Colonel Mansel served with the 10th in the Mediterranean; subsequently with the 53rd in the Peninsula, and was severely wounded at the battle of Toulouse.

78* Colonel Bradshaw's services:—Expedition to Madeira, in 1807; expedition to Walcheren, 1809, including the landing at Ter-Vere, siege and bombardment of Flushing; Peninsula from June 1811 to the end of the war, including siege, assault, and capture of Ciudad Rodrigo and Badajos; operations on the Bidassoa and Adour, blockade of Bayonne, and repulse of the sortie.

79 Colonel Dobbin served with the 19th in the Travancore war in 1809; at the capture of the Kandian territories in Ceylon in 1815. Also actively employed at the head of the Grenadier company throughout the Kandian campaign of 1818, and received the thanks of Sir Robert Brownrigge on three occasions in general orders, for a series of services against the insurgents.

80 Colonel John Drummond served in the Peninsula with the Coldstream Guards from Jan. 1813 to the end of that war in 1814.

81 Colonel Melville Browne served as Aide-de-camp to Sir Brent Spencer in the battles of Roleia, Vimiera, Busaco, Fuentes d'Onor, and the different affairs during the retreat of Massena from Portugal. Served also at the siege of Flushing in 1809, as Aide-de-camp to General Gore Browne.

82 Colonel Freeth served in the Peninsula and France from May 1809 to Jan. 1814, and was present at the following actions and sieges; viz.:—Fuentes d'Onor, capture of Ciudad Rodrigo and Badajoz, battles of Salamanca, Burgos, Vittoria, and Pyrenees, near Pamplona.

83 Colonel James Fleming served in India, Bourbon, and at the capture of the Isle of France.

84 Colonel Buckley served in the Peninsula with the Grenadier Guards, from March 1813 to the end of that war in 1814, including the passage of the Bidassoa, battle of the Nivelle, and investment of Bayonne. Served also the campaign of 1815, and was present at the battles of Quatre Bras and Waterloo, and taking of Peronne.

86 Colonel Byam served the campaigns of 1812, 13, 14, and 15, including the battles of Salamanca, Vittoria, Orthes, and Waterloo, besides minor affairs. Severely wounded by a grapeshot while carrying the regimental colour of the 38th at Salamanca, and slightly wounded at Waterloo.

88 Colonel Prendergast served in the Peninsula with the Scots Fusilier Guards from Dec. 1811 to March 1814, and was present at the battle of Salamanca, capture of Madrid, siege of Burgos and retreat from thence, affair at Osma, battle of Vittoria, sieges of Badajos and San Sebastian, attack at St. Jean de Luz, battle of the Nive, passage of the Adour, investment of Bayonne, siege of the Citadel, and repulse of the sortie.

90 Colonel Drake served with the army on the Elbe, under Lord Cathcart, in 1805 and 6; in Portugal and Spain, under Sir John Moore, 1808-9; with the expedition to Walcheren in 1809; in the Peninsula in 1810 and 11, as Aide-de-camp to Sir Brent Spencer; and in 1812 and 13 on the Staff of the Quarter-Master-General in the Peninsula.

90* Col. Custance served at Walcheren in 1809, and subsequently in the Peninsula, including the repulse of the French at Bejer, in front of Puerto de Banos pass, affairs in Roncesvalles pass, battle of Nivelle, attack on Cambo, crossing the Nive 9th Dec., action at St. Pierre d'Arubé near Bayonne, 13th Dec. (twice wounded and severely,) action at Sauveterre, passage of Gave d'Oleron and Gave de Pau, battle of Orthes, affair at Tarbes, action at Aire (wounded), and battle of Toulouse.

91 Sir John Rowland Eustace served in Upper Canada the campaigns of 1813 and 1814, in command of a troop of the 19th Light Dragoons attached to the division of the army under the immediate command of General Sir Gordon Drummond, and was engaged in the battle of Lundy's Lane near the Falls of Niagara on the 23d of July 1844, and commanded the whole of the cavalry outposts and piquets during the siege, was present at the storming of Fort Erie, and had the honour to be personally mentioned in the general orders of 1814 upon three different occasions. Accompanied the 1st battalion of the Grenadier Guards to Lower Canada in 1838, and was present with his regiment in the advance upon Napierville, and in the subsequent pursuit of the insurgents.

92 Colonel Stisted served in the Peninsula with the 1st Royal Dragoons, from June 1811 to the end of that war in 1814.

93 Sir Edward Cust joined the Duke of Wellington's army prior to the advance from Portugal in 1811, and continued with it up to the cantonments on the Adour in 1813, having been present with the 14th Light Dragoons at the battles of Fuentes d'Onor, Salamanca, Vittoria, the Pyrenees, Nivelle, and Nive, investment of Ciudad Rodrigo, siege of Badajoz, and generally in all the affairs of that period, until he quitted the Duke's army on promotion.

94 Colonel Daly served with the 24th on the expedition to Egypt in 1801. In April 1805 he embarked with the 56th regt. for Bombay, and he commanded four companies of the 2nd battalion employed in 1809, with a division in the field under Colonel Walker, at the storming of Malia, and at the reduction of other Forts in the Kattiwar District.

95 Colonel Salwey served the campaigns of 1813 and 14, with the Coldstream Guards, and was present at nearly all the actions in the Pyrenees, the crossing of the Bidassoa, capture of St. Jean de Luz, battle of the Nivelle, heights of Bidart, crossing the Adour, investment of Bayonne, and repulse of the sortie.

96 Colonel Dwyer served on the Staff of the late Marquis of Hastings, Commander-in-Chief in India, and was present during the Nepaul war, at the reduction of the Province of Kimaoon, and the storming of Almorah. He served also throughout the Pindarree war on the Staff, when he had charge of the communications of the combined armies.

97 Sir Henry Wyatt served the campaigns of 1814 and 15, with the 1st Life Guards, and was present at the battle of Toulouse, and capture of Paris.

98 Colonel Fraser served in the Peninsula with the 24th, from June 1809 to June 1813, including the action at Foz d'Arouce, battle of Busaco, battle of Fuentes d'Onor, on 3rd and 5th May, siege of Ciudad Rodrigo, covering the siege of Badajoz, battle of Salamanca, capture of Madrid, and siege of Burgos, where he was at the taking of the Horn Work, 19th Sept.; and he led the storming party to the breach formed by the mine on the 4th Oct. Employed in the field throughout the whole of the Kandian rebellion in Ceylon in 1817 and 18, as Aide-de-camp to the Commander of the Forces.

99 Colonel Roberts served in the Peninsula from May 1810 to Oct. 1812, and again from May 1813 to the end of that war in 1814, including the defence of Cadiz, battle of Barrosa, and capture of Seville. Medal for Barrosa, having commanded a field battery.

100 Sir Henry Fairfax served in the Peninsula with the Rifle Brigade in 1812, on the retreat from Madrid, and in the affair of San Munos.

100* Colonel Chatterton served in Portugal, Spain, Flanders, and France, from 1811 to 1818, including the affairs at Fuente Guinaldo, and Aldea de Ponte; the sieges of Ciudad Rodrigo, and Badajoz; actions at Usagre, Llerna, Salamanca, Heights of San Christoval, Rueda, Castrajon, to the battle of Salamanca; affairs at Tudela, Valladolid, and Celada del Camino, to the investment and siege of Burgos; the actions at Monasterio, Quintana Palla, Venta del Poso, and Cabezon, upon the retreat from Burgos to Salamanca; thence the out-posts at the passage of the Huebra, to Ciudad Rodrigo. Upon the advance of the army from Portugal, the action at Osma, battle of Vittoria, actions at Villa Franca and Tolosa, to the siege and capture of San Sebastian. The actions on crossing the Bidassoa, and carrying the enemy's fortified entrenchments. The battle of the Nivelle at St. Jean de Luz, at Anglet, and in front of Bayonne, battle of the Nive, passage of the Adour, and investment of Bayonne; occupation of Bordeaux, passage of the Garonne, and affair at Etauliers upon the passage of the Dordogne, battles of Quatre Bras and Waterloo, the advance to and capture of Paris, and with the army of occupation in France.

101 Colonel Vandeleur served in the Peninsula, France, and Flanders, and was severely wounded at the battle of Fuentes d'Onor.

102 Lord Howden served as Aide-de-camp to his Grace the Duke of Wellington during the years 1817 and 18, to the close of the occupation in France. Employed by Government on a special mission, and was present at the battle of Navarin in 1827 (wounded, and mentioned in Commander-in-chief's despatch); siege of Antwerp in 1832 (wounded); campaign in Spain, in Navarre and Basque Provinces, in 1834.

103 Colonel Douglas served at the capture of the Danish and Swedish West India Islands in 1801. On the expedition to the north of Germany in 1805 and 6. Peninsular campaigns from Feb. 1812 to March 1814, including the battles of Salamanca, Vittoria, and the Pyrenees (27th to 31st July); siege of San Sebastian from 24th Aug. to the 8th Sept., and battle of Nivelle. He has received a cross for Salamanca, Vittoria, Pyrenees, and Nivelle, having commanded a field battery.

105 Colonel Charles Stuart Campbell served in Egypt with the 26th in 1801; in Portugal and Spain in 1808-9, including the battle of Corunna, where he commanded the piquets of his brigade. Expedition to Walcheren and siege of Flushing in 1809. Served also in the Peninsula from 1811 to 1814, and commanded the 3rd Portuguese Regt. at the battle of Vittoria, as also at the siege and assault of San Sebastian—severely wounded in the thigh at the assault, the ball still remaining. Medal and a clasp.

106 Colonel Dugald Campbell served at the Ferrol in 1800; in Egypt in 1801, including the battles of the 8th, 13th, and 21st March (wounded). Served again in Egypt in 1807, including the bombardment of Rosetta. Present at the battle of Maida, 4th July 1806. Also at the capture of the islands of Ischia and Procida in 1809. Medal for services in Egypt.

108 Colonel Armytage served in the south of France with the Coldstream Guards from March to July 1814.

109 Colonel Clerke served with the old 94th at the defence of Cadiz, and also until the retreat from Santarem was closed at Fuentes d'Onor, having been present in the actions of Redinha, Condeixa, Foz d'Arouce, and Sabugal. Joined the 77th (also in the Peninsula) on promotion, and served with it in the action of El Bodon, sieges and assaults of Ciudad Rodrigo and Bada-

joz, including the storming of Fort Picurina. Severely wounded in the leg at the storming of the castle of Badajoz.

110 Colonel Wallace served the campaign of 1815, and was present at the battle of Waterloo.

111 Sir James Schoedde served the Egyptian campaign of 1801. Served also in the Peninsula from 1808 to the end of the war, including the battles of Roleia, Vimiera, Talavera, Busaco, Fuentes d'Onor, sieges of Ciudad Rodrigo and Badajoz, battles of Salamanca, Vittoria, Pyrenees, Nivelle, Nive, Orthes, and Toulouse, besides numerous minor actions and skirmishes. Medal for Nivelle. Commanded a brigade in China at the attack and capture of Chapoo, Woosung, Shanghai, and Chin Kiang Foo.

112 Colonel Clarke Kennedy served in the Peninsula from Sept. 1809 to Sept. 1813, including the battles of Fuentes d'Onor and Vittoria, besides various affairs of outposts; received two wounds at Waterloo. While leading his squadron in a successful charge against the Count D'Erlon's corps at Waterloo, perceiving an Eagle to the left, he changed the direction of his squadron, and ran the officer through the body who carried it. The Eagle belonged to the 105th French Regiment of Infantry, and is now deposited at Chelsea Hospital.

114 Colonel Craigie served the campaign of 1814 in Holland, including the attacks on Merxem, and bombardment of Antwerp. Served also in China, and commanded a column at Amoy, Chusan, and Chinhae.

115 Colonel Morris served in the American war with the 49th, and was present at the various operations at Fort George, and at the actions of Stoney Creek and Plattsburg. Accompanied the regiment on the China expedition, and commanded a brigade at the storming and capture of the heights above Canton, for which service he was made a *C.B.* Commanded a brigade at the attack and capture of the city of Amoy, and at the second capture of Chusan. Commanded the centre column of attack at the capture of the heights of Chinhae. Commanded the force at Ningpo, and repulsed the enemy with great slaughter in their attack on that city. Commanded a brigade at the attack and capture of the enemy's entrenched camp on the heights of Segoan, at the attack and capture of the city of Chapoo, and at the attack and capture of the enemy's position at Woosung.

116 Colonel Boldero served with the Grenadier Guards at Cadiz in 1810 and 11; in the Peninsula in 1812 and 13; in Holland in 1814; and the campaign of 1815, in which he served as Adjutant at the battles of Quatre Bras and Waterloo, and at the taking of Peronne.

117 The Hon. Colonel Ashburnham commanded a brigade of the Army of the Sutlej (Medal) at the battles of Ferozeshah and Sobraon.

118 Colonel Cureton served in the Peninsula from 1809 to the end of the war, and was present with the 14th Light Dragoons in the many actions and skirmishes that gallant corps was engaged in, including the battles of Talavera, Busaco, and Fuentes d'Onor; siege of Badajos in April 1812; battle of Salamanca, capture of Madrid, and battle of Vittoria. He served with the 40th at Orthes, Tarbes, and Toulouse. He was wounded in the right leg by a rifle ball in crossing the Mondego, near Coimbra, 1st Oct. 1810; received a severe sabre cut on the head (skull fractured), and another on the left hand at Fuentes d'Onor, 5th May 1811. He accompanied the 16th Lancers to India in 1822, and was present at the siege and capture of Bhurtpore, in 1825-6. Served as Assistant Adjutant-General of Cavalry in the campaign in Affghanistan under Lord Keane in 1839 and 40, and was present at the assault and capture of Ghuznee (Medal),—was specially selected to command the advance column of the army on its route through the Bolan Pass and entrance into Affghanistan; and was also selected to command a force of cavalry detached in advance of the army, to seize the enemy's guns and secure possession of the citadel of Cabool, in Aug. 1839, which he accomplished. Commanded a brigade of cavalry in the action of Maharajpore on the 29th Dec. 1843 (Medal), for which he was appointed a *C.B.* He again commanded a brigade of cavalry in the campaign on the Sutlej, and was engaged in the battles of Buddiwal, Aliwal, and Sobraon: in the two former he commanded the whole of the cavalry.

119 Colonel Pennefather commanded the Infantry Brigade at the battle of Meeanee (Medal), and was shot through the body: he was also at the destruction of the Fort of Imaumghur.

120 Colonel Brock served in the Peninsula with the 43rd Light Infantry from Aug. to Nov. 1808, June to Dec. 1811, and from Nov. 1812 to the end of that war in 1814, including the battles of Vimiera and Vittoria, action at Vera, passage of the Bidassoa, battles of the Nivelle and the Nive, actions at Arcangues and Tarbes, battle of Toulouse, and various skirmishes and affairs of outposts. Also in the attack on New Orleans; and afterwards at the capture of Paris. Served in the Coorg campaign in India; where a portion of his regiment (the 48th) bore a conspicuous and distinguished part. Severely wounded at the battle of Vimiera by a musket-shot, which passed completely through the ankle-bone, which it shattered most severely.

121 Colonel Reed served at the siege of Flushing in 1809; and in the Peninsula from June 1811 to March 1814, including the actions at, and heights above, Moresco, battle of Salamanca, capture of Madrid and the Retiro, action at Olmas, and battle of Vittoria, where he was severely wounded in the right shoulder.

122 Colonel James Jones served with the 22nd Light Dragoons in the East Indies, in 1802, 3, and 4, and in the Peninsula with the 87th regt. and on the staff from 1809 to 1814, and was wounded at Talavera.

123 Colonel Taynton served in Ireland during the Rebellion in 1798. In 1801 he was at the capture of the Danish Islands, and Island of St. Martin in the West Indies. In 1803 at the

attack and capture of St. Lucia and storming of the fortress of Morne Fortunée; also at the attack and capture of Tobago. Served on the staff of General Maitland at the attack and capture of the Dutch colony of Surinam. In 1807, he was at the second capture of the Danish West India Islands; in 1809 at the attack and capture of Martinique, including the siege of Fort Bourbon; also at the attack and capture of the Saintes Islands. From 1811 to 1813 he served in Sicily, and was employed as acting Deputy-Adjutant-General, and some time at the head of the Department.

124 Colonel Carlyon served with the 66th in the Nepaul war under Sir David Ochterlony.

125 Colonel Trafford served in the Peninsula, and was present at the battles of Talavera (wounded), Albuhera, Busaco, Vittoria, the Pyrenees, the Nivelle, the Nive, Orthes, and Toulouse.

126 Colonel George Tovey served in Calabria with the 20th, and was present at the battle of Maida. Served also in the Peninsula from July 1808 to Nov. 1809, and again from Oct. 1812 to the end of that war in 1814, including the battles of Vimiera, Talavera, Vittoria and the Pyrenees (25th July to 2nd August); siege of San Sebastian, battles of the Nivelle, the Nive (9th to 13th Dec.), and Orthes.

127 Colonel Angelo served with the expedition to Egypt in 1807; on the coast of Calabria in 1808; with the expedition to Walcheren in 1809; with the army to Catalonia in 1812 and 13, as an Assistant-Adjutant-General. Attached to the Austrian army, and acted as Aide-de-Camp to Major-General Count Nugent in the campaign against the Viceroy of Italy; present at the siege and capture of Trieste, Cattaro, and Ragusa, and in various services in the Adriatic.

128 Colonel Thwaites served on an expedition to the coast of Holland in 1796; in the East Indies in 1799; from that time on board H. M. S. *La Forte* till wrecked in the Red Sea. Crossed the Desert of Suez with Colonel Lloyd's Detachment, and joined the Vizier's Army in the advance to Cairo; then Sir David Baird's Army. He served in the Peninsula, in the 4th regiment, from 1811 to 1813, including the siege and assault of Badajos, the battles of Salamanca (wounded), Vittoria, and the Pyrenees (wounded).

129 Colonel Linton served the campaign of 1815 with the 6th Dragoons, and was present at the battle of Waterloo.

130 Colonel Coles served in South America with the 14th in 1807, including the operations previous to, and storming of, Monte Video. Served afterwards in the Peninsula from Aug. 1808 to Nov. 1811, and again from April 1813 to the end of that war in 1814; present with the 40th at the battles of Roleia, Vimiera, and Talavera; with the 4th Dragoons at Busaco, Albuhera, and Usagre; and with the 12th Light Dragoons at the passage of the Bidassoa, the Nive and the Adour.

131 Sir Michael Creagh accompanied the expedition under Sir David Baird to the Cape of Good Hope in 1806, wounded in the action of the Blue Berg, was desperately wounded by a cannon-shot in the left shoulder (which killed six of his men) at the attack on Bourbon in 1810; served in the Mahratta war, and during the Pindarree war of 1817 and 18. Commanded a strong detachment during that harassing war in the interior of Ceylon in 1819, when out of the flank companies of the regiment (200 strong) only 47 returned to the coast. Sir M. has served with his regiment in all quarters of the globe.

132 Colonel Eden served the campaign in Java in 1811 with the 22nd Light Dragoons, including the actions of the 10th and 26th Aug. Aide-de-camp to Sir Thomas Hislop at the battle of Maheidpore, and during the Mahratta war in 1817 and 18.

133 Colonel Story served in the Peninsula with the 3rd Dragoon Guards from Aug. 1809 to the end of that war in 1814, including the battle of Busaco, actions of Redinha, Campo Mayor and Los Santos, siege of Badajoz, battle of Albuhera, action of Usagre, sieges of Ciudad Rodrigo and Badajoz, action near Salamanca on the 26th May 1813, battle of Vittoria, blockade of Pampeluna, and battle of Toulouse.

134 Colonel Fraser served the campaign of 1815 with the 42nd, and was at the battles of Quatre Bras (slightly wounded), and at Waterloo (severely wounded).

135 Colonel Shee served the early part of the campaign of 1809 in Portugal; and the latter end of 1809 and the years 1810 and 11 with the Sicilian army. Served also the Peninsular campaigns of 1812, 13, and 14, with the Portuguese army.

136 Colonel Hartley served in the Peninsula with the 57th from Aug. 1813 to the end of that war in 1814, and was present at the battle of Nivelle. Served afterwards in Belgium.

137 Colonel Chester served in Holland in 1799, and was present in the action near Bergen 2nd Oct. Served also the campaign of 1808-9 in Spain, including the actions at Benevente, Villa Franca, and Lugo, and retreat to Corunna.

138 Colonel Geddes served with the 27th in Calabria in 1806; at the capture of the island of Procida in 1809; in Sicily in 1810; and subsequently in the Peninsula, including the battles of the Nivelle, the Nive, Orthes, and Toulouse, at which last he received a severe wound which broke the left thigh-bone near the hip-joint.

139 Colonel Gilmour served at the capture of Ischia, Zante, and Cephalonia, in 1809; and Santa Maura in 1810. Served afterwards on the eastern coast of Spain, and was present at the battle of Castalla; engaged with the enemy on several occasions covering the retreat; and employed in the batteries against Tarragona. After leaving Spain he went to Genoa, under Lord Wm. Bentinck.

140 Colonel Leslie served with the 29th on the secret expedition under Sir Brent Spencer and subsequently in the Peninsula from Aug. 1808 to Dec. 1811, and again from Feb. 1[illegible]

cluding the battles of Roleia and Vimiera, capture of Oporto, battle of Talavera, first siege Badajos, and battle of Albuhera, besides skirmishes and affrays at outposts. At the battle Talavera he was severely wounded in the right leg, where the ball still remains.

141 Colonel Wolrige was present at the attack on New Orleans on the 8th Jan. 1815.

142 Colonel George E. Jones served with the expedition to South America, in 1807; at the pture of the Isle of France, in 1810. Served also in Ava, and commanded the 89th in the neral action and attack of the enemy's entrenched lines before Rangoon, 7th December 24.

143 Colonel Persse served in the Peninsula from 1809 to the end of the war, and was se- rely wounded by a musket shot in the action of the 10th Dec. 1813, near Bayonne. In Aug. 14, he embarked for America as Aide-de-camp to Sir John Keane, and was present at New leans. At the siege and capture of Bhurtpore by Lord Combermere, he commanded the re- nent; and also during the campaign in Affghanistan under Lord Keane, including the siege d capture of Ghuznee, for which he has received a medal.

144 Colonel Beckwith served in the Peninsula with the 16th Light Dragoons, from July 1813 the end of that war in 1814, including the battle of the Nivelle, and battles of the Nive on 9th and 10th Dec. Served also the campaign of 1815, and was present at the retreat on 17th June and at the battle of Waterloo.

145 Colonel Robertson served with the 25th at the taking of Madeira in 1807; at the capture Guadaloupe in 1810, and again in 1815.

146 Colonel Robinson served with the 48th in the Peninsula from June 1809 to October 1813, luding the battles of Talavera and Busaco, Lines at Torres Vedras, pursuit of Massena, ion at Campo Mayor, siege of Ciudad Rodrigo, siege and storming of Badajos (shot through left arm at the assault, 6th April 1812); battle of Salamanca, retreat from Madrid, battles Vittoria and the Pyrenees (severely wounded, left leg fractured), 28th July 1813.

147 Colonel Maclean served with the 13th Light Dragoons in every action and affair in ich it was engaged in the Peninsula, from Dec. 1810 until wounded and taken prisoner at ches, 13th March 1814. Was present with his regiment during the Waterloo campaign; gaged in command of the rear-guard for the brigade on the 7th June, and throughout the ion on the 18th. Accompanied the 13th Dragoons to India in Feb. 1819; was employed in nmand of a cavalry brigade with the field force at the reduction of Kurnool, and served nterruptedly with his regiment for twenty-two years, when he returned with it to England, and placed on half-pay as 2nd Lieut.-Colonel.

48 Colonel Gawler served in the Peninsula with the 52nd from Nov. 1811 to the end of that r in 1814, including the siege and assault of Badajos, battles of Vittoria, Pass of Vera, the relle, the Nive, Orthes, and Toulouse, besides various minor affairs. Served also the cam- gn of 1815, and was present at the battle of Waterloo. Wounded below the right knee by usket-shot at the storming of Badajos, and in the neck by a musket-shot at San Munoz.

49 Colonel Kettlewell served at Copenhagen in 1807; and in Ceylon during the Rebellion, 817 and 18.

50 Colonel Ball served in the Peninsula with the 34th, from June 1809 to Nov. 1813, in- ling the battles of Busaco and Albuhera, siege of Badajos in May 1811, actions at Arroyo Molino and Almaraz, battle of Vittoria (wounded in the head), and actions at the Pass of ya (severely wounded in the left leg).

50* Colonel Monins served the campaign of 1815 with the 52nd Light Infantry, and was sent at the battle of Waterloo. Served afterwards with the army of occupation in France.

51 Colonel Cox served in the 95th Rifle Brigade at Copenhagen, and was present at some mishes near that city, and afterwards in the action of Kioge. He served afterwards in the insula from the landing at Mondego Bay in 1808, to the end of the war at Toulouse, in- ling skirmish at Obidas, battles of Roleia and Vimiera, retreat to Corunna, General Craw- d's march to Talavera, action at St. Milan, battles of Vittoria, Nivelle, and Nive; passage he Bidassoa, battle of Orthes, and Tarbes. Severely wounded in the right leg by a musket- at Vittoria; in the left side at Nivelle; and again in the right leg at Tarbes. He com- ded a division under Sir Benjamin D'Urban during the Caffre war at the Cape of Good e in 1835. Subsequently he was employed on particular service in Canada for five years ng both Rebellions, and is now employed on the Staff in Ireland.

52 Colonel Croker served in the East Indies from 1804 to 1824, including the siege of Gur- ri, 1807; campaign against the Seiks, 1808 and 9; campaign against the Nepaul States, 1814 15; campaign against Mahrattas and Pindarees, 1817 and 18. Commanded the 17th regi- t during the whole of the campaign in Affghanistan and Beloochistan, including the storm capture of the fortresses of Ghuznee and Khelat. Colonel Croker arrived in Bombay in nmand of the 17th regiment, in May 1836, being a solitary instance in the British army of fficer landing in the East Indies *twice* in the *same corps*.

53 Colonel Turnor served in Hanover with the 14th, in 1805 and 6. The campaign of -9, including the battle of Corunna. On the expedition to Walcheren, and at the siege of hing in 1809. Also the campaign of 1815, including the battle of Waterloo.

54 Colonel Falls served with the 20th on the expedition to Naples with the English and sian army in 1805. He was present at the battle of Maida in 1806; at the battle of Corunna 809; on the expedition to Walcheren the same year; subsequently in the Peninsula, at the e of the Pyrenees, at Roncesvalles, and Pampeluna (severely wounded), battles of the lle, and Orthes. Served afterwards on the expedition to Washington. In 1831 he was nded in the riots at Merthyr Tydvill, in South Wales.

	Cornet, 2d Lieut. or Ensign.	Lieut.	Captain.	Major.	Lieut.-Colonel.	When placed on half pay.
Phillip Walsh, *Major*, h. p. Irish Brigade	never	never	never	1 Oct. 94	1 Jan. 00	
Charles Augustus West,[1] *Lt.-Col.*, late 1 Royal Veteran Battalion, *Lieutenant-Governor of Landguard Fort*	20 Mar. 94	never	4 Feb. 97	never	5 May 04	
Henry Le Blanc,[2] *Lt.-Col.*, late 5 Royal Veteran Battalion, *Major of Chelsea Hospital*	9 July 92	22 May 95	1 June 99	12 June 06	5 Feb. 07	
Colin James Milnes, CB.,[3] late of 65 Foot	15 Mar. 93	1 Oct. 94	1 Feb. 98	2 Oct. 06	4 June 11	
Richard Harvey Cooke, CB.,[4] late of Grenadier Guards	20 Feb. 98	never	25 Nov. 99	never	7 Nov.	
John Mansel, CB.,[5] late of 53 Foot	Mar. 95	3 Sept. 95	4 April 00	28 Feb. 05	1 Jan. 12	
Hugh Halkett, CB. GCH.,[6] late of German Legion	18 April 94	15 July 95	21 Oct. 03	1 July 05	do	
Russell Manners, CB.,[7] late of 74 Foot	1 Sept. 91	9 June 94	3 May 01	11 Mar. 08	6 Feb.	
John Philip Hunt, CB.,[8] late of 11 Foot	8 Mar. 99	29 Nov. 99	17 Dec. 02	8 Sept. 08	27 April	
Charles Rowan, CB.,[9] late of 52 Foot	15 May 97	15 Mar. 99	25 June 03	9 May 11	do	
Rodolphe de May, *Lieut.-Col.*, h. p. Watteville's Regiment	never	never	1 May 01	13 Nov. 06	21 May	24 Oct.
John Bacon Harrison, CB.,[11] late of 50 Foot	13 Dec. 94	10 June 95	1 June 97	23 Feb. 09	19 June	
Charles Cother, CB.,[12] late of 83 Foot	16 Jan. 00	16 July 00	25 Mar. 03	9 Mar. 09	do	
Sir George Julius Hartmann, KCB. GCH.,[13] *Major*, h. p. German Legion	never	never	*9 Nov. 03	*12April 06	17 Aug.	24 Feb. 16
Gustavus Brown, CB.,[14] late of 95 Foot	4 Aug. 94		30 Dec. 97	25 July 10	do	
Sir *Richard Church*, CB. GCH.,[15] late of Greek Lt. Inf.	3 July 00	13 Jan. 03	7 Jan. 06	25 Feb. 11	19 Nov.	
Sir *James Malcolm*, KCB.,[17] late of Royal Marines	29 Nov. 79	18 April 93	1 Jan. 97	6 Feb. 06	4 June 13	
Charles Plenderleath, CB.,[18] late of 49 Foot	29 May 96	6 Mar. 97	3 July 99	16 Oct. 06	do	
John P. Hawkins, CB.,[20] late of 68 Foot	20 Dec. 99	23 May 00	24 Aug. 04	17 Sept. 12	21 June	
George Macdonell, CB.,[22] late of 79 Foot	15 Sept. 96	4 May 98	4 Sept. 05	6 Feb. 12	24 Feb. 14	
George M late of 69 Foot	12 Nov. 94	3 Sept. 95	21 Feb. 98	25 April 08	17 Mar.	
George late of Rifle Brigade	14 Sept. 94	7 Jan. 95	30 April 95	25 July 10	4 June	
Fiennes S of 6 Dragoons	19 Dec. 99	25 June 03	5 Oct. 04	25 May 09	4 June	
Sir *Henry Pynn*, CB.,[28] late of Portuguese Service	7 Aug. 99	28 Nov. 99	30 May 05	15 Nov. 09	4 June	
Fred. Robertson, CB. KCH.,[29] *Major*, h. p. Ger. Leg.			*25 Oct. 03	27 Jan. 11	18 June 15	24 Feb. 16
Jonathan Leach, CB.,[31] late of Rifle Brigade	15 Aug. 01	15 Oct. 01	7 April 04	21 June 13	do	
Geo. Davis Wilson, CB.,[32] late of 4 Foot	27 April 97	7 Aug. 99	7 Aug. 04	26 Dec. 13	18 June 15	
Hon. *G. L. Dawson Damer*, CB.,[34] late of 89 Foot	4 Dec. 06	31 Dec. 07	31 Dec. 12	10 Mar. 14	4 Dec.	
Geo. Francis Macleod, CB., late of Royal Engineers	never	1 July 01	1 July 06	6 Feb. 12	21 June 17	

	CORNET, ETC.	LIEUT.	CAPTAIN.	MAJOR.	LIEUT.-COLONEL.	WHEN PLACED ON HALF PAY.
Gabriel Burer, *Lieut.-Col.*, Unattached	never	30 Dec. 97	24 Nov. 03	1 July 13	3 July 17	22 Mar. 27
Geo. Ralph Payne Jarvis, *Major*, h. p. 36 Foot	8 Feb. 92	19 Dec. 93	14 Nov. 99	20 Dec. 10	12 Aug. 19	1811
P *John Wm. O'Donoghue*, CB.,[36] late Unattached	1 Oct. 94	23 April 00	12 June 06	31 Dec. 11	do	
P W *Hon.* R. Moore,[37] *Capt. & Lt.-Col.*, h. p. Colds. Gds.	21 Mar. 11	never	2 June 14	never	1 April 24	1 April 24
P W Edward Keane,[38] *Lt.-Col.*, Unattached	1 Dec. 03	21 Nov. 04	1 Dec. 06	18 June 15	17 June	29 Mar. 38
P Charles Purvis,[39] *Major*, h. p. Canadian Fencibles	3 June 96	31 Oct. 98	26 Feb. 01	7 May 12	27 May 25	11 June 18
P *Robert Macdonald*, CB.,[40] late of Royal Artillery	6 Jan. 95	6 Mar. 95	6 April 02	17 Aug.	do	
Benjamin Graves, *Major*, h. p. 12 Foot	April 95	19 Sept. 95	26 Aug. 04	24 Sept.	do	25 Jan. 18
P W *Francis Fuller*, CB.,[42] late of 59 Foot	9 July 03	5 Sept. 04	5 Oct. 09	17 July 17	19 Jan. 26	
William Leader Maberly, *Lt.-Col.*, Unattached	never	23 Mar. 15	14 May 18	19 May 25	30 Dec.	9 Mar. 32
P *Thomas Bell*, CB.,[44] late of 48 Foot	13 Nov. 99	17 Jan. 01	11 Sept. 05	26 Aug. 13	20 Sept.	
Thomas Perronet Thompson, *Lt.-Col.*, Unattached	23 Jan. 06	21 Jan. 08	7 July 14	9 June 25	24 Feb. 29	24 Feb. 29
James Dunbar Tovey, *Lt.-Col.*, Unattached	26 Oct. 99	3 July 00	9 Oct. 05	24 Jan. 19	11 Aug.	30 May 34
P W *Robert Macdonald*, CB.,[46] late of 35 Foot	10 Feb. 03	28 Oct. 03	8 Feb. 10	21 Sept. 13	25 Aug.	
Hugh John Cameron, *Major*, h. p. York Chasseurs	27 Nov. 95	25 Nov. 96	1 Aug. 04	4 June 13	22 July 30	12 Aug. 24
P W Patrick Campbell, CB.,[50] *Major*, Unattached	31 Aug. 97	1 Mar. 00	16 Aug. 04	21 June	do	14 May 18
Charles Hamilton Smith, KH., *Captain*, h. p. 15 Foot	never	30 Dec. 97	18 Jan. 06	13 Dec.	do	25 Oct. 21
James Lewis Basden, CB.,[53] *Lt.-Col.*, on retired full pay, 89 F.	12 Jan. 00	17 Mar. 01	4 Sept. 06	30 Dec. 14	do	
P James Poole Oates, KH.,[54] *Captain*, h. p. 88 Foot	3 Mar. 97	12 May 97	19 Oct. 04	3 Mar.	do	26 Mar. 18
P Charles Pratt,[56] *Major*, h. p. 96 Foot	10 Oct. 05	25 Aug. 07	28 Sept. 09	24 Mar.	do	1814
P George Spottiswoode,[57] *Major*, h. p. 71 Foot	4 Jan. 04	15 Aug. 04	19 June 06	31 Mar.	do	25 Feb. 16
P James Harvey, KH., *do.* h. p. 92 Foot	23 Feb. 99	7 Oct. 99	12 Oct. 04	12 April	do	1814
P Charles Campbell,[60] *do.* h. p. 94 Foot	27 Sept. 03	17 Mar. 04	14 July 08	do	do	25 Dec. 18
James Horton, *Major*, h. p. Meuron's Regt.	5 Aug. 99	16 May 01	23 July 07	18 May	do	30 Sept. 19
James Laing, *Major*, h. p. 61 Foot	Oct. 96	23 Nov. 96	7 Mar. 05	19 May	do	1814
John Bradish, *Captain*, h. p. 2 Ceylon Regt.		3 Nov. 94	2 June 03	4 June	do	25 Nov. 21
P Wm. Sall, KH.,[63] *Capt.* on retired full pay, R. Newf. Cos.	30 Oct. 94	26 Nov. 94	9 July 03	do	do	
Richard Bunce,[64] *Lieut.-Col.*, h. p. Royal Marines	27 Nov. 93	24 April 95	28 July	do	do	5 Aug. 33
P John M'Mahon,[65] *Major*, Unattached	25 Mar. 00	16 July 02	30 Aug. 08	do	do	29 Mar. 33
Robert Terry,[66] *Captain*, on retired full pay, 31 Foot	6 Aug. 99	7 Mar. 00	8 Oct.	do	do	
Colin Pringle, *Major*, h. p. German Legion			17 Nov.	do	do	25 Dec. 16
John Tho. Whelan,[67] *Captain*, h. p. R. Newf. Fen.		31 May 93	24 Nov.	do	do	25 June
P Patrick Grieve,[68] *Lt.-Col.*, on retired full pay, 75 Foot	9 July 03	1 Aug. 04	16 May 09	25 Nov. 19	9 Nov.	
P W John Cross, KH.,[69] *Lt.-Col.*, on retired full pay, 68 F.	9 July 05	29 May 06	31 Dec. 12	23 June 25	8 Feb. 31	

	ENSIGN, ETC.	LIEUT.	CAPTAIN.	MAJOR.	LIEUT.-COLONEL.	WHEN PLACED ON HALF PAY.
Lord Edward Hay, *Lt.-Col.*, Unattached	31 Oct. 16	24 Oct. 21	29 Jan. 24	19 Sept. 26	26 April 31	26 April 31
James W. Fairtlough,[70] *Lt.-Col.*, on retired full pay, 63 Foot	20 Aug. 02	24 May 04	14 Mar. 05	12 Aug. 19	17 Sept. 33	
Henry C. Streatfield,[71] *do.* on retired full pay, 87 Foot	Oct. 01	13 Nov. 01	7 Nov. 05	12 Aug. 19	4 Oct.	
Henry Senior,[72] *Lt.-Col.*, on retired full pay, 65 Foot	6 May 13	28 Dec. 15	24 April 23	12 Mar. 29	19 Sept. 34	
Charles Hughes,[73] *do.* on retired full pay, 24 Foot	25 May 96	11 May 97	28 Aug. 04	4 June 14	10 Oct. 35	
Ambrose Lane,[78] *Captain*, h. p. 44 Foot	1783	15 Sept. 94	18 Feb. 04	4 June 14	10 Jan. 37	25 [illegible] 21
John Charles Smith, *Lt.-Col.*, Unattached	31 Aug. 99	19 June 00	24 April	do	do	16 July 30
Nathaniel Bean, *Captain*, h. p. 49 Foot	25 Nov. 99	10 Sept. 01	2 June	do	do	16 Feb. 15
John Austen, KH.,[77] *Lt.-Col.*, Unattached	28 June 96	19 Jan. 97	4 Aug.	do	do	4 May 26
Jacob Watson,[78] *Major*, do.	15 Feb. 98	30 Aug. 99	5 Aug.	do	do	do
Henry Nooth,[79] *Captain*, h. p. 14 Foot	never	27 July 99	22 Aug.	do	do	26 Mar. 18
James M'Haffie, *do.* h. p. 60 Foot	7 Aug. 97	1 Feb. 98	24 Aug.	do	do	26 Nov. 18
Joseph Dacre Lacy,[80] *do.* h. p. 2 Garrison Batt.	5 Sept. 99	17 Oct. 99	27 Aug.	do	do	25 Dec. 16
George Dods, *Captain*, h. p. 1 Foot	1 Sept. 95	2 July 97	25 Oct.	do	do	20 June 16
George Jackman Rogers, *Major*, Unattached	5 Mar. 95	9 July 03	26 Oct.	do	do	11 May 26
Robert Blake Lynch, *Major*, do.	1 Nov. 96	1 April 97	23 Nov.	do	do	26 Feb. 28
William Burton [illegible] *Lieut.-Col.*, Royal Engineers	19 Nov. 06	1 May 07	15 April 12	23 June	do	
Francis Campbell, *Major*, Unattached	15 Mar. 99	30 Nov. 01	21 Nov. 05	25 July	do	11 May 26
[illegible]mas Blanshard, CB., *Lt.-Col.*, Royal Engineers	28 Sept. 07	1 April 08	21 July 13	29 Sept.	do	
John Robyns, KH.,[82] *Major*, R. Marines, on ret. full pay	13 Mar. 96	1 Jan. 99	19 June 07	27 Oct.	do	
John Falconer Briggs, KH.,[83] *Major*, h. p. 28 Foot	9 July 03	31 Oct. 05	18 Jan. 10	8 Dec.	do	25 Dec. 14
Peter Mathewson,[84] *Major*, h. p. Royal York Rangers	9 Feb. 03	4 May 04	15 June 08	27 April 15	do	25 Dec. 18
Hon. Edward Cadogan, *Major*, h. p. 8 West India Regt.	4 Dec. 06	26 Feb. 08	4 Jan. 10	25 May	do	19 Dec. 16
Cassius Matthew Clanchy,[87] *Major*, h. p. Portuguese Service	3 [illegible] 02	5 July 04	20 June 11	6 June	do	25 Dec.
[illegible] Charles Diggle, KH.,[88] *Major*, Unattached, *Gentleman Usher to the Queen*	31 Aug. 04	14 Feb. 05	24 May 10	18 June	do	23 June 43
[illegible] [illegible]rt Howard, *Major*, Unattached	25 May 03	14 Sept. 04	1 Sept. 13	do	do	18 May 26
Adam Giffard Downing, *Major*, h. p. 81 Foot	26 June 99	7 Mar.	Dec. 05	21 Dec.	do	25 Feb. 16
John Murray [illegible], *Major*, [illegible]	14 Nov. 04	29 Aug. 05	4 Sept. 12	20 Mar. 17	do	4 May 26
W. Reid, CB., *Lt.-Col.*, R. Engineers	10 Feb. 09	23 April 10	20 Dec. 14	do	do	
Edward Knox,[90] *Major*, [illegible]	26 Oct. 04	14 Mar. 05	5 Nov. 07	21 June	do	10 April 23
Sir John Scott Lillie, CB.,[91] *Lt.-Col.*, Unattached	3 Mar. 07	29 Mar. 10	11 Nov. 13	do	do	27 Mar. 28
Benjamin Orlando Jones,[93] *Major*, do.	29 May 05	23 Oct. 06	9 Sept. 12	4 Sept.	do	6 July 26
Tho. Peacocke,[94] *Major*, Unattached	3 April 06	25 Feb. 08	26 Aug. 13	do	do	25 Dec. 16
[illegible] de Lancey,[96] *Major*, Unattached	24 Jan. 05	18 Sept. 06	25 Feb. 08	24 Oct.	do	7 Dec. 38
William Hulme, *Lt.-Col.*, 96 Foot	25 Sept. 03	26 June 05	26 Aug. 13	23 Dec.	do	

	CORNET, ETC.	LIEUT.	CAPTAIN.	MAJOR.	LIEUT.-COLONEL.	WHEN PLACED ON HALF PAY.
P W William Tomkinson, *Captain*, h. p. **24 Dragoons**	9 July 07	6 Oct. 08	12 Mar. 12	21 Jan. 19	10 Jan. 37	8 Nov. 21
P John Neave Wells, CB.,[97] *Lt.-Col.*, R. Eng., on ret. full pay	6 Nov. 06	1 May 07	20 May	do	do	
P W *Sir* Digby Mackworth, *Bart.*,[98] KH., ***Major***, Unatt.	never	9 July 07	16 July	do	do	13 Aug. 30
P W John Browne,[99] *Major*, Unattached	21 Oct. 04	28 Feb. 05	25 May 15	do	do	10 Feb. 37
P W William Brereton, CB. KH., *Lt.-Col.*, R. Artillery	10 May 05	1 June 06	30 Sept. 16	do	do	
Samuel Fox, *Major*, Unattached	5 April 01	25 June 03	28 Mar. 05	12 Aug.	do	11 May 26
John Bazalgette,[100] *Maj.* Unat., *Dep.-Qr.-Mr.* ***Gen. in Nova Scotia***	29 July 96	26 April 99	17 Oct. 05	do	do	13 Aug. 30
Charles Collis, *Captain*, h. p. 84 Foot	23 Jan. 00	24 June 02	31 Oct.	do	do	9 Dec. 19
P Carlisle Spedding,[102] *Captain*, h. p. 32 Foot	12 June 99	7 Aug. 00	17 July 06	do	do	25 Aug. 21
William Green, KH., *Major*, Unattached	16 Feb. 97	25 July 99	26 July	do	do	19 Sept. 26
Daniel Baby, *Major*, do.	9 Nov. 97	10 May 99	6 Aug.	do	do	1 June
P Hugh M'Gregor,[103] *Captain*, h. p. 63 Foot	9 Feb. 04	25 Mar. 05	17 Aug.	do	do	25 Dec. 21
P Richard Cole,[104] *Major*, Unattached	23 Dec. 95	27 Feb. 96	25 Nov.	do	do	17 Aug. 26
John George Nathaniel Gibbes, *Captain*, h. p. Malta Regt.	15 Feb. 04	28 Mar. 05	2 Dec.	do	do	
P James Ballard Gardiner,[105] *Captain*, h. p. 74 Foot	3 Aug. 03	4 Jan. 05	20 July 09	17 Feb. 20	do	20 June 22
P George Nicholls, *Major*, Unattached	26 June 99	25 May 03	23 Feb. 09	5 July 21	do	11 May 26
P Anthony Emmett, ***Lieut.-Col.***, Royal Engineers	16 Feb. 08	24 June 09	21 July 13	do	do	
P William Crokat,[106] ***Major***, Unattached	9 April 07	30 June 08	31 Mar. 14	do	do	7 Nov. 26
P Robert Bateman,[107] ***Major***, Unattached	10 Mar. 04	3 July 05	5 Mar. 07	19 July	do	13 Aug. 30
P Peter Dudgeon,[108] ***Major***, do.	4 April 00	3 Sept. 01	19 Mar.	do	do	4 May 26
Gerard Quill,[109] *Major*, do.	9 April 00	5 Feb. 01	12 April	do	do	29 July 36
P Wm. Hanbury Davies,[110] ***Maj.*** do.	9 Sept. 99	18 May 00	16 July	do	do	20 July 30
P John Mitchell,[111] *Major*, do.	9 July 03	5 Dec. 04	1 Oct.	do	do	1 June 26
P Stephen Cuppage, ***Major***, Unattached	5 Nov. 03	30 June 04	15 Oct. 07	do	do	25 May 26
Charles Wright, KH., ***Captain***, late of ***R. Mil. College, Gentleman Usher*** *to the* ***Queen Dowager***	never	never	Dec.	do	do	
P Norcliffe Norcliffe, KH.,[114] *Major*, h. p. 18 Hussars	5 Feb. 07	25 April 08	29 Feb. 16	9 Aug.	do	22 May 23
Sir William Davison, KH., *Captain*, h. p. 2 Foot	never	never	25 Dec. 13	20 Oct.	do	25 Sept. 14
Robert Martin Leake, *Major*, Unattached	2 Oct. 05	11 Dec. 06	14 Feb. 11	18 July 22	do	26 Feb. 24
Abraham Josias Cloete, CB. KH., ***Major***, Unattached, ***Deputy-Quarter-Master-General, Cape of Good Hope***	29 June 09	17 May 10	5 Nov. 12	21 Nov.	do	16 Mar. 20
Charles Christopher Johnson,[117] ***Major*** h. p. 10 Foot, ***Assistant Quarter-Master-General at Athlone***	5 May 04	12 Sept. 05	18 Aug. 14	26 Dec.	do	30 Oct. 23
P Joseph Darby,[118] *Lt.-Col.*, R. Artillery, on retired full pay	1 July 02	12 Sept. 03	22 Mar. 09	22 July 30	do	
Richard Thomas King,[119] *do.* do. on retired full pay	8 Sept. 03	do	8 May 11	do	do	
Charles Dixon, *Lt.-Col.*, R. Engineers, on retired full pay	7 Oct. 06	1 Dec. 06	1 May 11	do	do	

	ENSIGN, ETC.	LIEUT.	CAPTAIN.	MAJOR.	LIEUT.-COLONEL.	WHEN PLACED ON HALF PAY.
William Henry Slade, *Lt.-Col.*, Royal Engineers	1 Nov. 06	1 May 07	4 Mar. 12	22 July 30	10 Jan. 37	
George Macdonald,[120] *Lieut.-Col.*, h. p. 16 Foot, *Lieutenant-Governor of Dominica*	5 Sept. 05	25 July 06	17 Aug. 15	13 Aug.	do	19 June 41
Richard Zachary Mudge,[121] *Lt.-Col.*, R. Eng., on ret. full pay	4 May 07	14 July 07	21 July 13	never	do	
Sherbourne Williams,[122] *Lt.-Col.*, do. do.	25 July 07	1 May 08	do	never	do	
Frederick English, *Lt.-Col.*, Royal Engineers	8 Sept. 07	1 April 08	do	never	do	
Alexander Brown, *Lt.-Col.*, do.		1 Aug. 08	do	never	do	
Ely Duodecimus Wigram, *Lt.-Col.*, Unattached	never	29 [illegible] 23	1 Aug. 26	never	13 [illegible]	10 Dec. 47
John Cox, KH.,[123] *Lt.-Col.*, Unattached	16 Mar. 08	8 June 09	23 Dec. 19	19 Aug. 28	17 Feb.	17 Feb. 37
James Robertson Craufurd, *Capt. & Lt.-Col.*, Gr. Gds.	14 June 21	29 Aug. 22	19 Sept. 26	never	18 Feb.	
William Stewart Balfour, *Lt.-Col.*, Unattached	8 Feb. 21	12 May 25	17 June 26	never	24 Feb.	25 Feb. 48
Henry N. Douglas, *Lt.-Col.*, 78 Foot......................	23 Sept. 03	23 May 05	14 Dec. 11	22 Oct. 25	28 April	
Hon. Chas. B. Phipps, *Lt.-Col.*, Unatt., *Equerry to the Queen*	never	17 Aug. 20	12 Oct. 26	never	26 May	22 Jan. 47
Henry John Murton,[125] *do.*, Royal Marines, on retired full pay	1 May 96	18 Feb. 04	20 Oct. 13	10 Jan. 37	10 July	
William Booth,[126] *Lt.-Col.*, h. p. 41 Foot	8 May	9 Mar. 09	3 May 21	28 June 27	11 July	13 Sept. 43
John George Robinson, *Capt. & Lt.-Col.*, Scots Fus. Gds.	never	23 Jan. 17	5 June 27	never	12 Aug.	
Richard Greaves,[127] *Major*, Unattached, *Military Secretary to the Lieut. General commanding in Ireland*	25 June 12	16 July 12	28 Oct. 24	8 May 28	29 Sept.	21 Jan. 37
Henry Fane, *Lt.-Col.*, h. p. 11 Dragoons	30 May 22	15 May 23	30 Dec. 26	24 April 35	17 Oct.	19 Jan. 38
John James Whyte, *Lt.-Col.*, Unattached....................	21 Aug. 23	22 Dec. 25	31 Dec. 27	5 April 33	2 Oct.	16 Apr. 47
Robert O'Hara,[128] *Lt.-Col.*, Unattached	29 Aug. 05	3 Dec. 07	4 April 11	14 May 29	10 Nov.	31 Dec. 41
Edward Charlton, KH.,[129] *Maj*, Unatt. *Dep.-Adj. Gen. at Ceylon*	26 Oct. 04	25 Sept. 06	22 June 09	22 July 30	17 Nov.	1 Dec. 37
Alexander Maclean Fraser,[130] *Lt.-Col.*, Unattached	8 Nov. 04	17 July 05	25 June 24	29 July 36	27 Nov.	10 Aug. 38
William Cuthbert Ward, *Lt.-Col.*, Royal Engineers	10 May 08	24 June 09	21 July 13	10 Jan. 37	9 Dec.	
*Marq. Guiseppe de Piro, CMG., *Lieut.-Col.*, Royal Malta Fencible Regiment, on retired full pay	never	never	never	25 April 25	29 Dec.	
Lord Charles Wellesley, *Lt.-Col.*, Unattached	16 Jan. 24	2 Nov. 28	26 Feb. 30	8 Sept. 31	do	21 Mar. 45
Joseph Walker,[131] *Lt.-Col.*, on retired full pay, R. Marines....	8 Dec. 98	18 Aug. 04	19 July 21	10 Jan. 37	1 Jan. 38	
Frederick Clinton, *Lt.-Col.*, h. p. 22 Dragoons............	never	19 Nov. 23	10 May 27	never	12 Jan.	3 April 46
Richard Airey, *Lt.-Col.*, Unattached	15 Mar. 21	4 Dec. 23	22 Oct. 25	9 May 34	10 Feb.	13 Feb. 47
James Gordon, *Lieut.-Col.*, Royal Engineers	11 July 08	24 June 09	1 Sept. 13	10 Jan. 37	31 Mar.	
Sir Wm. Alexander Maxwell, *Bart.*, *Lt.-Col.*, Unatt.	14 Dec. 09	15 Aug. 11	2 Feb. 15	31 Dec. 28	6 April	6 April 38
Francis Rawdon Chesney, *Lt.-Col.*, Royal Artillery..........	9 Nov. 04	20 Sept. 05	20 June 15	2 Dec. 36	27 April	
Thomas Hall,[133] *Lt.-Col.*, Unattached	26 Sept. 06	29 Aug. 07	16 Sept. 13	19 Jan. 26	23 June	12 June 40

	CORNET, ETC.	LIEUT.	CAPTAIN.	MAJOR.	LIEUT.-COLONEL.	WHEN PLACED ON HALF PAY.
P W Wm. Henry Elliott, KH., *Lt.-Col.*, 51 Foot	6 Dec. 09	13 Aug. 12	9 Nov. 20	12 July 31	27 June 38	
Peter Edwards, *Major*, Unattached	1 Oct. 07	3 June 09	17 Mar. 11	13 May 24	28 June	11 May 26
P William Freke Williams, KH.,[134] *Major*, Unattached, *Assistant Adjutant-General at Athlone*	30 Aug. 10	10 June 11	31 Oct. 14	9 April 25	do	
P W William Cartwright,[135] *Major*, Unattached	2 July 12	6 Jan. 14	16 Nov. 20	19 May	do	19 May 25
P W John Garland, KH.,[136] *Major*, do.	14 Mar. 05	4 Nov. 06	26 Nov. 13	26 May	do	26 May 25
William Miller, KH., *Major*, h. p. Royal Artillery	1 Oct. 01	13 June 03	1 Feb. 08	27 May	do	20 Aug. 26
P John Campbell, *Lt.-Col.*, on retired full pay, 97 Foot	9 July 03	17 Mar. 04	5 May	do	do	
P Hardress Robert Saunderson,[139] *Major*, Unattached	15 June 04	18 Feb. 06	do	do	do	30 Sept. 26
Wm. Henry Newton, KH., *Lt.-Col.*, R. Can. R. Regt.	20 June 00	25 Dec. 00	25 June	do	do	
Nicholas Lawson Darrah, *Lt.-Col.*, 97 Foot	16 Aug. 04	2 April 05	30 June	do	do	
W Arthur Gore,[140] *Major*, Unattached	22 Dec. 04	10 Oct. 05	14 July	do	do	4 May 26
P David Goodsman, *Major*, do.	12 Aug. 99	23 Mar. 00	28 Nov.	do	do	1 June 26
Loftus Owen, *Major*, do.	22 Dec. 99	1 Nov. 02	8 Dec.	do	do	10 June 26
Pringle Taylor, KH.,[142] *Major*, do.	15 Aug. 11	2 July 12	2 Jan. 20	16 June	do	4 July 34
W Thomas Robert Swinburne, *Major*, Unattached	24 June 13	never	26 Dec. 16	10 Sept.	do	10 Sept. 25
P W George Whichcote,[144] *Major*, do.	10 Jan. 11	8 July 12	22 Jan. 18	29 Oct.	do	29 Oct. 25
W James Arthur Butler,[145] *Major*, do.	23 June 13	never	18 April 16	19 Nov.	do	19 Nov. 25
Joseph Kelsall, *Lt.-Col.*, on retired full pay, 70 F.	17 Dec. 03	21 Feb. 05	11 Nov. 13	23 Nov. 32	do	
Richard Wm. Astell, *Capt. & Lt.-Col.*, Gren. Guards	never	20 Nov. 23	13 Sept. 27	never	7 July	
Robert Spark, *Lt.-Col.*, 93 Foot	May 07	3 Sept. 07	17 Feb. 20	25 Dec. 35	28 July	
P George Maunsell,[147] *Lt.-Col.*, Unattached	13 Mar. 06	25 Dec. 06	18 July 11	21 Nov. 28	15 Sept.	12 May 43
P. F. Wellesley Campbell, *Capt. & Lt.-Col.*, Scots Fus. Gds.	13 Jan. 25	14 July 25	3 July 29	never	9 do.	
Thomas Henry Johnston, *Lt.-Col.*, 66 Foot	21 Feb. 22	1 Oct. 25	24 Oct. 26	20 May 36	28 Dec.	
Henry Aitchison Hankey, *Lt.-Col.*, 1 Dr. Guards	26 June 23	10 Mar. 25	15 Aug. 26	27 Sept. 33	1 Mar. 39	
W John Campbell, *Major*, Unattached	23 Jan. 12	28 Mar. 14	2 April 18	22 April 26	29 Mar.	4 Sept. 43
Plomer Young, KH., *Lt.-Col.*, do., *Assist. Adj.-Gen. in Canada*	8 May 05	3 Sept. 06	20 April 15	12 Feb. 28	do	1 Sept. 40
Henry Dive Townshend, *Lieut.-Col.*, Unattached	16 July 12	14 Sept. 15	1 Nov. 21	10 Oct. 35	do	28 April 46
James Bucknall Bucknall Estcourt,[149] *Lt.-Col.*, Unatt.	13 July 20	9 Dec. 24	4 Nov. 25	21 Oct. 36	do	25 Aug. 43
George Phillpotts, *Lt.-Col.*, Royal Engineers	1 May 11	7 June 11	23 Mar. 25	28 June 38	do	
Thomas Wright, CB., *Lieut.-Col.*, 39 Foot	18 Dec. 12	22 April 14	14 July 25	12 Mar. 37	24 April	
Frederick Charles Griffiths, *Lt.-Col.*, Unatt., *Assistant Commandant at Maidstone*	17 June 24	16 Feb. 26	5 April 31	28 Oct. 37	3 May	3 May 39
William Blois, *Lt.-Col.*, 52 Foot, on retired full pay	3 May 15	30 Aug. 21	14 July 25	12 Aug. 34	11 May	

	2D LIEUT. ETC.	LIEUT.	CAPTAIN.	MAJOR.	LIEUT.-COLONEL.	WHEN PLACED ON HALF PAY.
Thomas Wood, *Capt. & Lt.-Col.*, Grenadier Guards	16 Nov. 20	12 June 23	25 June 25	28 June 38	28 June 39	
John Pennycuick, CB. KH., *Lt.-Col.*, 24 Foot..............	31 Aug. 07	15 Jan. 12	14 June 21	25 April 34	23 July	
Edward T. Tronson,[150] *Lt.-Col.*, on retired full pay, 13 Foot ..	28 Nov. 06	26 Jan. 08	2 Sept. 19	27 Mar. 35	do	
Richard Carruthers, CB., *Lt.-Col.*, 2 Foot..............	19 May 14	25 Jan. 25	16 April 29	19 Feb. 36	do	
Geo. James Muat M'Dowell,[151] *CB.*, late of 16 Lancers........	4 April 16	4 Dec. 17	14 Nov. 27	4 Aug. 37	do	
William Hassall Eden, *Lt.-Col.*, 56 Foot	31 Mar. 14	22 June 20	31 July 23	29 Aug. 26	10 Aug.	
𝔚 Peter Faddy,[152] *Lt.-Col.*, Royal Artillery, on retired full pay	8 Sept. 03	1 Nov. 03	5 Sept. 11	22 July 30	do	
Henry George Jackson, *Lt.-Col.*, R. Artillery	22 Dec. 03	1 May 04	31 Dec. 12	22 July 30	16 Aug.	
𝔚 [illegible] Forbes Macbean,[153] *do.* do. on retired full pay	15 Sept. 04	20 May 05	20 Dec. 14	10 Jan. 37	do	
Hugh Henry Rose, CB., *Lieut.-Col.*, Unattached	8 June 20	24 Oct. 21	22 July 24	30 Dec. 26	17 Sept.	17 Sept. 39
Joseph Clarke, *Lieut.-Col.*, 76 Foot	22 Mar. 10	10 June 13	24 Feb. 25	26 June 33	do	
Sir John Gaspard Le Marchant,[154] *Lt.-Col.*, Unatt., *Governor and Commander-in-Chief of Newfoundland*	26 Oct. 20	24 Oct. 21	30 June 25	14 Dec. 32	18 Oct. 39	29 Dec. 46
Charles Gascoyne, *Lieut.-Col.*, 72 Foot	7 Dec. 20	30 Jan. 23	31 Dec. 25	23 Aug. 31	22 Oct.	
𝔚 Charles Edward Gordon, *Lt.-Col.*, R. Artillery, *Assistant-Adjutant-General in Ireland*......................	8 Sept. 03	6 Dec. 03	17 Mar. 12	22 July 30	24 Nov.	
Matthew C. D. St. Quintin, *Lieut.-Col.*, 17 Lancers	29 June 20	8 Jan. 24	9 Nov. 26	15 April 37	31 Dec.	
Hon. Arthur Upton, *Capt. & Lt.-Col.*, Coldst. Guards	never	10 Feb. 25	16 May 29	never	31 Dec.	
Frederick Paget, *do.* do.	20 Mar. 23	24 Feb. 25	4 June 29	never	24 Jan. 40	
George Moncrieffe, *do.* Scots Fusilier Guards..	never	8 April 26	6 July 30	never	do	
Marcus John Slade, *Lt.-Col.*, 90 Foot	15 July 19	12 May 25	22 April 26	27 Sept. 31	7 Feb.	
Henry William Adams, CB., *Lieut.-Col.*, 49 Foot	31 July 23	31 Dec. 25	10 June 26	18 Jan. 39	13 Mar.	
Philip Warren Walker, *Lieut.-Col.*, Royal Artillery..........	3 Dec. 03	6 Dec. 03	1 June 12	22 July 30	16 Mar.	
Thomas Leigh Goldie, *Lt.-Col.*, 57 Foot	13 June 25	10 Dec. 25	24 Nov. 28	28 Dec. 38	20 Mar.	
George Henry MacKinnon, CB. *Lt.-Col.*, Unattached, *Colonel Commandant of British Kaffraria*	29 June 24	4 Nov. 24	21 Feb. 28	never	24 April	5 April 44
Charles Bagot, *Capt. & Lt.-Col.*, Grenadier Guards	5 Aug. 24	24 Feb. 25	30 Dec. 28	never	15 May	
Horatio Walpole,[156] *Lieut.-Col.*, h. p. 39 Foot	never	8 May 17	13 Jan. 25	17 Nov. 37	18 May	10 Aug. 47
Sir George A. F. Houstoun Boswall, *Bart.*, *Lt.-Col.*, Unatt ..	never	2 April 25	11 June 30	never	12 June	14 Aug. 46
Hon. James Yorke Scarlett, *Lt.-Col.*, 5 Dragoon Guards	26 Mar. 18	24 Oct. 21	9 June 25	11 June 30	3 July	
𝔚 John Singleton, KH.,[157] *Lt.-Col.*, 30 Foot, on retired full pay	11 Jan. 10	25 July 12	15 April 24	10 Jan. 28	17 July	
𝔚 Charles Blachley,[158] *Lt.-Col.*, R. Artillery, on retired full pay	3 Dec. 03	1 Mar. 04	21 June 12	22 July 30	20 July	
𝔚 Hassel Richard Moor,[159] *do.* do. on retired full pay	22 Dec. 03	1 May 04	1 Dec. 12	do	22 July	
Sir John Campbell, *Bart.*, *Lieut.-Col.*, 38 Foot	25 Nov. 21	1 July 24	11 July 26	29 Dec. 37	7 Aug.	
𝔚 Harry David Jones, *Lt.-Col.*, Royal Engineers	17 Sept. 08	24 June 09	12 Nov. 13	10 Jan. 37	7 Sept.	

	ENSIGN, ETC.	LIEUT.	CAPTAIN.	MAJOR.	LIEUT.-COLONEL.	WHEN PLACED ON HALF PAY.
Arthur Wellesley Torrens, *Lt.-Col.*, 23 Foot	never	14 April 25	12 June 30	never	11 Sept. 40	
P James Nisbet Colquhoun, *Lt.-Col.*, Royal Artillery	1 June 08	8 Sept. 10	6 Nov. 27	2 Dec. 36	10 Nov.	
Ralph Carr Alderson, *Lt.-Col.*, Royal Engineers	14 Dec. 11	1 July 12	29 July 25	28 June 38	do	
Geo. Gustavus Chas. William Du Plat, KH., *Captain*, Royal Engineers, *Consul General at Warsaw*	1 Aug. 14	1 July 15	8 Feb. 36	29 Mar. 39	do	
Benjamin Francis Dalton Wilson, *Lt.-Col.*, 35 Foot	27 Aug. 25	10 June 26	20 April 32	17 June 36	15 Dec.	
Samuel Brandram Boileau, *Lt.-Col.*, 22 Foot	4 Oct. 21	1 Aug. 26	25 Nov. 28	9 Dec. 36	18 Dec.	
Patrick Mac Dougall, *Lt.-Col.*, Unattached	2 Mar. 08	16 Feb. 11	28 July 14	19 Dec. 26	29 Dec.	29 Dec. 40
C David Marlay,[160] *Lt.-Col.*, R. Marines, on retired full pay	11 Jan. 01	4 Aug. 05	5 Jan. 26	never	13 Jan. 41	
Edward Sabine, *Lt.-Col.*, Royal Artillery	22 Dec. 03	20 July 04	24 Jan. 13	10 Jan. 37	25 Jan.	
P Anthony Marshall,[161] *do.*, R. Engineers, on retired full pay	1 Oct. 08	1 Aug. 09	28 Feb. 14	do	19 Feb.	
P Bartholomew Vigors Derinzy, KH., *Lt.-Col.*, 86 Foot	26 May 06	16 Mar. 08	25 Oct. 14	4 Jan. 33	26 Feb.	
P *Joseph Anderson*,[162] CB. KH., late of 50 Foot	27 June 05	6 Oct. 08	20 Jan. 14	16 Feb. 26	1 April 41	
P Wm. Dunn,[163] *Lt.-Col.*, R. Artillery, on retired full pay	22 Dec. 03	20 July 04	22 July 13	10 Jan. 37	do	
John Frederick Sales Clarke, *Lt.-Col.*, Unattached	19 Feb. 18	11 Oct. 21	14 July 25	30 Dec. 37	2 April	6 Nov. 46
Thomas Gordon Higgins, *Lt.-Col.*, Royal Artillery	4 Oct. 06	1 Feb. 08	29 July 25	28 June 38	do	
Hon. George Fred. Upton, *Capt. & Lt.-Col.*, Coldst. Gds.	24 Apr. 23	29 Oct. 25	12 Dec. 26	16 June 37	16 April	
Hon. Arthur Alexander Dalzell, *Lieut.-Col.*, 48 Foot	29 April 19	5 Feb. 24	26 June 27	5 Jan. 41	23 April	
P W William Havelock, KH., *Lt.-Col.*, 14 Dragoons	12 July 10	12 May 12	19 Feb. 18	31 Dec. 30	30 April	
Thomas Simson Pratt, CB.,[164] *Lt.-Col.*, h. p. 26 Foot, *Deputy-Adjutant-General at Madras*	2 Feb. 14	20 April 20	17 Sept. 25	25 Dec. 35	6 May	8 Oct. 43
W James Forlong, KH., *Lt.-Col.*, 43 Foot	11 Mar. 13	22 Dec. 14	20 Sept. 21	1 July 28	7 May	
Thomas Edwin Kelly, *Lt.-Col.*, Provisional Batt. at Chatham	1 April 06	11 Feb. 08	26 Dec. 22	10 Jan. 37	11 May	
Thomas Stevens, *Lt.-Col.*, Royal Marines	15 Jan. 01	15 Aug. 05	11 Mar. 26	never	14 May	
John Dixon, *Capt. & Lt.-Col.*, Grenadier Guards	never	10 Dec. 25	1 Dec. 30	never	18 May	
N. W. J. B. Micklethwait, *Capt. & Lt.-Col.*, Scots Fus. Gds.	never	12 Oct. 26	31 Dec. 30	never	18 May	
C Samuel Burdon Ellis, CB., *Lt.-Col.*, Royal Marines	1 Jan. 04	29 April 06	15 Nov. 26	6 May 41	26 May	
Andrew Brown, *Lt.-Col.*, 1 Foot	26 Oct. 20	17 Mar. 25	5 April 31	26 May 38	8 June	
William Thornton, *Capt. & Lt.-Col.*, Grenadier Guards	never	8 April 26	3 Dec. 30	never	do	
Hon. Edw. B. Wilbraham, *Lt.-Col.*, Unattached	never	28 April 25	13 Aug. 29	never	11 June	7 Aug. 46
W Orlando Felix,[165] *Maj.*, Unatt., *Dep-Qr-Mr-Gen. at Madras*	14 Aug. 10	10 Nov. 14	20 May 24	31 Oct. 26	18 June	31 Oct. 26
W Joseph Mark Harty, KH.,[166] *Lt.-Col.*, on ret. full pay 33F.	23 April 07	1 May 07	11 Mar. 13	20 Dec. 27	22 July	
Walter Trevelyan, *Capt. & Lt.-Col.*, Coldstream Guards	18 Nov. 17	25 Sept. 25	19 Sept. 26	28 Dec. 32	10 Aug.	
P Zachary Clutterbuck Bayly,[167] *do.*, R. Art., on ret. full pay	22 Dec. 03	27 July 04	28 Aug. 13	10 Jan. 37	17 Aug.	
Joseph Bradshaw, *Lt.-Col.*, 60 Foot	12 May 25	12 Dec. 26	2 Dec. 31	9 Dec. 36	27 Aug.	

	CORNET, ETC.	LIEUT.	CAPTAIN.	MAJOR.	LIEUT.-COLONEL.	WHEN PLACED ON HALF PAY.
George Buller, *Lt.-Col.*, Rifle Brigade	2 Mar. 20	28 Mar. 25	19 Aug. 28	31 Dec. 39	27 Aug. 41	
William Nelson Hutchinson, *Lt.-Col.*, 20 Foot	24 Feb. 20	25 Oct. 23	17 June 26	4 Dec. 32	7 Sept.	
Edwin Cruttenden, *Lt.-Col.*, R. Art., on retired full pay	14 Jan. 04	29 July 04	25 Oct. 13	10 Jan. 37	16 Sept.	
James Sinclair,[168] *Lt.-Col.*, R. Art., on retired full pay	9 June 04	15 Nov. 04	14 Feb. 14	10 Jan. 37	25 Sept.	
Arthur Charles Gregory, *Lt.-Col.*, 98 Foot	24 Oct. 21	1 Oct. 25	15 Aug. 26	18 Oct. 31	5 Oct.	
Henry Frederick Lockyer, KH., *Lt.-Col.*, 97 Foot	25 Mar. 13	19 Jan. 14	20 June 22	12 June 35	26 Oct.	
Simcoe Baynes, *Lt.-Col.*, Unattached	24 June 12	28 Dec. 15	24 June 24	2 Oct. 35	do	26 Oct. 41
Richard Edwards, *do.* Royal Marines	19 April 01	15 Aug. 05	16 May 26	never	30 Oct.	
Eyre John Crabbe, KH.,[169] *Lt.-Col.*, 74 Foot, on ret. full pay	11 June 07	11 Mar. 08	19 May 14	31 Jan. 28	6 Nov.	
Montague Cholmeley Johnstone, *Lt.-Col.*, 27 Foot	27 Feb. 23	16 Dec. 24	19 Sept. 26	27 July 38	16 Nov.	
Chas. Cornwallis Mitchell, KH.,[170] *Capt.*, h. p. Port. Serv.	2 Oct. 09	16 Mar. 13	4 Sept. 17	5 Jan. 26	23 Nov.	4 Sept. 17
Frederick Meade,[171] *Major*, Unattached	26 Mar. 05	30 Mar. 09	7 April 25	19 Jan.	do	28 Aug. 27
John Wildman,[172] *Major*, Unattached	3 June 13	11 Nov. 14	30 Mar. 20	11 Feb.	do	11 Feb. 26
Wm. Frederick Forster, KH.,[173] *Major*, Unattached, *Assistant-Adjutant-General in Ireland*	10 June 13	26 Nov. 13	26 June 17	18 Feb. 26	do	18 April
William Beetham,[174] *Major*, Unattached	5 Oct. 04	18 July 05	16 Jan. 12	8 April	do	8 Feb. 2
Frederick Johnston, *do.* do.	4 April 10	18 Feb. 13	21 Aug. 17	do	do	26 Feb.
Fred. Alex. Mackenzie Fraser, *Major*, Unatt., *Assistant-Quarter-Master-General in Canada*	4 Mar. 13	6 Feb. 14	24 April 16	22 April	do	1 July 39
William Bragge, *Major*, Unattached	24 May 10	11 Oct. 11	24 June 13	10 June	do	10 June 26
Albert Goldsmid,[176] *Major*, Unattached	30 May 11	20 Feb. 12	22 Feb. 16	do	do	do
George Walter Prosser, *do.* *Major and Superintendent of Studies at the Royal Military College*	6 Oct. 12	16 Sept. 13	24 Jan. 18	do	do	
Edward MacArthur,[177] *Major*, Unattached	27 Oct. 08	6 July 09	8 Feb. 21	do	do	10 June 2
Day Hort Macdowall,[179] *Major*, Unattached	15 April 13	10 Mar. 14	11 Sept. 17	18 July	do	21 Feb.
James Price Hely, KH.,[180] *Major*, Unattached	4 April 95	9 July 03	15 Feb. 10	1 Aug.	do	1 Aug.
Charles Robert Bowers,[182] *Major*, Unattached	18 Jan. 10	18 Oct. 10	8 Dec. 18	15 Aug.	do	15 Aug.
Robert Vandeleur, *Major*, Unattached	22 May 15	19 Oct. 15	24 Oct. 21	do	do	do
John Arnaud, KH., *do.* do.	2 July 07	13 Sept. 08	13 Jan. 14	29 Aug.	do	29 Aug.
Frederick Towers, *do.* do.	18 Nov. 13	18 April 15	8 July 20	do	do	do
Sir Thomas Livingstone Mitchell,[183] *Major*, Unattached	24 July 11	16 Sept. 13	3 Oct. 22	do	do	do
Robert Garrett, KH., *Lt.-Col.*, 46 Foot	6 Mar. 11	3 Sept. 12	7 July 14	19 Sept.	do	
Richard Connop, *Major*, Unattached	30 Dec. 13	15 Sept. 14	25 Sept. 17	do	do	19 Sept. 26
Thomas Molyneux Williams, KH., *Major*, Unattached	14 Feb. 11	28 Feb. 12	16 Sept. 19	do	do	do
Alexander Wilton Dashwood, *Major*, Unattached	23 April 18	1 Nov. 21	23 Oct. 23	do	do	do

	ENSIGN, ETC.	LIEUT.	CAPTAIN.	MAJOR.	LIEUT.-COLONEL.	WHEN PLACED ON HALF PAY.
Herbert Vaughan, *Major*, 90 Foot	4 July 18	20 July 20	13 Nov. 23	19 Sept. 26	23 Nov. 41	
George Green Nicolls, *Major*, Unattached	11 Aug. 14	2 Dec. 19	24 April 24	7 Nov.	do	7 Sept. 38
𝔚 William Nepean, *do.* do.	11 July 11	2 April 12	4 Oct. 21	14 Nov.	do	14 Nov. 26
𝔚 Arthur Hill Trevor, KH., *Lt.-Col.*, 59 Foot	1 April 09	1 Jan. 10	27 July 15	12 Dec.	do	
𝔓 Robert Carlile Pollock,[187] *Major*, Unattached	4 Mar. 08	11 July 11	5 Oct. 15	26 Dec.	do	26 Dec. 26
Richard Rich Wilford Brett, *Major*, do	23 Dec. 13	24 July 14	24 May 16	30 Dec.	do	20 Sept. 33
Charles Maxwell Maclean, *Major*, 72 Foot	29 Oct. 07	21 Dec. 09	24 July 23	1 Feb. 27	do	
𝔓 *Hon.* Arthur Fra. Southwell, *Major*, Unattached	2 June 08	27 Dec. 09	16 June 14	20 Mar.	do	20 Mar. 27
William Holmes Dutton, *Major*, Unattached	never	4 May 15	15 Aug. 22	do	do	5 July 27
𝔚 *Hon.* George Thomas Keppel, *Major*, Unattached	4 April 15	25 May 20	17 Feb. 25	do	do	20 Mar. 27
George Thomas Colomb, *Major*, Unattached, *Commandant of Royal Hibernian School*	8 Dec. 08	18 Oct. 10	23 June 14	27 April	do	27 April 27
𝔓 𝔚 William Burney, KH.,[189] *Major*, Cape Mounted Riflemen, on retired full pay	28 April 08	1 May 10	2 June 14	6 Sept.	do	
Fra. *Marquis of* Conyngham, KP. GCH., *Major*, Unattached	21 Sept. 20	24 Oct. 21	12 June 23	2 Oct.	do	2 Oct.
𝔓 Henry Arthur Magenis, *Lt.-Col.*, 87 Foot	1 Oct. 12	4 Mar. 13	9 Sept. 19	20 Nov.	do	
𝔓 𝔚 William Bruce, KH., *Major*, 48 Foot	1 Dec. 06	17 Jan. 08	14 Mar. 11	31 Dec.	do	
Sidney John Cotton, *Lt.-Col.*, 22 Foot	19 April 10	13 Feb. 12	1 Jan. 20	18 Jan. 28	do	
Gerald Rochfort,[191] *Major*, on retired full pay, 3 Foot	28 Feb. 05	25 Sept. 05	1 July 12	1 May	do	
𝔚 James Leslie,[192] *do.* Unattached	4 April 05	15 May 06	3 Jan. 11	15 May	do	11 June 29
Maurice Barlow, *Lt.-Col.*, 14 Foot	21 July 14	23 Mar. 15	20 Dec. 21	12 June	do	
Nicholas Wilson, KH., *Lt.-Col.*, 77 Foot	31 Oct. 09	7 Oct. 13	24 Oct. 21	30 Dec.	do	
𝔓 John Napper Jackson, *Major*, 99 Foot	1 July 05	1 Jan. 06	28 Feb. 12	11 June 29	do	
𝔓 𝔚 James Richard Rotton,[193] *Lt.-Col.*, Unattached	27 June 11	9 Jan. 12	18 Sept. 17	11 Aug.	do	7 June 44
Botet Trydell, *Lt.-Col.*, 83 Foot	19 Oct. 04	30 Oct. 06	17 Nov. 18	3 Dec.	do	
𝔚 John Clark, KH., *Major*, 54 Foot	2 June 14	27 Nov. 21	29 Aug. 26	25 Dec.	do	
Philip Dundas, *Lt.-Col.*, 47 Foot	22 Aug. 05	25 Aug. 07	16 Nov. 20	28 June 31	do	
James Gray,[194] *Lt.-Col.*, R. Artillery, on retired full pay	9 June 04	20 Dec. 04	1 May 14	10 Jan. 37	do	
𝔓 Robert Sloper Piper,[195] *Lt.-Col.*, R. Engineers, on ret. full pay	10 Jan. 09	21 Dec. 09	16 Mar.	do	do	
𝔓 Philip Barry, *Lt.-Col.*, Royal Engineers	10 Feb. 09	1 Mar. 10	1 Oct. 14	do	do	
James Fogo,[196] *Lt.-Col.*, Royal Artillery, on retired full pay	18 June 04	21 Dec. 04	4 Oct. 14	do	do	
𝔓 *Hon.* Wm. Arbuthnott,[197] *Lt.-Col.*, R. Art., on ret. full pay	16 July 04	do	20 Dec.	do	do	
𝔓 Henry Blachley,[198] *Lt.-Col.*, R. Artillery, on ret. full pay	10 Aug. 04	18 Sept. 05	do	do	do	
James Archibald Chalmer, *Lt.-Col.*, Royal Artillery	do	1 Mar. 05	do	do	do	
𝔚 Wm. Henry Stopford-Blair,[199] *Lt.-Col.*, h. p. R. Artillery	15 Sept. 04	2 July 05	1 April 15	do	do	20 Dec. 41
𝔓 George John Belson,[200] *Lt.-Col.*, R. Art., on retired full pay	29 Sept. 04	6 July 05	21 May	do	do	

	Ensign, etc.	Lieut.	Captain.	Major.	Lieut.-Colonel.	When placed on Half Pay.
Fred. Henry Turner, *Lt.-Col.*, Unattached	never	4 July 15	26 Oct. 26	never	23 Nov. 41	28 Nov. 45
Redmond William Brough, *Lt.-Col.*, h. p. 2 Foot, *Assistant Adjutant-General at Belfast*	10 Mar. 07	15 July 08	10 Jan. 22	20 May 35	26 Nov.	2 Mar. 46
Robert Franck Romer, *Lt.-Col.*, R. Art., on retired full pay, *Barrack Master at Guernsey*	9 Nov. 04	16 July 05	23 May 15	10 Jan. 37	23 Dec. 41	
[illegible] George Dry Hall,[illegible] *Lt.-Col.*, Unattached	4 Oct. 10	28 Nov. 11	2 June 25	24 Aug. 32	31 Dec. 41	1 Jan. 39
Charles F. Head,[illegible] *Major*, Unattached	11 April 11	3 June 13	10 Feb. 25	22 Mar. 33	do	2 Sept. 39
Henry Robert Milner, *Lt.-Col.*, 94 Foot	7 Feb. 22	3 Dec. 25	12 Dec. 26	5 July 33	do	
[illegible] Samuel Dilman Pritchard, *Lt.-Col.*, Unatt., *Assistant-Adjutant-General in* [illegible]	4 May 09	11 April 11	7 April 25	30 Aug. 33	do	1 Jan. 39
Edw. Hungerford Delaval Elers Napier, *Major*, Unattached	11 Aug. 25	11 Oct. 26	21 June 31	11 Oct. 39	do	14 Oct. 42
Edward Harvey, *Lt.-Col.*, [illegible]	24 Mar. 25	4 May 26	12 Oct. 30	30 April 41	do	25 April 48
Hon. Fra. Grosvenor [illegible], *Capt. & Lt.-Col.*, Gr. Guards	never	30 April 27	31 Dec. 30	never	do	
[illegible] Henry [illegible], *Lt.-Col.*, Ceylon Rifle [illegible]	21 Mar. 05	28 Nov. 05	31 Mar. 13	10 Jan. 37	7 Jan. 42	
David Anderson [illegible], *Lt.-Col.*, Royal Marine Artillery	15 April 01	15 Aug. 05	31 July 26	23 Nov. 41	12 Feb.	
[illegible] David James Ballingall, *do.* [illegible] Marines	1 July 03	do	do	do	do	
John Hewes,[205] *Lt.-Col.*, [illegible] Marines, on retired full pay	4 July 03	do	do	do	do	
Richard Carr Molesworth,[206] *Lt.-Col.*, R. Art., on ret. full pay	9 Nov. 04	17 July 05	20 June 15	10 Jan. 37	7 April	
James Robert Young, *Lt.-Col.*, 25 Foot	27 July 15	14 Dec. 18	13 May 26	31 Dec. 33	8 April	
[illegible] Willington,[illegible] *Lt.-Col.*, 84 Foot, on retired full pay	1 Oct. 12	2 Oct. 14	3 Dec. 25	28 June 38	do	
[illegible] William Bell, *do.* Royal Artillery	23 Nov. 04	2 Dec. 05	3 July 15	10 Jan. 37	13 April	
[illegible] Brodie Fraser, *do.* do	14 Dec. 04	3 Dec. 05	1 Aug. 15	do	do	
[illegible] Paris Perry, *Lt.-Col.*, 3 West India Regiment	8 Oct. 12	18 Feb. 13	8 June 26	8 Dec. 37	15 April	
John Michel, *Lt.-Col.*, 6 Foot	3 April 23	28 April 25	12 Dec. 26	6 Mar. 40	do	
[illegible] Percy [illegible], *Lt.-Col.*, Unattached	16 Mar. 20	19 Feb. 24	11 June 28	26 Oct. 41	do	30 June 43
[illegible] Severus W. Lynam Stretton, [illegible], 64 Foot	11 June 12	6 [illegible] 14	13 Aug. 25	2 Dec. 31	6 May	
John [illegible] Pringle, *Lt.-Col.*, Unattached	never	24 Dec. 25	15 June 30	never	13 May	29 Dec. 46
[illegible] Richard Westmore,[210] *do.* on retired full pay, 33 Foot	28 May 12	1 April 13	23 June 25	do	14 June	
Hon. Lauderdale Maule, *do.* 79 Foot	24 Aug. 26	21 July 31	22 May 35	11 May 39	do	
John [illegible] Chads,[211] *Major*, on ret. full pay, 1 W. India Regt.	4 May 09	1 Dec. 14	27 Jan. 20	22 April 36	1 July	
Charles Brownlow Cumberland, *Lieut.-Col.*, 96 Foot	21 Dec. 20	15 Oct. 25	10 June 26	19 Sept. 34	22 July	
Frederick [illegible], *Col.*, 32 Foot	13 May 24	22 Oct. 25	16 April 29	28 Sept. 39		
[illegible] [illegible] Louis, *do.* Royal Artillery	14 Dec. 04	28 Dec. 05	26 Oct. 15	10 Jan. 37	9 Aug.	
Edward [illegible] Archer, *[illegible]*, Unattached	3 May 12	30 Mar. 14	26 May 25	15 June 30	5 Aug.	5 April 31

	CORNET, ETC.	LIEUT.	CAPTAIN.	MAJOR.	LIEUT.-COLONEL.	WHEN PLACED ON HALF PAY.
John Messiter, *Lt.-Col.*, 28 Foot	18 July 15	3 July 23	19 Sept. 26	27 Sept. 33	24 Aug. 42	
Charles Craufurd Hay, *Lt.-Col.*, 19 Foot	27 June 24	24 Dec. 25	19 Sept. 26	16 June 37	30 Aug.	
Robert Pattisson,[212] *Major*, on retired full pay, 13 Foot	31 Mar. 08	4 Jan. 10	30 Oct. 31	22 July 42	4 Oct.	
Charles St. Lo Malet, *Lt.-Col.*, Unattached	6 Jan. 19	26 May 25	25 Feb. 26	10 Jan. 38	25 Oct.	16 Dec. 45
𝔓 James Macdougall, *Lt.-Col.*, 42 Foot	11 June 12	8 Sept. 13	10 Sept. 25	23 Oct. 35	1 Nov.	
Philip Hill, *Major*, Unattached	11 Mar. 24	17 Sept. 25	29 Aug. 26	13 May 36	do	10 Feb. 43
David Hay, *do.* 6 Dragoon Guards	6 Oct. 08	31 Oct. 11	5 Aug. 19	10 Jan. 37	do	
William Longworth Dames, *Major*, h. p. Rifle Brigade	26 July 20	24 Nov. 28	27 June 34	12 Oct. 41	do	6 Nov. 46
Lord Arthur Lennox, *Lt.-Col.*, h. p. 6 Foot	24 June 23	22 Oct. 25	1 Aug. 26	6 July 38	22 Nov.	25 Feb. 45
Charles Warren, CB., *do.* 55 Foot	24 Nov. 14	13 Nov. 18	1 Aug. 22	21 Nov. 34	23 Dec.	
Gore Browne, CB., *do.* 41 Foot	14 Jan. 24	11 July 26	11 June 29	19 Dec. 34	do	
𝔓 *Joseph Simmons*, CB.,[213] late of 41 Foot	16 April 12	23 Dec. 13	18 Feb. 27	22 Aug. 37	do	
George Henry Lockwood, CB., *Lt.-Col.*, 3 Light Dragoons	10 Mar. 25	10 Aug. 26	7 Sept. 32	6 Mar. 39	do	
George Alexander Malcolm, CB.,[214] *Major*, Unattached	31 Dec. 25	7 June 27	30 Dec. 31	13 Dec. 39	do	16 May 45
John Bloomfield Gough, CB., *Captain*, 3 Light Dragoons, *Quarter-Master-General, East Indies*	24 Feb. 20	1 Oct. 25	1 Aug. 26	26 May 41	do	
Norman Maclean, CB., *Major*, on retired full pay, 55 Foot	17 Sept. 07	23 Feb. 09	29 Mar. 27	23 Nov. 41	do	
Robert Henry Wynyard, CB., *Lt.-Col.*, 58 Foot	25 Feb. 19	17 July 23	20 May 26	25 July 41	30 Dec.	
Donald Campbell,[215] *Lt.-Col.*, R. Marines, on retired full pay	5 July 03	15 Aug. 05	31 July 26	23 Nov. 41	4 Jan. 43	
Henry Eyre, *Lieut.-Col.*, Unattached	28 Aug. 17	20 April 26	3 April 28	17 Feb. 37	17 Mar.	28 April 43
Harry Shakespear Phillips,[216] CB., *Lieut.-Col.*, Unattached	8 Jan. 24	12 May 25	14 Feb. 28	31 Aug. 38	31 Mar.	26 May 48
𝔓 Thomas Grantham, *Lieut.-Col.*, Royal Artillery	14 Dec. 04	29 Dec. 05	28 Oct. 15	10 Jan. 37	4 April	
Francis Haultain, *Lieut.-Col.*, Royal Artillery	do	23 Feb. 06	7 June 16	do	do	
John Gordon, *Lt.-Col.*, Royal Artillery, on retired full pay	10 May 05	1 June 06	5 Aug. 16	10 Jan. 37	6 April	
Wm. Fred. Elrington, *Capt. & Lt.-Col.*, Scots Fus. Guards	never	14 Nov. 26	30 Aug. 31	never	14 April	
Lord William Paulet, *Lieut.-Col.*, Unattached	1 Feb. 21	23 Aug. 22	12 Feb. 25	10 Sept. 30	21 April	31 Dec. 47
Henry Burnside, *Lieut.-Col.*, 61 Foot	8 Oct. 07	18 Feb. 08	13 Nov. 17	10 Jan. 37	9 May	
Thomas Arthur, *Lieut.-Col.*, 3 Dragoon Guards	23 June 25	19 Sept. 26	8 Feb. 31	15 Sept. 38	12 May	
John Christie Clithcrow, *Capt. & Lieut.-Col.*, Colds. Guards	11 April 25	8 April 26	22 July 30	never	30 May	
𝔓 Andrew Snape Hamond Aplin, *Lt.-Col.*, 86 Foot	5 July 10	24 Sept. 12	9 Mar. 25	28 June 38	16 June	
John H. Poole, CB., *Major*, 22 Foot	24 Mar. 14	30 Sept. 19	1 Nov. 30	18 Oct. 39	4 July	
𝔓 Philip M'Pherson, CB., *Major*, 17 Foot	2 Nov. 09	13 June 11	13 Mar. 27	23 Nov. 41	4 July	
Charles Wm. Ridley, *Capt. & Lt.-Col.*, Grenadier Guards	never	21 Feb. 28	14 June 31	never	14 July	
Willoughby Moore, *Lt.-Col.*, 6 Dragoons	7 Sept. 20	17 July 23	4 Mar. 26	17 July 40	28 July	

	CORNET, ETC.	LIEUT.	CAPTAIN.	MAJOR.	LIEUT.-COLONEL.	WHEN PLACED ON HALF PAY.
P Poole Vallancey England, *Lt.-Col.*, Royal Artillery	10 May 05	1 June 06	11 Mar. 17	10 Jan. 37	17 Aug. 43	
John Patton, *Lt.-Col.*, 12 Foot	18 Sept. 17	1 Mar. 21	10 Sept. 25	31 Oct. 34	18 Aug.	
Irwine Whitty, *Lt.-Col.*, Royal Artillery	12 July 05	1 June 06	23 Oct. 18	10 Jan. 37	do	
Henry Lewis Sweeting, *Lt.-Col.*, Royal Artillery	9 Aug. 05	1 June 06	1 May 19	10 Jan. 37	1 Sept.	
Peter Farquharson,[217] *Major*, h. p. 65 Foot, *Deputy Adjut.-General in Jamaica*	1 Sept. 07	1 May 10	2 June 25	24 Aug. 32	5 Sept.	12 Sept. 43
Duncan Alexander Cameron, *Lieut.-Col.*, 42 Foot	8 April 25	15 Aug. 26	21 June 33	23 Aug. 39	do	
Thomas Matheson, *Lieut.-Col.*, Unattached	17 Aug. 15	30 Oct. 23	2 Aug. 26	20 Oct. 37	17 Nov.	17 Nov. 43
George Bell, *Lt.-Col.*, 1 Foot	14 Mar. 11	17 Feb. 14	7 Aug. 28	29 Mar. 39	5 Dec.	
Robert Dampier Hallifax, *Lt.-Col.*, 75 Foot	31 July 23	23 June 25	8 April 26	30 July 36	12 Dec.	
Horatio Nelson Vigors,[218] *Lt.-Col.*, h. p., 13 Foot	12 April 27	11 Aug. 29	27 Mar. 35	20 Dec. 42	15 Dec.	9 Oct. 45
Robert Richardson, *Lt.-Col.*, Unattached	8 June 26	9 April 29	16 Aug. 33	18 June 41	22 Dec.	3 Sept. 47
Samuel Braybrooke, *Lt.-Col.*, Ceylon Rifle Regt.	17 Dec. 12	29 April 18	6 Mar. 23	27 Feb. 35	26 Jan. 44	
P CB Robert Law, KH., *Lt.-Col.*, R. Newfoundland Comps.	8 June 09	27 May 11	18 Oct. 21	29 Aug. 34	2 Feb.	
Hon. Aug. Fred. Foley, *Capt. & Lt.-Col.*, Gr. Gds.	never	30 Dec. 28	never	16 Mar. 32	16 Feb.	
P Edward James White,[220] *Lt.-Col.*, on ret. full pay, 70 Foot	30 Mar. 09	5 April 10	14 July 25	14 Dec. 32	23 Feb.	
P Robert Hunt,[221] *Lt.-Col.*, on retired full pay, 49 Foot	25 Jan. 98	6 Nov. 99	11 May 09	22 July 30	29 Mar.	
Gordon Drummond, *Capt. & Lt.-Col.*, Coldstream Gds.	never	10 June 26	3 Aug. 30	never	29 Mar.	
Thomas Scott Reignolds, CB., *Lt.-Col.*, 18 Foot	23 June 25	25 April 28	26 April 31	30 July 42	30 Mar.	
P James Humphreys Wood, *Lt.-Col.*, R. Artillery	13 Sept. 05	1 June 06	11 May 20	10 Jan. 37	1 April	
George Durnford, *Lt.-Col.*, R. Artillery, on retired full pay	1 Nov. 05	1 June 06	6 Aug. 21	10 Jan. 37	1 April	
Edw. Birch Reynardson, *Capt. & Lt.-Col.*, Gr. Guards	5 Nov. 29	12 June 30	12 Oct. 32	never	5 April	
Charles Dalton, *Lt.-Col.*, R. Artillery	1 Mar. 06	1 June 06	30 Dec. 22	10 Jan. 37	15 April	
Edward Wm. Bray, CB.,[222] *Major*, 39 Foot, on retired full pay	12 Jan. 05	20 April 08	6 April 19	10 Jan. 37	30 April	
James Stopford, CB., *Lt.-Col.*, 40 Foot	17 Sept. 25	2 Nov. 26	10 Sept. 30	11 Mar. 42	do	
Peter John Petit, CB., *Lt.-Col.*, 50 Foot	19 May 25	12 Feb. 28	28 May 33	30 Sept. 42	do	
Henry Havelock, CB., *Major*, 53 Foot, *Deputy Adjutant General at Bombay*	20 July 15	24 Oct. 21	5 June 38	4 Oct. 42	do	
Charles T. Van Straubenzee, *Major*, 3 Foot	28 Aug. 28	22 Feb. 33	10 Mar. 37	27 Aug. 43	do	
C John Rawlins Coryton, *Lt.-Col.*, R. Marines	6 July 03	15 Aug. 05	31 July 26	23 Nov. 41	6 May	
Henry C. Cobbe, *Lt.-Col.*, 2 West India Regt.	15 Feb. 31	23 Jan. 35	3 Nov. 37	20 Oct. 40	26 May	
Alex. Murray Tulloch, *Major*, Unatt. *Military Superintendent of Out-Pensioners*	9 April 26	30 Nov. 27	12 Mar. 38	29 Mar. 39	31 May	1 June 38
Hon. John St. Vincent Saumarez, *Lt.-Col.*, Unatt.	8 Jan. 24	28 Jan. 26	17 Dec. 29	10 June 40	31 May	31 May 44

	ENSIGN, ETC.	LIEUT.	CAPTAIN.	MAJOR.	LIEUT.-COLONEL.	WHEN PLACED ON HALF PAY.
Hugh Mitchell, *Lt.-Col.*, Royal Marines	9 July 03	15 Aug. 05	31 July 26	23 Nov. 41	10 July 44	
[illegible] Thomas Bunbury, CB., *Lt.-Col.*, 80 Foot	7 May 07	17 Aug. 09	25 Oct. 14	21 Nov. 34	26 July	
[illegible] Alexander M'Leod, *Lt.-Col.*, 61 Foot	3 Aug. 09	12 Dec. 11	31 Dec. 25	28 June 38	26 July	
Cosby Lewis Nesbitt, *Lt.-Col.*, 60 Foot	27 Mar. 24	2 June 25	18 Dec. 28	10 Aug. 41	26 July	
William George Gold, *Lt.-Col.*, 4 Foot	7 April 25	26 June 28	29 June 32	10 Feb. 43	26 July	
Hon. Robert Bruce, *Capt. & Lt.-Col.*, Gr. Gds., *Military Secretary to the Governor-General of Canada*	never	18 June 30	22 Feb. 33	never	2 Aug.	
Arthur Cunliffe Pole, *Lt.-Col.*, 63 Foot	7 Nov. 26	5 June 30	18 Oct. 33	1 Dec. 37	2 Sept.	
John Byrne, CB., *Lt.-Col.*, 53 Foot	1 Oct. 08	21 Dec. 09	19 April 21	26 Feb. 36	8 Oct.	
Edw. W. F. Walker, *Capt. & Lt.-Col.*, Scots Fus. Gds.	never	8 Mar. 27	18 Oct. 31	never	6 Dec.	
Hon. George Augustus Spencer, *Lt.-Col.*, 37 F.	12 Feb. 24	16 June 25	19 Dec. 26	17 Aug. 41	20 Dec.	
Charles John James Hamilton, *Capt. & Lt.-Col.*, Scots Fus. Gds.	never	5 June 27	6 Jan. 32	never	31 Dec.	
Richard Burne Rawnsley, *Lt.-Col.*, Royal Artillery	21 Mar. 06	22 Oct. 06	12 June 23	28 June 38	6 Jan. 45	
[illegible] Edward Thorp, *Lt.-Col.*, 89 Foot	7 Mar. 11	28 Jan. 13	13 Aug. 25	do	26 Feb.	
[illegible] William Redan Od, *Lt.-Col.*, Royal Engineers	25 April 09	29 May 10	20 Dec. 14	10 Jan. 37	18 Mar.	
Thomas A. Drought, *Lt.-Col.*, 15 Foot	11 Nov. 13	16 Oct. 17	10 Oct. 22	31 Dec. 30	21 Mar.	
Thomas Harte [illegible]nks, CB., *Lt.-Col.*, 10 Foot	7 July 25	26 Sept. 26	1 Mar. 39	29 Dec. 43	28 Mar.	
[illegible] Bird Hardinge, KH., *Lt.-Col.*, Royal Artillery	23 May 06	19 Dec. 06	17 July 23	28 June 38	5 April	
Joseph Hanwell, *Lt.-Col.*, Royal A[illegible]ry, on retired full pay	23 May 06	14 Jan. 07	17 July 23	28 June 38	10 April	
Charles Stuart, *Lt.-Col.*, 13 Foot	30 Dec. 26	31 Dec. 28	26 July 32	never	15 April	
Henry M'Manus, *Lt.-Col.*, h. p. Insp. Field [illegible]er	18 July 16	16 April 20	25 Oct. 27	23 Nov. 41	18 April	10 Mar. 48
James [illegible]x. Fullerton, *Major*, 9 La[illegible]rs	1 Aug. 22	30 Dec. 24	19 Sept. 26	23 Nov. 41	25 April	
William [illegible]ger, *Lt.-Col.*, Unattached	15 Dec. 17	9 April 25	31 Oct. 34	10 April 40	2 May	2 May 45
Hon. Augustus Almeric Spencer, *Lt.-Col.*, 44 [illegible]	8 April 25	5 July 27	6 April 31	21 July 43	17 May	
[illegible] Henry John Savage, *Lt.-Col.*, Royal [illegible]	30 Sept. 09	1 May 11	1 Dec. 15	10 Jan. 37	22 May	
[illegible] *Lt.-Col.*, 36 Foot	25 Dec. 13	13 April 20	19 Aug. 28	15 Dec. 40	22 May	
[illegible] Montresor, *Lt.-Col.*, Unattached	29 Mar. 21	25 Mar. 25	11 Mar. 26	23 Nov. 41	20 June	6 Feb. 46
[illegible] Henry Keane Bloomfield, *Lt.-Col.*, 11 Foot	30 Sept. 13	7 Aug. 17	1 April 24	28 June 38	27 June	
John [illegible], *Lt.-Col.*, [illegible]ttached	12 Nov. 18	6 Dec. 21	27 Aug. 25	28 June 38	27 June	23 June
Edward St. Maur, *Lt.-Col.*, 51 Foot	22 June 15	16 Nov. 20	29 May 23	1 July 37	4 July	
[illegible] [illegible]us Antonius [illegible]rs, *Lt.-Col.*, R. Engineers	30 Sept. 09	1 May 11	11 Nov. 16	10 Jan. 37	12 July	
Studholme John Hodgson,[223] *Lt.-Col.*, Unattached	30 Dec. 19	3 Feb. 25	30 Dec. 26	28 Dec. 38	8 Aug.	8 Aug.
Robert Andrews, *Lt.-Col.*, Royal Artillery	1 July 06	15 Oct. 07	26 Nov. 24	22 June 38	3 Sept.	
Charles Franklyn, *Lt.-Col.*, 84 Foot	17 July 23	8 April 26	10 July 28	28 Dec. 38	16 Sept.	
[illegible] Anthony Gardiner Sedley,[224] *Lt.-Col.*, h. p. 63 Foot	1 Aug. 11	16 July 12	22 May 35	2 Sept. 44	16 Sept.	23 Oct. 47
Harcourt Master,[225] *Lt.-Col.*, Unattached	30 July 18	6 Mar. 23	17 Sept. 25	28 June 38	26 Sept.	26 Sept. 45

	CORNET, ETC.	LIEUT.	CAPTAIN.	MAJOR.	LIEUT.-COLONEL.	WHEN PLACED ON HALF PAY.
Godfrey Charles Mundy,[226] *Major*, Unattached, *Deputy Adjutant-General in New South Wales*	25 Nov. 21	28 Aug. 23	13 May 26	31 Dec. 39	28 Nov. 45	31 Dec. 39
Francis Hugh George Seymour, *Lieut.-Colonel*, Unattached, *Equerry to H.R.H. Prince Albert*	never	12 July 27	24 Aug. 32	never	28 Nov.	10 Dec. 47
𝕻 Walter Elphinstone Lock, *Lt.-Col.*, Royal Artillery	1 July 06	1 Feb. 08	29 July 25	28 June 38	12 Dec.	
Henry Winchcombe Hartley, *Lt.-Col.*, 8 Foot	10 Sept. 18	1 Oct. 20	1 Oct. 25	28 June 38	16 Dec.	
𝕻 George Lenox Davis, CB., *Lt.-Col.*, 9 Foot	15 Sept. 08	15 Oct. 11	7 April 25	17 Oct. 37	19 Dec.	
William A. M'Cleverty,[227] *Major*, h. p., 48 Foot, *Deputy-Quarter-Master-General in New Zealand*	26 Mar. 24	26 Aug. 25	21 May 29	23 April 41	19 Dec.	
𝕻 Charles Barnwell, CB., *Lt.-Col.*, Inspecting Field Officer	30 July 07	30 Mar. 09	19 May 14	10 Jan. 37	22 Dec.	
Lewis Duncan Williams, *Major & Lt.-Col.*, 2 Life Guards	21 June 20	23 July 25	15 July 28	23 Nov. 41	30 Dec.	
Robert Blucher Wood, CB., *Lt.-Col.*, 80 Foot, *Assistant Adjutant-General in Dublin*	30 Dec. 34	12 Feb. 36	31 Dec. 41	17 May 44	do	
Charles Emilius Gold, *Lt.-Col.*, 65 Foot	20 Mar. 28	28 Oct. 31	5 Feb. 36	4 Oct. 44	do	
Charles Algernon Lewis, *Capt. & Lt.-Col.*, Grenadier Guards	13 Oct. 25	15 Aug. 26	12 April 33	never	do	
James Spence, CB., *Lt.-Col.*, 31 Foot	26 Nov. 08	20 Dec. 10	10 Feb. 25	28 June 38	5 Jan. 46	
Richard French, *do.* 52 Foot	9 June 25	30 Dec. 26	2 Mar. 32	11 May 39	16 Jan.	
William Campbell, *do.* 2 Dragoon Guards	6 Jan. 32	12 April 33	27 May 36	11 June 41	30 Jan.	
William Parlby, *do.* 10 Hussars	3 Oct. 16	6 May 24	19 Sept. 26	23 Nov. 41	30 Jan.	
George Congreve, CB., *do.* 29 Foot	8 April 25	12 Jan. 26	12 June 28	23 Nov. 41	11 Feb.	
Pennel Cole, *do.* Royal Engineers	1 Feb. 10	1 May 11	7 Feb. 17	10 Jan. 37	1 April	
𝕻 Edward Matson, *do.* do. *Assistant Adjutant-General to the Corps of Royal Engineers*	7 May 10	do	9 Jan. 21	do	do	
𝕻 James Conway Victor, *Lt.-Col.*, Royal Engineers	1 June 10	do	19 June 21	do	do	
𝕻 Crighton Grierson,[228] *Lt.-Col.*, R. Engineers, ret. on full pay	1 June 10	do	1 July 21	do		
Thomas Howard Fenwick, *Lt.-Col.*, Royal Engineers	21 July 10	do	2 Dec. 24	28 June 38	do	
Lewis Alexander Hall, *do.* do.	21 July 10	do	12 Jan. 25	do	do	
Patrick Yule, *do.* do.	1 May 11	11 May 11	25 Mar. 25	do	do	
𝖂𝕷 Philip Sandilands,[229] *Lt.-Col.*, R. Art., on retired full pay	4 Oct. 06	1 Feb. 08	29 July 25	do	do	
Browne Willis, *Lt.-Col.*, Royal Artillery	do	do	do	do	do	
Benjamin Hutcheson Vaughan-Arbuckle, *Lt.-Col.*, R. Art., on retired full pay	do	do	do	do	do	
𝖂𝕷 Thomas Fox Strangways, *Lt.-Col.*, Royal Artillery	18 Dec. 06	do	12 Dec. 26	23 Nov. 41	do	
𝕻 𝖂𝕷 John Stoyte, *Lt.-Col.*, 17 Foot	21 Mar. 11	4 July 13	27 Jan. 25	28 June 38	3 April	
John Thomas Hill, *do.* h. p. 21 Foot	13 Mar. 27	16 April 29	13 Feb. 35	12 Mar. 41	do	
William T. Shortt, *Major*, 62 Foot	25 Mar. 25	30 Dec. 26	26 Feb. 29	16 April 41	do	

	CORNET, ETC.	LIEUT.	CAPTAIN.	MAJOR.	LIEUT.-COLONEL.	WHEN PLACED ON HALF PAY.
John Longfield, *Lt.-Col.*, 8 Foot	23 June 25	26 Sept. 26	30 Jan. 35	19 Nov. 44	3 April 46	
Charles W. Morley Balders, C.B., *Major*, 5 Dragoon Guards	10 Nov. 25	25 Nov. 28	15 July 36	16 May 45	do	
Fred. William Hamilton, *Capt. & Lt.-Col.*, Grenadier Guards	never	12 July 31	1 Dec. 36	never	do	
P W Robert Pattison Holmes, *Lt.-Col.*, 23 Foot	14 Feb. 11	12 Dec. 11	4 Sept. 23	17 Dec. 30	14 April	
William Denny, *Lt.-Col.*, 71 Foot	10 Jan. 22	23 June 25	27 Sept. 33	24 April 38	do	
Charles Hastings Doyle, *Lt.-Col.*, Unattached, *Assistant Adjutant-General at Limerick*	23 Dec. 19	27 Sept. 22	16 June 25	28 June 38	do	15 April 47
Frederick Horn, *Lt.-Col.*, 20 Foot	26 Jan. 26	17 April 28	16 June 37	9 Aug. 39	do	
John F. Glencairn Campbell, *Lt.-Col.*, 91 Foot	25 Oct. 27	27 Aug. 29	23 Nov. 32	8 July 43	do	
Sterling Freeman Glover, *Lt.-Col.*, 12 Foot	21 Feb. 11	25 Nov. 13	31 May 33	18 Aug. 43	do	
P Robert Brookes, *Lt.-Col.*, 24 Foot	16 May 11	23 Aug. 13	27 Aug. 25	3 May 31	27 April	
Henry Frederick Bonham, *Lt.-Col.*, 10 Hussars	22 May 29	14 June 31	16 May 34	3 April 40	28 April	
John Harbridge Freer, *Lt.-Col.*, R. Artillery, on retired full pay	4 April 07	1 Feb. 08	1 April 27	23 Nov. 41	4 May	
Archibald White Hope, *Lt.-Col.*, do. do.	4 April 07	1 Feb. 08	5 July 27	23 Nov. 41	4 May	
Lord Fred. Paulet, *Capt. & Lt.-Col.*, Coldstream Guards	never	11 June 26	21 Sept. 30	never	8 May	
Manley Power, *Lt.-Col.*, Unattached	24 June 19	17 April 23	30 June 25	28 June 38	19 May	19 May 46
John Rowland Smyth, CB., *Lt.-Col.*, 16 Lancers	5 July 21	26 May 25	22 April 26	17 Aug. 41	19 June	
John Lewis Smith, *Lt.-Col.*, Royal Artillery, on retired full pay	10 June 07	1 Feb. 08	6 Nov. 27	23 Nov. 41	23 June	
P John Eyre, *Lt.-Col.*, Royal Artillery	10 June 07	11 Feb. 08	6 Nov. 27	23 Nov. 41	8 July	
John Fordyce, *Lt.-Col.*, 74 Foot	18 Dec. 28	11 May 32	5 Aug. 36	30 July 44	10 July	
William James D'Urban, *Major*, h. p. 26 Foot, *Dep. Quarter-Master-General, North America*	7 Oct. 19	25 Sept. 23	8 April 26	16 Oct. 35	31 July	31 July 46
P Henry John French,[220] *Major*, h. p. 85 Foot, *Deputy Qr.-Mr.-General, Leeward and Windward Islands*	27 Aug. 12	21 July 13	25 Sept. 23	23 May 36	do	do
Terence O'Brien, *Major*, h. p. 87 Foot, *Deputy Adjutant-General, Leeward and Windward Islands*	22 April 13	19 Jan. 15	20 Mar. 28	23 Nov. 41	do	do
John ffolliett Crofton,[221] *Lt.-Col.*, Unattached	18 Dec. 24	29 Aug. 26	17 July 35	15 April 42	7 Aug.	21 July 48
John Forbes, *Capt. & Lt.-Col.*, Coldstream Guards	20 Oct. 25	1 Aug. 26	10 Feb. 32	never	7 Aug.	
John Grattan, CB., *Major*, 18 Foot	8 July 13	4 Sept. 23	4 Mar. 36	26 May 41	14 Aug.	
Hon. James Lindsay, *Capt. & Lt.-Col.*, Grenadier Guards	never	16 Mar. 32	2 Dec.	never	do	
Hon. George Aug. Fred. Liddell, *do.* Scots Fus. Gds.	never	27 Nov. 28	24 April 35	never	8 Sept.	
William Sullivan, *Lieut.-Col.*, Unatt., *Assist. Adj.-General*	14 Oct. 24	8 April 26	21 June 31	27 Aug. 41	11 Sept.	11 Sept. [illegible]
Henry Cartwright, *Capt. & Lt.-Col.*, Grenadier Guards	never	26 July 32	2 June 37	never	2 Oct.	
Giles Vandeleur Creagh, *Major*, Unattached	6 Jan. 20	10 April 25	1 Aug. 26	27 Dec. 33	20 Oct.	17 Nov. 48

F

	CORNET, ETC.	LIEUT.	CAPTAIN.	MAJOR.	LIEUT.-COLONEL.	WHEN PLACED ON HALF PAY.
W John Hankey Bainbrigge,[232] *Major*, Unattached, *Fort Major and Adjutant of Guernsey*	25 Mar. 08	9 Mar. 09	9 Dec. 13	10 Jan. 37	20 Oct. 46	25 Dec. 14
Samuel E. Goodman, *Major*, 27 Foot	7 July 25	8 April 26	4 Oct. 33	28 Feb. 40	20 Oct.	
A. A. T. Cunynghame, *Capt. & Lt.-Col.*, Grenadier Guards	2 Nov. 30	22 May 35	17 Aug. 41	8 Aug. 45	3 Nov.	
Henry Penleaze, *Lt.-Col.*, Unattached	23 June 25	20 May 26	12 Feb. 30	never	4 Nov.	31 Mar. 48
St. Vincent William Ricketts, *Lt.-Col.*, 2 Dragoons	13 July 26	5 April 31	6 Nov. 35	7 April 43	6 Nov.	
P W Thomas Wright,[233] *Major*, h. p. Royal Staff Corps	5 May 04	3 Sept. 07	23 Dec. 13	25 June 30	9 Nov.	5 Nov. 30
W William James King, *do.* h. p. do.	16 May 05	29 May 09	17 Feb. 14	do	do	25 June 30
Hon. Nath. Henry Charles Massy, *Major*, Unattached	7 Oct. 20	7 July 25	20 May 26	16 July	do	25 Feb. 31
John Joseph Hollis, *Lt.-Col.*, 25 Foot	9 July 03	1 Dec. 04	30 Mar. 09	22 July	do	
Francis Louis Barrallier,[234] *Captain*, h. p. Rifle Brigade	14 Aug. 00	16 May 05	6 July	do	do	9 Aug. 33
P W James Henderson, KH.,[235] *Major*, Unattached	9 Feb. 94	1 Oct. 94	19 Oct.	do	do	28 Nov. 34
Peter Shadwell Norman, *Lt.-Col.*, 56 Foot	9 July 03	2 June 04	8 Mar. 10	do	do	
W Wm. Abraham Le Mesurier,[236] *Capt.*, h. p. 95 Foot, *Town Major of Alderney*	6 July 04	7 May 05	15 Mar.	do	do	19 Nov. 29
W John Swinburn,[237] *Major*, Unattached	28 Aug. 04	16 May 05	15 Aug.	do	do	22 Sept. 43
W Robert Kelly,[238] *Major*, do., *Fort-Major of Dartmouth*	22 Feb. 99	17 Oct. 00	16 Aug.	do	do	15 Jan. 29
George Stuart, *Captain*, h. p. 42 Foot	1 Mar. 03	1 Sept. 04	21 Feb. 11	do	do	11 Nov. 42
Thomas Kelly,[239] *do.* h. p. Cheshire Fencibles, *Fort Major of Tilbury Fort*	10 Mar. 95	25 June 03	28 Feb.	do	do	
W Charles Andrews Bayley,[240] CMG., *Captain*, Unattached, *Commandant of the Island of Gozo*	25 Nov. 04	16 May 05	15 Jan. 12	do	do	5 Oct. 26
W David England Johnston, *Lt.-Col.*, 5 Foot	9 Feb. 04	29 Dec. 04	12 Mar.	do	do	
Robert Edward Burrowes,[242] KH., *Major*, Unattached	3 Jan. 06	23 Aug. 09	5 July 15	22 July	do	6 Sept. 31
W Thomas Gloster,[243] *Major*, Unattached	1 April 07	17 Mar. 08	7 April 25	8 Oct.	do	8 Oct. 30
W Thomas George Harriott,[244] *Major*, h. p. R. Staff Corps	28 May 07	11 Oct. 11	13 Mar. 23	19 April 31	do	19 April 31
W John Walter, *Major*, 95 Foot	15 July 06	3 Sept. 07	24 Mar. 13	26 May	do	
P W James Kerr Ross,[245] KH., *Major*, Unattached	19 Mar. 07	4 May 08	22 Oct. 18	7 June	do	7 June 31
Eardley Wilmot, *Major*, Unattached	11 Mar. 19	11 July 22	12 May 25	21 June	do	21 June 31
Edward Basil Brooke, *Lt.-Col.*, 67 Foot	15 Dec. 17	9 April 25	11 July 26	5 July	do	
Edward George Walpole Keppel, *Major*, Unattached	4 June 18	29 Aug. 22	1 Sept. 25	23 Dec.	do	14 Oct. 36
P W John Fitz Maurice, KH.,[247] *Major*, Unattached, *Clerk of the Cheque to Yeomen of the Guard*	25 April 11	14 Jan. 13	16 June 25	30 Mar. 39	do	30 Mar. 39
Henry Dundas Maclean, *Major*, Unattached	never	5 Sept. 16	6 Nov. 24	20 April	do	
John Campbell, *Major*, 38 Foot	30 Mar. 15	11 Jan. 21	26 May 25	15 June	do	

	ENSIGN, ETC.	LIEUT.	CAPTAIN.	MAJOR.	LIEUT.-COLONEL.	WHEN PLACED ON HALF PAY.
P John Westlake,[249] *Major*, Unattached	12 Sept. 05	15 Jan. 07	8 July 13	28 May 33	9 Nov. 46	28 May 33
P John Crawford Young,[250] *Major*, Unattached	16 Aug. 04	13 Aug. 05	6 Oct. 13	6 Sept.	do	10 May 39
Frederick Hope, *Major*, Unattached	11 July 10	24 Oct. 21	9 June 25	4 Oct.	do	27 Sept. 42
P Lewis Alexander During,[251] *Major*, Unattached	25 Nov. 95	5 May 04	15 April 13	8 Nov.	do	13 Dec. 33
Joshua Simmonds Smith, *Major*, 1 Dragoon Guards	14 Aug. 17	25 May 22	19 April 27	31 Dec.	do	
Aralander Tennant, *Major*, 35 Foot	20 Oct. 08	10 June 13	10 June 26	1 Aug. 34	do	
William Nesbitt Orange, *Lt.-Col.*, 67 Foot	5 Feb. 14	19 Jan. 19	24 Oct. 21	15 Aug.	do	
Sir James John Hamilton, *Bart.*, *Major*, Unattached	10 July 23	12 May 25	8 April 26	28 Nov.	do	28 Nov. 34
Charles Deane, KH., *Major*, 1 Foot	5 Sept. 04	6 July 06	5 Dec. 18	19 June 35	do	
Henry Arthur O'Neill, *Major*, Unattached	11 Oct. 21	10 Sept. 24	4 Feb. 26	28 Aug.	do	25 Oct. 42
Hon. William Noel Hill,[253] *Major*, Unattached	13 Nov. 17	24 Oct. 21	14 Nov. 26	4 Dec.	do	30 Oct. 40
Henry [illegible], *Major*, Unattached	22 Mar. 21	31 July 23	11 July 26	4 Mar. 36	do	4 Mar. 36
John Stuart, *Major*, 6 Foot	22 Jan. 20	26 Mar. 23	13 Aug. 25	6 May	do	
P W Charles Sturt,[252] *Major*, [illegible]	17 Mar. 08	29 Dec. 08	27 July 20	20 May	do	24 April 38
P Fred. Chidley Irwin, KH.,[254] *Major*, Unattached, *Commandant the Troops in Western Australia*	25 Mar. 08	17 Aug. 09	27 Mar. 27	28 June	do	13 May 42
P W John Flamank,[256] *Major*, Unattached	2 Nov. 09	12 Dec. 11	17 May 21	16 Dec.	do	30 June 37
Wm. Matthew [illegible][257] *Lt.-Col.*, R. Eng., on retired full pay	14 Dec. 11	1 July 12	9 April 25	28 June 38	do	
P Daniel [illegible], *Lt.-Col.*, Royal Engineers	14 Dec. 11	1 July 12	7 June	do	do	
Frederick W. Whinyates, *Lt.-Col.*, Royal Engineers	14 Dec. 11	1 July 12	29 July	do	do	
P Alexander Watt Robe, *Lt.-Col.*, Royal Engineers	do	do	do	do	do	
John Alexander Forbes, *Lt.-Col.*, 92 Foot	5 Dec. 16	22 May 23	24 Dec.	do	do	
C P John Wilson,[258] *Lt.-Col.*, R. Mar., on retired full pay	10 July 03	13 Sept. 05	31 July 26	23 Nov. 41	do	
P Robert Mercer, *Lt.-Col.*, Royal Marines	11 July	18 Oct.	do	do	do	
Charles Otway, *Lt.-Col.*, Royal Artillery	1 July 07	5 Mar. 08	6 Nov. 27	do	do	
W William Cochrane Anderson, *Lt.-Col.*, Royal Artillery	3 Nov. 07	1 Aug.	do	do	do	
Reynolds Palmer, *Lt.-Col.*, Royal Artillery	17 Dec. 07	1 Oct.	do	do	do	
Richard Say Armstrong, *Lt.-Col.*, do.	do	22 Mar. 09	do	do	do	
Mark Evans, *do.* do.	4 April 08	1 May	do	do	do	
P Anthony R. Harrison, *do.* do.	1 June	27 Oct. 10	do	do	do	
Richard Parker, *Major & Lt.-Col.*, 1 Life Guards	2 Aug. 22	31 July 25	30 June	do	do	
George Tempest Rowland, *Lt.-Col.*, Royal Artillery	4 April 08	10 Sept. 09	31 Dec.	do	do	
James Brown, *Lt.-Col.*, 94 Foot	15 June 15	5 Oct. 20	28 Sept. 30	11 Feb. 42	do	
P Henry Richard Wright, *Lt.-Col.*, Royal Artillery	6 July 08	29 Dec. 10	11 July 29	1 Nov.	do	

	2D LIEUT., ETC.	LIEUT.	CAPTAIN.	MAJOR.	LIEUT.-COLONEL.	WHEN PLACED ON HALF PAY.
William Henry Bent, *Lt.-Col.*, Royal Marines	26 Nov. 08	11 Aug. 11	27 Oct. 29	9 Nov. 46	9 Nov. 46	
Charles Trollope, *Lt.-Col.*, 36 Foot	19 Nov. 25	10 Oct. 26	23 Aug. 31	16 June 43	20 Nov	
Robert Clarke, *Lt.-Col.*, Royal Artillery	26 Nov. 08	12 Aug. 11	6 Nov. 27	23 Nov. 41	28 Nov.	
James Whylock, *Lt.-Col.*, Royal Marines	25 April 04	24 Mar. 07	31 Aug. 27	28 Sept. 40	7 Dec.	
Andrew T. Hemphill, *Lt.-Col.*, 26 Foot	7 April 25	16 April 29	3 July 39	11 Feb. 46	8 Dec.	
Thomas Wearing, *Lt.-Col.*, Royal Marines	5 May 04	24 Apr. 07	20 Dec. 27	23 Nov. 41	18 Dec.	
Lord George Aug. Fred. Paget, *Lt.-Col.*, 4 Light Dragoons	25 July 34	1 Dec. 37	17 Aug. 41	30 Jan. 46	29 Dec.	
Brooke Taylor, *Lt.-Col.*, 85 Foot	15 May 27	15 June 30	28 Nov. 34	31 July 46	do	
Charles Ash Windham, *Capt. & Lt.-Col.*, Coldst. Guards	never	30 Dec. 26	31 May 33	9 Nov. 46	do	
Edward Rowley Hill, *Lt.-Col.*, 1 West India Regt.	23 Feb. 13	24 Feb. 14	26 Sept. 26	23 Nov. 41	1 Jan. 47	
Charles Wright, *Lt.-Col.*, Royal Engineers	1 July 12	1 Mar. 13	20 July 25	28 June 38	4 Feb.	
George William Key, *Lt.-Col.*, 15 Hussars	5 July 31	25 Aug. 33	16 Sept. 37	14 June 42	9 Feb.	
Augustus Cox, *Capt. & Lt.-Col.*, Grenadier Guards	never	27 July 32	8 Aug. 37	never	12 Feb.	
Frederick George Shewell, *Lt.-Col.*, 8 Hussars	28 Aug. 27	6 Sept. 31	26 Apr. 37	23 Aug. 44	19 Feb.	
Francis Ringler Thomson, *Lt.-Col.*, Royal Engineers	1 July 12	21 July 13	29 July 25	28 June 38	1 Mar.	
John Gordon Geddes, *Lt.-Col.*, Unattached	8 Nov. 15	27 Mar. 25	8 Apr. 26	23 Nov. 41	5 Mar.	4 Aug. 48
William Furneaux, *Lt.-Col.*, Royal Artillery	26 Nov. 08	18 Nov. 11	6 Nov. 27	do	19 Mar.	
Edward Pole, *Lt.-Col.*, 12 Lancers	7 July 25	19 Sept. 26	18 Nov. 31	30 July 44	30 Mar.	
Hale Young Wortham, *Lt.-Col.*, Royal Engineers	1 July 12	21 July 13	24 Sept. 25	28 June 38	16 Apr.	
Joshua Jebb, CB. *Lt.-Col.*, Royal Engineers, *Inspector General of*	1 July 12	do	26 Feb. 28	23 Nov. 41	do	
Arthur Shirley, *Lt.-Col.*, 7 Hussars	31 Aug. 30	1 Feb. 33	15 July 36	28 Aug. 46	do	
George Tait, *Lt.-Col.*, Royal Engineers	20 Mar. 13	21 July 13	16 Feb. 30	9 Nov.	do	
William Matthew Bigge, *Lt.-Col.*, 70 Foot	19 April 31	26 Feb. 36	21 June 39	2 May 45	23 April	
Francis Warde, *Lt.-Col.*, Royal Artillery	4 Mar. 09	8 Mar. 12	3 July 30	9 Nov. 46	7 May	
William Bates Ingilby, *Lt.-Col.*, Royal Artillery	1 April 09	9 Apr.	22 July 30	do	do	
Frederick Holt Robe, CB. *Major*, h. p. 87 Foot, *Deputy-Quarter-Master-General at the Mauritius*	22 Oct. 17	8 Apr. 25	22 Oct. 33	31 Dec. 41	28 May	
Thomas Orlando Cater, *Lt.-Col.*, Royal Artillery	1 April 09	16 Apr. 12	22 July 30	9 Nov. 46	do	
Robert Walpole, *Major*, h. p. Rifle Brigade, *Deputy-Quarter-Master-General in the Ionian Islands*	11 May 25	26 Sept. 26	24 Jan. 34	31 May 44	2 July	
Charles Du Pre Egerton, *Lt.-Col.*, Rifle Brigade	13 July 25	25 Nov. 28	31 July 35	14 Apr. 46	13 July	
*Francisco Busiett, *Lt.-Col.*, Royal Malta Fencibles	14 April 05		11 Feb. 22	10 Jan. 37	20 July	
James Smith Schonswar, *Lt.-Col.*, 5 Foot	5 Mar. 29	17 Dec. 30	6 May 36	2 Aug. 44	do	
Henry Pester, *Lt.-Col.*, Royal Artillery	1 May 09	16 June 12	22 July 30	9 Nov. 46	do	
Stephen Giles, *Lt.-Col.*, Royal Marines	3 Oct. 04	13 Jan. 08	31 Aug. 27	23 Nov 41	27 July	

	ENSIGN, ETC.	LIEUT.	CAPTAIN.	MAJOR.	LIEUT.-COLONEL.	WHEN PLACED ON HALF PAY.
Arthur Johnstone Lawrence, *Lt.-Col.*, Rifle Brigade	4 April 27	12 Feb. 30	24 Feb. 37	11 Sept. 46	1 Aug. 47	
Hon. George Cadogan, *Capt. & Lt.-Col.*, Grenadier Guards	never	22 Feb. 33	9 Jan. 38	never	6 Aug.	
Charles Ogle Streatfield, *Lt.-Col.*, Royal Engineers	20 Mar. 13	21 July 13	21 June 30	9 Nov.	1 Sept.	
John Heneage Grubbe, *Lt.-Col.*, 76 Foot	20 Aug. 18	24 Feb. 25	13 May 26	19 Jan. 39	3 Sept.	
William Blackburne, *Lt.-Col.*, 69 Foot	27 April 27	19 Nov. 30	6 Feb. 35	30 Oct. 40	do	
Francis Skelly, *Lt.-Col.*, 37 Foot	6 July 26	18 Sept. 28	21 Sept. 32	2 July 41	do	
John Charles Hope Gibsone, *Lt.-Col.*, 7 Dragoon Guards	8 Oct. 30	16 Aug. 33	24 July 35	25 Feb. 45	do	
George Cochrane, *Lt.-Col.*, Ceylon Rifle Regt.	22 Jan. 07	7 Feb. 08	13 Feb. 27	23 Nov. 41	28 Sept.	
Charles P. Ainslie, *Lt.-Col.*, Unattached	10 April 25	28 Jan. 26	16 Mar. 30	14 Oct. 42	22 Oct.	22 Oct. 47
Henry Daniell, *Capt. & Lt.-Col.*, Coldst. Guards	never	13 Aug. 29	27 Mar. 35	9 Nov. 46	29 Oct.	
Alex. Boswell Armstrong, *Lt.-Col.*, Cape Mounted Riflemen	30 Jan. 12	5 Feb. 14	15 Sept. 25	28 June 38	5 Nov.	
Freeman Murray, *Lt.-Col.*, h. p. 17 Foot	24 Feb. 25	8 Apr. 26	21 Dec. 32	20 Aug. 44	do	5 Nov. 47
Henry Horatio Kitchener, *Lt.-Col.*, h. p. 9 Foot	29 June 30	11 July 34	8 Jan. 41	27 Mar. 46	do	5 Nov. 47
Hon. Alex. Nelson Hood, *Capt. & Lt.-Col.*, Scots Fusilier Guards, *Groom in Waiting to the Queen*	never	30 Aug. 31	1 July 36	9 Nov.	do	
William Eyre, *Lt.-Col.*, 73 Foot	17 April 23	5 Nov. 25	20 Mar. 27	19 July 39	12 Nov.	
William Maxwell Mills, *Lt.-Col.*, 3 West India Regt.	20 July 32	17 Jan. 34	18 Sept. 40	25 July 45	do	
Sir Hew Dalrymple, *Bart.*, *Lt.-Col.*, 71 Foot	15 Feb. 31	4 Sept. 35	24 April 38	19 Mar. 47	do	
Francis William Dillon, *Lieut.-Col.*, 18 Foot	5 Dec. 05	6 Mar. 07	7 April 25	28 June 38	7 Dec.	
Edward Twopeny, *Lt.-Col.*, 78 Foot	27 Jan. 14	17 Aug. 20	22 Oct. 25	28 June 38	10 Dec.	
David Russell, *Lt.-Col.*, 84 Foot	10 Jan. 28	1 Oct. 29	5 April 33	7 July 45	do	
Hon. Robert Edward Boyle, *Capt. & Lt.-Col.*, Coldstream Guards, *Groom in Waiting to the Queen*	14 Nov. 26	16 July 29	23 Aug. 33	9 Nov. 46	do	
Arthur Edward Onslow, *Capt. & Lt.-Col.*, Scots Fus. Guards	never	11 Jan. 33	10 Nov. 37	never	do	
Joseph Ellison Portlock, *Lt.-Col.*, Royal Engineers	20 July 13	15 Dec. 13	22 June 30	9 Nov.	13 Dec.	
[illegible] Robert William Story, *Lt.-Col.*, Royal Artillery	6 Nov. 09	18 Mar. 13	27 May 31	do	21 Dec.	
George Butt Bury, *Lt.-Col.*, Royal Marines	10 Nov. 04	27 July 08	30 June 29	10 Nov. 40	27 Dec.	
Richard William Huey, *Lt.-Col.*, 68 Foot	26 Mar. 25	19 Dec. 26	11 June 30	13 Oct. 38	31 Dec.	
Robert Cole, *Lt.-Col.*, Unattached	21 Nov. 16	26 Dec. 22	14 Aug. 27	23 Nov. 41	31 Dec.	31 Dec. 47
James Irwin Willes, *Lt.-Col.*, Royal Marines	12 Nov. 04	27 July 08	15 Oct. 29	6 May 42	4 Jan. 48	
Horatio Shirley, *Lt.-Col.*, 88 Foot	12 May 25	31 Oct. 26	5 July 33	31 Dec. 41	18 Jan.	
Charles Carson Alexander, *Lt.-Col.*, Royal Engineers	20 July 13	15 Dec. 13	7 Oct. 31	9 Nov. 46	3 Feb.	
William Samuel Newton, *Capt. & Lt.-Col.*, Coldstream Guards	never	5 Dec. 34	31 Dec. 39	never	25 Feb.	
[illegible] Robert Hughes, *Lt.-Col.*, 1 West India Regt.	11 April 11	29 Oct. 12	13 Feb. 27	23 Nov. 41	1 Mar.	
Henry George Conroy, *Capt. & Lt.-Col.*, Grenadier Guards	never	21 June 33	12 Jan. 38	never	3 Mar.	
Robert Luxmoore, *Lt.-Col.*, 16 Foot	1 June 20	11 June 24	31 Aug. 30	18 April 45	10 Mar.	
Nicholas R. Brown, *Lt.-Col.*, 34 Foot	29 Mar. 21	2 June 25	2 May 37	23 Mar. 45	27 Mar.	

	ENSIGN, ETC.	LIEUT.	CAPTAIN.	MAJOR.	LIEUT-COLONEL.	WHEN PLACED ON HALF PAY.
William Fenwick Williams, *Captain*, Royal Artillery	14 July 25	16 Nov. 27	13 Aug. 40	22 May 46	31 Mar. 48	
Hugh Andrew Robert Mitchell, *Capt. & Lt.-Col.*, Gren. Gds.	never	4 Oct. 33	7 July 38	never	do	
James Hunter Blair, *Capt. & Lt.-Col.*, Scots Fusilier Guards	never	24 April 35	9 Nov. 38	never	do	
Egerton, Charles Wm. Miles Milman, *Captain & Lt.-Col.*, Coldstream Guards	never	do	5 Feb. 41	never	7 April	
John Wallace King, *Lt.-Col.*, 14 Light Dragoons	24 Mar. 25	14 Feb. 28	28 Dec. 32	14 Mar. 45	25 April	
George Augustus Vernon, *Capt. & Lt.-Col.*, Coldstream Gds.	2 July 20	12 April 31	28 Dec. 38	never	do	
Henry James Gillespie, *Lt.-Col.*, Royal Marines	11 Jan. 05	27 July 08	27 July 30	9 Nov. 46	17 May	
David McAdam, *Lt.-Col.*, Royal Marines	19 April 05	do	7 Dec. 30	do	27 May	
William Knox, *Lt.-Col.*, 13 Light Dragoons	12 Jan. 26	20 Mar. 27	14 Dec. 32	11 July 45	23 June	
Spencer Perceval, *Capt. & Lt.-Col.*, Coldstream Guards	never	13 Jan. 37	15 Oct. 41	never	do	
Edward Goulburn, *Capt. & Lt.-Col.*, Grenadier Guards	never	27 Dec. 33	14 July 38	never	18 July	
Henry Cooper, *Lt.-Col.*, 45 Foot	26 Feb. 29	5 April 31	13 Nov. 35	10 Sept. 45	19 July	
Randal Rumley, *Lt.-Col.*, 6 Foot	30 Dec. 24	8 Oct. 25	14 Aug. 27	23 Nov. 41	21 July	
George Dobson Young, *Lt.-Col.*, 10 Foot	6 April 19	25 Aug. 25	21 Jan. 41	5 Jan. 46	1 Aug.	
Charles Francis Seymour, *Capt. & Lt.-Col.*, Scots Fusilier Gds.	never	5 June 35	23 Nov. 38	never	1 Aug.	
Samuel John Luke Nicoll, *Lt.-Col.*, 30 Foot	27 April 32	8 June 38	10 April 40	5 Mar. 47	4 Aug.	
Henry Sandham, *Lt.-Col.*, Royal Engineers	20 July 13	15 Dec. 13	1 May 34	9 Nov. 46	9 Aug.	
Samuel Garmston, *Lt.-Col.*, Royal Marines	27 Sept. 05	24 Aug. 09	16 April 32	do	17 Aug.	
𝕭 John Harvey Stevens, *Lt.-Col.*, Royal Marines	28 Sept. 05	2 Sept. 09	do	do	do	
Henry Vaughan Brooke, *Lt.-Col.*, 32 Foot, *Military Secretary to the Commander-in-Chief at Bombay*	12 July 27	11 June 30	22 May 35	22 July 42	13 Sept.	
Henry Knight Storks, *Major*, Unattached	10 Jan. 28	2 Mar. 32	30 Oct. 35	7 Aug. 40	15 Sept.	23 May 45
𝕭 𝕶𝕳 Thomas Charlton Smith, *Major*, Unattached	24 June 13	5 Aug. 19	27 Mar. 35	30 Sept. 42	do	25 Aug. 46
William Sutton, *Major*, Cape Mounted Riflemen	5 June 27	16 Mar. 30	30 July 36	9 Nov. 46	do	
Sir Harry Darell, *Bart.*, *Major*, 7 Dragoon Guards	1 June 32	12 June 35	14 July 41	3 Sept. 47	do	
George Thos. Conolly Napier, *Major*, Cape Mounted Riflemen	23 Mar. 32	25 Aug. 37	16 Feb. 41	5 Nov. 47	do	
Hon. George Cecil Weld Forester, *Major*, Royal Horse Guards	27 May 24	1 Aug. 26	6 July 32	9 Nov. 46	19 Sept.	
Edward Cooper Hodge, *Lt.-Col.*, 4 Dragoon Guards	3 Aug. 26	3 July 28	19 Dec. 34	3 Dec. 41	3 Oct.	
Frederick Rodolph Blake, *Lt.-Col.*, 33 Foot	30 June 25	14 Aug. 27	23 Aug. 31	14 April 43	do	
Charles Cooke Yarborough, *Lt.-Col.*, 91 Foot	9 June 25	19 Sept. 26	4 Jan. 33	19 May 45	13 Oct.	
John Crofton Peddie, *Lt.-Col.*, 21 Foot	4 May 14	29 June 20	26 Nov. 25	28 June 38	20 Oct.	
Thomas Crombie, *Lt.-Col.*, Unattached	12 Aug. 24	8 Apr. 26	8 May 32	16 Nov. 41	do	20 Oct. 48
Charles Francis Maxwell, *Lt.-Col.*, 82 Foot	28 July 25	17 Aug. 26	16 Nov. 32	9 Nov. 46	27 Oct.	
𝕭 Archibald Macbean, *Lt.-Col.*, Royal Artillery	13 Dec. 10	23 July 14	28 Dec. 32	23 Nov. 41	1 Nov.	

	ENSIGN, ETC.	LIEUT.	CAPTAIN.	MAJOR.	LIEUT.-COLONEL.	WHEN PLACED ON HALF PAY.
B George James, *Lt.-Col.*, Royal Artillery	5 Mar. 10	25 Oct. 13	3 Sept. 31	9 Nov. 46	1 Nov. 48	
Charles Henry Nevett, *Lt.-Col.*, do.	do	17 Dec. 13	26 Oct. 31	do	do	
B CB John Bloomfield, *do.* do.	28 April 10	do	7 Feb. 32	do	do	
B Henry Palliser, *Lt.-Col.*, Royal Artillery	4 June 10	18 Feb. 14	27 Sept. 32	do	do	
Robert Longmore Garstin, *Lt.-Col.*, Royal Artillery	12 Dec. 11	20 Dec. 14	1 Aug. 33	do	do	
CB John Alexander Wilson, *Lt.-Col.*, do.	11 Sept. 12	20 Dec. 14	17 Oct. 33	do	do	
Richard Tomkyns, *do.* do.	do	29 Dec. 14	21 Nov.	do	do	
Henry Williams, *do.* do.	17 Dec. 12	20 May 15	17 Dec.	do	do	
CB Richard Goodwin Bowen Wilson, *Lt.-Col.*, Royal Artillery	do	20 June 15	8 July 34	do	do	
William Henry Charles Wellesley, *Lt.-Col.*, 81 Foot	29 June 30	5 Oct. 32	17 Jan. 40	14 April 48	3 Nov.	
Charles James Coote, *Lt.-Col.*, 69 Foot	21 June 31	19 Dec. 34	14 April 37	3 Sept. 47	10 Nov.	
Augustus Halifax Ferryman, *Lt.-Col.*, 44 Foot	27 June 34	30 June 37	16 April 41	22 Dec. 43	24 Nov.	
William John Ridley, *Capt. & Lt.-Col.*, Scots Fusilier Guards	never	19 June 35	24 May 39	never	do	
William Raikes Faber, *Lt.-Col.*, 2 West India Regiment	10 April 26	28 Aug. 28	22 May 35	23 Dec. 42	15 Dec.	
William Henry Law, *Lt.-Col.*, 83 Foot	29 April 13	28 Nov. 16	14 July 25	28 June 38	22 do	
Thomas James Galloway, *Lt.-Col.*, 70 Foot	13 Sept. 21	2 June 25	27 Dec. 27	23 Nov. 41	do	
George Duberly, *Lt.-Col.*, 64 Foot	28 Jan. 26	24 Dec. 29	23 Aug. 33	29 Sept. 43	do	
John Garvock, *Captain*, 31 Foot, *Extra Aide-de-Camp and Private Secretary to the Governor of the Cape of Good Hope*	4 Sept. 35	31 Dec. 39	25 Nov. 42	3 April 46	do	
Frederick Eld, *Major*, 90 Foot	23 Dec. 24	26 Sept. 26	27 Sept. 31	9 Nov. 46	do	
Sidney Beckwith, *Major*, Rifle Brigade	17 April 28	26 May 33	31 Dec. 39	13 July 47	do	

War Services of the Lieutenant-Colonels.

1 Lieut.-Colonel West served in Holland from Nov. 1794 to May 1796, and was present when the French attacked the British after crossing the Waal, and the different affairs in which his regiment (the 3rd Guards) was engaged; also the campaign of 1799 in Holland, including the action at the landing, and those of the 27th Aug., 10th and 19th Sept., and 2nd of Oct. Served the Egyptian campaign of 1801, and was employed in all the affairs after the landing, up to the surrender of Alexandria. Proceeded with the expedition to Hanover in 1805; to Zealand in 1807, and was present at the siege and surrender of Copenhagen. Embarked for the Peninsula in 1808, and was present at the passage of the Douro and capture of Oporto, action at Salamonde, battle of Talavera, and various minor affairs. Received a bayonet wound in the thigh in a skirmish, on the 2nd October 1799; and in a subsequent affair he was twice severely wounded,—on the left shoulder joint by a sabre cut, and on the right side by slug-shots.

2 Lieut.-Colonel Henry Le Blanc served in South America in 1806, and lost a leg.

3 Lieut.-Colonel Milnes commanded a detachment of the 10th, doing marine duty on board H. M. S. *Isis* in the North Sea, in 1795. Accompanied the Expedition from India to Egypt under Sir David Baird, in 1801. Employed with a detachment in Ceylon during the war with Kandy. Served with the 75th at the siege of Bhurtpore in 1805, and was engaged on three different assaults upon that fortress. Accompanied the 65th on the Expedition to the Persian Gulf in 1809; commanded the light division at the landing and attack on Ras-el-Khyma; commanded the storming party at the capture of Fort Schenass. Commanded the 65th at the capture of the Isle of France in 1810; also, on service in Kattywar in 1812, and was employed against Nownugghur. Commanded a brigade in Guzerat in 1814 and part of 1815; in Kattywar and Cutch in 1815 and 16; and in the Deccan war in 1817 and 18, commanded a division of the army against the Peishwa, near Poona, 16th Nov. 1817, crossed the river Moota Moola in the evening of that day, the progress of his division being obstinately opposed, but without effect, by the united force of His Highness's artillery, cavalry, and infantry, after which the enemy retired, leaving a great part of his camp standing, and considerable quantities of ammunition in the field.

4 Lieut.-Colonel Cooke served in the Peninsula, France, and Flanders, and was severely wounded at Waterloo. Medal for the assault and capture of San Sebastian.

5 Lieut.-Colonel Mansel served with the 53d in the attack at More Chabot and the siege of Morne Fortunée in St. Lucia in 1796; the whole of the Carib war in St. Vincent; at the reduction of Trinidad; and at the siege of Moro castle in the Island of Porto Rico in 1797. Returned from India in the spring of 1811, and joined the 2nd battalion of the 53d in the Peninsula; commanded the light companies of the 6th division throughout the campaigns of 1811 and 12, including the skirmish with the enemy's cavalry near Carpio, sieges of Ciudad Rodrigo, Badajos, and the Forts at Salamanca, battle of Salamanca (horse shot under him), and siege of Burgos. Commanded a Provisional Battalion, consisting of four companies of the Queen's, and a like number of the 53d, at the battle of Toulouse. Medal and a clasp for Salamanca and Toulouse.

6 Lieut.-Colonel Halkett served with the 2nd Light Infantry Battalion of the King's German Legion on the expedition to the North of Germany in 1805-6. Landed on the Island of Rugen in July 1807; was employed at the siege of Stralsund, and in August re-embarked at Rugen for Copenhagen, where the battalion formed part of the besieging corps. In April 1808 embarked with Sir John Moore's army for Gottenburg, and from thence to Portugal; belonged to the army which entered Spain with Sir John, and afterwards retired through Gallacia. Accompanied the expedition to Walcheren, and was present at the siege of Flushing. In Jan. 1811 embarked for Portugal; commanded the battalion at the battle of Albuhera, and was at the siege of Badajos in 1811; commanded the battalion during the campaign of 1812, including the siege of the forts at Salamanca, action of the heights of Moresco, battle of Salamanca, and retreat from Burgos when the Light Brigade K. G. L. formed the rear-guard with the cavalry, and repulsed the repeated charges of the enemy's cavalry. In April 1813 embarked for the North of Germany, and was employed in organizing the Hanoverian troops; commanded a brigade of the same in Count Walmoden's army, and was engaged at the battle of Goerde, as also on several other occasions. In Jan. 1814 commanded the centre of the corps which besieged and captured Gluckstadt. Commanded the right of the corps which was employed at the blockade of Harburg. Served also the campaign of 1815, and was present at the battle of Waterloo. He has received a medal and one clasp for the battles of Albuhera and Salamanca.

7 Lieut.-Colonel Manners served in India with the Bombay army during the second Mysore campaign, and was at Seringapatam and the siege of Pondicherry. Served also in the Peninsula, and was present at the battle of Busaco, pursuit of Massena, actions of Fos d'Arouce, Sabugal, and El Bodon; commanded the 74th at the battle of Fuentes d'Onor and at the siege of Ciudad Rodrigo,—commanded the flank companies at the assault; present at the first siege of Badajos, and succeeded to the command of the regt. at the last siege; present at the battle of Salamanca, capture of Madrid, and retreat from thence. Again commanded the regt. at the battle of Orthes, and was also present at the battle of Toulouse. He has received a cross.

8 Lieut.-Colonel Hunt accompanied the 52nd to the Ferrol, in 1800, and was present in the action of the Heights. Accompanied Sir John Moore as his Aide-de-camp on the expedition to Sweden, and afterwards to Portugal, in 1808, and served throughout that arduous campaign until the embarkation of the troops at Corunna. Served with the 2nd battalion during the Walcheren campaign. In Jan. 1811 embarked with the regt. for the Peninsula, and was present in the pursuit of Massena, action of Sabugal, battle of Fuentes d'Onor, and all the various affairs in which the light division was engaged in that campaign; during the last three months of which, and at the affair near Alfayates, he commanded the 2nd battalion. Commanded the 1st battalion at the siege and assault of Badajos, on which occasion the command of the second brigade of the light division devolved on him: for his conduct on this day he was promoted to the brevet rank of Lieut.-Colonel. Commanded the same brigade when the army went to repel Marshal Marmont from his predatory incursion into Portugal. Commanded the first battalion of the 52nd throughout the campaign of 1812, including the battle of Salamanca and action of San Munos. Served with the light division during the operations of Marshal Soult to relieve Pampeluna. On the 31st Aug. 1813, commanded the volunteers of the light division at the assault of San Sebastian, and was twice severely wounded: for his conduct on this occasion he was promoted to an effective Lieut.-Colonelcy in the 60th. Medal and two clasps.

9 Lieut.-Colonel Rowan served with the 52nd on the expedition to the Ferrol in 1800; in Sicily in 1806-7; and with Sir John Moore's expedition to Sweden, in 1808. Joined the army in Portugal two days after the battle of Vimiera, and served from that period in the reserve of Sir John Moore and in the battle of Corunna. Appointed Brigade-Major to the light brigade taken out by Major-General R. Craufurd, in 1809, to join the army in Portugal, and was present with the light division in several affairs near Almeidaand at the battle of Busaco. In 1811 appointed Assistant-Adjutant General to the light division, and was present at the battle of Fuentes d'Onor, siege and storming of Ciudad Rodrigo, siege and storming of Badajos,—slightly wounded at the assault, and received the brevet rank of Lieut.-Colonel for this service; battle of Salamanca, and the various affairs in which the light division was engaged from the middle of 1809 to the middle of 1813. Served also the campaign of 1815, and commanded a wing of the 52nd at the battle of Waterloo,—slightly wounded. Medal and two clasps.

11 Lieut.-Colonel Harrison served with the 50th in Corsica in 1795, and was present in several skirmishes near Ajaccio. Egyptian campaign of 1801, including the actions of the 8th and 21st March. Capture of Copenhagen in 1807. Campaign of 1808-9, including the battles of Roleia, Vimiera, and Corunna. At the capture of Walcheren in 1809. Served afterwards in the Peninsula, and was present at the battle of Fuentes d'Onor, storming of Fort Napoleon near Almaraz,—commanded the right wing of the regt. while escalading the above fort, for which he obtained the brevet rank of Lieut.-Colonel. Present at the affair with the enemy at Alba de Tormes on the retreat of the army from Madrid; commanded the regt. at the repulse of an attack at Bejar, present at the battle of Vittoria; commanded the regt. in the actions in the Pyrenees on the 26th, 27th, 28th, 29th, 30th, and 31st July 1813; also at the battle of St. Pierre near Bayonne, action at Aire, battles of Orthes and Toulouse. Medal and two clasps.

12 Lieut.-Colonel Cother covered the landing of the force under Sir David Baird at the Cape of Good Hope in 1806; was present in the general action at Blue Berg, and in all the operations that took place until the surrender of the colony. Was afterwards embarked on board the squadron under Sir Home Popham, doing duty as Marines, during which period the French frigate *La Volontaire* of 38 guns was taken. Covered the advance of the force under General Beresford at the reduction on the river Plate, and was engaged in every affair which took place at and in the vicinity of Buenos Ayres; and on the surrender of that place was taken prisoner, together with the whole force, and marched nearly 1000 miles into the interior. Landed in Portugal in 1808, and commanded the light companies of the brigade under General Ferguson at the battles of Roleia and Vimiera; was afterwards engaged in every affair with his regt. (the 71st) on the retreat to Corunna and in the action at that place. Landed again in Portugal in 1811, and was engaged at Arroyo de Molino, when General Gerard was surprised, and all his cannon and 1200 prisoners taken. Commanded one of the storming parties when the forts at Almaraz on the Tagus were taken, for which he obtained the brevet of Lieut.-Colonel. Commanded the 71st at the battle of Vittoria, on which occasion he received three musket-balls through his clothes, one in the saddle, and was also wounded by another. He also served eleven years in Ceylon, and commanded in the Eastern Provinces in the Kandian country during the rebellion in 1818. Medal for Vittoria.

13 Sir Julius Hartmann served with the Hanoverian artillery in the Netherlands in 1793 and 94, and was present at the battle of Famars, siege of Valenciennes, battles of Frixpoede and Hondscote, defence of and sortie from Menin, on which occasion he was made a prisoner. Commanded a troop of horse artillery of the King's German Legion on the expedition to the Continent in 1805, under Lord Cathcart. With the expedition to Gottenburg in 1808. Went to Portugal with the army under Sir John Moore, in command of the artillery K. G. L., and was present at the taking of Oporto, battles of Talavera and Busaco, action of Campo Mayor and taking of Olivença. Commanded artillery of the allied army at the battle of Albuhera and at the affair of Arroyo de Molino. Present at the siege of Badajos and at the forts of Salamanca. Commanded the artillery of the 4th and 5th divisions at the battle of Salamanca. Present at the taking of the Retiro at Madrid; commanded the reserve of artillery at the battle

of Vittoria; and the advance to San Sebastian; commanded the artillery of the left attack at the siege of that fortress; and the artillery of the left column at the passages of the Bidassoa, the Nivelle, the Nive, and the Adour, and also before Bayonne. Sir Julius has received a cross and two clasps.

14 Lieut.-Colonel Brown served in Holland in 1794, and was taken prisoner at the surrender of Grave. Served afterwards in the West Indies with the 60th from the commencement of 1796 to June 1809, and was present at the captures of St. Lucia and Grenada, the attack on Porto Rico, and surrender of Surinam. Proceeded to the Peninsula in 1810, and was attached to the Portuguese service; present at the battle of Busaco and attack on the forts of Salamanca; commanded the 9th Caçadores at the battle of Salamanca, siege of Burgos (from 19th Sept. to 21st Oct.), blockade of Pampeluna, actions in the Pyrenees near Pampeluna from 28th to 30th July; actions near Ordax on the 31st Aug. and 7th Oct., battles of the Nivelle and Nive, and action near Bayonne on the 13th Dec. During the above service he was three times wounded. He has received a cross.

15 Sir Richard Church served at the Ferrol in 1800; the Egyptian campaign of 1801, including the actions of the 8th, 13th, and 21st March, and taking of Alexandria. Served afterwards in Naples, Sicily, and Calabria, and was present at the battle of Maida, and defence of Capri, at which last he was wounded in the head. At the capture of Ischia in 1809; on the expedition to the Ionian Isles, and at the taking of Zante and Cephalonia. Severely wounded in an attack on Stellaura,—left arm shattered by a musket-shot.

17 Sir James Malcolm served on board the Channel fleet in the first American war. In action off Gibraltar in Oct. 1782, under Lord Howe. Also in Sir John Duckworth's action with the French fleet off St. Domingo, on the 6th Feb. 1806, when the whole of the enemy's line-of-battle ships were either taken or destroyed, and for which service he was made a Brevet-Major. In July 1812 appointed to the command of the 2nd battalion of Royal Marines, and served with it in the north of Spain until Jan. 1813. In the spring of that year he went with the battalion to America, and served the summer campaign of 1813 in the Chesapeak. In Oct. was ordered with the battalion to Canada; and, in conjunction with 200 of the Canadian Fencibles, joined the corps of observation on General Wilkinson's army. In May 1814, he led the battalion when they stormed the American fortress of Oswego. Commanded another battalion at the battles of Bladensburg and Baltimore, and in several affairs on the coast.

18 Lieut.-Colonel Plenderleath served with the 49th on the expedition to the Baltic, and was present at the battle of Copenhagen on the 2nd April 1801. Served afterwards in the American war, and commanded the regiment in the actions of Stoney Creek and Chrystler's Farm, as well as in affairs of less importance. He was severely wounded at Stoney Creek; and he has received a medal for Chrystler's Farm.

20 Lieut.-Colonel Hawkins served in the Peninsula with the 68th, and has received a medal and two clasps for the battles of Vittoria, the Pyrenees, and Nivelle.

22 Lieut.-Colonel Macdonell served in the American war, and has received a medal for the action at Chateauguay.

24 Lieut.-Colonel Muttlebury joined the 55th, then encamped before Nimeguen, and served the severe winter campaign of 1794-5 in Holland. In Admiral Christian's fleet during the dreadful gales which proved fatal to so large a proportion of ships; after which he was present at the taking of St. Lucia, where he was employed eleven months against the Brigands, during which period the 55th lost 25 officers and upwards of 600 men. Served with the reserve of the army under Sir Ralph Abercromby at the Helder in 1799. In November 1813 embarked with the 2nd battalion of the 69th for Holland, and was present at the bombardment of the French fleet at Antwerp and the storming of Bergen-op-Zoom,—for his conduct at the latter, although made prisoner, he was honoured with the brevet rank of Lieutenant-Colonel. Served also the campaign of 1815, including the battles of Quatre Bras and Waterloo,—early on the latter day he succeeded to the command of the regiment.

25 Lieut.-Colonel Wilkins served in Ireland during the Rebellion in 1798, and was wounded at New Ross. Landed with the force that occupied Madeira in 1801. From thence proceeded to the West Indies, where he was employed on the Staff. In 1809 joined the 95th, now the Rifle Brigade, and embarked with the corps on the Scheldt expedition. In 1810 commanded a detachment of the regiment in the defence of Cadiz, and a battalion in 1812 at the battle of Salamanca,—received a medal for the latter. Accompanied the army to Madrid, and aided in covering the retreat into Portugal. In 1813 advanced with the army to within range of the guns of Burgos, when the enemy abandoned the fortress. Was present at the battle of Vittoria, and in several minor affairs in following the retreating army to Pampeluna and San Sebastian. Volunteered his services at the storming of the latter, but the honour being subsequently claimed by a senior officer, he resumed the command of the 2nd battalion, and was sharply engaged with the enemy at the Bridge of Vera. Served in the campaign of 1815, including the advance on the 16th June, retreat on the 17th, and was in the command of the before-named battalion on the field of Waterloo, when, by a discharge of grape-shot from the enemy's artillery, both himself and horse were felled to the ground. In 1817 he joined the Army of Occupation in France, but from the serious effects of his wound was compelled to return to England.

26 Lieut.-Colonel Miller served the campaign of 1815 with the 6th Dragoons, and was severely wounded at Waterloo.

28 Sir Henry Pynn served in Ireland with the South Down Militia during the Rebellion, in 1798. Embarked with Sir Brent Spencer's Division in 1807, and was employed with the 82nd in Sicily; subsequently disembarked at the Mondego in 1808, and was present at the battles of Roleia and Vimiera. Attached to the Portuguese troops on the 15th Nov. 1809, and was present at the battle of Busaco. Commanded a corps of Light Infantry at the battle of Fuentes d'Onor and siege of Badajoz in 1811; commanded the 18th Portuguese Regiment in Lord Hill's corps d'armée covering the siege of Badajoz and storming of the Citadel in 1812; battle of Vittoria, action at the Pass of Maya; battles of the Pyrenees on the 28th and 30th July (severely wounded), action of Garris, battle of Orthes, action of Aire, and battle of Toulouse. Sir Henry has received a medal and two clasps.

29 Lieut.-Colonel Robertson served the campaigns of 1793, 94, and 95, in Flanders and Holland, under the Duke of York, and was present at the battle of Famars, siege of Valenciennes, and numerous other actions. Served on the expedition to the North of Germany under Lord Cathcart in 1805-6; and to Zealand in 1807. Also with that under Sir John Moore, first to Sweden, and afterwards to the Peninsula, where he was present in the action near Grijon, capture of Oporto, battles of Talavera and Busaco, retreat to the Lines before Lisbon, subsequent advance and pursuit of the French, siege of Ciudad Rodrigo, covering the siege of Badajoz, action at Canizal, battle of Salamanca, capture of Madrid, siege of Burgos, action of Osma, battle of Vittoria, actions of Villa Franca and Tolosa, siege of San Sebastian, passage of the Bidassoa, attack of the fortified position before St. Jean de Luz, actions before Bidart and Bayonne on the 9th, 10th, 11th, and 12th Dec., passage of the Adour, attack and capture of St. Etienne, investment of Bayonne, and repulse of the sortie. Commanded his regiment at the battle of Waterloo, and was severely wounded.

31 Lieut.-Colonel Leach, after serving with the 70th in the West Indies in 1803, 4, and 5, accompanied the Rifle Brigade on the expedition to Copenhagen in 1807, and was present at the battle of Kioge. He served subsequently in the Peninsula from 1808 to the end of that war in 1814, including the battles of Roleia, Vimiera, and Busaco, action of the Coa, retreat to the lines of Torres Vedras, battle of Fuentes d'Onor, sieges of Ciudad Rodrigo, and Badajoz, battle of Salamanca, retreat from Madrid, battle of Vittoria, various actions in the Pyrenees, passage of the Bidassoa and attack on the enemy's position at the Pass of Vera, battles of the Nivelle, battles of the Nive on the 9th, 10th, 11th, and 12th Dec., action at Tarbes, and battle of Toulouse, besides numerous affairs of van and rear guards and skirmishes. Served also the campaign of 1815, including the battles of Quatre Bras and Waterloo, at which last the command of the 1st battalion devolved on him. Colonel Leach has received several contusions, the first at Roleia, the next at the Coa, and again by a fragment of a shell at Waterloo. He obtained the brevet rank of Major for his conduct at Vittoria, and that of Lieut.-Colonel and Companionship of the Bath, for Waterloo.

32 Lieut.-Colonel Wilson served with the 4th on the expedition to the Helder in 1799, and was present in the actions of the 2nd and 6th October. Siege of Copenhagen in 1807. Expedition, first to Sweden and afterwards to the Peninsula, under Sir John Moore, including the retreat through Spain, and battle of Corunna (wounded). Accompanied it to Walcheren in 1809. Joined the army at the Lines of Torres Vedras in 1810, and was afterwards present in the pursuit of Massena, action of Sabugal, battle of Fuentes d'Onor, action at Barba del Puerco, storming of Badajoz (severely wounded). Aide-de-camp to Major-General Pringle at the battle of Salamanca, capture of Madrid and the Retiro, siege of Burgos and retreat therefrom, affair of Villa Muriel, battles of the Nivelle, the Nive, and St. Pierre, Orthes, and St. Palais. Served also the campaign of 1815; commanded the 4th at the battle of Waterloo, and was wounded. Medal for Badajoz.

34 Lieut.-Colonel the Honourable Dawson Damer accompanied Lord Cathcart to Russia as his Aide-de-camp in 1812. Attached to Sir Robert Wilson, and was present with the Russian Army at the retreat of the French Cavalry from Moscow. In 1813 present in the Allied Army at the battles of Lutzen, Bautzen, Wurtzen, and Culm. Attached to Count Walmoden, and was present at the operations before Hamburg and in Holstein in 1813. In the spring of 1814 entered France with the Allied Army, and was employed with the Corps d'Armée serving in the Low Countries. In the same year appointed Assistant-Quarter-Master-General to the army under the orders of the Prince of Orange; and in June 1815 was present in the same capacity at the battles of Quatre Bras and Waterloo.

36 Lieut.-Colonel O'Donoghue served in the attack at Ferrol in 1800; in South America, 1807, including the capture of Maldonado, siege and reduction of Monte Video. At the defence of Cadiz and Tarifa in 1810 and 11, including the defeat of the French in the assault of Tarifa in December 1811. Returned to the defence of Cadiz, in 1812, and after the French were compelled to raise the siege, he joined the Duke of Wellington's army then retiring from the siege of Burgos. Served the Mahratta campaigns of 1817-19; and in the Burmese War in 1824-25. Wounded in the right leg during the siege of Tarifa.

37 Lieut.-Colonel the Honourable Robert Moore served in the Peninsula with the Coldstream Guards from Jan. 1813 to the end of that war in 1814. Also the campaign of 1815, and was severely wounded at Waterloo.

38 Lieut.-Colonel Keane served with the 23d on the expedition to the north of Germany in 1805; in Portugal and Spain under Sir John Moore, including the retreat to, and the battle of, Corunna. Served afterwards in the Peninsula with the 7th Hussars, and as Aide-de-camp to Sir Hussey Vivian, from November 1813 to the end of the war in 1814, including the battles of Orthes and Toulouse. Also the campaign of 1815 in the same capacity, and was present at the battle of Waterloo and capture of Paris.

39 Lieut.-Colonel Purvis served in the Peninsula with the Royal Dragoons, and has received a medal for the battle of Vittoria.

40 Lieut.-Colonel Robert Macdonald, late of the Royal Artillery, has received a medal for the battle of Salamanca.

42 Lieut.-Colonel Fuller served with the 59th at the capture of the Cape of Good Hope in 1806; the Peninsular campaigns from Dec. 1812 to Feb. 1814, including the battle of Vittoria, siege of San Sebastian, and battle of the Nive, where he was wounded in the shoulder and thigh. Campaign of 1815, including the battle of Waterloo, storming of Cambray, and capture of Paris. Commanded the regiment at the siege and capture of Bhurtpore, in 1825-6, under Lord Combermere, and was slightly wounded in the arm. Medal for San Sebastian, having commanded the regiment there.

43 Lieut.-Colonel Taylor served in the Peninsula with the 9th, from Aug. 1808 to Feb. 1813, and again from Oct. 1813 to the end of the war in 1814, including the battles of Vimiera (wounded), Busaco, and Salamanca, retreat from Burgos, action of Villa Muriel (wounded), and repulse of the sortie from Bayonne.

44 Lieut.-Colonel Bell served with the 48th at the blockade of Malta, and siege of La Valetta. Also in the Peninsula from 1809 to the end of that war in 1814, including the passage of the Douro, battle of Albuhera (wounded), action at Aldea de Ponte, siege of Ciudad Rodrigo, siege and assault of Badajos (severely wounded), battles of Salamanca, the Pyrenees, Nivelle, Orthes, and Toulouse. He has received a cross for the four last-named battles, having on those occasions commanded the regiment.

46 Lieut.-Colonel Robert Macdonald, late of 35th regiment, served at the siege of Fort Bourbon and capture of Martinique in 1808-9. Present with the 3rd battalion of the Royals in the retreat from Burgos in 1812, and in the subsequent campaigns of 1813 and 14, including the action at Osma, battle of Vittoria, assault on the convent of San Sebastian 17th July, assault on the town 25th of July (severely wounded); and on the 31st Aug., although suffering from the effects of his wound, was present and engaged at the successful assault on San Sebastian, where he commanded two companies ordered to the breach in advance of the first brigade of the 5th division, and was at the surrender of the castle on the 8th of Sept. Engaged at the passage of the Bidassoa, battle of the Nivelle, battles of the Nive on the 10th, 11th, and 12th Dec., and repulse of the sortie from Bayonne. Served also the campaign of 1815, including the battles of Quatre Bras and Waterloo, where he was severely wounded.

50 Lieut.-Colonel Patrick Campbell served with the 52nd on the expedition to Ferrol and Cadiz, in 1800; in Sicily in 1806; on the expedition to Gottenburg in 1808; and subsequently in the Peninsula, France, and Flanders, during the whole of the war, including the retreat to Corunna, action of the Coa, battle of Busaco, retreat to the Lines of Torres Vedras, and all the actions in the advance to Sabugal, where he was severely wounded and sent to England for recovery. Rejoined the army in the advance to Madrid, and served in the subsequent retreat to Portugal, battle of Vittoria, attack on the heights of Vera, twice wounded at the head of the 52nd. Commanded also at the battles of the Pyrenees, the Nivelle (the 88th French regiment surrendered to the 52nd on this occasion) the Nive (9th to 13th Dec.), and a wing at Orthes (wounded), and was present at the battle of Toulouse. Served also the campaign of 1815, including the battle of Waterloo. Medal and a clasp for the battles of the Nivelle and the Nive.

53 Lieut.-Colonel Basden's services:—Mahratta war of 1803, 4, and 5, including the taking of Berhampore, Asseerghur, Arguam, Lasslgaum, Chawdore, Jaulnah, and Gawilleghur. American War in 1813 and 14, and was engaged at Long Woods (severely wounded in the thigh); Fort Erie, Black Rock, Buffalo, and battle of the Falls (wounded). Served also throughout the Burmese war.

55 Lieut.-Colonel Oates, during eight years' active service in the West Indies, was frequently engaged with the enemy, and twice severely wounded, viz. in the right side by a musket-ball at Cote de Fer, and in the left ankle in an attack near Port au Prince. Served also five years in the East Indies and in Egypt, and crossed the Desert under Sir David Baird. With the expedition to South America in 1807. Subsequently throughout the whole of the Peninsular war, including the battles of Talavera (severely wounded on the head by the bursting of a shell), Busaco, and Fuentes d'Onor; 2nd and 3rd sieges of Badajos,—severely wounded at the storming of Fort Picurina; battles of Vittoria, Nivelle, and Orthes,—severely wounded through the right thigh. Medal for services in Egypt.

56 Lieut.-Colonel Pratt served with the 82nd at the siege and capture of Copenhagen in 1807; in Portugal and Spain in 1808-9, including the battles of Roleia and Vimiera, retreat to, and battle of, Corunna. At Walcheren in 1809, and was severely wounded at the investment of Flushing. In 1813 he was appointed to the Quarter-Master-General's staff of the army on the eastern coast of Spain, and served with a portion of that army in Italy and in the south of France until the close of the war in 1814.

57 Lieut.-Colonel Spottiswoode served with the 71st in the Peninsula under Sir John Moore, and afterwards under the Duke of Wellington; he was with the storming party at Badajoz, and was severely wounded in the spine.

59 Lieut.-Colonel Charles Campbell served in the Peninsula with the old 94th from Jan. 1810 to the end of that war in 1814, including the defence of Cadiz, pursuit of Massena, actions of Redinha, Condeixa, and Sabugal; battle of Fuentes d'Onor, second siege of Badajos, action of El Bodon, siege and storm of Ciudad Rodrigo, siege and storm of Badajos, battle of Salamanca, capture of Madrid, battles of Vittoria, the Pyrenees (26th, 27th, and 28th July), Nivelle, and Orthes; affair of Vic Bigorre, and battle of Toulouse.

63 Lieut.-Colonel Sall served at the taking of Maldonado and Monte Video in 1807. Also in the Peninsula from 1813 to the end of that war in 1814, and was present at the repulse of the sortie from Bayonne.

64 Lieut.-Colonel Bunce served on board H. M. S. *Bedford*, at the battle of Camperdown, under Lord Duncan, and capture of the Dutch Fleet, 11th Oct. 1797. In 1799 landed from the fleet under Lord Nelson at the siege and capitulation of St. Elmo at Naples, surrender of the castles of Uovo and Nuovo and the siege and fall of Capua. Landed from the fleet at the siege of Malta in 1800. Served in Egypt, 1801. In May 1806, he commanded the seamen and marines landed from the squadron under Sir Sydney Smith at the attack and capture of the island of Capri, and was afterwards at the fall of Gaeta. Commanded the battalion of marines landed from the fleet under Sir Robert Stopford during the attack and capture of Java in 1811; attached to the advance under General Gillespie at the storming of the intrenched lines and fortifications of Cornelis, and received his thanks in public orders; also thanked in the field at the head of his battalion by Sir Samuel Auchmuty, the Commander-in-chief of the Forces. He was afterwards at the fall of Gresil and Sourabaya, two of the enemy's strongest sea-ports. Independent of the above, he has been frequently engaged in boat-actions. Medal for Java.

65 Lieut.-Colonel M'Mahon, being then a Lieut. in the Clare Militia, served at New Ross, Vinegar-hill, and at the re-capture of Wexford, in Ireland, from the rebels, in 1798; and also during the invasion of that country immediately afterwards by a French army. In 1800 he served with the 27th in the attack on Ferrol, and in the demonstration that was made on Quiberon Bay, Belleisle, and all along the coasts of France and Spain to Cadiz. Served in the Peninsula with the 5th (Rifle) battalion of the 60th, from 1808 to 1813, including the advance on Oporto in 1809, battle of Busaco, retreat to the Lines of Torres Vedras, advance from thence, investment and opening of the trenches before Badajos, battle of Albuhera, covering the third siege and the capture of Badajoz, storming the forts at Almaraz, capture of a strong column of the enemy at Arroyo de Molino, besides many minor affairs.

66 Lieut.-Colonel Terry served the campaign of 1799 in Holland with the 25th, including the battle of Egmont-op-Zee. Expedition to Egypt and surrender of Alexandria in 1801; capture of Madeira in 1807; capture of Guadaloupe and St. Martin's in 1810; re-capture of Guadaloupe in 1815.

67 Lieut.-Col. Whelan served in the American war with the Royal Newfoundland Fencibles.

68 Lieut.-Colonel Grieve served at the siege of Tarragona.

69 Lieut.-Colonel Cross served in the Peninsula from 1808 to the end of the war, with the exception of a short period in 1809, including the campaign and battle of Corunna, action at Almeida on the Coa, 24th July 1810; battle of Busaco, actions at Pombal, Redinha (wounded), Miranda de Corvo, Foz d'Arouce, and Sabugal; battle of Fuentes d'Onor, 3rd and 5th May 1811; siege of Ciudad Rodrigo, actions of San Munos and San Milan, battles of Vittoria, Lesaca Bridge, Bidassoa, Vera, 7th Oct., Nivelle, Nive (9th, 10th, and 11th Dec. 1813). Orthes, Tarbes, and Toulouse. Received a severe contusion on the 18th June at Waterloo. Col. Cross served in the Light Division as a volunteer, with the 1st battalion of the 52nd Light Infantry when effective in 2nd battalion, from 31st Dec. 1812 to July 1816.

70 Lieut.-Colonel Fairtlough served at the bombardment of Ter Vere, and siege and capture of Flushing in 1809. Also at the capture of Guadaloupe in 1815.

71 Lieut.-Colonel Streatfield served the Mahratta campaign of 1804, 5, and 6, including the assault of Bhurtpore, with the Grenadiers of the 65th, when out of 17 officers and 300 men who marched to the assault, 14 officers and 190 men were either killed or wounded. At the capture of the Isle of France in 1810. Served the Mahratta campaign of 1817 and 18, including the capture of Hatrass.

73 Lieut.-Colonel Senior was severely wounded in the action between H. M. packet *Lapwing* and the American privateer *Fox*, off Barbadoes, 30th Sept, 1813

75 Lieut.-Colonel Hughes served the Egyptian campaign of 1801 with the 24th. Engaged with a French squadron in the Mosambique channel, 3rd July 1810 Served the Nepaul campaigns of 1814, 15, and 16, and was wounded at Harriapore. Served also during the Mahratta war of 1816, 17, and 18. Medal for services in Egypt.

76 Lieut.-Colonel Lane served in the West Indies in 1796 and 7, and was present at the taking of St. Lucia. In 1801 he served the Egyptian campaign (Medal), including all the actions; and subsequently in the Peninsula, including the siege and storming of Badajoz, and battle of Salamanca.

77 Lieut.-Colonel Austen served with the 25th at the landing at the Helder in Aug. 1799, and was severely wounded at the battle of Egmont-op-Zee on the 2nd Oct. following. Served

in Egypt in 1801, including the surrender of Alexandria. Also at the capture of Guadaloupe, in 1810, and again in 1815.

78 Lieut.-Colonel Watson was 28 years in the 14th regt, the greater part of which time he served in the West and East Indies, and retired from active service in consequence of total loss of sight. He was at the capture of the Isle of France in 1810; of Java in 1811, including the investment and storming of Fort Cornelis, and storming the heights of Serondole; previous to which he was actively engaged on the coast when embarked in H. M. S. *Minden*, and at St. Nicholas Point commanded a detachment of the 14th and Royal Marines, and defeated a very superior French force of the enemy's best troops sent to attack that position. In 1812, he was at the storming of Djoqjocarta. In 1813, at the subjugation of the Piratical State of Sambas in the Island of Borneo, when he commanded the column which attacked the stockades leading up to the town, on which occasion he was wounded.

79 Lieut.-Colonel Nooth served with the 7th Fusiliers, on the expedition against Copenhagen, in 1807. With the 2nd battalion of the 14th, on the expedition under Sir David Baird, and was in the retreat of Sir John Moore's army, and at the battle of Corunna. Accompanied the battalion to Walcheren, and was present at the siege of Flushing.

80 Lieut.-Colonel Lacy served the campaign of 1799 in Holland, with the 56th, and was present in the actions of the 19th Sept., 2nd and 6th Oct.

82 Lieut.-Colonel Robyns served at the capture of Martinique in 1809. In Aug. 1813 he went to North America, and was actively employed in the Chesapeak under Sir George Cockburn. Commanded a battalion of Marines at the capture of Washington and action before Baltimore, where he was severely wounded. Served afterwards on the expedition against New Orleans.

83 Lieut.-Colonel Briggs served with the 28th at the siege and capture of Copenhagen in 1807; proceeded afterwards to Sweden, under Sir John Moore, and subsequently to Portugal, where he landed with his regiment immediately after the battle of Vimiera; he was afterwards present at the passage of the Douro, battles of Talavera, Busaco, Albuhera, the Nivelle, the Nive, Orthes, and Toulouse; the siege of Badajos, and Lord Hill's action before Bayonne, 13th Dec. 1813, besides all the minor affairs connected with the above-mentioned actions.

84 Lieut.-Colonel Mathewson joined the 75th Highland regt. in the East Indies in 1791; served the campaign in Mysore in that year, and was present and engaged before Seringapatam in Feb. 1792. He again served before Seringapatam in 1799. In the year following he served in Malabar and Canara, and was wounded when leading the Forlorn Hope at the assault of the Fortress of Jamaulabad. In 1801 he was actively employed during the campaign in the district of Cotiote; was often engaged, and at the reduction of several posts. In 1802-3 he was on service in Guzerat, and was present at the siege and reduction of Keria and of Brodera; also in field actions, and in that of the 6th Feb. 1803, on the banks of the river Mehie, he received a severe gun-shot wound in the left shoulder. He next served at the siege of Bhurtpore in 1805, and received a dangerous wound in the right breast from a spear when crossing the ditch at the assault on the 9th Jan.; he was also wounded by an explosion of gunpowder on the breach, when leading an assaulting party on the 21st February. In 1808 he was employed with his company of the Royal York Rangers on board the line-of-battle ships *York* and *Pompée* at the blockade of Martinique, and was actively employed at the reduction of that Island, having on landing a detached command, and he drew up and signed on the spot the capitulation of Pigeon Island on the 4th Feb. 1809. He was also actively engaged the same year at the capture of the Saintes. In 1810 he served at the capture of Guadaloupe; was engaged in the action of the 3rd Feb., and commanded that part of his regt. which on the following morning took possession of the Pont de Noziere, and captured the French force and guns at that post. As an Assistant-Quarter-Master-General, he accompanied, in the same month, the force sent to the capture of the Island of St. Martin, and continued to be employed on the Staff until he was again engaged at the capture of Guadaloupe in 1815, where, as Major of his regt., he was the first individual who landed, being in command of the advance on the 8th Aug., and on the following day he sustained a serious injury when in pursuit of the enemy down the hill of Palmiste and across the river Gallion.

87 Lieut.-Colonel Clanchy served in Hanover, under Lord Cathcart, in 1805 and 6; with the expedition to Madeira in 1807, and capture of the lines of Funchal. The Peninsular campaigns from Sept. 1808 to the end of that war in 1814, including the battle of Busaco, retreat to the Lines at Torres Vedras, and the subsequent advance and pursuit of the French army under Massena; actions of Pombal, Redinha, Condeixa, and Sabugal; first siege of Almeida and its subsequent blockade, battle of Fuentes d'Onor, retreat from Burgos, and scaling the heights of the Echalar.

88 Lieut.-Colonel Diggle served with the 52nd in Sicily, under Sir John Moore, and on the expedition to Gottenburgh. Subsequently he served in the Peninsula, and was present during the retreat and at the battle of Corunna; as also in the action of the Coa, battle of Busaco, and affairs when the Army fell back upon the Lines of Torres Vedras. He served also the campaign of 1813, 14, and 15, including the bombardment of Antwerp, affairs at Merxem, and battle of Waterloo, at which last he was severely wounded.

90 Lieut.-Colonel Knox served with the 1st Battalion of the 31st in Egypt in 1807, and was severely wounded at Rosetta. He afterwards served with the 2nd Battalion in the Peninsula, from 1808 to the spring of 1814, and was present at the battles of Talavera, Albuhera (severely

wounded), Busaco, Vittoria, the Pyrenees, the Nivelle, the Nive, and at St. Palais, where he was severely wounded, being shot through the body, and lost his right arm.

91 Sir John Scott Lillie served in the 6th regt. with the first expedition to Portugal in 1808, and was present at the battle of Vimiera, and capture of Lisbon. In 1809, as Captain in the Lusitanian Legion, in various engagements for the defence of Portugal during the important interval between the embarkation at Corunna and the return of the second expedition to Lisbon. Campaign of 1810—battle of Busaco, and retreat to the Lines at Torres Vedras. 1811—Actions of Pombal and Redinha, capture of Campo Mayor, sieges of Olivença and Badajoz. 1812—Battle of Salamanca, capture of Madrid, and retreat from Burgos. 1813—Actions at Aldea de Ponte, Osma, and Bridge of Subijana de Morellas (wounded), battle of Vittoria, blockade of Pampeluna, actions in the Pyrenees on the 24th, 25th, 26th, 28th, and 30th July, actions of Irun and St. Martial, capture of San Sebastian, passage of the Bidassoa, battles of the Nivelle (wounded) and the Nive. 1814—Battles of Orthes and Toulouse, at which last he was severely wounded and left for forty-eight hours on the field of battle, supposed to have been killed. Sir John has received a cross for the battles of the Pyrenees, Nivelle, Orthes, and Toulouse.

93 Colonel Orlando Jones accompanied the 36th to Hanover, and served the campaign of 1805-6. Embarked for the Peninsula in 1808, and served throughout the whole of that and the following campaigns without having been absent from his duty for a single day, and was present at the battles of Roleia and Vimiera. Attached to the Portuguese service in April 1809, and served at the battle of Busaco, occupation of the Lines at Lisbon, actions of Pombal, Redinha, Condeixa, Puente de Murcella, Casal Nova, Ceira, Guarda, Foz d'Arouce, Sabugal, and Fuentes d'Onor, storming the forts at Salamanca (wounded), battle of Vittoria, actions of Tolosa and Villa Franca (severely wounded), passage of the Bidassoa, battles of the Nivelle, Bayonne (9th Dec.), St. Jean de Luz (11th, 12th, and 13th Dec.), passage of the Adour, blockade of Bayonne and repulse of the sortie.

94 Lieut.-Colonel Peacocke served in the Mediterranean at the taking of the Islands of Ischia and Procida, and at the relief of Capri. In 1810 he joined the army in Portugal, and served with the 4th division throughout the campaigns in the Peninsula. 1810—Battle of Busaco, retreat to the Lines of Torres Vedras, affair of Dois Pontos. 1811—Actions of Pombal and Redinha, capture of Campo Mayor, siege of Olivença, battle of Albuhera. 1812—Siege of Ciudad Rodrigo, storming of Badajoz (severely wounded mounting the breach), capture of Madrid. 1813—Action of Aldea de Ponte, battle of Vittoria (horse shot under him), blockade of Pampeluna, affairs of Roncesvalles and Linçoins, battle of the Pyrenees, attack of the Heights above Saint Estevan. Passage of the Bidassoa, battle of the Nivelle. He has received the Portuguese Gold Cross for the Peninsular campaigns.

95 Lieut.-Colonel De Lancey served with the 9th Light Dragoons at Walcheren in 1809; and in the Peninsula during parts of 1811, 12, and 13.

97 Lieut.-Colonel Wells:—Campaign of Portugal and Spain in 1808 and 9, including action of Roleia, and the battles of Vimiera and Corunna; campaign in Holland in 1809, including the siege of Flushing; blockade of Cadiz, from March 1810, to the raising of the blockade in 1812, excepting about six months absence at Carthagena, and with the army in Estremadura, including the action of Barrosa, and the last siege of Badajoz in March and April 1812; served part of the campaign of 1813, until the army embarked at Bourdeaux in 1814, including the passage of the Bidassoa, blockade of Bayonne, and the taking of a work at Laredo. Campaign of 1815, in Belgium and France.

98 Lieut.-Colonel Sir Digby Mackworth, Bart., K.H., served six campaigns in the Peninsula and that of the Low Countries and France. Was Aide-de-camp to General Lord Hill in the Peninsula and in France, and when his Lordship was Commander of the Forces in Great Britain. Present at the battles of Talavera, Busaco, Albuhera, Pyrenees, and Toulouse, in the Peninsula, and at Waterloo. Received the Guelphic Order, and the thanks of His M. King William IV., for assisting in putting down the riots in Bristol and the Forest of Dean.

99 Lieut.-Colonel John Browne accompanied the 4th on the expedition first to Sweden and afterwards to the Peninsula, where he served until Nov. 1812, and was present in the Lines at Torres Vedras, pursuit of Massena, action of Redinha, battle of Fuentes d'Onor, siege of Badajoz in 1811 (severely wounded), siege and capture of Ciudad Rodrigo. Served also the campaign of 1815, including the battles of Quatre Bras and Waterloo, at which latter he was severely wounded.

100 Lieut.-Colonel Bazalgette sailed with the expedition from India to Egypt, under Sir David Baird, in 1801. Returned to India and served two campaigns in the Dooab and Ceded Districts, under General Campbell. Served also on the expedition to the Penobscot, in the United States of North America.

102 Lieut.-Colonel Spedding served in the Peninsula with the 4th Dragoons, and was present at the battles of Talavera, Busaco, Albuhera, and Salamanca; actions of Campo Mayor, Los Santos, and Usagre, besides other affairs.

103 Lieut.-Colonel M'Gregor served in the Peninsula in 1812, and was present during the operations of the covering army at the siege of Badajoz; also at the capture of Madrid, and at the battle of Salamanca.

104 Lieut.-Colonel Cole served in Italy and Sicily in 1805 and 6. On the 18th March 1807, when on passage to England, he was taken prisoner by a French ship-of-war, after an action of

two hours' duration. In 1808 he accompanied the 81st on the expedition to Corunna, and was in the whole of that service, as also at the battle of Corunna. In 1809 he sailed with the expedition to Walcheren, and was at the siege of Flushing. Subsequently he joined the army in Spain; and was present with the 81st at the battle of Castella, siege of Tarragona, retreat from Villa Franca, and investment of Barcelona. On the termination of the war of the Peninsula he accompanied his regiment to America; with which he afterwards returned in 1815, and joined the army in France, and marched with it to Paris, and served with the Army of Occupation. He has been twice wounded.

105 Lieut.-Colonel Gardiner served with the 50th on the expedition against Copenhagen in 1807. The campaigns in Portugal and Spain in 1808-9, including the battles of Roleia, Vimiera, and Corunna. The campaign at Walcheren in 1809, and those in the Peninsula from 1810 to 1813, including the battle of Vittoria, where he was severely wounded—compound fracture of the left thigh bone.

106 Lieut.-Colonel Crokat served in Sicily in 1807; in Portugal in 1808, under Sir Arthur Wellesley; in Spain and at Corunna under Sir John Moore; on the Walcheren expedition in 1809; subsequently in the Peninsula Severely wounded in the Pyrenees. He had charge of Napoleon at St. Helena when he died, and he brought home the despatches of his death.

107 Lieut.-Colonel Bateman sailed with the 5th on the expedition for Hanover in 1805; was shipwrecked off the Texel and made prisoner of war. Having been exchanged in March 1806, he sailed in June following with the expedition under Major-General Craufurd, which landed in South America, and he was present at the attack of Buenos Ayres. Served also in the Peninsula in 1810, 11, 13, and was severely wounded at the battle of Vittoria. Accompanied the regiment to America in 1814, and was present at Plattsburg.

108 Lieut.-Colonel Dudgeon served with the 58th in Egypt in 1801, and was present at the surrender of Grand Cairo and Alexandria. He served in Italy in 1805 and 6; and in the Peninsula from 1809 to 1813, including the Lines at Torres Vedras, covering the siege of Badajoz, battle of Salamanca, capture of Madrid, and siege of Burgos, at which last he was twice wounded, the second time most severely.

109 Lieut.-Colonel Quill, served with the 15th at the capture of the French West India Islands, in 1815, under Sir James Leith.

110 Lieut.-Colonel Davies served in South America, with the 47th, in 1806; and subsequently in the Peninsula, including the sieges of Cadiz, Tarragona, and Tarifa. Commanded three companies of the 47th at the breach of Tarifa, on the 31st Dec. 1811, when the French attempted to storm the town, but were driven back with great loss, together with the loss of all their artillery.

111 Lieut.-Colonel Mitchell served with the 3rd battalion of the Royals at Walcheren, in 1809, and was present at the siege of Flushing. Subsequently in the Peninsula from 1810 to 1812, including the battles of Busaco and Fuentes d'Onor, action of Sabugal, and those of Massena's retreat. Accompanied the expedition to Germany, under General Gibbs in 1813. Served as Deputy-Assistant-Quarter-Master-General in the campaign of 1814, in Holland; and in the same situation on the staff of the army in Flanders, and afterwards at the head-quarters of the Army of Occupation.

114 Lieut.-Colonel Norcliffe served in the Peninsula with the 4th Dragoons, and was present at the battles of Talavera, Busaco, and Albuhera; cavalry action of Usagre, and battle of Salamanca, in which last he was severely wounded and taken prisoner.

117 Lieut.-Colonel Johnson served with the 17th Light Dragoons in South America in 1806 and 7, at the siege and storming of Monte Video, and in the expedition of Buenos Ayres, during which service the regiment was armed with muskets and acted as infantry.

118 Lieut.-Colonel Darby served in Hanover in 1805; at the siege of Copenhagen in 1807; and the Corunna campaign in 1808-9.

119 Lieut.-Colonel King served in a mortar-boat in the Faro of Messina for two months in 1810. Advanced into the United States with Sir George Prevost's army, and commanded a battery against Plattsburg.

120 Lieut.-Colonel Macdonald accompanied the expedition to Hanover in 1805; joined the army in Sicily in 1806, and was employed with it in its various operations until 1810; in the latter year he went with the expedition to Naples, and was present at the capture of Ischia and Procida; returned to Sicily and employed against the French army in 1811; in 1812 was employed in Spain, including the battle of Castalla, and siege of Tarragona; embarked for Canada in 1814, and was present at the operations before Plattsburg. Received three wounds at Waterloo, viz., in the leg, in the neck, and through the body, wounding the lungs.

121 Lieut.-Colonel Mudge served in the Peninsula from March 1809 to June 1810.

122 Lieut.-Colonel Sherbourne Williams served at the capture of Guadaloupe in 1815.

123 Lieut.-Colonel John Cox served, with the exception of a few months, throughout the whole of the Peninsular war with the 95th (Rifle Brigade), commencing with the first affair, when his company formed part of the detachment which dislodged the French from the post of Obidos, 15th Aug. 1808. He was also engaged with the enemy in the following battles, sieges, affairs, &c., viz., Roleia, Vimiera, surrender of Lisbon, Bridge of Benevente, in front of Talavera, Barba del Puerca, Galligos, Barquillo, Almeida, Mora Morta, Sula, Busaco, Alemquier, Arada, Santarem, Pombal, Redinha, Condeixa, Caza Nova, Foz d'Arouce, Freixadas, Sabugal,

Almeida (10th to 14th April 1811), Marialva Bridge, Fuentes d'Onor, Naves d'Avar, Forcy, also Ciudad Rodrigo (siege and storming), San Milan, Vittoria, Echarrianos, Pampeluna, heights of Santa Barbara, Pass of Echallar, Vera, Pass of Vera, Nivelle, Nive, and Tarbes. Served also the campaign of 1815, including the affairs of out-posts on the 17th June, the battle of Waterloo, and capture of Paris. Wounded in the right shoulder by a musket-ball at Vimiera; compound fracture of the left arm by a musket-shot at the storming of Ciudad Rodrigo; left leg badly fractured by a musket-shot at Tarbes.

125 Lieut.-Colonel Murton served in the North Sea, and the Helder expedition in 1799; served in the Egyptian expedition and the East Indies in 1801; the West Indies (slightly wounded) in 1804; coast of France, and engaged with the enemy's flotilla and batteries, in 1805; the Mediterranean in 1806, engaged in cutting out the enemy's vessels from under batteries, and was voted a sword from the Patriotic Fund; in 1809, coast of Spain, and aiding the Guerillas; served in Holland in 1813. Medal for services in Egypt.

126 Lieut.-Colonel Booth's services :—Siege of Callinger (wounded at the assault). Nepaul war in 1814, including the sieges of Kolunga, Nahu, and Jetuck. Mahratta war in 1817, 18, including the sieges of Singhur, Latarak, Pourunder, and Wursetta. Burmese war in 1824-5, wounded at the storming of Martaban.

127 Lieut.-Colonel Greaves served with the 7th Fusiliers in America, in the campaign of 1814, and was also present in the attack on New Orleans, on the 8th Jan. 1815.

128 Lieut.-Colonel O'Hara served in Spain and Portugal from 1808 to 1811, including the battle of Vimiera and retreat to Corunna, battle of Talavera, action of the Coa, battle of Busaco, action of Sabugal, affairs of Redinha, Miranda de Corvo, and Foz d'Arouce; battle of Fuentes d'Onor, and siege of Badajoz.

129 Lieut.-Colonel Charlton served in the Peninsula with the 61st from June 1809 to Feb. 1810, and again from March 1813 to July 1814, including the battles of Talavera, the Pyrenees on the 28th, 29th, and 30th July, the Nivelle, Nive, Orthes, Tarbes, and Toulouse, besides various minor actions and affairs. Wounded on the 28th July in the Pyrenees, again at the Nive when in command of the Light Infantry Companies of the Left Brigade of the 6th division; twice severely wounded at Toulouse, the second wound received when commanding the 61st. Medal for Toulouse.

130 Lieut.-Colonel Alex. M. Fraser was employed in the expedition against Sambas, in the island of Borneo.

131 Lieut.-Colonel Walker served at Copenhagen.

133 Lieut.-Colonel Hall served at the capture of the Isle of France in 1810; on the expedition to Java in 1811, including the actions at Batavia and Weltevreiden, storming the entrenched lines at Fort Cornelis, storming the heights of Serandole, and capture of the fort of Samarang. Present also at the siege and storming of Bhurtpore in 1825-6.

134 Lieut.-Colonel W. F. Williams served in Senegal, Goree, and Sierra Leone during 1811 and 12; and in the Peninsula from Aug. 1813 to the end of that war, including San Sebastian, the passage of the Bidassoa, battles of Nivelle and Nive (11th, 12th, and 13th Dec.), and the investment of Bayonne. He embarked for Bordeaux in 1814 with the expedition to the Chesapeak under General Ross, and was wounded at the battle of Bladensburg, first slightly in the left arm, and again severely by a musket-ball through the left shoulder. He served subsequently for several years in the West Indies; and he was sent on a particular service to Canada during the insurrection in that country in 1838 and 39.

135 Lieut.-Colonel Cartwright served the campaigns of 1813 and 14 with the 61st, including the battles of the Pyrenees, Nivelle, Nive, Orthes, and Toulouse. Served the campaign of 1815 with the 10th Hussars, and was present at the battle of Waterloo.

136 Lieut.-Colonel Garland served in the Peninsula from 1809 to 1813, including the defence of Tarifa and Cadiz, battle of Fuentes d'Onor, pursuit of Massena, battle of Salamanca, sieges of Badajoz and Burgos, and action at Villa Muriel; the above service as Adjutant of the 30th. Served also the campaign of 1815 with the 73rd, including the battle of Quatre Bras, retreat on the following day, and battle of Waterloo, at which last he was severely wounded, being at that time senior officer of the 73rd, Lord Harris commanding the brigade.

139 Lieut.-Colonel Saunderson served at Malta and in Sicily. In the Light Battalion under Sir James Kempt on the expedition to Naples in 1806. Accompanied the 2nd battalion of the 39th to the Peninsula in 1809, and was present at the battle of Busaco, in the retreat to the Lines at Torres Vedras, and the advance from thence; re-capture of Campo Mayor, investment and opening of the trenches before Badajoz, battle of Albuhera (slightly wounded), capture of a strong division of the French army under General Gerard at Arroyo de Molino, where he was severely wounded by a musket-shot, which fractured his skull, and was sent to England for recovery. Rejoined the army in the Peninsula, and acted as Deputy-Judge-Advocate. After the battle of Toulouse embarked with a division of the army for Canada, where he was appointed to the Quarter-Master-General's Department, and was present at the affair of Plattsburg.

140 Lieut.-Colonel Gore served the campaign of 1815 with the 30th, and was slightly wounded at Waterloo.

142 Lieut.-Colonel Pringle Taylor proceeded in 1811 to join the 22nd Dragoons in the East Indies, where he served until their return to Europe and disbandment, 25th October 1820. He was in the field in 1815 and 16, and during the whole of the Mahratta war in 1817, 18, and 19;

the published official records show that his conduct was conspicuous in the Brigade Cavalry actions of Bucktowlie and of Nagnore (1817), and of Ashta (28th Feb. 1818), when he incurred, as Brigade-Major, the responsibility of ordering measures which terminated in the entire defeat of the Peishwa, the death of the gallant Gokla, and the rescue of the Rajah of Satarrah, the most influential events in terminating the war. At the siege of Capaul-droog, he commanded a battery at the storm (13th May 1819), he blew open the first gate with a galloper gun of the 22nd Dragoons, and heading the Forlorn Hope, he stormed in succession the five distinct circles of fortifications, every man and officer of his party being either killed or wounded; he received at the summit of that strong hill fort, at the moment of success in its capture, a shot through his lungs and body. The Governor-General of India specially recommended him to favourable consideration for his services in India. In 1823 and 24 he was employed in the Cape Cavalry against the Caffres. In 1841 he was relieved from a bullet which had been in his body since 1819.

144 Lieut.-Colonel Whichcote joined the 52nd as a volunteer in Dec. 1810, and served with it in the Peninsula, France, and Flanders, and was present in the actions of Sabugal, El Bodon, and Alfayates, siege and storm of Ciudad Rodrigo, and of Badajoz, battle of Salamanca, retreat from Burgos, battle of Vittoria, action at Vera, battles of the Nivelle, the Nive, Orthes, Tarbes, Toulouse, and Waterloo.

145 Lieut.-Colonel Butler served the campaign of 1815 with the 3rd Battalion of the Grenadier Guards, and was present in the battles of Quatre Bras and Waterloo (where he carried the colours), storming of Peronne, and capture of Paris.

147 Lieut.-Colonel Maunsell served with the 3rd Dragoon Guards in the Peninsula from April 1809, to the end of that war in 1814, including the battles of Talavera, the winter campaign of 1810 in the Lines of Lisbon, actions of Campo Mayor and Los Santos, battles of Busaco and Albuhera, action of Usagre, sieges of Ciudad Rodrigo and Badajoz, battles of Vittoria and Toulouse. Commanded a squadron at the brilliant cavalry affair of Usagre, where three French regiments were defeated by the 3rd Dragoon Guards.

149 Lieut.-Colonel Estcourt served in the expedition to the river Euphrates, from Jan. 1835 to June 1837; and as a mark of approbation of his conduct and exertions, he was promoted to the brevet rank of Lieut.-Colonel.

150 Lieut.-Colonel Tronson served in the West Indies from 1808 to 1812, including the capture of Martinique and siege of Fort Bourbon in 1809, and capture of Guadaloupe in 1810. The campaigns of 1813, 14, and 15, in Canada, including the operations against Plattsburg. Throughout the Burmese war, and was present at Kokein, 15th Dec. 1826, Pagoda Point, Napadie, Mehadie, Melloon, where the command of the 13th devolved upon him, and on the 9th Feb. 1826, at the storming of Pagamue, where he was wounded in the right leg, but continued to lead the left wing until most severely wounded in the left leg, where the ball still remains. Served the campaign in Affghanistan under Lord Keane, and commanded the 13th at the assault and capture of the Fortress and Citadel of Ghuznee, for which he obtained the brevet rank of Lieut.-Colonel. Commanded the regiment throughout the campaign in Kohistan, and at the sieges of Tootumdarrah, Jhoolghur (led and commanded the storming party), night attack at Baboo Koosh Ghur, Kardurrah, and Perwandurrah, when Dost Mahomed surrendered, and the force returned to Cabul.

151 Lieut.-Col. M'Dowell served at the siege and capture of Bhurtpore, in 1825-6; the campaign in Affghanistan under Lord Keane, including the siege and capture of Ghuznee; and he commanded the 16th Lancers in the action of Maharajpore. He served also in the campaign on the Sutlej in 1846, and commanded the 16th Lancers in the action of Buddiwal, and a Brigade of Cavalry in the battle of Aliwal.

152 Lieut.-Colonel Faddy, prior to entering the Royal Artillery, was a midshipman on board the *Asia*, at the capture of the Dutch Fleet in Saldanha Bay in 1795: present at the attack on Fort Jerome, St. Domingo, and at the siege and capture of the city of Santo Domingo in 1809; served in the Peninsula and France from July 1810 to June 1814, including the siege of San Sebastian, passage of the Adour, investment of Bayonne and repulse of the sortie, besides various minor affairs.

153 Lieut.-Colonel Macbean's services:—Siege of Copenhagen in 1807; expedition to Sweden, and subsequently to the Peninsula under Sir John Moore; expedition to Walcheren, and siege of Flushing; campaign of 1815, including the battle of Waterloo.

154 Sir Gaspard Le Marchant served as Adjutant-General to the Anglo-Spanish Legion, and Brigadier-General in the Spanish service during the years 1835, 6, and 7. Was present at the relief of Bilboa and affair before that town in Sept. 1835. Engaged on the heights of Arlaban, in Alava, on the 16th, 17th, and 18th Jan.; in raising the siege of San Sebastian, and storming the Lines 5th May; passage of the Urmea, and taking of Passages 28th May; in the general action before Alza Oct. 1836, besides several affairs in Guipuzcoa, as also in the general actions of the 10th, 13th, 15th, and 16th March before Hernani. For these services he received a medal.

156 Lieut.-Colonel Walpole served the campaign against the Rajah of Coorg, in 1834, with the 39th regiment.

157 Lieut.-Colonel Singleton served in the Peninsula from 1811 to 1813, and was slightly wounded at the siege of the forts at Salamanca, and twice severely wounded at the battle of Salamanca.

158 Lieut.-Colonel Charles Blachley served in the Peninsula from July 1809 to December 1812, including the battles of Busaco, Fuentes d'Onor, and Salamanca, and siege of Burgos.

159 Lieut.-Colonel Moor served in the Peninsula from June 1809 to June 1813, including the battles of Busaco, Fuentes d'Onor, and Salamanca; sieges of Ciudad Rodrigo and Badajoz, action at Castrajon, and twelve other affairs with the enemy.

160 Lieut.-Colonel Marlay served at the battle of Trafalgar.

161 Lieut.-Colonel Marshall served in the Peninsula from Jan. 1811 to Oct. 1813, including the first siege of Badajoz, siege and storm of Ciudad Rodrigo, siege and storm of San Sebastian. Slightly wounded at Ciudad Rodrigo 16th Jan. 1812; severely wounded twice by musket-shots at San Sebastian 31st August 1813, when leading the advance of the column of attack up the great breach.

162 Lieut.-Colonel Anderson's services:—Expedition to Calabria, including the battle of Maida and subsequent operations, and capture of the fortress of Catrone; expedition to Egypt in 1807; Peninsula from April 1809 to Jan. 1812, including the battles of Talavera (wounded) and Busaco, retreat to the lines of Torres Vedras, and various affairs there; with the advance at Espinhal, battle of Fuentes d'Onor, and many other affairs and skirmishes. Served at the capture of Gaudaloupe in 1815. Commanded a brigade at the battle of Punniar, and was severely wounded at its head when in the act of charging the enemy's guns.

163 Lieut.-Colonel Dunn served the campaign of 1805 in Italy; battle of Maida and capture of Scylla Castle in 1806; expedition to Egypt in 1807, including the attack on Alexandria and Rosetta, and battle of El Hamet (taken prisoner). Defence of Scylla Castle in 1808; Peninsular campaigns of 1810 and 11, including the siege of Ciudad Rodrigo, operations between the Aguada and Almeida, battles of the Coa, Busaco, and Albuhera; actions at Usagre and Aldea de Ponte, at which last he was severely wounded in the groin by a musket-ball, which remains unextracted. Served also in the American war in 1814, including the taking of Moose Island, and occupation of Castine.

164 Lieut.-Colonel Pratt served the campaign of 1814 in Holland, as a volunteer with the 56th regiment, and was present at the attack on Merxem, 2nd Feb., and the subsequent bombardment of Antwerp. He served with the 26th on the China expedition (Medal), and commanded the land forces at the assault and capture of the Forts of Chuenpee on the 7th Jan. 1841, and again at the assault and capture of the Bogue Forts on the 26th Feb. following. Commanded the 26th at the attacks on Canton from 24th May to 1st June; also at the night attack on Ningpo, at Segoan, Chapoo, Woosung, Shanghai, and at Chin Kiang Foo.

165 Lieut.-Colonel Felix served the campaign of 1815, and was slightly wounded at Quatre Bras.

166 Lieut.-Colonel Harty served with the 33rd at the capture of Bourbon and the Isle of France in 1810; the campaigns of 1813 and 14 in Germany and Holland, including both the attacks on Merxem, and the assault on Bergen-op-Zoom. Also the campaign of 1815, including the battle of Quatre Bras, the retreat on the following day, and battle of Waterloo,—slightly wounded.

167 Lieut.-Colonel Bayly served the campaign in Italy in 1805; battle of Maida and siege of Scylla in 1806; expedition to Egypt in 1807, including the capture of Alexandria and Rosetta. Capture of Ischia in 1809; attack on an armed ship and gun-boats in the bay of Scylla in 1810; with the Artillery on the eastern coast of Spain in 1813, and present at the investment of one of the sieges of Tarragona.

168 Lieut.-Colonel Sinclair's services:—Expedition to Zealand in 1807; expedition to Portugal and battle of Corunna; expedition to the Scheldt in 1809; Peninsular campaigns from Feb. 1811 to Aug. 1814, including the assault on Badajoz in 1812, affair of Villa Muriel, battles of Salamanca, Vittoria, and the Pyrenees; passage of the Bidassoa, Nivelle and Nive, and sortie from Bayonne, besides various minor affairs. Served also the campaign of 1815, including the battle of Waterloo.

169 Lieut.-Colonel Crabbe served in the Peninsula from Jan. 1810 to the 31st Dec. 1812, and again from June 1813 to the end of the war, including the whole of the retreat to the lines of Torres Vedras; battle of Busaco; the advance from the lines to Guarda; first siege of Badajoz; siege and storm of Ciudad Rodrigo; siege and storm of Badajoz; battle of Salamanca; capture of Madrid, and subsequent retreat through Spain; battles of Nivelle, Nive, Vic, Tarbes, Orthes, and Toulouse, and the whole of the various minor affairs during that period. Wounded 15th March 1811, at Foz d'Arouce, when commanding a party which drove a French piquet from the said village. Wounded again at Toulouse, when attacking the Tête de Pont.

170 Lieut.-Colonel C. C. Mitchell embarked for the Peninsula in 1810; commanded a company of Portuguese artillery at the siege and capture of Badajoz, and commanded a nine-pounder battery of field artillery at the battles of Vittoria and Toulouse, for which he has received a medal and one clasp.

171 Lieut.-Colonel Meade served with the 88th in the Peninsula in the campaigns of 1811, 12, 13, and 14, including the battle of Fuentes d'Onor, siege of Badajoz in 1811, battle of Salamanca (wounded), siege and storming of Badajoz, passage of the Nivelle and the Nive, battles of Orthes and Toulouse. In 1814 he accompanied his Regiment to America, and the following year joined the army of occupation in France. In 1821 he embarked for India on the Staff of Sir Thomas Reynell, and was at the siege and storming of Bhurtpore, for the capture of which fortress he received the rank of Major.

172 Lieut.-Colonel Wildman served in the Peninsula, France, and Flanders, with the 7th Hussars, and was present at the battle of Waterloo.

173 Lieut.-Colonel Forster served with the Scots Fusilier Guards before Bayonne in 1814.

174 Lieut.-Colonel Beetham served in the Egyptian expedition of 1807; also at the taking of Santa Maura.

176 Lieut.-Colonel Goldsmid served in the Peninsula with the 12th Light Dragoons, from 1812 to the end of that war in 1814, including the cavalry affairs at Castrajon, Quintara de Puerta, and Monasterio; battles of Salamanca and Vittoria, and siege of San Sebastian. Served also the campaign of 1815, and was present at the battle of Waterloo.

177 Lieut.-Colonel MacArthur was present as an Ensign in the 60th at the battle of Corunna. He afterwards served with the 39th in Sicily, and again in Spain, where he was engaged with the enemy at Vittoria, in the Pyrenees, at the Nivelle and the Nive, at Bayonne, Orthes, and Toulouse, and where he also served on the personal staff of the late Lt.-Gen. Sir Robert O'Callaghan. He accompanied his regiment from Bourdeaux to Canada, and afterwards served with it in the Army of Occupation in France.

179 Lieut.-Colonel Macdowall served the campaign of 1814 in Holland with the 52nd, including the actions at Merxem and bombardment of Antwerp.

180 Lieut.-Colonel Hely served with the 57th in the Peninsula; and having joined Lord Hill's division in 1809, he was afterwards present at the battle of Busaco, in the actions of Pombal and Redinha, the first siege of Badajoz, battle of Albuhera—where he was twice wounded, and held the command of the regiment after that action; battles of the Pyrenees, Nivelle, Nive, and that before Bayonne on the 13th Dec. 1813; affairs of Perache, Aire, and Tarbes, and battle of Toulouse. Sailed for Canada at the conclusion of this war; returned after the peace with America, landing at Ostend; marched to Paris, and served with the Army of Occupation until the breaking up of that force.

182 Lieut.-Colonel Bowers was slightly wounded at Waterloo.

185 Sir Thomas Livingstone Mitchell served with the 95th (Rifle Brigade) at the sieges of Ciudad Rodrigo and Badajoz; and on the Quarter-Master-General's staff until the termination of the Peninsular war, when he was sent back to Spain and Portugal on a special mission to make surveys of the fields of battle and positions of the armies.

187 Lieut.-Colonel Pollock served in Spain and Portugal with the 3rd battalion, 27th regt., from 1808 to the end of the war in 1814, including the battle of Busaco, retreat to the lines of Torres Vedras, actions of Redinha and Pombal, capture of Campo Mayor, siege and capture of Olivença, first siege of Badajoz and repulse of the sortie at San Christoval, battle of Albuhera, action of Fuente Guinalda, siege, storm, and capture of Badajoz (severely wounded), battle of Vittoria, blockade of Pampeluna, actions in the Pyrenees on the 24th, 25th, 26th, and 28th July (severely wounded), battles of the Nivelle, Nive, Orthes, and Toulouse: he was also present at the capture of Paris in 1815. In 1820 he embarked with the 90th for the Mediterranean, and was afterwards present at the disarming of Zante.

189 Lieut.-Colonel Burney served at the capture of Ischia and Procida, in 1809; defence of Cadiz in 1810; action of the Coa and Sabugal, battle of Fuentes d'Onor, retreat from Burgos. Served the campaign of 1814 in Holland, including the action at Merxem, bombardment of Antwerp, and storming of Bergen-op-Zoom. Engaged in the Burmese war at the attack of Padowa Pass and the fortified positions of Mahatee; storming the stockades and hills near, and taking the town and works of Arracan. Wounded on the 16th June 1815, at Quatre Bras, by a musket-shot in the left shin, and dangerously by a ball which entered the back part of the head.

191 Lieut.-Colonel Rochfort was at the capture of the Isle of France in 1810; and of Java in 1811, including capture of Cornelis, storming of Serandola and Fort Djocjocarta. Storming of redoubts at the island of Borneo; Nepaul campaign in 1814; siege and storm of Hattras; Mahratta campaigns of 1817 and 18; siege and storm of Bhurtpore 1825 and 6.

192 Lieut.-Colonel Leslie served with the 54th at the attack and capture of St. Domingo in 1809; in Stralsund under General Gibbs in 1813; the subsequent campaign in Holland under Lord Lynedoch, including the attack on Merxem, and bombardment of Antwerp. Campaign of 1815 under the Duke of Wellington; commanded and led the storming party at Cambray on the 24th June. Served at the Cape of Good Hope in 1819. Also in the Burmese war; commanded and led the left column at the Pass on the 26th March 1825; and on the following day commanded and led the 54th at the attack and capture of Mahatee, as also at the assault and capture of Arracan on the 1st April, and at the attack and capture of Ramree in May 1825.

193 Lieut.-Colonel Rotton served in the Peninsula from April 1812 to June 1813, including the battle of Salamanca. Present at Waterloo on the 16th, 17th, and 18th June. Served also at the siege and capture of Bhurtpore.

194 Lieut.-Colonel Gray accompanied the expedition which sailed under Sir David Baird, in 1805, and was present at the taking of the Cape of Good Hope, Jan. 1806. Accompanied the division sent from the Cape to co-operate with the expedition from India for the reduction of the Isle of France, having resigned the situation of Major of Brigade to the Royal Artillery at the Cape, to accompany the division as a volunteer. Wrecked in the *King George* transport, 1st Nov. 1805 (on which occasion Brigadier-General York was drowned), and saved several lives by his personal exertions, having been the last taken from the rocks by the boats of the *Leda* frigate.

195 Lieut.-Colonel Piper served six campaigns in the Peninsula, France, and Flanders, from March 1810 to the 27th Jan. 16. From 1810 to 12 was employed in the Lines of Lisbon and Almeida; and from Jan. 1812 to the conclusion of hostilities in 1815, held the command of a division of the Pontoon Train; (having been entrusted during that period with the organization and equipment of four several bridges;) threw the bridges of the Guadiana, Tagus, Bidassõa, Gave d'Oleron, Garronne, and Seine; served in the trenches at the last siege of Badajoz, from the morning of the 18th to the 23rd of March, when the bridges of communication below the town being destroyed and sunk, was dispatched (by order of the commander of the forces) to re-establish and remain with them—passing shot, shell, and ammunition during the nights, and provisions during the day time—for the remainder of the operations; received the thanks of Sir Rowland Hill at the passage of the Tagus in August same year, on the advance of his column to Madrid; and subsequently, when on route to Salamanca (in consequence of the enemy's cavalry intercepting the communication through the Sierra-do-Gato) was commanded by written instructions from the commander of the forces to retire with the bridges on Alcantra de la Reina and Badajoz. to Elvas, and finally to Abrantes; where, equipping a fresh train of boats for the operations of the ensuing year, advanced with the army from Sabugal and Freynada to the Ebro and Vittoria; passage of the Bidassõa in Oct. and latter part of the blockade of Pamplona; actions of the 9th and 11th Dec. 1813 at Bayonne; do. Toulouse in 1814; passed and repassed His Grace the Commander of the Forces and Staff during the operations of the day, from the right to the left bank of the river, on a fly-raft of three boats; and subsequently, advancing to Mongiscard on the Canal Royal du Midi, proceeded thence to Bordeaux. Proceeded to Ceylon, East Indies, 16 June 16. Served as commanding engineer in the Kandian Provinces, during the insurrections of 1817 and 18.

196 Lieut.-Colonel Fogo served in America during the whole war, including the battle of Plattsburg.

197 Lieut.-Colonel the Honourable William Arbuthnott served in the Peninsula, and was present at the passage of the Douro, and the battles of Oporto, Talavera, and Busaco.

198 Lieut.-Colonel Henry Blachley served in the Peninsula and France from Feb. 1812 to Aug. 1814, including the siege and capture of Badajoz, affair of Castrajon, battle of Salamanca, capture of Madrid and the Retiro, siege of Burgos, and retreat from thence, affair of Osma, battle of Vittoria, siege and capture of San Sebastian (both operations), passage of the Bidassoa and the Nivelle, actions of the 9th, 10th, 11th, and 12th Dec. 1813, in front of Bayonne, passage of the Adour, investment of Bayonne and repulse of the sortie, on which occasion he was wounded in the head by a musket-ball.

199 Lieut.-Colonel Stopford-Blair served on the expedition to South America in 1807. The campaign of 1815, including the battles of Quatre Bras and Waterloo (received a contusion), and capture of Paris.

200 Lieut.-Colonel Belson served in the Peninsula and South of France from July 1809 to the end of the war in 1814, including the retreat from Talavera, action in front of Almeida, action of the Coa, battle of Busaco, actions at Pombal, Redinha, Cazal Nova, Foz d'Arouce, and Sabugal; battle of Fuentes d'Onor, action on the heights of the Agueda, sieges of Ciudad Rodrigo and Badajoz, actions at Castrajon, San Munos, San Milan, and Osma; battle of Vittoria, action with the French, 28th June 1813, in the morning before they entered Pampeluna, in which he captured their last gun from Vittoria; actions in the Pyrenees, passage of the Nivelle, Nive, and Gâve d'Oleron; and battle of Orthes, besides various minor affairs and skirmishes.

202 Lieut.-Colonel Hall served in the Peninsula from 1812 to the end of that war in 1814, including the retreat from Burgos, passage of the Bidassoa, battles of the Nivelle and the Nive, investment of Bayonne, actions of Vic Bigorre and Tarbes, and battle of Toulouse. Served the campaign of 1815, including the battle of Waterloo (wounded), and with the Army of Occupation. Also in Canada, as Assistant-Quarter-Master-General during the disturbance of 1838; and as Military Secretary to the Governor-General in 1839 and 1840.

203 Lieut.-Colonel Head served with the 93rd during the expedition to the Southern States of America, and the campaign against New Orleans. Acted as Assistant-Quarter-Master-General to the Force assembled before Kolapore in the Southern Mahratta country in 1827. Employed in Canada on a particular service in the late insurrection.

205 Lieut.-Colonel Hewes served on board the *Rainbow*, of 24 guns in the West Indies, and was in a severe action with *La Nereide*, French frigate of 44 guns, off Cape Tiberon, and beat her off; employed on the coast of Catalonia and Corsica, and present at the cutting out *La Paix*, Genoese vessel armed with four guns, and moored to the batteries at Geraglio, near Cape Corse; he was at the attack on Leghorn in 1813, by Sir Josias Rowley, and present at the capture of Genoa by Lord Wm. Bentinck.

206 Lieut.-Colonel Molesworth served at the siege of Copenhagen in 1807.

208 Lieut.-Colonel Willington served in the East Indies from May 1813 to May 1823, including the campaigns of 1815 and 16 in Kattywar and Kutch; taking of Anjar; Deccan campaigns of 1817 and 18; campaign of 1819 in Kandiah; and in Kutch in 1820.

210 Lieut.-Colonel Westmore served the campaigns of 1813 and 14 in Germany and Holland, including both attacks on Merxem, and the assault on Bergen-op-Zoom; served at Waterloo on the 16th, 17th, and 18th June, and was severely wounded.

211 Lieut.-Colonel Chads served with the expedition to Walcheren in 1809.

212 Lieut.-Colonel Pattisson served with the 13th at the capture of Martinique in 1809, and of Guadaloupe in 1810; in Canada during the American war in 1813 and 14; in the Burmese war in 1824, 25, and 26, including the capture of Rangoon, storming the stockades at Kumaroot, Kokien (severely wounded), Napadee, Melloon, and Pagahm Mew; and he was also present at the repulse of the enemy before the Lines of Rangoon on the 1st Dec. 1824. Served also throughout the operations in Affghanistan and Beloochistan, and was present at the storm and capture of Ghuznée, operations in Kohistan, including the capture of Tootumdurrah and Jooighur; and he was afterwards at Jellalabad during its famous defence by Sir Robert Sale. He has received medals for Ghuznée and for Jellalabad.

213 Lieut.-Col. Simmons served in the Peninsula, as a volunteer with the 34th, and afterwards as an officer in the 23rd, and in the Rifle Brigade, from Sept. 1811 to the end of that war in 1814, including the storming of the forts at Almaraz, affairs of San Munos and San Milan, battle of Vittoria, actions at Yanzi Bridge and Echalar, storming Vera Heights, crossing the Bidassoa, battle of Nivelle, battles of the Nive, on the 10th, 11th, and 12th Dec. 1813. Served with the 41st throughout the Burmese war, and was present at the storming of Rangoon and Syrian Pagoda, led the head of the left column storming the trenches in front of the Dagon Pagoda, storming a strong stockade in front of the Dagon Pagoda. Commanded the left wing of the 41st regiment in the field against the Kolapore Rajah. Served with the regiment during the campaign of 1842 in Affghanistan, and commanded a column of attack in the action of the 28th April in the Pisheen Valley; present also in the actions near Candahar, at Goaine, and before Ghuznée; occupation and destruction of that fortress and of Cabool; expedition into Kohistan; storm, capture, and destruction of Istaliff, and in the various minor affairs in and between the Bolan and the Kyber Passes.

214 Lieut.-Colonel Malcolm served on the China expedition.

215 Lieut.-Colonel Donald Campbell served at Walcheren, in 1809.

216 Lieut.-Colonel Phillips served in the campaign on the Sutlej (medal), and commanded the 53rd in the battles of Buddiwal, Aliwal, and Sobraon, and a brigade in the army of the Sutlej during the occupation of the Punjaub.

217 Lieut.-Colonel Farquharson served at the capture of the Isle of France in 1810. Capture of the fort of Now Nuggar in Kallywar, Feb. 1814. On the borders of Scindia's country in 1814 and 15. Capture of forts of Joorin, August 1815, Anjar and Khuncoote, Feb., Dhingee and Dwarka, March 1816. Action and capture of Poona, 17th March 1817. At Ashtee, 21st Feb. 1818, the Mahratta General Gokla killed, and Satteria Reys captured. Storm of Kutch Booje Fort, March 1819. Capture of the forts of Rass-el-Kyma and Zama, 8th and 22nd Dec. 1819. Served also in Arabia in 1812, and was present in the action of Beni-Boo-Ali, 2nd March.

218 Lieut.-Colonel Vigors served throughout the campaigns of 1838 and 39 in Affghanistan. Commanded the two flank companies of the 13th Light Infantry, which formed a part of the force under Sir Robert Sale sent in pursuit of the ruler of Candahar, brother of the King of Cabool; crossed the rapid Helmond with eighteen men (the advance) on a small raft, landed close to the Fort of Girishk, which was found just vacated by the enemy. He commanded the left flank company of the 13th, with the forlorn hope, under Colonel Dennie, at the storm and capture of the fort of Ghuznée (medal), and was also present at the capture of Cabool, and in other minor affairs.

219 Lieut.-Colonel Richardson served in South Africa, in command of an expedition against the insurgent emigrant Boers, beyond the Orange River, in 1845. Also in command of the 7th Dragoon Guards in the Kaffir war of 1846-7.

220 Lieut.-Colonel White's services.—Campaign in Spain, under Sir John Moore, including the retreat to and battle of Corunna, where he was wounded. Siege of Flushing, and capture of Walcheren; campaigns in Canada, from Nov. 1813, to the end of the war.

221 Lieut.-Colonel Hunt served on the expedition to Hanover in 1805, and to Madeira in 1808; the campaign and battle of Corunna; and in the Peninsula, from Feb. 1812 to the end of the war in 1814; and subsequently in the American war.

222 Lieut.-Colonel Bray served the Mahratta campaigns of 1817, 18, and 19, and was present at the sieges and captures of Ryghur, Amulnier, and Asseerghur. He was on board the unfortunate ship *Kent*, which was burned in the Bay of Biscay, 1st March 1825. Commanded the 39th in the action of Maharajpore, and was severely wounded.

223 Lieut.-Colonel Hodgson served with the 45th in the Burmese war.

224 Lieut.-Colonel Sedley served in the Peninsula from Mar. 1812 to Dec. 1813, including the taking of the forts and the affair of the Guarena, battle of Salamanca, actions at Osma, Sabuganna de Morrilla, (severely wounded through the lungs), and Pyrenees, 31st Aug. Wounded on the 18th June at Waterloo. Served also in the Burmese war, during the latter part of which he was detached with the command of two companies to keep open the communication on the Irrawaddy between Rangoon and the army under Sir Archibald Campbell.

225 Lieut.-Colonel Master served with the 4th Light Dragoons during the campaign in Affghanistan, under Lord Keane, and was present at the siege and capture of Ghuznée.

226 Lieut.-Colonel Mundy served at the siege and storming of Bhurtpore as Aide-de-camp to Lord Combermere.

227 Lieut.-Colonel M'Cleverty served the campaign against the Rajah of Coorg, in April 1834, with the 48th regiment.

228 Lieut.-Colonel Grierson served at Cadiz during parts of 1812 and 1813, and afterwards on the eastern coast of Spain.

229 Lieut.-Colonel Sandilands served with the expedition to Walcheren; also the campaign of 1815, and was engaged on the 17th June with the Horse Artillery in covering the retiring movement from Quatre Bras, and on the 18th of June he was present at the battle of Waterloo.

230 Lieut.-Colonel French served in the Peninsula from Aug. 1813 to the end of the war, including siege of San Sebastian, passage of the Bidassoa, battles of the Nivelle and Nive, and investment of Bayonne. Served also in the American war, including the actions of Bladensburg, Baltimore, New Orleans, and Fort Bowyer.

231 Lieut.-Colonel Crofton was appointed Persian interpreter to the force under Brigadier-General Litchfield, in August 1832, and served with it throughout the arduous operations in Parkur, and against the tribes in the N. W. Desert, which ended in the taking of Balmeer.

232 Lieut.-Colonel Bainbrigge served with the 20th in the Peninsula, in 1808 and 9, and again in 1812 and 13, and was present at the battles of Vimiera, Corunna, Vittoria, and the Pyrenees, where he was twice wounded and lost an arm. Served also in the Walcheren expedition.

233 Lt.-Colonel Thomas Wright was slightly wounded at Waterloo.

234 Lt.-Colonel Barralier served at the capture of Martinique in 1809, as Acting Assistant Engineer; Aide-de-camp to Sir G. Beckwith at the first capture of Guadaloupe in 1810; and Acting Assist.-Quarter-Master-General at its second capture in 1815.

235 Lt.-Colonel James Henderson served with the 92d at the siege of Copenhagen and action at Kioge in 1807; with the expedition to Sweden, and afterwards to Portugal and Spain, under Sir John Moore in 1808-9, including the action at Lugo, and battle of Corunna. On the expedition to Walcheren in 1809. Served the campaigns of 1814 and 15 in France and Flanders with the 71st, including the affair of Tarbes, and battles of Toulouse and Waterloo, at which last he was severely wounded in the thigh by a grape-shot.

236 Lieut.-Colonel Le Mesurier served in the 24th at the capture of the Cape of Good Hope in 1806. In 1811, he joined the 2nd Battalion in the Peninsula, where he served until the end of that war in 1814, and was present at the sieges of Ciudad Rodrigo, Badajoz, battles of Salamanca, Vittoria, Pyrenees, Echalar, Nivelle, and Orthes (severely contused); and in the several affairs on the banks of the Dourdogne in front of Bordeaux, being on continual advance guard when that part of the army was moving forward on Angouleme.

237 Lt.-Colonel Swinburn served with the 43d at the siege of Copenhagen in 1807; the campaign of 1808 in Portugal,—wounded in the head on the retreat to Vigo. Subsequent campaigns in the Peninsula until 1812, including the action of the Coa, battle of Fuentes d'Onor, action of Sabugal, battle of Busaco, retreat to and occupation of the Lines of Torres Vedras, subsequent advance in pursuit of Massena, and actions of Pombal and Redinha—wounded in the hip. Joined the army at Toulouse in April 1814. Present at New Orleans in Jan. 1815. Subsequently joined the Duke of Wellington's army at Brussels, was present at the capture of Paris, and remained with the Army of Occupation until the end of 1818.

238 Lt.-Colonel Robert Kelly served in the Peninsula with the 5th battalion of the 60th, and was severely wounded in action with the enemy, 19th March 1814.

239 Lt.-Colonel Thomas Kelly served with the late 26th Lt. Dragoons during the latter part of the Carib war in St. Vincent. He afterwards accompanied his Regt. to Portugal and from thence to Egypt—the Transport in which he embarked was attacked by a Spanish Gun Boat, which, after a sharp conflict was beaten off. He served at the siege of Aboukir Castle, with the dismounted part of his Regt. He was also present in the action of the 21st March 1801, and in the affair of the advance of the army to the westward of Alexandria under Sir Eyre Coote. He was wounded in a night attack on the enemy's outposts on the 25th Aug., when, with a small detachment, he drove in the cavalry piquet, and captured the whole of the infantry piquets opposed to him, which were much more numerous than his own party. He has received the Egyptian medal.

240 Lt.-Colonel C. A. Bayley served in the Peninsula in 1808, 9, 10, 11, and part of 1812, and was present at the affair of Alberche, and battle of Talavera, as Adjutant of the 31st. Appointed Deputy-Assistant-Adjutant-General, in Jan. 1810, and attached to the 2d division under Lord Hill, in which capacity he served during the retreat to the lines of Torres Vedras, and subsequent advance and pursuit of Massena; also at the first siege of Badajoz, the affairs of Campo Mayor and Olivença, and other minor affairs during the operations in Estramadura, under Marshal Beresford. He was likewise present at the battle of Albuhera, and at the action of Arroyo de Molino, for which he received promotion.

242 Lt.-Colonel Burrowes served with the 12th at the capture of the Isle of France, in 1810, and commanded a detachment of that Regt. in boarding and capturing two French Privateers off the Isle de la Passe. Commanded a battalion of details with a force under Colonel the Honourable Leicester Stanhope in Kattywar, and was in advance at the storm and capture of the strong hill fortress of Meetialla.

243 Lt.-Colonel Gloster served in the Peninsula with the 61st from Oct. 1809 to the end of that war in 1814, including the battles of Busaco and Fuentes d'Onor, siege of the forts at Salamanca, battles of Salamanca, the Pyrenees (28th July to 2d Aug.), the Nivelle, the Nive

(9th to 13th Dec.), Orthes, and Toulouse. Wounded in the left arm at the battle of Salamanca, and through the right breast at Toulouse, the ball passing through the right lobe of the lungs and out at the back.

244 Lt.-Colonel Harriott served in the Royal Staff Corps at the defence of Cadiz, battle of Barrosa, passage of the Bidassoa, battles of the Nivelle and the Nive, actions near Bidart, affair of Tarbes, battle of Toulouse, capture of Paris, and with the army of occupation in France.

245 Lt.-Colonel Ross served the campaigns of 1811, 12, 13, 14, and 15 with the 92d, including the actions of Arroyo de Molino, taking of Almaraz, defence of Alba de Tormes, battle of Vittoria, affair at the pass of Maya, battles of the Pyrenees, wounded in the left leg by a musket-ball; battles of the Nivelle and the Nive, taking the Heights of La Costa, battle of Orthes, action at Aire, battles of Toulouse, Quatre Bras—wounded in the left foot by a musket-ball; and battle of Waterloo,—wounded in the right arm by a musket-ball.

247 Lt.-Colonel Fitz Maurice served in the Peninsula with the Rifle Brigade from April 1811 to the end of that war in 1814, including the action of Sabugal, battle of Fuentes d'Onor, sieges and assaults of Ciudad Rodrigo and Badajoz, action at San Milan, battle of Vittoria, actions at the Bridge of Yanzi and Vera, battles of the Nivelle and the Nive (9th, 10th, and 11th Dec.), action of Tarbes, and battle of Toulouse. Served also the campaign of 1815, including the battle of Quatre Bras. Leg broken at the storming of Badajoz, and severely wounded in the thigh by a musket-ball at Quatre Bras.

249 Lt.-Colonel Westlake served with the 26th on the expedition to the north of Spain, under Sir David Baird, in 1808, and subsequently in the retreat to Corunna, under Sir John Moore. On the expedition to Walcheren and siege of Flushing in 1809; and in the Peninsula from June 1811 to Aug. 1812. Slightly wounded at the siege of Flushing.

250 Lt.-Colonel Young served with the 91st in the Peninsula, from Aug. 1808 to Jan. 1809, including the battles of Roleia, Vimiera, Calcavellas, and Corunna. On the expedition to Walcheren in 1809; the Peninsular campaigns from Oct. 1812 to the end of that war in 1814, including the battles of the Nivelle, the Nive (10th, 11th, and 12th Dec.), Orthes, Tarbes, and Toulouse.

251 Lt.-Colonel During served in the Peninsula during the Corunna campaign, and subsequently from the latter part of 1812 to the end of that war in 1814, including the battles of Corunna, Vittoria, Pyrenees, the Nivelle, the Nive, Orthes, and Toulouse.

252 Lt.-Colonel the Honourable Wm. Noel Hill served in the Burmese war, in 1825 and 26, and was present in the actions of Prome and Tandwayn.

253 Lt.-Colonel Charles Stewart served in the Peninsula with the 71st, from Sept. 1810 to June 1813, including the action at Sobral, battle of Fuentes d'Onor (slightly wounded), and actions at Arroyo de Molino and Almaraz. Served also the campaign of 1815, and was present at the battle of Waterloo.

254 Lt.-Colonel Irwin served in the Peninsula from April 1809 to Feb. 1814, including the capture of Oporto, battles of Talavera and Fuentes d'Onor, siege of Badajoz, siege and storm of Ciudad Rodrigo, siege of Badajoz and capture of the castle by escalade (7th April 1812), battle of Salamanca, capture of Madrid and the Retiro, battles of Vittoria and the Pyrenees, besides various affairs and skirmishes on the advance and retreat of the army. Served also the Kandyan campaigns of 1817 and 18 in Ceylon.

256 Lt.-Colonel Flamank served in the Peninsula with the 51st, from Jan. 1811 to the end of that war in 1814, including the battle of Fuentes d'Onor, second siege of Badajoz, covering the sieges of Ciudad Rodrigo and third siege of Badajoz, affair in front of Moresco, battle of Salamanca, retreat from Burgos, battles of Vittoria and the Pyrenees (30th and 31st July), passage of the Bidassoa, battles of Nivelle and St. Pé, and battle of Orthes. Served also the campaign of 1815, including the battle of Waterloo and capture of Cambray.

257 Lieut.-Colonel Gosset served in Canada in 1813 and 1814.

258 Lt.-Colonel Wilson served in the battle of Trafalgar, and was sent with a guard on board the *Ildefonzo* (a Spanish ship of the line), and while he was thus situated the *Ildefonzo* was separated from the fleet and driven near to Cadiz; and, notwithstanding the circumstance of but thirty Englishmen being then on board, and Lieutenant Wilson the only commissioned English officer with five hundred Spaniards, the prize was nevertheless one of the four preserved for His Majesty's service. He served at the reduction of Les Saintes Islands in the West Indies; in the expedition to Walcheren; at the siege of Cadiz; in Portugal in 1810 and 11; in the action between the *Macedonian* and *United States*, and in the expedition against New Orleans; and he was one of the only two surviving officers from the wreck of the frigate *Boreas*. Served as adjutant of the Chatham Division.

	CORNET, 2d LIEUT. or ENSIGN.	LIEUT.	CAPTAIN.	MAJOR.	WHEN PLACED ON HALF PAY.
Hugh Goodwin, late of 48 Foot	27 Dec. 78	4 May 80	13 Oct. 94	9 July 03	
William White, *Major*, 5 R. Veteran Batt., on retired full pay	25 Mar. 80	24 Mar. 84	25 Oct. 94	1 Jan. 05	
Alexander Rose,[1] *Major*, 6 R. Veteran Batt. do.	14 Mar. 93	1 Oct. 94	2 July 96	10 Dec. 07	
John Williams, *Major*, h. p. Royal Marines	9 Mar. 81	1 July 82	31 Jan. 96	25 April 08	16 Sept. 12
Richard Henry Tolson, *Captain*, h. p. 25 Foot	7 Nov. 93	19 Jan. 95	3 May 00	1 Jan. 12	25 April 17
P George Langlands,[2] *Major*, 13 R. Vet. Batt., on retired full pay	2 Feb. 96	Dec. 02	23 Sept. 03	27 April	
Amand de Courten, *Captain*, h. p. Watteville's Regiment	never	never	1 May 01	4 June 13	1815
George Esdaile Elrington, *Captain*, 5 R. Vet. Batt., on retired full pay	28 Aug. 99	never	14 May	do	
Joseph Mignon May, *Captain*, h. p. Royal Marines	16 May 93	24 Mar. 95	1 Mar.	do	16 Aug. 16
Hon. Charles Murray, *do.* h. p. 17 Dragoons	3 Oct. 98	3 April 01	22 May	do	4 May 15
John Marjoram Close, *do.* h. p. Royal Artillery	6 Mar. 95	3 Oct. 95	25 Nov. 02	do	1 Sept. 19
Charles Emanuel May, *Major*, h. p. Meuron's Regiment	never	25 Sept. 98	11 June 07	17 June	25 Sept. 16
P James Lepper, *Captain*, h. p. 27 Foot	20 Feb. 00	25 Jan. 03	22 June 09	3 Mar. 14	4 Dec. 17
Richard Jones, *do.* h. p. 81 Foot		8 July 95	25 June 03	4 June	25 Dec. 17
William Sladden, *do.* h. p. Royal Marines	16 Nov. 93	24 April 95	27 July	do	22 June 16
John Philips, *do.* do.	1 Feb. 94	do	20 Oct.	do	13 Dec. 14
P Nicholas Philibert de Brem,[3] *Captain*, h. p. Chasseurs Britanniques	never	*1 May 01	25 Nov.	do	1814
P Nicholas Muller, *Captain*, h. p. Roll's Regiment	never	never	5 Jan. 04	do	1816
Robert Hart, *Captain*, h. p. Royal Marines	4 Feb. 94	2 Aug. 95	8 May	do	30 Jan. 17
William Milne, *do.* 2 R. Vet. Batt., on retired full pay	24 Aug. 99	May 04	22 May	do	
John Field Oldham, *do.* 8 R. Vet. Batt., on retired full pay	26 April 96	10 Feb. 97	4 Aug.	do	
Alexander Stewart, *do.* h. p. 4 Ceylon Regiment	28 Oct. 95	1 June 96	5 Aug.	do	18 June 18
W W. Philip Henry Fred. Mejer, *Major*, h. p. German Legion	never	never	22 Sept.	do	24 Feb. 16
George Lovell Spinluff,[4] *Captain*, late Veteran Comp. on ret. full pay	1 Feb. 98	17 May 99	1 Nov.	do	
W William *Baron* Decken, KH., *Captain*, h. p. German Legion	never	*4 Feb. 04	13 Dec. 06	18 June 15	24 Feb. 16
Bennet Holgate, *Major*, h. p. 40 Foot	12 May 04	23 Nov. 04	23 June 08	13 Nov. 17	9 Feb. 26
P William Medows Hamerton,[5] *Captain*, h. p. 67 Foot	26 Dec. 06	19 Mar. 07	16 Jan. 12	21 Jan. 19	22 April 19
Stopford Cane, *Captain*, h. p. 18 Foot	20 Jan. 96	5 Nov. 99	14 Feb. 05	12 Aug.	22 July 24
William Macdonald, *Captain*, h. p. Royal Marines	13 May 95	3 Oct. 96	15 Aug. 05	do	4 Feb. 23
P Thomas Wilson, *Captain*, h. p. 60 Foot	Oct. 00	7 Jan. 01	14 Nov. 05	2 Aug.	10 May 21
Christopher Wilkinson,[6] *Captain*, h. p. Royal Artillery	27 Oct. 98	1 Aug. 00	24 April 06	do	1 July 25
P W Charles Freeman Sandham,[7] *Captain*, h. p. Royal Artillery	27 Oct. 98	7 Nov. 00	1 June 06	do	7 June 22
P James Lane, *Captain*, h. p. Royal West India Rangers	1 July 01	18 April 05	30 Nov.	do	20 Jan. 20
Hy. Ross Gore, CB.,[8] *Captain*, h. p. 3 Foot, *Barrack-Master at Cashel*	13 Nov. 00	16 Mar. 03	4 Dec.	do	17 April 35
P John William Henderson, KH.,[9] *Captain*, h. p. 41 Foot	[1]9 July 00	25 July 01	12 Mar. 07	19 July 21	5 May 25

	CORNET, ETC.	LIEUT.	CAPTAIN.	MAJOR.	WHEN PLACED ON HALF PAY.
John Thornton, *Captain*, h. p. Cape Corps	29 Aug. 04	26 June 05	26 Nov. 07	19 July 21	14 June 27
Richard Staunton Sitwell, *Major*, do.	8 Oct. 02	3 April 05	22 Aug. 08	10 July 23	2 Aug. 26
Timothy Davies, *Major*, Unattached	4 Aug. 04	26 June 05	1 Feb. 10	28 Oct. 24	28 Dec. 26
Thomas Greatly,[12] *Captain*, h. p. Royal Artillery	15 Nov. 00	12 April 02	1 Feb. 08	27 May 25	22 Nov. 28
Hon. Sir Francis Charles Stanhope,[13] *Major*, Unattached	24 April 05	28 Aug. 06	18 Aug. 08	do	4 May 26
Joseph Brooksbank, *Major*, Unattached	17 Mar. 08	22 June 09	12 Oct. 20	24 Dec.	24 Dec. 25
Edward Jones,[15] *do.* do.	26 Aug. 07	15 Nov. 10	7 Feb. 22	10 June 26	28 Dec. 32
Charles Lowrie, *do.* do.	17 Dec. 02	14 July 04	11 June 12	29 Aug.	21 Nov. 28
James Adair,[16] *Major*, Unattached	7 Mar. 10	10 Oct. 11	25 Mar. 15	12 Dec.	1 Feb. 27
Sir Trevor Wheler, *Bart.*,[18] *Major*, Unattached	17 Nov. 08	11 July 11	10 April 17	5 Feb. 29	30 Nov. 30
Frederick Hammond, *Major*, Unattached	14 Nov. 16	20 Mar. 23	14 July 25	16 Mar. 30	1 Feb. 33
John Gowdie, *Major*, Unattached	10 Nov. 14	9 April 18	1 Nov. 21	11 June	10 Oct. 34
James Ryves,[21] *Captain*, Royal Marines, on retired full pay	13 Mar. 97	9 July 03	30 June 10	22 July	
Thomas Lewis Lawrence,[23] *do.* do. do.	15 M. 97	10 July 03	19 July	do	
Richard Steele Wilkinson,[24] *Captain*, h. p. Royal Marines	1 June 97	20 July 03	24 Sept.	do	5 April 39
James Johnston,[25] *Captain*, on retired full pay, 44 Foot	3 Dec. 03	5 Aug. 04	7 Mar. 11	do	
Richard Goate,[26] *Captain*, 35 Foot, on retired full pay	9 May 05	8 Jan. 07	27 June	do	
Archibald Smith, *Captain*, Unattached	9 April 07	18 Oct. 07	25 July	do	19 April 33
Richard Burges *Major*[28] *do.* h. p. Royal Artillery	8 Sept. 03	22 Sept. 03	11 Aug.	do	16 Oct. 32
Thomas Henry Shadwell Clerke, KH.,[29] *Captain*, on retired full pay, Depôt Staff	30 July 05	12 Mar. 07	22 Aug.	do	1 July 38
Joseph Williams, *Captain*, Royal Marines, on retired full pay	2 July 97	28 July 03	27 Aug.	do	
John Kitson,[30] *Major*, on retired full pay, 62 Foot	25 April 06	15 Jan. 07	3 Oct.	do	
Stephen Noel,[31] *Captain*, on retired full pay, 92 Foot	8 Aug. 00	25 July 03	19 Mar. 12	do	
William Taylor, *Captain*, Royal Marines, on retired full pay	16 ad. 98	10 Aug. 03	24 Mar.	do	
Moyle Sherer,[32] *do.* Unattached	ad 07	4 June 07	26 Mar.	do	6 July 32
Samuel Thorpe, KH.,[33] *Captain*, Unattached	2 April 07	14 Jan. 08	16 April	do	20 Feb. 35
Thomas Stirling Begbie,[35] *Captain*, Unattached	8 Oct. 07	10 Nov. 08	7 May	do	2 Nov. 32
Thomas Lemon, *Captain*, R. Marines, on retired full pay	30 ad. 98	19 Oct. 03	19 May	do	
John Macpherson,[38] *Captain*, Unattached	23 Sept. 99	2 July 03	2 July	do	6 Sept. 33
William Henry Hartman,[39] *Captain*, Unattached	9 July 03	28 Mar. 05	30 do.	do	16 Feb. 44
George Pinckney,[40] *Captain*, on retired full pay, 82 Foot	17 Sept. 01	22 Nov. 04	19 Nov.	do	
Honeyman Mackay,[41] *Major*, Unattached	5 Aug. 07	30 June 08	30 May 16	do	29 May 35
Philip Aubin,[42] *Major*, on retired full pay, 57 Foot	14 Feb. 11	29 April 13	22 June 26	12 April 31	
Thomas Rich. Plumbe Tempest, *Major*, Unattached	9 Nov. 15	30 Nov. 20	25 Dec. 25	12 July	6 July 38

	CORNET, ETC.	LIEUT.	CAPTAIN.	MAJOR.	WHEN PLACED ON HALF PAY.
James Dudgeon Brown,[43] *Major*, Unattached	13 May 13	24 Aug. 15	29 July 24	18 May 30	18 May 32
𝔓 William Seward,[44] *Major*, Unattached	26 Mar. 08	26 April 09	15 July 19	18 Oct.	12 Nov. 35
Samuel George Carter, *Major*, on retired full pay, 16 Foot	23 Mar. 04	27 Mar. 05	25 Dec. 14	8 Feb.	
𝔓 Geo. Fitz Gerald Stack, KH.,[45] *Major*, on retired full pay, 24 Foot	13 June 05	4 Dec. 06	25 May 15	26 Oct. 35	
George James Romney,[46] *Major*, Unattached	Dec. 06	15 Jan. 07	19 Aug. 19	1 April 36	10 Nov. 37
𝔓 Vance Young Donaldson,[47] *Major*, Unattached	14 Sept. 04	25 Dec. 05	24 June	10 Jan. 37	6 Mar. 40
𝔓 Henry Clements,[48] *Major*, on retired full pay, 16 Foot	7 April 05	26 Aug. 07	1 Sept.	do	
𝔓 John Doyle,[49] *Captain*, on retired full pay, 72 Foot	28 Sept. 04	13 Nov. 05	29 Sept.	do	
Henry Crause, *Captain*, Unattached	14 Nov. 05	12 Oct. 07	16 Dec.	do	28 July 43
𝔓 Roche Meade, KH.,[51] *Major*, Unatt., *Dep.-Assist. Adj.-General*	3 Aug. 09	23 Oct. 11	17 Feb. 14	do	31 May 39
James Hull Harrison,[52] *Captain*, Royal Marines, on retired full pay	6 Sept. 98	16 April 04	23 Feb.	do	
Julius Fleming, *Captain*, Royal Marines, on retired full pay	22 Sept. 98	8 Mar. 04	27 July	do	
𝔓 Geo. Henry Edward Murphy,[54] *Captain*, on retired full pay, 22 Foot	27 Nov. 05	2 July 07	25 Oct.	do	
𝔓 John Macphail, *Captain*, h. p. 7 Dragoons	2 Jan. 06	29 Sept. 08	do	do	29 May 40
O'Hara Baynes, *Captain*, h. p. R. Artillery	16 July 04	21 Dec. 04	28 Nov.	do	1 Aug. 27
𝔓 Richard Wheeler Hooper,[55] *Captain*, on retired full pay, 69 Foot	28 Aug. 07	4 Jan. 10	8 Dec.	do	
𝔓 Peter John Willats,[56] *Major*, on retired full pay, 48 Foot	31 Aug. 09	2 June 11	22 Dec.	do	
John Costley, *Captain*, Unattached	14 Feb. 05	1 Mar. 06	12 Jan. 15	do	15 Feb. 39
𝔓 John Casimer Harold, *Major*, 11 Foot	25 Sept. 06	28 May 07	16 Feb.	do	
𝔓 George Bolton,[59] *Captain*, h. p. 30 Foot	27 Mar. 06	11 Dec. 06	4 April	do	27 Oct. 37
𝔚 Thomas Reid,[60] *Major*, on retired full pay, 33 Foot	2 July 05	20 June 06	16 June	do	
William Cox,[61] *Captain*, on retired full pay, 54 Foot	1 May 06	8 Aug. 07	21 Sept.	do	
Barry Fox, *Captain*, h. p. Glengarry Fencibles	1 Jan. 07	10 Jan. 08	7 Dec.	do	22 Mar. 44
Samuel Charters,[62] *Captain*, h. p. Royal Artillery	14 Dec. 04	13 Feb. 06	15 Jan. 16	do	2 Feb. 28
James Mason,[63] *Captain*, on retired full pay, 77 Foot	11 July 05	5 Mar. 07	18 Jan.	do	
Robert Martin, *Major*, Ceylon Rifle Regt.	15 Aug. 04	28 Mar. 05	21 Nov.	do	
Charles Boyd, *Captain*, Unattached	15 Aug. 04	19 Dec. 05	12 July	do	3 May 39
𝔓 𝔚 Richard Handcock,[65] *Captain*, on retired full pay, 46 Foot	10 Sept. 05	5 Nov. 06	30 July 18	do	
Peter Sutherland,[66] *Captain*, on retired full pay, 72 Foot	1 Sept. 04	15 Jan. 07	20 May 19	do	
𝔓 Robert Muter, *Major*, Royal Canadian Rifle Regt.	5 Mar. 07	3 Mar. 08	27 May 19	do	
Henry James Michell Gregory,[67] *Captain*, Unattached	21 July 08	29 Dec. 09	5 Aug. 19	do	22 Dec. 46
𝔓 Frederick Wright,[68] *Captain*, R. Artillery, on retired full pay	13 Sept. 05	1 June 06	22 April 20	do	
William James Sutherland, *Major*, 21 Foot	3 May 14	22 Sept. 14	29 June	do	
Thomas Stewart,[69] *Captain*, Unattached	April 06	30 Oct. 06	9 Nov.	do	27 July 38
𝔓 John Crawfurd,[70] *Major*, Unattached	14 May 12	17 Sept. 13	17 May 21	do	16 April 41
𝔓 Henry Reid,[71] *Major*, h. p. 3 Ceylon Regiment	17 Mar. 08	26 July 09	26 July	do	27 Sept. 39

	Ensign, etc.	Lieut.	Captain.	Major.	When placed on half pay.
Henry Edward O'Dell, *Major*, St. Helena Regiment	8 July 06	25 Feb. 08	9 Jan. 22	10 Jan. 37	
William Chambré, *Major*, Unattached	9 July 11	27 May 12	10 Jan.	do	30 July 44
Hon. Arthur Charles Legge, *Captain*, Unattached	23 May 16	27 Feb. 17	17 Jan.	do	23 June 37
William Long,[73] *Captain*, h. p. 9 Foot	6 Oct. 08	14 June 10	31 Oct.	do	23 Mar. 38
Richard John Baron,[74] *Captain*, R. Engineers, on retired full pay	1 June 10	1 May 11	20 Dec.	do	
James Robert Colebrooke,[75] *do.* R. Artillery, on retired full pay	21 Mar. 06	3 June 06	31 Dec. 22	do	
Melville Dalyell, *Major*, Unattached	9 Dec. 19	19 May 25	19 Sept. 26	17 Feb.	23 Mar. 38
Henry Heghton Irving, *Major*, Unattached	1 Feb. 14	26 Dec. 16	3 June 24	11 July	12 May 43
George Gayton Palmer, *Captain*, R. Artillery, on retired full pay	20 Dec. 09	1 Oct. 13	26 Aug. 31	do	
William Sadlier, *Major*, 4 Foot	2 April 07	4 May 09	25 Aug. 25	4 Feb. 38	
George Browne,[76] *Major*, Unattached	10 June 13	30 Sept. 19	10 Feb. 32	15 June	25 Feb. 48
Frederick Mainwaring, *Major*, 51 Foot	5 April 10	15 April 13	4 Dec. 28	27 June	
John Bonamy,[77] *Captain*, on retired full pay, 6 Foot	19 Dec. 11	10 Feb. 14	24 Jan. 23	28 June	
John Marshall,[78] *Captain*, on retired full pay, 91 Foot	14 May 08	23 Nov. 09	20 Feb. 23	do	
Thomas James Adair, *Major*, 67 Foot	25 May 09	20 Feb. 11	27 Mar.	do	
Richard Manners,[79] *Captain*, on retired full pay, 59 Foot	13 April 09	8 Feb. 10	22 May	do	
William Augustus Raynes,[80] *Captain*, R. Art., on retired full pay *Barrack Master, Isle of Man*	25 April 06	22 Oct. 06	26 June	do	
John Henry Cooke,[81] *Captain*, Unattached, *Gentleman-at-Arms*	15 Mar. 09	19 April 10	31 Dec.	do	15 Dec. 40
Barton Parker Browne,[82] *Captain*, Unattached	8 April 13	22 June 15	5 May 24	do	10 May 39
Henry Boud, *Major*, 15 Hussars	25 May 09	1 Mar. 11	6 May	do	
John Birtwhistle,[83] *Major* Unattached	14 April 13	14 Jan. 19	13 May	do	12 Mar. 41
James T. Moore,[84] *Captain*, on retired full pay, 87 Foot	13 Oct. 08	18 Feb. 12	18 Aug.	do	
Ambrose Spong, *Captain*, on retired full pay, 60 Foot	15 Aug. 13	26 April 14	18 Nov.	do	
William Fraser, *Major*, 43 Foot	8 April 13	19 Jan. 14	9 Dec.	do	
John Clarke,[85] *Capt.*, on retired full pay, 66 F., *Knight of Windsor*	14 July 08	3 Oct. 09	13 Jan. 25	do	
James Algeo,[86] *Major*, Unattached	2 Sept. 06	4 Sept. 06	24 Feb.	do	9 May 45
Edmund Sheppard,[87] *Captain*, h. p. Royal Artillery	1 July 00	1 Feb. 08	2 Mar.	do	19 June 40
Isaac Richardson,[88] *Captain*, on retired full pay, 11 Foot	5 Dec. 05	1 Oct. 08	7 April	do	
Robert Brown, *Captain*, on retired full pay, 10 Foot	12 May 08	8 June 09	do	do	
William Cannon,[89] *Major*, on retired full pay, 97 Foot	26 Aug. 07	7 June 10	do	do	
Richard Tatton,[91] *Captain*, on retired full pay, 77 Foot	28 July 09	7 June 11	do	do	
James Jackson,[92] *do.* on retired full pay, 57 Foot	2 Mar. 09	19 June 11	do	do	
James Creagh, *Major*, 86 Foot	1 Jan. 10	4 Mar. 12	do	do	
William Graham,[93] *Captain*, Unattached	13 July 09	12 May 12	do	do	26 Mar. 41
William Henry Arthure, *Captain*, on retired full pay, 56 Foot	19 Feb. 07	21 Jan. 08	8 April	do	

	CORNET, ETC.	LIEUT.	CAPTAIN.	MAJOR.	WHEN PLACED ON HALF PAY.
Frederick Wm. Clements, *Captain*, Royal Canadian Rifle Regiment	16 Feb. 14	23 Feb. 15	8 April 25	28 June 38	
Nicholas Palmer, *Major*, 56 Foot	11 Nov. 13	3 May 21	26 May	do	
P Joseph Robert Raines, *Major*, 95 Foot	19 Sept. 05	28 May 07	2 June	do	
Henry Sykes Stephens, *Capt.*, Unatt., *Serjeant at Arms to the Queen*	14 June 15	8 Nov. 15	9 June	do	26 Oct. 41
P W John Lewis Black,[95] *Major*, Unattached	22 April 13	10 Mar. 14	16 June	do	3 Dec. 47
Lawrence Græme, *Captain*, Unatt., *Lieut.-Governor of Tobago*	16 Mar. 15	13 Dec. 21	do	do	16 Aug. 39
P Walter White,[96] *Major*, Unattached, *Town Major of Dublin*	16 June 08	7 Aug. 09	23 June	do	23 June 25
Thomas Bonnor, *Captain*, Ceylon Rifle Regiment	5 Oct. 15	24 Dec. 18	30 June	do	
Charles Barry, *Captain*, Unattached	23 Mar. 14	3 Feb. 15	21 July	do	12 Oct. 41
James M'Queen, *Major*, do.	31 Mar. 14	11 Feb. 19	do	do	14 June 42
Lewis Shuldham Barrington Robertson,[97] *Capt.*, R. Art., on ret. full pay	1 July 06	1 Feb. 08	29 July	do	
P Charles Rivers,[98] *Captain*, R. Engineers, on retired full pay	1 July 12	1 Mar. 13	do	do	
John M. Dalzell, *Major*, on retired full pay, 16 Foot	1 Mar. 09	10 Sept. 12	1 Sept.	do	
P W John Manley Wood, *Captain*, Unattached	19 May 14	6 Sept. 21	10 Sept.	do	3 April 46
Hunter Ward, *Major*, 48 Foot	9 Sept. 19	31 Dec. 22	do	do	
P Joseph Swinburne, *Major*, 83 Foot	16 Aug. 09	4 June 12	6 Oct.	do	
P W Samuel Waymouth,[100] *Major*, Unattached	18 May 12	28 Mar. 13	13 Oct.	do	26 Jan. 41
George Montagu, *Captain*, Unattached	8 Dec. 14	31 Oct. 22	22 Oct.	do	3 June 42
George Carpenter, *Major*, 41 Foot	1 Oct. 18	1 Mar. 20	29 Oct.	do	
Daniel Frazer, *Major*, 42 Foot	31 Oct. 11	13 June 16	5 Nov.	do	
Alexander Buchan,[101] *Captain*, Unattached	8 Jan. 09	3 Oct. 11	10 Nov.	do	25 April 39
George Hogarth, CB., *Major*, 26 Foot	22 May 17	13 Sept. 21	12 Nov.	do	
William Snow, *Captain*, Unattached	19 Dec. 15	19 Mar. 24	15 Dec.	do	3 Oct. 45
Peter Cheape, *Major*, 96 Foot	25 May 13	3 Aug. 15	24 Dec.	do	
Charles Smith, *Major*, Unattached	20 Oct. 13	21 April 14	31 Dec.	do	9 June 46
Charles Highmore Potts, *Captain*, 19 Foot	8 Feb. 16	13 Nov. 17	do	do	
Francis Westenra, *Major*, Unattached	31 July 17	24 Oct. 21	do	do	14 Mar. 45
John De Burgh, *Major*, 93 Foot	25 Nov. 19	7 April 25	19 Sept. 26	28 July	
Thomas Foster, *Captain*, Royal Engineers	1 Sept. 15	7 Sept. 19	10 Jan. 37	29 Mar. 39	
P John Maclean, *Major*, 46 Foot	2 May 11	10 Dec. 12	25 Dec. 30	12 April	
Wm. Robert Brudenell Smith, *Major*, Unattached	29 July 24	28 Jan. 26	20 Mar. 27	21 June	1 Mar. 44
Thomas Sidney Powell, *Major*, 57 Foot	13 May 26	31 May 31	13 Nov. 35	23 July	
Arthur Charles Lowe,[103] *Major*, Unattached	20 April 15	10 Aug. 15	3 April 27	21 Aug.	6 May 42
P W Edgar Gibson,[104] *do.* Unatt., *Barrack-Master at St. Lucia*	5 Dec. 12	26 Mar. 14	24 May 31	20 Sept.	13 Dec. 39
Alexander Sharrock, *Major*, on retired full pay, 29 Foot	7 Aug. 06	30 June 08	27 April 27	27 Sept.	

	ENSIGN, ETC.	LIEUT.	CAPTAIN.	MAJOR.	WHEN PLACED ON HALF PAY.
Edward Last, *Major*, 99 Foot	13 Oct. 14	20 Nov. 24	22 May 29	18 Oct. 39	
Oliver Robinson, *Captain*, 2 Foot	5 Oct. 20	24 Jan. 25	19 Feb. 36	18 Oct.	
Henry Samuel Davis, *Major*, 52 Foot	13 April 27	8 Oct. 30	17 July 35	13 Dec.	
P W Leonard Morse-Cooper,[108] ***Major***, Unattached	26 May 14	23 Jan. 17	25 Feb. 31	10 Jan. 40	10 Jan. 40
James Watson, *Major*, 14 Foot	22 Mar. 21	25 Dec. 22	14 Dec. 32	do	
Charles Wise, *Major*, Unattached	7 July 25	22 April 26	23 April 29	17 April	23 Sept. 45
John Jackson Lowth, *Major*, 38 **Foot**	3 July 24	11 Sept. 25	23 Mar. 32	12 June	
Francis Plunkett Dunne, *Major*, **Unattached**	29 May 23	23 June 25	30 Dec. 26	18 Sept.	18 Sept. 40
Thomas Edmund Campbell, *Major*, **Unattached**	30 June 25	13 May 26	17 Feb. 32	4 Nov.	28 Aug. 46
Robert Leonard,[108] *Capt.*, h. p. **R. Marines, *Paym. of Plymouth Div.***	27 Feb. 06	3 Mar. 12	28 April 34	do	25 Aug. 47
Frederick Spry, *Captain*, Royal **Marines, on retired full pay**	1 April 07	5 April 14	27 May 34	4 Nov.	20 April 47
Charles Robinson, *do.* Royal Marines	1 Aug. 06	11 May 13	do	5 Nov.	
John Buckley Casticau, *Captain*, Royal Marin**e Artillery**	22 Sept. 08	13 April 24	10 July 37	10 Nov.	
Edward Vicars, *Captain*, Royal Engineers	28 Mar. 22	8 April 26	28 July 40	do	
John Gordon, *Major*, 60 Foot	14 June 27	5 April 31	5 April 33	15 Dec.	
William Raban, *Major*, on retired full pay, 22 **Foot**	3 Jan. 11	2 June 13	14 Feb. 28	18 Dec.	
Robert Carmichael Smyth, *Major*, 93 Foot	8 July 18	5 May 25	8 April 26	18 May 41	
William Slater, *Major*, 82 Foot	9 Sept. 12	20 Jan. 14	25 Nov. 28	3 June	
P W Park Percy Ne**vill,**[109] ***Maj.*, h. p. 12 Foot, *Gentleman at Arms***	29 Mar. 10	17 July 11	27 Nov. 35	13 July	19 Nov. 44
P John Alves, *Major*, **Depôt Battalion Isle of Wight**	5 Nov. 07	25 Dec. 10	13 Mar. 27	17 Aug.	
Gilbert William Francklyn, ***Major*, 37 Foot**	30 April 27	23 Nov. 30	9 Dec. 36	27 Aug.	
P John Knight Janncey,[110] *Major*, **Unattached**	12 Mar. 07	10 Feb. 08	5 June 27	17 Sept.	17 Sept. 41
William Roberts, *Major*, 98 **Foot**	14 April 14	7 April 25	18 Oct. 31	5 Oct.	
Charles Robert Raitt, *Major*, **Unattached**	13 June 30	4 Oct. 33	22 June 38	29 Oct.	21 Mar. 45
W Charles Hill,[111] *Major*, 5**4 Foot, on retired full pay**	12 May 14	26 Nov. 21	5 Jan. 26	23 Nov.	
John Temple, *Major*, 60 Foot	14 May 18	21 Oct. 24	28 Jan.	do	
Richard Leslie Dundas, *Captain*, Unattached	17 June 19	17 Sept. 25	28 Jan.	do	30 Dec. 45
Edward Townsend, *Major*, 83 Foot	23 May 16	28 Oct. 24	18 Feb.	do	
P W George Frederick Paschal, ***Captain*, 70 Foot**	17 Mar. 12	19 Oct. 12	23 Mar.	do	
Thomas Hinton Hemmans, *Capta***in*, on retired full pay, 78 Foot**	15 May 11	2 Dec. 13	8 April	do	
George Hankey Smith, *Captain*, **73 Foot**	7 April 18	7 Feb. 22	do	do	
Guy Clarke, *Captai***n*, 77 Foot**	17 Feb. 20	17 July 23	do	do	
Robert Shafto Vicars, *Captain*, Unattached	10 Dec. 13	9 Aug. 21	22 April	do	12 May 43
William White Warburton, *Captain*, on retired full pay, 67 Foot	17 Aug. 09	2 April 12	5 May	do	

	2D LIEUT. ETC.	LIEUT.	CAPTAIN.	MAJOR.	WHEN PLACED ON HALF PAY.
Rawdon J. Pop. Vassall, *Major*, Unattached	6 June 22	22 Oct. 25	13 May 26	23 Nov. 41	23 May 48
ℬ Martin Crean Lynch,[113] *Captain*, 14 Foot, on retired full pay	11 Feb. 08	31 May 09	22 June	do	
Henry Francis Strange, *Major*, 25 Foot	23 May 15	7 April 25	29 June	do	
William Elliott, *Captain*, Unattached	6 Aug. 12	2 Sept. 13	6 July	do	27 Jan. 43
Thomas Unett, *Captain*, 19 Foot	27 Sept. 21	22 July 24	6 July	do	
Charles Ravenhill Wright,[114] *Captain*, 43 Foot, on retired full pay	25 Dec. 13	26 July 21	11 July	do	
Wm. Henry Adams, *Capt.*, Unatt., *Prof. of Fortification, R. Mil. Col.*	1 Feb. 21	11 Mar. 24	18 July	do	7 June 44
George Thomas Parke, *Major*, Unattached	3 Mar. 14	12 June 23	10 Aug.	do	6 Nov. 46
ℬ Edward Boyd, *Captain*, 29 Foot	16 July 11	1 July 12	17 Aug.	do	
George Lister Lister Kaye, *Major*, Unattached	25 Mar. 23	14 April 25	24 Aug.	do	31 Dec. 41
William Cockell,[116] *Major*, Unattached	26 Dec. 22	23 June 25	29 Aug.	do	20 Aug. 44
James Pattoun Sparks, *Captain*, 38 Foot	27 July 15	30 July 18	5 Sept.	do	
Henry Jervis, *Major*, 72 Foot	19 Dec. 11	29 Dec. 14	19 Sept.	do	
George Edward Thorold, *Major*, 92 Foot	24 June 24	9 June 25	do	do	
Alex. Houstoun, *Captain*, h. p. 4 F., *Staff Officer of Pensioners*	4 Dec. 23	19 Nov. 25	12 Dec.	do	1 July 42
Peter Beanet Reyne, *Major*, Ceylon Regiment	15 April 19	15 Dec. 22	21 Dec.	do	
George Johnston, *Captain*, Cape Mounted Riflemen	26 Jan. 19	24 June 24	30 Dec.	do	
Basil Herne Burchell, *Captain*, h. p. 57 Foot	25 Dec. 13	8 April 25	30 Dec.	do	22 July 42
Power Le Poer Trench, *Major*, 2 Dragoon Guards	12 Aug. 24	17 Dec.	do	do	
ℬ John Gould, *Captain*, 88 Foot	31 Aug. 07	22 Mar. 09	13 Feb. 27	do	
ℬ John De Lacy,[118] *Major*, Unattached	30 May 09	15 June 11	do	do	3 Jan. 45
John Thorne Weyland, *Captain*, Royal Canadian Rifle Regiment	31 July 06	1 Mar. 09	13 Mar.	do	
ℬ Joseph Smith, *Captain*, 14 Foot	16 Feb. 08	14 Mar. 11	do	do	
Richard Chetwode, *Captain*, h. p. 3 Dragoon Guards	24 May 20	15 Aug. 22	20 Mar.	do	25 Feb.
Ewan M'Pherson, *Captain*, 90 Foot	21 Jan. 13	5 Feb. 14	26 April	do	
John Parson Westropp, *Captain*, Unattached	11 Jan. 22	23 June 25	27 April	do	18 Feb. 42
George Marmaduke Reeves, *Captain*, 99 Foot	1 July 24	8 April 26	do	do	
Robert Henry Lowth, *Captain*, 86 Foot	4 Feb. 19	1 April 24	15 May	do	
Edward Charles Fletcher, *Captain*, h. p. 3 Dragoon Guards	30 Nov. 20	4 April 23	21 May	do	18 Mar. 42
George Hutchison, *Major*, 97 Foot	never	14 July 14	26 June	do	
ℭ Robert Gordon,[119] *Captain*, Royal Marines, on retired full pay	1 Jan. 04	13 May 06	31 Aug.	do	
ℬ William Elgee,[120] *Captain*, Royal Artillery, on retired full pay	1 July 07	20 May 08	6 Nov.	do	
James Smith Law, *do.* do. on retired full pay	3 Nov. 07	16 July	do	do	
ℬ John Pascoe,[121] *Captain*, Royal Artillery, on retired full pay	4 April 08	29 July	do	do	
ℬ George Spiller,[122] *do.* do. do.	2 May	7 Nov.	do	do	
ℬ Edward Jacob Bridges,[124] *Captain*, R. Artillery, on retired full pay	1 Oct.	14 Mar. 11	do	do	

	ENSIGN, ETC.	LIEUT.	CAPTAIN.	MAJOR.	WHEN PLACED ON HALF PAY.
𝔚 Willoughby Montagu,[123] *Captain*, h. p. Royal Artillery	26 Nov. 08	11 Aug. 11	6 Nov. 27	23 Nov. 41	6 Nov. 27
𝔓 Charles Campbell,[125] *Captain*, on retired full pay, 61 Foot	10 May 09	23 June 12	7 Nov.	do	
Burton Daveney, *Captain*, 1 Foot	27 April 20	7 July 25	8 Nov.	do	
Edward Bagot, *Major*, Unattached	23 Oct. 23	10 Dec. 25	do	do	11 Mar. 42
Foot	5 April 10	24 Oct. 11	13 Nov.	do	
nattached	6 July 14	12 June 19	9 Dec.	do	29 Nov. 44
𝔓 James Scargill, *Captain*, 97 Foot	12 April 10	21 Oct. 12	17 Jan. 28	do	
Robert Lewis, *Major*, 89 Foot	7 April 25	2 Mar. 26	12 Feb.	do	
Samuel Tryon, *Major*, Unattached, *Brigade Major at Nova Scotia*	23 Jan. 23	10 Sept. 25	19 Feb.	do	27 Dec. 42
William Dempster, *Captain*, 41 Foot, on retired full pay	9 Feb. 09	11 April 11	26 Feb.	do	
George Dawson,[128] *Major*, Unattached	7 May 11	7 Jan. 13	20 Mar.	do	29 Dec. 43
James Brand, *Major*, 16 Foot	11 Mar. 13	17 Aug. 30	25 April	do	
Charles Rayner Newman, *Major*, 14 Foot	28 Sept. 09	15 Aug. 11	1 May	do	
George Thurles Finucane, *Major*, Unattached, *Major of Brigade in the Ionian Islands*	22 Sept. 08	15 Mar. 10	17 June	do	3 May 39
Thomas Williams, *Major*, 4 Foot	12 Sept. 22	7 July 25	17 June	do	
Charlton O'Neill, *Captain*, on retired full pay, 97 Foot	12 Oct. 08	2 May 11	27 June	do	
John Joseph Grier, *Captain*, 93 Foot	11 Sept. 17	9 April 25	31 July	do	
𝔓 𝔚 Oliver D. Ainsworth,[130] *Major*, Unattached, *Brigade Major, Van Dieman's Land*	11 April 09	26 July 10	14 Aug.	do	16 June 43
𝔓 Alexander Campbell,[131] *Captain*, on retired full pay, 38 Foot	17 Dec. 13	26 Nov. 21	25 Sept.	do	
𝔓 Henry Dixon, *do.* do. 81 Foot	20 Aug. 12	21 Dec. 15	21 Nov.	do	
Mark Kerr Atherley, *Major*, 92 Foot	28 Aug. 23	13 Aug. 25	25 Nov.	do	
John Weech Randolph, *Major*, Unattached	25 Jan. 25	17 Nov. 25	9 Dec.	do	21 May 47
𝔓 James Poyntz,[132] *Captain*, on retired full pay, 30 Foot	14 April 14	19 July 15	28 Dec.	do	
John Gordon, *Major*, 47 Foot	28 Sept. 13	13 April 20	11 June 30	do	
Thomas Ogilvy, *Captain*, 2 Life Guards	9 Mar. 32	29 April 36	8 May 40	do	
John Augustus Udny, *Lieut. & Capt.*, Grenadier Guards	21 Sept. 30	13 Nov. 35	15 Dec.	do	
Charles Rochfort Scott,[133] *Captain*, h. p. Royal Staff Corps, *Assist. Qr.-Master General at Dublin*	2 Jan. 12	20 July 15	25 June 30	31 Dec.	25 June 30
George de Rottenburgh, *Captain*, Unattached, *Assistant Quarter Master General in Canada*	7 April 25	27 April 27	13 July 32	do	
Graves Chamney Swan, *Capt.*, Unatt., *Staff Officer of Pensioners*	14 July 25	25 Oct. 27	11 Oct. 33	do	
Richard Wilbraham, *Major*, 7 Foot	25 Mar. 28	25 May 33	22 July 36	do	
Edward Aldrich, *Captain*, Royal Engineers	15 Mar. 26	15 Feb. 30	30 Sept. 41	do	
William Harrison Askwith, *Captain*, Royal Artillery	18 Dec. 29	6 Nov. 30	23 Nov. 41	28 Jan. 42	

	CORNET, ETC.	LIEUT.	CAPTAIN.	MAJOR.	WHEN PLACED ON HALF PAY.
Henry Edmund de Burgh Sidley, *Major*, 86 Foot	4 May 15	21 Feb. 22	11 June 41	8 April 42	
𝔓 John Fraser,[134] *Major*, Unattached, *Fort Major of Jersey*	29 May 09	12 Feb. 12	17 Aug. 32	15 April	15 April 42
Anthony Blaxland Stransham, *Captain*, Royal Marines	1 Jan. 23	12 Oct. 32	12 Feb. 42	do	
James Hope Grant, CB., *Major*, 9 Lancers	29 Aug. 26	26 Feb. 28	29 May 35	22 April	
William Codd,[135] *Major*, Unattached	2 Mar. 20	25 Mar. 24	23 Mar. 33	6 May	30 May 43
Lacy Walter Yea, *do.* 7 Foot	6 Oct. 25	19 Dec. 26	30 Dec. 36	3 June	
Thomas Wheeler, *Major*, 28 Foot	24 May 14	18 Dec. 17	28 Sept. 32	24 Aug.	
Arthur Philip Savage Wilkinson, CB., **Major**, 13 Foot	25 Dec. 22	16 Dec. 24	6 Sept. 39	4 Oct.	
Hamlet Coote Wade,[136] CB., *Captain*, h. p. 1 Dragoon Guards	22 Feb. 27	9 Aug. 30	22 April 40	do	21 July 46
James Henry Fenwick, *Captain*, 13 Foot	25 Oct. 27	30 Oct. 31	15 Dec. 40	do	
𝔓 Thomas Canch,[120] *Major*, Unatt., ***Fort-Major of Edinburgh Castle***	28 Sept. 09	13 May 13	2 Nov. 30	1 Nov.	21 Feb. 40
John Douglas, *Captain*, 79 Foot	6 Sept. 33	8 July 36	8 June 41	do	
William James Myers, *Major*, h. p. Royal Staff Corps	9 June 25	7 Jan. 30	29 Dec. 35	22 Nov.	19 Mar. 47
Francis Hearle Stephens, *Major*, Unattached	23 Feb. 26	31 July 28	17 July 35	25 Nov.	25 Feb. 48
James Paterson, *Major*, 94 Foot	17 May 21	4 Dec. 23	5 April 31	23 Dec.	
William Greenwood, CB., *Captain*, Royal Artillery, on retired full pay	17 Dec. 12	22 May 15	22 Jan. 34	do	
Matthew Smith, *Major*, 29 Foot	16 Sept. 16	31 Dec. 23	8 Feb. 34	do	
𝔓 Arthur O'Leary, *Major*, 55 Foot	18 April 11	25 Jan. 14	27 Nov. 35	do	
Henry Charles Barnston Daubeney, CB., ***Major***, 55 Foot	12 Mar. 29	9 Aug. 31	28 Oct. 36	do	
James Whitcombe, *Captain*, Royal Marines	13 Mar. 09	11 Mar. 26	10 July 37	do	
Frankling Lushington, CB., *Major*, 37 Foot	16 July 29	1 Oct. 33	30 Oct. 38	do	
Francis Smith Hamilton, *Captain*, Royal Marines	2 May 11	2 Oct. 29	7 Nov. 38	do	
Francis Wigston, *Major*, 18 Foot	16 Mar. 26	1 June 32	18 Jan. 39	do	
Ferdinand White, CB., *Captain*, 8 Foot	2 Nov. 26	10 Nov. 31	7 Aug. 40	do	
Ferdinand Whittingham, CB., *Major*, 26 Foot	2 Nov. 32	19 Feb. 36	30 April 41	do	
William Yorke Moore, *Major*, 54 Foot	15 Dec. 25	12 Dec. 26	19 July 33	30 Dec.	
Cyprian Bridge, *Major*, 58 Foot	8 April 25	31 Jan. 28	16 Dec. 36	do	
Edward Bond, *Major*, 39 Foot	8 Mar. 27	16 Sept. 29	26 Feb. 36	31 Mar. 43	
Harry Smyth, *Major*, 68 Foot	10 July 23	13 Aug. 25	15 Oct. 29	21 April	
Joseph Childs, *Capt.*, R. Marines	21 April 09	25 Sept. 27	10 July 37	9 May	
Charles Augustus Arney, ***Major***, 58 Foot	5 Nov. 25	9 Aug. 31	1 July 37	12 May	
Edmund Richard Jeffreys, ***do.*** 88 Foot	16 June 25	11 Oct. 27	2 Feb. 38	do	
Frederick Darley George, CB., ***Captain***, 22 Foot	24 Mar. 25	30 April 27	30 Aug. 33	4 July	

	ENSIGN, ETC.	LIEUT.	CAPTAIN.	MAJOR.	WHEN PLACED ON HALF PAY.
Thomas Sydenham Conway, CB., *Captain*, 99 Foot	14 Feb. 28	26 April 31	9 Dec. 36	4 July 43	
James Lynn, *Captain*, Royal Engineers	22 Sept. 26	13 Nov. 31	1 May 43	28 July	
Charles Dunsmure, *Major*, 42 Foot	9 April 25	7 Nov. 26	30 Jan. 35	5 Sept.	
Edmund William Wilton Passy, *Major*, **56 Foot**	8 April 25	30 Dec. 26	23 Sept. 36	12 Sept.	
Frank Adams, *Major*, 28 Foot	30 Dec. 26	23 Mar. 32	31 Dec. 39	29 Oct.	
William Bell, *Major*, 12 Foot	3 April 27	8 Oct. 30	3 July 35	3 Nov.	
Alexander Barry Montgomery, *Major*, 1 **Foot**	25 Nov. 24	30 Oct. 26	16 Aug. 33	5 Dec.	
P Richard Martin Meredith, *Major*, 13 **Foot**	1 April 13	26 Jan. 15	2 Sept. 38	15 Dec.	
Thomas Le Marchant, *Major*, Unattached	14 June 27	11 June 30	17 Oct. 34	22 Dec.	25 Feb. 45
David Rae Smith, *Major*, 22 Foot	3 Nov. 25	13 Feb. 28	26 April 31	23 Feb. 44	
Thomas Shadforth, *Major*, 57 Foot	8 April 25	10 Oct. 26	12 April 31	29 Mar.	
Edmund James Elliot, *Major*, 79 Foot	5 April 31	10 Oct. 34	3 April 40	12 April	
Patrick M'Kie, *Major*, Unattached	3 Nov. 12	3 Nov. 14	3 Oct. 29	30 April	31 Dec. 47
Marmaduke George Nixon, *Major*, 39 **Foot**	5 April 31	25 Mar. 33	28 Dec. 38	30 April	
William Langley Tudor, *Major*, 50 Foot	9 April 25	26 Nov. 29	1 April 41	do	
Charles D. Campbell, *Captain*, 39 Foot	9 Aug. 27	3 May 33	24 April 43	do	
Thomas Graham, *Major*, 1 Foot	21 May 26	27 April 27	9 Aug. 33	3 May	
George Pindar, *Major*, 15 Foot	24 Aug. 26	31 Dec. 30	21 Oct. 36	24 May	
Herbert Mends, *do.* 2 West India Regiment	1 April 22	19 Feb. 24	19 Mar. 29	26 May	
Corbett Cotton, *do.* 49 Foot	9 April 25	29 Mar. 27	4 May 32	5 June	
Inigo Jones, *do.* 11 Hussars	8 July 28	17 Dec. 30	14 April 37	7 June	
William Jones, ***do.* 61 Foot**	10 April 25	12 Dec. 26	24 Nov. 35	26 July	
Charles Crutchley, ***Major*, 23 Foot**	8 April 26	22 July 30	11 Dec. 35	23 Oct.	
George Green, ***do.* 84 Foot**	7 April 25	29 June 27	10 Nov. 37	19 Nov.	
John Leslie Dennie, *do.* 94 Foot	25 April 28	22 Sept. 30	17 May 41	29 Nov.	
Edward Carter Giffard, *Major*, Unattached	23 Nov. 26	8 Feb. 31	9 Oct. 35	20 Dec.	5 Mar. 47
Peter Delancey, *Major*, 75 Foot	29 Jan. 26	30 April 29	8 Mar. 39	17 Jan. 45	
Thomas Graham Egerton, *Major*, 77 **Foot**	24 Dec. 29	9 Mar. 32	23 Jan. 35	7 Feb.	
P **Edward K**enny, *Major*, 89 Foot	17 June 13	1 Nov. 19	4 Dec. 32	26 Feb.	
Robert Alexander Cuthbert, *Major*, **15 Foot**	25 Sept. 23	7 July 25	28 May 29	31 Mar.	
George Staunton, *Major*, 31 Foot	5 Oct. 26	15 Feb. 31	8 June 39	28 Mar.	
Maximilian James Western, *Major*, 64 Foot	10 June 26	8 June 30	29 Dec. 35	11 April	

	Ensign, etc.	Lieut.	Captain.	Major.	When placed on half pay.
Charles Herbert, *Major*, 75 Foot	19 Nov. 25	10 Oct. 26	27 Sept. 33	25 April 45	
Maurice Griffin Dennis, *Major*, 60 Foot	9 May 26	5 July 27	15 Dec. 37	2 May	
George Edward Turner, *Captain*, R. Artillery, ***Master of the Horse to the Lord Lieutenant of Ireland***	20 Dec. 33	12 July 36	5 April 45	9 May	
William Henry Archer, *Major*, 16 Lancers	28 Dec. 32	17 July 35	1 June 38	16 May	
Lord Alfred Paget, *Major*, Unattached, ***Chief Equerry to the Queen***	6 July 32	14 Mar. 34	20 Oct. 40	16 May	16 May 45
Edward R. King, *Major*, 36 Foot	16 Feb. 26	31 July 28	4 Dec. 32	22 May	
William Edie, *Major*, 98 Foot	14 Jan. 26	18 Oct. 31	29 Nov. 33	13 June	
John O'Grady,[140] *Major*, Unattached	20 Sept. 10	22 Sept. 13	26 May 31	27 June	27 June 45
John Singleton, *Major*, 11 Foot	17 June 26	31 Dec. 27	15 Feb. 39	27 June	
Francis Burdett, *Major*, 17 Lancers	18 April 34	14 April 37	21 May 41	27 June	
[illegible] William Austin,[141] *Major*, Unattached	5 Sept. 11	6 April 13	26 Sept. 34	4 July	25 July 45
Arnold Charles Errington, *Major*, 51 Foot	4 Feb. 26	13 Sept. 31	14 July 37	25 July	
William Henry Goode, *Major*, 62 Foot	31 May 18	31 July 23	29 Dec. 40	5 Sept.	
Matthew Benjamin George Reed, *Major*, 84 Foot	26 Feb. 18	19 Nov. 25	26 Feb. 36	16 Sept.	
Alfred Francis W. Wyatt, *Major*, 65 Foot	12 Dec. 26	23 April 29	19 Sept. 34	23 Sept.	
Fred. George Aug. Pinckney, *Major*, 73 Foot	8 April 25	8 April 26	23 Dec. 36	23 Sept.	
Richard Gardiner, *Major*, 76 Foot	12 May 14	29 Sept. 25	5 April 33	11 Nov.	
[illegible] Archibald Robertson,[142] *Major*, Unattached	13 April 09	6 Jan. 14	30 Dec. 34	30 Dec.	30 Dec. 45
John Doyle O'Brien, *Major*, Unattached	15 Mar. 21	16 June 25	4 Dec. 35	do	18 July 48
Robert Alexander Lockhart, *Major*, 80 Foot	11 June 30	5 Oct. 32	13 July 38	do	
Hugh Dennis Crofton, *Major*, 20 Foot	13 Mar. 35	29 Dec. 37	9 Aug. 39	do	
George Browne, *Major*, 35 Foot	31 Dec. 33	14 July 37	8 April 42	do	
Cecil William Forester, *Major*, 52 Foot	1 Aug. 26	14 May 29	4 Dec. 35	16 Jan. 46	
Thomas Hurdle, *Captain*, Royal Marines	24 Jan. 12	16 April 31	13 Nov. 40	20 Mar.	
John Tritton, *Major*, 10 Hussars	14 Jan. 13	14 Aug. 15	7 Oct. 36	3 April	
John Richard Blagden Hale, *Captain*, 3 Dragoons	17 June 31	16 May 34	10 July 37	do	
Edward Harris Greathed, *Major*, 8 Foot	22 June 32	10 May 33	27 April 38	do	
Charles Fred. Havelock, *Captain*, 53 Foot	13 Dec. 21	7 May 27	12 Dec. 39	do	
Henry William Paget, *Major*, Unattached	14 Dec. 32	1 May 35	3 July 40	do	3 April 46
Arthur Borton, *Major*, 9 Foot	13 July 32	3 April 35	30 July 41	do	
Arthur St. George H. Stepney, *Captain*, 29 Foot	16 May 34	10 Nov. 37	15 April 42	do	
Hon. Charles R. Sackville West, *Captain*, 21 Foot	30 Aug. 33	5 June 35	do	do	
Edward Lugard, *Captain*, 29 Foot, *Assist. Adjutant-General in India*	31 July 28	31 Oct. 31	30 Dec. 43	do	
Samuel Fisher, *Captain*, 3 Dragoons	15 June 27	16 Aug. 31	22 Dec. 45	do	
George M'Leod Tew,[143] *Major*, Unattached	19 Aug. 13	30 Sept. 19	12 Jan. 34	10 April	25 Aug. 46

	CORNET, ETC.	LIEUT.	CAPTAIN.	MAJOR.	WHEN PLACED ON HALF-PAY.
KH Anthony Robert **L'Estrange, *Major*, 71 Foot**	7 Dec. 14	20 Dec. 21	7 Jan. 30	14 April 46	
P KH John Enoch,[144] ***Major*, Unatt., *Deputy-Assistant Quarter-Master General***	30 Mar. 09	15 Aug. 11	22 July 30	do	19 May 46
Henry William Harris, *Major*, 24 Foot	23 May 22	27 Sept. 24	30 Dec. 31	do	
Hon. Henry Robert Handcock, ***Major*, 97 Foot**	8 April 25	20 Mar. 27	24 Feb. 32	do	
Henry Hope Graham, *Major*, **59 Foot**	15 Oct. 29	7 Sept. 32	7 Nov. 34	do	
David Forbes, *Major*, 91 Foot	8 Oct. 29	23 Nov. 32	24 July 35	do	
James Maxwell Perceval, *Major*, 12 Foot	21 June 33	18 Mar. 36	18 May 38	do	
Charles Hind, *Major*, Unattached	8 Oct. 29	7 Feb. 34	22 Feb. 39	do	7 April 48
George Augustus Fred. Quentin, *Major*, 10 Hussars	14 June 31	1 June 32	12 Feb. 36	28 April	
Francis Saunderson Holmes, *Major*, 8 Foot	8 Feb. 33	6 July 35	26 Oct. 41	do	
Howell Paynter, *Major*, 24 Foot	26 April 28	6 Jan. 33	6 May 42	do	
Augustus Francis Ansell, *Major*, 74 Foot	13 Jan. 20	19 Sept. 26	14 Dec. 32	1 May	
George Fenton Fletcher Boughey, *Major*, 59 Foot	1 Nov. 31	11 July 34	1 June 38	do	
William O'Grady Haly, *Major*, 47 Foot	17 June 28	19 July 31	25 April 34	19 May	
Sir Edmund Stephen Thomas, *Bart.*, *Major*, 69 Foot	25 Nov. 28	28 Oct. 31	1 May 35	do	
Frederick Granville, *Major*, 23 Foot	17 Sept. 29	1 Nov. 33	28 April 37	do	
Henry Sebastian Rowan, *Captain*, Royal Artillery	20 June 32	14 Aug. 34	18 Aug. 43	22 May	
Julian Fred. A. Symonds, *Captain*, Royal Engineers	1 Aug. 33	24 Sept. 36	22 April 45	do	
Collingwood Dickson, *Captain*, Royal Artillery	18 Dec. 35	29 Nov. 37	1 April 46	do	
Hon. R. Charles Henry Spencer, *Captain*, Royal **Artillery**	do	30 Dec. 37	do	do	
William Arkwright, *Major*, 6 Dragoons	24 July 28	25 June 30	11 May 38	9 June	
Lachlan Duff Gordon, *Major*, 20 Foot	25 July 34	27 July 38	31 Dec. 39	do	
Thomas Hook Pearson,[145] *Major*, Unattached	14 Mar. 25	1 Aug. 26	16 Aug. 31	19 June	7 April 48
P Charles Lewis, *Major*, 80 Foot	9 June 13	30 Dec. 19	22 Mar. 32	do	
Edward Baker Bere,[146] *Captain*, h. p. 15 Hussars	13 Aug. 25	29 Aug. 26	6 Dec. 33	do	2 July 47
Lawrence Fyler, *Major*, 3 Light Dragoons	7 Sept. 26	10 July 28	7 Feb. 34	do	
John Daniel Dyson, *Major*, 3 Dragoon Guards	9 Dec. 31	22 Mar. 33	8 July 36	do	
William Mathias, *Captain*, 62 Foot	8 Feb. 31	29 Mar. 33	16 Mar. 38	do	
David FitzGerald Longworth, *Captain*, 31 Foot	3 May 31	27 Nov. 35	25 Sept. 39	do	
George Frederick Long, *Captain*, 50 Foot	27 Sept. 33	17 June 37	8 Feb. 42	do	
William Petrie Waugh, *Captain*, 10 Hussars	1 Nov. 33	29 May 35	31 Dec. 44	do	
Henry Bates, *Captain*, 98 Foot, *Aide-de-Camp to the Commander-in-Chief in India*	9 July 29	28 Nov. 33	8 Aug. 45	do	
William Biddlecomb Marlow, *Captain*, Royal Engineers	1 Sept. 15	23 Mar. 25	28 Mar. 37	7 July	
Henry Matson, *Captain*, 58 Foot	16 Sept. 13	2 June 14	30 Nov. 38	do	

	Ensign, etc.	Lieut.	Captain.	Major.	When placed on half-pay.
Archibald William Reed, *Captain*, 99 Foot	4 Sept. 35	25 July 37	17 July 41	7 July 46	
Richard Denny, *Captain*, 19 Foot	18 May 36	12 Oct. 38	30 Dec. 42	do	
William Bookley Langford, *Captain*, Royal **Marines**	22 Jan. 28	22 Mar. 36	21 Jan. 45	do	
Henry R. Eardley Wilmot, *Captain*, Royal **Artillery**	21 June 34	10 Jan. 37	4 Sept. 45	do	
Hon. Thomas O'Grady, *Major*, 74 Foot	30 Dec. 26	24 Nov. 29	3 Oct. 34	10 July	
Thomas James Valiant, *Major*, 40 Foot	29 May 28	17 Dec. 29	1 May 35	do	
John Thomas Griffiths, *Major*, 6 Foot	6 Sept. 14	17 May 21	1 Sept. 31	7 Aug.	
Henry Calley, *Major*, 10 Foot	29 July 36	2 Feb. 39	30 Aug. 42	7 Aug.	
James St. John Munro, *Major*, Unattached	29 Mar. 27	9 Aug. 32	17 Nov. 37	14 Aug.	14 Aug. 46
James Ferguson, *Major*, 79 Foot	27 July 32	7 Aug. 35	18 Sept. 40	25 Aug.	
John Claridge Burmester, *Captain*, **Royal Engineers**	9 June 34	10 Jan. 37	1 April 46	2 Oct.	
𝔚 William How Hennis, *Captain*, **Royal Artillery**	18 Dec. 13	1 Aug. 16	5 June 35	20 Oct.	
Robert Miller Mundy, *Captain*, h. **p. Royal Artillery**	21 June 33	28 Dec. 35	28 April 44	do	27 Sept. 47
Lewis Coker, *Captain*, 29 Foot	11 Aug. 37	27 Sept. 39	4 April 45	do	
Henry Darby Griffith, *Major*, 2 **Dragoons**	25 Nov. 28	25 Nov. 31	1 Aug. 34	6 Nov.	
Sir William Gordon, *Bart.*, *Major*, **66 Foot**	5 June 28	27 April 32	12 May 37	do	
W. Holland L. D. Cuddy, *Captain*, **55 Foot**	31 May 33	27 Nov. 35	24 Oct. 45	do	
Isaac Foster, *Captain*, **3 West India Regiment**	25 May 11	14 Sept. 18	15 April 29	9 Nov.	
Archibald Campbell,[146] ***Captain*, h. p. 2 Ceylon Regt., *Staff Officer of Pensioners***	26 April 10	29 July 13	11 June	do	11 Aug. 29
Robert Alex. Andrews, *Captain*, on retired full pay, 30 Foot	18 Aug. 14	27 Mar. 24	20 Aug.	do	
John Spence, *Major*, 5 Foot	7 Nov. 22	25 June 24	5 Nov.	do	
James Draper, *Major*, 64 F., *Dep. **Assist. Adjutant General in Dublin***	18 Dec. 23	19 Nov. 25	24 Dec.	do	
John Harris, *Captain*, 24 Foot	28 Aug. 07	21 July 09	11 May 30	do	
𝔓 Thomas John Taylor, *Captain*, **78 Foot**	12 Mar. 12	7 Sept. 14	17 May	do	
𝔓 Thomas Beckham,[149] *Captain*, **Unatt., *Staff Officer of Pensioners***	7 May 11	23 Feb. 13	8 June	do	8 Mar. 45
Samuel Ives Sutton, ***Captain*, h. p. Portuguese Service, *Staff Officer of Pensioners***	22 Sept. 25	16 Nov. 26	11 June	do	20 Oct. '37
Henry Richmond Jones, ***Captain*, 6 Dragoon Guards**	9 June 25	14 Nov. 26	12 June	do	
Sir James Edward Alexander, *Captain*, **14 Foot, *Aide-de-Camp to*** *the Commander of the Forces in **North America***	20 Jan. 25	26 Nov. 25	18 June	do	
David Burns, *Captain*, 19 Foot	17 Oct. 11	25 Jan. 16	20 July	do	
𝔓 Edward L'Estrange, *Captain*, 70 **Foot**	10 Nov. 08	19 April 10	9 Nov.	do	
Benoit Bender, *Captain*, 82 Foot	29 Dec.	4 April	26 Nov.	do	
Richard Henry John Beaumont M'Cumming, ***Captain*, 15 Foot**	16 Dec. 24	6 Oct. 25	do	do	
𝔓 William Atkin, *Captain*, R. Canadi**an Rifles**	9 Mar. 10	2 July 11	31 Dec.	do	

	Ensign, etc.	Lieut.	Captain.	Major.	When placed on Half-Pay.
Donald Stuart, *Captain*, 46 Foot	2 May 16	25 Feb. 20	1 April 31	9 Nov. 46	
Henry Francis Ainslie, *Captain*, 83 Foot	29 Jan. 24	7 Nov. 26	5 April	do	
John Rowley Heyland, *Captain*, 35 Foot	8 Jan. 24	7 Jan. 26	12 April	do	
William Henry Robinson, *Captain*, 72 Foot	8 Jan. 24	29 Aug. 26	21 June	do	
Richard Watkins Bamford, *Capt.*, Unatt., ***Staff Officer of Pensioners***	9 April 25	20 Mar. 28	12 July	do	13 July 39
George F. Mylius, *Captain*, 26 Foot	17 Oct. 24	28 Jan. 26	30 Aug.	do	
Thomas Josephus Deverell, *Major*, 67 Foot	7 Nov. 22	25 June 29	30 Aug.	do	
Martin Orr,[151] *Captain*, Unatt., *Staff Officer of* ***Pensioners***	never	28 June 10	31 Oct.	do	23 Feb. 38
William Bletterman Caldwell, *Major*, Unattached, ***Commandant of*** *Pensioners, Hudson's Bay*	29 Sept. 14	28 Oct. 24	9 Dec.	do	2 June 48
Thomas Maitland Wilson, *Major*, 96 Foot	15 April 24	13 May 26	23 Dec.	do	
Abraham Splaine, *Captain*, 81 Foot	28 Oct. 24	22 April 26	16 Mar. 32	do	
Robert Bush, *Captain*, 96 Foot	22 April 26	5 June 27	23 Mar.	do	
Henry Fred. Hawker, *Capt.*, h.p. 12 Foot, ***Staff Officer of Pensioners***	24 Oct. 11	22 Feb. 16	12 April	do	10 Jan. 34
William Taylor, *Captain*, Royal Marines	30 Sept. 05	4 Sept. 09	16 April	do	
James Alexander Robertson, *Major*, 82 Foot	6 Mar. 23	17 Sept. 25	8 June	do	
Charles Kelson, *Captain*, Ceylon Regiment	26 Sept. 11	4 Mar. 13	10 June	do	
Edward Trevor,[152] *Captain*, h. p. Royal Artillery, ***Staff Officer*** *of Pensioners*	4 June 10	17 Dec. 13	23 June	do	17 April 45
James Ward, *Captain*, 81 Foot	25 May 15	23 June 25	6 July	do	
John Norman, *Captain*, 54 Foot	2 July 12	9 Nov. 15	9 July	do	
Angus William Mackay, *Captain*, 21 Foot	24 July 02	30 June 08	27 July	do	
George Herbert Fred. Campbell, *Captain*, h. p. **R. Staff Corps**, *Staff Officer of Pensioners*	never	11 June 30	27 July	do	27 May 42
James Robert Brunker, *Captain*, 15 Foot	9 April 25	9 Sept. 28	14 Sept.	do	
Gervase Parker Bushe, *Major*, Unattached	8 April 26	26 Sept. 26	21 Sept.	do	10 Dec. 47
Jasper Byng Creagh,[154] *Capt.* h. p. 29 Foot	9 April 25	12 June 28	5 Oct.	do	12 Dec. 43
Charles Compton Pratt, *Captain*, Royal Marines	14 Oct. 05	14 May 10	12 Oct.	do	
Henry Ivatt Delacombe, *Captain*, do.	21 Oct. 05	30 June 10	do	do	
George Hunt Coryton, *Captain*, do.	9 Nov. 05	22 Sept. 10	do	do	
John Ashmore, *Captain*, do.	19 Nov. 05	19 Dec. 10	do	do	
Richard Lyde Hornbrook, *Captain*, do.	8 Feb. 06	9 Jan. 12	do	do	
John M'Mahon Kidd, *Major*, 87 Foot	21 July 25	8 Nov. 27	28 Dec.	do	
Hen. B. Harvey, *Capt.*, 87 F., *Aide-de-Camp to Lt.* ***Gov. of Portsmouth***	24 Dec. 25	24 Nov. 26	28 Dec.	do	
Edward A. G. Muller, *Captain*, 1 Foot	3 Feb. 20	11 Aug. 25	11 Jan. 38	do	
William Jonathan Clerke, *Captain*, 77 Foot	24 Feb. 25	10 June 26	18 Jan. 38	do	

	ENSIGN, &c.	LIEUT.	CAPTAIN.	MAJOR.	WHEN PLACED ON HALF-PAY.
Charles Frederick Parkinson, *Captain*, Unattached, *Aide-de-Camp to the Colonel on the Staff in South Wales*	10 Nov. 25	4 Sept. 28	22 Feb. 33	9 Nov. 46	
Abraham Bolton, *Captain*, 5 Dragoon Guards	18 Oct. 25	26 June 27	8 Mar.	do	
Walter Hamilton, *Major*, 78 Foot	28 Jan. 19	15 April 24	15 Mar.	do	
James Graham, *Captain*, 89 Foot	28 April 25	19 April 27	19 April	do	
Richard Leckonby Phipps, *Major*, Unattached	10 April 25	31 Dec. 28	3 May	do	19 May 48
Jaffray Nicholson, *Captain*, 99 Foot	20 Nov. 24	22 April 26	5 July	do	
Thomas Tulloch, *Captain*, 42 Foot	25 June 26	23 Oct. 28	12 July	do	
George Ogle Moore, *Captain*, 82 Foot	18 Sept. 28	3 Dec. 30	12 July	do	
Hon. Charles Robert Weld Forester, *Captain*, Unattached, *Assistant Military Secretary to the Lieut.-General commanding in Ireland*	18 Dec. 27	8 Aug. 30	23 Aug.	do	4 April 45
Walter Campbell, *Captain*, Unatt., *Staff Officer of Pensioners*	23 June 25	25 June 29	20 Sept.	do	5 April 39
Charles Fegen, *Captain*, Royal Marines	30 Nov. 05	26 Jan. 11	30 Sept.	do	
Edward Sterling Farmar, *Capt.*, Unatt., *Staff Officer of Pensioners*	3 Jan. 17	10 Jan. 22	18 Oct.	do	26 May 44
Richard Wolfe,[156] *Captain*, h. p. *Sub-Inspector of Militia*	7 Feb. 11	3 Dec. 12	10 Dec.	do	19 Mar. 37
John Ed. Orange,[157] *Capt.*, h.p., 34 F. Unatt., *Staff Officer of Pensioners*	10 April 25	15 Oct. 27	27 Dec.	do	30 July 44
John Hildebrand Oakes Moore, *Major*, 44 Foot	25 Oct. 27	26 April 31	31 Dec.	do	
Thomas Scott,[158] *Captain*, Royal Marines, on retired full pay	11 Feb. 06	15 Jan. 12	7 Jan. 34	do	
Luke Smyth O'Connor, *Major*, 1 West India Regiment	27 April 27	22 Mar. 31	17 Jan.	do	
James Piggott, *Captain*, St. Helena Regiment	6 April 15	9 April 25	14 Feb.	do	
Alfred Horne, *Captain*, 12 Foot	29 Nov. 25	27 Nov. 28	21 Feb.	do	
Gervas Stanford Deverill, *Captain*, 90 Foot	2 Nov. 26	18 Nov. 27	7 Mar.	do	
[illegible] Loftus Francis Jones,[159] *Major*, Unattached	7 Feb. 11	1 Oct. 12	9 Mar.	do	14 Jan. 48
Henry Phipps Raymond, *Major*, 1 Foot	9 April 25	17 May 27	21 Mar.	do	
Henry Sadleir Bruere, *Major*, 43 Foot	1 Sept. 25	19 Feb. 28	8 April	do	
Wm. Joshua Crompton, *Captain*, Unatt., *Staff Officer of Pensioners*	10 Sept. 25	12 Dec. 26	11 April	do	5 Dec. 40
Thomas Myddelton Biddulph, *Captain*, 1 Life Guards	7 Oct. 26	23 Feb. 29	16 May	do	
William Lewis Dawes, *Captain*, Royal Marines	22 Aug. 06	14 July 13	27 May	do	
C B John Alexander Philips, *Captain*, Royal Marines	26 Aug. 06	17 July 13	do	do	
William Joliffe, *Captain*, Royal Marines	4 May 07	18 April 14	27 May	do	
Thomas E. Lacy, *Captain*, Unattached, *Town Major of Gibraltar*	8 April 25	3 Oct. 26	11 July	do	8 Oct. 47
Philip Smyly, *Captain*, 99 Foot	27 Mar. 28	18 June 30	18 July	do	
[illegible] Burke Cuppage, *Captain*, Royal Artillery	17 Dec. 12	20 June 15	20 July	do	
Oswald Samuel Blachford, *Captain*, 15 Hussars	6 Dec. 27	13 Sept. 31	1 Aug.	do	
Robert Burn, *Capt.*, R. Art., *Brigade Major to R. Art. at Montreal*	17 Dec. 12	20 June 15	14 Aug.	do	
[illegible] Richard Beaumont Burnaby, *Captain*, Royal Artillery	17 Dec. 12	28 June 15	9 Sept.	do	
John Gray, *Captain*, Unatt., *Staff Officer of Pens. in New Zealand*	31 Aug. 24	4 May 26	12 Sept.	do	7 May 47

	ENSIGN, ETC.	LIEUT.	CAPTAIN.	MAJOR.	WHEN PLACED ON HALF-PAY.
Thomas Coryndon Luxmoore, *Captain*, Royal Engineers	1 Jan. 14	1 Aug. 14	6 Nov. 34	9 Nov. 46	
Edward Charles Soden, *Major*, 2 West India Regiment	1 Feb. 16	27 June 24	10 Nov.	do	
John Hungerford Griffin, *Captain*, Royal Artillery	5 July 13	28 Oct. 15	21 Nov.	do	
Brownlow Villiers Layard, *Major*, 9 Foot	24 July 23	20 Jan. 26	21 Nov.	do	
Thomas Arscott Lethbridge, *Captain*, Royal Artillery	5 July 13	17 Nov. 15	20 Dec.	do	
Charles Hugh Lyle Tinling, *Captain*, 74 Foot	30 Nov. 17	3 May 21	30 Dec.	do	
Wyndham Edward Hanmer, *Captain*, R. Horse Guards	26 Mar. 29	15 Mar. 31	9 Jan. 35	do	
[illegible] John Impett, *Captain*, 25 Foot	14 April 14	5 Oct. 20	30 Jan.	do	
William Faris, *Captain*, Royal Engineers	1 Jan. 14	1 Aug. 14	1 Mar.	do	
James Kennard Pipon, *Captain*, h. p. 68 Foot, *Assistant Military Secretary to Commander-in-Chief at Malta*	3 Aug. 26	9 Dec. 28	6 Mar.	do	31 Mar. 43
George Wynell Mayow, *Captain*, Unattached	9 June 25	12 Feb. 30	6 Mar.	do	8 Oct. 47
Henry Robert Thurlow, *Captain*, 90 Foot, *Aide-de-Camp to the Master General of the Ordnance*	11 Aug. 25	8 Jan. 29	27 Mar.	do	
Geo. Talbot, *Cap.* 43 F., *Aide-de-Camp to the Comm. of the Forces in Canada*	2 Feb. 26	9 Sept. 28	3 April	do	
James Campbell, *Major*, 87 Foot	6 July 26	31 July 28	10 April	do	
John Fras. DuVernet,[161] *Capt.*, h.p., R. African Corps, *Staff Officer of Pens.*	27 Mar. 25	8 April 26	24 April	do	4 April 45
Edward Littledale, *Major*, 1 Dragoons	24 Dec. 29	21 Dec. 32	1 May	do	
Charles Murray, *Major*, 16 Foot	1 Sept. 15	13 Oct. 21	5 May	do	
Robert Baillie, *Major*, Unattached	8 Oct. 25	3 Aug. 30	29 May	do	19 May 47
Richard Going, *Captain*, 1 Foot	9 April 26	2 Feb. 27	19 June	do	
Robert Sherbourne Murray, *Captain*, Unattached	21 June 27	29 Mar. 33	19 June	do	6 Oct. 48
Frederick Henry Baddeley, *Captain*, Royal Engineers	1 Jan. 14	1 Aug. 14	25 June	do	
William Calder, *Captain*, Unatt., *Staff Officer of Pensioners*	14 July 14	24 June 24	6 July	do	27 Jan. 37
Hugh Plunkett Bourchier,[163] *Captain*, h. p. 19 Dragoons, *Town Major of Kingston, Canada*	12 May 14	20 Nov. 23	7 Aug.	do	6 Dec. 39
John Bolton,[164] *Captain*, on retired full pay, 75 Foot	5 Nov. 13	26 Mar. 19	4 Sept.	do	
[illegible] Mountford Stoughton Heyliger Lloyd,[165] *Major*, Unattached	16 Dec. 13	2 Mar. 15	13 Sept.	do	26 May 48
William Barnes,[166] *Captain*, on retired full pay, 17 Foot	4 Feb. 13	23 July 14	14 Sept.	do	
William Calamy, *Captain*, Royal Marines	18 June 07	14 June 20	24 Sept.	do	
Thomas Holmes Tidy, *Captain*, 14 Foot	14 April 25	28 Sept. 26	2 Oct.	do	
Charles James, *Major*, 63 Foot	29 Nov. 27	20 Jan. 32	9 Oct.	do	
Daniel Riley,[167] *Captain*, on retired full pay, 24 Foot	13 Jan. 25	15 Dec. 25	25 Oct.	do	
James Stuart, *Captain*, h. p., 84 Foot, *Staff Officer of Pensioners*	20 April 15	15 Dec. 25	13 Nov.	do	31 Dec. 44
George Edward Aylmer, *Captain*, 93 Foot	28 Feb. 28	13 Aug. 30	24 Nov.	do	
Daniel Thorndike, *Captain*, Royal Artillery	1 May 15	8 May 19	28 Dec.	do	
Harry Stow, *Captain*, Royal Artillery	do	26 Dec. 19	4 Feb. 36	do	

	Ensign, etc.	Lieut.	Captain.	Major.	When placed on half-pay.
KH Henry Anderson, *Staff Captain at Chatham*	22 June 13	15 June 15	12 Feb. 36	9 Nov. 46	
Henry Douglas Cowper, *Captain*, 40 Foot	20 July 30	14 Dec. 32	4 Mar.	do	
Alexander Jardine, *Captain*, 75 Foot	22 April 26	25 Feb. 30	11 Mar.	do	
William Fraser, *Captain*, Royal Artillery	1 May 15	5 Mar. 20	18 Mar.	do	
Edward Foy, *Major*, 71 Foot	22 Nov. 27	15 June 30	do	do	
Henry Alexander Kerr, *Captain*, 1 Foot	17 Aug. 26	22 Mar. 32	do	do	
John Roche, *Captain*, Unattached	27 Oct. 26	29 Jan. 30	25 Mar.	do	14 Apr. 48
Charles Gostling, *Captain*, Royal Artillery	1 May 15	22 April 20	19 April	do	
James Clarke, *Major*, 1 West India Regiment	11 Jan. 21	19 July 27	21 April	do	
Mountjoy Francis Martin, *Captain*, 2 Life Guards	27 Dec. 27	22 Mar. 31	22 April	do	
Charles Henry Mee, *Captain*, Royal Artillery	1 May 15	11 May 20	27 April	do	
KH Thomas Deacon, *Captain*, 25 Foot	5 April 13	3 Aug. 15	29 April	do	
Thomas Budgen, *Captain*, Royal Engineers	1 Aug. 14	1 July 15	13 May	do	
William Henry Gillman, *Captain*, 68 Foot	1 July 28	14 May 31	do	do	
John Wegg, *Captain*, 56 Foot	18 Dec. 28	10 Mar. 33	20 May	do	
Theophilus Desbrisay, *Captain*, Royal Artillery	1 May 15	12 May 20	25 May	do	
B Wm. Harloe Phibbs,[160] *Capt.*, Unatt., *Staff Officer of Pensioners*	30 Oct. 10	24 June 13	3 June	do	11 May 38
Robert Clifford Lloyd, *Major*, 76 Foot	30 Dec. 26	8 June 30	do	do	
Vincent Joseph Biscoe, *Captain*, Royal Engineers	1 Aug. 14	1 July 15	11 June	do	
Jas. Fraser, *Capt.*, 35 F., *Aide-de-Camp to the Governor of the Mauritius*	5 April 31	1 Aug. 34	17 June	do	
Mitchell George Sparks, *Captain*, 10 Foot	4 Nov. 19	26 Dec. 23	28 June	do	
Charles Bertie Symons, *Captain*, Royal Artillery	10 July 15	2 Dec. 21	1 July	do	
Andrew Armstrong Barnes, *Major*, 25 Foot	21 July 25	28 May 29	do	do	
George Fred. Cooper Scott, *Captain*, 76 Foot	25 Oct. 27	3 May 31	do	do	
Thomas Congreve Robe, *Captain*, Royal Artillery	11 Dec. 15	30 Dec. 22	10 Aug.	do	
William Beales, *Captain*, h. p. 9 Drs., *Staff Officer of Pensioners*	24 June 13	13 Dec. 21	12 Aug.	do	30 Aug. 44
Thomas Abbott, *Major*, 3 West India Regiment	13 Aug. 12	7 April 14	18 Aug.	do	
Archibald Inglis Lockhart, *Captain*, 92 Foot	31 Dec. 28	11 June 30	19 Aug.	do	
William Shaw, *Captain*, 3 West India Regiment	15 Mar. 27	26 April 31	19 Aug.	do	
Wm. M'Pherson, *Captain*, Unatt., *Staff Officer of Pensioners*	22 Nov. 21	22 Sept. 25	17 Sept.	do	8 April 42
Henry Powell Wulff, *Captain*, Royal Engineers	1 Aug. 14	1 July 15	23 Sept.	do	
Thomas Moore, *Captain*, 12 Foot	30 Mar. 14	25 Nov. 21	30 Sept.	do	
John Forbes, *Captain*, Unatt., *Staff Officer of Pensioners*	21 Nov. 11	21 Oct. 13	13 Oct.	do	20 Dec. 44
Johnson Ford, *Captain*, 43 Foot	7 Sept. 26	25 June 29	21 Oct.	do	
George M'Beath, *Captain*, 68 Foot	15 Oct. 29	31 May 33	28 Oct.	do	
Hon. Horace Pitt, *Captain*, Royal Horse Guards	27 Feb. 30	6 July 32	11 Nov.	do	

	ENSIGN, ETC.	LIEUT.	CAPTAIN.	MAJOR.	WHEN PLACED ON HALF-PAY.
William Robert Haliday, *Captain*, 93 Foot	12 Feb. 30	3 Mar. 33	11 Nov. 36	9 Nov. 46	
C. James Fynmore,[171] *Captain*, Royal Marines, on retired full pay	1 Sept. 08	4 May 22	15 Nov.	do	
William Johnston, *Captain*, 65 Foot	7 Jan. 26	6 Nov. 27	22 Nov.	do	
John William Yerbury, *Major*, 3 Dragoons	12 Dec. 26	5 July 33	1 July 37	do	
Lorenzo Rothe, *Major*, 36 Foot	6 Mar. 28	21 Aug. 35	2 April 41	20 Nov.	
Gregory Lewis Way, *Major*, 29 Foot	17 Feb. 32	30 July 36	21 May 41	8 Dec.	
John Blackburn, *Major*, 85 Foot	15 June 32	1 Sept. 37	16 Nov. 41	29 Dec. 46	
Henry Fane, *do.* 4 Light Dragoons	1 Aug. 34	30 July 36	6 May 42	29 Dec.	
John Edward Dupuis, *Captain*, Royal Artillery	13 Feb. 25	8 Nov. 27	15 June 40	8 Jan. 47	
Michael William Smith, *Major*, 15 Hussars	19 Nov. 30	21 Feb. 34	23 Apr. 39	9 Feb.	
Rodolph de Salis, *do.* 8 Hussars	17 Dec. 30	28 June 33	13 July 38	19 Feb.	
William Robinson, *Captain*, Royal Engineers	22 Sept. 26	6 Oct. 31	24 Oct. 42	19 Feb.	
William Devonish Deverell,[173] *Major*, Unattached	4 May 15	16 Nov. 20	7 April 37	5 March	5 Mar. 47
James Harington Trevelyan, *Major*, Unattached	16 April 29	24 Aug. 32	7 April 37	do	28 Jan. 48
Hon. Robert Needham, *do.* 12 Lancers	23 Aug. 33	12 Dec. 34	2 July 41	30 March	
John Hamilton Esten, *do.* Rifle Brigade	30 Aug. 26	30 Mar. 32	31 May 39	14 April	
Trevor Chute, *Major*, 70 Foot	10 Aug. 32	28 Oct. 36	2 Aug. 39	23 April	
Charles Edward Michel, *Major*, 66 Foot	25 Nov. 28	23 Nov. 33	2 Feb. 38	25 June	
Richard Henry Fitz Herbert, *Major*, Rifle Brigade	3 July 27	11 Jan. 33	25 Oct. 39	2 July	
Thomas Westropp M'Mahon,[174] *do.* Unattached	24 Dec. 29	2 Dec. 31	9 June 38	13 July	13 July 47
*Carlo Cutajar, *do.* R. Malta Fencible Regiment	24 Feb. 22	23 Jan. 25	17 Feb. 37	20 July	
Philip M. Nelson Guy, *do.* 5 Foot	23 Sept. 24	12 June 28	29 Dec. 37	20 July	
Philip Charles Cavan, *do.* 30 Foot	19 Dec. 34	1 Mar. 39	23 Apr. 41	30 July	
James Campbell, *do.* 61 Foot	22 Feb. 27	1 Apr. 31	25 Dec. 38	31 July	
W. Sherbrook Ramsay Norcott, *do.* Rifle Brigade	13 June 22	16 June 25	21 Feb. 40	1 Aug.	
Robert Sanders, *do.* 19 Foot	26 May 37	26 Jan. 41	3 Feb. 43	6 Aug.	
Wm. Twistleton Layard, *do.* Ceylon Rifle Regiment	22 Feb. 33	22 Nov. 36	16 Aug. 39	28 Sept.	
William Carden Seton, *do.* 41 Foot	2 Mar. 32	22 July 36	22 May 40	15 Oct.	
Exham Schomberg Turner Swyny, *Major*, 63 Foot	1 Oct. 29	17 Oct. 33	8 Aug. 38	22 Oct.	
Henry Edward Doherty, *Major*, 14 Light Dragoons	31 Dec. 33	15 July 36	17 May 39	22 Oct.	
Phillpotts Wright Taylor, *do.* R. Canadian Rifle Regiment	16 Mar. 32	4 Mar. 36	30 Oct. 40	5 Nov.	
Daniel Gardner Freer, *do.* 17 Foot	20 Nov. 23	6 April 26	7 May 41	12 Nov.	
Benjamin Brown, *do.* 78 Foot	7 July 25	15 May 28	22 Mar. 44	do	
John MacDuff, *do.* 40 Foot	10 Feb. 14	26 June 27	18 April 32	18 Nov.	

	CORNET, ETC.	LIEUT.	CAPTAIN.	MAJOR.	WHEN PLACED ON HALFPAY.
William R. Mansfield, *Major*, 53 Foot	27 Nov. 35	31 Aug. 38	10 Feb. 43	3 Dec. 47	
George O'Halloran Gavin, *do.* 16 Lancers	13 Nov. 27	14 Oct. 29	26 May 37	10 Dec.	
Charles Hagart, *do.* 7 Hussars	15 June 32	12 Aug. 34	21 Oct. 37	do	
Donald Meent Cameron, *do.* 3 Foot	26 April 28	17 Mar. 39	13 Mar. 40	do	
William Irwin, *Major*, 88 Foot	15 Nov. 27	19 Nov. 30	26 April 39	18 Jan. 48	
George Francis White, *Major*, 31 Foot	27 Jan. 25	3 April 28	9 Nov. 41	21 Jan.	
William C. E. Napier, *Captain*, 25 Foot	28 Aug. 35	17 Nov. 37	29 April 42	18 Feb.	
William M. G. M'Murdo, *Captain*, 78 Foot	1 July 37	5 Jan. 41	7 July 43	do	
John Eardley Wilmot Inglis, *Major*, 32 Foot	2 Aug. 33	19 Jan. 39	29 Sept. 43	25 Feb.	
Eric Mackay Clarke, *Major*, 3 West India Regt.	20 Nov. 30	6 June 35	30 June 43	10 Mar.	
Richard D. Kelly, *Major*, 34 Foot	7 Mar. 34	30 July 36	24 Sept. 41	17 Mar.	
Arthur Cyril Goodenough, *Major*, 34 Foot	6 April 34	25 Nov. 36	26 Oct. 41	27 Mar.	
Hallam D'Arcy Kyle, *Major*, 45 Foot	12 July 33	23 June 37	24 May 39	7 April	
Charles Steuart, *Major*, 14 Light Dragoons	10 Dec. 25	5 Feb. 29	9 Nov. 38	25 April	
Henry Smyth, *Major*, 68 Foot	28 June 33	28 Oct. 36	2 Dec. 42	12 May	
John Burns, *Major*, 2 Foot	27 April 27	15 Mar. 33	18 May 38	23 May	
Henry William Stisted, *Major*, 78 Foot	4 Dec. 35	29 Sept. 38	29 April 42	26 May	
Charles Edmund Doherty, *Major*, 13 Light Dragoons	24 April 35	6 Jan. 37	4 Sept. 40	23 June	
Hector Harvest, *Major*, Unattached	20 April 15	7 April 25	28 June 38	18 July	18 July 48
Thomas Charles Timins, *Major*, 70 Foot	16 Mar. 32	28 Nov. 37	3 Feb. 43	do	
William R. Preston, *Major*, 45 Foot	24 Sept. 29	22 Feb. 33	18 Oct. 39	19 July	
Thomas Miller, *Major*, 10 Foot	9 Jan. 17	19 April 27	16 July 41	1 Aug.	
Stanhope William Jephson, *Major*, 2 Foot	26 Nov. 30	19 Feb. 36	28 Dec. 41	4 Aug.	
William Francis Hoey, *Major*, 30 Foot	28 Oct. 31	5 Sept. 35	22 July 42	do	
Robert Jocelyn Straton, *Major*, 77 Foot	10 Jan. 28	18 Jan. 33	26 April 39	18 Aug.	
Usher Williamson, *Major*, 27 Foot	29 Aug. 26	11 Nov. 31	28 Feb. 40	do	
John Brathwaite Bonham, *Major*, 50 Foot	1 Oct. 29	28 May 33	30 July 38	25 Aug.	
William Case, *Major*, 32 Foot	10 Feb. 32	9 Feb. 38	25 Feb. 42	13 Sept.	
William Fenwick, *Major*, 10 Foot	26 Dec. 34	8 June 39	15 April 42	do	
George Anthony Durnford, *Captain*, 27 Foot	3 Mar. 25	15 Dec. 25	6 Nov. 38	15 Sept.	
William Glendonwyn Scott, *Captain*, 91 Foot	30 Mar. 32	12 June 35	22 Feb. 39	do	
John Walpole, *Captain*, Royal Engineers	1 Aug. 16	24 Sept. 25	28 Nov. 39	do	
Charles Herrick Burnaby, *Captain*, Royal Artillery	9 June 25	14 Nov. 27	12 Aug. 40	do	
Thomas Donovan, *Captain*, Cape Mounted Riflemen	15 Mar. 27	16 May 33	19 Nov. 41	do	
Charles Seagram, *Captain*, 45 Foot	22 June 26	5 Mar. 31	15 April 42	do	
Charles Assheton FitzHarding Berkeley, *Lt. & Capt.* Scots Fus. Gds.	27 May 36	12 Aug. 37	14 April 43	do	

	ENSIGN, ETC.	LIEUT.	CAPTAIN.	MAJOR.	WHEN PLACED ON HALF PAY.
St. John Thomas Browne, *Captain*, Royal Artillery	20 June 32	11 July 34	18 May 43	15 Sept. 48	
William Hogge, *Captain*, 7 Dragoon Guards	30 Oct. 35	14 Jan. 42	27 June 45	do	
Charles Lennox Brownlow Maitland, *Lt. & Capt.* Grenadier Guards	never	9 April 41	27 Mar. 46	do	
Charles Colville Young, *Captain*, Royal Artillery	19 Dec. 34	29 Jan. '37	1 April 46	do	
John T. Bisset, *Captain*, Cape Mounted Riflemen	7 Feb. 40	16 Feb. 44	1 April 47	do	
Alexander Maxwell, *Major*, 46 Foot	19 June 35	28 Dec. 38	27 Sept. 42	19 Sept.	
John Douglas Johnstone, *Major*, 33 Foot	15 Aug. 27	16 Mar. 30	19 Oct. 38	3 Oct.	
William Charles Forrest, *Major*, 4 Dragoon Guards	11 Mar. 36	5 Jan. 39	7 Sept. 41	do	
Bertie Edward Murray Gordon, *Major*, 91 Foot	26 Oct. 32	24 July 35	23 April 41	13 Oct.	
Frederick George Ainslie, *Major*, 21 Foot	24 April 28	5 Oct. 32	26 June 38	20 Oct.	
Charles Howe Spence, *Major*, 60 Foot	20 April 25	28 Sept. 26	24 May 41	do	
Henry Farrant, *Major*, 81 Foot	9 July 30	13 Feb. 35	10 May 44	3 Nov.	
James W. Llewellyn Paxton, *Major*, 69 Foot	19 April 27	12 Oct. 30	6 July 38	10 Nov.	
Alexander G. Grant, *Major*, 85 Foot	4 Oct. 33	18 Dec. 35	5 Aug. 42	do	
Henry Renny, *Major*, 81 Foot	27 Dec. 33	7 Aug. 35	29 May 44	17 Nov.	
Nathan Smith Gardiner, *Major* 44 Foot	23 July 25	18 July 34	26 Jan. 41	24 Nov.	
Henry George Hart, *Major*, 49 Foot	1 April 29	19 July 32	1 Dec. 42	15 Dec.	
Henry Dalrymple White, *Major*, 6 Dragoons	11 May 38	8 Feb. 39	17 May 44	22 Dec.	
Edward Morant, *Major*, 12 Royal Lancers	20 Sept. 33	24 April 35	11 Nov. 42	do	
Nathaniel Massey Stack, 71 Foot	25 Nov. 28	29 Dec. 35	6 July 38	do	
John Henry Bringhurst, *Major*, 90 Foot	7 Sept. 32	17 Mar. 38	30 Sept. 42	do	
George A. L. Blenkinsopp, *Major*, 45 Foot	4 Sept. 35	31 May 39	29 Mar. 44	do	
Thomas Bunbury Gough, *Major*, 33 Foot	27 Dec. 27	25 Jan. 31	23 Nov. 38	do	

1 Major Ross accompanied the 78th to Holland, and was present at the sortie of Nimeguen, and in several other engagements on the Waal. He served afterwards with the 87th, at the attack on Porto Rico, and capture of Surinam, and in the Brigand War in St. Lucia. Also in South America, and was present at the siege and capture of Monte Video (where he scaled the walls in the command of three companies), and captured a stand of colours, and secured a quantity of arms: at the attack on Buenos Ayres he received three wounds, one of which carried his left eye out of its socket. He accompanied the Regt. to the Peninsula; but, from the state of his wounds, was obliged to return to England.

2 Major Langlands served in the Peninsula with the 74th, and has received a medal and a clasp for the assaults and captures of Ciudad Rodrigo and Badajos, slightly wounded at the former, and severely at the latter.

3 Major de Brem served the campaigns in Germany from 1792 to 1800; in Egypt, in 1801; in Naples in 1805; in Calabria in 1806; in Egypt in 1807; at the taking of Ischia in 1809; at the siege of Santa Maura in 1810; at the defeat of the French in Sicily, in the same year; in the campaigns of 1811, 12, 13, 14 in the Peninsula and South of France. Severely wounded in Germany on the 30th September 1796; and again at the battle of the Pyrenees, on the 30th July 1813.

4 Major Spinluff served at the capture of the Cape of Good Hope in 1806.

5 Major Hamerton accompanied the 7th Fusiliers to the Peninsula in Feb. 1809, and was present at the capture of Oporto, battles of Talavera and Busaco, lines of Torres Vedras, sieges of Ciudad Rodrigo and Badajos, battles of Salamanca (severely wounded), Vittoria, Roncesvalles, the heights of Pampeluna, and the Pyrenees, where he was again severely wounded. Served also the campaign of 1815, and was present at the capture of Paris.

6 Major Christopher Wilkinson served the campaign of 1799 in Holland, under the Duke of York. Accompanied the expedition to the north of Germany in 1805, under Lord Cathcart.

7 Major Sandham served the campaign of 1799 in Holland, including the actions of the 27th Aug., 10th and 19th Sept., and 2d Oct. Expedition to Copenhagen in 1807; to Sweden, and afterwards to Portugal and Spain, under Sir John Moore in 1808-9; subsequently to Walcheren, in 1809; the campaign in Holland, in 1814; and in Flanders and France, in 1815, including the battle of Waterloo.

8 Major Gore served with the 89th regt. in the American war, including the actions at Chrystler's Farm, 11th Nov. 1813, and Niagara, 25th July 1814, where he was taken prisoner and detained until the end of the war. He served also throughout the Burmese war, and commanded a detachment under Major Sale in defence of the lines of Rangoon, and the regt. five times in action during the campaign.

9 Major J. W. Henderson served with the 8th West India Regiment at the capture of the Danish West India Islands, in 1801; and was afterwards present at the suppression of the mutiny of that regiment at Prince Rupert's, in Dominica. Served with the 3d West India Regiment at the storming and capture of Morne Fortunée, in St. Lucia, and at the capture of Tobago. Joined the 50th after the storming of Almaraz, and served in the Peninsula and France until the peace of 1814. Severely wounded in the head at the capture of Aire, on the 2d March 1814.

12 Major Greatly served in South America, under General Whitelock, in 1807; in Portugal and Spain in 1808-9, including the cavalry action at Benevente, and battle of Corunna. Served also at the attack and capture of Guadaloupe in 1810.

13 Major the Honourable Sir Francis Stanhope served in the 11th Foot at the siege of Flushing, in 1809; and with the 1st Life Guards in the Peninsula and South of France, and was on the Staff at the battle of Toulouse.

15 Major Edward Jones served as Adjutant of the 77th at Walcheren in 1809; and in the Peninsula from July 1811 to the end of that war in 1814, including the action of El Bodon, also the sieges and assaults of Ciudad Rodrigo and Badajos. Severely wounded at the storming of Ciudad Rodrigo.

16 Major Adair served with the 27th in Sicily in 1810 and 11; in the Peninsula and France from 1812 to the close of that war in 1814, including the taking of Alcoy, covering the retreat from Biar, battle of Castalla, siege and subsequent blockade of Tarragona, and actions at Villa Franca. Subsequently in Flanders and France, including the occupation of Paris in 1815.

18 Sir Trevor Wheeler served in the Peninsula with the 16th Light Dragoons from June 1810 to the end of that war in 1814, including the pursuit of Massena from the lines, actions of Pombal, Redinha, Foz d'Arouce, and Sabugal; battle of Fuentes d'Onor, actions of Llerena and Castrejon, battle of Salamanca, retreat from Burgos, battles of Vittoria, the Nivelle, and the Nive, 9th to 12th Dec. Served also the campaign of 1815, including the battle of Waterloo.

22 Major Hore served in Egypt in 1801, and has received the medal.

23 Major Lawrence served in Egypt in 1801, and has received the medal.

24 Major R. S. Wilkinson served on board H. M. S. *Diomede*, in Lord Duncan's fleet off Camperdown, blockading the Dutch fleet in the Texel in 1798; after which proceeded to India and fell in with a large body of Malay pirates off Batavia, which were completely destroyed. On board the *Leander* at the capture of the *Ville de Milan* French frigate, and recapture of the *Cleopatra*, off Bermuda. Served also in the expedition on the north coast of Spain, under Sir James Malcolm and Captain Parke. Major Wilkinson has served in every quarter of the globe, and was taken prisoner by the Americans near Norfolk in Virginia while carrying despatches. Medal for services in Egypt.

25 Major James Johnston served at the taking of Madeira in 1807; capture of Guadaloupe

and dependencies, St. Martin's, and St. Eustatius in 1810; also one campaign against the Burmese.

26 Major Goate's services:—Expedition to Germany in 1805 under Lord Cathcart; storming the heights of Soril, siege of Fort Bourbon, and capture of Martinique in 1809; Nepaul war in 1815, and was engaged on the heights of Muckwanpore, 15th Dec.; capture of Hattrass in 1816; Mahratta and Pindaree campaigns of 1817 and 18; Burmese war in 1825 and 26.

28 Major Hunt served at Hanover, in 1805, and 1806; at Copenhagen in 1807; and in the Peninsula from Sept. 1810 to May 1812, including the siege of Ciudad Rodrigo.

29 Major Shadwell Clerke served the Peninsular campaigns of 1808, 9, 10, and first part of 1811, including the battles of Roleia and Vimiera, retreat to Corunna, actions at Lugo and before Corunna, battle of Corunna (contused on the forehead by a musket-ball), operations on the Coa during the siege and battle of Almeida, battle of Busaco, retreat to the lines of Torres Vedras, affair near Leria, and actions of Pombal and Redinha, at which last he was severely wounded in the right leg, which was afterwards amputated.

30 Major Kitson served throughout the Kandian war of 1817, 18, and 19.

31 Major Noel served in St. Domingo in 1796, 97, and 98, under Generals Boyer and Sir Brent Spencer, and was wounded in the right thigh, when the French attacked the Cordon of Posts. Served also at the capture of St. Lucia, Tobago, and the colonies of Demerara, Essequibo, and Berbice.

33 Major Sherer served in the Peninsula with the 34th from July 1809 to Dec. 1811, and from August 1812 to July 1813, including the battles of Busaco, Albuhera, Arroyo de Molino, Vittoria, and Maya in the Pyrenees.

35 Major Samuel Thorpe served with the 23rd in the Peninsula under Sir John Moore, including the action at Lugo and battle of Corunna. Capture of Walcheren in 1809. Subsequently in the Peninsula, including the siege of Olivença, siege of Badajoz in 1811, battle of Albuhera (twice wounded). Served with the 39th at the battle of Toulouse, when he was again severely wounded. Also in the American war at Plattsburg; and subsequently at the capture of Paris.

36 Major Begbie served in the Peninsula with the 82nd from Aug. 1808 to Nov. 1809, including the capture of Oporto and battle of Talavera.

38 Major Macpherson served in Hanover in 1805 and 6; at Buenos Ayres in 1807; in Portugal and Spain from July 1808 to Jan. 1809, including the battles of Roleia and Vimiera; action at Lugo, and battle of Corunna. With the expedition to Walcheren, and siege of Flushing, where he was wounded; the Peninsular campaigns from May to Dec. 1812, including the battle of Salamanca, where he was severely wounded.

39 Major Hartman served in the expedition to Hanover in 1805-6; at the siege of Copenhagen in 1807; in Sweden, Portugal, and Spain in 1808-9, including the advance and retreat of the army and in the battle of Corunna. Expedition to Walcheren, 1809; subsequent campaigns in the Peninsula and France, including the defence of Tarifa and affair of Casas Viejas, battle of Barrosa, actions of Arroyo del Molino and Almarez, battles of Vittoria, the Pyrenees (25th, 30th, and 31st July), Pass of Maya, Nivelle, Nive, Bayonne, and Orthes; affair at St. Palais, and battle of Toulouse.

40 Major Pinckney served with the 36th on the expedition to South America, including the taking of Maldonado and siege of Monte Video; in the Peninsula from June 1808 to May 1809, including the battles of Roleia and Vimiera. On the expedition to Walcheren in 1809; received the flag of truce at the outpost at the attack and capture of Ter Vere; present also at Middleburgh and Flushing.

41 Major Mackay served with the 68th on the expedition to Walcheren, and at the capture of Flushing in 1809. Also in the Peninsula from June 1811 to the end of that war in 1814, including the battle of Salamanca, retreat from Burgos, and battles of Vittoria (wounded in the head), the Pyrenees, the Nivelle, and Orthes.

42 Major Aubin served in the Peninsula from Nov. 1811 to the end of the war, including the battles of Vittoria, the Pyrenees, 25th, 28th, 30th, and 31st July; Nivelle, Nive, 9th, 11th, and 13th Dec. 1813, besides many other minor actions and skirmishes. Severely wounded through the left side, in action at Conches, 18th March 1814. Served subsequently in the American war.

43 Major Brown served the campaign of 1814 in Holland with the 21st, and was present at the storming of Bergen-op-Zoom.

44 Major William Seward served with the 9th in the Peninsula, from Aug. 1808 to Jan. 1809, and was present at the battle of Vimiera; on the expedition to Walcheren in 1809; and subsequently in the Peninsula, including the defence of Tarifa, battles of Barrosa (wounded), Vittoria, and the Nive, and blockade of Bayonne.

45 Major Stack served in the Peninsula with the 24th from June 1809 to Feb. 1813, and again from 2nd Dec. 1813 to the end of that war in 1814, including the battles of Talavera (wounded) and Busaco, actions at Espinal and Foz d'Arouce, repulse of a sortie at Ciudad Rodrigo, battle of Salamanca, capture of the Retiro at Madrid, taking of the hills and outworks before Burgos, siege of Burgos and storming of the breaches (severely contused) various skirmishes with the rear-guard and covering party at the bridge over the Carrion on the retreat, and battle of Orthes, where he was severely wounded by a ball, which shattered the left elbow-joint, and occasioned amputation of the arm. Served eight years in Canada, and received a severe contusion on the head in 1829, when on duty.

46 Major Romney served in the East Indies with the 17th from Dec. 1808 to May 1823, and

was present at the siege and capture of Gounourie in 1807; and the Mahratta campaign of 1817, including the affair at Jubblepore.

47 Major Donaldson served in the Peninsula with the 57th, from June 1809 to the end of that war in 1814, including the siege of Badajos in April 1811, battles of Albuhera, Vittoria, and the Pyrenees.

48 Major Clements served at the capture of the Cape of Good Hope in 1806; subsequently on the expedition to South America; the campaign of 1808-9 in Spain, and extra aide-de-camp to Sir John Moore at the battle of Corunna. On the expedition to Walcheren in 1809; the Peninsular campaigns from 1810 to 1814, including Cavares and Merida, Salamanca, Begar, Vittoria, Valley of Bastan, and the Pyrenees.

49 Major Doyle served with the expedition to South America, including the siege of and sortie from Monte Video, and storm by the enemy of Colonia. Served also in the south of France, from Dec. 1813 to the end of that war in 1814, including the blockade of Bayonne and repulse of the sortie, where he received a contusion on the left arm.

51 Major Meade served in the Peninsula from Sept. 1810 to Oct. 1811, including the battle of Fuentes d'Onor, and other minor affairs. On the staff of General Count Walmoden, in 1813, at the actions of Hasdorf in Mecklenburg, and Goerde in Hanover. Assisted also at the defence of Rostock by the Swedes, where his horse was killed, and his left arm disabled. Served the campaign in Holland, in 1814, including the attack on Merxem, bombardment of Antwerp, and attack on Bergen-op-Zoom.

52 Major Harrison served in the American war.

54 Major Murphy served in the Peninsula from Dec. 1808 until the end of the war, including actions at Albeigana and Grijo, passage of the Douro, capture of Coimbra, siege and capture of San Sebastian, passage of the Bidassoa, action at Bidart (wounded); battles of Nivelle, Nive, 9th, 10th (wounded), 11th, 12th, and 13th Dec.; blockade of Bayonne, action of St. Etienne, and battle of Toulouse. Medal for Toulouse.

55 Major Hooper served in the Peninsula from 1809 to 1811—when he was sent to England on account of his wounds—and was present at the battle of Busaco, lines at Torres Vedras, skirmishes on the retreat of Massena, actions at Campo Mayor and Bella Castel, first siege of Badajos, taking of Olivença, and battle of Albuhera, where he was severely wounded through the shoulder in a charge.

56 Major Willats served in the Peninsula from 1812 to the end of the war, including the siege and storming of Ciudad Rodrigo, siege and storming of Badajos from 19th Jan. to 6th April 1812; operations near and blockade of Bayonne.

59 Major George Bolton served the campaign in Spain, under Sir John Moore, with the 14th, and was present at the battle of Corunna. Also with the expedition to Walcheren, and at the siege of Flushing in 1809.

60 Major Thomas Reid served with the 33d at the capture of Bourbon and the Isle of France in 1810; the campaign of 1813 and 14 in Germany and Holland, including both attacks on Merxem and storming of Bergen-op-Zoom. Also the campaign of 1815, including the battle of Quatre Bras, retreat of the 17th June, and battle of Waterloo, where he was severely wounded.

61 Major Cox served at Travancore in 1809, and in Ava in 1825.

62 Major Charters served with the expedition to Hanover, under Lord Cathcart in 1805; the Walcheren expedition, in 1809; and campaign in Holland, under Lord Lynedoch, in 1814.

63 Major Mason served with the expedition to the coast of America, in 1813, and was engaged in several small actions. Present also at the capture of Moose Island, in the Bay of Fundy, in 1814.

65 Major Handcock accompanied the expedition to Hanover in 1805; joined the army in Sicily in 1806, and was employed with its various operations from 1806 to 1810; went with the expedition to Naples, and was present at the capture of Ischia and Procida; returned to Sicily and employed against the French army, in 1811. Served in Spain during 1812 and 13, including the battle of Castalla, siege of Tarragona, and affair of Villa Franca. Also the campaign of 1815, and was severely wounded at Waterloo.

66 Major Sutherland served with the 72d at the capture of the Cape of Good Hope in 1806; and accompanied the force from thence to co-operate at the capture of the Isle of France in 1810.

67 Major Gregory served in the American war in 1814 and 15, and commanded a gun-boat belonging to the Flotilla under Commander Owen, on Lake Ontario, for which he received the thanks of the Naval Commander-in-Chief.

68 Major Wright served at the capture of Madeira, in 1808; and the campaign in the Peninsula, under Sir John Moore, in 1808-9.

69 Major Stewart served with the 25th at the reduction of Martinique, St. Martin's, and St. Eustatius, in 1809: and of Guadaloupe in 1810, and again in 1815.

70 Major Crawfurd served in the Peninsula from Jan. 1812 to July 1814, including operations of the covering army during the siege of Badajos in 1812, as a volunteer 79th regt.; battle of Salamanca, capture of Madrid, battles of the Pyrenees, Nivelle, Nive, and Orthes (severe gun-shot wound).

71 Major Henry Reid served at Cadiz from March 1813 to the end of the war. Served also in the American war, including the affair at Hampden.

73 Major Long served with the 71st in the Peninsula, from Sept. 1813 to the end of that war in 1814, including the action at Cambo, battles of the Nive, before Bayonne (wounded), Orthes, Aire, Tarbes, and Toulouse. Also the campaign of 1815, including the battle of Waterloo.

74 Major [illegible] served in the Peninsula from Jan. 1813 to the end of that war in 1814.

75 Major Colebrook served on the expedition to Walcheren in 1809.

76 Major George Browne served the campaign of 1815, including the battles of Quatre Bras and Waterloo.

77 Major Bonamy served in the Peninsula with the 6th from Sept. 1813 to June 1814, including the battles of Nivelle, Nive, 9th, 10th, and 11th Dec. and Orthes.

78 Major Marshall served with the 91st on the expedition to Portugal in 1808, including the battles of Roleia and Vimiera, advance into Spain and retreat through Gallicia under Sir John Moore, action at Lugo, and battle of Corunna. Expedition to Walcheren in 1809. Subsequently in the Peninsula, including the battles of Vittoria, the Pyrenees (26th, 27th, 28th, and 30th July), the Nivelle, and the Nive, on the 9th, 10th, 11th, and 13th Dec. 1813, investment of Bayonne, and battle of Orthes. Slightly wounded at Pampeluna, 28th July 1813, and severely at Orthes.

79 Major Manners served in the Peninsula with the 59th from Aug. 1812 to May 1814, including the battle of Vittoria, siege and storming of San Sebastian in Aug. 1813, battle of the Nive on the 9th, 10th, and 11th December, 1813. Wounded at the storming of Bhurtpore on the 18th January 1826.

80 Major Raynes served at the siege of Copenhagen in 1807; with the expedition to Sweden, and subsequently to the Peninsula under Sir John Moore, including the retreat to Corunna. Served also subsequently in the Peninsula from March 1810, to the end of the war in 1814, including the defence of Cadiz, battle of Barrosa, defence of Tarifa, action at Seville, battles of Vittoria, Pyrenees, and Nivelle, passage of the Adour, and operations before Bayonne.

81 Major Cooke's services:—See page 116, note 2.

82 Major B. P. Browne served the campaign of 1815 with the 11th Dragoons, and was present the battle of Waterloo. Also at the siege and capture of Bhurtpore, under Lord Combermere, in 1825-6; and was a volunteer for the dismounted cavalry storming party.

83 Major Birtwhistle served the campaign of 1814 in the South of France with the 32nd. Also the campaign of 1815, including the battle of Quatre Bras (slightly wounded), retreat on the 17th June, and battle of Waterloo (severely wounded).

84 Major Moore was present with the 2nd battalion of the 87th in nearly every action in which it was engaged, the greater part of the time as adjutant, including the battle of Talavera (wounded in the right thigh, where the ball still remains) defence of Cadiz during the whole time, battle of Vittoria (two horses shot under him), the Pyrenees, Nivelle, Orthes (horse shot), Vic Bigorre (wounded), and Toulouse, besides various affairs of out-posts. Served also the Mahratta campaign of 1817 and 18; and in the Burmese war, in 1825 and 26.

85 Major John Clarke served in the Peninsula from March 1809 to the end of that war in 1814, including the battles of Oporto and Talavera, Lines of Torres Vedras, actions of Arroyo de Molino and Campo Mayor, battle of Albuhera, siege of Badajoz, battles of Vittoria, the Pyrenees (from 25th to 31st July, and 2nd Aug.), the Nivelle, the Nive, (9th and 13th Dec.), action of St. Palais, battle of Orthes, action at Aire, and battle of Toulouse, besides numerous skirmishes. At the battle of Albuhera, when in the command of a company of flankers, was struck down by a Polish Lancer, and taken prisoner, but made his escape in a charge of cavalry.

86 Major Algeo served in the Peninsula with the 77th from Aug. 1813 to the end of the war.

87 Major Sheppard served at Walcheren, in 1809; and in Canada from March 1814 to Dec. 1816, including the actions at Chippawa, Lundy's Lane, before Fort Erie, and the attack on Snake Hill.

89 Major Richardson served in the Peninsula with the 11th from Aug. 1809 to Oct. 1814, including the battle of Busaco, the subsequent retreat of the army to the lines before Lisbon, the advance and pursuit of the enemy when they broke up from Santarem, blockade of Almeida, and battle of Fuentes d'Onor.

90 Major Cannon served in the Peninsula with the old 94th from January 1810 to the end of the war, including the defence of Fort Matagorda in front of Cadiz in 1810, lines of Torres Vedras, battle of Fuentes d'Onor, first siege of Badajos, action at El Bodon, storm of Ciudad Rodrigo, (severely wounded in the chest); battles of Salamanca, Vittoria (slightly wounded in the right knee), Pyrenees, Nivelle, Orthes, and Toulouse.

91 Major Tatton served in the Peninsula from Aug. 1811 to the end of that war in 1814, and was present at the blockade of Bayonne.

92 Major Jackson served in the Peninsula from Dec. 1809 to 1814, and was severely wounded through the left breast and in both arms at the battle of Albuhera. Served subsequently in the American war.

93 Major Graham served at the siege of Flushing in 1809, and afterwards in the Peninsula, including the blockade of Bayonne. Subsequently in the American war, including the action at Bladensburg and capture of Washington, action near Baltimore, and those in front of New Orleans on the 20th Dec. 1814, and 8th Jan. 1815; also at the taking of Fort Bowyer.

95 Major Black served the campaign of 1815, including the battles of Quatre Bras and Waterloo, at which last he was slightly wounded. Also in the campaign on the Sutlej (Medal), including the battles of Buddiwal, Aliwal, and Sobraon.

96 Major White served with the 11th regt. on the expedition to Walcheren and at the siege of Flushing in 1809. He served afterwards in the Peninsula from July 1812 to the end of 1813.

97 Major Robertson served with the expedition to Walcheren in 1809, and was present at the siege of Flushing. Also at the taking of the Kandian country, in Ceylon, under Sir Robert Brownrigg.

98 Major Rivers landed at Passages in Dec. 1813, and joined the light division in Feb. 1814;

took charge of a division of the boats fitted out at Socoa for the passage of the Adour; then joined the force for the siege of Bayonne. Embarked for America in 1814.

100 Major Waymouth served in the Peninsula with the 2nd Life Guards from Nov. 1812 to the end of that war in 1814, including the battle of Vittoria, investment of Pampeluna, and the battles of the Pyrenees. Also the campaign of 1815, including the action at Quatre Bras, covering the retreat on the 17th June, and battle of Waterloo. Severely wounded and taken prisoner, when charging the French cuirassiers at Waterloo.

101 Major Buchan served the campaign of 1814 in Holland, including the reconnoitring of the position before Antwerp, action at Merxem, and bombardment of Antwerp.

103 Major Lowe served with the 16th Lancers at the siege of Bhurtpore in 1825-6, and was wounded.

104 Major Gibson served in the Peninsula with the 1st Light Infantry battalion of the King's German Legion, from Aug. 1813 to the end of that war in 1814, including the siege of San Sebastian, an action in the Pyrenees at the passage of the Bidassoa (wounded), and the subsequent actions in which the left wing of the army was engaged. Served also the campaign of 1815, and was present at the battle of Waterloo.

106 Major Morse Cooper served the campaign of 1814 as a Volunteer with the Royals, and was present at the investment of Bayonne, and repulse of the sortie. Also the campaign of 1815, including the battles of Quatre Bras and Waterloo. Served with the 11th Light Dragoons at the siege and capture of Bhurtpore in 1825-6. Slightly wounded at Bayonne, and severely at Waterloo, having received five wounds.

108 Major Leonard was at the storming of the enemy's works at the Island of Santa Maura, and at the siege of the fortress until its surrender in March 1810. Served in three boat actions when belonging to the *Magnificent*. When in the Perlea he was in action with one line-of-battle ship and two frigates, off Toulon, from eight until three o'clock, Nov. 1811. In a boat action and about the same time, engaged with the batteries and three armed schooners at the entrance of the Petit Pass, off Toulon.

109 Major Nevill (see Note 3, page 116).

110 Major Jauncey served on the expedition to Walcheren in 1809. Subsequently in the Peninsula from July 1812 to June 1814, including the battle of Castalla, siege of Tarragona retreat from thence, its second siege, retreat from Villa Franca after the battle of the Pass of Ordall, and investment of Barcelona in 1814. Expedition to Naples in 1815.

111 Major Hill served the campaign of 1815, including the retreat on the 17th June, battle of Waterloo, and storming of Cambray. Served also in Caffraria in 1820 and 21; and afterwards in the Burmese war, including the taking of Mahrattee, and Aracan.

112 Major Lynch served at the siege of Flushing. At Malta and the Ionian Islands under Lord Wm. Bentinck. At Genoa and in the South of France in 1814. At the siege and capture of Bhurtpore and was wounded at the assault 18th Jan. 1826.

114 Major Wright served in the American war.

116 Major Cockell served at the siege and capture of Bhurtpore, under Lord Combermere.

118 Major de Lacy served in the Peninsula from Aug. 1809 to the end of the war, including the battles of Busaco and Albuhera, sieges of Ciudad Rodrigo and Badajoz, battles of Salamanca, Vittoria, Pyrenees (28 July to 2 Aug.), Nivelle, Orthes, and Toulouse. Received a gun-shot wound in the right arm at Vittoria. Has served seven years in the West Indies since the peace.

119 Major Gordon served at the battle of Trafalgar.

120 Major Elgee served in the Peninsula and France from Feb. 1809 to the end of the war in 1814, including the battles of Talavera and Fuentes d'Onor, siege of Burgos (contused wound in the leg), and investment of Bayonne.

121 Major Pascoe served in the Peninsula and France from Aug. 1809 to Feb. 1814, including the battles of Salamanca, Vittoria, Nivelle, and Nive, passage of the Bidassoa, and other operations; sieges of Badajoz (first siege), Forts of Salamanca, Burgos, and San Sebastian. Army of Occupation from 1815 to 1818.

122 Major Spiller served at Walcheren, and was present at the siege of Flushing, and the attack and capture of Ter Vere.

123 Major Montagu served at the siege of Dantzic, in 1813; also the campaign of 1815, including the battle of Waterloo and capture of Cambray.

124 Major Bridges served at Walcheren in 1809, and in the Peninsula and France from July 1811 to Aug. 1814, including the defence of Cadiz in 1811; battles of Vittoria and the Pyrenees; passage of Bidassoa; Nivelle, Nive, and Adour; and the operations before Bayonne. Attached to the Prussian corps d'armée in 1815, under the command of Prince Augustus of Prussia, and employed in the reduction of Philippeville, Marienbourg, and Rocroy. Adjutant to the Royal Artillery, serving with the force employed in Portugal in 1826; and the Brigade-Major to the Royal Artillery in the Canadas in 1838.

125 Major Charles Campbell served at the siege of Flushing in 1809; and subsequently in the Peninsula, including the battle of Castalla, and siege of Tarragona, under Sir J. Murray.

127 Major Caine served in the Nepaul campaign of 1815, and was present in action at Jeelghur. In the Deccan war of 1817 and 18, including the action at Jhubbulpore, where he carried the regimental colour of the 17th in the attack of the heights defended by the Arabs. He was Major of Brigade at the assault and capture of Bhurtpore, and was present during the whole of the siege: wounded by a grape shot in the left foot whilst charging the enemy's guns on the day of the capture. He commanded the Grenadiers of the 26th at the capture of Chusan

(Medal) 5th July 1840, and was British Commissioner, and Military Magistrate of that island until its evacuation in Feb. 1841. Major Caine has been in Asia from the commencement of his service to the present period, having left India in 1840 with the China expedition; and he is now employed as Colonial Secretary and Auditor General of Hong Kong.

128 Major Dawson served in the Kandian war in Ceylon.

130 Major Ainsworth served at the siege of Flushing in 1809, and subsequently in the Peninsula, including the battle of Fuentes d'Onor, and 2nd siege of Badajoz, and battle of Nivelle. Served also the campaign of 1815, and was present at the battle of Waterloo.

131 Major Campbell served the campaign of 1814, in the south of France, including the investment of Bayonne. Served also throughout the Burmese war.

132 Major Poyntz served in the Peninsula as a volunteer with the 30th, from February to November 1811, including the occupation of the Lines at Torres Vedras, pursuit of Massena, actions of Sabugal, Almeida, and Barba del Puerco; and battle of Fuentes d'Onor.

133 Major Rochfort Scott served with the expedition against New Orleans, and was present at the attack on the American Lines on the 8th Jan. 1815, and at the capture of Fort Boyer. Served afterwards in France with the Army of Occupation, from July 1815 to December 1818; and with the allied Anglo-Turkish force in Syria, from Dec. 1840 to Nov. 1841.

134 Major Fraser served in the Peninsula with the 53rd from Aug. 1811 to the end of that war in 1814, including the siege and capture of the fortified convents at Salamanca, battle of Salamanca, siege of the castle of Burgos, battles of Vittoria, the Pyrenees, the Nivelle, and Toulouse. Severely wounded at Pampeluna on the 26th July 1813.

135 Major Codd served with the 48th, in the operations against the Rajah of Coorg in 1834.

138 Major Wade served throughout the campaigns in Affghanistan from 1838 to 1842 inclusive,—he was Adjutant of the 13th at the storm and capture of Ghuznee (medal), and Major of Brigade at the assault and capture of the town and forts of Tootumdurrah, storm of Jhoolghur, night attack at Baboo Koosh Ghur, destruction of Khardurrah, and assault of Perwandurrah. Present with the 13th at the storming of the Koord Cabool Pass (wounded), affair of Tezeen, forcing the Jugdulluck Pass, reduction of the fort of Mamoo Khail, heroic defence of Jellalabad and sorties on the 14th Nov. and 1st Dec. 1841, 11th March, 24th March, and 1st April, 1842; general action and defeat of Akbar Khan before Jellalabad (medal), storming the heights of Jugdulluck, general action of Tezeen, and recapture of Cabool (medal).

139 Major Canch served in the Peninsula with the 5th from Aug. 1808 to Dec. 1812, and again from Oct. 1813 to the end of that war in 1814, including the battles of Roleia, Vimiera, Talavera, and Busaco; retreat to the lines of Torres Vedras, actions of Leria, Pombal, Redinha, and Sabugal—contused wound on the groin; battle of Fuentes d'Onor, second siege of Badajoz—contused wound on the chest; actions of El Bodon and Aldea de Ponte, siege and capture of Ciudad Rodrigo—wounded in the right thigh at the assault; third siege and capture of Badajoz—contused wound in the neck at the assault; battle of Salamanca,—horse killed; capture of Madrid and the Retiro, battles of the Nivelle, the Nive, and Orthes; actions of Sauveterre and Vic Bigorre, and battle of Toulouse,—horse wounded. Served afterwards in the American war, and was present at the action at Plattsburg.

140 Major O'Grady was present with the 62nd in the operations in 1814, against the French in retreat from Leghorn, including the affairs of Savona and Spezzia, forcing their positions on the heights of Neroi, and capture of Genoa. In the same year he served in the American war, and was present at the taking of Castine. He served with the 48th at the capture of Coorg in the East Indies in 1834; with the Queen's Royals, during the campaign of 1844-5, in the Southern Concan and Sawant Warree country, including the investment and capture of the Forts of Monohur and Munsuntosh; and on particular service in the Kaffir war (South of Africa) during part of 1846-7.

141 Major Austin served in the Peninsula, from Oct. 1811 to April 1812, including the siege and storm of Ciudad Rodrigo. Campaign of 1814 in Holland, including the taking of the fortified village of Merxem. Campaign of 1815, including the battle of Waterloo.

142 Major Robertson served in the Peninsula with the old 94th from Jan. 1810 to the end of the war, including the defence of Cadiz, from Feb. to Sept. 1810, where he was employed as an Assistant Engineer; lines at Torres Vedras, actions at Pombal, Redinha, Cazal Nova, Foz d'Arouce, and Sabugal; battle of Fuentes d'Onor, second siege and blockade of Badajoz in June 1811; actions at El Bodon, and Aldea de Ponte, siege and storming of Ciudad Rodrigo, siege and assault of Badajoz, battle of Salamanca, advance upon and capture of Madrid, retreat to Portugal, battle of Nivelle, actions of La Bastide, Sauveterre, Vic Bigorre, and Tarbes; battles of Orthes (severely wounded in the left arm) and Toulouse.

143 Major Tew served with the 50th in the battle of Punniar (Medal). Also the campaign of 1845-6 on the Sutlej (Medal and three clasps) including the battles of Moodkee, Ferozeshah, Aliwal, and Sobraon (dangerously wounded).

144 Major Enoch served with the expedition to Walcheren and at the siege of Flushing, in 1809; in the Peninsula from 1810 to 1813, including the sieges of Badajoz and Olivenza, in 1811; battle of Albuhera, actions of Fuente Grinaldo, 25th, 26th, and 27th Sept. 1811; sieges of Ciudad Rodrigo and Badajoz, battle of Salamanca (severely wounded, and horse killed under him). Served also the campaign of 1815, including the battle of Waterloo, storming of Cambray and capture of Paris.

145 Major Pearson served at the siege of Bhurtpore, and was a volunteer for the dismounted cavalry storming party. He served also in the action at Maharajpore, 29 Dec. 1843 (Medal), and in the campaign on the Sutlej in 1846, including the battles of Buddiwal, Aliwal, and Sobraon: at Aliwal he commanded the right wing of the 16th Lancers, and subsequently the regt., as also of Sobraon

146 Major Bere served with the 16th Lancers during the campaign in Affghanistan under Lord Keane, and was present at the siege and capture of Ghuznee (Medal); and he commanded the party of the 16th Lancers, under Brigadier Cureton, sent to seize the guns and secure the possession of the citadel of Cabool, and was appointed at Cabool Assistant-Adjutant-General of Cavalry, and continued so until the reduction of Lord Keane's army in the Provinces. He served also the campaign on the Sutlej in 1846 (Medal), including the battles of Buddiwal, Aliwal (wounded), and Sobraon.

148 Major Archibald Campbell served in the Peninsula with the 4th Portuguese Regt. from 20th May 1810 to the end of that war in 1814, including the battle of Busaco, Lines of Torres Vedras, action of Campo Mayor, battle of Albuhera, 1st and 2nd sieges of Badajoz, action at Arroyo de Molino, battles of Vittoria, Pyrenees, Pampeluna (severely wounded in the side), Nive 9th Dec., and before Bayonne 13th Dec., taking the island of Holriague, battle of Orthes, action at Aire, and battle of Toulouse. Head severely injured 24th June 1813, when pursuing the enemy to Pampeluna.

149 Major Beckham served the Peninsular campaigns of 1812, 13 and 14.

151 Major Orr served in the Peninsula, with the 7th Fusiliers, from Feb. to Aug. 1811, and again from April 1812 to the end of that war in 1814, including the siege of Badajoz in April and May 1811, battle of Albuhera (wounded in the left knee and elbow), action of Osma, battles of Vittoria, affair of Roncesvalles, battles of Pampeluna, Nivelle, Orthes, and Toulouse, besides various minor affairs. He was also at the capture of Paris in 1815.

152 Major Trevor served the campaign of 1814 in Holland. Also the campaign of 1815, including the battle of Waterloo, and captures of Cambray and Paris.

154 Major Creagh served in the Anglo-Spanish Legion, and was engaged on the heights of Arlaban in Alava, on the 16th, 17th, and 18th January, 1836, besides several other affairs. He was also employed on a Particular Service in Canada at the outbreak of the Rebellion in 1837.

156 Major Wolfe served with the 59th at the taking of Palembang in Sumatra in 1813; the taking of Bali, and also the fortified Kittore at Macassar in 1814; the Decan campaign of 1817 and 18; and in the Kandian war in 1818.

157 Major Orange served in the Burmese war in 1825.

158 Major Scott was at the destruction of two ships of the line in the Bay of Cette, 26th Oct. 1809; in action with the French fleet off Toulon, 19th July, 1811; in the action at Navarino, 20th Oct. 1827.

160 Major L. F. Jones served in the Peninsula from June 1812 to the end of that war in 1814, including the battle of Salamanca, actions of San Munos and San Milan, battle of Vittoria, actions in the Pyrenees at the heights of Santa Barbara, Echalar, Vera bridge and heights, crossing the Bidassoa, battles of Nivelle (severely wounded) and Orthes, affairs of Tarbes and Tournefeuille, and battle of Toulouse. Served also during the whole of the operations against New Orleans.

161 Major Du Vernet served with the 45th in the Burmese war in 1825 and 26.

163 Major Bourchier served in France with the army under the Duke of Wellington from 1815 to 1818; and in Canada during the insurrection in 1838 and 39, and was employed at Prescot, under Colonel Young, in organizing the Militia of that section of the Province.

164 Major John Bolton served the Mahratta campaigns of 1817 and 18, and was present at the siege of Rhyghur.

165 Major Lloyd was at Waterloo 18th June, taking of Cambray, 24th June 1815, and capture of Paris. Served one campaign latter part of 1826 against the Rajah of Kolapore. Also the campaign in the Southern Mahratta Country in 1844 (including the storming of Punella), and that in the Concan in 1845.

166 Major Barnes served at the capture of Fort Anjul in Cutch 25th Dec. 1815; the Mahratta campaigns of 1817-18; escalade of the Fort of Booje in Cutch, March 1819; siege of Ras-el-Kymah and Zyah in Arabia, Dec. 1819; escalade of Dwarka Ohamandel, Dec. 1820; action of Beni-Boo-Ally in Arabia, March 12.

167 Major Riley was in an engagement with a French squadron in the Mosambique channe 3rd July 1810; served the Nepaul campaign of 1814 and 15.

169 Major Phibbs served in the Peninsula, with the 27th, from Nov. 1813 to the end of that war in 1814, including the battles of the Nivelle, Orthes, and Toulouse. Served afterwards in the American war, and was present at the taking of Plattsburg. Lost his left arm, and was shot through both legs at the battle of the Nivelle.

171 Major Fynmore, previously to entering the Royal Marines, served several years as midshipman in the navy, and was at the battle of Trafalgar and at Buenos Ayres in 1807. In 1809 and 10 he served in the Great Belt in command of a gun-boat employed in the protection of our convoys, and was engaged with the enemy's gun and row-boats. On the night of the 1st of Aug. 1810 cut out three merchant vessels under a heavy fire of field-pieces and musketry. Six weeks detached from H.M.S. *Vanguard* the same year, to intercept the communication between the Port of Rostock and Wismar; assisted at the capture of a convoy of five sail, and drove on shore and destroyed an armed row-boat. In 1816 he served at Algiers; and in 1821, 22, and 23, in the West Indies, and was engaged with piratical vessels on the coast of Cuba, five of which were captured.

173 Major Deverell served the Deccan campaigns of 1816, 17, and 18; in the Persian Gulf in 1819 and 20, including the capture of the Arab fortresses of Ras-el-Khyma and Zyah; and in the Burmese war, from Nov. 1825 until the peace in 1826, including the capture of Donabew, attacks on the height near Prome, of Maloon, and of several stockades.

174 Major M'Mahon served with the 9th Lancers in the campaign on the Sutlej in 1846, and was present at the battle of Sobraon (Medal).

OFFICERS WITH LOCAL RANK.

GENERALS.

Hon. Sir E. Paget, *GCB.* 29 Nov. 20 *East Ind.*
S. *Visc.* Combermere, *GCB. & GCH.* do. *do.*
Sir Jasper Nicolls, *KCB.* 18 Oct. 39 *do.*
Tredway Clarke 23 Nov. 41 *do.*
Hugh, *Lord* Gough, *GCB.* 8 March 43 *E. Ind.*

LIEUT.-GENERALS.

Count Wallmoden, *KCB.* 21 Jan. 13 *Continent.*
John, *Lord* Seaton, *GCB. GCMG. GCH.* 8 July, 36 *Upper & Lower Canada.*
Rt. Hon. Sir Ed. Blakeney, *KCB. & GCH.* 26 Aug. 36 *Ireland.*
Nath. Forbes, 10 Jan. 37 *E.I.*
Tho. Boles, 23 Nov. 41 *do.*
Sir Hugh Fraser, *KCB.* 23 Nov. 41 *E.I.*
Sir Hoptoun Stratford Scott, *KCB.* do. *do.*
G. *Marq. of* Tweeddale. *KT.* CB. 15 Apr. 42, *Madras*
Sir W. M. Gomm, *KCB.*, 22 July, *Mauritius.*

1846. 9 Nov. *East Indies.*

H. S. Osborne
Sir Jas. L. Caldwell, *GCB.*
G. Carpenter
Sir Dav. Leighton, *KCB.*
Jas. Welsh
Sir Jas. Russell, *KCB.*
Martin White
Rich. Podmore
Sir Rob. Houstoun, *KCB.*
Jn. Greenstreet
M. L. Pereira
Sir J. Rose, *KCB.*
Geo. R. Kemp
John Munro
J. A. P. Macgregor
Sir J. Prendergast
Sir Wm. Richards, *KCB.*
Alex. Duncan
Sir T. Whitehead, *KCB.*
Robert J. Latter
Thomas Stewart
Jerry F. Dyson
W. H. Perkins
Sir John Doveton, *KCB.*
Alex. Fair, *CB.*
D. M'Pherson
Sir J. L. Lushington, *GCB.*
R. W. D. Sealy
Wm. C. Fraser
Wm. Gilbert
Sir H. G. W. Smith, *Bt. GCB.* 3 Sept. 47 *Cape of Good Hope.*

MAJOR-GENERALS.

Sir James Cockburn, *Bt.* GCH. 22 Feb. 31
Sir H. Lindsay Bethune, *Bt.* 21 Dec. 35 *Asia*
Sir George Arthur, *Bart. KCH.* 22 Dec. 37. *Upper Canada.*
B. Kennett, 28 June 38 *E. Ind.*
Wm. Innes, *CB.* do. *do.*
John P. Dunbar do. *do.*
Christ. Hodgson do. *do.*
Rich. Whish do. *do.*
A. Andrews, *CB.* do. *do.*
Jas. Ahmuty, 28 June 38, *E. Indies*
James Cock. do. *do.*
C. M'Leod, *CB.* do. *do.*
E. W. Shuldham do. *do.*
W. Sandwith, *CB.* do. *do.*
Mossem Boyd do. *do.*
John M'Innes do. *do.*
J. F. Salter, *CB.* do. *do.*
Sir E. G. Stannus, *CB.* do. *do.*
Patrick Byers do. *do.*
E. Cartwright do. *do.*
H. G. A. Taylor, *CB.* do. *do.*
A. Richards, *CB.* do. *do.*
Sir J. Sutherland do. *do.*
Her. Bowen, *CB.* do. *do.*
Arch. Watson do. *do.*
John Wells Fast do. *do.*
Jas. Durant do. *do.*
Brook Bridges Parlby, *CB.* do. *do.*
Hen. Hodgson do. *do.*
F. D. Ballantine do. *do.*
Sir R. Hen. Cunliffe, *Bt. CB.* do. *do.*
Wm. Clapham do. *do.*
John Truscott do. *do.*
John Woulfe do. *do.*
E. M. G. Showers do. *do.*
F. W. Wilson, *CB.* do. *do.*
John H. Collett do. *do.*
Patrick Cameron do. *do.*
John Carfrae do *do.*
Rich. West do. *do.*
Geo. Jackson do. *do.*
S. Goodfellow do. *do.*
Jas. S. Fraser do. *do.*
P. De la Motte, *CB.* do. *do.*
Hen. Huthwaite do. *do.*
T. Wilson, *CB.* do. *do.*
F. Vinc. Raper do. *do.*
Geo. Swiney do. *do.*
Sir G. Pollock, *GCB.* do. *do.*
A. Lindsay, *CB.* do. *do.*
Sir Walter Raleigh Gilbert, *KCB.* do. *do.*
E. Frederick, *CB.* do. *do.*
Geo. B. Brooks do. *do.*
Hen. Bowdler do. *do.*
Peter Lodwick do. *do.*
J. Morse do. *do.*
Sueton. H. Todd do. *do.*
John Briggs do. *do.*
Harry Thomson do. *do.*
Sir C. F. Smith, *KCB.* 9 Oct. 40 *Part. Serv.*
J. Kennedy, *CB.* 23 Nov. 41 *E. Ind.*
Benj. Roope do. *do.*
C. W. Hamilton do. *do.*
E. P. Waters, *CB.* do. *do.*
W. M. Burton do. *do.*
W. S. Whish, *CB.* do. *do.*
W. Battine, *CB.* do. *do.*
G. Hunter, *CB.* do. *do.*
R. C. Andrée do. *do.*
Sir A. Galloway, *KCB.* do. *do.*
Edgar Wyatt do. *do.*
G. M. Steuart do. *do.*
Mark Cubbon do. *do.*
S. R. Strover do. *do.*
Horatio T. Tapp do. *do.*
Tho. Shubrick do. *do.*
Wm. H. Kemm do. *do.*
Thomas King do. *do.*
Wm. Monteith do. *do.*
Sir Wm. Morison, *KCB.* do. *do.*
Thomas Morgan do. *do.*
L. C. Russell, *CB.* do. *do.*
Duncan Macleod do. *do.*
Wm. Cullen do. *do.*
David Barr do. *do.*
John Ogilvie do. *do.*
Sir J. H. Littler, *GCB.* 23 Nov. *E. Ind.*
Wm. Vincent do. *do.*
Thomas Marrett do. *do.*
J. A. Hodgson do. *do.*
Samuel Smith do. *do.*
Tho. Hen. Paul do. *E. Ind*
Ezekiel Barton do. *do.*
H. T. Roberts, *CB.* do. *do.*
John T. Gibson do. *do.*
F. Farquharson do. *do.*
Right Hon. Sir H. Pottinger, *Bart. GCB. Governor & Commander-in-Chief at Madras,* 23 Nov. 41 *E.I.*
J. Caulfield, *CB.* do. *do.*
R. Tickell, *CB.* do. *do.*
Sir Fra. Cockburn 10 Feb. 43, *Bahamas*
Sir H. G. W. Smith, *Bart. GCB.* 7 Apr. 46. *East Indies.*

COLONELS.

A. Findlay, *KH.* 26 Oct. 30 *W. Coast of Africa*
Fra. Raw. Chesney 27 Nov. 34 *Asia*
W. Wylde, *CB.* 10 Feb. 37 *Spain*
Sir R. Doherty, 5 May, *West Coast of Africa*
H. H. Rose, *CB.* 17 Nov. 40 *Syria.*
Geo. Macdonald, 24 Dec. 41 *W. Coast of Africa*
T. Monteath, *CB., A.D.C. to the Queen,* 4 Oct. 42 *E. Ind.*
G. P. Wymer, *CB., A.D.C. to the Queen,* 23 Dec. *E. Ind.*
Wm. Pattle, *CB. A.D.C. to the Queen* 4 July 43 *E. Ind.*
John Geo. Bonner, 10 Nov. 43 *E. Ind.*
*Edward Hay, 1 March, 44 *East India Company's Depôt at Warley.*
H. M. Wheeler, *CB. Aide de Camp to the Queen,* 3 Apr. 46 *East Indies*
G. E. Gowan, *CB. A. de C. to the Queen,* 19 June 46 *do.*
P. Montgomerie, *CB. A. de C. to the Queen,* do. *do*

9 Nov. 1846. *East Indies.*

James Stuart, *CB.*
Charles Ovans
William Henry Hewitt
William Strahan
J. Home
G. Wm. Aylmer Lloyd, *CB.*
Fran. Haleman
Alex. Tulloch, *CB.*
Arch. Brown Dyce
Fred. Buckley
J. Wheeler Cleveland
Rob. Blackall
David Capon
Wm. Donald Robertson
Duncan Sim
Chas. Maddison Bird
Geo. Henry MacKinnon, *CB.* 16 June 48 *Kaffraria*

LIEUT.-COLONELS.

F. A. Daniell 1 Jan. 12 *E. Ind.*
John Croadill, CB. 4 June 13 *do.*
H. *Prince* Reuss 30 Dec. 13 *Continent*
Bissell Harvey, *KH.* 16 May 16 *Continent*
J. F. Fulton, *KH.* 24 Nov. 25 *Continent*
J. F. De Burgh 12 Jan. 26 *Continent*
W. L. Watson, CB. 19 do. *E. Ind.*
E. Hawkshaw 15 June *Continent*
Anth. S. King 3 Aug. *do.*
Sir H. Wheatley, *Bart. CB. GCH.* 14 Sept. *Continent*
Robert Nixon do. *do.*
Hen. Roberts 5 Oct. *do.*
Andrew Tilt 12 do. *do.*
T. G. Fitz Gerald 19 do. *do.*
Aug. Meade do. *do.*
Hon. J. Walpole 26 do. *do.*
Donald Mackay do. *do.*
Anth. Rumpler 9 Nov. *do*
Wm. Thornhill 16 Nov. *do.*
Fletcher Wilkie 30 do. *do.*
J. S. Hawkshaw 14 Dec. *do.*
L. A. Northey do. *do.*
Jas. Ormsby 28 do. *do.*
Hon. J. Browne do. *do.*
Sir Wm. Verner, *Bart.* 28 Dec. *Continent.*
J. Carr. Smith do. *do.*
D. Macpherson 30 do. *do.*
J. R. Udney do. *do.*
George Baker 31 Aug. 29 *Greece*
Jas. Nisb. Colquhoun 10 Feb. 37 *Spain*
Justin Sheil, *CB.* 2 June, 37 *Persia*
Rich. Wilbraham do. *do.*
G. P. Cameron, *CB.* do. *do.*
Geo. Woodfall do. *do.*
Ralph Carr Alderson 22 June 38 *Spain*
Peter L. Pew, 23 July 39 *East Indies*
Jas. D. Parsons, *CB.* do. *do.*
Geo. Warren do. *do.*
Sir C. M. Wade, *CB.* do.
H. F. Salter, do. *do.*
J. S. H. Weston, 13 Nov. 39 *East Ind.*
Jas. Nisbet Colquhoun, 9 Oct. 40 *Part. Serv.*
R. Carr Alderson, 9 Oct. 40 do. *do.*
T. G. Higgins 9 Oct 40 *Part. Serv.*
G. G. C. W. Du Plat, *KH.* do. *Turkish Dominions.*
E. H. D. E. Napier, 17 Nov. 40 *Part. Serv.*
T. W. O. M'Niven, do. *do.*
R. W. Wilson, *CB.* 26 May 41 *East Indies*
F. S. Hawkins, *CB.* do. *do.*
H. E. Somerville 30 Aug. *do.*
R. Nich. Penny, *CB.* 23 Nov. 41 *do.*
Sir E. A. Campbell, *CB.* do. *do.*
Charles Andrews Bayley *CMG.* 23 Nov. 41. *Medit.*
Francis Farrant, 11 Mar. 42 *Persia.*
G. Huish, *CB.* 23 Dec. *E. Ind.*
F. Blundell, *CB.* do. *do.*
C. W. Young, *CB.* do. *do.*
J. Campbell, *CB.* do. *do.*
W. F. Williams 3 Mar. 43 *Turkey & Persia*
A. T. Reid, *CB.* 4 July 43, *E. Ind.*
C. Waddington, *CB.* do. *do.*
M. Stack, *CB.* do. *do.*
W. Wyllie, *CB.* do. *do.*
W. J. Browne, *CB.* do. *do.*
P. F. Story, *CB.* 4 July, 43. *East Indies.*
A. Woodburn, *CB.* do. *do.*
J. Lloyd, *CB.* do. *do.*
J. Outram, *CB.* do. *do.*
J. T. Leslie, *CB.* do. *do.*
H. C. Barnard, 20 Apr. 44 *do.*
J. G. Drummond do. *do.*
Hope Dick do. *do.*
Owen Phillipps do. *do.*
Wm. Mactier, *CB.* do. *do.*
Wm. Garden, *CB.* do. *do.*
E. J. Smith do. *do.*
Jos. Nash, *CB.* 26 Ap. 44 *do.*
W. Geddes, *CB.* do. *do.*
Thomas Sanders do. 1 *do.*

H. J. White, 29 Ap. 44 *E.I.*
C. E. T. Oldfield, *CB.* do. *do.*
J. Alexander do. *do.*
J. T. Lane, *CB.* do. *do.*
3 Apr. 46. *East Indies.*
Hugh Sibbald, Bengal Inf.
L. S. Bird, do.
Wm. Alexander, Bengal Cav.
W. H. Wake, Bengal Inf.
David Birrell, do.
H. R. Osborn, do.
T. Polwhele, do.
J. H. Handscomb, do.
Patrick Grant, *CB.* do.
R. J. H. Birch, do.
F. Brind, Bengal Artillery
Geo. Campbell, do.
P. Innes, Bengal Inf.
J. G. W. Curtis, do.
19 June 46. *East Indies.*
W. J. Thompson, *CB.* Bengal Infantry
Sir H. M. Lawrence, *KCB.* Bengal Art.
F. Abbott, *CB.* Bengal Eng.
J. F. Bradford, Bengal Cav.
R. Y. Reilly, Bengal Eng.
G. S. Lawrenson, *CB.* Bengal Art.
J. Angelo, Bengal Cav.
C. Marshall, Bengal Inf.
C. Grant, Bengal Art.
H. M. Graves, Bengal Inf.
A. Jack, do.
J. T. Leslie, *CB.*, 13 July 47 *E. I. Co.'s Depot at Warley*
Sir E. A. Campbell, *CB.*, 13 July 47 *Newry*

MAJORS.

Rob. Blackall, 25 Apr. 08 *E. Indies.*
R. H. Fotheringham, 1 Jan. 12 *do.*
Chas. Marriott 4 Ju. 14 *do.*
Major H. Court 4 June 14 *do.*
W. J. Matthews do. *do.*
Sheff. Lutwidge do. *do.*
Ernest, *Baron* de Schmiedern, *KH.* 20 Sept. *Continent*
John Norton, *alias* Teyoninhokarawen, Capt. and Leader of the Indians of the Five Nations. 15 Feb. 16 *Canada*
Tho. Hall 12 Aug. 19 *E. Ind.*
H. C. W. Smyth 19 July 21 *do.*
D. D. Anderson 19 Jan. 26 *do.*
Sa. Sankey 10 Aug. *Continent*
Cha. Irvine 21 Sept. *do.*
Henry Light 26 do. *do.*
G. Tito Brice 9 Nov. *do.*
B. Lutyens do. *do.*
T. H. Morice, *KH.* *do.*
R. H. Garthwaite do. *do.*
Tho. Pipon 16 do. *do.*
Charles Wayth do. *do.*
Robert Abbey do. *do.*
P. D. Fellowes do. *do.*
Ch. Hames 30 Nov. *Continent*
G. J. Wolseley 14 D. *do.*
W. J. Rainey do. *do.*
W. Phipps do. *do.*
W. D. Spooner 28 do. *do.*
Wm. Thomson do. *do.*
John Gordon 30 do. *do.*
Wm. W. Swaine do. *do.*
Fra. B. Eliot do. *do.*
R. Axford, 16 Oct. 28 *Rec. for E. In. Comp. at Liverpool*
Geo. W. Gibson 10 Jan. 37 *E. Ind.*
John Lauris do. *do.*
John Brandon do. *do.*
Wm. Hough do. *do.*
John Mackenzie do. *do.*
Geo. F. Holland do. *do.*

G. J. B. Johnston, 19 Jan. 37 *East Indies*
Hugh R. Murray do. *do.*
Jas. R. Colnett do. *do.*
Peter Johnston do. *do.*
Rich. Gardner do. *do.*
A. Macintosh do. *do.*
Charles Rogers do. *do.*
G. A. Kempland do. *do.*
W. Henderson do. *do*
T. Timbrell, *CB.* do. *do.*
Robert Butler do. *do.*
William Stokes do. *do.*
James Malton do. *do.*
Wm. Macleod do. *do.*
J. R. Wornum do. *do.*
Benjamin Ashe do. *do.*
James Steel do. *do.*
H. C. Rawlinson, *CB.* 2 June *Persia*
John Laughten do. *do.*
Ed. Pat. Lynch, 2 June *Persia.*
*T. Ritherdon 16 F. 38 *E. I. Sem. at Addiscombe*
Francis Hugh M. Wheeler 28 June 38 *E. Ind.*
Jas. W. Douglas do. *do.*
Jas. Manson do. *do.*
John Ward do. *do.*
S. L. Thornton do. *do.*
W. Simonds do. *do.*
Tho. Williams do. *do.*
R. L. Anstruther do. *do.*
Edm. Herring do. *do.*
Alex. Davidson do. *do.*
John Hailes do. *do.*
Geo. Chapman do. *do.*
Griffiths Holmes do. *do.*
G. H. Woodrooffe do. *do.*
J. H. Mackinlay do. *do.*
Niel Campbell do. *do.*
Robert Kent do. *do.*
A. M'Kinnon do. *do.*
Wm. Sage do. *do.*
Wm. Ramsey do. *do.*
Cha. Thoresby do. *do.*
J. Bedford do. *do.*
Wm. Edw. Blair Leadbeater do. *do.*
Jer. B. Nottidge do. *do.*
George Lee do. *do.*
D. Montgomerie do. *do.*
A. M. Campbell do. *do.*
Lac. Hor. Smith do. *do.*
J. Farquharson do. *do.*
John Worthy do. *do.*
John Forbes do. *do.*
Tho. Biddle do. *do.*
H. Macfarquhar do. *do.*
John Hewison do. *do.*
R. G. Polwhele do. *do.*
John Chisholm do. *do.*
Wm. Foquett do. *do.*
James Allen do. *do.*
George Barker do. *do.*
John Fitzgerald do. *do.*
Jas. Oliphant do. *do.*
J. Monson Boyes do. *do.*
Wm. Fred. Steer do. *do.*
G. W. Bonham do. *do.*
Tho. Wilkinson do. *do.*
G. H. Robinson do. *do.*
Hugh C. Cotton do. *do.*
Cha. Sinclair do. *do.*
R. Somner Seton, do. *do.*
John Thos. Croft, do. *do.*
Charles Wahab do. *do.*
Stuart Corbett do. *do.*
Humphrey Hay do. *do.*
Malc. Nicolson do. *do.*
Henry Barkley Henderson do. *do.*
Tho. Best Jervis do. *do.*
Fred. S. Sotheby, *CB.* do. *do.*
J. R. Woodhouse do. *do.*
Niel Campbell 23 July 39 *E. I.*
G. Thomson, *CB.* do. *do.*
Crawford Hagart, 13 Nov. 40 *E. I.*
Wm. Coghlan do. *do.*
C. Rochfort Scott 17 Nov. *P. Ser.*

R. Wilbraham 17 Nov. 40 *P. S.*
Cha. H. Churchill do. *do.*
Lewis Brown, 2 April, 41 *East Indies.*
G. A. Mee, 26 May 41 *do.*
Phillip Anstruther *CB* *do.*
Henry Moore, *CB.* do. *do.*
A. J. Hadfield, 8 July 41 *do.*
Fred. Wright Hands 23 Nov. 41. *E. Ind.*
C. T. Thomas do. *do.*
Wm. Rollings do. *do.*
Fred. B. White do. *do.*
John Jervis do. *do.*
Albert Pinson do. *do.*
Geo. R. Wilton do. *do.*
Andrew Fraser do. *do.*
James Scott do. *do.*
Wm. Hyslop do. *do.*
G. A. Underwood do. *do.*
G. S. Blundell do. *do.*
Francis Jenkins do. *do.*
Chas. Hewetson, 23 Nov. 41 *E. Ind.*
John Fawcett do. *do.*
D. Thompson do. *do.*
Æneas Sheriff do. *do.*
Albany Troward do. *do.*
Humffrey Lyons do. *do.*
James Mellor do. *do.*
Rob. S. Yolland do. *do.*
John Fra. Bird do. *do.*
Jas. Briggs do. *do.*
James Croudace do. *do.*
Peter Hamond do. *do.*
Geo. Twemlow do. *do.*
A. G. Hyslop do. *do.*
Thomas Gidley do. *do.*
J. Somers Down do. *do.*
Jas. Fraser, *CB.* do. *do.*
Thomas Sewell do. *do.*
Fra. B. Lucas do. *do.*
H. Stilles Foord do. *do.*
James C. Tudor do. *do.*
Step. G. Wheeler do. *do.*
Richard Ord do. *do.*
F. J. Simpson do. *do.*
Ralph Thorpe, do. *do.*
William Cotton do. *do.*
James Wyllie do. *do.*
G. F. F. Vincent do. *do.*
Clifton Benbow do. *do.*
Wm. Forbes do. *do.*
G. M. C. Smyth do. *do.*
Charles Field do. *do.*
Cha. G. Dixon do. *do.*
Cha. Richards do. *do.*
Claud Douglas do. *do.*
W. E. Litchfield do. *do.*
W. M. N. Sturt do. *do.*
R. M. M. Cooke do. *do.*
William Payne do. *do.*
*L. C. A. Meyer, do. *Cavalry Depot at Maidstone.*
T. Seaton, *CB.* 4 Oct. 42 *E. Ind.*
J. B. Backhouse, *CB.* do. *do.*
H. P. Burn do. *do.*
E. R. Mainwaring do. *do.*
A. G. F. J. Younghusband do. *do.*
Geo. Hall Mac-Gregor, *CB.* do. *Affghanistan.*
John Peter Ripley, 23 Dec. 42 *E. Ind.*
W. H. Simpson, *CB.* do. *do.*
T. E. A. Napleton do. *do.*
G. Burney do. *do*
J. Halkett Craigie, *CB.* do. *do.*
J. Ferris, *CB.* do. *do.*
F. A. Reid, *CB.* do. *do.*
G. C. Ponsonby do. *do.*
W. Anderson, *CB.* do. *do.*
R. Shirreff do. *do.*
C. Blood do. *do.*
W. Riddell do. *do.*
T. H. Scott, *CB.* do. *do.*
T. T. Pears, *CB.* do. *do.*
R. C. Moore, *CB.* do. *do.*
D. F. Evans do. *do.*
J. Macadam do. *do.*
Fred. Mackeson, *CB.* do. *do.*

C. H. Delamain, *CB.* 4 July 43 *E. Ind.*
M. F. Willoughby, *CB.* do. *do.*
W. T. Whitlie, *CB.* do. *do.*
G. Fisher, *CB.* do. *do.*
F. N. B. Tucker do. *do.*
J. Jackson, *CB.* do. *do.*
A. Tucker, *CB.* do. *do.*
S. J. Stevens, *CB.* do. *do.*
E. Green, *CB.* do. *do.*
W. B. G. Blenkins, *CB.* do. *do.*
F. E. Manning, 30 Apr. 44 *E. In.*
Birney Browne do. *do.*
Henry Clayton, do. *do.*
H. J. Guyon do. *do.*
Jas. Saunders do. *do.*
J. H. M'Donald do. *do.*
R. Cautley do. *do.*
Philip Harris do. *do.*
Cha. Ekins do. *do.*
N. A. Parker do. *do.*
F. R. Evans do. *do.*
Tho. Young 30 Apr. 44 *E. Ind.*
Geo. Thomson, *CB.* 2 Aug. *Recruiting for the E. I. Co. at Cork.*
George Hutt, *CB.* 2 Jan. 44 *do.*
Robert Henderson, *CB.* 25 Jan. 45. *do.*
Joshua Tait, *CB.* do. *do.*
Wm. Mayne, 23 Sept. 45 *do.*
George Hall Mac Gregor, *CB.* 11 Nov. 45 *E. Indies*

27 Mar. 1846. *East Ind.*
T. F. Tait, Bengal Infantry.

3 Apr. 46. *East Indies.*
P. O'Hanlan, Bengal Cav.
Sebastian Nash, do.
R. Houghton, Bengal Inf.
H. Garbett, Bengal Art.
J. L. Taylor, Bengal Inf.
E. FitzGerald Day, Ben. Art.
W. B. Thomson, Beng. Inf.
R. Horsford, Bengal Art.
R. Napier, Bengal Eng.
F. W. Anson, Bengal Inf.
J. R. Pond, do.
G. Johnston, Bengal Inf.
Geo. Carr, do.
Patrick Hay, do.
W. B. Holmes, do.
Æneas J. Mackay do.
R. T. Sandeman, do.
Henry Palmer, do.
David Pott, do.
G. H. Swinley, Bengal Art.
A. Macdougall, Bengal Inf.
A. M. Becher, do.
J. F. Egerton, Bengal Art.
J. Christie, Bengal Cav.
19 June, 46. *East Indies.*
F. Makeson, Bengal Inf.
J. Turton, Bengal Art.
F. B. Boileau, do.
R. Hill, Bengal Infantry.
C. Corfield, do.
Colin Troup, do.
T. F. Flemyng, do.
A. L. Campbell, Beng. Cav.
M. E. Loftie, Bengal Inf.
W. E. Baker, Bengal Eng.
R. Waller, Bengal Art.
John Fordyce, do.
Cha. O'Brien, Bengal Inf.
Wm. Hoggan, do.
W. S. Pillans, Bengal Art.
H. T. Tucker, Beng. Inf.
A. G. Ward, do.
E. Christie, Bengal Art.
T. L. Harrington, Ben. Cav.
D. Seaton, Bengal Inf.
Henry Forster, CB.

2 Oct. 1846. *East Indies.*
W. F. Grant

9 Nov. 1846. *East Indies.*
Wm. Struthers
Edw. Servante
Thos. Pasley Hay
Robert Wroughton

Henry Templer
Geo. Thomson
Wm. Geo. Lennox
George Templer
Thos. Donnelly
Wm. Rawlins
Rob. Mignan
Rich. Rodney Ricketts
Cha. Edw. Faber
Cha. Jas. Green
J. Tho. Smith
J. Hen. Cramer
J. Gwennap Hume
John Liptrap
Jas. Stevens
Geo. Wright
Haughton James
Geo. Turnbull Marshall
John Byng
Walter Rutherford
Wm. Pitt Macdonald
Geo. Joseph Mant
Peter La Touche
Fran. Chas. Scott
John Swanson
Fred. Jos. Clerk
Arch. Neil Maclean
Alex. M'Donald Elder
J. Rob. Sandford
Kenneth Campbell
Jas. Roxburgh
George Thornton
Gilbert Jas. Richardson
Rich. Blood
J. Horatio Clarkson
Jas. Ramsay Birrell
Hen. Canning Boileau
Jos. Cosfield
Mark Blaxland
John Lewis
Edw. Stanton
Wm. Tanzia Savary
Edw. J. Watson
Alfred Borradaile
Fran. Forbes
Thos. Fisher
Peter Melvill Melvill
John Read Brown
Geo. Munro Arthur
Rob. Codrington
Geo. Buxham Arbuthnot
Charles Farmer
Rob. Hen. Miles
Wm. Reece
Francis Wheeler
Rob. Dennis White
John Platt
Jas. Leverton Revell
Benj. Crispin
David Carstairs
Wm. And. Ludlow
Arth. Cole Spottiswoode
Hen. Hall
Jos. Graham
And. Rowland
Arth. Cleghorn Wight
Hen. Power
Jas. Templeton Brett
Rich. Wheeler Sparrow
Rob. Campbell
Geo. Farmer
Geo. Nott
Chris. Simpson Maling
Wm. Sampo
Anth. Highmore Jellicoe
Alex. Adam
Sam. Rich. Hicks
Chas. Pogley

J. Studholm Hodgson
J. Edw. Parsons
Rob. Garrett
Jas. Walker Bayley
Wm. Barclay Goodfellow
John Hayne
John Watkins
John Kennedy M'Causland
Cha. J. Lewes
Geo. Rich. Talbot
Montague Wm. Perrean
Bulstrode W. Cumberlege
Edw. Walter
Wm. Beaumont
John Cooper
Rob. Marsh. Hughes
J. Edmondstone Landers
Cha. J. Oldfield
John Cumberlege
Wm. Carleston Ormsby
John Hutchings
Geo. Hen. Harper
Rich. Woodward
Alex. Corse Scott
David Davidson
Farquharson Tweedale
Wm. Hunter
John Hobson
Tho. John Nuthall
Hen. Hudleston
John Welchman
Arth. Knyvett
Walter Scott
J. Hen. Bowden Congdon
S. Fraser Hannah
Alfred Lewis
John Shepherd
Emanuel Roberts
Francis Eades
T. G. E. Gammell Kenny
Hen. Aug. Hornsby
Rich. Hall
Alex. Macleod
Alex. B. Le Mesurier
Cha. Brooke Morton
Tho. Lysaght
Rich. Angelo
J. Lealand Mowatt
Edw. J. Dickey
Christopher H. Naylor
Wm. Fergusson Beatson
George Rowley
Willoughby Trevelyan
John Back
Cha. Hunter
J. Skarden Ramsay
Edwin Hen. Atkinson
William Hill
Hen. Heaton Hobson
James Henderson Macbraire
Fred. Cha. Elwall
Fred. Coventry
Andrew Charlton
James Benwell
Wm. Brett
Cha. Lucas
Hen. Willoughby Trevelyan
Tho. Eaton Cosgrave
John Tho. Philpot
Fred. Wm. Birch
George Cox
Cha. Chester
Robert M'Nair
[illegible]
[illegible]
[illegible]
[illegible]

Rob. Wm. Honner
Geo. Sidney Wilkinson
Hen. Bower
Anthony Harrison
Sam. Auchinleck Grant
Wm. Meyrick Macaulay
Cha. Fran. Le Hardy
Alex. Shirrefs
Robert Garstin
David Archer
R. Hickley Richardson
Mich. John Rowlandson
Hen. Morland
Fred. Wm. Todd
William Halpin
Coghill Glendwr Ottley
John Blaxland
Fran. Ant. Clarke
John Hill
Rob. Grant Carmichael
Tho. Maynor
Cha. Woodfall
Francis Dudgeon
Gus. Cowper Rochfort
Rich. Lambert
Arthur Trotter
John Gordon
David Scotland
Hubert Marshall
John Wm. Hicks
Hamlyn Lavicourt Harris
Arnold Rawson Wilson
Rawson John Crozier
John Liddell
St. George Dan. Showers
John Wyn Strettell
Cha. Moray Macleane
Wm. Scott Adams
Rob. Nich. Faunce
John Free
Herbert Beaver
William Stewart
Stephen Williams
Henry Drummond
George St. Pat. Lawrence
Cha. Griffin
Cha. Commeline
Hen. Nelson Worsley
Somerset James Grove
George Le Grand Jacob
Henry Griffith
Henry Stamford
John Grant
E. Anstruther Farquharson
Hon. H. Burrard Dalzell
Edw. Madden
Edw. Hen. Ludlow
Hampden Nicholson Pepper
Philip Goldney
Tho. Ditmas
William Macgeorge
J. Chicheley Plowden
George Moyle Sherer
Fred. Lewis Nicolay
Lockyer Willis Hart
Aug. Sam. Hawkins
Alex. Rob. Rose
Edw. Darvall
Wm. Hen. Atkinson
Wm. Freeth
Rob. Long Shawe
Wm. Mitchell
James Drummond
Wm. Binfield Wemyss
James Pope
[illegible] Boscawen
[illegible]
[illegible]

Fred. Vaughan M'[illegible]
Wm. Russell
Donald Mackay S[illegible]
Wm. Elsey, 1 Jan
E. I. Depot a[illegible]
Henry Browne, 1[illegible]
John Jacob, 16Jan.
George Hall, 8 Oc[illegible]
George Balfour, d[illegible]
Fred. ConyersCott[illegible]
Eng. 11 Dec. 47. E[illegible]
Herbert Benj. Edwa[illegible]
Bengal Army, 1[illegible]
Lahore t[illegible]
Sir RichmondC.Sh[illegible]
BengalArt. 1 Dec.
Harvey Terrick Co[illegible]
gal Army, do.

CAPTAIN.

Christopher Vaugh[illegible]
18 July 48 *Huds[illegible]*
Company's t[illegible]

Recruiting for the [illegible]
Company's A[illegible]

CAPTAINS.

Richard Geo. Gran[illegible]
H. Vibart Glegg *E[illegible]*

*Wm. F. Hay, [illegible]
E. I. Co.'s Depot, [illegible]

Officers of the [illegible]
Helena Regt [illegible]
local rank at [illegible]
and Eastward [illegible]
of Good Hope.

Brigadier-G[illegible]
Charles Dallas....[illegible]

Lieut.-C[illegible]
C. R. G. Hodso[illegible]

Major
D. K. Pritchar[illegible]

Captain
T. M. Hunter...
G. A. Den Taaffe
J. B. Spiller...
D. Mc Mahon...
A. A. Younge...
W. O. Kenned[illegible]
W. K. Dovet[illegible]
W. Mason ...

Lieut[illegible]
G. W. Melli[illegible]
M. J. Johns[illegible]
S. F. Armstr[illegible]
W. P. Samp[illegible]
C. S. T. B[illegible]
J. R. C. M[illegible]
T. B. Knipe[illegible]
T. S. Reed...
J. B. Alex[illegible]
D. H. H. L[illegible]

F. N. [illegible]
H. Mar[illegible]
G. S. C[illegible]
C. Prit[illegible]
F. M. B[illegible]

YEOMEN OF THE GUARD.

Her Majesty's Body Guard.

(INSTITUTED BY HENRY VII., IN THE YEAR 1485.)

Captain.
The Marquess of Donegal.

Lieutenant.
Sir George Philip Lee.

Ensign.
Sir George Houlton.

Clerk of the Cheque and Secretary.
P W *Lieut.-Col.* John FitzMaurice, K.H.

Exons.

P W *Sir* William Bellairs.[1]
Late a Captain in the 15th Hussars.

Thomas Seymour Sadler.

P W John Kincaid.[2]
Late a Captain in the Rifle Brigade.

Richard Phibbs.[3]
Late a Captain in the 48th Foot.

6 Ushers and 100 Yeomen.

1 Sir William Bellairs entered the 10th Hussars in 1811, and retired from that Regt., as a Captain, in 1819. He served in the campaigns of 1813 and 14 in the Peninsula, and was present at the battle of Vittoria, the battles in the Pyrenees in front of Pampeluna on the 27th, 28th, 29th, and 30th July; blockade of Pampeluna from 18th to 31st Oct., when it surrendered, battle of Orthes, action at Tarbes, and battle of Toulouse, besides many minor affairs. Served also the campaign of 1815, including the action at Quatre Bras, the retreat the following day, and battle of Waterloo: horse killed on the retreat from Quatre Bras, and two wounded under him at Waterloo.

2 Captain Kincaid joined the Rifle Brigade in 1809, and retired from it as a Captain in 1831. He served on the Walcheren expedition in 1809; and subsequently in the Peninsula, including the retreat to the lines of Torres Vedras in 1810, occupation of them, pursuit of Massena, actions at Santarem, Pombal, Redinha, Casal Nova, Foz d'Arouce, and Sabugal, battle of Fuentes d'Onor, actions near Fuente Guinaldo and Aldea de Ponte, siege and storming of Ciudad Rodrigo,—led the storming party of the light division; siege and storming of Badajoz, actions on the heights of San Christoval and at Castrejon, battle of Salamanca, capture of Madrid, retreat from Salamanca, in which he was acting Brigade-Major to the 1st Brigade of the light division; actions at San Munos and San Milan, battle of Vittoria, and three days' severe skirmishing in following the enemy to Pampeluna, which ended in the capture of their last gun by the Rifle Brigade: battles of the Pyrenees, storming the heights of Echalar, storming the fortified heights of Bera, battles of the Nivelle and the Nive, together with those near Bayonne on the 9th, 10th, 11th, 12th, and 13th Dec. 1813; action at Tarbes, and battle of Toulouse, besides numerous minor affairs. Served also the campaign of 1815, and was present at the battle of Quatre Bras, the retreat on the following day, battle of Waterloo, and capture of Paris: at Waterloo his horse was wounded in five places and killed under him.

3 Captain Phibbs was present with the 48th Regt. at the attack and capture of Coorg (East Indies) in 1834.

and dependencies, St. Martin's, and St. Eustatius in 1810; also one campaign against the Burmese.

26 Major Goate's services:—Expedition to Germany in 1805 under Lord Cathcart; storming the heights of Soril, siege of Fort Bourbon, and capture of Martinique in 1809; Nepaul war in 1815, and was engaged on the heights of Muckwanpore, 15th Dec.; capture of Hattrass in 1816; Mahratta and Pindaree campaigns of 1817 and 18; Burmese war in 1825 and 26.

28 Major Hunt served at Hanover, in 1805, and 1806; at Copenhagen in 1807; and in the Peninsula from Sept. 1810 to May 1812, including the siege of Ciudad Rodrigo.

29 Major Shadwell Clerke served the Peninsular campaigns of 1808, 9, 10, and first part of 1811, including the battles of Roleia and Vimiera, retreat to Corunna, actions at Lugo and before Corunna, battle of Corunna (contused on the forehead by a musket-ball), operations on the Coa during the siege and battle of Almeida, battle of Busaco, retreat to the lines of Torres Vedras, affair near Leria, and actions of Pombal and Redinha, at which last he was severely wounded in the right leg, which was afterwards amputated.

30 Major Kitson served throughout the Kandian war of 1817, 18, and 19.

31 Major Noel served in St. Domingo in 1796, 97, and 98, under Generals Boyer and Sir Brent Spencer, and was wounded in the right thigh, when the French attacked the Cordon of Posts. Served also at the capture of St. Lucia, Tobago, and the colonies of Demerara, Essequibo, and Berbice.

33 Major Sherer served in the Peninsula with the 34th from July 1809 to Dec. 1811, and from August 1812 to July 1813, including the battles of Busaco, Albuhera, Arroyo de Molino, Vittoria, and Maya in the Pyrenees.

35 Major Samuel Thorpe served with the 23rd in the Peninsula under Sir John Moore, including the action at Lugo and battle of Corunna. Capture of Walcheren in 1809. Subsequently in the Peninsula, including the siege of Olivença, siege of Badajos in 1811, battle of Albuhera (twice wounded). Served with the 39th at the battle of Toulouse, when he was again severely wounded. Also in the American war at Plattsburg; and subsequently at the capture of Paris.

36 Major Begbie served in the Peninsula with the 82nd from Aug. 1808 to Nov. 1809, including the capture of Oporto and battle of Talavera,

38 Major Macpherson served in Hanover in 1805 and 6; at Buenos Ayres in 1807; in Portugal and Spain from July 1808 to Jan. 1809, including the battles of Roleia and Vimiera, action at Lugo, and battle of Corunna. With the expedition to Walcheren, and siege of Flushing, where he was wounded; the Peninsular campaigns from May to Dec. 1812, including the battle of Salamanca, where he was severely wounded.

39 Major Hartman served in the expedition to Hanover in 1805-6; at the siege of Copenhagen in 1807; in Sweden, Portugal, and Spain in 1808-9, including the advance and retreat of the army and in the battle of Corunna. Expedition to Walcheren, 1809; subsequent campaigns in the Peninsula and France, including the defence of Tarifa and affair of Casas Viejas, battle of Barrosa, actions of Arroyo del Molino and Almarez, battles of Vittoria, the Pyrenees (25th, 30th, and 31st July), Pass of Maya, Nivelle, Nive, Bayonne, and Orthes; affair at St. Palais, and battle of Toulouse.

40 Major Pinckney served with the 36th on the expedition to South America, including the taking of Maldonado and siege of Monte Video; in the Peninsula from June 1808 to May 1809, including the battles of Roleia and Vimiera. On the expedition to Walcheren in 1809; received the flag of truce at the outpost at the attack and capture of Ter Vere; present also at Middleburgh and Flushing.

41 Major Mackay served with the 68th on the expedition to Walcheren, and at the capture of Flushing in 1809. Also in the Peninsula from June 1811 to the end of that war in 1814, including the battle of Salamanca, retreat from Burgos, and battles of Vittoria (wounded in the head), the Pyrenees, the Nivelle, and Orthes.

42 Major Aubin served in the Peninsula from Nov. 1811 to the end of the war, including the battles of Vittoria, the Pyrenees, 25th, 28th, 30th, and 31st July; Nivelle, Nive, 9th, 11th, and 13th Dec. 1813, besides many other minor actions and skirmishes. Severely wounded through the left side, in action at Couches, 16th March 1814. Served subsequently in the American war.

43 Major Brown served the campaign of 1814 in Holland with the 21st, and was present at the storming of Bergen-op-Zoom.

44 Major William Seward served with the 9th in the Peninsula, from Aug. 1808 to Jan. 1809, and was present at the battle of Vimiera; on the expedition to Walcheren in 1809; and subsequently in the Peninsula, including the defence of Tarifa, battles of Barrosa (wounded), Vittoria, and the Nive, and blockade of Bayonne.

45 Major Stack served in the Peninsula with the 24th from June 1809 to Feb. 1813, and again from 2nd Dec. 1813 to the end of that war in 1814, including the battles of Talavera (wounded) and Busaco, actions at Espinal and Foz d'Arouce, repulse of a sortie at Ciudad Rodrigo, battle of Salamanca, capture of the Retiro at Madrid, taking of the hills and outworks before Burgos, siege of Burgos and storming of the breaches (severely contused) various skirmishes with the rear-guard and covering party at the bridge over the Carrion on the retreat, and battle of Orthes, where he was severely wounded by a ball, which shattered the left elbow-joint, and occasioned amputation of the arm. Served eight years in Canada, and received a severe contusion on the head in 1829, when on duty.

46 Major Romney served in the East Indies with the 17th from Dec. 1806 to May 1823, and

was present at the siege and capture of Gounourie in 1807; and the Mahratta campaign of 1817, including the affair of Jubblepore.

47 Major Donaldson served in the Peninsula with the 57th, from June 1809 to the end of that war in 1814, including the siege of Badajos in April 1811, battles of Albuhera, Vittoria, and the Pyrenees.

48 Major Clements served at the capture of the Cape of Good Hope in 1806; subsequently on the expedition to South America; the campaign of 1808-9 in Spain, and extra aide-de-camp to Sir John Moore at the battle of Corunna. On the expedition to Walcheren in 1809; the Peninsular campaigns from 1810 to 1814, including Cavares and Merida, Salamanca, Begar, Vittoria, Valley of Bastan, and the Pyrenees.

49 Major Doyle served with the expedition to South America, including the siege of and sortie from Monte Video, and storm by the enemy of Colonia. Served also in the south of France, from Dec. 1813 to the end of that war in 1814, including the blockade of Bayonne and repulse of the sortie, where he received a contusion on the left arm.

51 Major Meade served in the Peninsula from Sept. 1810 to Oct. 1811, including the battle of Fuentes d'Onor, and other minor affairs. On the staff of General Count Walmoden, in 1813, at the actions of Hasdorf in Mecklenburg, and Goerde in Hanover. Assisted also at the defence of Rostock by the Swedes, where his horse was killed, and his left arm disabled. Served the campaign in Holland, in 1814, including the attack on Merxem, bombardment of Antwerp, and attack on Bergen-op-Zoom.

52 Major Harrison served in the American war.

54 Major Murphy served in the Peninsula from Dec. 1808 until the end of the war, including actions at Albeigana and Grijo, passage of the Douro, capture of Coimbra, siege and capture of San Sebastian, passage of the Bidassoa, action at Bidart (wounded); battles of Nivelle, Nive, 9th, 10th (wounded), 11th, 12th, and 13th Dec.; blockade of Bayonne, action of St. Etienne, and battle of Toulouse. Medal for Toulouse.

55 Major Hooper served in the Peninsula from 1809 to 1811—when he was sent to England on account of his wounds—and was present at the battle of Busaco, lines at Torres Vedras, skirmishes on the retreat of Massena, actions at Campo Mayor and Bella Castel, first siege of Badajos, taking of Olivença, and battle of Albuhera, where he was severely wounded through the shoulder in a charge.

56 Major Willats served in the Peninsula from 1812 to the end of the war, including the siege and storming of Ciudad Rodrigo, siege and storming of Badajos from 19th Jan. to 6th April 1812; operations near and blockade of Bayonne.

59 Major George Bolton served the campaign in Spain, under Sir John Moore, with the 14th, and was present at the battle of Corunna. Also with the expedition to Walcheren, and at the siege of Flushing in 1809.

60 Major Thomas Reid served with the 33d at the capture of Bourbon and the Isle of France in 1810; the campaign of 1813 and 14 in Germany and Holland, including both attacks on Merxem and storming of Bergen-op-Zoom. Also the campaign of 1815, including the battle of Quatre Bras, retreat of the 17th June, and battle of Waterloo, where he was severely wounded.

61 Major Cox served at Travancore in 1809, and in Ava in 1825.

62 Major Charters served with the expedition to Hanover, under Lord Cathcart in 1805; the Walcheren expedition, in 1809; and campaign in Holland, under Lord Lynedoch, in 1814.

63 Major Mason served with the expedition to the coast of America, in 1813, and was engaged in several small actions. Present also at the capture of Moose Island, in the Bay of Fundy, in 1814.

65 Major Handcock accompanied the expedition to Hanover in 1805; joined the army in Sicily in 1806, and was employed with its various operations from 1806 to 1810; went with the expedition to Naples, and was present at the capture of Ischia and Procida; returned to Sicily and employed against the French army, in 1811. Served in Spain during 1812 and 13, including the battle of Castalla, siege of Tarragona, and affair of Villa Franca. Also the campaign of 1815, and was severely wounded at Waterloo.

66 Major Sutherland served with the 72d at the capture of the Cape of Good Hope in 1806; and accompanied the force from thence to co-operate at the capture of the Isle of France in 1810.

67 Major Gregory served in the American war in 1814 and 15, and commanded a gun-boat belonging to the Flotilla under Commander Owen, on Lake Ontario, for which he received the thanks of the Naval Commander-in-Chief.

68 Major Wright served at the capture of Madeira, in 1808; and the campaign in the Peninsula, under Sir John Moore, in 1808-9.

69 Major Stewart served with the 25th at the reduction of Martinique, St. Martin's, and St. Eustatius, in 1809: and of Guadaloupe in 1810, and again in 1815.

70 Major Crawfurd served in the Peninsula from Jan. 1812 to July 1814, including operations of the covering army during the siege of Badajos in 1812, as a volunteer 79th regt.; battle of Salamanca, capture of Madrid, battles of the Pyrenees, Nivelle, Nive, and Orthes (severe gun-shot wound).

71 Major Henry Reid served at Cadiz from March 1813 to the end of the war. Served also in the American war, including the affair at Hampden.

73 Major Long served with the 71st in the Peninsula, from Sept. 1813 to the end of that war in 1814, including the action at Cambo, battles of the Nive, before Bayonne (wounded), Orthes, Aire, Tarbes, and Toulouse. Also the campaign of 1815, including the battle of Waterloo.

74 Major Baron served in the Peninsula from Jan. 1813 to the end of that war in 1814.

75 Major Colebrook served on the expedition to Walcheren in 1809.

76 Major George Browne served the campaign of 1815, including the battles of Quatre Bras and Waterloo.

77 Major Bonamy served in the Peninsula with the 6th from Sept. 1813 to June 1814, including the battles of Nivelle, Nive, 9th, 10th, and 11th Dec. and Orthes.

78 Major Marshall served with the 91st on the expedition to Portugal in 1808, including the battles of Roleia and Vimiera, advance into Spain and retreat through Gallicia under Sir John Moore, action at Lugo, and battle of Corunna. Expedition to Walcheren in 1809. Subsequently in the Peninsula, including the battles of Vittoria, the Pyrenees (26th, 27th, 28th, and 30th July), the Nivelle, and the Nive, on the 9th, 10th, 11th, and 13th Dec. 1813, investment of Bayonne, and battle of Orthes. Slightly wounded at Pampeluna, 28th July 1813, and severely at Orthes.

79 Major Manners served in the Peninsula with the 59th from Aug. 1812 to May 1814, including the battle of Vittoria, siege and storming of San Sebastian in Aug. 1813, battle of the Nive on the 9th, 10th, and 11th December, 1813. Wounded at the storming of Bhurtpore on the 18th January 1826.

80 Major Raynes served at the siege of Copenhagen in 1807; with the expedition to Sweden, and subsequently to the Peninsula under Sir John Moore, including the retreat to Corunna. Served also subsequently in the Peninsula from March 1810, to the end of the war in 1814, including the defence of Cadiz, battle of Barrosa, defence of Tarifa, action at Seville, battles of Vittoria, Pyrenees, and Nivelle, passage of the Adour, and operations before Bayonne.

81 Major Cooke's services:—See page 116, note 2.

82 Major B. P. Browne served the campaign of 1815 with the 11th Dragoons, and was present the battle of Waterloo. Also at the siege and capture of Bhurtpore, under Lord Combermere, in 1825-6; and was a volunteer for the dismounted cavalry storming party.

83 Major Birtwhistle served the campaign of 1814 in the South of France with the 32nd. Also the campaign of 1815, including the battle of Quatre Bras (slightly wounded), retreat on the 17th June, and battle of Waterloo (severely wounded).

84 Major Moore was present with the 2nd battalion of the 87th in nearly every action in which it was engaged, the greater part of the time as adjutant, including the battle of Talavera (wounded in the right thigh, where the ball still remains) defence of Cadiz during the whole time, battle of Vittoria (two horses shot under him), the Pyrenees, Nivelle, Orthes (horse shot), Vic Bigorre (wounded), and Toulouse, besides various affairs of out-posts. Served also the Mahratta campaign of 1817 and 18; and in the Burmese war, in 1825 and 26.

85 Major John Clarke served in the Peninsula from March 1809 to the end of that war in 1814, including the battles of Oporto and Talavera, Lines of Torres Vedras, actions of Arroyo de Molino and Campo Mayor, battle of Albuhera, siege of Badajoz, battles of Vittoria, the Pyrenees (from 25th to 31st July, and 2nd Aug.), the Nivelle, the Nive, (9th and 13th Dec.), action of St. Palais, battle of Orthes, action at Aire, and battle of Toulouse, besides numerous skirmishes. At the battle of Albuhera, when in the command of a company of flankers, was struck down by a Polish Lancer, and taken prisoner, but made his escape in a charge of cavalry.

86 Major Algeo served in the Peninsula with the 77th from Aug. 1813 to the end of the war.

87 Major Sheppard served at Walcheren, in 1809; and in Canada from March 1814 to Dec. 1816, including the actions at Chippawa, Lundy's Lane, before Fort Erie, and the attack on Snake Hill.

89 Major Richardson served in the Peninsula with the 11th from Aug. 1809 to Oct. 1814, including the battle of Busaco, the subsequent retreat of the army to the lines before Lisbon, the advance and pursuit of the enemy when they broke up from Santarem, blockade of Almeida, and battle of Fuentes d'Onor.

90 Major Cannon served in the Peninsula with the old 94th from January 1810 to the end of the war, including the defence of Fort Matagorda in front of Cadiz in 1810, lines of Torres Vedras, battle of Fuentes d'Onor, first siege of Badajos, action at El Bodon, storm of Ciudad Rodrigo, (severely wounded in the chest); battles of Salamanca, Vittoria (slightly wounded in the right knee), Pyrenees, Nivelle, Orthes, and Toulouse.

91 Major Tatton served in the Peninsula from Aug. 1811 to the end of that war in 1814, and was present at the blockade of Bayonne.

92 Major Jackson served in the Peninsula from Dec. 1809 to 1814, and was severely wounded through the left breast and in both arms at the battle of Albuhera. Served subsequently in the American war.

93 Major Graham served at the siege of Flushing in 1809, and afterwards in the Peninsula, including the blockade of Bayonne. Subsequently in the American war, including the action at Bladensburg and capture of Washington, action near Baltimore, and those in front of New Orleans on the 20th Dec. 1814, and 8th Jan. 1815; also at the taking of Fort Bowyer.

95 Major Black served the campaign of 1815, including the battles of Quatre Bras and Waterloo, at which last he was slightly wounded. Also in the campaign on the Sutlej (Medal), including the battles of Buddiwal, Aliwal, and Sobraon.

96 Major White served with the 11th regt. on the expedition to Walcheren and at the siege of Flushing in 1809. He served afterwards in the Peninsula from July 1812 to the end of 1813.

97 Major Robertson served with the expedition to Walcheren in 1809, and was present at the siege of Flushing. Also at the taking of the Kandian country, in Ceylon, under Sir Robert Brownrigg.

98 Major Rivers landed at Passages in Dec. 1813, and joined the light division in Feb. 1814;

took charge of a division of the boats fitted out at Socoa for the passage of the Adour; then joined the force for the siege of Bayonne. Embarked for America in 1814.

100 Major Waymouth served in the Peninsula with the 2nd Life Guards from Nov. 1812 to the end of that war in 1814, including the battle of Vittoria, investment of Pampeluna, and the battles of the Pyrenees. Also the campaign of 1815, including the action at Quatre Bras, covering the retreat on the 17th June, and battle of Waterloo. Severely wounded and taken prisoner, when charging the French cuirassiers at Waterloo.

101 Major Buchan served the campaign of 1814 in Holland, including the reconnoitring of the position before Antwerp, action at Merxem, and bombardment of Antwerp.

103 Major Lowe served with the 16th Lancers at the siege of Bhurtpore in 1825-6, and was wounded.

104 Major Gibson served in the Peninsula with the 1st Light Infantry battalion of the King's German Legion, from Aug. 1813 to the end of that war in 1814, including the siege of San Sebastian, an action in the Pyrenees at the passage of the Bidassoa (wounded), and the subsequent actions in which the left wing of the army was engaged. Served also the campaign of 1815, and was present at the battle of Waterloo.

106 Major Morse Cooper served the campaign of 1814 as a Volunteer with the Royals, and was present at the investment of Bayonne, and repulse of the sortie. Also the campaign of 1815, including the battles of Quatre Bras and Waterloo. Served with the 11th Light Dragoons at the siege and capture of Bhurtpore in 1825-6. Slightly wounded at Bayonne, and severely at Waterloo, having received five wounds.

108 Major Leonard was at the storming of the enemy's works at the Island of Santa Maura, and at the siege of the fortress until its surrender in March 1810. Served in three boat actions when belonging to the *Magnificent*. When in the Perles he was in action with one line-of-battle ship and two frigates, off Toulon, from eight until three o'clock, Nov. 1811. In a boat action and about the same time, engaged with the batteries and three armed schooners at the entrance of the Petit Pass, off Toulon.

109 Major Nevill (see Note 3, page 116).

110 Major Jauncey served on the expedition to Walcheren in 1809. Subsequently in the Peninsula from July 1812 to June 1814, including the battle of Castalla, siege of Tarragona retreat from thence, its second siege, retreat from Villa Franca after the battle of the Pass of Ordall, and investment of Barcelona in 1814. Expedition to Naples in 1815.

111 Major Hill served the campaign of 1815, including the retreat on the 17th June, battle of Waterloo, and storming of Cambray. Served also in Caffraria in 1820 and 21; and afterwards in the Burmese war, including the taking of Mahrattee, and Aracan.

112 Major Lynch served at the siege of Flushing. At Malta and the Ionian Islands under Lord Wm. Bentinck. At Genoa and in the South of France in 1814. At the siege and capture of Bhurtpore and was wounded at the assault 18th Jan. 1826.

114 Major Wright served in the American war.

116 Major Cockell served at the siege and capture of Bhurtpore, under Lord Combermere.

118 Major de Lacy served in the Peninsula from Aug. 1809 to the end of the war, including the battles of Busaco and Albuhera, sieges of Ciudad Rodrigo and Badajos, battles of Salamanca, Vittoria, Pyrenees (28 July to 2 Aug.), Nivelle, Orthes, and Toulouse. Received a gun-shot wound in the right arm at Vittoria. Has served seven years in the West Indies since the peace.

119 Major Gordon served at the battle of Trafalgar.

120 Major Elgee served in the Peninsula and France from Feb. 1809 to the end of the war in 1814, including the battles of Talavera and Fuentes d'Onor, siege of Burgos (contused wound in the leg), and investment of Bayonne.

121 Major Pascoe served in the Peninsula and France from Aug. 1809 to Feb. 1814, including the battles of Salamanca, Vittoria, Nivelle, and Nive, passage of the Bidassoa, and other operations; sieges of Badajoz (first siege), Forts of Salamanca, Burgos, and San Sebastian. Army of Occupation from 1815 to 1818.

122 Major Spiller served at Walcheren, and was present at the siege of Flushing, and the attack and capture of Ter Vere.

123 Major Montagu served at the siege of Dantzic, in 1813; also the campaign of 1815, including the battle of Waterloo and capture of Cambray.

124 Major Bridges served at Walcheren in 1809, and in the Peninsula and France from July 1811 to Aug. 1814, including the defence of Cadiz in 1811; battles of Vittoria and the Pyrenees; passage of Bidassoa; Nivelle, Nive, and Adour; and the operations before Bayonne. Attached to the Prussian corps d'armée in 1815, under the command of Prince Augustus of Prussia, and employed in the reduction of Philippeville, Marienbourg, and Rocroy. Adjutant to the Royal Artillery, serving with the force employed in Portugal in 1826; and the Brigade-Major to the Royal Artillery in the Canadas in 1838.

125 Major Charles Campbell served at the siege of Flushing in 1809; and subsequently in the Peninsula, including the battle of Castalla, and siege of Tarragona, under Sir J. Murray.

127 Major Caine served in the Nepaul campaign of 1815, and was present in action at Jeelghur. In the Deccan war of 1817 and 18, including the action at Jhubbulpore, where he carried the regimental colour of the 17th in the attack of the heights defended by the Arabs. He was Major of Brigade at the assault and capture of Bhurtpore, and was present during the whole of the siege: wounded by a grape shot in the left foot whilst charging the enemy's guns on the day of the capture. He commanded the Grenadiers of the 26th at the capture of Chusan

"PENINSULA"—"WATERLOO."

Years' Serv. Full Pay.	Half Pay.	
56		***Colonel.***
		P W Henry William, *Marquis of* Anglesey,[1] KG. GCB. GCH. *Lieut.-Col.* *12 Sept. 1793; *Col.* 3 May, 96; *Major-Gen.* 29 April, 1802; *Lieut.-Gen.* 25 April, 08; *Gen.* 12 Aug. 19; *Field Marshal*, 9 Nov. 46; *Colonel* of the Royal Horse Guards 20 Dec. 42.
		Lieut.-Colonel.
37	0	P W Everard Wm. Bouverie,[2] *Cornet*, P 2 April, 12; *Lieut.* 15 Oct. 12; *Capt.* P 9 Sept. 19; *Brev.-Maj.* 6 May, 31; *Maj. & Lt.-Col.* P 4 Dec. 32; *Lt.-Col. & Col.* P 16 Sept. 45.
		Major.
25	0	*Hon.* George Cecil Weld Forester, *Cornet*, P 27 May, 24; *Lieut.* P 1 Aug. 26; *Capt.* P 6 July, 32; *Brev.-Maj.* 9 Nov. 46; *Maj. & Lt.-Col.* P 19 Sept. 48.

Full Pay.	Half Pay.	CAPTAINS.	CORNET.	LIEUT.	CAPTAIN.	BREVET-MAJOR.
20	0	Wyndham Edw. Hanmer	P 26 Mar. 29	P 15 Mar. 31	P 9 Jan. 35	9 Nov. 46
19	0	*Hon.* Horace Pitt	P 27 Feb. 30	P 6 July 32	P 11 Nov. 36	9 Nov. 46
19	0	R. H. R. Howard Vyse ..	P 30 Nov. 30	P 31 May 33	P 27 Sept. 42	
12	0	A. Bateman Periam Hood	P 30 June 37	P 22 July 42	P 3 Apr. 46	
9	0	Hugh Smith Baillie	P 3 April 40	P 24 Mar. 43	P 7 Aug. 46	
9	0	*Lord* Geo. John Manners	P 20 Oct. 40	P 4 Aug. 43	P 5 Feb. 47	
7	0	*Lord* Alex. F.C.G. Lennox	P 8 Feb. 42	P 25 June 44	P 30 Mar. 47	
7	0	Horace Dormer Trelawny	P 15 April 42	P 27 Sept. 44	P 19 Sept. 48	
		LIEUTENANTS.				
7	0	Robert Sheffield	P 22 July 42	P 28 Feb. 45		
6	0	*Hon.* Lewis Alex. Grant	P 24 Mar. 43	P 4 July 45		
6	0	*Hon.* Geo. Watson Milles	P 22 Sept. 43	P 3 Apr. 46		
5	0	Fra. Wm. FitzHardinge Berkeley	P 27 Sept. 44	P 7 Aug. 46		
7	0	Wm. Griffin Sutton, *adj.*	19 Aug. 42	15 Jan. 47		
5	0	Francis Howard Vyse ..	P 29 Nov. 44	P 5 Feb. 47		
4	0	*Lord* Otho A. FitzGerald, *s.*	P 10 Jan. 45	P 30 Mar. 47		
4	0	Duncan James Baillie ..	P 28 Feb. 45	P 28 Sept. 47		
6	0	Joseph Brunt, R.M.	24 Nov. 43	P 19 Sept. 48		
		CORNETS.				
4	0	Wm. James Hope Gambier	P 4 July 45			
4	0	Edward Breedon	P 16 Sept. 45			
3	0	*Lord* Geo. C. G. Lennox	P 3 Apr. 46			
3	0	Sackville Geo. Lane Fox	P 7 Aug. 46			
2	0	Thomas Leslie	P 5 Feb. 47			
2	0	Cha. Sidney Davers Mills	P 20 July 47			
2	0	*Hon.* Philip Sidney	P 28 Sept. 47			
1	0	John Wyndham Billington	P 19 Sept. 48			

Full Pay.	Half Pay.	
7	0	*Adjutant.—Lieut.* William Griffin Sutton, 15 Jan. 47.
18	0	*Quarter-Master.*—Herbert Turner, 1 Jan. 31.
22	0	*Surgeon.*—George Gulliver, 2 June, 43; *A.-S.* 12 June, 28; *H.-A.* 17 May, 27.
	0	*Assistant-Surgeon.*—Fergus Kerin, 18 Aug. 48.
35	1 2/12	*Veterinary-Surgeon.*—P John Siddall,[3] 10 Oct. 12.

Blue—*Facings* Scarlet.—*Agents*, Messrs. Cox & Co.

[*Returned from France, February*, 1816.]

1 Lord Anglesey joined the Duke of York's army in Flanders in 1794, in command of the 80th; in the retreat he had the temporary command of Lord Cathcart's Brigade. Accompanied the Duke on the Expedition to Holland in 1799, and commanded the cavalry in the action of the 2nd Oct.,—"late in the evening, the enemy's cavalry having been defeated in an attempt which they made upon the British Horse Artillery on the beach, and having been charged by the cavalry under Lord Paget, were driven with considerable loss nearly to Egmont op-Zee." In the retreat of that army he protected the rear with his cavalry, and some skirmishing having taken place in which several pieces of cannon fell into the hands of the enemy, his Lordship with one squadron attacked the force under General Simon, amounting to six times his own numbers, repulsed them, retaking the British, and capturing at the same time several pieces of the enemy's cannon. In 1808 he proceeded to the Peninsula in command of two brigades of cavalry; attacked and defeated a body of the enemy at Sahagun; and, during the retreat of Sir John Moore he brought up the rear, and was engaged with the enemy at Mayorga and Benevente. Commanded a division of the Army under the Earl of Chatham on the Walcheren Expedition, in 1809. Commanded the cavalry in the campaign of 1815; engaged in frequent charges on the enemy, in protecting the rear of the infantry on the retreat of the 17th June; and, towards the close of the battle of Waterloo he was struck on the right thigh by a cannon-shot,—leg amputated. His Lordship has received a Medal for Sahagun and Benevente.

2 Colonel Bouverie served in the Peninsula from October, 1812, to the end of that war in 1814, including the battle of Vittoria. Served also the campaign of 1815, and was wounded at Waterloo.

3 Mr. Siddall served the campaign of 1815, and was present at the battle of Waterloo.

"WATERLOO."

Years' Serv.		
62		
Full Pay.	Half Pay.	

Colonel.

62 — *Hon. Sir* William Lumley,[1] GCB. *Cornet*, 24 Oct. 1787; *Lieut.* 19 May 90; *Capt.* 4 Dec. 93; *Major*, 10 Mar. 95; *Lieut.-Col.* 25 May, 95; *Col.* 29 April, 1802; *Major-Gen.* 25 Oct. 09; *Lieut.-Gen.* 4 June, 14; *Gen.* 10 Jan. 37; *Col. 1st Dragoon Guards*, 30 April, 40.

Lieut.Colonel.

21 | 5 — Henry Aitchison Hankey, *Ens.* P 26 June, 23; *Lieut.* P 10 March, 25; *Capt.* P 15 Aug. 26; *Major*, P 27 Sept. 33; *Lieut.-Col.* 1 March, 39.

Major.

27 | 5 — Joshua Simmonds Smith, *Cornet*, P 14 Aug. 17; *Lieut.* 25 May, 22; *Capt.* P 19 April, 27; *Major*, P 31 Dec. 33; *Brevet Lieut.-Col.* 9 Nov. 46.

Full Pay	Half Pay		Cornet.	Lieut.	Captain.	Brevet-Major.
		Captains.				
18	0	Alfred Scott	P 27 Sept. 31	P 11 July 34	P 8 Mar. 39	
10	0	William Warner Allen ..	P 29 Nov. 39	P 30 Apr. 41	P 2 Aug. 44	
10	0	James Peach Peach	P 15 June 39	P 17 June 42	P 11 Dec. 46	
9	0	George Wm. Blathwayt	P 20 Nov. 40	P 5 Aug. 42	P 13 Aug. 47	
9	0	Lockhart Little	P 7 Aug. 40	P 16 Aug. 42	P 31 Mar. 48	
8	0	William Tuthill	P 11 June 41	P 19 Jan. 44	P 31 Mar. 48	
13	0	Richard A. Moore......	P 12 Feb. 36	P 10 July 37	P 26 May 48	
7	0	James S. Stirling Stuart	P 17 June 42	P 3 May 44	P 3 Oct. 48	
		Lieutenants.				
7	0	Charles Geo. O'Callaghan	P 6 May 42	P 22 Dec. 43		
7	0	Edw. Rob. Starkie Bence	P 16 Aug. 42	P 2 Aug. 44		
6	0	Charles Arkwright......	P 24 Feb. 43	P 27 June 46		
9	0	James Foster	15 Dec. 40	P 30 Dec. 45		
7	0	Henry Charles Morgan[6]	P 6 May 42	P 24 Jan. 46		
5	0	George Briggs	P 10 May 44	P 13 Aug. 47		
5	0	Mordaunt Fenwick	P 14 June 44	P 31 Mar. 48		
4	0	Jas. Rob. Steadman Sayer	P 23 May 45	P 31 Mar. 48		
3	0	Emanuel Bradbury, *adj.*	8 Dec. 46	25 May 48		
2	0	Bankes Tomlin	P 2 Mar. 47	P 26 May 48		
2	0	Hugh Hamilton.........	P 1 Oct. 47	P 3 Oct. 48		
		Cornets.				
1	0	John Kemp, R.M.......	P 10 Mar. 48			
1	0	G. H. Warrington Carew	P 31 Mar. 48			
1	0	Robert Thomas Thomson	P 1 Apr. 48			
1	0	William Jacob Birt	P 26 May 48			
1	0	Charles Edwin Wyatt ..	P 18 July 48			
1	0	George Paynter	P 3 Nov. 48			

5 Capt. Hammersley served in the Peninsula from Aug. 1812 to the end of that war in 1814, and was present at the battles of Vittoria and Toulouse, and the investment of, and the Heights before Pampeluna. Shot through the shoulder whilst protecting a house in the neighbourhood of Dublin, on duty in 1806, when in the Militia.

Full Pay	Half Pay	
36	1	*Paymaster.*—Fred. Hmmersley,[5] 26 Sept. 48; *Cornet*, P 23 Jan. 12; *Lieut.* P 9 April 12; *Capt.* 8 May 40.
3	0	*Adjutant.*—*Lieut.* Emanuel Bradbury, 8 Jan. 47.
11	0	*Quarter-Master.*—Joseph Missett, 30 March, 38.
11	0	*Surgeon.*—Edward William Stone, MD. 17 March 48; *Assist.-Surg.* 5 Oct. 38.
2	0	*Assistant-Surgeon.*—John Peile, 8 Jan. 47.
5	0	*Veterinary Surgeon.*—F. Delany, 25 Sept. 44.

Scarlet—*Facings* Blue.—*Agents*, Messrs. Cox & Co.—*Irish Agents*, Sir E. R. Borough, *Bt.*, Armit, & Co.

[*Returned from Canada, Aug.* 1843.]

1 Sir William Lumley commanded the 22nd Light Dragoons in Ireland during the rebellion in 1798; was severely wounded through the ankle joint at Antrim, and preserved the town from being burnt by the rebels. Subsequently served in the command of that corps in the first expedition to Egypt under Sir Ralph Abercromby. Appointed to the staff at the Cape of Good Hope in 1806, but was afterwards transferred to be second in command of the expedition under Sir Samuel Auchmuty to South America; commanded the advance on landing in the Rio de la Plata, and at the capture of Monte Video, and the subsequent disastrous proceedings at Buenos Ayres under Lieut.-General Whitelock. Commanded the advance and landing at the capture of the island of Ischia, 1809. Appointed to the staff in the Peninsula in 1810; joined the army in the North of Portugal, and served as Major-General in Lord Hill's division, and subsequently in the same division under Lord Beresford; commanded on the Christoval side at the first siege of Badajoz in 1811, and upon the raising of that siege he commanded the whole of the allied cavalry at the battle of Albuhera, and also at the cavalry action at Usagre. Sir William has received a medal for Albuhera.

6 Lt. Morgan was present at the battles of Moodkee and Ferozeshah, at which last he was severely wounded.

Years' Serv.

Colonel.

66 — *Sir* Thomas Gage Montresor,[1] KCH. *Ens.* 12 March, 1783; *Lieut.* 4 April, 83; *Capt.* 17 June, 94; *Major*, 12 April, 99; *Lieut.-Col.* 27 June, 1801; *Col.* 25 July, 10; *Major-Gen.* 4 June, 13; *Lieut.-Gen.* 27 May, 25; *Gen.* 23 Nov. 41; *Col.* 2nd Dragoon Guards, 20 Feb. 37.

Full Pay.	Half Pay.	
		Lieut.-Colonel.
17	0	William Campbell, *Cornet*, P 6 Jan. 32; *Lieut.* P 12 Apr. 33; *Capt.* P 27 May, 36; *Major*, P 11 June, 41; *Lieut.-Col.* P 30 Jan. 46.
		Major.
24	$1\frac{1}{12}$	Power Le Poer Trench, *Ensign*, P 12 Aug. 24; *Lieut.* P 17 Dec. 25; *Capt.* P 30 Dec. 26; *Brevet-Major*, 23 Nov. 41; *Major*, P 30 Jan. 46.

Full Pay.	Half Pay.		CORNET.	LIEUT.	CAPTAIN.	BREVET-MAJOR.
		CAPTAINS.				
15	0	Francis Meynell	P 17 Jan. 34	P 24 April 35	P 3 Dec. 41	
18	0	Hylton Brisco	P 11 Oct. 31	P 25 July 34	P 4 Aug. 43	
12	0	Robert Wm. Dallas	P 6 Oct. 37	P 13 Dec. 39	P 23 Sept. 45	
10	0	Fred. James Ibbetson ..	P 17 May 39	P 18 Dec. 40	P 30 Jan. 46	
7	$\frac{10}{12}$	Atwood Dalton Wigsell..	P 3 Dec. 41	P 24 Feb. 43	P 8 Jan. 47	
11	0	Charles Hugh Key	P 9 Mar. 38	P 23 April 39	P 28 Apr. 48	
		LIEUTENANTS.				
14	0	Francis Haviland, *adj.* ..	24 Nov. 35	29 Sept. 37		
9	0	Charles Edward Conyers, *s.*	P 18 Dec. 40	P 25 Nov. 42		
9	0	Charles William Calvert	P 6 Nov. 40	P 31 Mar. 43		
6	0	John Carstairs Jones....	P 15 Dec. 43	P 23 Sept. 45		
6	0	Charles Edward Walker	P 29 Dec. 43	P 14 Apr. 46		
4	0	Leycester Hibbert	P 23 Sept. 45	P 25 June 47		
5	0	Edmund Ruck Keene ..	P 20 Dec. 44	P 24 Dec. 47		
2	0	Thomas Belsey Tomlin ..	P 25 June 47	P 15 Aug. 48		
5	0	Bryan Thornhill........	25 June 44	7 Aug. 46		
		CORNETS.				
8	0	George Bushman, R.M.	30 Apr. 41			
1	0	John Fermor Godfrey ..	P 26 May 48			
1	0	John Griffith Price	P 7 July 48			
1	0	John Clements	P 15 Aug. 48			

Full Pay.	Half Pay.	
13	0	*Paymaster.*—Henry Bond Head, 30 May, 45; *Ens.* P 23 Dec. 36; *Lieut.* P 21 June, 39; *Capt.* P 21 Mar. 45.
14	0	*Adjutant.*—*Lieut.* Francis Haviland, 4 Dec. 35.
13	0	*Quarter-Master.*—John Haviland, 15 July, 36.
23	0	*Surgeon.*—Alexander George Home, M.D., 24 March, 43; *Assist.-Surg.* 18 Jan. 27; *Hosp.-Assist.* 6 Oct. 26.
3	0	*Assistant-Surgeon.*—Alexander Smith, M.D., 7 Aug. 46.
14	0	*Veterinary Surgeon.*—Opie Smith, 20 Feb. 35.

Scarlet—*Facings* Black.—*Agents*, Messrs. Charles Hopkinson & Co.

[*Returned from France, November*, 1818.]

1 Sir Thomas Montresor has been twenty-four years on regimental full-pay, during which period he served at Gibraltar in 17[illegible] and [illegible], in Flanders and Holland in 1793, 4, and 5; the Egyptian campaign of 1801; and subsequently many years in India.

"TALAVERA" — "ALBUHERA" — "VITTORIA" — "PENINSULA."

Years' Serv. 50 (Full Pay. | Half Pay.)

Colonel.

P W Charles Murray, *Earl* Cathcart,[1] KCB. *Ens.* May, 99; *Lieut.* 10 Aug. 99; *Capt.* 3 Feb. 03; *Major*, 14 May, 07; *Lieut.-Col.* 30 Aug. 10; *Col.* 12 Aug. 19; *Major-Gen.* 22 July, 30; *Lt.-Gen.* 23 Nov. 41; *Colonel* 3rd Dragoon Guards, 19 Nov. 46.

Lieut.-Colonel.

24 | 0 Thomas Arthur, *Cornet*, P 23 June, 1825; *Lieut.* P 19 Sept. 26; *Capt.* P 8 Feb. 31; *Major*, P 15 Sept. 38; *Lieut.-Col.* P 12 May, 43.

Major.

16 | 0 John Daniel Dyson, *Cor.* P 9 Dec. 31; *Lieut.* P 22 Mar. 33; *Capt.* P 8 July 36; *Major*, P 19 June, 46.

Full Pay.	Half Pay.	CAPTAINS.	CORNET.	LIEUT.	CAPTAIN.	BREVET MAJOR.
16	0	Edward Dyson	P 18 Oct. 33	P 27 Oct. 37	P 17 Mar. 43	
12	0	William Squire	P 24 Mar. 37	P 2 Aug. 42	P 19 June 46	
7	0	Tho. Tristram Spry Carlyon	P 27 Dec. 42	P 6 Dec. 44	P 1 Dec. 46	
11	0	Henry Hickman Bacon ..	P 8 June 38	P 8 Nov. 42	P 5 Nov. 47	
11	0	Edward Bagwell Purefoy	P 15 Sept. 38	P 10 Feb. 43	P 3 Dec. 47	
9	0	Peter Broughton	P 30 Oct. 40	P 17 Mar. 43	P 10 Nov. 48	
		LIEUTENANTS.				
7	0	A. Rudkin Robinson, *adj.*	22 July 42	11 May 43		
7	0	Henry Marsh	P 5 Aug. 42	P 12 May 43		
6	0	Richard Croker	P 10 Feb. 43	P 22 Nov. 44		
6	0	Thomas Edward Whitby	P 12 May 43	P 19 June 46		
5	0	Edmund Henry Turton ..	P 15 Mar. 44	P 24 July 46		
3	0	Arch. Douglas Monteath	P 24 July 46	P 3 Dec. 47		
2	0	William Hickes Slade ..	19 Mar. 47	P 23 May 48		
2	0	Henry Heywood Lonsdale	P 2 Apr. 47	P 10 Nov. 48		
		CORNETS.				
2	0	J.H. de Cardonnel Lawson	P 6 Nov. 47			
2	0	Wyndham Knatchbull ..	P 3 Dec. 47			
2	0	Jas. Winterbottom, *R.M.*	17 Dec. 47			
1	0	Augustus Hunt	P 23 May 48			
	0	Charles Denison Pedder...	P 7 July 46			

19 | 0 *Paymaster.*—Ernest Aug. Hawker, 19 Oct. 38; *Ens.* 30 Sept. 30, *Lieut.* July, 36.

7 | 0 *Adjutant.*—*Lieut.* Andrew R. Robinson, 2 Aug. 42.

8 | 0 *Quarter-Master.*—P John Heydon,[2] 30 April, 41.

42 | 0 *Surgeon.*—P George Alex. Stephenson,[3] 28 Oct. 18; *Assist. Surg.* 14 May, 07.

2 | 0 *Assistant Surgeon.*—Richard Carmichael Bourne, 13 July, 47.

1 | 0 *Veterinary Surgeon.*—Austin Cooper Shaw, 21 Aug. 48.

Scarlet — *Facings* Yellow. — *Agents*, Messrs. Cox and Co.

[*Returned from France, January*, 1816.]

1 Lord Cathcart served on the Helder expedition in 1799. Accompanied the Expedition under Sir James Craig, and served in Naples and Sicily, in 1805 and 6, as Assistant Quarter-Master-General. Served on the Scheldt expedition, and was present at the siege of Flushing, in 1809. Proceeded to the Peninsula in 1812, as an Assistant Quarter-Master-General, and was present at the battles of Barrosa, Salamanca, and Vittoria, for which he has received a medal and two clasps. Served also the campaign of 1815, and was present at the battle of Waterloo.

2 Quarter-Master Heydon's services:—expedition to Walcheren, siege of Flushing, and expedition to South Beveland, in 1809; Peninsular Campaigns of 1812 and 13.

3 Mr. Stephenson served in the Peninsula from March 1809 to the end of that war in 1814.

On the Standards and Appointments the HARP AND CROWN, *and the Star of* ST. PATRICK, with the motto "*Quis Separabit?*"
"PENINSULA."

Years' Serv. Full Pay	Half Pay	
63		*Colonel.*
		P *Sir* George Anson,[1] GCB. *Cornet*, 3 May, 1786; *Lieut.* 16 March, 91; *Capt.* 9 Sept. 92; *Major*, 25 Dec. 94; *Lieut.-Col.* 21 Dec. 97; *Col.* 1 Jan. 05; *Maj.-Gen.* 25 July 10; *Lieut.-Gen.* 12 Aug. 19; *Gen.* 10 Jan 37; *Col.* 4th Dragoon-Guards, 24 Feb. 27.
		Lieut.-Colonel.
23	0	Edward Cooper Hodge, *Cornet*, 3 Aug. 26; *Lieut.* P 3 July 28; *Capt.* P 19 Dec. 34; *Major*, P 3 Dec. 41; *Lt.-Col.* P 3 Oct. 48.
		Major.
13	0	William Charles Forrest, *Cornet*, P 11 Mar. 36; *Lieut.* P 5 Jan. 39; *Capt.* P 7 Sept. 41; *Major*, P 3 Oct. 48.

Full Pay	Half Pay	CAPTAINS.	CORNET.	LIEUT.	CAPTAIN.	BREVET MAJOR.
12	0	Thos. Oliver W. Coster ..	P 4 Aug. 37	P 23 Nov. 38	P 27 Mar. 46	
9	0	Francis Rowland Forster	P 7 Feb. 40	P 11 Mar. 42	P 29 Jan. 47	
13	0	Josias Rogers John Coles[3]	P 2 Sept. 36	P 22 Mar. 39	P 19 Mar. 47	
8	0	James Cunningham	P 21 May 41	P 7 April 43	P 8 Oct. 47	
8	0	Thomas Jones..........	P 23 July 41	P 19 May 43	P 30 June 48	
6	0	Fra. Hastings G. Nicolls	P 2 June 43	P 27 Mar. 46	P 3 Oct. 48	
		LIEUTENANTS.				
6	0	John Mullen, *adj.*	9 Mar. 43	26 Mar. 46		
6	0	Ernest Henry Lane	P 14 July 43	P 19 May 46		
5	0	Thos. Miller Clarke, R.M.	30 July 44	P 29 Jan. 47		
5	0	Michael M'Creagh......	26 July 44	P 19 Mar. 47		
5	0	Thomas Bigoe Williams	P 23 Aug. 44	P 2 Apr. 47		
3	0	Arth. Masterson Robertson	P 18 May 46	P 8 Oct. 47		
3	0	John Collingwood	P 19 May 46	P 30 June 48		
		CORNETS.				
2	0	Henry Thos. Richardson	P 29 Jan. 47			
2	0	John Rich. Smyth Wallis	P 19 Mar. 47			
2	0	John MacDonnell Webb	P 2 Apr. 47			
2	0	W. Wm. Rudyerd Williams	P 8 Oct. 47			
1	0	John Glasgow	P 7 July 48			
1	0	James Robert Scott	P 3 Oct. 48			

4 Capt. Ralston was embarked with a detachment of the 24th Light Dragoons in the outward bound Indian fleet, which maintained an action with a French squadron, under Admiral Linois, off the Mauritius, 6th Aug. 1805, and in which the enemy were beaten off. On the 6th Aug. 1809, he led the advanced squadron of his regiment in action with the rebels before Seringapatam, in which the latter were beaten and dispersed; and on the same date he commanded the outlying piquet in a night attack from the garrison of Seringapatam.

Full Pay	Half Pay	
39	6 1/12	*Paymaster.*—John Ralston,[4] 29 Dec. 25; *Cornet*, P 6 July 04; *Lieut.* 10 July 06; *Capt.* 26 May 14.
6	0	*Adjutant.*—*Lieut.* John Mullen, 10 March, 43.
1	0	*Quarter-Master.*—John Thompson, 3 Oct. 48.
16	0	*Surgeon.*—Chilley Pine,[5] 5 Dec. 43; *Assist.-Surg.* 2 Aug. 33.
4	0	*Assist.-Surgeon.*—James Flyter, 6 June 45.
21	0	*Veterinary Surgeon.*—James Rainsford, 25 Dec. 28.

Scarlet—*Facings* Blue.—*Agent*, Geo. Samuel Collyer, Esq.
[*Returned from Portugal, May*, 1813.]

1 Sir George Anson served in Holland under H. R. H. The Duke of York and Sir Ralph Abercromby. Served also the campaigns of 1809, 10, 11, 12, and 13 in the Peninsula; commanded the 16th Light Dragoons at the battle of Oporto; and a brigade of Light Cavalry at the battles of Talavera, Busaco, Salamanca, and Vittoria. Sir George has received a Medal and two Clasps for Talavera, Salamanca, and Vittoria.

3 Capt. Coles served with the 4th Light Dragoons in the campaign under Lord Keane in Scinde and Affghanistan in 1838-9, and was present at the taking of Ghuznée.

5 Mr. Pine served with the 26th on the China expedition, (medal) and was present at the first capture of Chusan, attack on Canton, attack and capture of Amoy, repulse of the night attack on Ningpo, attack and capture of Tscke, Chapoo, Shanghai Woosung, and Chin Kiang Foo. He acted as senior Medical Officer in the campaigns in New Zealand, from April 1845 to May 1846, and was present at the destruction of Pomare's Pah, attack on Heki's Pah, destruction of the Waikadi Pah, storming of Kawiti's Pah at Ohiawai, and capture of Kawiti's Pah at Ruapekapeka.

The motto "*Vestigia nulla retrorsum.*"—"SALAMANCA"—"VITTORIA"—"TOULOUSE"—"PENINSULA."

Years' Serv. Full Pay.	Half Pay.	
69		*Colonel.*
		ℙ *Sir* John Slade, *Bart.*[1] GCH., *Cornet,* 11 May, 1780; *Lieut.* 28 April, 83; *Capt.* 24 Oct. 87; *Major,* 1 March, 94; *Lieut.-Col.* 29 April, 95; *Col.* 29 April, 1802; *Major-Gen.* 25 Oct. 09; *Lieut.-Gen.* 4 June, 14; *Gen.* 10 Jan. 37; *Col.* 5th Dragoon Guards, 20 July 31.
		Lieut.-Colonel.
30	1 2/12	*Hon.* James Yorke Scarlett, *Cornet,* P 26 March, 18; *Lieut.* P 24 Oct. 21; *Capt.* P 9 June, 25; *Major,* P 11 June, 30; *Lieut.-Col.* P 3 July, 40
		Major.
17	0	Charles W. Morley Balders,[2] CB. *Cornet,* P 10 Nov. 25; *Lieut.* P 25 Nov. 28; *Capt.* P 15 July, 36; *Major,* P 16 May, 45; *Brevet-Lt.-Col.* 3 Apr. 46.

Full Pay.	Half Pay.		CORNET.	LIEUT.	CAPTAIN.	BREVET-MAJOR.
		CAPTAINS.				
24	0	Abraham Bolton........	P 12 Oct. 25	P 26 June 27	P 8 Mar. 33	9 Nov. 46
17	0	Robert Bell............	P 16 Nov. 32	P 27 June 34	P 9 Mar. 38	
14	0	John Ireland Blackburne	P 3 April 35	P 17 June 36	P 26 Oct 41	
12	0	James Charles Yorke....	P 13 Jan. 37	P 10 Aug. 38	P 11 July 45	
12	0	Arthur Prime	P 30 June 37	P 5 April 39	P 26 Sept. 45	
12	0	George Lloyd Robson....	P 28 Nov. 37	P 3 July 40	P 30 Mar. 47	
		LIEUTENANTS.				
11	0	Wm. Noel Algernon Hill	P 10 Aug. 38	P 26 Oct. 41		
10	0	George Rowan Hamilton	P 10 Aug. 39	P 3 June 42		
8	0	James Fort............	P 11 May 41	P 27 Jan. 43		
8	0	Charles Holder	P 26 Oct. 41	P 30 July 44		
24	0	ℙ James Henley, R. M.[3]	6 Jan. 25	P 28 Nov. 45		
9	0	Thomas Robbins, *adj.* ..	7 May 40	13 April 46		
4	0	Chardin Philip Johnson..	P 14 Mar. 45	P 14 April 46		
4	0	John Jenkins Thomas ..	P 11 July 45	P 30 Mar. 47		
9	0	W. Sandfd. Wills Sandford	P 14 Aug. 40	P 8 Aug. 45		
		CORNETS.				
4	0	John Fort	P 10 Oct. 45			
3	0	George Duckworth	P 12 June 46			
3	0	Charles Wilton Goad...	7 July 46			
2	0	Adolp. Wm. Desart Burton	P 30 Mar. 47			

Full Pay.	Half Pay.	
12	1 4/12	*Paymaster.*—Edmund Vernon MacKinnon, 30 June, 48; *Cornet & Sub-Lieut.* P 29 April, 36; *Lieut.* P 27 March, 40.
9	0	*Adjutant.*—*Lieut.* Thomas Robbins, 8 May, 40.
8	0	*Quarter-Master.*—Alexander Langford, 18 June, 41.
40	5 3/12	*Surgeon.*—James Barlow,[5] M.D. 29 July, 13; *Assist.-Surg.* 5 March, 07; *Hosp.-Assist.* 25 June, 03.
8	0	*Assistant-Surgeon.*—William Arden, 9 April 41.
6	0	*Veterinary Surgeon.*—George Fisher, 29 Dec. 43.

Scarlet—*Facings* Green.—*Agents,* Messrs. Cox & Co.
[*Returned from Spain, July,* 1814.]

1 Sir John Slade served in Portugal and Spain, under Sir John Moore, in command of the Hussar Brigade, including the different operations terminating with the battle of Corunna. Placed again on the staff in the Peninsula, in Aug. 1809, where he served until June, 1813, in command of a brigade of cavalry. Sir John has received a Medal and one Clasp for the battles of Corunna and Fuentes d'Onor.

2 Lieut.-Col. Balders served the campaign on the Sutlej in 1845-6 (Medal), and commanded the 3rd Light Dragoons in the battles of Moodkee and Ferozeshah (wounded).

3 Lieut. Henley served the campaign of 1814 in the Peninsula, including the battle of Toulouse.

5 Dr. Barlow's services:—Expedition to Copenhagen in 1807; capture of Martinique in 1809; campaign of 1815 in the Netherlands and France.

Years' Serv.		
54		
Full Pay.	Half Pay.	

Colonel.

54 — *Sir* Thomas Hawker,[1] KCH. *Cornet*, 12 May, 1795; *Lieut.* 5 April, 96; *Capt* 10 July, 99; *Major*, 23 Nov. 1804; *Lieut.-Col.* 2 Sept. 08; *Col.* 4 June, 14; *Major-Gen.* 27 May, 25; *Lieut-Gen.* 28 June, 38; *Col.* 6th Dragoon Guards, 5 June, 39.

Lieut.-Colonel.

43 | 0 — James Jackson,[2] KH. *Ens.* 9 Oct. 06; *Lieut.* 25 Jan. 08; *Capt.* P 25 June, 13; *Brevet-Major*, 18 June, 15; *Major*, P 26 April, 27; *Brevet-Lieut.-Col.* 25 May, 26; *Lieut.-Col.* P 2 March, 39; *Col.* 23 Nov. 41.

Major.

41 | 0 — David Hay, *Cornet*, 6 Oct. 08; *Lieut.* P 31 Oct. 11; *Capt.* P 5 Aug. 19; *Brevet-Major*, 10 Jan. 37; *Regtl.-Major*, P 14 April, 37; *Brevet-Lt.-Col.* 1 Nov. 42.

Full Pay	Half Pay		CORNET.	LIEUT.	CAPTAIN.	BREVET-MAJOR.
		CAPTAINS.				
24	0	Henry Richmond Jones..	P 9 June 25	P 14 Nov. 26	P 12 June 30	9 Nov. 46
18	0	*Hon.* A. G. F. Jocelyn ..	P 26 April 31	P 6 July 32	P 17 Aug. 41	
17	$\frac{2}{12}$	William Neville Custance	P 11 Oct. 31	P 26 June 35	P 16 Mar. 38	
16	0	Charles Sawyer	P 6 Sept. 33	P 8 April 36	P 8 Aug. 45	
8	0	Edward Hare Croker....	P 17 Aug. 41	P 9 June 43	P 5 Nov. 47	
6	0	Frederick Charles Polhill	P 31 Mar. 43	P 2 Aug. 44	P 24 Nov. 48	
		LIEUTENANTS.				
27	0	William S. Philips, R.M.	25 Oct. 22	16 Feb. 26		
14	0	Thomas Manders, *adj.*..	P 30 July 35	6 Oct. 38		
10	0	Henry Dawson	P 24 Aug. 39	P 24 Feb. 43		
6	0	Samuel James Morton ..	P 9 June 43	P 28 Nov. 45		
4	0	Thomas Heywood	P 28 Nov. 45	P 12 Feb. 47		
3	0	Edward M'Evoy	P 30 April 46	P 23 July 47		
6	0	John Forster	P 25 Aug. 43	3 Sept. 47		
3	0	Alex. A. Melfort Campbell	8 Sept. 46	P 28 Jan. 48		
5	0	Robert Bickerstaff......	P 8 Nov. 44	P 29 Dec. 46		
3	0	Brent Neville...........	P 8 May 46	P 19 Sept. 48		
		CORNETS.				
2	0	John Davis Sherston....	P 10 Dec. 47			
2	0	Wm. Brough Phillimore	P 31 Dec. 47			
1	0	Francis Richard Hawker	P 24 Nov. 48			

10 | 0 — *Paymaster.*—John Terry Liston, 1 Dec. 48; *Ens.* P 27 July, 32; *Lieut.* P Feb. 34; *Capt.* P 30 Nov. 48.

14 | 0 — *Adjutant.*—*Lieut.* Thomas Manders, 31 July, 35.

14 | 0 — *Quarter-Master.*—Thomas Smith, 26 June, 35.

39 | $5\frac{11}{12}$ — *Surgeon.*—John Heriot,[3] M.D. 16 April, 12; *Assistant-Surgeon*, 8 Nov. 04; *Hosp.-Assist.* 11 May, 04.

23 | $\frac{2}{12}$ — *Assistant-Surgeon.*—Henry Carline, 28 Sept. 26; *Hospital-Assistant*, 31 Aug. 26.

3 | 0 — *Veterinary Surgeon.*—Alfred Henry Cherry, 28 Sept. 46.

Scarlet—*Facings* White.—*Agents*, Messrs. Cox & Co.—*Irish Agents*, Messrs. Cane & Co.

[*Returned from Buenos Ayres*, 1806.]

1 Sir Thomas Hawker was present in the actions in North Holland, the Helder expedition, in the 10th, 19th September, 2nd and 6th October, 1799; and was present in command of the 20th Light Dragoons in every action in which the British troops were engaged on the eastern coast of Spain, in 1812 and 1813; he has subsequently served on the Staff, in India, as Major-General.

2 Colonel Jackson served in the Peninsula, from April, 1809, to the end of that war in 1814, including the battles of Oporto, Talavera, and Busaco; action at Redinha, battle of Fuentes d'Onor, first siege of Badajoz, action at El Bodon, siege and capture of Ciudad Rodrigo, siege and capture of Badajoz, battles of Salamanca, Vittoria, Maya Pass, Pampeluna, 15th July, Pyrenees, 30th July, Nivelle, Nive, and Bayonne. Present at Waterloo, and with the army of occupation in France. Served in India and Arabia from 1819 to 1822, including the capture of Beni-Boo-Ali, as Military Secretary to Sir Lionel Smith, and, for which service, he was recommended by the Marquis of Hastings for the rank of Lieut.-Colonel.

3 Dr. Heriot served in the Peninsula from June, 1809, to the end of the war, including the battles of Talavera and Salamanca, siege of Burgos, and battles of Vittoria, the Pyrenees, and Orthes.

Years' Serv.		
49		
Full Pay.	Half Pay.	

Colonel.

P W *Hon.* Henry Murray,[1] CB. *Cornet,* 16 May, 00; *Lt.* 11 June, 01; *Capt.* 24 Aug. 02; *Major,* 26 March, 07; *Lt.-Col.* 2 Jan. 12; *Col.* 22 July, 30; *Major-Gen.* 28 June, 38; *Col.* 7th Dragoon Guards, 18 Dec. 47.

Lieut.-Colonel.

19 | 0 — John Charles Hope Gibsone,[2] *Cornet,* P 8 Oct. 30; *Lieut.* P 16 Aug. 33; *Capt.* P 24 July 35; *Major,* P 25 Feb. 45; *Lieut.-Col.* P 3 Sept. 47.

Major.

17 | 0 — *Sir* Harry Darell,[3] *Bart., Ensign,* P 1 June, 32; *Lieut.* P 12 June, 35; *Capt.* P 14 July, 41; *Major,* P 3 Sept. 47; *Brevet Lt.-Col.* 15 Sept. 48.

Full Pay	Half Pay		CORNET.	LIEUT.	CAPTAIN.	BREV.-MAJ.
		CAPTAINS.				
14	0	Henry Schonswar[4]......	P 24 July 35	P 24 April 40	P 22 Dec. 43	
14	0	William Hogg..........	P 30 Oct. 35	P 14 Jan. 42	P 27 June 45	15 Sept. 48
7	0	Antoine Sloet Butler[6]....	P 8 April 42	P 10 Mar. 43	P 19 Mar. 47	
11	0	Arth. Cavendish Bentinck	P 2 Nov. 38	P 31 Oct. 40	P 2 Mar. 47	
20	0	John Hamilton Gray[7] ..	P 24 Nov. 29	15 Sept. 37	22 June 47	
7	0	Charles Edward Petre ..	P 22 July 42	P 25 Feb. 45	P 12 Sept. 48	
		LIEUTENANTS.				
6	0	Philip Bunbury[8]	P 16 Mar. 43	P 6 Feb. 46		
6	0	Annesley Paul Gore	P 7 April 43	P 8 Jan. 47		
6	0	John Thomas Cramer[9] ..	P 22 Dec. 43	P 2 Mar. 47		
7	0	Cha. John Berners Plestow	P 20 Dec. 42	P 10 Mar. 47		
4	$\frac{3}{12}$	Arnold More Knight[10] ..	P 14 Feb. 45	29 Jan. 46		
3	0	Nicholas De la Cherois..	P 6 Feb. 46	P 12 Sept. 48		
		CORNETS.				
3	0	Nugent Chichester......	P 6 Nov. 46			
2	0	John Gray,[11] *adj.*	1 Jan. 47			
2	0	Robert Young, R. M.....	P 8 Jan. 47			
2	0	William Stuckey Wood..	P 2 Mar. 47			
2	0	William Middleton	P 19 Mar. 47			
2	0	Fitzroy George Smith ..	P 31 Dec. 47			
1	0	Thomas William Goff ..	P 12 Sept. 48			

15 | $1\frac{7}{12}$ — *Paymaster.*—John Terry Liston, 1 Dec. 48; *Ens.* P 27 July 32; *Lt.* P 7 Feb. 34; *Capt.* P 30 Nov. 48.

2 | 0 — *Adjutant.*—*Cornet* John Gray,[11] 1 Jan. 47.

6 | 0 — *Quarter-Master.*—Henry Magill,[12] 10 March, 43.

14 | 0 — *Surgeon.*—George Northern Foaker, 15 Dec. 45; *Assist.-Surg.* 1 May 35.

1 | 0 — *Assist.-Surgeon.*—James Thomson, M.D., 11 Feb. 48.

3 | 0 — *Veterinary Surgeon.*—Benjamin Chaning Rouse Gardiner, 19 May, 46.

Scarlet—*Facings* black.—*Agents,* Messrs. Cox & Co.

[*Returned from the Cape of Good Hope, 7 June* 1848.]

1 Major-General the Hon. Henry Murray served in Naples, Sicily, and Calabria, in 1806-7. Accompanied the expedition to Egypt in March 1807, and was present, as an Aide-de-camp, at the attack on Alexandria, siege and storming of Rosetta, and on every other occasion when our troops were engaged. Served at Walcheren in 1809, including the siege and surrender of Flushing. Went with the 18th Hussars to the Peninsula in Jan. 1813; present at the crossing of the Esla, and commanded the regiment in support of the 10th Hussars at the action of Morales de Toro. Served also in the campaign of 1815, including the battle of Quatre Bras; commanded the rear regiment of the Column on the retreat during the following day; and, at the battle of Waterloo, he led the 18th Hussars in the brilliant charge of Sir Hussey Vivian's Brigade, at the conclusion of the action.

2 Lieut.-Colonel Gibsone served throughout the Kaffir war of 1846-7, and was present on almost every occasion in which the troops were engaged with the enemy; and he had the command of and led the charge of Cavalry in the decisive affair of the Gwanga, on the 8th June, 1846, when a large body of the enemy was encountered and utterly broken, leaving upwards of 400 dead on the field, on which occasion his services were warmly acknowledged in the public despatches, and his name particularly mentioned in General Orders.

3 Sir Harry Darell served with the 18th Royal Irish on the China Expedition, and was present at the first taking of Chusan. He served also with the 7th Dragoon Guards during the whole of the Kaffir war, and commanded the squadron of his regiment at the Gwanga, on the 8th June, 1846, and received two severe wounds during the charge and attack.

4 Captain Schonswar served against the insurgent Boers in South Africa in 1845, and likewise in the Kaffir war in 1846 and 1847.

6 Captain Butler served with the 7th Dragoon Guards against the insurgent Boers in South Africa, in 1845. Also in the Kaffir war of 1846-47.

7 Capt. Gray was honourably mentioned in the public despatch as the officer who captured the cannon in the action with the South African insurgent Boers on the 30th April, 1845, on which occasion he was acting Aide-de-Camp to the officer commanding the Field Force. Served in the Kaffir war of 1846.

8 Lieut. Bunbury served throughout the Kaffir war, and was wounded in the charge at the Gwanga, on the 8th June, 1846.

9 Lieut. Cramer served with the 7th Dragoon Guards against the insurgent Boers in South Africa in 1845. Also in the Kaffir war of 1846.47, and had his horse shot in the affair at Trompeter's Drift, while commanding the Rear Guard.

10 Lieut. Knight served the Campaign on the Sutlej (medal) in 1845-6, and was present with the 16th Lancers in the battles of Buddiwal, Aliwal, and Sobraon.

11 Cornet Gray served in the expedition against the insurgent Boers beyond the Orange River, Cape of Good Hope, and was present in the affair of the 30th April 1845. He served also throughout the Kaffir war of 1846.

12 Quarter-Master Magill served in the expedition against the insurgent Boers beyond the Orange River, Cape of Good Hope, in 1845. He served also throughout the Kaffir war of 1846.

On the Standards an Eagle.—" PENINSULA"—" WATERLOO."

Years' Serv.	
55	
Full Pay.	Half Pay.

Colonel.

55 — P W *Sir* Arthur Benjamin Clifton,[1] KCB. KCH. *Cornet,* 6 June, 1794; *Lieut.* 7 Aug. 1794; *Capt.* 27 Feb. 1799; *Major,* 17 Dec. 1803; *Lieut. Col.* 25 July, 1810; *Col.* 12 Aug. 1819; *Major Gen.* 22 July 30; *Lieut.-Gen.* 23 Nov. 41 *Col.* 1st Dragoons, 30 Aug. 42.

Lieut.-Colonel.

35 | $\frac{1}{12}$ — P W Thomas Marten,[2] KH. *Cornet & Sub-Lieut.* 22 Nov. 13; *Lieut.* P 23 June, 17; *Capt.* P 4 May, 22; *Major,* P 12 Dec. 26; *Lieut.-Col.* 29 May, 35; *Col.* 9 Nov. 46.

Major.

20 | 0 — Edward Littledale, *Ens.* P 24 Dec. 29; *Lieut.* P 21 Dec. 32; *Capt.* P 1 May 35; *Brev.-Major* 9 Nov. 46; *Major,* P 25 Feb. 48.

Full Pay	Half Pay		CORNET.	LIEUT.	CAPTAIN.	BREVET-MAJOR.
		CAPTAINS.				
17	0	John Yorke............	P 21 Dec. 32	P 5 Dec. 34	P 14 Dec. 41	
14	0	Robert Wardlaw........	P 5 June 35	P 28 July 40	P 14 Oct. 42	
13	0	Chas. C. Waldo Sibthorp	P 28 Oct. 36	P 7 Sept. 41	P 13 Oct. 43	
10	0	Walter B. Barttelot	P 1 Mar. 39	P 14 Dec. 41	P 7 Feb. 45	
8	0	Thomas Thoroton	P 14 Dec. 41	P 23 June 43	P 25 Feb. 48	
9	0	Hugh Gough	P 30 Oct. 40	P 14 Oct. 42	P 13 Oct. 48	
		LIEUTENANTS.				
17	0	John Chamberlain, R.M.	1 June 32	P 10 July 35		
10	0	Herbert Morgan........	P 23 June 39	P 19 Aug. 42		
7	0	Wm.de Cardonnel Elmsall	P 1 July 42	P 13 Oct. 43		
7	0	*Sir* Cha.W.C. Burton, *Bt.*	P 1 July 42	26 July 44		
7	0	Aug. Henry De Trafford	P 14 Oct. 42	P 7 Feb. 45		
6	0	Henry Croft	P 13 Oct. 43	P 11 Dec. 46		
6	0	Joseph John Henley	P 27 Oct. 43	P 25 Feb. 48		
4	0	George Henry Littledale	P 7 Feb. 45	P 13 Oct. 48		
		CORNETS.				
3	0	William Harrisson, *adj.*	14 Apr. 46			
3	0	Michael Stocks	P 11 Dec. 46			
1	0	George Campbell	P 25 Feb. 48			
1	0	John Collman Davenport	9 June 48			
1	0	James Ainslie	P 13 Oct. 48			

2 Colonel Marten served the campaign of 1814, in the Peninsula, with the household brigade. Also the campaign of 1815, including the battle of Waterloo.

5 Dr. Bartley served in the Peninsula, and was present at the battle of Salamanca.

18 | 0 — *Paymaster.*—Lawrence Luke Esmonde White, 29 Sept. 43; *Ens.* P 18 Jan. 31; *Lieut.* P 26 June, 35.

3 | 0 — *Adjutant.*—*Cornet* William Harrisson, 14 Apr. 46.

15 | 0 — *Quarter-Master.*—W John Partridge, 18 July, 34.

38 | $\frac{1}{12}$ — *Surgeon.*—P John Metge Bartley,[5] M.D. 31 Aug. 26; *Assist.-Surg.* 27 Dec. 10.

8 | 0 — *Assist.-Surgeon.*—John Grogan, M. B. 16 April, 41.

12 | 0 — *Veterinary Surgeon.*—Matthew Poett, 21 April, 37.

Scarlet—*Facings* Blue.—*Agents,* Messrs. Cox & Co.

[*Returned from France, January,* 1816.]

1 Sir Arthur Clifton's services:—Campaigns of 1809, 10, 11, 12, 13, 14, and 15. Commanded a squadron in covering and supporting four Spanish guns at the battle of Talavera, and employed in different subsequent operations; battle of Busaco, pursuit of Massena from Santarem, taking from him prisoners and baggage; battle of Fuentes d'Onor, actions at Navé d'Aver, El Bodon, Fuente Guinaldo, and Aldea de Ponte; several affairs during the retreat of the army from Salamanca to Ciudad Rodrigo; charged with a squadron a body of French Infantry under General Clausel, near Salamanca, killing or taking nearly a hundred of the enemy; battle of Vittoria, blockade of Pampeluna, several affairs in the Pyrenees, battle of Toulouse, skirmishing with the enemy and covering the retreat on the 17th of June, and battle of Waterloo. Sir Arthur has received a Medal and one Clasp for Fuentes d'Onor and Vittoria.

On the Standards an Eagle.—" WATERLOO."

Years' Serv.		
57		***Colonel.*** *Sir* Wm. Kier Grant,[1] KCB. GCH. *Ens.* 30 May, 1792; *Lieut.* 18 Feb. 93; *Capt.* 6 July, 94; *Major*, 6 Jan. 96; *Lieut.-Col.* 3 Dec. 1800; *Col.* 25 July, 10; *Major-Gen.* 4 June, 13; *Lieut.-Gen.* 27 May, 25; *Gen.* 23 Nov. 41; *Col.* 2d Dragoons, 24 Aug. 39.
Full Pay.	Half Pay.	
23	0	***Lieut.-Colonel.*** St. Vincent William Ricketts, *Cornet*, P 13 July, 26; *Lieut.* P 5 April, 31; *Capt* P 6 Nov. 35; *Major*, P 7 April, 43; *Lieut.-Col.* P 6 Nov. 46.
20	$\frac{3}{12}$	***Major.*** Henry Darby Griffith, *Cornet*, P 25 Nov. 28; *Lieut.* P 25 Nov. 31; *Capt.* P 1 Aug. 34; *Major*, P 6 Nov. 46.

Full Pay	Half Pay	CAPTAINS.	CORNET.	LIEUT.	CAPTAIN.	BREV.-MAJ.
14	0	Donald John M. Macleod	P 10 July 35	P 23 Feb. 38	P 28 Dec. 41	
13	0	Geo. Aug. Filmer Sulivan	P 29 July 36	P 26 Feb. 41	P 5 April 44	
15	0	George Calvert Clarke ..	P 30 May 34	P 7 Oct. 36	P 20 Sept. 39	
7	0	Andrew Robertson......	P 14 Jan. 42	P 10 Mar. 43	P 7 Aug. 46	
7	0	*Sir* Geo. Fra. Hampson, *Bt.*	P 5 Aug. 42	P 18 April 45	P 24 Sept. 47	
9	0	Samuel Toosey Williams, *s.*	P 26 June 40	29 Apr. 42	P 24 Dec. 47	
		LIEUTENANTS.				
10	0	Frederick Philips, R.M.	P 11 May 39	P 29 Dec. 43		
6	0	Henry Sales Scobell	P 7 April 43	P 16 May 45		
6	0	Fred. Drummond Hibbert	P 29 Dec. 43	P 7 Aug. 46		
5	0	William Wallace Hozier	P 5 April 44	P 6 Nov. 46		
5	0	Edward Amphlett	P 28 June 44	P 25 June 47		
4	0	Henry Dalton Wittit Lyon	P 18 April 45	P 24 Sept. 47		
		CORNETS.				
4	0	David C. R. C. Buchanan	P 16 May 45			
3	0	William Miller, *adj.*	7 July 46			
3	0	John Arthur Freeman ..	P 7 Aug. 46			
4	0	W. Cunninghame Bontine	P 28 Mar. 45			
2	0	Devereux P. Cockburn..	P 25 June 47			
2	0	Francis Sutherland	P 24 Sept. 47			
1	0	Thomas Price Gratrex ...	P 25 Apr. 48			

Full Pay	Half Pay	
34	0	*Paymaster.*—[illegible] William Crawford, 24 March, 29; *Cornet*, 17 Aug. 15; *Lieut.* 25 June, 19.
3	0	*Adjutant.*—*Cornet* William Miller, 7 July 46.
14	0	*Quarter-Master.*—[illegible] Michael Nelson, 25 Dec. 35; *Ens.* 4 Dec. 35.
23	$1\frac{1}{12}$	*Surgeon.*—Robert Dundin Smyth, 6 Nov. 40; *Assist.-Surg.* 12 Oct. 25; *Hosp.-Assist.* 19 May 25.
8	0	*Assistant-Surgeon.*—John Ramsay Brush,[4] MD., 8 June, 41.
10	0	*Veterinary Surgeon.*—Thomas Jex, 4 Oct. 39.
		Scarlet—*Facings* Blue.—*Agents*, Messrs. Charles Hopkinson and Co.—*Irish Agents*, *Sir* E. R. Borough, *Bart.*, Armit and Co.

[*Returned from France, January*, 1816.]

1 Sir Wm. Kier Grant served in Flanders, and was present at Famars, siege of Valenciennes, &c. in 1793. In 1794 he was present in the actions of the 17th, 24th, and 26th of April, the 10th, 17th, 18th, and 22nd of May. Joined the Russian and Austrian army in Italy early in 1799, and served the campaigns of that and the two following years, including the battles of Novi, Rivoli, Mondovi, Savilliano, Marengo, &c.; the sieges of Alexandria, Sarraval, Tortona, Cunio, Savona, Genoa, &c. Sir Wm. served subsequently fifteen years in the East Indies, six years as Adjutant-General, the rest as a Major-General on the staff, during which he was a considerable time commander of the forces in the Island of Java, and Second member of Council. Commanded the force in the following service, viz.: in 1817 and 18 Guzerat field-force, which formed a division of the army of the Deccan; 1819, capture of Rarree and conquest of the Sawuntwarree State; also, the capture of Bhooj and conquest of the principality of Cutch; in the Persian Gulf against the Joasmee pirates, including the capture of Ras-el-Khyma and Zyah, Arab fortresses.

4 Doctor Brush served with the 26th on the China expedition (Medal), and was present at the repulse of the night attack on Ningpo, at the attack and capture of Chapoo, Woosung, Shanghae, and Chin Kiang Foo, and at the landing before Nankin.

Emb. for the East Indies, July, 1837.] **3rd (*The King's Own*) Regt. of Lt. Dragoons.** [Serving Beng

The White Horse, within the Garter on the 2nd and 3rd Standards, with the Motto, "*Nec aspera terrent*" "SALAMANCA"—"VITTORIA"—"TOULOUSE"—"PENINSULA"—"CABOOL, 1842"—"MOODKEE" "FEROZESHAH"—"SOBRAON."

Years' Serv. Full Pay.	Half Pay.	
51		***Colonel.*** — *Lord* Charles Somerset Manners, KCB.[1] *Cornet*, 7 Feb. 98; *Lieut.* 1 June, 9[…] *Capt.* 21 Aug. 1800; *Major*, 13 Oct. 08; *Lieut.-Col.* 1 Aug. 11; *Col.* 6 N[…] 17; *Major-Gen.* 27 May, 25; *Lt.-Gen.* 28 June, 38; *Col.* 3rd Drs. 8 Nov. […]
44	1/12	*Lieut.-Colonels.*—Michael White, CB.[3] *Cornet*, P 15 Aug. 04; *Lt.* P 14 May, 0[…] *Capt.* 7 Nov. 15; *Brvt.-Maj.* 10 Jan. 37; *Maj.* 4 Jan. 39; *Lt.-Col.* P 13 D[…] 39; *Col.* 3 Apr. 46.
40	5	Charles Middleton, s.[4] *Ens.* 19 Sept. 04; *Lieut.* 28 Apr. 06; *Capt.* P 18 July, 1[…] *Brev.-Maj.* 8 Feb. 19; *Maj.* P 16 June, 25; *Lt.-Col.* P 19 Nov. 25; *Col.* 28 Ju. […]
24	0	Geo. Henry Lockwood, CB.[5] *Cornet*, P 10 Mar. 25; *Lt.* P 10 Aug. 26; *Capt.* P […] Sept. 32; *Maj.* 6 March, 39; *Brevet Lt.-Col.* 23 Dec. 42; *Lt.-Col.* 9 Nov. 4[…]
23	0	*Majors.*—John Wm. Yerbury,[7] *Cornet*, P 12 Dec. 26; *Lieut.* P 5 July 33; *Ca[pt.]* 1 July 37; *Major*, 9 Nov. 46.
23	0	Lawrence Fyler,[6] *Cornet*, P 7 Sept. 26; *Lieut.* P 10 July 28; *Capt.* P 7 Feb. 3[…] *Brev.-Major*, 19 June, 46; *Major*, P 7 April, 48.

Full Pay	Half Pay		Cornet.	Lieut.	Captain.	Brev.-Ma[j.]
		Captains.				
18	0	John Rich. Blagden Hale[8]	P 7 June 31	P 16 May 34	P 10 July 37	3 Apr. 4[6]
29	1/12	J B Gough,[9] CB. s. l.c. 23 D. 49	24 Feb. 20	P 1 Oct. 25	P 1 Aug. 26	26 May 4[1]
16	0	Walter Unett[7]	P 23 Aug. 33	P 31 Mar. 37	P 1 Nov. 42	
19	0	George Forbes[10]	10 Dec. 30	15 Feb. 34	P 24 Jan. 45	
20	0	W. E. FitzEdward Barnes[11]	19 Nov. 29	P 24 July 35	P 16 May 45	
22	0	Samuel Fisher[12]	15 June 27	P 16 Aug. 31	22 Dec. 45	3 Apr. 4[6]
16	0	Henry Aime Ouvry	P 17 Oct. 33	P 4 Sept. 35	P 2 May 45	
22	0	Wm. Howe Hadfield	25 Oct. 27	P 20 Sept. 31	3 Apr. 46	
15	0	James Cowell[15]	P 18 July 34	P 17 Mar. 37	P 9 June 48	
		Lieutenants.				
15	0	Edward Geo. Swinton[14]	P 6 June 34	7 Oct. 36		
12	0	John Sullivan[16]	9 July 37	31 Dec. 39		
12	0	Henry Wood[7]	P 10 July 37	P 16 Nov. 41		
12	0	Edmund Roche[17]	P 11 July 37	29 April 42		
12	0	George Cookes[11]	P 14 July 37	P 29 April 42		
9	0	Jonas Hamilton Travers[7]	P 28 Feb. 40	13 June 43		
10	0	Edward B. Cureton[18]	21 June 39	19 Dec. 43		
11	0	John Blackburne Hawkes[19]	P 2 Mar. 38	P 27 Sept. 39		
8	0	Thomas Penton[11]	P 16 Nov. 41	P 26 Jan. 44		
5	0	John Rathwell,[21] R. M.	1 Mar. 44	22 Dec. 45		
4	0	William Henry Orme[22]	P 24 Jan. 45	3 Apr. 46		
4	0	Charles Russell Colt[23]	P 16 May 45	9 Nov. 46		
4	0	Edw. Joseph Thackwell, s.	2 Sept. 45	P 29 Dec. 46		
5	0	William Gray Draper	P 19 Jan. 44	P 11 Dec. 46		
3	0	Thomas Heathcote Stisted	3 Apr. 46	P 10 Dec. 47		
4	0	Geo. E. F. Kauntze,[25] *adj.*	19 Dec. 45	P 28 Jan. 48		
3	0	George Thomas Gough	4 Apr. 46	P 9 June 48		
3	0	Frank Chaplin	P 8 May 46	P 10 Nov. 48		
5	0	Robert Hodgson[24]	20 Dec. 44	21 Dec. 48		
		Cornets.				
3	0	James Macqueen[26]	14 April 46			
3	0	T. C. Belmore St. George	P 29 Dec. 46			
1	0	George Thorne Ricketts	P 28 Jan. 48			
1	0	Thos. Shepherd Townend	P 5 May 48			
1	0	Robert Macneill	P 16 June 48			
1	0	Fred. Tho. Ongley Hopson	P 15 Aug. 48			
1	0	Gordon Brassey	P 10 Nov. 48			

3 Colonel White served at the ca[p]ture of Hattrass in 1817, and dur[ing] the Mahratta campaigns of 1817 [and] 18; also at siege and captur[e of] Bhurtpore in 1825-6. Commanded [a] Brigade throughout the campaign [of] 1842 in Affghanistan, for which [he] was appointed a CB. Again co[m]manded a Brigade of Cavalry in [the] actions of Moodkee and Ferozesh[ah] (wounded); and the 3rd Drs in [the] battle of Sobraon.

4 Colonel Middleton served in [the] West Indies with the Royals, in 18[…] and 6; on the Staff with the ar[my] which proceeded from Madras to [the] Northern Mahratta country bey[ond] the Nerbudda River, in 1809 and […] with the 22nd Light Dragoons [in] Java during 1811, 12, and 13, [and] was present at the affairs of the […] and 21st, and at the cavalry a[ction] which finally settled the conque[st of] that valuable Island on the […] Aug. 1811, after the Fortress [and] Lines of Cornelis had been [taken.] Employed also at the taking of […] Jocarta, and all the subsequent operations which [took] place on that Island under the gallant Gillespie. [Served] in the field with the 22d Lt. Dragoons in 1815 and […] and during the whole of the Mahratta war of 1817, […] and 19, and was present with the division of the la[te Sir] Thomas Munro at the capture of the Forts of Dum[…] Dorwar, Bedamme, Belgaum, and Shallapore, at wh[ich] last place he was severely wounded.

5 Lt.-Col. Lockwood commanded the 3rd Light [Drs.] throughout the campaign of 1842 in Affghanistan u[nder] General Pollock (medal and CB.), and was present [at] forcing the Khyber Pass, storming the heights of [Jug]dulluck, action of Tezeen and Huftkotul, occupa[tion of] Cabool, siege and capture of Istaliff.

		Paymaster.—
4	0	*Adjutant.—Lieut.* Geo. E. F. Kauntze, 30 Mar. 48.
8	0	*Quarter-Master.*—Abraham Crabtree,[16] 25 Nov. 42; *Cornet*, 17 Sept. 41.
40	0	*Surgeon.*—Jas. Henderson,[27] M.D. 20 Apr. 26; *A.-S.* 22 Mar. 10; *H.-A.* 5 Aug.[…]
12	0	*Assistant-Surgeons.*—Henry Franklin,[11] 20 Dec. 37.
9	0	Francis Laing,[11] 6 Nov. 40.
20	0	*Veterinary Surgeon.*—George Edlin,[16] 17 Dec. 29.

Blue—*Facings* Scarlet.
Agents, Messrs. Cox & [Co.]

1 Lord Charles Manners served the campaign of 1808 in Spain, including the cavalry engagement at Benevente. At Wal[cheren] as Aide-de-Camp to Lord Chatham, and was present at the siege of Flushing. Acted as Aide-de-Camp to the Duke of [Wel]lington from 1811 until the army entered Madrid in 1812; when he assumed the command of the Regiment, and remained [in] it until the war closed in 1814. His Lordship has received a medal and two clasps for Salamanca, Vittoria, and Toulouse.

6 Major Fyler served with the 16th Lancers during the campaign in Affghanistan under Lord Keane, including the [storm] and capture of Ghuznee (Medal). Also at the battle of Maharajpore (Medal) 29 Dec. 1843, and in the campaign on the [Sutlej] in 1846, including the battles of Buddiwal and Aliwal, at which last he was severely wounded by a musket shot w[hile] charging a body of infantry.

12 Major Fisher did duty with the 11th Drs. as a volunteer at the siege and capture of Bhurtpore in 1825-6. He served [with] the 3rd Drs. the campaign of 1842 in Affghanistan; as also in the battle of Moodkee (severely wounded), and Ferozeshah[…]

[For Notes 9, 13, 15, 17, 18, 21, 24, 27, 28, and 29, see opposite page.

14 Lt. Swinton served the campaign on the Sutlej in 1845-6, and was present at the battles of Moodkee (severely wounded), Ferozeshah, and Sobraon.

[…] occupation of Cabool. He served also the campaign on the Sutlej (medal) in 1845-6, and was present at the battles of Moodkee (wounded), Ferozeshah (wounded), and Sobraon (severely wounded).

"TALAVERA" "ALBUHERA" "SALAMANCA" "VITTORIA" "TOULOUSE" "PENINSULA."
"AFFGHANISTAN" "GHUZNEE."

Years' Serv. 51	
Full Pay.	Half Pay.

Colonel.

Sir George Scovell,[1] KCB. *Adjutant*, 5 April, 98; *Cornet*, 20 June, 98; *Lieut.* 4 May, 00; *Capt.* 10 March, 04; *Major*, 30 May, 11; *Lieut.-Col.* 17 Aug. 12; *Col.* 27 May, 25; *Major-Gen.* 10 Jan. 37; *Lt.-Gen.* 9 Nov. 46; *Col.* 4th Light Dragoons, 18 Dec. 47.

Lieut.-Colonel.

14 | 10/12 | *Lord* George Augustus Fred. Paget, *Cornet & Sub-Lt.* P 25 July, 34, *Lieut.* P 1 Dec. 37; *Capt.* P 17 Aug. 41; *Major*, P 30 Jan. 46; *Lieut.-Col.* P 29 Dec. 46.

Major.

15 | 3/12 | Henry Fane,[3] *Ensign*, P 1 Aug. 34; *Lieut.* P 30 July 36; *Capt.* P 6 May 42; *Maj.* P 29 Dec. 46.

Full Pay	Half Pay	CAPTAINS.	CORNET.	LIEUT.	CAPTAIN.	BREV.-MAJ.
14	0	John T. Douglas Halkett	P 23 Jan. 35	6 July 37	P 25 Oct. 42	
14	0	Alexander Low	P 2 Oct. 35	P 6 July 38	P 14 July 43	
9		George John Brown	P 17 April 40	P 14 July 43	P 30 Jan. 46	
9		Robert Portal	P 17 Jan. 40	P 8 May 45	P 9 June 46	
9	0	Fenwick Boyce Barron ..	P 8 May 40	P 26 Sept. 45	P 29 Dec. 46	
7	0	Archibald Grant	P 24 June 42	P 31 Oct. 45	P 8 Dec. 48	
		LIEUTENANTS.				
16	0	J. H. Turner Warde, R.M	P 21 June 33	P 22 May 35		
11	0	Martin Kirwan	P 23 Nov. 38	P 24 June 42		
7	0	Herbert Dawson Slade ..	P 25 Oct. 42	P 9 June 46		
5	0	C. Berkeley Molyneux, *s.*	20 Sept. 44	1 April 47		
10	0	John Williams Wallington	P 20 Sept. 39	P 7 June 44		
10	0	Thomas Hutton	P 21 June 39	P 6 May 42		
4	0	Edward Tredcroft	P 31 Oct. 45	P 8 Dec. 48		
		CORNETS.				
3	0	Francis Clare Ford......	P 8 May 46			
3	0	Hugh Mallet	P 19 May 46			
3	0	Charles Brandreth	P 9 June 46			
3	0	Henry Astley Sparke ..	P 29 Dec. 46			
2	0	George Ellis, *adjutant* ..	7 May 47			
1	0	Edward Hylton Jolliffe ..	P 8 Dec. 48			

3 Major Fane served the campaign in Affghanistan, and was present at the storm and capture of Ghuznee (Medal).

4 Mr. Graves served with the 4th Lt. Drs. during the campaign in Affghanistan under Lord Keane, and was present at the siege and capture of Ghuznee (Medal).

21 | 0 | *Paymaster.*—Geo. Charles Dalbiac, 11 Feb. 42; *Cor.* 31 July, 28; *Lt.* 10 May, 31.
2 | 0 | *Adjutant.*—*Cornet* George Ellis, 5 May 48.
7 | 0 | *Quarter-Master.*—Thomas Tarleton, 18 Feb. 42.
23 | 0 | *Surgeon.*—John Stewart Graves,[4] 2 July, 41; *A. S.* 28 Sept. 26; *H. A.* 22 Feb. 26.
3 | 0 | *Assist.-Surg.*—John Reid, 14 Aug. 46.
11 | 0 | *Veterinary Surgeon.*—John Byrne, 14 Dec. 38.

Blue, *Facings* Scarlet.—*Agents*, Messrs. C. Hopkinson & Co.—*Irish Agents*, Messrs. Cane & Co.

[Returned from the East Indies, March 1842.]

1 Sir George Scovell served the campaign under Sir John Moore, terminating with the battle of Corunna, at which he was present as Deputy-Assistant-Quarter-Master-General. Afterwards in the Peninsula in the same department at the head-quarters under the Duke of Wellington, from Feb. 1809 to the end of that war in 1814, and was present at the passage of the Douro and pursuit of Marshal Soult; battles of Talavera, Busaco, and Fuentes d'Onor; sieges of Ciudad Rodrigo and Badajoz, battle of Salamanca, siege of Burgos, battles of Vittoria, the Pyrenees, Nivelle, and Nive; passage of the Adour, and battle of Toulouse. Served also the campaign of 1815, including the battle of Waterloo. Sir George has received a cross and one clasp.

---

9 Lt.-Col. Gough served as Deputy Quarter-Master-General of the army during the war in China, and received the brevet rank of Major and of Lieut.-Colonel, together with the Companionship of the Bath, for his conduct in action, he having been present in almost every engagement during the expedition. He was afterwards present in the battle of Maharajpore, as Military Secretary to the Commander-in-Chief in India; and he commanded a Brigade of Cavalry at the battles of Moodkee and Ferozeshah, and officiated as Quarter-Master-General in the battle of Sobraon, and was very severely wounded.

15 Capt. Cowell served throughout the campaign of 1842 in Affghanistan (Medal) under General Pollock. He was present as Aide-de-Camp to Sir Joseph Thackwell in the action at Maharajpore on the 29th Dec. 1843, and has received the Bronze Star. He served also the campaign on the Sutlej, and was present in the battles of Moodkee, Ferozeshah, and Sobraon.

17 Lieut. Roche served the campaign of 1838-9, with Lord Keane's army in Beloochistan and Affghanistan, as Aide-de-Camp to Sir Joseph Thackwell, and at periods as Assistant Adjutant-General of Division; and was present at the capture of Ghuznee (Medal), and in some skirmishes. He served with the 3rd Lt. Drags. in the force under Sir Geo. Pollock (Medal), at the battle of the Khyber Pass, and at the relief of Jellalabad, in 1842; and as A. Q. M. Gen. of the Cavalry Division of the Army of the Sutlej from 9th Jan. 1846 to the breaking up of the army, and was present at the battle of Sobraon (Medal).

18 Lt. Cureton was present with the 16th Lancers, in the action at Maharajpore, 29th Dec. 1843 (Medal); and with the 3rd Drags. at the battles of Moodkee (severely wounded) and Sobraon.

21 Lt. Rathwell was present at the battles of Moodkee, Ferozeshah (wounded), and Sobraon.

24 Cornet Hodgson was present at the siege and capture of Bhurtpore, and was a volunteer for the dismounted cavalry storming party. He was also present in the action of Maharajpore (medal), and at the battle of Sobraon.

27 Dr. Henderson served at the capture of Guadaloupe in 1810; two years in the American war; and during the whole of the Burmese war. Also the campaign of 1842 in Affghanistan.

28 Cornet Macqueen served with the 16th Lancers during the campaign in Affghanistan under Lord Keane, including the siege and capture of Ghuznee (Medal). He was afterwards present at the battle of Maharajpore (Medal); and he also served the campaign on the Sutlej (Medal), including the actions at Buddiwal, Aliwal, and Sobraon.

29 Lt. Orme was present at Moodkee and Ferozeshah, at which last he was severely wounded in the arm.

The Castle of Inniskilling.
" WATERLOO."

Years' Serv. Full Pay.	Years' Serv. Half Pay.	
		Colonel.
54		*Sir* George Pownoll Adams,[1] KCH. *Cornet*, 5 Oct. 1795; *Lieut.* 12 March, 96; *Capt.* 11 Oct. 97; *Major*, 5 Feb. 02; *Lieut.-Col.* 8 Dec. 04; *Col.* 4 June, 13; *Major-Gen.* 12 Aug. 19; *Lieut.-Gen.* 10 Jan. 37; *Col.* 6th Dragoons 26th Oct. 40.
		Lieut.-Colonel.
24	$5\frac{1}{12}$	Willoughby Moore, *Cornet*, P 7 Sept. 20; *Lieut.* P 17 July, 23; *Capt.* P 4 Mar. 26; *Major*, P 17 July, 40; *Lieut.-Col.* P 28 July, 43.
		Major.
11	0	Henry Dalrymple White, *Cornet*, P 11 May 38; *Lieut.* P 8 Feb. 39; *Capt.* P 17 May 44; *Major*, P 21 Dec. 48.

Full Pay	Half Pay		CORNET.	LIEUT.	CAPTAIN.	BREVET-MAJOR.
		CAPTAINS.				
15	0	Charles Cameron Shute	P 19 July 34	P 13 May 39	P 5 Mar. 47	
12	0	Robert Moore Peel........	P 2 Dec. 37	P 2 July 41	P 25 June 47	
10	0	Francis Sutton	P 23 Aug. 39	P 3 June 42	P 8 Oct. 47	
8	0	Whitehall Dod	P 26 Nov. 41	P 28 July 43	P 25 Feb. 48	
7	0	Thomas Fraser Grove ..	P 2 Sept. 42	P 10 Nov. 43	P 18 Aug. 48	
6	0	Fred. W. John FitzWygram	P 28 July 43	P 17 May 44	P 21 Dec. 48	
		LIEUTENANTS.				
6	0	William Martyn Powell..	P 10 Nov. 43	P 8 Oct. 44		
5	0	Conyers Tower	P 7 June 44	P 6 June 45		
6	0	*Sir* W. C. Morshead, *Bart.*	P 2 June 43	P 9 June 46		
5	0	Arthur Lowther, *adj.*.....	P 31 May 44	P 5 Mar. 47		
5	0	William Doyle, R. M. ..	13 Dec. 44	P 11 June 47		
3	0	Robert George Manley ..	P 9 June 46	P 25 June 47		
4	0	*Hon.* H. L. Boyle Rowley	P 29 Nov. 45	P 8 Oct. 47		
4	0	H. R. Salusbury Trelawny	P 4 July 45	P 22 Dec. 46		
2	0	Arthur Royds..........	P 25 June 47	P 18 Aug. 48		
3	0	Robert Dennistoun	P 3 Nov. 46	P 24 Sept. 47		
6	0	Henry W. Walters......	P 21 July 43	P 28 April 48		
		CORNETS.				
1	0	Miles Stringer	P 16 June 48			
1	0	*Sir* E. Synge Hutchinson, *Bt.*	P 18 Aug. 48			

Full Pay	Half Pay	
18	0	*Paymaster.*—Charles Francis Gregg, 26 Mar. 41; *Ens.* P 16 Dec. 31; *Lieut.* P 14 Feb. 34.
5	0	*Adjutant.*—*Lieut.* Arthur Lowther, 23 June 48.
6	0	*Quarter-Master.*—James Marshall, 14 April, 43.
24	0	*Surgeon.*—James Sidey, M.D. 2 July, 41; *Assist.-Surg.* 12 Jan. 26; *Hosp.-Assist.* 1 Dec. 25.
8	0	*Assist.-Surg.*—Cosmo Gordon Logie, M.D. 5 Oct. 41.
19	0	*Veterinary Surgeon.*—Herbert Hallen, 3 Aug. 30.

Scarlet—*Facings* Yellow.—*Agents*, Messrs. Cox & Co.—*Irish Agents*, *Sir* R. P. Borough, *Bt.* Armit, & Co.

[*Returned from France, January*, 1816.]

1 Sir George Pownoll Adams served in Ireland during the rebellion in 1798. Also under Lord Lake in the East Indies, where he was actively employed for several years.

"PENINSULA"—"WATERLOO."

Years' Serv. Full Pay.	Half Pay.					
50		*Colonel.* Sir William Tuyll,[1] KCH. *Cor.* 22 Oct. 99; *Lieut.* 18 July, 01; *Capt.* 7 April, 04; *Major,* 20 Nov., 06; *Lieut.-Col.* 13 June, 11; *Col.* 27 May, 25; *Major Gen.* 10 Jan., 37; *Lt.-Gen.* 9 Nov. 46; *Col.* 7th Hussars, 10 Mar. 46.				
19	0	*Lieut.-Colonel.* Arthur Shirley, *Cornet,* P 31 Aug. 30; *Lieut.* P 1 Feb. 33; *Capt.* P 15 July, 36; *Major,* P 28 Aug. 46; *Lt.-Col.* P 16 April 47.				
17	0	*Major.* Charles Hagart, *Cornet,* P 15 June 32; *Lieut.* P 12 Aug. 34; *Capt.* P 21 Oct. 37; *Major,* P 10 Dec. 47.				
			CORNET.	LIEUT.	CAPTAIN.	BREVET-MAJOR.
		CAPTAINS.				
12	0	James Macaul Hagart ..	P 26 May 37	P 16 May 45	P 11 Sept. 46	
8	0	*Sir* Wm. Russell, *Bart., s.*	P 2 July 41	P 27 Feb. 46	P 16 Apr. 47	
10	0	Charles Bowles[2]	P 16 Aug. 39	P 1 Nov. 42	P 17 Apr. 47	
8	0	Hen. *Marq. of* Worcester, *s*	P 17 Aug. 41	P 7 July 43	P 13 Aug. 47	
4	0	Wm., *Visc.* St. Lawrance	P 9 May 45	P 28 Aug. 46	P 10 Dec. 47	
4	0	Edward Henry Cooper ..	P 16 May 45	P 11 Sept. 46	P 15 Aug. 48	
		LIEUTENANTS.				
4	0	William Babington	P 11 Nov. 45	P 9 Oct. 46		
4	0	Wm. Ridley Cha. Cooke	P 13 Nov. 45	P 15 Jan. 47		
4	0	Alfred Sartoris	P 30 Dec. 45	P 16 Apr. 47		
3	0	William Dascon Bushe ..	P 27 Feb. 46	P 17 Apr. 47		
3	0	Francis Arthur Farrell ..	P 9 Oct. 46	P 15 Aug. 48		
2	0	*Hon.* Charles Harbord ..	P 15 Jan. 47	P 3 Oct. 48		
8	0	Thomas Pedder	P 16 April 41	2 July 45		
		CORNETS.				
2	0	Joseph Trenerry, *Adj.* ..	2 July 47			
3	0	Wm. Percival Heathcote	P 22 May 46			
2	0	Charles Craufurd Fraser .	P 3 Dec. 47			
2	0	Henry William Meredyth	P 10 Dec. 47			
1	0	Fred. Myddleton West ..	P 15 Aug. 48			
18	0	*Paymaster.*—Edward George Cubitt, 16 Feb. 44; *Ens.* P 9 Dec. 31; *Lieut.* 28 April, 37.				
2	0	*Adjutant.*—*Cornet* Joseph Trenerry, 3 Sept. 47.				
8	0	*Quarter-Master.*—John Evans Parry, 12 Oct. 41.				
22	0	*Surgeon.*—Stephen Lawson, 2 June 43; *A. S.* 29 July 30; *H. A.* 29 Nov. 27.				
1	0	*Assistant-Surgeon.*—Robert Wilson, M.D., 25 Aug. 48.				
2	0	*Veterinary Surgeon.*—Thomas Siddell, 3 Feb. 47.				

Blue.—*Agents,* Messrs. Cox & Co.—*Irish Agents, Sir* E. R. Borough, *Bt.* Armit, & Co.

[Returned from Canada Dec. 1842.]

1 Sir Wm. Tuyll served during part of the campaigns of 1793, 94, and 95, in the Netherlands; at the Helder, in 1799; and in Portugal, Spain, and Walcheren, in 1808 and 9, as Aide-de-camp to the present Marquis of Anglesey.

2 Captain Bowles served throughout the campaign of 1842 in Affghanistan (medal) in the 3rd Light Dragoons. He served also in the campaign on the Sutlej, including the battle of Sobraon (Medal).

8th (*The King's Royal Irish*) *Regiment of Lt. Dragoons.* (*Hussars.*) [Head Quarters at Newbridge.

Harp and Crown. "*Pristinæ virtutis memores.*"—"LESWARREE"—"HINDOOSTAN."

Years' Serv. Full Pay.	Half Pay.	
54		*Colonel.* Sir John Browne,[1] KCH. *Cornet*, 27 May, 95; *Lieut.* 17 May, 96; *Capt.* 1 June, 97; *Major*, 16 Feb. 09; *Lieut.-Col.* 14 March, 11; *Col.* 19 July, 21; *Major-Gen.* 22 July, 30; *Lieut.-Gen.* 23 Nov. 41; *Col.* 8th Hussars, 4 April, 43.
22	0	*Lieut.-Colonel.* Frederick George Shewell, *Cornet*, P 28 Aug. 27; *Lieut.* 6 Sept. 31; *Capt.* P 28 Apr. 37; *Major*, P 23 Aug. 44; *Lieut.-Col.* P 19 Feb. 47.
19	0	*Major.* Rodolph de Salis, *Cornet*, P 17 Dec. 30; *Lieut.* P 28 June, 33; *Capt.* P 18 July, 38; *Major*, P 19 Feb. 47.

Full Pay	Half Pay		CORNET.	LIEUT.	CAPTAIN.	BREV.-MAJ.
		CAPTAINS.				
15	0	Charles Joseph Longmore	P 30 May 34	P 17 Aug. 38	P 23 Aug. 44	
10	0	*Hon.* James Sandilands..	P 2 Mar. 39	P 31 Jan. 40	P 1 Aug. 45	
10	0	Arth. Jas. *Lord* Killeen	P 17 Sept. 39	P 5 Mar. 41	P 23 Jan. 46	
8	0	John Thompson........	P 5 Mar. 41	P 12 May 43	P 22 Dec. 46	
11	0	Henry Francis Cust,[2] *s*....	P 30 Mar. 38	P 31 Dec. 39	P 19 Feb. 47	
6	0	Edward Walter	P 4 Feb. 43	P 30 Mar. 44	P 10 Dec. 47	
		LIEUTENANTS.				
16	0	Joseph Reilly, R.M.	P 26 Apr. 33	27 Mar. 34		
8	0	Edward Seager, *adj*.....	P 17 Sept. 41	29 June 43		
6	0	Edward Thomkinson ..	P 12 May 43	P 12 Apr. 44		
12	0	George Lockwood	P 11 July 37	P 28 Aug. 40		
7	0	Charles John Bourchier..	P 22 Apr. 42	P 29 Dec. 43		
4	0	*Hon.* Shapland Fra. Carew	P 21 Mar. 45	P 9 Jan. 46		
6	0	Price Built Manners Wood	P 22 Sept. 43	P 24 Sept. 45		
9	0	James Sadler Naylor	17 July 40	P 22 July 45		
3	0	William Davis	P 9 Jan. 46	P 22 Dec. 46		
9	0	George Chetwode	P 8 May 40	P 10 Mar. 43		
3	0	Fra. Edmund Macnaghten	P 27 Oct. 46	P 23 May 48		
		CORNETS.				
3	0	Daniel Hugh Clutterbuck	P 22 Dec. 46			
1	0	John Gough Calthorpe ..	P 23 May 48			
10	0	*Paymaster.*—Henry Duberly, 12 Nov. 47; *Ens.* P 28 Sept. 39; *Lt.* 15 April 42.				
8	0	*Adjutant.*—*Lieut.* Edward Seager, 5 Oct. 41.				
10	0	*Quarter-Master.*—James Landers, 29 Nov. 39.				
14	1 1/12	*Surgeon.*—Gideon Dolmage, 5 April 44; *Assist.-Surg.* 10 Dec. 33.				
4	0	*Assistant-Surgeon.*—Henry Somers, M.D. 17 Oct. 45.				
6	0	*Veterinary Surgeon.*—Edward Simpson Grey, 24 April, 43.				

Blue.—*Agents*, Messrs. Cox & Co.—*Irish Agents*, Sir E. R. Borough, *Bt.* Armit, & Co.

[*Returned from the East Indies, May*, 1823.]

1 Sir John Browne served on the expedition to South America under General Whitelock; on that to Portugal under the Duke of Wellington, including the battles of Roleia and Vimiera; and subsequently on Sir John Moore's expedition to Spain, including the affairs with the French cavalry at Sahagun and Benevente, retreat to Corunna, and battle of Corunna. He was afterwards attached to the Portuguese army, and received five wounds in action with the enemy on the 18th Feb. 1811. He was also attached for five months to a division of the Spanish army in Estramadura under General Mendizabel.

2 Captain Cust was present at the battle of Maharajpore, and has received the Bronze Star.

---

4 Lt.-Col. Fullerton commanded the 9th Lancers at the battles of Punniar (Medal), and also in the campaign on the Sutlej, including the battle of Sobraon (medal).

5 Major Grant served in China as Brigade-Major to Lord Saltoun, and was present at the assault and capture of Chin Kiang Foo and at the landing before Nankin. He served with the 9th Lancers at Sobraon (medal).

6 Capt. Little, Lts. Donovan, Humbley, Anderton, Hawtrey, French, King, Bird and Clifton, served in the campaign on the Sutlej in 1846, and were present at the battle of Sobraon (medal).

7 Capt. Spottiswoode served as Brigade Major of Cavalry in the battles of Punniar (medal) and Sobraon (medal).

8 Capt. Reed commanded the right squadron of the 9th Lancers in the action of Punniar (medal); and he served in the campaign on the Sutlej, including the battle of Sobraon (medal).

10 Captain Campbell was present at Punniar (medal), and at Sobraon (medal).

12 Capt. Pratt served with the 16th Lancers in the campaign in Affghanistan, under Lord Keane in 1839 and 40. Was present at the assault and capture of Ghuznee (medal). Volunteered with the squadron detached under Brigadier Cureton in advance of the army, to seize the enemy's guns, and secure possession of the citadel of Cabul in August 1839, which was accomplished. Appointed Major of Brigade with the army of reserve in 1842 and 43. Served as Asst.-Adjt.-Gen. to the Cavalry Division with the army of Gwalior under Lord Gough in 1843-44, and was present at the battle of Maharajpore (medal).

14 Lts. Anson, Campbell, and Hamilton, Qr.-Master Allan, Doctor Staunton served with the 9th Lancers in the campaign on the Sutlej in 1846, and were present at the battle of Sobraon (medal).

15 Lt. Francis served with the 16th Lancers at the actions of Buddiwal and Aliwal; and as aide-de-camp to Sir Joseph Thackwell at Sobraon (medal).

16 Lt. MacFarlane was at the battle of Sobraon (medal), previous to which he received a sword thrust through the arm in a skirmish close to the Seik entrenchments.

19 Surgeon Grant served with the 16th at the battle of Sobraon (medal).

20 Capt. Yule served in the 16th Lancers during the campaign in Affghanistan under Lord Keane, and was present at the siege and capture of Ghuznee (medal). Also the campaign on the Sutlej in 1846 (medal); including the battles of Buddiwal, Aliwal, and Sobraon.

Embarked for India, May 1842.] **9th (*The Queen's Royal*) *Regt. of Lt. Drs.* (*Lancers.*)** [Serving in Bengal.

"PENINSULA."—"PUNNIAR."—"SOBRAON."

Years' Serv. Full Pay.	Half Pay.	
54		*Colonel*.—P [illegible] James Wallace Sleigh,[1] CB. *Cornet*, Feb. 95; *Lieut*. 29 Apr. 95; *Capt*. 25 Oct. 98; *Maj*. 14 June, 05; *Lt.-Col*. 14 Dec. 09; *Col*. 12 Aug. 19; *Major-Gen*. 22 July, 30; *Lt.-Gen*. 23 Nov. 41; *Col*. 9th Lancers, 24 Aug. 39.
42	6/12	*Lt.-Colonels*.—Alex. Campbell,[2] CB. KH. *Cor*. 24 Aug. 06; *Lt*. P 4 Sep. 06; *Capt*. P 18 Aug. 12; *Maj*. P 9 Aug. 21; *Brev.-Lt.-Col*. 16 July, 30; *Lt.-Col*. P 28 Jan. 42; *Col*. 9 Nov. 46.
30	4	John Scott,[3] CB. *Cornet*, P 4 May, 15; *Lieut*. P 26 Oct. 15; *Capt*. P 28 June, 21; *Major*, P 9 Nov. 26; *Lieut.-Col*. 31 Aug. 30; *Col*. 19 June, 46.
27	0	*Majors*.—Jas. Alex. Fullerton,[4] *Cornet*, P 1 Aug. 22; *Lt*. P 30 Dec. 24; *Capt*. P 19 Sept. 26; *Brev-Maj*. 23 Nov. 41; *Maj*. P 28 Jan. 42.; *Brev. Lt.-Col*. 25 Apr. 45.
23	0	James Hope Grant,[5] CB. *Cornet*, P 29 Aug. 26; *Lieut*. P 26 Feb. 28; *Capt*. P 29 May, 35; *Major*, 22 April, 42.

Full Pay	Half Pay	CAPTAINS.	CORNET.	LIEUT.	CAPTAIN.	BREV.-MAJ.
18	0	Archibald Little[6]	P 4 Oct. 31	P 31 Aug. 32	P 24 Feb. 37	
16	0	Andrew Spottiswoode[7]..	P 10 May 33	P 29 April 36	P 11 Oct. 39	
17	6/12	Edward Rudston Read[8]	P 18 Nov. 31	P 12 Dec. 34	P 27 Aug. 41	
18	0	John Rose Holden Rose[9]	P 19 July 31	P 11 Jan. 33	P 29 April 42	
22	0	John Cameron Campbell[10]	25 Oct. 27	P 16 Mar. 32	28 Apr. 46	
15	0	*Hon*. Charles Powys[11] ..	P 28 Feb. 34	P 1 July 36	P 13 July 47	
21	4/12	Edward James Pratt[12] ..	14 Feb. 28	P 20 Jan. 32	20 Sept. 44	
14	0	Robert Abercromby Yule[20]	P 3 July 35	P 26 May 37	P 2 July 47	
14	0	William Drysdale[13]	P 29 Dec. 35	P 31 Aug. 38	P 29 Oct. 47	
		LIEUTENANTS.				
13	0	Cha. H. Douglas Donovan[6]	19 Feb. 36	P 3 Aug. 41		
14	0	Oct. Henry St. Geo. Anson[14]	27 Nov. 35	8 Dec. 38		
14	0	Wm. Well. W. Humbley[6]	27 Mar. 35	15 Dec. 38		
13	0	WmR Newport Campbell[14]	P 10 June 36	15 July 41		
12	0	Fred. Courtney Trower[13]	P 30 June 37	13 May 42		
10	0	Thomas John Francis[15]..	P 14 June 39	P 1 July 42		
7	0	Alexander Hawtrey[6]	P 24 April 42	P 31 May 44		
7	0	Wm. Hamilton,[14] *adj*. ..	29 April 42	23 Oct. 45		
6	0	Fra. John M'Farlane[16] ..	P 6 Jan. 43	P 24 Oct. 45		
7	0	Lucius John French[6]....	P 13 Dec. 42	28 Apr. 46		
9	0	Henry Nelthorpe	P 20 Oct. 40	P 17 Jan. 45		
6	0	Robert William King[6]..	P 23 June 43	17 Mar. 47		
9	0	John Head	P 15 Dec. 40	19 Nov. 42		
6	0	Wm. Wilberforce Bird[6]..	P 24 Nov. 43	P 6 Aug. 47		
5	0	Chandos Fred. Clifton[6]..	P 31 May 44	P 29 Oct. 47		
3	0	John Henry King	P 23 Jan. 46	P 31 Dec. 47		
3	0	Charles Abbott Delmar ..	P 8 May 46	P 23 May 48		
4	0	George Pinckney Atkinson	P 8 Aug. 45	P 31 Mar. 48		
2	0	Henry Andrew Sarel....	P 13 July 47	P 15 Dec. 48		
		CORNETS.				
3	0	Richard Shaw, R. M.....	3 Apr. 46			
2	0	Frederick Ellis	P 13 Aug. 47			
2	0	Edmund D'Arcy Hunt ..	P 29 Oct. 47			
1	0	A. Eastfield Wilkinson ..	P 11 Feb. 48			
1	0	Henry Scott	P 12 May 48			
1	0	Robert Sutherland......	P 23 May 48			
1	0	Alex. J. Hardy Elliott ..	18 July 48			
1	0	W. Wedderburn Arbuthnot	P 15 Dec. 48			

3 Colonel Scott was present with the French army under Marshal Gerard, at the siege of Antwerp, in Dec. 1832; and, by permission of the Marshal, he accompanied the troops upon every occasion during the siege. In Oct. 1838, he was appointed to the command of the cavalry of the Bombay division of the army of the Indus, as Brigadier; served in that rank during the campaigns of 1838 and 39, in Scinde and Affghanistan, and was present at the attack and capture of Ghuznee. During the latter part of 1839, he commanded a detached column, consisting of the whole of the artillery, (excepting 4 guns,) the cavalry, and one battalion of infantry: this column was destined to secure the subjugation of Upper Scinde, and to co-operate with the main column under Sir Tho. Willshire, directed against Khelat. In the action at Maharajpore on the 29th Dec. 1843, he commanded a Brigade of Cavalry, as also at the battle of Sobraon.

9 Capt. Rose commanded a half squadron of the 3rd Light Dragoons at the forcing of the Khyber Pass, and was also at the relief of Jellalabad, and at the re-capture of Cabool, in Affghanistan, in 1842 (medal). At the battle of Punniar, near Gwalior, he commanded the left squadron of the 9th Lancers (medal). He was also at Sobraon (medal).

17 Paymaster Barlow served in the Peninsula from Aug. 1810 to April 1812; the campaign against Nepaul in 1815; and the Mahratta campaigns of 1817 and 18; and was present at the battle of Jubblepore, 19th Dec. 1817. He was present with the 10th at the battle of Sobraon (medal).

Full Pay	Half Pay	
39	0	*Paymaster*.—P Cuthbert Barlow,[17] 3 Jan. 28; *Ens*. 7 Jan. 10; *Lieut*. 13 Jan. 14.
7	0	*Adjutant*.—*Lieut*. William Hamilton,[14] 29 April, 42.
7	0	*Quarter-Master*.—Andrew Allan,[14] 13 May, 42.
23	0	*Surgeon*.—Rob. Joynt Gordon Grant,[19] 2 Jul. 41; *A.-S*. 14 Feb. 28; *H.-A*. 7 Sep. 26.
9	0	*Assistant-Surgeons*.—Walter George Leonard Staunton,[14] 29 May, 40.
9	0	Eneas Macintosh Macpherson, 21 Aug. 40.
14	0	*Veterinary Surgeon*.—Richard John Gedaliah Hurford,[18] 17 July, 35.

Blue—*Facings* Scarlet.—*Agent*, George Samuel Collyer, Esq.

1 General Sleigh served in Flanders in 1795; in the actions in North Holland and the Helder, 10th and 19th Sept., and 2d and 6th Oct. 1799. In the Peninsula in 1811 and 12. Commanded the 11th Dragoons at Waterloo, towards the close of which the command of the 4th Brigade devolved on him. In 1819 he accompanied his regiment to India, and commanded the Cavalry division at the siege of Bhurtpore in 1825 & 6.

2 Colonel Campbell was present at the capture of the Cape of Good Hope with Sir David Baird's army, in 1806; and he served subsequently in India in the 25th Lt. Dragoons until 1811. In 1842 he proceeded again to India with his regiment, and commanded the 1st Cavalry Brigade of the army of Gwalior, in the action at Punniar, on the 29th Dec. 1843; and the 2nd Cavalry Brigade in the battle of Sobraon, 10 Feb. 1846.

11 Capt. the Hon. C. Powys, prior to entering the army, served five years and three months in the Royal Navy, and was present in H.M.S. *Blonde*, at the taking of the Morea Castle, in the Gulf of Lepanto, in 1828.

13 Captain Drysdale served with the 4th Light Dragoons, and Lieut. Trower with the 16th Lancers, during the campaign in Affghanistan under Lord Keane, and were present at the siege and capture of Ghuznee. (Medal.) These officers were also present with the 9th Lancers in the action at Punniar, 29th Dec. 43 (medal); and afterwards at Sobraon (medal).

18 Mr. Hurford served with the 16th Lancers during the campaign in Affghanistan under Lord Keane, including the siege and capture of Ghuznee (medal). He was also in the action at Maharajpore, 29th Dec. 1843 (medal); and afterwards at Sobraon (medal).

HeadQuarters at Poonah.] 10th (*The Prince of Wales's own*) *Royal Reg. of Lt. Drs.* (*Hussars.*) [Emb. for Bombay, 5 May 46.

"PENINSULA."—"WATERLOO."

Colonel.

Years' Serv. 46 — *Hon.* Henry Beauchamp Lygon,[1] *Cornet*, 9 July, 1803; *Lieut.* 24 May, 04; *Capt.* 15 Jan. 07; *Major*, 14 May, 12; *Lt.-Col.* 18 June, 15; *Col.* 24 Mar. 22; *Major-Gen.* 10 Jan. 37; *Lt.-Gen.* 9 Nov. 46; *Col.* 10th Hussars, 23 June, 43.

Lieut.-Colonels.

Full Pay	Half Pay	
20	0	Henry Fred. Bonham, *Cornet*, P 22 May, 29; *Lieut.* P 14 June, 31; *Capt.* P 16 May, 34; *Major*, 3 Apr. 46; *Lieut.-Col.* P 28 Apr. 46.
33	1/12	William Parlby, *Cornet*, P 3 Oct. 16; *Lieut.* P 6 May, 24; *Capt.* P 19 Sept. 26; *Brevet-Major*, 23 Nov. 41; *Major*, P 26 Sept. 45; *Lt.-Col.* P 30 Jan. 46.
36	1/2	*Majors.*—John Tritton,[2] *Cornet*, 14 Jan. 13; *Lt.* 14 Aug. 15; *Capt.* 7 Oct. 36; *Major*, 3 Apr. 46.
18	0	George Aug. Fred. Quentin, *Cornet*, P 14 June, 31; *Lieut.* P 1 June, 32; *Capt.* P 12 Feb. 36; *Major*, P 28 Apr. 46.

Full Pay	Half Pay	CAPTAINS.	CORNET.	LIEUT.	CAPTAIN.	BREVET-MAJOR.
11	0	John Wilkie	P 11 May 38	P 29 May 40	P 17 May 44	
10	0	Broadley Harrison, *s.* ..	P 11 Oct. 39	P 7 Sept. 41	P 7 June 44	
11	0	*Lord* Geo. A. Beauclerk	P 28 Aug. 38	P 5 Feb. 41	P 6 Dec. 44	
16	0	William Petrie Waugh[3]..	P 1 Nov. 33	P 29 May 35	P 31 Dec. 44	19 June 46
22	0	Thomas Lloyd	P 15 Mar. 27	P 12 Oct. 30	3 Apr. 46	
11	0	*Sir* Thomas Munro, *Bart.*	P 7 July 38	P 27 Aug. 41	P 28 Apr. 46	
11	0	Methuen Stedman......	P 1 June 38	P 21 Feb. 40	P 4 Apr. 45	
11	0	William Murray........	P 9 Mar. 38	P 29 May 40	P 6 Nov. 46	
7	0	Charles Freville Surtees..	P 28 Jan. 42	P 7 Feb. 45	P 10 Dec. 47	
		LIEUTENANTS.				
10	0	George Webb, *adj.*......	28 June 39	30 Dec. 41		
7	0	*Hon.* F.C.G. FitzClarence, *s*	22 April 42	P 23 May 45		
5	0	C. H. S. G. *Lord* Garvagh	P 17 May 44	P 20 Mar. 46		
12	0	Thomas Sargent Little ..	9 Dec. 37	19 Oct. 39		
10	0	Malcolm R. Laing Meason[5]	P 21 June 39	P 26 Oct. 41		
9	0	Robert Charles Holmes..	P 20 Nov. 40	P 2 Apr. 44		
8	0	Richard Playne Smith ..	P 26 Oct. 41	P 3 Apr. 46		
8	0	Charles Potts Rosser	P 8 Jan. 41	3 Apr. 46		
5	0	Theodore Wirgman, R.M.	P 29 Nov. 44	3 Apr. 46		
5	0	John Wycliffe Thompson	P 22 Nov. 44	P 3 Apr. 46		
4	0	Wm. Macfarlane Wardrop	P 7 Feb. 45	P 3 Apr. 46		
8	0	Richard Everard Blake[7]	P 24 Jan. 41	27 May 42		
9	0	Arthur John Loftus	P 15 Dec. 40	3 May 44		
3	0	John Walrond Clarke ..	P 20 Mar. 46	P 1 Dec. 46		
6	0	Charles MacMahon	P 4 Aug. 43	P 2 Feb. 47		
13	0	John Percy Smith[6]	P 8 July 36	21 Aug. 39		
3	0	Butler Mildmay Giveen	4 Apr. 46	P 11 June 47		
3	0	Benjamin Aylett Branfill	5 Apr. 46	P 10 Dec. 47		
3	0	John Drummond	6 Apr. 46	P 15 Dec. 48		
		CORNETS.				
3	0	Robert Clements	3 Apr. 46			
3	0	Edw. Jas. Stopford Blair	7 Apr. 46			
3	0	Theodore Williams	P 8 Apr. 46			
3	0	Edward Stacey	P 1 Dec. 46			
2	0	Henry Alexander	P 3 Sept. 47			
2	0	John Rawlinson Cuthbert	P 10 Dec. 47			
1	0	Henry Fraser Dimsdale	P 11 Feb. 48			
1	0	Francis B. Hallowell Carew	P 15 Dec. 48			

Full Pay	Half Pay	
11	0	*Paymaster.*—Richard John Elrington, 2 Feb. 44; *Ens.* P 24 March, 38; *Lieut.* [P 29 May, 39.
10	0	*Adjutant.*—*Lieut.* George Webb, 20 Sept. 39.
3	0	*Quarter-Master.*—John Fenn, 19 May, 46.
23	0	*Surgeon.*—Murdoch John Maclaine Ross,[9] 8 Feb. 42; *Assist.-Surg.* 15 Feb. 27; *Hosp.-Assist.* 28 Feb. 26.
4	0	*Assistant-Surgeons.*—Thomas Fraser, M.D., 16 Dec. 45.
8	0	John Edward Stephens,[10] M.D., 5 Oct. 41.
9	0	*Veterinary Surgeon.*—James Robertson, 2 Oct. 40.

Blue.—*Agent*, Messrs. Cox & Co.

5 Lieut. Meason served with the 40th in Lower and Upper Scinde and Beloochistan in 1840-41; and throughout the second Affghan campaign under Gen. Nott,—at Candahar during the winter of 1841-42; on the advance to Cabool he was severely wounded at Goaine. He was also present at the battle of Maharajpore. He has received the medal inscribed "Candahar, Cabool," and the Bronze Star for Maharajpore.

7 Lieut. Blake carried the Queen's colour of the 22nd at the battles of Meeanee and Hyderabad (medal). He served also with that regt. in the subsequent operations in the southern Mahratta country, including the investment and capture by storm of the forts of Punella and Powanghur.

9 Mr. Ross served in the 16th Lancers the campaign in Affghanistan under Lord Keane, and was present at the capture of Ghuznee, for which he has received a medal.

10 Doctor Stephens was present at the battle of Maharajpore (medal), and also in the battles of Moodkee, Ferozeshah, and Sobraon.

Lieut.-Gen. the Honourable Henry B. Lygon, served in the Peninsula with the 16th Dragoons, from March 1809 to Sept. 1810, and again from Feb. 1814 to the end of that war, including the capture of Oporto, battle of Talavera, and passage of the Coa. Severely wounded in the neck, 28th Aug 1810, in Massena's advance to the battle of Busaco.

2 Major Tritton served with the late 24th Dragoons at the siege and capture of Hattras, and the Mahratta campaigns of 1817 and 18; with the 11th Lt. Drs. at the siege and capture of Bhurtpore in 1825-6; and with the 3rd Lt. Drs. the campaign of 1842 in Affghanistan. He served as D. A. Adj. General of the cavalry of the army of the Sutlej in 1845-6, and was present at the battles of Moodkee, Ferozeshah, and Sobraon.

3 Major Waugh served with the 16th Lancers at the battle of Maharajpore (medal), 29th Dec. 1843; and on the Staff in the battles of Buddiwal, Aliwal, and Sobraon.

6 Lieut. John Percy Smith served the campaign in Affghanistan under Lord Keane, with the 16th Lancers, and was present at the siege and capture of Ghuznee (Medal).

The *Sphinx*, with the words, "EGYPT"—"SALAMANCA"—"PENINSULA"—"WATERLOO"—"BHURTPORE."

Years' Serv. Full Pay	Half Pay	
43		*Colonel.*
		Sir Henry Wyndham,[1] *Ens.* 27 March 06; *Capt.* 8 June 09; *Major*, 9 Aug. 13; *Lieut.-Col.* 20 Jan. 14; *Col.* 27 May 25; *Major-Gen.* 10 Jan. 37; *Lieut.-Gen.* 9 Nov. 46; *Col.* 11th Hussars, 19 Nov. 47.
		Lieut.-Colonel.
22	3 1/12	James Thomas, *Earl of* Cardigan, *Cornet*, P 6 May, 24; *Lieut.* P 13 Jan. 25; *Capt.* P 9 June, 26; *Major*, P 3 Aug. 30; *Lieut.-Col.* 3 Dec. 30; *Col.* 9 Nov. 46.
		Major.
21	0	Inigo William Jones, *Cornet*, P 8 July, 28; *Lieut.* P 17 Dec. 30; *Capt.* P 14 Apr. 37; *Major*, P 7 June, 44.

Full Pay	Half Pay	Captains.	Cornet.	Lieut.	Captain.	Brevet-Major.
20	0	John Douglas	P 18 June 29	P 25 Oct. 33	P 11 May 39	
12	1 1/12	Edmund Peel	P 18 Mar. 36	P 17 July 40	P 3 Nov. 46	
7	0	William Stephen Sandes, *s.*	P 3 June 42	P 5 Dec. 43	P 30 Mar. 47	
7	0	*Hon.* Gerard James Noel	P 8 July 42	P 29 Dec. 43	P 13 July 47	
6	0	William Foster	P 5 Dec. 43	P 26 Sept. 45	P 1 Aug. 48	
17	0	John Bunce Pilgrim	P 4 Dec. 32	P 16 Sept. 37	P 14 June 42	
		Lieutenants.				
6	0	Jas. Tho. Wightman, R.M.	24 Feb. 43	P 5 Apr. 44		
6	0	Thomas Yorke Dallas	P 29 Dec. 43	P 21 Apr. 46		
5	0	Wm. G. Baker Cresswell	P 5 April 44	P 10 July 46		
5	0	Frederick Henry Sykes	P 23 July 44	P 3 Nov. 46		
3	0	Arthur Brisco	P 10 July 46	P 13 July 47		
2	0	William Ennis, *Adj.*	22 Jan. 47	27 Jan. 48		
2	0	Edwin Adolphus Cook	P 30 Mar. 47	P 28 Jan. 48		
2	0	Lester Garland	P 13 July 47	P 1 Aug. 48		
2	0	Geo. H. Lutton Boynton	P 11 June 47	P 16 June 48		
2	0	Walter Stephens Brinkley	P 24 Sept. 47	P 10 Nov. 48		
		Cornets.				
1	0	Mathew Wharton Wilson	P 28 Jan. 48			
1	0	Eyre Coote	P 1 Aug. 48			
1	0	James Miller	P 10 Nov. 48			

Full Pay	Half Pay	
10	0	*Paymaster.*—Joseph Hely,[2] 1 Dec. 48; *Ens.* 16 Feb. 39; *Lieut.* 11 Nov. 45.
2	0	*Adjutant.*—*Lieut.* William Ennis, 22 Jan. 47.
2	0	*Quarter-Master.*—John Gilleland, 5 March, 47.
23	0	*Surgeon.*—Patrick O'Callaghan, M.D. 3 Feb. 43; *Assist.-Surg.* 21 Feb. 28; *Hosp.-Assist.* 18 July, 26.
6	0	*Assist-Surgeon.*—Richard Pyper, 24 Nov. 43.
17	0	*Veterinary Surgeon.*—John William Gloag, 29 June, 32.

Blue.—*Agents*, Messrs. Cox & Co.

[*Returned from the East Indies, June* 1838.]

1 Lieut.-General Wyndham served the Peninsular campaigns of 1808, 9, 11, and 13, including the actions of Roleia, Vimiera, Benevente, Albuhera, Usagre, Morales de Toro, Vittoria, and the Pyrenees. Served also the campaign of 1815, and was severely wounded at Waterloo.

2 Lieut. Hely served as a captain in the 1st Lancers of the late Anglo-Spanish Legion, in 1835 and 36, and was engaged at the castle of Guevara, the stronghold of the Carlists; and afterwards at Mendegus, Asua, and heights of Arlaban in Alava on the 16th, 17th, and 18th Jan. 1836; also at the passage of the Urumea on the 28th May, and commanded the squadron which took Passages on that day. Again on the right of the lines when Alza was attacked; together with constant skirmishes in front of Vittoria.

The *Sphinx*, with the words, "EGYPT"—"PENINSULA"—"WATERLOO."

Years' Serv. Full Pay.	Half Pay.	
60		*Colonel.* **P** *Sir* Henry John Cumming,[1] KCH. *Cornet*, 12 May, 1790; *Lieut.* 9 Feb. 93; *Capt.* 21 Feb. 94; *Major*, 25 Oct. 98; *Lieut-Col.* 17 Feb. 1803; *Col.* 1 Jan. 12; *Major-Gen.* 4 June, 14; *Lieut.-Gen.* 22 July, 30; *Col.* 12th *Lancers*, 20 Jan. 37.
24	0	*Lieut-Colonel.* Edward Pole, *Cornet*, P 7 July, 25; *Lieut.* P 19 Sept. 26; *Capt.* P 18 Nov. 31; *Major*, P 30 July, 44; *Lieut.-Col.* P 30 March, 47.
16	0	*Major.* Edward Morant, *Cornet*, P 20 Sept. 33; *Lieut.* P 24 Apr. 35; *Capt.* P 11 Nov. 42; *Major*, P 22 Dec. 48.

Full Pay	Half Pay	CAPTAINS.	CORNET.	LIEUT.	CAPTAIN.	BREVET-MAJOR.
16	0	Wm. Heathcote Tottenham	P 13 Dec. 33	P 23 Oct. 35	P 7 July 43	
11	0	David Arthur Monro....	P 28 Dec. 38	P 1 June 41	P 1 May 46	
10	0	Thomas Henry Clifton ..	P 26 Apr. 39	P 2 July 41	P 30 Mar. 47	
9	0	Rich. Hugh Smith Barry	P 15 Dec. 40	P 26 Nov. 41	P 3 Sept. 47	
8	0	Charles Sutton	P 13 July 41	P 7 July 43	P 28 Apr. 48	
8	0	C. Sabine Aug. Thellusson	P 26 Nov. 41	P 30 July 44	P 22 Dec. 48	
		LIEUTENANTS.				
7	0	Tho. Cockayne Maunsell	P 11 Nov. 42	P 16 Jan. 46		
8	0	John De Montmorency Prior	31 Dec. 41	30 Apr. 46		
6		Henry George Sutton ..	P 5 Dec. 43	P 1 May 46		
5	0	John Almerus Digby....	P 30 July 44	P 30 Mar. 47		
3	0	Thomas Geo. Alex. Oakes	P 16 Jan. 46	P 3 Sept. 47		
3	0	John Wilson Fox	P 1 May 46	P 26 Nov. 47		
2	0	Charles Goring	P 30 Mar. 47	P 31 Mar. 48		
2	0	Charles Edward Grogan	P 16 Apr. 47	P 28 Apr. 38		
1	0	Frederick Arden	P 17 Mar. 48	P 22 Dec. 48		
		CORNETS.				
2	0	Arthur W. Williams, R.M.	P 5 Nov. 47			
1	0	Constable Curtis........	P 31 Mar. 48			
1	0	Charles Marr, *adj*.......	P 25 May 48			

Full Pay	Half Pay	
11	0	*Paymaster.*—Blayney Townly Walshe,[2] 3 Oct. 48; *Ens.* P 26 Aug. 38; *Lieut.* 31 Dec. 39.
1	0	*Adjutant.*—*Cornet* Charles Marr, 26 May, 48.
1	0	*Quarter-Master.*—Michael Blake, 18 July 48.
14	0	*Surgeon.*—George Anderson, 16 Dec. 45; *A.-S.* 12 June 35.
6	0	*Assistant-Surgeon.*—Robert Villiers George, M.D. 10 Nov. 43.
2	0	*Veterinary Surgeon.*—William Thacker, 14 July 47.

Blue—*Facings* Scarlet.—*Agent*, George Samuel Collyer, Esq.—*Irish Agents*, Messrs. Cane & Co.

[*Returned from Portugal, March* 1828.]

1 Sir Hen. John Cumming served with the 11th Dragoons in Flanders, and was present in every action that occurred, including the sieges of Valenciennes and Dunkirk; and battles of Famars and Cateau: also the winter campaign of 1794 in Holland, and that to the Helder in 1799. Served also two years in the Peninsula, in command of the 11th Light Dragoons, including the action of El Bodon, (wounded by a sabre cut in the arm,) and battle of Salamanca, for which latter he has received a medal.

2 Paymaster Walshe served with the 9th throughout the campaign of 1842 in Affghanistan (Medal) under *Sir* George Pollock, including the storming the Khyber Pass, taking the Fort of Mamoo Khail, storming the heights of Jugdulluck, action in the Tezeen Valley, clearing the heights of Huff Kotul, and storming the Town of Istaliff.

On the chacoes and appointments, the Motto, "*First in Æternum.*"—"PENINSULA"—"WATERLOO."

Years' Serv.	
46	
Full Pay.	Half Pay.

Colonel.

46 — Hon. Edward Pyndar Lygon,[1] CB. *Sub-Lieut.* 1 June, 03; *Lieut.* 7 Nov. 05; *Captain*, 15 Feb. 08; *Lieut.-Colonel*, 27 April, 15; *Colonel*, 27 April, 22; *Major-General*, 10 Jan. 37; *Lt.-Gen.* 9 Nov. 46; *Colonel*, 13th Light Dragoons, 29 Jan. 45.

Lieut.-Colonel.

23 | 3/12 — William Knox, *Ensign*, P 12 Jan. 26; *Lieut.* P 20 Mar. 27; *Capt.* P 14 Dec. 32; *Major*, P 11 July, 45; *Lt.-Col.* P 23 June 1848.

Major.

14 | 0 — Charles Edmund Doherty, *Cornet*, P 24 Apr. 35; *Lieut.* P 6 Jan. 37; *Capt.* P 4 Sept. 40; *Major*, P 23 June 1848.

Full Pay.	Half Pay.		CORNET.	LIEUT.	CAPTAIN.	BREV-MAJ.
		CAPTAINS.				
14	0	Sam. Auchmuty Dickson	P 22 May 35	P 28 Sept. 39	P 29 Sept. 43	
14	0	Wm. Richard Ormsby Gore	P 29 Dec. 35	P 12 Apr. 39	P 19 May 46	
7	0	Henry Holden	P 22 Apr. 42	P 30 Dec. 45	P 19 Mar. 47	
8	0	Rob. H. Johnston Stewart	P 26 Feb. 41	P 14 Nov. 45	P 24 Sept. 47	
5	0	Felton Fred. Wm. Hervey, *s.*	P 8 Oct. 44	P 12 Sept. 46	P 29 Oct. 47	
4	0	Robert Higginson Borrowes	P 14 Feb. 45	P 19 Mar. 47	P 23 June 48	
		LIEUTENANTS.				
7	0	John Augustin Oldham	P 1 Apr. 42	23 June 43		
4	0	Thomas Howard Goad ..	4 July 45	P 13 Aug. 47		
4	0	Thomas Irwin, *adj*	24 Oct. 45	23 Sept. 47		
4	0	Soame Gambier Jenyns	P 30 Dec. 45	P 24 Sept. 47		
3	0	Arthur Tremayne	P 11 Sept. 46	P 29 Oct. 47		
3	0	Cecil M. B. Dunn Gardner	P 9 Oct. 46	P 23 June 48		
2	0	Luke White	P 19 Mar. 47	P 8 Dec. 48		
		CORNETS.				
2	0	Randall Wilmer Hatfield	P 16 April 47			
2	0	Hugh Mosman	P 13 Aug. 47			
2	0	*Hon.* J. W. H. Hutchinson	P 8 Oct. 47			
2	0	Percy Shawe Smith	P 29 Oct. 47			
1	0	Algernon Massingberd ..	P 23 June 48			

15 | 0 — *Paymaster.*—Edmund Bentley Frith, 7 Sept. 41; *Ens.* P 31 Oct. 34; *Lieut.* P 3 Nov. 37.

{4 | 0 — *Adjutant.*—*Lieut.* Thomas Irwin, 24 Oct. 45.

2 | 0 — *Quarter-Master.*—Thomas Anderson, 2 April, 47.

25 | 0 — *Surgeon.*—James Young,[4] M.D. 18 Oct. 39; *Assist.-Surg.* 14 Aug. 24; *Hosp. Assist.* 18 May 24.

5 | 0 — *Assist.-Surg.*—George Thomas Woodman, M.D. 29 Nov. 44.

19 | 0 — *Veterinary Surg.*—John Legrew, 9 July, 30.

Blue—*Facings* Buff.—*Agents*, Messrs. Cox & Co.—*Irish Agents*, Sir E. R. Borough, *Bt.*, Armit, & Co.

[Returned from the East Indies, May 1840.]

1 Lieut.-General the Honourable Edward P. Lygon served in the Peninsula with the 2nd Life Guards, from Nov. 1812 to the end of that war in 1814, including the battle of Vittoria. Served also the campaign of 1815, and was present at the battle of Waterloo.

4 Dr. Young served in Africa from 1824 to 1827 inclusive, and was present at the battle of Doodwa, against the Ashantees, 7 Aug. 26.

Emb. for India, 24 May 1841. | **14th (*The King's*) Regt. of Light Dragoons.** | Serving in Bengal.

The "PRUSSIAN EAGLE"—"DOURO"—"TALAVERA"—"FUENTES D'ONOR"—"SALAMANCA"—"VITTORIA"—"ORTHES"—"PENINSULA."

Years' Serv. Full Pay	Half Pay					
53		*Colonel.* P W Sir Edward Kerrison, *Bart.*[1] KCB. & GCH. *Cornet*, 23 June, 1796; *Lieut.* 1 Feb. 98; *Capt.* 18 Oct. 98; *Major.* 12 May, 1803; *Lieut.-Col.* 4 April, 05; *Col.* 4 June, 13; *Major-Gen.* 12 Aug. 19; *Lieut.-Gen.* 10 Jan. 37; *Col.* 14th Light Dragoons, 18 June, 30.				
39	0	*Lieut.-Colonels.*—P W Wm. Havelock,[2] KH. *Ens.* 12 July, 10; *Lieut.* 12 May, 12; *Capt.* P 19 Feb. 18; *Major*, P 31 Dec. 30; *Lieut.-Col.* 30 April, 41.				
24	0	John Wallace King, *Cornet*, P 24 March, 25; *Lieut.* P 14 Feb. 28; *Capt.* P 28 Dec. 32; *Major*, P 14 March, 45; *Lieut.-Col.* P 25 April, 48.				
16	0	*Majors*—Henry Edward Doherty, *Cornet*, P 31 Dec. 33; *Lieut.* P 15 July 36; *Capt.* P 17 May 39; *Major*, P 22 Oct. 47.				
24	0	Charles Steuart, *Cornet*, 10 Dec. 25; *Lieut.* P 5 Feb. 29; *Capt.* P 9 Nov. 38; *Major*, P 25 April, 48.				
		CAPTAINS.	CORNET.	LIEUT.	CAPTAIN.	BREV.-MAJ.
11	0	Wm. Clarke, *QrM.* 15 Sep. 37	24 April 38	4 Jan. 41	P 25 Nov. 42	
10	0	John Hesketh Goddard..	P 26 July 39	P 15 Jan. 41	P 16 May 45	
19	0	William Wilmer[5]	P 15 June 30	11 Apr. 33	P 31 Dec. 39	
14	0	Arthur Scudamore[7]	P 29 May 35	18 Feb. 38	P 22 Oct. 47	
11	0	Wm. Augustus Gaussen	P 17 Aug. 38	8 Apr. 42	P 1 Oct. 47	
14	0	Richard Herbert Gall ..	P 3 July 35	7 Dec. 38	P 31 Mar. 48	
12	0	John Forster FitzGerald[7]	P 24 Mar. 37	31 May 39	P 25 Apr. 48	
11	½	Thomas Garratt	9 Mar. 38	29 Dec. 40	P 23 May 48	
13	0	Charles Wm. Thompson[8]	P 26 Feb. 36	P 17 Jan. 40	P 1 Dec. 48	
		LIEUTENANTS.				
23	0	James Chambre	P 27 July 26	P 12 Feb. 29		
12	0	John Augustus Todd,[7] *r.*	P 28 Apr. 37	P 14 June 39		
11	0	Rich. Buckley Prettejohn	P 23 Feb. 38	P 18 Oct. 39		
8	0	Wm. Nettleship[10]	P 15 Jan. 41	P 25 Nov. 42		
8	0	Robert Johnston Brown	P 31 Dec. 41	P 16 May 45		
8	0	Richard P. Apthorp, *adj.*	P 30 Apr. 41	5 Nov. 46		
7	0	William M'Mahon, *s.*....	P 26 Nov. 42	P 6 Nov. 46		
4	0	Robert Townly Woodman	P 25 Apr. 45	19 Feb. 47		
10	0	Arthur Need	P 13 Oct. 39	P 17 June 42		
4	0	William English........	P 16 May 45	23 Apr. 47		
3	0	James Wentworth Bennett	P 1 May 46	P 25 June 47		
3	0	John Theodore Ling	P 4 Apr. 46	P 9 Apr. 47		
8	0	Taylor Lambard Mayne..	P 6 Aug. 41	P 20 Dec. 42		
3	0	Herbert Edwards	P 6 Nov. 46	P 22 Oct. 47		
3	0	Thomas Barrett	P 11 Dec. 46	P 21 Jan. 48		
6	0	Henry Elmhirst Reader	24 Nov. 43	9 Aug. 45		
3	0	Ambrose Lloyd	P 22 Dec. 46	P 31 Mar. 48		
2	0	Samuel Kerr Ibbetson ..	P 19 Feb. 47	P 25 Apr. 48		
2	0	Augustus John Cureton..	2 Mar. 47	P 27 Oct. 48		
2	0	Wm. Dundas Boyd	P 23 Mar. 47	P 1 Dec. 48		
		CORNETS.				
2	0	*Hon.* Rich. W. Chetwynd	23 April 47			
2	0	William Spilling........	P 25 June 47			
2	0	William D'Urban Blyth..	P 22 Oct. 47			
1	0	Stanley Ollivant Black ..	P 21 Jan. 48			
1	0	John Dudgeon	P 31 Mar. 48			
2	0	Michael Cusac Smith ..	P 10 Dec. 47			
1	0	Thomas Edward Gordon	P 27 Oct. 48			
1	0	Frederick Vansittart	P 1 Dec. 48			
37	0	*Paymaster.*—P Sam. Rofe,[12] 3 Sept. 12.				
8	0	*Adjutant.*—*Lieut.* R. Pretyman Apthorp, 25 Nov. 42.				
1	0	*Quarter-Master.*—George Shenton, 7 April, 48.				
13	0	*Surgeon.*—Archibald Stewart,[13] 12 Feb. 47; *Assist.-Surg.* 19 Feb. 36.				
4	0	*Assistant-Surgeons.*—Robert Bridgeman Wigstrom, 23 May, 45.				
5	0	Charles Hamilton Fasson,[14] 12 July, 44.				
11	0	*Veterinary Surgeon.*—J. G. Philips, 28 Aug. 38.				

2 *Lieut.-Col.* Havelock served in the Peninsula from July 1810 to the end of that war in 1814, including the battles of Busaco, Sabugal, Salamanca, and Vittoria; passage of the Bidassoa, battle of the Nivelle, affairs near Bayonne, battles of Orthes and Toulouse. Served also the campaign of 1815, and was wounded at Quatre Bras.

5 Capt Wilmer served with the 16th Lancers throughout the campaign in Affghanistan in 1838 and 39, including the siege and capture of Ghuznee (Medal). He was also present in the action of Maharajpore (Medal) 29th Dec. 1843.

8 Capt. Thompson served as a Captain in the Anglo Spanish Legion, and was engaged at Hernani 30th Aug. 1835; the operations on the heights of Arlaban, 16th, 17th, and 18th Jan. 1836; and the action before San Sebastian, 5th May, 1836, in which he was severely wounded in the hip and the hand.

14 Mr. Fasson served with the 53rd in the campaign on the Sutlej, and was present at Buddiwal and Aliwal (Medal).

Blue—*Facings* Scarlet.—*Agent*, Messrs. Cox & Co.

1 Sir Edward Kerrison served at the Helder in 1799; including the battles of the 19th Sept., 2d and 6th Oct. Campaign of 1808-9 in Spain, under Sir John Moore, including the battle of Corunna. Commanded the 7th Hussars in the campaigns of 1813, 14, and 15, and was present at the battles of Orthes and Waterloo, for which he has received medals. Sir Edward was severely wounded (his arm having been broken in two places) in Spain, 25 Dec. 1808; and slightly wounded at Waterloo, where he had also a horse shot under him.

7 Capts. Scudamore and FitzGerald, and Lieut. Todd served with the 4th Light Dragoons during the campaign in Affghanistan under Lord Keane, and were present at the siege and capture of Ghuznee (Medal).

10 Lieut. Nettleship served as a Captain in the Anglo-Spanish Legion, during the years 1835, 36, and 37, and was present at the relief of Bilboa, operations on the heights of Arlaban in Alava, 16th, 17th, and 18th Jan. 1836; action before San Sebastian, 5th May; action on the Ametza Heights, 1 Oct.; operations on the 10th, 12th, 14th, 15th, and 16th March, 1837; siege of Irun, and various skirmishes.

12 Paymaster Rofe served in the Peninsula from Oct. 1812 to the end of the war.

13 Mr. Stewart served with the 9th Lancers in the campaign on the Sutlej in 1846, and was present at the battle of Sobraon (Medal).

Emb. for India, 11 July, 1839.] **15th (*The King's*) Regt. of Lt. Drs. (*Hussars*).** [Serving at Bangalore, Madras.

"EMSDORF"—"EGMONT-OP-ZEE"—"VILLIERS EN COUCHE"—"SAHAGUN"—"VITTORIA"—"PENINSULA"—"WATERLOO."

Years' Serv. 55 — Full Pay. | Half Pay.

Colonel.—P Sir Robert Thomas Wilson,[1] *Cornet*, Apr. 1794; *Lieut.* 31 Oct. 94; *Capt.* 21 Sept. 96; *Major*, 28 June, 1800; *Lieut.-Col.* 27 Feb. 02; *Col.* 25 July, 10; *Major-Gen.* 4 June, 13; *Lieut.-Gen.* 27 May, 25; *Gen.* 23 Nov. 41; *Col.* 15th Hussars, 29 Dec. 35.

38 | 5 4/12 | *Lieut.-Colonels.*—P Lovell Benjamin Lovell,[2] KH. *Cornet*, P18 Dec. 05; *Lieut.* P19 May, 08; *Capt.* P12 Dec. 11; *Brevet-Major*, 21 Jan. 19; *Regtl.-Major*, P28 Oct. 24; *Lieut.-Col.* P21 Nov. 28; *Col.* 23 Nov. 41.

18 | 0 | George William Key, *Cornet*, P5 July, 31; *Lieut.* 25 Aug. 33; *Capt.* P16 Sept. 37; *Major*, P14 June, 42; *Lieut.-Col.* 9 Feb. 47.

40 | 3/12 | *Majors.*—Henry Bond,[3] *Cornet*, P25 May, 09; *Lieut.* 1 March, 11; *Capt.* P6 May, 24; *Brevet-Major*, 28 June, 38; *Major*, 24 Nov. 43.

19 | 0 | Michael William Smith, *Ens.* 19 Nov. 30; *Lieut.* P21 Feb. 34; *Capt.* P23 Apr. 39; *Major*, 9 Feb. 47.

Full Pay	Half Pay	CAPTAINS.	CORNET.	LIEUT.	CAPTAIN.	BREV.-MAJ.
23	2	Charles H. T. Hecker....	P29 Aug. 26	P 3 Jan. 28	2 June 39	
20	0	Oswald Sam. Blachford	P 6 Dec. 27	P13 Sept. 31	P 1 Aug. 34	9 Nov. 46
18	0	Richard Knox..........	P28 June 31	20 Apr. 34	9 Mar. 42	
17	0	Francis Woodley Horne	P31 Aug. 32	P 6 Sept. 33	P 19 Aug. 42	
22	2 4/12	Richard Francis Poore ..	P 22 July 24	P 3 Dec. 25	7 July 43	
15	0	John Brett............	P10 Oct. 34	P14 Apr. 37	9 Feb. 45	
12	0	Thomas J. Kearney	27 Jan. 37	8 May 40	3 Sept. 47	
12	0	Henry Keown..........	P 22 Aug. 37	P 20 Mar. 39	P 25 Feb. 48	
10	0	*Lord* Spencer S. Compton	P 1 Nov. 39	P 20 Oct. 43	P 20 Dec. 46	
		LIEUTENANTS.				
21	0	P. D'Ormieux Von Streng[5]	P 11 Nov. 28	17 Apr. 34		
16	0	John Macartney........	P27 Sept. 33	P19 Dec. 34		
14	0	George Horne, *adjutant*	P 19 June 35	P28 Aug. 38		
10	0	Lewis Edward Nolan, R.M.	P15 Mar. 39	P19 June 41		
10	0	Henry Brett	P21 June 39	P11 Feb. 42		
15	0	Tho. R. Crawley, *s.*	19 Dec. 34	9 Mar. 42		
10	0	Charles Bill	P29 Nov. 39	1 April 43		
10	0	Henry Lee,[9] *s.*	P 12 Oct. 39	P 29 July 44		
7	0	Jas. L. Sandys Lumsdaine	P 22 April 42	9 Feb. 45		
7	0	Charles Walpole Hinxman	25 Oct. 42	P30 May 45		
7	0	George Stoney Swinney	P 14 June 42	12 Apr. 46		
7	0	Horace Trower	P 30 Aug. 42	3 Apr. 46		
7	0	John Clancy	P22 Apr. 42	P23 Sept. 45		
6	0	James Boyd Miller......	P 7 July 43	7 Jan. 47		
5	0	Gust. Adolphus Hartman	P10 May 44	9 Feb. 47		
5	0	William Veall Greetham	P31 May 44	P30 July 47		
4	0	Henry John Wale	20 June 45	P 25 Feb. 48		
3	0	Thos. Conolly Pakenham	26 June 46	P 17 Mar. 48		
2	0	James H. D'Arcy Hutton	P 30 July 47	P 15 Dec. 48		
		CORNETS.				
2	0	Frederick Wm. Goldfrap	P 24 Dec. 47			
1	0	James Edwards Vivian ..	P 25 Feb. 48			
1	0	David Henry Howell....	P26 Feb. 48			
1	0	Thompson Donovan	P 17 Mar. 48			
1	0	Charles William Kendall	P 5 May 48			
1	0	Edward Harnett	P 2 June 48			
1	0	John Puget............	P12 Sept. 48			
1	0	William Oliver Bird	P 15 Dec. 48			

2 Colonel Lovell served at the taking of Monte Video under Sir Sam. Auchmuty in 1807, and subsequently in the Peninsula, including the battles of Talavera, the Coa, Busaco, Fuentes d'Onor (wounded), Salamanca, Vittoria, the Pyrenees, Nive, Orthes, and Toulouse; actions or skirmishes near Talavera, Sexmiro, Val de la Mula, La Meares, Freixeda, Guarda, Coimbra, Valle, Venda de Sierra, Pombal, Redinha, Miranda de Corvo, Coa, Galligos, Nave d'Aver, Espiga, near Fuentes d'Onor, Llerena, near Salamanca, St. Christoval, Rueda, Castrillos, Foncastin, Matylla, at Burgos, Osma, Huarte, Pampeluna, Vale de Bastan, Pass of Maya, Lines of Ainho, Cambo, Hasparren, Helite, Garris, Sauveterre, St. Gladie, Buelbo, Garliu, San Roman—total, ten general actions, forty minor actions or skirmishes, besides attending seven sieges; and was at the siege of Oporto, being one of the Military Reporters under Lord Wm. Russell.

5 Lieut. Von Streng served with the 13th Light Infantry in Affghanistan, and was present at both attacks on Ghuznee, and for which he has received the Medal.

7 Dr. Mouat served in the Burmese war.

10 | 0 | *Paymaster.*—James Gustavus Hamilton Holmes, 24 Feb. 37; *Ens.* P11 June, 30; *Lieut.* 2 Aug. 33;

14 | 0 | *Adjutant.*—*Lieut.* George Horne, 1 April, 43.

5 | 0 | *Quarter-Master.*—Walter Clarkson, 1 Sept. 48; *Cornet*, 20 Aug. 44.

37 | 0 | *Surgeon.*—Jas. Mouat,[7] M.D. 15 Feb 27; *Assist.-Surg.* 1 Oct. 12; *Hosp.-Assist.* 16 July, 12.

7 | 0 | *Assistant-Surgeons.*—Joseph Jee, 15 April 42.

7 | 0 | Jas. Richard Moline,[10] 7 Oct. 42.

10 | 0 | *Veterinary Surgeon.*—Thomas Hurford, 25 Jan. 39.

Blue—*Agents*, Messrs. Cox & Co.

1 Sir Robert Wilson served in Flanders and Holland in 1793, 4, and 5; in the rebellion in Ireland in 1798; in Holland in 1799; the Egyptian campaign of 1801; capture of the Cape of Good Hope in 1806; raised and commanded the Lusitanian Legion in 1808 and 9 in Spain and Portugal. Served several campaigns with the Russian army in Russia, Poland, Germany, and France; and with the Austrian army in Italy.

3 Major Bond served in the 17th Lt. Drs. at the taking of Anjar in Cutch in 1816: also throughout the Mahratta campaign of 1817 and 18. He was present with the 11th Lt. Drs. at the siege and capture of Bhurtpore in 1825-6. Accompanied the 3rd Lt. Drs. into Affghanistan with the force under Sir Geo. Pollock, and was present at the forcing of the Khyber Pass, and in every engagement in the advance of the army on Cabool: also commanded the Rear Guard on three different occasions,—engaged the enemy at Tezeen and Jugdulluck, and safely covered and protected the whole of the baggage of the army, notwithstanding the repeated attacks of the enemy.

9 Lt. Lee was present with the 16th Lancers in the action at Maharajpore, 29th Dec. 1843.

10 Assist.-Surg. Moline served with the 22nd during the campaigns of 1844-45, in the southern Mahratta country, and was present in the operations against the Fort Buddurghur.

"TALAVERA"—"FUENTES D'ONOR"—"SALAMANCA"—"VITTORIA"—"NIVE"
"PENINSULA"—"WATERLOO"—"BHURTPORE"—"AFFGHANISTAN"—
"GHUZNEE"—"MAHARAJPORE."—"ALIWAL."—"SOBRAON."

Years' Serv. 68 Full Pay.	Half Pay.	
		Colonel.—Sir John Ormsby Vandeleur,[1] GCB. *Ens.* 29 Dec. 1781; *Lt.* 21 July, 83; *Capt.* 7 Mar. 92; *Major*, 1 Mar. 94; *Lieut.-Col.* 1 Jan. 98; *Col.* 25 Apr. 1808; *Major-Gen.* 4 June, 11; *Lieut.-Gen.* 19 July, 21; *Gen.* 28 June 38; *Col.* 16th Lancers 18 June 30.
25	3 4/12	*Lieut.-Colonel.*—John Rowland Smyth, CB.,[2] *Cornet*, P5 July, 21; *Lieut.* P26 May, 25; *Capt.* P22 April, 26; *Major*, P17 Aug. 41; *Brevet-Lt.-Col.* 19 June, 46; *Lieut.-Col.* P10 Dec. 47.
22	0	*Majors.*—George O'Halloran Gavin,[3] *Cornet*, P13 Nov. 27; *Lt.* P14 Oct. 29; *Capt.* P26 May 37; *Major*, P10 Dec. 47.
17	0	William Henry Archer, *Cornet*, P28 Dec. 32; *Lieut.* P17 July, 35; *Capt.* P1 June, 38; *Major*, P16 May, 45.

Full Pay	Half Pay		CORNET.	LIEUT.	CAPTAIN.	BREV.-MAJ.
		CAPTAINS.				
15	0	Thomas Pattle[5]	P13 June 34	P23 Dec. 36	P 7 May 47	
12	0	Kingsmill Manley Power[6]	P24 Feb. 37	P17 Aug. 38	P24 Nov. 48	
11	0	Ernle Warriner	P 2 Nov. 38	P13 July 41	P 1 May 46	
13	0	Charles John Foster[7]	P 8 Apr. 36	21 Dec. 38	P10 Dec. 47	
5	0	Edward Shelley	P 6 Dec. 44	3 Apr. 46	P 7 Apr. 48	
8	0	James Coster	P 1 May 41	P25 Apr. 45	P 1 Sept. 48	
		LIEUTENANTS.				
10	0	Patrick Dynon,[9] *adjutant*	29 May 39	16 June 42		
3	0	Fred. Loftus Dashwood	31 Mar. 46	P23 Apr. 47		
3	0	Walter Scott Lockhart Scott	1 Apr. 46	P 7 May 47		
3	0	Tho. Rob. Chas. Dimsdale	P19 May 46	P 2 July 47		
5	0	Richard Heaviside	P16 Feb. 44	30 Apr. 47		
7	0	Jas. G. Archer-Burton[10]	P27 May 42	P16 May 45		
2	0	William Thomas Dickson	P23 Apr. 47	P25 Feb. 48		
2	0	Thomas Woolaston White	P 7 May 47	P 7 Apr. 48		
2	0	Francis William Grant	P 2 July 47	P 1 Sept. 48		
		CORNETS.				
2	0	Martin Kisbee, R.M.	8 Oct. 47			
1	0	Lancelot Halton	P25 Feb. 48			
1	0	Robert Goff	P 7 Apr. 48			
1	0	*Hon.* A. A. S. Annesley	P 1 Sept. 48			

5 Capt. Pattle served with the regiment during the campaign in Affghanistan under Lord Keane, and was present at the siege and capture of Ghuznee (Medal). Also the campaign on the Sutlej in 1846 (Medal), including the battles of Buddiwal, Aliwal, (wounded) and Sobraon.

Full Pay	Half Pay	
13	0	*Paymaster.*—George Frederick Rosser,[13] 28 May, 47; *Ens.* 20 Aug. 36.
10	0	*Adjutant.*—*Lieut.* Patrick Dynon,[9] 12 Dec. 39.
2	0	*Quarter-Master.*—George Lamb,[14] 4 June, 47.
24	0	*Surgeon.*—Arthur Wood, MD.[15] 21 Aug. 40; *A.-S.* 19 Nov. 26; *H.-A.* 22 Dec. 25.
3	0	*Assist.-Surgeon.*—Usher Williamson Evans, M.D. 3 Apr. 46.
		Veterinary Surgeon.—

Scarlet—*Facings* Blue.—*Agents*, Messrs. Cox & Co.

[*Returned from Bengal*, Dec. 1846.]

1 Sir John Vandeleur served on the Continent under the Duke of York, in 1794 and 95, including the battles of the 2d and 18th May, and 1st June, besides several minor affairs. Commanded a brigade of Cavalry in India, under Lord Lake, and was present at the battles of Leswarree, Futtyghur, and Afzulghur; and the sieges of Agra and Bhurtpore. Commanded a brigade in the campaigns of 1811, 12, 13, 14, and 15, and was present at the siege of Ciudad Rodrigo (wounded when leading his division to the breach), and battles of Salamanca, Vittoria, Nive, and Waterloo, for which he has received decorations.

2 Lieut. Col. Smyth served with the 16th Lancers at the siege of Bhurtpore, under Lord Combermere. He was also present with the Regt. in the action of Maharajpore, 29 Dec. 43; and in the campaign on the Sutlej in 1846, including the battles of Buddiwal and Aliwal, in the last of which he commanded the Regt. until severely wounded in the thigh by a musket-ball whilst charging the enemy's infantry and guns.

3 Maj. Gavin served with the 16th Lancers during the campaign in Affghanistan under Lord Keane, including the siege and capture of Ghuznee (medal). He was also present at the battle of Maharajpore, 9th Dec. 1843 (medal).

6 Capt. Power served with the 9th Lancers in the battle of Punniar (Medal). Also in the campaign on the Sutlej in 1846, including the battle of Sobraon (Medal).

7 Captain Foster served with the 16th Lancers during the campaign in Affghanistan under Lord Keane, including the siege and capture of Ghuznee (medal). He served also at the battle of Maharajpore, 9th Dec. 1843 (medal); and in the campaign on the Sutlej in 1846 (medal), including the battles of Buddiwal, Aliwal (as Aide-de-Camp to Brigadier Cureton), and Sobraon.

9 Lieut. Dynon served with the 16th Lancers during the campaign in Affghanistan under Lord Keane, including the siege and capture of Ghuznee (medal). He served also at the battle of Maharajpore (medal), 9th Dec. 1843; and in the campaign on the Sutlej in 1846 (medal), including the battles of Buddiwal, Aliwal, and Sobraon.

10. Lieut. Archer-Burton served the campaign on the Sutlej (medal) with the 3rd Lt. Dragoons, and was present at the battles of Moodkee, Ferozeshah, and Sobraon.

13 Paymaster Rosser was present at the siege and capture of Bhurtpore, in 1825-6. He served with the army of the Indus, under Lord Keane, in 1838 and 39, and was present at the capture of Ghuznee (medal). He was also present in the action at Maharajpore, 29th Dec. 1843, (Medal); and also at Buddiwal, Aliwal, and Sobraon.

14 Qr.-Mast. Lamb served with the 16th Lancers during the campaign in Affghanistan under Lord Keane, including the siege and capture of Ghuznee (Medal). Also at the battle of Maharajpore (Medal) 29th Dec. 1843; and in the campaign on the Sutlej (Medal) in 1846, including the battle of Buddiwal, Aliwal, and Sobraon.

15 Doctor Wood served with the 9th Lancers in the Gwalior campaign in 1843 [Medal]; also the campaign on the Sutlej in 1846, and was present at the battle of Sobraon (Medal).

"*Death's Head*," with the Motto, "*Or Glory.*"

Years' Serv.		
12		*Colonel.*
		His Royal Highness, Prince George W. F. C. *of* Cambridge, KG. GCMG. *Colonel*, 3 Nov. 37; *Major-Gen.* 7 May, 45; Colonel of the 17th Lancers, 25 April, 42.
Full Pay.	Half Pay.	*Lieut.-Colonel.*
29	0	Matthew C. D. St. Quintin, *2nd Lieut.* P 29 June, 20; *Lieut.* P 8 Jan. 24; *Capt.* P 9 Nov. 26; *Major*, P 15 April, 37; *Lieut.-Col.* P 31 Dec. 39.
		Major.
15	0	Francis Burdett, *Cornet*, P 18 April, 34; *Lieut.* P 14 April, 37; *Capt.* P 21 May, 41; *Major*, P 27 June, 45.

Full Pay	Half Pay		Cornet.	Lieut.	Captain.	Brevet-Major.
		Captains.				
13	0	John Davy Brett	P 4 Mar. 36	P 1 Mar. 39	P 15 April 42	
13	0	Aug. Saltren Willett	P 9 Dec. 36	P 31 Dec. 39	P 14 June 42	
10	0	Abraham Hamilton	P 1 Nov. 39	P 21 May 41	P 10 Jan. 45	
9	0	Henry Roxby Benson ..	P 31 Jan. 40	P 15 April 42	P 27 June 45	
11	0	J. Elphinstone Fleeming	24 Mar. 38	P 26 Nov. 41	P 23 May 48	
6	0	Edw.C.Arneman Haworth	P 31 Mar. 43	P 10 Jan. 45	P 22 Dec. 48	
		Lieutenants.				
6	0	Richard Douglas Hay Lane	P 10 Nov. 43	P 27 June 45		
5	0	William Ince Anderton..	P 12 July 44	P 28 Nov. 45		
7	0	William Morris[1]........	P 18 June 42	14 May 45		
4	0	John Charles Watts Russell	P 10 Jan. 45	P 7 May 47		
4	0	Wm. H. Kennedy Erskine	P 28 Nov. 45	P 23 May 48		
3	0	Howard St. George, *adj*..	P 19 June 46	15 June 48		
4	0	William Fred. Richards[2]	P 24 Jan. 45	P 31 Dec. 47		
2	0	William Fred. Webb	P 11 June 47	P 13 Oct. 48		
2	0	Robert White	P 15 Oct. 47	P 22 Dec. 48		
		Cornets.				
1	0	John Pratt Winter	P 16 June 48			
1	0	Thomas Taylor, R.M. ..	26 May 48			
1	0	Joseph Haythorne Reed	P 13 Oct. 48			
1	0	Aug.Fred.Cavendish Webb	P 22 Dec. 48			

Full Pay	Half Pay	
5	0	*Paymaster.*—John Stephenson, 30 Apr. 47; *Cor.* 16 Feb. 44; *Lt.* 25 Sept. 45.
3	0	*Adjutant.—Lieut.* Howard St. George, 26 May, 48.
18	0	*Quarter-Master.*—William Hall, 10 May, 31.
23	0	*Surgeon.*—James Brown Gibson, M.D. 2 July 41; *Assist.-Surg.* 12 Jan. 29; *Hosp.-Assist.* 14 Dec. 26.
4	0	*Assist.-Surgeon.*—Henry Kendall, M.D., 16 Dec. 45.
4	0	*Veterinary Surgeon.*—William C. Lord, 26 Jan. 45.

Blue—*Facings* White.

Agents, Messrs. Cox & Co.—*Irish Agents*, *Sir* E. R. Borough, *Bt.*, Armit & Co.

[*Returned from the East Indies, May,* 1823.]

1 Lieut. Morris served with the 16th Lancers at the battle of Maharajpore (medal). Also in the campaign on the Sutlej (medal), and was present at Buddiwal, Aliwal (wounded), and Sobraon.

2 Lieut. Richards served with the 9th Lancers in the campaign on the Sutlej in 1846, and was present at the battle of Sobraon (medal).

1st (or Grenadier) Regiment of Foot Guards.

"LINCELLES"—"CORUNNA"—"BARROSA"—"PENINSULA"—"WATERLOO."

Years' Serv. Full Pay.	Half Pay.	
		Colonel.
62	0	P W Arthur, *Duke of* Wellington,[1] KG. GCB. & GCH. *Ens.* 7 March, 87; *Lieut.* 25 Dec. 87; *Capt.* 30 June, 91; *Major*, 30 April, 93; *Lieut.-Col.* 30 Sept. 93; *Col.* 3 May, 96; *Major-Gen.* 29 April, 1802; *Lieut.-Gen.* 25 April, 08; *Gen.* (in Spain and Portugal) 31 July, 11; *Field Marshal*, 21 June, 13; *Col.* Grenadier Guards, 22 Jan. 27.
		Lieut.-Colonel.
36	0	John Home, *Ens.* P 19 Jan. 13; *Lieut. & Capt.* P 30 June, 15; *Capt. & Lieut.-Col.* P 10 May, 27; *Major & Col.* P 11 Sept. 40.; *Lt.-Col.* 15 April, 45.
		Majors.
37	0	1 P W Charles F. Rowley Lascelles,[2] *Ens.* P 10 Sept. 12; *Lieut. & Capt.* 9 June, 14; *Capt. & Lt.-Col.* P 21 Feb. 28; *Col.* 23 Nov. 41; *Major & Col.* 4 July 43.
38	0	2 *Sir* Ord Honyman,[3] *Bart. Cornet*, 12 Dec. 11; *Lieut. & Capt.* 4 July, 15; *Capt. & Lieut.-Col.* P 28 Sept. 30; *Major & Colonel*, P 2 Oct. 46.
35	0	3 Godfrey Thornton, *Ens.* P 20 Jan. 14; *Lieut. & Capt.* P 11 Oct. 21; *Capt. & Lieut.-Col.* P 3 Dec. 30; *Col.* 9 Nov. 46; *Major*, P 6 Aug. 47.
		Captains and Lieut.-Colonels.
35	0	3 Henry William Barnard, *s. Ens.* 9 June, 14; *Capt.* P 15 Aug. 22; *Capt. & Lieut.-Col.* P 17 May, 31; *Col.* 9 Nov. 46.
34	3/12	2 Philip Spencer Stanhope, *Ens.* 30 March, 15; *Lieut. & Capt.* P 17 July, 23; *Capt. & Lieut.-Col.* P 16 March, 32; *Col.* 9 Nov. 46.
29	2 1/12	1 John Julius Wm. Angerstein, *Ens. & Lieut.* P 9 April, 18; *Lieut. & Capt.* P 2 April, 25; *Capt. & Lieut.-Col.* P 12 Sept. 34; *Col.* 9 Nov. 46.
30	0	3 William Fludyer, *Ens.* 30 Dec. 19; *Ens. & Lieut.* P 25 Oct. 21; *Lieut. & Capt.* P 7 July, 25; *Capt. & Lieut.-Col.* P 2 Dec. 36; *Col.* 9 Nov. 46.
27	10/12	2 Jas. Robertson Craufurd, *Ens.* 14 June, 21; *Ens. & Lieut.* P 29 Aug. 22; *Lieut. & Capt.* P 19 Sept. 26; *Capt. & Lieut.-Col.* P 16 Feb. 37.
26	0	3 Richard Wm. Astell, *Ens. & Lieut.* P 20 Nov. 23; *Lieut. & Capt.* P 13 Sept. 27; *Capt. & Lieut.-Col.* P 7 July, 38.
25	3 4/12	1 Thomas Wood, *Cornet*, P 16 Nov. 20; *Lieut.* P 12 June 23; *Capt.* P 25 June 25; *Brev.-Maj.* 28 June 38; *Capt. & Lieut.-Col.* P 28 June, 39.
25	0	1 Charles Bagot, 2nd *Lieut.* 5 Aug. 24; *Ens. & Lieut.* 24 Feb. 25; *Lieut. & Capt.* P 30 Dec. 28; *Capt. & Lieut.-Col.* P 15 May, 40.
24	14 3/12	2 P Ernest Frederic Gascoigne,[4] *Ens.* 2 May, 11; *Lieut.* 13 May, 13; *Capt.* 6 July, 15; *Major*, P 19 May, 25; *Lieut.-Col.* P 3 June, 28; *Col.* 23 Nov. 41.
24	0	1 John Dixon, *Ens. & Lieut.* P 10 Dec. 25; *Lieut. & Capt.* P 1 Dec. 30; *Capt. & Lieut.-Col.* P 18 May, 41.
23	0	3 William Thornton, *Ens. & Lieut.* P 8 Apr. 26; *Lieut. & Capt.* P 3 Dec. 30; *Capt. & Lieut.-Col.* P 8 June 41.
22	0	2 *Hon.* Francis Grosvenor Hood, *Ens. & Lieut.* P 30 Apr. 27; *Lieut. & Capt.* P 31 Dec. 30; *Capt. & Lieut.-Col.* P 31 Dec. 41.
21	0	1 Charles William Ridley, *Ens. & Lieut.* P 21 Feb. 28; *Lieut. & Capt.* P 14 June, 31; *Capt. & Lieut.-Col.* P 14 July 43.
21	0	3 *Hon.* Augustus Frederick Foley, *Ens. & Lieut.* P 30 Dec. 28; *Lieut. & Capt.* P 16 Mar. 32; *Capt. & Lieut.-Col.* P 16 Feb. 44.
20	0	3 Edward Birch Reynardson, *Ens.* P 5 Nov. 29; *Ens. & Lieut.* P 12 June 30; *Lieut. & Capt.* P 12 Oct. 32; *Capt. & Lieut.-Col.* P 5 April 44.
19	0	1 *Hon.* Robert Bruce, *s. Ens. & Lieut.* P 18 June 30; *Lieut. & Capt.* P 22 Feb. 33; *Capt. & Lieut.-Col.* P 2 Aug. 44.
23	1	2 Charles Algernon Lewis, *Cornet*, P 13 Oct. 25; *Lieut.* P 15 Aug. 26; *Capt.* P 12 Apr. 33; *Capt. & Lieut.-Col.* P 30 Dec. 45.
18	0	3 Frederick William Hamilton, *Ens. & Lieut.* 12 July 31; *Lieut. & Capt.* 1 Dec. 36; *Capt. & Lieut.-Col.* P 3 April, 46.
17	0	2 *Hon.* James Lindsay, *Ens. & Lieut.* P 16 Mar. 32; *Lieut. & Capt.* P 2 Dec. 36; *Capt. & Lieut.-Col.* P 14 Aug. 46.
17	0	1 Henry Cartwright, *Ens. & Lieut.* P 26 July 32; *Lieut. & Capt.* P 2 June 37; *Capt. & Lieut.-Col.* P 2 Oct. 46.
19	0	1 Arthur Augustus Thurlow Cunynghame,[5] *2d Lieut.* P 2 Nov. 30; *Lieut.* 22 May 35; *Capt.* P 17 Aug. 41; *Major*, P 8 Aug. 45; *Lieut.-Col.* P 3 Nov. 46.
17	0	3 Augustus Cox, *Ens. Lieut.* P 27 July 32; *Lieut. & Capt.* P 8 Aug. 37; *Capt. & Lieut.-Col.* P 12 Feb. 47.
16	0	1 *Hon.* George Cadogan, *Ens. & Lieut.* P 22 Feb. 33; *Lieut. & Capt.* P 9 Jan. 38; *Capt. & Lieut.-Col.* P 6 Aug. 47.
16	0	2 Henry George Conroy, *Ens. & Lieut.* P 21 June 33; *Lieut. & Capt.* P 12 Jan. 38; *Capt. & Lt.-Col.* P 3 Mar. 48.
16	0	2 Hugh Andrew Robert Mitchell, *Ens. & Lieut.* P 4 Oct. 33; *Lieut. & Capt.* P 7 July 38; *Capt. & Lieut.-Col.* P 31 March 48.
16	0	1 Edward Goulburn, *Ens. & Lieut.* P 27 Dec. 33; *Lieut. & Capt.* P 14 July 38, *Capt. & Lieut.-Col.* P 18 July 48.

Years' Serv. Full Pay.	Half Pay.	Lieuts. and Captains.	Cor. 2d Lt. or Ensign.	Ensign and Lieut.	Lieut. and Captain.
15	0	1 *Hon.* Alex. Gordon	....	P 2 May 34	P 15 May 40
14	0	1 Henry Torrens D'Aguilar	....	29 May 35	P 12 June 40
14	0	3 Robert Cavendish Spencer Clifford	....	P 5 June 35	P 14 Aug. 40
14	0	3 John Arthur Lambert, *adjutant*	....	P 10 July 35	P 11 Sept. 40
19	0	1 Hervey Hopwood	21 Sept. 30	P 24 July 35	P 30 Oct. 40
14	0	3 John Augustus Udny, *Major*, 23 Nov. 41.	....	P 13 Nov. 35	P 15 Dec. 40
13	0	1 *Hon.* Henry Hugh Manvers Percy, *adj.*	....	P 1 July 36	P 29 Dec. 40
12	0	2 John Temple West	....	P 18 Feb. 37	P 16 April 41
12	0	1 *Hon.* Henry Townshend Forester	....	23 Feb. 37	P 18 May 41
12	0	2 George Grey Rous	....	P 24 Feb. 37	P 8 June 41
17	0	2 Studholme Brownrigg	P 20 July 32	9 May 35	P 29 Dec. 40
12	0	1 Edward G. Wynyard	12 May 37	P 9 Jan. 38	P 25 Oct. 42
11	0	2 Edward William Pakenham	....	P 12 Jan. 38	P 14 July 43
11	0	3 Harry Brereton Trelawny	....	P 13 July 38	P 16 Feb. 44
11	0	1 *Hon.* Richard W. Penn Curzon	....	P 14 July 38	P 5 April 44
9	0	1 John Reeve	....	P 1 May 40	P 14 Feb. 45
9	0	3 *Hon.* Mortimer West	....	P 12 June 40	P 16 May 45
9	0	2 Ralph Bradford, *adjutant*	....	P 30 Oct. 40	P 19 Dec. 45
9	0	1 Michael Bruce	....	P 15 Dec. 40	P 30 Dec. 45
14	0	2 *Hon.* Charles Hugh Lindsay, *s.*	P 5 June 35	P 3 July 40	9 May 45
8	0	1 C. L. Brownlow Maitland, *s. Maj.* 15 Sept. 48	....	P 9 April 41	P 27 Mar. 46
8	0	1 *Lord* Arthur Hay[7]	....	P 30 April 41	P 3 Apr. 46
9	0	2 Henry Edward Montresor	15 Dec. 40	P 18 May 41	P 18 May 46
8	0	3 His Serene Highness, *Prince* William Augustus Edward of Saxe Weimar	1 June 41	P 8 June 41	P 19 May 46
11	0	3 Charles Kemeys Kemeys Tynte	P 10 Nov. 38	P 16 Apr. 42	P 26 Sept. 45
8	0	3 *Sir* Coutts Lindsay, *Bart.*	....	P 31 Dec. 41	P 14 Aug. 46
7	0	3 *Hon.* Henry Aldworth Neville	....	P 2 Sept. 42	P 2 Oct. 46
7	0	2 Campbell Munro	....	P 3 Sept. 42	P 20 Oct. 46
8	0	3 Wm. Drogo, *Viscount* Mandeville	3 Dec. 41	P 21 Jan. 42	P 1 Dec. 46
7	0	2 Jas. Fred. Dudley Crichton Stuart	....	P 25 Oct. 42	P 12 Feb. 47
10	0	1 *Hon.* Charles Reginald Pakenham	14 June 39	P 12 Oct. 41	P 20 Oct. 46
10	0	1 Richard Lloyd	P 26 July 39	15 April 42	P 30 July 47
7	0	2 *Hon.* Egremont William Lascelles	....	P 23 Nov. 42	P 6 Aug. 47
7	0	3 *Hon.* George Stephens Gough	16 Aug. 42	P 24 Mar. 43	P 3 Mar. 48
9	0	2 *Lord* Frederick John FitzRoy	P 18 Sept. 40	P 14 July 43	P 31 Mar. 48
9	0	2 Villiers La Touche Hatton	17 July 40	P 10 Feb. 43	P 22 June 47
7	0	1 Henry Frederick Ponsonby, *s.*	27 Dec. 42	P 16 Feb. 44	P 18 July 48
		Ensigns and Lieuts.			
6	0	2 Cuthbert George Ellison	23 Nov. 43	P 5 April 44	
5	0	2 John Francis Cust	26 July 44	P 2 Aug. 44	
5	0	2 Beaumont William Hotham	....	P 20 Aug. 44	
5	0	2 William Henry Beaumont de Horsey	....	P 22 Nov. 44	
4	0	2 George Wentworth Alex. Higginson	....	P 14 Feb. 45	
4	0	3 Augustus Henry Lane Fox	....	P 16 May 45	
5	0	1 William Edward Hope Vere	P 23 Feb. 44	P 23 May 45	
4	0	1 Albert Evelyn Rowley	6 July 45	P 7 July 45	
4	0	2 Herbert Lowther Wilson	....	26 Sept. 45	
5	0	2 Frederick Augustus Thesiger	P 31 Dec. 44	P 28 Nov. 45	
4	0	2 *Hon.* Arthur Frederick Egerton, *s.*	....	P 30 Dec. 45	
4	0	2 James Carnegie	4 July 45	P 23 Jan. 46	
3	0	1 James Evelyn	....	P 27 Mar. 46	
3	0	3 Sidney Burrard	....	P 3 April 46	
3	0	1 *Hon.* Edw. M. G. Stuart Wortley	....	P 18 May 46	
3	0	3 William Samuel Morant	....	P 19 May 46	
3	0	3 Charles Vannotten Pole	....	P 14 Aug. 46	
3	0	3 Alexander Kinloch	....	P 27 Oct. 46	
3	0	3 Edward Sherard Burnaby	....	P 3 Nov. 46	
3	0	1 John Davie Ferguson Davie	....	P 1 Dec. 46	
5	0	1 William Gordon Cameron	24 May 44	P 12 Feb. 47	
6	0	3 Charles Russell	P 25 Aug. 43	P 9 June 46	
3	0	3 Cameron Neville Hogge	1 Dec. 46	P 6 Aug. 47	
2	0	1 William Thomas Francis Wallace	20 July 47	P 3 Mar. 48	
1	0	1 Frederick Charles Keppel	....	P 31 Mar. 48	
1	0	1 William John Christie	....	P 1 April 48	
1	0	1 Charles Pierrepoint Lane Fox	....	P 18 July 48	
1	0	Arch. Henry Plantag. Stuart Wortley	....	18 Aug. 48	

Years' Serv. Full Pay.	Years' Serv. Half Pay.	
		Adjutants.
14	0	3 *Capt.* John Arthur Lambert, 24 March, 48.
9	0	2 *Capt.* Ralph Bradford, 14 Aug. 46.
13	0	1 *Capt. Hon.* Henry Hugh Manvers Percy, 11 June, 47.
		Quarter-Masters.
34	0	2 P W John Payne,[8] 31 Aug. 15.
20	0	1 Richard France, 24 Dec. 29.
19	0	3 John Lilley, 8 June, 30.
		Surgeon-Major.
25	0	James Dennis Wright, 7 Feb. 45; *Surg.* 11 May, 32; *Assist.-Surg.* 11 Nov. 24.
		Battalion-Surgeon.
24	0	2 Geo. Brown, 26 June, 40; *Asst.-Surg.* 12 Jan. 26; *Hosp.-Assist.* 21 April, 25
25	4/12	1 Francis Cornelius Huthwaite, 7 Feb. 45; *Assist.-Surgeon,* 10 Nov. 25; *Hosp.-Assist.* 16 Nov. 23.
		Assistant-Surgeons.
11	0	2 George Eleazar Blenkins, 13 April, 38.
9	0	1 Charles Nicoll, 26 June, 40.
8	0	3 James John Marjoribanks Wardrop, 21 May 41.

***Solicitor.*—John Parkinson, 19 July, 31.**

1st Battalion returned from Portugal, 1828.
2d Battalion returned from Canada, Oct. 1842.
3d Battalion returned from France, Nov. 1818.
Facings Blue.—*Agents,* Messrs. Cox & Co.

War Office, 29th July, 1815.

The Prince Regent, as a mark of His Royal Approbation of the distinguished gallantry of the Brigade of Foot Guards in the Victory of Waterloo, has been pleased, in the name and on the behalf of His Majesty, to approve of all the Ensigns of the Three Regiments of Foot Guards having the Rank of Lieutenants, and that such Rank shall be attached to all the future Appointments to Ensigncies in the Foot Guards, in the same manner as the Lieutenants in those Regiments obtain the Rank of Captain.

His Royal Highness has also been pleased to approve of the First Regiment of Foot Guards being made a Regiment of Grenadiers, and styled "*The First, or Grenadier Regiment of Foot Guards,*" in commemoration of their having defeated the Grenadiers of the French Imperial Guards upon this memorable occasion.

---

1 The Duke of Wellington has received a cross and nine clasps for Roleia and Vimiera, Talavera, Busaco, Fuentes d'Onor, Ciudad Rodrigo, Badajos, Salamanca, Vittoria, Pyrenees, Nivelle, Nive, Orthes, and Toulouse. To sketch an outline of the pre-eminent services of the greatest soldier of the age, would far exceed the limits of this work.

2 Colonel Lascelles served in the Peninsula in 1814. Also the campaign of 1815, including the battles of Quatre Bras and Waterloo, and taking of Peronne.

3 Sir Ord Honyman served the campaign of 1814 in Holland, and was present at the bombardment of Antwerp, and storming of Bergen-op-Zoom, where he commanded the leading sub-division of the storming party of the Grenadier Guards.

4 Colonel Gascoigne served in the Peninsula from July 1813 to May 1814, including the passage of the Bidassoa, battles of the Nivelle and Nive, and the investment of Bayonne. Served afterwards in the American war, and was present at the battle of Bladensburg and capture of Washington, where he was severely wounded.

5 Lt.-Colonel Cunynghame served as Aide-de-Camp to Lord Saltoun during the latter part of the war in China (medal), and was present at the siege and capture of the city of Chin Kiang Foo, and at the investment of Nankin.

7 Lord Arthur Hay served as Aide-de-Camp to Lord Hardinge at the battle of Sobraon (medal).

8 Quartermaster Payne served in Sicily in 1806 and 7; in 1808 and 9 in Spain, and present in the actions of Sahagun, Benevente, Lugo, and Corunna; subsequently at Walcheren. He served also the campaigns of 1812, 13, 14, and 15, in the Peninsula, France, and Flanders, and was present in the actions of the Pyrenees, siege and capture of San Sebastian, passage of the Bidassoa and of the Nive, action at the Mayor's House, sortie and investment of Bayonne, battles of Quatre Bras and Waterloo, capture of Peronne and of Paris and subsequently with the army of occupation.

"LINCELLES."—The *Sphinx*, with the words "EGYPT"—"TALAVERA"—"BARROSA"—"PENINSULA"—"WATERLOO."

Years' Serv.		
51		***Colonel.***
Full Pay.	Half Pay.	*His Royal Highness* A. F. *Duke of Cambridge*, KG. GCB. GCMG GCH. *Lieut.-Gen.* 24 Aug. 1798; *Gen.* 25 Sept. 03; *Field-Marshal*, 26 Nov. 13; *Colonel*, Coldstream Guards, 5 Sept. 05.
		Lieut.-Colonel.
38	0	1 Thos. Chaplin,[1] *Ens.* P 18 April, 11; *Lieut. & Capt.* 6 Oct. 14; *Lieut.-Col.* P 15 Aug. 26; *Col.* 23 Nov. 41; *Major*, P 8 May, 46; *Lieut.-Col.* P 25 April 48.
		Majors.
36	0	2 Henry John Wm. Bentinck, *Ens.* 25 Mar. 13; *Lieut. & Capt.* 18 Jan. 20; *Capt. & Lieut.-Col.* P 16 May, 29; *Col.* 23 Nov. 41; *Major*, 9 Nov. 46.
29	0	1 Chas. Murray Hay, *Ens.* P 20 April, 20; *Ens. & Lieut.* P 1 Nov. 21; *Lieut. & Capt.* P 24 Dec. 25; *Capt. & Lieut.-Col.* P 22 June, 32; *Col.* 9 Nov. 46; *Major*, P 25 April 48.
		Captains & Lieut.-Colonels.
27	1	2 Wm. John Codrington, *Ens.* P 22 Feb. 21; *Ens. & Lieut.* P 24 April, 23; *Lt. & Capt.* P 20 July, 26; *Capt. & Lt.-Col.* P 8 July, 36; *Col.* 9 Nov. 46.
24	0	1 *Hon.* Arthur Upton *Ens. & Lieut.* P 10 Feb. 25; *Lieut. & Capt.* P 16 May, 29 *Capt. & Lieut.-Col.* P 31 Dec. 39.
26	0	1 Frederick Paget, *Ensign*, 20 Mar. 23; *Ens. & Lieut.* 24 Feb. 25; *Lieut. & Capt.* P 4 June 29; *Capt. & Lieut.-Col.* P 24 Jan. 40.
26	$\frac{3}{12}$	2 *Hon.* George Frederick Upton, *Ens.* P 24 April, 23; *Lieut.* P 29 Oct. 25; *Capt.* P 12 Dec. 26; *Major*, P 16 June, 37; *Lieut.-Col.* P 16 April, 41.
24	0	1 John Christie Clitherow, *2nd Lieut.* 11 April, 25; *Ens. & Lieut.* P 8 April, 26; *Lieut. & Capt.* 22 July 30; *Capt. & Lieut.-Col.* P 30 May, 43.
23	0	2 Gordon Drummond, *Ens. & Lieut.* P 10 June 26; *Lieut. & Capt.* P 3 Aug. 30; *Capt. & Lieut.-Col.* P 29 March 44.
23	0	1 *Lord* Frederick Paulet, *Ens. & Lieut.* 11 June 26; *Lieut. & Capt.* P 21 Sept. 30; *Capt. & Lieut.-Col.* P 8 May, 46.
24	0	1 John Forbes, *Ensign*, P 20 Oct. 25; *Ens. & Lieut.* P 1 Aug. 26; *Lieut. & Capt.* P 10 Feb. 32; *Capt. & Lieut.-Col.* P 7 Aug. 46.
23	0	2 Charles Ash Windham, *Ens. & Lieut.* P 30 Dec. 26; *Lieut. & Capt.* P 31 May, 33; *Brevet-Major*, 9 Nov. 46; *Capt. & Lieut.-Col.* P 29 Dec. 46.
20	0	2 Henry Daniell, *Ens. & Lieut.* P 13 Aug. 29; *Lieut. & Capt.* P 27 Mar. 35; *Brevet-Major*, 9 Nov. 46; *Capt. & Lieut.-Col.* P 29 Oct. 47.
22	$\frac{5}{12}$	2 *Hon.* Robert Edward Boyle, *Ens.* P 14 Nov. 26; *Lieut.* P 16 July 29; *Capt.* P 23 Aug. 33; *Brevet-Major*, 9 Nov. 46; *Capt. & Lieut.-Col.* 10 Dec. 47.
15	0	2 William Samuel Newton, *Ens. & Lieut.* P 5 Dec. 34; *Lieut. & Capt.* P 31 Dec. 39; *Capt. & Lieut.-Col.* P 25 Feb. 48.
14	0	2 Egerton Charles Wm. Miles Milman, *Ens. & Lieut.* P 24 April 35; *Lieut. & Capt.* P 5 Feb. 41; *Capt. & Lieut.-Col.* P 7 April 48.
20	0	1 George Augustus Vernon, *Ens.* 2 July 29; *Lieut.* P 12 April 31; *Capt.* P 28 Dec. 38; *Capt. & Lieut.-Col.* P 25 April 48.
25	$6\frac{7}{12}$	1 Walter Trevelyan, *2nd Lieut. R. Engineers*, 18 Nov. 17; *Lieut.* 25 Sept. 25; *Capt.* P 19 Sept. 26; *Major*, P 28 Dec. 32; *Lieut.-Col.* 10 Aug. 41.
12	0	2 Spencer Perceval, *Ens. & Lieut.* P 13 Jan. 37; *Lieut. & Capt.* P 15 Oct. 41; *Capt. & Lt.-Col.* P 23 June 48.

1 Colonel Chaplin was severely wounded at St. Sebastian.

Years' Serv. Full Pay.	Years' Serv. Half Pay.	Lieutenants and Captains.	Cornet, 2d Lieut. or Ensign.	Ensign and Lieut.	Lieut. and Captain.
12	0	1 Matthew Edward Tierney	....	P 10 Mar. 37	P 27 Jan. 43
12	0	1 *Hon.* Thomas Vesey Dawson	....	P 11 Aug. 37	P 30 May 43
15	0	1 Henry Wedderburn Cumming	P 22 Aug. 34	P 16 Mar. 38	P 30 Dec. 42
11	0	1 Thomas Montagu Steele	12 Jan. 38	P 20 July 38	P 29 Mar. 44
13	0	1 William Mark Wood	P 22 July 36	24 May 41	P 20 Aug. 44
15	0	2 William Eccles	P 28 Feb. 34	P 28 Oct. 36	P 8 April 42
10	0	2 Charles H. White	11 Jan. 39	P 31 Dec. 39	P 8 May 46
10	0	1 William Baring	P 15 Feb. 39	P 21 May 41	P 9 June 46
11	0	2 Charles Lygon Cocks	P 28 July 38	P 24 Jan. 40	P 7 Aug. 46
10	0	2 Poulett G. H. Somerset, *adjutant*	P 29 Mar. 39	P 1 May 40	28 Dec. 46
9	0	1 James Charles Murray Cowell	....	25 Sept. 40	P 11 June 47
10	0	1 James Halkett, *adjutant*	P 7 June 39	P 23 April 41	1 July 47
9	0	2 Dudley Wilmot Carleton	P 10 April 40	P 11 June 41	P 13 July 47
10	0	2 *Lord* Aug. Charles Lennox FitzRoy	17 May 39	P 27 Aug. 41	P 30 July 47
13	0	2 Charles Sedley Burdett	P 21 Oct. 36	25 June 41	P 29 Oct. 47
9	0	1 Francis William Newdigate	30 Dec. 40	P 13 May 42	P 10 Dec. 47
6	0	2 Lionel Daniel Mac Kinnon	....	P 30 May 43	P 25 Feb. 48
7	0	2 *Sir* Geo. Ferd. Radziwill Walker, *Bt.*	P 27 Dec. 42	P 29 Mar. 44	P 7 April 48
6	0	2 George Warrender	P 29 Dec. 43	P 2 May 45	P 31 Dec. 47
5	0	1 William Gregory Dawkins	P 2 Aug. 44	P 6 Sept. 44	P 25 April 48
4	0	1 Hylton Jolliffe	....	P 8 Aug. 45	P 23 June 48
6	0	1 George Thomas Duncombe	P 4 Aug. 43	P 7 June 44	P 24 Sept. 47
10	0	2 Clement William Strong	18 Jan. 39	6 May 42	P 1 Sept. 48
		Ensigns and Lieuts.			
3	0	2 Ullick Canning *Lord* Dunkellin, *s.*	....	P 27 Mar. 46	
3	0	2 Francis Augustus Plunkett Burton	....	P 8 May 46	
4	0	1 *Hon.* Percy Robert Basil Feilding	P 8 Aug. 45	P 7 Aug. 46	
5	0	2 Edward Heneage Dering	P 24 May 44	P 18 Sept. 46	
3	0	2 William Henry Reeve	....	P 29 Dec. 46	
2	0	1 *Hon.* Granville Chas. Cornwallis Eliot	....	P 11 June 47	
2	0	1 Charles Baring	....	P 2 July 47	
2	0	2 Henry Montolieu Bouverie	2 Apr. 47	P 13 July 47	
2	0	1 Henry Armytage	....	P 30 July 47	
2	0	2 *Hon.* Henry William John Byng	....	27 Aug. 47	
2	0	1 Charles Rodney Morgan	....	P 29 Oct. 47	
2	0	2 Arthur John Bethell Thellusson	....	P 10 Dec. 47	
3	0	1 Thomas Francis Rolt	27 Oct. 46	P 28 Jan. 48	
1	0	1 Robert Desmond Sulivan	....	P 25 Feb. 48	
1	0	2 Horrace William Cust	....	P 7 April 48	
1	0	1 David Robertson Williamson	....	P 25 April 48	
2	0	2 Philip Sambrook Crawley	P 2 Mar. 47	P 23 June 48	

Full Pay	Half Pay	
		Adjutants.
10	0	2 *Captain* Poulett George Henry Somerset, 8 May, 46.
10	0	1 *Captain* James Halkett, 11 June 47.
		Quarter-Masters.
13	0	1 William Morse, 2 June, 36.
12	0	2 Thomas Lee, 25 July, 37.
		Surgeon-Major.
24	0	Edward Greatrex, 2 Sept. 45; *Surg.* 14 April, 43; *Assist.-Surg.* 16 Nov. 26; *Hosp.-Assist.* 24 Nov. 25.
		Battalion-Surgeon.
11	0	2 Wm. Thomas Christopher Robinson, 2 Sept. 45; *Assist.-Surg.* 23 Mar. 38.
		Assistant-Surgeons.
17	0	1 James Munro, M.D. 2 Nov. 32.
4	0	2 Joseph Skelton, 2 Sept. 45.

Solicitor.—William George Carter, 29 Jan. 24.

Facings Blue—*Agents*, Messrs. Cox & Co.

[*1st Battalion returned from France, July*, 1814.]

[*2d Battalion returned from Canada 29th Oct.* 1842.]

"LINCELLES"—The "*Sphynx*," with the words, "EGYPT"—"TALAVERA"—"BARROSA" "PENINSULA"—"WATERLOO."

Years' Serv. Full Pay.	Years' Serv. Half Pay.	
		Colonel.
		His Royal Highness **Francis Albert Augustus Charles Emanuel,** ***Duke of*** **Saxony,** ***Prince of*** **Saxe-Coburg and Gotha, KG. KT. KP. GCB. GCMG.** ***Field Marshal,*** **8 Feb. 40;** ***Colonel*** **of the Scots Fusilier Guards, 25 April, 42.**
		Lieut.-Colonel.
37	0	Berkeley Drummond,[1] *Ens.* 5 March, 12; *Lieut. & Capt.* 4 July, 15 *Capt. & Lt.-Col.* P 21 Dec. 26; *Major & Col.* 23 Nov. 41; *Lt.-Col.* P 31 Dec. 44.
		Majors.
35	$\frac{2}{12}$	1 William Thomas Knollys,[2] *Ens.* 9 Dec. 13; *Lieut. & Capt.* 25 Sept. 17; *Capt. & Lt.-Col.* P 31 Dec. 27; *Col.* 23 Nov. 41; *Major & Col.* P 6 Dec. 44.
35	$\frac{2}{12}$	2 Henry Colvile, *Ens.* P 29 Dec. 13; *Lt. & Capt.* P 6 Nov. 17; *Capt. & Lieut.-Col.* P 6 July, 30; *Major & Col.* P 31 Dec. 44.
		Captains and Lieut.-Colonels.
35	0	1 Henry, *Lord* Rokeby,[3] *Ens.* 21 April 14; *Lieut. & Capt.* P 12 June, 23; *Capt. & Lieut.-Col.* P 21 Sept. 32; *Col.* 9 Nov. 46.
29	0	2 George Dixon, *Ens. & Lieut.* P 20 Jan. 20; *Capt.* P 8 April, 26; *Capt. & Lieut.-Col.* P 20 May, 36; *Col.* 9 Nov. 46.
27	$5\frac{2}{12}$	2 John George Robinson, *Ens. & Lieut.* 23 Jan. 17; *Lieut. & Capt.* P 5 June, 27; *Capt. & Lieut.-Col.* P 12 Aug. 37.
24	0	2 Patrick FitzRoy Wellesley Campbell, *2nd Lieut.* 13 Jan. 25; *Ens. & Lieut.* P 14 July, 25; *Lieut. & Capt.* P 3 July, 29; *Capt. & Lieut.-Col.* P 9 Nov. 38.
27	$\frac{4}{12}$	1 George Morton Eden, *Ens.* P 18 July, 22; *Lieut.* P 10 Sept. 25; *Capt.* P 12 Dec. 26; *Major,* P 11 Oct. 31; *Lieut.-Col.* P 20 May, 36; *Col.* 9 Nov. 46.
23	0	1 George Moncrieffe, *Ens. & Lieut.* P 8 April, 26; *Lieut. & Capt.* P 6 July, 30; *Capt. & Lieut.-Col.* P 24 Jan. 40.
23	0	2 Nathaniel Waldegrave John Branthwayt Micklethwait, *Ens. & Lieut.* P 12 Oct. 26; *Lieut. & Capt.* P 31 Dec. 30; *Capt. & Lieut.-Col.* P 18 May, 41.
23	0	2 William Frederick Elrington, *Ens. & Lieut.* P 14 Nov. 26; *Lieut. & Capt.* P 30 Aug. 31; *Capt. & Lieut.-Col.* P 14 April, 43.
22	0	2 Edward Walter Forestier Walker, *Ens. & Lieut.* P 8 Mar. 27; *Lieut. & Capt.* P 18 Oct. 31; *Capt. & Lieut.-Col.* P 6 Dec. 44.
22	0	1 Charles John James Hamilton, *Ens. & Lieut.* P 5 June, 27; *Lieut. & Capt.* P 6 Jan. 32; *Capt. & Lieut-Col.* P 31 Dec. 44.
21	0	1 *Hon.* George Augustus Fred. Liddell, *Ens. & Lieut.* P 27 Nov. 28; *Lieut. & Capt.* P 24 April 35; *Capt. & Lieut.-Col.* P 8 Sept. 46.
18	0	1 *Hon.* Alexander Nelson Hood, *Ens. & Lieut.* P 30 Aug. 31; *Lieut. & Capt.* P 1 July 36; *Brevet-Major,* 9 Nov. 46; *Capt. & Lieut.-Col.* P 5 Nov. 47.
16	0	2 Arthur Edw. Onslow, *Ens. & Lieut.* P 11 Jan. 33; *Lieut. & Capt.* P 10 Nov. 37; *Capt. & Lieut.-Col.* P 10 Dec. 47.
14	0	2 James Hunter Blair, *Ens. and Lieut.* P 24 April 35; *Lieut. and Capt.* P 9 Nov. 38; *Capt. & Lieut.-Col.* P 31 March, 48.
14	0	2 Charles Francis Seymour,[4] *Ens. & Lieut.* P 5 June, 35; *Lieut. & Capt.* P 23 Nov. 38; *Capt. & Lieut.-Col.* P 1 Aug. 48.
14	0	1 William John Ridley, *Ens. & Lieut.* P 19 June 35; *Lieut. & Capt.* P 24 May 39; *Capt. & Lieut.-Col.* P 24 Nov. 48.

1 Colonel Berkeley Drummond's services:—Campaign of 1814 in Holland, including the storming of Bergen-op-Zoom. Campaign of 1815, including the battles of Quatre Bras and Waterloo.

2 Colonel Knollys served in the South of France, from 6th March, 1814, to the end of the war; was present at the blockade of Bayonne and repulse of the Sortie, on which occasion Sir Henry Sullivan and ten officers of the Guards were killed or died of their wounds.

3 Lord Rokeby served the campaign of 1815, including the battles of Quatre Bras and Waterloo.

4 Lieut.-Colonel Seymour served as senior Aide-de-camp to Lieut.-Gen. Sir George Berkeley throughout the operations in Kaffraria in 1846-7.

Years' Serv. Full Pay.	Years' Serv. Half Pay.	LIEUTENANTS AND CAPTAINS.	CORNET, 2D LIEUT. OR ENSIGN.	ENSIGN AND LIEUT.	LIEUT. AND CAPTAIN.
19	0	2 Robert Moorsom	3 Aug. 30	P 21 Sept. 32	P 12 Aug. 37
13	0	2 *Hon.* Charles Grantham Scott	....	P 12 Feb. 36	P 1 Nov. 39
15	0	2 Charles Tyrwhitt	P 1 Aug. 34	P 26 Feb. 36	P 15 Nov. 39
13	0	2 Edward John Stracey	....	P 3 June 36	P 14 Feb. 40
15	0	1 Francis Seymour	P 2 May 34	P 16 June 37	P 4 Sept. 40
12	0	2 *Lord* Jas. C. Plantagenet Murray..	....	P 26 May 37	P 1 July 42
12	0	1 Fred. Charles Arthur Stephenson, *adj.*	....	25 July 37	P 13 Jan. 43
13	0	1 C. A. Fitz-H. Berkeley, *s.* (*Maj.* 15 Sep. 48)	P 27 May 36	P 12 Aug. 37	P 14 April 43
12	0	1 Thomas Harcourt Powell	....	P 22 Aug. 37	P 6 Dec. 44
12	0	1 John Hamilton Elphinstone Dalrymple	....	P 10 Nov. 37	P 31 Dec. 44
10	0	2 Henry Percival de Bathe	....	P 1 Nov. 39	P 14 Feb. 45
10	0	2 *Sir* Archibald Keppel Macdonald, *Bt.*	P 12 July 39	P 15 Nov. 39	P 28 Nov. 45
9	0	1 Wm. Yates Peel	....	P 14 Feb. 40	P 7 July 46
9	0	1 George William Mercer	....	P 27 Mar. 40	P 8 Sept. 46
8	0	1 Henry Poole Hepburn............	....	P 19 Feb. 41	P 2 Oct. 46
11	0	1 *Hon.* Hew Hamilton Haldane Duncan	P 6 July 38	P 18 May 41	P 22 Jan. 47
9	0	2 Francis Haygarth, *adj.*	P 14 Feb. 40	P 21 May 41	30 Sept. 47
9	0	2 *Hon.* Richard Charteris	P 2 Oct. 40	P 7 Oct. 42	P 14 May 47
6	0	2 Henry Green Wilkinson	....	P 13 Jan. 43	P 10 Dec. 47
6	0	1 *Hon.* Edw. Keppel Wentworth Coke	....	P 7 April 43	P 4 Feb. 48
7	0	1 *Hon.* John Strange Jocelyn	P 7 Oct. 42	P 14 April 43	P 31 Mar. 48
8	0	2 Wm. Fred. *Viscount* Chewton[1]	18 July 41	P 25 Aug. 43	P 13 Aug. 47
5	0	2 Charles Thomas Wemyss	....	11 April 44	P 24 Nov. 48
12	0	Patrick L. C. Paget, *s*............	11 Aug. 37	P 6 Aug. 41	P 12 Dec. 43
		ENSIGNS AND LIEUTENANTS.			
5	0	1 *Lord* Brownlow Thos. Montague Cecil	....	P 12 April 44	
5	0	2 John Floyd Peel	....	P 6 Dec. 44	
7	0	2 William Biddulph Parker	20 May 42	P 20 Aug. 44	
6	0	1 *Lord* Adolphus F. C. W. Vane, *s.* ..	P 7 April 43	P 28 Nov. 45	
4	0	1 *Lord* Robert Conolly Taylor	....	P 19 Dec. 45	
3	0	1 *Hon.* William Frederick Scarlett ..	P 14 April 46	P 12 June 46	
5	0	2 Francis Fortescue	P 7 June 44	P 7 July 46	
3	0	2 Augustus William Henry Meyrick	....	P 8 Sept. 46	
4	0	2 William Aitchison................	P 21 Mar. 45	P 2 Oct. 46	
3	0	1 Robert Nigel Fitzhardinge Kingscote	....	P 27 Oct. 46	
2	0	1 George Thomas Francis Shuckburgh	....	P 5 Nov. 47	
2	0	1 Hugh FitzHardinge Drummond....	13 Aug. 47	P 10 Dec. 47	
1	0	2 *Hon.* Augustus Henry Vernon	....	P 4 Feb. 48	
1	0	2 John Dugdale Astley	....	P 31 Mar. 48	
3	0	2 *Hon.* Wenman Clarence Walpole Coke	P 31 July 46	P 7 April 48	
1	0	1 William Gascoyne Bulwer	P 14 April 48	P 1 Aug. 48	
3	0	1 William George Stevenson	P 31 July 46	P 31 Mar. 48	
1	0	2 Duncombe Fred. Batt Buckley	....	P 24 Nov. 48	
		Adjutants.			
12	0	1 *Captain* Fred. Charles Arthur Stephenson, 14 Feb. 45.			
9	0	2 *Captain* Francis Haygarth, 11 Sept. 46.			
		Quarter-Masters.			
16	0	2 [illegible] Joseph Aston,[2] 9 Aug. 33.			
12	0	1 [illegible] George Copeland,[3] 7 April, 37.			
		Surgeon-Major.			
31	1/12	Wm. Henry Judd, 22 July, 45; *Surg.* 12 July, 27; *Assist.-Surg.* 1 Jan. 18.			
		Battalion-Surgeon.			
26	0	2 Thomas Richardson, 22 July, 45; *Assist.-Surg.* 4 Dec. 23.			
		Assistant-Surgeons.			
22	0	1 John Bowling, 12 July, 27.			
7	0	2 John Ashton Bostock,[4] M.D. 8 Feb. 42.			
		Solicitor.—Wilmer Wilmer, 27 Dec. 33.			

Facings Blue.—*Agents, Sir* John Kirkland & Co.

[*1st Battalion embarked for the Peninsula Dec.* 1808, *and returned from France July*, 1814.]

[*2d Battalion embarked for the Netherlands Nov.* 1813, *and returned from France Jan.* 1816. *Served in Portugal from Dec.* 1826 *to March*, 1828.

1 Lord Chewton served with the Militia in the suppression of the insurrection in Canada; and with the 53rd in the campaign on the Sutlej in 1846, including the battle of Sobraon (medal).

2 Quarter-Master Aston served the campaign of 1814 in Holland, including the bombardment of Antwerp, and storming of Bergen-op-Zoom. Present at Quatre Bras and Waterloo.

3 Quarter-Master Copeland served in the Peninsula, from March, 1813, to the end of the war, including the battle of Vittoria, siege of San Sebastian, passage of the Bidassoa, the Nive, and the Adour, investment of Bayonne, and repulse of the sortie. Present at Quatre Bras and Waterloo.

4 Doctor Bostock served in the Buffs at the battle of Punniar, and has received the Bronze Star.

The King's Cypher within the Collar of *St. Andrew*, and the *Crown* over it. In the second colour the *Thistle & Crown*.—"St Lucia."—"Egmont-op-Zee."—*The Sphinx*, "Egypt"—"Corunna"—"Busaco"—"Salamanca"—"Vittoria"—"St. Sebastian"—"Nive"—"Peninsula"—"Niagara"—"Waterloo"—"Nagpore"—"Maheidpoor"—"Ava."

Years' Serv. 66 (Full Pay | Half Pay)

Colonel.

Rt. Hon. Sir James Kempt,[1] GCB. GCH., *Ens.* 31 Mar. 1783; *Lieut.* 18 Aug. 84; *Capt.* 30 May, 94; *Major*, 18 Sept. 94; *Lieut.-Col.* 28 Aug. 99; *Col.* 9 March, 09; *Major-Gen.* 1 Jan. 12; *Lieut.-Gen.* 27 May, 25; *Gen.* 23 Nov. 41; *Col.* of the Royals, 7 Aug. 46.

Lieut.-Colonels.

29 | 0 | 1 Andrew Brown, *Ens.* 26 Oct. 20; *Lieut.* 17 March, 25; *Capt.* P 5 April, 31; *Major*, P 26 May, 38; *Lieut.-Col.* P 8 June, 41.

30 | 8 7/12 | 2 George Bell,[2] *Ens.* 14 Mar. 11; *Lieut.* 17 Feb. 14; *Capt.* P 7 Aug. 28; *Brevet-Major*, 29 Mar. 39; *Major*, 14 July, 43; *Lieut.-Col.* P 5 Dec. 43.

Majors.

41 | 3 4/12 | 1 Charles Deane,[3] KH. *Cornet*, 5 Sept. 04; *Lieut.* P 6 July, 06; *Capt.* P 5 Dec. 18; *Major*, P 19 June, 35; *Brevet-Lt.-Col.* 9 Nov. 46.

25 | 0 | 1 Alexander Barry Montgomery, *Ens.* 25 Nov. 24; *Lieut.* 30 Oct. 26; *Capt.* P 16 Aug. 33; *Major*, P 5 Dec. 43.

23 | 0 | 2 Thomas Graham, *Ens.* 21 May 26; *Lieut.* P 27 April 27; *Capt.* P 9 Aug. 33; *Major*, P 3 May 44.

24 | 0 | 2 Henry Phipps Raymond, *Ens.* 9 Apr. 25; *Lieut.* P 17 May 27; *Capt.* P 21 Mar. 34; *Brevet-Maj.* 9 Nov. 46; *Major*, P 17 Dec. 47.

Full Pay	Half Pay	CAPTAINS.	ENSIGN.	LIEUT.	CAPTAIN.	BREV.-MAJ.
29	0	2 Burton Daveney	27 April 20	P 7 July 25	P 8 Nov. 27	23 Nov. 41
29	0	2 Edw. A. G. Muller[5]	3 Feb. 20	11 Aug. 25	P 11 Jan. 33	9 Nov. 46
23	0	2 Richard Going	9 April 26	P 2 Feb. 27	P 19 June 35	9 Nov. 46
23	0	1 Henry Alex. Kerr	P 17 Aug. 26	22 Mar. 32	P 18 Mar. 36	9 Nov. 46
19	0	2 Trevor Davenport	8 June 30	P 22 Mar. 33	P 10 Mar. 37	
18	0	1 Francis Gregor Urquhart .	P 18 Nov. 31	P 16 Aug. 33	P 14 April 37	
16	0	2 Henry Richard Marindin	P 11 Jan. 33	P 18 Mar. 36	P 30 April 41	
16	0	2 Thomas Scott Hawkins ..	P 29 Mar. 33	P 17 Sept. 36	P 23 June 43	
25	0	2 Tyrrell Matthias Byrne ..	30 June 24	23 Mar. 26	16 June 43	
24	0	1 Charles Curtis	10 Feb. 25	19 Feb. 27	14 July 43	
16	0	1 William Little Stewart ..	P 12 April 33	13 Jan. 37	P 28 July 43	
16	0	1 Henry Draper Neville[8] ..	P 16 Aug. 33	P 20 Jan. 37	P 5 Dec. 43	
16	0	1 *Hon.* Cha. Dawson Plunkett	P 11 Oct. 33	P 10 Mar. 37	P 29 Dec. 43	
16	0	1 Frederick R. Mein	22 Oct. 33	P 14 April 37	P 3 May 44	
15	0	1 Edward Robert Wetherall	P 27 June 34	P 22 Aug. 37	P 19 Dec. 45	
22	0	1 William Webster	20 Feb. 27	P 24 Aug. 32	5 Feb. 46	
22	1/12	1 John Matcham Isaac[9]	4 Nov. 26	3 Sept. 29	11 July 45	
14	0	2 Francis Locker Whitmore	P 7 Aug. 35	10 May 39	P 3 Sept. 47	
13	0	2 James Pollock Gore......	P 6 Feb. 36	P 20 Dec. 39	P 29 Oct. 47	
14	0	2 John Edward Sharp	P 24 April 35	P 9 Feb. 38	P 17 Dec. 47	

1 Sir James Kempt accompanied Sir Ralph Abercromby upon the Expedition to Holland in 1799, as aide-de-camp, and was present in all the actions except that of the 10th Sept., when he was absent in England with dispatches. Accompanied Sir Ralph to the Mediterranean in June, 1800 as Military Secretary and aide-de-camp, and served with him until his death. Continued to serve in the same situations with Lord Hutchinson, and was present in all the battles in Egypt, and at the capture of Cairo and Alexandria. Commanded a Light Battalion upon the Expedition to Naples in 1805. Went to Calabria in the same year, and commanded the Light Brigade at the battle of Maida. Joined the army in the Peninsula, under the Duke of Wellington, Dec. 1811, and was appointed to the command of a brigade in the 3rd Division; served at the siege of Badajoz; commanded the attack on Fort Picurina, and the brigade which led the attack and carried the castle of Badajoz by escalade, on which occasion he was severely wounded in the foot. Removed to a brigade in the Light Division in Feb. 1812, and served in command of it until the conclusion of that war in 1814 and was present at the battle of Vittoria, the attack on the heights of Vera, battles of Nivelle (slightly wounded in the arm), Nive, Orthes, and Toulouse, besides several other less important affairs. Commanded a division in the campaign of 1815, and was severely wounded at the battle of Waterloo. Sir James has received the Egyptian Medal, and a Cross and 3 Clasps for Maida, Badajos, Vittoria, Nivelle, Nive, Orthes, and Toulouse.

2 Lt.-Col. Bell served in the Peninsula from July 1811 to the end of that war in 1814, and was engaged in the action of Arroyo du Molino, battle of Vittoria, battles in the Pyrenees, on the 7th, 25th, 30th, and 31st July, 1813, battles of the Nivelle, the Nive, Bayonne, Orthes, Tarbes, and Toulouse, besides a great many affairs and skirmishes. He afterwards served in the East Indies, in the Burmese war, and in the West Indies. He was actively employed during the rebellion in Canada, particularly in the capture of St. Charles, and St. Eustache; he afterwards commanded the small Fort and garrison of Coteau-du-Lac, an important position on the River St. Lawrence, and received the thanks of the Commander of the Forces for his exertions in recovering the guns and shot from the bottom of the River, and mounting them in position when it was reported impracticable; the guns were 24-pounders, sixteen of which and 4,000 round shot he recovered in the depth of a Canadian winter.

3 Lt.-Col. Deane served the campaign of 1809 against the Rajah of Lahore. He served also at the siege of Hattras and other forts in 1817; the Mahratta and Pindarree campaigns of 1817 and 18, under the immediate command of the Marquis of Hastings; and in the Burmese war in 1825-6.

5 Major Muller served in the Burmese war.

8 Captain Neville served in Canada during the rebellion of 1837 and 1838, and was engaged with the rebels at St. Charles and at St. Eustache.

9 Capt. Isaac served with the Cape Mounted Rifles i several affairs and skirmishes with the border Tribes at the Cape of Good Hope, between 1830 and 1839.

Years' Serv. Full Pay.	Half Pay.		Ensign.	Lieut.
		Lieutenants.		
15	0	1 David Green..............	P 30 Dec 34	P 2 Feb. 38
12	0	2 Joseph D. Windham	P 10 Mar. 37	P 11 June 41
11	0	1 Andrew Anderson	P 19 Oct. 38	19 Aug. 41
10	0	2 Cha. Evered Poole, *r*.......	P 10 May 39	P 17 Dec. 41
10	0	2 Arthur Newland	P 18 Sept. 39	P 15 Apr. 42
9	0	1 Wm. Kent Allix, *Adj.*	28 July 40	P 23 June 43
9	0	1 Cha. Edgecumbe Davenport	P 11 Sept. 40	14 July 43
9	0	1 Spencer Geo. Aug. Thursby	P 15 Dec. 40	P 28 July 43
8	0	2 Spencer Vansittart	P 30 April 41	P 5 Sept. 43
8	0	1 George Gwavas Carlyon	P 7 Sept. 41	P 29 Dec. 43
8	0	1 Frederick Carter	P 17 Dec. 41	P 23 Feb. 44
8	0	1 Jesse Lloyd	3 Dec. 41	P 17 Mar. 43
8	0	1 Frederick Wells	12 Oct. 41	2 Aug. 44
8	0	1 Thomas Henry Breedon	P 26 Oct. 41	P 19 May 43
7	0	2 Hugh Lynedoch Barton ..	P 15 Apr. 42	P 19 Dec. 45
7	0	2 John Alex. Gavin Campbell	P 2 Aug. 42	P 11 Apr. 45
6	0	2 Roger James Aytoun	P 23 June 43	15 Jan. 47
5	0	2 Wm. Henry Sharpe Sharpe	P 23 Feb. 44	P 9 April 47
5	0	1 Richard George Coles......	P 3 May 44	P 14 May 47
5	0	2 Thomas Edward Bidgood, *Adj*	P 25 June 44	P 22 June 47
4	0	2 William James Gillum	P 14 Feb. 45	P 2 July 47
4	0	2 George Taaffe	P 19 Dec. 45	P 3 Sept. 47
3	0	1 Hastings Fowler Jones	P 21 Apr. 46	P 22 Oct. 47
3	0	2 Edward Hamilton Finney ..	P 1 May 46	P 17 Dec. 47
6	0	2 Wm. Fortescue Scott	15 July 43	18 Feb. 48
5	0	1 James White Minchin......	P 30 July 44	P 10 Dec. 47
		Ensigns.		
4	0	2 Henry Francis Bythesea....	P 26 Sept. 45	
3	0	2 John Cadwalader Pugh	P 25 Aug. 46	
3	0	1 Brock Carter	3 Nov. 46	
3	0	1 George Rowland..........	P 30 Nov. 46	
3	0	2 Henry Howard Barber	P 1 Dec. 46	
3	0	2 Bingham H. Edw. Muller ..	29 Dec. 46	
2	0	1 Charles Minchin	P 5 Feb. 47	
2	0	2 Henry Whichcote Turner ..	30 Mar. 47	
2	0	1 James Frederick Webster ..	P 9 April 47	
2	0	2 Francis Beaumaris Bulkeley	P 22 June 47	
2	0	1 John Alexander Christie	P 2 July 47	
2	0	2 Gilbert Andrew Amos	4 Sept. 47	
2	0	2 James Aytoun	P 22 Oct. 47	
2	0	1 Donald Harvey Munro	19 Nov. 47	
2	0	1 Charles James Phillipps	P 17 Dec. 47	
1	0	1 Alexander Draper	18 Feb. 48	

3 Quarter-master Thompson served with the 2nd Battalion Royal Regt. throughout the Mahratta war, with the army in the Deccan, under Sir John Doveton, in the years 1817, 18, and 19. Also during the Burmese war, from Jan. 1825 until its conclusion in 1826.

4. Dr. Knox was actively employed during the rebellion in Canada in 1837, 38, and 39, was present in sole medical charge of the troops in the action of St. Charles.

Full Pay	Half Pay	
28	0	*Paymasters.*—1 James Espinasse, 8 Feb. 39; *Ens.* 8 Feb. 21; *Lieut* 7 April, 25; *Capt.* 11 July, 37.
7	0	2 William John Bampfield, 30 June 48; *Ens.* 18 Mar. 42; *Lieut.* [12 Sept. 46
9	0	*Adjutants.* 1 *Lieut.* Wm. Kent Allix, 30 May 45.
5	0	*Adjutants.* 2 *Lieut.* Thomas Edward Bidgood, 18 Feb. 48.
		Quarter-Masters.
8	0	1 Charles Broadley, 11 Feb. 42; *Ens.* 3 Aug. 41.
4	0	2 Michael Thompson,[3] 31 Oct. 45.
		Surgeons.
15	0	2 George Gordon Robertson, MD., 25 June 44; *Assist.-Surg.* 12 Aug. 34.
16	0	1 Alexander Knox,[4] M.D., 15 Mar. 44; *Assist.-Surg.* 12 Apr. 33.
9	0	*Assistant-Surgeons.*—1 Luke Barron, MD., 10 July, 40.
5	0	*Assistant-Surgeons.*—2 William Thomas Hoskin, M.D. 1 March, 44.
4	0	*Assistant-Surgeons.*—1 James Mee, 28 March 45

Facings Blue—*Agent*, John Lawrie, *Esq.*—*Irish Agents*, Messrs. Cane & Co.

[*1st Battalion embarked for Foreign Service*, 11 *Nov.* 39. *Serving in New Brunswick.* *Depôt at Aberdeen.*]

[*2d Battalion returned from Barbadoes*, 25 *Feb.* 46. Head quarters at Dublin.]

"*The Paschal Lamb*," with the mottos "*Pristinæ virtutis memor*," and "*Vel exuviæ triumphant*." The *Queen's Cypher* within the Garter, having the Crown over it. On the Grenadiers' Caps, the *King's Crest* and the *Queen's Cypher* and *Crown*; and on the Drums the *Queen's Cypher*. The *Sphinx*, with the words "EGYPT"—"VIMIERA"—"CORUNNA"—"SALAMANCA"—"VITTORIA"—"PYRENEES"—"NIVELLE"—"TOULOUSE"—"PENINSULA"—"AFFGHANISTAN"—"GHUZNEE"—"KHELAT."

Years' Serv.		
47		*Colonel.* P W Alex. George, *Lord* Saltoun,[1] KCB. *Ens.* 28 April 02; *Lt.* 2 Sept. 02; *Capt.* 7 Sept. 04; *Lt.-Col.* 25 Dec. 13; *Col.* 27 May 25; *Major-Gen.* 10 Jan. 37; *Lt.-Gen.* 9 Nov. 46; *Col.* of the Queen's Royals, 7 Aug. 46.
Full Pay.	Half Pay.	
35	0	*Lieut.-Colonel.*—Richard Carruthers,[2] CB. *Ens.* 19 May 14; *Lt.* 25 Jan. 25; *Capt.* P 16 April, 29; *Major,* P 19 Feb. 36; *Brevet-Lieut.-Col.* 23 July, 39; *Lieut.-Col.* 1 Jan. 47.
22	0	*Majors.*—John Burns, *Ens.* P 27 Apr. 27; *Lieut.* P 15 March 33; *Capt.* P 18 May 38; *Major,* P 23 May 48.
19	0	Stanhope William Jephson,[3] *Ens.* P 26 Nov. 30; *Lieut.* P 19 Feb. 36; *Capt.* P 28 Dec. 41; *Major,* P 4 Aug. 48.

Full Pay	Half Pay	CAPTAINS.	ENSIGN.	LIEUT.	CAPTAIN.	BREV.-MAJ.
29	0	Oliver Robinson[5]	5 Oct. 20	24 Jan. 25	P 19 Feb. 36	13 Nov. 39
13	0	Tho. W. E. Holdsworth[6]	P 15 Jan. 36	P 14 Dec. 38	P 16 Aug. 42	
12	0	Thomas Addison[7]	15 Sept. 37	31 Jan. 39	P 16 Dec. 45	
9	0	Demetrius W. G. James	P 31 Jan. 40	P 15 Dec. 40	P 9 June 46	
14	0	William Domvile	P 24 Apr. 35	P 18 Aug. 38	P 25 Aug. 46	
13	0	Geo. Edw. Alex. Tobin[11]	P 30 Dec. 36	15 Dec. 40	P 11 Feb. 48	
9	0	Wm. Joseph Oldham[9]	29 May 40	P 3 Aug. 41	P 26 May 48	
16	21 1/12	Hector Munro[10]	5 Sept. 11	20 May 13	18 Dec. 45	
8	0	Edward Selby Smyth[13]	P 26 Jan. 41	29 May 43	P 4 Aug. 48	
7	0	Charles Edmund Thornton	P 30 Dec. 42	P 20 Aug. 44	P 19 Sept. 48	
		LIEUTENANTS.				
14	0	Godfrey Piercy[12]	P 24 July 35	16 April 38		
14	0	Henry Cole Faulkner, *r.*	P 13 Nov. 35	P 18 May 39		
11	0	Frederick Connor	P 29 Sept. 38	27 Jan. 40		
13	0	John Henry Grant[11]	2 Apr. 36	15 Dec. 40		
7	0	Alexander Gillespie	P 16 Aug. 42	P 16 Dec. 45		
7	0	Cha. FitzGerald Studdert[14]	P 22 April 42	P 24 Nov. 43		
6	0	William Wynn Kirkby[9]	P 20 Jan. 43	1 Jan. 47		
5	0	Miles Fisher Monckton	P 12 Jan. 44	P 10 July 46		
7	0	Richard Hill Rocke, *Adj.*	7 Jan. 42	P 30 May 43		
6	0	Raymond Inglis	22 Nov. 43	P 11 Feb. 48		
4	0	Frederick Mathias	P 16 Dec. 45	P 26 May 48		
4	0	William Henry Poulett	P 30 May 45	P 4 Aug. 48		
3	0	Cecil Squire	P 9 June 46	P 19 Sept. 48		
		ENSIGNS.				
6	0	Brooks M'Carty	9 June 43			
3	0	Robert Holdsworth	P 25 Sept. 46			
2	0	Fra. Lionel Oct. Atty	1 Jan. 47			
2	0	George Gollop	P 30 Apr. 47			
1	0	Richard Bury Russell	P 11 Feb. 48			
1	0	John Charles Weir	P 9 June 48			
1	0	James Harwood Rocke	P 4 Aug. 48			
1	0	John Tolcher	P 19 Sept. 48			
11	0	*Paymaster.*—Oliver Nicolls, 25 Nov. 45; *Ens.* P 13 Jan. 38; *Lieut.* 16 July 41.				
7	0	*Adjutant.*—*Lieut.* Richard Hill Rocke, 4 Aug. 48.				
3	0	*Quarter-Master.*—John Mansfield, 27 Oct. 46.				
14	0	*Surgeon.*—George Roche Smith, 14 April 48; *Assist.-Surg.* 13 Sept. 35.				
9	0	*Assistant-Surgeon.*—Edward Scott Docker, 29 Dec. 40.				

14 Lt. Studdert served in the 9th Lancers during the campaign in 1843-4 against Gwalior, including the battle of Punniar (Medal), and the investment and surrender of Gwalior.

10 Captain Munro served in the American war with the 49th Regt. and was present in the actions at Prescot, Chrystler's Farm, and Plattsburg, besides various skirmishes.

9 Captain Oldham and Lieut. Kirkby served the campaign in the Southern Mahratta country in 1844 (including the storm of the fortress of Punella), and that in the Concan in 1845.

Facings Blue.—*Agent,* Messrs. Cox & Co.—*Irish Agents, Sir* E. R. Borough, *Bart.,* Armit, & Co. [*Returned from Bombay,* 1 *Jan.* 1846.]

1 Lord Saltoun served in Sicily, in 1806 and 7; Sir John Moore's campaign in 1808-9, including the battle of Corunna. Expedition to Walcheren, 1809. Went to Cadiz in April 1811, and remained with the army until the end of the Peninsular war in 1814, and was present at the storming of Seville, passage of the Bidassoa, battle of the Nivelle, actions of the 9th, 10th, and 12th Dec. 1813 in front of Bidart, passage of the Adour, blockade of Bayonne and repulse of the sortie. Served also the campaign of 1815, including the battles of Quatre Bras and Waterloo, and the storming of Peronne. In Dec. 1841 he embarked in command of reinforcements for China, and commanded a Brigade at the attack and capture of Chin Kiang Foo.

2 Lt. Colonel Carruthers served the campaign in Affghanistan and Beloochistan, and commanded the Regt. at the assault and capture of the fortress of Ghuznee (Medal), and at the assault and capture of the fortress and citadel of Khelat. He commanded the Forces, as a Brigadier, in the Southern Concan and Sawant Warree Country during the campaign of 1844 and 45.

11 Capt. Tobin and Lt. Grant served the campaign of 1844 and 45 in the Southern Concan and Sawant Warree Country, including the storming of several stockades, and the investment and capture of the Forts of Monohur and Munsuntosh.

13 Capt. Smyth served as Brigade Major to the Forces in the Southern Concan and Sawant Warree Country during the campaign of 1844 and 45, including the storming of several stockades, and the investment and capture of the Forts of Monohur and Munsuntosh.

5 Major Robinson served the campaign in Affghanistan and Beloochistan, including the storm and capture of Ghuznee (severely wounded) and of Khelat. Medal for Ghuznee.

6 Captain Holdsworth served the campaign in Affghanistan and Beloochistan, including the storm and capture of Ghuznee (Medal) and of Khelat (severely wounded). He served also the campaign in the Southern Mahratta country in 1844 (including the storm of the Fortress of Punella), and that in the Concan in 1845.

[illegible]

12 Lieut. Piercy served the campaign in Affghanistan and Beloochistan, including the storm and capture of Ghuznee (Medal) and of Khelat. He served also the campaign of 1844-5 in the Southern Concan and Sawant Warree country, including the storming of several stockades, and the investment and capture of the Forts Monohur and Munsuntosh.

The *Dragon* "Douro" "Talavera" "Albuhera" "Pyrenees" "Nivelle" "Nive" "Peninsula" "Punniar."

Years' Serv. 55

Colonel.

Full Pay / Half Pay

Sir Henry King,[1] CB. KCH. *Cornet*, 25 March, 94; *Lieut.* 12 Aug. 95; *Capt.* 3 May, 00; *Major*, 5 Feb. 07; *Lieut.-Col.* 31 Dec. 11; *Col.* 27 May, 25; *Major-Gen.* 10 Jan. 37; *Lt.-Gen.* 9 Nov. 46; *Col.* of the Buffs, 18 March, 45.

Lieutenant-Colonel.

53 | 0 | *Sir* James Dennis,[2] KCB. *Ens.* 2 Sept. 96; *Lt.* 12 Apr. 97; *Capt.* 6 Aug. 03; *Brevet-Major*, 13 Oct. 12; *Brevet-Lieut.-Col.* 27 May, 25; *Regtl.-Major*, 25 Apr. 28; *Regtl.-Lieut.-Col.* 4 June, 38; *Col.* 28 June, 38.

21 | 0 | *Majors.*—Charles T. Van Straubenzee,[3] *Ens.* P 28 Aug. 28; *Lieut.* P 22 Feb. 33; *Capt.* P 10 Mar. 37; *Major*, 27 Aug. 43; *Brevet-Lt.-Col.* 30 April, 44.

21 | 0 | Donald Mcent Cameron,[4] *Ens.* 26 April 28; *Lieut.* P 17 March 30; *Capt.* P 13 March 40; *Major*, P 10 Dec. 47.

Full Pay	Half Pay		Ensign.	Lieut.	Captain.	Brev.-Maj.
		Captains.				
10	0	James Talbot Airey,[5] *s.*	11 Feb. 30	P 3 May 33	P 22 July 42	
22	0	Harry Blair	9 Dec. 27	9 Nov. 31	30 Dec. 43	
20	0	George Bridge	16 April 29	21 Sept. 32	28 Jan. 44	
15	0	Hall Plumer Chamberlain	P 14 Feb. 34	P 3 June 36	P 13 Feb. 46	
14	0	Peter Browne	20 Feb. 35	7 Dec. 38	P 20 Nov. 46	
11	0	Charles A. Cobbe	P 6 July 38	P 28 Jan. 42	P 8 Dec. 46	
11	0	Charles William Green	7 April 38	P 13 Mar. 40	P 14 May 47	
9	0	Fred. Francis Maude,[6]	P 13 Mar. 40	P 27 Aug. 41	P 10 Dec. 47	
8	0	Hugh Smith,[4] *s.*	P 8 Jan. 41	1 Nov. 42	P 10 Dec. 47	
10	0	James Wm. Richardson[4]	P 15 Nov. 39	8 April 42	P 31 Dec. 47	
		Lieutenants.				
14	0	Wm. John Dorehill,[4] *r.*	P 16 Jan. 35	10 Mar. 38		
13	0	Kenneth Mackenzie[4]	P 3 June 36	P 31 May 39		
11	0	Alex. Hamilton Robson[4]	P 25 Dec. 38	P 29 May 40		
10	0	Thomas Kains[4]	P 29 Nov. 39	20 May 42		
7	0	James Swetenham[7]	P 22 July 42	P 8 Aug. 45		
5	0	Walter Pownall	P 6 Dec. 44	P 18 Oct. 45		
5	0	Charles Hood	P 26 June 44	P 20 Nov. 46		
5	0	Garnett Warburton	P 5 July 44	P 31 July 46		
4	0	George James Ambrose	P 4 July 45	5 Nov. 46		
4	0	Henry John King	P 8 Aug. 45	P 23 Apr. 47		
4	0	R. G. Amherst Luard, Adj.	6 July 45	P 14 May 47		
3	0	Cortlandt Taylor	P 13 Feb. 46	P 10 Dec. 47		
3	0	Octavius Cobb Rooke	P 20 Nov. 46	P 10 Dec. 47		
2	0	Augustus Edward Ellice	P 9 Apr. 47	P 31 Dec. 47		
		Ensigns.				
4	0	John Henry Lukis	16 Sept. 45			
2	0	Fred. Richard Berguer	P 23 Apr. 47			
2	0	John Lewes	P 14 May 47			
2	0	Smith Ramadge	15 May 47			
2	0	Rob. Sandford Warburton	P 8 Oct. 47			
2	0	Charles Kavanagh	P 31 Dec. 47			
1	0	Alexander Strange	16 June 48			

6 Capt. Maude was present in the battle of Punniar (Medal) as Adjutant of the Buffs, and had his horse killed under him.

5 Captain Airey acted as Aide-de-Camp to Sir Robert Sale at the storming of the Khoord Cabool Pass in Oct. 1841, and had his horse shot under him. He served as Aide-de-Camp to Major Gen. Elphinstone, in Affghanistan, from January 1841, and was present in every skirmish or sortie made by the garrison from the cantonments during the insurrection at Cabool, and was afterwards given up as a hostage. He acted as Aide-de-Camp to Sir John M'Caskill at the storming of Istaliff, and was present with the Buffs at the battle of Punniar (medal).

5 | 0 | *Paymaster.*—Fred. Geo. Syms, 25 June 47; *Ens.* 22 Mar. 44; *Lieut.* 7 May 47.

4 | 0 | *Adjutant.*—*Lieut.* Richard George Amherst Luard, 24 Dec. 47.

11 | 0 | *Quarter-Master.*—Joseph Cartmail, 12 July, 39; *Ens.* 7 Dec. 38.

15 | 0 | *Surg.*—Robert Stevenson,[4] MD., 2 Feb. 44; *Assist.-Surg.* 14 March, 34.

3 | 0 | *Assistant-Surgeon.*—George Fenton Cameron, M.D., 7 July, 46.

Facings Buff.—*Agent*, Charles R. M'Grigor, Esq.—*Irish Agents, Sir* E. R. Borough, *Bt.*, Armit, & Co.

[Returned from Bengal, May, 1845.]

1 Sir Henry King served at the siege of Porto Rico, and capture of Trinidad, in 1797. Whilst quartered at Marin, to windward of Martinique, he was ordered to proceed in a small vessel to St. Pierre, with a detachment of twenty-six men, to form a guard for the Governor, Sir Wm. Keppel; encountered a French privateer off the Diamond Rock, mounting four long nines, with seventy men on board, which, after a sharp action of twenty minutes, was beaten off with a loss of ten men killed, and fifteen wounded; Sir Henry having only one man killed, and himself wounded in the shoulder. Served the Egyptian campaign of 1801, including the action at the landing at Aboukir Bay, siege of the castle, and actions of the 21st March and 9th May at Rahmanie, at which latter he commanded a squadron of the 26th Light Dragoons, and lost his right leg. Expedition to Walcheren, and siege of Flushing, 1809. Appointed Commandant of Tarifa in 1810, and for his services at its defence, his commission as Lieut. Colonel was antedated to the day of the assault, 31st Dec. 1811. Joined Lord Wellington's army a few days after the battle of Salamanca; commanded the 82nd at the battle of Vittoria, and towards the close of the action the command of the brigade devolved on him. Sir Henry has received the Egyptian medal, and a medal for the battle of Vittoria.

2 Sir James Dennis served with the 49th on board H. M. S. *Monarch*, at the battle of Copenhagen in 1801, and was wounded in both hands and contused. Served in the last American war, including battle of Queenstown (wounded), storming of Fort George, action at Stoney Creek (wounded in two places with musket balls, and also contused by having his horse shot, which fell on him), and action of the Rapids at Hoopies Creek. Commanded a division at the battle of Maharajpore, 29th Dec. 1843 (a Bronze Star), for which he was appointed a K.C.B. Sir James received the Brevet rank of Major for his services at Queenstown, on which occasion he commanded that post during the operations which took place prior to the arrival of General Brock.

3 Lt-Col. Straubenzee served the campaign against the Rajah of Coorg in 1834. In the action of Maharajpore (Medal) on the 29th Dec. 1843, he succeeded to the command of the 39th regt.

4 The following Officers were present with the Regt. at the battle of Punniar, 29th Dec. 1843, and have received the Bronze Star for the same, viz.—Major Cameron, Captains Maude, Smith, and Richardson, Lieuts. Dorehill (wounded on right side of chest), Mackenzie, Robson, (had his horse shot under him) and Kains, and Doctor Stevenson.

7 Lt. Swetenham was severely wounded in the right leg, and slightly on the left side, whilst carrying the Regimental Colour of the Buffs at the battle of Punniar, on the 29th Dec. 1843; he has received the Bronze Star.

"*The Lion of England*"—"CORUNNA"—"BADAJOZ"—"SALAMANCA"—"VITTORIA" "ST. SEBASTIAN"—"NIVE"—"PENINSULA"—"BLADENSBURG"—"WATERLOO."

Years' Serv. 56 Full Pay.	Half Pay.	
		Colonel.—𝔓 *Sir* Thomas Bradford,[1] GCB. GCH. *Ens.* 20 Oct. 1793; *Lieut.* 9 Dec. 93; *Capt.* 15 April, 94; *Major*, 9 Sept. 95; *Lieut.-Col.* 1 Jan. 1801; *Col.* 25 July, 10; *Major-Gen.* 4 June, 13; *Lieut.-Gen.* 27 May, 25; *Gen.* 23 Nov. 41; *Col.* 4th Regt. 7 Feb. 46.
24	0	*Lieutenant-Colonel.*—William George Gold,[2] *2nd-Lt.* 7 April 25; *Lt.* 26 Jun. 28; *Capt.* p 29 June, 32; *Major*, p 10 Feb. 43; *Lt.-Col.* 26 July, 44.
42	0	*Majors.*—𝔓 William Sadlier,[3] *Ens.* 2 April, 07; *Lieut.* 4 May, 09; *Capt.* 25 Aug. 25; *Major*, 4 Feb. 38.
27	0	Thomas Williams, *Ens.* p 12 Sept. 22; *Lieut.* p 7 July, 25; *Capt.* p 17 June 28; *Brev.-Maj.*, 23 Nov. 41; *Major*, 1 June, 45.

Full Pay	Half Pay	CAPTAINS.	ENSIGN.	LIEUT.	CAPTAIN.	BREV.-MAJ.
22	0	Thomas Faunce[4]	5 April 27	p 12 Nov. 29	p 23 June 37	
19	0	Farquhar M. Campbell ..	3 Aug. 30	p 6 Dec. 33	p 6 Oct. 37	
16	0	Fred. Leopold Arthur, *s.*	p 6 Dec. 33	p 3 July 35	p 8 June 38	
16	0	George Kennedy........	p 24 Dec. 33	p 1 July 36	p 15 Mar. 39	
14	0	Charles Staniforth Hext	p 9 Oct. 35	p 6 Oct. 37	p 25 Feb. 45	
20	0	Wm. Charles Sheppard	11 June 29	10 Nov. 34	1 June 45	
9	0	John Josiah Hort	20 Nov. 40	p 30 Sept. 42	p 29 Dec. 46	
9	0	Hercules Atkin Welman[5]	p 17 Jan. 40	16 Mar. 43	3 Feb. 47	
13	0	William Wilby	p 27 May 36	p 7 Oct. 37	p 10 Dec. 47	
10	0	William Bellingham	8 Mar. 39	p 25 Feb. 42	p 29 Jan. 47	
		LIEUTENANTS.				
12	0	Jas. Alex. Madigan......	23 June 37	p 14 Dec. 38		
13	0	W. Wyndham Bond, *Adj.*	p 4 Nov. 36	9 Mar. 39		
11	0	John Lennox MacAndrew	p 14 Dec. 38	p 8 May 40		
10	0	John Cowell Bartley	p 26 Apr. 39	p 20 Oct. 40		
11	0	G. Latham Thomson[6]....	p 27 July 38	9 April 41		
9	0	David Francis Chambers	p 31 Jan. 40	6 May 42		
8	0	John Gray Bolton	26 Jan. 41	30 July 42		
9	0	Henry Batson Ramsbottom	p 20 Oct. 40	p 28 June 44		
9	0	Theobald Pepper Roberts	p 15 Dec. 40	2 Aug. 44		
8	0	Henry FitzGerald	p 16 Nov. 41	12 Sept. 44		
6	0	John Hallowes	p 10 Mar. 43	p 11 Oct. 44		
5	0	Dominic Jacotin Gamble	p 19 April 44	p 25 Feb. 45		
5	0	Arthur Vaughan D. Harris	p 23 July 44	18 Nov. 45		
5	0	George Fred. Coryton ..	2 Aug. 44	p 14 Apr. 46		
		ENSIGNS.				
4	0	Arthur Ridgway Poyntz	16 Sept. 45			
3	0	Francis Edwin Maunsell..	p 12 June 46			
3	0	Thomas Knott..........	28 Aug. 46			
3	0	George Augustus Morgan	22 Dec. 46			
3	0	Edward Mulso Purvis ..	22 Apr. 46			
2	0	Octavius Yorke Cocks ..	p 30 Mar. 47			
4	0	Charles Collins	11 Nov. 45			

4 Captain Faunce served in command of the Light Company, at the re-capture of the Fort of Nepaunee, 21st Feb. 1841.

5 Capt. Welman served the campaign on the Sutlej in 1845-6 (Medal) as Adjutant of the 80th, including the battles of Moodkee, Ferozeshah, and Sobraon.

6 Lieut. Thomson served in the Caffre War, under Sir Benjamin D'Urban.

7 Capt. Burn served the campaign in the Eastern Islands, and was at the taking of Macassar in 1814. Served the Mahratta campaign of 1817 and 18, and was severely wounded at Bhurtpore in 1826.

8 Dr. Logan served with the 53rd the campaign on the Sutlej (Medal), and was present at Buddiwal, Aliwal, and Sobraon.

Full Pay	Half Pay	
38	$\frac{1}{12}$	*Paymaster.*—James Burn,[7] 6 Feb. 35; *Ens.* 1 Oct. 11; *Lieut.* 16 June, 13; [*Capt.* 19 Dec. 34.
13	0	*Adjutant.*—*Lieut.* Wadham Wyndham Bond, 13 Oct. 48.
		Quarter-Master.—
21	0	*Surgeon.*—Thos. Galbraith Logan,[8] M.D., 30 Aug., 42; *Assist.-Surg.* 29 July, 30; [*Hosp.-Assist.* 8 May, 28.
8	0	*Assistant-Surgeon.*—Richard Gamble, M.D., 8 June, 41.

Facings Blue.—*Agents*, Messrs. Cox & Co.

[Returned from Madras, 25 Sept. 48.]

1 Sir Thomas Bradford served in Ireland during the Rebellion in 1798. He was employed as an Assistant Adjutant-General with the Army in Hanover under Lord Cathcart in 1805; also in the same capacity the following year to the troops under Sir S. Auchmuty destined to reinforce General Beresford in the River Plate; in September, however, he was appointed Deputy Adjutant-General and Chief of that Department to the troops serving in South America: during this campaign he was present at the siege of Monte Video and the attack previous to it, as also that on Buenos Ayres. In June 1808 he was appointed to the Adjutant General's Department of the Army in Portugal, and was present at the battles of Vimiera and Corunna. He commanded a Brigade of the Portuguese Army from the end of 1811 to the general peace in 1814, and was engaged at the battle of Salamanca, siege of Burgos, battle of Vittoria, assault of Tolosa, attack of the outworks of San Sebastian and siege of that fortress, actions of the Nive on the 9th, 10th, 11th, and 12th Dec. 1813 near Biaritz, passage of the Adour, investment of Bayonne and repulse of the sortie, at which he was severely wounded. Sir Thomas has received a cross and one clasp for Corunna, Salamanca, Vittoria, San Sebastian, and Nive.

2 Lt. Col. Gold served in the campaign on the Sutlej (Medal) with the 53d, including the battles Buddiwal, Aliwal, and Sobraon (wounded), in the first of which he commanded the Regiment.

3 Major Sadlier served in Sicily from July 1806 to June 1812, and was present at the capture of the Islands of Ischia and Procida. Served subsequently in the Peninsula, including the battle of Castalla and siege of Tarragona, action at Villa Franca, besides various minor affairs; served also in the American war, including the attack on Plattsburg.

"*Quo fata Vocant,*" *surmounting* St. George and the Dragon. *On the corners of the 2nd colour the* Rose *and* Crown; *on the caps the* King's Crest; *also* St. George killing the Dragon. "WILHELMSTAHL"—"ROLEIA"—"VIMIERA"—"CORUNNA"—"BUSACO"—"CIUDAD RODRIGO"—"BADAJOZ"—"SALAMANCA"—"VITTORIA"—"NIVELLE"—"ORTHES"—"TOULOUSE"—"PENINSULA."

Years' Serv. 56 Full Pay.	Half Pay.		2D LIEUT.	LIEUT.	CAPTAIN.	BREV.-MAJ.
		Colonel.				
		Sir Jasper Nicolls,[1] KCB. *Ens.* 24 May, 1793; *Lieut.* 25 Nov. 94; *Capt.* 12 Sept. 99; *Major*, 6 July, 1804; *Lieut.-Col.* 29 Oct. 07; *Col.* 4 June, 14; *Maj.-Gen.* 19 July, 21; *Lt.-Gen.* 10 Jan. 37; *Col.* 5th Fusiliers, 4 April, 43.				
43	2 4/12	*Lieut.-Colonel.*— David England Johnson,[2] *Ens.* 9 Feb. 04; *Lt.* 29 Dec. 04; *Capt.* 12 March, 12; *Brevet-Major*, 22 July, 30; *Major*, P 29 Dec. 37; *Lieut.-Col.* 9 Nov. 46.				
20	0	r. James Smith Schonswar, *Cornet*, P 5 Mar. 29; *Lieut.* P 17 Dec. 30; *Capt.* P 6 May, 36; *Maj.* P 2 Aug. 44; *Lt-Col.* 20 July 47.				
27	0	*Majors.*—John Spence,[3] *Ens.* 7 Nov. 22; *Lieut.* 25 June, 24; *Capt.* P 5 Nov. 29; *Maj.* 9 Nov. 46.				
25	0	r. Philip M. Nelson Guy, *Ens.* P 23 Sept. 24; *Lieut.* P 12 June 28; *Capt.* P 29 Dec. 37; *Maj.* 20 July 47.				
		CAPTAINS.				
20	0	r. John Woodward......	P 5 Nov. 29	P 10 May 33	P 12 June 40	
16	0	Fra. Richard Pyner	22 Nov. 33	P 9 Feb. 38	P 15 Dec. 40	
18	0	r. Walt. Craufurd Kennedy	27 Oct. 31	10 Nov. 34	P 21 Feb. 40	
13	0	r. Henry F. F. Johnson..	22 Nov. 36	P 23 April 39	P 20 Jan. 43	
17	0	James Egbert Simmons[4]	20 Jan. 32	29 May 35	P 23 July 41	
14	0	r. Wm. Seymour Scroggs	P 12 June 35	P 21 June 39	9 Nov. 46	
12	1/12	Felix Ashpitel..........	P 28 Apr. 37	P 24 Apr. 40	P 24 Oct. 45	
10	0	William Chester Master	P 23 April 39	P 26 Oct. 41	P 29 Dec. 46	
10	0	r. George Bryan Milman	P 24 May 39	20 Sept. 42	P 29 Jan. 47	
15	0	r. Griffin Nicholas	8 April 34	26 May 36	22 Dec. 45	
13	0	r. Henry Edmunds......	P 8 April 36	P 15 Mar. 30	P 20 Oct. 46	
9	0	John Wallace Colquitt ..	P 17 Jan. 40	P 30 Dec. 42	P 20 July 47	
		LIEUTENANTS				
9	0	r. Jas. Archibald Forrest, r.	P 6 Mar. 40	P 20 Jan. 43		
8	0	William Lyons, *Adj.*	15 Jan. 41	12 Sept. 43		
7	0	George Renny	1 Nov. 42	1 May 44		
7	0	r. Thomas Bellew	P 22 April 42	P 30 Dec. 45		
7	0	r. Ferdin. W. L'Estrange	27 Dec. 42	9 Jan. 46		
6	0	Hambly Knapp	P 20 Jan. 43	P 27 Mar. 46		
6	0	Arthur Watson Palmer..	24 Feb. 43	P 31 July 46		
6	0	John Swaine Hogge	P 9 June 43	9 Nov. 46		
5	0	r. Garthshore Stirling Home	24 Feb. 44	23 Dec. 46		
5	0	r. Arthur England Johnson	26 July 44	24 Dec. 46		
8	0	John Henry Chads	9 Jan. 41	12 May 44		
3	0	Leopold FitzGerald	P 13 Feb. 46	P 20 July 47		
3	0	r. Francis Henry Pender	P 27 Mar. 46	P 30 July 47		
7	0	William Hill Forster[5] ..	P 22 July 42	22 Dec. 45		
14	0	John Urban Vigors[6]	P 27 Feb. 35	P 20 Nov. 38		
		2ND LIEUTENANTS.				
3	0	George John Stewart....	P 31 July 46			
3	0	r. C. Carter, *Adj.*	13 Nov. 46			
3	0	r. Joseph W. Tate Dickson	1 Dec. 46			
3	0	Albert Ernest Ross	22 Dec. 46			
3	0	r. John Flood..........	23 Dec. 46			
3	0	Wm. Henry Petty Meard	24 Dec. 46			
3	0	George Bennett	P 29 Dec. 46			
2	0	John William Madden ..	P 29 Jan. 47			
2	0	r. William Leach	P 21 July 47			
2	0	r. Legh Richmond Parry	P 30 July 47			
1	0	r. Samuel Lindsay Maylo	P 10 Mar. 48			
4	0	*Paymaster.*—Wm. R. C. Potter, 30 July 47; *2d Lieut.* P 30 Dec. 45; *Lieut.* [P 20 Dec. 46.				
8	0	*Adjutants.*—*Lieut.* Wm. Lyons, 12 Sept. 43.				
3	0	r. *2d Lieut.* Charles Carter, 20 July 47.				
2	0	*Quarter-Masters.*—r. Bernard M'Donald, 20 July 47.				
2	0	Robert Webster, 23 July 47.				
10	0	*Surgeons.*—Wm. Ord Mackenzie, M.D., 8 Jan. 47; *Assist.-Surg.* 4 Jan. 39.				
10	0	r. Wm. Sall, M.D., 13 July 47; *Assist.-Surg.* 10 May 39.				
3	0	*Assist.-Surgeons.*—Robert Fraser Robb, M.D., 7 Aug. 46.				
2	0	r. Dudley Hanley, M.D., 20 July 47.				

Facings Bright Green.—*Agents*, Messrs. Cox & Co.

[Returned from Gibraltar, 12 May, 1843.]

2 Lt.-Col. Johnson embarked with his regiment on the expedition to Hanover in 1805, and was shipwrecked and taken prisoner. Accompanied the expedition to South America in 1806, and was present at the storming of Buenos Ayres. Served afterwards in the Peninsula from June 1808 to Jan. 1809, and from June 1809 to December 1812, including the battles of Roleia, Vimiera, Lugo, Corunna, Busaco, Redinha, Sabugal (wounded), Fuentes d'Onor, El Bodon, first siege of Badajoz, and assault and capture of the citadel, siege and storming of Ciudad Rodrigo (severely wounded at the assault), and battle of Salamanca.

3 Major Spence served against the Ashantees from November 1822 to 1825.

4 Captain Simmons served the campaign in Affghanistan and Beloochistan, as Adjutant of the Queen's Royals, including the storm and capture of Ghuznee (Medal) and Khelat; at the storm of each of these fortresses he was severely wounded.

1 Sir Jasper Nicolls served in the Mahratta war, and was at the battle of Argaum, and at the siege and storm of Gawiel Ghur. Joined Lord Cathcart's army in Hanover, in 1805. Accompanied the expedition under General Craufurd to South America, in 1806, and commanded a column at the assault on Buenos Ayres, in July 1807. Embarked for Spain in 1808, and commanded the 14th at the battle of Corunna. Proceeded to Walcheren in 1809. Employed in the Nepaul war, and commanded a force, and conquered the province of Kumaoon, April 1815. Served as a Brigadier in the Pindarree war, and for a time commanded the centre division. At the siege of Bhurtpore, he commanded the second division of Infantry, consisting of three brigades, which division carried the left breach on the 18th Jan. 1826. Medal for Corunna.

5 Lieut. Forster served the campaign on the Sutlej in 1845-6 (Medal), with the 9th, and was present at the battles of Moodkee, Ferozeshah (contused wound), and Sobraon.

6 Lieut. Vigors served the campaign of 1842 in Affghanistan (Medal), including the storming of the Khyber Pass, taking the Fort of Mamookkail, storming the heights of Jugdulluck, action in the Tezeen valley, storming the Tezeen heights, and taking of Istaliff. He served also the campaign of 1845-6 on the Sutlej (Medal), including the battles of Moodkee, Ferozeshah (wounded), and Sobraon.

Emb. for C. of G. Hope, 28 Aug. 1846. Reserve Batt. at Fermoy.] 6th (*The Royal 1st Warwickshire*) Regt. of Foot.

"*The Antelope.*"—On the three corners of the second colour, "*The Rose and Crown.*"—And on the Grenadiers' caps, "*The King's Crest.*"—"ROLEIA"—"VIMIERA"—"CORUNNA"—"VITTORIA"—"PYRENEES"—"NIVELLE"—"ORTHES"—"PENINSULA"—"NIAGARA."

Years' Serv. Full Pay.	Half Pay.	
76		*Colonel.—Sir* George Nugent,[1] *Bart.* GCB. *Ensign*, 5 July, 1773; *Lieut.* 23 Nov. 75; *Capt.* 28 April, 78; *Major*, 3 May, 82; *Lieut.-Col.* 8 Sept. 83; *Col.* 1 Mar. 94; *Major.-Gen.* 3 May, 96; *Lieut.-Gen.* 25 Sept. 1803; *Gen.* 4 June, 13; *Field Marshal*, 9 Nov. 46; *Col.* 6th Regt. 26 May, 06.
26	$\frac{8}{12}$	*Lieutenant-Colonels.*—John Michel, *Ensign*, P 3 Apr. 23; *Lieut.* P 28 Apr. 25; *Capt.* P 12 Dec. 26; *Major*, P 6 Mar. 40; *Lieut.-Col.* P 15 April, 42.
23	$1\frac{2}{12}$	Randal Rumley, *Cornet*, P 30 Dec. 24; *Lieut.* P 8 Oct. 25; *Capt.* P 14 Aug. 27; *Brev.-Major*, 23 Nov. 41; *Major*, 26 July, 44; *Lieut.-Col.* P 21 July, 48.
35	0	*Majors.*—r. John Thomas Griffiths, *Ensign*, 6 Sept. 14; *Lieut.* P 17 May, 21; *Capt.* 1 Sept. 31; *Major*, 7 Aug. 46.
25	4	John Stuart, *Ens.* 22 Jan. 20; *Lt.* 26 March, 23; *Capt.* P 13 Aug. 25; *Major*, P 6 May, 36; *Brevet Lieut.-Col.* 9 Nov. 46.

Full Pay	Half Pay	CAPTAINS.	ENSIGN.	LIEUT.	CAPTAIN.	BREV.-MAJ.
16	0	Robt. W. M'Leod Fraser	5 July 33	P 17 July 35	P 15 Apr. 42	
16	0	Morris James Hall......	P 15 Mar. 33	7 Jan. 36	P 1 Nov. 42	
12	0	r. J. Elphinston Robertson	P 8 April 37	P 21 June 39	P 27 Oct. 43	
12	0	r. George Finlay[5]	P 17 Nov. 37	P 15 Apr. 42	P 19 Nov. 44	
10	0	Edward F. Crowder[5]....	15 June 39	P 1 Nov. 42	P 2 May 45	
9	0	r. Reginald Peel	P 5 June 40	P 14 April 43	P 28 Nov. 45	
19	0	r. John Craven Mansergh	26 Nov. 30	11 July 34	31 July 46	
18	0	Edward Staunton	17 May 31	4 Dec. 34	31 July 46	
14	0	Edward James Blanckley	22 May 35	17 Jan. 38	7 Aug. 46	
7	0	Henry Balguy	P 29 Apr. 42	P 20 Oct. 43	P 12 Nov. 47	
7	0	r. Charles Henry Dowker	P 7 Jan. 42	P 7 July 43	P 21 July 48	
7	0	r. Edward John Otway ..	29 May 42	P 29 Sept. 43	P 1 Aug. 48	
		LIEUTENANTS.				
7	0	r. William Albert Stratton	27 May 42	P 19 Nov. 44		
8	0	*Hon.* A. G. C. Chichester, *ad.*	P 19 Feb. 41	P 22 Nov. 42		
7	0	r. David Henry Elrington	P 7 Oct. 42	P 2 May 45		
7	0	Thomas Henry Somerville	25 Oct. 42	P 28 Nov. 45		
7	0	Godfrey Armytage	P 1 Nov. 42	P 29 Nov. 45		
9	0	George Grant Webb[6]....	20 Mar. 40	P 28 Dec. 41		
6	0	r. Wm. Edward Robertson	P 14 April 43	P 9 June 46		
6	0	r. Henry Pratt Gore....	P 21 July 43	P 10 June 46		
7	0	r. Philip Augustus Mosse	16 Apr. 42	31 July 46		
5	0	r. Thomas Fred. Puleston	P 19 Nov. 44	31 July 46		
8	0	Wm. FrazerGeo. Servantes	2 July 41	7 Aug. 46		
4	0	Charles Parker Catty ..	P 2 May 45	29 Jan. 47		
4	0	Richard Thompson	8 Aug. 45	P 12 Nov. 47		
3	0	r. Frederick William Gore	P 9 June 46	P 7 Apr. 48		
3	0	Robert Provo Norris....	P 10 June 46	P 21 July 48		
		ENSIGNS.				
3	0	r. John Richard Blake ..	P 27 Feb. 46			
5	0	r. W. Lee,[7] *ad.* Q-M. 28June44	28 July 46			
3	0	r. C. H. T. Bruce de Ruvignes	30 July 46			
3	0	r. Henry John Newton King	31 July 46			
3	0	John Hen. Ford Eskington	28 Aug. 46			
3	0	Fra. W. H. M'Cleland ..	3 Nov. 46			
2	0	r. Augustus Davies......	P 4 June 47			
2	0	Alexander Shuldham ..	P 8 Oct. 47			
2	0	Edward Lloyd	P 12 Nov. 47			
1	0	Nicholas Appleby Spoor	P 7 Apr. 48			
1	0	Hugh Augustus Crofton	P 21 July 48			

Full Pay	Half Pay	
		Paymaster.—John Mackintosh, 14 Aug. 46; *2nd Lieut.* 5 July, 08; *Lieut.* 15 Aug. 05.
5	0	*Adjutants.*—r. *Ensign* William Lee,[7] 28 July 46.
8	0	*Lieut. Hon.* Augustus George Charles Chichester, 22 Oct. 47.
3	0	*Quarter-Masters.*—John Croker, 28th July, 46.
3	0	r. George Pollard, 28 July, 46.
23	0	*Surgeons.*—John Murtagh,[5] MD., 2 July, 41; *Asst.-Surg.* 11 Feb. 30; *Hosp.-Asst.* 5 Dec. 26.
24	0	r. Peter Robertson, M.D. 2 July, 41; *A. S.*, 12 Jan. 26; *H. A.*, 24 Nov. 25.
5	0	*Assistant-Surgeons.*—r. John William Mostyn, M.D., 8 March, 44.
3	0	Henry Vereker Bindon, 12 June 46.

Facings Blue.—*Agents*, Messrs. Cox and Co.—*Irish Agents*, *Sir* E. R. Borough, *Bt.*, Armit, & Co.

5 Captains Finlay and Crowder, and Doctor Murtagh, with the effective men of the wing of the 6th Regt. stationed at Aden, formed part of an expedition of 500 men under the command of Lieut. Col. Pennycuick, which destroyed the Arab posts of Sheik Medi and Sheik Othman, and skirmished between those places on the 8th Oct. 1841.

6 Lieut. Webb served with the Left Wing of the Queen's Royals during the campaign of 1844 and 45 in the Southern Concan and Sawunt Warree Country, including the storming of several stockades, and the investment and capture of the Forts of Monohur and Munsuntosh.

7 Ensign Lee served with the Royal Marines at the capture of the Island of Carabusa, together with several piratical vessels in its harbour, in 1828-9.

1 Sir George Nugent served in the first American war, from Sept. 1777 until its termination in 1783, and was employed on the Expedition up Hudson's River for the relief of General Burgoyne's army; present also at the capture of Forts Montgomery and Clinton, by assault, and on various other desultory services. Accompanied the brigade of Guards to the Continent, in March, 1793, and served the campaign of that year: present at the siege of Valenciennes, actions of St. Amand, Lincelles, &c. and on the army going into winter quarters he returned home for the purpose of raising a regt., the 85th. In Sept. 1794, he accompanied his regt. to Walcheren, where he held the local rank of Brigadier-General; and, in Oct. joined the army of the Duke of York, and obtained the command of a brigade of the line, cantoned in and near to the town of Tiel in the Waal. Commanded the Northern District in Ireland during the whole of the Rebellion.

Emb. for Foreign Serv. 6th Nov. 1839.] *7th Regt. of Foot, (Royal Fusiliers.)* [At Nova Scotia. Depot at Youghal.

In the centre of the colours, The "*Rose*" within the "*Garter*" and the "*Crown*" over it. And in the corners of the second Colour, The "*White Horse.*" "MARTINIQUE"—"TALAVERA"—"ALBUHERA"—"BADAJOZ"—"SALAMANCA"—"VITTORIA"—"PYRENEES"—"ORTHES"—"TOULOUSE"—"PENINSULA."

Years' Serv.		
55		
Full Pay.	Half Pay.	
		Colonel.
		Right Hon. Sir Edward Blakeney,[1] KCB. GCH. *Cornet* 28 Feb. 1794; *Lieut.* 24 Sept. 94; *Capt.* 24 Dec. 94; *Major,* 17 Sept. 1801; *Lieut.-Col.* 25 April, 08: *Col.* 4 June, 14; *Major-Gen.* 27 May, 25; *Lieut.-Gen.* 28 June, 38; *Col.* 7th Fusiliers, 20 Sept. 32.
		Lieut.-Colonel.
34	1 11/12	Frederic Farquharson, *Ens.* 17 Sept. 13; *Lieut.* 25 May, 14; *Capt.* P 23 Sept. 19; *Major,* P 29 June, 30; *Lieut.-Col.* P 7 Sept. 32; *Col.* 9 Nov. 46.
		Majors.
23	1/12	Lacy Walter Yea, *Ens.* P 6 Oct. 25; *Lieut.* P 19 Dec. 26; *Capt.* P 30 Dec. 36; *Major,* P 3 June, 42.
19	2 1/12	Richard Wilbraham,[2] *2nd Lieut.,* P 25 Mar. 28; *Lieut.* 25 May, 33; *Capt.* P 22 July, 36; *Brev.-Major,* 31 Dec. 41; *Major,* P 19 Jan. 44.

Full Pay	Half Pay	CAPTAINS.	ENSIGN.	LIEUT.	CAPTAIN.	BREVET-MAJOR.
15	0	T. St. V. H. C. Troubridge	P 24 Jan. 34	P 30 Dec. 36	P 14 Dec. 41	
15	0	Robert Stuart..........	P 23 May 34	11 June 37	P 2 Sept. 42	
15	1 1/12	Arthur John Pack......	P 9 Aug. 33	P 5 May 37	P 23 June 43	
13	0	Charles Stewart Cochrane	P 8 April 36	P 17 Aug. 38	P 12 Jan. 44	
12	0	*Hon.* W. Lygon Pakenham	P 25 Aug. 37	P 31 Aug. 38	P 26 Jan. 44	
13	0	*Hon.* Charles Luke Hare	P 18 Mar. 36	P 7 Dec. 38	P 23 Aug. 44	
12	0	Wm. Lewis Grant......	P 7 April 37	P 28 July 40	P 23 May 45	
12	0	Wm. R. Browne........	29 Sept. 37	P 5 Mar. 41	P 27 Mar. 46	
10	0	Herb. Wat. Wms. Wynn	P 5 July 39	P 24 Sept. 41	P 28 Apr. 46	
10	0	Albany French Wallace,[3]	P 5 Apr. 39	P 29 Dec. 40	P 1 Oct. 47	
		LIEUTENANTS.				
10	0	Frederick Mills, *d. adjt.*	P 25 Jan. 39	P 1 April 42		
8	0	Edm. H. Wilson Bellairs	P 16 Nov. 41	P 16 Aug. 42		
9	0	Geo. Christian Wilson, *r.*	15 Dec. 40	P 19 May 43		
9	0	*Hon.* William Monck, *Adj.*	P 28 Aug. 40	P 29 April 42		
11	0	Plomer J. Young	11 May 38	P 1 Nov. 39		
6	0	Henry Aylmer Porter ..	P 30 May 43	P 14 June 44		
8	0	John Donovan Verner ..	P 24 Sept. 41	P 23 Aug. 44		
10	0	Robert Kaye	16 Nov. 39	27 Sept. 44		
7	0	Fred. John G. Whitehead	P 25 Nov. 42	P 8 Oct. 44		
6	0	George Rashleigh Edgell	P 14 July 43	P 20 Dec. 44		
7	0	Dugald Stewart Miller ..	P 27 Sept. 42	P 8 Aug. 45		
6	0	Charles Edward Watson	P 13 Oct. 43	P 8 Aug. 45		
6	0	Augustus Alex. Ruxton ..	P 25 Aug. 43	P 24 Oct. 45		
5	0	W. H. Dominic Fitz Gerald	P 8 Oct. 44	P 27 Mar. 46		
10	0	Thomas Beckwith Speedy[4]	15 Mar. 39	23 Oct. 41		
5	0	William Jesse Hoare, *d.pm.*	P 12 Jan. 44	P 1 May 46		
4	0	Montagu Wigley Bell ..	P 12 July 45	P 9 Apr. 47		
6	0	Harry Lee Carter	P 14 Apr. 43	P 1 May 46		
5	0	Richard William Aldworth	P 19 Aug. 44	P 22 Oct. 47		
5	0	C. Fra. Berens Dawkins	P 31 Dec. 44	P 5 Nov. 47		
6	0	James Duncan Longden	31 Mar. 43	P 3 Nov. 46		

2 Major Wilbraham served the Syrian campaign of 1840-41, including the advance on Gaza and affair near Askelon.

3 Capt. Wallace served with the 26th in China (Medal), and was present at Chusan, Canton, sea batteries of Amoy, Golongso, defence of Ningpo, at Tsche, Chapoo, Woosung, Shanghae, Chin Kiang Foo, and Nanking.

4 Lt. Speedy served the campaigns of 1841 and 42, in the 13th Light Infantry, and was present at the storming of the Khoord Cabool Pass, affair of Tezeen, forcing the Jugdulluck Pass, reduction of the Fort of Mamoo Khail, defence of Jellalabad and sorties on the 14th Nov. and 1st Dec. 1841, 11th March, 24th March, and 1st April 1842, and general action and defeat of Akbar Khan. Medals for Jellalabad and Cabool.

Full Pay	Half Pay	
19	0	*Paymaster.*—Thomas Gilley, 11 May, 38; *Lieut. & Adj.* 9 Nov. 30.
9	0	*Adjutant.*—*Lieut. Hon.* William Monck, 20 March, 46.
2	0	*Quarter-Master.*—John Hogan, 1 Oct. 47.
17	0	*Surgeon.*—John Mitchell, M.D. 12 Jan. 44; *Assist.-Surg.* 13 Nov. 32.
6	0	*Assistant Surgeons.*—Thomas Moore Sunter, M.B., 6 Oct. 43.
3	0	William Sedgwick Saunders, 6 Nov. 46.

Facings Blue.—*Agents,* Messrs. Cox & Co.—*Irish Agents, Sir* E. R. Borough, *Bt.,* Armit, & Co.

1 Sir Edward Blakeney accompanied the expedition under Major Gen. White to the West Indies, and was present at the capture of Demerara, Berbice, and Essequibo, in 1796: in the course of this service he was three times taken prisoner by Privateers and suffered severe hardships. In 1799 he accompanied the expedition to Holland, and was present in the actions of the 10th and 19th Sept., and also in those of the 2nd and 6th October. In 1807 he sailed with the Royal Fusiliers to the Baltic; joined Lord Cathcart's expedition, and was present at the capture of the Danish Fleet and surrender of Copenhagen. In 1809 he was present at the capture of Martinique. In 1811 he sailed for Lisbon in command of the Fusiliers, and during that and the following campaigns of 1812, 13, and 14, he was present at the battles of Busaco and Albuhera—severely wounded through the thigh; action at Aldea de Ponte, sieges of Ciudad Rodrigo and Badajos—severely wounded through the arm at the assault; battles of Vittoria, Pampeluna, Pyrenees, and Nivelle, besides various minor actions. In 1814 he joined the force against New Orleans, and was present at the assault of the lines before that place. In 1815 he joined the army in Belgium, and was present at the capture of Paris. Sir Edward has received a cross and one clasp for Martinique, Albuhera, Badajos, Vittoria, and Pyrenees.

The "*White Horse,*" on a red ground within the "*Garter,*" and the "*Crown*" over it. In the three corners of the second colour, the "*Royal Cypher and Crown.*" "*Nec aspera terrent.*" The "*Sphinx,*" with the words "EGYPT"—"MARTINIQUE"—"NIAGARA."

Years' Serv. Full Pay.	Years' Serv. Half Pay.	Captains.	Ensign.	Lieut.	Captain.	Brev.-Maj.
60		*Colonel.*				
		Sir Gordon Drummond,[1] GCB. *Ens.* 21 Sept. 1789; *Lt.* 31 Mar. 91; *Capt.* 31 Jan. 92; *Maj.* 28 Feb. 94; *Lt.-Col.* 1 March, 94; *Col.* 1 Jan. 98; *Maj.-Gen.* 1 Jan. 05; *Lt.-Gen.* 4 June, 11; *Gen.* 27 May, 25; *Col.* 8th Foot, 24 Apr. 46.				
		Lieut.-Colonels.				
28	2 10/12	Henry Winchcombe Hartley, *Ens.* 10 Sept. 18; *Lieut.* 1 Oct. 20; *Capt.* P 1 Oct. 25; *Brevet-Major,* 28 June 38; *Major,* P 26 Oct. 41; *Lt.-Col.* P 16 Dec. 45.				
24	0	John Longfield, *Ens.* P 23 June 25; *Lieut.* P 26 Sept. 26; *Capt.* P 30 Jan. 35; *Major,* P 19 Nov. 44; *Lieut.-Col.* 3 Apr. 46.				
17	0	*Majors.*—Edward Harris Greathed, *Ens.* P 22 June, 32; *Lieut.* P 10 May, 33; *Capt.* P 27 Apr. 38; *Maj.* P 3 Apr. 46.				
16	0	Francis Saunderson Holmes, *Ens.* P 8 Feb. 33; *Lieut.* 6 July 35; *Capt.* P 26 Oct. 41; *Major,* P 28 Apr. 46.				
		CAPTAINS.				
16	0	Stephenson Brown	P 8 Mar. 33	P 4 Sept. 35	P 6 May 42	
16	0	Fred. Douglas Lumley	P 22 Oct. 33	8 Jan. 38	P 25 Oct. 42	
14	0	John Hinde	P 28 Feb. 35	P 30 June 37	P 4 July 45	
21	0	James Speedy	15 May 28	23 May 32	14 Jan. 44	
10	0	James Johnston	P 7 June 39	P 13 May 42	P 21 Apr. 46	
12	0	A. Cunningh. Robertson[2]	P 15 Sept. 37	P 20 Aug. 41	P 11 Nov. 45	
14	0	Edwin Gream Daniell[3]	P 2 Oct. 35	P 7 Sept. 38	P 25 Nov. 45	
23	0	Ferdinand White,[6] CB.	P 2 Nov. 26	10 Nov. 31	P 7 Aug. 40	23 Dec. 42
10	0	William Bayly[8]	26 Jan. 39	23 June 42	29 May 48	
		LIEUTENANTS.				
8	0	George Edward Baynes	P 2 July 41	P 12 Dec. 43		
8	0	Richard Wilson Hartley	P 26 Oct. 41	P 27 Sept. 44		
7	0	John Hen. Edw. de Robeck	P 6 May 42	P 19 Nov. 44		
7	0	Alfred Ingilby Garnett	P 13 May 42	P 4 July 45		
7	0	Ellis James Charter	P 25 Oct. 42	P 16 Dec. 45		
6	0	Robert Stuart Baynes, *adj.*	P 28 July 43	P 27 Mar. 46		
8	0	John Ball Campbell	2 July 41	29 Sept. 43		
8	0	Richard Wm. Woods[5]	P 27 Aug. 41	30 Dec. 43		
7	0	Thomas George Souter[5]	21 May 42	28 Jan. 44		
9	0	Thomas Dowse	27 Mar. 40	2 Sept. 45		
8	0	Charles Power Cobbe	13 July 41	3 Apr. 46		
7	0	Daniel Beere	4 May 42	3 Apr. 46		
7	0	Thomas Aldridge	21 May 42	3 Apr. 46		
7	0	Ersk. Nimmo Sandilands	21 May 42	3 Apr. 46		
5	0	George Corry	26 July 44	3 Apr. 46		
5	0	Shaftoe Craster Craster	P 27 Sept. 44	3 Apr. 46		
4	0	Edward Rawlings Hannam	P 4 July 45	P 3 Apr. 46		
6	0	Robert Becher Stowards	23 Dec. 43	P 21 Apr. 46		
5	0	William Henry Herrick	5 Jan. 44	P 28 Apr. 46		
7	0	B. Kennicott M'Dermott[4]	1 Nov. 42	13 Nov. 46		
4	0	M'Kay Rynd	P 16 Dec. 45	P 5 Mar. 47		
7	0	Charles Covell Neame	20 May 42	P 14 Feb. 45		
3	0	Horace Ximenes	P 27 Mar. 46	29 May 48		
		ENSIGNS.				
3	0	W. Huddleston Macadam	P 23 Jan. 46			
4	0	John Biggs	P 2 Sept. 45			
3	0	Wm. Waldegrave Pogson	P 27 Mar. 46			
3	0	George Fuller Walker	14 Apr. 46			
3	0	Allan John Robertson	28 Apr. 46			
2	0	John Vere Wm. Hen. Webb	29 Jan. 47			
2	0	Thomas Beattie Grierson	P 21 May 47			
2	0	Alexander Ross Bayly	2 Apr. 47			
32	4 4/12	*Paymaster.*—Bartholomew Hartley,[7] 30 Oct. 35; *Ens.* 15 Jan. 13; *Lieut.* 26 May, 14; *Capt.* 17 April, 35.				
6	0	*Adjutant.*—*Lieut.* Robert Stuart Baynes, 29 May 48.				
7	0	*Quarter-Master.*—John Ross, 8 Nov. 42.				
13	0	*Surgeon.*—John Chas. Graham Tice, M.D., 23 Jan. 46; *Assist.-Surg.* 15 Jan. 36.				
8	0	*Assistant-Surgeons.*—James Richard Ffennell, 20 Nov. 41.				
3	0	Richard Domenichetti, M.D., 3 Apr. 46.				
3	0	Henry Clinton Martin, 20 March, 46.				

2 Captain Robertson served in the Anglo-Spanish Legion from July 1835 to June 1837. Received a medal for the action of 5th May, 1837; the cross of the 1st class of San Fernando, for the actions of the 15th and 16th March, 1837; and another medal for the storming of Irun, 17th May following: severely wounded in the face by a splinter in the general action on the heights of Ametza, 1st Oct. 1836.

3 Captain Daniell served with the 55th in China (Medal), and was present at Amoy, Chusan, and Chinhae, including the repulse of the night attack.

4 Lieut. M'Dermott served with the Buffs at the battle of Punniar (medal).

5 Lieuts. Woods and Souter were present with the Buffs in the action of Punniar, and have received the Bronze Star.

6 Major White served, as a Captain in the 40th, throughout the operations in Candahar and Affghanistan in 1841 and 42 (Medal), and also at the battle of Maharajpore (Medal).

7 Paymaster Hartley served at the surrender of Martinique; and taking of Guadaloupe in 1815.

8 Capt. Bayly was present at the battle of Plattsburg in 1814.

Facings Blue.—*Agents,* Messrs. Cox & Co.

1 Sir Gordon Drummond served in Holland in 1794 and 95, and was present in Nimeguen during the siege, and at the sortie. Accompanied the expedition to Egypt in 1801, and was present in the battles of the 13th and 21st March; also at the battle of Rhamanieh, and at the surrender of Grand Cairo and of Alexandria. Sir Gordon saw much service in the American war, and commanded in the action near the Falls of Niagara, where he was severely wounded.

The figure of "Britannia," "ROLEIA," "VIMIERA," "CORUNNA," "BUSACO," "SALAMANCA," "VITTORIA," "ST. SEBASTIAN," "NIVE," "PENINSULA," "CABOOL, 1842," "MOODKEE," "FEROZESHAH," "SOBRAON."

Years' Serv. Full Pay	Half Pay					
49		*Colonel.*—P *Sir* James Archibald Hope,[1] K.C.B. *Ens.* 12 Jan. 00; *Lt.* 3 June, 01; *Capt.* 18 Feb. 06; *Major,* 6 March, 11; *Lt.-Col.* 21 June, 13; *Col.* 22 July, 30; *Major.-Gen.* 23 Nov. 41; *Col.* 9th F. 18 Feb. 48.				
41	0	*Lieut.-Colonel.*—P George Lenox Davis,[2] CB., *Ens.* 15 Sept. 08; *Lieut.* 15 Oct. 11; *Capt.* 7 April, 25; *Major,* P 17 Oct. 37; *Lieut.-Col.* 19 Dec. 45.				
21	5 1/12	*Majors.*—Brownlow Villiers Layard,[3] *Ens.* 24 July, 23; *Lieut.* 20 Jan. 26; *Capt.* P 21 Nov. 34; *Brev.-Major,* 9 Nov. 46; *Major,* 3 Sept. 47.				
17	0	Arthur Borton,[4] *Ens.* P 13 July, 32; *Lieut.* P 3 April, 35; *Capt.* 30 July, 41; *Brev.-Major,* 3 April, 46; *Major,* P 19 Sept. 48.				
		CAPTAINS.	**ENSIGN.**	**LIEUT.**	**CAPTAIN.**	**BREV.-MAJ.**
10	0	John Harvey	P 5 Jan. 39	P 16 April 41	P 22 Dec. 43	
14	0	Charles Elmhirst,[6]	P 14 Aug. 35	P 17 Oct. 37	22 Dec. 45	
14	0	Duncan Munro Bethune[5]	17 Apr. 35	21 Mar. 38	22 Dec. 45	
14	0	William Shelton[6]	22 May 35	P 30 Oct. 38	31 Mar. 46	
13	0	Fred. D. Lister[6]	16 Sept. 36	P 22 Feb. 39	P 14 Apr. 46	
10	0	Charles Hamilton Fenton[9]	P 12 Apr. 39	22 Apr. 42	P 23 Jan. 46	
11	0	Charles Henry Leslie[16]	P 20 July 38	16 July 41	P 14 Apr. 46	
13	0	George Cubitt	P 1 July 36	P 26 Apr. 39	P 12 Nov. 47	
10	0	Alexander Taylor[12]	21 June 39	30 July 41	P 23 May 48	
6	0	George Harrington Hawes[8]	24 Nov. 43	4 Jan. 46	P 19 Sept. 48	
		LIEUTENANTS.				
15	0	Lionel Hook,[10] *adj.*	5 Sept. 34	4 Dec. 38		
11	0	Chas. Spencer Gaynor[10]	9 Nov. 38	27 Mar. 40		
11	0	Archibald Bluntish[11]	7 Dec. 38	P 28 July 40		
9	0	Robert Daunt[13]	P 28 July 40	P 16 Aug. 42		
8	0	Tho. E. Bowerbank Dent[10]	P 19 Feb. 41	P 21 July 43		
8	0	Frederic Percy Lea, *r.*	P 24 Sept. 41	19 Aug. 43		
8	0	William Burden[6]	26 Oct. 41	13 Oct. 43		
7	0	Edwin Morton[8]	P 29 April 42	14 Feb. 44		
5	0	Wm. Thomas DeWilton	P 11 Oct. 44	29 Jan. 47		
6	0	Sydney Darling	30 May 43	4 July 45		
3	0	Andrew Sievwright	1 Apr. 46	P 1 Sept. 48		
3	0	Henry Ralph Browne	3 Apr. 46	P 19 Sept. 48		
6	0	John Hanham	P 22 Dec. 43	P 23 Dec. 45		
		ENSIGNS.				
3	0	William Parker Terry	2 Apr. 46			
3	0	Charles Wm. Loinsworth	4 Apr. 46			
3	0	Samuel B. M. Skinner	5 Apr. 46			
2	0	Frederick Smith	P 20 Oct. 47			
2	0	Thomas Rice Hamilton	P 12 Nov. 47			
1	0	Henry John Wilkinson	P 23 May 48			
1	0	Arthur Oswald Richards	P 1 Sept. 48			
1	0	James Legh Thursby	P 19 Sept. 48			
22	17 8/12	*Paymaster.*—Robt. Bluntish,[10] 14 Dec. 09.				
15	0	*Adjutant.—Lieut.* Lionel Hook,[10] 22 Dec. 45.				
42	0	*Quarter-Master.*—P James Scott,[16] 17 Dec. 07.				
11	0	*Surgeon.*—James Mouat, 3 Nov. 48; *Assist.-surg.* 14 Dec. 38.				
5	0	*Assist.-Surgeon.*—David Anderson,[8] M.D., 23 July, 44.				

Facings Yellow.—*Agents,* Sir John Kirkland & Co.—*Irish Agents, Sir* E. R. Borough, *Bt.*; Armit & Co. [*Returned from Bengal,* 10 *July,* 1847.]

3 Major Layard served during the siege, and carried the colors of the 14th Regt. at the storming of Bhurtpore under Lord Combermere, 18th Jan. 1826.

6 Captains Elmhirst, Shelton and Lister (wounded at Istaliff), and Lt. Burden served the campaign in Affghanistan under General Pollock, and have received the Medal for the re-capture of Cabool.

10 Lts. Hook, Gaynor, and Dent, and Paymaster Bluntish, served the campaign of 1842 in Affghanistan (Medal); and that on the Sutlej in 1845-6 (Medal), including the battles of Moodkee, Ferozeshah, & Sobraon.

11 Lieut. Bluntish served the campaign of 1842 in Affghanistan (Medal); and that on the Sutlej (Medal), including the battles of Moodkee and Sobraon.

12 Lieut. Hanham served the campaign on the Sutlej in 1845-46 (Medal), and was present at the battles of Moodkee, (wounded) Ferozeshah, and Sobraon.

1 Sir James Hope served with the expedition to Hanover in 1805-6; to Zealand in 1807, including the siege of Copenhagen; to Sweden in 1808; in Portugal and Spain in 1808-9, including the action at Lugo and battle of Corunna. With the expedition to Walcheren in 1809; the Peninsular campaigns from 1810 to the end of that war in 1814, including the battle of Barrosa, siege of Ciudad Rodrigo, covering the siege of Badajos, affairs in front of Salamanca and at Osma, battle of Vittoria, siege of San Sebastian, passages of the Bidassoa, Gave d'Oleron, and Gave de Pau; battles of the Nivelle, Nive, Orthes, & Toulouse. Sir Jas. has received a cross & a clasp for the battles of Vittoria, Nivelle, Nive, Orthes, & Toulouse.

2 Lieut.-Colonel Davis served with the 9th in the Peninsula from Sept. 1808 until taken prisoner, on the retreat of Sir John Moore, 9 Jan. 1809, at Lugo, where he was left dangerously ill, and he was retained a prisoner of war in France until 1814. In 1842 he served the campaign in Affghanistan (Medal), and was present at the forcing of the Khyber, the Jugdulluck, the Tezeen, and the Haft Kotil Passes, and the assault and capture of Istaliff. He served also in the campaign on the Sutlej, and commanded the 9th at the battle of Sobraon (Medal).

4 Major Borton served the campaign in Affghanistan in 1842 (Medal) under General Pollock; and that on the Sutlej in 1845-6 (Medal) including the battles of Moodkee, and succeeded to the command of the regt. at Ferozeshah (severely wounded).

5 Capt. Bethune served the campaign in Affghanistan in 1842 (Medal),—as adjutant of the 9th at the forcing of the Khyber Pass, and as aide-de-camp to Sir John M'Caskill at the action of Mamookail, forcing the Tezeen Pass, re-capture of Cabool, storm, capture, and destruction of Istaliff. He served also the campaign on the Sutlej in 1845-6 (Medal), as aide-de-camp to Sir John M'Caskill at the battle of Moodkee, where the Major-General was killed,—as aide-de-camp to Brigadier Wallace (who was killed), at Ferozeshah (charger shot),—and in command of the light company of the 9th at Sobraon.

8 Capt. Hawes, Lt. Morton and Dr. Anderson, served the campaign on the Sutlej in 1845-6 (Medal), including the battles of Moodkee, Ferozeshah & Sobraon.

9 Captain Fenton served with the 53rd in the campaign on the Sutlej in 1846 (Medal), including the battles of Buddiwal, Aliwal, and Sobraon.

12 Capt. Taylor served the campaign of 1842 in Affghanistan (Medal); and that on the Sutlej (Medal), including the battles of Moodkee and Ferozeshah (severely wounded).

13 Lt. Daunt served the campaign in Affghanistan (Medal); and that on the Sutlej (Medal), including the battles of Moodkee, Ferozeshah, and Sobraon (wounded).

16 Captain Leslie served with the 80th the campaign on the Sutlej in 1845-6 (Medal), including the battles of Moodkee, Ferozeshah, and Sobraon.

16 Qr.-Master Scott served in Holland, in 1799, and was present in the action of the 19th Sept. Served also in the Peninsula from Aug. 1808 to Aug. 1809, and again from Jan. 1813 to June 1814, including the battle of Vimiera, capture of Oporto, battle of Vittoria, siege of San Sebastian, battles of the Nive on the 9th, 10th, and 11th Dec. 1813.

Years' Serv. Full Pay	Half Pay	The "*Sphinx*," with the words, "EGYPT"—"PENINSULA"—"SOBRAON."				
52		*Colonel*.—P *Sir* Thomas M'Mahon,[1] *Bt.* KCB. *Ens.* 2 Feb. 97; *Lieut.* 24 Oct. 99; *Capt.* 8 Oct. 03; *Major*, 6 Nov. 06; *Lieut.-Col.* 4 May 09; *Col.* 4 June, 14; *Major-Gen.* 27 May, 25; *Lieut.-Gen.* 28 June, 38; *Col.* 10th Foot, 28 Sept. 47.				
24	0	*Lieut.-Colonels.*—Thomas Harte Franks,[2] CB. *Ens.* P7 July, 25; *Lieut.* P26 Sept. 26; *Capt.* P1 Mar. 39, *Major*, P29 Dec. 43; *Lt.-Col.* P28 March, 45.				
30	0	George Dobson Young,[4] *Ens.* 6 April 19; *Lieut.* 25 Aug. 25; *Capt.* 21 Jan. 41; *Major*, 5 Jan. 46; *Lieut.-Col.* 1 Aug. 48.				
29	3 1/12	*Majors.*—Thomas Miller, *Ens.* 9 Jan. 17; *Lieut.* 19 April 27; *Capt.* 16 July 41; *Major*, 1 Aug. 48.				
15	0	William Fenwick,[3] *Ens.* 26 Dec. 34; *Lieut.* P8 June 39; *Capt.* P15 April 42; *Major*, 13 Sept. 48				
		CAPTAINS.	ENSIGN.	LIEUT.	CAPTAIN.	BREV.-MAJ.
13	0	Hy. Errington Longden[3]	16 Sept. 36	P 7 Aug. 40	P 26 Mar. 43	
23	0	John Cassidy Stock[3]	23 Mar. 26	1 Feb. 29	12 July 42	
29	9/12	Mitchell George Sparks[6]	4 Nov. 19	26 Dec. 23	28 June 36	9 Nov. 46
10	0	Samuel Hobson[3].........	P 22 Nov. 39	P 1 April 42	P 25 June 44	
17	0	Richard Mordesley Best	P 20 April 32	P 16 Jan. 35	P 7 June 39	
23	0	Charles Dunbar[7]........	P 3 Aug. 26	9 Nov. 32	5 Sept. 45	
18	0	Malcolm MacGregor	P 6 Sept. 31	P 12 Dec. 34	29 Nov. 41	
10	0	George Frederick Moore..	25 Oct. 39	9 Nov. 41	P 21 May 47	
12	0	Henry Macmanus Sall ..	8 Dec. 37	1 Sept. 40	12 Sept. 48	
11	0	Henry Radford Norman[3]	P 23 Feb. 38	8 April 42	4 Oct. 48	
		LIEUTENANTS.				
11	0	John R. Graham Pattison[3]	28 June 38	8 April 42		
11	0	Robert George Jephson[3]	P 19 Oct. 38	8 April 42		
9	0	J. VanHarthalsMontagu[3] *r*	P 17 April 40	P 22 April 42		
10	0	Charles Doyle Patterson[3]	21 June 39	4 Oct. 41		
8	0	Alexander Montgomerie[3]	P 24 Sept. 41	P 25 Nov. 42		
8	0	Marshall Valentine Bull[3]	P 16 Nov. 41	P 16 Dec. 42		
9	0	John Bendyshe[3]	P 14 Feb. 40	2 Jan. 43		
7	0	John Sweeting Herbert[3]	8 April 42	10 Nov. 43		
7	0	Stewart C. C. Galloway[3]	28 May 42	P 25 June 44		
10	0	George Lewis Dive Amiel[3]	P 20 Dec. 39	P 1 July 42		
7	0	John Miller[3]	8 Nov. 42	4 June 45		
6	0	John William Medhurst[3]	P 20 Jan. 43	15 Sept. 45		
6	0	John Thomas Chandler[3]	24 Mar. 43	P 10 Oct. 45		
5	0	Edwin Dashwood[3]	P 5 Jan. 44	11 Feb. 46		
6	0	John Mapes Webb Ensor	P 22 Dec. 43	22 Dec. 45		
4	0	Richard Cormick Clifford	17 Oct. 45	1 Jan. 47		
6	0	John Edw. Hussey Taylor	P 27 Oct. 43	9 Oct. 46		
4	0	Cuthbert Barlow	18 April 45	P 10 Dec. 47		
6	0	Richard Taylor	17 Aug. 43	17 Nov. 44		
4	0	John Montresor Smyth..	23 Sept. 45	P 7 July 48		
4	0	Charles Nedham	28 Feb. 45	1 Aug. 48		
4	0	Patrick Browne Lucas ..	P 10 Oct. 45	4 Oct. 48		
4	0	C. R. Berkeley Calcott ..	11 Oct. 45	22 Dec. 48		
		ENSIGNS.				
4	0	Joseph Chas. Goodfellow	12 Oct. 45			
4	0	Richard Henry Travers ..	P 9 Dec. 45			
3	0	Geo. T. Whitaker,[3] *adj.*..	8 May 46			
1	0	W. H. P. Gordon Bluett	P 23 May 48			
2	0	John Edmund Whaite ..	18 Dec. 47			
2	0	Thomas Pianta Denne ..	P 5 Nov. 47			
1	0	J. Lee Stanwell Aldersey	P 20 Oct. 48			
1	0	Fred. Browne Sandwith	P 1 Dec. 48			
1	0	Augustus Barton White	22 Dec. 48			
14	0	*Paymaster.*—Edward Lee,[8] 12 Sep. 48; *Ens.* P12 June, 35; *Lieut.* P13 Apr. 39; *Capt.* 1 Aug. 48.				
3	0	*Adjutant.*—*Ens.* George Thomson Whitaker,[3] 24 Aug. 46.				
1	0	*Quarter-Master.*—James Murphy, 3 March 48.				
14	0	*Surgeon.*—Edward Mockler, 7 Aug. 46; *Assist.-Surg.* 25 Sept. 35.				
10	0	*Assistant-Surgeons.*—James Gordon Inglis, M.D., 29 Mar. 39.				
8	0	James Macbeth,[3] M.D., 3 Dec. 41.				
6	0	Vere Webb, 13 Oct. 43.				

Facings Yellow.—*Agents*, Messrs. Cox & Co.

1 Sir Thomas M'Mahon served at the blockade of Malta in 1800. In the Peninsula in 1809, 10, 11, and part of 1812, including the operations against Marshal Massena, occupation of the positions defending Lisbon, pursuit of Massena, and other desultory services. Early in 1813 he proceeded to Calcutta, and was appointed Adjutant-General to Her Majesty's forces in India. In 1817 and 18 he served in the field with the Marquis of Hastings, when his Lordship took command of the army in person, and executed his brilliant and triumphant operations against the whole force of the confederated Mahratta States, which were in succession annihilated.

2 Lieut.-Col. Franks commanded the 10th in the battle of Sobraon (Medal).

3 Major Fenwick, Captains Longden, Stock, Hobson, Lieuts. Norman, Pattison, Jephson, Montagu, Patterson, Montgomerie, Bull, Bendyshe, Herbert, Galloway Amiel, Miller, Medhurst, and Chandler, Ensign Whitaker, and Assist.-Surgeon Macbeth, served with the 10th in the campaign on the Sutlej, and were present in the battle of Sobraon (Medal).

4 Lt.-Col. Young served with the 31st throughout Gen. Pollock's campaign of 1842 in Affghanistan (Medal), including the action of Mazeena, Tezeen, and Jugdulluck, the occupation of Cabool, and the different engagements leading to it. He served also in the campaign on the Sutlej, and was dangerously wounded in the battle of Moodkee (Medal).

5 Major Montizambert served with the 41st in the campaign of 1842 in Affghanistan, and was present in the actions of Goaine and before Ghuznee, occupation and destruction of that fortress and of Cabool. Expedition into Kohistan, storm, capture and destruction of Istaliff, and in the various minor affairs in and between the Bolan and the Khyber Passes.

6 Major Sparks has received the Medal for services in China, having been present with the 49th before Nankin.

7 Captain Dunbar served with the 18th in China, and was present at Canton, Amoy, Chusan, Chinhae, Ningpo, Chapoo, Shanghai, Woosung, and Chin Kiang Foo.

8 Captain Lee served with the 40th in Scinde and Affghanistan from Feb. 1839 to Nov. 1842, and was severely wounded at Candahar on the 12th Jan. 1842. He was present with the 10th in the battle of Sobraon (Medal).

"Salamanca"—"Pyrenees"—"Nivelle"—"Nive"—"Orthes"—"Toulouse"—"Peninsula."

Years' Serv. Full Pay.	Half Pay.		Ensign.	Lieut.	Captain.	Brev.-Maj.
55		*Colonel.* Sir John Wilson,[1] KCB. *Ens.* 26 Mar. 1794; *Lieut.* 19 Aug. 95; *Capt.* 18 Jan. 99; *Major*, 27 May, 1802; *Lieut.-Col.* 22 Dec. 08; *Col.* 4 June, 14; *Maj.-Gen.* 27 May, 25; *Lieut.-Gen.* 28 June, 38; *Col.* 11th Regt. 10 May, 41.				
36	0	*Lieut.-Colonel.*—Henry Keane Bloomfield,[2] *Ens.* 30 Sept. 13; *Lieut.* P 7 Aug. 17; *Capt.* P 1 April, 24; *Brevet-Major*, 28 June, 38; *Major*, P 26 Feb. 41; *Lieut.-Col.* P 27 June, 45.				
39	4	*Majors.*—John Casemir Harold,[3] *Ens.* 25 Sept. 06; *Lieut.* 26 May, 07; *Capt.* 16 Feb. 15; *Brevet-Major*, 10 Jan. 37; *Major*, 6 Nov. 41.				
23	1/12	John Singleton, *Ens.* P 17 June, 26; *Lieut.* P 31 Dec. 27; *Capt.* P 15 Feb. 39; *Major*, P 27 June, 45.				
		Captains.				
31	0	Edward Moore	21 May 18	7 Apr. 25	7 Feb. 39	
17	0	Alexander Cockburn	P 4 Dec. 32	P 27 May 36	P 13 Dec. 42	
16	0	Edward Lynch Blosse	P 15 Nov. 33	P 25 Jan. 39	P 5 Sept. 43	
14	0	Augustus Fred. Jenner	P 9 Oct. 35	P 21 June 39	P 5 April 44	
12	0	William Kenny	P 3 Nov. 37	P 15 Dec. 40	P 30 July 44	
12	0	Lewis Charles Conran	P 17 Mar. 37	2 Apr. 41	P 7 June 44	
23	0	John James Grant	9 Mar. 26	P 12 Feb. 28	22 Mar. 44	
23	1	Robert Webster	10 April 25	26 Nov. 30	29 Dec. 43	
14	0	William Henry Thornton	3 Oct. 35	1 Nov. 38	26 Feb. 45	
8	0	Owen Florance Louis Ward	P 26 Feb. 41	P 13 Dec. 42	P 9 Oct. 46	
		Lieutenants.				
8	0	John Walpole D'Oyly	P 17 Sept. 41	P 5 Sept. 43		
7	0	Lawre. Hartshorne Scott	25 Oct. 42	P 13 Oct. 43		
7	0	James Pattison	P 22 Nov. 42	P 26 Apr. 44		
7	0	J. R. T. Hastings Parker	P 13 Dec. 42	P 26 May 44		
11	0	John Robert Wilton	29 Dec. 38	3 Dec. 41		
6	0	Henry Maynard Ball	P 21 July 43	P 6 Dec. 44		
6	0	John Alexander Hunter	P 5 Sept. 43	P 27 June 45		
7	0	John T. Tho. Boyd, *Adj.*	P 21 Jan. 42	4 July 45		
5	0	Winter Goode	P 26 Apr. 44	P 28 Aug. 46		
5	0	John Roe	P 26 May 44	P 9 Oct. 46		
5	4/12	Richard Maunsell	P 29 Sept. 43	P 4 July 45		
5	0	Joseph Stewart Travers	27 May 44	15 Mar. 48		
5	0	Richard Wingfield Cardiff	P 6 Dec. 44	P 1 Dec. 48		
		Ensigns.				
5	0	Mathias S. Crooke	P 20 Aug. 44			
4	0	Henry John Maclean	30 May 45			
5	0	Geo. J. Arnolds Cameron	23 Feb. 44			
3	0	Harry Clayton Hague	P 28 Aug. 46			
3	0	Philip Doyne Vigors	P 9 Oct. 46			
2	0	John MacHenry	P 2 Apr. 47			
1	0	David Simpson	2 June 48			
1	0	George Todington Osborn	P 1 Dec. 48			
41	3/12	*Paymaster.*—Alexander Boyd,[6] 8 Feb. 21; *Ens.* 14 Sept. 08; *Lieut.* 9 Aug. 09.				
7	0	*Adjutant.*—*Lieut.* John Theodore Thomas Boyd, 10 March, 48.				
11	0	*Quarter-Master.*—J. J. Grant, 5 Oct. 38.				
24	0	*Surgeon.*—John Strange Chapman,[7] 5 Oct. 41; *A.-S.* 28 Sep. 26 *H.A.* 15 Dec. 25.				
7	0	*Assistant-Surgeons.*—Thomas Guy, MD. 28 Jan. 42.				
4	0	Thornton Marshall, 11 April, 45.				

Facings, Green.—*Agent*, Charles R. M'Grigor, Esq.

2 Lt.-Col. Bloomfield served the campaign of 1815, including the battle of Waterloo, storming of Cambray, and capture of Paris.

3 Major Harold served the campaign and battle of Corunna, Expedition to Walcheren and siege of Flushing.

6 Paymaster Boyd accompanied the expedition to Walcheren, and was present at the siege of Flushing.

1 Sir John Wilson served in the West Indies in 1796, and was present at the capture of St. Lucia, including the siege of Morne Fortunée. Also at the taking of St. Vincent, including the operations against the forts in that island. In July following he was made prisoner of war, and carried into Guadaloupe. In Jan. 1797, he was captured again in the British Channel. In 1798 he was at the taking of Minorca. In 1800, he embarked on an expedition against Cadiz. In 1801, to Egypt, and was present in the actions of the 13th and 21st March, and during the whole of that campaign. He proceeded to the Peninsula in 1808, and was severely wounded at the battle of Vimiera. In Jan. 1809, he joined the Lusitanian legion, and acted with this corps during an arduous period of service, in which it was repeatedly engaged with the enemy, being employed in covering Ciudad Rodrigo and Almeida. In June 1810, he was attached to the Portuguese army, and during the subsequent operations against Marshal Soult, as well in the north of Portugal as on the eastern frontier, he commanded an advanced corps of Marshal Beresford's army. In April 1811, he was appointed second in command to General Silveira in the province of Tras os Montes, and acted as such during a period of the operations against Puebla da Senabria, when the place was taken by that general. In Sept. following, he was appointed to the command of the advanced guard of General Bargeliar's Corps d'Armee, and employed on Marshal Massena's rear during his invasion of Portugal, being repeatedly engaged with the enemy. In April 1812, took the field again in command of the Militia of the Province of Minho, and was engaged in active operations against Marshal Marmont, on the frontiers of the Beira. In June 1813, he joined the army at his own request, and was appointed to the command of the 1st Portuguese Brigade of Infantry, with which he served at the siege of San Sebastian, the passage of the Bidassoa, and battle of the Nivelle; and on the 18th Nov. following, being engaged with his Brigade, he was again severely wounded. Sir John has received a medal for San Sebastian.

7 Mr. Chapman served throughout the campaign in Affghanistan under Lord Keane, and was present at the storm and capture of the fortress and citadel of Ghuznee, for which he has received a medal.

"MINDEN"—"GIBRALTAR"—with the *Castle* and *Key*—"*Montis Insignia Calpe*"—"SERINGAPATAM"—"INDIA."

Years' Serv. 62 Full Pay.	Half Pay.					
		Colonel.—Hon. Robert Meade, *Ens.* 7 Nov. 1787; *Lieut.* 15 May, 93; *Capt.* 23 Sept. 93; *Major*, 30 Oct. 94; *Lieut.-Col.* 10 Mar. 95; *Col.* 29 April, 02; *Major-Gen.* 25 Oct. 09; *Lieut.-Gen.* 4 June, 14; *Gen.* 10 Jan. 37; *Col.* 12th Regt. 9 Oct. 23.				
31	$\frac{1}{12}$	*Lieut.-Colonels.*—John Patton, *Ens.* 18 Sept. 17; *Lieut.* P 1 Mar. 21; *Capt.* P 10 Sept. 25; *Major*, P 31 Oct. 34; *Lieut.-Col.* P 18 Aug. 43.				
38	$\frac{1}{12}$	r. Sterling Freeman Glover, *Ens.* 21 Feb. 11; *Lt.* 25 Nov. 13; *Capt.* P 31 May, 33; *Major*, P 18 Aug. 43; *Lt.-Col.* 14 April 46.				
22	0	*Majors.*—William Bell, *Ens.* P 3 April 27; *Lieut.* P 8 Oct. 30; *Capt.* P 3 July, 35; *Major*, 2 Nov. 43.				
16	0	r. James Maxwell Perceval, *Ens.* P 21 June, 33; *Lieut.* P 18 Mar. 36; *Capt.* P 18 May, 38; *Major*, P 14 April, 46.				
		Captains.	**Ensign.**	**Lieut.**	**Captain.**	**Brev-Maj.**
24	0	Alfred Horne	P 19 Nov. 25	P 27 Nov. 28	P 21 Feb. 34	9 Nov. 46
15	0	r. Thomas Brooke	P 31 Oct. 34	P 29 July 36	P 15 May 40	
30	6$\frac{1}{12}$	r. Thomas Moore	30 Mar. 14	25 Nov. 21	30 Sept. 36	9 Nov. 46
19	0	John Francis Kempt	P 16 June 30	19 May 37	29 Apr. 42	
15	0	Hew Dalrymp. Fanshawe, s	4 July 34	P 25 May 38	P 13 May 42	
23	0	r. Patrick Francis Blake	26 Jan. 26	30 July 29	5 May 42	
12	0	Perrott Thornton	P 13 Jan. 37	P 22 Mar. 39	P 12 May 43	
12	0	r. Bennett Watk. Gillman	P 23 Aug. 37	16 Oct. 40	P 18 Aug. 43	
14	0	Francis Gilbert Hamley	P 7 Aug. 35	P 25 July 37	2 Nov. 43	
9	0	r. Geo. Curzon Bisshopp	P 12 June 40	P 13 May 42	P 23 June 48	
13	0	William James Hutchins	2 Dec. 36	1 Dec. 40	20 Dec. 46	
19	0	r. Charles Robert Storey	P 16 June 30	29 Jan. 36	9 June 48	
		Lieutenants.				
15	0	r. William Robert Lewis	P 21 Feb. 34	26 June 38		
13	0	Henry D. Persse, r.	22 April 36	13 Mar. 40		
8	0	r. James Clarke Hearn	P 30 Apr. 41	P 16 Aug. 42		
7	0	r. Richard Atkinson	P 18 Mar. 42	P 17 Feb. 43		
7	0	Henry Segrave	P 29 Apr. 42	P 12 May 43		
7	0	James Wm. Espinasse	P 30 Apr. 42	P 18 Aug. 43		
7	0	Wm. Edward Crofton, *adj.*	15 Apr. 42	5 Jan. 46		
7	0	John Reynolds Palmer	1 May 42	6 Jan. 46		
6	0	Wm. Henry Queade	9 June 43	P 27 June 45		
7	0	r. Edward Foster, *adj.*	2 May 42	14 Apr. 46		
7	0	r. Thomas Dundas	27 Dec. 42	P 14 Apr. 46		
6	0	r. Geo. Richard Littlehale	P 12 May 43	P 21 July 46		
4	0	Thomas George Vereker	P 23 May 45	P 11 Dec. 46		
4	0	Thomas Garner	P 25 Nov. 45	P 31 Dec. 47		
2	$\frac{7}{12}$	Samuel Fairtlough	25 Aug. 46	P 22 Oct. 47		
4	0	r. Edward Herrick	16 Dec. 45	P 23 June 48		
		Ensigns.				
3	0	Hans White	P 3 Apr. 46			
3	0	r. Henry Albert Norris	P 21 July 46			
3	0	r. Henry Cole	9 Sept. 46			
3	0	r. Frederick Bagnell	20 Oct. 46			
3	0	Henry Robson	P 27 Oct. 46			
3	0	George Newton Fendall	11 Dec. 46			
2	0	r. Robert Nasmyth Irving	2 Mar. 47			
2	0	r. Benjamin Samuel Adams	P 31 Dec. 47			
1	0	Thomas White Goodrich	P 23 June 48			
2	0	*Lord* Frederick Montagu	P 23 Apr. 47			
30	7$\frac{1}{12}$	*Paymaster.*—Robert Willington Kyffin, 17 Sept. 41; *Ens.* 14 May 12; *Lieut.* [23 Dec. 13; *Capt.* 11 Sept. 40.				
7	0	*Adjutants.—Lieut.* Wm. Edw. Crofton, 29 March 44.				
7	0	r. *Lieut.* Edward Foster, 14 April, 46.				
6	0	*Quarter-Masters.*—John Cowell, 20 Oct. 43.				
3	0	r. Alexander Nesbitt, 11 Dec. 46.				
13	0	*Surgeons.*—r. William Dick, MD. 7 Aug. 46; *Assist.-Surg.* 13 May 36.				
10	0	Wm. Duncan, 1 Dec. 48; *Assist-Surg.* 8 Nov. 39.				
4	0	*Assistant-Surgeons.*—r. John Small, 30 Dec. 45.				
5	0	Peter Mackey,[1] M.D. 30 July, 44.				

Facings Yellow—*Agents*, Messrs. Cox & Co.

[1st Battalion returned from the Mauritius, 1 March 1848.]

1 Doctor Mackey served with the 9th in the campaign on the Sutlej (Medal) in 1845-6, including the battles of Moodkee and Ferozeshah.

6 Captain Burslem served the campaigns of 1838, 39, and 40 in Affghanistan, with the 13th, and was present at the storm and capture of Ghuznee (medal), assault and capture of the town and forts of Tootumdurrah, storm of Jhoolghur, night attack at Baboo Koosh Ghur, destruction of Khardurrah, and assault of Perwandurrah.

11 Capt. Stapylton and Lieut. Talbot served the campaigns of 1841 and 42, and were present in every action from the Khoord Cabool Pass to Cabool, and detailed in note 7.

5 Captains Jennings and Holcombe, Lieutenant Wade, and Doctor Robertson served with the 13th throughout the campaigns in Affghanistan from 1838 to 1842 inclusive, and were present at the storm and capture of Ghuznée (medal), assault and capture of the town and forts of Tootumdurrah, storm of Jhoolghur, night attack at Baboo Koosh Ghur, destruction of Khardurrah, assault of Perwandurrah, storming of the Khoord Cabool Pass, affair of Tezeen, forcing the Jugdulluck Pass, reduction of the fort of Mamoo Khail, heroic defence of Jellalabad and sorties on the 14th Nov. and 1st Dec. 1841, 11th March, 24th March, and 1st April, 1842; general action and defeat of Akbar Khan before Jellalabad, storming the heights of Jugdulluck, general action of Tezeen, and recapture of Cabool (medal). Capt. Jennings was severely wounded retiring into Jugdulluck with the rear guard, 26th Oct. 1841, and slightly wounded in the general action before Jellalabad, 7th April 1842. Capt. Holcombe was severely wounded [illegible]

The "*Sphinx*," with the words, "EGYPT," "MARTINIQUE," "AVA," "AFFGHANISTAN," "GHUZNI[illegible]
A *Mural Crown*, superscribed "JELLALABAD," "CABOOL, 1842."

Years' Serv. 55 Full Pay.	Half Pay.	
		Colonel.
		P [illegible] *Sir* William Maynard Gomm,[1] KCB. *Ens.* 24 May, 94; *Lieut.* Nov. 94; *Capt.* 25 June, 03; *Major,* 10 Oct. 11; *Lieut.-Col.* 17 Aug. 12; C[illegible] 16 May, 29; *Maj-Gen.* 10 Jan. 37; *Lt.-Gen.* 9 Nov. 46; *Col.* 13th, 10 Mar. [illegible]
28	0	*Lieut.-Colonel.*—Charles Stuart, *Ens.* P 30 Dec. 26; *Lt.* P 31 Dec. 28; *Lieut.* [illegible] *Capt.* P 16 July, 32; *Capt. & Lieut.-Col.* 15 April, 45.
30	5 11/12	*Majors.*—P Richard Martin Meredith,[2] *Ens.* 1 April, 13; *Lieut.* 26 Jan. 1[illegible] *Capt.* 2 Sept. 38; *Major,* 15 Dec. 43.
27	0	A. P. S. Wilkinson,[3] CB. *Ens.* 25 Dec. 22; *Lieut.* 16 Dec. 24; *Capt.* 6 Sept. 3[illegible] *Brev.-Maj.* 4 Oct. 42; *Major,* P 3 Nov. 46.

Full Pay	Half Pay	Captains.	Ensign.	Lieut.	Captain.	Brev.-Ma[j.]
22	0	James Henry Fenwick[4] ..	25 Oct. 27	30 Oct. 31	P 15 Dec. 40	4 Oct. [illegible]
21	0	Peter Redmond Jennings[5]	P 5 Aug. 28	P 22 June 32	13 Jan. 42	
19	0	Alex. Essex F. Holcombe[5]	P 3 Dec. 30	12 Sept. 34	22 July 42	
18	0	George King[4]	13 April 31	P 16 Jan. 35	2 Aug. 42	
17	0	Rollo Gillespie Burslem[6]	13 April 32	P 27 Mar. 35	20 Dec. 42	
18	0	John Stewart Wood,[7] *s.*	12 April 31	P 21 Aug. 35	30 June 43	
17	0	*Hon.* E. J. W. Forester[4]	P 28 Dec. 32	9 Apr. 38	23 May 45	
14	0	George Mein,[8] *s.*	19 June 35	21 April 39	P 3 Nov. 46	
11	0	John William Cox[9]	26 June 38	22 Apr. 40	P 9 Apr. 47	
10	0	Granville G. C. Stapylton[11]	15 June 39	13 Jan. 42	P 28 Apr. 48	
		Lieutenants.				
13	0	George Wade,[5] *adj.*	27 May 36	6 Sept. 39		
11	0	Fred. Van Straubenzee,[10] *r.*	P 17 Aug. 38	30 Apr. 41		
9	0	George Talbot[11]	7 Feb. 40	22 July 42		
9	0	Gerald Fitz Gerald King	P 3 Nov. 40	14 Oct. 42		
7	0	George Henry Tyler	23 July 42	14 Apr. 46		
5	0	Russell Charles Stanhope	P 23 Feb. 44	P 27 Feb. 46		
7	0	Charles Rowley Platt ..	P 30 Sept. 42	26 July 44		
6	0	Melville Browne	24 Feb. 43	P 9 Apr. 47		
6	0	Henry Hogge	P 22 Dec. 43	P 24 Sept. 47		
4	0	John Busby	P 3 Oct. 45	P 24 Oct. 47		
5	0	James Nicol	24 May 44	P 28 Apr. 48		
		Ensigns.				
4	0	Edward Lynch	P 30 May 45			
3	0	Hugh Maurice Jones ..	P 22 Apr. 46			
3	0	Kenneth Rob. Murchison	P 28 Apr. 46			
3	0	Robert Peel	P 21 July 46			
3	0	William Henry Kerr ...	P 31 July 46			
3	0	Stanton Senior	P 3 Nov. 46			
2	0	Alfred P. F. C. Somerset	22 Jan. 47			
2	0	Rbt. Blackall Montgomery	P 24 Sept. 47			
2	0	Henry Stone	P 24 Dec. 47			
1	0	Wilson Henry Jones....	P 28 Apr. 48			

4 Major Fenwick, Capt. Ki[ng], and the Hon. Capt. Forester serv[ed] throughout the campaigns in Af[f]ghanistan from 1838 to 1842 incl[u]sive, including the storm and captu[re] of Ghuznee (medal), storming [the] Khoord Cabool Pass, affair of T[e]zeen, forcing the Jugdulluck Pa[ss], reduction of the fort of Mam[oo] Khail, defence of Jellalabad a[nd] sorties on the 14th Nov. and [1st] Dec. 1841, 11th March, 24th Mar[ch] and 1st April, 1842, general act[ion] and defeat of Akbar Khan be[fore] Jellalabad (medal), storming [the] heights of Jugdulluck, gen[eral] action of Tezeen, and recapture of Cabool (meda[l]). Capt. Forester served as an aide-de-camp to Sir W[il]loughby Cotton in 1838, 39, and 40, and at Ghuznee.

12 Paymaster Carew served with the 17th Lance[rs] the campaign on the Nerbudda in 1814; in [illegible] and Kutch, including the siege of Anjar in 18[illegible] Dwarkar, 1816; the campaign against the Pindar[ees] 1817 and 18; in Candeish, 1820; and in K[illegible] 1821. He served in the 13th Lt. Inf. with the Arm[y of] the Indus, during 1838, 39, and 40, and was at [the] capture of Ghuznee, for which he has received a m[edal].

Full Pay	Half Pay	
31	7 1/12	*Paymaster.*—Harry Carew,[12] 1 Feb. 31; *Ens.* 1 Jan. 11; *Lieut.* 19 March, [illegible]
13	0	*Adjutant.*—*Lieut.* George Wade,[5] 26 June 46.
1	0	*Quarter-Master.*—Duncan M'Naughten, 15 Aug. 48. [*Hosp.-Assist.* 29 Dec. [illegible]
24	0	*Surgeon.*—John Robertson,[5] MD. 14 Dec. 41; *Assist.-Surgeon,* 13 March, [illegible]
8	0	*Assistant-Surgeon.*—Frederick William Tupper, 8 June 41.

Facings Blue.—*Agts.*, Messrs. Cox & Co.—*Irish Agts.*, *Sir* E. R. Borough, *Bt.*, Armit & C[o.]

[Returned from India, 18 July 45.]

1 Sir William Gomm served in the expedition to the Helder, in 1799, including the action of the [illegible] Sept. at Bergen. Expedition on the coast of France and Spain, under Sir James Pulteney, in 1800. Ex[]pedition to Hanover, in 1805; and that to Stralsund and Copenhagen, in 1807. Campaign of 1808–9, in[]cluding the battles of Roleia, Vimiera, and Corunna. Expedition to Walcheren, and siege of Flushing [in] 1809. Proceeded again to the Peninsula, in 1810, where he served during the remainder of the war th[e] principal part of the time as an Assistant-Quarter-Master-General, including the battles of Busaco a[nd] Fuentes d'Onor, assault and capture of Badajoz, battle of Salamanca; action at Villa Muriel, battle [of] Vittoria, siege of San Sebastian, and battle of the Nive. Served also the campaign of 1815, including t[he] battle of Waterloo. Sir William has received a cross and one clasp.

2 Major Meredith served in the Peninsula from Nov. 1813 to June 1814, and was actively employ[ed] from the Pyrenees to the battle of Toulouse, at which he was present. Served in Canada in 1814 and [was] present at capture of Rangoon, May 1824.

3 Major Wilkinson served with the 13th throughout the Burmese war, including the landing at Cheduba, storming the Stockade, and capture of the Island; affair of Kumaroot, storming seven Stockades at [illegible]root, attack and capture of Syriam, actions near Rangoon on the 1st, 5th, and 7th Dec. 1824; storming [of] Kokien (wounded); expedition to Bassein, and capture of Negrais, Bassein, and Lamina; actions at [illegible]bike and Napadee, storming of Melloon, and battle of Pagahm Mew. He also served throughout [the] campaigns in Affghanistan from 1838 to 1842 inclusive, including the expedition to Girishk, storm a[nd] capture of Ghuznee (medal), storming of the Khoord Cabool Pass, affair of Tezeen, forcing the Jugdulluck Pass, reduction of the fort of Mamoo Khail, heroic defence of Jellalabad, and sorties on the 14th Nov. a[nd] 1st Dec. 1841, 11th March, 24th March, and 1st April, 1842; general action and defeat of Akbar Khan be[fore] Jellalabad on the 7th April 1842 (medal), in which action he commanded the centre column after the [death] of Colonel Dennie. Commanded the 13th in storming the heights of Jugdulluck, in the general action [of] Tezeen, and at the recapture of Cabool (medal), for which he has received the Companionship of the B[ath].

10 Lieut. Straubenzee served the campaigns of 1840, 41, and 42, and was [illegible]

7 Captain Wood served the campaign against the Rajah of Coorg in 1834, and was at the storming of the several stockades leading to the capture of the Huggal Pass. He served also throughout the campaigns in Affghanistan,—in 1838 and 39 as aide-de-camp to Sir Robert Sale, and in 1840, 41, and 42 as adjutant to the 13th, and was present at the storm and capture of Ghuznee (medal), assault and capture of the town and forts of Tootumdurrah, storm of Jooighur (wounded), night attack at Baboo Koosh Ghur, destruction of Kardurrah, assault of Purwandurrah, storming the Khoord Cabool Pass, affair of Tezeen, forcing the Jugdulluck Pass, reduction of the fort of Mamoo Khail, defence of Jellalabad (wounded 17th March 1842) and sorties on the 14th Nov. and 1st Dec. 1841, 11 March, 24th March, and 1st April 1842; general action and defeat of Akbar Khan before Jellalabad (medal)—horse sabred under him; storming the Jugdulluck Pass, general action at Tezeen, and recapture of Cabool (medal).

8 Capt. Mein served with the 13th in Affghanistan in 1838, 39, 40, and 41, and was present at the storm and capture of Ghuznee (medal), assault and capture of the town and forts of Tootumdurrah, storm of Jooighur, night attack at Baboo Koosh Ghur, destruction of Khardurrah, assault of Perwandurrah, and storming the Khoord Cabool Pass, where he was dangerously wounded and sent into Cabool, and was consequently present with the force under Major-General Elphinstone during the insurrection at Cabool, and on the disastrous retreat, until taken prisoner at Tezeen on the 9th Jan. 1842; he was released with the other Cabool captives in September following.

9 Capt. Cox served the campaigns of 1840, 41, and 42, and was present at Tootumdurrah, Jhooighur, Baboo Koosh Ghur, Khardurrah, storming the Khoord Cabool Pass, and in all the following actions, detailed in note 5.

On the Bear-skin Caps of the Grenadiers and Drummers, the *White Horse*, "*Nec aspera terrent.*"—"TOURNAY"—"CORUNNA"—"JAVA"—"WATERLOO"—"BHURTPORE." The *Royal Tiger*, superscribed "INDIA."

Years' Serv.		
Full Pay.	Half Pay.	
66		***Colonel.*** *Sir* James Watson,[1] KCB., *Ens.* 24 June, 1783; *Lieut.* 18 April, 92; *Capt.* 11 Mar. 95; *Major*, 3 Dec. 02; *Lieut.-Col.* 15 May, 06; *Col.* 4 June, 14; *Maj-Gen.* 19 July, 21; *Lieut.-Gen.* 10 Jan. 37; *Col.* 14th Regt. 24 May, 37.
34	$\frac{7}{12}$	*Lieut.-Colonel.*—Maurice Barlow, *Ens.* P21 July, 14; *Lieut.* 23 March, 15; *Capt.* P20 Dec. 21; *Major*, P12 June, 28; *Brevet-Lieut.-Col.* 23 Nov. 41; *Lieut.-Col.* 24 Dec. 47.
28	0	*Majors.*—James Watson,[3] *Ens.* 22 Mar. 21; *Lieut.* P25 Dec. 22; *Capt.* P14 Dec. 32; *Major*, P10 Jan. 40.
40	0	Cha. Rayner Newman,[5] *Ens.* 28 Sept. 09; *Lieut.* 15 Aug. 11; *Capt.* P1 May, 28; *Brev.-Major*, 23 Nov. 41; *Major*, 24 Dec. 47.

Full Pay	Half Pay		ENSIGN.	LIEUT.	CAPTAIN.	BREV.-MAJ.
		CAPTAINS.				
24	0	Tho. Holmes Tidy[6]	14 April 25	P28 Sept. 26	P 2 Oct. 35	9 Nov. 46
27	14	[illegible] Joseph Smith[7]	16 Feb. 08	14 Mar. 11	13 Mar. 27	23 Nov. 41
23	0	John Watson	20 July 26	P17 May 27	P11 Aug. 37	
18	6	*Sir* Jas. E. Alexander,[8] *s.*	P20 Jan. 25	P26 Nov. 25	P18 June 30	9 Nov. 46
24	0	Ralph Budd	10 Mar. 25	P16 Mar. 26	1 June 41	
18	0	John Dwyer	P19 July 31	21 Nov. 34	22 Jan. 46	
15	0	Edward Archdall	6 Sept. 34	P25*Nov. 36	P 3 Apr. 46	
15	0	William Douglas	P23 May 34	1 Aug. 38	18 Sept. 46	
24	0	George Black	9 April 25	12 July 27	16 July 41	
14	0	Edward Prothero, *s.*	P 2 Oct. 35	P26 April 39	24 Dec. 47	
		LIEUTENANTS.				
14	0	William Blundell	P30 Oct. 35	P10 Jan. 40		
13	0	Rob. Wm. Romer	P30 Sept. 36	15 Jan. 40		
10	0	John Peter Hall........	P26 April 39	P23 April 41		
10	0	David Tho. Armstrong, *r.*	22 Nov. 39	P28 Jan. 42		
10	0	John M'Culloch O'Toole[11]	21 June 39	P24 June 42		
9	0	Loftus Hare	P31 Jan. 40	18 Nov. 45		
7	0	William Cosmo Trevor ..	11 Mar. 42	22 Jan. 46		
7	0	Frederick Hammersley..	P 1 July 42	P21 Apr. 46		
7	0	Robert Macdonald, *adj.*	20 May 42	20 June 46		
5	0	Charles Cecil Newman ..	26 July 44	2 Oct. 46		
4	0	Browning Drew	P 7 Mar. 45	P 8 Jan. 47		
4	0	Henry Townsend	30 Dec. 45	24 Dec. 47		
7	0	Jon. Willington Shelton	3 Nov. 42	23 May 45		
		ENSIGNS.				
3	0	Simeon Charles Lousada	P 3 Apr. 46			
3	0	George Slater	21 Apr. 46			
3	0	William Hanbury Hawley	P10 July 46			
3	0	Charles Francis Fuller ..	2 Oct. 46			
3	0	C. J. Smith Dodsworth..	P27 Oct. 46			
2	0	Thomas Segrave........	P 8 Jan. 47			
2	0	W. R. Benningham M'Gwire	24 Dec. 47			
1	0	John Barlow	P 1 Aug. 48			

11 Lieut O'Toole served with the 49th on the China expedition, and was present at the attack and capture of Amoy, the second capture of Chusan, attack and capture of Chinhae, occupation of Ningpo and repulse of the night attack, attack and capture of Segoan, Chapoo, Woosung, and Chin Kiang Foo, and the demonstration before Nankin.

5 Major Newman was at the siege and storming of Bhurtpore.

6 Major Tidy served at the siege and capture of Bhurtpore.

7 Major Smith served with the 27th in Sicily when Murat threatened it with invasion; and, for nearly three years in the Peninsula, including the battle of Castalla, and the attack at the Col d'Ordal.

8 Sir J. Alexander served four years in the Madras cavalry previous to being transferred to H. M. Dragoons; was present with the armies in the field during the late Burman, Persian, Turkish, Portuguese, and Caffre wars.

10 Quarter-Master Goddard was at Waterloo, 18th June, and storming of Cambray, 24th June, 1815. Present at the siege of Hattrass. Served the campaign of 1817 and 18, in the Deccan. Present at the siege and storming of Bhurtpore, 1826.

Full Pay	Half Pay	
30	$2\frac{10}{12}$	*Paymaster.*—Peter Valentine Wood, 2 Aug. 31; *Ens.* 17 Sept. 07; *Lieut.* 3 Jan. 11; *Capt.* 13 Feb. 28.
7	0	*Adjutant.*—*Lieut.* Robert Macdonald, 2 Oct. 46.
26	0	*Quarter-Master.*—[illegible] Samuel Goddard,[10] 20 March. 23
23	0	*Surgeon.*—Wm. Wallace, M.D., 2 July, 41; *A.S.* 8 Mar. 27; *H.A.* 17 Aug. 26.
8	0	*Assist.-Surg.*—John Elliott Carte, M.D. 31 Dec. 41.

Facings Buff.—*Agents*, Messrs. Downes & Son.

[Returned from Nova Scotia, 28 June 1847.]

1 Sir James Watson served with the 14th Regt. on the Continent under the Duke of York in 1793 and 94; at the reduction of the islands of St. Lucie and Trinidad in 1796 and 97. Commanded the 14th regiment at the capture of the Isles of France and Java, including the assault and capture of Djocjocarta; commanded the expedition that captured the piratical state of Sambas in Borneo in 1813; at the capture of the fort of Hattras, and in the Pindarree and Mahratta wars; actively assisted at the reduction of the fortress of Dhomone Mundela (where he led the storming party), Gurra Kotah, and Asseerghur. Medal for Java.

3 Major Watson served at the siege and storming of Bhurtpore.

"MARTINIQUE"—"GUADALOUPE."

Years' Serv.		
57		***Colonel.***
		Sir Phineas Riall,[1] KCH. *Ens.* 31 Jan. 1792; *Lieut.* 28 Feb. 94; *Capt.* 31 May, 94; *Major*, 8 Dec. 94; *Lieut.-Col.* 1 Jan. 1800; *Col.* 25 July, 10; *Major-Gen.* 4 June, 13; *Lieut.-Gen.* 27 May, 25; *Gen.* 23 Nov. 41; *Col.* 15th Foot, 24 Apr. 46.
Full Pay.	**Half Pay.**	***Lieut.-Colonel.***
35	$\frac{4}{12}$	Thomas A. Drought, *Ens.* 11 Nov. 13; *Lieut.* P 16 Oct. 17; *Capt.* P 10 Oct. 22; *Major*, P 31 Dec. 30; *Lieut.-Col.* P 21 March 45.
		Majors.
23	0	George Pinder, *Ens.* P 24 Aug. 26; *Lieut.* P 31 Dec. 30; *Capt.* P 21 Oct. 36; *Major*, P 24 May, 44.
26	$\frac{1}{12}$	Robert Alexander Cuthbert, *Ens.* P 25 Sept. 23; *Lieut.* P 7 July 25; *Capt.* P 28 May 29; *Major*, P 21 March 45.

Full Pay.	Half Pay.	CAPTAINS.	ENSIGN.	LIEUT.	CAPTAIN.	BREV.-MAJ.
24	0	James Robert Brunker ..	9 April 25	9 Sept. 28	P 14 Sept. 32	9 Nov. 46
25	0	R. H. J. B. M'Cumming	P 16 Dec. 24	P 6 Oct. 25	P 26 Nov. 30	9 Nov. 46
19	0	John A. Cole	14 Jan. 30	26 May 33	P 14 Dec. 38	
18	0	John Hope Wingfield ..	P 17 May 31	P 4 Oct. 33	P 18 Jan. 39	
19	0	Fitz William Walker....	P 31 Dec. 30	P 17 June 36	P 21 June 39	
16	0	Henry Grierson	P 9 Aug. 33	P 24 Feb. 37	P 6 May 42	
13	0	Daniel Capel	P 29 April 36	P 14 Dec. 38	P 22 Sept. 43	
13	0	*Hon.* Francis Colborne, *s.*	P 1 Oct. 36	P 18 Jan. 39	P 24 May 44	
14	0	William Fulton	P 10 Apr. 35	P 11 Oct. 39	P 12 Apr. 44	
12	0	Charles Edward Astell ..	P 24 Feb. 37	P 22 June 39	P 3 Oct. 48	
		LIEUTENANTS.				
12	0	James Allix Wilkinson ..	10 Mar. 37	P 4 Aug. 40		
11	0	Algr. Robinson Sewell, *adj.*	P 16 Feb. 38	P 18 Sept. 40		
11	0	William Boyle, *d. adj.* ..	6 Dec. 38	P 21 May 41		
10	0	Edward Pardoe	P 18 Jan. 39	P 22 Apr. 42		
10	0	John Smith............	P 12 July 39	P 23 June 43		
10	0	C. Theodore de Montenach	P 13 July 39	P 22 Sept. 43		
8	$\frac{4}{12}$	William West Turner[2] ..	19 Feb. 41	P 27 Dec. 42		
9	0	Johnson Wilkinson	P 4 Aug. 40	P 24 May 44		
7	0	William Drake Hague ..	P 6 May 42	P 13 June 45		
6	0	Charles Wm. Clayton East	P 23 June 43	P 6 Nov. 46		
6	0	Henry W. Walters	P 21 July 43	P 28 April 48		
5	$\frac{2}{12}$	Digby Gerahty	P 4 Aug. 43	P 13 Mar. 46		
5	0	Christopher Sayers......	5 Jan. 44	P 3 Oct. 48		
		ENSIGNS.				
4	0	Augustus Fred. Warburton	P 13 June 45			
5	0	Frederick Henry Mylius	11 July 45			
2	0	Alfred Todd	P 25 June 47			
1	0	James Walmsley	P 31 Mar. 48			
1	0	Joseph Tuite	P 28 April 48			
1	0	Wm. Robert Thompson..	P 29 April 48			
1	0	Andrew John Cowper ..	P 18 Aug. 48			
1	0	Francis Powell Hopkins	P 3 Oct. 48			

[2] Lieut. Turner served with the 26th in China, and was present at the defence of Ningpo, action of Tseke, attack and ture of Chapoo, Shanghae, Woosung, and Chin Kiang Foo.

Full Pay.	Half Pay.	
19	5	*Paymaster.*—Robert MacGregor, 20 Oct. 48; *Ens.* 6 Oct. 25; *Lt.* 8 Aug. 27; *Capt.* 12 May 48.
11	0	*Adjutant.*—*Lieut.* Algernon Robinson Sewell, 16 May, 45.
11	0	*Quarter-Master.*—Robert Imray, 8 June, 38.
28	$5\frac{2}{12}$	*Surgeon.*—Wm. Dobson, 29 Mar. 39; *Assist.-Surg.* 22 Sept. 25; *Hosp.-Assist.* 6 May, 15.
10	0	*Assist.-Surgeons.*—Thomas Henry O'Flaherty, 15 Nov. 39.
4	0	James Alexander Wishart, M.D., 9 Dec. 45.

Facings Yellow—*Agents, Sir* John Kirkland & Co.

[1] Sir Phineas Riall has received a medal and one clasp for Martinique and Guadaloupe. Served in America in 1813, and was severely wounded at the battle of Chippawa.

Years' Serv. Full Pay.	Half Pay.					
64		**Colonel.**				
		☩ Wm. Carr, *Viscount* Beresford,[1] GCB. GCH. *Ens.* 27 Aug. 1785; *Lieut.* 25 June, 89; *Capt.* 24 Jan 91; *Major,* 1 March, 94; *Lieut.-Col.* 11 Aug. 94; *Col.* 1 Jan. 00; *Major-Gen.* 25 April, 08; *Lieut.-Gen.* 1 Jan. 12; *Gen.* 27 May, 25: *Col.* 16 Regt. 15 March, 23.				
		Lieut.-Colonel.				
29	0	Robert Luxmoore, *Ens.* 1 June, 20; *Lieut.* 11 June 24; *Capt.* P 31 Aug. 30; *Major,* P 18 April, 45; *Lieut.-Col.* P 10 March, 48.				
36	1/12	*Majors.*—James Brand, *Ens.* 11 March, 13; *Lieut.* 17 Aug. 20; *Capt.* 25 April, 28; *Brev.-Major,* 23 Nov. 41; *Major,* 19 Aug. 42.				
34	0	Charles Murray,[3] *2d Lieut.* 1 Sept. 15; *Lieut.* 13 Oct. 21; *Capt.* 5 May 35; *Brev.-Major,* 9 Nov. 46; *Major,* P 10 March, 48.				
			ENSIGN.	LIEUT.	CAPTAIN.	BREV.-MAJ.
		Captains.				
23	0	William Ashmore	P 18 Feb. 26	P 27 Apr. 27	29 Dec. 40	
23	10 4/12	Alexander Munro	6 Oct. 15	26 Apr. 28	1 July 41	
15	0	*Hon.* James Colborne, *s.*	P 21 Mar. 34	26 June 38	P 23 July 41	
23	0	John Willett Payne Audain	14 Dec. 26	2 Oct. 28	27 May 42	
22	1 10/12	Henry Copinger.........	28 Apr. 25	6 Mar. 28	8 July 42	
18	0	Charles Hawker.........	22 Feb. 31	P 20 July 32	P 25 Aug. 43	
17	0	John Henderson.........	P 20 Jan. 32	28 Nov. 34	P 10 Nov. 43	
23	4/12	Francis Lucas[4]	P 1 Oct. 25	24 Oct. 27	19 Nov. 44	
10	0	Chas. Lorenzo de Winton	P 15 Feb. 39	2 July 41	P 10 Mar. 48	
13	0	George Douglas	20 May 36	P 30 Aug. 39	P 14 Nov. 45	
		Lieutenants.				
19	0	Chas. Jeffries Carter	18 June 30	28 Dec. 31		
10	0	John Octavius Chichester	P 26 Oct. 39	27 May 42		
9	0	George Patrick Goldie ..	P 24 Apr. 40	8 July 42		
9	0	Charles Armstrong	P 25 Apr. 40	19 Aug. 42		
9	0	Geo. Fred. Macdonald, *r.*	P 8 May 40	P 25 Aug. 43		
9	0	Henry Alfred Macdonald	30 Dec. 40	P 10 Nov. 43		
7	0	George John Peacocke ..	8 July 42	P 24 Oct. 45		
6	0	L. Stanhope Rich. Lovell	22 Dec. 43	P 3 Nov. 46		
5	0	Geo. De la Poer Beresford	P 19 April 44	P 2 Mar. 47		
7	0	Thomas C. Higginson ..	10 Apr. 42	8 July 46		
3	0	James William Bostock[5]	P 1 May 46	P 20 Oct. 48		
		Ensigns.				
4	0	Charles Coote Grant, *adj*	P 9 May 45			
4	0	William Armstrong.....	P 24 Oct. 45			
4	0	Thomas Lyons.........	P 31 Oct. 45			
4	0	Fred. Wardell Ruxton ..	P 19 Dec. 45			
3	0	John Parker	P 3 Nov. 46			
3	0	Henry Evans Quin......	24 Aug. 46			
2	0	Cook Sibbs Flower......	P 20 July 47			
1	0	William Stackpoole	P 14 April 48			
1	0	John Crosby Vaughan....	22 Dec. 48			
18	0	*Paymaster.*—Wm. Alphonso Kirk, 22 Nov 44; *Ens.* 30 Dec. 31; *Lt.* 8 Feb. 34.				
4	0	*Adjutant.*—*Ensign* Charles Coote Grant, 31 Dec. 47.				
1	0	*Quarter-Master.*—John Banyard, 3 March, 48.				
10	0	*Surgeon.*—Benjamin Usher Hamilton, M.D. 23 March 47; *Assist.-Surg.* 22 Feb. 39.				
4	0	*Assistant-Surgeons.*—Edward John Kennedy, M.D. 14 Nov. 45.				
2	0	Henry Fowle Smith, 23 March 47.				

3 Major Murray served in the Kandian war in Ceylon, in 1817 and 18.

4 Captain Lucas, with the effective men of the wing of the 6th Regt. stationed at Aden, formed part of an expedition of 500 men under the command of Lieut.-Col. Pennycuick, which destroyed the Arab posts of Sheik Medi and Sheik Othman, and skirmished between those places on the 6th Oct. 1841.

5 Lieut. Bostock served as acting Aide-de-Camp to Brigadier Campbell commanding the 2nd Cavalry Brigade of Cavalry of the Army of the Sutlej, and was present at the battle of Sobraon (Medal).

Facings Yellow—*Agents, Sir* John Kirkland & Co.

1 Lord Beresford has received a Cross and seven Clasps for Corunna, Busaco, Albuhera, Badajos, Salamanca, (severely wounded) Vittoria, Pyrenees, Nivelle, Nive, Orthes, and Toulouse.

The *Royal Tiger*, superscribed "HINDOOSTAN"—"AFFGHANISTAN"—"GHUZNEE"—"KHELAT.

Years' Serv. 57 Full Pay.	Half Pay.					
		Colonel.				
		P W *Sir* Peregrine Maitland,[1] KCB. *Ens.* 25 June, 1792; *Lieut. & Capt.* 30 April, 94; *Capt. & Lieut.-Col.* 25 June, 1803; *Col.* 1 Jan. 12; *Major-Gen.* 4 June, 14; *Lieut.-Gen.* 22 July 30; *Col.* 17th Regt. 2 Jan. 43.				
		Lieut.-Colonel.				
38	7/12	P W John Stoyte,[2] *Ens.* 21 Mar. 11; *Lieut.* 4 July, 13; *Capt.* P 27 Jan. 25; *Brev.-Major*, 28 June, 38; *Major*, 8 Jan. 41; *Lt.-Col.* 3 Apr. 46.				
28	12	*Majors.*—P Philip M'Pherson, CB.[3] *Ens.* 2 Nov. 09; *Lt.* 13 June, 11; *Capt.* 13 Mar. 27; *Brev.-Maj.* 23 Nov. 41; *Brev.-Lt.-Col.* 4 July, 43; *Maj.* 1 Aug. 44.				
24	1 8/12	Daniel Gardiner Freer, *Ens.* 20 Nov. 23; *Lieut.* P 8 April, 26; *Capt.* 7 May, 41; *Major*, P 12 Nov. 47.				
			ENSIGN.	LIEUT.	CAPTAIN.	BREV.-MAJ.
		CAPTAINS.				
16	0	Legendre Ch. Bourchier[4]	P 5 Apr. 33	P 12 Feb. 36	P 20 July 38	
24	0	P W David Cooper[5]	11 Aug. 25	1 May 28	16 Nov. 41	
14	0	Oliver Paget Bourke[4] ..	P 11 Dec. 35	P 27 Oct. 37	7 Nov. 44	
13	0	Thos. Ormaby Ruttledge[4]	P 29 Apr. 36	P 23 Apr. 38	9 Sept. 46	
13	0	Edward Henry Cormick[4]	P 20 July 36	P 11 Jan. 39	17 Sept. 47	
8	0	William Reader	16 July 41	P 5 Dec. 43	P 2 July 47	
9	0	E.F.N. *Lord* Burghersh, *s.*	20 Nov. 40	P 27 Jan. 43	P 13 July 47	
12	0	John L. Croker[4]	18 Mar. 37	5 June 39	P 5 Nov. 47	
12	0	Edward Croker	P 27 Oct. 37	21 Oct. 39	P 10 Mar. 48	
12	0	William Edwards[6]	P 1 Dec. 37	P 28 Dec. 41	13 Dec. 47	
		LIEUTENANTS.				
12	0	John Pennefather Perceval	17 Feb. 37	16 May 39		
11	0	Wm. Gordon	P 20 July 38	P 3 Apr. 40		
10	0	Alex. M'Kinstry	P 22 Feb. 39	P 25 Sept. 40		
10	0	Johnson Bourne, *r.*	P 11 Jan. 39	P 19 Nov. 41		
10	0	Rich. John Ross O'Conor	P 12 Apr. 39	1 Feb. 42		
9	0	Lethbridge Charles Moore[4]	3 Apr. 40	6 Aug. 42		
10	0	John Ballard Gardiner[10]	25 Oct. 39	19 Aug. 42		
12	0	Campbell Sawers, *adj.* ..	P 14 Apr. 37	30 Oct. 40		
9	0	William A. Armstrong ..	P 1 Nov. 40	28 July 43		
7	0	William Belfield[10]	P 13 May 42	P 29 July 43		
3	0	Archibald W. Dickson ..	P 20 Mar. 46	P 29 Dec. 46		
4	0	Henry Thwaites........	P 1 Aug. 45	8 Oct. 47		
3	0	Philip M'Pherson	27 Oct. 46	P 10 Mar. 48		
2	0	David Latouche Colthurst	P 20 July 47	P 10 Nov. 48		
		ENSIGNS.				
6	0	John Nolan............	P 29 July 43			
5	0	Richard Bolton Neynoe..	2 Aug. 44			
2	0	Acton De Veulle	P 19 Nov. 47			
1	0	Fred. J. Sandys Lindesay	P 10 Mar. 48			
2	0	William Pollard........	P 2 Mar. 47			
1	0	Clement H. Jno. Heigham	P 10 Nov. 48			
1	0	George Tito Brice	22 Dec. 48			
15	23	*Paymaster.*—Wm. Sanford Hall, 10 July, 40; *Ens.* 19 Dec. 11; *Lt.* 22 Apr. 13.				
12	0	*Adjutant.*—*Lieut.* Campbell Sawers, 10 March, 48.				
8	0	*Quarter-Master.*—John Mulhall,[4] 17 Aug. 41.				
20	1 1/12	*Surg.*—George Archer, M.D., 20 Jan. 43; *A.-S.* 2 Nov. 30; *H.-Asst.* 1 Nov. 27				
8	0	*Assist.-Surgeon.*—Nesbitt Heffernan, M.B. 11 June, 41.				

Facings White.—*Agents*, Messrs. Cox & Co.

[Returned from Bombay 6 Aug. 1847.]

3 Lt.-Col. M'Pherson embarked for the Peninsula in May 1809, as a volunteer in the 43rd, and served as such in the advance up to Talavera and the retreat from thence, to 2nd Nov. 1809, when he was promoted to an Ensigncy in the 43rd, from which time he served with the *Light Division* until the end of that war, in 1814, including the following battles, sieges, &c., viz., Coa, Mortiagoa, skirmish near and battle of Busaco, Coimbra, Alenquer, Pombal, Redinha, Miranda de Corvo, *Foz d'Aronce*, Sabugal, Fuentes d'Onor, Espeja, Soita, Ciudad Rodrigo, Badajoz, Mar and Apr. 1812, Carvalhinos, Petiegua, Salamanca, Nivelle, Bayonne, Nive, Tarbes, Tournefeuille and Toulouse. Contused on the head in the trenches at Badajoz by the bursting of a shell. Served as aide-de-camp to Sir Charles Napier throughout the operations in Scinde, including the battles of Meeanee and Hyderabad.

1 Sir Peregrine Maitland served with the 1st Guards in Flanders, and was present in several actions: also at Ostend in 1798. He was employed in Spain in 1808-9, and was present in the actions of Lugo and Corunna; he served also in the expedition to the Scheldt in 1809. He commanded a Brigade of Guards at the passage of the Nive (Medal) and also at the battle of Waterloo.

2 Lt.-Col. Stoyte was present at the storming of Badajos 6th April, 1812; operations in front of and battle of Salamanca, severely wounded at Salamanca, lost one finger, and wounded through the left hand and in the breast while carrying the colours, the standard of which was shot away; wounded through the right hand and taken prisoner at Bergen-op-Zoom; present on the 16th and 18th June at Waterloo.

4 Captains Bourchier, Bourke, Ruttledge, Cormick, J. L. Croker, E. Croker, and Lieutenant Moore, and Quarter-master Mulhall served with the regiment during the campaign in Affghanistan and Beloochistan, and were present at the storm and capture of Ghuznee, 23 July 1839, and storm and capture of Khelat, 13 Nov. following. The citadel of Ghuznee was assaulted by the 17th, led by Lieut.-Col. Croker; and the first British standard, viz. the Regimental Colour of the 17th Regiment, was planted on the Citadel of Ghuznee by Capt. John L. Croker. Capt. Bourchier received a severe and also a slight wound in the right arm at Khelat.

5 Capt. Cooper served in the Peninsula with the 3rd Foot Guards from Sept. 1810 to July 1813, including the retreat from Busaco to the Lines of Torres Vedras, occupation of them, advance through Portugal, battle of Fuentes d'Onor, siege of Ciudad Rodrigo, battle of Salamanca, capture of Madrid, siege of Burgos. Also the campaign of 1815, including the battles of Quatre Bras and Waterloo, and the capture of Paris.

6 Capt. Edwards served as Extra Aide-de-Camp to Sir Charles Napier during Sir Charles' campaign against the Mountain and Desert Tribes situated on the right bank of the Indus, early in 1845.

10 Lieuts. Gardiner and Belfield, with a detachment of the 17th, served with Lieut.-Col. Outram's Light brigade in the Southern Mahratta Campaign of 1844-5, and was present at all its operations, including the capture of Ghetra 21st, and storming of Monohur Stockades and Fort 24th January 1845, at which place this detachment formed the storming party and suffered very severely.—Lt. Gardiner who commanded it was wounded in the head, and he received the thanks of the Governor in Council, and the Commander in Chief in Public Orders for his services.

On the three corners of the second Colour, the *Lion of Nassau*, "*Virtutis Namurcensis Præmium.*" *The Sphinx*, "EGYPT." "CHINA," "*The Dragon.*"

Years' Serv. 62 | *Colonel.*—Matthew, *Lord* Aylmer,[1] GCB. *Ens.* 19 Oct. 87; *Lieut.* 26 Oct. 91; *Capt.* 8 Aug. 94; *Major*, 9 Oct. 00; *Lieut.-Col.* 25 Mar. 02; *Col.* 25 July, 10; *Major-Gen.* 4 June, 13; *Lieut.-Gen.* 27 May, 25; *Gen.* 23 Nov. 41; *Col.* 18th Regt. 23 July 32.

Lieut.-Colonels.

Full Pay.	Half Pay.	
24	0	Thomas Scott Reignolds,[2] CB. *Ens.* 23 June 25; *Lieut.* 25 April 28; *Capt.* P 26 April 31; *Major*, 30 July 42; *Lieut.-Col.* 30 March 44.
44	0	Francis William Dillon,[3] *Ens.* 5 Dec. 05; *Lieut.* 6 Mar. 07; *Capt.* 7 Apr. 25; *Brevet-Major*, 28 June, 38; *Major*, 23 Nov. 41, *Lieut.-Col.* 7 Dec. 47.
34	1 10/12	*Majors.*—John Grattan,[4] CB. *Ens.* P 8 July, 13; *Lt.* 4 Sept. 23; *Capt.* 4 Mar. 36; *Brev.-Major*, 26 May, 41; *Major*, 19 May, 42; *Brev. Lt.-Col.* 14 Aug. 46.
23	0	Francis Wigston,[5] *Ens.* P 16 Mar. 26; *Lieut.* P 1 June, 32; *Capt.* P 18 Jan. 39; *Brev.-Major*, 23 Dec. 42; *Major*, 7 Dec. 47.

Full Pay.	Half Pay.	CAPTAINS.	ENSIGN.	LIEUT.	CAPTAIN.	BREV.-MAJ.
20	0	Clement A. Edwards[6] ..	11 June 29	P 28 Nov. 34	P 13 Mar. 40	
16	0	T. B, *Lord* Cochrane[7] ...	P 27 Sept. 33	P 12 May 37	P 12 Oct. 41	
16	0	John Clark Kennedy[7] ..	P 25 Oct. 33	P 10 Mar. 37	P 3 Dec. 41	
12	0	Geo. Fred. Stevenson Call[8]	P 7 Apr. 37	P 20 Sept. 39	P 30 Dec. 42	
21	0	John Bruce	31 July 28	P 12 Apr. 31	19 Aug. 42	
15	0	James Wm. Graves[9]	24 Oct. 34	31 May 39	26 Jan. 44	
21	0	Archibald Neil Campbell	14 Aug. 28	8 April 31	1 Nov. 42	
15	0	William Tyrrell Bruce,[11]	P 4 July 34	P 15 Apr. 36	15 May 47	
15	0	John Joseph Wood......	19 Sept. 34	23 Oct. 39	7 Dec. 47	
10	0	Thomas Henry Ashton ..	P 27 Sept. 39	P 31 Dec. 41	P 3 Mar. 48	
		LIEUTENANTS.				
14	0	George Hilliard[12]	P 13 Feb. 35	do.		
13	0	Thomas Martin,[11] *r.*	27 May 36	27 Oct. 39		
10	0	Anth. W. S. F. Armstrong[13]	P 21 June 39	26 Jan. 41		
10	0	Isaac Henry Hewitt[14] ..	P 12 July 39	13 May 41		
10	0	Wm. Peter Cockburn[8] ..	P 21 June 39	20 June 41		
10	0	Henry Duncan Burrell[15]	24 Oct. 39	17 Aug. 41		
9	0	Charles Woodwright[11] ..	P 13 Mar. 40	12 Sept. 41		
8	0	Edmond Wm. Sargent[16].	18 May 41	26 July 42		
8	0	John Elliot...........	P 2 July 41	20 Aug. 42		
8	0	Matthew Jones Hayman[7]	P 14 July 41	20 Aug. 42		
8	0	Henry Allsop Ward	17 Aug. 41	24 Oct. 42		
8	0	Henry James Mason....	26 Nov. 41	P 21 Apr. 43		
7	0	Frederick Lillie	19 Aug. 42	14 Sept. 43		
7	0	Wm. Henry Graves	25 Nov. 42	2 Feb. 44		
7	0	Richard Henry Farrer ..	30 Dec. 42	17 May 44		
8	0	Joseph George Wilkinson	1 June 41	26 July 44		
8	0	George Swaby	P 16 April 41	19 May 43		
7	0	William Blake Graham..	31 Dec. 42	5 Sept. 45		
6	0	Charles Frederick Kelly	2 Apr. 43	P 5 Feb. 47		
5	0	Robert Doran, *Adjutant*	26 Jan. 44	P 6 Aug. 47		
6	0	Richard Trevor Irwin ..	1 April 43	8 Jan. 47		
7	0	Charles Compton Abbott	22 July 42	24 May 44		
2	0	Alexander Minter	17 Jan. 47	P 5 May 48		
		ENSIGNS.				
5	0	Robert Halahan	17 May 44			
3	0	Bernard M'Cabe[18]	8 May 46			
2	0	John Edward Swindley..	15 Jan. 47			
2	0	John Canavan..........	16 Jan. 47			
3	0	Fred. Herbert Suckling..	P 7 July 46			
2	0	Francis Eteson	P 6 Aug. 47			
2	0	George Augustus Elliot..	P 10 Dec. 47			
1	0	Thos. Robinson Gibbons	P 5 May 48			

2 Lt.-Col. Reignolds served with the 49th on the China expedition (Medal), and was present at the storming of the heights and forts above Canton, taking of Amoy, second capture of Chusan, storming of the fortified heights of Chinhae, taking of Ningpo, attack and capture of the enemy's entrenched camp on the heights of Segoan (severely wounded), capture of Chapoo (wounded), Woosung, and Chin Kiang Foo, and landing before Nankin.

3 Lt.-Col. Dillon served in the expedition to St. Domingo in 1809. Served also in China (Medal), and was present at the first capture of Chusan, storm and capture of the heights above Canton, and of the sea-batteries on Amoy, and subsequent capture of the city.

4 Lt.-Col. Grattan was actively employed on the frontiers during the rebellion in Canada in 1838. He served in China with the 18th (Medal), and was present at the storming of the heights above Canton, and led the advance against the enemy's entrenched camp, for which he was selected by Sir Hugh Gough as the bearer of his despatches, promoted to the rank of major, and appointed brigade major of Fort St. George by Lord Hill. On his return to China—on board the *Madagascar*—in charge of Lord Auckland's despatches, the ship having caught fire during a gale of wind, he with a few others narrowly escaped the fate of fifty-seven souls who perished upon that occasion; he fell into the hands of the Chinese, and was detained 108 days in captivity; after which he was at the attack of Segoan, and commanded the 18th (after the fall of Lt.-Col. Tomlinson) at Chapoo, Woosung, and Shanghai, and he was present at the storming of Chin Kiang Foo and the landing before Nankin.

5 Major Wigston was at Canton, Amoy, Chusan, Chinhae, Ningpo, Segoan, Chapoo, & Chin Kiang Foo (Medal).

6 Capt. Edwards was at Canton, Amoy, Chapoo, Shanghai, Woosung and Chin Kiang Foo (Medal).

7 Captains Lord Cochrane and Kennedy, Lt. Hayman, and Surgeon Stewart, served with the 18th on the China expedition (Medal), and were present at the demonstration before Nankin.

8 Capt. Call and Lieut. Cockburn were at Canton and Amoy (Medal).

Full Pay.	Half Pay.	
35	0	*Paymaster.*—John MacKenzie Kennedy,[19] 30 Oct. 28; *Ens.* 24 Feb. 14; *Lieut.* P 6 Feb. 23.
5	0	*Adjutant.*—*Lieut.* Robert Doran, 12 Nov. 47.
5	0	*Quarter-Master.*—George Peel,[17] 23 July 44.
11	0	*Surgeon.*—James Stewart,[7] 5 Aug. 46; *Assist.-Surg.* 17 April, 38.
4	0	*Assist.-Surgs.*—Joseph Hamilton Dwyer, A.B. 14 Nov. 45.
3	0	William Kelman Chalmers, M.D. 13 Nov. 46.
3	0	Frederick Burton Phillipson, 25 Sept. 46.

Facings Blue.
Agents, Messrs. Cox & Co.

1 Lord Aylmer served in the expedition to St. Domingo in 1793 and 1794; was present in the first and second attacks upon Tiburon; at the storming of Fort de l'Acul, near *Leogane* (wounded); at the affair of Bombard, near Cape Nicola Mole; and at the reduction of Port au Prince. Present at the descent near Ostend, in May 1798; remained as prisoner in France for six months. Present in 1799 at the battle of the Helder; at the attack on the British lines on the 10th Sept., battles of 19th Sept., and 2nd Oct. 1799, in Holland. Served in the Coldstream Guards in the North of Germany under Lord Cathcart in 1805. Present at the siege of Copenhagen. Served on the Staff of the Army throughout the Peninsular war, as Assistant, and Deputy Adjutant-General, and commanding a Brigade. Was present at the passage of the Douro, and has received a cross and one clasp for the following actions:—Talavera, Busaco, Fuentes d'Onor, Vittoria, and the Nive.

16 Lt. Sargent was at Woosung, Shanghai, and Chin Kiang Foo (Medal). [For Notes 9, 11, 12, 13, 14, 15, 17, 18, 19, see next page.

Emb. for For. Serv. 11 Sept. 1840.] 19th (The 1st Yorkshire North Riding) Regt. of F. [Serving in North America. Depot at Mullingar.

Years' Serv.	
69	
Full Pay.	Half Pay.

Colonel.

P Sir Warren Marmaduke Peacocke,[1] KCH. KC., *Ens.* 12 Dec. 80; *Lieut.* 22 May, 82; *Capt.* 14 April, 83; *Major*, 1 March, 94; *Lieut.-Col.* 1 Jan. 98; *Col.* 25 Apr. 08; *Maj.-Gen.* 4 June, 11; *Lt.-Gen.* 19 July, 21; *Gen.* 28 June, 38; *Col.* 19th Regt. 31 May, 43.

Lieut.-Colonel.

Full Pay	Half Pay	
25	0	Charles Craufurd Hay, *Ens.* 27 June, 24; *Lieut.* P 24 Dec. 25; *Capt.* P 19 Sept. 26; *Major*, P 16 June, 37; *Lieut.-Col.* P 30 Aug. 42.
13	0	*Majors.*—Henry Calley, *Ens.* P 29 July 36; *Lieut.* P 2 Feb. 39; *Capt.* P 30 Aug. 42; *Major*, P 7 Aug. 46.
12	0	Robert Sanders, *Ens.* P 26 May 37; *Lieut.* 26 Jan. 41; *Capt.* P 3 Feb. 43; *Major*, P 6 Aug. 47.

Full Pay	Half Pay	CAPTAINS.	ENSIGN.	LIEUT.	CAPTAIN.	BREVET-MAJOR.
30	$3\frac{1}{12}$	Chas. Highmore Potts ..	8 Feb. 16	P 13 Nov. 17	P 31 Dec. 25	28 June 38
38	0	David Burns[2]	17 Oct. 11	25 Jan. 16	20 July 30	9 Nov. 46
22	$5\frac{7}{12}$	Thomas Unett..........	P 27 Sept. 21	P 22 July 24	P 6 July 26	23 Nov. 41
10	0	Hugh John M. Campbell	31 May 39	P 30 Aug. 42	P 4 April 45	
9	0	Henry Edward M'Gee ..	P 4 Sept. 40	P 3 Feb. 43	P 8 Aug. 45	
11	0	James Ker	P 30 Mar. 38	P 12 Oct. 41	P 7 Aug. 46	
9	0	John Lewis Richard Rooke	P 11 Sept. 40	P 20 Aug. 44	P 2 April 47	
8	0	Robert Warden	P 12 Oct. 41	P 4 April 45	P 6 Aug. 47	
13	0	Richard Denny[3]	P 13 May 36	P 12 Oct. 38	P 30 Dec. 42	7 July 46
7	0	John Margitson	P 24 June 42	P 8 Aug. 45	P 15 Aug. 48	
		LIEUTENANTS.				
14	0	James Cochrane........	5 June 35	P 28 Dec. 38		
15	0	George Tuite	P 7 Feb. 34	31 May 39		
12	0	Edw. John Ellerman....	P 10 Feb. 37	P 4 Sept. 40		
12	0	Henry Butler Stoney ..	P 5 May 37	P 11 Sept. 40		
10	0	John Phillipps	P 2 Feb. 39	P 20 May 42		
6	0	George Bingham Jenings	P 21 July 43	P 4 April 45		
7	0	Charles Kyd Skeete	P 30 Aug. 42	P 24 Oct. 45		
6	0	John Hay Moore, *d. adj.*	P 3 Feb. 43	P 7 Aug. 46		
6	0	Rob. Onesiphorus Bright	P 9 June 43	P 2 April 47		
5	0	Wm. Henry Lee Warner	P 20 Aug. 44	P 6 Aug. 47		
4	0	Henry Braddell	P 18 Apr. 45	P 6 Aug. 47		
14	0	R. Barrett, *ad.* (Q.M. 30 Oct. 35)	13 June 45	14 Aug. 48		
4	0	William Harris	P 8 Aug. 45	P 15 Aug. 48		
		ENSIGNS.				
4	0	Godfrey Wm. Hugh Massey	P 24 Oct. 45			
3	0	Geo. Varnham Macdonald	13 Nov. 46			
2	0	Fred. Charles Ashworth..	P 2 April 47			
2	0	Henry Hill Dawson	P 6 Aug. 47			
2	0	Hugh Francis Massy	P 7 Aug. 47			
1	0	George Lidwill	P 18 Feb. 48			
1	0	Oswald Aug. Grimston ..	23 June 48			
1	0	Tho. Goodricke Peacocke	P 15 Aug. 48			
24	0	*Paymaster.*—Thos. R. Travers, 23 Nov. 38; *Ens.* 7 April, 25; *Lieut.* P 10 June, 26.				
14	0	*Adjutant.*—*Lieut.* Richard Barrett,[4] 13 June, 45.				
4	0	*Quarter-Master.*—Alexander Hendry,[5] 2 Sept. 45.				
19	$2\frac{1}{12}$	*Surgeon.*—Wm. Odell, 21 April 43; *Assist.-Surg.* 9 Nov. 30; *Hosp.-Assistant*, 14 Feb. 28.				
6	0	*Assistant-Surgeons.*—Thomas Longmore, 3 Feb. 43.				
8	0	Thomas Waller Barrow,[6] 8 June, 41.				

Facings Green.—*Agents*, Messrs. Cox & Co.—*Irish Agents*, Sir E. R. Borough, *Bt.*, Armit, & Co.

2 Major Burns served throughout the Kandian campaign of 1818; and received the thanks of Sir Robert Brownrigg on three occasions, in general orders, for a series of services against the insurgents.

3 Major Denny commanded the Light Company of the 58th at the destruction of Pomare's Pah on the 30th April, 1845; at Mawe on 8th May; at the attack and destruction of the Waikadi Pah on the 16th May; at the storming of Kawiti's Pah at Ohiawai on the 1st July and destruction of the same on the 10th July; again at the destruction of Arratua's Pah on the 16th July; and he was actively engaged at the storming of Kawiti's Pah on the 11th Jan. 1846.

4 Lieut. Barrett served in the Kandian Territories, Ceylon, during the whole of the Rebellion of 1817 and 18, and commanded an outpost during part of the above period.

5 Quarter-Master Hendry served the campaign of 1815, and was present at the battles of Quatre Bras and Waterloo, and capture of Paris.

6 Mr. Barrow served in the Queen's Royal Regt. in the campaign of 1844 in the Southern Mahratta country (including the storming of the fortress of Punella), & that in the Concan in 1845.

1 Sir Warren Peacocke was in the actions of Antrim and Ballynahinch in the rebellion in Ireland in 1798. At the landing in Egypt and all the actions there in 1801. On the Expedition to Hanover in 1805, and on that to Denmark in 1807. At the passage of the Douro in 1809; and commanded at Lisbon during the remainder of the Peninsular war.

9 Captain Graves served with the 18th in China (medal) from September 1840 to June 184[illegible] and was present at the [illegible] and capture of the heights above Canton, attack and capture of Amoy, second capture of Chusan, attack and capture of the heights of Chinghae, occupation of Ningpo and repulse of the night attack, attack and capture of the enemy's entrenched camp on the heights of Segoan, attack and capture of Chapoo, Woosung, Shangai, and Chin Kiang Foo, and demonstration before Nankin. He was also present at the operations in the Canton River, under Major General D'Aguilar in April 1847, and was selected as the officer to remain in command at the Factories when the force was withdrawn, for the purpose of organising and drilling the Associated Gentlemen Volunteers at Canton.

11 Capt. Bruce, Lts. Martin and Woodwright, were at Amoy, Chapoo, Shanghai, Woosung, & Chin Kiang Foo (Medal).

12 Lt. Hilliard was at the Bogue Forts, Canton (wounded), Amoy, Chapoo, Shanghai, Woosung, & Chin Kiang Foo (Medal).

13 Lt. Armstrong was at Canton, Amoy, Chusan, Chinhae, Ningpo, Segoan, and Chin Kiang Foo (Medal). He commanded the guard at the West Gate of Ningpo on the morning of the 10th March 1841, when the enemy in force attacked that post, which, notwithstanding the overwhelming disparity of numbers, was bravely maintained and the enemy repulsed with severe loss (Medal).

14 Lieut. Hewitt was at Canton, Amoy, Chusan, Chinhae, Ningpo, Segoan, Chapoo, Shanghai, Woosung, and Chin Kiang Foo (Medal).

15 Lieut. Burrell served with the 18th in China (medal) at Amoy, Chusan, Chinhae, Ningpo, Segoan, Chapoo, Shanghai, Woosung, and Chin Kiang Foo.

17 Quarter-master Peel served throughout the whole of the China expedition (Medal).

18 Ens. M'Cabe served the campaign on the Sutlej in the 31st regt. (Medal).

19 Paymaster Kennedy served as paymaster of the 22nd in Scinde, under Sir Charles Napier, in 1843 (Medal).

"MINDEN"—"EGMONT-OP-ZEE"—The *Sphinx*, with the words "EGYPT"—"MAIDA"—"VIMIERA" "CORUNNA"—"VITTORIA"—"PYRENEES"—"ORTHES"—"TOULOUSE"—"PENINSULA."

Years' Serv. Full Pay.	Half Pay.	
57		*Colonel.*
		𝔓 *Sir* James Stevenson Barns,[1] KCB. *Ens.* 11 July, 92; *Lieut.* 2 Jan. 94; *Capt.* 27 Feb. 96; *Major*, 17 Sept. 02; *Lieut.-Col.* 6 Nov. 06; *Col.* 4 June, 14; *Major-Gen.* 19 July, 21; *Lieut.-Gen.* 10 Jan. 37; *Col.* 20 F. 25 April, 42.
		Lieut.-Colonels.
29	0	William Nelson Hutchinson, *Ens.* 24 Feb. 20; *Lieut.* 25 Oct. 23; *Capt.* P 17 June, 26; *Major*, P 4 Dec. 32; *Lieut.-Col.* P 7 Sept. 41.
23	0	r. Frederick Horn, *Ens.* P 26 Jan. 26; *Lieut.* P 17 April, 28; *Capt.* P 16 June, 37; *Major*, P 7 Sept. 41; *Lt.-Col.* 14 April 46.
14	0	*Majors.*—Hugh Dennis Crofton, *Ens.* P 13 Mar. 35; *Lieut.* 29 Dec. 37; *Capt.* P 9 Aug. 39; *Major*, P 30 Dec. 45.
15	0	r. Lachlan Duff Gordon, *Ens.* P 25 July, 34; *Lieut.* P 27 July, 38; *Capt.* P 31 Dec. 39; *Major*, P 9 June, 46.

Full Pay	Half Pay	CAPTAINS.	ENSIGN.	LIEUT.	CAPTAIN.	BREV.-MAJ.
14	0	r. *Lord* Mark Kerr, *s.* ..	P 19 June 35	P 14 Sept. 38	P 26 June 40	
13	0	Fred. Charles Eveleigh ..	P 1 July 36	P 10 Nov. 37	P 12 Mar. 41	
14	0	James B. Sharpe	27 Nov. 35	P 12 April 39	P 7 Sept. 41	
29	3/12	r. Patrick Hennessy	24 Apr. 20	19 May 25	20 Aug. 41	
24	0	r Scrope Reynett Berdmore	25 Jan. 25	11 Oct. 27	15 Apr. 42	
13	0	r. Geo. B. Cham. Crespigny	P 29 Jan. 36	P 20 July 39	P 17 June 42	
22	0	Henry Crawley	11 Oct. 27	11 June 30	9 Oct. 43	
12	0	Richard Leigh Lye......	P 3 Nov. 37	P 9 Aug. 39	P 30 Dec. 45	
11	0	r. George Steevens......	P 3 Aug. 38	P 17 Apr. 40	14 Apr. 46	
12	0	John A. Vesey Kirkland, *s.*	P 22 Aug. 37	P 27 July 38	P 6 Sept. 44	
7	0	r. Edward Lewis Knight	P 21 July 42	P 30 June 43	P 3 Apr. 46	
10	0	r. Maurice Cane........	15 June 39	P 7 Sept. 41	P 1 Sept. 48	
		LIEUTENANTS.				
10	0	E. Gilling Hallewell, *adj.*	P 31 Dec. 39	15 Apr. 42		
9	0	Geo. Fred. Weller Poley	P 17 Apr. 40	15 Apr. 42		
8	0	Wm. Pollexfen Radcliffe	P 12 Mar. 41	P 2 Aug. 42		
13	0	Christophilus Garstin ..	P 14 May 36	15 Dec. 40		
8	0	r. George Tomson......	P 7 Sept. 41	9 Oct. 43		
8	0	John Richard Jackson ..	P 5 Nov. 41	3 Jan. 44		
7	0	Wm. Thomas Wayte Wood	P 15 June 42	P 23 Aug. 44		
7	0	r. Charles Richard Butler	10 Jan. 42	P 21 Mar. 45		
7	0	Edmund Francis Anstey	P 1 Nov. 42	P 30 Dec. 45		
6	0	r. Andrew Beatty	13 Oct. 43	P 9 June 46		
6	0	r. William Henry Dowling	20 Oct. 43	8 Sept. 46		
3	0	Mansfield Turner	P 13 Feb. 46	P 29 Jan. 47		
5	0	r. John Everard Deane ..	23 Feb. 44	P 4 Feb. 48		
6	0	Henry James	P 31 Mar. 43	P 3 Oct. 45		
6	0	r. John Gittens Maycock	P 2 June 43	P 4 April 45		
5	0	r. James George Hay ..	P 31 Dec. 44	P 1 Sept. 48		
		ENSIGNS.				
6	0	r Charles William Robinson	17 Nov. 43			
4	0	r. Nathaniel Steevens ..	P 19 Dec. 45			
3	0	George Huish Adams ..	14 Apr. 46			
3	0	Jas. Wallace Dunlop Adair	21 Apr. 46			
2	0	William Henry McNeill..	P 1 Oct. 47			
2	0	Charles Frederick Turner	5 Nov. 47			
1	0	r. Charles Lutyens	P 4 Feb. 48			
1	0	r. George Shuldham Peard	P 5 Feb. 48			
1	0	r. Francis Padfield, *adj.*...	P 7 Apr. 48			
1	0	Henry Towry Law......	P 25 Aug. 48			

Full Pay	Half Pay	
36	0	*Paymaster.*—Charles South, 23 Aug. 37; *Ens.* 9 Dec. 13; *Lieut.* P 17 Dec. 18.
10	0	*Adjutants.*—*Lieut.* Edmund G. Hallewell, 1 March, 44.
8	0	r. *Ens.* Francis Padfield, 22 Dec. 48.
8	0	*Quarter-Masters.*—David Bilham, 17 Sept. 41.
3	0	r. Joseph M'Gee, 8 Sept. 46.
12	0	*Surgs.*—Isidore Anthony Blake, M.B., 20 Oct. 46; *Assist.-Surg.* 15 Sept. 37.
10	0	r. John Gillespie Wood, M.D., 10 Dec. 47; *Assist.-Surg.* 11 Jan. 39.
8	0	*Assistant-Surgeons.*—Robert John Cole, M.D. 27 Aug. 41.
7	0	r. Edward Howard, 29 April, 42.

Facings Yellow.—*Agents*, *Sir* John Kirkland & Co.

1 Sir James Barns served with the Royals under Gen. O'Hara, at Toulon, until its evacuation, and was present at the defence of Fort Mulgrave, and also at the sortie from Toulon, 30 Nov. 1793. He served the whole of the campaign in Corsica in 1794, terminating with the surrender of Calvi, including the storming of Convention Redoubts, capture of St. Fiorenzo, Bastia, and the siege of Calvi. In 1799, he served the campaign in Holland, including the actions of the 10th Sept. 2nd and 6th Oct. (wounded). Accompanied the expedition to the Ferrol in 1800; and that to Egypt in 1801, and served the whole of the campaign until the surrender of Alexandria. Served in the expedition to Walcheren in 1809; and in Spain and Portugal from March, 1810, until the conclusion of that war in 1814, and has received a cross for Busaco, Salamanca (severely wounded), St. Sebastian, and the Nive, on which occasions he commanded the 3rd Battalion of the

The Thistle within the Circle of St. Andrew, "*Nemo me impune lacessit.*" The King's Cypher and Crown.

Years' Serv. Full Pay	Half Pay	
54		*Colonel.*—P W *Right Hon. Sir* Frederick Adam,[1] GCB. GCMG. *Ens.* 4 Nov. 1795; *Lt.* 2 Feb. 96; *Capt.* 30 Aug. 99; *Maj.* 9 July, 03; *Lt.-Col.* 28 Aug. 04; *Col.* 20 Feb. 12; *Maj.-Gen.* 4 June 14; *Lt.-Gen.* 22 July, 30; *Gen.* 9 Nov. 46; *Col.* 21st Fusil. 31 May, 43.
35	0	*Lieut.-Colonel.*—John Crofton Peddie, *2nd Lieut.* 4 May 14; *Lieut.* P 29 June 20; *Capt.* P 26 Nov. 25; *Brevet-Major,* 28 June, 38; *Major,* 5 Dec. 43; *Lieut.-Col.* P 20 Oct. 48.
34	1 1/12	*Majors.*—William James Sutherland, *2nd Lieut.* 3 May 14; *Lieut.* P 22 Sept. 14; *Capt.* P 29 June, 20; *Brevet-Major,* 10 Jan 37; *Major,* 31 Dec. 42.
21	0	Frederick George Ainslie, *2nd Lieut.* P 24 April 28; *Lieut* P 5 Oct. 32; *Capt.* P 26 June 38; *Major,* P 20 Oct. 48.

Full Pay	Half Pay	CAPTAINS.	2d LIEUT.	LIEUT.	CAPTAIN.	BREV.-MAJ.
41	6	Angus Wm. Mackay[3] ..	P 24 July 02	P 30 June 08	27 July 32	9 Nov. 46
17	0	John Ramsay Stuart	P 20 Jan. 32	9 Aug. 35	P 10 Jan. 40	
17	0	Thos. Bythesea Mortimer	P 16 Nov. 32	2 July 37	P 24 Sept. 41	
16	0	*Hon.* C. R. Sackville West[4]	P 30 Aug. 33	P 5 June 35	P 15 Apr. 42	3 Apr. 46
15	0	Robert Spring[6]	P 14 Feb. 34	P 4 Dec. 35	11 Feb. 46	
10	0	Fred. Paul Haines,[7] *s.* ..	P 21 June 39	P 15 Dec. 40	16 May 46	
11	0	William J. Verner	6 Apr. 38	P 15 Oct. 41	22 Feb. 46	
14	0	Lewis Chamberlayne Irwin	P 10 Apr. 35	P 28 Feb. 40	5 Nov. 47	
13	0	Arthur Lake Johnston ..	P 22 July 36	30 Dec. 38	P 20 Oct. 48	
10	0	Willoughby, H. Carter ..	P 4 Oct. 39	P 2 July 41	P 2 June 48	
		FIRST LIEUTENANTS.				
18	0	Wm. Francis Ring, *r.* ..	28 Oct. 31	8 May 35		
13	0	Arthur Geo. Shawe	1 April 36	23 Aug. 39		
11	0	John Watson	P 18 Aug. 38	31 May 40		
11	0	Robert Nicholson	P 7 Sept. 38	13 June 40		
11	0	John Patrick Stuart *adj.*	30 Dec. 38	3 Oct. 40		
9	0	Fra. E. Newport Tinley	P 28 Aug. 40	P 25 Sept. 41		
9	0	Wm. Savage	7 Aug. 40	25 Oct. 42		
8	0	Thomas Wm. Prevost ..	18 June 41	P 5 April 44		
8	0	Arthur Edgecumbe Tuke	P 24 Sept. 41	10 Aug. 44		
8	0	Henry Frederick Evans..	P 26 Oct. 41	11 May 45		
8	0	Edward Clemison	P 16 Nov. 41	19 Dec. 45		
7	0	George Caldwell Dickins	P 27 May 42	21 Apr. 46		
3	0	Edward Thomas Barnard	P 23 Jan. 46	P 20 Oct. 48		
3	0	Wm. Thomas M'Grigor ..	28 Apr. 46	P 1 Dec. 48		
		SECOND LIEUTS.				
5	0	Charles Beevor Daveney	P 31 Dec. 44			
3	0	Jos. FitzThomas Shadwell	P 26 June 46			
2	0	Thomas Francis Hobbs ..	15 Jan. 47			
2	0	John Thomas Dalyell ..	14 May 47			
1	0	John Wm. Charles Fagge	P 1 Aug. 48			
1	0	William John Legh	P 20 Oct. 48			
1	0	Geo. James B. Burttelot	P 1 Dec. 48			

3 Major Mackay served the campaign of 1807 in Egypt. Made prisoner of war in an engagement with the enemy in Calabria 16th June, 1809, and detained as such until 18 May, 1814. Present at New Orleans, 8 Jan. 1815.

4 The Hon. Major West served on Sir Hugh Gough's staff throughout the campaign on the Sutlej (Medal),—as Aide-de-camp in the battles of Moodkee and Ferozeshah, and as Officiating Military Secretary during the remainder of the campaign and in the battle of Sobraon.

6 Capt. Spring served with the 53d in the campaign on the Sutlej in 1846 (Medal), including the actions at Buddiwal, Aliwal, and Sobraon.

Full Pay	Half Pay	
15	0	*Paymaster.*—Geo. Pott Erskine, 3 Nov. 43; *Ens.* P 11 July 34; *Lt.* P 1 Mar. 39
11	0	*Adjutant.*—*Lieut.* John Patrick Stuart, 1 Dec. 48.
8	0	*Quarter-Master.*—James Mahood, 25 Feb. 41.
10	0	*Surgeon.*—Francis Charles Annesley, 15 Aug. 48; *Assist.-Surg.* 17 Sept. 39.
9	0	*Assistant-Surgeon.*—John Summers, M.D. 29 May, 40.

Facings Blue.—*Agent,* John Lawrie, Esq.

[*Returned from Bengal,* 11*th May,* 1848.]

1 Sir Frederick Adam served in Holland, and was present in the actions of the 27th August, 10th September, and 2nd October, 1799; took part in the actions of the 8th, 13th, and 21st March, 1801, in Egypt. Sir Frederick was severely wounded near Alicant, 12th April, 1813; at the pass of Ordall he received two wounds, one which broke his left arm, and another which shattered his left hand; and he was also severely wounded at Waterloo.

7 Captain Haines' services:—On the formation of the Army of the Sutlej he was appointed to officiate as Military Secretary to the Commander-in-Chief, Sir Hugh Gough (vice Colonel Gough, who became a Brigadier of Cavalry), and in that capacity he was present at the battles of Moodkee and Ferozeshah, 18th and 21st Dec. 1845. In the latter engagement he was severely wounded by grape shot at the attack on the enemy's works, his horse being killed under him at the same moment. At the recommendation of Lord Gough he was promoted to a company in the 10th Foot without purchase, he being then a Lieut. in the 4th Regt.

20 Ensign Hughes served throughout the operations in Scinde (Medal), including the destruction of Imaumghur and the battles of Meeanee and Hyderabad. He was also present at Panulla and Powughur.

21 Doctor Currie served with the 16th Lancers at the battle of Maharajpore 29th Dec. 1843 (Medal). Also in the campaign on the Sutlej in 1846 Medal, including the actions at Buddiwal, Aliwal, and Sobraon.

22 Dr. Anderson was at Hyderabad (Medal), Panulla, Powughur, Munnohur, and Munsuntosh.

23 Dr. M'Grath served with the 2nd Queen's Royals during the campaign in the Southern Mahratta country in 1844-5, including the surrender of the Fort of Budurghur storming of Panulla, and capture of Powughur; he was also at the taking of Stockades below the Hussmunt Ghaut in the Concan.

"Scinde," "Meeanee," "Hyderabad."

Years' Serv. 55 Full Pay.	Half Pay.	
		Colonel.—Sir Charles Jas. Napier,[1] GCB. *Ens.* 31 Jan. 94; *Lieut.* 8 May, 94; *Capt.* 22 Dec. 03; *Major*, 29 May, 06; *Lt.-Col.* 27 June, 11; *Col.* 27 May. 25; *Maj.-Gen.* 10 Jan. 37; *Lt.-Gen.* 9 Nov. 46; *Col.* 22 Regt. 21 Nov. 43.
20	2	*Lieut.-Colonels.*—Samuel Brandram Boileau, *Ens.* p 4 Oct. 21; *Lieut.* p 1 Aug. 26; *Capt.* p 25 Nov. 28; *Major*, p 9 Dec. 36; *Lieut.-Col.* p 18 Dec. 40.
38	1 8/12	Sydney John Cotton, *Cor.* 19 Apr. 10; *Lt.* 13 Feb. 12; *Capt.* p 1 Jan. 20; *Major* 18 Jan. 28; *Brevet Lieut.-Col.* 23 Nov. 41; *Lieut.-Col.* 8 Jan. 43.
35	0	*Majors.*—John H. Poole,[3] CB. *Ens.* 24 Mar. 14; *Lieut.* 30 Sept. 19; *Capt.* 1 Nov. 30; *Major*, p 18 Oct. 39; *Brevet Lieut.-Col.* 4 July, 43.
24	0	David Rae Smith,[4] *Ens.* p 3 Nov. 25; *Lieut.* 13 Feb. 28; *Capt.* p 26 April 31; *Major*, 23 Feb. 44.

Full Pay	Half Pay		Ensign.	Lieut.	Captain.	Brev.-Maj.
		Captains.				
24	0	Fred. Darley George,[5] CB.	p 24 Mar. 25	p 30 April 27	p 30 Aug. 33	4 July 43
21	0	T. Sydenham Conway,[6] CB.	14 Feb. 28	p 26 April 31	p 9 Dec. 36	4 July 43
17	0	Thomas Chute[7]	p 24 Feb. 32	p 9 Dec. 36	18 Feb. 43	
16	0	John Heatly,[9] s.	20 Sept. 31	28 Mar. 34	p 17 Nov. 43	
17	0	James Ramsay,[10] s.	18 May 32	p 19 May 34	30 Mar. 44	
27	6 4/12	Thomas White	7 Dec. 15	25 Aug. 24	5 Oct. 38	
12	0	Edward Dunbar[11]	p 27 Oct. 37	p 20 Oct. 40	p 11 Oct. 44	
11	0	Francis Pym Harding[12]	p 16 Mar. 38	p 18 Dec. 40	29 Jan. 47	
23	0	Fred. Browne Russell ..	2 Nov. 26	18 Feb. 30	13 Sept. 42	
15	0	Joseph Edwin Thackwell[13]	p 6 June 34	23 Oct. 39	p 26 May 48	
		Lieutenants.				
12	0	Fred. Geo. Tho. Deshon[14]	29 Dec. 37	5 Jan. 41		
10	0	John Brennan[15] *adj.*	17 Sept. 39	30 Apr. 41		
9	0	Joseph Maycock	p 20 Oct. 40	29 Apr. 42		
8	0	Herbert Geo. Bowden,[16] *r.*	30 Apr. 41	p 30 May 43		
10	0	Alexander Miller[17]	15 Mar. 39	28 Nov. 40		
8	0	William Carrow[14]	p 31 Dec. 41	p 15 Dec. 43		
11	0	Robert Blackall[18]	p 19 Jan. 38	6 Mar. 40		
10	0	Robert Colvill Jones[19] ..	p 9 Aug. 39	8 Feb. 41		
6	0	William Henry Budd[11] ..	p 10 Feb. 43	p 11 Oct. 44		
7	0	Wm. Richard Goddard[11]	1 Nov. 42	7 Dec. 44		
7	0	John Higgin Graham ..	6 May 42	p 7 Mar. 45		
6	0	Thomas Stack[15]	18 Feb. 43	18 Nov. 45		
8	0	William Mayne	17 Aug. 41	28 Sept. 43		
6	0	John Baldwin..........	p 29 Dec. 43	p 22 May 46		
5	0	Geo. P. Edw. Morrison ..	28 June 44	p 8 Sept. 46		
6	0	Hen. Allen Murray Deane	p 5 Dec. 43	p 1 Dec. 46		
5	0	Arthur Grueber Walch ..	16 Feb. 44	11 Dec. 46		
3	0	EdwSimeonWebberSmith	21 Apr. 46	p 30 July 47		
7	0	Frederick George Moore	4 Nov. 42	20 Nov. 45		
3	0	William Couch	20 Oct. 46	p 19 Nov. 47		
3	0	Thomas Young	p 22 May 46	p 26 May 48		
3	0	Lynch Stapleton Cotton	p 8 Sept. 46	p 27 May 48		
4	0	Hen. Vansit. Pennefather	28 Feb. 45	18 Aug. 48		
		Ensigns.				
3	0	A. J. B. L. Butt........	31 Mar. 46			
3	0	William Hughes[20]	9 Sept. 46			
3	0	Francis George King....	14 Apr. 46			
2	0	Nicholas Henry M'Grath	p 30 July 47			
1	0	D. Pleydell Bouverie....	p 12 May 48			
1	0	Arthur Lloyd Monck ..	18 Aug. 48			
2	0	John William Poole	6 Nov. 47			
1	0	Henry Charles Fraser ..	22 Dec. 48			

Full Pay	Half Pay	
9	0	*Paymaster.*—Thos. Hanson Ratcliff, 3 Sept. 47; *Ens.* 3 Apr. 40; *Lt.* p 16 Aug. 42.
10	0	*Adjutant.*—*Lieut.* John Brennan, 26 May, 48.
8	0	*Quarter-Master.*—William Young,[4] 16 Dec. 41; *Ens.* 10 Nov. 41.
13	0	*Surgeon.*—Samuel Currie, M.D.,[21] 12 Feb. 47; *Assist.-Surg.* 14 Oct. 36.
9	0	*Assist.-Surg.*—John Anderson,[22] M.D. 8 May, 40.
8	0	Thomas M'Grath,[23] M.D. 8 June, 41.
3	0	Daniel Paterson Barry, 7 Aug. 46.

Facings Buff.—*Agents*, [Messrs. Cox & Co.

3 Lt.-Col. Poole served throughout the operations in Scinde (medal) under Sir Charles Napier and commanded the 22nd at the battle of Meeanee, and a brigade at the battle of Hyderabad. He was also previously at the destruction of the Fort of Imaumghur in the Desert. He served the campaign in the Southern Mahratta country in 1844-5, including the investment and capture of the Forts Panulla and Powughur.

4 Major Smith, and Quarter Master Young served the campaign in the Southern Mahratta country, in 1844-5, and were present at the investment and capture of the Forts of Panulla and Powughur.

5 Maj. George served throughout the operations in Scinde (Medal) under Sir Charles Napier, including the destruction of Imaumghur, and the battles of Meeanee and Hyderabad, at which last he commanded the 22nd regt. He served also the campaign in the Southern Mahratta country in 1844-5, and was present at the investment and capture of the forts of Panulla and Powughur, and in the operations against the Forts Munnahur and Munsuntosh in the Southern Concan.

6 Maj. Conway served throughout the operations in Scinde (Medal) including the battles of Meeanee and Hyderabad; and he commanded the Light Company (detached) at the previous defence of the Residency at Hyderabad. He served also the campaign in the Southern Mahratta country, and was present at the investment and capture of Panulla and Powughur.

7 Captain Chute served throughout the operations in Scinde (Medal, including the destruction of Imaumghur, and the battles of Meeanee and Hyderabad (severely wounded.)

9 Capt. Heatly served with the 49th, and as Dep. Asst. Adj. Gen., throughout the operations in China, and was present at Chusan, Canton, Amoy, Chusan, Chinhae, Ningpo, Chapoo, Woosung, Chin Kiang Foo, & Nankin.

1 Sir Charles Napier served in the Irish rebellion, in 1798; and in the insurrection, in 1803. Commanded the 50th throughout the campaign terminating with the battle of Corunna, when he was made prisoner after receiving five wounds, viz. leg broken by a musket-shot, sabre-cut on the head, in the back by a bayonet, ribs broken by a cannon-shot, and several severe contusions from the butt-end of a musket. Returned to the Peninsula the latter part of 1809, where he remained until 1811, and was present at the action of the Coa (had two horses shot under him), battle of Busaco (shot through the face, also jaw broken and eye injured), battle of Fuentes d'Onor, second siege of Badajoz, and a great number of skirmishes. In 1813 he served in a floating expedition on the coast of the United States of North America; landed a great number of times at Craney Island, and other places. Served also the campaign of 1815, and was present at the storming of Cambray. Commanded the force employed in Scinde, and on the 17th Feb. 1843, with only 2,800 British troops, he attacked and defeated, after a desperate action of three hours' duration, 22,000 of the enemy, strongly posted at Meeanee. On the 21st Feb. Hydrabad surrendered to him; and on the 24th March, with 5,000 men, he attacked and signally defeated 20,000 of the enemy, posted in a very strong and difficult position at Dubba near Hydrabad, thus completing the entire subjugation of Scinde. Early in 1845, with a force consisting of about 5000 men of all arms, he took the field against the mountain and desert tribes situated on the right bank of the Indus to the north of Shikarpore, and after an arduous campaign he effected the total destruction of these robber tribes. Sir Charles has received a medal for Corunna.

11 Capt. Dunbar, Lts. Budd and Goddard, served the campaign in the Southern Mahratta country, and were present at the investment and capture of Panulla and Powughur, and in the operations against the forts Munnahur and Munsuntosh. Capt. Dunbar served in Upper and Lower Scinde in 1842-3.

12 Capt. Harding served with the Lt. Company at defence of the Residency at Hyderabad, and was afterwards severely wounded at the battle of Meeanee (Medal).

13 Capt. Thackwell served in Scinde, and was present at the battle of Hyderabad, including the investment and capture of Forts Panulla and Powughur.

14 Lts. Deshon and Carrow were at Hyderabad (Medal), Panulla, Powughur, Munnahur, and Munsuntosh.

15 Lts. Brennan and Stack served throughout the operations in Scinde (Medal) including the destruction of Imaumghur and the battles of Meeanee and Hyderabad (severely wounded). They were afterwards present at Panulla, Powughur, Munnahur, and Munsuntosh.

16 Lieut. Bowden served throughout the operations in Scinde (Medal), including ... wounded in the breast. He was afterwards present at the investment and capture of the Forts of Panulla and Powughur.

17 Lieut. Miller served with the 26th on the China expedition, and was present at the defence of Ningpo, at Tsekee, attack and capture of Chapoo, Shanghai, Woosung, and Chin Kiang Foo.

18 Lt. Blackall served with the 49th in China, and was present at the first taking of Chusan.

r. b. Emb. for Foreign Serv. 13 May, 1842.] **23rd (*Royal Welsh Fusiliers*) Regt. of Foot.** [r. b. Serving in North America.

In the centre of the Colour the *Prince of Wales's Feathers*, with the motto, "*Ich Dien.*"—In the second and third corners, the *Rising Sun* and the *Red Dragon*, and in the fourth corner, the *White Horse*, with the Motto, "*Nec aspera terrent.*"—"MINDEN"—the *Sphinx*, with the words "EGYPT"—"CORUNNA"—"MARTINIQUE"—"ALBUHERA"—"BADAJOZ"—"SALAMANCA"—"VITTORIA"—"PYRENEES"—"NIVELLE"—"ORTHES"—"TOULOUSE"—"PENINSULA"—"WATERLOO."

Years' Serv.		
66		*Colonel.*
Full Pay.	Half Pay.	
		P *Sir* James Willoughby Gordon,[1] *Bt.* GCB. GCH. *Ens.* 17 Oct. 1783; *Lieut.* 5 Mar. 89; *Capt.* 2 Sept. 95; *Major.* 9 Nov. 97; *Lieut.-Col.* 21 May, 1801; *Col.* 25 July, 10; *Major-Gen.* 4 June, 13; *Lieut.-Gen.* 27 May, 25; *Gen.* 23 Nov. 41; *Col.* 23rd Fusiliers, 23 April, 23.
24	0	*Lieut.-Colonels.*—Arthur Wellesley Torrens, *Ens. & Lieut.* 14 April, 25; *Lieut. & Capt.* 12 June, 30; *Capt. & Lieut.-Col.* P11 Sept. 40.
38	0	r. P Wat. Robert Pattison Holmes,[2] *2nd Lieut.* 14 Feb. 11; *Lieut.* P12 Dec. 11; *Capt.* P4 Sept. 23; *Major,* 17 Dec. 30; *Lt.-Col.* 14 Apr. 46.
23	0	*Majors.*—Charles Crutchley, *2nd Lieut.* P8 Apr. 26; *Lieut.* 28 July, 30; *Capt.* P11 Dec. 35; *Major,* P22 Oct. 44.
20	0	r. Frederick Granville, *2nd Lieut.* P17 Sept. 29; *Lieut.* P1 Nov. 33; *Capt.* P28 Apr. 37; *Major,* P19 May, 46.

Full Pay	Half Pay		2nd Lieut.	Lieut.	Captain.	Brev.-Maj.
		Captains.				
19	0	r. Harry Geo. Chester ..	26 Oct. 30	7 Aug. 35	P11 Sept. 40	
24	0	r. Fred. J. Phillott......	7 Apr. 25	P12 Dec. 26	15 Apr. 42	
16	0	r. HobartGrant Anderdon	P15 Nov. 33	P24 Mar. 37	P31 Mar. 43	
15	0	Daniel Lysons[5]	P26 Dec. 34	P23 Aug. 37	P29 Dec. 43	
13	0	Fra. A. Disney Roebuck	P13 May 36	P10 Apr. 40	P17 Jan. 45	
12	0	r. Arth.W.WilliamsWynn	P24 Mar. 37	P11 Sept. 40	P28 Mar. 45	
10	0	r. Arthur James Herbert	P5 Apr. 39	15 Apr. 42	P8 Aug. 45	
10	0	Francis Edward Evans ..	P5 Apr. 39	15 Apr. 42	P11 Nov. 45	
14	0	r. Edward Battye, s.....	P31 July 35	P4 Aug. 37	14 Apr. 46	
9	0	Thomas Parker Rickford	P11 Sept. 40	P22 Apr. 42	P19 May 46	
8	0	Wm. Pitcairn Campbell	6 Aug. 41	P4 Aug. 43	P16 Apr. 47	
		First Lieutenants.				
7	0	r. Edward W. D. Bell ..	15 Apr. 42	P17 Nov. 43		
9	0	John Charles Conolly ..	P30 Oct. 40	P22 July 42		
7	0	Francis R. Campbell....	16 Apr. 42	P29 Mar. 44		
7	0	Peregrine L. Phillips ..	P22 Apr. 42	P20 Aug. 44		
7	0	Fred. Thomas Brock....	20 May 42	P22 Oct. 44		
7	0	r. Grismond Philipps ..	3 June 42	P17 Jan. 45		
6	0	r. Robert Bruce........	P31 Mar. 43	P28 Mar. 45		
6	0	r. Charles Edward Hopton	P4 Aug. 43	P30 May 45		
6	0	Henry Hall Dare, *Adj.*..	P20 Oct. 43	P8 Aug. 45		
6	0	r. John Vincent........	P17 Nov. 43	P11 Nov. 45		
7	0	Robert Taylor Raynes	17 Apr. 42	14 Apr. 46		
5	0	Fred. Biscoe Tritton	P22 Mar. 44	P8 May 46		
5	0	r. *Hon.* W. Matt. Plunkett	P29 Mar. 44	P19 May 46		
5	0	r. Lewis Agassiz........	P20 Aug. 44	P16 Apr. 47		
5	0	Cornelius Graham Sutton	P22 Oct. 44	P15 Oct. 47		
		Second Lieuts.				
4	0	r. A. F. *Lord* Greenock, *adj.*	P30 May 45			
4	0	George Morrison Marsh..	P8 Aug. 45			
4	0	r. Edward Howell	P11 Nov. 45			
3	0	r. RobertVaughanDickens	1 May 46			
3	0	r. Edmund Crofts	P8 May 46			
3	0	John Cornewall Brady ..	P19 May 46			
3	0	r *Sir* HORChamberlain *Bt*	25 Aug. 46			
3	0	r. George Henry Hughes	P28 Aug. 46			
2	0	Richard Milford........	P16 Apr. 47			
2	0	Francis M. Hall Dare ..	P15 Oct. 47			
1	0	r. Trevor Hope Edwardes	P26 Sept. 48			

Full Pay	Half Pay	
22	13 11/12	*Paymaster.*—P Wat. Geo. Dunn,[6] 15 Mar. 31; *2nd Lt.* 15 Apr. 13; *Lt.* 18 July, 15.
6	0	*Adjutants.*—*Lieut.* Henry Hall Dare, 19 June, 46.
4	0	r. *2nd Lt.* Alan Fred., *Lord* Greenock, 25 Aug. 46.
5	0	*Quarter-Masters.*—Charles Grant, 5 July, 44.
3	0	r. Robert Fortune, 25 Aug. 46.
23	0	*Surgeons.*—Edw. Bradford, 24 Sept. 41; *Asst.-S.* 20 Mar. 28; *Hos.-A.* 5 Dec. 26.
15	0	r. Robert Smith, 8 Dec. 45; *Assist.-Surg.* 26 Sept. 34.
5	0	*Assist.-Surgeons.*—William Godfrey Watt, 1 March, 44.
4	0	r. Douglas Grantham, 24 Oct. 45.

Facings Blue.—*Agents,* Messrs. Cox & Co.

[*1st Battalion Returned from Nova Scotia,* 5 *Oct.* 48.]

5 Captain Lysons served in Canada during the late insurrection, and was honourably mentioned in Col. Gore's despatches at St. Denis.

6 Paymaster Dunn served in the Peninsula in 1814. Present at Waterloo 18th June. Storming of Cambray (commanded ladder party 23d Fusiliers), and capture of Paris.

1 Sir Willoughby Gordon went up in Lord Hood's Fleet to the siege of Toulon, as a Volunteer in 1793. Present at the taking of the French Force at Bantry Bay, in 1796. Commanded the 85th, when it took possession of and occupied Madeira. In the spring of 1812 he was appointed Quarter-Master-General to the Forces serving in the Peninsula under the Duke of Wellington, and was with the Army at the capture of Madrid, at Burgos, and the subsequent retreat to Portugal.

2 Lt. Col. Holmes served in the Peninsula, from 1812 to the end of the war, including the sieges of Ciudad Rodrigo and Badajoz, in 1812; battles of Nivelle, Nive, Orthes, and Toulouse. Present at Waterloo, storming of Cambray, and capture of [illegible]

The *Sphinx*, with the words, "EGYPT"—"CAPE OF GOOD HOPE"—"TALAVERA"—"FUENTES D'ONOR"—"SALAMANCA"—"VITTORIA"—"PYRENEES"—"NIVELLE"—"ORTHES"—"PENINSULA."

Years' Serv. Full Pay.	Half Pay.	
51		*Colonel.*—Robert Ellice,[1] *Ens.* 8 Nov. 98; *Lt.* 5 Jan. 99; *Capt.* 4 May, 01; *Major*, 12 May, 08; *Lt.-Col.* 16 Mar. 09; *Col.* 12 Aug. 19; *Major-Gen.* 22 July, 30; *Lt.-Gen.* 23 Nov. 41; *Col.* 24th Regt. 2 Nov. 42.
36	1 8/12	*Lieut.-Colonels.*—[illegible] Robert Brookes,[2] *Ens.* 16 May, 11; *Lieut.* 23 Aug. 13; *Capt.* 27 Aug. 25; *Major*, 3 May, 31; *Lt.-Col.* 27 April 46.
38	4 3/12	John Pennycuick,[3] CB. KH. *Ens.* 31 Aug. 07; *Lt.* 15 Jan. 12; *Capt.* P 14 June, 21; *Maj.* P 25 Apr. 34; *Brev.-Lt.-Col.* 23 July, 39; *Lt.-Col.* P 12 June, 40.
27	0	*Majors.*—Henry William Harris,[4] *Ens.* P 23 May, 22, *Lieut.* 27 Sept. 24; *Capt.* P 30 Dec. 31; *Major*, P 14 Apr. 46.
21	0	Howell Paynter, *Ens.* 26 April, 28; *Lieut.* 6 Jan. 33; *Capt.* P 6 May, 42; *Major*, P 28 April, 46.

Full Pay	Half Pay	CAPTAINS.	ENSIGN.	LIEUT.	CAPTAIN.	BREV.-[illegible].
42	0	John Harris[5]	28 Aug. 07	21 July 09	11 May 30	9 Nov. 46
24	0	Aug. Geo. Blachford....	P 12 Nov. 25	P 12 Dec. 26	17 Aug. 41	
24	0	Wm. Gustavus Brown ..	7 July 25	11 May 30	10 May 44	
23	2/12	Charles Lee...........	8 Apr. 25	P 30 Dec. 28	12 Apr. 44	
10	0	Charles Henry Ellice, *s.*	never	10 May 39	P 8 Aug. 45	
14	0	Robert William Travers..	23 Jan. 35	P 27 Mar. 40	3 Apr. 46	
12	0	Charles Robinson Harris	P 17 Feb. 37	8 Jan. 41	P 14 Apr. 46	
12	0	Edmund Wodehouse	P 24 Mar. 37	P 15 Jan. 41	P 28 Apr. 46	
11	0	Louis Howe Bazalgette..	26 June 38	P 24 Sept. 41	7 Apr. 48	
9	0	John Saunders Shore....	P 27 Mar. 40	P 6 May 42	P 20 Oct. 48	
		LIEUTENANTS.				
9	0	Francis Spring	P 28 Feb. 40	P 22 April 42		
8	0	John Henry Lutman	8 Jan. 41	P 16 June 43		
8	0	Geo. Ellis Lloyd Williams	P 23 Apr. 41	22 Aug. 44		
11	2/12	Francis Charles Skurray	P 7 Oct. 37	8 April 42		
9	0	Sweton Grant	15 May 40	19 Jan. 44		
7	0	Andrew John Macpherson	19 Apr. 42	26 July 44		
7	0	Richard Aubin Croker ..	P 13 Feb. 42	5 Oct. 44		
7	0	George Frederick Berry..	7 Jan. 42	P 25 Apr. 45		
8	0	Charles Mackechnie	P 16 Apr. 41	3 Apr. 46		
8	0	George Phillips	3 Dec. 41	do.		
7	0	Walter Cumming	20 May 42	do.		
6	0	John Bulkeley Thelwall	P 4 Aug. 43	do.		
6	0	William Hartshorn, *adj.*	29 Dec. 43	do.		
5	0	Cammillo Montebello Drew	10 May 44	do.		
4	0	William Selby	P 27 June 45	P 28 Apr. 46		
4	0	Francis Clark..........	P 11 Apr. 45	P 9 Oct. 46		
9	0	Oliver Thomas Graham ..	10 Jan. 40	10 May 41		
6	0	Henry Parr T. Woodington	P 19 May 43	P 25 Aug. 46		
3	0	Orlebar Bletsoe Payne ..	3 Apr. 46	7 Apr. 48		
3	0	John Acton Woodgate ..	4 Apr. 46	7 Apr. 48		
3	0	Thomas Maling Greensill	5 Apr. 46	P 20 Oct. 48		
3	0	William Phillips.......	6 Apr. 46	P 20 Oct. 48		
7	0	Henry Macdonald Burns	20 May 42	23 June 48		
		ENSIGNS.				
3	0	Hector C. Barthol. Collis	7 Apr. 46			
3	0	Wm. Douglas Hall Baillie	P 14 Apr. 46			
3	0	Henry John Hinde......	13 Nov. 46			
3	0	Rob. G. A. de Montmorency	P 25 Aug. 46			
1	0	James Charles W. Kippen	P 31 Mar. 48			
1	0	Alexander Pennycuick ..	18 July 48			
1	0	Fred. Wm. Adam Parsons	10 Aug. 48			
1	0	Richard Henry Holland	P 20 Oct. 48			
16	0	*Paymaster.*—Geo. Abercromby Ferrier, 29 Mar. 42; *Ens.* P 12 April, 33; *Lieut.* [P 1 June, 38.				
6	0	*Adjutant.*—*Lieut.* William Hartshorn, 25 Oct. 44.				
7	0	*Quarter-Master.*—James Price, 16 Aug. 42.				
17	0	*Surgeon.*—George Kincaid Pitcairn, M.D. 6 Oct. 43; *Assist.-Surg.* 23 Nov. 32.				
3	0	*Assist.-Surgeons.*—William Hanbury, 3 Apr. 46.				
3	0	William James Furlonge, M.D. 3 Apr. 46.				
8	0	James Grant, M.D.[6] 12 Oct. 41.				

Facings Green.—*Agents*, Messrs. Cox & Co.

2 Lieut.-Colonel Brookes served in the Peninsula from July, 1811, to the end of the war, including the following battles, sieges, &c., viz.: Badajos, Salamanca, Burgos, Palencia, Osma, Vittoria, San Sebastian, Aug. and Sept. 1813, Santa Clara (wounded), Bidassoa (wounded), Nivelle, Nive, 9th, 10th (wounded), and 11th Dec. and blockade of Bayonne; he was acting Engineer during the siege of San Sebastian; and he accompanied a detachment of Volunteers in a night attack and capture of the Island of Santa Clara by a combined force of seamen and troops. Proceeded to North America with the force that embarked from Bourdeaux, and served there until the termination of the American war; and subsequently with the army of occupation in France.

4 Major H. W. Harris served in the Burmese war, and was present in the engagements at Paddoo, and Mahatee; severely wounded in the body and neck by musket shots at the attack of the Hills of Arracan.

5 Major John Harris was in the engagement with the *Bellona* and *Minerva*, French frigates, and a corvette, in the Mosambique channel, 3rd July, 1810; served the Nepaul campaigns of 1814 and 15, including the taking of Harriapore; in the Mahratta war in 1817; in Lower Canada in 1837, at the taking of Grande Brulee. In Upper Canada in 1838. Commanded the 24th regt. before Navy Island with the local rank of Major.

6 Doctor Grant served with the Queen's Royals the campaign of 1844-5 in the Southern Concan and Sawunt Warree Country, including the storming of several stockades, and the investment and capture of the Fort of Monohur and Munsuntosh.

1 Lieut.-General Ellice served on the expedition to South America, and was present at the capture of Buenos Ayres.

3 Lieut.-Col. Pennycuick served on the Expedition to Java, including the actions at Weldevrieden, Fort Cornelis, Djogjocarta, and Probolingo; wounded in the breast in an attack upon the enemy's field artillery, within the lines of Cornelis, 26th Aug. 1811. Served also at the Capture of Balli and Macassar, in 1814; in the Burmese War, in 1825 and 26; the campaign in Affghanistan and Beloochistan, in 1839, including the storm and capture of the fortresses of Ghuznee and Khelat, at which last he led the advance at the assault. Marched into Arabia in command of 500 men from the garrison of Aden; destroyed the Aughgents of Sheik Medi and Sheik Othman, and skirmished between those places on the 5th and 6th Oct. 1841.

Emb.^d for For. Ser. 21 Dec. 1839.] **25th (*The King's own Borderers*) Regt. of Ft.** [Serving at Madras.

The *King's Crest* in two corners of the Colour, "*In Veritate Religionis confido.*" The *Arms of Edinburgh*, "*Nisi Dominus frustra;*" with the *White Horse* in the third corner of the Colour. "*Nec aspera terrent.*" "MINDEN"—"EGMONT-OP-ZEE." The *Sphinx*. "EGYPT."—Flank Companies, "MARTINIQUE."

Years' Serv.		
63		*Colonel.*
Full Pay.	Half Pay.	
		Sir Henry Fred. Campbell,[1] KCB. & GCH. *Ens.* 20 Sept. 86; *Lieut. & Capt.* 25 April, 93; *Capt. & Lieut.-Col.* 6 April, 96; *Col.* 25 Sept. 03; *Major-Gen.* 25 July, 10; *Lieut.-Gen.* 4 June, 14; *Gen.* 10 Jan. 37; *Col. 25th Regt.* 20 Oct. 31.
		Lieut.-Colonels.
30	$4\frac{1}{12}$	James Robert Young, *Ens.* 27 July, 15; *Lieut.* 14 Dec. 18; *Capt.* P 13 May, 26; *Major,* P 31 Dec. 33; *Lieut.-Col.* 8 April, 42.
45	$\frac{6}{12}$	John Joseph Hollis, *Ens.* 9 July 03; *Lt.* 1 Dec. 04; *Capt.* 30 Mar. 09; *Br.-Maj.* 22 July 30; *Maj.* 8 Apr. 42; *Brev.-Lt.-Col.,* 9 Nov. 46; *Lt.-Col.* 19 June 48.
33	1	*Majors.*—Henry Francis Strange,[3] *Ens.* 23 May 15; *Lieut.* 7 April 25; *Capt.* P 29 June 26; *Brev.-Major,* 23 Nov. 41; *Major,* 20 Oct. 42.
24	0	Andrew Armstrong Barnes, *Ens.* 21 July 25; *Lieut.* 28 May 29; *Capt.* P 1 July 36; *Brev.-Major,* 9 Nov. 46; *Maj.* 19 June 48

Full Pay	Half Pay		ENSIGN.	LIEUT.	CAPTAIN.	BREV.-MAJ.
		CAPTAINS.				
24	0	Samuel Wells	9 Apr. 25	P 8 Oct. 29	P 15 Sept. 37	
16	0	Samuel B. Hamilton....	20 Sept. 33	P 14 July 37	P 12 Jan. 39	
20	0	George Holt	10 Aug. 23	12 Sept. 25	30 Oct. 40	
14	0	Wm. C. E. Napier[4]	28 Aug. 35	P 17 Nov. 37	P 29 April 42	18 Feb. 48
14	0	Edward Ramsden Priestley	27 Nov. 35	P 13 Jan. 38	P 20 Oct. 43	
32	$3\frac{7}{12}$	John Impett[5]	14 April 14	P 5 Oct. 20	30 Jan. 35	9 Nov. 46
12	0	Stanhope Mason Gildea..	P 29 Apr. 37	P 11 May 38	P 19 May 46	
26	$10\frac{6}{12}$	Thomas Deacon[6]....	5 Apr. 13	3 Aug. 15	29 Apr. 36	9 Nov. 46
11	0	James Ogilvy..........	P 31 Mar. 38	P 15 Dec. 40	19 June 48	
6	0	*Hon.* Fra. Wm. H. Fane, *s.*	24 Feb. 43	26 July 44	P 1 Aug. 48	
		LIEUTENANTS.				
10	0	Stewart Northey	P 18 Jan. 39	P 21 May 41		
10	0	Robert Mascie Taylor ..	P 11 Jan. 39	P 3 Aug. 41		
18	0	Henry T. Walker, *adj.*..	28 Oct. 36	P 4 July 39		
12	0	Robert Murphy Nicolls	9 July 37	4 Oct. 39		
11	0	Fred. J. B. Priestley	2 Mar. 38	8 April 42		
11	0	Robert Cairnes Bruce ..	P 30 Mar. 38	do.		
11	0	Samuel Percy Lea......	P 6 July 38	do.		
10	0	Wm. H. Tylden Pattenson	P 23 Aug. 39	do.		
8	0	Delancey Barclay Johnston	15 Oct. 41	P 21 July 43		
7	0	George Bent	10 April 42	P 13 Oct. 43		
7	0	Charles D. Pogson	9 April 42	P 10 May 44		
8	0	Cha. Jas. Stewart Wallace	5 Nov. 41	P 20 Dec. 44		
7	0	George E. Lane[6]	27 May 42	22 July 45		
6	0	Charles Fred. Browne ..	19 May 43	9 June 46		
6	0	Henry Exley Jones	P 27 Oct. 43	9 June 46		
5	0	George Needham	P 3 May 44	9 June 46		
4	0	Frederick Wm. Breedon	P 16 May 45	29 Jan. 47		
6	0	Robert Briscoe	27 Oct. 43	P 30 Dec. 45		
5	0	Thomas Edwin Blomfield	24 May 44	P 8 Oct. 47		
5	0	William Thomas Potts ..	29 Mar. 44	P 5 Nov. 47		
3	0	William George Turner ..	P 19 May 46	25 April 48		
4	0	Astley Campbell Smith..	P 11 Nov. 45	11 June 48		
3	0	Horatio Priestley	28 Aug. 46	19 June 48		
		ENSIGNS.				
3	0	William Trail Arnold....	P 20 Nov. 46			
2	0	Henry Veitch..........	P 19 Feb. 47			
2	0	George Gould..........	P 8 Oct. 47			
2	0	Standish Grady Maunsell	P 5 Nov. 47			
2	0	William Henry Newenham	17 Dec. 47			
1	0	Charles Cramond Dick ..	25 April 48			
1	0	John Henry Nott	P 12 Sept. 48			
1	0	William Vere Lane	12 Sept. 48			

1 Sir Henry Frederick Campbell served in Holland from Feb. to May, 1793; in Flanders from June to Dec. 1794, and was present in the action at Boxtel. Embarked for Portugal in Dec. 1808, in command of the 2d Brigade of Guards, and was present at the passage of the Douro and capture of Oporto, action at Salamonde, and battle of Talavera, where he was severely wounded, and returned to England in consequence. Rejoined the army in Portugal, in June, 1811, and resumed the command of the 2nd Brigade of Guards, with which he was present at the siege of Ciudad Rodrigo. On the advance of the British Army across the Agueda into Spain, he commanded the 1st Division, and with it was present at the battle of Salamanca, capture of Madrid, and siege of Burgos. Medal and one clasp for Talavera and Salamanca.

5 Major Impett served the campaign of 1815 with the 71st, and was present at the battle of Waterloo.

6 Maj. Deacon served with the 2nd battalion of the 73rd on the expedition to Stralsund, under Sir Sam. Gibbs, in 1813, and to the north of Germany, under Count Walmoden, and was present at the battle of Goerde. Subsequently in Holland, under Lord Lynedoch, during the operations of the winter campaign of 1813-14. Campaign of 1815,—severely wounded at Waterloo. Commanded one of the disturbed districts of the Kandian provinces, and other operations, in Ceylon, during the rebellion of 1817 and 18.

Full Pay	Half Pay	
19	0	*Paymaster.*—Wm. Brumell, 30 Sept. 42; *Ens.* 11 June, 30; *Lieut.* 10 Oct. 34.
13	0	*Adjutant.—Lieut.* Henry Torrens Walker, 15 Dec. 43.
27	0	*Quarter-Master.*—John Potts, 10 Jan. 22.
15	0	*Surgeon.*—James M'Gregor, 13 Dec. 44; *Assist.-Surg.* 24 July 34.
11	0	*Assist.-Surgs.*—Edward John Burton, M.D. 11 May 38.
3	0	Jonas King Carr, M.D. 24 July 46.
1	0	James Fraser, M.D. 20 Oct. 48.

[*Facings* Blue.

[*Agents,* Messrs. Cox & Co.

3 Major Strange served with the 26th on the China expedition (Medal), and was present at the defence of Ningpo, at Tsekee, Chapoo, Woosung, Shanghae, Chin Kiang Foo, and Nankin.

4 Major Napier served as aide-de-camp to Sir Charles Napier during his campaign against the mountain and desert tribes situated on the right bank of the Indus, early in 1845.

6 Lt. Lane served with the 40th in the action of Maharajpore, and has received the Bronze Star.

The *Sphinx*, "EGYPT."—"CORUNNA."—"CHINA."—*The Dragon.*

Years' Serv.		
55		*Colonel.*
		ℙ ℭ𝔅 John, *Lord* Seaton,[1] GCB. GCMG. GCH., *Ens.* 10 July, 1794; *Lt.* 4 Sept. 95; *Capt.* 12 Jan. 00; *Major*, 21 Jan. 08; *Lt.-Col.* 2 Feb. 09; *Col.* 4 June, 14; *Major-Gen.* 27 May, 25; *Lieut.-Gen.* 28 June, 38; *Col.* 26 F. 28 March, 38.
Full Pay.	Half Pay.	*Lieut.-Colonel.*
24	0	Andrew T. Hemphill, *Ens.* 7 Apr. 25; *Lieut.* 16 Apr. 29; *Capt.* 3 July, 39; *Major*, 11 Feb. 46; *Lt.-Col.* P 8 Dec. 46.
30	1 2/12	*Majors.*—George Hogarth,[3] CB., *Ens.* P 22 May 17; *Lieut.* P 13 Sept. 21; *Capt.* P 12 Nov. 25; *Brev.-Major*, 28 June 38; *Major*, 28 Aug. 41.
17	0	Ferdinand Whittingham,[6] CB. *Ens.* 2 Nov. 32; *Lieut.* P 19 Feb. 36; *Capt.* P 30 Apr. 41; *Brev.-Major*, 23 Dec. 42; *Major*, P 1 Oct. 47.

Full Pay.	Half Pay.	CAPTAINS.	ENSIGN.	LIEUT.	CAPTAIN.	BREV.-MAJ.
25	0	George F. Mylius[5]	17 Oct. 24	P 28 Jan. 26	P 30 Aug. 31	9 Nov. 46
20	0	Bernard Granville Layard	P 13 Aug. 29	12 Jan. 33	17 June 41	
14	0	Francis Carey	P 22 May 35	P 2 Sept. 37	P 7 July 43	
16	0	Henry Edgar[8]	P 27 Sept. 33	P 24 Nov. 35	10 Dec. 44	
16	0	John Wm. Johnstone[9]	P 31 May 33	25 Feb. 37	P 20 Dec. 44	
12	0	John Rodgers[10]	P 31 Mar. 37	P 18 May 38	P 4 Apr. 45	
14	0	George Frend,[11]	P 24 Nov. 35	P 14 July 37	5 Dec. 43	
13	0	William Smith Nicholson	P 4 Mar. 36	19 Dec. 38	P 2 Sept. 45	
15	0	Charles Cameron[12]	16 May 34	1 July 37	31 July 46	
10	0	William Hopson Hopson	P 4 July 39	P 28 Dec. 41	P 24 Dec. 47	
		LIEUTENANTS.				
15	0	Walter Brisbane Park[14]	26 Dec. 34	15 June 39		
14	0	Wm. Thomas Betts[10]	24 Nov. 35	15 Nov. 39		
9	0	Arthur August. Longmore	P 8 May 40	P 31 Dec. 41		
7	0	Thomas Andrews	P 27 Dec. 42	25 June 44		
8	0	Bertie Mathew Roberts	22 May 41	P 23 June 43		
7	0	Jacob Geo. Mountain, *adj.*	25 Oct. 42	P 19 May 46		
8	0	Robert Mordaunt Dickens	18 June 41	26 June 46		
5	0	Thomas William Andrews	P 2 Feb. 44	14 Aug. 46		
5	0	Richard Wollaston Clerke	P 12 April 44	P 22 Dec. 46		
5	0	Charles Edward Preston	26 July 44	P 19 Mar. 47		
5	0	*Hon.* Alex. E. G. Sinclair	P 20 Dec. 44	P 9 April 47		
5	0	Christo. Edw. Blackett	21 Dec. 44	P 1 Oct. 47		
5	0	Robert Thomas Hearn	19 Aug. 44	29 May 47		
		ENSIGNS.				
3	0	William Robert Bell	P 19 May 46			
3	0	Henry James Noyes	26 June 46			
3	0	Rodney Mylius	14 Aug. 46			
2	0	William Esdaile Thomas	P 19 Mar. 47			
2	0	Chamb. Henry Hinchliff	P 9 April 47			
2	0	William Edward Wallace	P 3 Sept. 47			
2	0	James Brown Young	P 15 Oct. 47			
2	0	Sylvester W. F. M. Wilson	P 12 Nov. 47			

11 Capt. Frend served as aide-de-camp to Sir Hugh Gough at Maharajpore (medal), in which action he was severely wounded, and had his right arm amputated in the field.

12 Captain Cameron served throughout the China expedition (medal), and was present at Chusan, Canton, Amoy, defence of Ningpo, at Chapoo, Woosung, Shanghae, and Nanking.

14 Lt. Park served in China (medal), at Amoy, Golongso, defence of Ningpo, at Tseke, Chapoo, Woosung, Shanghae, Chin Kiang Foo, and Nanking.

Full Pay.	Half Pay.	
11	0	*Paymaster.*—Robert Collins Craigie, 3 Nov. 43; *Ens.* P 2 Feb. 38; *Lt.* P 16 Nov. 41.
7	0	*Adjutant.*—*Lieut.* Jacob George Mountain, 14 Aug. 46.
2	0	*Quarter-Master.*—Charles Kent,[10] 2 April 47.
10	0	*Surgeon.*—William Augustus Heise, M.D., 4 Feb. 48; *Asst.-Surg.* 18 Oct. 39.
1	0	*Assist.-Surgeon.*—Frederick Clarke, 27 Oct. 48.
		Facings Yellow.—*Agents*, Messrs. Cox & Co.—*Irish Agents*, *Sir* E. R. Borough, *Bt.*, Armit, & Co.

[Returned from Bengal, 4th July, 1843.]

1 Lord Seaton has received a cross and three clasps for Corunna, Albuhera, Ciudad Rodrigo, (where he was severely wounded), Nivelle, Nive, Orthes, and Toulouse.

3 Major Hogarth served in China (medal), at the defence of Ningpo, at Chapoo, Woosung, Shanghae, Chin Kiang Foo, and Nanking. He commanded the left wing of the 26th on a detached command at the assault and capture of the city of Chin Kiang Foo.

5 Maj. Mylius served throughout the China expedition (medal), and was present at the first capture of Chusan, the operations before Canton from the 24th to the 31st May 1841, at Woosung, Shanghae, Chin Kiang Foo, and Nanking.

6 Major Whittingham served as Aide de Camp to Sir Hugh Gough throughout the operations of 1842 in China (medal), and was present at Segoan, Chapoo, Woosung, Shanghae, and Chin Kiang Foo.

8 Capt. Edgar served in China (medal) at the defence of Ningpo, at Chapoo, Woosung, Shanghai, Chin Kiang Foo, and Nanking.

9 Captain Johnstone served throughout the China expedition (medal), and was present at Chusan, Canton (wounded in the left wrist), defence of Ningpo, at Tsake, Chapoo, Woosung, Shanghae, Chin Kiang Foo, and Nanking.

10 Captain Rodgers, Lt. Betts, and Qr.-Master Kent, served throughout the China expedition (medal), and were present at Chusan, Canton, defence of Ningpo, at Chapoo, Woosung, Shanghae, Chin Kiang Foo, and Nanking.

A Castle with Three Turrets; St. George's colours flying in a blue Field. The White Horse. "*Nec aspera terrent.*" "ST. LUCIA." The *Sphinx*, with the words "EGYPT"—"MAIDA"—"BADAJOZ"—"SALAMANCA"—"VITTORIA"—"PYRENEES"—"NIVELLE"—"ORTHES"—"TOULOUSE"—"PENINSULA"—"WATERLOO."

Years' Serv. Full Pay.	Half Pay.	
49		***Colonel.***
		P *Sir* William F. P. Napier,[1] KCB. *Ens.* 14 June, 00; *Lieut.* 18 Apr. 01; *Capt.* 2 June, 04; *Major*, 30 May, 11; *Lieut.-Col.* 22 Nov. 13; *Col.* 22 July, 30; *Major-Gen.* 23 Nov. 41; *Col.* 27th Regt. 5 Feb. 48.
		Lieut.-Colonel.
26	0	Montague Cholmeley Johnstone, *Ens.* P 27 Feb. 23; *Lieut.* P 16 Dec. 24; *Capt.* P 19 Sept. 26; *Major*, P 27 July, 38; *Lieut.-Col.* P 16 Nov. 41.
		Majors.
24	0	Samuel E. Goodman, *2nd Lieut.* 7 July 25; *Lieut.* P 8 April 26; *Capt.* P 4 Oct. 33; *Major*, P 28 Feb. 40; *Brevet Lt.-Col.* 20 Oct. 46.
23	0	Usher Williamson, *Ensign*, P 29 Aug. 26; *Lieut.* P 11 Nov. 31, *Capt.* P 28 Feb. 40; *Major*, P 18 Aug. 48.

Full Pay	Half Pay	CAPTAINS.	ENSIGN.	LIEUT.	CAPTAIN.	BREVET-MAJOR.
24	0	Geo. Anthony Durnford	3 Mar. 25	P 15 Dec. 25	6 Nov. 38	15 Sept. 48
20	0	Thomas Percival Touzel	10 Sept. 29	P 4 Oct. 33	P 16 Nov. 41	
18	0	Henry D. Cholmeley	P 13 July 31	P 13 Dec. 33	P 3 June 42	
17	0	Andrew Vincent Watson	P 21 Dec. 32	P 18 May 38	P 20 Oct. 43	
24	0	Walter Butler..........	P 15 Dec. 25	P 19 Sept. 26	20 Sept. 44	
16	0	Frederick King	P 13 Dec. 33	P 17 Aug. 38	P 20 Oct. 46	
12	0	Herman Stapylton......	P 4 Aug. 37	P 19 Mar. 41	P 1 Dec. 46	
13	0	Francis Wm. Johnstone..	P 19 Aug. 36	P 23 July 41	P 9 June 48	
12	0	Bartholomew Tunnard[5]	P 26 Dec. 37	P 16 Nov. 41	18 Aug. 48	
9	0	Oliver Langley	P 19 Mar. 40	P 22 Mar. 44	P 22 Dec. 48	
		LIEUTENANTS.				
12	0	Edw. Nassau Molesworth	P 1 Dec. 37	P 2 Apr. 41		
12	0	Benjamin Midgley, *adj.*	11 Dec. 37	16 Apr. 41		
10	0	John Samuel Manly	15 Feb. 39	P 20 Oct. 43		
8	0	Fred. Charles Herring ..	P 16 Nov. 41	5 Aug. 46		
7	0	*Hon.* F. Beau. Pakenham	P 8 Feb. 42	P 20 Oct. 46		
7	0	Brabazon Noble........	P 3 June 42	P 20 Nov. 46		
6	0	C. A. W. Wedderburne..	P 5 Dec. 43	P 1 Dec. 46		
5	0	Thomas William Mostyn	2 Feb. 44	P 20 July 47		
5	0	John Rich. Hedges Becher	P 31 May 44	P 24 Sept. 47		
5	0	Barclay Thomas........	31 Dec. 44	19 Nov. 47		
4	0	Edward Barnes	25 July 45	P 9 June 48		
3	0	Alexander Chancellor ..	P 20 Oct. 46	P 18 Aug. 48		
3	0	William Archibald Kidd	P 20 Nov. 46	P 22 Dec. 48		
		ENSIGNS.				
3	0	William Crozier	29 Dec. 46			
2	0	Charles Warren........	23 April 47			
2	0	Charles Conrad Brine ..	P 20 July 47			
2	0	Wm. Cameron Somerville	P 24 Sept. 47			
2	0	James Henry Creagh ..	19 Nov. 47			
1	0	William Douglas Phelips	P 9 June 48			
1	0	John Anderson Gordon..	P 12 Sept. 48			
1	0	*Sir* Sir Jas. L. Cotter, *Bt*	P 22 Dec. 48			

5 Capt. Tunnard was severely wounded in a night attack upon a large body of the Cape-Dutch Emigrant Boors at the Congella Camp, Port Natal, 23rd May, 1842.

6 Mr. Mostyn served in the Peninsula, from Jan. 1811 until the end of the war, including the siege of Badajoz, April 1812, battles of Salamanca, Vittoria, and the Pyrenees; storming of San Sebastian with the Volunteer party; battles of Orthes and Toulouse. Served in the American war, including the action at Plattsburg. Present on the 18th June at Waterloo.

Full Pay	Half Pay	
41	4/12	*Paymaster.*—Victor Raymond, 9 March, 26; *Ens.* 11 Feb. 08; *Lieut.* 16 Nov. 09; *Capt.* 7 April, 25.
12	0	*Adjutant.*—*Lieut.* Benj. Midgley, 11 Dec. 37.
18	0	*Quarter-Master.*—Geo. Thompson, 13 Sept. 31.
39	0	*Surgeon.*—P W Thos. Mostyn,[6] 6 Oct. 25; *Assist.-Surg.* 19 Dec. 11; *Hosp.-Assist.* 9 Nov. 10.
7	0	*Assist.-Surgeon.*—William Nelson Irwin, 2 Dec. 42.

Facings Buff.—*Agent*, John Lawrie, Esq.

[*Returned from the Cape of Good Hope*, 18 *April* 48.]

1 Sir William Napier served at the siege of Copenhagen and battle of Kioge, in 1807; Sir John Moore's campaign of 1808-9; the subsequent Peninsular campaigns from 1809 to the end of that war in 1814, and was present in many of the soul-stirring scenes which he has described with so much ability in his admirable "History of the Peninsular War," including the action of the Coa (wounded), battle of Busaco, actions of Pombal, Redinha, and Casal Nova—severely wounded at the head of six companies supporting the 52nd; action of Foz d'Aronce, battle of Salamanca, passage of the Huebra, actions of Vera when Soult attempted to relieve San Sebastian, and again when the Allies passed the Bidassoa; battles of the Nivelle and Nive—wounded in defending the churchyard of Arcangues; battle of Orthes. Medal and two clasps for Salamanca, Nivelle, and Nive, at which battles he commanded the 43rd Light Infantry, and also in many minor actions. Served also in the campaign of 1815.

The Sphinx, with the words "EGYPT"—"CORUNNA"—"BARROSA"—"ALBUHERA"—"VITTORIA"—"PYRENEES"—"NIVELLE"—"NIVE"—"ORTHES"—"PENINSULA" "WATERLOO."

Years' Serv. 57

Colonel.

Full Pay.	Half Pay.	
		P *Hon. Sir* Edward Paget,[1] GCB. *Cornet & Sub-Lieut.* 23 Mar. 92; *Capt.* 7 Dec. 92; *Major,* 14 Nov. 93, *Lieut.-Col.* 30 April, 94; *Col.* 1 Jan. 98; *Major-Gen.* 1 Jan. 1805; *Lieut.-Gen.* 4 June, 11; *Gen.* 27 May, 25; *Col.* 28th Regt. 26 Dec. 15.
34	0	*Lieut.-Colonel.*—John Messiter, *Ens.* 16 July, 15; *Lieut.* P 3 July, 23; *Capt.* P 19 Sept. 26; *Major,* P 27 Sept. 33; *Lieut.-Col.* 24 Aug. 42.
35	$\frac{1}{12}$	*Majors.*—Thomas Wheeler, *Ensign,* 24 May, 14; *Lieut.* P 18 Dec. 17; *Capt.* 28 Sept. 32; *Major,* 24 Aug. 42.
23	0	Frank Adams, *Ens.* P 30 Dec. 26; *Lieut.* 23 Mar. 32; *Capt.* P 31 Dec. 33; *Major,* 29 Oct. 43.

Full Pay.	Half Pay.	CAPTAINS.	ENSIGN.	LIEUT.	CAPTAIN.	BREV.-MAJ.
16	0	Robt. Julian Baumgartner	P 27 Sept. 33	P 30 June 37	P 23 April 41	
24	0	Mottram Andrews......	9 April 25	P 24 July 28	24 Aug. 42	
20	0	Henry Furey Wakefield[2]	P 17 Dec. 29	29 July 32	30 Dec. 43	
10	0	Percy Archer Butler....	P 1 Mar. 39	2 May 42	P 4 Apr. 45	
12	0	Alexander Fraser	P 11 Aug. 37	P 12 July 39	P 8 Oct. 44	
12	0	John Guise Rogers Aplin	P 7 Oct. 37	P 23 April 41	20 Nov. 45	
13	0	George Butler Stoney ..	P 13 May 36	P 11 Jan. 39	19 Dec. 44	
9	0	John Tayler Gorle[3]	P 7 Aug. 40	P 28 Dec. 41	P 28 Mar. 45	
13	0	Henry J. Coote[4]	23 Sept. 36	P 17 Sept. 39	7 Dec. 44	
11	0	Robert Henry Lindsell ..	P 13 Jan. 38	P 15 Nov. 39	11 June 48	
		LIEUTENANTS.				
10	0	Samuel Rawson........	P 31 May 39	13 Sept. 42		
11	0	John Dane	P 11 May 38	28 July 40		
10	0	Charles A. Thompson, *r.*	4 Jan. 39	P 30 Apr. 41		
10	0	Fred. Lussan Loinsworth	P 14 June 39	14 Oct. 42		
8	0	Henry Webb, *adjutant*..	18 June 41	14 Oct. 42		
9	0	Charles Steevens	P 7 Aug. 40	P 28 Dec. 41		
8	0	Henry William Dennie..	18 Dec. 41	30 Dec. 42		
10	0	William Roberts	29 May 42	28 Feb. 44		
7	0	John Dundas Malcolm..	31 Oct. 42	29 Mar. 44		
7	0	Sussex L. A. B. Messiter	5 Nov. 42	P 24 May 44		
5	0	Edward Collins	P 24 May 44	P 21 May 47		
3	0	Henry R. Crewe Godley	P 25 Sept. 46	P 21 July 48		
5	0	John Meacham	19 Apr. 44	22 Dec. 48		
		ENSIGNS.				
5	0	Charles Greenwood Walsh	25 May 44			
3	0	Philip Hen. Prender. Aplin	21 Apr. 46			
5	0	Henry Baxter[5]	22 Oct. 44			
2	0	William Gordon Shute ..	P 26 Nov. 47			
3	0	Fred. Dickinson Bourne	P 5 Apr. 46			
2	0	Simpson Heckett	31 Dec. 47			
1	0	Edward Thomas Stehelin	19 Sept. 48			
1	0	Vesey Traell	22 Dec. 48			

3 Capt. Gorle served with the 10th regiment the campaign on the Sutlej (Medal) and was present in the battle of Sobraon.

4 Captain Coote served with the 22nd throughout the operations in Scinde (medal) under Sir Charles Napier, and was present at the destruction of Imaumghur, and in the battles of Meeanee and Hyderabad (severely wounded). He was mentioned in orders as being the first man who entered the enemy's entrenched position, and also as having taken the first colour from the enemy at the battle of Hyderabad.

6 Paymaster Benson served in the Peninsula, from July, 1812, to the end of the war, including the battles of Vittoria, the Pyrenees, (wounded in the arm), Pampeluna, Nivelle, Nive, Orthes, and Toulouse. Served also in the American war, and was severely wounded in the right breast by a rifle ball at Plattsburg.

Full Pay.	Half Pay.	
29	8	*Paymaster.*—P Geo. Thos. Benson,[6] 20 May, 36; *Ens.* 13 Feb. 12; *Lt.* 25 Aug. 13.
8	0	*Adjutant.*—*Lieut.* Henry Webb, 21 May, 43.
5	0	*Quarter-Master.*—Adam Cowan, 23 July, 44.
34	$3\frac{1}{12}$	*Surgeon.*—P[illegible] Wm. Henry Young,[7] 4 Sept. 28; *A.-S.* 4 Feb. 13; *H.-A.* 19 Dec. 11.
7	0	*Assist.-Surg.*—Benjamin Wm. Marlow, MD., 25 Oct. 42.

Facings Yellow.—*Agents,* Messrs. Cox & Co.

[*Returned from Bombay,* 19*th May* 1848.]

1 Sir Edward Paget served in the campaign in Flanders and Holland in 94. He was present in the naval action off Cape St. Vincent, 14 Feb. 97; in the actions of the 8th, 13th, and 21st March, in Egypt (in the latter he was wounded), the investment of Cairo and Alexandria. Sir Edward lost his right arm in the action at Oporto, 12th May 09, and has received a Medal for Corunna.

2 Captain Wakefield served with the 40th in Lower and Upper Scinde in 1839 and 40. He commanded the Grenadier Company during the whole of the operations in Candahar and in Affghanistan, in 1841 and 42, and has received the Medal for Candahar, Ghuznee, and Cabool. He was also present in the action of Maharajpore, and has received the Bronze Star.

5 Ensign Baxter served with the 40th at the capture of Fort Manora and surrender of Kurrachee in Lower Scinde in 1839; relief of the force sent against the Fort and Town of Kajjack, investment of Candahar in 1841-2, relief of Khelat-i-Ghiluc; the second Affghan campaign in 1842, including the actions of Kalleeshuk, Kuubakuk, Panjwarie, Tillookhan, Baba Wallie, and Gowine, storming the heights of Bellool, capture of Ghuznee, affairs of Benee Bedam and Mydeun, and those with the rear-guard from Toorkab to Gundamuck, at the Tezeen Pass, and from Lundikhana to Ali Musjid (Medal inscribed "Candahar, Ghuznee, Cabool 1842") He was also present at the battle of Maharajpore (Medal).

7 Mr. Young served in the Peninsula, from March, 1811 to Feb. 1813, including the last siege of Badajoz, and battle of Salamanca. Served also the campaigns of 1813, 14, and 15, in Germany, Holland, and the Netherlands, including the attack on Bergen-op-Zoom, and battle of Waterloo.

"ROLEIA"—"VIMIERA"—"TALAVERA"—"ALBUHERA"—"PENINSULA"—"FEROZESHAH"—"SOB

Years' Serv. 56 Full Pay.	Half Pay.	Colonel.
		John, *Earl of* Strafford,[1] GCB. & GCH. *Ens.* 30 Sept. 1793; *Lt.* 1 93; *Capt.* 24 May, 94; *Lieut.-Col.* 14 March, 1800; *Col.* 25 July, *Major-Gen.* 4 June, 13; *Lieut.-Gen.* 27 May, 25; *Gen.* 23 Nov. 41; *Col. Regt.* 28 Jan. 28.
		Lieut.-Colonels.
24	0	George Congreve,[2] CB. *Ens.* 8 Apr. 25; *Lieut.* P 12 Jan. 26; *Capt.* P 12 J 28; *Brev.-Major,* 23 Nov. 41; *Major,* 8 April, 42; *Lieut.-Col.* 11 Feb.
28	6 1/12	Armine Simcoe Henry Mountain,[2*] CB., *s. Ens.* 20 July, 15; *Lieut.* P 3 Dec. *Capt.* P 26 May, 25; *Maj.* P 30 Dec. 26; *Lt.-Col.* 23 June, 40; *Col.* 19 Ju
39	4/12	*Majors.*—Matthew Smith,[3] *Ens.* 16 Sept. 16; *Lt.* 31 Dec. 23; *Capt.* 8 Feb. *Brevet-Major* 23 Dec. 42; *Major* 22 Dec. 45.
17	0	Gregory Lewis Way, *Ens.* P 17 Feb. 32; *Lieut.* 30 July 36; *Capt.* P 21 May *Major,* P 8 Dec. 46.

Full Pay	Half Pay		ENSIGN.	LIEUT.	CAPTAIN.	BREV.-M
		CAPTAINS.				
15	0	Arth. St. Geo. H. Stepney[4]	P 16 May 34	P 10 Nov. 37	P 15 Apr. 42	3 Apr
25	13 4/12	Edward Boyd[5]	16 July 11	1 July 12	17 Aug. 26	23 Nov
24	0	John D. Young,[6] *s.*	16 Aug. 25	P 7 Jan. 27	5 Nov. 41	
12	0	John Power[7]	P 5 May 37	P 12 July 39	P 29 Dec. 43	
12	0	Lewis Coker[8]	11 Aug. 37	P 27 Sept. 39	P 4 Apr. 45	20 Oct.
10	0	Kenneth Murchison[6]	1 Feb. 39	20 May 41	22 Dec. 45	
21	0	Edward Lugard,[9] *s.*	31 July 28	P 31 Oct. 31	30 Dec. 43	3 Apr.
14	0	John Æneas Duncan[10] ..	P 7 Aug. 35	26 Oct. 39	30 July 46	
15	0	Æneas William Fraser[11]	P 6 June 34	P 4 Mar. 36	27 Sept. 44	
11	0	Edw. Henry Westropp[12]	P 2 Nov. 38	8 Apr. 42	5 Aug. 47	
		LIEUTENANTS.				
11	0	Carey Handfield[13]	14 Dec. 38	8 Apr. 42		
8	0	*Hon.* Horace M. Monckton	P 23 April 41	P 29 Apr. 42		
7	0	C. E. M'Donnell,[14] *adj.*	P 21 Apr. 42	P 29 June 43		
8	0	William Francis Stehelin[13]	30 April 41	20 Dec. 42		
9	0	Hugh George Colvill,[15] *r.*	10 Jan. 40	3 Aug. 41		
7	0	Henry George Walker[8] ..	P 20 Apr. 42	31 Dec. 43		
7	0	Henry Torrens Metge[16] ..	28 Jan. 42	25 Sept. 44		
7	0	St. Geo. Mervyn Nugent[14]	P 25 Oct. 42	P 31 Dec. 44		
6	0	Lindsay Farrington[13]	23 June 43	27 Sept. 44		
6	0	John Mackenzie Lyle[13] ..	P 19 May 43	P 2 Sept. 45		
5	0	Augustus Alexander Dick[7]	P 31 Dec. 44	20 Mar. 46		
4	0	Valens Tonnochy[16]	P 2 Sept. 45	20 Mar. 46		
4	0	Frederick Kneebone	19 Dec. 45	20 Mar. 46		
7	0	Edward Thos. FitzGerald	23 July 42	20 Dec. 43		
8	0	Henry Philips Onslow ..	19 Nov. 41	30 July 46		
7	0	Wm. Septimus Simmons	1 Apr. 46	25 Nov. 46		
3	0	Charles Hugh Levinge ..	2 Apr. 46	P 19 Feb. 47		
4	0	Edward Browne Hart ..	9 Dec. 45	5 Aug. 47		
3	0	Richard John Evans	4 Apr. 46	P 28 Sept. 47		
3	0	John Sheridan Henderson	3 Apr. 46	10 Dec. 47		
3	0	Edmond H. C. Pery	P 22 May 46	P 1 Aug. 48		
6	0	Rob. C. Dalrymple Bruce	10 Nov. 43	14 April 46		
4	0	John Thomas James	P 18 Apr. 45	P 10 Mar. 48		
		ENSIGNS.				
3	0	Wm. Lancey Davies Smith	14 Apr. 46			
5	0	Alexander Robt. Mowbray	23 Aug. 44			
3	0	George Augustus Ferris..	P 8 Dec. 46			
2	0	George Henry Nevill....	19 Feb. 47			
3	0	James Fraser Draper	20 Mar. 46			
2	0	William D. Chapman ..	10 Dec. 47			
2	0	Edward Hazlefoot Paske	P 14 Apr. 47			
1	0	De Vic Valpy..........	P 20 Oct. 48			
12	0	*Paymaster.*—James Herbert Clay, 31 May 44; *Ens.* P 5 May 37; *Lt.* 9 Ap				
7	0	*Adjutant.*—*Lieut.* Charles Eustace MacDonnell,[14] 20 Mar. 46.				
7	0	*Quarter-Master.*—Chas. Sutherland Dowson, 10 Dec. 47; *Ens.* 9 June, 42;				
14	0	*Surgeon.*—Richard Dane, MD., 21 July, 46; *Assist.-Surg.* 17 July, 35.				
7	0	*Assist.-Surgeons.*—William Green Trousdell, 8 April, 42.				
3	0	Alexander Mackay Macbeth, 21 July 46.				
8	0	Ludovic Charles Stewart, 8 June 41.				

Facings Yellow.—*Agents,* Messrs. Cox

[Continuation of Note 1.] affair before Bayonne on the Dec. 1813, when the 2nd Di was attacked by six Divisions French Army commanded by shal Soult: in this action he horse shot under him. On the Feb. at the commencement of Campaign of 1814, he was en with the Rear Guard of the at Espelette; and on the follo day was employed in the at the heights above Garris. in the subsequent actions of and Aire; and he repulsed th my at Garlin. He was also en with his brigade at the bat Toulouse. He commanded a B of Guards at the battle of Wa His Lordship has received a and one clasp for Vittoria, Py Nivelle, Nive, and Orthes.

2 Lt.-Col. Congreve comm the 29th in the Campaign Sutlej, and was severely wou the battle of Ferozeshah (M

2* Col. Mountain (see page

3 Major Smith served as M Brigade with the army under Pollock during the campaign in Affghanistan (medal), an present (as D. A. Adj.-Gen. Inf. Div.) at the forcing of the ber Pass, action at Mamoo forcing the Tezeen and Huft Passes, attack and capture of Istaliff (received the brevet rank of Major).

4 Maj. Stepney served with the 29th in the Ca on the Sutlej (Medal): the Command of the Re devolved on him when Lt.-Col. Congreve was w at the battle of Ferozeshah, and which comm retained during the night of the 21st and the m the 22nd Dec. 1845, and during the remainder active part of the campaign until severely woun a grape-shot at the conclusion of the battle of So

1 Lord Strafford served with the 33rd in Flanders and in Holland in 1794 and 95, and was wounded at Geldermals served with the 3rd Guards in the expeditions to Hanover in 1805; to Copenhagen in 1807; and to Walcheren in 18 the latter he was with the Reserve under Sir J. Hope, and commanded his advance, composed of the Grenadier Batt the Guards and a detachment of the 95th Rifles; in this command he charged a detachment of Dutch troops, taki officers and upwards of a hundred men prisoners. In 1811 he joined the Brigade of Guards in Portugal; and in Se of that year he was nominated to the command of a Brigade, in the 2nd Division under Lord Hill. He was present in all the movements and affairs with the enemy in the South of Spain—and during the period of the Siege of Ciudad R he was detached in command to Idanha Nova with his own Brigade and some cavalry to observe the movements of of the enemy commanded by Gen. Foy, at Coria. Upon Lord Hill joining the main body of the Army on the dismant of the Campaign of 1813, he was engaged in the several actions of Vittoria, of the Pyrenees, of Pampeluna, in which he was wounded; in the crossing of the Nivelle and attack of the fortified camp,—wounded and had two horses sho him; at Cambo, in driving the enemy's out-posts and reconnoitring the Tete-de-Pont; in the passage of the Nive (

9 Maj. Lugard served as a Maj. of Brigade throughout the campaign of 1842 in Affghanistan under Gen. Pollock, and was present in the actions of Mazeena, Tezeen, and Jug dulluck, the occupation of Cabool, and the different engagements leading to it (medal). He served throughout the Campaign on the Sutlej (medal);—as Dep. Assist. Adj. Gen. to Sir Harry Smith at the battles of Moodkee (wounded), Ferozeshah (wounded), and Sobraon;—as Adj Gen. of the whole Force commanded by Sir Harry at the affair of Buddewal, and in the battle of Aliwal; and he officiated as

the Sutlej (Medal), and were present at the battles of Ferozeshah and Sobraon.

14 Lts. MacDonnell and Nugent served with the 29th in the Campaign on the Sutlej (Medal), and were present at the battles of Ferozeshah and Sobraon (severely wounded).

15 Lt. Colvill served with the 39th in the action of Maharajpore (medal), 29th Dec. 1843, and was very severely wounded.

16 Lts. Medge and Tonnochy were present at Sobraon (Medal).

Years' Serv. 45

The Sphinx, with the words "EGYPT"—"BADAJOZ"—"SALAMANCA"—"PENINSULA"—"WATERLOO."

Colonel.

Full Pay.	Half Pay.	
		Ⓟ George, *Marquis of* Tweeddale,[1] KT. CB. *Ens.* June, 1804; *Lt.* 12 Oct. 04; *Capt.* 14 May, 07; *Major,* 14 May, 12; *Lt.-Col.* 21 June, 13; *Col.* 27 May, 25; *Major-Gen.* 10 Jan. 37; *Lt.-Gen.* 9 Nov. 46; *Col.* 30th Foot, 7 Feb. 46.
17	0	*Lieut.-Col.*—Samuel John Luke Nicoll, *2d Lieut.* P 27 Apr. 32; *Lieut.* P 8 June 38; *Capt.* P 10 Apr. 40; *Major,* P 5 March 47; *Lt.-Col.* P 4 Aug. 48.
15	0	*Majors.*—Philip Chas. Cavan, *Ens.* P 19 Dec. 34; *Lieut.* P 1 Mar. 39; *Capt.* P 23 April 41; *Major,* P 30 July 47.
18	0	William Francis Hoey, *Ens.* P 28 Oct. 31; *Lieut.* 5 Sept. 35; *Capt.* P 22 July 42; *Maj.* P 4 Aug. 48.

Full Pay.	Half Pay.	CAPTAINS.	ENSIGN.	LIEUT.	CAPTAIN.	BREV.-MAJ.
21	0	Charles Sillery	24 Nov. 28	20 July 30	P 15 Mar. 39	
15	0	James Thomas Mauleverer[6]	P 18 Apr. 34	P 19 Aug. 36	P 28 July 43	
22	0	William Hodder Heard..	16 Sept. 27	10 Dec. 33	20 Sept. 44	
13	0	Robert Dring O'Grady ..	P 30 July 36	P 26 Apr. 39	P 5 Mar. 47	
10	0	Robert William Smith ..	P 15 Mar. 39	P 23 April 41	P 28 May 47	
9	0	James Brodie Patullo ..	P 24 Apr. 40	10 Oct. 42	P 30 July 47	
11	0	John Tryon Still	11 May 38	P 13 Dec. 42	P 21 July 46	
9	0	Charles Dudley Oliver ..	P 30 Oct. 40	P 23 Feb. 44	P 26 May 48	
8	0	John Henry Keogh	P 26 Jan. 41	P 28 June 44	P 4 Aug. 48	
8	0	Armar Lowry..........	P 2 April 41	20 Sept. 44	P 15 Dec. 48	
		LIEUTENANTS.				
13	0	John Tongue, *r.*........	P 2 Dec. 36	P 8 Nov. 39		
10	0	Paget Bayly	P 8 Mar. 39	P 26 Jan. 41		
8	0	Edm. Aug. Whitmore, *adj.*	P 6 Aug. 41	10 July 46		
8	0	James Rose	P 16 Nov 41	28 Dec. 46		
5	0	Fred. Augustus Edwardes	P 8 Oct. 44	P 29 Dec. 46		
5	0	Thomas Henry Pakenham	P 12 July 44	P 19 Mar. 47		
5	0	Tho. Wm. Roger Coventry	P 28 June 44	P 28 May 47		
4	0	Arthur Wellesley Conolly	7 July 45	P 25 June 47		
3	0	Thomas William Cator ..	29 Dec. 46	P 30 July 47		
3	0	Wm. W. Hastings Greene	P 30 Dec. 46	P 26 May 48		
2	0	Graham Le Fevre Dickson	P 5 Mar. 47	P 1 Aug. 48		
2	0	Fra. Topping Atcherley..	P 4 June 47	P 4 Aug. 48		
2	0	Wm. Robert Hepburn ..	P 30 July 47	P 15 Dec. 48		
		ENSIGNS.				
3	0	Mark Walker	25 Sept. 46			
2	0	James St. Clair Hobson..	10 Jan. 47			
2	0	John Dillon Ross Lewin	28 May 47			
2	0	T. Mapleson FitzPatrick	P 10 Dec. 47			
1	0	Matthew Pennefather ..	P 26 May 48			
1	0	James Crosby Anderson	P 1 Aug. 48			
1	0	*Hon.* John Colborne	5 Aug. 48			
1	0	G. F. Coventry Pocock..	P 15 Dec. 48			

6 Captain Mauleverer served with the 17th throughout the campaign in Affghanistan and Beloochistan, under Lord Keane, and was present at the storm and capture of Ghuznee and of Khelat. Medal for Ghuznee.

Full Pay.	Half Pay.	
24	0	*Paymaster.*—R. Ch. Macdonald, 8 May, 35; *Ens.* 10 April, 25; *Lieut.* P 13 Dec. 27.
8	0	*Adjutant.*—*Lieut.* Edmund Augustus Whitmore, 28 Dec. 46.
2	0	*Quarter-Master.*—Timothy Morris, 28 May 47; *Ens.* 15 Jan. 47.
12	0	*Surgeon.*—Thomas D'Arcey, 27 Oct. 46; *Assist.-Surg.* 29 Dec. 37.
8	0	*Assistant-Surgeon.*—Augustus Purefoy Lockwood, 17 Sept. 41.

Facings Yellow.—*Agents,* Messrs. Cox & Co.

[*Returned from New Brunswick,* 6th *Jan.* 1844.]

1 Lord Tweeddale served in the Peninsula as an Assistant-Quarter-Master-General, and has received a medal for the battle of Vittoria, in which action he was wounded, as also at Busaco. Served also in the American war, and was again wounded.

2* Colonel Mountain served as Deputy-Adjutant-General throughout the war in China (medal), and was present at the first capture of Chusan, storming of the heights and forts above Canton, action of the 30th May, taking of Amoy, 2nd capture of Chusan, storming of the fortified heights of Chinhae, taking of Ningpo, and sortie at the repulse of the night attack, action of Tsehe, capture of Chapoo (three severe wounds), assault and capture of Chin Kiang Foo, and investment of Nanking.

---

9 Capt. Plunkett served with the 31st throughout the campaign of 1842 in Affghanistan (Medal), including the actions of Mazeena, Tezeen, and Jugdulluck, the occupation of Cabool, and the different engagements leading to it. He served also in the campaign on the Sutlej (Medal), and was present at Moodkee and Ferozeshah (severely wounded).

10 Lt. Law served with the 31st throughout the campaign of 1842 in Affghanistan (Medal), including the actions of Mazeena, Tezeen, and Jugdulluck, the occupation of Cabool, and the different engagements leading to it. He served also throughout the campaign on the Sutlej (Medal), including the battles of Moodkee, Ferozeshah, Buddiwal, Aliwal, and Sobraon (severely wounded).

11 Capt. Robertson and Lt. Noel served throughout the campaign on the Sutlej (Medal), including the battles of Moodkee, Ferozeshah, Buddiwal, Aliwal, and Sobraon.

12 Lieut. Elmslie served throughout the campaign on the Sutlej (Medal), and was present in the battles of Moodkee, Ferozeshah, Buddiwal, Aliwal, and Sobraon, at which last he was shot through the shoulder.

13 Lt. [illegible] served throughout the campaign on the Sutlej (Medal), and was present in the battles of Moodkee, Ferozeshah, Buddiwal, Aliwal. and Sobraon (wounded).

"TALAVERA" — "ALBUHERA" — "VITTORIA" — "PYRENEES" — "NIVELLE" — "NIVE" — "ORTHES" — "PENINSULA" — "CABOOL, 1842" — "MOODKEE" — "FEROZESHAH" — "ALIWAL" — "SOBRAON."

Years' Serv. Full Pay.	Half Pay.	
56		*Colonel.—Hon.* Henry Otway Trevor,[1] CB. *Ens.* 27 April 93; *Lieut. and Capt.* 23 June 95; *Capt. and Lieut.-Col.* 25 Oct. 06; *Col.* 4 June 14; *Maj.-Gen.* 19 July 21; *Lieut.-Gen.* 10 Jan. 37; *Col.* 31st Regt. 12 July 47.
41	0	*Lieut.-Colonel.*—James Spence,[2] CB. *Ens.* 26 Nov. 08; *Lieut.* P 20 Dec. 10; *Ct.* 10 Feb. 25; *Brev.-Maj.* 28 June, 38; *Maj.* 30 Dec. 43; *Lt.-Col.* 5 Jan. 46.
14	0	John Garvock[6] *s. Ens.* P 4 Sept 35; *Lieut.* 31 Dec. 39; *Captain*, P 25 Nov. 42; *Brev.-Maj.* 3 Apr. 46; *Lieut.-Col.* 22 Dec. 48.
23	0	*Majors.*—George Staunton, [4] *Ens.* P 5 Oct. 26; *Lieut.* P 15 Feb. 31; *Capt.* P ... June, 39; *Major*, P 28 March, 45.
24	0	George Francis White,[5] *Ens.* 27 Jan. 25; *Lt.* 3 Apr. 28; *Capt.* 9 Nov. 41; *Major* P 21 Jan. 48.

Full Pay	Half Pay		Ensign.	Lieut.	Captain.	Brev.-Maj.
		Captains.				
21	0	Thomas Conyngham Kelly	3 Apr. 28	P 31 Aug. 30	6 May 43	
18	0	David FitzG. Longworth[7]	P 3 May 31	P 27 Nov. 35	P 25 Sept. 39	19 June 4…
20	0	Frederick Spence	24 Dec. 29	P 1 Nov. 31	28 June 44	
19	0	Robert John Eagar[8]	11 June 30	P 25 Jan. 38	P 8 Oct. 44	
18	0	James Croft Brooke[8]	P 31 Oct. 31	2 Sept. 33	31 Mar. 46	
13	0	Joseph Greenwood. *s.*[8] ...	P 6 May 36	27 Oct. 39	31 Mar. 46	
11	0	Harry Piesley L'Estrange	P 28 Dec. 38	P 19 Mar. 41	20 Mar. 46	
13	0	Thomas Henry Plasket[9]..	P 21 Oct. 36	29 Oct. 39	P 23 Apr. 47	
8	0	James Peter Robertson[11]	P 29 Oct. 41	P 30 Sept. 42	P 21 Jan. 48	
		Lieutenants.				
10	0	Edward Wm. Bray,[8]	21 June 39	21 Jan. 41		
9	0	Robert Law[10]	8 Feb. 40	27 July 42		
10	0	Graham Elmslie[12]	P 23 Aug. 39	P 24 June 42		
7	0	Poole Gabbett[13]........	P 22 April 42	9 Nov. 43		
8	0	Thomas Scarman[15]	26 Oct. 41	5 Dec. 43		
7	0	John Stillman Gould,*r*...	P 30 Sept. 42	28 June 44		
7	0	Arthur Pilkington[16]	8 Nov. 42	11 Sept. 45		
6	0	Edward Andrew Noel[11]..	P 7 July 43	P 2 May 45		
7	0	Robert Mackenzie	27 Dec. 42	19 Dec. 45		
9	0	Aug. Samuel Bolton,[17] *adj.*	29 Dec. 40	16 Sept. 45		
6	0	Henry Prim Hutton[18] ..	9 Nov. 43	25 Dec. 45		
4	0	Edward B. Stirling Carver	P 25 July 45	P 23 Apr. 47		
3	0	Cha. Jas. Orton Swaffield	27 Feb. 46	P 21 Jan. 48		
		Ensigns.				
3	0	Henry Brenchley	2 Apr. 46			
3	0	George Walter Baldwin	4 Apr. 46			
3	0	Samuel Christian	5 Apr. 46			
2	0	Amyatt Ernle Brown....	20 Mar. 47			
2	0	S. Fra. Glossop Bytheses	17 Sept. 47			
2	0	Thomas Edward Pedder	P 19 Mar. 47			
1	0	Richard John Leeson ..	P 28 Jan. 48			
1	0	Arthur Cassidy	P 17 Nov. 48			

15 Lt. Scarman carried the colours of the 39th in the action of Maharajpore, and was wounded in the left leg by a grape shot; shortly after which he received a severe wound in the left arm.

19 Doctor Hart served in the campaigns of 1810 and 11 in the Peninsula and was present at Busaco, Redinha, and Fuentes... bal. He served also throughout the campaign of 1842 in Affghanistan under General Pollock, and was present at the actions of Mazeena, Tezeen, and Jugdulluck, and the occupation of Cabool, and the different engagements leading to it (medal).

16 Lieut. Pilkington served in the campaign on the Sutlej (Medal), with the 31st, and was present at Moodkee and Ferozeshah, at which last he was severely wounded by a grape shot through the ancle.

Full Pay	Half Pay	
12	0	*Paymaster.*—Julius Brockman Travers, 9 May, 45; *2nd Lieut.* 8 July, 37; …
9	0	*Adjutant.—Lieut.* Augustus Samuel Bolton,[17] 22 Dec. 45. [8 Apr. …
8	0	*Quarter-Master.*—Samuel Bennison,[20] 13 July, 41. [*Assist.* 4 Dec. …
33	6 1/12	*Surgeon.*—P Henry Hart,[19] M.D. 21 Sept. 30; *Assist.-Surg.* 31 Jan. 11; *H.*…
5	0	*Assist.-Surgeon.*— Hampden Hugh Massey, MD. 22 Nov. 44.

Facings Buff.—*Agents,* Messrs. Cox and Co.—*Irish Agents, Sir* E. R. Borough, [*Bt.*, Armit, & Co.]

[*Returned from Bengal 6th Dec.* 1846.]

1 Lieut.-Gen. the Hon. H. O. Trevor served in Flanders in 1793, 94, and 95, and at Copenhagen in 1807. Embarked 31st Dec. 1808, with the first battalion of the Coldstream Guards for the Peninsula, where he served until May 1811, and again, from May to Nov. 1812; commanded the regt. at the battle of Salamanca, for which he has received a medal.

2 Lt.-Col. Spence was present with the 31st in the action of Stuola, near Genoa, on the 13th April 1814, and in the subsequent attacks upon the city of Genoa until its surrender, as also at the surrender of Corsica in the same year. In 1815 he served with the army in Naples. On the 1st March, 1825, he was present at that lamentable catastrophe, the burning of the *Kent*, in the Bay of Biscay. He commanded the 31st throughout the campaign on the Sutlej, at the battles of Moodkee (soon after its commencement), Ferozeshah, (for which he was appointed a *C.B.*) Buddiwal, and Aliwal, and the first brigade of Sir Harry Smith's division at the battle of Sobraon; and was one of only five officers out of thirty who escaped unwounded in all the actions. Had his horse shot under him at Ferozeshah and Sobraon.

4 Major Staunton served with the 10th in the campaign on the Sutlej (Medal), and was present at the battle of Sobraon.

5 Major White served in the campaign on the Sutlej (Medal) with the 31st, including the battles of Moodkee and Ferozeshah. He was also at Buddiwal.

6 Lt.-Col. Garvock served as a Major of Brigade in Sir Harry Smith's division throughout the campaign (medal), and was present at the battles of Moodkee, Ferozeshah (horse shot under him), Buddiwal, Aliwal, and Sobraon, where he was himself severely wounded, and his horse struck in three places. He also acted as Adjutant-General and Quarter-Master General to Sir Harry Smith in the action with and defeat of the rebel Boers at Bloem Plaats (South Africa), 29th Aug. 1848.

7 Major Longworth joined the 40th early in 1842 at Candahar, and accompanied General Nott's force to Ferozepore viâ the Khyber Pass, and was present at the second occupation of Ghuznee and of Cabool (Medal), and also at the engagement of Goaine. He served the campaign on the Sutlej in the 31st, and was present at Moodkee, Ferozeshah, Buddiwal, Aliwal, and Sobraon, at which last he commanded the regiment, and had his horse shot. He was one of only five officers out of thirty who escaped unwounded in all the actions.

17 Lieut. Bolton served the campaign on the Sutlej (Medal). He acted as Aide-de-camp to Sir …

8 The following officers served with the 31st throughout the campaign of 1842 in Affghanistan under Major-General Pollock, and were present in the actions of Mazeena, Tezeen, and Jugdulluck, the occupation of Cabool, and the different engagements leading to it, viz.—Captains Eagar, Brooke, and Greenwood, Lieuts. Bray, Atty, and Quarter-master Bennison. Captain Brooke was wounded on the 16th Sept. near Jugdulluck.

18 Lt. Hutton served the campaign on the Sutlej (Medal), and carried the colours of the 31st in the battles of Moodkee and Ferozeshah (wounded); he was also present at Buddiwal, Aliwal, and Sobraon.

20 Quartermaster Bennison was present at that lamentable catastrophe, the burning of the *Kent*, East Indiaman, in the Bay of Biscay, on the 1st March, 1825. He served with the 31st throughout the campaign of 1842 in Affghanistan (Medal) under Major-General Pollock, including the actions of Mazeena, Tezeen, and Jugdulluck, the occupation of Cabool, and the different engagements leading to it. He served also the campaign on the Sutlej (Medal), and was present in the battles of Moodkee, Ferozeshah, Buddiwal, Aliwal, and Sobraon, and was one of only five officers who escaped being wounded.

"ROLEIA"—"VIMIERA"—"CORUNNA"—"SALAMANCA"—"PYRENEES"—"NIVELLE"—"NIVE"—"ORTHES"—"PENINSULA"—"WATERLOO."

Years' Serv. 54 Full Pay.	Half Pay.		Ensign.	Lieut.	Captain.	Brev.-Maj.
		Colonel.—B Sir John Buchan,[1] KCB. *Ens.* 29 July, 95; *Lieut.* 21 Oct. 95; *Capt.* 15 March, 1802; *Major,* 30 June, 04; *Lieut.-Col.* 30 March, 09; *Col.* 12 Aug. 19; *Major.-Gen.* 22 July, 30; *Lieut.-Gen.* 23 Nov. 41; *Col.* 32nd Regt. 12 June, 43.				
25	0	*Lieut.-Colonels.*—Frederick Markham,[2] *Ens.* P13 May, 24; *Lieut.* P22 Oct. 25; *Capt.* P16 April, 29; *Major,* P28 Sept. 39; *Lieut.-Col.* P22 July, 42.				
22	0	Henry Vaughan Brooke, *s.* *Ens.* P12 July, 27; *Lt.* P11 June, 30; *Capt.* P22 May, 35; *Major,* P22 July, 42; *Lt.-Col.* 13 Sept. 48.				
16	0	*Majors.*—John Eardley Wilmot Inglis, *Ens.* 2 Aug. 33; *Lieut.* 19 Jan. 39; *Capt,* P29 Sept. 43; *Major,* P25 Feb. 48.				
17	0	William Case, *Ens.* 10 Feb. 32; *Lieut.* 9 Feb. 38; *Capt.* P25 Feb. 42; *Major,* 13 Sept. 48.				
		Captains.				
10	0	Jas. D. Carmichael Smyth	P12 July 39	11 May 41	P18 Apr. 45	
12	0	Edw. W. D. Lowe	20 May 37	P12 Mar. 41	P23 May 45	
10	0	John Pelling Pigott	P15 Feb. 39	P28 Jan. 42	P19 Dec. 43	
20	0	Arthur Lowry Balfour	P 6 Aug. 29	P29 Mar. 33	P31 May 39	
9	0	Charles Thomas King	10 July 40	P27 May 42	P25 Feb. 48	
8	0	Frederick Yard	P12 Mar. 41	P22 July 42	P25 Feb. 48	
25	8 4/12	William Bell	30 Nov. 15	26 Apr. 28	2 July 41	
11	0	George Samuel Moore	9 Feb. 38	P25 June 41	24 May 48	
11	0	Harry Wainright Hough[4]	P20 July 38	P10 Jan. 40	10 April 46	
7	0	Andrew Gram Brine	15 April 42	P18 Apr. 45	13 Sept. 48	
		Lieutenants.				
7	0	Thomas Maunsell	P27 May 42	P23 May 45		
6	0	Henry John Davies	7 April 43	P13 Feb. 46		
7	0	Houstoun Stewart	P 6 May 42	P16 Dec. 45		
10	0	George Jeffrey[6]	4 June 39	18 June 41		
9	0	Robert Stacy Colls[7]	14 Feb. 40	24 Apr. 43		
7	0	William Cumming	8 Apr. 42	P 3 May 44		
5	0	Charles Richardson	P15 Mar. 44	P23 Jan. 46		
7	0	James Henry Wemyss	P13 May 42	3 Apr. 46		
7	0	John Moore	P 1 Nov. 42	3 Apr. 46		
6	0	Wm. Airde Birtwhistle	P12 Dec. 43	3 Apr. 46		
5	0	John William Boissier	P31 Dec. 44	3 Apr. 46		
19	0	Samuel Reed	15 June 30	26 July 33		
4	1/12	Charles Clapcott	P18 Apr. 45	P12 June 46		
4	0	R. Edw. L. H. Williams	P23 May 45	23 Sept. 47		
7	0	William Patterson	17 April 42	14 April 46		
4	0	Henry D. O'Callaghan, *s.*	P19 Dec. 45	P10 Dec. 47		
5	0	W. Garforth, *ad.* (QM. 28 Ju. 44)	3 Apr. 46	24 Feb. 48		
3	0	Bowen Van Straubenzee	4 Apr. 46	P23 Feb. 48		
3	0	William Power	6 Apr. 46	P25 Feb. 48		
3	0	Alfred Bassano	3 Apr. 46	24 May 48		
4	0	William Rudman[8]	22 Dec. 45	P11 Feb. 48		
4	0	Henry William Sibley	17 Oct. 45	9 Feb. 48		
3	0	John Swinburn	5 Apr. 46	13 Sept. 48		
		Ensigns.				
2	0	Edward Chippindall	P10 Dec. 47			
2	0	John Birtwhistle	P11 Dec. 47			
2	0	Samuel Hill Lawrence	12 Dec. 47			
1	0	Walter Lawrence Ingles	21 Jan. 48			
1	0	John Hedley	P25 Feb. 48			
1	0	Harley Kingsmill Drury	26 Feb. 48			
1	0	William James Anderson	15 Aug. 48			
1	0	John Alexander Shortt	20 Oct. 48			
34	2 5/12	*Paymaster.*—[illegible] G. Moore,[9] 19 Oct 26; *Ens.* 1 Oct. 12; *Lieut.* 6 Dec. 13.				
5	0	*Adjutant.*—*Lieut.* William Garforth, 3 April, 46.				
1	0	*Quarter-Master.*—John Giddings, 13 Sept. 48.				
15	0	*Surgeon.*—Charles Scott, M.D. 9 May, 45; *Assist.-Surg.* 7 Nov. 34				
7	0	*Assist.-Surgeons.*—Edward Moorhead, M.D. 2 Aug. 42.				
3	0	Alexander Peile Cahill, M.D. 3 April, 46.				
3	0	John Dunlop, M.D. 3 April, 46.				

Facings White—*Agents,* Messrs. Cox & Co.

2 Lieut.-Col. Markham was severely wounded in Canada, 23 Nov. 1837.

4 Capt. Hough served with the 50th, in the battle of Punniar (medal); also the campaign on the Sutlej (medal) in 1845-6, including the battles of Moodkee, Ferozeshah, Aliwal, and Sobraon (severely wounded).

6 Lieut. Jeffrey served as a captain in the Anglo-Spanish Legion, and was present during the operations on the heights of Alava on the 16th, 17th, and 18th Jan.; in the actions in front of San Sebastian on the 5th May (severely wounded), and 1st Oct. (severely wounded), 1836; 10th, 12th (wounded), 14th, 15th, and 16th March, 10th and 17th May, 1837. He has received two medals.

7 Lieut. Colls served with the 39th in the battle of Maharajpore, and has received the bronze star.

8 Lieut. Rudman served with the 62nd in the campaign on the Sutlej (medal), including the battles of Ferozeshah and Sobraon.

9 Paymaster Moore served the campaign of 1814 in Holland, including the action at Merxem, and bombardment of Antwerp. Present at Waterloo.

1 Sir John Buchan was actively employed in the Mysore war, and was present at the battle of Mallavelly and assault of Seringapatam. In 1800 and 1801 he was employed with the Flank Companies of his regiment (the old 94th), in the operations against the Southern Poligars; on which occasion he relinquished a staff situation to join his company in the field. Subsequently to this he held different detached commands in Ceylon during the Kandian war. In 1810 he held a command at the attack and capture of Guadaloupe. Served afterwards in the Peninsula with the Portuguese army, from 1811 to the end of the war, including the battles of Vittoria, Pyrenees, Nivelle, Nive, Orthes and Toulouse. Sir John has received a medal for Seringapatam, and a cross and one clasp for Guadaloupe, Vittoria, Pyrenees, Nivelle, and Nive.

"SERINGAPATAM"—"WATERLOO."

Years' Serv. Full Pay	Half Pay	
52		*Colonel.*
		P W Henry D'Oyly,[1] *Ens.* 2 Aug. 97; *Lt. & Capt.* 25 Nov. 99; *Major*, 4 June, 11; *Capt. & Lieut.-Col.* 27 May 13; *Col.* 12 Feb. 30; *Major-Gen.* 28 June, 38; *Col.* 33rd Foot, 28 Sept. 47.
		Lieutenant-Colonel.
24	0	Frederick Rodolph Blake, *Ens.* P 30 June, 25; *Lieut.* P 14 Aug. 27; *Capt.* P 23 Aug. 31; *Major*, 14 April, 43; *Lt.-Col.* P 3 Oct. 48.
		Majors.
22	0	John Douglas Johnstone, *Ens.* P 15 Aug. 27; *Lieut.* 16 Mar. 30; *Capt.* P 19 Oct. 38; *Major*, P 3 Oct. 48.
22	0	Thos. Bunbury Gough, *Ens.* P 27 Dec. 27; *Lieut.* P 25 Jan. 31; *Capt.* P 23 Nov. 38; *Major*, 22 Dec. 48.

Full Pay	Half Pay		Ensign.	Lieut.	Captain.	Brev.-Maj.
		Captains.				
19	0	Henry Wm. Bunbury ..	P 29 June 30	P 30 Aug. 33	P 18 Aug. 38	
14	0	George V. Mundy	never	27 Feb. 35	P 1 May 40	
17	0	George Erskine	17 Aug. 32	P 3 June 36	14 April 43	
14	0	Edward Augustus Milman	P 27 Nov. 35	P 28 Dec. 38	P 27 Sept. 44	
13	0	Edward Winnington	P 22 Jan. 36	4 Jan. 39	P 31 Jan. 45	
13	0	Chas. P. B. Walker	P 27 Feb. 36	21 June 39	P 22 Dec. 46	
13	0	Charles Mills	P 3 June 36	P 25 Sept. 40	P 15 Aug. 48	
11	0	Robert Gregory Wale ..	30 Oct. 38	27 Aug. 41	P 25 Aug. 48	
10	0	John B. Collings........	21 June 39	22 Jan. 42	P 3 Oct. 48	
9	0	Edw. Westby Donovan..	10 Jan. 40	14 June 42	22 Dec. 48	
		Lieutenants.				
9	0	William Pretyman, *adj.*	P 8 May 40	P 5 Aug. 42		
9	0	Henry Ulick Burke	P 17 July 40	P 30 Aug. 42		
9	0	Henry Charles Fitzgerald	P 25 Sept. 40	9 Oct. 42		
8	0	John Ed. Taubman Quayle	P 7 Sept. 41	7 Nov. 43		
7	0	Richard Lacy	11 Mar. 42	P 27 Sept. 44		
8	0	George Henry Cazalet ..	26 Nov. 41	P 20 Aug. 44		
7	0	Henry Disney Ellis	14 June 42	P 31 Jan. 45		
7	0	Wm. Mortimer Pechell..	P 5 Aug. 42	8 Dec. 46		
7	0	Thomas Wickham	P 25 Oct. 42	P 22 Dec. 46		
5	0	Nathaniel Kemp........	P 27 Sept. 44	P 15 Aug. 48		
3	0	Basil Fanshawe	P 14 Apr. 46	P 3 Oct. 48		
3	0	Frederic Smith Vacher ..	8 Dec. 46	P 20 Oct. 48		
3	0	J. Cochrane	13 Apr. 46	22 Dec. 48		
		Ensigns.				
2	0	Charles Carter Barrett ..	P 22 Jan. 47			
2	0	Frank Corbett	P 30 Mar. 47			
1	0	Walter George Nugent ..	P 15 Aug. 48			
1	0	Charles Edward Mansfield	P 1 Sept. 48			
1	0	George James Pennock ..	P 3 Oct. 48			
1	0	William Henry Parry ..	P 20 Oct. 48			
1	0	Valentine Bennett	P 17 Nov. 48			
1	0	Alex. Bruce Wallace....	22 Dec. 48			

Full Pay	Half Pay	
24	14 1/12	*Paymaster.*—Patrick M'Grath, 4 Oct. 31; *Ens.* 7 Feb. 11; *Lieut.* 14 Jan. 13.
9	0	*Adjutant.*—*Lieut.* William Pretyman, 15 Aug. 48.
7	0	*Quarter-Master.*—Joseph Jones, 25 Oct. 42.
11	0	*Surgeon.*—James Townsend Oswald Johnston, M.D., 29 Dec. 46; *Assist.-Surg.* 3 Aug. 38
9	0	*Assist.-Surgeon.*—James Carroll Dempster, M.D. 29 Dec. 40.

Facings Red.—*Agents*, Messrs. Cox & Co.

[*Returned from North America, May* 1848.]

1 Major-General D'Oyly served in the campaign in North Holland, in 1799, under Sir Ralph Abercromby, and the Duke of York, and was taken prisoner in the action of the 19th Sept. He served with the army in the North of Spain under Sir John Moore, in 1808—9, and was at the battle of Corunna. Accompanied the expedition to Walcheren in 1809. Served at Cadiz during the siege in 1811 and 12, under Lord Lynedoch, and Sir George Cooke, to whom he was Aide-de-camp, and was sent home with despatches, announcing the raising of the siege in 1812. Served also in Flanders, under Lord Lynedoch, in 1814; and subsequently with the army under the Duke of Wellington in Flanders and France, and was severely wounded at the battle of Waterloo.

2 Lieut.-Colonel Whannell served the campaigns of 1813 and 14 in Germany and Holland, including the attacks on Merxem, bombardment of the French fleet at Antwerp, and the attack on Bergen-op-Zoom.

"ALBUHERA"—"ARROYO DOS MOLINOS"—"VITTORIA"—"PYRENEES"—"NIVELLE"—"NIVE"—"ORTHES"—"PENINSULA."

Years' Serv. (Full Pay / Half Pay)

Colonel.

67 — ℗ *Sir* Thomas Makdougall Brisbane,[1] *Bart.* GCB. GCH. *Ens.* 10 Jan. 1782; *Lieut.* 30 July, 91; *Capt.* 12 April, 93; *Major*, 5 Aug. 95; *Lieut.-Col.* 4 April, 1800; *Col.* 25 July, 10; *Major.-Gen.* 4 June, 13; *Lieut.-Gen.* 27 May, 25; *Gen.* 23 Nov. 41; *Col.* 34th Regt. 16 Dec. 26.

Lieutenant-Colonel.

28 | 0 — Nicholas R. Brown, *Ens.* 22 Mar. 21; *Lieut.* 2 June 25; *Capt.* 2 May, 37; *Major*, 23 Mar. 45; *Lieut.-Col.* 27 March 48.

Majors.

15 | 0 — Richard D. Kelly, *Ens.* 7 Mar. 34; *Lieut.* P 30 July, 36; *Capt.* P 24 Sept. 41; *Major*, P 17 Mar. 48.

15 | 0 — Arthur Cyril Goodenough, *Ens.* P 8 April 34; *Lieut.* P 25 Nov. 36; *Capt.* P 26 Oct. 41; *Major*, 27 March 48.

Full Pay	Half Pay		Ensign.	Lieut.	Captain.	Brev.-Maj.
		Captains.				
15	0	Frederick H. Lang......	11 July 34	P 4 Aug. 37	P 13 Dec. 42	
14	0	John Simpson..........	P 13 Mar. 35	P 3 Nov. 37	P 26 Jan. 44	
13	0	John Gwilt ....,........	P 25 Nov. 36	P 10 Aug. 38	P 14 Feb. 45	
17	0	Charles F. Hervey	2 Nov. 32	P 30 Dec. 34	23 Mar. 45	
8	0	Robert Christopher Packe	P 1 June 41	P 3 Feb. 43	P 12 Feb. 47	
8	0	James Maxwell	P 24 Sept. 41	P 13 Oct. 43	P 22 June 47	
16	0	Alex. John H. Lumsden..	P 3 May 33	P 19 Dec. 34	10 July 46	
8	0	Henry Hugh Oxley	P 15 Oct. 41	P 12 Dec. 43	P 17 Mar. 48	
15	0	Thomas Bourke	P 9 May 34	2 May 37	27 Mar. 48	
7	0	Wm. Leopold Talbot....	P 20 May 42	P 26 Jan. 44	P 14 Apr. 48	
		Lieutenants.				
12	0	Fra. Chas. Harvey, *s*.....	P 29 Sept. 37	P 24 Sept. 41		
7	0	Edw. Fred. Agnew, *d. adj.*	21 May 42	P 22 Mar. 44		
7	0	Edward Wilmot Sitwell	P 13 Dec. 42	P 30 July 44		
6	0	Cha. Wm. Goldf. Burrill	P 3 Feb. 43	P 14 Feb. 45		
6	0	Charles Wilson Randolph	P 10 Feb. 43	23 Mar. 45		
6	0	*Sir* Geo. H. S. Douglas, *Bt.*	P 3 Nov. 43	P 19 May 46		
6	0	M. Gaussen Best, *adj.* ..	P 12 Dec. 43	P 21 July 46		
5	0	William Warry	P 26 Jan. 44	P 12 Feb. 47		
5	0	John Robinson, *d. pm.* ..	P 22 Mar. 44	P 22 June 47		
4	0	Joseph Jordan	P 14 Feb. 45	27 Mar. 48		
3	0	Edmund Probyn	P 19 May 46	P 16 June 48		
4	0	Henry Jardine Street ..	P 14 Nov. 45	P 3 Nov. 46		
2	0	Henry Edward Bale	P 12 Feb. 47	P 21 July 48		
		Ensigns.				
3	0	Charles Thorold	P 21 July 46			
2	0	John Peel	P 22 June 47			
1	0	David Steuart	P 17 Mar. 48			
1	0	George Edward Westhead	P 7 Apr. 48			
1	0	Granville William Puget	P 14 Apr. 48			
1	0	Robert Campbell	P 12 May 48			
1	0	Dudley Persse	P 16 June 48			
1	0	Henry Dalton Probyn ..	P 21 July 48			

21 | 0 — *Paymaster.*—Chas. Boyse Roche, 30 Nov. 38; *Ens.* 18 Jan. 28; *Lieut.* 21 June, 32.

6 | 0 — *Adjutant.*—*Lieut.* Mawdistly Gaussen Best, 18 Sept. 46.

5 | 0 — *Quarter-Master.*—Thomas Williamson, 22 Nov. 44.

12 | 0 — *Surgeon.*—William Denny, 7 Aug. 46; *Assist.-Surg.* 13 Jan. 47.

3 | 0 — *Assist.-Surgeons.*—O'Connor D'Arcey, M.D. 2 Oct. 46.

1 | 0 — James Edmund Clutterbuck, M.D. 22 Dec. 48.

Facings Yellow.—*Agents*, Messrs. Cox & Co.—*Irish Agents*, Messrs. Cane & Co.

[1] Sir Thomas Brisbane joined the Duke of York's army in the beginning of the war, and was present in every action except that of the 22nd May 93, when he was confined from a wound received in the action of the 18th of the same month. He was subsequently present at the taking of various islands, forts, &c. in the West Indies. Sir Thomas has received a cross and one clasp for Vittoria, Pyrenees, Nivelle, Orthes, and Toulouse, where he was wounded.

"MAIDA."

Years' Serv.	
Full Pay.	Half Pay.

Colonel.

47 — P W Sir George Henry Fred. Berkeley,[1] KCB. *Cornet*, 21 Jan. 02; *Lieut.* 27 Aug. 03; *Capt.* 1 May, 05; *Major*, 28 Jan. 08; *Lieut.-Col.* 13 June, 11; *Col.* 27 May, 25; *Maj.-Gen.* 10 Jan. 37; *Lt.-Gen.* 9 Nov. 46; *Col.* 35th Regt. 11 July, 45.

Lieut.-Colonel.

23 | $\frac{6}{12}$ — Benjamin Francis Dalton Wilson, *Ens.* P 27 Aug. 25; *Lieut.* P 10 June, 26; *Capt.* P 20 April, 32; *Major*, P 17 June, 36; *Lieut.-Col.* P 15 Dec. 40.

Majors.

40 | 1 — Aralander Tennant,[2] *Ens.* P 20 Oct. 08; *Lieut.* 10 June, 13; *Capt.* P 10 June, 26; *Major*, P 1 Aug. 34; *Brevet Lt.-Col.* 9 Nov. 46.

16 | 0 — George Browne, *Ens.* P 31 Dec. 33; *Lieut.* P 14 July 37; *Capt.* 8 April 42; *Major*, P 30 Dec. 45.

Full Pay	Half Pay	CAPTAINS.	ENSIGN.	LIEUT.	CAPTAIN.	BREV.-MAJ.
18	0	James Fraser, *s.*	P 5 April 31	P 1 Aug. 34	P 17 June 36	9 Nov. 46
21	1	Edward H. Hutchinson	P 20 Mar. 27	P 10 Sept. 29	P 8 June 38	
23	$\frac{10}{12}$	James Tedlie	P 19 May 25	P 5 June 27	23 July 38	
18	0	Charles Beamish	P 26 Apr. 31	P 20 Mar. 35	P 31 Dec. 39	
16	0	Frederick English	P 22 Mar. 33	P 17 June 36	P 15 Dec. 40	
23	0	Theophilus Faris	P 8 Apr. 26	P 25 Aug. 29	29 May 45	
24	0	George Bayly	10 Feb. 25	17 Apr. 30	8 May 46	
12	0	Thomas Teulon	P 29 Dec. 37	P 15 Dec. 40	P 31 Dec. 47	
10	0	Robert Henry Price	P 31 Dec. 39	P 3 May 44	P 23 June 48	
17	0	Neil Snodgras Buchanan	P 21 Dec. 32	P 25 Dec. 35	P 28 July 38	
		LIEUTENANTS.				
10	0	Wm. Thomas Harris	P 27 Sept. 39	P 7 July 43		
9	0	Archibald Tisdall	26 June 40	P 20 Sept. 44		
9	0	Fred. George Elkington	P 4 Sept. 40	P 31 Dec. 44		
7	0	William Ranby Goate	15 April 42	29 May 45		
7	0	Edward Bowen Cooke	P 16 Aug. 42	8 May 46		
6	0	Henry S. Bowman, *adj.*	13 Oct. 43	1 Apr. 47		
5	0	M. Villiers Sankey Morton	P 3 May 44	P 2 Apr. 47		
5	0	Augustus William Ord	P 20 Sept. 44	P 6 Aug. 47		
5	0	Charles Miller Layton	P 6 Dec. 44	P 31 Dec. 47		
4	0	James Bickerstaff	P 11 Nov. 45	P 12 May 48		
3	0	Samuel Fritche Blyth	28 Apr. 46	P 23 June 48		
7	0	Wm. John James Smith	20 May 42	7 Sept. 43		
5	0	Wm. Henry Ballingall	P 5 Apr. 44	11 Oct. 46		
		ENSIGNS.				
3	0	James Spratt	8 May 46			
3	0	Francis Lloyd Digby	P 9 June 46			
3	0	Richard Lane Warren	10 July 46			
2	0	Henry Edward Moore	P 3 Sept. 47			
2	0	John Harris	P 31 Dec. 47			
1	0	William Wright	12 May 48			
1	0	William Glynne Massey	P 16 June 48			
1	0	Richard Longfield Craster	P 23 June 48			

2 Lt.-Col. Tennant served at the siege of Flushing, in 1809.

5 Doctor Fairbairn served with the 41st throughout the campaign of 1842 in Affghanistan, and was present at the engagements on the 28th March and 28th April in the Pisheen Valley; in those near Candahar, at Gosine, and before Ghuznee; occupation and destruction of that fortress and of Caboul; expedition into Kohistan, storm, capture, and destruction of Istaliff; and the various minor affairs in and between the Bolan and the Khyber Passes.

12 | 0 — *Paymaster.*—Wm. Shearman, 31 Jan. 45; *2d Lt.* P 21 Apr. 37; *Lt.* 5 May, 42.

6 | 0 — *Adjutant.*—*Lieut.* H. Samuel Bowman, 13 Oct. 43.

9 | 0 — *Quarter-Master.*—George Cole, 15 Dec. 40.

10 | 0 — *Surgeon.*—James Walker Chambers, M.D., 6 Aug. 47; *Assist.-Surg.* 4 Oct. 39.

8 | 0 — *Assistant-Surgeons.*—William Home Fairbairn,[5] M.D., 11 June, 41.

Facings Blue.—*Agents*, Messrs. Cox & Co.—*Irish Agents*, Sir E. R. Borough, Bt., Armit & Co.

[Returned from the Mauritius, 8 April 1848.]

1 Sir George Berkeley served in Egypt in 1807, and was present at the taking of Alexandria. In 1809 he was appointed Assistant Adjutant-General to the army in Portugal, and was present in the actions of the 10th, 11th, and 12th May, 1809, passage of the Douro, battles of Talavera, Busaco, Fuentes d'Onor, siege of Badajos in 1811, also its subsequent siege, storm, and capture; battle of Salamanca, capture of Madrid, siege of Burgos, action at Villa Muriel, battle of Vittoria, siege and capture of San Sebastian, passage of the Bidassoa, battles of the Nivelle and Nive. Served also the campaign of 1815, including the battle of Waterloo, at which he was severely wounded. Sir George has received a cross and three clasps.

"Firm."—"HINDOOSTAN"—"ROLEIA"—"VIMIERA"—"CORUNNA"—"SALAMANCA"—"PYRENEES"—"NIVELLE"—"NIVE"—"ORTHES"—"TOULOUSE"—"PENINSULA."

Years' Serv. 71		
Full Pay.	Half Pay.	
		Colonel.—*Sir* Roger Hale Sheaffe,[1] *Bart. Ens.* 1 May, 1778; *Lieut.* 27 Dec. 80; *Capt.* 6 May, 95; *Major,* 13 Dec. 97; *Lieut.-Col.* 22 March, 98; *Col.* 25 April 1808; *Major-Gen.* 4 June, 11; *Lieut.Gen.* 19 July, 21; *General,* 28 June, 38; *Col.* 36 *Regt.* 21 Dec. 29.
23	2 6/12	*Lieut.-Colonels.*—Charles Ashmore, *Ens.* 25 Dec. 13; *Lieut.* 13 April, 20; *Capt.* P 19 Aug. 28; *Major,* P 15 Dec. 40; *Lieut.-Col.* 22 May, 45.
23	4/12	r. Charles Trollope, *Ens.* P 19 Nov. 25; *Lieut.* P 10 Oct. 26; *Capt.* P 23 Aug. 31; *Major,* P 16 June, 43; *Lt.-Col.* 20 Nov. 46.
23	0	*Majors.*—Edward R. King, *2nd Lieut.* 16 Feb. 26; *Lieut.* 31 July, 28; *Capt.* P 4 Dec. 32; *Major,* 22 May 45.
21	0	r. Lorenzo Rothe, *Ens.* P 6 Mar. 28; *Lt.* P 21 Aug. 35; *Capt.* P 2 April, 41; *Major,* 20 Nov. 46.

Full Pay	Half Pay	CAPTAINS.	ENSIGN.	LIEUT.	CAPTAIN.	BREV.-MAJ.
13	0	r. James Nugent	P 15 April 36	11 Jan. 39	P 22 Sept. 43	
13	0	Tho. Mathias Luz Weguelin	P 23 Dec. 36	P 28 June 39	P 29 Dec. 43	
12	0	Edward Charles Butler..	P 13 Jan. 37	P 5 Mar. 41	P 23 Aug. 44	
12	0	r. William Ward Abbott	P 24 Mar. 37	P 2 April 41	P 31 Jan. 45	
19	0	r. John Pratt..	P 8 June 30	8 June 35	22 May 45	
19	0	John Fleury	P 16 July 30	P 6 May 36	3 Apr. 46	
12	0	r. Charles Wilson Carden	P 20 Oct. 37	1 Dec. 41	P 3 Apr. 46	
12	0	Robert Hallowell Carew	P 28 Nov. 37	P 13 May 42	20 Nov. 46	
7	0	Alex. M'Geachy Alleyne	P 14 May 42	P 17 May 44	P 31 Mar. 48	
19	1/12	Lewis Alex. Patrick Boyd	21 May 29	P 9 Oct. 35	30 Mar. 47	
8	0	Henry Archibald Cubitt	12 Mar. 41	21 Sept. 43	4 Sept. 48	
6	0	Frederick Palmer	P 16 June 43	16 Feb. 46	P 24 Nov. 48	
		LIEUTENANTS.				
8	0	r. Richard Lloyd	P 2 April 41	P 22 Sept. 43		
8	0	r. John Arthur Brockman	20 May 42	P 7 June 44		
7	0	r. Wm. Ryland Rainsford	P 6 Jan. 43	P 31 Jan. 45		
6	0	r. Roger Barnston, *adj.*..	7 July 43	3 Apr. 46		
5	0	Wm. Hamilton Fortescue	P 2 Feb. 44	P 21 Apr. 46		
6	0	Geo. Rob. Jas. Marshall	23 Sept. 43	26 June 46		
5	0	r. Daniel Tom	P 7 June 44	26 June 46		
4	0	Geo. L. Rawdon Berkeley	P 31 Jan. 45	P 25 Aug. 46		
7	0	Cecil Rivers	P 20 May 42	29 Dec. 46		
6	0	John Rotton, *adj.*......	P 7 Jan. 43	P 22 Jan. 47		
4	0	John Shaw Kennedy, *s.*..	7 Feb. 45	P 5 Nov. 47		
3	0	Henry Keane Grant	P 3 Apr. 46	P 25 Feb. 48		
3	0	Charles Hallowell Carew	28 Apr. 46	20 Oct. 48		
3	0	Thomas Morgan........	26 June 46	P 24 Oct. 48		
3	0	Chas. James Hale Monro	26 June 46	P 25 Oct. 48		
3	0	Wm. Hy. Acland Dashwood	26 June 46	P 8 Dec. 48		
		ENSIGNS.				
3	0	r. Bernard Robert Shaw	P 10 July 46			
3	0	r. John Edmund Harvey	P 14 Aug. 46			
3	0	r. Thomas Rice	P 25 Aug. 46			
3	0	Richard Harbord	P 22 Dec. 46			
2	0	r. George Massey Robbins	P 2 Apr. 47			
1	0	Flint William Stacey....	P 25 Feb. 48			
1	0	William Tyler Stuart....	20 Oct. 48			
1	0	Alfred Macdonald......	P 24 Nov. 48			
1	0	John Welman Helyar....	P 25 Nov. 48			
1	0	John Crawford Langford.	P 8 Dec. 48			

3 Doctor Jopp served with the Queen's Royals during the campaign of 1844-45 in the Southern Concan and Sawant Warree country, including the storming of several stockades, and the investment and capture of the Forts of Monohur and Munsuntosh.

Full Pay	Half Pay	
29	10 1/12	*Paymaster.*—Humphrey Hen. Carmichael, 24 Feb. 14; *Ens.* 24 Sept. 03; *Lieut.* 27 Nov. 06; *Capt.* 31 Dec. 12.
6	0	*Adjutants.*—r. *Lieut.* Roger Barnston, 20 Nov. 46.
6	0	*Lieut.* John Rotton, 20 Oct. 48.
14	0	*Quarter-Masters.*—William Stuart, 10 July, 35.
3	0	r. Patrick Owens, 20 Nov. 46.
24	0	*Surgeons.*—John James Russell, M.D. 11 June, 41; *Assist.-Surg.* 25 April, 26; *Hosp.-Assist.* 16 June, 25.
10	0	r. James Jopp,[3] M.D. 1 Jan. 47; *Assist.-Surg.* 22 Feb. 39.
4	0	*Assist.-Surgeons.*—William Mills Dowding, 9 May, 45.
2	0	r. Francis Smith, 1 Jan. 47.

Facings Grass Green.—*Agents,* Messrs. Price & Boustead.

1 Sir Roger Sheaffe served in Holland in 1799; and in the expedition to the Baltic, in 1801, under Sir Hyde Parker and Lord Nelson. The Americans having invaded Upper Canada at Queenstown on the 13th Oct. 1812, and General Brock, commanding in the province, having fallen in a gallant effort with an inadequate force to oppose them, they posted themselves on a woody height above Queenstown. Major-General Sheaffe, on whom the command devolved, assembled some regular troops and militia, with a few Indians, and on the same day attacked and completely defeated them, their commanding General delivering his sword to Major-General Sheaffe, and surrendering his surviving troops on the field of battle—their number

"MINDEN"—"TOURNAY"—"PENINSULA."

Years' Serv. 56 Full Pay.	Half Pay.					
		Colonel. Hon. Sir Alexander Duff,[1] GCH. *Ens.* 23 May, 1793; *Lieut.* 15 Jan. 94; *Capt.* 16 Jan. 94; *Major,* 28 Mar. 94; *Lieut.-Col.* 14 April, 98; *Col.* 25 April, 1808; *Major-Gen.* 4 June, 11; *Lieut.-Gen.* 19 July, 21; *Gen.* 28 June, 38; *Col.* 37th Regt. 20 July, 31.				
25	0	*Lieut.-Colonels.*—*Hon.* George Augustus Spencer, *Ens.* P12 Feb. 24; *Lieut.* P16 June, 25; *Capt.* P19 Dec. 26; *Major,* 17 Aug. 41; *Lieut.-Col.* P20 Dec. 44.				
23	0	Francis Skelly, *Ens.* P6 July, 26; *Lieut.* 18 Sept. 28; *Capt.* P21 Sept. 32; *Major,* P2 July, 41; *Lieut.-Col.* 3 Sept 47.				
22	0	*Majors.*—Gilbert Wm. Francklyn, *Ens.* P30 April, 27; *Lieut.* 23 Nov. 30; *Capt.* P9 Dec. 36; *Major,* P27 Aug. 41.				
20	0	Franklin Lushington,[2] C.B. *Ens.* P16 July, 29; *Lieut.* 10 Oct. 33; *Capt.* P30 Oct. 38; *Brev.-Major,* 23 Dec. 42; *Major,* P5 Nov. 47.				
		CAPTAINS.	ENSIGN.	LIEUT.	CAPTAIN.	BREV.-MAJ.
14	0	John Owen Lewis	P11 July 35	9 July 38	P29 Oct. 41	
13	0	Eliott Thomas Seward ..	P 9 Dec. 36	P15 Feb. 39	P17 June 42	
12	0	William Hamilton......	26 May 37	P21 June 39	P 4 July 45	
12	0	Edward D. Atkinson....	P 6 Oct. 37	P28 July 40	P20 Feb. 46	
11	0	John Hunter Mushet ..	P19 Oct. 38	P21 Feb. 40	P 1 May 46	
12	0	Arthur M. Alex. Bowers	P29 Dec. 37	P 2 July 41	P26 June 46	
11	0	Henry John Curteis	P 6 April38	P27 Aug. 41	P 2 Oct. 46	
11	0	Herbert Russell Manners	28 Aug. 38	7 Jan. 42	13 Nov. 46	
15	0	Thomas William Gells ..	P28 Nov. 34	P28 April 37	P 1 July 42	
11	0	Steph. Fra. Cha. Annesley	P 6 July 38	P17 Aug. 41	P22 Oct. 47	
		LIEUTENANTS.				
9	0	Robert Prescott Harrison	P28 July 40	P17 June 42		
8	0	Raymond Richard Pelly	P26 Jan. 41	20 May 44		
8	0	John Clutterbuck	P29 Oct. 41	P 4 July 45		
7	0	Joseph Jones, *adjutant*..	7 Jan. 42	29 Dec. 45		
7	0	Wm. Joseph Bazalgette..	P17 June 42	P30 Dec. 45		
6	0	Charles Luxmoore......	P17 Nov. 43	P 1 May 46		
5	0	James Henry Wyatt	P20 Sept. 44	P26 June 46		
4	0	Thomas Michaelson Machel	P 4 April 45	P 2 Oct. 46		
4	0	Edward Joseph N. Burton	P13 June 45	P20 Nov. 46		
4	0	John Leversage George..	P 4 July 45	P 2 Mar. 47		
4	0	G. D. Dillon Pilkington	P30 Dec. 45	P20 July 47		
7	0	Henry Thomas[4]........	11 Apr. 42	22 Dec. 45		
7	0	Robt. Gordon Cumming[5]	29 July 42	22 Dec. 45		
		ENSIGNS.				
3	0	Charles Samuel Blois....	P20 Feb. 46			
3	0	Thomas Jackson	P 1 May 46			
3	0	John Grattan Anderson..	31 July 46			
3	0	Joseph Hobson	P20 Nov. 46			
2	0	Wm. Pole Collingwood..	P23 Mar. 47			
2	0	Francis Hubble Douce ..	P 9 Apr. 47			
1	0	William Baker	P28 April 48			
1	0	Raynsford Taylor	P 8 Dec. 48			
11	0	*Paymaster.*—Henry Piercy,[6] 13 Aug. 47; *Ens.* P9 March 38; *Lt.* 14 Nov. 39.				
7	0	*Adjutant.*—*Lieut.* Joseph Jones, 2 April, 42.				
12	0	*Quarter-Master.*—Richard Hamilton, 2 Nov. 37.				
24	0	*Surgeon.*—Alex. Browne, M.D. 22 Nov. 39; *Assist.-Surg.* 3 Aug. 26; *Hosp.-Assist.* 16 June, 25.				
6	0	*Assistant-Surgeons.*—Alexander Forteath, M.D. 10 Feb. 43.				
3	0	James William Fleming, 27 Oct. 46.				

Facings Yellow.—*Agent*, Charles R. M'Grigor, Esq.

1 Sir Alex. Duff served in Flanders; accompanied the expedition from the East Indies to Egypt, where he served until the peace of 1802. Sir Alex. commanded the centre column in the attack upon Buenos Ayres.

2 Major Lushington served the campaign of 1842 in Affghanistan (Medal), and was severely wounded.

4 Lieut. Thomas served the campaign on the Sutlej in 1845-6 (Medal) with the 9th, including the battles of Moodkee, Ferozeshah, and Sobraon.

5 Lieut. Cumming served the campaign on the Sutlej in 1845—6 (Medal) with the 9th, and was present at the battles of Moodkee and Sobraon.

6 Paymaster Piercy served the campaign of 1844 and 45 in the southern Concan and Sawunt Warree country, in the Queen's Royals, and was present at the storming of several stockades, and at the investment of the forts of Monohur and Munsuntosh.

Emb. for For. Service, 4 Sept. 1840.] **38th (*The 1st Staffordshire*) *Regt. of Foot*.** [Serving in Nova Scotia. Depot at Castlebar.

"MONTE VIDEO"—"ROLEIA"—"VIMIERA"—"CORUNNA"—BUSACO"—"BADAJOZ"—"SALAMANCA"—"VITTORIA"—"ST. SEBASTIAN"—"NIVE"—"PENINSULA"—"AVA."

Years' Serv.		
53		*Colonel.*
		Hon. Hugh Arbuthnott,[1] CB. *Ens.* 18 May, 96; *Lt.* 15 Sept. 96; *Capt.* 20 March, 99; *Major,* 23 Nov. 04; *Lt.-Col.* 9 May, 11; *Col.* 19 July, 21; *Major-Gen.* 22 July, 30; *Lt.-Gen.* 23 Nov. 41; *Col.* 38th Regt. 4 April 43.
Full Pay.	Half Pay.	*Lieut.-Colonel.*
26	1 4/12	Sir John Campbell,[2] *Bart. Ens.* 25 Nov. 21; *Lieut.* 1 July, 24; *Capt.* P 11 July, 26; *Major,* P 29 Dec. 37; *Lieut.-Col.* P 7 Aug. 40.
25	0	*Majors.*—John Jackson Lowth[3], *Ens.* 3 July, 24; *Lieut.* 11 Sept. 25; *Capt.* P 23 Mar. 32; *Major,* P 12 June, 40.
20	14	John Campbell, *Ens.* 30 March, 15; *Lieut.* P 11 Jan. 21; *Capt.* P 26 May 25; *Major,* P 15 June, 32; *Brevet Lt.-Col.* 9 Nov. 46.

Full Pay	Half Pay	CAPTAINS.	ENSIGN.	LIEUT.	CAPTAIN.	BREV.-MAJ.
34	0	James Pattoun Sparks ..	27 July 15	30 July 18	5 Sept. 26	23 Nov. 41
18	0	Jos. Samuel Adamson ..	P 15 Mar. 31	P 27 Sept. 33	P 1 Dec. 37	
24	0	Charles Irvine..........	9 April 25	P 17 May 27	P 4 May 39	
23	0	John Gage Lecky	P 22 April 26	P 26 Mar. 29	P 10 April 40	
17	0	John W. S. Smith[4]......	3 Feb. 32	4 Aug. 37	P 7 Aug. 40	
28	0	Frederick Tudor[5]	26 Nov. 21	18 Sept. 24	29 Sept. 40	
13	0	Valentine Fred. Story ..	P 25 Nov. 36	30 Oct. 40	P 26 May 44	
24	0	Thomas Southall[6]	2 Dec. 25	25 Sept. 28	3 Jan. 45	
15	0	Thomas Anderson, ...	16 May 34	P 29 Dec. 37	22 Aug. 48	
12	0	Cockayne Frith	22 Aug. 37	P 4 May 39	P 6 Oct. 48	
		LIEUTENANTS.				
12	0	Robert Charles Sinclair..	P 23 Aug. 37	P 21 Sept. 39		
11	0	John Robert Jackson....	11 May 38	P 7 Aug. 40		
11	0	Wm. James Loftus......	P 9 Nov. 38	P 8 Nov. 42		
10	0	Robert Scott	31 May 39	P 14 Apr. 43		
10	0	Arthur Layard	P 1 Mar. 39	P 29 Dec. 40		
10	0	James Jarvis	P 21 Sept. 39	P 5 Dec. 43		
9	0	Henry Holden, *adj.*	P 7 Aug. 40	22 Mar. 44		
7	0	Edw. Thos. Gloster, *d. ad.*	P 13 May 42	3 Jan. 45		
6	0	Gustavus Hume	P 30 May 43	P 9 June 46		
6	0	Roderick Hugonin[7]	P 21 July 43	P 26 June 46		
6	0	Samuel Hackett........	P 20 Oct. 43	P 3 Dec. 47		
6	0	Fiennes Arthur Quartley	6 Dec. 43	22 Aug. 48		
5	0	George Green	22 Mar. 44	P 6 Oct. 48		
		ENSIGNS.				
4	0	Cha. F. Torrens Daniell	3 Jan. 45			
3	0	Henry Fisher	14 Apr. 46			
3	0	Ludford Harvey Daniel ..	P 9 June 46			
3	0	Charles Edward Johns ..	P 26 June 46			
2	0	Charles Wm. Watkins ..	P 15 Oct. 47			
2	0	Horatio Page Vance	P 3 Dec. 47			
1	0	James Thomas Craster ..	19 Sept. 48			
1	0	A. Campbell Snodgrass..	P 6 Oct. 48			
23	4/12	*Paymaster.*—Wm. F. Vernon, 9 July, 30; *Ens.* 1 June, 26; *Lieut.* 5 July, 27.				
9	0	*Adjutant.*—*Lieut.* Henry Holden, 17 Nov. 48				
9	0	*Quarter-Master.*—James Twibill, 8 May, 40; *Ens.* 7 May, 40.				
11	0	*Surgeon.*—Frederick Foaker, 23 March 47; *Assist.-Surg.* 19 Oct. 38.				
8	0	*Assist.-Surgeons.*—Edward Le Blanc,[7] 24 May, 41.				
5	0	Robert Browne, 1 March, 44.				

Facings Yellow.—*Agents,* Cox & Co.—*Irish Agents,* Messrs. Cane & Co.

2 Sir John Campbell served throughout the Burmese war, from 15th April, 1824, to its conclusion in Feb. 1826, as Aide-de-camp to Sir Archibald Campbell.

3 Major Lowth served with the 38th in the Burmese war, and was present at the affairs of Sembike and Napadie, and attack and capture of Melloon and of Pagham Mew.

5 Captain Tudor served throughout the Burmese war.

6 Captain Southall served in the Burmese war from Nov. 1825, to its conclusion in 1826.

1 Lieut.-General the Honourable Hugh Arbuthnott served with the 49th at the Helder, in 1799; also on the expedition to the Baltic, and battle of Copenhagen, in 1801. In July 1807, embarked with the expedition to Zealand, and was present at the siege and capture of Copenhagen. Accompanied the expedition to Sweden, and afterwards to Portugal and Spain under Sir John Moore, and was present at the battle of Corunna. Served also in the Peninsula under the Duke of Wellington, and commanded the 52nd at the battle of Busaco, for which he has received a medal.

4 Captain Smith commanded a detachment of the 38th Regiment in co-operation with a Naval expedition under Captain Lock in the ascent, in boats, of the river St. Juan de Nicaragua, central America, in 1848, including the assault and capture of the port of Serapiqui, and surrender of the Forts of Castello Viejo and St. Carlos. He also accompanied Captain Lock to the town of Granada, and was present at the deliberations and conclusion of a treaty with the Nicaragua commissioners

7 Lieut. Hugonin and Assist.-Surgeon Le Blanc served with a detachment of the 38th Regiment in co-operation with a Naval expedition under Capt. Lock in the ascent, in boats, of the river St. Juan de Nicaragua, central America, in 1848, including the assault and capture of the port of Serapiqui, and surrender of the Forts of Castello Viejo and St. Carlos.

"Primus in Indis."—"PLASSEY"—"GIBRALTAR"—with the Castle and Key, "Montis Insignia Ca[lpe]"—"ALBUHERA"—"VITTORIA"—"PYRENEES"—"NIVELLE"—"NIVE"—"ORTHES"—"PENINSULA"—"MAHARAJPORE."

Years' Serv. Full Pay.	Half Pay.	
72		**Colonel.** ℗ *Sir* Frederick Philipse Robinson,[1] GCB. *Ens.* Feb. 1777; *Lieut.* 1 Sept. *Capt.* 3 July, 94; *Major,* 1 Sept. 94; *Lieut.-Col.* 1 Jan. 1800; *Col.* 25 July, *Major-Gen.* 4 June, 13; *Lieut.-Gen.* 27 May, 25; *Gen.* 23 Nov. 41; *Col.* 3[9th] Regt. 15 June, 40.
36	1/12	*Lieut.-Colonel.*—Thomas Wright,[2] CB. *Ens.* 18 Dec. 12; *Lieut.* 22 April, *Capt.* P 14 July, 25; *Major,* P 10 March, 37; *Lieut.-Col.* 24 Apr. 39.
22	0	*Majors.*—Edward Bond,[4] *Ens.* P 8 Mar. 27; *Lieut.* P 16 Sept. 29; *Capt.* P Feb. 36; *Major,* P 31 March, 43.
18	0	Marmaduke George Nixon,[5] *Ens.* 5 April, 31; *Lieut.* 25 Mar. 33; *Capt.* P Dec. 38; *Brev.-Major,* 30 Apr. 44; *Major,* 7 Aug. 46.

Full Pay	Half Pay		ENSIGN.	LIEUT.	CAPTAIN.	BREV.-M[AJOR].
		CAPTAINS.				
26	0	Henry Francis Stokes[8] ..	24 July 23	1 Aug. 25	24 Apr. 39	
17	0	Robert Newport Tinley[9]	4 April 32	P 19 July 33	P 15 Dec. 40	
18	0	Arthur Herbert[10]	P 18 Jan. 31	2 Sept. 34	P 31 Dec. 41	
22	0	Charles D. Campbell[10] ..	P 9 Aug. 27	3 May 33	24 April 43	30 April
17	0	Henry Aug. Strachan[12] ..	21 Sept. 32	2 June 35	5 June 43	
15	0	William Munro,[14]	P 20 June 34	P 1 April 36	2 July 44	
14	0	William Clarges Wolfe ..	P 30 Oct. 35	P 10 Mar. 37	7 Aug. 46	
12	0	Thomas Wright Hudson	P 16 June 37	30 Oct. 40	7 Dec. 45	
10	0	Thomas Edw. Wilbraham	P 8 Mar. 39	P 21 May 41	20 Mar. 46	
13	0	Francis James Hugonin ..	P 12 Aug. 36	P 26 April 39	P 2 Oct. 46	
		LIEUTENANTS.				
13	0	J. Fitz Roy Dalrymple ..	P 2 Dec. 36	P 8 Dec. 37		
13	0	Humphrey Gray,[10]	25 Mar. 36	1 July 38		
12	0	William Hardinge[10]	P 10 Mar. 37	24 Apr. 39		
11	0	Chas. Tho. Hamilton[10] r..	P 17 Feb. 38	P 19 July 39		
11	0	Robert Hamilton Currie[10]	P 28 Dec. 38	P 14 Feb. 40		
15	0	Theodore M. Haultain[10] *adj*	27 June 34	20 Oct. 40		
10	0	Wm. Newport Tinley[10] ..	P 15 Nov. 39	P 11 June 41		
9	0	℗ Francis Gee[15]	18 Sept. 40	5 June 43		
8	0	Simon George Newport[10]	3 Aug. 41	2 July 44		
8	0	Henry Droz Gaynor[10] ..	P 31 Dec. 41	2 Aug. 44		
7	0	James Johnston	22 April 42	P 29 Dec. 43		
6	0	William Leckie	10 Nov. 43	16 April 45		
8	0	William Greenham	27 Aug. 41	11 Dec. 46		
5	0	James Agnew	22 Oct. 44	P 23 June 48		
		ENSIGNS.				
5	0	George Wolfe	27 Sept. 44			
4	0	John Popkin Traherne ..	4 July 45			
3	0	William Henry Wilson ..	9 June 46			
2	0	Michael C. Wall	P 30 Mar. 47			
2	0	Hugh Robert Hibbert ..	P 28 Sept. 47			
1	0	Benson Harrison	P 23 June 48			
1	0	Lewis Stafford Northcote	P 24 June 48			

Full Pay	Half Pay	
43	0	*Paymaster.*—G. Augustus Durnford,[13] 13 Feb. 27; *Ens.* 28 June, 06; *Lieut.* Mar. 10; *Capt.* 13 Feb.
15	0	*Adjutant.*—*Lt.* Theodore M. Haultain, 19 Mar. 47.
12	0	*Quarter-Master.*—Jones Duke, 10 Jan. 37.
17	0	*Surgeon.*—Charles Hugh James,[10] 18 Aug. 43; *Assist.-Surg.* 5 Oct. 32.
7	0	*Assist.-Surgeon.*—Henry Armstrong, 17 June, 42.

Facings Green.—*Agents,* Messrs. Cox and Co.

[*Returned from Bengal* 9 *June,* 1847.]

2 Lieut.-Col. Wright served [in the] campaign against the Rajah of Co[org] in 1834, and received a very se[vere] injury in the right leg in leading [the] advanced attack at the taking of [the] stockade of Periapatam, the fron[tier] stockade of the Coorg territory. [In] 1839 he was employed in the op[era]tions against Kurnool, and was [se]verely and dangerously wounde[d in] the affair of Zerapore on the 1[...] of Oct. He commanded a Brig[ade] in the battle of Maharajpore (M[e]dal) on the 29th Dec. 1843 in wh[ich] action his horse was shot under [him] in taking the battery at Chounda.

4 Major Bond served with [the] 53rd in the campaign on the Su[tlej] (Medal), and was present at Bud[di]wal, Aliwal, and Sobraon.

1 Sir Frederick Robinson served five years in the first American war, including the battle of Horse Neck, assault [and] capture of Stoney Point by the Americans (wounded and taken prisoner), and battle of New London. Subsequently at [the] capture of Martinique, St. Lucia, and Guadaloupe, in 1794, including the storming of Fleur d'Epée and the Heights of P[al]miste. Joined the army under the Duke of Wellington, in 1812, and was present at the action of Osma, and battle of V[it]toria, and commanded the Brigade which carried the village of Gamazza Mayo without firing a shot. In July and Aug[ust] following he was present at the 1st and 2nd assaults on San Sebastian (severely wounded), passage of the Bidassoa, the gr[eat] reconnoissance before Bayonne, battle of the Nive (severely wounded), blockade of Bayonne and repulse of the Sortie [on] which day he succeeded to the command of the 5th Division. In June, 1814, embarked in command of a Brigade, for Ameri[ca] commanded the two Brigades intended to attack the works of Plattsburg, but received orders to retire, after having for[ced] the passage of the Saranac. In Nov. following, appointed Commander-in-Chief and Provisional Gov. of the Upper Provin[ce] which appointment he held till June 1816. Sir Fred. has received a medal & two clasps for Vittoria, San Sebastian, & the Ni[ve].

5 Major Nixon served the campaign against the Rajah of Coorg in 1834; and in the action of Maharajpore on [the] 29th Dec 1843, he served as Major of Brigade to the 5th Brigade.

8 Captain Stokes served in the 38th throughout the Burmese war; and with the 39th in the action of Maharajpore.

9 Captain Tinley served the campaign against the Rajah of Coorg in 1834. In the action at Maharajpore, 29th Dec. 1843, was severely wounded.

10 Major Campbell, Capt. Herbert, Lieuts. Gray, Hardinge, Hamilton, Currie, Haultain, Tinley, Flynn, Newport, Gaynor, and Dr. James, served with the Regt. at the action of Maharajpore on the 29th Dec. 1843; Major Camp[bell] Captain Herbert, and Lieuts. Currie and Newport, were slightly wounded; and Lieut. H. Gray was very severely wou[nded].

12 Capt. Strachan served the campaign against the Rajah of Coorg, in 1834.

13 Capt. Durnford served at the capture of the Isle of France in 1810; in the expedition to Java in 1811; capture of Kand[y] 1815; in the Kandyan rebellion in 1817 and 18; and in the action of Maharajpore, 29th Dec. 43.

14 Capt. Munro served as Adjutant of the 39th in the action at Maharajpore, and was severely wounded (medal).

15 Lt. Gee served in the Peninsula from 1811 to 1814, and was present at Vittoria, Stewart's Rock near Maya, Pyre[nees,] Pampeluna, Nivelle, Nive, Bayonne, Garris, Orthes, and Toulouse. He was also present in the action at Maharajpore the 29th Dec 1843.

*** The 39th Regt. was raised in 1701; it proceeded from Ireland to Portugal in 1704; to Spain and battle of Almanza, 1710; between 1710 and 1727, at Gibraltar, Minorca, and Ireland,—and again to Gibraltar when besieged in 1727. Went to Jamaica in 1730; in Ireland and England, 1732 to 1744; on board the Fleet as Marines in 1748. Embarked for India early in 1754, where it remained until 1758, and was present at the battle of Plassey. Returned to Ireland in 1758; Gibraltar 1769; England [illegible] ndies in 1794; returned to Ireland in 1795, in which year it went again to the West Indies, and remained there until 1803, when it returned to England, and was formed into two Battalions. The 2nd Battalion remained at home until June, 1809, when it proceeded to the Peninsula and was present at the 1st siege of Badajoz, and battles of Busaco, Albuhera, and Arroyo de Molino: it was disbanded on the 24th Dec. 1815. The 1st Battalion served in the Mediterranean until 1811, when it also joined the Duke of Wellington's army in the Peninsula, and was present at the following actions: viz.—Vittoria, Pyrenees, Nivelle, Nive, repulse of the French army before Bayonne on the 13th Dec. 1813, Garris, Orthes, Aire, Vic Bigorre, Tarbes, and Toulouse. At the close of the campaign of 1814, it embarked for Canada. In Aug. 1815, it joined the Duke of Wellington's army at Paris, and remained in France until 1818, when it returned to England. Embarked for New South Wales in 1826; landed at Madras in 1832; employed in the capture of the Coorg Territory, in April 1834; and in the operations against Kurnool in 1839. In 1841 it was transferred to the Bengal Presidency, and was conspicuously engaged in the action at Maharajpore on the 29th Dec. 1843. Returned to England 9 June 1847.

The *Sphinx*, with the word "EGYPT" on the caps of the Flank Companies. "MONTE VIDEO"—"ROLEIA"—"VIMIERA"—"TALAVERA"—"BADAJOZ"—"SALAMANCA"—"VITTORIA"—"PYRENEES"—"NIVELLE"—"ORTHES"—"TOULOUSE"—"PENINSULA"—"WATERLOO"—"CANDAHAR," "GHUZNEE and CABOOL, 1842," "MAHARAJPORE."

Years' Serv. Full Pay.	Half Pay.	
55		***Colonel.***
		℗ ⚜ *Sir* Alexander Woodford,[1] KCB. GCMG. *Ens.* 6 Dec. 94; *Lieut.* 15 July, 95; *Capt.* 11 Dec. 99; *Capt. & Lieut.-Col.* 8 Mar. 10; *Col.* 4 June, 14; *Major-Gen.* 27 May, 25; *Lieut.-Gen.* 28 June, 38; *Col.* 40th Foot, 25 April, 42.
36	4/12	*Lieut.-Col.*—℗ Severus Wm. Lynam Stretton,[3] *Ens.* 11 June 12; *Lieut.* 6 Jan. 14; *Capt.* P 13 Aug. 25; *Major,* P 2 Dec. 31; *Lieut.-Col.* P 6 May 42.
21	0	*Majors.*—Thomas James Valiant, *Ens.* 29 May, 28; *Lieut.* P 17 Dec. 29; *Capt.* P 1 May, 35; *Major,* P 10 July, 46.
26	9 4/12	John MacDuff,[5] *Ens.* 10 Feb. 14; *Lt.* 26 June, 27; *Capt.* P 13 April, 39; *Major,* 13 Nov. 47.

Full Pay	Half Pay	CAPTAINS.	ENSIGN.	LIEUT.	CAPTAIN.	BREV.-MAJ.
19	0	Henry Douglas Cowper..	P 20 July 30	P 14 Dec. 32	P 4 Mar. 36	9 Nov. 46
16	0	John Martin Bladen Neill[10]	P 22 Mar. 33	P 9 Jan. 35	P 11 Mar. 42	
18	0	James Todd[9]	P 22 Feb. 31	4 July 34	22 July 45	
11	0	Arthur Leslie	P 20 Nov. 38	P 6 May 42	P 3 April 46	
18	0	Thomas L. K. Nelson[9], *s.*	25 Nov. 31	29 Jan. 36	P 10 July 46	
15	0	Wm. Augustus Fyers[10] ..	P 17 Oct. 34	P 20 May 36	P 7 May 47	
10	0	John W. Thomas[9]	7 June 39	P 7 Sept. 41	P 14 May 47	
10	0	Robert Carey[10]	15 Nov. 39	10 Nov. 41	P 14 May 47	
9	0	Jn. Anstruther M'Gowan[9]	P 21 Feb. 40	4 Mar. 42	P 31 Dec. 47	
10	0	Fra. Brockman Morley[13]	P 5 Apr. 39	27 May 42	P 18 Aug. 48	
		LIEUTENANTS.				
10	0	Edw. Hungerford Eagar[9]	P 13 April 39	16 July 41		
9	0	Frederick Huey[13]	P 5 June 40	5 Mar. 42		
8	0	John Cormick[13]	P 27 Aug. 41	P 25 Oct 42		
8	0	Richard Dawson[14]	P 21 May 41	14 April 43		
8	0	Samuel Snelling[9]	26 Oct. 41	30 Dec. 43		
7	0	Fred. Montagu Hockings	20 May 42	P 10 July 46		
5	0	Aldborough Rich. Rundle	23 Feb. 44	P 31 July 46		
5	0	Lewis Alexander Forbes, *r.*	P 27 Sept. 44	P 17 Oct. 45		
6	0	Hans Thomas Fell White	P 12 May 43	P 14 May 47		
4	0	R. John Lechmere Coore	P 27 June 45	P 14 May 47		
5	0	Richard Mahony Hickson	P 13 Dec. 44	29 Jan. 47		
3	0	Thomas Wilson	P 10 July 46	P 31 Dec. 47		
4	0	Francis Barry Drew, *adj.*	P 23 May 45	17 Aug. 48		
2	0	Robert Hare	P 7 May 47	P 18 Aug. 48		
		ENSIGNS.				
2	0	Rogers Parker Hibbert ..	P 14 May 47			
2	0	Thomas George Gardiner	P 15 May 47			
2	0	Henry Christopher Wise .	26 Nov. 47			
2	0	Henry Fowler.........	P 31 Dec. 47			
1	0	John Pinckney	P 14 Apr. 48			
1	0	George Owen Bowdler ..	26 May 48			
1	0	David Pennefather......	P 18 Aug. 48			

5 Major MacDuff acted as a Field Officer in the 40th during the operations in Candahar and in Affghanistan in 1841-42 (medal); and he commanded the Grenadier Company in the action at Maharajpore (medal).

Full Pay	Half Pay	
37	0	*Paymaster.*—Charles Scarlin Naylor,[15] 8 May, 35; *Ens.* 1 Sept. 12; *Lieut.* 25 Dec. 15; *Capt.* 9 May, 34.
4	0	*Adjutant.*—*Lieut.* Francis Barry Drew, 11 Feb. 48.
7	0	*Quarter-Master.*—Thomas Walter Hives,[9] 25 Oct. 42.
9	0	*Surgeon.*—Joseph Burke,[16] 22 Dec. 48; *Assist.-Surg.* 10 Jan. 40.
1	0	*Assist.-Surg.*—Edward Wm. Clemishaw Kingdom, M.D., 25 Feb. 48.

Facings Buff.—*Agents,* Messrs. Cox & Co.—*Irish Agents, Sir* E. R. Borough, Bt., Armit & Co.

[*Returned from India, Feb.* 1846.]

1 Sir Alexander Woodford served in the 9th in North Holland, and was severely wounded on the 19th Sept. 1799. Served in the Coldstream Guards at the capture of Copenhagen in 1807. Served on the Staff in Sicily, in 1808, 9, and 10. Commanded the Light Battalion of the Brigade of Guards, at the siege of Ciudad Rodrigo, capture of Badajos, battle of Salamanca, capture of Madrid, and at the siege of Burgos. Commanded first battalion Coldstream Guards at the battle of Vittoria, capture of San Sebastian, at the Nivelle, the Nive, and investment of Bayonne. Commanded the second battalion at the battle of Waterloo, surrender of Paris, and during the occupation in France. Sir Alexander has received a medal and two clasps for the battles of Salamanca, Vittoria, and the Nive.

3 Lt. Col. Stretton served the campaigns of 1812 and 13 in the Peninsula, with the 68th Light Infantry, and was severely wounded at the battle of Vittoria by two gun shots lodged in the body, one of which has not been extracted.

9 Captains Todd, T. L. K. Nelson, Thomas and M'Gowan (severely wounded at Gundamuck), Lieutenants Eagar (severely wounded at Beni Badam) and Snelling, and Quartermaster Hives, served throughout the operations in Candahar and in Affghanistan in 1841 and 42, and have received the medal. These officers were also present in the action of Maharajpore, 29th Dec. 1843, and have received the Bronze Star: Lt. Eagar was slightly wounded, and Capts. T. L. K. Nelson and Thomas were severely wounded. Capt. Nelson was Adjutant of the Regt. during the second Affghan campaign, in 1842, as well as at Maharajpore, where he had a horse shot under him.

10 Captains Bladen Neill, Fyers, and Carey served throughout the operations in Candahar and in Affghanistan in 1841 and 42, and have received the medal.

16 Mr Burke served with the 50th the campaign on the Sutlej (medal), including the battles of Moodkee, Ferozeshah, Aliwal, and Sobraon.

13 Capt. Morley, Lieuts. Huey (severely wounded), and Cormick, were present in the action of Maharajpore, and have received the bronze star.

14 Lt. Dawson was attached to the 22nd at the battle of Hyderabad, and has received the medal. He was afterwards present with the 40th at Maharajpore, in which action he was wounded, and has received the Bronze Star.

15 Captain Naylor served at the siege and capture of Loghur, Koaree, Ryghur, and several small Hill Forts in the Southern Mahratta Country in 1818. Served in the Serwent Warree State, and was severely wounded in both legs (compound fracture of the right) at the assault of Roree, 13th Feb. 1819. Served also in the Burmese war in 1825 and 1826; and at the capture of Kurrachee in Lower Scinde in 1839.

41st (*The Welsh*) *Regiment of Foot.*

[Head Quarters
[at Buttevant.

he Colours and Appointments, the *Prince of Wales's Plume*, with the motto, "*Gwell Angau na Chywilydd*."—"DETROIT"—"QUEENSTOWN"—"MIAMI"—"NIAGARA"—"AVA."
"CANDAHAR, GHUZNEE, and CABOOL, 1842."

Serv.	
8	*Colonel.*
Half Pay.	⚔ Charles Ashe A'Court,[1] CB. KH. *Ens.* 17 Dec. 01; *Lieut.* 2 Sept. 02; *Capt.* 25 July, 04; *Major*, 26 Feb. 11; *Lieut.-Col.* 19 May, 18; *Col.* 22 July, 30; *Major-Gen.* 23 Nov. 41; *Col.* 41st Foot, 5 Feb. 48.
	Lieut.-Colonel.
0	Gore Browne,[2] CB. *Ens.* 14 Jan. 24; *Lt.* P 11 July, 26; *Capt.* P 11 June, 29; *Major*, P 19 Dec. 34; *Brevet-Lt.-Col.* 23 Dec. 42; *Lt.-Col.* P 22 July, 45.
3 5/12	*Majors.*—George Carpenter, *Ens.* 1 Oct. 18; *Lieut.* 1 Mar. 20; *Capt.* P 29 Oct. 25; *Brevet-Major*, 28 June, 38; *Major*, P 22 July, 45.
0	William Carden Seton, *Ens.* P 2 Mar. 32; *Lieut.* P 22 July, 36; *Capt.* P 22 May, 40; *Major*, P 15 Oct. 47.

		ENSIGN.	LIEUT.	CAPTAIN.	BREV.-MAJ.
	CAPTAINS.				
0	Henry Law Maydwell, *s.*	21 Aug. 35	28 Sept. 38	P 15 April 42	
0	Robert Butler[4]	12 April 31	P 25 Oct. 33	P 1 Mar. 44	
0	George Bagot, *s.*	26 July 35	P 7 Oct. 37	4 July 45	
0	Robert Pratt,[5]	P 16 June 37	P 27 June 39	P 23 Sept. 45	
0	Augustus J. W. Northey	P 14 July 37	P 3 July 40	P 27 Sept. 44	
0	James Eman[6]	25 Mar. 36	10 Aug. 38	9 Oct. 46	
0	Chas. Timothy Tuckey[5]	P 28 June 39	2 Oct. 41	P 3 Nov. 46	
0	Grenville G. Wells	P 20 Dec. 39	P 22 Nov. 42	P 19 Mar. 47	
0	John Harvey Thursby ..	P 26 Aug. 36	P 18 Apr. 41	P 5 Apr. 44	
0	George Montagu Hicks ..	P 16 Nov. 41	P 20 Jan. 43	P 15 Oct. 47	
	LIEUTENANTS.				
0	Edwin Robert Wethered	P 5 Aug. 42	P 24 May 44		
0	Thomas Clough Taylor ..	P 30 Sept. 42	R 20 Aug. 44		
0	Julius Edmund Goodwyn	P 5 Jan. 44	P 6 June 45		
0	Wm. Samuel Greatheed	P 26 Jan. 44	P 23 Sept. 45		
0	Rich. Oliver Fra. Steward	P 29 Sept. 43	P 26 Sept. 45		
0	Joseph Gostling Egginton	P 30 Sept. 42	P 9 Dec. 45		
0	Rob. Fra. Lascelles Jenner	P 4 April 45	P 7 July 46		
0	Henry Warter Meredith	P 6 June 45	P 3 Nov. 46		
0	*Hon.* Richard Handcock	P 12 Apr. 44	P 3 Apr. 46		
0	Reginald Heber Rawlins	P 23 Sept. 45	P 19 Mar. 47		
0	F. G. H. Games Williams	P 7 July 46	P 14 May 47		
0	George Skipwith	P 3 Nov. 46	P 15 Oct. 47		
0	William Hunt	P 19 Nov. 44	25 Aug. 46		
	ENSIGNS.				
0	William Johnstone, *adj.*	30 Dec. 45			
0	Charles Pelgue Bertram	P 5 Feb. 47			
0	Henry Dixon	P 6 Feb. 47			
0	Robert Cary Barnard	P 19 Mar. 47			
0	Chas. Yelverton Balguy	P 14 May 47			
0	Thomas Acres Peirce ..	P 15 Oct. 47			
0	George William Alexander	P 19 Nov. 47			
0	Marcus Antonius Waters	P 26 May 48			

9 Mr. Stewart served with the 41st in Affghanistan in 1842, and was present in the engagements of the 30th Aug. at Goaine, and the 5th Sept. before Ghuznee, the occupation and destruction of that fortress and of Cabool, and the various minor affairs in and between the Bolan and Khyber Passes (Medal). He served also with the 31st during the campaign on the Sutlej (Medal), and was present in the battles of Moodkee and Ferozeshah.

1/12 *Paymaster.*—Thos. Miller Creagh, 21 June 39; *Ens.* 23 Feb. 25; *Lt.* 6 Mar. 26.
0 *Adjutant.*—*Ensign* William Johnstone, 20 Oct. 46.
0 *Quarter-Master.*—Archibald Elliott, 21 July, 48; *Ens.* 31 March, 48.
1/12 *Surgeon.*—⚔ Wm. Mortimer Wilkins,[8] 23 Dec. 36; *Assist.-Surg.* 22 June, 25; [*Hosp.-Assist.* 10 Jan. 14.
0 *Assist.-Surg.*—David Stewart,[9] 3 Dec. 41.
Facings White.—*Agents*, Messrs. Cox & Co.—*Irish Agents*, *Sir* E. R. Borough, [*Bt.*, Armit, & Co.
[*Returned from the East Indies*, 13 *July*, 1843.]

-General A'Court was detached on a separate command in 1806 to the Adriatic, to attack the islands of Tremiti; e same year he assisted at the siege of Scylla. In 1807 he served in Egypt, and was present at the capture of ria, and in the action near Rosetta. At the siege and capture of Santa Maura he was in charge of the Quarter-General's department: he was also at the siege of Capri in the same year. He was Aide-de-camp to the Adjutant-when the enemy landed in Sicily, in 1809, and commanded the advance-guard to which nearly 1800 prisoners sur-, and he personally captured the enemy's standard. Served afterwards on the staff in Sicily, Spain, and Italy, and ent at the siege of Tarragona, action at Villa Franca, and retreat from thence; subsequently at the occupation of , capture of Genoa, siege of Savona, and lastly at the surrender of Naples in 1815.

Col. Browne commanded the 41st during the whole of the campaign of 1842 in Affghanistan, and was present in the nts with the enemy on 28 March and 28 April in the Pisheen Valley; in that of the 29 May near Candahar, 30 Aug. e, 5 Sept. before Ghuznee, occupation and destruction of that fortress and of Cabool, expedition into Kohistan, storm, and destruction of Istaliff, and in the various minor affairs in and between the Bolan and the Khyber Passes.

tain Butler,—the same service as detailed in Note 2, except 29 May near Candahar.

tain Eman,—the same service as Lt.-Col. Browne, detailed in Note 2.

tains Pratt and Tuckey,—the same as Note 2, except the action of the 28th March.

Wilkins served the campaign of 1814 in the Peninsula; in the Kandian war in Ceylon, during 1817 and 18; and n of a Light Battalion at the siege of Kolapore in 1827. Services in Affghanistan the same as in Note 2.

Emb. for Foreign Serv. 12 Jan. 1841.] **42d (*The Royal Highland*) Regt. of Foot.** [Serving at Bermuda. Reserve Batt. do.

St. Andrew, "*Nemo me impune lacessit.*"—The *Sphinx*, with the words "EGYPT"—"CORUNNA"—"FUENTES D'ONOR"—"PYRENEES"—"NIVELLE"—"NIVE"—"ORTHES"—"TOULOUSE"—"PENINSULA"—"WATERLOO."

Years' Serv. 54 — Full Pay. | Half Pay.

Colonel.

P *Sir* John Macdonald,[1] GCB. *Ens.* 15 Apr. 95; *Lieut.* 2 Feb. 96; *Capt.* 22 Oct. 02; *Major*, 28 Feb. 05; *Lieut.-Col.* 17 Mar. 08; *Col.* 4 June, 14; *Maj-Gen.* 27 May, 25; *Lieut.-Gen.* 28 June, 38; *Col.* 42nd Highlanders, 15 Jan. 44.

24 | 0 | *Lieut.-Colonels.*—Duncan Alex. Cameron, *Ens.* 8 April, 25; *Lieut.* P 15 Aug. 26; *Capt.* P 21 June, 33; *Major*, P 23 Aug. 39; *Lieut.-Col.* P 5 Sept. 43.

36 | $1\frac{1}{12}$ | r. P James Macdougall,[2] *2nd Lt.* 11 June, 12; *Lt.* 8 Sept. 13; *Capt.* P 10 Sept. 25; *Major*, 23 Oct. 35; *Brevet-Lieut.-Col.* 1 Nov. 42; *Lt.-Col.* 14 Apr. 46.

24 | 0 | *Majors.*—Charles Dunsmure, *Ens.* 9 Apr. 25; *Lieut.* P 7 Nov. 26; *Capt.* P 30 Jan. 35; *Major*, P 5 Sept. 43.

36 | $2\frac{1}{12}$ | r. Daniel Frazer, *Ens.* 31 Oct. 11; *Lieut.* 13 June 16; *Capt.* P 5 Nov. 25; *Brev.-Maj.* 28 June 38; *Maj.* 14 Apr. 46.

Full Pay	Half Pay	CAPTAINS.	ENSIGN.	LIEUT.	CAPTAIN.	BREV.-MAJ.
24	0	Geo. Burrell Cumberland	11 Apr. 25	31 Dec. 28	P 30 Mar. 38	
23	0	Thomas Tulloch........	P 25 June 26	23 Oct. 28	P 12 July 33	9 Nov. 46
19	0	r. Jn. Cameron Macpherson	P 10 Sept. 30	P 21 June 33	P 6 Mar. 40	
17	0	*Hon.* Robert Rollo	P 10 Aug. 32	P 25 Sept. 35	P 5 Nov. 41	
17	0	r. Alexander Cameron ..	24 Feb. 32	P 30 Jan. 35	15 Apr. 42	
17	0	r. H. Maurice Drummond	P 4 Dec. 32	P 15 Dec. 37	P 3 June 42	
16	0	Charles Murray	P 21 June 33	P 30 Mar. 38	P 5 Sept. 43	
14	0	r. George W. Macquarie	P 25 Sept. 35	P 31 May 39	P 25 Oct. 44	
12	0	Archibald Colin Campbell	P 24 Feb. 37	P 23 Aug. 39	P 6 Dec. 44	
15	0	r. John Hinton Daniell[4]	P 14 Mar. 34	18 Nov. 36	P 29 Nov. 44	
11	0	r. Farquhar Campbell ..	P 30 Nov. 38	P 16 May 40	P 3 Nov. 46	
10	0	Thomas Robert D. Hay,	P 2 Aug. 39	P 5 Nov. 41	P 17 Nov. 48	
		LIEUTENANTS.				
14	0	r. G. Maclaine Ross, *pm.*	8 May 35	9 Aug. 39		
10	0	Robert Bligh Sinclair ..	P 27 Sept. 39	15 Apr. 42		
9	0	r. Augustus Paterson ..	P 10 Jan. 40	15 Apr. 42		
9	0	Thomas Hugh Cockburn	P 6 Mar. 40	15 Apr. 42		
9	0	r. Andrew Pitcairn, *adj.*	P 15 May 40	P 15 Apr. 42		
9	0	Alexander Ramsay	P 16 May 40	P 3 June 42		
8	0	John Walter Wedderburn	P 26 Oct. 41	P 5 Sept. 43		
8	0	*Hon.* G. H. Essex Grant, *s.*	P 5 Nov. 41	P 30 Aug. 44		
7	0	r. Ernest F. G. Clavering	P 15 Apr. 42	P 25 Oct. 44		
7	0	r. Archd. Macra Chisholm	17 Apr. 42	14 Apr. 46		
7	0	r. Gilbert Innes Menzies	18 Apr. 42	28 Aug. 46		
5	0	r. Chas. Campbell Graham	P 30 Aug. 44	24 May 47		
5	0	Wm. John Cuninghame	P 25 Oct. 44	P 13 Aug. 47		
5	0	John Wm. Powlett Orde	P 6 Dec. 44	P 12 Nov. 47		
3	0	Rowl. Aynsworth Frazer	14 Apr. 46	P 16 June 38		
3	0	r. John Chetham M'Leod	21 Apr. 46	P 17 Nov. 48		
		ENSIGNS.				
3	0	William Lear Macnish ..	28 Aug. 46			
3	0	Rob Campbell Cuninghame	29 Aug. 46			
3	0	r. James Erskine Paterson	P 20 Oct. 46			
2	0	r. James William Balfour	P 2 Mar. 47			
2	0	Henry Montgomery	P 3 Mar. 47			
2	0	r. John Drysdale........	22 June 47			
2	0	Charles Maitland	P 12 Nov. 47			
1	0	William James Robertson	P 16 June 48			
1	0	William Crofton Ward ..	18 Aug. 48			
1	0	John Gordon Campbell ..	P 17 Nov. 48			

2 Lt.-Col. Macdougall served the campaigns of 1813 and 14, in the Peninsula, including the affair of San Marcial, battles of Nivelle, Nive, 9th, 10th, 11th, 12th, and 13th Dec., Orthes, and Toulouse.

4 Capt. Daniell served with the 49th in China (Medal),—at Amoy, Chusan, Chinhae, Ningpo, Segoan, Chapoo, Woosung, and Chin Kian Foo.

17 | 0 | *Paymast.*—J. Wheatley, 12 Oct. 38; *Ens. & Adjt.* 20 July, 32; *Lieut.* 3 Apr. 35.

9 | 0 | *Adjutants.*—

9 | 0 | r. *Lieut.* Andrew Pitcairn, 28 Aug. 46.

9 | 0 | *Quarter-Masters.*—[illegible] Edward Paton, 19 June, 40.

6 | 0 | r. Charles Fraser, 28 Aug. 46; *Ens.* 4 Sept. 43.

23 | 0 | *Surgeons.*—Jas. M'Gregor, M.D., 26 Feb. 41; *A.-S.* 12 Apr. 26; *H.-A.* 5 Jan. 26.

12 | 0 | r. Hugh Mackey, 7 Aug. 46; *Assist.-Surg.* 17 Feb. 37.

7 | 0 | *Assistant-Surgeons.*—Wm. Mure Muir, M.D., 22 Nov. 42.—*Facings* Blue.

4 | 0 | Robert Henry King, 22 July 45.—*Agents*, Messrs. Cox & Co.

1 Sir John Macdonald served with the 89th in Ireland during the Rebellion of 1798, and was present at the battles of Ross, Vinegar Hill, and other principal actions. In 1799 and 1800 he was at the siege of La Valetta and capture of Malta. He served in Egypt in the three following years, and was present in the action on the landing on the 8th March, and also in the two other general actions fought on the 13th and 21st March, 1801. In 1807 he was employed as military secretary to Lord Cathcart, whilst his Lordship commanded the King's German Legion as a distinct army in Swedish Pomerania, as well as during the subsequent attack upon and capture of Copenhagen and the Danish fleet. In 1809 he served in the Walcheren expedition, and had charge of the Adjutant-General's department of the reserve commanded by Sir John Hope. The following year he was employed as Deputy Adjutant-General to the force allotted to the defence of Cadiz, under Lt.-Gen. Graham, and was present at the battle of Barrosa. In 1813 and 14 he was employed in charge of the left wing of the Peninsular army, and in that capacity was present in the actions of the 9th, 10th, 11th, and 13th Dec. 1813, upon the Nive, and in the affairs which attended the closing of the blockade of Bayonne, and at the action brought on by the general sortie from that fortress. Sir John has received a medal for services in Egypt, and a medal and one clasp for Barrosa and the Nive.

43rd (*The Monmouthshire*) *Regt. of Foot.* (*Light Infantry.*)

"VIMIERA"—"CORUNNA"—"BUSACO"—"FUENTES D'ONOR"—"CIUDAD RODRIGO"—"BADAJOZ"—"SALAMANCA"—"VITTORIA"—"NIVELLE"—"NIVE"—"TOULOUSE"—"PENINSULA."

Years' Serv. Full Pay.	Half Pay.					
46		*Colonel.*				
		Hon. Sir Hercules Robert Pakenham,[1] KCB. *Ens.* 23 July, 03; *Lieut.* 3 Mar. 04; *Capt.* 2 Aug. 05; *Major,* 30 Aug. 10; *Lt.-Col.* 27 April, 12; *Col.* 27 May 25; *Maj.-Gen.* 10 Jan. 37; *Lt.-Gen.* 9 Nov. 46; *Col.* 43 F. 9 Sep. 44.				
		Lieut.-Colonel.				
36	3/12	James Forlong,[2] KH. *Ens.* P 11 Mar. 13; *Lieut.* P 22 Dec. 14; *Capt.* P 20 Sept. 21; *Major,* P 1 July, 28; *Lieut.-Col.* 7 May, 41.				
33	3 4/12	*Majors.*—William Fraser,[3] *Ens.* 8 April, 13; *Lieut.* 19 Jan. 14; *Capt.* P 9 Dec. 24; *Brevet-Major,* 28 June, 38; *Major,* 7 May, 41.				
24	0	Henry Sadleir Bruere, *Ens.* P 1 Sept. 25; *Lieut.* P 19 Feb. 28; *Capt.* P 8 Apr. 34; *Brevet-Major,* 9 Nov. 46; *Major,* 11 Apr. 48.				
		CAPTAINS.	ENSIGN.	LIEUT.	CAPTAIN.	BREV.-MAJ.
23	0	George Talbot, *s.*	2 Feb. 26	P 9 Sept. 28	P 3 Apr. 35	9 Nov. 46
23	0	Johnson Ford	P 7 Sept. 26	P 25 June 29	P 21 Oct. 36	9 Nov. 46
15	0	John Chidley Coote	P 4 July 34	P 15 Sept. 37	P 31 Dec. 41	
15	0	Henry Skipwith	P 24 Oct. 34	P 25 Jan. 39	P 5 Aug. 42	
14	0	*Hon.* T. G. Cholmondeley	P 3 Apr. 35	P 31 Dec. 39	P 21 July 43	
14	0	Robert Lambert	P 1 May 35	P 15 May 40	P 25 Aug 43	
13	0	Robert Newton Phillips	P 27 May 36	P 2 Oct. 40	P 12 Jan. 44	
11	0	Owen Arth. Ormsby Gore	P 20 Nov. 38	P 16 Feb. 41	P 9 June 46	
9	0	*Hon.* P. Egerton Herbert	17 Jan. 40	P 7 Sept. 41	P 19 June 46	
12	0	James M. Primrose	6 Jan. 37	7 May 41	11 Apr. 48	
		LIEUTENANTS.				
9	0	Dawson Cornelius Greene	P 3 July 40	P 14 Jan. 42		
9	0	Henry Ayshford Sanford	7 Aug. 40	P 5 Aug. 42		
9	0	Henry Parry Denniss	P 21 Aug. 40	P 27 Dec. 42		
9	0	Fred. Sadleir Bruere	P 11 Sept. 40	P 21 July 43		
8	0	Walter John Paul	P 16 Feb. 41	P 25 Aug. 43		
8	0	James Abercromby Dick	P 1 June 41	P 24 Oct. 45		
8	0	Richard Henry Weyland	P 3 Aug. 41	28 Dec. 45		
8	0	Fra. Hutchinson Synge	P 7 Sept. 41	P 9 June 46		
7	0	Graham Colvile	P 5 Aug. 42	11 June 47		
7	0	Fred. Green Wilkinson, *adj.*	P 27 Dec. 42	P 13 Aug. 47		
4	0	William Milnes	6 June 45	25 Apr. 48		
		ENSIGNS.				
4	0	Horace Fred. Hill	20 June 45			
4	0	Charles Carew de Morel	P 24 Oct. 45			
3	0	*Hon.* Henry Wrottesley	9 June 46			
3	0	*Hon.* Henry Wm. C. Ward	P 19 June 46			
3	0	Arth. Edw. Val. Ponsonby	26 June 46			
2	0	Henry J. Parkin Booth	11 June 47			
2	0	Lumley Graham	P 13 Aug. 47			
2	0	John Francis Girardot	P 3 Sept. 47			
2	0	Charles, *Lord* Lurgan	P 5 Nov. 47			
1	0	*Hon.* Lewis Watson Milles	P 28 Apr. 48			
13	0	*Paymaster.*—Daniel Henry Mackinnon,[4] 27 Oct. 48; *Cor.* P 1 July 36; *Lieut.* P 23 Mar. 38; *Capt.* P 15 Oct. 47.				
7	0	*Adjutant.*—*Lieut.* Fred. Green Wilkinson, 25 April 48.				
1	0	*Quarter-Master.*—Joseph Denton, 15 Aug. 48.				
11	0	*Surgeon.*—Patrick Davidson, M.D., 27 Oct. 46; *Assist.-Surg.* 12 Jan. 38.				
2	0	*Assistant-Surgeon.*—John Lawrence Johnston, 31 Dec. 47.				

3 Major Fraser was severely wounded at the battle of the Nive.

Facings White.—*Agents,* Messrs. Cox & Co.

[*Returned from Nova Scotia,* 5 April, 46.]

1 Sir Hercules Pakenham served at the siege and capture of Copenhagen, in 1807, also the Peninsular campaigns of 1808, 9, 10, 11, and 12, including the battles of Roleia, Vimiera (wounded), Busaco, and Fuentes d'Onor, siege and storm of Ciudad Rodrigo, two sieges and storm of Badajos, severely wounded at the assault. Sir Hercules has received a cross.

2 Lieut.-Col. Forlong served the campaigns of 1813 and 14, in Germany and Holland, including the actions at Merxem, bombardment of Antwerp, and storming of Bergen-op-Zoom. Served also the campaign of 1815, and was severely wounded at Quatre-Bras,—right collar bone fractured and ball lodged in the right breast.

4 Captain Mackinnon served with the 16th Lancers throughout the campaign in Affghanistan, under Lord Keane, and was present at the siege and capture of Ghuznee (Medal). He served also in the campaign on the Sutlej (Medal) in 1846, including the battles of Buddiwal, Aliwal, and Sobraon.

The *Sphinx*, "EGYPT."—"BADAJOZ"—"SALAMANCA"—"PENINSULA"—"BLADENSBURG"—"WATERLOO"—"AVA."

Years' Serv. 56 — Full Pay | Half Pay

Colonel.

Hon. Sir Patrick Stuart, GCMG. *Cornet & Sub-Lieut.* 26 Sept. 93; *Lieut.* 6 June, 94; *Capt.* 12 April, 96; *Major,* 1 Feb. 03; *Lieut.-Col.* 25 Sept. 06; *Col.* 4 June, 14; *Major-Gen.* 19 July, 21; *Lieut.-Gen.* 10 Jan. 37; *Col.* 44th Regt. 7 April, 43.

Lieut.-Colonels.

24 | 0 | *Hon.* Augustus Almeric Spencer, *Ens.* 8 Apr. 25; *Lieut.* P 5 July, 27; *Capt.* P 6 Apr. 31; *Major,* P 21 July, 43; *Lieut.-Col.* 17 May, 45.

15 | 0 | *r.* Augustus Halifax Ferryman, *Ens.* P 27 June, 34; *Lieut.* 30 June, 37; *Capt.* P 16 April, 41; *Major,* P 22 Dec. 43; *Lieut.-Col.* P 24 Nov. 48.

Majors.

22 | 0 | *r.* John Hildebrand Oakes Moore, *Ens.* 25 Oct. 27; *Lieut.* P 26 April 31; *Capt.* P 31 Dec. 33; *Brevet-Major,* 9 Nov. 46; *Major,* P 31 Dec. 47.

22 | 2 1/12 | Nathan Smith Gardiner,[2] *Ens.* P 23 July 25; *Lieut.* 18 July 34; *Capt.* P 26 Jan. 41; *Maj.* P 24 Nov. 48.

Full Pay	Half Pay	CAPTAINS.	ENSIGN.	LIEUT.	CAPTAIN.	BV.-MAJ.
8	0	*r.* William Steevens	26 Feb. 41	P 12 Feb. 42	P 27 Sept. 44	
14	0	Cha. W. Dunbar Staveley, *s.*	P 6 Mar. 35	P 4 Oct. 39	P 6 Sept. 44	
14	0	*r.* William MacMahon ..	P 6 Nov. 35	28 Feb. 40	17 May 45	
16	0	Francis Mostyn Owen ..	P 1 Nov. 33	P 6 Nov. 35	P 21 Mar. 45	
8	0	*r.* H. Hamon John Massy	P 2 April 41	P 11 Nov. 42	P 3 Oct. 45	
9	0	Robert Feilden	P 20 Nov. 40	18 Nov. 42	P 27 Feb. 46	
8	0	*r.* Andrew Browne	P 30 Apr. 41	14 Oct. 42	P 8 Sept. 46	
7	0	John Le Marchant Carey	27 Oct. 42	P 15 Mar. 44	P 2 Apr. 47	
23	0	*r.* William Spring	P 30 Dec. 26	P 1 June 32	16 Dec. 45	
9	0	*r.* Fred. Sykes Daubeney[3]	20 Nov. 40	P 13 May 42	P 28 Apr. 48	
9	0	Alex Cruickshank Lindsay	P 31 Jan. 40	P 8 Feb. 42	P 27 Mar. 46	
7	0	Bowes Fenwick	P 29 Jan. 42	P 12 July 44	P 24 Nov. 48	
		LIEUTENANTS.				
7	0	John Robinson	26 Oct. 42	P 22 Dec. 43		
6	0	William Faussett	7 July 43	P 23 Aug. 44		
7	0	*r.* Astley Greene........	24 Oct. 42	17 May 45		
6	0	John Stanley Howard ..	P 13 Oct. 43	P 25 July 45		
6	0	William Hanmer	P 22 Dec. 43	P 3 Oct. 45		
5	0	*r.* William Parker	29 Mar. 44	P 30 Dec. 45		
5	0	*Hon.* C. W. Herbert Agar	P 30 Mar. 44	P 27 Feb. 46		
4	0	*r.* Geo. Lethbridge Ottley	23 May 45	P 6 Nov. 46		
4	0	William Henry Hotham	P 25 July 45	P 8 Dec. 46		
6	0	George N. Micklethwait[4]	P 10 Feb. 43	26 July 44		
4	0	*r.* Godfrey Cooper	P 27 June 45	P 2 Apr. 47		
4	0	Edward Ogle Streatfield	P 3 Oct. 45	P 10 Dec. 47		
4	0	*r.* William Hy. Mansfield	P 14 Nov. 45	P 28 Apr. 48		
3	0	*r.* Richard Preston	P 27 Feb. 46	P 24 Nov. 48		
		ENSIGNS.				
4	0	*r.* John C. Hamilton Parks	P 30 Dec. 45			
3	0	George Barchard	P 2 Oct. 46			
3	0	William Fletcher	P 6 Nov. 46			
3	0	*r.* George White	P 8 Dec. 46			
2	0	John Colpoys, *adj.*......	19 Mar. 47			
2	0	John William Dunne....	P 23 Apr. 47			
1	0	*r.* William Thomas Baker	7 Jan. 48			
1	0	*r.* Tamworth Geo. Ferrers	P 25 Feb. 48			
1	0	*r.* James Pope, *adj.*	31 Mar. 48			
1	0	Charles Pye Pye	P 28 Apr. 48			
1	0	Samuel Cooper	P 24 Nov. 48			

Paymaster.—

2 | 0 | *Adjutants.*—*Ensign* John Colpoys. 9 Apr. 47.

1 | 0 | *r. Ensign* James Pope, 31 March 48.

6 | 0 | *Quarter-Masters.*—Thomas Walsh, 27 Oct. 43.

8 | 0 | *r.* Daniel Doherty, 23 July 41.

12 | 0 | *Surgeons.*—Edward Robertson, M.D., 18 Sept. 46; *Assist.-Surg.* 11 Aug. 37.

28 | 8 1/12 | Daniel Armstrong, 30 Oct. 38; *A.S.* 22 Dec. 14; *H.A.* 6 Sept. 13.

8 | 0 | *Assistant-Surgeons.*—Egerton James Pratt, 11 June, 41.

1 | 0 | *r.* Jenkin Humfray Llewelyn, 17 March, 48.

Facings Yellow.—*Agents,* Messrs. Cox & Co.

3 Capt. Daubeney served with the 55th in China (Medal), and was present at the escalade and capture of Chin Kiang Foo, where he carried the Regimental Colour, which was shot in two places.

4 Lt. Micklethwaite served with the 53rd in the campaign on the Sutlej in 1846 (medal), and was present at Buddiwal, Aliwal, and Sobraon.

2 Major Gardiner served with the 22nd throughout the operations in Scinde under Sir Charles Napier including the destruction of the Fort of Imaumghur battles of Meanee and Hyderabad (Medal).

"Rolеia"—"Vimiera"—"Talavera"—"Busaco"—"Fuentes D'Onor"—"Ciudad Rodrigo"—"Badajoz"—"Salamanca"—"Vittoria"—"Pyrenees"—"Nivelle"—"Orthes"—"Toulouse"—"Peninsula"—"Ava."

Years' Serv. 46

Full Pay.	Half Pay.	Colonel.
		P ⊠ *Sir* Colin Halkett,[1] GCB. GCH. *Lieut.-Col.* 17 Nov. 1803; *Col.* 1 Jan. 12; *Major-Gen.* 4 June, 14; *Lt.-Gen.* 22 July, 30; *Gen.* 9 Nov. 46; *Col.* 45th Regt. 12 July 47.
40	$\frac{8}{12}$	*Lieut.-Colonels.*—P Edmund French Boys,[2] *Ens.* P 17 Nov. 08; *Lieut.* 3 Apr. 10; *Capt.* P 8 June 15; *Major,* 3 Feb. 29; *Lt.-Col.* 21 June 32; *Col.* 9 Nov. 46.
20	0	r. Henry Cooper, *Ens.* P 26 Feb. 29; *Lieut.* P 5 Apr. 31; *Capt.* P 13 Nov. 35; *Major,* 10 Sept. 45; *Lt.-Col.* 19 July 48.
16	0	*Majors.*—Hallam D'Arcy Kyle, *Ens.* P 12 July 33; *Lieut.* P 23 June 37; *Capt.* P 24 May 39; *Major,* P 7 April 48.
20	0	r. William R. Preston, *Ens.* P 24 Sept. 29; *Lieut.* P 22 Feb. 33; *Capt.* P 18 Oct. 39; *Major,* 19 July 48.

Full Pay.	Half Pay.	Captains.	Ensign.	Lieut.	Captain.	Brev.-Maj.
28	$\frac{4}{12}$	r. John Butler Wheatstone	1 May 21	31 Mar. 26	16 Nov. 41	
23	0	Charles Seagram	22 June 26	5 Mar. 31	15 Apr. 42	15 Sept. 48
11	0	Henry John Shaw	P 23 Mar. 38	P 7 June 39	P 1 July 42	
22	0	r. George Bligh Moultrie	P 31 Dec. 27	P 31 Dec. 30	P 11 July 37	
14	0	r. Geo. A. L. Blenkinsopp[3]	P 4 Sept. 35	P 31 May 39	P 29 Mar. 44	22 Dec. 48
11	0	r. Henry Thomas Vialls	P 25 Dec. 38	20 Nov. 40	P 30 Aug. 44	
21	0	r. Donald William Tench	31 July 28	P 2 Dec. 31	1 Oct. 44	
15	0	r. Robert Bates	6 June 34	P 25 Dec. 38	15 Oct. 45	
10	0	Henry Woodbine Parish	P 9 Mar. 39	15 Apr. 42	P 6 Feb. 46	
10	0	Stephen Bilton Gordon..	7 June 39	15 Apr. 42	19 July 48	
10	0	Robert Jones Garden ..	21 June 39	P 16 Apr. 42	P 1 Aug. 48	
19	0	Henry Downe Griffith ..	13 June 30	6 Apr. 36	P 20 Oct. 43	
		Lieutenants.				
10	0	Wm. Cairnes Armstrong	P 6 Sept. 39	P 1 July 42		
9	0	r. W. Edmund Bewes, *pm.*	19 June 40	P 22 July 42		
7	0	George Wm. Morris	P 16 Apr. 42	P 28 July 43		
7	0	Robert Miller.........	21 May 42	P 29 Mar. 44		
7	0	r. James M'Crea, *adj.* ..	23 May 42	P 30 Aug. 44		
7	0	Geo. Adam Crooks Kippen	20 May 42	1 Oct. 44		
7	0	r. Rob. A. F. Graves Colleton	22 May 42	7 Feb. 45		
7	0	r. Rob. Beckford Johnstone	27 May 42	10 Sept. 45		
7	0	r. Henry Leach	P 22 July 42	15 Oct. 45		
6	0	r. Courtney P. T. Stacey	P 28 July 43	P 7 July 46		
7	0	George Burrell	11 Feb. 42	P 21 Apr. 43		
6	0	William Dawson	12 Sept. 43	29 Jan. 47		
5	0	George Stacpole Coxon..	P 29 Mar. 44	20 Jan. 47		
4	0	r. Trevor Goff	P 25 July 45	P 7 Apr. 48		
4	0	Arthur Smyth..........	P 9 Dec. 45	P 1 Aug. 48		
		Ensigns.				
4	0	r. E. S. Fra. Geo. Dawson	25 Nov. 45			
4	0	r. William Fleming .. .	30 Dec. 45			
3	0	r. Fred. Robert Grantham	P 6 Feb. 46			
3	0	Charles Duncan Cameron	P 19 May 46			
2	0	r. George Lamont Hobbs	29 Jan. 47			
2	0	Charles Lewis Griffin ..	19 Mar. 47			
2	0	r. Robert Graham Howard	P 23 Apr. 47			
1	0	Drury Richard Barnes ..	P 7 Apr. 48			
1	0	Alexander Walker......	1 Aug. 48			
1	0	William Hodnett Rowland	P 2 Aug. 48			

Full Pay.	Half Pay.	
30	$6\frac{4}{12}$	*Paymaster.*—Monkhouse Graham Taylor, 26 Aug. 36; *Ens.* P 10 June, 13; *Lieut.* P 5 Sept. 22.
7	0	*Adjutants.*—r. *Lieut.* James M'Crea, 22 Jan. 47.
10	0	*Quarter-Masters.*—Edwin Walters, 13 Dec. 39; *Ens.* 31 May, 39.
2	0	r. Luke FitzGibbon, 15 Oct. 47.
20	$1\frac{4}{12}$	*Surgeons.*—Duncan Menzies, 24 June, 42; *A.-S.* 29 July, 30; *H.-A.* 1 Nov. 27.
14	0	r. Francis Robert Waring, 15 Dec. 45; *Assist.-Surg.* 8 May, 35.
7	0	*Assist.-Surgeons.*—Thomas Best, 22 April, 42.
4	0	r. Francis Oliver Barker, 14 Feb. 45.

Facings Green.—*Agents,* Messrs. Price and Boustead.

1 Sir Colin Halkett has received a cross for Albuhera, Salamanca, Vittoria, and the passage of the Nive, and was severely wounded at Waterloo.

2 Colonel Boys served in the Peninsula from 1809 to 1811, and again from 1813 to the end of the war, including the action at Sabugal, and battles of Fuentes d'Onor (wounded), Orthes, and Toulouse (wounded). Served also in the Burmese war.

3 Major Blenkinsopp commanded the detachment 91st Regiment in the action with and defeat of the Rebel Boers at Bloem Plaats (South Africa) 29th Aug. 1848.

"DOMINICA."

Years' Serv. Full Pay	Years' Serv. Half Pay	
59		*Colonel.*
		John, *Earl of* Stair,[1] KT. *Ens.* 28 Feb. 1790; *Lt.* 30 April, 92; *Capt.* 26 April, 93; *Lieut.-Col.* 6 Dec. 98; *Col.* 25 April, 1808; *Major-Gen.* 4 June, 11; *Lieut.-Gen.* 19 July, 21: *Gen.* 28 June, 38; *Col.* 46th Regiment, 31 May, 43.
		Lieutenant-Colonel.
23	14$\frac{4}{12}$	P Robert Garrett,[2] KH. *Ens.* P 6 March, 11; *Lt.* 3 Sept. 12; *Capt.* P 7 July, 14; *Major,* P 19 Sept. 26; *Brevet-Lt.-Col.* 23 Nov. 41; *Lt.-Col.* P 16 May 45.
		Majors.
33	5$\frac{4}{12}$	P John Maclean,[3] *Ens.* 2 May, 11; *Lieut.* 10 Dec. 12; *Capt.* 25 Dec. 30; *Major,* P 12 April, 39.
14	0	Alexander Maxwell, *Ens.* P 19 June 35; *Lieut.* P 28 Dec. 38; *Capt.* P 27 Sept. 42; *Major,* P 19 Sept. 48.

Full Pay	Half Pay		Ensign.	Lieut.	Captain.	Brev.-Maj.
		Captains.				
33	0	Donald Stuart[6]	2 May 16	25 Feb. 20	1 Apr. 31	9 Nov. 46
20	0	Wm. Thomas Bremner	P 3 Dec. 29	P 21 June 31	P 5 April 39	
27	0	William Child	13 Nov. 22	11 Aug. 26	2 Apr. 41	
14	0	Arthur George Vesey	P 29 May 35	P 25 Aug. 37	P 22 July 42	
13	0	David Fyffe	P 11 June 36	2 Apr. 41	P 16 May 45	
10	0	Arthur Wombwell	P 5 Apr. 39	P 29 Oct. 41	P 8 May 46	
15	0	William Henry O'Toole	P 12 Dec. 34	31 May 39	8 Jan. 47	
9	0	Colin Fred. Campbell	1 May 40	10 Mar. 42	P 13 Aug. 47	
8	0	Algernon Robert Garrett	1 June 41	P 27 Sept. 42	P 28 Apr. 48	
9	0	James Hill Albouy	P 10 Apr. 40	P 3 Dec. 41	P 19 Sept. 48	
		Lieutenants.				
10	0	Henry Steele, *ad.*	1 Feb. 39	27 May 42		
8	0	Henry Fuller Sandwith	P 30 Oct. 41	26 Apr. 44		
7	0	Chas. Robert Shervinton	20 May 42	6 July 45		
7	0	Robert William Piper	28 May 42	P 11 July 45		
7	0	William Hardy	P 27 Sept. 42	P 8 May 46		
6	0	John Edward Lyons	P 3 Mar. 43	P 6 Nov. 46		
5	0	James George Clarke	26 Apr. 44	22 Feb. 47		
5	0	John H. Chambers	31 May 44	30 Mar. 47		
5	0	Albert Nicholas	P 6 Dec. 44	P 13 Aug. 47		
4	0	George Fred. Dallas	P 16 May 45	P 28 Apr. 48		
4	0	John Crymes	P 28 Nov. 45	P 21 July 48		
3	0	Cha. Somerville M'Alester	P 6 Nov. 46	P 10 Nov. 48		
2	0	J. J. Williams Fredericks	P 23 July 47	P 24 Nov. 48		
		Ensigns.				
2	0	Edward Wemyss	5 Feb. 47			
2	0	Dacre J. Barrett Lennard	P 30 Mar. 47			
2	0	Henry Ridge Wolrige	31 Mar. 47			
2	0	Charles Edward Eustace	P 24 Sept. 47			
1	0	William Henry Bennett	P 28 Apr. 48			
1	0	William Reginald Hesketh	P 21 July 48			
1	0	Alfred C. N. Smyth Pigott	P 19 Sept. 48			
1	0	Edward Meurant	P 10 Nov. 48			

6 Major Stuart served at the siege and capture of Kittoor in the East Indies in Dec. 1824.

9 Paymaster Corcoran served the Coorg campaign in the East Indies, with the 48th, in 1834.

Full Pay	Half Pay	
11	0	*Paymaster.*—Alexis Corcoran,[9] 8 July 42; *Ens.* 30 Nov. 38; *Lt.* 8 April, 42.
10	0	*Adjutant.*—*Lieut.* Henry Steele, 5 Nov. 47.
3	0	*Quarter-Master.*—Samuel Scoltock, 13 March 46.
23	0	*Surgeon.*—Wm. Irwin Breslin, M.D. 2 July, 41; *Assist.-Surg.* 8 March, 27; *Hosp.-Assist.* 9 Feb. 26.
3	0	*Assistant-Surgeon.*—George Richard Woolhouse, 7 Aug. 46.

Facings Yellow.

Agents, Messrs. Cox & Co.

[*Returned from North America,* 8 *May* 1848.]

1 Lord Stair went to Flanders in 1794, and served on the Continent until the return of the British army, in 1795. In October, 1805, he accompanied the Expedition to Hanover. In July, 1807, he went to Zealand, and was present at the siege of Copenhagen.

2 Lieut.-Col. Garrett served in the Peninsula with the 6th Division in 1811, and with the 4th Division in 1812 and 13, and was present in all the actions, sieges, and smaller affairs in which those two Divisions were respectively engaged from Fuentes d'Onor in May 1811, until the end of 1813, when he was sent to England for recovery from his wounds. He received two wounds at the attack of the Forts at Salamanca, on which occasion the command of the Light Company of the Queen's and some Artillery devolved upon him, he being the only surviving officer of the column he attacked with; and he was again severely wounded in the Pyrenees.

3 Major Maclean served with the 43rd in the Peninsula from June 1812 to the end of that war in 1814, including the action of the 14th Nov. 1812 on retreat from Salamanca, battles of Vittoria, the Nivelle wounded), the Nive, and Toulouse. Present also in the action before New Orleans on the 8th Jan. 1815.

"*Primus in Indis.*"—"Plassey"—"Gibraltar"—with the *Castle and Key*, "*Montis Insignia* C[illegible]—"Albuhera"—"Vittoria"—"Pyrenees"—"Nivelle"—"Nive"—"Orthes"—"Peninsu[illegible]"Maharajpore."

Years' Serv.		
72		
Full Pay.	Half Pay.	*Colonel.*
		℗ *Sir* Frederick Philipse Robinson,[1] GCB. *Ens.* Feb. 1777; *Lieut.* 1 Sept. [illegible] *Capt.* 3 July, 94; *Major*, 1 Sept. 94; *Lieut.-Col.* 1 Jan. 1800; *Col.* 25 July, [illegible] *Major-Gen.* 4 June, 13; *Lieut.-Gen.* 27 May, 25; *Gen.* 23 Nov. 41; *Col.* 3[illegible] Regt. 15 June, 40.
36	1/12	*Lieut.-Colonel.*—Thomas Wright,[2] CB. *Ens.* 18 Dec. 12; *Lieut.* 22 April, [illegible] *Capt.* P 14 July, 25; *Major*, P 10 March, 37; *Lieut.-Col.* 24 Apr. 39.
22	0	*Majors.*—Edward Bond,[4] *Ens.* P 8 Mar. 27; *Lieut.* P 16 Sept. 29; *Capt.* P[illegible] Feb. 36; *Major*, P 31 March, 43.
18	0	Marmaduke George Nixon,[5] *Ens.* 5 April. 31; *Lieut.* 25 Mar. 33; *Capt.* P[illegible] Dec. 38; *Brev.-Major*, 30 Apr. 44; *Major*, 7 Aug. 46.

Full Pay.	Half Pay.		Ensign.	Lieut.	Captain.	Brev.-M[illegible]
		Captains.				
26	0	Henry Francis Stokes[8] ..	24 July 23	1 Aug. 25	24 Apr. 39	
17	0	Robert Newport Tinley[9]	4 April 32	P 19 July 33	P 15 Dec. 40	
18	0	Arthur Herbert[10]	P 18 Jan. 31	2 Sept. 34	P 31 Dec. 41	
22	0	Charles D. Campbell[10] ..	P 9 Aug. 27	3 May 33	24 April 43	30 April
17	0	Henry Aug. Strachan[12] ..	21 Sept. 32	2 June 35	5 June 43	
15	0	William Munro,[14]	P 20 June 34	P 1 April 36	2 July 44	
14	0	William Clarges Wolfe ..	P 30 Oct. 35	P 10 Mar. 37	7 Aug. 46	
12	0	Thomas Wright Hudson	P 16 June 37	30 Oct. 40	7 Dec. 45	
10	0	Thomas Edw. Wilbraham	P 8 Mar. 39	P 21 May 41	20 Mar. 46	
13	0	Francis James Hugonin ..	P 12 Aug. 36	P 26 April 39	P 2 Oct. 46	
		Lieutenants.				
13	0	J. Fitz Roy Dalrymple ..	P 2 Dec. 36	P 8 Dec. 37		
13	0	Humphrey Gray,[10]	25 Mar. 36	1 July 38		
12	0	William Hardinge[10]	P 10 Mar. 37	24 Apr. 39		
11	0	Chas. Tho. Hamilton[10] r..	P 17 Feb. 38	P 19 July 39		
11	0	Robert Hamilton Currie[10]	P 28 Dec. 38	P 14 Feb. 40		
15	0	Theodore M. Haultain[10] *adj.*	27 June 34	20 Oct. 40		
10	0	Wm. Newport Tinley[10] ..	P 15 Nov. 39	P 11 June 41		
9	0	℗ Francis Gee[15]	18 Sept. 40	5 June 43		
8	0	Simon George Newport[10]	3 Aug. 41	2 July 44		
8	0	Henry Droz Gaynor[10] ..	P 31 Dec. 41	2 Aug. 44		
7	0	James Johnston........	22 April 42	P 29 Dec. 43		
6	0	William Leckie	10 Nov. 43	16 April 45		
8	0	William Greenham	27 Aug. 41	11 Dec. 46		
5	0	James Agnew	22 Oct. 44	P 23 June 48		
		Ensigns.				
5	0	George Wolfe	27 Sept. 44			
4	0	John Popkin Traherne ..	4 July 45			
3	0	William Henry Wilson ..	9 June 46			
2	0	Michael C. Wall	P 30 Mar. 47			
2	0	Hugh Robert Hibbert ..	P 28 Sept. 47			
1	0	Benson Harrison	P 23 June 48			
1	0	Lewis Stafford Northcote	P 24 June 48			

2 Lieut.-Col. Wright served [illegible] campaign against the Rajah [illegible] in 1834, and received a [illegible] injury in the right leg in [illegible] advanced attack at the [illegible] stockade of Periapatam, [illegible] stockade of the Coorg terri[illegible] 1839 he was employed [illegible] tions against Kurnool, and [illegible] verely and dangerously [illegible] the affair of Zorapore on [illegible] of Oct. He commanded [illegible] in the battle of Maharajp[illegible] dal) on the 29th Dec. 1843 [illegible] action his horse was shot [illegible] in taking the battery at [illegible]

4 Major Bond served [illegible] 53rd in the campaign on the [illegible] (Medal), and was present at B[illegible] wal, Aliwal, and Sobraon.

43	0	*Paymaster.*—G. Augustus Durnford,[13] 13 Feb. 27; *Ens.* 28 June, 06; *Lie*[illegible] [Mar. 10; *Capt.* 13 Fe[illegible]
15	0	*Adjutant.*—*Lt.* Theodore M. Haultain, 19 Mar. 47.
12	0	*Quarter-Master.*—Jones Duke, 10 Jan. 37.
17	0	*Surgeon.*—Charles Hugh James,[10] 18 Aug. 43; *Assist.-Surg.* 5 Oct. 32.
7	0	*Assist.-Surgeon.*—Henry Armstrong, 17 June, 42.

Facings Green.—*Agents*, Messrs. Cox and Co.

[*Returned from Bengal* 9 *June*, 1847.]

1 Sir Frederick Robinson served five years in the first American war, including the battle of Horse Neck, [illegible] capture of Stoney Point by the Americans (wounded and taken prisoner), and battle of New London. Subsequ[illegible] capture of Martinique, St. Lucia, and Guadaloupe, in 1794, including the storming of Fleur d'Epée and the Hospi[illegible] Joined the army under the Duke of Wellington, in 1812, and was present at the action of Osma, and bat[illegible] toria, and commanded the Brigade which carried the village of Gamarra Mayor without firing a shot. In July [illegible] following he was present at the 1st and 2nd assaults on San Sebastian (severely wounded), passage of the Bidassoa, reconnoissance before Bayonne, battle of the Nive (severely wounded), blockade of Bayonne and repulse of the [illegible] which day he succeeded to the command of the 5th Division. In June, 1814, embarked in command of a Brigade, for [illegible] commanded the two Brigades intended to attack the works of Plattsburg, but received orders to retire, after [illegible] the passage of the Saranac. In Nov. following, appointed Commander-in-Chief and Provisional Gov. of the Upper [illegible] which appointment he held till June 1816. Sir Fred. has received a medal & two clasps for Vittoria, San Sebastian, & [illegible]

5 Major Nixon served the campaign against the Rajah of Coorg in 1834; and in the action of Maharajpore [illegible] 29th Dec. 1843, he served as Major of Brigade to the 5th Brigade.

8 Captain Stokes served in the 38th throughout the Burmese war; and with the 39th in the action of Maharajpore.

9 Captain Tinley served the campaign against the Rajah of Coorg in 1834. In the action at Maharajpore, 29th D[illegible] was severely wounded.

10 Major Campbell, Capt. Herbert, Lieuts. Gray, Hardinge, Hamilton, Currie, Haultain, Tinley, Flynn, [illegible] Gaynor, and Dr. James, served with the Regt. at the action of Maharajpore on the 29th Dec. 1843. Major [illegible] Captain Herbert, and Lieuts. Currie and Newport, were slightly wounded; and Lieut. M. Gray was only severely [illegible]

12 Capt. Strachan served the campaign against the Rajah of Coorg, in 1834.

13 Capt. Durnford served at the capture of the Isle of France in 1810; in the expedition to Java in 1811 [illegible] of [illegible] 1813; in the Kandyan rebellion in 1817 and 18; and in the action of Maharajpore, 29th Dec. 43.

14 Capt. Munro served as Adjutant of the 39th in the action at Maharajpore, and was severely wounded [illegible]

15 Lt. Gee served in the Peninsula from 1811 to 1814, and was present at Vittoria, Stewart's Heights[illegible] Pampeluna, Nivelle, Nive, Bayonne, Garris, Orthes, and Toulouse. He was also present in the action at Mahar[illegible] the 29th Dec. 1843.

*** The 39th Regt. was raised in 1701; it proceeded from Ireland to Portugal in 1704; to Spain and battle of Almanza, 1710; between 1710 and 1727, at Gibraltar, Minorca, and Ireland,—and again to Gibraltar when besieged in 1727. Went to Jamaica in 1730; in Ireland and England, 1789 to 1744; on board the Fleet as Marines in 1748. Embarked for India early in 1754, where it remained until 1758, and was present at the battle of Plassey. Returned to Ireland in 1758; Gibraltar 1769; England and Ireland until 1793. Went to the West Indies in 1794; returned to Ireland in 1795, in which year it went again to the West Indies, and remained there until 1803, when it returned to England, and was formed into two Battalions. The 2nd Battalion remained at home until June, 1809, when it proceeded to the Peninsula and was present at the 1st siege of Badajoz, and battles of Busaco, Albuhera, and Arroyo de Molino: it was disbanded on the 24th Dec. 1815. The 1st Battalion served in the Mediterranean until 1811, when it also joined the Duke of Wellington's army in the Peninsula, and was present at the following actions: viz.—Vittoria, Pyrenees, Nivelle, Nive, repulse of the French army before Bayonne on the 13th Dec. 1813, Garris, Orthes, Aire, Vic Bigorre, Tarbes, and Toulouse. At the close of the campaign of 1814, it embarked for Canada. In Aug. 1815, it joined the Duke of Wellington's army at Paris, and remained in France until 1818, when it returned to England. Embarked for New South Wales in 1826; landed at Madras in 1832; employed in the capture of the Coorg Territory, in April 1834; and in the operations against Kurnool in 1839. In 1841 it was transferred to the Bengal Presidency, and was conspicuously engaged in the action at Maharajpore on the 29th Dec. 1843. Returned to England 9 June 1847.

The *Sphinx*, with the word "EGYPT" on the caps of the Flank Companies. "MONTE VIDEO"—"ROLEIA"—"VIMIERA"—"TALAVERA"—"BADAJOZ"—"SALAMANCA"—"VITTORIA"—"PYRENEES"—"NIVELLE"—"ORTHES"—"TOULOUSE"—"PENINSULA"—"WATERLOO"—"CANDAHAR," "GHUZNEE and CABOOL, 1842," "MAHARAJPORE."

Years' Serv. Full Pay.	Half Pay.	
55		*Colonel.* Sir Alexander Woodford,[1] KCB. GCMG. *Ens.* 6 Dec. 94; *Lieut.* 15 July, 95; *Capt.* 11 Dec. 99; *Capt. & Lieut.-Col.* 8 Mar. 10; *Col.* 4 June, 14; *Major-Gen.* 27 May, 25; *Lieut.-Gen.* 28 June, 38; *Col.* 40th Foot, 25 April, 42.
36	1/12	*Lieut.-Col.*—Severus Wm. Lynam Stretton,[3] *Ens.* 11 June 12; *Lieut.* 6 Jan. 14; *Capt.* P 13 Aug. 25; *Major*, P 2 Dec. 31; *Lieut.-Col.* P 6 May 42.
21	0	*Majors.*—Thomas James Valiant, *Ens.* 29 May, 28; *Lieut.* P 17 Dec. 29; *Capt.* P 1 May, 35; *Major*, P 10 July, 46.
26	9 4/12	John MacDuff,[5] *Ens.* 10 Feb. 14; *Lt.* 26 June, 27; *Capt.* P 13 April, 39; *Major*, 13 Nov. 47.

Full Pay	Half Pay	CAPTAINS.	ENSIGN.	LIEUT.	CAPTAIN.	BREV.-MAJ.
19	0	Henry Douglas Cowper	P 20 July 30	P 14 Dec. 32	P 4 Mar. 36	9 Nov. 46
16	0	John Martin Bladen Neill[10]	P 22 Mar. 33	P 9 Jan. 35	P 11 Mar. 42	
18	0	James Todd[9]	P 22 Feb. 31	4 July 34	22 July 45	
11	0	Arthur Leslie	P 20 Nov. 38	P 6 May 42	P 3 April 46	
18	0	Thomas L. K. Nelson[9], *s.*	25 Nov. 31	29 Jan. 36	P 10 July 46	
15	0	Wm. Augustus Fyers[10]	P 17 Oct. 34	P 20 May 36	P 7 May 47	
10	0	John W. Thomas[9]	7 June 39	P 7 Sept. 41	P 14 May 47	
10	0	Robert Carey[10]	15 Nov. 39	19 Nov. 41	P 14 May 47	
9	0	Jn. Anstruther M'Gowan[9]	P 21 Feb. 40	4 Mar. 42	P 31 Dec. 47	
10	0	Fra. Brockman Morley[12]	P 5 Apr. 39	27 May 42	P 18 Aug. 48	
		LIEUTENANTS.				
10	0	Edw. Hungerford Eagar[9]	P 13 April 30	16 July 41		
9	0	Frederick Huey[12]	P 5 June 40	5 Mar. 42		
8	0	John Cormick[12]	P 27 Aug. 41	P 25 Oct. 42		
8	0	Richard Dawson[14]	P 21 May 41	14 April 43		
8	0	Samuel Snelling[9]	26 Oct. 41	30 Dec. 43		
7	0	Fred. Montagu Hockings	20 May 42	P 10 July 46		
5	0	Aldborough Rich. Rundle	23 Feb. 44	P 31 July 46		
5	0	Lewis Alexander Forbes, *r.*	P 27 Sept. 44	P 17 Oct. 45		
6	0	Hans Thomas Fell White	P 12 May 43	P 14 May 47		
4	0	R. John Lechmere Coore	P 27 June 45	P 14 May 47		
5	0	Richard Mahony Hickson	P 13 Dec. 44	29 Jan. 47		
3	0	Thomas Wilson	P 10 July 46	P 31 Dec. 47		
4	0	Francis Barry Drew, *adj.*	P 23 May 45	17 Aug. 48		
2	0	Robert Hare	P 7 May 47	P 18 Aug. 48		
		ENSIGNS.				
2	0	Rogers Parker Hibbert	P 14 May 47			
2	0	Thomas George Gardiner	P 15 May 47			
2	0	Henry Christopher Wise	26 Nov. 47			
2	0	Henry Fowler	P 31 Dec. 47			
1	0	John Pinckney	P 14 Apr. 48			
1	0	George Owen Bowdler	26 May 48			
1	0	David Pennefather	P 18 Aug. 48			

5 Major MacDuff acted as a Field Officer in the 40th during the operations in Candahar and in Affghanistan in 1841-42 (medal); and he commanded the Grenadier Company in the action at Maharajpore (medal).

Full Pay	Half Pay	
37	0	*Paymaster.*—Charles Scarlin Naylor,[15] 8 May, 35; *Ens.* 1 Sept. 12; *Lieut.* 25 Dec. 15; *Capt.* 9 May, 34.
4	0	*Adjutant.*—*Lieut.* Francis Barry Drew, 11 Feb. 48.
7	0	*Quarter-Master.*—Thomas Walter Hives,[9] 25 Oct. 42.
9	0	*Surgeon.*—Joseph Burke,[16] 22 Dec. 48; *Assist.-Surg.* 10 Jan. 40.
1	0	*Assist.-Surg.*—Edward Wm. Clemishaw Kingdom, M.D., 25 Feb. 48.

Facings Buff.—*Agents*, Messrs. Cox & Co.—*Irish Agents*, *Sir* E. R. Borough, [*Bt.*, Armit & Co.

[*Returned from India*, *Feb.* 1846.]

1 Sir Alexander Woodford served in the 9th in North Holland, and was severely wounded on the 19th Sept. 1799. Served in the Coldstream Guards at the capture of Copenhagen in 1807. Served on the Staff in Sicily, in 1808, 9, and 10. Commanded the Light Battalion of the Brigade of Guards, at the siege of Ciudad Rodrigo, capture of Badajoz, battle of Salamanca, capture of Madrid, and at the siege of Burgos. Commanded first battalion Coldstream Guards at the battle of Vittoria, capture of San Sebastian, at the Nivelle, the Nive, and investment of Bayonne. Commanded the second battalion at the battle of Waterloo, surrender of Paris, and during the occupation in France. Sir Alexander has received a medal and two clasps for the battles of Salamanca, Vittoria, and the Nive.

3 Lt.-Col. Stretton served the campaigns of 1812 and 13 in the Peninsula, with the 68th Light Infantry, and was severely wounded at the battle of Vittoria by two gun shots lodged in the body, one of which has not been extracted.

9 Captains Todd, T. L. K. Nelson, Thomas and M'Gowan (severely wounded at Gundamuck), Lieutenants Eagar (severely wounded at Beni Badam) and Snelling, and Quartermaster Hives, served throughout the operations in Candahar and in Affghanistan in 1841 and 42, and have received the medal. These officers were also present in the action of Maharajpore, 29th Dec. 1843, and have received the Bronze Star: Lt. Eagar was slightly wounded, and Capts. T. L. K. Nelson and Thomas were severely wounded. Capt. Nelson was Adjutant of the Regt. during the second Affghan campaign in 1842, as well as at Maharajpore, where he had a horse shot under him.

10 Captains Bladen Neill, Fyers, and Carey served throughout the operations in Candahar and in Affghanistan in 1841 and 42, and have received the medal.

12 Capt. Morley, Lieuts. Huey (severely wounded), and Cormick, were present in the action of Maharajpore, and have received the bronze star.

14 Lt. Dawson was attached to the 22nd at the battle of Hyderabad, and has received the medal. He was afterwards present with the 40th at Maharajpore, in which action he was wounded, and has received the Bronze Star.

15 Captain Naylor served at the siege and capture of Loghur, Koaree, Ryghur, and several small Hill Forts in the Southern Mahratta Country in 1818. Served in the Serwent Warree State, and was severely wounded in both legs (compound fracture of the right) at the assault of Boree, 13th Feb. 1819. Served also in the Burmese war in 1825 and 1826; and at the capture of Kurrachee in Lower Scinde in 1839.

16 Mr Burke served with the 50th the campaign on the Sutlej (medal), including the battles of Moodkee, Ferozeshah, Aliwal, and Sobraon.

"EGMONT-OP-ZEE"—"COPENHAGEN"—"QUEENSTOWN."—"CHINA," "*The Dragon.*"

Years' Serv. 45

Full Pay.	Half Pay.	
		Colonel.—Sir Edward Bowater,[1] KCH. *Ens.* 31 Mar. 04; *Lt. & Capt.* 28 Aug. 09; *Capt. & Lt.-Col.* 25 July, 14; *Col.* 12 Oct. 26; *Maj-Gen.* 10 Jan. 37; *Lt.-Gen.* 9 Nov. 46; *Col.* 49th Foot, 24 Apr. 48.
26	4/12	*Lieut.-Colonel.*—Henry William Adams,[2] CB. *Ens.* 31 July, 23; *Lieut.* P 31 Dec. 25; *Capt.* P 10 June, 26; *Major,* P 18 Jan. 39; *Lt.-Col.* P 13 Mar. 40.
24	0	*Majors.*—Corbet Cotton, *Ens.* 9 April, 25; *Lieut.* P 29 March, 27; *Capt.* P 4 May, 32; *Major,* 5 June, 44.
20	0	Henry George Hart, *Ens.* 1 Apr. 29; *Lieut.* 19 July 32; *Capt.* 1 Dec. 42; *Major,* P 15 Dec. 48.

Full Pay.	Half Pay.		ENSIGN.	LIEUT.	CAPTAIN.	BREV.-MAJ.
		CAPTAINS.				
20	0	John Myers Montgomery[4]	24 Dec. 29	2 Jan. 33	P 24 June 42	
21	0	John Thornton Grant[3] ..	28 Apr. 28	12 Nov. 30	30 July 42	
18	0	Henry Garner Rainey[3] ..	12 Apr. 31	8 June 33	P 27 Dec. 42	
14	0	Charles Thomas Powell[5]	P 20 Nov. 35	P 10 Feb. 37	P 15 Dec. 43	
12	0	David M'Adam[6]	28 Apr. 37	24 July 39	P 8 May 46	
10	0	Wm. H. Clinton Baddeley[7]	P 11 Oct. 39	P 7 Sept. 41	P 9 June 46	
8	0	Charles Stuart Glasbrook	P 7 Sept. 41	P 27 Dec. 42	P 25 Aug. 46	
12	0	George Francis Stuart ..	P 23 June 37	P 5 Apr. 39	P 12 May 43	
7	0	Richard Thompson	P 25 Feb. 42	P 17 Nov. 43	P 23 May 48	
8	0	Henry S. M. D. Fulton..	8 Jan. 41	1 Nov. 42	P 15 Dec. 48	
		LIEUTENANTS.				
10	0	Cha. Philip Jo. Stopford[5] *r.*	P 17 Sept. 39	P 25 Jan. 41		
7	0	Leopold Bellairs	28 Dec. 42	P 30 July 44		
7	0	James Hesketh Biggs ..	P 30 Dec. 42	13 Aug. 44		
6	0	J. Wells Armstrong, *adj.*	P 18 Aug. 43	P 29 Nov. 44		
13	0	David Seton	P 30 Dec. 36	2 Apr. 41		
5	0	Charles Jones Powell....	P 5 Apr. 44	P 8 May 46		
5	0	Francis James Bampfylde	P 20 Aug. 44	P 9 June 46		
5	0	John Hynde King	25 June 44	P 7 July 46		
5	0	Cha. Garner Richardson	P 4 Oct. 44	P 25 Aug. 46		
4	0	Cadwalladar Adams	P 2 Sept. 45	P 23 Mar. 47		
6	0	M. W. De la Poer Beresford	24 Feb. 43	19 Dec. 44		
5	4/12	George Chichester	P 29 Nov. 44	P 23 May 48		
4	0	Wm. Whitaker Maitland	P 16 May 45	P 15 Dec. 48		
		ENSIGNS.				
4	0	Herbert Rocke	P 23 May 45			
3	0	William Bellairs........	P 8 May 46			
3	0	John Nason	9 May 46			
3	0	T. Edwyn Houghton Platt	P 9 June 46			
3	0	James William Dewar ..	P 7 July 46			
1	0	John Augustus Conolly..	P 25 Feb. 48			
1	0	Fanshawe Wm. Gostling	P 23 May 48			
1	0	George Henry Lamb....	P 15 Dec. 48			

Full Pay.	Half Pay.	
14	0	*Paymaster.*—Henry Seymour Michell,[3] 9 April 47; *Ens.* P 22 May 35; *Lieut.* 22 Mar. 39.
6	0	*Adjutant.*—*Lieut.* James Wells Armstrong, 25 Aug. 46.
12	0	*Quarter-Master.*—Henry Mayne,[8] 23 June, 37.
10	0	*Surgeon.*—John Davies, 27 Oct. 48; *Assist.-surg.* 22 Nov. 39.
3	0	*Assist. Surg.*—Henry Beckwith, 3 Nov. 46.

Facings Green.—*Agents,* Messrs. Cox & Co.—*Irish Agents, Sir* E. R. Borough, Bt., Armit & Co.

[*Returned from Bengal,* 24 *Aug.* 1843.]

4 Capt. Montgomery was at Canton, Amoy, Chusan, Chinhae (severely wounded), Ningpo, and Segoan (wounded). He served ten years in the Navy prior to entering the Army.

5 Capt. Powell and Lt. Stopford served in the 22nd throughout the operations in Scinde under Sir Chas. Napier, including the battles of Meeanee and Hydrabad (Medal). Capt. Powell was also at the destruction of the Fort of Imaumghur.

6 Capt. M'Adam was at the first taking of Chusan, and at Woosung, Chin Kiang Foo, and Nankin.

7 Capt. Baddeley was at Amoy, Chusan (2nd capture), Ningpo, Segoan, Chapoo, Woosung, and Chin Kiang Foo, at which last he was twice wounded—once dangerously by a ball which fractured the thigh bone.

8 Qr.-Master Mayne,—the same as Note 3, except the first taking of Chusan.

1 Sir Edward Bowater served with the 3rd Guards, at the siege and taking of Copenhagen, in 1807; and subsequently in the Peninsula from Dec. 1808 to Nov. 1809, and again from Dec 1811 to the end of that war in 1814, including the passage of the Douro and taking of Oporto, battles of Talavera and Salamanca, capture of Madrid, siege of Burgos, battle of Vittoria, siege of San Sebastian, passage of the Bidassoa, and battle of the Nive (Mayor's house). Served also the campaign of 1815, including the battles of Quatre Bras and Waterloo. Wounded at Talavera, and again at Waterloo.

2 Lieut.-Col. Adams commanded the 18th in the following operations in China, viz., the first taking of Chusan, storming and taking the Heights above the city of Canton, capture of Amoy, second capture of Chusan, storming and taking the fortified Heights of Chinhae, and capture of the city of Ningpo.

3 Captains Grant and Rainey, and Paymaster Michell, served throughout the whole of the operations in China, commencing with the first taking of Chusan, and terminating with the demonstration before Nankin, including the storm and capture of the heights above Canton, attack and capture of Amoy, second capture of Chusan, attack and capture of the heights of Chinhae, occupation of Ningpo, repulse of the night attack on Ningpo, attack and capture of the enemy's entrenched camp on the heights of Segoan, attack and capture of Chapoo, Woosung, and Chin Kiang Foo. Capt. Grant was wounded at Chin Kiang Foo.

23 Lt. Bigge served on the Sutlej (Medal), at Moodkee, Ferozeshah, Aliwal (wounded), and Sobraon.

24 Lt. Barnes served on the Sutlej (Medal),—at Moodkee and Ferozeshah (severely wounded).

27 Lieut. Sleeman served on the Sutlej (Medal), at Aliwal and Sobraon (wounded).

28 Lt. Purcell, with a detachment of the 50th, was wrecked on the Andaman Islands in Nov. 1844, where he remained for 55 days, suffering great privation. He served on the Sutlej (Medal), and was at Buddiwal, and severely wounded at Aliwal while carrying the colours.

31 Paymaster Dodd served in the Burmese war, including the actions of the 26th, 27th, and 29th March, 1825. Present also at the battle of Punniar (Medal).

32 Quar.-Master Fair served with the 44th in the retreat from Cabool, and was taken prisoner at Gundamuck after receiving four wounds. He served with the 50th at the battle of Punniar (Medal), and the campaign on the Sutlej (Medal), including the battles of Moodkee, Ferozeshah, Aliwal, and Sobraon.

The *Sphinx* with the words "EGYPT"—"VIMIERA"—"CORUNNA"—"ALMARAZ"—"VITTORIA"—"PYRENEES"—"NIVE"—"ORTHES"—"PENINSULA"—"PUNNIAR"—"MOODKEE"—"FEROZESHAH"—"ALIWAL"—"SOBRAON."

Years' Serv. 58

Full Pay.	Half Pay.	
		Colonel.—Sir John Gardiner,[1] KCB. *Ens.* 23 Nov. 91; *Lieut.* 12 July, 93; *Capt.* 17 May, 96; *Major*, 18 Dec. 06; *Lieut.-Col.* 29 Oct. 09; *Col.* 12 Aug. 19; *Maj.-Gen.* 22 July, 30; *Lt.-Gen.* 23 Nov. 41; *Col.* 50th Regt. 20 Jan. 44.
24	0	*Lieut.-Colonel.*—Peter John Petit,[2] CB. *Ens.* P 19 May 25; *Lt.* 12 Feb. 28; *Capt.* P 28 May 33; *Maj.* P 30 Sep. 42; *Brev. Lt.-Col.* 30 Apr. 44; *Lt.-Col.* P 19 Sep. 48.
20	0	*Majors.*—John Brathwaite Bonham,[3] *Ens.* P 1 Oct. 29; *Lieut.* P 28 May 33; *Capt.* P 20 July 38; *Major*, P 25 Aug. 48.
24	0	William Langley Tudor,[4] *Ens.* 9 Apr. 25; *Lieut.* P 26 Nov. 29; *Capt.* 1 April 41; *Brev.-Major*, 30 April 44; *Major*, P 19 Sept. 48.

Full Pay	Half Pay	CAPTAINS.	ENSIGN.	LIEUT.	CAPTAIN.	BREV.-MAJ.
16	0	William Knowles[5]	P 9 Aug. 33	P 20 July 38	P 25 June 41	
17	0	Richard Waddy[8]	17 Aug. 32	4 May 36	18 Nov. 41	
16	0	George Frederick Long[9]	P 27 Sept. 33	P 17 June 37	P 8 Feb. 42	19 June 44
19	3	John Lucas Wilton[11]	P 13 Mar. 27	16 Mar. 32	15 July 45	
8	0	John Olaus Moller......	18 June 41	P 3 Feb. 43	P 30 Dec. 45	
8	0	Henry Edwin Weare.....	22 Oct. 41	P 22 Dec. 43	P 26 May 48	
5	0	John Edw. Leveson Gower	P 23 July 44	P 31 July 46	P 12 May 48	
12	0	Wm. Scott Carter[15]	P 7 Apr. 37	23 Sept. 40	P 25 Aug. 48	
9	0	Heathfield Jas. Frampton[16]	4 Aug. 40	P 20 Aug. 41	P 19 Sept. 48	
8	0	Robert Bridges Bellers[18]	P 12 Mar. 41	P 30 Sept. 42	P 6 Oct. 48	
		LIEUTENANTS.				
13	0	James Griffith Smyth[12]..	P 4 June 36	16 Feb. 40		
13	0	Benj. Grey Mackenzie,[8]..	22 Apr. 36	P 17 Feb. 38		
11	0	Henry William Wily[13] ..	27 June 38	15 Nov. 39		
13	0	Edw. Cowell Mullen[14] ..	P 26 Aug. 36	17 July 40		
9	0	Charles Abney Mouat[17]..	6 Mar. 40	16 Sept. 41		
8	0	Fred. Torrens Lyster,[19] *adj.*	20 June 41	P 1 Nov. 42		
8	0	Charles Hen. Tottenham[20]	P 21 June 41	8 Sept. 43		
8	0	Edward John Chambers[21]	P 20 Aug. 41	30 Dec. 43		
7	0	William Percival Elgee[23]	P 27 May 42	6 Oct. 44		
7	0	Richard Moore Barnes[24]	P 1 Nov. 42	5 July 45		
5	0	John Purcell[27]	29 Mar. 44	7 Feb. 46		
5	0	Cha. Hildebrand Slessor[28]	21 Dec. 44	11 Feb. 46		
3	0	Wm. A. Douglas Anderson	1 Apr. 46	P 25 Aug. 48		
3	0	William Bellers	26 June 46	P 19 Sept. 48		
3	0	Edward George Hibbert	P 29 Apr. 46	P 6 Oct. 48		
5	0	Herman Ernest Galton..	P 20 Dec. 44	P 20 Nov. 48		
		ENSIGNS.				
3	0	Parr William Kingsmill	7 Aug. 46			
2	0	Walter Devereux Shirley	P 13 Aug. 47			
1	0	Robert Carter	11 Feb. 48			
1	0	Tindall Hebden	P 19 Sept. 48			
1	0	John MacMahon	P 3 Nov. 48			

2 Lieut.-Col. Petit commanded the 50th at the battle of Punniar (Medal), and had his horse shot under him. He served also during the operations on the Sutlej (Medal), and commanded the 50th in the battles of Moodkee Ferozeshah (two horses shot under him), and Sobraon (dangerous wounded); was also present at Aliwal.

3 Major Bonham was present with the 50th in the battle of Punniar (Medal). He served also the campaign on the Sutlej (Medal), in 1845-6, including the battles o Moodkee, Ferozeshah, Aliwal, an Sobraon (dangerously wounded).

4 Major Tudor served as Aide-de-camp to General Grey in the action of Punniar (Medal).

5 Capt. Knowles was present with the 50th in the battle of Punniar (Medal). He served also the campaign on the Sutlej (Medal), in 1845-6, including the battles of Moodkee Ferozeshah (wound.), & Aliwal (dangerously wounded, right leg amputated.)

8 Capt. Waddy and Lieut. Mackenzie were present at the battle of Punniar (medal).

9 Major Long served the campaigns on the Sutlej (Medal), in the 50th, including the battles of Moodkee (wounded), Ferozeshah, Aliwal, and Sobraon, in which last he succeeded to its command.

13 Lieutenant Wily served the campaign on the Sutlej (Medal), including the battles of Moodkee, Ferozeshah, Aliwal, and Sobraon.

Full Pay	Half Pay	
25	0	*Paymaster.*—John Beach Dodd,[31] 25 Sept. 40; *Ens.* 24 May 24; *Lieut.* 31 Oct. 25.
8	0	*Adjutant.*—*Lieut.* Frederick Torrens Lyster, 25 Aug. 48.
1	0	*Quarter-Master.*—Alexander Fair,[32] 7 July 48.
11	0	*Surgeon.*—Arthur Charles Webster, 30 June 48; *Assist.-Surg.* 6 April 38.
1	0	*Assist.-Surg.*—Andrew Acres Stoney, 22 Dec. 48.

Facings Blue.—*Agents*, Messrs. Cox & Co.

[*Returned from Bengal, 6 June* 1848.]

1 Sir John Gardiner served in Lord Moira's expedition in Flanders and Holland in 1794 and 95. Actively employed in the West Indies, from 1795 to 1802. Accompanied the expedition to Walcheren in 1809. Served in the Peninsula during 1813 and 14, and commanded a brigade at the battles of the Nivelle and Orthes, for which he has received a medal and clasp. Commanded the Infantry Brigade that took possession of Bourdeaux, and in the various operations which took place in the neighbourhood of that town until the embarkation of the army for America.

11 Capt. Wilton served with the 50th in the campaign on the Sutlej (Medal), including the battle of Aliwal, where he was severely burnt by an explosion of one of the enemy's tumbrils, and battle of Sobraon, where he was very severely wounded having received a shot in the hip, and three severe sabre wounds in the right arm and shoulder.

12 Lieut. Smyth was present with the 50th in the battle of Punniar (Medal). He served also the campaign on the Su (Medal), in 1845-6, including the battles of Moodkee, Ferozeshah, Aliwal, and Sobraon (severely wounded).

14 Lieut. Mullen was present with the 50th in the battle of Punniar (Medal). He served also the campaign on the (Medal), as Adjutant of the 50th, including the battles of Moodkee and Ferozeshah (severely wounded).

15 Capt. Carter served the campaign on the Sutlej (Medal), including the battles of Moodkee (wounded), Ferozeshah Aliwal, and Sobraon.

16 Capt. Frampton was present in the battle of Punniar (Medal). He served also the campaign on the Sutlej (Medal), including the battles of Moodkee, Ferozeshah, and Aliwal, in which last he was dangerously wounded, and had his left arm amputated.

17 Lieut. Mouat was present in the battle of Punniar (Medal). He served also the campaign on the Sutlej (Medal), including the battles of Moodkee, Ferozeshah (wounded), Aliwal, and Sobraon (severely wounded).

18 Capt. Bellers was present at Punniar (Medal); also on the Sutlej (Medal) including the battles of Moodkee, Ferozeshah, Aliwal (wounded), and Sobraon.

20 Lieut. Tottenham was present with the 50th in the battle of Punniar (Medal). He served also the campaign on the Sutlej (Medal), including the battles of Moodkee, Ferozeshah, Aliwal, and Sobraon (wounded); at Ferozeshah he acted as Aide de-camp to Brigadier Ryan; at Sobraon he was attached to the Adjutant General's staff; and subsequently, until the breaking up of the army of the Sutlej, he acted as Aide-de-camp to Sir Harry Smith.

21 Lieut. Chambers was at Punniar (Medal); also on the Sutlej Medal), at Moodkee, and Ferozeshah (severely wounded).

For Notes 23, 24, 27, 28, 31, and 32, see preceding page.

[illegible] served in the wars of Succession in Portugal and in Spain, from 1833 to 1841, as Captain of Infantry and Cavalry, and was present in Oporto during the Siege, and at the Siege and Capture of Irun, Fontarabia, Morella, Berga, and Castellote, (severely wounded). Was on the Staff of General Don Diego Leon, commanding his escort, and extra aide-de-camp. He was twice decorated with the Order of St. Ferdinand for charges of cavalry at Allo and Berga, and with the medals for the siege and capture of Irun and Morella. He served with the 50th in the battle of Punniar (medal).

[Emb. for Foreign Serv. 15 July 1836.] 51st (*The 2nd Yorkshire West Riding*) or [Serving at Bangalore, Madras.

The King's Own Light Infantry Regt.

"MINDEN"—"CORUNNA"—"SALAMANCA"—"VITTORIA"—"PYRENEES"—"NIVELLE"—"ORTHES"—"PENINSULA"—"WATERLOO."

Years' Serv.		
55		*Colonel.*
		🅟 *Sir* Benjamin D'Urban,[1] GCB.KCH., *Cornet*, April, 1794; *Lieut.* 1 July, 94; *Capt.* 2 July, 94; *Major* 21 Nov. 99; *Lieut.-Col.* 1. Jan. 1805; *Col.* 4 June, 13; *Major-Gen.* 12 Aug. 19; *Lt.-Gen.* 10 Jan. 37; *Col.* 51st, 25 Dec. 29.
Full Pay.	Half Pay.	
40	0	*Lieut.-Colonels.*—🅟 🅦 Wm. Henry Elliott,[2] KH. *Ens.* P 6 Dec. 09; *Lt.* P 13 Aug. 12; *Capt.* P 9 Nov. 20; *Major* P 12 July, 31; *Lieut.-Col.* P 27 June, 38.
34	0	Edw. St. Maur, *Ens.* P 22 June, 15; *Lieut.* P 16 Nov. 20; *Capt.* P 29 May, 23; *Major* P 1 July, 37; *Lt.-Col.* 4 July, 45.
39	0	*Majors.*—🅟 🅦 Fred. Mainwaring,[3] *Ens.* 5 April, 10; *Lieut.* 15 April, 13; *Capt.* 4 Dec. 28; *Major* P 27 June, 38.
23	0	Arnold Charles Errington, *Ens.* P 4 Feb. 26; *Lieut.* 13 Sept. 31; *Capt.* P 14 July, 37; *Major*, P 25 July, 45.

Full Pay	Half Pay		ENSIGN.	LIEUT.	CAPTAIN.	BREV.-MAJ.
		CAPTAINS.				
21	0	Percy Rice	14 Aug. 28	P 28 Nov. 34	P 2 Sept. 37	
18	0	Wm. Henry Hare	P 9 Aug. 31	P 25 Dec. 35	P 27 June 38	
18	0	Richard D. Baker	13 Sept. 31	P 16 Dec. 36	P 5 Oct. 41	
18	0	Augustus Thomas Rice...	P 11 Oct. 31	P 10 Mar. 37	P 15 Oct. 41	
22	1 1/12	Edward Lionel Wolley ..	P 29 Dec. 25	4 Jan. 33	P 31 Dec. 41	
16	0	William H. H. Anderson	20 Sept. 33	28 Aug. 36	P 6 June 45	
14	0	*Hon.* David Erskine	P 31 July 35	P 27 June 38	P 25 July 45	
10	0	Thomas M'Lean Farmer..	7 June 39	P 8 Jan. 41	P 7 July 46	
11	0	William Douglas Scott ..	27 June 38	8 Apr. 42	P 20 July 47	
18	0	B.C.Graham Crookshank[5]	25 Mar. 36	29 Dec. 38	18 July 48	
		LIEUTENANTS.				
12	0	Augustus Henry Irby ..	P 15 July 37	P 5 Oct. 41		
10	0	Arthur Miller Harris....	P 26 July 39	P 23 June 43		
9	0	Rich. Atherton Ffarington	P 3 July 40	P 23 June 43		
8	0	David Stephenson	P 26 Feb. 41	P 27 Sept. 44		
8	0	Edward Cecil Singleton	P 31 Dec. 41	P 31 Dec. 44		
10	0	Henry Fletcher Marston[4]	8 Mar. 39	8 Aug. 41		
10	0	John Henry Dickson	15 Nov. 39	20 May 42		
7	0	Louis Henry Bedford ..	27 May 42	P 22 Dec. 43		
7	0	William Jeffries Pegus ..	17 Apr. 42	4 July 45		
7	0	William H. Kemp	20 May 42	do.		
7	0	Alexander Philip Rossi..	21 May 42	do.		
6	0	James Wm. Mansfield ..	P 23 June 43	do.		
6	0	Robert Neville..........	P 24 June 43	do.		
6	0	Samuel Alexander Madden	P 7 July 43	do.		
5	0	Geo. Warburton Drought	P 27 Sept. 44	P 22 July 45		
6	0	John George Don Marshall	14 July 43	P 25 July 45		
4	0	Henry Bruen Westropp	P 11 July 45	P 20 July 47		
5	0	Wm. Lemp. Fred. Sheaffe	6 Dec. 44	6 Aug. 47		
4	0	Samuel George Carter ..	13 June 45	18 July 48		
9	0	William Graham Cassidy[6]	27 Mar. 40	6 Apr. 42		
		ENSIGNS.				
4	0	R. Gordon Sanders Mason	4 July 45			
4	0	Archibald Robertson....	5 July 45			
4	0	George Oliver Nunn	8 July 45			
4	0	John Willoughby Bateman	P 22 July 45			
4	0	Edward O'Callaghan....	10 Oct. 45			
2	0	John Anderson	P 25 June 47			
2	0	John Frederick Trydell..	23 Mar. 47			
4	0	Charles Sergison Nott ..	25 Nov. 45			
2	0	Richard Pilmer	26 Mar. 47			
1	0	Alex. Nenon Armstrong	23 May 48			

2 Lieut.-Col. Elliott embarked with the regiment for Lisbon, 26 Jan. 1811, and was present at the battle of Fuentes d'Onor, covering the siege of Ciudad Rodrigo, second siege of Badajoz, affair near Val Moresco, battle of Salamanca, capture of Madrid and the Retiro, covering the siege of Burgos, retreat into Portugal during which operation he served as Aide-de-Camp to Col. Mitchell, 51st regt., commanding the brigade, and received a contusion on the shoulder when in the act of delivering an order to an officer in advance. In June 1813, he was appointed an Aide-de-Camp to Major-General Inglis, and was present at the battles of the Pyrenees, 30th and 31st July—received a flesh wound, and had a horse killed; action at Lesaca, passage of the Adour, battle of Nivelle, attack of the heights of St. Pé, and battle of Orthes. Appointed Major of Brigade to the 1st Brigade, 7th division, and served as such until the end of that war. Served also the campaign of 1815, including the battle of Waterloo, capture of Cambray, and capitulation of Paris.

3 Major Mainwaring served in the Peninsula, from March 1811 to Jan. 1814, including the battle of Fuentes d'Onor, 2nd siege of Badajos, affair near Val Moresco, battle of Salamanca, retreat from Burgos, capture of Madrid and the Retiro, battles of Vittoria, Pyrenees, and Nivelle. Served also the campaign of 1815, and was present at the battle of Waterloo.

4 Lieut. Marston served with the 41st Regt. the campaign of 1842 in Affghanistan, and was present in the engagements with the enemy on the 28th April in the Pisheen Valley; in that of the 29th May near Candahar, 30th Aug. at Goaine, 5th Sept. before Ghuznee, occupation and destruction of that fortress and of Cabool, expedition into Kohistan, storm, capture, and destruction of Istaliff, and in the various minor affairs in and between the Bolan and the Khyber Passes.

Full Pay	Half Pay	
14	0	*Paymaster.*—Hugh Somerville Sawyer Burney, 31 July, 46; *Ens.* P 29 Dec. 35; [*Lt.* P 14 June, 39.
		Adjutant.—
5	0	*Quarter-Master.*—Robert Shean, 20 Aug. 44.
23	0	*Surgeon.*—John Hartley Sinclair, M.D. 2 July, 41; *Assist.-Surg.* 21 Dec. 26; *Hosp.-Assist.* 14 April, 26.
6	0	*Assist.-Surgeons.*—George Cunningham Micklebam, 16 June, 43.
4	0	William Abbott Anderson, 28 Feb. 45.
1	0	Thomas Crawford, M.D. 18 Feb. 48.

Facings Blue.—*Agents*, *Sir* John Kirkland & Co.

1 Sir Benjamin D'Urban has received a cross and five clasps for Busaco, Albuhera, Badajoz, Salamanca, Vittoria, Pyrenees, Nivelle, Nive, and Toulouse. He served in the Peninsula and France from the autumn of 1808 to the end of the war in 1814, and was never absent. In the end of 1808 and beginning of 1809—having been then on the Quartermaster-General's Staff of the Forces in Portugal—he was employed by Sir John Cradock in observation of the French corps on the Frontiers of Castille and Estremadura,—and, in the execution of this duty, he was with Sir Robert Wilson in his operations between Ciudad Rodrigo and Salamanca,—and after-

[For continuation, see bottom of next page.

"HINDOOSTAN"—"VIMIERA"—"CORUNNA"—BUSACO"—"FUENTES D'ONOR" "CIUDAD RODRIGO"—"BADAJOZ"—"SALAMANCA"—"VITTORIA"— "NIVELLE"—"NIVE"—"ORTHES"—"TOULOUSE"—"PENINSULA"— "WATERLOO."

Years' Serv. Full Pay	Years' Serv. Half Pay	
55		**Colonel.**
		𝕻 *Sir* Archibald Maclaine,[1] CB. *Ens.* 16 Apr. 94; *Lieut.* 29 April, 95; *Capt.* 22 Dec. 04; *Major,* 4 Oct. 10; *Lieut.-Col.* 25 Jan. 13; *Col.* 22 July, 30; *Major-Gen.* 23 Nov. 41; *Col.* 52nd F. 8 Feb. 47.
24	0	*Lieut.-Colonel.*—Richard French, *Ens.* P 9 June, 25; *Lieut.* P 30 Dec. 26; *Capt.* P 2 Mar. 32; *Major,* P 11 May, 39; *Lieut.-Col.* 16 Jan. 46.
22	0	*Majors.*—Henry Samuel Davis, *Ens.* 13 Apr. 27; *Lieut.* P 8 Oct. 30; *Capt.* P 17 July 35; *Major,* P 13 Dec. 39.
23	0	Cecil William Forester, *Ens.* P 1 Aug. 26; *Lieut.* 14 May 29; *Capt.* P 4 Dec. 35; *Major,* 16 Jan. 46.

Full Pay	Half Pay	CAPTAINS.	ENSIGNS.	LIEUT.	CAPTAIN.	BREV.-MAJ.
23	1/12	Joshua Allen Vigors	P 19 Sept. 26	P 17 Sept. 29	P 19 Oct. 38	
14	0	George Campbell	P 13 Mar. 35	21 Dec. 38	P 26 Jan. 41	
14	1/12	Cha. Jas. Conway Mills..	P 26 Dec. 34	P 28 Aug. 38	P 25 June 41	
12	0	Charles Albert Denison, *s.*	P 22 Sept. 37	P 11 May 39	P 26 Oct. 41	
11	0	William Corbett........	P 23 Nov. 38	P 31 Jan. 40	P 19 June 46	
10	0	Fred. John Wilson......	P 1 June 39	P 25 June 41	P 13 July 47	
10	0	RobertOctaviusCumming	22 Feb. 30	3 Sept. 41	P 25 Feb. 48	
9	0	M. Van Kerkwyk Bowie	P 1 Feb. 40	P 22 July 43	P 14 Apr. 48	
8	0	John Hen. Fraser Stewart	P 15 Jan. 41	P 2 Feb. 44	P 16 June 48	
8	0	Geo. Aug. Joc. M'Clintock	P 27 Aug. 41	P 4 April 45	P 18 Aug. 48	
		LIEUTENANTS.				
8	0	Maxwell Du Pré Stronge	P 25 June 41	P 16 Dec. 45		
7	0	Hugh Montgom. Archdall	15 Apr. 42	P 6 Feb. 46		
7	0	Arthur Lennox Peel	P 2 Sept. 42	P 1 May 46		
6	0	Cha.Hen.RouseBoughton	P 28 July 43	P 19 June 46		
5	0	Andrew George Corbet..	P 12 Apr. 44	P 23 Apr. 47		
5	0	William Fuller, *adj.*	25 June 44	12 July 47		
5	0	James Johnes Bourchier	P 28 June 44	P 13 July 47		
5	0	*Hon.* Ernest Geo. Curzon	P 13 Dec. 44	P 18 Feb. 48		
4	0	Charles Cornwallis Ross ..	P 16 Dec. 45	P 25 Feb. 48		
3	0	George Charles Synge ..	P 16 Jan. 46	P 14 Apr. 48		
3	0	Thomas Henry Vyvyan..	P 6 Feb. 46	P 16 Apr. 49		
3	0	George Parker Heathcote	P 1 May 46	P 18 Aug. 48		
		ENSIGNS.				
3	0	Charles Pye Blathwayt ..	P 19 June 46			
2	0	Arthur French Lloyd....	P 9 Apr. 47			
2	0	Chidley Downes Coote ..	P 3 Sept. 47			
1	0	Carisbrooke James Lyon	P 18 Feb. 48			
1	0	Charles Anthony Bacon..	P 25 Feb. 48			
1	0	*Hon.* D. John Monson ...	P 16 June 48			
1	0	Cecil Lennox Peel......	P 1 Aug. 48			
1	0	*Hon.* Henry Flower	P 18 Aug. 48			
1	0	Charles Henry Lambert	P 13 Oct. 48			

2 Paymaster Dickson served in the Peninsula from April 1813 to the close of that war, and was present at the second siege of Tarragona, action at Ordal, and investment of Barcelona. Served throughout the whole of the Burmese war. Also in Affghanistan in 1841 and 42, and has received a Medal for the latter.

Full Pay	Half Pay	
34	2	*Paymaster.*—𝕻 Francis Dickson,[2] 26 July, 27; *Ens.* 12 Mar. 12; *Lieut.* 27 Jan. 14.
5	0	*Adjutant.*—*Lieut.* William Fuller, 20 Aug. 44.
4	0	*Quarter-Master.*—William Knott, 25 Feb. 45.
22	0	*Surgeon.*—Wm. Cruickshank, M.D. 6 Jan. 43; *Assist.-Surg.* 5 Nov. 29; *Hosp.-Assist.* 22 Nov. 27.
5	0	*Assistant-Surgeon.*—Raphael Woolman Read, 31 May, 44.

Facings Buff.—*Agent,* Charles R. M'Gregor, Esq.

[*Returned from Canada 12th August,* 1847.]

1 Sir Archibald Maclaine's services:—Mysore campaign of 1799 against Tippoo Sultan, including the battle of Mallavelly, siege and storming of Seringapatam, where he received three wounds, from the effects of which he was confined in hospital for upwards of a year. Capture of the Danish settlement of Tranquebar, and the Polygar war in 1801, including the battle of Arlingy, and affair of Serungapore, where he was wounded. Mahratta war of 1802, 3, and 4, against Scindia, Holkar, and the Bara Rajah, including the storm of Julnaghur, siege and storming of Gawilghur, siege of Asseerghur (wounded), and battle of Argaum. Ordered home in 1804, in consequence of severe wounds received in the different actions from 1799 to 1804. Peninsular campaigns of 1810, 11, and 12, including the defence of Cadiz, the defence of Matagorda (an outwork of Cadiz, and a ruined redoubt when taken possession of from the enemy), from 22nd February to 22nd April 1810, during which long period Sir Archibald, then a captain in the old 94th regiment, with a very small force under his command, most gallantly kept at bay 8,000 of the enemy under Marshal Soult, who conducted the siege, and did not evacuate until ordered to do so by Lieut.-General Sir Thomas Graham, his men being nearly all either killed or wounded. Served also at the battle of Barrosa (dangerously wounded, and his horse killed,) and capture of Seville.

---

wards with the Spanish Army of General Cuesta, upon the Tagus and Guadiana, and at the battle of Medelin. He was then selected to be Quartermaster-General of the Portuguese Army, of which Marshal Beresford had recently taken the command; and, returning to Portugal, joined it accordingly. In this appointment he continued to serve throughout the war,—occasionally employed, however, in charge of a corps of Portuguese cavalry, which he commanded at Salamanca and Vittoria: in the other actions above mentioned, for which he received decorations, he was in the performance of his duties on the Staff.

"NIEUPORT"—"TOURNAY"—"ST. LUCIA"—"TALAVERA"—"SALAMANCA"—"VITTORIA"—"PYRENEES"—"NIVELLE"—"TOULOUSE"—"PENINSULA"—"ALIWAL"—"SOBRAON."

Years' Serv. Full Pay.	Half Pay.	*Colonel.*				
45		P W *Lord* Fitz Roy James Henry Somerset,[1] GCB. *Cornet*, 9 June, 04; *Lt.* 30 May, 05; *Capt.* 5 May, 08; *Maj.* 9 June, 11; *Lieut.-Col.* 27 Apr. 12; *Col.* 28 Aug. 15; *Maj.-Gen.* 27 May, 25; *Lt.-Gen.* 28 June, 38; *Col.* 53rd F. 19 Nov. 30.				
39	2 1/12	*Lieut.-Colonels.*—John Byrne,[2] CB. *Ens.* 1 Oct. 08; *Lieut.* 21 Dec. 09; *Capt.* P 19 Apr. 21; *Brev.-Maj.* 26 Feb. 36; *Major*, 6 May 43; *Lt.-Col.* P 8 Oct. 44.				
34	0	Henry William Breton, *Ens.* 16 Mar. 15; *Lieut.* P 27 July, 20; *Capt.* P 21 July, 25; *Major*, P 31 Dec. 28; *Lieut.-Col.* P 11 July 34; *Col.* 9 Nov. 46.				
33	7/12	*Majors.*—Henry Havelock,[3] CB., *s* 2d *Lt.* 20 July, 15; *Lt.* P 24 Oct. 21; *Capt.* 5 June 38; *Brev.-Major*, 4 Oct. 42; *Maj.* 30 June 43; *Brev. Lt. Col.* 30 April 44.				
14	0	William R. Mansfield,[4] *Ens.* 27 Nov. 35; *Lieut.* P 31 Aug. 38; *Capt.* P 10 Feb. 43; *Major*, P 3 Dec. 47.				
		Captains.	**Ensign.**	**Lieut.**	**Captain.**	**Brev.-Maj.**
14	0	Charles Lempriere[7]	P 4 Dec. 35	P 12 Oct. 38	P 31 Mar. 43	
24	4/12	Wm. H. H. Forbes Clarke[8]	25 Nov. 24	1 May 26	29 Sept. 43	
24	0	Robert Boyd Brown[10]	P 16 June 25	P 10 Aug. 26	12 Dec. 43	
15	0	John C. Lambton Carter	28 Mar. 34	P 23 Sept. 36	29 Mar. 44	
18	0	George Alexander Tytler[11]	P 28 Oct. 31	P 13 Mar. 35	P 6 June 45	
32	0	Thomas Ffrench[12]	4 Dec. 17	26 Apr. 28	31 Oct. 40	
11	0	George E. Hillier[13]	14 Dec. 38	P 16 Apr. 41	19 Mar. 47	
28	0	Charles Fred. Havelock[14]	P 13 Dec. 21	7 May 27	12 Dec. 39	3 Apr. 46
9	0	John Chester[15]	P 2 Oct. 40	P 1 July 42	P 3 Dec. 47	
14	0	John MacNeale Walter	P 31 July 35	3 July 39	29 Sept. 47	
		Lieutenants.				
8	0	Robert Townley Parker[10]	P 3 Aug. 41	P 10 Feb. 43		
8	0	John Shiffner	P 15 Oct. 41	P 31 Mar. 43		
7	0	A. Bowen Owen Stokes[15]	P 29 Apr. 42	P 28 July 43		
7	0	William Payn[10]	P 27 May 42	P 12 Jan. 44		
7	0	Fred. Gordon Steward[10]	28 May 42	P 28 June 44		
10	0	Charles Fra. Wedderburne	P 31 May 39	P 26 Jan. 41		
9	0	Thomas Mowbray	5 June 40	25 Feb. 42		
9	0	James Morphett[10]	15 Dec. 40	1 Nov. 42		
8	0	Macartney Hume Oldfield	26 Nov. 41	P 15 Mar. 44		
10	0	George Robert Hopkins[10]	28 Aug. 39	26 July 41		
7	0	John Breton[16]	P 2 Dec. 42	26 July 44		
8	0	Alex. James Sutherland[10]	15 Jan. 41	24 May 44		
5	0	William Hunt Grubbe[10]	27 July 44	16 Feb. 46		
5	0	Henry Buck[10]	28 July 44	22 Feb. 46		
7	0	Hon. Archibald Robertson	P 8 Apr. 42	P 8 Aug. 45		
4	0	Henry F. Hastings Parker	P 2 May 45	19 Mar. 47		
3	0	John Wm. Follows,[17] *adj.*	31 Mar. 46	P 4 June 47		
5	0	William George Spiller	23 Aug. 44	14 Sept. 47		
7	0	Fra. W. Durley Waddilove	P 22 July 42	P 21 Apr. 46		
7	0	George Herbert Cox	17 Apr. 42	7 July 43		
3	0	William Ross Fuller	P 14 Apr. 46	P 3 Dec. 47		
3	0	George John Ashton	P 23 Jan. 46	31 Mar. 48		
3	0	James Winsmore Corfield	28 Aug. 46	P 16 June 48		
		Ensigns.				
4	0	Francis Stanford	25 Nov. 45			
3	0	Alex. James Johnston	23 Apr. 46			
2	0	John Alexander Dalzell	30 Jan. 47			
2	0	Edward Moore	19 Mar. 47			
2	0	Avary Jordan Davern	29 Jan. 47			
2	0	Edward Dyne Fenton	P 13 Aug. 47			
2	0	George Wedderburn	P 3 Dec. 47			
1	0	Bendyshe Walton	P 16 June 48			
20	7 11/12	*Paymaster.*—W William Telford,[19] 20 Oct. 48; *Ens.* 5 Dec. 11; *Lt.* 26 Aug. 13; *Capt.* 2 Apr. 41.				
3	0	*Adjutant.*—*Lieut.* John Wm. Follows,[17] 27 May, 46.				
2	0	*Quarter-Master.*—William Peel, 20 July, 47.				
17	0	*Surgeon.*—Nelson Dartnell,[18] 19 Jan. 44; *Assist.-Surg.* 4 Dec. 32.				
2	0	*Assistant-Surgeons.*—Gordon Kenmure Hardie, M.D. 12 Feb. 47				
5	0	Edward Baily Tuson, 20 Aug. 44.				
3	0	James Simpson Grant, M.D. 25 Sept. 46.				

Facings Red.
Agents, Messrs. Cox & Co.

8 Captain Clarke served with the 47th in the Burmese war; with the 53rd on the Sutlej (Medal), and was present at Buddiwal, Aliwal, and Sobraon.

10 Capt. Brown, Lieuts. Parker, Payn, Steward, Morphett, Hopkins, Sutherland, Grubbe, and Buck, served in the campaign on the Sutlej (Medal), and were present at Buddiwal, Aliwal, and Sobraon.

11 Captain Tytler served with the army of the Indus in the Affghanistan campaign of 1839, and was present at the storm and capture of Ghuznee (Medal) and occupation of Cabool. He served as Baggage Master of General Pollock's army during the campaign of 1842 in Affghanistan (Medal), and was present in the following actions:—Forcing the Khyber Pass on the 5th April, Mamookhail, Jugdulluck Pass, Tezeen and Huft Kotul Passes, and re-capture of Cabool. He served with the 53d in the campaign on the Sutlej (Medal) in 1846, and was present at Buddiwal, Aliwal, and Sobraon; at Buddiwal he acted as a Brigade Major, and had a horse shot under him.

12 Capt. Ffrench served with the 26th in China (Medal), and was at Chusan, Ningpo, Chapoo, Shanghai, Woosung, Chin Kiang Foo, and Nankin.

1 Lord Fitz Roy Somerset performed the arduous and responsible duty of Aide-de-Camp and Military Secretary to His Grace the Duke of Wellington throughout the campaigns in Spain, Portugal, France, and Flanders, and was present at the battles of Roleia, Vimiera, Talavera, and Busaco (wounded); the attack and capture of Oporto, pursuit of Marshal Soult, retreat to the lines of Torres Vedras, occupation of them, operations in the pursuit of Marshal Massena, battle of Fuentes d'Onor, 1st siege of Badajos, the brilliant affair of El Bodon, siege and capture of Ciudad Rodrigo, siege and capture of Badajos, battle of Salamanca, capture of Madrid and the Retiro, driving the enemy from Valladolid to Burgos, siege of that castle, various affairs on the retreat from Burgos to the frontiers of Portugal, advance in 1813, battles of Vittoria and the Pyrenees, actions of 1813, passage of the Bidassoa, the Nivelle, and the Nive; advance in 1814, battles of Orthes and Toulouse, and every other affair which took place; also the battle of Quatre Bras, retreat of the 17th June, and battle of Waterloo,—severely wounded, right arm amputated. His Lordship has received a cross and [illegible] for [illegible]

2 Lt.-Col. Byrne was severely wounded when in command of the 31st at the battle of Moodkee. (Medal.)

3 Lt. Col. Havelock served in the Burmese war in 1824, 25, and 26, as Dep. Assist. Adjt.-General, and was present at the capture of Kemmendine, Kumaroot, and Melloon, and in the action of Pagham Mew. Served with the army of the Indus and in Affghanistan in 1839, 41, and 42, as Aide-de-Camp to Sir Willoughby Cotton, Persian Interpreter to Maj. Gen. Elphinstone and to Sir Robt. Sale, and Dep. Assist. Adjt.-Gen. in Sir Geo. Pollock's force, in which army he was attached to the infantry division of four brigades commanded by Sir John M'Caskill;—present at the storm and capture of Ghuznee, in the several actions in forcing the passes between Cabool & Jellalabad in 1841, and at the defence of the latter place in 1841 and 42. Commanded the right column in the attack on Mahommed Akbar's camp on the 7th April 1842, for which and preceding services he was promoted to the rank of Major by Brevet, and appointed a Companion of the Bath. He was also present in the action at Tezeen, at the re-capture of Cabool, and was senior officer of the Staff during the succeeding operations in the Kohistan under Sir John M'Caskill, and at the attack on and capture of Istaliff. Served as Persian Interpreter to Sir Hugh Gough in the action of Maharajpore (Medal); and also throughout the campaign on the Sutlej (Medal), including the battles of Moodkee, Ferozeshah, and Sobraon.

6 Major Mansfield served in the campaign on the Sutlej (Medal) in 1846, and was present at Buddiwal, Aliwal, and Sobraon, at which last he acted as Aide-de-camp to the Commander-in-chief.

7 Capt. Lempriere was at Buddiwal.

[Emb. for Foreign Service 17 Oct. 45.] — **54th (The West Norfolk) Regt. of Foot.** [Serving at Antigua. Depot at Jersey.

The *Sphinx*, with the words "MARABOUT"—"EGYPT"—"AVA."

Years' Serv. 45 Full Pay.	Half Pay.	
36	1 1/12	*Colonel.*—℗ Ulysses, *Lord* Downes,[1] KCB. *Ens.* 31 March 04; *Lt.* 12 Nov. 04; *Capt.* 4 Sept. 06; *Major*, 31 Mar. 11; *Lt.-Col.* 5 Sept. 12; *Col.* 27 May 25; *Major-Gen.* 10 Jan. 37; *Lt.-Gen.* 9 Nov. 46, *Col.* 54th F. 4 April 45.
35	0	*Lt.-Colonel.*—℗ [illegible] Mildmay Fane,[2] *Ens.* 11 June, 12; *Lt.* 25 Sept. 13; *Capt.* P 28 July, 14; *Maj.* P 2 Mar 20; *Lt.-Col.* P 12 June, 23; *Col.* 28 June, 38.
24	0	*Majors.*—[illegible] John Clark,[3] KH. *Ens.* 2 June, 14; *Lieut.* 27 Nov. 21; *Capt.* P 29 Aug. 26; *Major*, P 25 Dec. 29; *Brevet Lieut.-Col.* 23 Nov. 41.
		William Yorke Moore, *Ens.* P 15 Dec. 25; *Lieut.* P 12 Dec. 26; *Capt.* P 19 July, 33; *Major*, P 30 Dec. 42.

Full Pay	Half Pay	CAPTAINS.	ENSIGN.	LIEUT.	CAPTAIN.	BREV.-MAJ.
34	2 4/12	℗ John Norman[4]	2 July 12	9 Nov. 15	9 July 32	9 Nov. 46
21	0	John Rose Wheeler, *s.*	30 July 28	P 25 Dec. 29	P 15 Dec 40	
21	0	Henry Brown	P 14 Aug. 28	P 31 Dec. 29	P 6 Aug. 41	
17	0	Bowland Moffat	P 22 June 32	P 7 Aug. 35	P 27 Aug. 41	
13	0	Seton Lionel Smith	12 Feb. 36	P 19 July 39	P 30 Dec. 42	
11	0	Alfred Robert Margary	P 26 June 38	20 Oct. 40	P 27 Oct. 43	
22	0	John Brett Chalk	P 12 July 27	23 Feb. 31	6 Dec. 44	
20	0	Launcelot Edward Wood	P 21 May 29	P 22 June 32	24 May 46	
11	0	John Arthur Skurray	P 3 Aug. 38	P 27 Aug. 41	9 Oct. 46	
8	0	John William Hay	never	P 6 Aug. 41	P 5 Nov. 47	
		LIEUTENANTS.				
10	0	George Poulett	P 22 Mar. 39	P 8 Feb. 42		
10	0	George Cumming Miller	P 19 July 39	P 1 Apr. 42		
9	0	John Charles Hill Jones	P 16 Dec. 40	P 30 Dec. 42		
8	0	Edward Neville	1 June 41	P 29 Sept. 43		
8	0	Francis Fane, *s.*	P 27 Aug. 41	P 12 Dec. 43		
8	0	John Floyd	P 17 Sept. 41	2 Aug. 44		
7	0	William Freeland Brett	P 1 Apr. 42	6 Dec. 44		
7	0	Lawrence Trent Cave, *s.*	P 23 July 42	P 6 Feb. 46		
7	0	J. Sinclair Thomson, *adj.*	P 25 Nov. 42	13 June 46		
7	0	John S. Ferguson Fowke	P 30 Dec. 42	14 June 46		
6	0	Thos. Hungerford Powell	P 29 Sept. 43	P 14 Aug. 46		
5	0	Pridaux William Gillum	P 28 Oct. 43	P 31 Dec. 47		
6	0	Alfred Wright	10 Nov. 43	21 Apr. 46		
		ENSIGNS.				
5	0	W. Edw. Freeman O'Brien	6 Dec. 44			
4	0	Fra. Wm. Tho. Caulfield	17 Jan. 45			
3	0	Henry Elliott Bayly	14 Apr. 46			
3	0	John Fred. Flamank	7 July 46			
3	0	Arthur Hunt	10 Oct. 46			
2	0	William Frederick Hart	17 Sept. 47			
2	0	George Daniel Kinahan	28 Sept. 47			
2	0	Edward Thomas Shiffner	P 31 Dec. 47			

3 Lieut.-Col. Clark served the campaign of 1815, including the battle of Waterloo and storming of Cambray. Served also the campaigns of 1824 and 25 in Ava, including the taking of Rangoon, Kimendine, Kamaroot, and Mahattee. Led the attack upon the fortified heights at Aracan, and was severely wounded in the neck, arm, and left side.

4 Major Norman was present at the battle of Vittoria, and severely wounded and taken prisoner in the Maya Pass, in the Pyrenees.

6 Capt. Bartley served the Corunna campaign, and subsequently in the Peninsula from March, 1811, to the end of the war and was engaged at Almaraz, Alba de Tormes Baighar, Vittoria, Pyrenees, 25th, 26th, and 27th July, Pampeluna 28th and 30th July.

Full Pay	Half Pay	
41	7/12	*Paymaster.*—℗ George Bartley,[6] 23 June, 25: *Ens.* 25 Oct. 07; *Lt.* 13 Apr. 09; [*Capt.* 9 Dec. 21.
7	0	*Adjutant.*—*Lieut.* James Sinclair Thomson, 24 May, 46.
3	0	*Quarter-Master.*—William Marriott, 11 Sept. 46; *Ens.* 12 June 46.
10	0	*Surgeon.*—Charles Dawson, M.D., 9 Oct. 46; *Assist.-Surg.* 11 Jan. 39.
4	0	*Assistant-Surgeons.*—Francis Hastings Baxter, M.D., 11 July, 45.
4	0	Thomas Moorhead, M.D., 24 Oct. 45.

Facings Green.—*Agents*, Messrs. Cox & Co.

1 Lord Downes was appointed Aide-de Camp to Sir John Cradock, whom he accompanied to Portugal in Nov. 1808, where Sir John held the chief command until May 1809, when he was succeeded by the Duke of Wellington, with whom Lord Downes continued as Aide de Camp and Assistant Military Secretary during the whole war, and was present at the battles of Talavera (slightly wounded), Busaco, Fuentes d'Onor, and El Bodon; sieges of Ciudad Rodrigo and Badajos, battles of Salamanca, Vittoria, and the Pyrenees; siege of San Sebastian, battles of the Nivelle, Nive, and Toulouse (slightly wounded). His Lordship has received a cross and one clasp.

2 Col. Fane served in the Peninsula from Dec. 1812 to March 1814, including the battle of Vittoria, assault and capture of San Sebastian, and battles of the Nive on 9 and 13 Dec. 13. Served also the campaign of 1815, including the battles of Quatre Bras and Waterloo, at the former of which he was severely wounded.

13 Capt. Hillier acted as Aide de-camp to Brigadier Careton in the action of Maharajpore, and has received the Bronze Star. He served as Aide de camp to the Governor General with the Army of the Sutlej, and was severely wounded in the action at Moodkee (Medal).

14 Major Havelock served with the 16th Lancers at the siege and capture of Bhurtpore, in 1825-6; and in that on the Sutlej, including the battle of Sobraon (Medal). Served with the Army of the Indus, during the campaign in Affghanistan in 1839 under Lord Keane as Brigade Major to the Cavalry Division, and was present at the siege and capture of Ghuznee (Medal). He acted in the same capacity during the campaign in Affghanistan in 1842 under General Pollock, and was present in the action at Tezeen, and at the recapture of Cabool (Medal). He served also as D. A. Quartermaster General to the Cavalry Division in the campaign on the Sutlej (Medal), including the battles of Moodkee, Ferozeshah, and Sobraon, and was most severely wounded in the lungs at Ferozeshah

15 Capt. Chester and Lieut. Stokes served in the campaign on the Sutlej (Medal), and was present at Buddiwal Aliwal, and Sobraon (severely wounded).

16 Lt. Breton served in the campaign on the Sutlej (Medal), and was present at Buddiwal, Aliwal, and Sobraon (wounded).

17 Lieut. Pollows served in the campaign of 1845-6 on the Sutlej (Medal), and was engaged in the battles of Aliwal and Sobraon.

18 Mr. Dartnell served with the 4th Lt. Dragoons during the campaign in Affghanistan under Lord Keane, and was present at the siege and capture of Ghuznee (Medal).

19 Capt. Telford served in the Peninsula from March 1812 to the end of the war, including the battle of Salamanca, retreat from Burgos, action of Villa Muriel, affair at Osma, battle of Vittoria, carrying of the outworks of San Sebastian 17th July, and first assault on the body of the fortress 25th July; also second assault and capture 31st Aug. 1813; battles of the

"CHINA."—"The Dragon."

Years' Serv. Full Pay	Years' Serv. Half Pay	
57		**Colonel.** John Millet Hamerton, C.B.[1] *Cornet*, 31 Oct. 93; *Lieut.* 31 Jan. 94; *Capt.* 28 Oct. 96; *Maj.* 15 June 04; *Lieut.-col.* 4 June 11; *Col.* 27 May 19; *Maj.-Gen.* 10 Jan. 37; *Lieut.-Gen.* 9 Nov. 46; *Col.* 55th Regt. 15 Dec. 48.
35	0	*Lieut.-Colonel.*—Charles Warren,[2] CB. *Ens.* 24 Nov. 14; *Lt.* 13 Nov. 18; *Capt.* P 1 Aug. 22; *Major*, 21 Nov. 34; *Brevet Lt.-Col.* 23 Dec. 42; *Lt.-Col.* P 25 Nov. 45.
33	5 1/12	*Majors.*—Arthur O'Leary,[3] *Ens.* 18 Apr. 11; *Lieut.* 25 Jan. 14; *Capt.* 27 Nov. 35; *Brevet-Maj.* 23 Dec. 42; *Maj.* 11 Nov. 45.
20	0	Henry Charles Barnston Daubeney,[4] CB. *Ens.* 12 Mar. 29; *Lt.* 9 Aug. 31; *Capt.* P 28 Oct. 36; *Brev.-Maj.* 23 Dec. 42; *Major*, P 25 Nov. 45.

Full Pay	Half Pay	CAPTAINS.	ENSIGN.	LIEUT.	CAPTAIN.	BREV.-MAJ.
23	0	John Baillie Rose[5]	P 8 Apr. 26	18 May 32	P 7 Feb. 40	
19	0	John Coats[6]	P 2 Nov. 30	3 June 32	P 10 Apr. 40	
22	0	Hector M'Caskill	29 Nov. 27	4 June 32	P 15 Dec. 40	
14	0	Fred. Amelius Whimper[5]	P 23 Jan. 35	P 23 Mar. 38	P 5 Oct. 41	
16	0	W. Holland L. D. Cuddy[7]	P 31 May 33	27 Nov. 35	P 24 Oct. 45	6 Nov. 46
16	0	Henry Thomas Butler[7] ..	P 1 Nov. 33	P 18 Mar. 36	11 Nov. 45	
12	0	Edmund Pitman[8]	P 27 Jan. 37	P 28 Sept. 39	P 11 Dec. 46	
11	0	Daniel M'Coy	25 May 38	P 15 Nov. 39	P 9 Apr. 47	
11	0	George King[7]	P 19 Oct. 38	P 7 Feb. 40	5 Nov. 47	
14	0	Clifford Felix Henry	P 25 Dec. 35	30 Nov. 38	P 29 Jan. 47	
		LIEUTENANTS.				
13	0	W. Haviland Fairtlough[7]	P 12 Aug. 36	29 Dec. 38		
13	0	William Snowe[10]	5 Aug. 36	27 Aug. 38		
10	0	John George Schaw,[10] r.	P 14 June 39	P 15 Dec. 40		
11	0	John Frend,[7] *adj.*	P 7 Sept. 38	20 Feb. 41		
10	0	Henry Reynolds Werge	P 31 Dec. 39	8 April 42		
7	0	Edw. John Tho. Montresor	P 27 May 42	P 24 Oct. 45		
6	0	Thomas Smith Lloyd ..	26 Oct. 43	P 25 Nov. 45		
6	0	Reginald Yonge Shipley	P 5 Dec. 43	P 11 Dec. 46		
5	0	Alfred C. Cure	30 July 44	P 9 Apr. 47		
7	0	Robert Smith........	P 20 Dec. 42	14 Apr. 46		
4	0	Robert William Torrens	P 16 Sept. 45	P 5 Nov. 47		
4	0	Thomas Southwell Brown	14 Nov. 45	P 26 May 48		
4	0	Thomas Ryan..........	23 Sept. 45	28 Aug. 48		
		ENSIGNS.				
4	0	Charles M. G. Quantrille	P 27 June 45			
4	0	Henry Peploe Feilden ..	P 24 Oct. 45			
4	0	Augustus Leacock Marsh	P 30 Dec. 45			
2	0	William Shiell	P 15 Jan. 47			
2	0	Robert Hume.........	P 9 Apr. 47			
1	0	Wm. Geo. Cunningham...	P 26 May 48			
1	0	William Macdonnell	18 Aug. 48			
1	0	William Barnston	22 Dec. 48			

Full Pay	Half Pay	
13	0	*Paymaster.*—Henry Hyacinth Warren,[10] 13 Dec. 44; *Ens.* P 9 Dec. 26; *Lt.* [4 Feb. 32.
11	0	*Adjutant.*—*Lieut.* John Frend,[7] 4 July 44.
10	0	*Quarter-Master.*—James Wm. Grigg,[7] 22 June, 39.
22	0	*Surgeon.*—Alex. Campbell,[12] 30 Sept. 42; *A. Surg.* 29 July. 30; *H. A.* 27 Feb. 27.
8	0	*Assist.-Surgeon.*—Henry Clinton Foss,[13] 26 Feb. 41.

[*Returned from China*, 10 *Aug.* 1844.]

Facings Green.—*Agents*, Messrs. Barron and Smith.—*Irish Agent*, J. Atkinson, Esq.

1 Lieut.-General Hamerton served on the Continent under the Duke of York, in 1794. Embarked for the West Indies in 1795, and was at the capture of St. Lucia the following year. Served in Egypt in 1801. Commanded the 1st battalion of the 4th regt. in Spain; and the 2nd battalion in the campaign of 1815, and was wounded in the battle of Waterloo.

2 Lt.-Col. Warren served the campaign against the Rajah of Coorg in 1834, and was severely wounded at Somwar Pettah on the 3rd April; he succeeded to the command of the Right Wing of the 55th on Lt.-Col. Mill being killed. He commanded the 55th at Chin Kiang Foo in China, and was again severely wounded in a personal encounter with three Tartars, two of whom he himself killed.

3 Major O'Leary served the campaigns of 1811, 12, and 13, in the Peninsula, including the siege of Ciudad Rodrigo, battle of Salamanca, siege of Burgos, and retreat therefrom. Served in the Nepaul war, and was severely wounded in an attack on the heights of Harriapore, 1st March, 1816. Served in the Mahratta war in 1817 and 18. Also in China at Amoy, Chusan, and Chinhae, including repulse of the night attack.

4 Major Daubeney served the campaign against the Rajah of Coorg in 1834. On the China expedition he commanded the Light Company of the 55th at the repulse of the enemy's night attack on Chinhae, and also at Chapoo; and he was Major of Brigade to Sir James Schoedde at Woosung, Shanghai, and Chin Kiang Foo.

5 Captain Rose served with the 55th, and Captain Whimper with the 98th, at Chin Kiang Foo, in China.

6 Captain Coats served in China, at Amoy, Chusan, and Chin Kiang Foo.

7 Major Cuddy, Capts. Butler and King, Lieuts. Fairtlough and Frend, and Quarter-Master Grigg served in China, at Amoy, Chusan, Chinhae (including repulse of night attack), Chapoo, Woosung, Shanghae, and Chin Kiang Foo. Major Cuddy was severely wounded at Chin Kiang Foo whilst leading the advance guard at the escalade of the city.

8 Capt. Pitman served in China, at Amoy, Chusan, Chinhae, and Chin Kiang Foo.

10 Lieuts. Snowe and Schaw, and Paymaster Warren served in China, at Amoy, Chusan, and Chinhae—including repulse of the night attack.

12 Surgeon Campbell served with the 22nd in the campaign in Scinde under Sir Charles Napier, and was present at the destruction of the Fort of Imaumghur, and at the battle of Meeanee (Medal). He served also the campaign of 1844 in the Southern Mahratta country, and was present at the investment and storming of Punalla and Powughur.

13 Assist.-Surg. Foss served with the 16th in the campaign on the Sutlej and was present at the battle of Sobraon (medal).

Years' Serv. 46 — Full Pay | Half Pay

"Moro"—"Gibraltar"—With the *Castle and Key*, "*Montis Insignia Calpe.*"

Colonel.—John *Earl of* Westmorland,[1] GCB. GCH., *Ens.* 17 Dec. 03; *Lt.* 5 Jan. 04; *Capt.* 3 May, 05; *Maj.* 20 Dec. 10; *Lt.-Col.* 12 Dec. 11; *Col.* 4 June, 14; *Maj.-Gen.* 27 May, 25; *Lt.-Gen.* 28 June, 38; *Col.* 56th Regt. 17 Nov. 42.

32 | 2[illegible] — *Lieut.-Colonels.*—William Hassall Eden, *Ens.* P31 March, 14; *Lieut.* P22 June, 20; *Capt.* P13 July, 23; *Major,* P29 Aug. 26; *Lieut.-Col.* P10 Aug. 39.

46 | 0 — r. Peter Shadwell Norman, *Ens.* 9 July 03; *Lt.* 2 June 04; *Cap.* 8 Mar. 10; *Brev.-Maj.* 22 July 30; *Maj,* 15 July 37; *Brev. Lt.-Col.* 9 Nov. 46; *Lt.-Col.* 20 Nov. 46.

24 | 0 — *Majors.*—Edmund Wm. Wilton Passy, *Ens.* 8 Apr. 25; *Lieut.* P30 Dec. 26; *Capt.* P23 Sept. 36; *Major,* P12 Sept. 43.

36 | 0 — r. Nicholas Palmer,[2] *Ens.* 11 Nov. 13; *Lieut.* 3 May, 21; *Capt.* P26 May, 25; *Brevet-Major,* 28 June, 38; *Major,* 20 Nov. 46.

Full Pay	Half Pay		Ensign.	Lieut.	Captain.	Brev.-Maj.
		Captains.				
21	0	John Wegg	P18 Dec. 28	10 Mar. 33	P20 May 36	9 Nov. 46
18	0	r. Wm. Adam Conran...	P11 Oct. 31	P20 May 36	P30 Dec. 42	
13	0	Soulden Oakeley........	P28 June 36	P 6 Sept. 39	P22 Dec. 43	
12	0	r. Arthur William Byles	17 Nov. 37	15 Apr. 41	P20 Aug. 44	
14	0	Samuel Symes Cox	P13 Nov. 35	P12 June 40	P26 Apr. 44	
10	0	r. George William Paty..	P 6 Sept. 39	P18 Feb. 42	P 6 Feb. 46	
9	0	George Raban	31 Jan. 40	P30 Dec. 42	P 3 Apr. 46	
17	0	r. Rich. Walter Lacy....	23 Mar. 32	15 Sept. 37	1 May 46	
8	0	Richard Anderson	8 Jan. 41	P 7 Apr. 43	P29 Dec. 46	
10	0	r. John James Bull	P 8 June 39	P16 Nov. 41	P29 Dec. 43	
8	0	James S. Hawker Farrer	2 Apr. 41	P 2 June 43	P28 Apr. 48	
10	0	Thomas Wallace Fraser ..	30 Aug. 39	10 Dec. 41	3 Oct. 48	
		Lieutenants.				
8	0	Edward Fred. Hare, *adj.*	9 Jan. 41	P12 May 43		
8	0	Wm. George Margesson	P16 July 41	P12 Sept. 43		
7	0	Hugh Whitchurch Austin	28 Jan. 42	P22 Dec. 43		
7	0	r. Fox Maule Ramsay, *adj.*	P18 Feb. 42	P 7 June 44		
6	0	r. George Scott Hanson..	P 7 Apr. 43	P 6 Feb. 46		
6	0	Alex. George Woodford	P 2 June 43	P 3 Apr. 46		
8	0	r. Allan Macdonald	16 Nov. 41	1 May 46		
6	0	William Fred. Ward	P18 Aug. 43	1 May 46		
5	0	r. Henry C. Lananze....	P 7 June 44	1 May 46		
5	0	John Pye Pye..........	P20 Aug. 44	19 May 46		
4	0	r. Henry John Tolcher ..	P28 Nov. 45	P29 Dec. 46		
4	0	r. Francis Wm. Fellows ..	P16 Dec. 45	29 Oct. 47		
3	0	William Watkin Bassett	P 6 Feb. 46	P28 Jan. 48		
3	0	r. Francis Henniker Sykes	P27 Feb. 46	P28 Apr. 48		
3	0	r. William Clutterbuck ..	P 3 Apr. 46	3 Oct. 48		
5	0	George Leslie..........	22 Nov. 44	P 7 July 46		
		Ensigns.				
3	0	r. George Thorne	29 Apr. 46			
3	0	r. John Keys Humfrey ..	30 Apr. 46			
3	0	Hugh Eccles	1 May 46			
3	0	Morton Robert Eden....	19 May 46			
2	0	r. William Cairncross ..	29 Oct. 47			
3	0	r. Fred. Robinson Bernard	3 Apr. 46			
1	0	Marcell Conran	P28 Jan. 48			
1	0	Geo. L. W. D. Flamstead	P28 Apr. 48			
1	0	C. E. Johnson Palmer ..	P 4 Aug. 48			
11	0	George E. L. C. Bissett..	20 Oct. 48			

2 Major Palmer served the campaign of 1814 in Holland, including the attack upon the village of Merxem, 13th Jan., also second attack and capture 2d Feb., when his regt. captured two guns; bombardment of the French fleet in the Scheldt, from 3d to 6th Feb. Actively engaged at Fort Frederick on the Scheldt, 22d March, in impeding the passage of French line of battle ships to Fort Lillo, for the purpose of throwing provisions and assistance into the garrison. Again employed on the same duty 25th March following.

5 | 0 — *Paymaster.*—Stephen Lawson, 6 Jan. 43; *Ens.* 26 Dec. 34; *Lieut.* 22 Jan. 39.

8 | 0 — *Adjutants.*—*Lieut.* Edward Frederick Hare, 19 May, 46.

7 | 0 — r. *Lieut.* Fox Maule Ramsay, 20 Nov. 46.

5 | 0 — *Quarter-Masters.*—William Dougherty, 3 May, 44.

3 | 0 — r. Joseph Swaine, 20 Nov. 46.

24 | 0 — *Surgeons.*—Michael Ryan, M.D. 9 Apr. 41; *Assist.-Surg.* 16 June, 25; *Hosp.-Assist.* 10 Mar. 25.

11 | 0 — r. Geo. Alex. Cowper, M.D. *Surg.* 22 Dec. 46; *As.-Surg.* 30 Mar. 38.

3 | 0 — *Assistant-Surgeons.*—William Deeble, 27 Oct. 46.

3 | 0 — r. Jas. Henry May, 22 Dec. 46.

Facings Purple.—*Agents,* Messrs. Cox & Co.

1 Lord Westmorland served in 1805—6, as Aide-de-Camp to Lieut.-General Don on the expedition to Hanover. In 1806—7, as Assistant-Adjutant-General in Sicily; on board Admiral Sir J. Duckworth's fleet in the action at the passage of the Dardanelles, and the destruction of the Turkish fleet, lying off the castles; in the actions before Constantinople at the island of Prota, and at the repassage of the fleet through the Dardanelles. In Egypt as Assistant-Adjutant-General with the force under Major-General Wauchope, at the first storming of the town of Rosetta, and in the retreat; and subsequently in the second attack and siege of that place, with the force under Major-General Sir W. Stewart. In 1808, served in Portugal as Assistant-Adjutant-General in the army commanded by Sir Arthur Wellesley, in the affair in the front of Obidos, and in the battles of Roleia and Vimiera. In 1809, served as extra Aide-de-Camp to Lord Wellington, and was present at the battle of Talavera. In 1810, with the 3rd Dragoon Guards, in the campaign in Portugal, including the retreat to Torres Vedras, battle of Busaco, and advance to Santarem. In Sept. 1813, proceeded on a mission as Military Commissioner to the head-quarters of the allied armies, under Prince

[For continuation of note, see next page.

"ALBUHERA"—"VITTORIA"—"PYRENEES"—"NIVELLE"—"NIVE"—"PENINSULA."

Colonel.

Years' Serv.	
51	
Full Pay.	Half Pay.

𝔓 Henry, *Viscount* Hardinge,[1] GCB. *Ens.* 8 Oct. 1798; *Lieut.* 25 Mar. 1802; *Capt.* 7 Apr. 04; *Major,* 13 Apr. 09; *Lieut.-Col.* 30 May, 11; *Col.* 19 July, 21; *Maj.-Gen.* 22 July, 30; *Lieut.-Gen.* 23 Nov. 41; *Col.* 57th Regt. 31 May, 43.

Lieut.-Colonel.

23 | 1 1/12 | Thomas Leigh Goldie, *Ens.* P 13 June 25; *Lt.* P 10 Dec. 25; *Capt.* P 24 Nov. 28; *Major,* P 28 Dec. 38; *Brev. Lt.-Col.* 20 Mar. 40; *Lieut.-Col.* P 25 June 47.

Majors.

24 | 0 | Thomas Shadforth, *Ens.* 8 Apr. 25; *Lieut.* P 10 Oct. 26; *Capt.* P 12 Apr. 31; *Major,* 29 March, 44.

20 | 3 4/12 | Thomas Sidney Powell,[3] *Ensign,* P 13 May, 26; *Lieut.* P 31 May, 31; *Capt.* P 13 Nov. 35; *Brev.-Major,* 23 July, 39; *Major,* P 21 July, 48.

Full Pay	Half Pay		ENSIGN.	LIEUT.	CAPTAIN.	BREV.-MAJ.
		CAPTAINS.				
19	0	Henry Gahan..........	P 13 June 30	P 15 June 32	P 6 Mar. 40	
18	0	Henry Montagu Smyth..	7 June 31	P 20 Mar. 35	24 May 45	
23	0	William Fred. Harvey ..	P 11 April 26	P 13 Aug. 29	5 Aug. 42	
15	0	Langford Frost	12 Aug. 34	9 Sept. 37	11 Oct. 45	
14	0	Edward Stanley	8 May 35	10 June 38	29 Dec. 45	
12	0	Henry J. Warre, *s.*	3 Feb. 37	1 June 41	P 8 Jan. 47	
12	0	John Auchmuty........	17 Nov. 37	P 6 Mar. 40	P 2 Mar. 47	
10	0	John Alfred Street.[4]	P 29 Nov. 39	P 5 Oct. 41	7 Jan. 48	
10	0	Henry Braddel Croker ..	P 25 Jan. 39	P 15 Dec. 40	18 May 48	
13	0	George K. Massy Dawson	P 30 July 36	P 6 Nov. 40	P 25 Nov. 42	
		LIEUTENANTS.				
11	0	Loftus Cassidy..........	P 9 Nov. 38	11 June 41		
12	0	Clement Swetenham	31 Mar. 37	2 July 41		
11	0	David Edw. Armstrong..	25 Dec. 38	11 Sept. 41		
9	0	William Inglis	7 Feb. 40	P 31 Dec. 41		
9	0	Robert Hunt	4 Sept. 40	12 Feb. 42		
9	0	Rob.Wm.S.Raper Hunton	P 30 Oct. 40	20 May 42		
8	0	Robert Abraham Logan	26 Oct. 41	P 3 Mar. 43		
7	0	George Armstrong, *adj*..	8 Nov. 42	P 2 Mar. 47		
3	0	Hector Monro	23 Jan. 46	P 29 Jan. 47		
5	0	Charles Edmund Law[5] ..	P 2 Feb. 44	P 8 May 46		
5	0	Jason Hassard	3 Oct. 44	18 May 48		
5	0	John H. Lothian	P 31 Dec. 44	23 May 48		
3	0	James Stewart	29 Jan. 46	10 Nov. 48		
		ENSIGNS.				
2	0	Henry Butler	P 2 Mar. 47			
2	0	William Fowler Jones ..	19 Mar. 47			
2	0	James Franklyn Bland ..	P 10 Dec. 47			
1	0	Edw. C. Geils Kenny....	2 June 48			
1	0	Charles William St. Clair	18 July 48			
1	0	Gerrard John Forsyth ..	P 21 July 48			
1	0	John Augustus O'Neill..	P 3 Nov. 48			
1	0	George Herman Norman	24 Nov. 48			

3 Major Powell served as Aide-de-Camp and Persian Interpreter to Lord Keane throughout the campaign of 1838-9 in Affghanistan, and has received a medal for Ghuznee.

4 Captain Street served in the 26th with the expedition to the North of China in 1842 (Medal), and was present at the attack and capture of Chin Kiang Foo, and at the landing before Nankin.

5 Lieut Law served with the 9th Lancers in the campaign on the Sutlej in 1846, and was present at the battle of Sobraon (Medal).

6 Dr. Gordon served with the 16th Lancers at the battle of Maharajpore 29 Dec. 43, and has received the Bronze Star.

10 | 0 | *Paymaster.*—Mark Matthews, 28 July 43; *Ens.* 29 May 39; *Lt.* 23 Nov. 40.

7 | 0 | *Adjutant.*—*Lieut.* George Armstrong, 23 May 48.

7 | 0 | *Quarter-Master.*—David Morrow, 30 June 43; *Ens.* 7 Jan. 42; *Lt.* 24 Feb. 43.

8 | 0 | *Surgeon.*—Charles Alexander Gordon,[6] M.D. 10 July 46; *Assist.-Surg.* 8 June 41.

8 | 0 | *Assistant-Surgeon.*—James Jackson, 11 June 41.

Facings Yellow.—*Agents,* Messrs. Cox & Co.—*Irish Agents,* Messrs. Cane & Co.

[*Returned from Madras* 23 *Sept.* 46.]

1 Lord Hardinge served throughout the whole of the Peninsular war, nearly the whole of the time as Deputy Quarter Master General of the Portuguese army, and was present at the battles of Roleia and Vimiera (wounded), retreat to, and battle of Corunna, passage of the Douro, battle of Busaco, lines of Torres Vedras, battle of Albuhera, 1st and 2d sieges of Badajoz, siege and capture of Ciudad Rodrigo, 3d siege of Badajoz, battles of Salamanca, Vittoria (severely wounded), Pampeluna, the Pyrenees, Nivelle, Nive, and Orthes. Served also the campaign of 1815, and was severely wounded at Ligny, 16 June,—left hand amputated. As Governor General of India he was engaged in the battles of Moodkee, Ferozeshah, and Sobraon. His lordship has received a cross and five clasps.

Schwarzenberg, in Germany. Served at the siege of Huningues, and the campaign of 1814 in France, including the taking of Langres, the battles of La Rothiere and Brienne, capture of Troyes, affairs of Mormant and Nangis, in front of Bray, defence of Troyes, when attacked by Bonaparte 23rd Feb.; battle of Bar-sur-Aube, the subsequent affair upon the Barce, re-capture of Troyes, battles of Arcis-sur-Aube and of Fere Champenoise, advance upon and battle of Paris, and capture of that city. As His Majesty's Envoy Extraordinary and Minister Plenipotentiary at the Court of Tuscany, served with the Austrian army in the campaign against Naples, in 1815, including the battles of Tolentino and Macerata. Signed, in conjunction with Field Marshal Bianchi, who commanded the Austrian army, the Military convention by which the kingdom of Naples was restored to its Sovereign, King Ferdinand.

"GIBRALTAR"—with the *Castle and Key*, "*Montis Insignia Calpe*."—The *Sphinx*, with the words "EGYPT"—"MAIDA"—"SALAMANCA"—"VITTORIA"—"PYRENEES"—"NIVELLE"—"ORTHES"—"PENINSULA."

Years' Serv. Full Pay.	Half Pay.					
50		*Colonel.*				
		⅌ George Charles D'Aguilar,[1] CB. *Ens.* 24 Sept. 99; *Lieut.* 1 Dec. 02; *Capt.* 30 March, 08; *Major*, 1 April, 13; *Lieut.-Col.* 20 May, 13; *Col.* 22 July, 30; *Major-Gen.* 23 Nov. 41; *Col.* 58th Regiment, 5 Feb. 48.				
30	0	*Lieut.-Colonel.*—Robert Henry Wynyard,[2] CB. *Ens.* 25 Feb. 19; *Lieut.* P 17 July 23; *Capt.* P 20 May 26; *Major*, 25 July 41; *Lieut.-Col.* P 30 Dec. 42.				
24	0	*Majors.*—Cyprian Bridge,[3] *Ens.* 8 April, 25; *Lieut.* P 31 Jan. 28; *Capt.* P 16 Dec. 36; *Major*, P 30 Dec. 42.				
23	11/12	Charles Augustus Arney, *Ens.* P 5 Nov. 25; *Lieut.* P 9 Aug. 31; *Capt.* P 1 July, 37; *Major*, P 12 May, 43.				
		CAPTAINS.	ENSIGN.	LIEUT.	CAPTAIN.	BREV.-MAJ.
16	0	Geo. Ponsonby Hume ..	P 28 June 33	P 16 Dec. 36	P 20 Sept. 39	
31	5	Henry Matson[4]	16 Sept. 13	2 June 14	30 Nov. 38	7 July 46
15	0	Joseph Henry Laye[5]....	P 2 May 34	1 Dec. 37	P 26 Mar. 41	
23	4/12	Jonas Pasley Hardy	29 Sept. 25	3 Nov. 26	25 June 41	
14	0	Cha. Lavallin Nugent ..	P 21 Aug. 35	4 Feb. 38	P 16 Nov. 41	
21	0	Andrew Hamilton Russell	18 Jan. 28	23 July 34	P 31 Dec. 41	
24	0	Wm. Wild Jos. Cockcraft[5]	8 Apr. 25	P 22 Apr. 26	20 July 39	
13	0	Charles Wm. Thompson[7]	P 23 Dec. 36	P 3 May 39	P 12 May 43	
13	0	Charles Dresing	P 19 Feb. 36	2 June 38	2 July 45	
9	0	William Temple Parratt	P 5 Sept. 40	P 9 June 43	P 24 Oct. 45	
		LIEUTENANTS.				
13	0	Alexander Macleod Hay[5]	P 22 July 36	19 Oct. 38		
11	0	Henry Colin Balneavis[8]	7 July 38	P 26 Mar. 41		
11	0	John Alex. Cha. Petley[5]	P 12 Oct. 38	P 26 June 41		
11	0	John M'Lerie,[9]	28 Dec. 38	27 June 41		
13	0	Alfred Rush	P 15 July 36	13 July 41		
10	0	Isaac Rhodes Cooper, *adj.*	P 23 Apr. 39	P 16 Nov. 41		
10	0	Mich. Lionel Westropp[10]	P 20 Sept. 39	29 Dec. 42		
8	0	Cha. St. John S. Herbert	P 26 Mar. 41	P 27 Jan. 43		
8	0	George Hyde Page[6]	P 23 Apr. 41	P 12 May 43		
8	0	J.D.M. Bidwell Edwards[5]	30 Apr. 41	P 23 June 43		
8	0	Leslie Jenkin Thompson	17 Sept. 41	18 Aug. 47		
7	0	Fra. Robert Chester Master	P 22 Nov. 42	8 Dec. 47		
5	0	George Henry Wynyard[11]	3 May 44	P 8 Dec. 48		
		ENSIGNS.				
4	0	Thomas John Grant	9 May 45			
4	0	Michael Tighe.........	30 Dec. 45			
1	0	John Rae Johnstone	23 May 48			
1	0	Arthur Cooper	P 27 May 48			
1	0	Gladwin John H. Wynyard	15 Aug. 48			
1	0	Sedborough Mayne	18 Aug. 48			
1	0	John Hayman Ward	P 12 Sept. 48			
1	0	James Duncan	P 8 Dec. 48			
19	0	*Paymaster.*—⅌ Tho. Richardson Timbrell,[12] 25 Oct. 42; *Qr.-Master*, 19 Nov. 30.				
10	0	*Adjutant.*—*Lieut.* Isaac Rhodes Cooper, 7 Jan. 48.				
2	0	*Quarter-Master.*—William Moir, 15 Oct. 47				
11	0	*Surgeon*—Arthur Saunders Thomson, M.D. 6 Aug. 47; *Assist.-Surg.* 19 Oct. 38.				
10	0	*Assist.-Surgeons.*—Richard Bannatine, 17 Sept. 39.				
6	0	Thomas Moore Philson,[5] M.D., 6 Oct. 43.				

Facings Black.—*Agents*, Messrs. Cox & Co.

7 Capt. Thompson served throughout the whole of the operations in New Zealand from April to June 1845 under Lieut.-Col. Hulme, and from June 1845 to Jan. 1846 under Colonel Despard.

8 Lieut. Balneavis was present at the assault on Kawiti's Pah at Ohiawai on the 1st July 1845; at the destruction of Arratua's Pah on the 16th July; and at the storming of Kawiti's Pah at Ruapekapeka on the 11th Jan. 1847.

9 Lt. McLerie was present, as Adjutant of the 58th, at all the actions against the rebels in the Northern part of New Zealand during the campaigns from May 1845 to Jan. 1847. At the affair at Mawie he commanded a detachment composed of marines and a company of the 96th regiment.

10 Lt. Westropp was present at the destruction of Pomari's Pah on the 30th April 1845; at the attack on Heki's Pah on the 8th May; at the destruction of Waikadi's Pah on the 16th May; at the storming of Kawiti's Pah at Ohiawai on the 1st July and at its destruction on the 10th July; he was also present at the capture of Kawiti's Pah on the 11th Jan. 1846.

11 Lieut. Wynyard commanded and led a storming party from the left stockade into the breach at Kawiti's Pah on the 11th Jan. 1846.

1 Major-General D'Aguilar served eight years in India during the wars of Scindia and Holkar, and was present at the siege and storm of Baroach in Guzerat in Aug. 1803; at the reduction of Powanghur in Malwa in 1804; the capture and occupation of Oogein, the capital of Scindia, in 1805; also at the several assaults upon the Fortress of Bhurtpore in 1805, in the last of which he was wounded. Served subsequently in Walcheren at the siege of Flushing. Also in Sicily, the Greek Islands, and on the eastern coast of Spain, where he was present in 1813 at the action of Biar, and defeat of Marshal Suchet at Castalla. Joined the army in the Netherlands under the Duke of Wellington in 1815, and was present at the capture of Paris. Major-General D'Aguilar has served 26 years on the General Staff, of which eight as Assistant-Adjutant-General at the Horse Guards (principally under the Duke of York), and twelve as Adjutant-General of the army in Ireland. He commanded the expedition which, in 1847, assaulted and took the forts of the Bocca Tigris in the Canton River, those of the Staked Barrier, and those of the city of Canton, spiking 879 pieces of heavy ordnance.

2 Lieut.-Colonel Wynyard served with the force under Col. Despard in New Zealand from Oct. 1845 until Jan. 1847 in command of the 58th, and entered the breach with the stormers in the assault on Kawiti's Pah, at Ruapekapeka on the 11th Jan. 1846.

3 Major Bridge served with the 58th throughout the whole of the operations in New Zealand. He commanded the regiment in the action at Mawie under Lieut.-Colonel Hulme; conducted a night attack in boats up the Waikadi River and completely routed a rebel tribe, commanded the 58th on the second expedition, re-captured a hill at the head of the regiment on the morning of the 1st July 1845 at Ohiawai, and led on the storming parties at the assault on that afternoon, and was at the capture of the Pah on the 11th July. He was also present at the capture of the Kawiti's Pah, at Ruapekapeka on the 11th Jan. 1846.

4 Major Matson joined the force in New Zealand under Colonel Despard in August 1845, and served as Acting Deputy Quartermaster-General, and was present at the assault and capture of Kawiti's Pah at Ruapekapeka on the 11th Jan. 1846.

5 Captains Lay and Cockcraft, Lieuts. Hay, Petley, and Edwards, and Doctor Philson served in the expedition against Kawiti's Pah, at Ruapekapeka.

6 Lieut. Page was present at the storming of Kawiti's Pah, 11th Jan. 1846, and he defeated the Natives in a night attack on his post on the River Hutt, 16th May following. He was actively engaged throughout the whole of the military operations in the Southern Provinces of New Zealand.

12 Paymaster Timbrell was present, as a volunteer, with the old 94th, at battles of the Nive on the 9th, 10th, 11th, and 13th Dec. 1813; and at the action at Sauveterre, battles of Orthes and Toulouse, and other minor affairs in the South of France, as an Ensign, with the 87th Regiment.

"CAPE OF GOOD HOPE" — "CORUNNA" — "JAVA" — "VITTORIA" — "ST. SEBASTIAN" — "NIVE" — "PENINSULA" — "BHURTPORE."

Years' Serv. Full Pay.	Half Pay.	
55		*Colonel.*
		Sir John Harvey,[1] KCB. KCH. *Ens.* 18 Sept. 94; *Lieut.* 15 July 95; *Capt.* 8 Jan. 04; *Major,* 28 Jan. 08; *Lieut.-Col.* 25 June, 12; *Col.* 27 May, 25; *Major-Gen.* 10 Jan. 37; *Lt.-Gen.* 9 Nov. 46; *Col.* 59th F. 3 Dec. 44.
		Lieut.-Colonel.
26	14	[illegible] Arthur Hill Trevor,[2] KH. *Ens.* 1 April 09; *Lt.* P 1 Jan. 10; *Capt.* P 27 July 15; *Major,* P 12 Dec. 26; *Brevet-Lieut.-Col.* 23 Nov. 41; *Lt.-Col.* P 2 Feb. 44.
20	0	*Majors.*—Henry Hope Graham, *Ens.* P 15 Oct. 29; *Lieut.* P 7 Sept. 32; *Capt.* P 7 Nov. 34; *Major,* P 14 Apr. 46.
18	0	George Fenton Fletcher Boughey, *Ens.* P 1 Nov. 31; *Lieut.* P 11 July, 34; *Capt.* P 1 June, 38; *Major,* P 1 May, 46.

Full Pay	Half Pay	CAPTAINS.	ENSIGN.	LIEUT.	CAPTAIN.	BREV.-MAJ.
19	0	Arnold E. Burmester....	31 Aug. 30	P 7 Mar. 34	P 16 Mar. 38	
15	0	Wm. Wynne Lodder....	P 7 Mar. 34	P 5 June 35	P 6 Feb. 41	
22	0	Henry Butler..........	P 15 May 27	7 Sept. 32	P 19 Mar. 41	
15	0	*Hon.* Jas. Pierce Maxwell	P 6 June 34	P 5 May 37	P 25 June 41	
12	0	*Hon.* Adolph. E. P. Graves	never	3 Feb. 37	P 13 May 42	
16	0	Henry B. F. Dickinson..	5 July 33	P 23 Dec. 36	P 4 Aug. 40	
14	0	Henry William Gordon..	28 Aug. 35	P 14 Aug. 40	P 11 July 45	
18	0	Adam John Laing Peebles	12 Apr. 31	P 13 June 34	1 Oct. 45	
11	0	Francis Fuller	P 16 Mar. 38	P 25 June 41	P 14 Apr. 46	
10	0	Charles Townshend Wilson	P 11 Oct. 39	P 30 Dec. 42	P 1 May 46	
		LIEUTENANTS.				
12	0	Thomas Peebles, *adj*.....	P 17 Mar. 37	P 6 Feb. 41		
9	0	Joseph de Montmorency	P 14 Aug. 40	P 14 Apr. 43		
8	0	George Newcomen.......	P 5 Feb. 41	P 12 Jan. 44		
8	0	William Bridges........	P 19 Nov. 41	P 19 Jan. 44		
8	0	Edward Gamage Byam, *r.*	P 25 June 41	P 23 Aug. 44		
7	0	Mathew Pennefather Lloyd	P 30 Dec. 42	P 11 July 45		
7	0	Robert William Wade ..	P 15 April 42	15 Dec. 45		
7	0	James Leyne	20 May 42	1 Oct. 45		
6	0	Charles Kendal Bushe ..	P 14 Apr. 43	P 14 Apr. 46		
5	0	Charles Stuart Baker ..	29 Mar. 44	P 8 Jan. 47		
9	0	John King	P 10 July 40	P 29 Apr. 42		
5	0	Edwyn Fra. B. S. Stanhope	P 12 Apr. 44	15 Oct. 47		
5	0	Thomas Wm. John Lloyd	21 Dec. 44	20 Dec. 46		
		ENSIGNS.				
4	0	Edward Fred. Chadwick	10 Oct. 45			
4	0	Jas. Stanhope Pat. Clarke	P 26 Sept. 45			
3	0	Godfrey Goodman Mosley	P 1 May 46			
2	0	Steph. Remnant Chapman	P 8 Jan. 47			
2	0	John George Chapman ..	P 23 Mar. 47			
2	0	Henry Kean	29 Oct. 47			
1	0	Fred. Anthony Trevor ..	P 15 Aug. 48			
1	0	James Alfred Caulfield ..	P 10 Nov. 48			

Full Pay	Half Pay	
17	0	*Paymaster.*—Anthony Walshe, 10 Sept. 41; *Ens.* P 2 Nov. 32; *Lt.* 23 Jan. 37.
12	0	*Adjutant.*—*Lieut.* Tho. Peebles, 1 April, 42.
8	0	*Quarter-Master.*—William Macdonald, 21 May, 41.
24	0	*Surgeon.*—Tho. Williams, M.D., 26 Jan. 41; *Assist.-Surg.* 28 Sept. 26; *Hosp.-Assist.* 3 Nov. 25.
2	0	*Assist.-Surgeon.*—Thomas Connor O'Leary, 6 Aug. 47.

Facings White.—*Agents,* Messrs. Cox & Co.—*Irish Agents, Sir* E. R. Borough, [Bt., Armit & Co.

[*Returned from Barbadoes,* 17*th Dec.* 1843.]

1 Sir John Harvey served the severe winter campaign of 1794-95, in Holland, under the Duke of York, and carried the colours of the 80th in the action of the 31st December. In 1795, he served on the coast of France, at Isle Dieu and Quiberon. Proceeded to the Cape of Good Hope in 1796, where he was present during the short service which led to the surrender of the Dutch fleet at Saldanha Bay. In Feb 1801, proceeded from India to Egypt, under *Sir David Baird.* Returned to India in 1802, and served the campaigns of 1803, 4, 5, and 6, under Lord Lake, including the siege of Bhurtpore, and subsequent operations against the Mahratta Chief Holkar. Employed as Deputy-Adjutant-General, in Upper Canada, during the campaigns of 1813 and 14, including the first action of Fort George, surprise and defeat of the enemy at Stoney Creek, defeat of the enemy at Chrysler's Farm (medal), capture of Fort Niagara, Black Rock, Buffalo, and Oswego, battle of Lundy's Lane, siege and assault of Fort Erie, and sortie on the 17th September following. Severely wounded at the siege of Fort Erie, 6th Aug. 1814.

2 Lieut.-Col. Trevor served with the 33rd in Germany and Holland in 1813 and 14, including both attacks on Merxem, operations in front of Antwerp, and the storming of Bergen-op-Zoom. Served also the campaign of 1815, including the action at Quatre Bras, retreat on the following day, battle of Waterloo, advance to and capture of Paris.

"Celer et audax."

"Roleia"—"Vimiera"—"Martinique"—"Talavera"—"Fuentes d'Onor"—"Albuhera"—"Ciudad Rodrigo"—"Badajoz"—"Salamanca"—"Vittoria" "Pyrenees"—"Nivelle"—"Nive"—"Orthes"—"Toulouse"—"Peninsula."

Years' Serv. Full Pay.	Half Pay.	
		Colonel-in-Chief.
		Field Marshal *His Royal Highness* A. F. *Duke of* Cambridge, 22 Jan. 27.
		Colonels Commandant.
52		1 𝔓 *Sir* William Gabriel Davy,[1] CB. KCH. *Ens.* March, 97; *Lieut.* 22 May, 97; *Capt.* 1 Jan. 02; *Major*, 5 Feb. 07; *Lieut.-Col.* 28 Dec. 09; *Col.* 12 Aug. 19; *Major-Gen.* 22 July, 30; *Lieut.-Gen.* 23 Nov. 41; *Col.* 60th Rifles, 2 Nov. 42.
66		2 𝔓 *Sir* Wm. Cornwallis Eustace,[2] CB. KCH. *Lieut.* 27 Sept. 83; *Capt.* 24 Dec. 02; *Major*, 17 March, 08; *Lieut.-Col.* 23 Aug. 10; *Col.* 12 Aug. 19; *Major-Gen.* 22 July, 30; *Lieut.-Gen.* 23 Nov. 41; *Col.* 60th Rifles, 7 April, 43.
		Lieut.-Colonels.
26	3 4/12	1 *Hon.* Henry Dundas,[3] CB. *Ens. & Lieut.* 18 Nov. 19; *Capt.* P 1 April, 24; *Major*, P 11 July, 26; *Lieut.-Col.* P 3 Dec. 29; *Col.* 23 Nov. 41.
25	0	2 Cosby Lewis Nesbitt, *2nd Lieut.* 27 Mar. 24; *Lieut.* P 2 June, 25; *Capt.* P 18 Dec. 28; *Major*, 10 Aug. 41; *Lieut.-Col.* 26 July, 44.
24	0	1 Joseph Bradshaw, *Ens.* P 12 May, 25; *Lieut.* P 12 Dec. 26; *Capt.* P 2 Dec. 31; *Major*, P 9 Dec. 36; *Lt.-Col.* P 27 Aug. 41.
23	0	*Majors.*—1 Maurice Griffin Dennis, *Ens.* 9 May, 26; *Lieut.* 5 July, 27; *Capt.* P 15 Dec. 37; *Major*, P 2 May, 45.
22	0	1 John Gordon, *Ens.* P 14 June 27; *Lieut.* P 5 April 31; *Capt.* P 5 April 33; *Major*, P 15 Dec. 40.
18	12 10/12	2 John Temple, *2nd Lieut.* P 14 May 16; *Lieut.* P 21 Oct. 24; *Capt.* P 28 Jan. 26; *Brevet-Major*, 23 Nov. 41; *Major*, P 28 Jan. 48.
24	0	2 Charles Howe Spence, *2nd Lieut.* 20 April 25; *Lieut.* P 28 Sept. 26; *Capt.* 24 May 41; *Major*, P 20 Oct. 48.

Full Pay	Half Pay	Captains.	2d Lieut.	Lieut.	Captain.	Brevet-Major.
34	1 1/12	2 Joseph Robinson	21 Apr. 14	P 18 Nov. 24	7 June 39	
22	0	1 Henry Bingham	P 30 April 27	P 28 Sept. 32	25 June 41	
21	0	2 John Jones..........	P 12 June 28	P 2 Dec. 31	P 16 July 41	
21	0	1 Wm. Fanshawe Bedford	P 18 Dec. 28	P 28 June 33	P 23 July 41	
20	0	1 *Hon.* H. Lyttle. Powys	P 2 April 29	P 19 Sept. 34	17 Aug. 41	
15	0	2 Andrew Carden, *s.* ..	P 14 Mar. 34	P 4 Dec. 35	P 30 Dec. 40	
16	0	1 Fra. Roger Palmer ..	P 15 Mar. 33	P 24 April 35	P 11 Mar. 42	
18	0	2 John Kenn. Mackenzie	P 16 Dec. 31	P 16 Sept. 36	23 Apr. 42	
14	0	2 Henry Holbech	P 29 May 35	4 Mar. 41	P 25 June 44	
15	0	1 Webbe Butler........	P 19 Sept. 34	P 15 Dec. 40	26 July 44	
11	0	1 James Douglas	P 17 Aug. 38	P 16 July 41	P 20 Sept. 44	
11	0	2 *Hon.* Adrian Hope ..	P 23 Nov. 38	P 23 Apr. 41	P 20 Dec. 44	
12	0	1 Henry John Darell....	P 5 May 37	P 2 July 41	P 12 Jan. 44	
11	0	2 C.W. Hamilton Sotheby	P 25 Dec. 38	17 Aug. 41	P 14 Aug. 46	
22	4/12	1 William James Yonge	P 27 July 26	P 17 May 27	10 July 46	
10	0	1 R. F. Waldo Sibthorp	P 20 Sept. 39	P 10 Sept. 41	P 5 Mar. 47	
9	0	2 William Grenfell	P 3 July 40	P 14 Oct. 41	P 22 June 47	
13	0	2 Douglas Jones	P 30 Dec. 36	26 Nov. 41	P 28 Jan. 48	
9	0	2 Ashton Mosley	P 28 Aug. 40	P 11 Mar. 42	P 25 Feb. 48	
9	0	1 Henry Friend Kennedy	P 11 Sept. 40	7 Apr. 42	P 20 Oct. 48	

1 Sir William Davy commanded the 5th battalion of the 60th at the battles of Roleia, Vimiera, and Talavera, for which he has received a medal and one clasp.

2 Sir William Eustace was at the battles of Ross and Vinegar Hill, and at Wexford, and all through the Irish rebellion, in 1798. Went to Naples with Sir James Craig; from thence to Sicily and Calabria, and was present at the action on landing in St. Eufemia Bay, the battle of Maida, and siege of Scylla. He was on board the *Loire* frigate when she captured the *Gannemede*. Commanded the Chasseurs Britanniques at the battle of Fuentes d'Onor, the siege of San Christoval, battle of Salamanca, capture of Madrid, defence of Olmos in front of Burgos, various engagements on the retreat from thence, actions in the Pyrenees (severely wounded 31st August), and various other affairs, in one of which he was wounded, and in another he had a horse killed under him. Medal and one clasp for Fuentes d'Onor and Salamanca.

3 Colonel the Honourable Henry Dundas commanded the 83rd during the suppression of the insurrection in Lower Canada in 1837; and also in repelling the attacks of the American Brigands who landed near Prescott, Upper Canada, in 1838.

Years' Serv. Ful. Pay.	Half Pay.		2nd Lieut.	Lieut.
		1st Lieutenants.		
13	0	1 Charles Napier North	20 May 36	28 Dec. 38
13	0	2 John Francis Jones[3]	P 21 Oct. 36	P 12 Apr. 39
9	0	1 George Clapcott..........	29 Dec. 40	P 31 Mar. 43
8	0	2 Godfrey Rhodes, *r*.........	P 19 Mar. 41	P 25 June 44
8	0	2 George Waldegrave Bligh	12 Mar. 41	26 July 44
8	0	2 Stephen Kenny, *adj*.......	8 June 41	do.
8	0	1 Gibbes Rigaud	P 11 June 41	do.
8	0	1 Ed. FitzGerald Campbell, *adj*	2 July 41	do.
8	0	2 Eustace Henry Rose	P 16 July 41	do.
8	0	2 Peter Burton Roe	P 23 July 41	do.
8	0	1 William Percival Salmon ..	P 27 Aug. 41	do.
8	0	2 James Fraser	P 10 Sept. 41	do.
7	0	2 John Warburton	17 June 42	P 20 Sept. 44
7	0	1 William Hutchinson	8 April 42	P 26 April 44
6	0	2 Randle Joseph Feilden	P 31 Mar. 43	P 25 Feb. 45
6	0	1 Dunbar Douglas Muter ..	14 April 43	P 17 Jan. 45
6	0	1 Henry Francis Williams ..	19 May 43	P 20 Dec. 44
10	0	1 John Archibald Mac Queen	30 Aug. 39	6 June 45
6	0	1 Cha. Alex. Boswell Gordon	P 21 April 43	P 13 June 45
9	0	1 John Maguire[4]	P 7 Feb. 40	4 July 43
5	0	2 Henry Edward Warren....	P 5 Jan. 44	P 30 Dec. 45
7	0	1 Alfred FitzGerald	8 Nov. 42	P 13 Feb. 46
8	0	1 Arthur Hill Hastead Mercer	P 30 Apr. 41	1 Nov. 42
5	0	1 Frederick Arthur St. John	23 July 44	P 5 Mar. 47
7	0	1 Francis Andrews	27 May 42	19 Dec. 45
5	0	1 Francis Dawson..........	26 July 44	7 June 47
5	0	1 Lyon Conway Travers	29 July 44	P 22 June 47
5	0	1 John Prevost Battersby ..	30 July 44	P 28 Jan. 48
5	0	1 John Lambert Edw. Baynes	31 July 44	P 25 Feb. 48
5	0	1 Bernard Ward	1 Aug. 44	P 5 May 48
5	0	2 John Henry Payne	P 20 Aug. 44	P 12 Sept. 48
16	0	H. Anthony O'Molony[7] ..	P 24 Dec. 33	10 Mar. 37
		2nd Lieutenants.		
5	0	1 Hunter Richardson Farnden	27 July 44	
4	0	1 Vincent Tongue	P 14 Feb. 45	
4	0	2 Richard Harcourt Robinson	P 25 Feb. 45	
4	0	2 Arthur Charles Greville ..	P 4 April 45	
4	0	1 Robert Wilmot Brooke	P 30 Dec. 45	
3	0	2 Richard Freer............	22 May 46	
3	0	2 Francis Charteris Fletcher	P 31 July 46	
3	0	2 Edward Bowles..........	P 14 Aug. 46	
3	0	2 Charles William Earle	24 Dec. 46	
2	0	1 Robert J. E. Robertson ..	P 5 Mar. 47	
2	0	1 Thomas Nicholson.......	P 22 June 47	
3	0	1 George Clarke	1 Aug. 46	
2	0	2 William Mure	P 22 Oct. 47	
2	0	2 John Du Cane	P 5 Nov. 47	
1	0	1 Ch. Wm. Pownall Lillingston	P 28 Jan. 48	
1	0	1 Conyngham Jones........	P 25 Feb. 48	
1	0	1 William Tedlie	P 5 May 48	
1	0	2 Bryan Viney Douglas Smith	P 12 Sept. 48	
1	0	2 Henry James Robertson ..	P 20 Oct. 48	
1	0	1 Henry Cockburn	10 Nov. 48	

Ful. Pay.	Half Pay.	
40	$\frac{1}{12}$	*Paymasters.*—1 [illegible] Edward Coxen,[5] 9 Feb. 26; *2nd Lieut.* 5 April, 09; *Lieut.* 28 June, 10; *Capt.* 8 April, 25.
21	0	2 William Henry Fitzgerald, 20 Sept. 39; *Ens.* 17 Jan. 28; *Lieut.* P 31 May, 33.
8	0	*Adjutants.*—2 *First Lieut.* Stephen Kenny, 9 May, 43.
8	0	1 *First Lieut.* Edward Fitzgerald Campbell, 12 May 48.
7	0	*Quarter-Masters.*—1 Thomas Berrey, 29 Mar. 42.
2	0	2 Richard Power, 24 May 47.
23	0	*Surgeons.*—1 Charles Robert Boyes, M.D. 2 July 41; *Asst.-Surg.* 28 Nov. 27; *Hosp.-Ass.* 17 Aug. 26.
23	0	2 Augustus Henry Cowen,[6] 2 July 41; *A. S.* 29 July 30; *H. A.* 2 Nov. 26.
8	0	*Assistant-Surgeons.*—1 Thomas Cowan, MD. 17 Sept. 41.
5	0	1 William Joseph Macfarlane, 16 Feb. 44.
5	0	2 Frederick John Folliott Payne, 31 May, 44.
4	0	George Augustus Frederick Shelton, M.B. 3 Jan. 45.

[*1st Battalion embarked for India, July,* 1845. *Serving in Scinde.*]
[*2nd Battalion returned from North America, 5th June,* 47.]

Regimentals Green—*Facings* Scarlet.—*Agents*, Messrs. Cox & Co.
Irish Agents, Sir E. R. Borough, *Bt.*, Armit, and Co.

3 Lieut. J. F. Jones served in the 17th during the campaign in Affghanistan and Beloochistan, under Lord Keane, and was engaged at the storm and capture of Ghuznee and of Khelat. Accompanied the expedition from Aden which destroyed the Arab posts of Sheik Medi and Sheik Othman, and skirmished between those places on the 5th Oct. 1841.

4 Lt. Maguire served with the 55th in China (Medal), at Amoy, Chusan, and Chinhae.

5 Capt. Coxen served at the siege of Flushing in 1809, and subsequently in the Peninsula, including the lines of Torres Vedras, actions at Pombal, Redinha, Mirando de Corvo, Ponte de Rheux, Sabugal, and Almeida; battle of Fuentes d'Onor, siege and storm of Ciudad Rodrigo, siege and storm of Badajoz, battle of Salamanca, capture of Madrid, actions at Zamarnos and San Milan, battle of Vittoria, actions of Lesaca, Vera bridge and heights; battle of Nivelle, Nive, (from 9th to 13th Dec.) and Orthes; and affair at Tarbes. Served also the campaign of 1815, and was severely wounded in the knee at Waterloo.

6 Mr. Cowen served with the Force employed against the Rajah of Coorg, in April 1834.

7 Lieut. O'Molony served the campaign on the Sutlej (Medal) with the 80th, including the battles of Moodkee, Ferozeshah, Aliwal, and Sobraon.

Embarked for India, 1 July 45. **61st (*The South Gloucestershire*) Regt. of Foot.** [Serving in Bengal.]

The *Sphinx*, with the words, "EGYPT"—"TALAVERA"—"SALAMANCA"—"PYRENEES"—"NIVELLE"—"NIVE"—"ORTHES"—"TOULOUSE"—"PENINSULA"—Flank Companies, "MAIDA."

Years' Serv.		
61		*Colonel.* Hastings Fraser,[1] CB. *Ens.* 9 April, 1788; *Lieut.* 3 Nov. 90; *Capt.* 7 Dec. 97; *Major* 28 July, 1802; *Lieut.-Col.* 7 Sept. 04; *Col.* 4 June, 13; *Major.-Gen.* 12 Aug. 19; *Lieut.-Gen.* 10 Jan. 37; *Col.* 61st Regiment, 1 Sept. 48.
Full Pay.	Half Pay.	
41	1/12	*Lieut.-Colonels.*—Henry Burnside,[2] *Ens.* 8 Oct. 07; *Lieut.* 18 Feb. 08; *Capt.* P 13 Nov. 17; *Bt.-Maj.* 10 Jan. 37; *Maj.* 28 June, 38; *Lt.-Col.* 9 May, 43.
40	0	Alexander M'Leod,[3] *Ens.* 3 Aug. 09; *Lieut.* P 12 Dec. 11; *Capt.* P 31 Dec. 25; *Brevet-Major*, 28 June, 38; *Major*, 7 Jan. 42; *Lt.-Col.* 26 July 44.
24	0	*Majors.*—William Jones, *Ens.* 10 Apr. 25; *Lieut.* P 12 Dec. 26; *Capt.* P 24 Nov. 35; *Major*, 26 July 44.
22	0	James Campbell, *Ens.* 22 Feb. 27; *Lieut.* 1 Apr. 31; *Capt.* P 25 Dec. 38; *Major*, 31 July 47.

Full Pay	Half Pay	CAPTAINS.	ENSIGN.	LIEUT.	CAPTAIN.	BREV.-MAJ.
23	0	Wm. Henry Vicars	P 26 Sept. 26	P 12 Apr. 31	7 Jan. 42	
15	0	Francis John Stephens	P 12 Sept. 34	24 May 37	P 26 Jan. 44	
14	0	Charles Clement Deacon	P 28 Aug. 35	P 2 Dec. 37	26 July 44	
13	0	Thomas Hussey Burgh	P 29 July 36	P 20 Nov. 38	P 22 July 45	
12	0	Thomas N. Dalton	22 Sept. 37	14 Dec. 40	23 April 46	
24	1/12	Charles J. Otter[5]	20 Dec. 24	12 Nov. 27	9 Mar. 39	
21	0	William Alex. Dely[6]	31 July 28	21 April 33	22 Oct. 47	
8	0	James Massey	P 5 Mar. 41	2 June 43	19 Nov. 47	
11	0	Tho. Philip H. Fitzmayer	28 Dec. 38	16 July 41	20 Nov. 47	
7	0	John Patrick Redmond	7 Jan. 42	P 29 Sept. 43	20 May 48	
		LIEUTENANTS.				
9	0	Hen. Hugh M'K. Fleming[7]	29 May 40	P 29 April 42		
7	0	Wm. Edw. Durand Deacon	3 June 42	P 26 Jan. 44		
7	0	Frederick Huson	20 May 42	30 Jan. 44		
7	0	Alexander William Gordon	P 11 Mar. 42	P 3 May 44		
9	0	Robert Cecil Dudgeon	P 28 Aug. 40	26 July 44		
7	0	Edward Thomas Wickham	P 19 Aug. 42	26 July 44		
7	0	William James Hudson	P 20 Aug. 42	26 July 44		
7	0	H. E. Hillm. Burnside, *adj.*	27 Dec. 42	26 July 44		
6	0	Andrew Grant	2 June 43	23 Aug. 44		
8	0	Archibald Armstrong	20 Nov. 41	7 Dec. 45		
5	0	Drought Rich. Croasdaile	3 May 44	23 April 46		
5	0	C. Rowland Richardson[10]	P 16 Feb. 44	23 Dec. 45		
7	0	John Fred. Woolhouse	2 Aug. 42	P 21 July 46		
5	0	Edward Shawe Powys	26 July 44	3 Oct. 46		
5	0	James St. George Lewin	27 July 44	14 Dec. 46		
5	0	Rich. Gunn Brackenbury	23 Aug. 44	P 29 Dec. 46		
5	0	George Alexander Bace	28 July 44	3 May 47		
7	0	William Charles Dilkes	27 May 42	31 Mar. 46		
4	0	Fred. Rob. Eyre Burnside	P 27 June 45	19 Nov. 47		
4	0	Robert Greig	P 22 July 45	20 Nov. 47		
3	0	David Reid	31 Mar. 46	P 25 Feb. 48		
3	0	William Henry Wall	20 Oct. 46	20 May 48		
2	0	Charles Bisset Fenwick	P 14 May 47	P 18 Aug. 48		
		ENSIGNS.				
3	0	John Nagel	P 29 Dec. 46			
3	0	Thos. Harrison Harrison	30 Dec. 46			
2	0	Edward Ring Berry	29 Jan. 47			
2	0	Thomas Maitland Moore	20 July 47			
2	0	Julius G. Mangen Strode	17 Dec. 47			
2	0	Jas. Henry Huffey Parks	11 June 47			
1	0	Thomas Gabbett	P 26 May 48			
1	0	Henry Brackenbury	18 Aug. 48			

Full Pay	Half Pay	
40	0	*Paymaster.*—Archer Toole,[9] 1 May, 28; *Ens.* 11 May, 09; *Lieut.* 30 Jan. 12.
7	0	*Adjutant.*—*Lieut.* Henry Edward Hillman Burnside, 23 March, 47.
9	0	*Qr.-Master.*—Michael Wall, 16 Feb. 41; *Ens.* 6 Nov. 40.
13	0	*Surgeon.*—Patrick Gammie,[11] 2 March, 47; *Assist. Surg.* 17 June, 36.
10	0	*Assistant-Surgeons.*—David Lucas, 20 Dec. 39.
5	0	William Holmes Jephson, M.D. 12 July 44.
12	0	Frederick Hobson Clark, 15 Sept. 37.

Facings Buff.—*Agents*, Messrs. Cox & Co.

3 Lieut.-Col. M'Leod served the whole of the campaigns of 1810 & 11, first half of 1812, and the latter part of 1814, in the Peninsula, including the battles of Busaco and Fuentes d'Onor, 3d and 5th May 1811, and all the other operations.

5 Capt. Otter served with the 14th at siege and capture of Bhurtpore in 1825-6. When in the 4th Regt. he commanded the storming party in the attack on the Fort of Buddami, Southern Mahratta country, in June 1841.

6 Captain Dely served the campaign against the Rajah of Coorg in 1834, with the 48th.

7 Lieutenant Fleming served with the 41st throughout the campaign of 1842 in Affghanistan, and was present in the engagements of the 28th March and 28th April in the Pisheen Valley; also in the actions near Candahar, at Goaine, and before Ghuznee; occupation and destruction of that fortress and of Cabool; expedition into Kohistan; storm, capture, & destruction of Istaliff, and the various minor affairs in and between the Bolan and the Khyber Passes. He has received the Medal.

9 Paymaster Toole served in the Peninsula from Feb. 1810 to March 1814, including the battles of Busaco, and Fuentes d'Onor; siege of Forts at, and battle of Salamanca (severely wounded in the left arm); battles of the Pyrenees (28th, 29th, 30th and 31st July) and Nivelle, where he was severely wounded in the right leg.

10 Lt. Richardson served the campaign on the Sutlej (Medal), with the 9th, and was present at the battles of Moodkee, Ferozeshah, & Sobraon.

1 Lt. Gen. Fraser served the three campaigns of 1790, 91 and 92, in the East Indies, including the siege and storming of Bangalore, the assault of Tippoo's fortified camp, and the subsequent siege of Seringapatam. In 1793 he served at the siege and capture of Pondicherry. In 1797 he sailed on the projected Manilla expedition to Penang. In 1799 he took the field against Tippoo Sultan, and was present at the battle of Mallavelly, and the siege and assault of Seringapatam. Served during the whole of the Polygar war in 1801.

2 Lt.-Col. Burnside served at the capture of Martinique, and siege of Fort Desaix, March 1809; capture of Guadaloupe in 1810; and campaigns of 1813 and 14 in Canada.

11 Mr. Gammie served the campaign on the Sutlej (medal), and was present with the 80th at the battles of Moodkee and Ferozeshah, and in medical charge of the 31st at Buddiwal, Aliwal, and Sobraon.

"NIVE"—"PENINSULA."—"FEROZESHAH."—"SOBRAON."

Years' Serv. Full Pay	Half Pay	
56		*Colonel.* 𝕻 *Sir* John Forster Fitzgerald,[1] KCB. *Ens.* 29 Oct. 93; *Lieut.* 31 Jan. 94; *Capt.* 9 May, 94; *Major,* 25 Sept. 03; *Lieut.-Col.* 25 July, 10; *Col* 12 Aug. 19; *Major-Gen.* 22 July, 30; *Lt.-Gen.* 23 Nov. 41; *Col.* 62nd, 21 Nov. 43.
31	4 1/12	*Lieut.-Colonel.*—𝖂 Thomas Reed[2], CB. *Cornet,* 26 Aug. 13; *Lt.* P 2 May, 15; *Capt.* P 19 Feb. 24; *Maj.* P 15 June, 26; *Lt.-Col.* P 11 Aug. 29; *Col.* 23 Nov. 41.
24	0	*Majors.*—Wm. T. Shortt,[3] *Ens.* 25 March, 25; *Lieut.* P 30 Dec. 26; *Capt.* P 20 Feb. 29; *Major,* 16 April, 41; *Brevet Lt.-Col.* 3 Apr. 46.
30	1/12	William Henry Goode,[4] *Ens.* 21 May 18; *Lieut.* P 31 July 23; *Capt.* 29 Dec. 40; *Maj.* 5 Sept 45.

Full Pay	Half Pay		ENSIGN.	LIEUT.	CAPTAIN.	BREV.-MAJ.
		CAPTAINS.				
20	0	William Ambrose Pender	P 25 June 29	3 Mar. 33	P 12 Jan. 38	
18	0	Wm. Mathias[5] ……..	P 8 Feb. 31	P 29 Mar. 33	P 16 Mar. 38	19 June 46
17	0	George Edward Olpherts	P 20 Jan. 32	12 Oct. 33	P 16 April 41	
25	0	Charles Wm. Sibley[6]….	27 Nov. 24	16 Oct. 26	19 Aug. 42	
16	0	Robt. Ambrose Shearman[7]	P 20 Sept. 33	29 Aug. 35	22 Dec. 45	
12	0	Charles Young[8]………	P 28 Nov. 37	P 22 Nov. 39	8 Oct. 47	
11	0	Lennard Barrett Tyler ..	P 23 Mar. 38	18 July 40	9 Feb. 48	
10	0	William F. Dickson ….	25 Jan. 39	5 July 41	P 11 Feb. 48	
10	0	John Burton Forster[9] ..	P 22 Nov. 39	31 Dec. 41	P 17 Mar. 48	
6	0	R. Humphrey Haviland[14]	P 4 Aug. 43	P 16 Sept. 45	P 8 Dec. 48	
		LIEUTENANTS.				
9	0	Charles Lambert,[10] *adj.*	20 Nov. 40	7 Sept. 42		
8	0	Arthur Murray, *r*…….	31 Dec. 41	P 4 Aug. 43		
8	0	Geo. Perceval Drought[7]	P 2 July 41	P 10 May 44		
6	0	MurdockJohnGregorson[12]	17 Mar. 43	P 27 June 45		
7	0	William Lenox Ingall[13]..	27 Dec. 42	23 July 45		
5	0	Robert Allan Cox[11] ….	16 Feb. 44	22 Dec. 45		
5	0	John M. M. Hewett[16] ..	30 July 44	22 Dec. 45		
6	0	Robert Hedley	P 29 Sept. 43	3 Apr. 46		
4	0	W. B. C. S. Wandesforde[20]	P 4 July 45	P 14 Apr. 46		
3	0	Charles Fleming Steuart	P 12 June 46	P 26 May 48		
4	0	James Daubeny, ……	4 July 45	P 28 April 46		
8	0	John Southcote Mansergh	P 11 June 41	P 9 May 43		
4	0	George Vautier Seale….	P 16 Sept. 45	P 8 Dec. 48		
		ENSIGNS.				
4	0	Timothy Walsh[17] ……	28 Nov. 45			
3	0	Richard Augustus Wood	1 Apr. 46			
3	0	Richard John Edw. Reed	2 Apr. 46			
2	0	John O'Callaghan ……	P 8 Jan. 47			
1	0	Henry Smith Adlington	P 11 Feb. 48			
1	0	Wm. Henry Hopkinson..	P 25 Feb. 48			
1	0	Geo. Hampden Wilkieson	P 8 Dec. 48			
1	0	George O'Donnell ……	22 Dec. 48			

12 Lieut. Gregorson was [illegible] wounded at Ferozeshah (medal).

13 Lt. Ingall served the [illegible] paign on the Sutlej (medal [illegible] ing the battles of Feroze[illegible] (wounded) and Sobraon.

14 Capt. Haviland served the campaign on the Sutlej [illegible] including the battles of Ferozeshah and Sobraon (severely wounded).

15 Lt. Roberts was [illegible] wounded at Ferozeshah [illegible].

16 Lt. Hewett served the [illegible] paign on the Sutlej (medal), [illegible] ing the battles of Ferozeshah (wounded) and Sobraon.

18 Surgeon Wood was present [illegible] the battle of Ferozeshah (medal).

19 Assist.-Surgeon Banon served with the army [illegible] the Sutlej, and was taken prisoner by the Sikhs at [illegible] affair of Buddiwal; and after a captivity of twenty days—twelve of which in irons—he was relieved [illegible] advance of the British force on Lahore.

17 Ensign Walsh served with the 48th in the cam paign against the Rajah of Coorg, in April 1834 [illegible] served with the 55th in China (medal), and was [illegible] sent at the following engagements, viz., at Ar[illegible] Chusan, Chinhae, (including the repulse of the [illegible] attack), Chapoo, Woosung, Shanghai, and storm of Chin-Kiang-Foo.

Full Pay	Half Pay	
31	0	*Paymaster.*—C. H. J. Lane, 24 Jan. 29; *Ens.* 26 Mar. 18; *Lieut.* P 27 May, 24
5	0	*Adjutant.*—*Lieut.* John M. M. Hewett,[16] 15 Dec. 48.
2	0	*Quarter-Master.*—Thomas Boyd, 10 Sept. 47.
17	0	*Surgeon.*—Robert Wood,[18] 3 July 43; *Assist.-Surg.* 31 Aug. 32.
9	0	*Assistant-Surgeon.*—Rich. Geo. Davys Banon,[19] 30 Oct. 40.

Facings Buff.—*Agents,* Messrs. Cox & Co.

[Returned from Bengal, 20 July, 47.]

1 Sir John F. Fitzgerald commanded a light battalion and a brigade in the Peninsula, and has received a cross [illegible] Badajoz, Salamanca, Vittoria, and the Pyrenees.

2 Colonel Reed served the campaign of 1815, including the battle of Waterloo. He commanded a brigade of the Army [illegible] the Sutlej at the battle of Ferozeshah, and was slightly wounded.

3 Lt.-Col. Shortt commanded the 62nd throughout the campaign on the Sutlej (medal), including the battles of Ferozeshah (wounded), and Sobraon.

4 Major Goode served with the 10th in the campaign on the Sutlej (medal), and was present in the battle of Sobraon.

5 Major Mathias served in the campaign on the Sutlej (medal), and commanded a detachment of her Majesty's troops [illegible] the affair of Buddiwal, and in the action at Aliwal, and he was second in command of the 62nd at the battle of Sobraon.

6 Captain Sibley served in the Burmese war. Also at the battle of Ferozeshah (medal), and was severely wounded.

7 Captain Shearman and Lieut. Drought served in the campaign on the Sutlej (medal), and were present at Budd[illegible] Aliwal, and Sobraon.

8 Captain Young served in the campaign on the Sutlej, and was present in the battle of Sobraon (medal).

9 Captain Forster served in the campaign on the Sutlej (medal), including the battles of Ferozeshah and Sobraon; [illegible] former of which he acted as a Major of Brigade, and had a horse shot under him.

10 Lieut. Lambert served in the campaign on the Sutlej (medal), and was present at the affair of Buddiwal, in the [illegible] at Aliwal as Adjutant of a detachment of her Majesty's troops, and at the battle of Sobraon as Adjutant of the 62nd Regt.

11 Lieut. Cox served in the campaign on the Sutlej (medal), including the battles of Ferozeshah and Sobraon.

20 Lieut. Wandesforde served with the 80th in the campaign on the Sutlej, and was severely wounded at the battle of Sobraon (Medal)

"EGMONT-OP-ZEE"—"MARTINIQUE"—"GUADALOUPE."

Years' Serv. Full Pay	Years' Serv. Half Pay	
54		*Colonel.* — P *Sir* Henry Watson,[1] CB. *Cornet*, 6 May, 95; *Lieut.* 10 Feb. 96; *Capt.* 25 June 03; *Major*, 18 Jan. 10; *Lieut.-Col.* 17 Aug. 12; *Col.* 22 July 30; *Major-Gen.* 28 June 38; *Col.* 63rd Regt. 17 May 47.
23	0	*Lieut.-Colonel.*—Arthur Cunliffe Pole, *Ens.* P 7 Nov. 26; *Lieut.* 5 June, 30; *Capt.* P 18 Oct. 33; *Major*, P 1 Dec. 37; *Lieut.-Col.* 2 Sept. 44.
20	0	*Majors.*—Exham Schomberg Turner Swyny, *Ens.* 1 Oct. 29; *Lieut.* P 17 Oct. 33; *Capt.* P 8 Aug. 38; *Major*, P 22 Oct. 47.
22	0	Charles James, *2nd Lieut.* P 29 Nov. 27; *Lieut.* P 20 Jan. 32; *Capt.* P 9 Oct. 35; *Brevet Major*, 9 Nov. 46; *Major*, P 10 Dec. 47.

Full Pay	Half Pay	CAPTAINS.	ENSIGN.	LIEUT.	CAPTAIN.	BREV.-MAJ
19	0	Andrew Timbrell Allan ..	29 Sept. 30	P 28 Dec. 32	P 31 Dec. 41	
16	0	Thomas Harries	P 19 July 33	P 2 May 34	P 26 Jan. 44	
18	16	Charles Higginbotham ..	P 29 June 15	20 Sept. 33	30 June 44	
15	0	Patrick Lindesay	P 21 Feb. 34	P 5 Feb. 36	16 Sept. 45	
14	0	Gustavus Nicolls Harrison	P 5 June 35	P 1 Dec. 37	P 3 Apr. 46	
12	0	Charles Edward Fairtlough	P 12 May 37	P 31 Dec. 39	25 Aug. 46	
11	0	Edw. Jas. Ingleby Fleming	P 26 Jan. 38	17 Aug. 41	P 28 April 46	
12	0	William Fred. Carter ..	P 1 Dec. 37	2 April 41	4 June 47	
11	0	Henry B. Phipps[2]	17 Aug. 38	31 Oct. 40	P 2 Mar. 47	
38	0	George Gardine Shaw[3] ..	P 30 May 11	21 Dec. 13	31 May 39	
12	0	Henry Lees	P 27 Dec. 37	8 Apr. 41	15 Dec. 48	
		LIEUTENANTS.				
9	0	Fra. Charles Annesley ..	P 15 Dec. 40	P 13 May 42		
9	0	W. G. Langrishe Crowther	20 Oct. 40	25 May 42		
8	0	Wm. Frederick Lowrie..	2 April 41	20 April 43		
9	0	Power Le Poer Bookey..	P 15 Dec. 40	P 25 Nov. 42		
7	0	George Aug. Bannatyne..	P 13 May 42	30 June 44		
7	0	James Fairtlough	P 8 Nov. 42	P 30 July 44		
6	0	James Shortall Macauley	18 Aug. 43	18 Nov. 44		
6	0	Arthur J. Le Grand	P 5 Sept. 43	16 April 45		
5	0	H. Mulleneux Walmsley, *ad*	P 28 June 44	25 Sept. 45		
3	0	Francis Douglas Grey[4] ..	9 May 46	P 13 Aug. 47		
7	0	William Henry Emerson[5]	P 2 Apr. 42	P 31 Mar. 43		
10	0	Henry Roe Evans[6]	P 4 May 39	22 July 42		
4	0	D. C. Aug. Delhoste	16 Sept. 45	15 Dec. 48		
		ENSIGNS.				
2	0	G. C. Widdrington Curtois	23 Mar. 47			
2	0	Chas. Le Mesurier Carey	P 13 Aug. 47			
2	0	Cecil Charles Pole	P 22 Oct. 47			
2	0	Edw. R. Charles Sheldon	P 3 Dec. 47			
1	0	John Jeken Cockburn ..	17 Mar. 48			
1	0	F. T. Logan Paterson ..	26 May 48			
1	0	Vincent Mackesy	22 Dec. 48			
1	0	John Dalbiac Luard	22 Dec. 48			

Full Pay	Half Pay	
16	0	*Paymaster.*—John Thorp, 8 Oct. 44; *Ens.* P 27 Sept. 33; *Lieut.* P 5 June 35.
5	0	*Adjutant.*—*Lieut.* Hugh Mulleneux Walmsley, 8 March 47.
9	0	*Quarter-Master*—Edward Joyce, 9 Oct. 40; *Ens.* 4 Sept. 40.
22	0	*Surg.*—Alexander Sheriffe Macdonell,[7] 2 Dec. 42; *Assist.-Surg.* 29 July 30; *Hospital-Assist.* 15 Nov. 27.
7	0	*Assist.-Surgeon.*—Robert Lewins, M.D., 13 Dec. 42.

Facings Green.—*Agents*, Messrs Cox & Co.

[Returned from Madras, August 1847.]

1 Sir Henry Watson served in the Peninsula, and was present at the passage of the Douro and battle of Oporto, capture of Campo Mayor, siege of Olivença, actions of Los Santos and Usagre, battle of Albuhera—in command of the 7th Portuguese cavalry: battle of Fuentes d'Onor, battle of Salamanca—in command of the 1st Portuguese cavalry, at the head of which regt. he was severely wounded in a charge on the leading regt. of Thomiere's division formed in square, which they succeeded in routing and dispersing. Previous to this battle he had been employed in rear of the French army, while they occupied the banks of the Douro, to harass their foraging parties. At the battle of Toulouse he commanded all the Portuguese cavalry excepting the 4th regt. In 1809 he was appointed to instruct and form the Portuguese cavalry. He has received a medal for Salamanca.

2 Captain Phipps served with the 26th in China (Medal).

3 Captain Shaw served at the siege and capture of Hattras, and throughout the Mahratta campaigns of 1817 and 1818. Also at the siege and capture of the Forts of Punella and Powughur in the Southern Mahratta country in 1844-5.

4 Lieut. Grey served as an Ensign in the 24th Bengal N. I. during the campaign on the Sutlej, and was present at the battle of Ferozeshah (Medal).

5 Lieut. Emerson served with the 10th in the campaign on the Sutlej in 1846, and acted as Aide-de-Camp to Brigadier Stacey at the battle of Sobraon (Medal).

6 Lieut. Evans served with the 10th in the campaign on the Sutlej, and was wounded at the battle of Sobraon (Medal).

7 Mr. Macdonell served the campaign on the Sutlej (Medal) with the 80th, including the battles of Moodkee, Ferozeshah, and Sobraon.

"ST. LUCIA"—"SURINAM."

Years' Serv. Full Pay	Half Pay	
		Colonel.
51		Sir Richard Bourke,[1] KCB. *Ens.* 22 Nov. 1798; *Lt. & Capt.* 25 Nov. 99; *Major,* 27 Aug. 1805; *Lieut.-Col.* 16 Sept. 06; *Col.* 4 June, 14; *Major.-Gen.* 19 July, 21; *Lieut.-Gen.* 10 Jan. 37; *Col.* 64th Regt. 29 Nov. 37.
		Lieut.-Colonels.
24	0	James Stopford,[2] CB. *Ens.* P 17 Sept. 25; *Lieut.* P 2 Nov. 26; *Capt.* P 10 Sept. 30; *Major,* P 11 March, 42; *Brevet-Lt.-Col.* 30 April, 44; *Lieut.-Col.* 13 Nov. 47.
23	0	George Duberly, *Ens.* P 28 Jan. 26; *Lieut.* P 24 Dec. 29; *Capt.* P 23 Aug. 33; *Major,* P 29 Sept. 43.
		Majors.
23	0	Maximilian James Western, *Ens.* P 10 June, 26; *Lieut.* P 8 June, 30; *Capt.* P 29 Dec. 35; *Major,* P 11 April, 45.
26	0	James Draper, *Ens.* 18 Dec. 23; *Lieut.* P 19 Nov. 25; *Capt.* P 24 Dec. 29; *Brevet-Major,* 9 Nov. 46, *Major,* 22 Dec. 48.

Full Pay	Half Pay		Ensign.	Lieut.	Captain.	Brev.-Maj.
		Captains.				
19	0	Wm. John James	P 20 July 30	P 20 Apr. 32	P 1 Dec. 37	
15	0	Fred. Arthur Errington	P 21 Feb. 34	P 1 July 36	P 6 May 42	
18	0	Harry Altham Cumberlege	P 2 Dec. 31	22 Apr. 35	P 22 Mar. 44	
11	0	Fra. Henry Kilvington, *s.*	P 20 July 38	P 8 Jan. 41	12 Mar. 48	
13	0	Charles Pattison	P 7 Oct. 36	P 30 Aug 39	P 10 Dec. 47	
10	0	Thomas Stirling	P 23 Apr. 39	P 6 May 42	P 28 Apr. 48	
9	0	Charles Scott Jeffery	P 17 Nov. 40	P 29 Sept. 43	P 21 July 48	
11	0	Geo. W. Powlett Bingham	P 16 Feb. 38	8 April 42	P 12 Sept. 48	
11	0	Frederick Holland	P 26 June 38	15 May 40	P 1 Dec. 48	
7	0	*Hon.* J. Lyon Browne, *r.*	P 14 Jan. 42	P 8 Nov. 44	22 Dec. 48	
		Lieutenants.				
7	0	Isaac Temple Twining	20 May 42	P 17 Jan. 45		
6	0	John Buchanan Burne, *adj.*	P 29 Sept. 43	P 27 Mar. 46		
6	0	William Helsham Candler	P 3 Nov. 43	P 13 Feb. 46		
5	0	Neville Hill Shute	P 22 Mar. 44	P 25 Sept. 46		
6	0	Robert Mockler	12 Sept. 43	12 Jan. 48		
6	0	Henry Francis	P 23 June 43	14 Sept. 45		
4	0	Alfred Picton Bowlby	31 Oct. 45	12 Mar. 48		
3	0	Josiah Marshall Heath	P 1 May 46	P 31 Dec. 47		
3	0	Robert Du Cane	P 3 Apr. 46	P 28 Apr. 48		
3	0	Charles Thompson	P 19 June 46	P 2 June 48		
2	0	William John Chads	P 12 Nov. 47	P 12 Sept. 48		
7	0	Wm. Fletcher Jas. Morphy	26 May 42	10 Nov. 43		
10	0	Sidney Cotton	25 Oct. 39	14 Oct. 42		
6	0	Richard Charles M'Crea[3]	28 July 43	9 Jan. 46		
5	0	Matthew Fanning	1 Feb. 44	14 Apr. 46		
5	0	Geo. Hamilton Twemlow	P 11 Oct. 44	16 May 46		
5	0	Arthur Edward Mulloy	P 17 May 44	P 20 Oct. 46		
5	0	Archibald E. C. Forster	10 May 44	22 Dec. 46		
4	0	Doveton D. Greentree	P 9 May 45	9 Jan. 47		
3	0	Chas. Fred. Brockman	15 Apr. 46	P 15 Oct. 47		
4	0	Godfrey Lyon Knight	28 Feb. 45	17 Mar. 48		
2	0	Walter Johnston	P 8 Oct. 47	P 12 Oct. 48		
3	0	John Henry Capel Loft	14 Apr. 46	22 Dec. 48		
		Ensigns.				
1	0	William Bell	21 Jan. 48			
1	0	William Davies Shipley	P 3 Mar. 48			
1	0	Horatio Glynn Grylls	P 28 Apr. 48			
1	0	John Austen Moultrie	P 29 Apr. 48			
1	0	Augustus Applewhaite	P 2 June 48			
1	0	Francis Fothergill Hood	P 21 July 48			
1	0	H. Hammerton Alexander	P 12 Sept. 48			
1	0	Frederick J. Hutchinson	22 Dec. 48			

Full Pay	Half Pay	
10	0	*Paymaster.*—James Howes, 1 Oct. 47; *Quarter-Master,* 6 Sept. 30.
6	0	*Adjutant.*—*Lieut.* John Buchanan Burne, 16 June, 48.
3	0	*Quarter-Master.*—John Sears, 1 Oct. 47; *Ens.* 8 May 46; *Lt.* P 19 March 47.
23	0	*Surgeon.*—Wm. Smith, 2 July, 41; *Assist.-Surg.* 28 Sept. 26; *Hosp.-Assist.* [9 Mar. 26.
1	0	*Assistant-Surgeon.*—Henry Crisp, 3 Nov. 48.
1	0	Wm. Henry Shortt, 4 Feb. 48.
1	0	Andrew Leith Adams, MD. 1 Dec. 48.

[*Returned from North America* 20 *July,* 43.]

Facings Black.—*Agents,* Messrs. Cox & Co.—*Irish Agents,* Messrs. Cane & Co.

1 Sir Richard Bourke served in Holland in 1799, and was present in the actions of the 27th Aug. 10th and 19th Sept. 2nd and 6th Oct. where he received a severe wound through both jaws. Served as Quarter-Master-General in South America, and was present in the actions of the 19th and 20th Jan. 1807; at the siege and storming of Monte Video, and in the expedition against Buenos Ayres.

2 Lt. Col. Stopford served with the 40th throughout the operations in Candahar and in Affghanistan during 1841 and 42; and he commanded the Regt. in the action of Maharajpore, 29th Dec. 1843, until severely wounded in the side,—he had also a horse cut down under him.

3 Lt. M'Crea served with a detachment of the 17th with Lt. Col. Outram's Light Brigade, in the Southern Mahratta Campaign of 1844–5, and was present in all its operations, including the capture of Gotra and storming of [illegible] stockades.

The *Royal Tiger*, superscribed "INDIA"—"ARABIA."

Years' Serv.		
70		*Colonel.*
Full Pay.	Half Pay.	Thomas Grosvenor,[1] *Ens.* 1 Oct. 1779; *Lieut. & Capt.* 20 Oct. 84; *Capt. & Lt.-Col.* 25 April, 93; *Col.* 3 May, 96; *Major-Gen.* 29 April, 1802; *Lt.-Gen.* 25 April, 08; *Gen.* 12 Aug. 19; *Field Mars.* 9 Nov. 46; *Col.* 65 Regt. 8 Feb. 14.
21	0	*Lieut.-Colonel.*—Charles Emilius Gold, *Ens.* P 20 Mar. 28; *Lt.* P 28 Oct. 31; *Capt.* P 5 Feb. 36; *Major*, P 4 Oct. 44; *Lieut.-Col.* 30 Dec. 45.
23	0	*Majors.*—Alfred Francis W. Wyatt, *Ens.* P 12 Dec. 26; *Lieut.* P 23 Apr. 29; *Capt.* P 19 Sept. 34; *Major*, P 23 Sept. 45.
32	7	James Patience,[3] *Ens.* 5 April, 10; *Lieut.* 24 Oct. 11; *Capt.* 13 Nov. 27; *Brev.-Major*, 23 Nov. 41; *Major*, 30 Dec. 45.

Full Pay	Half Pay	CAPTAINS.	ENSIGN.	LIEUT.	CAPTAIN.	BREV.-MAJ.
21	0	Geo. Freeman Murray ..	26 Apr. 28	P 29 June 32	P 5 Jan. 39	
21	0	Jas. Lewis Smith	P 21 Sept. 28	P 22 Oct. 33	P 17 Apr. 40	
25	12 3/12	P Rickard O'Connell[4] ..	12 May 12	15 July 13	16 July 41	
16	0	J. FitzHerbert de Teissier[5]	P 13 Sept. 33	1 Apr. 36	P 6 May 42	
19	0	William Pym Young ..	P 26 Oct. 30	P 27 Nov. 35	12 Sept. 43	
18	0	Richard Newenham	P 14 June 31	P 5 Feb. 36	P 4 Oct. 44	
14	0	St. Leger Barry	P 27 Nov. 35	10 Jan. 39	P 6 Dec. 44	
13	0	Peter Wolfe	P 22 July 36	P 17 Apr. 40	P 23 Sept. 45	
22	1 8/12	William Johnston[6]	P 7 Jan. 26	P 6 Nov. 27	P 22 Nov. 36	9 Nov. 46
21	2 7/12	Oliver Barker D'Arcey ..	P 8 Apr. 26	P 9 Dec. 31	19 Dec. 45	
		LIEUTENANTS.				
10	0	Christopher Rhatigan, *adj.*	26 Apr. 39	30 Dec. 41		
9	0	Duncan Bazalgette	P 31 Jan. 40	P 31 Dec. 41		
8	0	Charles Alfred Cuthbert	P 19 Mar. 41	12 Sept. 43		
7	0	Thomas Robert M'Coy ..	28 May 42	P 23 June 43		
8	0	Benj. W. Rawson Trafford	P 21 May 41	P 8 Nov. 44		
8	0	Thomas Barnard	16 July 41	P 6 Dec. 44		
8	0	Robert Henry MacGregor	P 31 Dec. 41	P 13 June 45		
8	0	John Gordon	5 Oct. 41	4 July 45		
7	0	George Meyler	P 7 Oct. 42	P 23 Sept. 45		
7	0	Henry Ferdinand Turner	8 Feb. 42	8 Dec. 45		
6	0	John Hervey Elton Elwes	P 6 Oct. 43	P 16 Dec. 45		
6	0	James Paul[7]	8 Nov. 43	19 Dec. 45		
7	0	Chas. Philip O'Connell ..	1 July 42	4 July 45		
		ENSIGNS.				
5	0	Rich. B. Twyford Thelwall	P 8 Nov. 44			
5	0	Fra. Percival Drought ..	P 6 Dec. 44			
5	0	John Ewen	7 Dec. 44			
4	0	James Barton	P 13 June 45			
4	0	Richard Maxwell Slegg ..	P 23 Sept. 45			
3	0	Wm. Fred. Tho. Marshall	13 Mar. 46			
3	0	John W. Hughes Williams	P 21 July 46			
1	0	Thomas George Strange...	22 Dec. 48			

4 Capt O'Connell served in the Peninsula with the 43d Lt. Infantry from April 1812, to the end of that war in 1814, including the capture of Badajos, where he was severely wounded as a volunteer with the storming party; battle of Salamanca, capture of Madrid and the Retiro, retreat from Madrid, action at San Munos, battles of Vittoria and the Pyrenees, action at Lesaca, attack on the heights of Vera, passage of the Bidassoa, and many other minor affairs Severely wounded at the capture of Badajos on the night of the 6th April, 1812, where he served as a volunteer with the storming party.

10 Quarter-Master Paul served against the Pirates in the Persian Gulf, and destruction of Ras-el-Khyma, in 1809; at the capture of the Isle of France in 1810; in the Kattywar country in 1811-12, and taking the Fort of Now Nugger; in the Guzerats and Kutch in 1814, 15, and 16, and taking the forts of Angar, Kincoote, and Dwarka; Mahratta war in the Deccan, 1817 and 18. Capture of Poona and Cutch; storming the hill forts of Booj; Expedition to the Persian Gulf, including the capture of the forts of Ras-el-Khyma and Zaya, 1819. Expedition to Arabia in 1821, including the action at Beni-Boo-Ali, and destruction of the Pirates.

Full Pay	Half Pay	
13	0	*Paymaster.*—J. Williams Marshall, 3 Apr. 46; *Ens.* P 2 Sept. 36; *Lt.* P 19 Mar. 41.
10	0	*Adjutant.*—*Lieut.* C. Rhatigan, 30 Dec. 41.
10	0	*Quarter-Master.*—Thomas Paul,[10] 26 Apr. 39; *Ens.* 25 Jan. 39.
13	0	*Surgeon.*—Robert Keating Prendergast, 14 Apr. 46; *Assist.-Surg.* 7 Oct. 36.
4	0	*Assistant-Surgeons.*—Thomas Esmonde White, M.D., 26 Sept. 45.
4	0	William Ker Park, 31 Oct. 45.

Facings White.—*Agents*, Messrs. Cox & Co.

1 Field Marshal Grosvenor accompanied his regiment (the 3rd Foot Guards) to Holland in 1793, and afterwards into Flanders. In 1799 he went with the expedition to the Helder, and was present in the affair at the lines of Zuype (wounded), the battle of Alkmaer, and the actions of the 17th Sept. and 6th and 9th Oct. Commanded the picquets and out-posts at the siege of Copenhagen on the day of the sortie, when the Danes were repulsed. At the siege of Flushing, he was next in command to Sir Eyre Coote.

3 Major Patience was present at the surrender of Martinique, and at the capture of Les Saintes and Guadaloupe, in 1815.

5 Capt. de Teissier served in Scinde, in command of a detachment, protecting the stores and ammunition of the army, tracked up the Indus Served also in the Light Company of the 17th during the campaign in Affghanistan and Beloochistan, and was present at the storm and capture of the fortresses of Ghuznee and Khelat, for which he has received the Medal.

6 Major Johnston served with the 49th throughout the whole of the operations in China, except the capture of Segoan, and was present at the attack and capture of Chusan (both operations), storm and capture of the heights above Canton, attack and capture of Amoy and Chinhae, occupation of Ningpo and repulse of the night attack, attack and capture of Segoan, Chapoo, Woosung, and Chin Kiang Foo, and demonstration before Nankin.

7 Lieut. Paul served with the 31st throughout the campaign of 1845-6 on the Sutlej (medal), and was present in the battles of Moodkee, Ferozeshah, (wounded), Buddiwal, Aliwal, and Sobraon.

"DOURO"—"TALAVERA"—"ALBUHERA"—"VITTORIA"—"PYRENEES"—"NIVELLE"—"NIVE"—"ORTHES"—"PENINSULA."

Years' Serv. Full Pay.	Half Pay.					
62		*Colonel.*				
		Richard Blunt,[1] *Ens.* 31 Jan. 1787; *Lieut.* 23 Feb. 91; *Capt.* 12 July, 93; *Major,* 17 May, 96; *Lieut.-Col.* 23 Aug. 99; *Col.* 25 Oct. 1809; *Major-Gen.* 1 Jan. 12; *Lt.-Gen.* 27 May, 25; *Gen.* 23 Nov. 41; *Col.* 66th Regt. 25 Mar. 35.				
26	1 1/12	*Lieut.-Colonel.*—Tho. Henry Johnston, *Ens.* P 21 Feb. 22; *Lieut.* P 1 Oct. 25; *Capt.* P 24 Oct. 26; *Major,* P 20 May, 36; *Lieut.-Col.* P 28 Dec. 38.				
21	1/12	*Majors.*—*Sir* William Gordon, *Bart., Ens.* P 5 June 28; *Lieut.* P 27 Apr. 32; *Capt.* P 12 May 37; *Major,* P 6 Nov. 46.				
21	0	Charles Edward Michel; *Ens.* P 25 Nov. 28; *Lieut.* 23 Nov. 33; *Capt.* P 2 Feb. 38; *Major,* P 25 June, 47.				
		Captains.	ENSIGN.	LIEUT.	CAPTAIN.	BREV.-MAJ.
17	0	Geo. Grattan Biscoe	P 7 Apr. 32	P 12 Feb. 36	P 27 Sept. 39	
22	0	John Johnston	P 24 May 27	P 9 Mar. 32	2 Apr. 41	
23	0	George Maxwell........	P 23 Feb. 26	29 May 28	21 Oct. 43	
15	0	Henry John Turner	P 9 May 34	P 22 Nov. 36	P 29 Dec. 43	
14	0	Edw. Montagu Davenport	P 24 Apr. 35	6 Aug. 38	P 31 Dec. 44	
13	0	Fred. Charles Trench....	P 22 Nov. 36	P 28 Dec. 38	P 24 Jan. 45	
12	0	James Hunter Blair Birch	P 15 Dec. 37	P 15 Dec. 40	P 6 Nov. 46	
8	0	HardressDeL.Saunderson	2 April 41	P 30 June 43	P 24 Dec. 47	
8	0	Astley Paston Cooper ..	P 12 Oct. 41	P 20 Oct. 43	P 1 Aug. 48	
7	0	Francis William Astley..	P 4 Mar. 42	P 29 Dec. 43	P 12 Sept. 48	
		Lieutenants.				
10	0	James Hamilton Ross,*adj.*	P 21 June 39	1 Nov. 42		
8	0	George Charles Downman	29 Oct. 41	28 Dec. 43		
7	0	Wm. M. S. Caulfield, *s.*	28 May 42	P 31 Dec. 44		
7	0	Tom Benson	P 8 Nov. 42	P 8 Aug. 45		
4	0	Robert Conner	P 11 July 45	P 6 Nov. 46		
4	0	John Clifton Hawkes....	P 24 Jan. 45	14 Mar. 47		
4	0	Nicholas Kendall	P 11 Nov. 45	P 28 Sept. 47		
3	0	Walter S. Pearce Serocold	P 10 July 46	P 24 Dec. 47		
3	0	Wildman Yates Peel	P 30 Nov. 46	P 1 Aug. 48		
3	0	Frederick Wainwright ..	23 May 46	12 Sept. 48		
3	0	Webster Thomas Gordon	P 1 Dec. 46	P 12 Sept. 48		
2	0	David Robert Ross	2 Apr. 47	26 Oct. 48		
5	0	Charles William Aylmer.	21 Dec. 44	P 28 Aug. 46		
		Ensigns.				
2	0	George Watson	P 9 Apr. 47			
2	0	Richard White	P 25 June 47			
2	0	Arch. Hamilton Dunbar	P 28 Sept. 47			
2	0	Charles Perrin	P 24 Dec. 47			
	0	John Walker	P 25 Nov. 45			
1	0	William Bowles........	P 12 Sept. 48			
1	0	George Glascott Newton	3 Nov. 48			
1	0	Richard Horner Paget ..	1 Dec. 48			
34	6 4/12	*Paymaster.*—Kenneth Tolmie Ross, 11 Aug. 25; *Ens.* 22 June, 09; *Lieut.* 8 Oct. 12.				
10	0	*Adjutant.*—*Lieut.* James Hamilton Ross, 21 Oct. 43.				
7	0	*Quarter-Master.*—Mathew Relley, 27 Sept. 42.				
10	0	*Surgeon.*—Robert G. Montgomery, M.D., 19 Nov. 47; *Assist.-Surg.* 5 July 30.				
5	0	*Assistant-Surgeons.*—Walter Simpson, MD. 23 Feb. 44.				
3	0	Joseph Thomas La Presle, 22 Dec. 46.				

Facings Green.—*Agents,* Messrs. Cox & Co.—*Irish Agents,* Messrs. Cane & Co.

1 General Blunt served in Lord Moira's expedition, and in Flanders in 1794 and 95, and was actively employed in the West Indies, from 1795 until 1802. He has since served in Hanover, Madeira, and in the Peninsula.

"BARROSA"—"PENINSULA"—The *Royal Tiger*, superscribed, "INDIA."

Colonel.

Years' Serv.		
50		ℙ John Clitherow,[1] *Ens.* 19 Dec. 99; *Lieut. & Capt.* 24 Feb. 03; *Capt. & Lieut.-Col.* 8 Oct. 12; *Col.* 25 July, 21; *Major-Gen.* 22 July, 30; *Lieut.-Gen.* 23 Nov. 41; *Col.* 67th F. 15 Jan. 44.
Full Pay.	Half Pay.	
31	4/12	*Lieut.-Colonels.*—Edward Basil Brooke, *2nd Lieut. Royal Artillery*, 15 Dec. 17; *Lt.* 9 April, 25; *Capt.* P 11 July 26; *Major*, P 5 July, 31; *Lt.-Col.* 9 Nov. 46.
27	8 1/12	r. William Nesbitt Orange,[3] *Ens.* 5 Feb. 14; *Lieut.* 19 Jan. 19; *Capt.* P 24 Oct. 21; *Major*, P 15 Aug. 34; *Brevet Lt.-Col.*, 9 Nov. 46; *Lt.-Col.* 3 Sept. 47.
40	0	*Majors.*—ℙ Thomas James Adair,[4] *Ens.* 25 May 09; *Lieut.* 20 Feb. 11; *Capt.* P 27 Mar. 23; *Brevet Major*, 28 June 38; *Major*, 9 Nov. 46.
27	0	r. Thomas Josephus Deverell, *Ens.* 7 Nov. 22; *Lieut.* 25 June 29; *Capt.* P 30 Aug. 31; *Brevet Major*, 9 Nov. 46; *Major*, 3 Sept. 47.

Full Pay	Half Pay	CAPTAINS	ENSIGN.	LIEUT.	CAPTAIN.	BREV.-MAJ.
30	0	Thomas Byrne	4 Nov. 19	5 Mar. 23	22 Jan. 39	
17	0	r. Samuel Hood Murray	P 22 June 32	P 8 Dec. 37	P 1 Nov. 42	
15	0	John Porter	P 28 Mar. 34	P 29 Dec. 37	P 6 Oct. 43	
14	0	Charles Barnard Hague..	P 5 Sept. 35	P 30 Dec. 37	P 5 Dec. 43	
11	0	Frederick Wm. Lane,[5] s.	P 19 Jan. 38	P 6 Dec. 39	P 13 Oct. 43	
13	0	r. Henry Collette........	P 26 Aug. 36	22 Jan. 39	P 23 Feb. 44	
12	0	Thomas P. Onslow......	17 Nov. 37	P 25 May 39	P 11 July 45	
16	0	William Pilsworth......	P 24 May 33	18 Mar. 38	9 Nov. 46	
12	0	r. Capel Coape	P 29 Dec. 37	P 11 Oct. 39	29 Dec. 46	
16	0	r. Stonehouse G. Bunbury, s	P 28 June 33	P 25 Dec. 38	30 Dec. 46	
10	0	r. Walter Caulfield Pratt.	P 25 May 39	15 Sept. 42	P 13 Aug. 47	
10	0	r. William Hayter Hussey	P 8 Nov. 39	P 29 Sept. 43	P 10 Sept. 47	
		LIEUTENANTS.				
9	0	r. Robert Follett Synge[6]	P 20 Oct. 40	26 Sept. 42		
7	0	Robert Hudson Wood ..	P 11 Mar. 42	P 5 Dec. 43		
7	0	Francis Richard Taylor..	28 May 42	16 May 45		
6	0	r. Dugald Stewart Miller	P 24 Feb. 43	P 11 July 45		
7	0	r. Thomas Basil Tuite ..	P 3 Dec. 42	P 23 Aug. 44		
5	0	John Cuthbert Murray..	P 23 Feb. 44	9 Nov. 46		
5	0	r. William Du Vernet[7] ..	22 Mar. 44	29 Jan. 46		
5	0	James Graham, *Adj.*....	3 May 44	29 Dec. 46		
5	0	Fitzmaurice Pratt	P 20 Dec. 44	20 Dec. 46		
4	0	Daniel Thompson	P 11 July 45	P 16 Apr. 47		
4	0	r. *Count* W. Const. Rivarola	P 1 Aug. 45	P 6 Aug. 47		
3	0	William D'Arcy........	10 July 46	P 13 Aug. 47		
3	0	Robert Blakeney	P 3 Nov. 46	P 10 Sept. 47		
3	0	John William Percy	21 Apr. 46	P 30 Mar. 47		
4	0	Henry S. G. S. Knight ..	2 Sept. 45	3 June 47		
		ENSIGNS.				
3	0	r. Edward Daubeney....	29 Dec. 46			
3	0	r. Alfred Addington Jones	29 Dec. 46			
3	0	William Cumming Sheils	31 Dec. 46			
2	0	r. James Anderson, *Adj.*	19 Feb. 47			
2	0	r. Henry Leslie Hunt ..	P 16 Apr. 47			
2	0	r. Edm. Holden Steward	P 6 Aug. 47			
2	0	William Serjeant Arnold	P 13 Aug. 47			
2	0	Vivian Arthur Webber..	P 10 Sept. 47			
1	0	r. Robert Philip Armstrong	P 25 Feb. 48			
1	0	r. William Vesey Munnings	P 10 Mar. 48			
1	0	Charles Matthews	P 30 June 48			

6 Lieut. Synge served with the Cameronians on the China expedition (medal), and carried the colours of the regiment at the repulse of the night attack on Ningpo, the attack and capture of Chapoo, the taking of Shanghae and Woosung, the storming of Chin Kiang Foo, and the operations before Nankin.

7 Lt. Du Vernet was on board the ill-fated *Runnymede*, when that ship was cast away on the Andaman Isles, near Humason, in Nov. 1844, with detachments of the 10th and 50th regts. on board, where he remained for fifty-four days surrounded by Cannibals and suffering great privations. He served afterwards with the 50th in the campaign on the Sutlej (medal), and was present at Buddiwal and Ahwal, at which last he received a slight wound in the right knee from a grape-shot, after which he was severely wounded in the left foot by the bursting of a shell.

9 Paymaster Robinson served at the siege of Asseerghur, March and April, 1819.

Full Pay	Half Pay	
32	0	*Paymaster.*—James Robinson,[9] 26 Dec. 37; *Ens.* 20 Nov. 17; *Lieut.* 24 April, 20.
5	0	*Adjutants.*—*Lieut.* James Graham, 22 Jan. 47.
2	0	r. *Ensign* James Anderson, 3 Sept. 47.
10	0	*Quarter-Masters.*—George Crispin, 25 Oct. 39; *Ens.* 22 Mar. 39.
2	0	r. Thomas McGrath, 3 Sept. 47.
22	0	*Surgeons.*—James Shiels, M.D. 2 July, 41; *Assist.-Surg.* 29 July, 30; *Hosp.-Assist.* 25 Jan. 27.
10	0	r. John Samuel Charlton, 3 Sept. 47; *Assist.-Surg.* 1 Mar. 30.
2	0	*Assistant-Surgeons.*—Thomas Blatherwick, 4 June, 47.
3	0	r. John Henry Dundas, 6 Feb. 46.

Facings Yellow.—*Agents*, Messrs. Cox & Co.

1 Lieut. General Clitherow served the Egyptian campaign of 1801; the expedition to Hanover in 1805; and that to Walcheren, in 1809. In the Peninsula from Dec. 1809 to Dec. 1812, including the battles of Busaco, Fuentes d'Onor (severely wounded), and Salamanca, and siege of Burgos (severely wounded). Served also in France, in 1815. Medal for services in Egypt.

3 Lt.-Col. Orange served on the frontiers of Niagara in 1814 and 15. Served also at the siege and capture of Logmur Issapore, Koarry, and Rhyghur, in the Southern Concan country in India in 1818.

4 Major Adair served in Spain from Sept. 1810 to the end of the war, including the siege of Cadiz, battle of Barrosa, Fort San Philip, Balaguere, Villa Franca, Tarragona and Barcelona. Served also the Nepaul campaigns of 1817 and 18, and subsequently in the Deccan, including the siege and reduction of Rhyghur, Amulnier, and Asseerghur. Twice severely wounded by matchlock balls in the left arm, and right side at the siege of Asseerghur on the evening of the 18th March, 1819, in repulsing a sortie made by the garrison of the fort into the town.

5 Captain Lane served with the 49th on the China Expedition, and was present at the attack and capture of Amoy, Chusan [illegible] severely wounded, left arm amputated on the field

"SALAMANCA"—"VITTORIA"—"PYRENEES"—"NIVELLE" "ORTHES"—"PENINSULA."

Years' Serv. Full Pay.	Half Pay.	
54		*Colonel.* ₱ Charles Nicol,[1] CB., *Ens.* 24 June, 95; *Lt.* 31 Aug. 95; *Capt.* 30 Nov. 95; *Major,* 3 April, 06; *Lt.-Col.* 13 June, 11; *Col.* 27 May, 25; *Major-Gen.* 10 Jan. 37; *Lt.-Gen.* 9 Nov. 46; *Col.* 68th F. 7 Dec. 44.
24	0	*Lieut.-Colonel.*—Richard William Hucy, *Ens.* 26 March, 25; *Lieut.* P 19 Dec. 26, *Capt.* P 11 June, 30, *Major,* P 13 Oct. 38; *Lieut.-Col.* P 31 Dec. 47.
26	0	*Majors.*—Harry Smyth, *Ens.* P 10 July 23; *Lieut.* P 13 Aug. 25; *Capt.* P 15 Oct. 29; *Major,* 21 April, 43.
16	0	Henry Smyth, *Ens.* P 28 June 33; *Lieut.* P 28 Oct. 36; *Capt.* P 2 Dec. 42; *Major,* P 12 May 48.

Full Pay	Half Pay	CAPTAINS.	ENSIGN.	LIEUT.	CAPTAIN.	BREV.-MAJ.
21	0	Wm. Henry Gillman....	P 1 July 28	14 May 31	P 13 May 36	9 Nov. 46
20	0	Geo. Macbeath	P 15 Oct. 29	P 31 May 33	P 28 Oct. 36	9 Nov. 46
16	0	Herbert Blount	P 8 Nov. 33	P 15 Sept. 37	P 23 July 44	
14	0	Heneage Griffith Wynne	P 10 July 35	P 13 Oct. 38	P 30 Jan. 46	
11	0	Alfred Tipping	P 22 June 38	P 30 May 43	P 7 May 47	
8	0	Henry Harpur Greer....	P 10 Sept. 41	P 20 Aug. 44	P 31 Dec. 47	
6	0	Fra. C. P. Amedèe Stuart	P 30 May 43	P 30 Jan. 46	P 31 Mar. 48	
5	0	Samuel Wm. Hen. Hawker	19 Jan. 44	21 Apr. 46	P 14 Apr. 48	
19	10/12	John Edward Lewis	P 12 Jan. 30	23 Jan. 35	13 July 47	
13	0	Henry Needham[2]	16 Sept. 36	27 Nov. 38	30 Dec. 43	
		LIEUTENANTS.				
7	0	Tho. Whitmore Storer, *adj.*	P 2 Dec. 42	P 23 Jan. 46		
5	0	Horatio Harbord Morant	P 20 Aug. 44	P 3 Nov. 46		
4	0	*Hon.* Dan. Greville Finch	P 2 May 45	P 22 Dec. 46		
4	0	Henry G. R. Carmichael	P 16 Dec. 45	P 7 May 47		
4	0	George Hugh Alington ..	P 30 Dec. 45	P 14 May 47		
4	0	Edmund David Lyon....	P 14 Nov. 45	P 8 Oct. 47		
6	0	John Cassidy	19 May 43	P 14 Apr. 46		
3	0	Fred. Stuckley Savage ..	P 30 Jan. 46	P 31 Dec. 47		
3	0	Stephen Croft..........	P 28 Aug. 46	P 14 Apr. 48		
3	0	C. Ughtred Shuttleworth	P 18 Sept. 46	P 12 May 48		
7	0	Thos. De Courcy Hamilton	P 30 Sept. 42	10 Apr. 47		
		ENSIGNS.				
3	0	Ralph Westropp........	P 3 Nov. 46			
3	0	Wm. Francis W. Garforth	P 22 Dec. 46			
2	0	William Henry Seymour	P 7 May 47			
2	0	Charles Samuel Nicol ..	P 14 May 47			
2	0	*Hon.* Eyre C. Hy. Massey	P 8 Oct. 47			
2	0	Charles Edmonstone Kirk	P 5 Nov. 47			
2	0	Thomas H. L. H. Phipps	P 31 Dec. 47			
1	0	J. H. *Visc.* Russborough	P 31 Mar. 48			
1	0	Harrison W. John Trent	P 14 Apr. 48			
1	0	Thomas Tryon	P 12 May 48			

Full Pay	Half Pay	
20	0	*Paymaster.*—Morris Robinson Campbell, 20 Aug. 41; *Ens.* 2 July, 29; *Lieut.* 19 Dec. 35.
7	0	*Adjutant.*—*Lieut.* Thomas Whitmore Storer, 30 March, 47.
1	0	*Quarter-Master.*—Thomas Tunks, 14 Apr. 48.
15	0	*Surgeon.*—Thomas Hunter, M.D., 23 July, 44; *Assist.-Surg.* 18 April, 34.
4	0	*Assistant-Surgeon.*—Robert William Woolcombe, 28 March 45.

Facings Green.—*Agents,* Messrs. Cox & Co.—*Irish Agent,* John Atkinson, *Esq.*

[*Returned from Canada, June,* 1844.]

1 Lieut.-General Nicol commanded the 66th at the battles of Vittoria, the Pyrenees, Nivelle, and Nive. Commanded a division of the army, under Sir David Ochterlony, in the Nepaul war. He has received a medal for the battle of the Nive.

2 Captain Needham served with the 50th in the battle of Punniar (Medal); also the campaign on the Sutlej (Medal) in 1845-6, including the battles of Moodkee (severely wounded) and Sobraon (dangerously wounded).

"JAVA"—"BOURBON"—"WATERLOO"—"INDIA."

Years' Serv. 56 Full Pay.	Half Pay.	
		Colonel.
		P *Sir* Ralph Darling,[1] GCH. *Ens.* 15 May, 1793; *Lieut.* 2 Sept. 95; *Capt.* 6 Sept. 96; *Major,* P2 Feb. 1800; *Lt.-Col.* P17 July, 01; *Col.* 25 July 10; *Maj.-Gen.* 4 June, 13; *Lt.-Gen.* 27 May, 25; *Gen.* 23 Nov. 41; *Col.* 69th Foot, 5 Feb. 48.
		Lieut.-Colonels.
22	0	*r.* William Blackburne, *Ens.* P27 Apr. 27; *Lieut.* P19 Nov. 30; *Capt.* P6 Feb. 35; *Major,* P30 Oct. 40; *Lt.-Col.* 3 Sept. 47.
18	0	Charles James Coote, *Ens.* P21 June 31; *Lieut.* P19 Dec. 34; *Capt.* P14 Apr. 37; *Major,* 3 Sept. 47; *Lieut.-Col.* P10 Nov. 48.
		Majors.
21	0	*Sir* Edmund Stephen Thomas, *Bt.,* *Ens.* P25 Nov. 28; *Lieut.* P28 Oct. 31; *Capt.* P1 May 35; *Major,* P19 May, 46.
21	1 1/12	*r.* James W. Llewellyn Paxton, *Ens.* P19 Apr. 27; *Lieut.* P12 Oct. 30; *Capt.* P6 July 38; *Major,* P10 Nov. 48.

Full Pay	Half Pay	CAPTAINS.	ENSIGN.	LIEUT.	CAPTAIN.	BREV.-MAJ.
31	0	Henry D. O'Halloran ..	1 Nov. 18	P28 June 27	P 1 Sept. 38	
32	4 4/12	P Henry Bridger Tudor[4]	16 May 13	19 Oct. 20	27 April 40	
16	0	William Walker........	2 Aug. 33	P 1 May 35	P 1 Nov. 40	
16	0	*r.* David Elliot Mackirdy	P 5 Apr. 33	P30 Dec. 36	P26 June 41	
14	8/12	Arthur Lowry Cole	P22 Aug. 34	P20 Nov. 38	P 7 Sept. 41	
14	0	*r.* Cecil Edward Bewes ..	P 7 Aug. 35	P 4 Oct. 39	P27 Oct. 43	
18	0	Wm. J. B. M'Leod Moore	1 Nov. 31	4 Jan. 36	18 Sept. 46	
13	0	*r.* Charles Fred. Law....	P 7 Oct. 36	P 8 Nov. 39	P 9 Oct. 46	
14	0	James Handasyde Edgar	P 9 Oct. 35	P28 June 39	29 Jan. 47	
11	0	*r.* Percival Fenwick	P28 Sept. 38	P 1 Nov. 40	P14 May 47	
15	2 1/12	George Floyd Duckett ..	P 4 May 32	P29 Aug. 34	P 5 July 39	
8	0	Charles John Carmichael	29 Jan. 41	P 8 Aug. 45	P10 Nov. 48	
		LIEUTENANTS.				
9	0	Charles William Parker	20 Oct. 40	23 May 45		
9	0	Aug. Barnard Hankey ..	P30 Oct. 40	P20 June 45		
8	0	*r.* Edward Bowen, *Adj*...	1 June 41	P 2 Sept. 45		
5	0	*r.* F. Wentworth Bennett	P20 Aug. 44	P19 May 46		
7	0	*r.* F. George Wm. Fearon	27 May 42	24 May 45		
7	0	*r.* Gordon Henry Evans, *r.*	8 Nov. 42	18 Sept. 46		
4	0	Denis Dunne, *adj*	23 May 45	18 Sept. 46		
8	0	*r.* Charles Eyre Butler ..	P24 Sept. 41	24 Sept. 46		
4	0	*r.* George Bagot........	P20 June 45	P25 Sept. 46		
4	0	Thomas Harvey	P 9 Aug. 45	P14 May 47		
8	0	*r.* Rodney Payne O'Shea	16 July 41	20 Apr. 44		
4	0	William Shepherd Milner	P28 Nov. 45	3 Sept. 47		
3	0	*r.* William George Daniel	4 Apr. 46	P24 Dec. 47		
3	0	Francis Gamble Blood ..	12 June 46	P14 Apr. 48		
3	0	James Smyth	P25 Sept. 46	P12 Sept. 48		
3	0	Richard Fitzgerald	18 Sept. 46	P10 Nov. 48		
		ENSIGNS.				
3	0	*r.* Charles Gilborne	17 Sept. 46			
2	0	Alex. Edgar M'Gregor ..	2 Apr. 47			
2	0	*r.* William Tracey	11 June 47			
2	0	John Lindsay Maclean ..	13 July 47			
2	0	*r.* Henry Chas. Strickland	3 Sept. 47			
2	0	Henry Beauchamp Brady	P24 Dec. 47			
1	0	George Fred. Gildea	P14 Apr. 48			
3	0	Herbert Charles Gray ..	20 Nov. 46			
1	0	Edward Marcon	13 Sept. 48			
1	0	Wm. L. Barnard Straton	P10 Nov. 48			

4 Capt. Tudor served in the Peninsula from May 1813 to the end of the war.

5 Captain Robinson served with the 55th in the operations against the Rajah of Coorg in April, 1834, and was wounded.

Full Pay	Half Pay	
28	0	*Paymaster.*—F. Henry Dalgety, 1 March, 39; *Ens.* 11 Jan. 21; *Lt.* 23 Mar. 26.
4	0	*Adjutants.*—*Lieut.* Denis Dunne, 30 April, 47.
8	0	*r. Lieut.* Edward Bowen, 3 Sept. 47.
12	0	*Quarter-Masters.*—James Hollis, 3 Nov. 37.
2	0	*r.* Robert Smyth, 3 Sept. 47.
10	0	*Surgeons.*—*r.* John Bathurst Thomson, M.D. 3 Sept. 46; *A.-S.* 11 Jan. 39.
10	0	Henry James Schooles, M.D., 1 Oct. 47; *Assist.-Surg.* 28 June 39.
2	0	*Assist.-Surgeons.*—*r.* Arthur Stewart Willocks, 3 Sept. 47.
1	0	William Watson Somerville, M.D. 22 Dec. 48.

Facings Green.—*Agents,* Messrs. Cox & Co.

1 Sir Ralph Darling's services:—In 1795, the slaves in the island of Granada, assisted by the French from Guadaloupe, having revolted and murdered the Governor and upwards of forty of the principal inhabitants, he was employed with his Regt. (the 45th) in quelling the insurrection. In Jan. 1797, volunteered on the expedition against Trinidad, and was present at the destruction of the Spanish ships of war, and at the surrender of the island. In July 1799, proceeded with the expedition against the Dutch settlement of Surinam, and was employed in the arrangements for the capitulation, and present at the surrender of that colony. In April 1801, proceeded with the expedition against the Danish and Swedish islands, St. Croix, St. Thomas, St. Martin, and St. Bartholomew, and was present at their reduction. In September 1808, his Regt. (the 51st) being ordered on active service, he resigned his staff employment (Principal Assist. Adjt.-General) and took the command of it. Joined the army under Sir John Moore, in Spain, and was present during the advance and retreat, the action at Lugo, and battle of Corunna, for which last he received a Medal. In July 1809, was appointed Dep. Adjt.-General to the Force sent to the Scheldt under

"NIVE"—"PENINSULA."—"FEROZESHAH."—"SOBRAON."

Years' Serv. Full Pay.	Half Pay.	
56		*Colonel.* Sir John Forster Fitzgerald,[1] KCB. *Ens.* 29 Oct. 93; *Lieut.* 31 Jan. 94; *Capt.* 9 May, 94; *Major,* 25 Sept. 03; *Lieut.-Col.* 25 July, 10; *Col* 12 Aug. 19; *Major-Gen.* 22 July, 30; *Lt.-Gen.* 23 Nov. 41; *Col.* 62nd, 21 Nov. 43.
31	4 8/12	*Lieut.-Colonel.*—Thomas Reed[2], CB. *Cornet,* 26 Aug. 13; *Lt.* P 2 May, 15; *Capt.* P 19 Feb. 24; *Maj.* P 15 June, 26; *Lt.-Col.* P 11 Aug. 29; *Col.* 23 No. 41.
24	0	*Majors.*—Wm. T. Shortt,[3] *Ens.* 25 March, 25; *Lieut.* P 30 Dec. 26; *Capt.* P 26 Feb. 29; *Major,* 16 April, 41; *Brevet Lt.-Col.* 3 Apr. 46.
30	1/12	William Henry Goode,[4] *Ens.* 21 May 18; *Lieut.* P 31 July 23; *Capt.* 29 Dec. 40; *Maj.* 5 Sept 45.

Full Pay	Half Pay	CAPTAINS.	ENSIGN.	LIEUT.	CAPTAIN.	BREV.-MAJ.
20	0	William Ambrose Pender	P 25 June 29	3 Mar. 33	P 12 Jan. 38	
18	0	Wm. Mathias[5]	P 8 Feb. 31	P 29 Mar. 33	P 16 Mar. 38	19 June 46
17	0	George Edward Olpherts	P 20 Jan. 32	12 Oct. 33	P 16 April 41	
25	0	Charles Wm. Sibley[6]....	27 Nov. 24	16 Oct. 26	19 Aug. 42	
16	0	Robt. Ambrose Shearman[7]	P 20 Sept. 33	29 Aug. 35	22 Dec. 45	
12	0	Charles Young[8].........	P 28 Nov. 37	P 22 Nov. 39	8 Oct. 47	
11	0	Lennard Barrett Tyler ..	P 23 Mar. 38	18 July 40	9 Feb. 48	
10	0	William F. Dickson	25 Jan. 39	5 July 41	P 11 Feb. 48	
10	0	John Burton Forster[9] ..	P 22 Nov. 30	31 Dec. 41	P 17 Mar. 48	
6	0	R. Humphrey Haviland[14]	P 4 Aug. 43	P 16 Sept. 45	P 8 Dec. 48	
		LIEUTENANTS.				
9	0	Charles Lambert,[10] *adj.*	20 Nov. 40	7 Sept. 42		
8	0	Arthur Murray, *r*........	31 Dec. 41	P 4 Aug. 43		
8	0	Geo. Perceval Drought[7]	P 2 July 41	P 10 May 44		
6	0	MurdockJohnGregorson[12]	17 Mar. 43	P 27 June 45		
7	0	William Lenox Ingall[13]..	27 Dec. 42	23 July 45		
5	0	Robert Allan Cox[11]	16 Feb. 44	22 Dec. 45		
5	0	John M. M. Hewett[16] ..	30 July 44	22 Dec. 45		
6	0	Robert Hedley	P 29 Sept. 43	3 Apr. 46		
4	0	W. B. C. S. Wandesforde[20]	P 4 July 45	P 14 Apr. 46		
3	0	Charles Fleming Steuart	P 12 June 46	P 26 May 48		
4	0	James Daubeny, ...	4 July 45	P 28 April 46		
8	0	John Southcote Mansergh	P 11 June 41	P 9 May 43		
4	0	George Vautier Seale....	P 16 Sept. 45	P 8 Dec. 48		
		ENSIGNS.				
4	0	Timothy Walsh[17]	28 Nov. 45			
3	0	Richard Augustus Wood	1 Apr. 46			
3	0	Richard John Edw. Reed	2 Apr. 46			
2	0	John O'Callaghan	P 8 Jan. 47			
1	0	Henry Smith Adlington	P 11 Feb. 48			
1	0	Wm. Henry Hopkinson..	P 25 Feb. 48			
1	0	Geo. Hampden Wilkieson	P 8 Dec. 48			
1	0	George O'Donnell	22 Dec. 48			

12 Lieut. Gregorson was se[verely] wounded at Ferozeshah (medal).

13 Lt. Ingall served the cam[paign] on the Sutlej (medal), [includ]ing the battles of Feroze[shah] (wounded) and Sobraon.

14 Capt. Haviland served [the] campaign on the Sutlej (meda[l]) including the battles of Fero[zeshah] and Sobraon (severely wounde[d]).

15 Lt. Roberts was se[verely] wounded at Ferozeshah (meda[l]).

16 Lt. Hewett served the cam[paign] on the Sutlej (medal), [includ]ing the battles of Ferozes[hah] (wounded) and Sobraon.

18 Surgeon Wood was present at the battle of Ferozeshah (meda[l]).

19 Assist.-Surgeon Banon served with the army [on] the Sutlej, and was taken prisoner by the Sikhs a[t the] affair of Buddiwal; and after a captivity of twenty days—twelve of which in irons—he was released [on the] advance of the British force on Lahore.

17 Ensign Walsh served with the 48th in the cam[paign] against the Rajah of Coorg, in April 1834 — served with the 55th in China (medal), and was present at the following engagements, viz., at Chusan, Chinhae, (including the repulse of the [night] attack), Chapoo, Woosung, Shanghai, and storming Chin-Kiang-Foo.

Full Pay	Half Pay	
31	0	*Paymaster.*—C. H. J. Lane, 24 Jan. 29; *Ens.* 26 Mar. 18; *Lieut.* P 27 May, 2[illegible]
5	0	*Adjutant.*—*Lieut.* John M. M. Hewett,[16] 15 Dec. 48.
2	0	*Quarter-Master.*—Thomas Boyd, 10 Sept. 47.
17	0	*Surgeon.*—Robert Wood,[18] 3 July 43; *Assist.-Surg.* 31 Aug. 32.
9	0	*Assistant-Surgeon.*—Rich. Geo. Davys Banon,[19] 30 Oct. 40.

Facings Buff.—*Agents,* Messrs. Cox & Co.

[Returned from Bengal, 20 July, 47.]

1 Sir John F. Fitzgerald commanded a light battalion and a brigade in the Peninsula, and has received a cross f[or] Badajos, Salamanca, Vittoria, and the Pyrenees.

2 Colonel Reed served the campaign of 1815, including the battle of Waterloo. He commanded a brigade of the Army [of] the Sutlej at the battle of Ferozeshah, and was slightly wounded.

3 Lt.-Col. Shortt commanded the 62nd throughout the campaign on the Sutlej (medal), including the battles of Feroze[shah] (wounded), and Sobraon.

4 Major Goode served with the 10th in the campaign on the Sutlej (medal), and was present in the battle of Sobraon.

5 Major Mathias served in the campaign on the Sutlej (medal), and commanded a detachment of her Majesty's troops [at] the affair of Buddiwal, and in the action at Aliwal, and he was second in command of the 62nd at the battle of Sobraon.

6 Captain Sibley served in the Burmese war. Also at the battle of Ferozeshah (medal), and was severely wounded.

7 Captain Shearman and Lieut. Drought served in the campaign on the Sutlej (medal), and were present at Buddi[wal], Aliwal, and Sobraon.

8 Captain Young served in the campaign on the Sutlej, and was present in the battle of Sobraon (medal).

9 Captain Forster served in the campaign on the Sutlej (medal), including the battles of Ferozeshah and Sobraon, [in the] former of which he acted as a Major of Brigade, and had a horse shot under him.

10 Lieut. Lambert served in the campaign on the Sutlej (medal), and was present at the affair of Buddiwal, in the [action] at Aliwal as Adjutant of a detachment of her Majesty's troops, and at the battle of Sobraon as Adjutant of the 62nd Regt.

11 Lieut. Cox served in the campaign on the Sutlej (medal), including the battles of Ferozeshah and Sobraon.

20 Lieut. Wandesforde served with the 80th in the campaign on the Sutlej, and was severely wounded at the [battle of] Sobraon (Medal)

"EGMONT-OP-ZEE"—"MARTINIQUE"—"GUADALOUPE."

Years' Serv.						
54		*Colonel.*				
Full Pay.	Half Pay.	P *Sir* Henry Watson,[1] CB. *Cornet*, 6 May, 95; *Lieut.* 10 Feb. 96; *Capt.* 25 June 03; *Major*, 18 Jan. 10; *Lieut.-Col.* 17 Aug. 12; *Col.* 22 July 30; *Major-Gen.* 28 June 38; *Col.* 63rd Regt. 17 May 47.				
23	0	*Lieut.-Colonel.*—Arthur Cunliffe Pole, *Ens.* P7 Nov. 26; *Lieut.* 5 June, 30; *Capt.* P18 Oct. 33; *Major*, P1 Dec. 37; *Lieut.-Col.* 2 Sept. 44.				
20	0	*Majors.*—Exham Schomberg Turner Swyny, *Ens.* 1 Oct. 29; *Lieut.* P17 Oct. 33; *Capt.* P8 Aug. 38; *Major*, P22 Oct. 47.				
22	0	Charles James, *2nd Lieut.* P29 Nov. 27; *Lieut.* P20 Jan. 32; *Capt.* P9 Oct. 35; *Brevet Major*, 9 Nov. 46; *Major*, P10 Dec. 47.				
		CAPTAINS.	ENSIGN.	LIEUT.	CAPTAIN.	BREV.-MAJ
19	0	Andrew Timbrell Allan..	29 Sept. 30	P28 Dec. 32	P31 Dec. 41	
16	0	Thomas Harries........	P19 July 33	P 2 May 34	P26 Jan. 44	
18	16	Charles Higginbotham ..	P29 June 15	20 Sept. 33	30 June 44	
15	0	Patrick Lindesay	P21 Feb. 34	P 5 Feb. 36	16 Sept. 45	
14	0	Gustavus Nicolls Harrison	P 5 June 35	P 1 Dec. 37	P 3 Apr. 46	
12	0	Charles Edward Fairtlough	P12 May 37	P31 Dec. 39	25 Aug. 46	
11	0	Edw. Jas. Ingleby Fleming	P26 Jan. 38	17 Aug. 41	P28 April 46	
12	0	William Fred. Carter ..	P 1 Dec. 37	2 April 41	4 June 47	
11	0	Henry B. Phipps[2]......	17 Aug. 38	31 Oct. 40	P 2 Mar. 47	
38	0	George Gardine Shaw[3] ..	P30 May 11	21 Dec. 13	31 May 39	
12	0	Henry Lees	P27 Dec. 37	8 Apr. 41	15 Dec. 48	
		LIEUTENANTS.				
9	0	Fra. Charles Annesley ..	P15 Dec. 40	P13 May 42		
9	0	W.G. Langrishe Crowther	20 Oct. 40	25 May 42		
8	0	Wm. Frederick Lowrie..	2 April 41	20 April 43		
9	0	Power Le Poer Bookey..	P 15 Dec. 40	P25 Nov. 42		
7	0	George Aug. Bannatyne..	P13 May 42	30 June 44		
7	0	James Fairtlough	P 8 Nov. 42	P30 July 44		
6	0	James Shortall Macauley	18 Aug. 43	18 Nov. 44		
6	0	Arthur J. Le Grand	P 5 Sept. 43	16 April 45		
5	0	H. Mulleneux Walmsley, *ad*	P 28 June 44	25 Sept. 45		
3	0	Francis Douglas Grey[4] ..	9 May 46	P13 Aug. 47		
7	0	William Henry Emerson[5]	P 2 Apr. 42	P31 Mar. 43		
10	0	Henry Roe Evans[6]	P 4 May 39	22 July 42		
4	0	D. C. Aug. Delhoste	16 Sept. 45	15 Dec. 48		
		ENSIGNS.				
2	0	G. C. Widdrington Curtois	23 Mar. 47			
2	0	Chas. Le Mesurier Carey	P13 Aug. 47			
2	0	Cecil Charles Pole	P22 Oct. 47			
2	0	Edw. R. Charles Sheldon	P 3 Dec. 47			
1	0	John Jeken Cockburn ..	17 Mar. 48			
1	0	F. T. Logan Paterson ..	26 May 48			
1	0	Vincent Mackesy	22 Dec. 48			
1	0	John Dalbiac Luard	22 Dec. 48			
16	0	*Paymaster.*—John Thorp, 8 Oct. 44; *Ens.* P27 Sept. 33; *Lieut.* P5 June 35.				
5	0	*Adjutant.*—*Lieut.* Hugh Mulleneux Walmsley, 8 March 47.				
9	0	*Quarter-Master*—Edward Joyce, 9 Oct. 40; *Ens.* 4 Sept. 40.				
22	0	*Surg.*—Alexander Sheriffe Macdonell,[7] 2 Dec. 42; *Assist.-Surg.* 29 July 30; *Hospital-Assist.* 15 Nov. 27.				
7	0	*Assist.-Surgeon.*—Robert Lewins, M.D., 13 Dec. 42.				

Facings Green.—*Agents*, Messrs Cox & Co.

[Returned from Madras, August 1847.]

1 Sir Henry Watson served in the Peninsula, and was present at the passage of the Douro and battle of Oporto, capture of Campo Mayor, siege of Olivença, actions of Los Santos and Usagre, battle of Albuhera—in command of the 7th Portuguese cavalry: battle of Fuentes d'Onor, battle of Salamanca—in command of the 1st Portuguese cavalry, at the head of which regt. he was severely wounded in a charge on the leading regt. of Thomiere's division formed in square, which they succeeded in routing and dispersing. Previous to this battle he had been employed in rear of the French army, while they occupied the banks of the Douro, to harass their foraging parties. At the battle of Toulouse he commanded all the Portuguese cavalry excepting the 4th regt. In 1809 he was appointed to instruct and form the Portuguese cavalry. He has received a medal for Salamanca.

2 Captain Phipps served with the 26th in China (Medal).

3 Captain Shaw served at the siege and capture of Hattras, and throughout the Mahratta campaigns of 1817 and 1818. Also at the siege and capture of the Forts of Punella and Pownghur in the Southern Mahratta country in 1844-5.

4 Lieut. Grey served as an Ensign in the 24th Bengal N. I. during the campaign on the Sutlej, and was present at the battle of Ferozeshah (Medal).

5 Lieut. Emerson served with the 10th in the campaign on the Sutlej in 1846, and acted as Aide de-Camp to Brigadier Stacey at the battle of Sobraon (Medal).

6 Lieut. Evans served with the 10th in the campaign on the Sutlej, and was wounded at the battle of Sobraon (Medal).

7 Mr. Macdonell served the campaign on the Sutlej (Medal) with the 80th, including the battles of Moodkee, Ferozeshah, and Sobraon.

"ST. LUCIA"—"SURINAM."

Years' Serv. Full Pay.	Half Pay.	
51		*Colonel.*
		⚜ Sir Richard Bourke,[1] KCB. *Ens.* 22 Nov. 1798; *Lt. & Capt.* 25 Nov. 99; *Major,* 27 Aug. 1805; *Lieut.-Col.* 16 Sept. 06; *Col.* 4 June, 14; *Major.-Gen.* 19 July, 21; *Lieut.-Gen.* 10 Jan. 37; *Col.* 64th Regt. 29 Nov. 37.
		Lieut.-Colonels.
24	0	James Stopford,[2] CB. *Ens.* P 17 Sept. 25; *Lieut.* P 2 Nov. 26; *Capt.* P 10 Sept. 30; *Major,* P 11 March, 42; *Brevet-Lt.-Col.* 30 April, 44; *Lieut.-Col.* 13 Nov. 47.
23	0	George Duberly, *Ens.* P 28 Jan. 26; *Lieut.* P 24 Dec. 29; *Capt.* P 23 Aug. 33; *Major,* P 29 Sept. 43.
		Majors.
23	0	Maximilian James Western, *Ens.* P 10 June, 26; *Lieut.* P 8 June, 30; *Capt.* P 29 Dec. 35; *Major,* P 11 April, 45.
26	0	James Draper, *Ens.* 18 Dec. 23; *Lieut.* P 19 Nov. 25; *Capt.* P 24 Dec. 29; *Brevet-Major,* 9 Nov. 46, *Major,* 22 Dec. 48.

Full Pay.	Half Pay.	CAPTAINS.	ENSIGN.	LIEUT.	CAPTAIN.	BREV.-MAJ.
19	0	Wm. John James	P 20 July 30	P 20 Apr. 32	P 1 Dec. 37	
15	0	Fred. Arthur Errington..	P 21 Feb. 34	P 1 July 36	P 6 May 42	
18	0	Harry Altham Cumberlege	P 2 Dec. 31	22 Apr. 35	P 22 Mar. 44	
11	0	Fra. Henry Kilvington, *s.*	P 20 July 38	P 8 Jan. 41	12 Mar. 48	
13	0	Charles Pattison	P 7 Oct. 36	P 30 Aug 39	P 10 Dec. 47	
10	0	Thomas Stirling	P 23 Apr. 39	P 6 May 42	P 28 Apr. 48	
9	0	Charles Scott Jeffery	P 17 Nov. 40	P 29 Sept. 43	P 21 July 48	
11	0	Geo. W. Powlett Bingham	P 16 Feb. 38	8 April 42	P 12 Sept. 48	
11	0	Frederick Holland......	P 26 June 38	15 May 40	P 1 Dec. 48	
7	0	*Hon.* J. Lyon Browne, *r.*	P 14 Jan. 42	P 8 Nov. 44	22 Dec. 48	
		LIEUTENANTS.				
7	0	Isaac Temple Twining ..	20 May 42	P 17 Jan. 45		
6	0	John Buchanan Burne, *adj.*	P 29 Sept. 43	P 27 Mar. 46		
6	0	William Helsham Candler	P 3 Nov. 43	P 13 Feb. 46		
5	0	Neville Hill Shute	P 22 Mar. 44	P 25 Sept. 46		
6	0	Robert Mockler	12 Sept. 43	12 Jan. 48		
6	0	Henry Francis	P 23 June 43	14 Sept. 45		
4	0	Alfred Picton Bowlby ..	31 Oct. 45	12 Mar. 48		
3	0	Josiah Marshall Heath ..	P 1 May 46	P 31 Dec. 47		
3	0	Robert Du Cane	P 3 Apr. 46	P 28 Apr. 48		
3	0	Charles Thompson	P 19 June 46	P 2 June 48		
2	0	William John Chads	P 12 Nov. 47	P 12 Sept. 48		
7	0	Wm. Fletcher Jas. Morphy	28 May 42	10 Nov. 43		
10	0	Sidney Cotton	25 Oct. 39	14 Oct. 42		
6	0	Richard Charles M'Crea[3]	28 Jul 43	9 Jan. 46		
5	0	Matthew Fanning	1 Feb. 44	14 Apr. 46		
5	0	Geo. Hamilton Twemlow.	P 11 Oct. 44	16 May 46		
5	0	Arthur Edward Mulloy..	P 17 May 44	P 20 Oct. 46		
5	0	Archibald E. C. Forster..	10 May 44	22 Dec. 46		
4	0	Doveton D. Greentree ..	P 9 May 45	9 Jan. 47		
3	0	Chas. Fred. Brockman..	15 Apr. 46	P 15 Oct. 47		
4	0	Godfrey Lyon Knight ..	28 Feb. 45	17 Mar. 48		
2	0	Walter Johnston	P 8 Oct. 47	P 12 Oct. 48		
3	0	John Henry Capel Loft ..	14 Apr. 46	22 Dec. 48		
		ENSIGNS.				
1	0	William Bell	21 Jan. 48			
1	0	William Davies Shipley..	P 3 Mar. 48			
1	0	Horatio Glynn Grylls ..	P 28 Apr. 48			
1	0	John Austen Moultrie ..	P 20 Apr. 48			
1	0	Augustus Applewhaite ..	P 2 June 48			
1	0	Francis Fothergill Hood	P 21 July 48			
1	0	H. Hammerton Alexander	P 12 Sept. 48			
1	0	Frederick J. Hutchinson	22 Dec. 48			

Full Pay.	Half Pay.	
10	0	*Paymaster.*—James Howes, 1 Oct. 47; *Quarter-Master,* 6 Sept. 39.
6	0	*Adjutant.*—*Lieut.* John Buchanan Burne, 16 June, 48.
3	0	*Quarter-Master.*—John Sears, 1 Oct. 47; *Ens.* 8 May 46; *Lt.* P 19 March 47.
23	0	*Surgeon.*—Wm. Smith, 2 July, 41; *Assist.-Surg.* 28 Sept. 26; *Hosp.-Assist.* [9 Mar. 26.
1	0	*Assistant-Surgeon.*—Henry Crisp, 3 Nov. 48.
1	0	Wm. Henry Shortt, 4 Feb. 48.
1	0	Andrew Leith Adams, MD. 1 Dec. 48.

1 Sir Richard Bourke served in Holland in 1799, and was present in the actions of the 27th Aug. 10th and 19th Sept. 2nd and 6th Oct. where he received a severe wound through both jaws. Served as Quarter-Master-General in South America, and was present in the actions of the 19th and 20th Jan. 1807; at the siege and storming of Monte Video, and in the expedition against Buenos Ayres.

2 Lt. Col. Stopford served with the 40th throughout the operations in Candahar and in Affghanistan during 1841 and 42; and he commanded the Regt. in the action of Maharajpore, 29th Dec. 1843, until severely wounded in the side,—he had also a horse cut down under him.

3 Lt. M'Crea served with a detachment of the 17th with Lt. Col. Outram's Light Brigade, in the Southern Mahratta Campaign of 1844–5, and was present in all its operations, including the capture of Gotra and storming of Monoghur stockades.

[*Returned from North America* 20 *July,* 43.]

Facings Black.—*Agents,* Messrs. Cox & Co.—*Irish Agents,* Messrs. Cane & Co.

The *Royal Tiger*, superscribed "INDIA"—"ARABIA."

Years' Serv. 70 Full Pay.	Half Pay.	
		Colonel.
		Thomas Grosvenor,[1] *Ens.* 1 Oct. 1779; *Lieut. & Capt.* 20 Oct. 84; *Capt. & Lt.-Col.* 25 April, 93; *Col.* 3 May, 96; *Major-Gen.* 29 April, 1802; *Lt.-Gen.* 25 April, 08; *Gen.* 12 Aug. 19; *Field Mars.* 9 Nov. 46; *Col.* 65 Regt. 8 Feb. 14.
21	0	*Lieut.-Colonel.*—Charles Emilius Gold, *Ens.* P 20 Mar. 28; *Lt.* P 28 Oct. 31; *Capt.* P 5 Feb. 36; *Major,* P 4 Oct. 44; *Lieut.-Col.* 30 Dec. 45.
23	0	*Majors.*—Alfred Francis W. Wyatt, *Ens.* P 12 Dec. 26; *Lieut.* P 23 Apr. 29; *Capt.* P 19 Sept. 34; *Major,* P 23 Sept. 45.
32	7	James Patience,[3] *Ens.* 5 April, 10; *Lieut.* 24 Oct. 11; *Capt.* 13 Nov. 27; *Brev.-Major,* 23 Nov. 41; *Major,* 30 Dec. 45.

Full Pay	Half Pay	CAPTAINS.	ENSIGN.	LIEUT.	CAPTAIN.	BREV.-MAJ.
21	0	Geo. Freeman Murray ..	26 Apr. 28	P 29 June 32	P 5 Jan. 39	
21	0	Jas. Lewis Smith	P 21 Sept. 28	P 22 Oct. 33	P 17 Apr. 40	
25	$12\frac{2}{12}$	B Rickard O'Connell[4] ..	12 May 12	15 July 13	16 July 41	
16	0	J. FitzHerbert de Teissier[5]	P 13 Sept. 33	1 Apr. 36	P 6 May 42	
19	0	William Pym Young ..	P 26 Oct. 30	P 27 Nov. 35	12 Sept. 43	
18	0	Richard Newenham	P 14 June 31	P 5 Feb. 36	P 4 Oct. 44	
14	0	St. Leger Barry	P 27 Nov. 35	10 Jan. 39	P 6 Dec. 44	
13	0	Peter Wolfe	P 22 July 36	P 17 Apr. 40	P 23 Sept. 45	
22	$1\frac{8}{12}$	William Johnston[6]	P 7 Jan. 26	P 6 Nov. 27	P 22 Nov. 36	9 Nov. 46
21	$2\frac{7}{12}$	Oliver Barker D'Arcey ..	P 8 Apr. 26	P 9 Dec. 31	19 Dec. 45	
		LIEUTENANTS.				
10	0	Christopher Rhatigan, *adj.*	26 Apr. 39	30 Dec. 41		
9	0	Duncan Bazalgette	P 31 Jan. 40	P 31 Dec. 41		
8	0	Charles Alfred Cuthbert	P 19 Mar. 41	12 Sept. 43		
7	0	Thomas Robert M'Coy ..	28 May 42	P 23 June 43		
8	0	Benj. W. Rawson Trafford	P 21 May 41	P 8 Nov. 44		
8	0	Thomas Barnard	16 July 41	P 6 Dec. 44		
8	0	Robert Henry MacGregor	P 31 Dec. 41	P 13 June 45		
8	0	John Gordon	5 Oct. 41	4 July 45		
7	0	George Meyler	P 7 Oct. 42	P 23 Sept. 45		
7	0	Henry Ferdinand Turner	8 Feb. 42	8 Dec. 45		
6	0	John Hervey Elton Elwes	P 6 Oct. 43	P 16 Dec. 45		
6	0	James Paul[7]	8 Nov. 43	19 Dec. 45		
7	0	Chas. Philip O'Connell..	1 July 42	4 July 45		
		ENSIGNS.				
5	0	Rich. B. Twyford Thelwall	P 8 Nov. 44			
5	0	Fra. Percival Drought ..	P 6 Dec. 44			
5	0	John Ewen	7 Dec. 44			
4	0	James Barton..........	P 13 June 45			
4	0	Richard Maxwell Slegg..	P 23 Sept. 45			
3	0	Wm. Fred. Tho. Marshall	13 Mar. 46			
3	0	John W. Hughes Williams	P 21 July 46			
1	0	Thomas George Strange...	22 Dec. 48			

4 Capt O'Connell served in the Peninsula with the 43d Lt. Infantry from April 1812, to the end of that war in 1814, including the capture of Badajos, where he was severely wounded as a volunteer with the storming party; battle of Salamanca, capture of Madrid and the Retiro, retreat from Madrid, action at San Munos, battles of Vittoria and the Pyrenees, action at Lesaca, attack on the heights of Vera, passage of the Bidassoa, and many other minor affairs. Severely wounded at the capture of Badajos on the night of the 6th April, 1812, where he served as a volunteer with the storming party.

10 Quarter-Master Paul served against the Pirates in the Persian Gulf, and destruction of Ras-el-Khyma, in 1809; at the capture of the Isle of France in 1810; in the Kattywar country in 1811.12, and taking the Fort of Now Nuggur; in the Guzerats and Kutch in 1814, 15, and 16, and taking the forts of Angar, Kincoote, and Dwarka; Mahratta war in the Deccan, 1817 and 18. Capture of Poona and Cutch; storming the hill forts of Booj; Expedition to the Persian Gulf, including the capture of the forts of Ras-el-Khyma and Zaya, 1819. Expedition to Arabia in 1821, including the action at Beni-Boo-Ali, and destruction of the Pirates.

Full Pay	Half Pay	
13	0	*Paymaster.*—J. Williams Marshall, 3 Apr. 46; *Ens.* P 2 Sept. 36; *Lt.* P 19 Mar. 41.
10	0	*Adjutant.*—*Lieut.* C. Rhatigan, 30 Dec. 41.
10	0	*Quarter-Master.*—Thomas Paul,[10] 26 Apr. 39; *Ens.* 25 Jan. 39.
13	0	*Surgeon.*—Robert Keating Prendergast, 14 Apr. 46; *Assist.-Surg.* 7 Oct. 36.
4	0	*Assistant-Surgeons.*—Thomas Esmonde White, M.D., 26 Sept. 45.
4	0	William Ker Park, 31 Oct. 45.

Facings White.—*Agents,* Messrs. Cox & Co.

1 Field Marshal Grosvenor accompanied his regiment (the 3rd Foot Guards) to Holland in 1793, and afterwards into Flanders. In 1799 he went with the expedition to the Helder, and was present in the affair at the lines of Zuype (wounded), the battle of Alkmaer, and the actions of the 17th Sept. and 6th and 9th Oct. Commanded the picquets and out-posts at the siege of Copenhagen on the day of the sortie, when the Danes were repulsed. At the siege of Flushing, he was next in command to Sir Eyre Coote.

3 Major Patience was present at the surrender of Martinique, and at the capture of Les Saintes and Guadaloupe, in 1815.

5 Capt. de Teissier served in Scinde, in command of a detachment, protecting the stores and ammunition of the army, tracked up the Indus. Served also in the Light Company of the 17th during the campaign in Affghanistan and Beloochistan, and was present at the storm and capture of the fortresses of Ghuznee and Khelat, for which he has received the Medal.

6 Major Johnston served with the 49th throughout the whole of the operations in China, except the capture of Segoan, and was present at the attack and capture of Chusan (both operations), storm and capture of the heights above Canton, attack and capture of Amoy and Chinhae, occupation of Ningpo and repulse of the night attack, attack and capture of Segoan, Chapoo, Woosung, and Chin Kiang Foo, and demonstration before Nankin.

7 Lieut. Paul served with the 21st throughout the campaign of 1845-6 on the Sutlej (medal), and was present in the battles of Moodkee, Ferozeshah, (wounded), Buddiwal, Aliwal, and Sobraon.

"DOURO"—"TALAVERA"—"ALBUHERA"—"VITTORIA"—"PYRENEES"—
"NIVELLE"—"NIVE"—"ORTHES"—"PENINSULA."

Years' Serv.		
62		*Colonel.*
Full Pay.	Half Pay.	℗ Richard Blunt,[1] *Ens.* 31 Jan. 1787; *Lieut.* 23 Feb. 91; *Capt.* 12 July, 93; *Major*, 17 May, 96; *Lieut.-Col.* 23 Aug. 99; *Col.* 25 Oct. 1809; *Major-Gen.* 1 Jan. 12; *Lt.-Gen.* 27 May, 25; *Gen.* 23 Nov. 41; *Col.* 66th Regt. 25 Mar. 35.
26	1 1/12	*Lieut.-Colonel.*—Tho. Henry Johnston, *Ens.* P 21 Feb. 22; *Lieut.* P 1 Oct. 25; *Capt.* P 24 Oct. 26; *Major*, P 20 May, 36; *Lieut.-Col.* P 28 Dec. 38.
21	1/12	*Majors.*—Sir William Gordon, *Bart.*, *Ens.* P 5 June 28; *Lieut.* P 27 Apr. 32; *Capt.* P 12 May 37; *Major*, P 6 Nov. 46.
21	0	Charles Edward Michel; *Ens.* P 25 Nov. 28; *Lieut.* 23 Nov. 33; *Capt.* P 2 Feb. 38; *Major*, P 25 June, 47.

Full Pay	Half Pay	CAPTAINS.	ENSIGN.	LIEUT.	CAPTAIN.	BREV.-MAJ.
17	0	Geo. Grattan Biscoe	P 7 Apr. 32	P 12 Feb. 36	P 27 Sept. 39	
22	0	John Johnston	P 24 May 27	P 9 Mar. 32	2 Apr. 41	
23	0	George Maxwell........	P 23 Feb. 26	29 May 28	21 Oct. 43	
15	0	Henry John Turner	P 9 May 34	P 22 Nov. 36	P 29 Dec. 43	
14	0	Edw. Montagu Davenport	P 24 Apr. 35	6 Aug. 38	P 31 Dec. 44	
13	0	Fred. Charles Trench....	P 22 Nov. 36	P 28 Dec. 38	P 24 Jan. 45	
12	0	James Hunter Blair Birch	P 15 Dec. 37	P 15 Dec. 40	P 6 Nov. 46	
8	0	HardressDeL.Saunderson	2 April 41	P 30 June 43	P 24 Dec. 47	
8	0	Astley Paston Cooper ..	P 12 Oct. 41	P 20 Oct. 43	P 1 Aug. 48	
7	0	Francis William Astley..	P 4 Mar. 42	P 29 Dec. 43	P 12 Sept. 48	
		LIEUTENANTS.				
10	0	James Hamilton Ross, *adj.*	P 21 June 39	1 Nov. 42		
8	0	George Charles Downman	29 Oct. 41	28 Dec. 43		
7	0	Wm. M. S. Caulfield, *s.*	28 May 42	P 31 Dec. 44		
7	0	Tom Benson	P 8 Nov. 42	P 8 Aug. 45		
4	0	Robert Conner	P 11 July 45	P 6 Nov. 46		
4	0	John Clifton Hawkes....	P 24 Jan. 45	14 Mar. 47		
4	0	Nicholas Kendall	P 11 Nov. 45	P 28 Sept. 47		
3	0	Walter S. Pearce Serocold	P 10 July 46	P 24 Dec. 47		
3	0	Wildman Yates Peel	P 30 Nov. 46	P 1 Aug. 48		
3	0	Frederick Wainwright ..	23 May 46	12 Sept. 48		
3	0	Webster Thomas Gordon	P 1 Dec. 46	P 12 Sept. 48		
2	0	David Robert Ross	2 Apr. 47	26 Oct. 48		
5	0	Charles William Aylmer .	21 Dec. 44	P 28 Aug. 46		
		ENSIGNS.				
2	0	George Watson	P 9 Apr. 47			
2	0	Richard White	P 25 June 47			
2	0	Arch. Hamilton Dunbar	P 28 Sept. 47			
2	0	Charles Perrin	P 24 Dec. 47			
	0	John Walker	P 25 Nov. 45			
1	0	William Bowles........	P 12 Sept. 48			
1	0	George Glascott Newton	3 Nov. 48			
1	0	Richard Horner Paget ..	1 Dec. 48			

Full Pay	Half Pay	
34	6 [illegible]	*Paymaster.*—Kenneth Tolmie Ross, 11 Aug. 25; *Ens.* 22 June, 09; *Lieut.* 8 Oct. 12.
10	0	*Adjutant.*—*Lieut.* James Hamilton Ross, 21 Oct. 43.
7	0	*Quarter-Master.*—Mathew Reilley, 27 Sept. 42.
10	0	*Surgeon.*—Robert G. Montgomery, M.D., 19 Nov. 47; *Assist.-Surg.* 5 July 39.
5	0	*Assistant-Surgeons.*—Walter Simpson, MD. 23 Feb. 44.
3	0	Joseph Thomas La Presle, 22 Dec. 46.

Facings Green.—*Agents*, Messrs. Cox & Co.—*Irish Agents*, Messrs. Cane & Co.

1 General Blunt served in Lord Moira's expedition, and in Flanders in 1794 and 95, and was actively employed in the West Indies, from 1795 until 1803. He has since served in Hanover, Madeira, and in the Peninsula.

"BARROSA"—"PENINSULA"—The *Royal Tiger*, superscribed, "INDIA."

Years' Serv. Full Pay.	Half Pay.	
50		*Colonel.* ℗ John Clitherow,[1] *Ens.* 19 Dec. 99; *Lieut. & Capt.* 24 Feb. 03; *Capt. & Lieut-Col.* 8 Oct. 12; *Col.* 25 July, 21; *Major-Gen.* 22 July, 30; *Lieut-Gen.* 23 Nov. 41; *Col.* 67th F. 15 Jan. 44.
31	$\frac{4}{12}$	*Lieut.-Colonels.*—Edward Basil Brooke, *2nd Lieut. Royal Artillery*, 15 Dec. 17; *Lt.* 9 April, 25; *Capt.* P 11 July 26; *Major*, P 5 July, 31; *Lt.-Col.* 9 Nov. 46.
27	$8\frac{8}{12}$	r. William Nesbitt Orange,[3] *Ens.* 5 Feb. 14; *Lieut.* 19 Jan. 19; *Capt.* P 24 Oct. 21; *Major*, P 15 Aug. 34; *Brevet Lt.-Col.*, 9 Nov. 46; *Lt.-Col.* 3 Sept. 47.
40	0	*Majors.*—℗ Thomas James Adair,[4] *Ens.* 25 May 09; *Lieut.* 20 Feb. 11; *Capt.* P 27 Mar. 23; *Brevet Major*, 28 June 38; *Major*, 9 Nov. 46.
27	0	r. Thomas Josephus Deverell, *Ens.* 7 Nov. 22, *Lieut.* 25 June 29; *Capt.* P 30 Aug. 31; *Brevet Major*, 9 Nov. 46; *Major*, 3 Sept. 47.

Full Pay	Half Pay	CAPTAINS	ENSIGN.	LIEUT.	CAPTAIN.	BREV.-MAJ.
30	0	Thomas Byrne	4 Nov. 19	5 Mar. 23	22 Jan. 39	
17	0	r. Samuel Hood Murray	P 22 June 32	P 8 Dec. 37	P 1 Nov. 42	
15	0	John Porter	P 28 Mar. 34	P 29 Dec. 37	P 6 Oct. 43	
14	0	Charles Barnard Hague..	P 5 Sept. 35	P 30 Dec. 37	P 5 Dec. 43	
11	0	Frederick Wm. Lane,[5] s.	P 19 Jan. 38	P 6 Dec. 39	P 13 Oct. 43	
13	0	r. Henry Collette........	P 26 Aug. 36	22 Jan. 39	P 23 Feb. 44	
12	0	Thomas P. Onslow.......	17 Nov. 37	P 25 May 39	P 11 July 45	
16	0	William Pilsworth......	P 24 May 33	18 Mar. 38	9 Nov. 46	
12	0	r. Capel Coape	P 29 Dec. 37	P 11 Oct. 39	29 Dec. 46	
16	0	r. Stonehouse G. Bunbury, s	P 28 June 33	P 25 Dec. 38	30 Dec. 46	
10	0	r. Walter Caulfield Pratt.	P 25 May 39	15 Sept. 42	P 13 Aug. 47	
10	0	r. William Hayter Hussey	P 8 Nov. 39	P 29 Sept. 43	P 10 Sept. 47	
		LIEUTENANTS.				
9	0	r. Robert Follett Synge[6]	P 20 Oct. 40	26 Sept. 42		
7	0	Robert Hudson Wood ..	P 11 Mar. 42	P 5 Dec. 43		
7	0	Francis Richard Taylor..	28 May 42	16 May 45		
6	0	r. Dugald Stewart Miller	P 24 Feb. 43	P 11 July 45		
7	0	r. Thomas Basil Tuite ..	P 31 Dec. 42	P 23 Aug. 44		
5	0	John Cuthbert Murray..	P 23 Feb. 44	9 Nov. 46		
5	0	r. William Du Vernet[7] ..	22 Mar. 44	29 Jan. 46		
5	0	James Graham, *Adj*.....	3 May 44	29 Dec. 46		
5	0	Fitzmaurice Pratt	P 20 Dec. 44	29 Dec. 46		
4	0	Daniel Thompson	P 11 July 45	P 16 Apr. 47		
4	0	r. *Count* W. Const. Rivarola	P 1 Aug. 45	P 6 Aug. 47		
3	0	William D'Arcy........	10 July 46	P 13 Aug. 47		
3	0	Robert Blakeney	P 3 Nov. 46	P 10 Sept. 47		
3	0	John William Percy	21 Apr. 46	P 30 Mar. 47		
4	0	Henry S. G. S. Knight ..	2 Sept. 45	3 June 47		
		ENSIGNS.				
3	0	r. Edward Daubeney....	29 Dec. 46			
3	0	r. Alfred Addington Jones	29 Dec. 46			
3	0	William Cumming Shells	31 Dec. 46			
2	0	r. James Anderson, *Adj.*	19 Feb. 47			
2	0	r. Henry Leslie Hunt ..	P 16 Apr. 47			
2	0	r. Edm. Holden Steward	P 6 Aug. 47			
2	0	William Serjeant Arnold	P 13 Aug. 47			
2	0	Vivian Arthur Webber..	P 10 Sept. 47			
1	0	r. Robert Philip Armstrong	P 25 Feb. 48			
1	0	r. William Vesey Munnings	P 10 Mar. 48			
1	0	Charles Matthews	P 30 June 48			

6 Lieut. Synge served with the Cameronians on the China expedition (medal), and carried the colours of the regiment at the repulse of the night attack on Ningpo, the attack and capture of Chapoo, the taking of Shanghae and Woosung, the storming of Chin Kiang Foo, and the operations before Nankin.

7 Lt. Du Vernet was on board the ill-fated *Runnymede*, when that ship was cast away on the Andaman Isles, near Humson, in Nov. 1844, with detachments of the 10th and 50th regts. on board, where he remained for fifty-four days surrounded by Cannibals and suffering great privations. He served afterwards with the 50th in the campaign on the Sutlej (medal), and was present at Buddiwal and Aliwal, at which last he received a slight wound in the right knee from a grape-shot, after which he was severely wounded in the left foot by the bursting of a shell.

9 Paymaster Robinson served at the siege of Asseerghur, March and April, 1819.

Full Pay	Half Pay	
32	0	*Paymaster.*—James Robinson,[9] 26 Dec. 37; *Ens.* 20 Nov. 17; *Lieut.* 24 April, 20.
5	0	*Adjutants.*—*Lieut.* James Graham, 22 Jan. 47.
2	0	r. *Ensign* James Anderson, 3 Sept. 47.
10	0	*Quarter-Masters.*—George Crispin, 25 Oct. 39; *Ens.* 22 Mar. 39.
2	0	r. Thomas McGrath, 3 Sept. 47.
22	0	*Surgeons.*—James Shiels, M.D. 2 July, 41; *Assist.-Surg.* 20 July, 30; *Hosp.-Assist.* 25 Jan. 27.
10	0	r. John Samuel Charlton, 3 Sept. 47; *Assist.-Surg.* 1 Mar. 39.
2	0	*Assistant-Surgeons.*—Thomas Blatherwick, 4 June, 47.
3	0	r. John Henry Dundas, 6 Feb. 46.

Facings Yellow.—*Agents*, Messrs. Cox & Co.

1 Lieut. General Clitherow served the Egyptian campaign of 1801; the expedition to Hanover in 1805; and that to Walcren, in 1809. In the Peninsula from Dec. 1809 to Dec. 1812, including the battles of Busaco, Fuentes d'Onor (severely wounded), and Salamanca, and siege of Burgos (severely wounded). Served also in France, in 1815. Medal for services in Egypt.

3 Lt.-Col. Orange served on the frontiers of Niagara in 1814 and 15. Served also at the siege and capture of Lognur Issapore, Koarry, and Rhyghur, in the Southern Concan country in India in 1818.

4 Major Adair served in Spain from Sept. 1810 to the end of the war, including the siege of Cadiz battle of Barrosa, Fort San Philip, Balaguere, Villa Franca, Tarragona and Barcelona. Served also the Nepaul campaigns of 1817 and 18, and subsequently in the Deccan, including the siege and reduction of Rhyghur, Amulnier, and Asseerghur. Twice severely wounded by matchlock balls in the left arm, and right side at the siege of Asseerghur on the evening of the 19th March, 1819, in repulsing a sortie made by the garrison of the fort into the town.

5 Captain Lane served with the 49th on the China Expedition, and was present at the attack and capture of Amoy, Chusan [illegible]

[1st Batt. emb. Foreign Serv. 21 Feb. 48. / r. b. do. do. 13 Dec. 47.] **76th Regiment of Foot.** [1st Batt. at Corfu / r. b. at Zante.

Serv. / Half Pay.	
	The *Elephant*, circumscribed "HINDOOSTAN"—"NIVE"—"PENINSULA."
	Colonel.
2	P *Sir* Robert Arbuthnot,[1] KCB. *Cornet*, 1 Jan. 97; *Lieut.* 1 June, 97; *Capt.* 20 Aug. 02; *Major*, 13 Aug. 09; *Lieut.-Col.* 22 May, 11; *Col.* 19 July, 21; *Major-Gen.* 22 July, 30; *Lt.-Gen.* 23 Nov. 41; *Col.* 76th Regt. 31 May, 43.
1 10/12	*Lieut.-Colonels.*—Joseph Clarke, *Ens.* 22 March, 10; *Lieut.* P10 June, 13; *Capt.* P24 Feb. 25; *Major*, 26 June, 33; *Lieut.-Col.* 17 Sept. 39.
4/12	r. John Heneage Grubbe, *Ens.* P20 Aug. 18; *Lieut.* P24 Feb. 25; *Capt.* P13 May, 26; *Major*, P19 Jan. 30; *Lt.-Col.* 3 Sept. 47.
0	*Majors.*—Richard Gardiner, *Ens.* 12 May 14; *Lieut.* 29 Sept. 25; *Capt.* P5 April 33; *Major*, 11 Nov. 45.
0	r. Robert Clifford Lloyd, *Ens.* P30 Dec. 26; *Lieut.* P8 June 30; *Capt.* P3 June 36; *Brev.-Major*, 9 Nov. 46; *Major*, 3 Sept. 47.

	CAPTAINS.	ENSIGN.	LIEUT.	CAPTAIN.	BREV.-MAJ.
0	r. G. F. Cooper Scott....	25 Oct. 27	P 3 May 31	P 1 July 36	9 Nov. 46
0	Robt. Shepherd	P10 July 23	P13 May 26	5 Jan. 37	
0	r. Henry Brewster......	P18 Oct. 33	P19 Aug. 36	P 9 Nov. 39	
0	Collingwood Fenwick ..	P 4 Sept. 35	P 7 April 37	P 3 April 40	
0	Chas. S. S. Evans Gordon	12 Oct. 32	P 3 June 36	P20 Dec. 4.	
0	r. Henry Dalton Smart..	P31 Dec. 33	P25 Aug. 37	8 Jan. 43	
0	Morley S. Tynte Dennis	P18 Sept. 35	P23 Nov. 37	P10 Nov. 43	
12 3/12	r. P Archibald Campbell[2]	7 Mar. 11	5 Mar. 12	P27 Oct. 37	
0	John B. Flanagan	8 Feb. 31	28 Aug. 35	11 Nov. 45	
0	r. John Gore Ferns	3 May 31	23 Feb. 38	14 Apr. 46	
0	Thomas Tydd..........	P 3 June 36	P19 Oct. 38	3 Sept. 47	
0	John Geo. C. Disbrowe..	....	2 Feb. 44	P31 Mar. 48	
	LIEUTENANTS.				
0	Arch. Rutherfoord......	P19 Aug. 36	P 1 Feb. 39		
0	Wm. Wood Senhouse....	P 7 April 37	20 July 39		
0	Henry Hearne Lacy, *Adj.*	P 1 Feb. 39	P16 Apr. 41		
0	r. Charles O'Donoghue..	29 Aug. 39	P20 Dec. 42		
0	William Hugh Barton ..	P 8 Nov. 39	P 6 Oct. 43		
0	r. Wilford Brett, *Adj.* ..	P29 May 40	P13 Jan. 43		
0	Robert H. H. Keightley	2 Apr. 41	11 Nov. 45		
0	r. John Edward Large ..	P10 Nov. 43	1 May 46		
0	r. John William Preston	26 Jan. 44	P13 Nov. 46		
0	Benjamin Rising	26 July 44	P 8 Dec. 46		
0	Thomas Crawford Poole	P 15 Dec. 40	P 10 May 44		
0	r. JamesCumming Clarke	P28 Mar. 45	P 4 June 47		
0	John Cumming Clarke ..	11 Nov. 45	3 Sept. 47		
0	Wm. Charles Bancroft, *s.*	25 June 44	21 April 46		
0	r John Richard Lovett ..	P28 Nov. 45	P 2 Mar. 47		
0	r Robert Hyde Page	P30 July 44	P13 Aug. 47		
	ENSIGNS.				
0	r. Andrew Gammell	16 Apr. 46			
0	r. William Price Hill ..	18 Apr. 46			
0	r. John Dunlop	1 May 46			
0	James Fox Bland	P 8 Dec. 46			
0	WalterMontfordWestropp	P 4 June 47			
0	r.G.Henry John Heigham	P22 June 47			
0	JohnH.HoustonGammell	P15 Oct. 47			
0	George Wardlaw	P 5 Nov. 47			
0	John Geddes	25 Aug. 48			
0	R. Hamilton Montgomerie	1 Sept. 48			

2 Captain Campbell served with the 77th in the Peninsula, from Aug. 1812 to the end of that war in 1814, and was present at the blockade of Bayonne and repulse of the sortie.

0	*Paymaster.*—William Doran, 8 March, 44; *Ens.* 15 Nov. 33; *Lieut.* 16 April, 36; *Capt.* 3 March 43.
0	*Adjutants.*—*Lieut.* Henry Hearn Lacy, 1 May, 46.
0	r. *Lieut.* Wilford Brett, 3 Sept. 47.
6 1/12	*Quarter Masters.*—John William Preston, 12 June, 28; *Ens.* 11 June, 12; *Lieut.* 19 Dec. 16.
0	r. Henry Tyler, 3 Sept. 47.
0	*Surgeons.*—Robert Thomas Scott, 7 Aug. 46; *Assist.-Surg.* 15 July 36.
1	r. Henry Cooper Reade, 3 Sept. 47; *Assist.-Surg.* 31 May, 39.
0	*Assistant-Surgeons.*—James Crerar, 3 Sept. 47.
0	r. George Anderson Wilkinson, 17 Dec. 47.

Facings Red.—*Agents, Sir* John Kirkland & Co.

· Robert Arbuthnot served in Ireland during the rebellion, in 1798, including the battle of Bally- k on the 8th Sept., against the French. At the capture of the Cape of Good Hope, in 1806. ded from thence to South America, on the staff of Lord Beresford, and was present in the battle s to the surrender of Buenos Ayres, and at two engagements before its re capture by the Spa- ; he was subsequently thirteen months a prisoner. On his return from South America he served staff of Lord Beresford in the Island of Madeira, and afterwards in the Peninsula, from 1808 to l of that war in 1814, with the exception of the first part of 1813, and has received a cross and lasps for Busaco, Albuhera, Badajoz, Nivelle, Nive, Orthes, and Toulouse. Independent of the he was also present at the battle of Corunna, passage of the Douro, lines of Torres Vedras, siege duction of Olivença, first siege of Badajoz, third siege and storm of Badajoz; the siege and storming dad Rodrigo, passage of the Adour, and in a great many operations of less importance.

On the Colours and Appointments, the *Plume of the Prince of Wales.*
"SERINGAPATAM"—"CIUDAD RODRIGO"—"BADAJOZ"—
"PENINSULA."

Years' Serv. Full Pay.	Half Pay.					
56		*Colonel.*				
		Sir John Macleod,[1] CB. KCH. *Ens.* 9 Mar. 1793; *Lieut.* 2 May, 94; *Capt.* 24 June, 95; *Major,* 9 June, 99; *Lieut.-Col.* 1 Jan. 05; *Col.* 4 June, 13; *Major-General,* 12 Aug. 19; *Lieut.-Gen.* 10 Jan. 37; *Col.* of the 77th, 17 Feb. 40.				
39	1 1/12	*Lieut.-Colonel.*—Nicholas Wilson, KH. *Ens.* 31 Oct. 09; *Lieut.* 7 Oct. 13; *Capt.* P 24 Oct. 21; *Major,* P 30 Dec. 28; *Brevet Lieut.-Col.* 23 Nov. 41; *Lieut.-Col.* 4 Aug. 48.				
20	0	*Majors.*—Thomas Graham Egerton, *Ens.* 24 Dec. 29; *Lieut.* P 9 Mar. 32; *Capt.* P 23 Jan. 35; *Major,* P 7 Feb. 45.				
21	0	Robert Jocelyn Straton, *Ens.* 10 Jan. 28; *Lieut.* P 18 Jan. 33; *Capt.* P 26 Apr. 39; *Major,* P 18 Aug. 48.				
		CAPTAINS.	ENSIGNS.	LIEUT.	CAPTAIN.	BREVET-MAJOR.
25	4 1/12	Guy Clarke	17 Feb. 20	P 17 July 23	P 8 Apr. 26	23 Nov. 41
24	0	Wm. Jonathan Clerke	24 Feb. 25	P 10 June 26	P 18 Jan. 33	9 Nov. 46
25	0	Alexander Tomkins	28 June 24	P 24 Dec. 25	P 8 Dec. 37	
21	0	George Dixon	P 30 Dec. 28	P 26 Dec. 34	P 29 Nov. 39	
27	0	Paris Wm. Aug. Bradshaw	P 26 Dec. 22	24 Feb. 25	30 Oct. 40	
18	0	Henry Jervis White	P 23 Dec. 31	11 Sept. 35	P 11 Nov. 42	
18	0	William Forbes	P 2 Dec. 31	11 Aug. 35	P 7 Feb. 45	
10	0	Edw. Hen. Lowther Crofton	P 10 May 39	P 11 Nov. 42	P 23 May 45	
10	0	James Butler Fellowes, *s.*	P 31 May 39	15 Apr. 42	P 7 Apr. 48	
10	0	Alexander Aitken	1 Feb. 39	8 Nov. 43	P 18 Aug. 48	
		LIEUTENANTS.				
13	0	Bartholomew O'Brien	P 15 Apr. 36	P 13 July 38		
12	0	John Hackett	17 Nov. 37	28 Aug. 39		
9	0	Patrick M'Carthy, *Adj.*	15 Dec. 40	22 July 44		
8	0	Geo. Harry Smith Willis	P 23 Apr. 41	P 30 Aug. 44		
8	0	George Cary	P 28 Dec. 41	9 Nov. 43		
7	0	Henry Robert Carden	P 11 Nov. 42	P 7 Feb. 45		
7	0	Thomas Oriel Forster	P 25 Nov. 42	P 14 Feb. 45		
5	0	Francis Kennedy	26 July 44	P 23 May 45		
6	0	Robert Mostyn	10 Nov. 43	P 29 Dec. 46		
6	0	Henry Jobling Wallack[3]	P 22 July 43	P 25 June 44		
5	0	G. St. Leger Gordon Gordon	P 30 Aug. 44	P 18 Aug. 48		
4	0	Thomas Elliott	P 7 Feb. 45	P 12 Sept. 48		
5	0	William Bertram	P 29 Mar. 44	P 7 July 46		
		ENSIGNS.				
4	0	W. Wentworth Grant Dilke	P 14 Feb. 45			
4	0	Henry Kent	P 8 Aug. 45			
3	0	William Ronalds	P 29 Dec. 46			
1	0	William Henry Weston	P 26 May 48			
1	0	Wm. H. C. George Pechell	P 1 Aug. 48			
1	0	Wm. Felix Tollemache	P 18 Aug. 48			
1	0	William Rickman	P 12 Sept. 48			
1	0	Bentinck Duncan Gilby	17 Nov. 48			
30	6	*Paymaster.*—William Galway, 29 Sept. 43; *Ens.* 4 Nov. 13; *Lieut.* 27 July 20; *Capt.* 2 Apr. 41.				
9	0	*Adjutant.*—*Lieut.* Patrick M'Carthy, 15 Dec. 40.				
1	0	*Quarter-Master.*—John Remington Breading, 23 June, 48.				
13	0	*Surgeon.*—Joseph Samuel Prendergast, M.D. 22 May 46; *Assist.-Surgeon,* 10 Feb. 36.				
5	0	*Assistant-Surgeon.*—Christopher Macartney, M.B., 2 Feb. 44.				

[*Returned from North America,* 25 June 48.]

Facings Yellow.—*Agent,* Charles R. M'Grigor, Esq.

1 Sir John Macleod served in the arduous campaign of 1794 in Holland, under the Duke of York, and was present at the attack and taking of Fort St. André, the bombardment and sortie of Nimeguen, the attack and defeat of the enemy at Beirren-Mansel, Guilder-Mansel, and Thuil. Commanded the brigade which carried the village of Merxem, 14th Jan. 1814, and was severely wounded.

3 Lieut. Wallack served the campaign on the Sutlej in 1845-6 (medal) with the 9th, and was present at the battles of Moodkee, Ferozeshah, and Sobraon.

Emb. for For. Serv. Apr. 1842.] 78th (Highland) Regt. of F. (or Ross-shire Buffs.) [Serving at Belgaum, Bombay.

"*Cuidich'n Rhi.*"—The *Elephant*, superscribed "ASSAYE"—"MAIDA"—"JAVA."

Record of the Service of the 78th Highlanders. Raised by letter of Service dated 7th March 1793; inspected and passed July 1793; proceeded to Holland September 1794; returned to England May 1795; proceeded to Quiberon August 1795; returned January 1796; proceeded to the Cape of Good Hope 1796; to Calcutta February 1797; to Bombay February 1803; to Goa February 1807; to Java August 1811; returned to England July 1817; proceeded to Ireland November 1817; embarked for Ceylon April 1826; returned to England February 1838. Embarked for India April 1842.

Year's Serv. Full Pay.	Half Pay.	
61		*Colonel.*
		℞ Paul Anderson,[1] CB. *Ens.* 31 March, 1788; *Lieut.* 31 March, 91; *Capt.* 1 July, 95; *Major*, 25 June, 1801; *Lieut.-Col.* 17 Oct. 05; *Col.* 4 June, 13; *Major-Gen.* 12 Aug. 19; *Lieut.-Gen.* 10 Jan. 37; *Col.* 78th Highlanders 9 Feb. 37.
46	0	*Lieut.-Colonels.*—Henry N. Douglas,[2] *Ens.* 23 Sept. 03; *Lieut.* 23 May, 05; *Capt.* 14 Dec. 11; *Major*, P 22 Oct. 25; *Lieut.-Col.* P 28 April, 37.
35	0	Edward Twopeny, *Ens.* 27 Jan. 14; *Lieut.* P 17 Aug. 20; *Capt.* P 22 Oct. 25; *Brev.-Major*, 28 June 38; *Major*, 8 April, 42; *Lieut.-Col.* P 10 Dec. 47.
30	0	*Majors.*—Walter Hamilton, *Ens.* P 28 Jan. 19; *Lieut.* P 15 Apr. 24; *Capt.* P 15 Mar. 33; *Brevet-Major*, 9 Nov. 46; *Major*, P 10 Dec. 47.
14	0	Henry William Stisted,[3] *Ens.* P 4 Dec. 35; *Lieut.* P 29 Sept. 38; *Capt.* P 29 Apr. 42; *Major*, P 26 May, 48.

Full Pay	Half Pay	CAPTAINS.	ENSIGNS.	LIEUT.	CAPTAIN.	BREV.-MAJ.
34	3 5/12	℞ Thomas John Taylor[5]	12 Mar. 12	7 Sept. 14	17 May 30	9 Nov. 46
21	0	Colin Campbell M'Intyre	9 Apr. 25	P 17 July 28	P 28 Apr. 37	
20	0	Henry Hamilton	P 13 Aug. 29	P 29 Nov. 33	P 29 April 42	
12	0	Wm. M. G. M'Murdo[6] ..	1 July 37	5 Jan. 41	7 July 43	18 Feb. 48
24	0	Joseph Richard Lamert ..	10 Apr. 25	13 Dec. 32	29 Dec. 43	
16	0	John Fowden Haliburton	P 15 Feb. 33	P 28 Apr. 37	24 Oct. 44	
22	1 1/12	Peter Grehan[7]	P 8 April 26	26 Nov. 30	P 18 Sept. 40	
14	0	Fred. Edmund Caldwell	P 9 Oct. 35	P 18 May 38	P 10 Dec. 47	
13	0	George Henry Hunt	P 8 Jan. 36	P 9 Nov. 38	12 May 48	
10	0	Jas. Duncan MacAndrew	P 15 Mar. 39	P 21 May 41	P 6 Oct. 48	
		LIEUTENANTS.				
10	0	Thomas Molyneux Keogh	P 21 June 39	P 4 Mar. 42		
9	0	William Henry Ridge ..	P 13 Mar. 40	P 5 Mar. 41		
12	0	Græme Alex. Lockhart	P 8 Dec. 37	8 April 42		
10	0	H. Douglas Gordon, *adj.*	P 18 Jan. 39	do.		
9	0	Alex. Mackenzie	P 7 Feb. 40	do.		
9	0	Douglas Hastings	20 Mar. 40	do.		
10	0	Edward Fellowes	P 23 April 39	P 29 April 42		
12	0	Michael Edward Smith ..	P 3 Nov. 37	P 20 Dec. 39		
10	0	Robert B. Arthur Purvis	P 11 May 39	P 15 May 40		
8	0	Lawrence Pl. Bouverie, *r.*	P 7 Sept. 41	28 Dec. 42		
10	0	Wm. Buck C. Aug. Parker	16 Oct. 39	P 17 Feb. 43		
7	0	Wm. M'Gregor Archer ..	P 1 April 42	24 Oct. 44		
7	0	HowardDouglasCampbell	9 April 42	29 Nov. 44		
6	0	Wm. Æneas Moncrieffe ..	P 17 Mar. 43	P 17 Jan. 45		
4	0	William Cumming Rose	17 Jan. 45	P 12 June 46		
7	0	George Floyer Sydenham	P 29 April 42	9 Nov. 46		
8	0	Robert Douglas[9]	2 April 41	28 Dec. 42		
4	0	Thomas Anderson	23 May 45	P 10 Dec. 47		
3	0	Robert Bogle	P 14 Apr. 46	P 11 Dec. 47		
3	0	Donald Stuart	P 12 June 46	P 23 May 48		
4	0	HerbertTaylorMacpherson	28 Feb. 45	13 July 48		
2	0	Duncan D. Grahame	P 5 Mar. 47	P 26 Sept. 48		
2	0	Joseph Webster	P 10 Dec. 47	P 6 Oct. 48		
		ENSIGNS.				
3	0	Horatio Gillmore	31 Mar. 46			
3	0	Joseph P. H. Crowe	27 Oct. 46			
2	0	John Hunter	21 May 47			
2	0	John Simon Fran. Dick ..	P 11 Dec. 47			
2	0	Henry B. Harrison Rocke	P 10 Dec. 47			
1	0	Edmund Alex. Delisser	P 26 Sept. 48			
1	0	A. Wickham Pym Weekes	P 6 Oct. 48			
1	0	Henry Preston Elrington	P 20 Oct. 48			
24	1/12	*Paymaster.*—Edward Evans, 30 July, 44; *Ens.* 24 March 25; *Lieut.* 5 Jan. 27;				
10	0	*Adjutant.—Lieut.* Hamilton Douglas Gordon, 16 June, 48. [*Capt.* 24 Nov. [illegible]				
11	0	*Quarter-Master.*—Joseph Webster, 31 May, 39; *Ens.* 23 Nov. 38.				
14	0	*Surgeon.*—Archibald Alexander, 3 Oct. 45; *Assistant-Surgeon*, 20 Feb. 35.				
6	0	*Assist.-Surgeons.*—David Reid M'Kinnon, 12 Dec. 43.				
3	0	James Leitch, M.D. 23 Jan. 46.				
2	0	James M'Nab, M.D. 2 March, 47. [*Facings* Buff.—*Agents*, Messrs. Cox & Co.]				

3 Major Stisted served with the Queen's Royals during the campaign in Affghanistan and Beloochistan under Lord Keane, including the storm and capture of Ghuznee (wounded) and of Khelat. Medal for Ghuznee.

5 Major Taylor served the campaigns of 1813 and 1814, [illegible] the investment of Pampeluna, the battles of the Pyrenees on the 28th, 29th and 30th July, 1813, [illegible] of Bayonne, action of the River Bidassoa 31st Aug. 1813, battle of Orthes, affair of Vic and Tarbes, and battle of Toulouse where he was severely wounded.

6 Major M'Murdo served as Assistant Quarter-Master-General to the Army under Sir Charles Napier during the campaign in Scinde in 1843, and was present as such at the destruction of the Fort of Imaumghur, in the battle of Meeanee,—in which his horse was shot under him; skirmish with the enemy while conducting Major Stack's brigade from Muttaree to form a junction with Sir Charles Napier's force at Hydrabad; and battle of Hydrabad, where he received a sabre wound in the right [illegible]. His gallantry in single combat [illegible] cited the highest encomiums from Sir Charles Napier in his despatches, and he was afterwards rewarded by promotion to an Unattached Company. He again served as Assistant Quarter-master General to Sir Charles Napier's Army [illegible] the campaign against the Mountain and Desert tribes situated on the right bank of the Indus, early in [illegible].

7 Captain Grehan served with the Queen's Royals throughout the campaign in Affghanistan and Beloochistan under Lord Keane, and was present at the storm and capture of Ghuznee (Medal) and of Khelat.

1 General Anderson was at the storming of Convention redoubts, Moselle Fort, and the siege of Calvi, [illegible] served subsequently in the West Indies, and received a severe contusion in the side in the storming of Morne [illegible] Lucia; served as Aide-de-Camp to Sir John Moore in the expedition to Holland; and afterwards in the expedition to Egypt, where he was severely wounded by a shot in the arm, in the action of 21st March; served in the expedition to Walcheren, and was present at the siege of Flushing. Medal for Corunna.

2 Lieut.-Col. Douglas served the Campaign in Java, including the investment and storming of Fort Cornelis in August, and storming the Heights of Serondole in September, 1811, investment and storming of the Fortifications of [illegible] in [illegible] 1812. Commanded the detachment which took possession of the Island of Banca, and on his return was appointed to [illegible], which he resigned to accompany his regiment in the expedition to the Island of Bally in [illegible] and [illegible] Col. Douglas's services at the storming of Djocjocarta were noticed in the London Gazette, he having [illegible] which took the Sultan prisoner.

9 Lt. Douglas served with the Buffs at the battle of Punniar (medal).

Emb. for Foreign Serv. 1 Jan. 1841.] *79th Regt. of Foot (Cameron Highlanders).* [Serving in N. America, Depôt, Nenagh.

"EGMONT-OP-ZEE,"—The *Sphinx*, with the words "EGYPT"—"FUENTES D'ONOR"—"SALAMANCA"—"PYRENEES"—"NIVELLE"—"NIVE"—"TOULOUSE"—"PENINSULA"—"WATERLOO."

Years' Serv.		
53		*Colonel.*
		P W *Sir* James Macdonell,[1] KCB. KCH. *Ens.* 25 Jan. 96; *Lt.* 2 Feb. 96; *Capt.* 10 Sept. 03; *Maj.* 17 Apr. 04; *Lt.-Col.* 7 Sept. 09; *Col.* 12 Aug 10; *Maj.-Gen.* 22 July, 30; *Lt.-Gen.* 23 Nov. 41; *Col.* 79th 14 July, 42.
Full Pay.	Half Pay.	*Lieut.-Colonel.*
23	1/12	*Hon.* Lauderdale Maule, *Ens.* P 24 Aug. 26; *Lieut.* 21 July, 31; *Capt.* P 22 May, 35; *Major,* P 11 May, 39; *Lieut.-Col.* P 14 June, 42.
18	0	*Majors.*—Edmund James Elliot, *Ens.* P 5 April 31; *Lt.* P 10 Oct. 34; *Capt.* P 3 April 40; *Major,* P 12 April 44.
17	0	James Ferguson, *Ens.* P 27 July 32; *Lieut.* P 7 Aug. 35; *Capt.* P 18 Sept. 40; *Major,* P 25 Aug. 46.

Full Pay	Half Pay	CAPTAINS.	ENSIGN.	LIEUT.	CAPTAIN.	BREV.-MAJ.
16	0	John Douglas	P 6 Sept. 33	P 8 July 36	P 8 June 41	1 Nov. 42
15	0	Wm. Monro	P 10 Oct. 34	P 29 Dec. 37	P 14 June 42	
14	0	Richard C. H. Taylor ..	11 Dec. 35	P 29 Mar. 39	P 23 Aug. 44	
11	0	Robert Douglas Clephane	P 8 June 38	P 18 Sept. 40	P 11 Apr. 45	
10	0	William M'Call	P 29 Mar. 39	P 8 June 41	P 14 Nov. 45	
10	0	Thomas John Reeve	P 11 May 39	P 28 Dec. 41	P 9 June 46	
9	0	Andrew Hunt..........	P 22 Feb. 40	P 15 June 42	P 25 Aug. 46	
9	0	Thomas Bromhead Butt.	P 3 April 40	P 2 Aug. 42	P 2 Apr. 47	
9	0	Wm. Chauval Hodgson..	P 18 Sept. 40	P 10 Feb. 43	P 11 June 47	
7	0	Wm. Arthur Mainwaring	P 14 June 42	P 12 Apr. 44	P 27 Oct. 48	
		LIEUTENANTS				
8	0	James Robertson	P 29 Jan. 41	P 14 April 43		
8	0	Henry Mackay, *Adj.*....	18 June 41	11 Apr. 44		
8	0	Henry Murray	P 1 June 41	23 Aug. 43		
7	0	William Forrest, *d. adj.*..	P 14 Oct. 42	P 30 May 45		
6	0	Henry Wotton Campbell	P 14 April 43	P 4 July 45		
5	0	Oliver Graham	P 12 Apr. 44	P 14 Nov. 45		
4	0	Keith Ramsay Maitland	P 4 July 45	P 25 Aug. 46		
7	0	Alex. Cockburn M'Barnett	19 Aug. 42	28 Nov. 45		
3	0	George Murray Miller ..	P 30 Jan. 46	P 2 Apr. 47		
3	0	Adam Maitland	P 9 June 46	P 11 June 47		
3	0	W. Cuningh. Cuninghame	P 26 June 46	P 31 Dec. 47		
3	0	Edward William Cuming	P 24 July 46	P 31 Mar. 48		
4	0	William Scott	P 11 Nov. 45	P 25 Apr. 48		
3	0	Charles Millns Harrisson	P 3 Nov. 46	P 27 Oct. 48.		
		ENSIGNS.				
4	0	John Snodgrass Chalmers	P 11 Apr. 45			
2	0	James Webster	P 2 Apr. 47			
2	0	Francis Augustus Grant, *s.*	P 11 June 47			
2	0	Francis Joseph Harrisson	22 June 47			
2	0	Andrew Hill	P 31 Dec. 47			
1	0	Robert Tod Boothby	P 31 Mar. 48			
1	0	John Scott	P 27 Oct. 48.			

3 Paymaster Cornes served with the 53rd in the campaign on the Sutlej in 1846 (medal), and commanded the rear-guard at Buddiwal when cut off by the enemy's cavalry, and effected his retreat in an orderly manner in the face of the entire Seik cavalry,—his conduct on this occasion afterwards elicited the Duke of Wellington's "cordial approbation and thanks for the gallantry and judgment he displayed in protecting the baggage and sick in the movement towards Loodiana, when attacked by a large force of the enemy on the 21st January." He was also present at the battles of Aliwal and Sobraon. At Buddiwal he was wounded in the leg, and his horse was shot under him.

Full Pay	Half Pay	
8	0	*Paymaster.*—John Cornes,[3] 5 Nov. 47; *Quarter-Master,* 25 June 41; *Cornet,* 2 Oct. 46; *Lieut.* P 23 March 47.
8	0	*Adjutant.*—*Lieut.* Henry Mackay, 19 June, 41.
11	0	*Quarter-Master.*—P W Alexander Cruickshanks,[4] 12 Oct. 38.
12	0	*Surgeon.*—John Grant, 10 July 46; *Assist.-Surg.* 9 June 37.
8	0	*Assist.-Surgeons.*—Thomas Goldie Scot, M.D. 14 Dec. 41.
4	0	Henry Day Fowler, 19 Dec. 45.

Facings Green.—*Agents,* Messrs. Cox & Co.—*Irish Agents, Sir* E. R. Borough, *Bt.,* [Armit, & Co.

1 Sir James Macdonell served with the expedition to Naples and Calabria, in 1805 and 6, including the battle of Maida, for which he has received a medal. Served afterwards in Portugal, Spain, France, and Flanders.

4 Quarter-Master Cruickshanks served at the siege and capture of Copenhagen, in 1807; on the expedition to Gottenborgh, in 1808; the campaign of 1808-9, in the Peninsula; expedition to Walcheren, siege and capture of Flushing, 1809; campaigns of 1810, 11, 12, 13, 14, and 15, in the Peninsula, France, and Flanders, including the defence of Cadiz and Isla-de-Leon, from Feb. to Aug. 1810; battles of Busaco and Fuentes d'Onor—taken prisoner of war while in defence of the village; covering the siege of Badajos, in March and April 1812; battles of the Nivelle, Nive, Toulouse (wounded in the left leg), Quatre Bras, and Waterloo. Served with the army of occupation until 1818.

---

14 Lt. Holdich served as Aide-de-Camp to Sir Harry Smith throughout the campaign on the Sutlej (medal), and was present in the battles of Moodkee, Ferozeshah (wounded), Buddiwal, Aliwal, and Sobraon (severely wounded). He served also as Aide-de-Camp to Sir Harry in the action with and defeat of the Rebel Boers at Bloem Plaats (South Africa) 29 Aug. 1848.

The Sphinx, with the words "EGYPT"—"MOODKEE"—"FEROZESHAH"—"SOBRAON"

Colonel.

Years' Serv. Full Pay.	Half Pay.	
50		Sir Edmund Keynton Williams,[1] KCB. *Ens.* 30 Aug. 99; *Lieut.* 18 April 00; *Capt.* 25 Sept. 07; *Major,* 8 Oct. 12; *Lieut.-Col.* 21 June 13; *Col.* 22 July 30; *Major-Gen.* 23 Nov. 41; *Col.* 80th Foot 24 Oct. 48.
36	6	*Lieut.-Colonels.*—Thomas Bunbury,[2] CB. *Ens.* 7 May, 07; *Lieut.* 17 Aug. 09; *Capt.* 25 Oct. 14; *Major,* P21 Nov. 34; *Lt.-Col.* 26 July 44.
15	0	Robert Blucher Wood,[4] CB. *Cornet,* P30 Dec. 34; *Lieut.* P12 Feb. 36; *Capt.* P31 Dec. 41; *Major,* P17 May, 44; *Lieut.-Col.* P30 Dec. 45.
19	0	*Majors.*—Robert Alex. Lockhart,[5] *Cornet* P11 June 30; *Lieut.* P5 Oct. 32; *Capt.* P13 July 38; *Major* P30 Dec. 45.
33	3½	Charles Lewis,[6] *Ens.* 9 June 13; *Lt.* 30 Dec. 19; *Capt.* 22 Mar. 32; *Brev.-Maj.* 19 June 46; *Maj.* 3 Feb. 47.

Full Pay	Half Pay	CAPTAINS.	ENSIGN.	LIEUT.	CAPTAIN.	BREV.-MAJ.
19	0	Robert George Hughes ..	P29 June 30	P 6 July 32	P 3 Dec. 41	
22	0	Richard Talbot Sayers[7] ..	P19 Apr. 27	P25 May 32	16 Mar. 43	
20	15½	James Deaves Morris	14 Apr. 14	25 June 18	18 Mar. 43	
11	0	Lambert L. Montgomery[7]	P22 June 38	P17 Jan. 40	P28 July 43	
13	0	Samuel Tolfrey Christie	P22 Jan. 36	P13 July 38	28 Aug. 45	
11	0	Alex. William Riley[7]	P26 June 38	P19 Feb. 41	22 Dec. 45	
11	0	Anthony Ormsby[9]	P13 July 38	P 2 July 41	25 Dec. 45	
18	0	Robert Hawkes	P 2 Dec. 31	8 July 37	P11 Oct. 44	
16	0	Henry Crickitt Tyler....	P 3 May 33	P 1 May 35	P27 June 46	
g9	0	Edward Hardinge[12]	P11 Jan. 40	P31 Dec. 41	P22 Dec. 48	
		LIEUTENANTS.				
12	0	John Cumming[11]	P23 Sept. 37	P 8 May 40		
7	0	Theodore Rich. Hickson	1 Apr. 42	15 July 43		
10	0	George Dean Pitt, *s.*	11 Oct. 39	19 Jan. 44		
9	0	Charles Duperier[13]	29 Dec. 40	26 July 44		
8	0	Astell Thomas Welsh ..	P21 May 41	26 July 44		
8	0	Edward Alan Holdich,[14] *s.*	P 2 July 41	do.		
8	0	George Samuel Young[7] ..	16 July 41	do.		
7	0	William Hunter[15]	20 May 42	do.		
6	0	Wm. Fred. Adams Colman[7]	15 June 43	10 Mar. 45		
6	0	Henry Geo. John Bowler[7]	16 June 43	13 July 45		
7	0	Benjamin Hallowell Boxer	21 May 42	28 Aug. 45		
5	0	*Hon.* Arth. E. Hardinge[16] ..	P 7 June 44	22 Dec. 45		
5	0	Hamilton Charles Smith	P 8 Oct. 44	24 Dec. 45		
6	0	William Calvert Dunn ..	P15 Dec. 43	P 3 Apr. 46		
3	0	William Deane Freeman	P30 Jan. 46	9 Oct. 46		
7	0	Robert Cassels Oliphant	15 Apr. 42	13 Nov. 46		
3	0	*Hon.* John Howe M. Browne	27 Feb. 46	11 Dec. 46		
4	0	George Bodle, *Adj.*	23 May 45	21 Feb. 46		
4	0	Bliss John Hume	11 Nov. 45	P17 Mar. 48		
4	0	Matthew Kirkland......	22 Dec. 45	20 Oct. 48		
3	0	James John Dudgeon ...	20 Mar. '46	P22 Dec. 48		
4	0	Frederick Miller........	16 May 45	P 4 April 46		
4	0	Charles Frederick Amiel	P16 May 45	P25 Sept. 46		
		ENSIGNS.				
3		Donald Maclean Fraser..	8 May 46			
3		Thomas Airey,[19]	21 April 46			
3		William Paterson	11 Dec. 46			
2		Thomas William Hunt ..	21 May 47			
2		Jas. L. Winniett Nunn ..	29 Oct. 47			
1	0	Robert D. David Lecky	P21 Jan. 48			
3	0	Edward John Mathias ..	18 Sept. 46			
1	0	Cecil Rice	1 Dec. 48			

Full Pay	Half Pay	
23	0	*Paymaster.*—Tho. Bloomfield Hunt,[21] 1 Aug. 37; *Ens.* P19 Jan. 26; *Lt.* 25 Oct. 3[illegible]
4	0	*Adjutant.*—*Lieut.* George Bodle, 21 May 47.
3	0	*Quarter-Master.*—George Crawford, 21 May, 47; *Ens.* 18 Sept. 46.
16	0	*Surgeon.*—John Robert Taylor,[22] 14 June, 42; *Assist.-Surg.* 31 May, 33.
7	0	*Assist.-Surgs.*—Miah William Murphy, 22 July, 42.
3	0	David Stuart Erskine Bain, 23 Jan. 46.
2	0	Henry Carr Lucas, 2 Mar. 47.

Agents, Messrs. Cox & Co.
Facings Yellow.

5 Major Lockhart served the campaign on the Sutlej (medal) with the 80th, including the battles of Moodkee, Ferozeshah (severely wounded) and Sobraon.

6 Major Lewis served in the Peninsula from Aug. 1813 to the end of that war in 1814. Also the campaigns of 1825 and 26 in Burmah, as Brigade Major. He served the campaign on the Sutlej [illegible] with the 80th, including the battles of Moodkee, Ferozeshah, & [illegible]

7 Captains Sayers, Montgomery and Riley, Lieuts. Young, Colman, Bowler, and Bodle, served the campaign on the Sutlej (medal) with the 80th, including the battles of Moodkee, Ferozeshah, and Sobraon. Lt. Young was wounded in the hand at Sobraon.

9 Capt. Ormsby served the campaign on the Sutlej (medal), including the battles of Aliwal and Sobraon. He was also present at Buddiwal.

11 Lt. Cumming served in China with the 26th (medal), and was present at the first capture of Chusan, and at the action of Chuen [illegible]

12 Captain Hardinge was present with the 39th in the action at Maharajpore on 29th Dec. 1843 (medal). He served the campaign on the Sutlej (medal) with the 80th, including the battles of Moodkee and Sobraon.

13 Lt. Duperier served with the 26th in China (medal) at Ningpo, Chapoo, Shanghae, Woosung, and Chin Kiang Foo (wounded).

[For Note 14, see preceding page.

1 Sir Edmund Williams served the campaign of 1799 in Holland, including the actions of the 2nd and 6th Oct. (wounded). Present at the battle of Maida, in 1806; and at the taking of Ischia, in 1809. Served also throughout the war in the Peninsula, including the battle of Busaco (wounded), siege of Badajoz, in 1811, battle of Salamanca [illegible] once severely), siege of Burgos, battle of Vittoria, action at Tolosa, the entire siege of St. Sebastian, including the first, second (wounded), and third assaults; passage of the Bidassoa, battles of the Nivelle and Nive, passage of the Adour, and investment of Bayonne (wounded). Sir Edmund has received a cross and one clasp.

2 Lt.-Col. Bunbury served in the Peninsula from 1808 to the end of the war, including capture of Oporto, battles of Talavera and Barrosa. He was Major of Brigade to the force which defended Tarifa (at the [illegible] ment of which he had his horse shot under him), at the capture of Seville, defence of the Bridge of Puente Largo near Aranjuez. He was present at the battles of the Nivelle and of the Nive (severely wounded), [illegible] ment of Bayonne, and commanded the 6th Caçadores at the battle of Toulouse. He commanded the [illegible] and was employed on various services for four years in New Zealand, from the establishment of the settlement until 1844,—towards the close of which year he was wrecked on one of the Andaman Islands, and he commanded the troops and crews of the transports *Briton* and *Runnymede,* for [illegible] where, under the most trying yet providential circumstances, the lives of about 600 troops and [illegible] ing women and children, were preserved. He commanded the 80th throughout the campaign on the [illegible] (medal) including the battles of Moodkee (wounded), Ferozeshah (horse shot under him) and [illegible]

"MAIDA"—"CORUNNA"—"PENINSULA."

Years' Serv. 55

Colonel.

Full Pay.	Half Pay.	
		Thomas Evans,[1] CB. *Ens.* 3 Dec. 94; *Lieut.* 1 Oct. 95; *Capt.* 19 Nov. 03; *Major,* 6 Feb. 12; *Lt.-Col.* 13 Oct. 12; *Col.* 22 July, 30; *Major-Gen.* 28 June, 38; *Col.* 81st Regt. 12 July, 47.
19	0	*Lieut.-Colonel.*—William Henry Charles Wellesley, *Ens.* P29 June 30; *Lieut.* P5 Oct. 32; *Capt.* P17 Jan. 40; *Major,* P14 April 48; *Lieut.-Col.* P3 Nov. 48.
19	0	*Majors.*—Henry Farrant, *Ens.* 9 July 30; *Lieut.* 13 Feb. 35; *Capt.* 10 May 44; *Major,* P3 Nov. 48.
16	0	Henry Renny, *Ens.* P27 Dec. 33; *Lieut.* P7 Aug. 35; *Capt.* 29 May 44; *Major,* P17 Nov. 48.

Full Pay.	Half Pay.	CAPTAINS.	ENSIGNS.	LIEUT.	CAPTAIN.	BREV.-MAJ.
25	0	Abraham Splaine	P28 Oct. 24	P22 Apr. 26	P16 Mar. 32	9 Nov. 46
26	7 1/12	James Ward	25 May 15	P23 June 25	P 6 July 32	9 Nov. 46
22	0	John Hamilton Stewart	23 July 27	2 Aug. 34	2 July 41	
15	0	*Hon.* Rob. A. Geo. Dalzell	P21 Mar. 34	P11 Sept. 35	P30 July 44	
15	0	Henry Edward Sorell ..	P16 May 34	P 6 Nov. 35	13 Nov. 46	
17	0	George W. Raikes	P14 Dec. 32	P23 Oct. 35	P22 Dec. 46	
13	0	Anchitel F. F. Boughey..	P30 July 36	P12 June 40	5 Apr. 47	
10	0	John Arthur Gildea	P23 Aug. 39	P30 Apr. 41	P14 April 48	
7	0	Thomas Deane Perry ..	P 6 May 42	P30 July 44	P 3 Nov. 48	
6	0	Henry Austen[2]	7 April 43	P22 Jan. 47	P17 Nov. 48	
		LIEUTENANTS.				
12	0	Fred. Edw. Sorell, *adj.* ..	P11 Aug. 37	1 Jan. 41		
11	0	John Oldright..........	21 Sept. 38	28 Mar. 41		
10	0	John Bourchier	24 Aug. 39	2 July 41		
10	0	James Woods..........	31 Dec. 39	P 6 May 42		
9	0	Francis Lepper	P 7 Feb. 40	P20 Oct. 43		
8	0	Charles James Skerry ..	10 Sept. 41	29 May 44		
7	0	Wm. Benjamin Browne..	P16 Aug. 42	P18 April 45		
6	0	Charles Ellison Goodwin	24 Mar. 43	13 Nov. 46		
6	0	Robert Bruce Chichester	P20 Oct. 43	5 Apr. 47		
5	0	Fred. Sidney De Vere Lane	10 May 44	P10 Dec. 47		
5	0	Thomas Howard Fenwick	P30 July 44	P14 April 48		
4	0	Hedworth John Liddell	P18 Apr. 45	P 3 Nov. 48		
4	0	Percy G. Botfield Lake..	10 Oct. 45	P17 Nov. 48		
		ENSIGNS.				
3	0	William Fergusson Currie	P22 Dec. 46			
2	0	Thomas Hignell.........	22 Jan. 47			
2	0	William Egerton Todd ..	21 May 47			
2	0	Malachi Hanley	28 May 47			
2	0	George Betts	P10 Dec. 47			
1	0	Charles Hunter	P14 April 48			
1	0	Richard Henry Willcocks	P 3 Nov. 48			
1	0	Henry Louis Villiers	P17 Nov. 48			
19	0	*Paymaster*—Wm. Fred. Nixon, 8 Jan. 41; *Ens.* 3 Aug. 30; *Lieut.* P22 Jan. 36.				
12	0	*Adjutant.*—*Lieut.* Fred. Edward Sorell, 13 Nov. 46.				
5	0	*Quarter-Master.*—James Correll, 28 June, 44.				
15	0	*Surgeon.*—George Taylor, 30 May, 45; *Assist.-Surg.* 16 May, 34.				
6	0	*Assist.-Surgeon.*—Charles Frederick Stephenson, M.D. 20 Oct. 43.				

2 Captain Austen served as a volunteer on board H. M. S. *Bellerophon* at the siege and capture of Acre and throughout the Syrian campaign (Medal.)

Facings Buff.—*Agents,* Messrs. Cox & Co.

[*Returned from Canada,* 24 *Sept.* 47.]

1 Maj.-Gen. Evans's services:—Entered the army in 1793 as a volunteer, and enlisted 150 men for the service. Operations in the West Indies and Ireland, in 1794 and 95; capture of Demerara and Berbice, in 1796. Captured returning from South America, and kept a close prisoner in France, in 1797. Operations at Minorca and Guernsey, in 1798 and 99; ditto on the Coast of Spain, Malta, and Marmorice, in 1800. Egyptian campaign of 1801 (medal), including the actions of the 8th, 13th, and 21st of March: battle of Rahmanie on the Nile, and reduction of that fortress, sieges and surrender of Cairo and Alexandria (as Lieut. and Adjutant of the 8th). Operations at Gibraltar, in 1802 and 3; ditto in the West Indies (as Captain in the 8th and Aide de-camp to Sir Gordon Drummond), in 1804, 5, and 6. Operations in Nova Scotia, in 1807 and 8; ditto in the Canadas (as Aide-de-camp and Military Secretary to Sir G. Drummond), in 1809, 10, and 11. Campaigns of 1812, 13, and 14, in Upper Canada (as Brigade Major, discharging duties of Deputy-Adjutant-General, and in command of the 8th), including the preparation of the force against Detroit and Michilimackinac, the defence of Fort George, and destruction of the enemy's attacking batteries, and directing the reinforcements on Queenston, which enabled Major-General Sheaffe to defeat and capture the American army, after General Brock's fall in a gallant attempt on the enemy with inadequate means. Assault on Sackett's Harbour, expulsion of the enemy's army from Forty Mile Creek, and capture of his army material, with many prisoners; battle of Chippewa, covering the army's retirement on Fort George, and retrograde on Twenty Mile Creek, until resuming the offensive. Night attack on the enemy's investing force of Fort George, on which the American commander, General Swift, was slain. Battle of Lundy's Lane, two repulses of the enemy's sorties, with severe loss, on the 5th and 13th Aug. 1814, before Fort Erie, by the pickets under his command; assault of Fort Erie, and the series of affairs on the Niagara frontier. For these services, and conducting the 2nd battalion of the King's regiment from New Brunswick to Canada, through the Wilderness, General Evans has had honourable mention made of his name in the London Gazettes, and in General Orders on ten several occasions; and so unremitted have been this officer's services in all quarters, that out of forty-five years of practical work, two only were in England. Wounded in three places at Sackett's Harbour; sword struck from his grasp and shivered at Lundy's Lane; contused and had his horse shot at Fort Erie.

On the Colours and Appointments, the *Prince of Wales's Plume*.—"ROLEIA"—"VIMIERA"—"VITTORIA"—"PYRENEES"—"NIVELLE"—"ORTHES"—"PENINSULA"—"NIAGARA."

Serv.	
	Colonel.
6	*Sir* Andrew Pilkington,[1] KCB. *Ens.* 7 Mar. 83; *Lieut.* 24 Jan. 91; *Capt.* 2 Mar. 95; *Major*, 31 Mar. 04; *Lieut.-Col.* 5 Oct. 09; *Col.* 12 Aug. 19; *Major-Gen.* 22 July, 30; *Lieut.-Gen.* 23 Nov. 41; *Col.* 82nd Regt. 10 May, 41.
Half Pay.	*Lieut.-Colonel.*
0	Charles Francis Maxwell, *Ens.* P 28 July 25; *Lieut.* P 17 Aug. 26; *Capt.* P 16 Nov. 32; *Brev.-Maj.* 9 Nov. 46; *Major*, 10 July, 47; *Lt.-Col.* P 27 Oct. 48.
	Majors.
11 8/12	William Slater, *Ens.* 9 Sept. 12; *Lieut.* 20 Jan. 14; *Capt.* P 25 Nov. 28; *Major*, 3 June, 41.
0	James Alex. Robertson, *Ens.* P 6 Mar. 23; *Lieut.* P 17 Sept. 25; *Capt.* P 8 June 32; *Brev.-Maj.* 9 Nov. 46; *Major*, P 27 Oct. 48.

Serv.		ENSIGN.	LIEUT.	CAPTAIN.	BREV.-MAJ.
	CAPTAINS.				
0	George Ogle Moore	18 Sept. 28	P 3 Dec. 30	P 12 July 33	9 Nov. 46
13 8/12	Benoit Bender[4]	P 29 Dec. 08	4 Apr. 10	26 Nov. 30	9 Nov. 46
0	Wm. Jas. Whittuck	P 3 Dec. 30	P 28 Aug. 35	P 21 June 39	
0	Edw. Blagden Hale	P 2 Aug. 33	P 29 Jan. 36	P 5 Feb. 41	
0	David Watson..........	P 12 July 33	P 24 Oct. 35	3 June 41	
0	Jas. P. Bowyer Puleston	P 24 Oct. 35	P 26 Apr. 39	P 27 May 42	
0	Fred. William Diggle....	P 14 Oct. 36	P 21 June 39	10 July 47	
0	John Allen Lloyd Philipps	P 31 Dec. 41	P 20 Sept. 43	P 8 Dec. 46	
0	John Montresor, ...	14 Dec. 38	P 12 Mar. 41	P 13 June 45	
0	E.R.W. Wingfield Yates, *s.*	P 24 Mar. 37	P 2 Aug. 39	P 27 Oct. 48	
	LIEUTENANTS.				
0	Osborne West..........	P 11 May 38	P 13 Dec. 39		
0	Cha. T. Vesey Isaac	30 Oct. 38	26 Dec. 40		
0	Geo. Edm. Halliday......	P 23 Aug. 39	P 15 Apr. 42		
0	Octavius Fred. Timins ..	P 28 Aug. 40	P 30 May 43		
0	Charles Graves	P 5 Mar. 41	19 Aug. 42		
0	Frederick Edward Tighe	P 28 July 43	P 23 Jan. 46		
0	Henry Bruce, *Adj.*......	3 June 41	3 Apr. 47		
0	Stanley Slater	16 Apr. 42	4 Apr. 47		
0	Samuel Peters Jarvis....	P 14 June 45	15 Jan. 47		
0	Charles Pringle Beague..	P 23 Sept. 45	P 2 Mar. 47		
4/12	John Lawrie	P 22 Dec. 43	P 7 Nov. 47		
0	Charles Joseph Harford..	P 16 Jan. 46	P 27 Oct. 48		
0	Wm. Roberts Farmar[5] ..	P 25 Feb. 45	11 April 46		
	ENSIGNS.				
0	Herbert Morris	P 19 June 46			
0	*Hon.* Alfred Bury	26 June 46			
0	William Alex. Baillie	28 Aug. 46			
0	Daniel Stratton Collings	P 30 Mar. 47			
0	Thomas Smith	28 May 47			
0	John Gordon	3 Sept. 47			
0	William Barron	P 26 Nov. 47			
0	John Sprot	P 10 Sept. 48			

4 Major Bender served in Canada from Dec. 1808 to Jan. 1815, and was present in the action of Maguaga, taking of Detroit, taking several Block houses on the Miamie River, actions at the River Raisin and Miamie, storming of Sandusky and Fort Niagara, engagement of 2nd Jan. 1814, actions at Black Rock and at Buffalo.

Serv.	
0	*Paymaster.*—Luke FitzGerald Bernard, 8 Dec. 48; *Ens.* P 6 Aug. 41; *Lieut.* P 3 May 44.
0	*Adjutant.*—*Lieut.* Henry Bruce, 3 June, 41.
0	*Quarter-Master.*—Robert Hare, 11 Feb. 48.
0	*Surgeon.*—Thomas David Hume, M.D. 2 July, 41; *Assist.-Surg.* 11 Oct. 27; *Hosp. Assist.* 26 Oct. 26.
0	*Assistant-Surgeon.*—Geo. Thos. Finlay, 22 Dec. 48.

Facings Yellow.—*Agent*, John Lawrie, Esq.

[*Returned from North America*, 8 *June*, 48.]

Andrew Pilkington served on board the Channel Fleet in 1793 and 94. Commanded a company of the Queen's on board the *Royal George*, in Lord Howe's action of 1st June, 1794, and received two splinter wounds. Employed Vest Indies in 1793, 96, and 97, including the capture of Trinidad. In Ireland during the rebellion in 1798; with the ons to the Helder in 1799 and 1805. In 1814, commanded a brigade at the reduction of the islands in Passamaquoddy On passage to India in 1800, he was severely wounded in the defence of the *Kent* East Indiaman against a large privateer.

ut Farmar served with the 50th on the Sutlej (medal), at Buddiwal and Aliwal, at which last he was severely l in the right thigh by a grape shot while carrying the colours.

"CAPE OF GOOD HOPE"—"TALAVERA"—"BUSACO"—"FUENTES D'ONOR"—"CIUDAD RODRIGO"—"BADAJOZ"—"SALAMANCA"—"VITTORIA"—"NIVELLE"—"ORTHES"—"TOULOUSE"—"PENINSULA."

Years' Serv.		
Full Pay.	Half Pay.	*Colonel.*
49		🄿 *Sir* Frederick Stovin,[1] KCB. KCMG. *Ens.* 22 March 1800; *Lieut.* 7 Jan. 01; *Capt.* 24 June 02; *Major,* 27 April 12; *Lt.-Col.* 26 Aug. 13; *Col.* 22 July 30; *Major-Gen.* 23 Nov. 41; *Col.* 83rd Regiment, 1 Sept. 48.
43	$1\frac{2}{12}$	*Lieut.-Colonels.*—Botet Trydell,[2] *Ens.* 19 Oct. 04; *Lt.* 30 Oct. 06; *Capt.* 17 Nov. 18; *Major,* P 3 Dec. 29; *Brev.-Lt.-Col.* 23 Nov. 41; *Lt.-Col.* 2 Aug. 24.
31	$4\frac{8}{12}$	🄿 Wm. Henry Law,[3] *Ens.* 29 April, 13; *Lieut.* P 28 Nov. 16; *Capt.* P 14 July, 25; *Brevet-Major,* 28 June, 38; *Major,* 2 Apr. 41; *Lt.-Col.* 22 Dec. 48.
40	0	*Majors.*—🄿 Joseph Swinburne,[4] *Ens.* 16 Aug. 09; *Lieut.* 4 June, 12; *Capt.* 6 Oct. 25; *Brev.-Major,* 28 June, 38; *Major,* 2 Aug. 42.
31	$2\frac{1}{12}$	Edward Townsend, *Ens.* 23 May 16; *Lieut.* P 28 Oct. 24; *Capt.* P 18 Feb. 26; *Brev.-Major,* 23 Nov. 41; *Major,* 22 Dec. 48.

Full Pay	Half Pay	CAPTAINS.	ENSIGN.	LIEUT.	CAPTAIN.	BREV.-MAJ.
25	0	Henry Francis Ainslie....	29 Jan. 24	P 7 Nov. 26	P 5 April 31	9 Nov. 46
19	0	Edward D'Alton.........	13 June 30	P 2 Aug. 33	P 20 Sept. 39	
18	0	Henry Lloyd...........	P 5 Apr. 31	P 8 April 34	P 10 April 40	
24	0	John Kelsall............	P 14 July 25	P 30 April 27	4 Oct. 41	
25	0	William Garstin	28 Oct. 24	29 May 28	2 Aug. 42	
16	0	D. W. P. Labalmondiere	21 June 33	P 25 May 38	P 7 June 44	
16	0	Thomas Richard De Rinzy	P 2 Aug. 33	14 Nov. 38	P 22 July 45	
15	0	Edward Steele..........	P 18 April 34	P 15 Mar. 39	P 19 Mar. 47	
11	0	Charles Wilson Austen..	P 14 Dec. 38	P 15 Dec. 40	P 1 Dec. 48	
14	0	Septimus Alphonso F. Cary	P 3 April 35	20 May 40	22 Dec. 48	
		LIEUTENANTS.				
13	0	Thomas Spring, *r.*	P 14 May 36	2 Apr. 41		
11	0	David Anderson.........	28 Dec. 38	15 May 41		
10	0	John Thos. Downman ...	P 1 Feb. 39	P 19 Nov. 41		
10	0	*Hon.* William Gage	P 22 Mar. 39	2 Aug. 42		
8	0	John William Crowe....	2 July 41	P 3 Apr. 46		
8	0	William Nott, *Adj.*	19 Nov. 41	21 May 46		
6	0	John Dennis Swinburne	25 Mar. 43	3 Oct. 46		
5	0	Thomas Adams	P 20 Aug. 44	P 19 Mar. 47		
6	0	Rob. H. Payne Crawfurd	P 27 Jan. 43	P 11 July 45		
4	0	John Sharman Molony..	P 23 May 45	29 June 48		
4	0	Henry De Renzy Pigott	P 22 July 45	P 19 Sept. 48		
4	0	William Mills Molony ..	P 8 Aug. 45	P 1 Dec. 48		
7	0	Samuel Read	31 Oct. 42	28 Feb. 44		
7	0	Edw. M. H. Mainwaring[5]	28 Jan. 42	26 Mar. 46		
5	0	Thomas Parker Wright..	2 Feb. 44	7 Aug. 46		
5	0	James Verling Ellis	29 Mar. 44	P 8 Sept. 46		
4	0	John Norris M'Kelvey ..	P 25 Feb. 45	P 11 Dec. 46		
4	0	John Meade	10 May 45	9 Jan. 47		
4	0	Mowbray Baumgartner..	P 4 April 45	P 26 Nov. 47		
3	0	Wm. Kavanagh Bookey	P 3 April 46	22 Dec. 48		
3	0	Wm. John Nunn	P 22 May 46	do		
2	0	Stephen Wm. Metge	P 12 Feb. 47	do		
2	0	Herbert Stanley Cooper	P 19 Mar. 47	do		
		ENSIGNS.				
1	0	William Hall	1 Aug. 48			
1	0	Frederick Dickinson	18 Aug. 48			
3	0	Fran. Hen. Digby Marsh	31 Mar. 46			
1	0	Usher William Alcock ..	P 17 Mar. 48			
1	0	Marm. N. Richardson ..	P 27 Oct. 48			
1	0	Thomas Rowland	22 Dec. 48			
1	0	Thomas Graham........	do			
1	0	Richard Thomas Sweeny	P 1 Dec. 48			

Full Pay	Half Pay	
26	10	*Paymaster.*—Richard Brough, 7 Oct. 24; * *Lieut.* 25 Dec. 13.
8	0	*Adjutant.*—*Lieut.* William Nott, 19 Nov. 41.
6	0	*Quarter-Master.*—William Calburn,[5] 16 Sept. 45; *Ens.* 22 Dec. 43.
23	0	*Surgeon.*—George Ledingham, M.D. 2 July, 41; *Assist.-Surg.* 8 Nov. 27; *Hosp.-Assist.* 31 Aug. 26.
7	0	*Assist.-Surgeons.*—John Harry Ker Innes, 8 April 42.
2	0	William Nettleton Boyce, 12 Feb. 47.
1	0	James Hamilton Bewes, 22 Dec. 48.

Facings Yellow.—*Agents,* Messrs. Cox & Co.—*Irish Agents, Sir* E. R. Borough, *Bt.,* [Armit, & Co.,

[*Returned from Canada, July* 1843.]

2 Lieut.-Colonel Trydell served at the capture of the Cape of Good Hope, in 1806; and was present at the battle of Blueberg. He served also in the Kandian Insurrection of 1817 and 18, in Ceylon.

3 Lt.-Col. Law served in the Peninsula from Sept. 1813 to the end of the war, including the battles of Nivelle and Nive.

4 Major Swinburne served in the Peninsula from 1809 to the end of the war, including the battles of Oporto, Talavera (wounded in the right arm and foot), and Busaco; actions at Pombal, Leria, Condeixa, Fleur-de-lis, Guarda, and Sabugal; battle of Fuentes d'Onor, first siege of Badajos, action at Elbodon, sieges of Ciuda Rodrigo and Badajos, battles of Salamanca, Vittoria, Pyrenees, and Nivelle; action at Salvaterre, battle of Orthes (wounded in the neck), action at Vic Bigorre and battle of Toulouse.

5 Quarter-Master Calburn served with the Buffs at the battle of Punniar (Medal).

5 Lieut. Mainwaring served in the Queen's in the campaign in the southern Mahratta country in 1844 (including the storming of the fortress of Punella), and that in the Concan in 1845.

1 Sir Frederick Stovin served at the Ferrol, in 1800; in Germany, in 1805; at the siege and capture of Copenhagen, in 1807; with the expedition to Sweden, in 1808; in Spain and Portugal, in 1808-9, including the retreat to and battle of Corunna. With the expedition to Walcheren and at the capture of Flushing, in 1809; subsequently in the Peninsula, and was second in command at the first defence of Tarifa; Aide-de-camp to Sir Thomas Picton at the siege and capture of Ciudad Rodrigo and Badajos. Assistant Adjutant-General to the 3rd division at the battle of Salamanca, capture of Madrid and the Retiro, retreat therefrom and subsequent advance, passage of the Ebro, battles of Vittoria, Pyrenees, Nivelle, and Orthes, action at Vic Bigorre, and battle of Toulouse. Served also at New Orleans, where he was wounded. Sir Frederick

Emb. for the East Indies, April, 1840.

84th (*York and Lancaster*) Regt. of Foot.

[Serving at Secunderabad, Madras.

The *Union Rose*, "NIVE"—"PENINSULA"—"INDIA."

Years' Serv.		
63		*Colonel.*
		Sir Loftus Wm. Otway,[1] CB. *Cornet*, 17 May, 1796; *Lieut.* 2 Sept. 96; *Capt.* 27 Oct. 98; *Major*, 24 Feb. 1803; *Lieut.-Col.* 28 Mar. 05; *Col.* 4 June, 13; *Major-Gen.* 12 Aug. 19; *Lieut Gen.* 10 Jan. 37; *Col.* 84th Rég. 30 Dec. 40.
Full Pay.	Half Pay.	
26	0	*Lieut.-Cols.*—Charles Franklyn, *Ens.* P17 July, 23; *Lieut.* P8 April, 26; *Capt.* P10 July, 28; *Major*, P28 Dec. 38; *Lieut.-Col.* 16 Sept. 45.
21	0	David Russell, *Cornet*, P10 Jan. 28; *Lieut.* P1 Oct. 29; *Capt.* P5 April, 33; *Major*, 7 July, 45; *Lieut.-Col.* P10 Dec. 47.
27	4	*Majors.*—Matthew Benjamin George Reed, *Ens.* P26 Feb. 18; *Lieut.* P19 Nov. 25; *Capt.* P26 Feb. 36; *Major*, 16 Sept. 45.
24	0	George Green,[2] *Ens.* 7 April, 25; *Lieut.* 29 June 27; *Capt.* P10 Nov. 37; *Major*, P19 Nov. 44.

Full Pay.	Half Pay.		ENSIGN.	LIEUT.	CAPTAIN.	BREV.-MAJ.
		CAPTAINS.				
23	0	James Alexander West ..	P 6 July 26	28 Feb. 28	8 April 42	
21	0	Thomas Bridge..........	P26 June 28	30 Aug. 31	18 Nov. 42	
24	7 1/12	Thomas Fred. Richardson	25 Dec. 17	26 April 28	14 Oct. 42	
16	0	Matthew Cassan.........	P13 Dec. 33	19 May 38	13 Mar. 44	
15	0	Thomas Davison.........	P23 May 34	P 2 Nov. 38	7 July 45	
23	11 1/2	Wm. Justin MacCarthy..	15 June 15	30 Sept. 30	29 March 44	
14	0	George Francis Harrison	P26 June 35	P28 Dec. 38	16 Sept. 45	
13	0	Wm. Murray Mitchell ..	P 5 Mar. 36	P 1 Nov. 39	7 Dec. 45	
18	0	William Radcliffe	P27 Sept. 31	P24 Apr. 35	P 7 June 44	
11	0	Charles F. Seymour	9 Jan. 38	29 Aug. 40	P10 Dec. 47	
		LIEUTENANTS.				
11	0	Thos. Lightfoot.........	1 June 38	P 30 Oct. 40		
13	0	Henry Fred. Saunders,[4] *r.*	30 July 36	27 Dec. 37		
11	0	*Hon.* John W. Monck, *Adj.*	P 28 Dec. 38	8 April 42		
11	0	Thomas Edmonds Holmes	P 28 Dec. 38	do.		
10	0	Geo. Fred. Macbean.....	4 Jan. 39	do.		
10	0	Spier Hughes..........	P31 Dec. 39	do.		
9	0	Wm. Frederick Macbean	P 31 Oct. 40	30 Sept. 42		
10	0	Charles Alex. Halfhide[5]	20 June 39	25 June 41		
7	0	Arthur Moore Cassan....	P 7 April 42	29 Dec. 43		
7	0	Robert Wallen Jones	10 April 42	12 Nov. 44		
7	0	Walter C. E. Snow......	11 April 42	22 Nov. 44		
7	0	Cornelius Chas. Rolleston	20 May 42	7 July 45		
7	0	Robert Crosse Stewart ..	25 Oct. 42	16 Sept. 45		
7	0	Thomas Horan[7]	27 May 42	P23 Sept. 45		
6	0	Geo. B. Vaughan Arbuckle	29 Dec. 43	P17 Oct. 45		
7	0	Fred. Augustus Davidson	24 July 42	3 May 44		
5	0	David O'Brien	22 Nov. 44	20 May 46		
4	0	Daniel Maunsell.......	P28 Mar. 45	2 Oct. 46		
4	0	Eugene Currie	P 8 Aug. 45	P27 Oct. 46		
5	0	Francis H. Garner......	P 3 May 44	10 July 47		
7	0	Wm. M'Geachy Keats ..	P14 Oct. 42	21 April 46		
4	0	James Edmund Leahy...	P31 Oct. 45	P10 Dec. 47		
4	0	Bowes Mein	28 Mar. 45	P 24 Dec. 47		
		ENSIGNS.				
4	0	Benjamin Sandwith	19 Dec. 45			
3	0	Richard Hansted Barwell	2 Oct. 46			
3	0	Thomas H. P. Kennan ..	P27 Oct. 46			
3	0	Fred. John G. Saunders	P29 Dec. 46			
2	0	Edwin Fletcher Foster ..	P23 Apr. 47			
3	0	Geo. Fred. Tod Whitlock	P11 Dec. 46			
2	0	Edm. K. V. Arbuckle ..	P10 Dec. 47			
2	0	T. Young (Qr.-M. 9 April 47.)	21 July 48			

Full Pay.	Half Pay.	
23	0	*Paymaster.*—Geo. Henry Eddy, 28 Apr. 37; *Ens.* P29 Aug. 26; *L.* 20 Feb. 35.
11	0	*Adjutant.*—*Lieut. Hon.* John Willington Monck, 17 Dec. 47.
4	0	*Quarter-Master.*—John Faircloth, 23 May, 48; *Ens.* 16 Sept. 45; *L.* 17 Jan. 47.
16	0	*Surgeon.*—John Marshall, 30 Aug. 42; *Assist.-Surg.* 29 March, 33.
2	0	*Assistant-Surgeons*, Francis William Innes, M.D. 10 Feb. 37.
7	0	Christopher Ninian English, M.D. 8 April, 42.
5	0	Thomas Stack, M.D., 22 Nov. 44.

Facings Yellow.—*Agents*, Messrs. Cox & Co.

1 Sir Loftus Otway served in Ireland during the rebellion in 1798, and was present in the action at Vinegar Hill. Proceeded to the Peninsula in 1808 as a Major in the 18th Hussars, and on the 13th of Dec., at Rueda, he surprised and captured the whole of the French Cavalry out-lying piquet. On the 16th following, near to Valladolid, whilst *en decouvert*, he encountered Col. Antignac, commandant of the 22d Chasseurs à Cheval, at the head of a strong force; charged and routed him; took the Colonel prisoner, and more of his Chasseurs than he had Dragoons to guard them, and brought them all into Head-quarters, horses, men, arms, and baggage. At Benevente, whilst commanding the out lying piquet, he was opposed to Lieut.-General Le Fevre, for nearly an hour, at the head of six squadrons of the Imperial Guard; charged and broke his advanced guard, whose commanding officer was killed, and whose sword he took. In the affair of Campo Mayor he gained the rear of the enemy, and captured between five and six hundred men and their entire battering train (sixteen 24-pounders), and brought them part of the way back, but was obliged to abandon his capture, with the exception of sixteen prisoners and one tumbril, the enemy being in possession of the road by which he was to return. At Albuhera he commanded the three regts. of Portuguese Cavalry, which covered the left flank of the army.

2 Major Green served in the Burmese war.

4 Lieut. Saunders served nearly four years on the Western coast of Africa, and was present with the Expeditionary force in the Interior in 1837. Employed on a mission to convey despatches to the French at Senegal, in 1839.

5 Lieut. Halfhide served with the 49th throughout the whole of the operations in China except the capture of Segoan, and was present at the attack and capture of the Chusan (both operations), storm and capture of the heights above Canton, attack and capture of Amoy and Chinhae, occupation of Ningpo and repulse of the night attack, attack and capture of Chapoo, Woosung, and Chin Kiang Foo, and demonstration before Nankin.

7 Lieut. Horan served with the 41st during the whole of the campaign of 1842 in Affghanistan, and was present in the engagements with the enemy on 28 March and 28 April in the Pisheen Valley; in that of the 29th May near Candahar, 30th Aug. at Goaine, 5th Sept. before Ghuznee, occupation and destruction of that fortress and of Cabool, expedition into Kohistan, storm, capture, and destruction of Istaliff, and in the various minor affairs in and between the Bolan and the Khyber Passes.

"Aucto splendore resurgo."

"FUENTES D'ONOR"—"NIVE"—"PENINSULA"—"BLADENSBURG."

Years' Serv.		
55		
Full Pay.	Half Pay.	
		Colonel.
		✠ *Sir* John Wright Guise,[1] *Bart.* KCB. *Ens.* 4 Nov. 94; *Lieut.* and *Capt.* 25 Oct. 98; *Capt.* and *Lieut.-Col.* 25 July 05; *Col.* 4 June 13; *Major-Gen.* 12 Aug. 19; *Lieut.-Gen.* 10 Jan. 37; *Col.* 85th Lt. Infantry, 1 June 47.
		Lieut.-Colonel.
22	0	Brook Taylor, *Ens.* P 15 May, 27; *Lieut.* P 15 June, 30; *Capt.* P 28 Nov. 34; *Major*, 31 July, 46; *Lieut.-Col.* P 29 Dec. 46.
		Majors.
17	0	John Blackburn, *Ens.* P 15 June 32; *Lieut.* P 1 Sept. 37; *Capt.* P 16 Nov. 41; *Major*, P 29 Dec. 46.
16	0	Alexander G. Grant, *Ens.* P 4 Oct. 33; *Lieut.* P 18 Dec. 35; *Capt.* P 5 Aug. 42; *Major*, P 10 Nov. 48.

Full Pay	Half Pay		ENSIGN.	LIEUT.	CAPTAIN.	BREV.-MAJ.
		CAPTAINS.				
15	0	Cholmeley Edward Dering	P 9 May 34	17 April 38	P 2 Sept. 42	
15	0	John William Grey	P 16 May 34	P 1 June 38	P 31 Mar. 43	
22	0	William Todd..........	P 30 Aug. 27	P 2 Mar. 32	13 Aug. 44	
14	0	*Hon.* J. E. Hovel Thurlow	P 4 Sept. 35	P 19 Mar. 41	P 2 Aug. 44	
15	0	Ralph Allen Chas. Daniell	P 11 April 34	P 2 Feb. 38	P 20 Oct. 43	
16	0	Robert Ladbroke Day ..	P 18 Oct. 33	P 7 Aug. 35	P 19 May 46	
11	0	Thomas Edmond Knox ..	26 Jan. 38	P 24 June 42	31 July 46	
10	0	Evelyn Latimer Parratt	P 4 Oct. 39	P 31 Mar. 43	P 28 Dec. 46	
8	0	Thomas Hobbins Ward..	P 10 Sept. 41	P 8 July 42	P 10 July 46	
9	0	Conw. Fred. Cha. Seymour	P 21 Feb. 40	P 27 Oct. 43	P 10 Nov. 48	
		LIEUTENANTS.				
11	0	Pat. W. Sydenham Ross, *s.*	P 9 Nov. 38	P 2 Sept 42		
9	0	Hugh Massy	P 13 Mar. 40	P 12 Jan. 44		
8	0	John Augustus Keyt, *r.*	21 May 41	1 Apr. 44		
8	0	William Williamson	P 16 Nov. 41	P 22 Nov. 44		
7	0	Robert Maunsell	P 24 June 42	P 28 Mar. 45		
6	0	Charles Warburton......	P 31 Mar. 43	13 Jan. 46		
6	0	Wm. Alexander Filder ..	P 27 Oct. 43	P 28 Dec. 46		
5	0	*Hon.* Wm. Stuart Knox	P 12 Jan. 44	P 29 Dec. 46		
5	0	George Thompson, *Adj*...	P 23 Feb. 44	31 Mar. 47		
5	0	Charles Hamilton Aide..	17 May 44	1 Apr. 47		
5	0	George Warde.........	P 22 Nov. 44	P 10 Nov. 48		
		ENSIGNS.				
4	0	Edmund Yates Peel	31 Jan. 45			
4	0	James Gubbins	19 Dec. 45			
3	0	Alexander V. Bond......	P 24 July 46			
3	0	Frederick Sitwell	P 8 Sept. 46			
3	0	*Sir* H. H. Edwardes, *Bt.*	P 28 Dec. 46			
3	0	Frederick Thistlethwayte	P 29 Dec. 46			
2	0	*Hon.* Cavendish Browne	P 5 Nov. 47			
1	0	*Hon.* Edmund John Boyle	P 12 Sept. 48			
1	0	Nelson Rycroft	P 13 Oct. 48			
1	0	John Armitage	P 10 Nov. 48			

Full Pay	Half Pay	
33	1	*Paymaster.*—George Ash Thompson, 27 Jan. 20; *Ens.* 16 Mar. 15; *Lieut.* P 22 May, 17.
5	0	*Adjutant.*—*Lieut.* George Thompson, 25 Aug. 46.
8	0	*Quarter-Master.*—William Neil, 25 April, 41.
17	0	*Surgeon.*—George Clerihew, M.D., 5 Dec. 43; *Assist.-Surg.* 2 Nov. 32.
5	0	*Assistant-Surgeon.*—John Alex. William Thompson, M.D. 19 Nov. 44.

Facings Blue.—*Agents*, Messrs. Cox & Co.—*Irish Agents*, *Sir* E. R. Borough, *Bart.*, Armit, & Co.

[*Returned from the West Indies*, 25 *Apr.* 46.]

1 Sir John Guise served with the 3rd Guards at Ferrol, Vigo, and Cadiz, in 1800; the Egyptian campaign of 1801 (medal), including the actions of the 8th and 21st March, and 17th August, attack of the fortress of Marabout on the following day, action of the 22nd August, investment and capture of Alexandria. Expedition to Hanover in 1805-6. Proceeded to the Peninsula in 1809, and commanded the light battalion of the Guards with a Rifle company of the 60th attached, on the retreat to the lines in 1810, battle of Busaco, and subsequent retreat, lines of Torres Vedras, several actions on the advance from thence in 1811, and battle of Fuentes d'Onor. Present also at the sieges and captures of Ciudad Rodrigo and Badajoz. Commanded the 1st battalion of the 3rd Guards at the battle of Salamanca, capture of Madrid, siege of Burgos and retreat from thence, advance in 1813, battle of Vittoria, siege and capture of San Sebastian, passage of the Bidassoa, battles of the Nive, passage of the Adour, investment of Bayonne and repulse of the sortie—during the latter part of the action he commanded the 2nd brigade of Guards in consequence of Sir E. Stopford being wounded. Sir John has received a cross.

Emb. for the East Indies, May, 1842.] **86th (The Royal County Down) Regt. of Foot.** [Stationed at Bombay.

On the Colours & Appointments, the *Harp* and *Crown*, with the Motto "*Quis Separabit?*" "INDIA"—The *Sphinx*, with the words "EGYPT"—"BOURBON"—On the Buttons, the *Irish Harp* and *Crown*.

Years' Serv. Full Pay	Half Pay	
56		*Colonel.*
		P John Maister,[1] *Ens.* 13 Nov. 93; *Lieut.* 14 Jan. 94; *Capt.* 30 Mar. 95; *Major*, 20 June 01; *Lieut.-Col.* 20 Aug. 07; *Col.* 4 June 14; *Major-Gen.* 19 July 21; *Lieut.-Gen.* 10 Jan. 37; *Col.* 86th Regiment, 25 Aug. 43.
		Lieutenant-Colonels.
39	4 2/12	P Bartholomew Vigors Derinzy,[2] KH. *Ens.* 26 May, 06; *Lieut.* 16 Mar. 08; *Capt.* 25 Oct. 14; *Major*, 4 Jan. 33; *Lieut.-Col.* P 26 Feb. 41.
39	0	P Andrew Snape Hamond Aplin,[3] *Ens.* 5 July, 10; *Lt.* 24 Sept. 12; *Capt.* 9 Mar. 25; *Brev.-Major*, 28 June, 38; *Major*, P 7 July, 38; *Lieut.-Col.* 16 June, 43.
39	0	*Majors.*—James Creagh, *Ens.* 1 Jan. 10; *Lieut.* 4 March, 12; *Capt.* 7 April, 25; *Brevet-Major*, 28 June, 38; *Major*, P 18 Jan. 39.
34	4/12	Henry Edm. De Burgh Sidley, *Cornet*, 4 May 15; *Lieut.* 21 Feb. 22; *Capt.* P 11 June 30; *Major*, 8 April, 42.

Full Pay	Half Pay		Ensign.	Lieut.	Captain.	Brev.-Maj.
		Captains.				
27	3 3/12	Robert Henry Lowth ..	P 4 Feb. 19	P 1 April 24	P 15 May 27	23 Nov. 41
18	0	Joseph Edwards........	P 11 Oct. 31	P 4 Dec. 35	P 11 May 41	
21	0	William Stuart	6 Mar. 28	P 28 Sept. 30	8 Apr. 42	
22	0	Giles Keane	21 June 27	P 22 Feb. 31	23 Oct. 42	
19	2 1/12	Wm. Harding Woodgate	13 Dec. 27	P 11 Oct. 31	14 Nov. 43	
26	0	Abra. Collis Anderson, *s.*	12 June 23	9 July 29	27 Aug. 43	
26	8/12	Donough O'Brien	12 Sept. 22	2 July 29	31 Oct. 40	
8	0	Thomas Andrews Rawlins	P 17 Nov. 41	P 29 Dec. 43	P 5 Feb. 47	
13	0	John Perkins Mayers ..	P 29 July 36	P 23 Apr. 39	P 27 Jan. 43	
13	0	Harvey Wel. Pole Welman[6]	2 April 36	28 Dec. 38	9 Jan. 46	
		Lieutenants.				
10	0	Alexander Lecky, *r.*	P 18 May 39	P 2 Apr. 42		
11	0	Joshua Henry Kirby	P 10 Aug. 38	8 Apr. 42		
11	0	John Rees Croker[5]......	P 25 Dec. 38	do.		
9	0	Charles George Butler[4]..	P 3 Nov. 40	do.		
8	0	Charles Osborne Creagh[4]	18 June 41	P 5 Aug. 42		
9	0	Francis Boynton Cowper	11 Sept. 40	15 Apr. 42		
8	0	Wm. Henry Weaver	P 28 Dec. 41	23 Feb. 43		
10	0	Charles Darby[4]	6 Sept. 39	P 30 July 42		
7	0	James Boyd, *Adj.*	8 Apr. 42	13 Nov. 43		
7	0	John Jerome	9 Apr. 42	14 Nov. 43		
7	0	Francis Russell Creed ..	P 6 May 42	21 Nov. 43		
7	0	John James Matthews ..	P 5 Aug. 42	P 3 May 44		
6	0	Edward Baker Weaver ..	25 Feb. 43	24 July 46		
7	0	Wm. H. Howard Ellison	29 Apr. 42	1 Aug. 44		
7	0	Andrew Baxter[8]	27 Dec. 42	1 July 45		
6	0	James John Gordon	27 Jan. 43	11 Nov. 45		
7	0	William Henry Beatty ..	16 Apr. 42	8 Sept. 46		
5	0	George Wm. Robinson ..	22 Mar. 44	2 Sept. 47		
5	0	John Spier	30 July 44	1 May 46		
3	0	O. Robert Hamond Orlebar	P 13 Mar. 46	P 10 Dec. 47		
5	0	John Richardson Stuart	23 Mar. 44	13 Dec. 47		
6	0	Ormond Fitzgerald	6 Jan. 43	1 Apr. 47		
3	0	Hen. Marshman Havelock	31 Mar. 46	P 23 June 48		
		Ensigns.				
4	0	George Sherman Nunn..	9 May 45			
3	0	Ralph FitzGibbon Lewis	27 Oct. 46			
2	0	Hampden Cole Bowen ..	P 23 Mar. 47			
3	0	*Hon.* Wm. Hen. Lysaght	13 Nov. 46			
2	0	Maxwell Lepper	P 13 Aug. 47			
2	0	Edward Leet	P 10 Dec. 47			
2	0	Hopton Bassett Scott ..	24 Dec. 47			
1	0	Henry Edward Jerome ..	21 Jan. 48			

2 Lieut.-Colonel Derinzy's services:—Campaign and battle of Corunna (severely wounded in both knees); expedition to Walcheren, including the siege and capture of Flushing (wounded in left arm.) In the Peninsula campaigns, from Dec. 1810 to the end of that war in 1814, including the affairs of Pombal and Redinha, re-capture of Campo Mayor, capture of Olivença, 1st siege of Badajoz, battle of Albuhera, siege and capture of Ciudad Rodrigo, siege and capture of Badajoz, battle of Salamanca, affair of Aldea de Ponte, retreat from Madrid, affairs of Osma and Jocaunna, battle of Vittoria, blockade of Pampeluna, affairs of Roncesvalles, Zubiri, &c., battles of Pampeluna, 28th July, and of the Pyrenees, 30 July, affairs of Echalar, St. Estevan, &c. capture of San Sebastian, passage of the Bidassoa, battle of the Nivelle (dangerously wounded through the body, reported killed); battle of the Nive, affairs of Bastide de la Clarence, and Gave d'Oleron. Twice wounded, musket-ball in left arm, and by a splinter of a shell in the chest at the battle of Toulouse, but did not quit the field. Medal for Toulouse.

Full Pay	Half Pay	
16	0	*Paymaster.*—Charles Fade Heatly, 17 Dec. 47; *Ens.* 19 Apr. 33; *Lieut.* 7 July 37.
7	0	*Adjutant.*—*Lieut.* James Boyd, 8 April, 42.
23	0	*Quarter-Master.*—Joseph Jerome, 23 March, 26.
23	0	*Surgeon.*—Alexander Thom, 2 July, 41; *Assist.-Sur.* 8 Mar. 27; *H. A.* 2 Nov. 26.
8	0	*Assistant-Surgeons.*—James Coghlan, 5 Oct. 41.
5	0	Mark Stanley Todd, 22 Nov. 44.
1	0	James Kellie, M.D., 5 May, 48.

Facings Blue.—*Agents*, Messrs. Cox & Co.

1 Lieut.-Gen. Maister served in the Helder expedition in 1799, and was present in the actions of the 10th Sept., 2nd and 6th Oct., in which last he received four wounds. Served also in the Peninsula.

3 Lieut. Col. Aplin served in the Peninsula, from Feb. 1811 to the end of the war, including the battle of Salamanca, siege of Burgos, and capture of Madrid. Served also throughout the Burmese war, and was present in numerous engagements with the enemy.

6 Capt. Welman served with the 17th Regt. during the campaign of 1838 & 39 in Affghanistan and Beloochistan under Lord Keane, & was present at the storm & capture of Ghuznee (Medal), and of Khelat, at which last he was with the advance party.

8 Lieut. Baxter served in China in the 26th Regt. from the commencement to the termination of hostilities, and was present at Chusan, Canton, Amoy, Chinhae, defence of Ningpo, Segoan, Chapoo, Woosung, Chin Kiang Foo, and Nankin.

"MONTE VIDEO"—"TALAVERA."—An Eagle, with a Wreath of Laurel above the Harp, in addition to the Arms of the Prince of Wales, in commemoration of their distinguished Services on various occasions, and particularly at the Battle of "BARROSA"—"TARIFA"—"VITTORIA"—"NIVELLE" "ORTHES"-"TOULOUSE"—"PENINSULA"-"AVA."

Years' Serv.		
55		**Colonel.**
Full Pay.	Half Pay.	℘ Hugh, *Lord* Gough,[1] GCB. *Ens.* 7 Aug. 94; *Lieut.* 11 Oct. 94; *Capt.* 25 June, 03; *Major*, 8 Aug. 05; *Lieut.-Col.* 29 July, 09; *Col.* 12 Aug. 19; *Major-Gen.* 22 July, 30; *Lieut-Gen.* 23 Nov. 41; *Col.* 87th Fusiliers, 15 Mar. 41.
		Lieut.-Colonel.
33	3 1/12	℘ Henry Arthur Magenis,[2] *Cornet*, 1 Oct. 12; *Lieut.* 4 March, 13; *Capt.* P 9 Sept. 19; *Maj.* P 20 Nov. 27; *Brev. Lt.-Col.* 23 Nov. 41; *Lt.-Col.* 18 Apr. 45.
23	0	*Majors.*—James Campbell, *Ens.* P 6 July 26; *Lieut.* P 31 July 28; *Capt.* P 10 April 35; *Brevet-Major*, 9 Nov. 46; *Major*, 28 May 47.
23	7/12	John M'Mahon Kidd, *Ens.* P 21 July 25; *Lieut.* P 8 Nov. 27; *Capt.* P 28 Dec 32; *Brevet Major*, 9 Nov. 46; *Major*, P 13 July, 47.

Full Pay	Half Pay	CAPTAINS.	2ND LIEUT.	LIEUT.	CAPTAIN.	BREV. MAJ.
24	0	Henry B. Harvey, *s.*	P 24 Dec. 25	P 24 Nov. 28	P 28 Dec. 32	9 Nov. 46
18	0	William Boyd	P 22 Feb. 31	P 17 Oct. 34	P 26 Apr. 44	
14	0	Alexander Murray[5]	P 24 Apr. 35	23 Oct. 39	P 20 Aug. 44	
18	0	Richard Serrell O'Brien	25 Nov. 31	19 Aug. 36	18 Apr. 45	
16	0	William Percy Lea	P 22 Feb. 33	P 21 Apr. 37	31 July 46	
13	0	Robert Edwin Rich	P 10 June 36	P 18 Sept. 40	P 14 Aug. 46	
12	0	Charles F. Campbell	15 Sept. 37	P 28 Aug. 40	2 Oct. 46	
11	0	Louis H. Hamilton	6 Apr. 38	P 17 Jan. 40	22 Dec. 46	
7	0	William Henry Taylor	P 30 Dec. 42	P 7 June 44	P 23 June 48	
6	0	Alexander Hugh Cobbe	16 June 43	P 10 Jan. 45	P 21 July 48	
		FIRST LIEUTENANTS.				
7	0	William Elford Adams	20 May 42	11 Apr. 44		
6	0	Albemarle Dewar	P 25 Aug. 43	18 April 45		
7	0	James Bailie, *Adj.*	P 20 Dec. 42	P 14 Feb. 45		
5	0	John Halkett le Couteur	P 3 May 44	27 Mar. 46		
5	0	John FitzGerald	P 7 June 44	P 10 July 46		
5	0	Edw. W. Johnston Fulcher	P 20 Dec. 44	P 14 Aug. 46		
4	0	Henry Smyth Bawtree	P 10 Jan. 45	P 8 Sept. 46		
4	0	Edward Thomas King	18 April 45	28 May 47		
3	0	Edward Stanley	P 27 Mar. 46	P 13 July 47		
3	0	Hugh Lloyd	P 10 July 46	P 28 Sept. 47		
3	0	Thomp. Macky M'Clintock	P 14 Aug. 46	P 8 Oct. 47		
3	0	William Murphy	P 8 Sept. 46	P 23 June 48		
3	0	*Hon.* Aug. Mur. Cathcart	25 Sept. 46	21 July 48		
		SECOND LIEUTS.				
3	0	Austin Peter O'Malley	15 Aug. 46			
3	0	Edw. Beauchamp Maunsell	P 2 Oct. 46			
2	0	William Wiltshire	P 13 July 47			
2	0	William Baldwin	P 30 July 47			
2	0	Henry James Stephenson	P 28 Sept. 47			
2	0	George Neeld Boldero	P 8 Oct. 47			
1	0	Jasper Lucas	P 23 June 48			
1	0	John Peyton	P 21 July 48			

5 Captain Murray served in the 18th on the China expedition (Medal), and was present at Canton, Amoy, Chusan, Chinhae, Ningpo, Segoan, Chapoo (wounded), Shanghai, Woosung, and Chin Kiang Foo.

6 Paymaster Bedford served as Major and Deputy Assistant Adjutant General to the Anglo-Spanish Legion, during 1835 and part of 1836; and was engaged in the village of Mendigur, and heights of Arlaban, in Alava, on the 16th, 17th, and 18th Jan. 1836.

Full Pay	Half Pay	
21	1 7/12	*Paymaster.*—William Devaynes Bedford,[6] 28 April 37; *Ens.* P 6 April 26; [*Lt.* P 31 Jan. 27.
7	0	*Adjutant.*—*Lieut.* James Bailie, 15 Aug. 48.
2	0	*Quarter-Master.*—Robert Gibson, 2 April 47.
10	0	*Surgeon.*—William Leslie Langley, M.D. 23 March, 47; *A.-S.* 11 Jan. 39.
2	0	*Assist.-Surgeon.*—Christopher Wright Wray, 23 March, 47.

Facings Blue.—*Agent*, Charles R. M'Grigor, Esq.

[*Returned from the Mauritius*, 25 Sept. 43.]

1 Lord Gough served at the capture of the Cape of Good Hope, and the Dutch Fleet in Saldanha Bay, 1795. Served afterwards in the West Indies, including the attack on Porto Rico, the brigand war in St. Lucia, and capture of Surinam. Proceeded to the Peninsula in 1809, and commanded the 87th at the battles of Talavera, Barrosa, Vittoria, and Nivelle, for which engagements he has received a cross. He also commanded the regiment at the defence of Cadiz and of Tarifa (slightly wounded in the head). At the battle of Talavera his horse was shot under him, and he himself was afterwards severely wounded in the side by a shell,—for his conduct in this action the Duke of Wellington subsequently recommended that his Lieut.-Colonelcy should be ante-dated to the date of his despatch, thus making him the first officer who ever received Brevet rank for services performed in the field at the head of a regiment. At Barrosa his regiment captured the Eagle of the 8th French Regiment; and at Vittoria they captured the Baton of Marshal Jourdan. At the Nivelle he was again severely wounded. Commanded the Land Force at Canton—for which he was made a GCB.—and during nearly the whole of the operations in China,—for which service he was created a Baronet. On the 29th Dec. 1843, with the right wing of the army of Gwalior, he defeated a Mahratta force at Maharajpore, and captured 56 guns, &c. In 1845 and 46 the Army under his personal command defeated the Seik Army at Moodkee, Ferozeshah, and Sobraon, for which and previous services he was raised to the Peerage.

2 Lieut.-Colonel Magenis served with the 7th Fusiliers in the Peninsula and at New Orleans.

[Emb. for For. Serv. 30 Nov. 1840.] **88th Regt. of Foot (Connaught Rangers.)** [Serving at Trinidad. Depôt at Kinsale.

On the Colours and appointments the *Harp and Crown*, with the motto, "*Quis Separabit?*" The *Sphinx*, with the words "EGYPT"—"TALAVERA"—"BUSACO"—"FUENTES D'ONOR"—"CIUDAD RODRIGO"—"BADAJOZ"—"SALAMANCA"—"VITTORIA"—"NIVELLE"—"ORTHES"—"TOULOUSE"—"PENINSULA."

Years' Serv. Full Pay	Half Pay		Ensign.	Lieut.	Captain.	Brev.-Maj.
62		*Colonel.*				
		℘ *Sir* John Alex. Wallace,[1] *Bt.* KCB. *Ens.* 26 Dec. 1787; *Lieut.* 6 Apr. 90; *Capt.* 8 June, 96; *Major,* 9 July, 1803; *Lieut.-Col.* 28 Aug. 04; *Col.* 4 June, 13; *Major-Gen.* 12 Aug. 19; *Lieut.-Gen.* 10 Jan. 37; *Col.* 88th Regiment, 20 Oct. 31.				
		Lieut.-Colonel.				
24	0	Horatio Shirley, *2nd Lieut.* P 12 May, 25; *Lieut.* P 31 Oct. 26; *Capt.* P 5 July, 33; *Major,* P 31 Dec. 41; *Lieut.-Col.* 18 Jan. 48.				
24	0	*Majors.*—Edmund Richard Jeffreys, *Ens.* 16 June, 25; *Lieut.* P 11 Oct. 27; *Capt.* P 2 Feb. 38; *Major,* P 12 May, 43.				
22	0	William Irwin, *Ens.* P 15 Nov. 27; *Lieut.* 19 Nov. 30; *Capt.* P 26 Apr. 39; *Major,* 18 Jan. 48.				
		Captains.				
15	0	Robert Wm. Balfour....	P 31 Oct. 34	P 16 Mar. 38	P 25 Sept. 40	
20	0	William Mackie........	5 Feb. 29	P 14 June 33	2 Dec. 40	
14	0	Henry Beckwith Sawrey	P 6 Nov. 35	P 1 Mar. 39	P 31 Dec. 41	
28	13 4/12	℘ John Gould[2]........	31 Aug. 07	22 Mar. 09	13 Feb. 27	23 Nov. 41
11	0	Geo. Vaughan Maxwell, *s.*	P 2 Feb. 38	P 26 Apr. 39	P 6 Dec. 44	
10	0	Edward Norton........	P 25 Jan. 39	P 27 Mar. 40	P 29 Jan. 46	
15	0	Edw. John Vesey Brown	P 12 Sept. 34	29 Dec. 40	P 6 Nov. 46	
10	0	Edward Bayley........	P 5 Apr. 39	7 June 41	P 6 Aug. 47	
10	0	Edward Herbert Maxwell	P 26 Apr. 39	P 16 Nov. 41	P 8 Oct. 47	
10	0	John B. Johnson Brooke, *s.*	P 11 Oct. 39	P 31 Dec. 41	18 Jan. 48	
		Lieutenants.				
13	0	Jas. Birley Leatham....	P 5 Feb. 36	9 Jan. 39		
10	0	J. Hardman Burke, *d.adj.*	P 1 Nov. 39	P 3 Mar. 43		
9	0	Bryan Holme Holme....	P 21 Feb. 40	P 12 May 43		
8	0	Edw. Rowland Forman, *s.*	P 15 Oct. 41	P 29 Dec. 43		
9	0	Joshua Grant Crosse....	P 25 Sept. 40	P 30 Aug. 44		
8	0	Edmund Corbett......	28 Dec. 41	P 6 Dec. 44		
8	0	Edmund Gilling Maynard	P 31 Dec. 41	P 23 Jan. 46		
6	0	Thomas Gore..........	P 3 Mar. 43	P 19 Feb. 47		
5	0	Samuel Dunning, *adj.*..	16 Feb. 44	7 Oct. 47		
5	0	Benj. Banbury Mauleverer	P 30 Aug. 44	P 8 Oct. 47		
5	0	Lee Steere Steere......	P 6 Dec. 44	18 Jan. 48		
3	0	Henry Ernst..........	23 Jan. 46	P 14 April 48		
3	0	H. J. Le Marchant Baynes	14 Apr. 46	P 12 Sept. 48		
		Ensigns.				
3	0	John Salmon Bayley....	P 6 Nov. 46			
2	0	Jackson Wray........	P 19 Feb. 47			
2	0	William James Harrison	P 7 May 47			
2	0	Henry William Grogan..	P 6 Aug. 47			
2	0	John Edward Riley....	P 8 Oct. 47			
1	0	Arthur Dillon Maule....	3 Mar. 48			
1	0	Richard Grace........	P 14 Apr. 48			
1	0	William Daunt........	13 Sept. 48			
		Paymaster.—				
5	0	*Adjutant.*—*Lieut.* Samuel Dunning, 1 July, 44.				
0	0	*Quarter-Master.*—Thomas Hamilton Mills, 16 Feb. 44; *Ens.* 2 June, 43.				
12	0	*Surgeon.*—James Guy Piers Moore, 12 June, 46; *Assist.-Surg.* 3 March, 37.				
5	0	*Assist.-Surgeons.*—John Shaw Willes,[3] M.D. 15 March, 44.				
1	0	Frederick York Shegog, M.D. 18 Aug. 48.				

Facings Yellow.—*Agents,* Messrs. Cox & Co.—*Irish Agents, Sir* E. R. Borough, *Bt.,* [Armit, & Co.

1 Sir J. A. Wallace was at the battle of Seringapatam, the storming of Pagoda Hill, and of Tippoo's lines and camp, and the siege of Seringapatam, storming of Kistnagurrie, &c. &c. In 1798 served at the reduction of Minorca; from thence he joined the army under the command of Sir Ralph Abercromby, and was at the landing at Aboukir in Egypt, 8th March; the battles of the 13th and 21st, before Alexandria; at Rhamanieh, Rosetta, and Grand Cairo. He has received a Medal and two Clasps for Busaco, Fuentes d'Onor, and Salamanca.

2 Major Gould served with the 76th on the expedition to Walcheren and at the siege of Flushing in 1809; Peninsula campaigns from June 1813 to the end of that war in 1814, including the siege of San Sebastian, action of San Marcial, passage of the Bidassoa, battles of the Nivelle and Nive, and all the operations round Bayonne. Served afterwards in the Amer.can war, and was present in the action at Plattsburg.

3 Dr. Willes, with a detachment of the 17th, served with Lt.-Col. Outram's Light Brigade in the Southern Mahratta campaign of 1844-5, and was present in all its operations, including the capture of Gotra, and storming of Monohur Stockades and Fort. He received the thanks of the Governor in council, and the Commander-in-Chief in public orders for his services.

The *Sphinx*, with the words "EGYPT"—"JAVA"—"NIAGARA"—"AVA."

Years' Serv.		
58		
Full Pay.	Half Pay.	
		Colonel.
		P *Sir* Charles Bulkeley Egerton,[1] GCMG. KCH. *Ens.* 16 Nov. 1791: *Lieut.* 21 Mar. 93; *Capt.* 22 April, 95; *Major*, 1 June, 98; *Lieut.-Col.* 14 Nov. 1802; *Col.* 4 June, 11; *Major-Gen.* 4 June, 14; *Lieut.-Gen.* 22 July, 30; *Gen.* 9 Nov. 46; *Col.* 89th Regt. 26 Sept. 37.
		Lieut.-Colonel.
35	3	P Edward Thorp,[3] *Ens.* 7 Mar. 11; *Lieut.* 28 Jan. 13; *Capt.* P13 Aug. 25; *Brev.-Major*, 28 June. 38; *Major*, 21 May, 41; *Lt.-Col.* 20 Feb. 45.
24	0	*Majors.*—Robert Lewis,[4] *Ens.* 7 Apr. 25; *Lieut.* P2 Mar. 26; *Capt.* P12 Feb. 28; *Brev.-Major*, 23 Nov. 41; *Major*, 16 June, 43.
30	0	P Edward Kenny,[5] *Ens.* 17 June 13; *Lieut.* 1 Nov. 19; *Capt.* P4 Dec. 32; *Major*, 26 Feb. 45.

Full Pay	Half Pay		ENSIGN.	LIEUT.	CAPTAIN.	BREV.-MAJ.
		CAPTAINS.				
24	0	James Graham[6]........	22 Apr. 25	19 Apr. 27	P19 Apr. 38	9 Nov. 46
17	0	Caledon Rich. Egerton ..	15 June 32	P28 Mar. 34	P15 Mar. 39	
15	0	*Hon.* Charles Daly	P25 July 34	P17 Feb. 37	P31 Dec. 39	
17	0	Fred. Chas. Aylmer	P4 Dec. 32	P25 July 34	20 May 40	
19	0	John Spence	30 Sept. 30	P12 Apr. 33	14 April 43	
17	0	John Duntze Macdonald	13 July 32	P13 June 34	16 June 43	
14	0	Arthur Pigott	P24 Apr. 35	2 July 38	P25 Aug. 43	
14	0	Henry Crawford	P9 Oct. 35	8 Nov. 38	P23 Jan. 46	
10	0	Henry W. Palmer	11 Jan. 39	P22 July 42	P25 Feb. 48	
8	0	Arundel Edmund Hill ..	7 Sept. 41	P27 Oct. 43	P3 Oct. 48	
		LIEUTENANTS.				
11	0	Rob. B. Hawley, *Adj.* ..	28 Aug. 38	P31 Dec. 39		
9	0	F. Y. John Stewart	P15 May 40	16 June 43		
10	0	George Marshall Knipe, *r.*	P22 Feb. 39	20 May 42		
6	0	John Macdonald Cuppage	10 Nov. 43	P8 Aug. 45		
8	0	Leslie Skynner[7]	P26 Oct. 41	14 July 43		
7	0	John Lewes Phillipps ..	P22 July 42	P19 Dec. 45		
5	0	Chas. Henry E. Holloway	11 Oct. 44	P1 Oct. 47		
4	0	Butler Dunboyne Moore	P17 Jan. 45	P22 Oct. 47		
4	0	Tho. R. J. G. Thompson	11 July 45	P3 Mar. 48		
5	0	Hans Robert White	P22 Dec. 43	19 Dec. 45		
7	$\frac{5}{12}$	Thomas Hobbs Williams	20 May 42	14 Apr. 46		
2	0	Alexander Campbell	P7 May 47	P16 June 48		
3	0	Edward Jonathan Head	P20 Feb. 46	P3 Oct. 48		
		ENSIGNS.				
3	0	Edward Buller Thorp ..	12 June 46			
2	0	Carrick Darby	P3 Sept. 47			
2	0	William Drummond	P1 Oct. 47			
2	0	John Atkinson	P22 Oct. 47			
3	0	Leopold Brown	28 Apr. 46			
1	0	Alfred Nixon	P3 Mar. 48			
1	0	Charles Heycock	P31 Mar. 48			
1	0	Robert Selby	P3 Oct. 48			

5 Major Kenny served in the Peninsula, from June 1813, to the end of the war, including the action at Osma, battle of Vittoria, siege and capture of San Sebastian, passage of the Bidassoa (severely wounded above the left hip); St. Jean de Luz, and the series of actions between the 9th and 13th Dec 1813 in front of the intrenched camp near Bayonne. Served also in Ava, and was present in most of the operations throughout the war.

6 Major Graham joined the 54th regt. in Burmah, as a volunteer, in Dec. 1824, and was present at the carrying the entrenched Fords of the Mahattee river, 27th March, and at the attack on the fortified heights of Arracan, 29th March, 1825; at the latter he was wounded in the side and face.

9 Dr. M'Dermott served at New Orleans, 8th Jan. 1815; also the subsequent campaign in Flanders, including the operations in connection with the battle of Waterloo.

Full Pay	Half Pay	
14	0	*Paymaster.*—Robert Browne Thomas Boyd, 26 Mar. 41; *Ens.* P20 Feb. 36; [P *Lieut.* 15 Feb. 39.
11	0	*Adjutant.*—*Lieut.* Robert B. Hawley, 27 Oct. 46.
1	0	*Quarter-Master.*—William Watson, 25 April, 48.
30	$5\frac{1}{12}$	*Surgeon.*—Michael M'Dermott,[9] M.D. 5 April, 39; *Assist.-Surg.* 25 Dec. 28; *Hosp.-Assistant.* 7 Feb. 14.
3	0	*Assistant-Surgeon.*—Richard Gilborne, 2 Oct. 46.

Facings Black.—*Agents*, Messrs. Cox & Co.—*Irish Agents*, Messrs. Cane & Co.

[*Returned from North America* 28 Apr. 47.]

1 Sir C. B. Egerton commanded a detachment on board a line-of-battle ship, in Lord Howe's action of the 1st June, 1794. Served at the blockade of Malta, and surrender of Valetta, 5th Sept. 1800; from thence proceeded with Sir Ralph Abercromby's expedition to Egypt, and was present in the actions of the 13th and 21st March, 1801. Served with the army in Spain and Portugal in 1810 and 1811.

3 Lt.-Col. Thorp served in the Peninsula, from Jun ,1811, to the end of the war, including the affairs of El Bodon and Alfayate, siege and storming of Ciudad Rodrigo, battles of the Pyrenees, crossing the Bidassoa, St. Jean de Luz, different actions investing Bayonne, and repulse of the sortie.

4 Major Lewis served in the Burmese war.

7 Lieut. Skynner served with the 55th in China, and has received the Medal.

" MANDORA."—The *Sphinx* with the word, " EGYPT"—" MARTINIQUE"— " GUADALOUPE."

Years' Serv. Full Pay.	Half Pay.		Ensign.	Lieut.	Captain.	Brev.-Maj.
		Colonel.				
57		Sir Alexander Leith,[1] KCB. *Ens.* 8 Aug. 92; *Lieut.* Oct. 94; *Capt.* 27 Nov. 94; *Major*, 1 Aug. 04; *Lieut.-Col.* 7 Feb. 11, *Col.* 10 July, 21; *Major-Gen.* 22 July, 30; *Lieut.-Gen.* 23 Nov. 41; *Col.* 90th Light Infantry, 2 Sept. 41.				
		Lieut.-Colonel.				
26	3 4/12	Marcus John Slade,[2] *Ens.* 15 July, 19; *Lieut.* P 12 May, 25; *Capt.* P 22 April, 26; *Major*, P 27 Sept. 31; *Lieut.-Col.* P 7 Feb. 40.				
17	14	*Majors.*—Herbert Vaughan, *Ens.* P 4 July 18; *Lieut.* 20 July 20; *Capt.* P 13 Nov. 23; *Major*, P 19 Sept. 26; *Brevet Lieut.-Col.* 23 Nov. 41.				
25	0	Frederick Eld,[2] *Ens.* P 23 Dec. 24; *Lieut.* P 26 Sept. 26; *Capt.* P 27 Sept. 31; *Brevet-Major*, 9 Nov. 46: *Major*, 29 Sept. 47; *Brev. Lt.-Col* 22 Dec. 48.				
		CAPTAINS.				
24	0	Hen. Rob. Thurlow, *s.*	P 11 Aug. 25	8 Jan. 29	P 27 Mar. 35	9 Nov. 46
23	0	Gervas S. Deverill	P 2 Nov. 26	P 13 Nov. 27	P 7 Mar. 34	9 Nov. 46
24	0	John Blaquiere Mann, *s.*	10 Feb. 25	P 17 Nov. 25	2 June 38	
17	0	John Henry Bringhurst[2]	P 7 Sept. 32	17 Mar. 38	P 30 Sept. 42	22 Dec. 48
11	0	Thomas Ross	P 23 Mar. 38	P 18 May 41	P 4 June 47	
15	0	Duncan Campbell	P 8 April 34	P 1 Feb. 39	3 Oct. 46	
11	0	William P. Purnell	24 Mar. 38	P 25 June 41	P 16 June 48	
8	0	Wm. Benjamin Bastard[3]	P 19 Mar. 41	P 2 Dec. 42	P 16 June 48	
10	0	Henry Lecky[2]	P 25 Jan. 39	P 30 Sept. 42	P 13 Oct. 48	
9	0	Robert Grove[2]	P 7 Feb. 40	P 7 Mar. 45	P 24 Nov. 48	
		LIEUTENANTS.				
9	0	David Davies[2]	11 Apr. 40	24 Apr. 45		
9	0	William Victor Johnson[2]	12 June 40	P 25 Apr. 45		
8	0	Thomas Smith	P 16 July 41	P 16 Sept. 46		
6	0	Purcell O'Gorman, *Adj.*	P 3 Feb. 43	2 May 46		
6	0	Richard Rodes Wyvill[2]	P 14 April 43	P 4 June 47		
5	0	Thomas James Meredith[2]	P 16 Feb. 44	10 Mar. 48		
4	0	James Perrin	P 7 Mar. 45	P 16 June 48		
4	0	Michael Foster Ward	P 25 Apr. 45	P 12 Sept. 48		
4	0	John Christopher Guise	P 6 June 45	P 13 Oct. 48		
2	0	*Hon.* William Harboard	never	P 22 Jan. 47		
4	0	John Hardy Thursby	P 16 Sept. 45	P 24 Nov. 48		
		ENSIGNS.				
4	0	Henry M'Mahon Eagar	P 9 May 45			
2	0	Hebert M. Vaughan	23 Jan. 47			
2	0	William Pattison Tinling	P 4 June 47			
2	0	Vere Henry Close	11 June 47			
2	0	Rob. Dymock Vaughton	P 2 July 47			
1	0	Frederick Beatty	10 Mar. 48			
1	0	Harry Denison	P 16 June 48			
1	0	Henry Butler	P 12 Sept. 48			
1	0	Henry Hope Crealock	P 13 Oct. 48			
1	0	Henry Flower Every	P 24 Nov. 48			
10	0	*Paymaster.*—James William Bambrigge Peddie, 1 Sept. 18; *Ens.* 25 Oct. 30; *Lt.* P 16 Feb. 44.				
6	0	*Adjutant.*—*Lieut.* Purcell O Gorman, 10 March 48.				
4	0	*Quarter-Masters.*—Samuel Williams,[2] 18 April, 45.				
24	0	*Surgeon.*—Robert Ellson, 16 Feb. 41; *Assist.-Surg.* 20 Oct. 25; *Hosp.-Assist.* 14 April, 25.				
7	0	*Assistant-Surgeon.*—William Maclise,[2] 27 Dec. 42.				

Facings Buff.—*Agent*, Charles R. M'Grigor, Esq.

1 Sir Alexander Leith served in Flanders with the 42nd, particularly at the defence of Nieuport. Served with the 31st at the attack of the post of the Vigie, and at the subsequent capture of St. Lucia, in 1796. In North Holland in 1799, and was severely wounded and lost an eye at the battle of Alkmaar. Egyptian campaign of 1807, including the attack on Rosetta. Served afterwards in the Peninsula, from April 1812 to July 1814, and commanded the 31st at the battles of Vittoria, the Pyrenees on the 25th, 28th, and 30th July, the Nivelle, the Nive, and St. Pierre (severely wounded), storming the heights of Garris, battle of Orthes, action of Aire, and battle of Toulouse. Sir Alexander has received a cross and one clasp.

2 Lieut.-Cols. Slade and Eld; Major Bringhurst; Capts. Lecky, and Grove; Lieuts. Davies, Johnson, Wyvill, and Meredith; Quarter-Master Williams and Assist.-Surgeon Maclise, served with the 90th in Kaffirland, during the whole of the war of 1846 7.

3 Captain Bastard served with the 53rd in the campaign on the Sutlej (Medal) in 1846, including the actions at Budiwal, Aliwal, and Sobraon.

r. b. Foreign Service, 27 May 42.] 91st (*The Argyllshire*) *Regt. of Foot.* [Head Quarters at Gosport. r. b. at the Cape of Good Hope.

"ROLEIA"—"VIMIERA"—"CORUNNA"—"PYRENEES"—"NIVELLE"—"NIVE"—"ORTHES"—"TOULOUSE"—"PENINSULA."

Years' Serv. Full Pay	Half Pay	
68		*Colonel.*—Gabriel Gordon,[1] *Ens.* 6 Jan. 1781; *Lieut.* 26 Nov. 84; *Capt.* 10 July, 94; *Maj.*, 16 May, 1800; *Lt.-Col.* 9 March, 02; *Col.* 4 June, 11; *Maj.-Gen.* 4 June, 14; *Lt.-Gen.* 22 July, 30; *Gen.* 9 Nov. 46: *Col.* 91st Regt. 19 Apr, 37.
22	0	*Lieut.-Colonels.*—r. John Francis Glencairn Campbell, *Ens.* 25 Oct. 27; *Lieut.* P 27 Aug. 29; *Capt.* P 23 Nov. 32; *Maj.* 8 July, 43; *Lt.-Col.* 14 Apr. 46.
24	0	Charles Cooke Yarborough, *Ens.* P 9 June 25; *Lieut.* P 19 Sept. 26; *Capt.* P 4 Jan. 33; *Major*, 19 May 45; *Lieut.-Col.* P 13 Oct. 48.
20	0	*Majors.*—r. David Forbes, *Ens.* P 8 Oct. 29; *Lieut.* P 23 Nov. 32; *Capt.* P 24 July 35; *Major*, 14 Apr. 46.
17	0	Bertie Edward Murray Gordon, P *Ens.* 26 Oct. 32; *Lieut.* P 24 July 35; *Capt.* P 23 April 41; *Major* P 13 Oct. 48.

Full Pay	Half Pay	CAPTAINS.	ENSIGN.	LIEUT.	CAPTAIN.	BREV.-MAJ.
17	0	r. Wm. Glendonwyn Scott	P 30 Mar. 32	P 12 June 35	P 22 Feb. 39	15 Sept. 48
17	0	r. Edward W. C. Wright	21 Dec. 32	P 13 Nov. 35	P 2 July 41	
14	17 8/12	r. Colin Campbell	P 10 Apr. 35	P 2 Feb. 38	P 12 Oct. 41	
18	5	r. P JohnGeo. Rawstorne[4]	22 July 13	18 Aug. 14	10 Oct. 38	
28	0	John Ward[5]	8 Apr. 16	8 Sept. 28	15 Apr. 42	
21	0	r. John Campbell Cahill	28 Feb. 28	8 May 35	14 Oct. 42	
14	0	Henry J. Savage	5 June 35	P 11 May 38	8 July 43	
14	0	r. James Christie	P 24 July 35	P 22 Feb. 39	P 13 Oct. 43	
15	0	r. Robert Fred. Middlemore	19 Dec. 34	P 12 July 39	19 May 45	
14	0	r. John Brown, s.	6 Nov. 35	31 Dec. 39	14 Apr. 46	
12	0	Edward Missenden Love	P 23 June 37	P 17 Aug. 38	P 20 Dec. 42	
11	0	Fred. J. Bayly..........	30 Oct. 38	P 23 April 41	P 13 Oct. 48	
		LIEUTENANTS.				
12	0	r. J. M. Pennington[6]....	P 26 Dec. 37	P 9 Oct. 40		
10	0	Wm. Tho. Laird Patterson	P 22 Feb. 39	P 12 Oct. 41		
13	0	Richard Sweet Cole	P 12 Aug. 36	P 25 Dec. 38		
9	0	Robert Stein	P 9 Oct. 40	15 Apr. 42		
10	0	r. Edward John Dickson	P 27 Sept. 39	P 14 Oct. 42		
8	0	James Day Cochrane[7] ..	P 31 Dec. 41	P 13 Oct. 43		
8	0	r. Robert Henry Howard	P 12 Oct. 41	13 Jan. 45		
7	0	r. Joseph Owgan	16 Apr. 42	P 21 Mar. 45		
8	0	Alfred James Melvin....	18 Oct. 41	10 May 45		
7	0	r Hen Christopher Metcalfe	P 29 Apr. 42	P 25 July 45		
6	0	John Trotter Bethune ..	P 13 Oct. 43	P 19 Feb. 47		
7	0	Philip Antrobus........	P 23 Apr. 42	P 2 Feb. 44		
4	0	r. Craven Lloyd	P 25 July 45	P 13 July 47		
6	0	r. John MacPherson....	20 Oct. 43	P 6 Oct. 48		
4	0	*Count* George Rivarola..	16 Sept. 45	P 13 Oct. 48		
		ENSIGNS.				
4	0	r. Douglas Ernest Manners	18 April 45			
8	0	r. J. Gordon, *adj.* Q. M. 26 Jan. 41	22 Jan. 47			
2	0	r. Edw. Geo. Mainwaring	9 Apr. 47			
2	0	Robert Whitle	28 Apr. 47			
2	0	Edw. Jas. Somers Ray ..	29 Apr. 47			
2	0	John Alex. Saunders	30 Apr. 47			
2	0	David Knox Horsburgh..	P 13 July 47			
2	0	Robert Henry Crampton[9]	P 5 Nov. 47			
1	0	William Barron Stanton	P 28 Jan. 48			
1	0	Frederick Boehmer	1 Aug. 48			
1	0	Alex. Watson Mackenzie	P 6 Oct. 48			
1	0	Penrose John Dunbar ..	P 8 Dec. 48			

9 Ens. Crampton was dangerously wounded in the action with the Rebel Boers at Bloem Plaats.

7 Lt. Cochrane served with the 91st in the operation against the Caffer Tribes, Cape of Good Hope, and was severely wounded (shot through the body and left hand, and contused on the groin), on the 18th April 1846, when covering the rear of Colonel Somerset's division, during the retreat from the Amatoli Mountains to Block Drift.

8 Mr. Power served with the 7th Dr. Gds. on the expedition against the insurgent Boers at the Cape of Good Hope in 1845, and in the Kaffir war of 1846-7,—the latter part of which as Surgeon R. B. 91st Regt.

Full Pay	Half Pay	
24	0	*Paymaster.*—G. Had. Dalrymple, 31 Jan. 40; *Ens.* P 5 Nov. 25; *Lieut.* 6 Dec. 27.
8	0	*Adjutants.*—r. *Ensign* John Gordon, 22 Jan. 47.
1	0	*Ensign* Frederick Boehmer, 1 Aug. 48.
3	7/12	*Quarter-Masters.*—William Blackburne, 1 Aug. 48; *Ens.* 20 Oct. 46.
2	0	r. James Paterson, 1 Oct. 47.
23	0	*Surgeons.*—John Forrest, M.D. 2 July, 41; *A. S.* 9 Feb. 26; *H. A.* 10 Nov. 25.
12	0	r. William John Power,[8] 7 Aug. 46; *Assist. Surg.* 14 July, 37.
6	0	*Assist.-Surgs.*—r. Alexander Barclay, M.D. 22 Dec. 43.
5	0	William Munro, MD. 6 Dec. 44.

Facings Yellow.—*Agents*, Messrs. Barron & Smith.

[1st *Battalion returned from the Cape of Good Hope*, 26 *April* 48.]

1 General Gordon has received a medal and one clasp for Martinique and Guadaloupe.

4 Captain Rawstorne served in the Peninsula, from Aug. 1813 to the end of the war, and was present at the battle of Orthes.

5 Capt. Ward served with the 91st in the Kaffir War of 1846-7.

6 Lieut. Pennington commanded the detachment of the 91st in the action with and defeat of the Rebel Boers at Bloem Plaats, 29 Aug. 1848.

" EGMONT-OP-ZEE"—" MANDORA"—The *Sphinx*, with the words " EGYPT"—" CORUNNA"—" FUENTES D'ONOR"—" ALMARAZ"—" VITTORIA"—" PYRENEES"—" NIVE"—" ORTHES"—" PENINSULA"—" WATERLOO."

Years' Serv.		
53		*Colonel.*
		℗ *Sir* William Macbean,[1] KCB. *Ens.* 20 Feb. 1796; *Lieut.* 1 Oct. 96; *Capt.* 25 Oct. 04; *Major,* 16 Feb. 09; *Lieut.-Col.* 30 May, 11; *Col.* 19 July, 21; *Major-Gen.* 22 July, 30; *Lieut.-Gen.* 23 Nov. 41; *Col.* 92nd Highlanders, 31 May, 43.
Full Pay.	**Half Pay.**	*Lieut.-Colonel.*
31	$1\frac{4}{12}$	John Alex. Forbes, *Ens.* P 5 Dec. 16; *Lieut.* P 22 May, 23; *Capt.* P 24 Dec. 25; *Brev.-Major,* 28 June, 38; *Major,* P 17 Sept. 39; *Lieut.-Col.* 9 Nov. 46.
		Majors.
25	$\frac{4}{12}$	Geo. Edw. Thorold, *Ens.* 24 June, 24; *Lieut.* P 9 June, 25; *Capt.* P 19 Sept. 26; *Brevet-Major,* 23 Nov. 41; *Major,* 1 Nov. 42.
25	$\frac{5}{12}$	Mark Kerr Atherley, *Ens.* P 28 Aug. 23; *Lieut.* P 13 Aug. 25; *Capt.* P 25 Nov. 28; *Brev.-Major,* 23 Nov. 41; *Major,* 9 Nov. 46.

Full Pay	Half Pay		ENSIGN.	LIEUT.	CAPTAIN.	BREV.-MAJ.
		CAPTAINS.				
21	0	Arch. Inglis Lockhart ..	P 31 Dec. 28	P 11 June 30	P 19 Aug. 36	9 Nov. 46
26	0	Rob. Macleod Sutherland	25 Dec. 23	7 Aug. 24	5 Oct. 41	
18	0	Ken. Douglas Mackenzie, *s*	P 25 Nov. 31	P 19 Aug. 36	P 27 Sept. 44	
14	0	Edward Eldridge Haines	P 26 June 35	P 1 Feb. 39	P 3 Apr. 46	
11	0	Arch. Hamilton Tattnall	P 10 Aug. 38	25 Aug. 41	P 9 June 46	
8	0	Cha. Edw. Stuart Gleig..	1 June 41	P 24 June 42	9 Nov. 46	
8	0	Charles Gordon	P 14 Dec. 41	P 17 Mar. 43	P 22 June 47	
6	0	Chris. Monteith Hamilton	P 3 Feb. 43	P 27 Sept. 44	P 12 Nov. 47	
8	0	William Charles Lyon ..	15 July 41	P 27 Jan. 43	P 28 Jan. 48	
6	0	James George Hay	P 30 June 43	P 20 June 45	P 23 June 48	
		LIEUTENANTS.				
5	0	Forbes Macbean........	P 27 Sept. 44	P 8 Aug. 45		
8	0	Hugh Scott............	P 16 April 41	P 4 Oct. 44		
10	0	M. MacNaughten Smith	P 31 May 39	8 April 42		
5	0	A. Welling. Cameron, *Adj.*	6 Dec. 44	P 27 Mar. 46		
8	0	Edward Peter Mann, *r.*	15 Nov. 41	30 Mar. 46		
4	0	Robert Bethune	P 17 Jan. 45	P 3 Apr. 46		
4	0	WO'B. Hastings Buchanan	P 2 May 45	P 21 Apr. 46		
4	0	Robert William Duff....	P 20 June 45	P 9 June 46		
4	0	G. W. H. *Visc.* Kirkwall	P 8 Aug. 45	9 Nov. 46		
3	0	*Hon.* Walter Charteris ..	P 6 Feb. 46	P 22 June 47		
3	0	Alastair M'Ian M'Donald, *s*	P 27 Mar. 46	P 12 Nov. 47		
3	0	John Cunningham......	P 3 Apr. 46	P 31 Dec. 47		
3	0	Geo. Wm. Holmes Ross	P 21 Apr. 46	P 23 June 48		
		ENSIGNS.				
3	0	Colin Campbell	1 May 46			
3	0	David Erskine	P 8 Sept. 46			
3	0	Walter John Macdonald	13 Nov. 46			
3	0	John Henry St. John ..	20 Nov. 46			
2	0	James Wemyss Anderson	P 22 June 47			
2	0	Donald Patrick Campbell	P 12 Nov. 47			
2	0	George Henry Renny ..	P 31 Dec. 47			
1	0	William Miller	P 23 June 48			
	0	*Paymaster.*—				
5	0	*Adjutant.—Lieut.* Arthur Wellington Cameron, 9 June, 46.				
8	0	*Quarter-Master.*—Donald M'Queen 6 Dec. 44; *Ens.* 14 Nov. 41. [15 June 26.				
23	0	*Surgeon.*—Thomas Foss, 2 July 41; *Assist.-Surg.* 18 Jan. 27; *Hosp.-Assist.*				
2	0	*Assistant-Surgeon.*—Charles Robert Robinson, 12 Nov. 47.				

Facings Yellow.—*Agents,* Messrs. Cox & Co.—*Irish Agents,* Messrs. Cane & Co.

[*Returned from the West Indies, February,* 1844.]

1 Sir Wm. Macbean served the campaign of 1794 in Holland, as a Cadet in the service of the Seven United Provinces. Served in Ireland, during the rebellion, in 1798, including the action at Vinegar Hill and capture of Wexford. Landed with the army in Portugal in Aug. 1808, and served throughout the Peninsular war, including the battles of Roleia, Vimiera, Corunna, Busaco, and Salamanca; siege, assault, and capture of San Sebastian, passage of the Bidassoa, battles of the Nivelle and Nive, and investment of Bayonne, at which last he was severely wounded, as also in opposing a French division on its advance to Lamego, in 1810. Served also in the war in Ava. Sir William has received a cross for Busaco, Salamanca, San Sebastian and the Nive.

"CAPE OF GOOD HOPE."

Years' Serv. 50 — Full Pay. | Half Pay.

Colonel.

(50) ℗ *Sir* James Douglas,[1] KCB. *Ens.* 10 July, 1799; *Lieut.* 19 June, 1800; *Capt.* 16 Sept. 02; *Major*, 16 Feb. 09; *Lieut.-Col.* 30 May, 11; *Col.* 19 July, 21; *Major-Gen.* 22 July, 30; *Lt.-Gen.* 23 Nov. 41; *Col.* 93rd Regt. 15 June, 40.

Lieutenant-Colonel.

48 | 0 | Robert Spark,[2] *Ens.* May, 07; *Lieut.* 3 Sept. 07; *Capt.* 17 Feb. 20; *Major*, P 25 Dec. 35; *Lieut-Col.* P 28 July, 38.

30 | 0 | *Majors.*—John De Burgh, *Ens.* P 25 Nov. 19; *Lieut.* 7 April, 25; *Capt.* P 19 Sept. 26; *Major* P 28 July, 38.

30 | $1\frac{1}{12}$ | Robert Carmichael Smyth, *2nd Lieut.* 8 July 18; *Lieut.* 5 May, 25; *Capt.* P 8 April, 26; *Major*, P 18 May, 41.

Full Pay	Half Pay		ENSIGN.	LIEUT.	CAPTAIN.	BREV.-MAJ.
		CAPTAINS.				
27	$5\frac{4}{12}$	John Joseph Grier	11 Sept. 17	9 Apr. 25	P 31 July 28	23 Nov. 41
21	0	George Edward Aylmer ..	28 Feb. 28	P 13 Aug. 30	P 24 Nov. 35	9 Nov. 46
19	0	William Robt. Haliday ..	P 12 Feb. 30	P 3 Mar. 33	P 11 Nov. 36	9 Nov. 46
19	0	Wm. Bernard Ainslie ..	P 28 Sept. 30	P 24 Nov. 35	P 29 Sept. 37	
15	0	Robert Murray Banner ..	P 19 Dec. 34	P 30 Dec. 36	P 26 Feb. 41	
15	0	*Ld.* Cosmo Geo. Russell, *s.*	P 12 Aug. 34	P 6 July 38	P 27 Aug. 41	
14	0	Charles Henry Gordon ..	P 24 Nov. 35	P 28 July 38	P 13 May 42	
23	0	W. MacDonald, *QM.* 16 No. 26	23 Aug. 27	P 13 Jan. 34	3 Dec. 47	
14	0	Alex. Sebastian Leith Hay	P 25 Dec. 35	P 26 Apr. 39	P 31 Mar. 48	
11	0	John Alexander Ewart ..	27 July 38	15 April 42	P 12 May 48	
		LIEUTENANTS.				
15	0	John F. A. Hartle, *Adj.*	21 Feb. 34	P 11 Nov. 36		
13	0	George Studdert	P 3 June 36	P 19 July 39		
13	0	Francis H. Crawford	14 Oct. 36	P 15 Dec. 40		
13	0	Evan D. Macpherson	P 11 Nov. 36	P 26 Feb. 41		
12	0	Edward Hunter Blair ..	P 29 Sept. 37	P 18 May 41		
11	0	George Seton	P 28 July 38	P 13 May 42		
10	0	Colin Maxwell	P 26 Apr. 39	P 27 Sept. 42		
9	0	Robert Lockhart Ross ..	P 15 Dec. 40	27 June 45		
4	0	Warner Westenra Carden	27 June 45	P 4 June 47		
4	0	Robert Eglinton Seton ...	P 4 July 45	P 17 Dec. 47		
4	0	Wm. Fra. Aug. Eliott ..	P 14 Nov. 45	P 11 Feb. 48		
3	0	John Alex. Fraser	13 Apr. 46	P 31 Mar. 48		
5	0	Stephen Blake	P 4 Oct. 44	P 21 July 46		
		ENSIGNS.				
3	0	Hen. A. Bolton Mackenzie	14 Apr. 46			
3	0	Wm. G. Alex. Middleton	24 July 46			
3	0	Alexander Young	P 2 Oct. 46			
2	0	Wm. Donald Macdonald	P 4 June 47			
2	0	John Millar Bannatyne ..	P 17 Dec. 47			
1	0	James Dalzell...	P 11 Feb. 48			
1	0	Fred. William Burroughs	P 31 Mar. 48			
1	0	W. G. Drummond Stewart	P 2 June 48			

Paymaster.—

15 | 0 | *Adjutant.*—*Lieut.* John F. A. Hartle, 28 Jan. 48.

5 | 0 | *Quarter-Master.*—Donald Sinclair, 22 March, 44.

35 | $1\frac{1}{12}$ | *Surgeon.*—℗ John Campbell,[4] M.D., 27 Dec. 33; *Assist.-Surg.* 27 July, 15; *Hosp.-Assist.* 25 Mar. 13.

2 | 0 | *Assist.-Surgeon.*—James Webster, M.D. 28 Sept. 47.

Facings Yellow.—*Agents*, Messrs. Cox and Co.

[*Returned from North America*, 31 *Aug.* 48.]

4 Dr. Campbell served the campaigns of 1813 and 14 in the Peninsula, including the battle of Orthes; served also at New Orleans.

1 Sir James Douglas served in the Peninsula with the Portuguese army, and has received a cross and three clasps for the battles of Busaco, Salamanca, Pyrenees, Nivelle, Nive, Orthes, and Toulouse.

2 Lt.-Col. Spark served in the American war in 1814 and 15, and was wounded at New Orleans 8th January 1815.

† K

Years' Serv. Full Pay.	Half Pay.	
46		*Colonel.*
		₱ *Sir* William Warre,[1] CB., *Ens.* 5 Nov. 03; *Lieut.* 2 June 04; *Capt.* 25 April 06; *Major,* 30 May 11; *Lt.-Col.* 13 May 13; *Col.* 22 July 18; *Major-Gen.* 23 Nov. 41; *Col.* 94th Foot, 28 Sept. 47.
24	3 2/12	*Lieut.-Colonels.*—Henry Robert Milner, *Ens.* P 7 Feb. 22; *Lieut.* P 8 Dec. 25; *Capt.* P 12 Dec. 26; *Major,* P 5 July, 33; *Lieut.-Col.* P 31 Dec. 41.
33	7/12	James Brown, *Ens.* P 15 June, 15; *Lieut.* 5 Oct. 20; *Capt.* 28 Sept. 30; *Major,* 11 Feb. 42; *Lieut.-Col.* 9 Nov. 46.
21	0	*Majors.*—John Leslie Dennis,[3] *Ens.* 25 Apr. 28; *Lieut.* 22 Sept. 30; *Capt.* 17 May, 41; *Major,* P 29 Nov. 44.
28	0	James Paterson,[4] *Ens.* P 17 May 21; *Lieut.* P 4 Dec. 23; *Capt.* P 5 April 31; *Brev.-Maj.,* 23 Dec. 42; *Major,* 31 July 46.

Full Pay	Half Pay		Ensign.	Lieut.	Captain.	Brev.-Maj.
		Captains.				
31	6 8/12	Henry Nicholls	25 July 11	P 15 Sept. 14	9 Feb. 38	
15	0	George Maunsell	P 11 July 34	P 8 Dec. 37	P 31 Dec. 41	
14	0	Thomas Fownes Scale	P 8 May 35	P 27 Apr. 38	P 16 Aug. 42	
24	0	Lawrence Desborough	10 Apr. 25	3 Aug. 27	14 Oct. 42	
14	0	Henry George Buller	P 26 June 35	P 8 June 38	5 June 44	
13	0	Wm. H. Kirby	14 Oct. 36	P 28 Dec. 38	7 Dec. 45	
12	0	George A. K. D'Arcy	P 21 Apr. 37	26 Sept. 39	9 Nov. 46	
12	0	William Henry Dore	P 8 Dec. 37	P 27 Sept. 39	17 Dec. 46	
16	0	Alexander Crie Meik	P 10 May 33	14 Sept. 35	29 May 47	
11	0	Septimus Lyster[6]	P 28 Dec. 38	18 Aug. 41	P 6 Oct. 48	
		Lieutenants.				
14	0	Edward Smyth Mercer	P 6 Mar. 35	P 11 June 36		
13	0	Adam Campbell	19 April 36	19 Feb. 38		
11	0	James Stewart Menzies	P 10 Feb. 38	24 Oct. 39		
11	0	George Dorehill	P 20 Nov. 38	25 Sept. 40		
11	0	Gilbert Mahon	P 9 Nov. 38	24 July 41		
10	0	Alexander Maclean, *Adj.*	15 Mar. 39	P 28 Jan. 42		
9	0	Henry John Wahab	P 22 May 40	P 16 Aug. 42		
8	0	Thomas Henry Stoddard	26 Oct. 41	5 June 44		
8	0	Joseph Alfred Sykes	P 31 Dec. 41	2 Aug. 44		
9	0	Justin Edw. D. MacCarthy	16 Dec. 40	29 Mar. 44		
7	0	Isaac S. B. Phipps Boileau	29 Apr. 42	P 29 Dec. 43		
7	0	R. W. Newman Vaughan, *s.*	P 16 Aug. 42	P 25 Apr. 45		
10	0	Charles Augustus Daniell[7]	P 18 Jan. 39	P 10 Apr. 40		
5	0	Henry Hamilton Pratt	P 25 June 44	9 Nov. 46		
8	0	George Noble Bredin	6 Aug. 41	30 Sept. 43		
5	0	Herbert Taylor M'Crea	2 Aug. 44	17 Dec. 46		
5	0	James Buchanan	20 Aug. 44	25 Aug. 47		
5	0	Norcliffe Bendyshe Walton	22 Nov. 44	P 17 Dec. 47		
4	0	David Hunter Blair	P 4 Apr. 45	P 12 Nov. 47		
4	0	Rice Davies Knight	P 25 Apr. 45	P 25 Feb. 48		
3	0	Richard Hull Lewis	29 Dec. 46	P 3 Mar. 48		
4	0	M. L. Varnham Reynolds	2 Sept. 45	P 10 Mar. 48		
1	0	Charles William St. John	11 Feb. 48	P 6 Oct. 48		
		Ensigns.				
3	0	Whiteford John Bell	13 Nov. 46			
4	0	Francis Dalmahoy Wyatt	11 April 45			
2	0	Samuel Sexton	P 17 Dec. 47			
1	0	Henry Vansit. Stonehouse	P 25 Feb. 48			
1	0	Wm. D. H. Guinness Day	P 3 Mar. 48			
3	0	Charles Twysden Scale	P 10 July 46			
1	0	Philip Primrose	18 Aug. 48			
1	0	Richard Raphael Meade	P 6 Oct. 48			

3 Major Dennis served with the 49th in China, and was present at Chusan (both operations), Canton, and Amoy; after which he was employed as military magistrate at Chusan.

4 Major Paterson commanded the Grenadiers of the Cameronians on the China expedition, and was present at the operations before Canton from the 24th to the 31st May 1841, defence of Ningpo, at Segoan, Chapoo, Woosung, Shanghae, Chin Kiang Foo, and Nanking.

6 Capt. Lyster served in the War of Succession in Spain as Lieut. of Infantry, and was present in the operations before San Sebastian, and was severely wounded through the body in the attack upon the fortified heights of Arambura near Henani. He was also present at the assault and capture of Irun (medal) and Fontarabia.

7 Lieut. Daniell served with the 26th in China, at Amoy, Chusan, and at Chin Kiang Foo.

Full Pay	Half Pay	
7	0	*Paymaster.*—John Mills Hewson, 28 Sept. 47; *Ens.* 18 March 42; *Lt.* 29 Dec. 43.
10	0	*Adjutant.—Lieut.* Alexander Maclean, 10 Sept. 44.
2	0	*Quarter-Master.*—Thomas FitzGerald, 23 Jan. 47.
39	0	*Surgeon.*—₱ William Thompson, M.D. 19 Jan. 38; *Assist.-Surg.* 18 Oct. 10.
8	0	*Assist.-Surgeons.*—Edward Menzies, 29 Oct. 41.
3	0	William Westall, M.D., 21 July, 46.
2	0	John Clay Purves, M.D. 9 April 47.

Facings Green.—*Agents,* Messrs. Cox & Co.

1 Sir William Warre served the campaign of 1808-9, on the staff of Sir Ronald Ferguson and Lord Beresford, and was present at the battles of Roleia and Vimiera, subsequent retreat, and battle of Corunna. In March 1809 accompanied Lord Beresford to Lisbon, as his first Aide-de-camp, and assisted in training the Portuguese troops. Served in the field under his lordship's orders until May 1813, and was present at the passage of the Douro, when he was sent to command the peasantry and to destroy the bridges in rear of the French army under Marshal Soult, the accomplishment of which enabled the advance-guard of the British to overtake and defeat the rear of the French at Salamonde, who lost here their remaining guns, baggage, &c. Present also during the retreat from the Coa to the lines of Torres Vedras, 2d siege of Badajos, siege and storming of Ciudad Rodrigo, 3d siege and storming of Badajos, siege of the Forts and battle of Salamanca.

Emb. for Foreign Serv. 25 Oct. 1888. [illegible]

95th (*The Derbyshire*) Regt. of Foot.

[Serving in China. Depôt at Londonderry.

Years' Serv.		
53		
Full Pay.	Half Pay.	
		Colonel.
		P Sir Richard Armstrong,[1] CB. *Ens.* 23 June, 96; *Lieut.* 5 Nov. 99; *Capt.* 9 July, 03; *Major*, 30 May, 11; *Lieut.-Col.* 26 Aug. 13; *Col.* 22 July, 30; *Major-Gen.* 23 Nov. 41; *Col.* 95th Foot, 29 March, 48.
		Lieut.-Colonel.
39	7 3/12	P James Campbell,[2] KH. *Ens.* 17 Sept. 03; *Lieut.* 25 Aug. 04; *Capt.* P 31 Mar. 08; *Major*, P 3 June, 19; *Lieut.-Col.* P 10 July, 24; *Col.* 28 June, 38.
43	0	*Majors.*—P John Walter,[3] *Ens.* P 15 July, 06; *Lieut.* 3 Sept. 07; *Capt.* P 24 Mar. 13; *Major*, 26 May, 31; *Brevet-Lieut.-Col.* 9 Nov. 46.
41	2 5/12	P Joseph Robert Raines,[4] *Ens.* 19 Sept. 05; *Lieut.* 28 May, 07; *Capt.* 2 June, 25; *Brevet-Major*, 28 June, 38; *Major*, 20 Apr. 46.

Full Pay.	Half Pay.	CAPTAINS.	ENSIGN.	LIEUT.	CAPTAIN.	BREV.-MAJ.
18	0	John G. Champion	2 Aug. 31	P 8 May 35	P 2 Feb. 38	
26	9 3/12	Wm. Armstrong Rogers	7 July 14	2 June 30	14 May 42	
16	0	Alfred Thomas Heyland	P 4 Apr. 33	P 8 July 36	P 13 Dec. 42	
14	0	Henry Hume	P 9 May 35	P 1 Dec. 37	P 19 Jan. 44	
14	0	Henry O. Chester Master	P 18 Sept. 35	P 2 Feb. 38	P 2 Feb. 44	
12	0	John Fitz Thomas Dennis	P 4 Aug. 37	P 30 Oct. 38	P 25 Nov. 45	
9	0	John Henry Carew	P 10 July 40	P 13 Dec. 42	P 11 Sept. 46	
7	0	Thomas Davis	20 May 42	P 2 Feb. 44	P 3 Mar. 48	
13	0	George Cornwall	P 8 July 36	P 9 Mar. 38	9 June 48	
7	0	William Minchin	P 29 Apr. 42	P 1 Mar. 44	P 15 Dec. 48	
		LIEUTENANTS.				
13	0	*Hon.* E. Sidney Plunkett	P 17 June 36	P 11 May 41		
11	0	Geo. James Dowdall, *adj.*	P 8 June 38	14 May 42		
7	0	Julius Aug. Robert Raines	28 Jan. 42	5 April 44		
7	0	James George Eddington	P 3 June 42	P 25 June 44		
7	0	Wm. Rowland Maxwell	P 20 Dec. 42	14 Apr. 46		
6	0	George Courtenay Vialls	P 20 Jan. 43	P 22 May 46		
6	0	Henry Swettenham	23 June 43	9 July 45		
5	0	John Neptune Sargent ..	P 19 Jan. 44	P 11 Sept. 46		
5	0	Thomas Browne Feneran	19 April 44	P 8 Dec. 46		
6	0	Lionel Fraser.........	24 Nov. 43	P 7 May 47		
5	0	Edward Spicer Charlton	23 Mar. 44	P 3 Mar. 48		
4	0	Henry Foster	P 25 Nov. 45	9 June 48		
3	0	John Herbert Armstrong	P 22 May 46	P 15 Dec. 48		
		ENSIGNS.				
3	0	George Cavendish Taylor	P 11 Sept. 46			
3	0	S. Blomefield Kekewich	P 8 Dec. 46			
2	0	Alex. J. John Macdonald	23 Apr. 47			
2	0	Anthony Morgan	P 7 May 47			
2	0	Rich. L. Otway Pearson	3 Dec. 47			
1	0	George Wightman	31 Mar. 48			
1	0	Robert Graham Polhill..	P 16 June 48			
1	0	Geo. L. Carmichael Smyth	P 15 Dec. 48			

Full Pay.	Half Pay.	
26	0	*Paymaster.*—[illegible] F. Feneran,[5] 15 Dec. 37; *Quarter-Master*, 1 Dec. 23.
11	0	*Adjutant.*—*Lieut.* George James Dowdall, 7 March, 45.
8	0	*Quarter-Master.*—William Holt, 3 Dec. 41.
13	0	*Surgeon.*—Archibald Gordon,[9] M.D., 12 Sept. 48; *Assist.-Surg.* 28 June 36.
8	0	*Assistant-Surgeons.*—Huntley George Gordon, M.D. 31 Dec. 41.
6	0	Edmonds Robert Richardson, 30 June, 43.

Facings Yellow.—*Agents*, Messrs. Cox & Co.—*Irish Agents*, *Sir* E. R. Borough, *Bt.*, Armit, and Co.

1 Sir Richard Armstrong served in the Peninsula from Aug. 1808 to the end of that war in 1814, including the capture of Oporto, battle of Busaco, actions at Pombal and Redinha, defence of Alba de Tormes, battles of Vittoria, the Pyrenees (severely wounded through the arm), and Toulouse, besides a great many minor actions and skirmishes. Served also the campaigns of 1825 and 26 in Burmah as a Brigadier: stormed and carried Stockades near Prome, on the 1st and 5th Dec. 1825. Sir Richard has received a medal and two clasps for the battles of Busaco, Vittoria, and the Pyrenees.

2 Colonel Campbell served during part of the Rebellion in Ireland, in 1798 and 99, and was present in the actions at Ballynamuck, Granard, and Wilson's Hospital—wounded in the hand in the latter affair. Volunteered in the expedition to Hanover, in 1805-6, and resigned a Staff situation for that purpose; served with the expedition until the French army was expelled from that country. Campaign in Spain, in 1808-9, expedition to Walcheren; campaign of 1815, including the surrender of Cambray and Paris.

3 Lieut.-Colonel Walter served in the Peninsula from October, 1813, to the end of that war, in 1814, including the passage of the Bidassoa, battle of Nivelle 10th Nov., and Nive 9th, 10th, 11th, 12th, and 13th December, 1813; and investment of Bayonne in 1814. Served also the campaign of 1815, and was present at the surrender of Paris.

4 Major Raines served at the battles of Roleia, Vimiera, and Corunna, besides minor affairs during the retreat; served also at Walcheren.

5 Paymaster Feneran served the campaign of 1814 in Holland. Also the campaign of 1815, including the battle of Waterloo.

9 Doctor Gordon served with the 53rd in the campaign on the Sutlej (Medal) in 1846, including the actions at Buddiwal, Aliwal, and Sobraon.

Years' Serv.		
55		**Colonel.**
Full Pay.	Half Pay.	*Sir* Lewis Grant,[1] KCH. *Lieut.* 15 Feb. 1794; *Capt.* 11 June, 96; *Major*, 8 Sept. 02; *Lieut.-Col.* 18 Feb. 1804; *Col.* 4 June 13; *Major-Gen.* 12 Aug. 19; *Lieut.-Gen.* 10 Jan. 37; *Col.* 96th Regt. 9 April, 39.
29	0	*Lieut.-Colonels.*—Charles Brownlow Cumberland, *Ens.* P 21 Dec. 20; *Lieut.* P 15 Oct. 25; *Capt.* P 10 June, 26; *Major*, P 19 Sept. 34; *Lieut.-Col.* P 22 July, 42.
46	1/12	William Hulme,[2] *Ens.* 25 Sept. 03; *Lieut.* 26 June, 05; *Capt.* 26 Aug. 13; *Brevet-Major*, 23 Dec. 17; *Regtl.-Major*, 9 March, 34; *Brevet-Lieut.-Col.* 10 Jan. 37; *Lt.-Col.* 18 Aug. 48.
30	6	*Majors.*—Peter Cheape, *Ens.* 25 May, 13; *Lieut.* 3 Aug. 15; *Capt.* P 24 Dec. 25; *Brev.-Major*, 28 June, 38; *Major*, P 22 July, 42.
25	0	Thomas Maitland Wilson, *Ens.* P 15 Apr. 24; *Lieut.* P 13 May 26; *Capt.* P 23 Dec. 31; *Brev. Maj.* 9 Nov. 46; *Major*, 18 Aug. 48.

Full Pay	Half Pay		ENSIGN.	LIEUT.	CAPTAIN.	BREV.-MAJ.
		CAPTAINS.				
23	1/12	Robert Bush	P 22 Apr. 26	P 5 June 27	P 23 Mar. 32	9 Nov. 46
17	0	Edward Hill	P 29 Dec. 32	P 23 June 37	P 27 July 38	
16	0	John Snodgrass	13 Dec. 33	1 Dec. 36	P 15 Dec. 40	
15	0	Wm. Archibald Eyton ..	P 14 Feb. 34	P 30 June 37	P 22 July 42	
14	0	Edward W. Scovell	29 Dec. 35	P 2 Nov. 38	P 13 Dec. 42	
23	0	Edward Regan Gregg[3] ..	6 Apr. 26	28 Sept. 27	20 Oct. 42	
13	0	Richard Roundell Currer	16 Sept. 36	P 27 Sept. 39	P 20 Oct. 46	
13	0	Edward Croker[4]	P 4 Mar. 36	P 17 Nov. 37	P 19 Mar. 47	
22	0	James Clyde	P 5 June 27	P 23 Mar. 32	1 Aug. 48	
11	0	Frederick Pierce	P 18 Aug. 38	P 29 Jan. 41	18 Aug. 48	
		LIEUTENANTS.				
11	0	Richard Roney, *r.*	P 14 Sept. 38	30 April 41		
9	0	John Napier Magill	P 18 Sept. 40	P 22 July 42		
8	0	Robert Mounsey Lambert	P 29 Jan. 41	P 13 Dec. 42		
7	0	R. F. W. Cumberland, *adj.*	20 May 42	P 25 Nov. 45		
9	0	Herbert Vaughan Mundell	2 Nov. 40	30 Dec. 45		
7	0	Ernest Fred. Griffiths ..	8 July 42	P 14 Apr. 46		
7	0	John William Lloyd	P 22 July 42	P 2 Oct. 46		
5	0	Cha. Oct. Eardley Wilmot	29 Mar. 44	P 20 Oct. 46		
5	0	Geo. Fred. Campbell Bray	22 Mar. 44	27 Jan. 46		
4	0	John Vize O'Donnell ..	P 25 Nov. 45	P 11 Feb. 48		
9	0	James Henry Archer....	P 15 Dec. 40	P 22 Dec. 43		
7	0	William Rogers	30 Dec. 42	25 July 44		
5	0	John Salmon Gordon ..	30 July 44	P 20 Mar. 46		
7	0	John Smith Cannon	28 Jan. 42	14 Apr. 46		
4	0	John Whiteside[5]........	19 Dec. 45	P 12 Nov. 47		
7	0	Fred. Dobson Middleton[6]	30 Dec. 42	18 Aug. 48		
7	0	Edward Oliver Barker ..	P 31 Dec. 42	18 Aug. 48		
6	0	Christophilus Garstin[6] ..	P 27 Jan. 43	18 Aug. 48		
4	0	Frederick Jessop Jones ..	P 2 Sept. 45	18 Aug. 48		
4	0	E. D. Justin Mac Carthy	P 2 Sept. 45	18 Aug. 48		
3	0	William Munnings Lees..	P 14 Apr. 46	18 Aug. 48		
3	0	Fred. Goulburn Allman..	7 Aug. 46	12 Sept. 48		
3	0	Patrick James John Grant	14 Apr. 46	P 28 Apr. 48		
		ENSIGNS.				
3	0	Octavius Lowry	P 2 Oct. 46			
3	0	Charles Anderson	P 20 Oct. 46			
3	0	James Wm. S. Moffatt ..	3 Nov. 46			
1	0	William Alfred Swift	P 11 Feb. 48			
3	0	Watkin Tench Little....	22 May 46			
2	0	George B. Cumberland..	P 13 Aug. 47			
1	0	George Henry Cochrane	2 Aug. 48			
1	0	Alfred John Ford	18 Aug. 48			

3 Captain Gregg served with the 26th throughout the China expedition, and was present at the operations before Canton, at the attack on the sea batteries of Amoy and capture of the strongly fortified island of Goolangsoo, where, with a detachment of twelve men, he drove a large body of the enemy from a battery. He was also at the defence of Ningpo, at Chapoo, Woosung, Shanghae, Chin Kiang Foo, and Nankin.

4 Capt. Croker served as Assist. Quarter-Master-General in the action at Zorapore near Kurnaul on the 16th October, 1839; and also in a like capacity in the action at Maharajpore, 29 December 1843 (Medal).

5 Lt. Whiteside served throughout the campaign under Gen. Pollock in Affghanistan in 1842 (Medal) and that on the Sutlej in 1845-6 (Medal), including the battles of Moodkee, Ferozeshah, and Sobraon.

6 Lts. Middleton and Garstin served with the 58th on the expedition against Kawiti's Pah at Ruapekapeka, in New Zealand.

7 Paymaster Griffiths served the campaigns of 1813 and 14 in the Peninsula. Served also in the American war, including the capture of Washington, battle before Baltimore, the several operations on the coast, the several attacks upon the enemy's lines before New Orleans, and taking of Fort Bowyer. In the batteries upon the banks of the Mississippi at the blowing up of a man-of-war schooner.

Full Pay	Half Pay	
24	12 1/12	*Paymaster.*—Edwin Griffiths,[7] 11 Jan. 38; *2nd Lt.* 6 Jan. 13; *Lt.* 12 Nov. 13.
7	0	*Adjutant.*—*Lieut.* R. F. W. Cumberland, 9 April 47.
1	0	*Quarter-Master.*—William Thompson, 25 Feb. 48 [3 Nov. 25.
24	0	*Surgeon.*—Wm. Lucas, 2 July, 41; *Assist.-Surg.* 25 May 26; *Hosp.-Assist.*
8	0	*Assistant-Surgeons.*—Richard De Lisle, 27 Aug. 41.
5	0	William MacAndrew, M.D., 6 Dec. 44.
3	0	John James Clifford, M.D., 7 Aug. 46.

Facings Yellow.—*Agent*, Charles R. M'Grigor, Esq.

1 *Sir Lewis Grant* was on board H. M. ship *Orion*, in the action with the French fleet 23d June, 95. Was subsequently at the capture of various places in the West Indies.

2 Lieut.-Col. Hulme served in the Pindarree campaign, and commanded the flank companies in the general action of the 21st Dec. 17, for which he obtained the brevet rank of Major; he again commanded them when the fort of Talneir was stormed 28th Feb. 1818.

Emb. for Foreign Serv. 30 Jan. 41.] **97th (*The Earl of Ulster's*) *Regt. of Foot.*** [1st Bn. ser. at Nova Scotia r. b. Bn. at Jamaica.

"Quò fas et gloria ducunt."

Years' Serv.		
50		*Colonel.*
Full Pay.	Half Pay.	
		P Sir Henry Frederick Bouverie,[1] KCB. GCMG. *Ens.* 5 Aug. 99; *Lieut. & Capt.* 19 Nov. 00; *Capt. & Lieut.-Col.* 28 June, 10; *Col.* 4 June, 14; *Maj.-Gen.* 27 May, 25; *Lieut.-Gen.* 28 June, 38; *Col.* 97th Foot, 21 Nov. 43.
33	3 7/12	*Lieut.-Colonels.*—P Henry Fred. Lockyer,[2] KH., *Ens.* P 25 Mar. 1813; *Lt.* 19 Jan. 14; *Capt.* P 20 June 22; *Major,* P 12 June, 35; *Lieut.-Col.* 26 Oct. 41.
40	5 1/12	r. Nicholas Lawson Darrah,[3] *2nd Lieut.* 16 Aug. 04; *Lieut.* 2 April, 05; *Capt.* P 30 June, 08; *Brevet-Maj.* 27 May, 25; *Regtl.-Maj. & Brev.-Lt.-Col.* 28 June, 38; *Lt.-Col.* 14 Apr. 46.
35	0	*Majors.*—George Hutchison, *Lieut.* 14 July, 14; *Capt.* P 26 June. 27; *Brevet-Major,* 23 Nov. 41; *Major,* 27 Sept. 42.
24	0	r. *Hon.* Henry Robert Handcock, *Ens.* 8 April 25; *Lieut.* P 20 Mar. 27; *Capt.* P 24 Feb. 32; *Major,* 14 Apr. 46.

Full Pay	Half Pay		Ensign.	Lieut.	Captain.	Brev.-Maj.
		Captains.				
17	0	Aug. Fred. Welsford	P 24 Feb. 32	P 25 July 34	P 19 Jan. 38	
16	0	Robt. Colvill	P 27 Dec. 33	P 10 Feb. 37	P 29 May 40	
24	0	John M'Caskill	25 Jan. 25	27 June 28	26 Oct. 41	
13	0	r. Tho. Onslow W. Ingram	P 13 May 36	P 9 Mar. 38	P 15 Apr. 42	
29	10 4/12	r. P James Scargill[5]....	12 Apr. 10	21 Oct. 12	17 Jan. 28	23 Nov. 41
14	0	Isaac Moore	20 Feb. 35	29 June 38	20 Feb. 44	
12	0	r. Geo. Mauleverer Gowan	P 10 Feb. 37	P 17 May 39	P 25 Apr. 45	
13	0	r. Marc Antoine Obert ..	12 Mar. 36	P 10 Jan. 40	P 6 Feb. 46	
17	0	r. John Hutton	27 April 32	28 Dec. 38	14 Apr. 46	
17	0	Richard Pattinson[6]	P 16 Nov. 32	P 18 Apr. 34	P 23 Apr. 47	
10	0	r. Thomas Williams Evans	P 14 June 39	P 6 May 42	11 April 48	
13	0	James Dupre Brabazon..	29 April 36	29 Jan. 41	20 Oct. 48	
		Lieutenants.				
11	0	Robert Dillon..........	P 8 June 38	P 29 Nov. 39		
10	0	r. Edmund C. Legh	5 July 39	15 Apr. 42		
10	0	Fowler Burton, *adjutant*	P 30 Aug. 39	15 Apr. 42		
9	0	Thomas Biggs	P 2 Oct. 40	15 Nov. 43		
8	0	Sydney Cosby Jackson..	P 10 Sept. 41	P 25 June 44		
6	0	Septimus Moore Hawkins	P 2 June 43	P 30 Aug. 44		
7	0	Archibald Richard Harenc	P 15 Apr. 42	P 25 Apr. 45		
7	0	Edward D. Harvest	17 Apr. 42	P 6 Feb. 46		
9	0	r. John F. Ferris[7]	20 Nov. 40	14 Apr. 46		
7	0	r. Wm. George Bindon, *adj.*	18 Apr. 42	P 9 June 46		
6	0	r. Hedley S. J. Vicars ..	22 Dec. 43	P 6 Nov. 46		
5	0	Thomas Venables	P 28 June 44	P 8 Dec. 46		
5	0	r. Charles Henry Lumley	P 30 Aug. 44	P 10 Dec. 47		
4	0	Lawrence Wm. Reynolds	P 25 Apr. 45	P 21 July 48		
6	0	Henry George Woods ..	13 Oct. 43	20 Oct. 48		
8	0	George Webb	24 Sept. 41	7 Dec. 42		
		Ensigns.				
3	0	r. Thomas Edward Jones	P 6 Feb. 46			
3	0	r. Edward Kent Jones ..	21 Apr. 46			
3	0	r. Charles Edw. Stainforth	8 Sept. 46			
3	0	Richard Francis Holmes	26 Sept. 46			
3	0	r. William Fred. Norman	P 6 Nov. 46			
3	0	Osborne Barwell Cannon	P 6 Nov. 46			
2	0	r. James Vaughan Arthure	P 13 July 47			
2	0	r. Wm. Richard Annesley	P 10 Dec. 47			
1	0	Thomas Henry Pipon ..	P 21 July 48			
1	0	Ernest Randolph Mackesy	20 Oct. 48			

Full Pay	Half Pay	
13	0	*Paymaster.*—George Griffin, 24 March, 43; *Ens.* 16 Dec. 36; *Lt.* 22 Feb. 39.
10	0	*Adjutants.*—*Lieut.* Fowler Burton, 23 Sept. 45.
7	0	r. *Lieut.* William George Bindon, 8 Sept. 46.
3	0	*Quarter-Masters.*—John Desmond, 12 June, 46.
3	0	r. Patrick Carroll, 7 Aug. 46.
33	4 2/12	*Surgeons.*—W. Austin, M.D. 21 Nov. 28; *A.-S.* 4 Mar. 13; *H.-A.* 21 Nov. 11.
14	0	r. John Drope M'Illree, 8 Dec. 45; *Assist.-Surg.* 20 Feb. 35.
8	0	*Assistant-Surgeons.*—r. John Ewing, 21 May, 41.
3	0	Charles Vidler Cay, 12 June, 46.

Facings Sky Blue.—*Agents,* Messrs. Cox & Co.

5 Major Scargill served with the 9th at the defence of Tarifa, from May to Dec. 1811. Also in the South of France from March to May 1814, including the blockade of Bayonne and repulse of the sortie.

6 Capt. Pattinson served the campaign of the Indus under Lord Keane, as Aide-de-Camp to Brigadier Arnold, 16th Lancers, including the siege and capture of Ghuznee (Medal). He served as Major of Brigade of Cavalry in the campaign of Gwalior and on the Sutlej, including the battles of Maharajpore (Medal), Buddiwal (horse killed), Aliwal, and Sobraon (Medal). He acted as Assist.-Adjutant-General of Cavalry under Brigadier Cureton during Sir Harry Smith's operations in the Upper Sutlej.

7 Lieut. Ferris served in the Burmese war in 1825 and 26.

1 Sir Henry Bouverie served with the Coldstream Guards in Egypt during the campaign of 1801, including the action at the landing, and those of the 13th and 21st March, for which he has received a medal. Aide-de-Camp to the Earl of Rosslyn at the siege of Copenhagen, in 1807. Aide-de-Camp to the Duke of Wellington at the passage of the Douro, and at the battle of Talavera. Assistant Adjutant-General at the battles of Salamanca and Vittoria, siege and assault of San Sebastian, battles of the Nive and Orthes, for which he has received a cross and one clasp.

2 Lieut.-Colonel Lockyer served in the Peninsula, from Aug. 1813 to the end of the war, including the battles of Nivelle, Nive, Orthes, Aire, (severely wounded on left wrist and elbow joint), and Toulouse.

3 Lieut.-Col. Darrah served in Scylla castle when besieged in 1806; and before the same place in 1808. At Milli, in Sicily, when a descent was made by the troops of Murat, king of Naples. Served also the campaign of 1814 in Holland, including the attack on Bergen-op-Zoom.

Emb. for Foreign Serv. Dec. 1841. | **98th Regiment of Foot.** | [Serving in Bengal.

On the Colours and Appointments "CHINA" and the device of "*The Dragon.*"

Years' Serv. Full Pay.	Half Pay.	
51		*Colonel.* ℙ *Sir* Willoughby Cotton,[1] GCB. & KCH. *Ens.* 31 Oct. 1798; *Lieut. & Capt.* 25 Nov. 99; *Capt. & Lieut-Col.* 12 June, 1811; *Col.* 25 July, 21; *Major-Gen.* 22 July, 30; *Lieut.-Gen.* 23 Nov. 41; *Col.* 98th Regt. 1 Aug. 39.
39	2 5/12	*Lieut.-Colonels.*—ℙ Colin Campbell,[2] CB. *Ens.* 26 May, 08; *Lt.* 28 June 09; *Capt.* 9 Nov. 13; *Major,* P 26 Nov. 25; *Lieut.-Col.* P 26 Oct. 32; *Col.* 23 Dec. 42.
24	4	Arthur Charles Gregory, *Ens.* P 24 Oct. 21; *Lieut.* P 1 Oct. 25; *Capt.* P 15 Aug. 26; *Major,* P 18 Oct. 31; *Lieut.-Col.* P 5 Oct. 41.
29	6 4/12	*Majors.*—William Roberts,[3] *Ens.* 14 April, 14; *Lieut.* 7 April, 25; *Capt.* P 18 Oct. 31; *Major,* P 5 Oct. 41.
23	0	William Edie,[4] *Ens.* P 14 Jan. 26; *Lieut.* P 18 Oct. 31; *Capt.* P 29 Nov. 33; *Major,* P 13 June, 45.

Full Pay	Half Pay	CAPTAINS.	ENSIGN.	LIEUT.	CAPTAIN.	BREV.-MAJ.
14	0	Thos. Heaton Lovett[4]	P 5 June 35	P 27 Apr. 38	P 3 Dec. 41	
13	0	Daniel Rainier[4]	P 4 Mar. 36	P 11 May 38	P 27 May 42	
16	0	Thomas Charles Ormsby[4]	P 22 Mar. 33	20 Oct. 37	17 Mar. 43	
13	0	John Morton Jeffery[4]	P 28 June 36	P 22 June 38	P 31 Mar. 43	
12	0	Edmund Haythorne,[4] *s.*	12 May 37	P 4 Oct. 39	11 Sept. 44	
10	0	Francis Grantham,[4]	P 26 Apr. 39	P 16 April 41	P 10 July 46	
10	0	Charles Colby[4]	P 30 Aug. 39	P 18 June 41	P 10 July 46	
14	0	William Coates	P 6 Feb. 35	23 Oct. 39	18 Aug. 47	
20	0	Henry Bates,[7] *s.*	9 July 29	28 Nov. 33	P 8 Aug. 45	19 June 46
11	0	Warren Auchmuty, *s.*	P 16 Feb. 38	25 Aug. 40	P 9 April 47	
		LIEUTENANTS.				
9	0	Frederick Shelton	P 24 Jan. 40	P 18 Dec. 40		
8	0	Francis Peyton[4]	P 29 Jan. 41	P 27 May 42		
14	0	James Dutton Smyth	P 29 Dec. 35	P 30 Dec. 37		
8	0	Lawrence Shadwell,[4] *adj.*	P 16 April 41	17 Mar. 43		
8	0	Edward Grantham,[4]	P 5 Oct. 41	17 Mar. 43		
8	0	Augustus Fred. Steele[4]	P 18 Nov. 41	17 Mar. 43		
7	0	Thomas Clement Dunbar	1 Apr. 42	P 31 Mar. 43		
8	0	Henry T. Richmond	21 Nov. 41	9 June 43		
8	0	S. Hen. Hutchins Edwards	26 Nov. 41	18 Dec. 43		
7	0	Richard Young	22 July 42	28 July 44		
7	0	Molyneux Batt	28 Dec. 42	11 Sept. 44		
6	0	Martin Dillon	18 Mar. 43	14 Nov. 44		
6	0	Octavius Latouche	P 31 Mar. 43	P 24 Jan. 45		
6	0	Robert Reid	P 23 June 43	P 25 Jan. 45		
7	0	Robert John Hughes	7 Jan. 42	30 Aug. 43		
5	0	Campbell Barber Browne	23 Feb. 44	P 10 July 46		
5	0	John Reardon	31 Dec. 44	P 10 July 46		
5	0	Geo. D. Dickson Cleveland	P 10 May 44	P 2 Sept. 45		
4	0	William Croker	P 25 Jan. 45	P 22 June 47		
6	0	Henry Wallace Stroud	19 Mar. 43	18 Aug. 47		
6	0	Charles Hill Fresson	9 June 43	7 Jan 48		
4	0	Daniel Antoine Baby	28 Feb. 45	P 1 Aug. 48		
2	0	Richard Clancy	P 22 June 47	P 1 Dec. 42		
		ENSIGNS.				
4	0	James Stewart	27 Feb. 45			
4	0	Horatio Nelson Kippen	P 18 Apr. 45			
3	0	Peter Edward Quin	22 May 46			
2	0	Montague Browne	19 Nov. 47			
2	0	Don. Macleod Farrington	P 17 Dec. 47			
1	0	Charles Henry Dagg	18 July 48			
1	0	Frederick Moller	P 1 Aug. 48			
1	0	Thomas Templeman	P 1 Dec. 48			

Full Pay	Half Pay	
33	7	*Paymaster.*—Edward Hunter,[4] 27 Mar. 40; *Ens.* 13 July, 09; *Lieut.* 11 A[illegible] 13; *Capt.* 18 May, 38.
8	0	*Adjutant.*—*Lieut.* Lawrence Shadwell, 21 July, 48.
11	0	*Quarter-Master.*—James Fagan[4], 19 Jan. 38.
14	0	*Surgeon.*—Charles Cowen,[5] 16 Feb. 44; *Assist.-Surg.* 27 March, 35.
8	0	*Assistant-Surgeons.*—Edgar Dumaresq Batt,[4] 12 Oct. 41.
4	0	John Collis Brown, 25 April, 45.
7	0	Benjamin Swift, M.D., 8 April 42.

Facings White.—*Agents,* Messrs. Cox & Co.

3 Major Roberts was present at the assault and capture of Chin Kiang Foo; and he commanded the 98th at the landing before Nankin.—medal for China.

4 The following officers served in the 98th with the expedition to the North of China in 1842, (medal) and were present at the attack and capture of Chin Kiang Foo, and at the landing before Nankin, viz.—Major Edie, Captains Lovett, Rainier, Ormsby, Jeffery, Haythorne, Grantham, and Colby; Lieuts. Peyton, Shadwell, E. Grantham, and Steele; Captain Hunter, Quarter-Master Fagan, and Assist.-Surg. Batt.

5 Mr. Cowen served with the [illegible] in China (medal), and was present during the operations against Canton, and at the attack and capture of Chapoo, Shanghai, Woosung, and Chin Kiang Foo.

7 Major Bates served as Aide-de-camp to Sir Robert Dick (who was killed) in the battle of Sobraon.

1 Sir Willoughby Cotton served with the 3rd Guards on the expedition to Copenhagen in 1806; and that to Copenhagen in 1807, where he was appointed Deputy-Assistant-Adjutant-General to the [illegible] the Duke of Wellington, and was present at the battle of Kioge. In 1809 he accompanied the Duke to [illegible] and served as Deputy-Assistant-Adjutant-General to the Light Division during the whole of the [illegible] of the retreat to Torres Vedras and the subsequent advance, the former containing a series of [illegible] the battle of the Coa. Returned to England on promotion in June 1811, and rejoined the Peninsular [illegible] in 1813; he was present at the battle of Vittoria, commanded the Light Companies at the passage [illegible] Adour, and the piquets of the 2nd brigade of Guards at the repulse of the sortie from Bayonne. [illegible] manded a division of Sir Archibald Campbell's army in the Burmese war; and also of [illegible] under Keane in Affghanistan, and was present at the assault and capture of Ghuznee (Medal).

[illegible] the battle of Barrosa, defence of Tarifa, expedition for the relief of [illegible] Passage of the Bidassoa and [illegible] outworks 17th July, and body of the fortress 25th July, 1813; on these assaults led the columns of attack. Passage of the Bidassoa [illegible] two severe wounds at the assault of San Sebastian, one through the right hip, and one through the left thigh. Severely wounded at the assault of the intrenched position on the Bidassoa by a musket shot through the right thigh. Commanded the 98th at the assault and capture of the city of Chin Kiang Foo.

Years' Serv.		
55		
Full Pay.	Half Pay.	
		Colonel.
		Sir Howard Douglas,[1] *Bt.* GCB. GCMG. *2nd Lieut.* 1 Jan. 94; *Lieut.* 30 May, 94; *Capt.* 2 Oct. 99; *Maj.*, 12 Oct. 04; *Lt.-Col.* 31 Dec. 06; *Col.* 4 June, 14; *Major-Gen.* 19 July, 21; *Lt.-Gen.* 10 Jan. 37; *Col.* 99th Regt. 15 Mar. 41.
50	0	*Lieut.-Colonel.*—Henry Despard,[2] CB., *Ens.* 25 Oct. 1799; *Lieut.* 25 June, 03; *Capt.* P 19 Nov. 06; *Major,* P 12 Aug. 19; *Lt.-Col.* P 13 Aug. 29; *Col.* 9 Nov. 46.
40	3 10/12	*Majors.*—John Napper Jackson,[3] *Ens.* 1 July, 05; *Lieut.* 1 Jan. 06; *Capt.* 28 Feb. 12; *Major,* 11 June, 29; *Brevet Lieut.-Col.* 23 Nov. 41.
28	6 6/12	Edward Last,[4] *Ens.* 13 Oct. 14; *Lieut.* P 20 Nov. 24; *Capt.* P 22 May 29; *Major,* P 18 Oct. 39.

Full Pay	Half Pay	CAPTAINS.	ENSIGN.	LIEUT.	CAPTAIN.	BREV.-MAJ.
23	2 3/12	Geo. Marmaduke Reeves	1 July 24	P 8 Apr. 26	P 27 Apr. 27	23 Nov. 41
25	0	Jaffray Nicholson	P 20 Nov. 24	P 22 Apr. 26	P 5 July 33	9 Nov. 46
21	0	Philip Smyly	P 27 Mar. 28	P 18 June 30	P 18 July 34	9 Nov. 46
20	0	Edw. Maurice O'Connell, *s.*	P 22 May 29	P 9 Dec. 31	P 28 Apr. 37	
34	2 11/12	John Armstrong[5]	29 Oct. 12	19 Apr. 14	29 Sept. 37	
24	0	Henry James Day	10 Feb. 25	11 June 29	16 July 41	
14	0	Archibald Wm. Reed[6]	P 4 Sept. 35	P 25 July 37	P 17 July 41	7 July 46
30	6 6/12	Ewan M'Pherson[7]	21 Jan. 13	5 Feb. 14	P 26 Apr. 27	23 Nov. 41
14	0	Richard Ramsbottom	P 7 Aug. 35	P 1 June 38	P 16 Aug. 42	
12	0	William J. Hamilton	20 Apr. 37	5 July 39	P 12 Sept. 48	
		LIEUTENANTS.				
13	0	Isaac Hindley H. Gall	22 Nov. 36	7 Oct. 39		
12	0	Rupert Barber Deering, *s.*	P 3 Mar. 37	17 Oct. 39		
12	0	Charles Blamire	P 25 July 37	16 July 41		
11	0	Patrick Johnston,[8] *ad.*	P 20 Nov. 38	P 18 July 41		
10	0	Frederick Montgomerie	P 20 Sept. 39	P 18 Feb. 42		
10	0	Robert Henry De Winton[9]	P 18 Oct. 39	P 16 Aug. 42		
8	0	Charles Edward Leigh[10]	P 18 June 41	P 27 Dec. 42		
10	0	Lempster R. Elliot[11]	9 Aug. 39	P 28 Dec. 41		
8	0	G. J. De Winton De Winton	P 18 July 41	12 July 45		
7	0	Edmund W. Isdell	P 18 Feb. 42	P 5 Nov. 47		
7	0	Bernard Henry O'Reilly	P 16 Aug. 42	P 10 Dec. 47		
8	0	Robert Mends	P 31 Dec. 41	3 March 48		
5	0	William Forward Austen	P 6 Sept. 44	P 12 Sept. 48		
		ENSIGNS.				
3	0	Fred. William Despard	29 Jan. 46			
2	0	James Grime	15 Jan. 47			
3	0	Robert Baylis	21 April 46			
2	0	Wm. H. D. Reeves Welman	P 10 Dec. 47			
1	0	Augustus Fred. Smith	28 Jan. 48			
1	0	Robert William Benison	23 May 48			
1	0	Francis Seymour Gaynor	P 1 Aug. 48			
1	0	Allan Macdonald	P 12 Sept. 48			

12 Paymaster Pratt served in the American war in 1814; volunteered to pass through the American fleet on Lake Ontario, in command of Bateaux, with provisions for the Niagara Frontiers. Present at the siege of Fort Erie, and thanked in public orders by Sir Gordon Drummond, for assisting to take a foraging party at Sugar-Loaf. Present also at the defence of the Tête-de-pont, on the Chippeway Creek.

13 Quarter-master Macdonald served at Walcheren, and was present at the siege of Flushing. Served afterwards in the Peninsula, including the battle of Busaco, Lines of Torres Vedras, and subsequent advance from thence; battle of Salamanca, capture of Madrid, siege of Burgos, and retreat from thence, action at Osma, battle of Vittoria, siege and capture of San Sebastian (wounded), passage of the Bidassoa and storming the heights (wounded), passage of the Nive 9th (wounded) 10th and 11th Dec., investment of Bayonne, and repulse of the sortie, (severely contused on the head from the fragment of a shell), besides various minor actions and skirmishes.

Full Pay	Half Pay	
14	23	*Paymaster.*—Edward Pratt,[12] 18 Oct. 30; *Ens.* 3 Dec. 12; *Lieut.* 20 May, 14.
11	0	*Adjutant.*—*Lieut.* Patrick Johnston, 9 Oct. 46.
15	0	*Quarter-Master.*—Alexander Macdonald,[13] 13 June, 34; *Ens.* 16 May, 34.
15	0	*Surgeon.*—Henry Hadley,[14] MD. 27 June, 45; *Assist.-Surg.* 28 Nov. 34.
8	0	*Assistant-Surgeons.*—George Thomas Galbraith,[15] MD. 5 Oct. 41.
2	0	Henry Higgins Jones, MD. 10 Dec. 47.

Facings Yellow.—*Agent,* George Samuel Collyer, Esq.

1 Sir Howard Douglas served in Portugal and Spain in 1808 and 9, and was present at the battle of Corunna. Served afterwards at Walcheren, including the siege and bombardment of Flushing. Returned to the Peninsula in 1811, and continued there during that year and to the end of the campaign of 1812, having in that time been employed on a special mission extending throughout the north of Spain, and was present at the operations on the Orbigo and Esaler, and in the combined naval and military operations on the north coast of Spain in the early part of 1812, the attack and reduction of Lequetio, and afterwards at the siege of Astorga; the operations on the Douro, including the blockade of Zamona, the attack and reduction of the enemy's Ports on the Douro, and the siege of Burgos.

2 Colonel Despard was engaged at the reduction of four strong forts, and in the assault and capture by storm of the fortress of Chumeer in the East Indies, in 1807 and 8; also at the siege of Gunourie. In 1809 he served the campaign against the Seiks; also the campaign of 1817 and 18 in the Deccan, as a Major of Brigade, including the battle of Jubbulporé. He commanded the troops in New Zealand from June 1845 to January 1846; he was at the attack of the Pah at Oharawai on the 1st July 1845 and its subsequent capture; and he commanded the combined naval and military force engaged in the operations against the Pah of Ruapekapeka, and its subsequent capture by assault on the 11th January 1846.

3 Lieut.-Col. Jackson served in the Peninsula from 1810 to the end of the war in 1814, including the siege of Cadiz, Lines at Torres Vedras, Massena's retreat from Portugal, actions and affairs at Pombal, Redinha, Leira, Condeixa, Fleur-de-Lis, Guarda, Foz d'Arouce, and Sabugal; battle of Fuentes d'Onor, 3rd and 5th May, siege of Badajoz in June and July, 1811, actions at El Bodon and Guinaldo, siege and storm of Ciudad Rodrigo, third siege of Badajoz and storm of the Castle by escalade, 6th April, 1812; battle of Salamanca, capture of Madrid, the Retiro, and Fort La China, and in command of an escort of the third Division in charge of the garrison of Fort La China on route to Ciudad Rodrigo. Retreat to Portugal, Oct. and Nov. 1812, battles of Vittoria, Pyrenees, Nivelle, and Orthes; actions at Vic Bigorre and Tarbes, battle of Toulouse, and the whole of the various minor affairs during that period.

4 Major Last commanded the troops in the southern district of New Zealand during the greater part of the operations against the hostile natives in 1846. He assisted in driving back the rebels who attacked the detachment under Lieut. Page (58th regt.) at Boulcott's farm in the valley of the Hutt on the 16th May 1846; was present at the capture of Te Rauparaha and several other influential chiefs; and commanded the combined force at the affair of the Horokiwi, obliging the rebels to retreat and ultimately to disperse.

5 Capt. Armstrong was present at the affair at the Horokiwi on the 6th Aug. 1846.

6 Major Reed was present at the assault and capture of Ruapekapeka, for which he obtained the Brevet rank of Major. He was also engaged with the hostile natives in the valley of the Hutt 16th June 1846.

7 Major M'Pherson served the campaign of 1813 in Holland, including the actions at Merxem and bombardment of Antwerp.

8 Lieut. Johnston was present at Ohaeawai and Ruapekapeka.

9 Lieut. R. H. De Winton served in the whole of the operations against the hostile natives in the southern district of New Zealand in 1846.

10 Lieut. Leigh was present at Ruapekapeka; and he served also through the campaign in the south.

11 Lieut. Elliot volunteered with the 58th on that regt. proceeding to New Zealand, and served throughout the northern and southern campaigns of 1845 and 1846; was present at Okaihau, Ohaeawai, Ruapekapeka, and Horokiwi, and in several skirmishes in the north.

14 Dr. Hadley served with the 40th regt. at the taking of the fort of Munora and Kurrachee, in Lower Scinde, in Fe[illegible] 1835; and served in the subsequent campaign against the Beloochees and action at Dadur, in Upper Scinde, in 1840.

15 Dr. Galbraith was present at Ohaeawai and Ruapekapeka. He was the senior medical officer present during the greater part of the operations in the southern district of New Zealand: at several skirmishes in the valley of the Hutt; and at the Horokiwi on the 6th Aug. 1846.

"Copenhagen"—"Monte Video"—"Rolera"—"Vimiera"—"Corunna"—"Busaco"—"Barrosa"—"Fuentes d'Onor"—"Ciudad Rodrigo"—"Badajoz"—"Salamanca"—"Vittoria"—"Nivelle"—"Nive"—"Orthes"—"Toulouse"—"Peninsula"—"Waterloo."

Years' Serv.		
		Colonel-in-Chief.
		P W *Field Marshal* Arthur, *Duke of* Wellington, KG. GCB. GCH. 19 Feb. 20.
		Colonels Commandant.
55		1 P W *Sir* Andrew Francis Barnard,[1] GCB. GCH. *Ens.* 26 Aug. 1794; *Lieut.* Sept. 94; *Capt.* 13 Nov. 94; *Major*, 1 Jan. 1805; *Lieut.-Col.* 28 Jan. 08; *Col.* 4 June, 13; *Major-Gen.* 12 Aug. 19; *Lieut.-Gen.* 10 Jan. 37; *Col.* 1st Battalion Rifle Brigade, 25 Aug. 22.
44		P W *Sir* Henry George Wakelyn Smith,[2] *Bart.* GCB., *2nd Lieut.* 8 May, 05; *Lieut.* 15 Aug. 05; *Capt.* 28 Feb. 12; *Major*, 29 Sept. 14; *Lieut.-Col.* 18 June, 15; *Col.* 10 Jan. 37; *Major-Gen.* 9 Nov. 46: *Col.* 2nd Battalion Rifle Brigade, 16 April, 47.
Full Pay.	Half Pay.	*Lieutenant-Colonels.*
28	11/12	1 George Buller,[3] CB. *2nd Lt.* 2 Mar. 20; *Lt.* 28 Mar. 25; *Capt.* P 19 Aug. 28; *Major*, P 31 Dec. 39; *Lieut.-Col.* P 27 Aug. 41.
24	0	2 Charles Du Pré Egerton, *2nd Lieut.* P 13 July, 25; *Lieut.* P 25 Nov. 28; *Capt.* P 31 July 35; *Major*, 14 Apr. 46; *Lieut.-Col.* 13 July, 47.
22	1/12	r.2 Arthur Johnstone Lawrence, *2nd Lieut.* P 4 Apr. 27; *Lieut.* P 12 Feb. 30; *Capt.* P 24 Feb. 37; *Major*, P 11 Sept. 46; *Lieut.-Col.* 1 Aug. 47.
		Majors.
23	0	2 John Hamilton Esten, *2nd Lieut.* P 30 Aug. 26; *Lieut.* P 30 Mar. 32; *Capt.* P 31 May, 39; *Major*, 14 April, 47.
22	0	1 Richard Henry FitzHerbert, *2nd Lieut.* P 3 July, 27; *Lieut* P 11 Jan. 33; *Capt.* P 25 Oct. 39; *Major*, 2 July, 47.
21	0	1 Sidney Beckwith,[4] *2nd Lieut.* 17 Apr. 28; *Lieut.* 26 May, 33; *Capt.* P 31 Dec. 39; *Major*, 13 July, 47; *Brevet Lieut.-Col.* 22 Dec. 48.
27	0	r.2 Wm. Sherbrook Ramsay Norcott, *2nd Lieut.* 13 June, 22; *Lieut.* 16 June, 25; *Capt.* 21 Feb. 40; *Major*, 1 Aug. 47.

Full Pay	Half Pay	Captains.	2nd Lieut.	Lieut.	Captain.
18	0	r.2 Wm. Henry Frankland	P 7 June 31	P 4 Dec. 35	P 8 Aug. 41
16	0	r.2 Wilmot Henry Bradford	P 24 May 33	P 26 Aug. 36	P 27 Aug. 41
16	0	r.2 Wm. Henry Beresford	P 25 Jan. 33	P 3 Aug. 38	P 15 Apr. 42
16	0	1 Alfred H. Horsford	12 July 33	P 23 Apr. 39	P 5 Aug. 42
15	0	1 Edward Rooper	24 Jan. 34	P 5 July 39	P 2 Sept. 42
13	0	1 Edward Arthur Somerset	29 Jan. 36	9 July 40	P 31 Jan. 45
13	0	r.2 William Shipley Warren	P 6 May 36	10 July 40	P 25 April 45
13	0	2 Robert Crawfurd	P 22 July 36	P 2 Oct. 40	P 10 Oct. 45
12	0	1 Alex. Macdonell	P 23 June 37	P 11 May 41	P 24 Oct. 45
10	0	r.2 Frederick Robert Elrington	P 7 June 39	23 Nov. 41	P 22 May 46
10	0	1 *Lord* Alexander George Russell	P 11 July 39	15 Apr. 42	P 7 Aug. 46
10	0	2 Joseph Wilkinson	30 Dec. 39	15 April 42	12 Jan. 47
9	0	1 Charles John Woodford	28 Feb. 40	P 3 June 42	14 Apr. 47
9	0	1 Henry Hardinge	P 19 June 40	P 5 Aug. 42	P 7 May 47
8	0	2 Wm. Harry, *Earl of* Erroll, *s.*	never	18 May 41	P 2 July 47
9	0	2 Maximil. Montague Hammond,	15 Dec. 40	P 7 Apr. 43	P 24 Sept. 47
8	0	1 Spencer Stewart	P 11 May 41	P 16 June 43	P 24 Sept. 47
20	0	2 Frederick Augustus Wetherall,[5] *s.*	10 Dec. 29	P 14 Dec. 32	1 Aug. 44
8	0	r.2 Peregrine Charles Baillie Hamilton	P 2 July 41	P 6 Oct. 43	P 12 Nov. 47
8	0	1 Julius Richard Glyn[6]	16 July 41	P 13 Oct. 43	P 9 June 48
8	0	1 Albert de Lautour	P 27 Aug. 41	P 5 July 44	31 Aug. 48
8	0	2 Aubrey Agar Cartwright	P 15 Oct. 41	P 31 Jan. 45	P 22 Dec. 48

1 Sir Andrew Barnard served at St. Domingo from April to Aug. 1796; served in the expedition under Sir Ralph Abercromby to the West Indies, and was at the reduction of Morne Fortunée. In 1799, served in the expedition to the Helder, and was present in the actions of the 27th Aug., 10th Sept, and 2d and 6th Oct. Sir Andrew has received a cross and four clasps for Barrosa (severely wounded), Ciudad Rodrigo, Badajoz, Salamanca, Vittoria, Nivelle (severely wounded), Orthes, and Toulouse. Slightly wounded at Waterloo.

2 Sir Harry Smith served with the Rifle Brigade at the siege, storm, and taking of Monte Video under Sir S. Auchmuty; and at the assault upon Buenos Ayres under Brigadier-General Craufurd. Employed with the troops in Spain under Sir John Moore, from the battle of Vimiera to the embarkation of the troops at Corunna. Embarked for the Peninsula under Major-General Robert Craufurd in 1809; was seriously wounded in the action upon the bridge of the Coa near Almeida. Commanded a company in the pursuit of Massena from the Lines of Lisbon; at the actions of Redinha, Condeixa, and Foz d'Aronce. Appointed Brigade-Major to the 2nd Light Brigade in the Light Division, and was present in the action of Sabugal, battle of Fuentes d'Onor, siege and storm of Ciudad Rodrigo, siege and storm of Badajoz, battles of Salamanca and Vittoria, attack of the heights of Vera, and passage of the Bidassoa, battle of Sarre, attack upon the position of St. Jean de Luz and heights of Arcangues, battle of Orthes, affair at Tarbes, and battle of Toulouse. Appointed Assistant-Adjutant-General to the troops under Major-General Ross destined against Washington, and was present at the battle of Bladensburg and destruction of Washington. Brought home despatches, and went out again immediately under Sir Edward Pakenham, and was present at the attack upon the enemy's lines near New Orleans. After the death of Sir Edward he was appointed Military Secretary to Sir John Lambert, commanding the army, and was present at the siege and taking of Fort Bowyer. Appointed Assist. Quarter-Master-General to the 6th Division of the Army under the Duke of Wellington, and was present at the battle of Waterloo. In 1828 he was appointed D. Q. M. Gen. at the Cape of Good Hope, and commanded a division under Sir Benjamin D'Urban throughout the operations against the Kaffir tribes in 1834 and 1835. In 1840 he proceeded to the East Indies as Adjutant-General, and was nominated a *K.C.B.* for the action of Maharajpore, in which battle he was present as Adjutant-General; and for his distinguished services in the campaign on the Sutlej and brilliant victory over the Sikhs at Aliwal, he was nominated a *G.C.B.* and afterwards created a Baronet. Finally, as Governor and Commander-in-chief at the Cape of Good Hope, he attacked and defeated the rebel Boers at Boem Plaats 29th Aug. 1848.

3 Lt. Colonel Buller held a command in the action with and defeat of the rebel Boers at Boem Plaats 29th Aug. 1848, and was severely wounded above the knee—the same shot killing his horse.

[*For Notes 4, 5, and 6, see next page.*

Full Pay.	Half Pay.	LIEUTENANTS.	2ND LIEUT.	LIEUT.
10	0	2 Thomas Cochrane Inglis	P 14 June 39	P 14 April 43
7	0	1 John Peter Need	20 May 42	P 10 Oct. 45
7	0	r.2 William Robert Churchill Spencer	21 May 42	P 24 Oct. 45
7	0	2 Hercules Walker	22 May 42	P 30 Dec. 45
7	0	1 George Palmer Evelyn	28 May 42	P 31 Dec. 45
7	0	2 Edward Newdigate	29 May 42	14 Apr. 46
7	0	2 Robert Henry Baird	o 1 July 42	P 22 May 46
6	0	1 Charles Plumer Pennington	P 21 Apr. 43	P 24 July 46
6	0	r.2 Henry Davie Ferguson Davie	P 16 June 43	P 7 Aug. 46
6	0	2 *Hon.* Gilbert Elliot, *adjutant*	P 7 July 43	P 11 Sept. 46
6	0	r.2 Charles Edward Barry Baldwin	P 6 Oct. 43	23 Apr. 47
5	0	1 John Cole Nicholl	P 5 July 44	P 7 May 47
6	0	r.2 William James Colville	22 Nov. 43	P 14 May 47
5	0	r.2 *Hon.* William Draper Mortimer Best	P 17 May 44	P 2 July 47
5	0	1 Charles Vernon Oxenden	P 23 Aug. 44	P 13 July 47
4	0	2 Arthur De Vere *Visc.* Malden	31 Jan. 45	P 23 July 47
4	0	1 Charles Henry Spencer Churchill	P 10 Oct. 45	P 24 Sept. 47
4	0	1 Edmund Manningham Buller	11 Oct. 45	P 24 Sept. 47
4	0	2 *Hon.* James Stuart	P 24 Oct. 45	P 15 Oct. 47
4	0	1 Augustus Wykeham Clifton	P 14 Nov. 45	P 12 Nov. 47
4	0	1 *Hon.* Leicester Curzon	P 29 Nov. 45	P 12 Nov. 47
4	0	1 Arthur William Godfrey	P 30 Dec. 45	P 9 June 48
4	0	1 George Henry William Walker	P 31 Dec. 45	P 22 Dec. 48
		SECOND LIEUTENANTS.		
3	0	r.2 John Ross	14 Apr. 46	
3	0	1 Herbert Somerset Hamilton Cornewall	P 28 Apr. 46	
3	0	1 William Bagenall Brewster, *adj.*	P 7 July 46	
3	0	1 *Hon.* Henry Clifford	P 7 Aug. 46	
3	0	r.2 Peter MacDonald *adj*(*Q.M.* 19 *May* 46)	8 Sept. 46	
3	0	1 Wyndham William Knight	P 11 Sept. 46	
2	0	r.2 Alfred Manners Drummond	P 19 Mar. 47	
2	0	r.2 George Horsey Waddington	P 23 Apr. 47	
2	0	r.2 Arthur Nixon	30 Apr. 47	
2	0	1 Robert Baillie	P 7 May 47	
2	0	2 Francis Walter Balfour	P 14 May 47	
2	0	2 Henry Tryon	P 2 July 47	
2	0	1 Coote Buller	P 13 July 47	
2	0	2 Frederick Henry Ramsden	P 14 July 47	
2	0	2 Arthur Frederick Warren	P 23 July 47	
2	0	1 James Rowles	P 24 Sept. 47	
2	0	1 Henry Gore Lindsay	P 25 Sept. 47	
2	0	1 Adam Steuart	P 1 Oct. 47	
2	0	2 Charles Edward Bott	P 15 Oct. 47	
2	0	1 J. C. R., *Lord* Clanmorris	P 12 Nov. 47	
2	0	r.2 Henry Wrixon Becher	P 13 Nov. 47	
1	0	r 2 Charles William Doberty	P 9 June 48	
1	0	2 William Thomas Markham	P 22 Dec. 48	
1	0	1 Hugh Guion Macdonald	22 Dec. 48	

1 Paymaster Lindam serv in the campaign on the Sut in 1846 (Medal), and was verely wounded (lost left l at the battle of Sobraon.

Full Pay.	Half Pay.	
11	0	*Paymasters.*—2 John Newbury, 23 Aug. 44; *Ens.* 28 Dec. 38; *Lt.* 21 Aug. 4
7	0	1 Charles James Lindam,[1] 8 Oct. 47; *Ens.* 8 Nov. 42; *Lieut.* P 28 Mar. 4
3	0	*Adjutants.*—r.2 *Second Lieut.* Peter MacDonald, 8 Sept. 46.
6	0	2 *First Lieut. Hon.* Gilbert Elliot, 23 April, 47.
3	0	1 *Second Lieut.* William Bagenall Brewster, 19 June 48.
10	0	*Quarter-Masters.*—1 Richard Taylor, 29 March, 39.
3	0	r.2 Thomas Gough, 14 Aug. 46.
3	0	2 William Stillwell, 27 Oct. 46.
22	0	*Surgeons.*—1 Evans Garnons Lloyd, 6 Aug. 41; *A.-S.* 18 Oct. 27; *H.-A.* 25 Jan. 2
14	0	2 Arthur Anderson, M.D. 16 Dec. 45; *Assist.-Surg.* 16 Oct. 35.
15	0	r. 2 Thomas Alexander, 30 May 45; *Assist.-Surg.* 10 Oct. 34.
8	0	*Assist.-Surgs.*—2 John Fraser, M.D. 20 Aug. 41.
4	0	r. 2 John Liddell Robinson, 22 July, 45.
2	0	1 James Edward Scott, M.B. 11 June, 47.
1	0	1 John Riggs Miller Lewis, *M.D.* 11 Feb. 48.

Regimentals Green.—*Facings* Black.—*Agents,* Messrs. Cox & Co.

[1st *Battalion embarked for Foreign Service,* 10 *Nov.* 1840. *At the Cape of Good Hope. Depôt at Bristol.*]

[2nd *Battalion embarked for Bermuda,* 14*th Sept.* 1841. *Now serving in Canada.*]

[r. 2nd *Battalion embarked for Foreign Service* 25*th July* 1842. *Serving in Canada.*

4 Lieut.-Col. Beckwith commanded the Infantry in the action with and defeat of the rebel Boers at Bloem Plaats.

5 Captain Wetherall served the campaign of 1839 in Affghanistan and Beloochistan with the 17th, and was present at storm and capture of Ghuznee (Medal) and of Khelat.

6 Capt. Glyn served as Field Adjutant to the force under Sir Harry Smith in the action with and defeat of the rebel Bo at Bloem Plaats.

"DOMINICA"—"MARTINIQUE"—"GUADALOUPE."

Years' Serv. 49 Full Pay.	Half Pay.					
30	$6\frac{7}{12}$	*Colonel.*—⚑ *Sir* George Thomas Napier,[1] KCB. *Ens.* 25 Jan. 00; *Lt.* 13 June, 00; *Capt.* 5 Jan. 04; *Major,* 30 May, 11; *Lt.-Col.* 6 Feb. 12; *Col.* 27 May, 25; *Maj.-Gen.* 10 Jan. 37; *Lt.-Gen.* 9 Nov. 46; *Col.* 1st W. I. Regt. 29 Feb. 44.				
		Lt.-Cols.—⚑ Edward Rowley Hill,[3] *Ens.* 23 Feb. 13; *Lt.* 24 Feb. 14; *Capt.* P 26 Sept. 26; *Brev.-Maj.* 23 Nov. 41; *Maj.* P 6 May, 42; *Lt.-Col.* 1 Jan. 47.				
26	$12\frac{1}{12}$	⚑ Robert Hughes,[4] *Ens.* 11 April 11; *Lieut.* 29 Oct. 12; *Capt.* 13 Feb. 27; *Brevet-Major,* 23 Nov. 41; *Major,* 3 Mar. 43; *Lieut.-Col.* 1 Mar. 48.				
22	0	*Majors.*—Luke Smyth O'Connor, *Ens.* P 27 April 27; *Lieut.* 22 Mar. 31; *Capt.* P 17 Jan. 34; *Brev.-Major,* 9 Nov. 46; *Major,* 1 Jan. 47.				
25	3	James Clarke, *Ens.* 11 Jan. 21; *Lt.* P 19 July, 27; *Capt.* 21 April, 36; *Br.-Maj.* 9 Nov. 46; *Maj.* 1 Mar. 48.				
		CAPTAINS.	**ENSIGN.**	**LIEUT.**	**CAPTAIN.**	**BREV.-MAJ.**
24	0	George Robeson........	21 July 25	17 April 28	1 June 39	
21	0	George Waller Meehan..	17 April 26	14 April 36	15 Apr. 42	
17	0	Augustus Wm. Murray	P 28 Dec. 32	P 28 Nov. 37	P 25 Nov. 42	
13	0	Richard Olpherts[5]......	P 2 Dec. 36	P 21 June 39	P 15 Mar. 44	
17	$13\frac{4}{12}$	Robert Horatio Minty, *s*	21 May 18	19 Apr. 36	6 Dec. 44	
23	$\frac{8}{12}$	John Powell	29 Sept. 25	7 Oct. 32	10 Nov. 44	
12	0	Alex. Wm. Mackenzie...	3 Feb. 37	1 June 39	1 Jan. 47	
6	0	Richard D'Oyly Fletcher	P 21 Apr. 43	P 19 Apr. 44	P 9 Apr. 47	
6	0	Charles Walter Grange[6]	P 3 Nov. 43	P 2 May 45	P 31 Dec. 47	
12	0	Edmund Hayter Bingham	P 10 Mar. 37	1 June 39	1 Mar. 48	
13	0	Ninian Craig	P 25 Mar. 36	26 Oct. 39	21 Mar. 48	
10	0	Robert Hughes	2 June 39	18 June 41	6 Apr. 48	
		LIEUTENANTS.				
10	0	James Henry Robeson, *s.*	23 Nov. 39	15 Apr. 42		
8	0	James Aggas, *s.*........	8 Jan. 41	do.		
10	0	Richard Doris, *s.*	25 Oct. 39	22 July 42		
8	0	Thomas Wm. Stowart ..	20 June 41	22 Nov. 42		
7	0	Henry Anton	14 Jan. 42	3 Mar. 43		
7	0	George Herbert Robeson	19 Apr. 42	31 Jan. 44		
7	0	W. John Chamberlayne, *s.*	25 Nov. 42	6 Dec. 44		
6	0	George Allan	3 Mar. 43	3 Jan. 45		
15	$19\frac{4}{12}$	John Ross	25 May 15	11 Sept. 17		
5	0	William Sankey, *s.*	P 19 Apr. 44	P 8 Aug. 45		
5	0	John Moore Tittle......	31 Jan. 44	9 Sept. 45		
5	0	Haydon Lloyd Cafe	P 27 Sept. 44	P 9 Dec. 45		
4	0	Anthony Tunstall	P 2 May 45	P 3 Apr. 46		
5	0	Thomas Clark, *adj.*	26 Apr. 44	23 July 46		
4	0	George Jones	11 July 45	P 24 July 46		
4	0	Henry Jones	3 Jan. 45	28 June 47		
3	0	Stanley Douglas Stubbs	P 24 July 46	P 29 Oct. 47		
2	0	Henry Ratcliffe Searle ..	P 28 May 47	P 31 Dec. 47		
4	0	George Philan	17 Jan. 45	1 Mar. 48		
4	0	Wm. Newcomen Watts..	P 9 Dec. 45	21 Mar. 48		
4	0	John Fanning..........	30 Dec. 45	6 Apr. 48		
3	0	Richard Doyle Barrett..	14 Apr. 46	9 Apr. 48		
3	0	Alexander Morphy	28 Apr. 46	14 June 48		
		ENSIGNS.				
2	0	Samuel Head	1 Jan. 47			
2	0	Julius William Thompson	P 9 Apr. 47			
2	0	Richard Philip Fletcher	P 29 Oct. 47			
2	0	Courtenay Thos. Hammill	30 Oct. 47			
1	0	Oliver George Stokes....	P 14 Jan. 48			
1	0	Waring Alex. Biddle....	P 18 Feb. 48			
1	0	James Wright..........	14 Apr. 48			
1	0	William James Ross	12 May 48			
1	0	Angus William Mackay..	23 May 48			
1	0	Arthur Wellesley Castray	23 June 48			
1	0	Edmund Patterson	12 Sept. 48			
8	0	*Paymaster.*—Alexander Smith, 3 Dec. 47; *Quartermaster,* 18 Nov. 41.				
5	0	*Adjutant.*—*Lieut.* Thomas Clark, 21 July, 46.				
1	0	*Quarter-Master.*—Charles Stokeley, 17 March, 48. [*H.A.* 10 Dec. 10.				
28	$16\frac{6}{12}$	*Surg.*—⚑ John Edmonstone Stewart,[7] 2 Nov. 30; *Assist.-Surg.* 25 June, 12;				
5	0	*Assistant-Surgeons.*—George William Powell, 20 Aug. 44.				
3	0	John Madden, 2 Oct. 46. [*Facings* White.				
3	0	Thomas Frederick Wall, 20 Nov. 46. *Agents,* Cox & Co.				

3 Lt.-Col. Hill served in the Peninsula from Sept. 1812 to the end of that war in 1814, including the affair of San Munos and retreat from Burgos, as a volunteer; battle of Vittoria, passage of the Bidassoa, battles of Nivelle and Toulouse.

4 Lt.-Col. Hughes served in the Peninsula from 1809 to 1814, including the first siege of Badajos, and the battles of Busaco, Vittoria (wounded), Salamanca, and the Pyrenees, besides various minor actions and skirmishes. Present at Waterloo on the 16th, 17th and 18th June, and was wounded on the 18th.

5 Capt. Olpherts served in the 40th throughout the campaign at Candahar and in Affghanistan with the army under Sir Wm. Nott.

6 Capt. Grange served as an officer of Militia in Canada during the suppression of the insurrection, and was present at the siege of Navy Island.

7 Mr. Stewart served in the Peninsula from March, 1811 to Feb. 1813, and was present at the retreat from Burgos.

1 Sir George Napier accompanied the expedition to Sweden, and from thence to Portugal, in 1808, when he became Aide-de-camp to Sir John Moore, in which capacity he served the Corunna campaign, and was at the battle of Corunna, and the affairs which preceded it. Served afterwards with the 52nd in the campaigns of 1809, 10, and 11, when he was made Brevet-Major—he and his brother, Major-Gen. Wm. Napier, being two out of eleven chosen by Lord Wellington for promotion on the occasion of Massena's retreat. He gained the brevet of Lieut.-Col. for leading the storming party at the smaller breach of Ciudad Rodrigo, where he lost his right arm, having had the same arm broken at the action of Casal Nova, and had it wounded again during the siege of Ciudad Rodrigo, two days before he lost it in the breach. He was also wounded at the battle of Busaco, while in the act of striking [illegible] at a French grenadier at the head of the enemy's attacking column. In 1813, he rejoined the 52nd, and was present at the battle of Orthes, the action of Tarbes, and the battle of Toulouse. Medal for Ciudad Rodrigo.

Years' Serv. Full Pay	Half Pay	
46		**Colonel.**—℗ Sir Robert John Harvey,[1] C.B., *Ens.* 8 Oct. 03; *Lt.* 24 Mar. 04; *Capt.* 2 Jan. 06; *Maj.* 25 July, 11; *Lt.-Col.* 21 June, 13; *Col.* 22 July, 30; *Major-Gen.* 23 Nov. 41; *Col.* 2d W. I. Regt. 15 June, 48.
18	0	*Lieutenant-Colonels.*—Henry C. Cobbe, *Ens.* 15 Feb. 31; *Lieut.* P 23 Jan. 35; *Capt.* P 3 Nov. 37; *Major*, P 20 Oct. 40; *Lt.-Col.* 26 May, 44.
23	0	William Raikes Faber,[2] *2nd Lt.* P 10 April, 26; *Lt.* P 28 Aug. 28; *Capt.* P 22 May, 35; *Brev.-Maj.* 23 Dec. 42; *Maj.* P 17 Nov. 43; *Lt.-Col.* P 15 Dec. 48.
26	1 1/12	*Majors.*—Herbert Mends,[3] *Ens.* 1 April, 22; *Lieut.* 19 Feb. 24; *Capt.* 19 Mar. 29; *Major*, 26 May, 44.
33	0	Edw. Charles Soden, *Ens.* 1 Feb. 16; *Lieut.* 27 June 24; *Capt.* 10 Nov. 34; *Brev.-Major*, 9 Nov. 46; *Major*, 29 July 47.

Full Pay	Half Pay	CAPTAINS.	ENSIGN.	LIEUT.	CAPTAIN.	BREV.-MAJ.
27	8 1/12	Richard Elliott	28 July 14	30 Nov. 26	7 Aug. 39	
24	0	Stephen John Hill	10 Nov. 25	13 Feb. 28	15 April 42	
21	0	Henry Wase Whitfeild	13 Feb. 28	28 Oct. 31	15 April 42	
11	0	George Howell	P 11 May 38	P 14 Feb. 40	P 2 Aug. 42	
22	14	[illegible] Abraham P. Kenyon	24 June 13	24 June 13	26 May 44	
14	0	John Miller	P 29 Dec. 35	25 Jan. 39	15 Mar. 46	
7	0	Charles C. Rookes	P 11 Mar. 42	P 31 Dec. 42	P 20 Mar. 46	
12	0	William Anderson, *s.*	10 July 37	25 Oct. 39	9 Nov. 46	
12	0	Jas. Delamain Mends	P 3 Nov. 37	26 Oct. 39	29 July 47	
11	0	John Warren Glubb, *s.*	16 Mar. 38	8 Mar. 40	26 Oct. 47	
15	0	Charles Durie	1 Aug. 34	P 6 July 38	9 Jan. 48	
6	0	John Crosbie Harnett	9 Nov. 43	P 4 April 45	P 3 Oct. 48	

Full Pay	Half Pay	LIEUTENANTS.	ENSIGN.	LIEUT.
10	0	Wm. M'Carthy Murray, *s.*	22 Feb. 39	4 Aug. 41
10	0	John Harger	25 Oct. 39	15 April 42
10	0	Stephen Blaney Gordon	26 Oct. 39	do
10	0	George Bennett	27 Oct. 39	do.
9	0	Wm. Elliot Mockler, *s.*	8 May 40	do.
11	0	John Harpur (*Q.-M.* 5 Mar. 38)	15 Dec. 40	18 Aug. 42
8	0	John Cornelius M'Pherson	14 Dec. 41	29 Dec. 42
7	0	Robert Scott	15 April 42	10 Nov. 43
7	0	Arthur Wellesley Joyce	17 April 42	28 Mar. 44
7	0	Arthur Hunt	18 April 42	26 May 44
8	0	Charles Thomas Dumaresq	2 April 41	P 20 Oct. 43
6	0	John M'Court	1 Jan. 43	1 July 45
11	0	John Gaggin Cox	1 June 38	31 Dec. 39
5	0	George James Ivey	1 Nov. 44	15 Jan. 47
4	0	David Aikman Patterson	P 4 April 45	29 July 47
4	0	Alex. John Blair Child	2 Sept. 45	26 Oct. 47
5	0	Edmund John Gardiner	21 Dec. 44	P 5 Nov. 47
8	0	Augustus Wedderburn	P 26 Feb. 41	P 2 Dec. 42
1	0	Robert Grigg	7 Jan. 48	P 3 Oct. 48
3	0	Henry A. Whitmore Ayton	14 Aug. 46	13 Oct. 48
3	0	Patrick M'Loughlin	17 Sept. 46	do.
3	0	Fred. Blanco Forster	12 Nov. 46	do.

Full Pay	Half Pay	ENSIGNS.	ENSIGN.
3	0	George Ellis	13 Nov. 46
2	0	Thomas Gibbings	15 Jan. 47
2	0	M. Sackville Eaton	19 Feb. 47
2	0	R. S. Wilkinson Jones	13 Aug. 47
2	0	George Ross Caldwell	P 1 Oct. 47
2	0	Charles John Patterson	P 2 Oct. 47
2	0	Wm. Tho. James Simmons	8 Oct. 47
6	0	T. Birley, *Ad. Q.-M.* 20 Oct. 43	29 Dec. 47
1	0	Wm. Benjamin Crispin	21 July 48
1	0	John Smith Swanzy	P 3 Oct. 48
1	0	Fred. Cipriano Palacios	P 13 Oct. 48
1	0	James Lambert Byrne	14 Oct. 48
1	0	Forward Rumley	15 Oct. 48

Full Pay	Half Pay	
2	0	*Paymaster.*—℗ Allan Robertson,[7] 14 May 47.
6	0	*Adjutant.*—*Ens.* Thomas Birley, 29 Dec. 47.
1	0	*Quarter-Master.*—Charles Frederick Johnson, 2 June, 48.
10	0	*Surgeon.*—Wm. Henry Brownson, M.D., 18 Feb. 48; *Assist.-Surg.* 17 Sept. 39.
2	0	*Assist.-Surgeons.*—William Legge Reid, M.D. 23 March 47.
1	0	Patrick Joseph Clarke, 17 Mar. 48.
3	0	Thomas Parr, 21 July 46.

Facings Yellow.—*Agent*, Charles R. MacGrigor, Esq.

3 Major Mends served many years on the Western Coast of Africa, and was present at the first attack made upon the Ashantees near the village of Dooguah, 26th Sept. 1823, under Sir Charles M'Carthy. Present also at the destruction of the native Dutch town of Succondee, 17th Feb. 1824, and employed in the boats of H. M. ships of war skirmishing with the natives of that town and the Ashantees on the following morning. In action against the Ashantees, 21st May, 1824; and at the defeat of their army on the heights in rear of Cape Coast Castle, 11th July following. On the 4th Feb. 1826, whilst in command of Dixcove Fort, he was attacked by about 6000 natives, the garrison consisting of only one corporal and nineteen privates, (natives) R. Afr. corps; with these he defended the post, and forced the enemy to retreat with much loss in killed and wounded. Besides the above he has been in various skirmishes with the natives.

7 Paymaster Robertson served as 2nd Lieut. of Royal Marines in the Baltic in 1809-10, and was present in several actions with gun-boats, privateers and batteries. He joined the 3rd Battalion 1st Foot, as Ensign, at Torres Vedras in 1811 on the retreat of the French army from Santarem, and was present in the action of Sabugal, blockade of Almeida, and battle of Fuentes d'Onor. In 1813 he joined the 4th Battalion with the force in Germany under General Gibbs, and was at the blockade of Hamburgh in 1814; after which marched into Holland, and, whilst detached with the Grenadiers, was at the assault of Bergen-op-Zoom, where he was twice wounded by musket-balls, and taken prisoner.

2 Lt.-Colonel Faber served with the 49th throughout the war with China (Medal), and was present at the first and second capture of Chusan, storm and capture of the heights above Canton, attack and capture of Amoy and of Chinhae, occupation of Ningpo, and repulse of the night attack, attack and capture of the enemy's entrenched camp on the heights of Segoan, of Chapoo, and of Woosung, and investment of Nankin.

1 Sir Robert Harvey served as Assistant-Quarter-Master-General of the British and of the Portuguese armies in Portugal, Spain, and France, from 1809 to the close of the war in 1814, and was present at the battles of the passage of the Douro and Busaco, second siege of Badajos, siege and storm of Ciudad Rodrigo and Badajos, battle of Salamanca, siege of Burgos, battles of Vittoria, Pyrenees slightly wounded, Nivelle, Nive, Orthes, and Toulouse, besides numerous minor affairs. From 1809 to 1811 he was employed in procuring intelligence of the enemy in advance of the army, in organizing nine Portuguese Guerilla Corps, the officers of which presented him with an elegant sword in testimony of his services with them; and in assisting the attempt of the enemy's passage of the Tagus at Chamusca. From 1811 to 1814, he was the organ of communication between the Duke of Wellington and the Portuguese troops. Medal for the battle of Orthes.

Full Pay.	Half Pay.	55
		P Colonel.—Sir Guy Campbell,[1] *Bart.*, CB. *Ens.* 9 Dec. 94; *Lieut.* 4 April 96; *Capt.* 14 Sept. 04; *Maj.* 1 April 13; *Lt.-Col.* 26 Aug. 13; *Col.* 22 July 30; *Maj.-Gen.* 23 Nov. 41; *Col.* 3rd West India Regt. 24 Oct. 47.
37	0	*Lieut.-Colonels.*—P Francis Perry,[2] *Ens.* 8 Oct. 12; *Lieut.* 18 Feb. 13; *Capt.* 8 June, 26; *Major*, 8 Dec. 37; *Lieut.-Col.* 15 April, 42.
17	0	William Maxwell Mills, *Ens.* P20 July, 32. *Lieut.* P17 Jan. 34; *Capt.* P18 Sept. 40; *Major*, P25 July, 45; *Lt.-Col.* P 12 Nov. 47.
31	5 7/12	*Majors.*—Thomas Abbott,[3] *Ens.* 18 Aug. 12; *Lieut.* 7 Apr. 14; *Capt.* 18 Aug. 36; *Brev.-Major*, 9 Nov. 46; *Major*, 2 July, 47.
19	0	Eric Mackay Clarke,[10] *Ens.* 20 Nov. 30; *Lieut.* 6 June, 35; *Capt.* P 30 June, 43; *Major*, P10 March, 48.

Full Pay.	Half Pay.	CAPTAINS.	ENSIGN.	LIEUT.	CAPTAIN.	BREV.-MAJ.
22	0	William Shaw[4]	15 Mar. 27	26 Apr. 31	19 Aug. 36	9 Nov. 46
18	0	Alexander Findlay	5 July 31	22 May 33	17 June 37	
23	10 8/12	James Palmer	20 Apr. 15	6 June 16	25 Aug. 39	
35	3	Isaac Foster[5]	25 May 11	14 Sept. 18	15 Apr. 29	9 Nov. 46
15	0	James Travers	28 Nov. 34	29 July 36	15 Apr. 42	
13	0	Wm. St. Leger Angelo	20 May 36	20 Oct. 37	25 July 44	
8	0	Edward Poitier	P 10 June 41	24 Mar. 43	P 8 Sept. 46	
13	0	James Waddell	P 5 Feb. 36	2 May 38	1 May 40	
9	0	William Knox Orme,[6]	P 13 Mar. 40	P31 Dec. 44	P 11 June 47	
29	0	Thomas Prendergast[7]	17 Oct. 20	22 Apr. 25	13 June 40	
14	0	Geo. W. Conyngham Stuart	P 27 Mar. 35	P 19 Jan. 38	P 20 June 45	
20	9 4/12	Geo. W. Molyneux Lovett[8]	27 April 20	30 Nov. 24	10 July 46	
		LIEUTENANTS.				
13	0	Rich. Plunket Ireland	23 Dec. 36	28 Dec. 38		
12	0	Henry Wm. H. Graham, *ad.*	3 Nov. 37	13 April 40		
11	0	Clayton S. Hext Hingston	28 June 38	11 Sept. 40		
10	0	Peter John Macdonald, *s.*	25 Oct. 39	18 June 41		
10	0	Geo. B. Triscott Colman, *s.*	31 Dec. 39	7 Jan. 42		
8	0	Henry Charles Watson	P 18 June 41	29 Dec. 42		
7	0	James Francis Birch, *s.*	7 Jan. 42	30 Dec. 42		
7	0	Thomas M'Curdy	P29 Mar. 42	2 June 43		
7	0	Charles Daniel Addison	21 July 42	21 July 43		
5	0	Rowland Webster, *s.*	12 Jan. 44	P 25 July 45		
5	0	William Samuel Cumming	2 Feb. 44	21 Apr. 46		
4	0	John O'Flanagan	P 24 Jan. 45	1 Oct. 46		
4	0	Robert Willock Davies	27 Feb. 45	7 Aug. 47		
7	0	E. Couren, *Qr. Mas.* 2 Dec. 42.	17 Oct. 45	P 5 Nov. 47		
3	0	Henry Crofton	P 8 Sept. 46	P 19 Nov. 47		
8	0	Ralph Dudgeon	19 Mar. 41	2 Aug. 44		
5	0	Strange Beetson Hartigan	30 July 44	7 Apr. 48		
5	0	Frederick William Dowse	23 Feb. 44	27 Mar. 46		
4	0	John Halahan	11 July 45	2 June 48		
4	0	Henry Wheeler	16 Dec. 45	31 Aug. 48		
2	0	John Nicholson	P 19 Nov. 47	P 1 Sept. 48		
5	0	Charles Roberts,[9]	26 Jan. 44	22 Dec. 45		
		ENSIGNS.				
3	0	George Sotheby Tyler	28 Apr. 46			
3	0	William Ivers Lutman	P25 Sept. 46			
2	0	William John Russwurm	5 Feb. 47			
2	0	Robert William Harley	8 Oct. 47			
1	0	William Henry Walsh	11 Feb. 48			
1	0	John Hardy	P 7 Apr. 48			
2	0	Robt. Horsley, *Q.M.* 16 Ap. 47	2 June 48			
1	0	Francis Brown Dixon	P 4 Aug. 48			
1	0	Paul Furnell	P 1 Sept. 48			
1	0	William Hamilton	19 Sept. 48			
1	0	James Bolton Knott	8 Dec. 48			

Full Pay.	Half Pay.	
5	0	*Paymaster.*—Fred. Jesse Hills, 5 Feb. 47; *Ens.* 30 Jan. 44; *Lieut.* P9 May 45.
2	0	*Adjutant.*—*Lieut.* H. W. H. Graham, 1 July, 42.
7	0	*Quarter-Master.*—Roger Magrath, 2 June, 48; *Ens.* 15 Apr. 42; *Lt.* 2 June, 43.
0	0	*Surgeon.*—George Douglas Dods, M.D. 13 Aug. 47; *Assist.-Surg.* 22 Nov. 39.
2	0	*Assist.-Surgs.*—Henry Shearly Sanders, 5 March 47.
1	0	William Johnstone Fyffe, 8 Dec. 48.
1	0	George Hyde, 8 Dec. 48.

Facings Blue.—*Agent*, Edw. S. Codd, Esq.

2 Lt.-Col. Perry joined the army in Portugal as a volunteer in 1811, and was present at the siege and capture of Ciudad Rodrigo and of Badajoz, as well as in various minor affairs up to the battle of Salamanca, where he lost an arm. Subsequently he proceeded to the East Indies in the 89th, and served in various operations there up to 1818, after which he was present at the suppression of the Kandian rebellion in Ceylon.

3 Major Abbott served with the expedition to New Orleans. Very favourably mentioned in a public despatch to the Secretary for the Colonies for important services rendered whilst in command of the troops employed on an expedition into the interior of Africa in 1837; and also in defeating a projected attack on the Colony of Sierra Leone in 1840, by the numerous tribes on the frontier.

4 Major Shaw was present at the retaking of Barra Point on the River Gambia, 11th Nov. 1831; and at the attack upon Essow, 17th Nov following.

5 Maj. Foster served four years as a midshipman in the Royal Navy on the East India station, prior to entering the army. Was present at the capture of five ships having troops on board, going into Java Roads. Served in the Travancore war, in 1809; landed at Cochin with party under Capt. Foote, to assist the troops in storming the rear of that place; was afterwards wounded in the Straits of Malacca, when boarding some Malay prows. In the Kandian campaign of 1818, he was taken prisoner, and was rescued just at the period when the rebels were in the act of suspending him to a tree.

6 Captain Orme served with the 16th Lancers in the action of Maharajpore (Medal). Also in the campaign on the Sutlej (Medal), and was present in the actions at Buddiwal and Aliwal, in which last he received a severe bayonet wound when charging the Sikh infantry.

7 Capt. Prendergast served throughout the Burmese war, and was present at the taking of Prome, storming the enemy's works on the 1st, 2nd and 5th Dec. 1825, and 19th Jan. 1826, and battle of Pagham Mew.

9 Lieut. Roberts served with the 62d in the campaign on the Sutlej, and was severely wounded at the battle of Ferozeshah (Medal).

1 Sir Guy Campbell landed at Lisbon as a Captain in the 6th Regt. in June 1808, and was present at the battles of Roleia, Vimiera, advance into Spain, the subsequent retreat to and battle of Corunna. In July 1809 he served with the expedition to Walcheren as D.A. Adj.-Gen. to the Reserve under Sir John Hope. In 1810 he was appointed Military Secretary to Gen. Campbell, Governor of Gibraltar, and served as acting Assist. Adjt.-General with the troops detached thence to Cadiz under General Bowes when the Duke D'Albuquerque fell back on that city. In Oct. 1812, the 6th being ordered to Portugal, he gave up his appointment as Aide-de camp and Military Secretary at Gibraltar, and joined it at Rio Tinto. He was present as Major of the 6th at the battle of Vittoria, and succeeded to the command of the Regiment on the [illegible] Roncesvalles. He again commanded it at the attack of the Heights of Echalar (severely wounded, and promoted [illegible] rank of Lt.-Col. on the Field), and at the battles of the Pyrenees (Medal) in July and Aug. He also commanded [illegible] of Maya on the 17th Oct. 1813,—when being relieved, he returned to England on account of his wounds. [illegible] was appointed an Assistant Adjutant General to the Army in Flanders and attached to Picton's Division, [illegible] present at the battles of Quatre Bras and Waterloo, for which he received the Cross of a C.B. [illegible]

Ceylon Rifle Regiment.

Lieut.-Colonels.

Years' Serv. Full Pay.	Half Pay.	
37	0	Samuel Braybrooke,[1] *2nd Lieut.* 17 Dec. 12; *Lieut.* 29 April, 18; *Capt.* March, 23; *Major,* P 27 Feb. 35; *Lieut.-Col.* 26 Jan. 44.
43	1[illegible]	[illegible] Henry Simmonds,[2] *Ens.* 21 Mar. 05; *Lieut.* 28 Nov. 05; *Capt.* P 31 M 13; *Brevet-Major,* 10 Jan. 37; *Major,* P 2 Dec. 37; *Lieut.-Col.* 7 Jan.
37	5	George Cochrane,[4] *Ens.* 22 Jan. 07; *Lt.* 7 Feb. 08; *Capt.* 13 Feb. 27; *Br Major,* 23 Nov. 41; *Major,* 8 Jan. 47; *Lt.-Col.* P 28 Sept. 47.
31	0	*Majors.*—Peter Bennet Reyne, *2nd Lieut.* 28 Sept. 18; *Lieut.* 15 Dec. *Capt.* P 21 Dec. 26; *Brev.-Maj.* 23 Nov. 41; *Major,* 20 June, 45.
41	3[illegible]	Robert Martin,[3] *Ens.* 15 Aug. 04; *Lt.* 28 Mar. 05; *Capt.* 21 Nov. 16; *Bre Maj.* 10 Jan. 37; *Major,* 8 Jan. 47.
16	0	William Twistleton Layard, *2nd Lieut.* P 22 Feb. 33; *Lieut.* P 22 Nov. 36; *Ca* P 16 Aug. 39; *Major,* P 28 Sept. 47.

Full Pay	Half Pay	CAPTAINS.	2ND LIEUT.	LIEUT.	CAPTAIN.	BREV.-M.
32	6	Charles Kelson[5]	26 Sept. 11	4 Mar. 13	10 June 32	9 Nov.
24	9[illegible]	Thomas Bonnor	P 5 Oct. 15	24 Dec. 18	P 30 June 25	28 June
29	7[illegible]	[illegible] Thomas Lillie[6] ..	1 Oct. 12	17 July 15	7 Dec. 38	
34	[illegible]	William Driberg[7]	2 June 15	8 Aug. 22	17 June 42	
27	0	Rodney Mylius, s.......	16 May 22	30 May 24	9 Oct. 42	
21	0	Francis Brownrigg Bayly	2 Jan. 28	8 May 35	2 May 45	
19	0	James Mitchell Macdonald	26 Oct. 30	P 29 July 36	P 9 May 45	
15	0	George Bulkeley Tattersall	P 16 May 34	P 28 Apr. 37	8 June 45	
15	0	William Price..........	P 13 June 34	8 May 38	20 June 45	
15	0	Henry Charles Bird	P 13 June 34	22 May 38	P 2 Sept. 45	
13	0	Edward John Holworthy	P 12 Feb. 36	P 25 Jan. 39	P 17 Oct. 45	
15	0	Nicholas Fenwick	P 14 Nov. 34	P 17 Sept. 38	23 Jan. 46	
19	17[illegible]	George Richard Campsie	5 Nov. 12	14 July 14	8 Jan. 47	
14	0	Benj. Bloomfield Keane	8 May 35	P 11 Jan. 39	do.	
13	0	Henry Gibbs Remmett ..	P 8 July 36	P 28 June 39	do.	
13	0	Henry Alexander Raitt ..	P 22 Nov. 36	P 5 July 39	do.	
12	0	Wm. Henry Underwood	P 28 April 37	P 14 Mar. 40	do.	
10	0	Henry Lucas	P 5 July 39	P 27 Sept. 42	P 12 Feb. 47	
12	0	Robert Watson[9]........	7 July 37	29 Jan. 42	2 Mar. 47	
24	2	Albert Watson	17 July 23	14 Jan. 30	11 Apr. 45	
10	0	William Chas. Vanderspar	P 16 Aug. 39	9 Oct. 42	P 28 Sept. 47	
11	0	William Bagenall	2 Nov. 38	P 29 April 42	1 Dec. 48	
		FIRST LIEUTENANTS.				
9	0	Henry Skinner	P 15 Dec. 40	29 Mar. 43		
8	0	Chas. Theophilus Clement	P 24 Sept. 41	30 May 43		
7	0	John Anthony Layard ..	20 May 42	P 23 Aug. 44		
7	0	John Dwyer	22 May 42	P 7 Dec. 44		
7	0	Geo. Thomson Dawson..	17 June 42	P 31 Dec. 44		
7	0	Henry John Bews......	22 July 42	16 April 45		
7	0	Henry Bird............	P 27 Sept. 42	P 18 April 45		
6	0	Cornelius Chas. Durnford	10 Feb. 43	8 June 45		
6	0	Edw. Frederick Tranchell	30 May 43	20 June 45		
6	0	James Alexander Fraser	27 Oct. 43	P 8 Aug. 45		
5	0	Vincent Wing..........	P 12 July 44	P 2 Sept. 45		
5	0	Donald Duncan Graham	P 23 Aug. 44	P 16 Sept. 45		
11	0	Henry Ashmore Evatt ..	P 22 June 38	22 Aug. 41		
5	0	Frederick Arthur Walter	26 Jan. 44	23 Jan. 46		
7	0	David Stewart[10]........	7 Nov. 42	P 11 Nov. 45		
7	0	Horace George Hayes ..	P 24 June 42	P 25 Nov. 45		
5	0	George Sidney Dwyer ..	24 Aug. 44	25 Oct. 46		
4	0	John Henderson	P 18 April 45	2 Dec. 46		
7	0	Alexander Paterson Smith	16 April 42	27 Dec. 43		
7	0	Cha. Gasper Dav. Annesley	1 Nov. 42	11 Oct. 45		
7	0	George Shaffner Pearson	24 July 42	8 Jan. 47		
7	0	Samuel Sharpe	8 Nov. 42	do		
6	0	William Robert Gray....	7 April 43	do		
6	0	John Jermyn Symonds ..	12 May 43	do		
6	0	F. T. F. A. MacDonnell	12 Sept. 43	do		
6	0	James Armar Butler	P 13 Oct. 43	9 Jan. 47		
6	0	Thomas Cochrane	25 April 45	do		

4 Lt.-Col. Cochrane serve the capture of Martinique, Les Saintes in 1809, and Gua loupe in 1810, and also in 1

5 Major Kelson served the late 103rd in the Ameri war, and was present in action of Lundy's Lane, at storming of Fort Erie on morning of the 15th Aug. 1 and at the repulse of the so on the 9th Sept. following,

6 Capt. Lillie served in Peninsula from Dec. 1812 to end of the war, including crossing of the Zadino; batt Vittoria; blockade of Pan luna from 5th to 18th Ju pass of Roncesvalles, 28th J battle of Pampeluna, 28th J Nivelle, Nive (9th to 13th D Orthes (severely wounded), Toulouse. Present at Wa loo on the 18th June, and at storming of Cambray.

7 Captain Driberg, prio entering the army, served years and a half as midsh man in the royal navy; 1808, 9, and 10 on the I India station; in 1812 and in the blockading squadr off Flushing, Cherbourg Texel, and in the Baltic. 1815 he served as voluntee the Kandian campaign in C lon.

1 Lt.-Col. Braybrooke served at the capture of the Kandian territories in 1815, and in the Kandian rebellion in 1817 an

2 Lieut.-Col. Simmonds served in the Peninsula from Feb. 1808 to Feb. 1813, including the affairs of Talavera and Alber battles of Talavera, Busaco, and Albuhera; covering the siege of Badajoz in 1812, engaged every day during the retreat f Madrid and Salamanca; the retreat to Portugal, and subsequent pursuit of Massena from the lines, besides several minor af

3 Major Martin, prior to entering the regular army, served nearly two years in the Nottingham Fencibles; subsequ he served eight years in the field in Sicily; the campaign of 1807 in Egypt; taking of Genoa in 1814; two campaigns in United States of North America, including the taking of Castine and its dependencies on the River Penobscot.

9 Captain Watson served the campaign of 1814 and 15 in Holland and the Netherlands, including the action Merxem, and bombardment of Antwerp.

10 Lieut. Stewart was present with the "Buffs" in the battle of Punniar, and has received the Bronze Star.

Years' Serv. Full Pay.	Half Pay.		2nd Lieut.	1st Lieut.
		First Lieutenants.		
4	0	George Adolphus Tranchell	20 June 45	9 Jan. 47
5	0	William Leman Braybrooke, *adj.*	29 Mar. 44	10 Jan. 47
4	0	John MacDougall	1 Aug. 45	5 Feb. 47
8	0	Frederick Nassau Dore[1]	26 Oct. 41	14 Jan. 44
4	0	Geddes Sansoni Twynam	P 18 Oct. 45	P 23 July 47
4	0	Alfred John Douglas Smith	P 16 Dec. 45	P 28 Sept. 47
5	0	Richard Snowden Payne	29 Mar. 44	P 7 May 47
4	0	Charles Caldwell Grantham	16 Sept. 45	23 Oct. 47
3	0	Windsor Henry Humphreys	P 24 July 46	P 29 Oct. 47
2	0	Charles Peregrine Teesdale	P 7 Jan. 47	P 18 Dec. 47
2	0	John Warden M'Farlane	8 Jan. 47	P 28 April 48
2	0	Marr Ward	12 Jan. 47	P 7 July 48
2	0	John Brown	5 Feb. 47	P 1 Aug. 48
2	0	Charles Stanhope Smelt	9 Jan. 47	4 Aug. 48
2	0	James Owen Bovill	P 23 Mar. 47	P 20 Oct. 48
		Second Lieutenants.		
2	0	Richard Percival Wigmore	10 Jan. 47	
2	0	John Inman	11 Jan. 47	
2	0	William Joseph Gorman	13 Jan. 47	
2	0	William Derbishire	14 Jan. 47	
2	0	Richard Henry Brook	15 Jan. 47	
2	0	Alexander Maxwell Rutherford	16 Jan. 47	
2	0	William Dobyns	17 Jan. 47	
2	0	James Cox	18 Jan. 47	
2	0	Robert Atherton	19 Jan. 47	
2	0	Edmund Bagenall	P 12 Feb. 47	
2	0	William Charles Bruce	2 Apr. 47	
2	0	Andrew Campbell Knox Lock	P 26 Sept. 47	
2	0	Charles Cliffe	P 29 Oct. 47	
2	0	Walter Henry Long	P 18 Dec. 47	
1	0	Robert Seymour Croxton Sillery	7 Jan. 48	
1	0	George Charles Henry Waters	21 Jan. 48	
1	0	Thomas Miller	11 Feb. 48	
1	0	Charles Rouch	P 7 July 48	
1	0	Valentine Baker	P 1 Aug. 48	
1	0	Ralph Thickness	P 20 Oct. 48	
1	0	John Alexander Campbell	10 Nov. 48	
4	0	George Fead Lamert	17 Oct. 45	
16	0	*Paymaster.*—James Edward Boggis, 8 Sept. 46; *Ens.* P 12 July 33; *Lt.* P 17 Oct. 34; *Capt.* 26 July 44.		
5	0	*Adjutants.*—*Lieut.* William Leman Braybrooke, 7 April, 48. *Lieut.*		
3	0	*Quarter-Masters.*—Andrew Coakley, 11 Dec. 46.		
2	0	Richard Bunn, 3 Dec. 47.		
16	0	*Surgeons.*—James Stuart, 22 Dec. 43; *Assist.-Surg.* 5 July, 33.		
10	0	John Newton, 29 Jan. 47; *Assist.-Surg.* 4 Oct. 39.		
5	0	*Assist.-Surgs.*—Henry Forbes Dakers, 13 Dec. 44.		
2	0	Fenwick Martin Tweddell, 8 Jan. 47.		
2	0	John Rambaut, 29 Jan. 47.		

Regimentals *Green*—*Facings* Black.—*Agents, Sir* John Kirkland & Co.

1 Lieut. Dore served with the Buffs in the battle of Punniar (medal).

"CAPE OF GOOD HOPE."

Lieutenant-Colonels.

Years' Serv. Full Pay.	Half Pay.	
37	1	P [illegible] Henry Somerset,[1] CB. KH. *Cornet*, 5 Dec. 1811; *Lieut.* 30 Dec. 12; *Capt.* 6 Oct. 15; *Major*, P25 March, 23; *Lt.-Col.* P17 July, 24; *Col.* 28 June, 38.
36	1	Alexander Boswell Armstrong,[2] *2nd Lt.* 30 Jan. 12; *Lieut.* 5 Feb. 14; *Capt.* 15 Sept. 25; *Brevet-Major*, 28 June, 38; *Major*, 16 Feb. 44; *Lt.-Col.* 5 Nov. 47.
17	0	*Majors.*—George Thomas Conolly Napier,[3] *Ens.* 23 Mar. 32; *Lieut.* P25 Aug 37; *Capt.* P16 Feb. 41; *Major*, 5 Nov. 47; *Brevet-Lt.-Col.* 15 Sept. 48.
21	4/12	William Sutton, *l. c.* 15 Sept. 48; *Ens.* P5 June, 27; *Lieut.* P16 Mar. 30; *Capt.* P30 July, 36; *Brev.-Major*, 9 Nov. 46; *Major*, P6 Oct. 48.

Full Pay.	Half Pay.	CAPTAINS.	ENSIGN.	LIEUT.	CAPTAIN.	BREV.-MAJ.
22	0	Thomas Donovan	15 Mar. 27	16 May 33	19 Nov. 41	15 Sept. 48
12	0	John Robert O'Reilly[5] ..	30 Apr. 37	3 Mar. 39	19 April 46	
13	0	Charles Henry Somerset, *s.*	P30 July 36	20 Sept. 39	8 Jan. 47	
12	0	John Armstrong[6]	P28 Oct. 37	7 Feb. 40	8 Jan. 47	22 Dec. 48
14	0	Thomas Hare..........	27 Mar. 35	6 Nov. 38	1 Apr. 47	
10	0	Frederick Campbell	2 Mar. 39	P16 Feb. 41	1 Apr. 47	
9	0	John T. Bisset, *s.*	7 Feb. 40	16 Feb. 44	1 Apr. 47	15 Sept. 48
8	0	John Borrow	P16 Feb. 41	P23 Feb. 44	1 Apr. 47	
10	20	George Johnston	26 Jan. 19	P24 June 24	P30 Dec. 26	23 Nov. 41
21	0	Frederick Philip Glubb..	2 Oct. 28	P10 May 33	8 Dec. 46	
21	0	Duncan Fraser	P13 Feb. 28	10 Dec. 33	6 Nov. 41	
4	0	George Jackson Carey ..	P22 July 45	1 Apr. 47	P 6 Oct. 48	
		LIEUTENANTS.				
5	0	Joseph Salis,[7] R. M.	10 May 44	8 Jan. 47		
5	0	John M'Donnell	P28 June 44	do.		
4	0	James Fischal Boyes, *adj.*	3 Jan. 45	22 Jan. 47		
7	0	William Macdonald Mill[8]	17 Apr. 42	1 Apr. 47		
7	0	Robert Fred. Aug. Lavers	20 May 42	do.		
3	0	John Harvey	25 Aug. 46	do.		
6	0	John Bourke	P30 June 43	9 Sept. 45		
2	0	Richard Jennings Bramly	P 5 Mar. 47	P31 Mar. 48		
6	0	Charles Harland Bell....	24 Mar. 43	2 Sept. 44		
2	0	Henry James Palmer ..	12 Jan. 47	P 1 Aug. 48		
2	0	Edward Lister Green ..	22 Jan. 47	P 6 Oct. 48		
2	0	John Sandham Warren[9]	1 Apr. 47	P20 Oct. 48		
		ENSIGNS.				
2	0	Edward Monckton Jones	8 Jan. 47			
2	0	Wm. Benj. Croft Goodison	11 Jan. 47			
2	0	Geo. Stoddart Whitmore	23 Jan. 47			
2	0	Francis Smyth	3 Apr. 47			
2	0	George Lloyd Studdert..	4 Apr. 47			
2	0	Murray Babington Steele[7]	5 Apr. 47			
2	0	James C. Grant Kingsley	6 Apr. 47			
2	0	Bedford Davies	P23 July 47			
1	0	Patrick Robertson......	7 April 48			
1	0	Ralph Lovel Thursby ..	P 1 Aug. 48			
1	0	Thomas John Lucas	P 6 Oct. 48			
1	0	Hen. Geo. Edwd. Somerset	13 Oct. 48			

7 Lieut. Salis and Ensign Steele were dangerously wounded in the action with the rebel Boers at Bloem Plaats 29th Aug. 1848.

8 Lieut. Mill was severely wounded in the action with the rebel Boers at Bloem Plaats.

9 Lieut. Warren served in the campaign on the Sutlej (Medal), and was attached to the 53rd, and with them in the engagements at Buddiwal and Aliwal: he was present with his own regt.—the 73rd Bengal Native Infantry—in the battle of Sobraon.

Full Pay.	Half Pay.	
4	0	*Paymaster.*—Benj. Dunbar Wemyss, 21 May, 47; *Ens.* 28 Feb. 45; *Lt.* P8 Sep. 46.
4	0	*Adjutant.*—*Lieut.* James Fischal Boyes, 25 April 48.
8	0	*Quarter-Master.*—Michael Rorke, 10 May, 44; *Ens.* 19 Nov. 41.
24	0	*Surgeon.*—Wm. Cruickshank Eddie, 26 Mar. 41; *Assist.-Surg.* 12 Jan. 26; *Hospital Assistant*, 1 May, 25.
6	0	*Assist.-Surg.*—Robert Marshall Allen, 30 June, 43.
10	0	*Veterinary Surgeon.*—John Kingsley, 29 March, 1839.

Regimentals Green.—*Facings* Black.—*Agents*, *Sir* John Kirkland & Co.

1 Col. Somerset served the campaigns of 1813, 14, and 15, including the battles of Vittoria, Orthes, Toulouse, and Waterloo. During a protracted service on the frontiers of the Cape of Good Hope, he held a command in the various arduous operations against the Kaffir tribes.

2 Lieut.-Col. Armstrong served at the capture of Genoa in 1814, and subsequently in the American war, including the capture of Washington, attack before Baltimore 13th Sept. 1814; and on New Orleans, 8th Jan. 1815, where he was wounded and taken prisoner. Present when Graham's Town was attacked by about ten thousand Caffres, 22d April, 1819, and who were repulsed with great slaughter by three hundred men under the command of Col. Willshire.

3 Lieut.-Col. Napier commanded the Cape Mounted Riflemen at the action of the Gwanga, and throughout the late Kaffir war: for these services he obtained the Brevet rank of Lieut.-Colonel.

5 Captain O'Reilly served throughout the last Caffre war, and was shot through both thighs, 15th Jan. 1835, in an attack made by Col. Somerset on a large body of Caffres in the Bushman's River Poort, who had invaded the Colony; on which occasion a most handsome General Order was issued on the gallantry evinced by Lieut. O'Reilly.

6 Major Armstrong commanded the Cape Mounted Riflemen in the action with and defeat of the rebel Boers at Bloem Plaats 29th Aug. 1848, and was treacherously wounded (severely) by a man to whom he

Years' Serv. Full Pay.	Half Pay.	
		Colonel.—The Lieut.-General Commanding the Forces in Canada, for the time being.
26	23$\frac{4}{12}$	*Lieut.-Col.*—Wm. Henry Newton,[1] KH., *Cornet* 20 June 1800; *Lieut.* P 25 Dec. 00; *Capt.* 25 June 08; *Brevet-Major* 27 May 25; *Major* 11 May 26; *Brevet-Lt.-Col.* 28 June 38; *Lieut.-Col.* 18 Dec. 45.
23	19$\frac{8}{12}$	*Majors.*—Robert Muter,[3] *Ens.* 5 Mar. 07; *Lieut.* 3 Mar. 08; *Capt.* P 27 May 19; *Brevet-Major* 10 Jan. 37; *Major* 18 Dec. 45.
17	0	Phillpotts Wright Taylor, *Ens.* P 16 Mar. 32; *Lieut.* P 4 Mar. 36; *Capt.* P 30 Oct. 40; *Major,* P 5 Nov. 47.

Full Pay	Half Pay		ENSIGN.	LIEUT.	CAPTAIN.	BREV.-MAJ.
		CAPTAINS.				
18	17$\frac{10}{12}$	Frederick Wm. Clements	16 Feb. 14	23 Feb. 15	8 April 25	28 June 38
32	10$\frac{6}{12}$	John Thorne Weyland[5]	31 July 06	1 Mar. 09	13 Mar. 27	23 Nov. 41
24	15	William Atkin[6]	9 Mar. 10	2 July 11	31 Dec. 30	9 Nov. 46
13	0	Pat. Leonard M'Dougall	13 Feb. 36	P 11 May 39	P 7 June 44	
11	0	Edward Stopford Claremont, *s.*	P 9 Feb. 38	16 July 41	P 14 Nov. 45	
22	13	George Vallancy Hamilton[8]	2 Feb. 14	29 Oct. 29	6 Mar. 43	
14	0	Percy Hill	P 24 April 35	P 5 Oct. 38	P 23 Jan. 46	
23	11$\frac{4}{12}$	William Thomas Colman	7 Sept. 15	13 June 30	3 Dec. 41	
8	0	James Nicol Holmes	17 July 41	P 5 July 44	P 5 Nov. 47	
16	0	Digby St. Vincent Hamilton	P 30 Aug. 33	30 Nov. 37	9 Nov. 46	
		LIEUTENANTS.				
20	13$\frac{4}{12}$	Robert Douglas	12 Oct. 15	10 Aug. 26		
13	0	Francis Hawtrey Cox	P 26 Feb. 36	P 28 Dec. 38		
12	0	William Hervey FitzGerald[11]	P 5 May 37	5 Jan. 41		
8	0	John Neville Peto	P 13 July 41	P 21 July 42		
13	0	Richard Hollis	1 July 36	12 Jan. 38		
8	0	William Henry Kingsmill	19 July 41	P 14 Nov. 45		
8	0	Reginald Macdonell,[14] *adj.*	20 July 41	17 Dec. 45		
8	0	John Barnard Geale	21 July 41	18 Dec. 45		
12	0	George Deare	P 15 Dec. 37	P 1 Feb. 39		
7	0	Henry Calveley Cotton	P 16 Apr. 42	P 14 July 45		
8	0	William Henry Sharpe	22 July 41	14 Apr. 46		
8	0	John Weyland	23 July 41	do		
7	0	Edward Benjamin Wilson	14 Jan. 42	14 Apr. 46		
7	0	Simeon Henry Stuart	P 2 Dec. 42	do		
5	0	William Henry Eliot	25 June 44	do		
5	0	Spencer Peel	P 5 July 44	do		
8	0	Matthew White	2 April 41	26 June 46		
8	0	James John Lloyd	P 16 April 41	P 19 May 46		
4	0	William Causabon Frend	P 14 Nov. 45	P 30 June 48		
6	0	John Christopher Minnitt	P 6 Oct. 43	14 Apr. 46		
		ENSIGNS.				
3	0	Henry George Augustus Powell	23 Jan. 46			
3	0	Robert Berney Ficklin	P 3 Apr. 46			
3	0	Patrick Hopkins	14 Apr. 46			
3	0	Robert Le Marchant Gray	15 Apr. 46			
3	0	George Granville Gower Munro	16 Apr. 46			
3	0	John Henry Blake	18 Apr. 46			
2	0	Walter James Brittain	15 Jan. 47			
2	0	Kenneth Mackenzie Moffatt	P 5 Nov. 47			
2	0	George Ernest Bulger	6 Nov. 47			
3	0	W. Aug. Myrton Cunynghame	8 May 46			

Full Pay	Half Pay	
34	0	*Paymaster.*—Wm. Henry Wardell, 16 Dec. 28; *Ens.* 15 Aug. 15; *Lieut.* P 21 Feb. 22.
8	0	*Adjutant.*—*Lieut.* Reginald Macdonell, 13 June 45.
14	0	*Quarter-Master.*—James Baxter, 15 July 35.
23	0	*Surgeon.*—John Maitland, M.D., 3 Dec. 41; *A.-Surg.* 12 June, 28; *H.-A.* 16 Dec. 26.
9	0	*Assistant-Surgeons.*—A. B. Cleland, M.D., 21 Feb. 40.
8	0	Philip Whiteside Maclagan, M.D. 15 Jan. 41.

Regtls.-Green.—*Facings* Scarlet.
Agents, Sir John Kirkland & Co.

6 Captain Hamilton served in the Queen's Royals during the campaign of 1844-5 in the southern Concan and Sawunt Warree country, including the storming of several stockades, and the investment and capture of the forts of Monohur and Munsuntosh.

6 Major Atkin served at Walcheren in 1809, and in the Peninsula with the 2d Light Infantry of the King's German Legion, from Dec. 1810 to the end of that war in 1814, including the attack on Guarda Heights, battle of Albuhera, sieges of Olivenca, Ciudad Rodrigo, Badajoz, and forts at Salamanca, battle of Salamanca, capture of Madrid and the Retiro, siege of Burgos and covering the retreat from thence, when the two Light Infantry battalions of the German Legion repulsed a large body of French cavalry; battle of Vittoria, action at Tolosa, siege of San Sebastian, actions in the Pyrenees, passage of the Bidassoa (wounded), battles of Nivelle and Nive, investment of Bayonne (wounded) and repulse of the sortie, besides various minor affairs. Present also at the capture of Paris in 1815.

11 Lieut. FitzGerald served in the Anglo-Spanish Legion during 1835 36 and 37. He was severely wounded in the action of the 5th May near St. Sebastian, and has received two crosses and a medal for his conduct and services.

14 Lieut. Macdonell, as an officer of a Local Corps, was actively employed in suppressing the late insurrection in Canada.

1 Lieut.-Colonel Newton received a commission at the early age of twelve, in consequence of the services of his father, then commanding a Regt. of Light Dragoons. Served in the West Indies in the campaign of 1810, under Sir Geo. Beckwith, as a Regimental Officer; was afterwards appointed Assistant Quarter-Master-General and Major of Brigade in St. Thomas, and Grenada. Joined his Regt. on their being ordered on service to the Coast of America in 1814, where he served with the Division under Sir John Sherbrooke. Joined the army under the Duke of Wellington, in June 1815; was appointed one of the Staff Commandants in Belgium, and was present at the taking of Landrecy by the Prussians.

3 Major Muter served in the Peninsula with the 7th Fusiliers, and was present at the passage of the Douro, capture of Oporto, the subsequent operations against Marshal Soult in the North of Portugal, and battle of Talavera, where being dangerously wounded on the evening of the 28th July 1809, and taken prisoner while in hospital, he was detained a prisoner of war until the Peace in 1814. He served also at the attack upon New Orleans 8th Jan. 1815, and commanded the right advanced piquet on the night the army retired from its position— the piquets were exposed at intervals to a heavy cannonade.

5 Major Weyland served the campaigns in Upper Canada from 1812 to 1815, including the actions at Fort George and Stoney Creek, at which last he was severely wounded.

Years' Serv. Full Pay.	Half Pay.	
		Lieutenant-Colonel.
37	9 1/12	John Ross,[1] *Ens.* 1 July, 03; *Lt.* 1 Nov. 05; *Capt.* 15 April, 13; *Major,* P 5 Nov. 25; *Lt.-Col.* 9 Dec. 36; *Col.* 9 Nov. 46.
35	8 1/12	*Major.*—Henry Edward O'Dell,[2] *Ens.* 8 July, 06; *Lieut.* 25 Feb. 08; *Capt.* 9 Jan. 23; *Brevet-Major,* 10 Jan. 37; *Major,* 30 Aug. 43.

Full Pay.	Half Pay.	*Captains.*	ENSIGN.	LIEUT.	CAPTAIN.	BREVET-MAJOR.
30	1 1/12	Gilbert Woollard	20 Nov. 17	27 May 22	27 Mar. 40	
27	0	George Adams Barnes, *s.*	12 Dec. 22	P 23 Sept. 24	30 Oct. 40	
10	0	James Keating	26 Apr. 39	9 Aug. 39	30 Aug. 43	
31	3 4/12	James Piggott[3]	6 Apr. 15	9 Apr. 25	14 Feb. 34	9 Nov. 46
29	0	C. H. Marechaux	9 Dec. 20	6 Apr. 26	5 Aug. 42	
		Lieutenants.				
12	0	Wm. Forbes Macbean....	7 July 37	7 Jan. 42		
11	0	Thomas Jones..........	9 Mar. 38	7 Jan. 42		
10	0	Frederick Rice Stack....	1 June 39	7 Jan. 42		
7	0	Henry Robert Cowell ..	15 April 42	1 Mar. 44		
6	0	Joseph Hayes, *adj.*	10 Feb. 43	17 Aug. 48		
6	0	John Henry Prendervill̇e	10 Nov. 43	18 Aug. 48		
		Ensigns.				
4	0	John Gandy	P 21 Mar. 45			
4	0	Robert Alexander Loudon	P 16 Sept. 45			
3	0	John Denham Saunder ..	14 April 46			
1	0	William Henry Hole	P 26 May 48			
1	0	Richard Williams Thomas	18 Aug. 48			
6	0	*Adjutant.*—*Lieut.* Joseph Hayes, 30 Dec. 45.				
7	0	*Quarter-Master.*—Wm. Miller, 7 Jan. 42.				
21	0	*Surg.*—John Wardrop Moore, 10 Feb. 43; *A.-S.* 29 July, 30; *H.-A.* 8 May, 28.				
6	0	*Assistant Surgeon.*—John Mullins, 13 Oct. 43.				

2 Major O'Dell served with the 5th on the expedition to South America in 1807. Also in the Peninsula in Sir Thomas Picton's Division, from 1809 to the end of that war in 1814, including the battle of Busaco, lines at Torres Vedras, actions of Pombal, Redinha, Condeixa, Foz d'Arouce, Leria, Robleda, Guarda, and Sabugal, battle of Fuentes d'Onor, action of El Bodon, first siege of Badajoz, siege and capture of Ciudad Rodrigo and of Badajoz, battle of Salamanca (severely wounded), capture of Madrid and the Retiro, retreat from Burgos, battles of Vittoria, the Nivelle, the Nive, Orthes, and Toulouse. Embarked for America in 1814, and was present at the affair at Plattsburg.

3 Major Piggott served with the 26th at the first taking of Chusan in China.

Facings Buff.—*Agents, Sir* John Kirkland & Co.

1 Colonel John Ross served with the 51st in the Peninsula under Sir John Moore, and was present in the action at Lugo, the retreat to, and battle of, Corunna. On the expedition to Walcheren and siege of Flushing, in 1809. Peninsular campaigns from Jan. 1811 to the end of that war in 1814, including the battle of Fuentes d'Onor, siege of Badajoz and storming of Fort San Christoval in 1811, covering the sieges of Ciudad Rodrigo and Badajoz, affair at Moresco, battle of Salamanca, capture of the Retiro at Madrid, siege of Burgos and retreat from thence, action at San Munos, battle of Nivelle, and carrying the heights of St. Pé, and battle of Orthes. Served also the campaign of 1815, including the battle of Waterloo and taking of Cambray. Wounded in action at Lesaca, 31st August 1813.

Royal Newfoundland Companies.

Years' Serv. Full Pay.	Half Pay.	
		Lieutenant-Colonel.
39	8/12	Robert Law,[1] KH. *Ens.* 8 June, 1809; *Lieut.* 27 May, 11; *Capt.* P 18 Oct. 21; *Major,* P 29 Aug. 34; *Lieut.-Col.* 2 Feb. 44.

Full Pay.	Half Pay.	CAPTAINS.	ENSIGN.	LIEUT.	CAPTAIN.	BREVET-MAJOR.
27	12 3/12	Richard Saunders	4 Nov. 09	25 Oct. 10	26 Oct. 41	
7	0	Hugh Best Chambers ..	21 Jan. 42	P 19 Oct. 43	P 19 June 46	
12	0	W. Witchurch Lyttleton	P 14 Apr. 37	P 23 Apr. 39	P 11 Apr. 45	
		LIEUTENANTS.				
11	0	William Jenkins, *s.*	23 Feb. 38	29 Dec. 40		
10	0	John Gillespie, *Adj.* ..	31 May 30	7 Jan. 42		
8	0	Walter Saxton Bold	6 Aug. 41	25 Nov. 42		
6	0	Henry Christ. Marriott ..	P 5 Sept. 43	P 19 June 46		
3	0	Martin Petrie..........	14 April 46	P 7 Jan. 48		
6	0	Charles Frederick Tyler	12 Dec. 43	P 28 Sept. 47		
		ENSIGNS.				
5	0	William John Coen	23 Feb. 44			
3	0	Charles Henry Martin...	27 April 46			
1	0	Thomas Johns...........	P 7 Jan. 48			
10	0	*Adjutant.*—*Lieut.* John Gillespie, 5 Nov. 47.				
11	0	*Surgeon.*—Cathrine Campbell Hamilton Grant, 22 Dec. 46; *A.-Sur.* 30 Mar. 38.				
7	0	*Assistant-Surgeon.*—Jas. Chas. Martin, 11 Nov. 42.				

Facings Blue.—*Agents, Sir* John Kirkland & Co.

1 Lt.-Col. Law served with the 71st Regt. on Sir J. Moore's retreat at Lugo and Corunna, in 1808-9; at the siege of Flushing, in 1809; subsequently in the Peninsula, including the affair at Sobral, Massena's retreat, battle of Fuentes D'Onor, 3d and 5th May 1811 (wounded in two places); covering 1st and 2d sieges of Badajoz, actions at Arroya de Molino and Almaraz, defence of Alba de Tormes, battles of the Pyrenees and capture of enemy's convoy at Elisonda, in July 1813; battle of the Nive, affair at Cambo, employed in an armed boat at Urt on the river Adour, battle near Bayonne 13th Dec. 1813, affairs at Hellette, Arrivarette, St. Palais, and Aire; battle of Orthes, and affair at Tarbes, where he was severely wounded. Served also the campaign of 1815, including the battle of Waterloo—severely wounded and horse killed by a cannon-shot. Served afterwards with the army of occupation in France.

Provisional Battalion at Chatham.

Years' Serv.		
Full Pay.	Half Pay.	
		Lieutenant-Colonels.
34	10 4/12	𝔓 Thomas Weare,[1] KH. *Ens.* 14 Sept. 04; *Lieut.* 25 June 05; *Captain,* 19 April 1810; *Brev.-Maj.* 21 June 13; *Major,* 1 June 26; *Brevet-Lieut.-Col.* 22 July 30; *Lieut.-Col.* 13 Apr. 38; *Col.* 23 Nov. 41.
42	1 7/12	Thomas Edwin Kelly,[2] *Ens.* 1 April 06; *Lieut.* 11 Feb. 08; *Capt.* 28 Dec. 22; *Brevet-Major,* 10 Jan. 37; *Major,* P24 Feb. 37; *Lieut.-Col.* 11 May 41.
		Staff Captain.
18	0	Henry Jackson, *Ens.* P5 April, 31; *Lt.* P20 Sept. 33; *Capt.* 27 Dec. 42.
		Acting Adjutant.—Ens. Lowry, 96 F.
		Acting Quarter-Master.—Lieut. W. W. Bond, 4 F.
40	0	*Surgeon.*—John Freeborn Pink, 10 Nov. 37; *A.-S.* 27 Apr, 20; *H. A.* 9 July 09.

Agents, Sir John Kirkland & Co.

1 Colonel Weare served with the British and Russian army in Italy, in 1805; in Egypt, in 1807, against the Turks, including the second attack on Rosetta, the capture of guns and camels on the right bank of the Nile, and the retreat to Alexandria. At the reduction of the Islands of Ischia and Procida, in 1809; at the taking of the Ionian Isles, in 1809 and 10; and during the siege of Santa Maura as an acting Engineer Officer. In the Peninsula as aide-de-camp to Gen. Sir John Oswald commanding the 5th Division, during the campaigns of 1812, 13, and 14, including the severe affair at Villa Muriel, the whole retreat from Burgos, the advance of 1813, affair of Osma, battle of Vittoria, both assaults and during the whole siege of San Sebastian, battle of the Nivelle, and some of the affairs at the Mayor's House in front of Bidart on the Bayonne road.

2 Lieut. Colonel Kelly served on the expedition to Copenhagen, in 1807; at the capture of Martinique in 1909, and Gaudaloupe in 1810; the campaigns of 1813, 14, and 15, in Lower Canada, including the actions at Chateauguay and Plattsburg.

Infantry Depôt Battalion, in the Isle of Wight.

Years' Serv.		
Full Pay.	Half Pay.	
27	15 7/12	*Lieut.-Colonel.*—𝔓 Jeremiah Taylor,[1] *Ens.* 28 Feb. 05; *Lieut.* 1 Oct. 07; *Capt.* 2 Oct. 17; *Major,* 1 April 24; *Lieut.-Col.* 22 Mar. 27; *Col.* 23 Nov. 41.
38	3 4/12	*Major.*—𝔓 John Alves,[2] *Ens.* 5 Nov. 07; *Lieut.* 25 Dec. 10; *Capt.* 13 Mar. 27; *Major,* 17 Aug. 41.
40	0	*Paymaster.*—𝔓 Edward Fugion,[3] 23 Dec. 19; *Ens.* 4 May, 09; *Lt.* 25 July, 11.
		Acting Adjutant.—Lieut. R. B. Deering, 99 F.
		Acting Quartermaster.—Lieut. Paterson, 42 F.

Agents, Sir John Kirkland & Co.

1 Col. Taylor served in the Peninsula with the 9th, from Aug. 1808 to Feb. 1813, and again from Oct. 1813 to the end of the war in 1814, including the battles of Vimiera (wounded), Busaco, and Salamanca, retreat from Burgos, action of Villa Muriel (wounded), and repulse of the Sortie from Bayonne.

2 Major Alves served the whole of the campaigns in Spain, Portugal, and France, of 1810, 11, 12, 13, and 14, with the 74th in Picton's division, without having ever been absent from it for a single day, including the battle of Busaco, retreat to the lines of Torres Vedras, occupation of them, and subsequent advance in pursuit of Massena, actions at Pombal, Redinha, Foz d Arouce, Guarda, and Sabugal, battle of Fuentes d'Onor, siege of Badajoz in June 1811, actions at El Bodon and Aldea de Ponte, siege and storm of Ciudad Rodrigo, siege, storm and escalade of the Castle of Badajoz in March and April, 1812, battle of Salamanca, capture of Madrid and the Retiro, affairs on the retreat from Madrid to Salamanca and Portugal in Nov. 1812, subsequent advance and passage of the Ebro, battle of Vittoria, blockade of Pampeluna, the battles in the Pyrenees on the 27th, 28th, and 30th July, battles of the Nivelle, the Nive, and Orthes, actions of Vic Bigorre and Tarbes, and battle of Toulouse.

3 Paymaster Fugion served in the Peninsula from July 1809 to the end of that war in 1814, including the battle of Salamanca, siege of Burgos, and battle of Orthes.

Colonel.

Count Sir Francis Rivarola, KCMG. KCH. *Ens.* 4 April, 1795; *Lieut.* 21 Feb. 98; *Capt.* 18 March, 04; *Major,* 6 Feb. 07; *Lieut.-Col.* 7 March, 11; *Col.* 19 July, 21; *Major-Gen.* 22 July, 30; *Lieut.-Gen.* 23 Nov. 41.

Lieut.-Colonel.—*Francisco Busiett,[1] 20 July, 47.

Major.—*Carlo Cutajar, 20 July, 47.

Captains.
*Salvatore Calleja, 17 Feb. 40.
*Mederico de Marchesi Alessi, 10 July, 40.
*Antonio Maltei, 11 April, 45.
*Guglielmo Petit, 10 May, 45.
*Salverio Gatt, 12 Feb. 47.
*Felice Rizzo, 20 July, 47.

Lieutenants.
*Giuseppe Gouder, 2 Jan. 40.
*Georgio Virtu, 17 Feb. 40.
*Nicola Metrovich, 10 July 40.
*William Gatt, 11 April, 45.
*Giuseppe Cavarra, 10 May, 45.
*Giuseppe Sesino, 20 July, 47.

Ensigns.
*Filippo Eynaud, 2 Jan. 40.
*Loreto Bonavita (*Adj.*) 17 Feb. 40.
*Giuseppe de Piro, 10 July, 40.
*James Lazzarini, 11 April, 45.
*Saveriode Piro, 10 May, 45.
*Henry Montanaro, 12 Feb. 47.
*Filipps Giacomo Testaferrata, 20 July, 47.

Paymaster.—Vincenzo Rizzo, 25 Feb. 17.

Adjutant.—**Ensign* Loreto Bonavito, 12 Feb. 47.

Quarter-Master.—*Paolo Salamone, 25 Jan. 39.

Surgeon.—J. Montanaro, 3 Aug. 38.

Assistant-Surgeon.—Ludovico Bernard, M.D. 27 Jan. 43.

Facings Blue.—*Agents, Sir* John Kirkland & Co.

1 Lt.-Col. Busiett was actively employed in various operations against the French prior to his entry into the British service, and was severely wounded by a bayonet thrust in the right side of his neck, and taken prisoner at the capture of Fort Urbano. Served afterwards during the operations at Malta in 1800. Served in Sicily in 1807; in Calabria in 1808; after which he was taken prisoner at the capture by the French of the Island of Capri.

---

8 Col. Campbell served with the 51st, at the capture of Kandy in Ceylon, in 1803; the campaign of 1808-9 in Spain, including the battle of Corunna. Also the campaigns of 1811, 12, 13, 14, and 15, under the Duke of Wellington, including the second siege of Badajoz, battles of Vittoria, the Pyrenees on the 26th and 28th July), heights of Lesaca, Nivelle, and St. Pé, Orthes, and Waterloo, and storming of Cambray.

9 Lt.-Col. Barnwell landed in the Peninsula with the Duke of Wellington's army on the 1st Aug. 1808, as an ensign in the 45th, and did not return until the breaking up of that army at Bourdeaux in 1814, and was present and engaged at the battles of Roleia and Vimiera, advance under Sir A. Cameron across the Douro to join Sir John Moore; retreat from Almeida to Lisboa, the retreat to Portugal after the battle of Talavera; battle of Busaco, and retreat to the lines of Lisbon; affairs on Massena's retreat, action of Sabugal, battle of Fuentes d'Onor, first siege of Badajos, action of Fuente Guinaldo, siege and storm of Ciudad Rodrigo and of Badajos, battle of Salamanca, capture of Madrid, affairs on the retreat from Madrid to Portugal, battle of Vittoria, blockade of Pampeluna, battles of the Pyrenees, crossing of the Bidassoa, storming of the enemy's fortified entrenchments on the 7th and 9th Oct. 1813, battles of the Nivelle, Orthes (horse shot), and Toulouse. He was also present with the 9th at the forcing of the Khyber Pass on the 5th April 1842 (Cabool Medal), and in the campaign on the Sutlej (Medal), including the battles of Moodkee, Ferozeshah, commanded a Brigade (horse shot), and Sobraon.

10 Paymaster Jellicoe served at the capture of Heligoland in 1807. Frequently engaged in boats in the North Seas and Baltic, and in several affairs with Danish gun boats and the Russians during 1808, 9, and 11. Served two years on the island of Anholt, and commanded a company at the defeat of the Danes in their attack of the island in 1811,—the garrison taking prisoners more than double their own numbers. Served afterwards in the Peninsula.

11 Paymaster Thompson accompanied the 81st Regt. throughout all its services.

12 Captain Middleton served in the Peninsula and France from 13th March, 1810, to 18th July, 1814, including the battle of Barrosa, siege of Ciudad Rodrigo, where he volunteered with the storming party; siege of Badajos, battles of Salamanca, Vittoria, Nivelle, Nive, Orthes, and Toulouse; besides various affairs of outposts.

13 Paymaster Sabine served with the 21st at the siege of Scylla in 1809. He was attached to the Grenadier Battalion at the Faro of Messina in 1810, and exposed to the daily fire from Murat's batteries. In 1813 he was at the taking of the Island of Pouza; and in the action before Genoa on the 17th April 1814 he was severe'y wounded on the head while leading a company of the 21st to dislodge the enemy from their strong position in the village of San Martino.

14 Lieut. M'Nair served during the American war in the campaigns of 1813 and 14 on the borders of Lake Ontario, and on the Niagara frontier, including the investment of Fort George, action at Black Rock and capture of the Town of Buffalo; siege of Fort Erie, and the action at the sortie, 17th Sept. 1814, besides other affairs. Prisoner of war about six months.

15 Lt. Courtenay served in the Peninsula from 1811 until severely wounded in the Pyrenees, in 1813.

16 Paymaster Matthews served in the Nepaul war in 1814 and 15; at the capture of Hattrass; in the Mahratta war in 1817 and 18; at the capture of Bhurtpore; and the campaign of 1842 in Affghanistan, under General Pollock.

17 Lieut. Spence served the campaigns of 1813 and 14, in Spain and France, with the 84th, and was present at the passage of the Bidassoa, battle of Nivelle and Nive, and actions near Bayonne.

18 Lieut. Pieters served in the American war in Canada in 1814 and 15; also in the late rebellion in Canada.

19 Lieut. B. H. Edwards served in the Peninsula from 1811 to the end of that war in 1814, including the siege and storming of Badajos (wounded) with the 9th Portuguese regiment of the Line; and in the 43rd Light Infantry at the battles of Salamanca, Vera, Nivelle (wounded), Nive, Tarbes, and Toulouse.

20 Paymaster Hood served the campaign of 1814 in the Peninsula; and he was afterwards

Inspecting Field Officers.

Years' Serv. Full Pay.	Years' Serv. Half Pay.	
53	0	𝕻 Nicholas Hamilton,[1] KH. *Ens.* 15 June, 1796; *Lieut.* 9 Dec. 96; *Capt.* 25 June, 03; *Major,* 18 June, 12; *Brev.-Lt.-Col.* 27 May, 25; *Col.* 28 June, 38.
50	3 7/12	Chesborough Grant Falconar,[2] KH. *Ens.* P1 Sept. 95; *Lieut.* 1 Nov. 99; *Capt.* 26 Dec. 05; *Brevet-Major,* 12 Aug. 19; *Regt.-Major,* P26 June, 23; *Lieut.-Col.* P22 Oct. 25; *Col.* 28 June, 38.
44	18/12	John Wharton Frith,[3] *Ens.* P17 July, 04; *Lieut.* 27 Feb. 05; *Capt.* 29 Jan. 12; *Major,* 22 July, 30; *Lieut.-Col.* P16 Dec. 36; *Col.* 9 Nov. 46.
37	0	𝕻 Frederick Maunsell,[4] *Ens.* 16 March, 12; *Lieut.* P28 Jan. 13; *Capt.* P24 June, 19; *Major,* P14 Aug. 27; *Lieut.-Col.* 23 May, 36; *Col.* 9 Nov. 46.
50	7/12	John Gregory Baumgardt,[5] CB. *Ens.* 1 Aug. 98; *Lieut.* 20 March 01; *Capt.* 10 Jan. 10; *Major,* P21 Oct. 24; *Lieut.-Col.* P9 June 25; *Col.* 28 June 38.
42	3 7/12	*Sir* Richard Doherty,[6] *Ens.* P10 Sept. 03; *Lieut.* 22 Nov. 04; *Capt.* 21 May 12; *Major,* P16 Sept. 24; *Lieut.-Col.* P26 Sept 26; *Col.* 23 Nov. 41.
29	12	William Bush,[7] KH. *Cornet,* P7 Jan. 08; *Lieut.* P20 June 09; *Capt.* P22 July 13; *Major,* P8 April 26; *Lieut.-Col.* P22 May 29; *Col.* 9 Nov. 46.
42	8 6/12	𝕻 [illegible] Jas. Campbell,[8] KH. *Ens.* P12 June 99; *Lt.* 25 Dec. 00; *Capt.* 1 Aug. 05; *Brev.-Maj.* 12 Aug. 19; *Maj.* P17 May 21; *Lt.-Col.* P12 July 31; *Col.* 9 Nov. 46.
38	4 4/12	𝕻 Charles Barnwell,[9] CB. *Ens.* 30 July, 07; *Lieut.* 30 March, 09; *Capt.* 19 May, 14; *Brevet-Maj.* 10 Jan. 37; *Maj.* 23 Nov. 41; *Lt.-Col.* 29 Dec. 45.

Paymasters.

Years' Serv. Full Pay.	Years' Serv. Half Pay.	
40	0	Nicholas Maunsell, 21 Aug. 1813; *Ens.* 27 Apr. 09; *Lieut.* 2 Nov. 09.
42	0	𝕻 Richard Jellicoe,[10] 24 Feb. 1814; *2nd Lieut.* 17 June 07.
33	10 5/12	𝕻 John Woodgate, 25 June, 1829; *Ens.* 17 Oct. 05; *Lieut.* 11 Feb. 08; *Capt.* 20 Feb. 12.
28	5 5/12	Henry Balthaser Adams, 30 Oct. 1828; *Ens.* 23 Feb. 15; *Lieut.* 12 June, 17; *Capt.* 17 Sept. 25.
21	4/12	Charles Henry Peirse, 23 Aug. 39; *Ens.* P6 Dec. 27; *Lieut.* 18 July, 30.
41	0	𝕻 John Middleton,[12] 25 Nov. 26; *Ens.* 10 Mar. 08; *Lt.* 4 Oct. 09; *Capt.* 7 Apr. 25.
36	0	John Henry Matthews,[16] 21 Oct. 13.
45	5 5/12	𝕻 Arnold Thompson,[11] 22 Aug. 05; *Ens.* 6 Sept. 98; *Lieut.* 9 July 03.
16	27 2/12	John Sabine,[13] 25 Sept. 46; *Ens.* 6 June, 05; *Lieut.* 14 April, 08.
38	2/12	𝕻 George Hood,[20] 25 Oct. 28; *Ens.* P21 Feb. 11; *Lieut.* P28 May 12.

Full Pay	Half Pay	ADJUTANTS.	ENSIGN.		LIEUT.		ADJUTANT.	
48	1	Thomas Shields	4 Feb.	00	3 Aug.	01	28 July	03
24	12 3/12	Robert M'Nair[14]	22 Oct.	12	24 Mar.	14	14 July	37
18	19 1/12	John O'Neill, *Staff Adj. at Edinburgh*	9 Apr.	12	29 Feb.	16	8 Feb.	42
17	1 8/12	Charles Pratt Hamilton	29 June	30	P13 Mar.	35	24 Feb.	43
11	28 7/12	𝕻 William Allan Courtenay[15]	14 June	09	23 Aug.	13	22 Nov.	44
23	16 1/12	𝕻 James Banbury Hamilton	25 Sept.	09	P23 July	12	6 Dec.	44
18	16 7/12	Charles Pieters[18]	4 Aug.	14	9 Sept.	19	2 Apr.	47
20	17 4/12	𝕻 Benjamin Hutchins Edwards[19]	14 May	12	21 Oct.	13	7 Mar.	47
6	0	Robert Alexander Dagg	2 Jan.	43	15 Mar.	46	17 Sept.	47
13	0	𝕻 John Spence[17]	22 April	36	11 Jan.	40	10 Mar.	48

1 Colonel Hamilton served the campaign of 1799 in Holland, and was present in the different battles; with the expedition to South America, including the attack on Buenos Ayres, and all the skirmishes which took place before and after that event; in the Peninsula under Sir John Moore, including the battles of Roleia Vimiera, and Corunna. Severely wounded (lost a leg) in action at Flushing, 7th Aug. 1809.

2 Colonel Falconar's services:—first Egyptian campaign; campaigns of 1805-6 in Italy, including battle of Maida, siege of Scylla, and capture of Catrone. Second Egyptian campaign, including the siege of Rosetta, and action at El Hamet. Campaign of 1814, in Holland, including action at Merxem and bombardment of Antwerp. Campaign of 1815, in Flanders. Besides the above, various other desultory services and skirmishes. Medal for services in Egypt.

3 Colonel Frith was present in several affairs consequent upon the operations carried on by the division of the army under Colonel Chalmers in the Travancore war, particularly on the 15th January 1809, and the storming of the enemy's lines on the 21st Feb. following. Served also at the capture of the Isle of Bourbon, and of the Isle of France in 1810.

4 Colonel Maunsell served in the Peninsula from Aug. 1813 to the end of that war in 1814, including the siege of San Sebastian, passage of the Bidassoa, battles of Nivelle, 10th Nov., and Nive, 9th, 10th, and 11th Dec. Served also in the American war, and was slightly wounded at Bladensburg, 24th Aug., and severely at New Orleans, 23d Dec. 1814.

5 Col. Baumgardt was present and served during the whole of Generals Lord Lake and Sir G. Hewitt's campaigns in India in 1803, 4 5, 6, and 7, including the battles of Laswarree, Futtighur, and several minor actions; the sieges of Agra, Dheig, Bhurtpore, and Hattras. Served during the whole of the Mahratta campaign in 1817 and 18. Suppressed a very serious insurrection in Bombay, when Commandant of that Garrison in 1833. Served also during the Affghanistan campaign in 1838 and 1839, and commanded the storming columns against the fortress of Khelat.

6 Sir Richard Doherty served at the capture of Martinique in 1809, and of Guadaloupe in 1810.

7 Col. Bush served at Walcheren in 1809.

9 (For this and remaining notes, see bottom of preceding page.)

Royal Regiment of Artillery.

The Royal Arms and supporters, with a Cannon, and the Motto "*Ubique*" over the Gun, and "*Quo fas et gloria ducunt*" below it.—"WATERLOO."—Rocket Troop, "LEIPSIC." "CHINA," with the device of "*The Dragon.*"

The figures in the first Column, prefixed to the Names, denote the Battalions to which the Officers belong.—H.B. Horse Brigade.—G.C. Gentleman Cadet.

Colonel-in-Chief.—Field Marshal *The Marquis of* Anglesey, KG. GCB. GCH. Master-General of the Ordnance.

Years' Serv. Full Pay.	Half Pay.		Colonels-Commandant.	Second Lieut.	First Lieut.	Captain.	Brevet-Major.	Reg.-Major.	Brevet-Lt.Col.	Reg.-Lt.-Col.	Brevet-Colonel.	Reg.-Colonel.	Colonel Comm.	Major-General.	Lieut.-General.
57	0	6	Alexander Watson 1	19 June 92	17 Jan. 93	9 Jan. 97	....	20 June 09	....	1 May 14	....	29 July 25	14 Mar. 42	10 Jan. 37	9 Nov. 46
56	0	5	Edward Vaughan Worsley	23 Jan. 93	15 Aug. 93	1 April 97	....	4 Sept. 09	4 June 14	20 Dec. 14	....	do	9 May 42	do	do
56	0	H.B.	*Sir* Thomas Downman, CB. KCH. 2	24 April 93	11 Sept. 93	1 Nov. 97	....	23 Jan. 10	17 Dec. 12	do	27 May 25	do	28 Sept. 43	do	do
56	0	1	Henry Evelegh 3	do	1 Jan. 94	3 Nov. 97	25 July 10	8 May 11	....	do	....	do	6 Feb. 45	do	do
56	0	10	*Hon.* William Henry Gardner 4	18 Sept. 93	1 Jan. 94	16 July 99	4 June 11	20 Dec. 14	....	do	....	do	1 April 46	do	do
56	0	7	Frederick Walker 5	do	do	do	do	do	....	3 July 15	....	do	18 May 46	do	do
55	0	3	Joseph Webbe Tobin	1 Jan. 94	14 Aug.	4 Feb. 00	1 Jan. 12	do	19 July 21	6 Aug. 21	....	31 Dec. 27	16 Aug. 46	do	do
55	0	9	Rich. Secker Brough 6	....	2 Sept. 94	1 Jan. 98	25 July 10	31 Dec. 22	12 Aug. 19	4 Sept. 23	....	21 Nov. 33	17 Aug. 46	23 Nov. 41	
55	0	2	James Power	....	30 Sept. 94	22 Feb. 99	4 June 11	12 June 23	12 Aug. 19	26 Dec 24	....	5 June 35	6 Dec. 46	do	
54	0	8	Thomas John Forbes	6 Mar. 95	13 April 95	9 Sept. 02	4 June 13	17 Oct. 23	....	22 July 25	....	10 Jan. 37	8 Dec. 47	9 Nov. 46	
54	0	4	J. Webber Smith, CB. 7, *Dir. Gen. of Art.*	do	3 Oct. 95	25 Nov. 02	4 June 13	26 Dec. 24	21 Sept. 13	do	22 July 30	do	2 June 48	23 Nov. 41	
54	0	11	Alexander Munro, KH. 8	6 Mar. 95	27 Jan. 96	2 May 03	4 June 14	29 July 25	....	29 July 25	....	4 May 46	1 Nov. 48	9 Nov. 46	
54	0	12	*Sir* Hew Dal. Ross, KCB. 9 *Dep. Adj. Gen.*	do	10 May 96	1 Sept. 03	31 Dec. 11	29 July 25	21 June 13	do	....	....	do	23 Nov. 41	
			Rem. from Corps, having Rank of *Maj.-Gen.*												
54	0		Robert Henry Birch 10	9 Mar.	25 July 96	12 Sept.	4 June 14	do	....	12 Dec. 26	....	do		9 Nov. 46	
54	0		James Armstrong 11	do	31 July 96	do	do	do	....	13 Oct. 27	....	do		do	
54	0		Thomas Paterson 12	1 Dec.	3 June 97	6 Dec.	do	5 Nov. 25	....	6 Nov.	....	do		do	
53	0		Nat. Wilmot Oliver 13	2 June	13 Feb. 98	2 [illegible] 04	do	14 Nov. 26	....	do	....	do		do	
53	0		Rich. John Jas. Lacy 14	8 Aug.	17 Mar. 98	20 July	do	The Re-	....	31 Dec.	....	do		do	
52	0		*Sir* Robert William Gardiner, KCB. KCH. 15	7 April 97	16 July 99	12 Oct. 04	27 April 12	gimental	3 Mar. 14	30 Dec. 28	22 July 30	do		23 Nov. 41	
49	0		Wm. Greenshields Power, CB. KH. 37	31 May 00	11 Feb. 02	13 June 07	21 Sept. 13	rank of	21 Jan. 17	12 June 25	10 Jan. 37	23 June 37		9 Nov. 46	
46	0		Alexander Macdonald, CB. 57	Dec. 03	1 May 04	1 Oct. 12	18 June 15	Major was	21 June 17	20 July 40	do	24 Nov. 39		do	
			COLONELS.					abolished							
52	0	6	Frederick Campbell 20 *s.*	12 Jan. 97	16 July 99	29 July 04	4 June 14	6th Nov.	....	23 Nov. 28	....	11 June 38		....	
52	0	1	George Turner, CB. 23	14 Jan.	do	do	do	1827.	....	25 Nov.	....	23 June		....	
52	0	H.B.	Richard Fra. Cleveland 25	24 Feb.	do	9 Oct.	do		....	9 Dec.	....	10 Aug. 39		....	
52	0	2	Peter Margetson Wallace 26	10 May	do	15 Nov.	do		....	30 Dec.	....	23 Nov. 41		....	
52	0	3	Richard Jones 27	12 May	do	5 Dec.	do		....	31 Dec.	....	do		....	
52	0	9	John Edw. Jones, 28 *Assist.-Adjt.-General*	14 July	do	20 Dec.	do		....	do	....	do		....	
52	0	5	Thomas Alston Brandreth, CB. 29	19 July	do	do	do		....	27 Oct. 29	....	do		....	
52	0	1	Thomas Hutchesson 30	1 Dec.	2 Oct.	10 Apr. 05	12 Aug. 19		....	22 July 30	....	do		....	
51	0	H.B.	Edw. Cha. Whinyate, CB. KH. 31	1 Mar. 96	do	8 July	18 July 15		....	do	....	do		....	
51	0	7	John Mitchell, CB. 32	do	do	20 Sept.	29 Sept. 14		....	do	....	do		....	
51	0	8	Arthur Hunt 34	11 Nov.	18 Apr. 01	1 June 06	12 Aug. 19		....	26 Oct. 31	....	do		....	
47	2 [illegible]/12	10	George Cobbe 35	9 Oct. 99	7 Sept.	2 June	do		....	20 [illegible] 34	....	1 Apr. 46		....	
45	4 [illegible]/12	10	Alex. Cavalie Mercer 36	20 Dec.	1 Dec.	3 Dec.	do		....	5 June 35	....	do		....	

Years' Serv. Full Pay.	Half Pay.		COLONELS.	SECOND LIEUT.	FIRST LIEUT.	CAPTAIN.	BREVET MAJOR.	BREVET LT.-COL.	REGIMTL. LT.-COL.	BREVET COLONEL.	REGIMTL. COLONEL.
42	6$\frac{4}{12}$	4	Jas. Stokes Bastard	15 Nov. 00	12 May 02	1 Feb. 08	27 May 25	....	27 April 36	....	9 Nov. 46
48	0	5	Tho. Gore Browne[38]	23 Feb. 01	12 Nov. 02	do	do	....	1 July 36	....	do
48	0	9	Duncan Grant[39]	do	23 Nov.	do	do	....	12 July	....	do
48	0	8	Henry Alex. Scott[40]	28 Apr.	20 Apr. 03	do	do	....	10 Aug.	....	do
48	0	7	Thomas Dyneley, CB.[41]	1 Dec.	1 July	28 May	18 June 15	....	10 Jan. 37	23 Nov. 41	do
47	0	3	Henry Charles Russel	1 Apr. 02	12 Sept.	15 July	27 May 25	....	do	....	do
47	0	6	William Cator[43]	7 May	do	1 May 09	12 April 14	22 July 30	do	....	do
46	0	8	Cha. Cornwallis Dansey, CB.[44]	19 July 03	do	1 Oct. 09	22 July 30	....	do	....	do
46	0	4	Adam Fife Crawford[45]	17 Aug.	do	3 Aug. 10	do	....	do	....	20 July 47
46	0	11	Henry Wm. Gordon[46]	do	do	do	do	....	do	....	1 Nov. 48
46	0	11	*Sir Wm. Macb. Geo. Colebrooke*, KH.[47]	do	do	27 Sept.	1 June 13	22 July 30	do	9 Nov. 46	do
46	0	11	Wm. Daniel Jones[48]	8 Sept. 03	do	8 May 11	22 July 30	....	10 Jan. 37	....	do
46	0	12	Wm. Bolden Dundas, CB.[49]	do	do	11 July	21 Jan. 19	10 Jan. 37	23 June 37	....	do
46	0	12	Courtenay Cruttenden[50]	do	24 Oct.	11 Aug.	22 July 30	....	28 June 38	....	do
			LIEUT.-COLONELS.								
46	0	H. B.	Wm. Wylde, CB.[52]	do	6 Dec.	16 Mar. 12	16 July 30	19 Aug. 36	20 Nov. 39	9 Nov. 46	
46	0	9	Charles Edward Gordon[53]	do	do	17 Mar.	22 July 30	....	24 Nov.		
46	0	5	Philip Warren Walker[54]	3 Dec.	do	1 June	do	....	16 Mar.		
46	0	5	*Alexander Maclachlan*[55]	do	do	17 June	do	1 June 32	11 April 40	9 Nov. 46	
46	0	1	Henry George Jackson[58]	22 Dec.	do	31 Dec.	22 July 30	16 Aug. 39	12 Aug.		
46	0	9	*Edward Sabine*[59]	do	20 July	24 Jan. 13	10 Jan. 37	....	25 Jan.		
45	0	9	James Arch. Chalmer,[60] *Assist. Director Gen.*	10 Aug. 04	1 Mar. 05	20 Dec. 14	do	....	23 Nov. 41		
42	2$\frac{1}{12}$	3	Francis Rawdon Chesney[62]	9 Nov. 04	20 Sept.	20 June 15	2 Dec. 36	27 April 38	13 April 42		
42	2$\frac{11}{12}$	H.B.	William Bell[63]	23 Nov.	2 Dec.	3 July	10 Jan. 37	....	do		
41	3$\frac{1}{12}$	6	George Brodie Fraser	14 Dec.	3 Dec.	1 Aug.	do	....	do		
41	3$\frac{4}{12}$	H.B.	Matthew Louis[64]	do	28 Dec.	26 Oct.	do	....	2 Aug.		
42	2$\frac{11}{12}$	7	Thomas Grantham[65]	do	29 Dec.	28 Oct.	do	....	4 April 43		
41	3$\frac{1}{12}$	7	Francis Haultain	do	23 Feb. 06	7 June 16	do	....	do		
38	6$\frac{4}{12}$	H.B.	Wm. Brereton, CB. KH.[66]	10 May 05	1 June	30 Sept.	21 Jan. 19	10 Jan. 37	17 Aug.		
38	6$\frac{4}{12}$	6	Poole Vallancey England[67]	do	do	11 Mar. 17	10 Jan. 37	....	17 Aug.		
38	5$\frac{1}{12}$	10	Irwine Whitty[68]	12 July	do	23 Oct. 18	do	....	18 Aug.		
38	5$\frac{1}{12}$	10	Henry Lewis Sweeting[69]	9 Aug.	do	1 May 19	do	....	1 Sept.		
39	4$\frac{11}{12}$	5	Jas. Humphreys Wood[70]	13 Sept. 05	do	11 May 20	do	....	1 April 44		
41	2$\frac{7}{12}$	3	Charles Dalton[71]	1 Mar. 06	do	30 Dec. 22	do	....	15 April		
41	2$\frac{1}{12}$	7	Richard Burne Rawnsley	21 Mar.	22 Oct.	12 June 23	28 June 38	....	6 Jan. 45		
41	2	2	Rich. Hardinge, KH.[73]	23 May	19 Dec.	17 July	do	....	5 April		
42	[illegible]	8	Robert Andrews	1 July	15 Oct. 07	26 Nov. 24	do	....	8 Sept.		
42	[illegible]	8	Walter Elphinstone Lock[75]	1 July	1 Feb. 08	20 July 25	do	....	12 Dec.		

Years' Service. Full Pay.	Half Pay.		LIEUTENANT COLONELS.	SECOND LIEUT.	FIRST LIEUT.	CAPTAIN.	BREVET-MAJOR.	BREVET-LIEUT. COL.	REGIMENT. LIEUT. n.	BREVET COLONEL.
42	$1\frac{1}{12}$	6	Browne Willis	4 Oct. 06	1 Feb. 08	29 July 25	28 June 38	....	1 April 46	
41	$1\frac{3}{12}$	4	[illegible]. Gordon Higgins [75]	do	do	do	do	2 April 41	do	
43	0	2	[illegible] [illegible]as Fox Strangways [76]	18 Dec.	do	12 Dec. 26	23 Nov. 41	....	do	
42	0	8	[illegible] John Eyre [77]	10 June 07	11 Feb. 08	6 Nov. 27	do	....	8 July	
42	$\frac{1}{12}$	2	Charles Otway	1 July	5 Mar. 08	6 Nov. 27	do	....	9 Nov. 46	
41	$\frac{7}{12}$	9	[illegible] Wm. [illegible]ane Anderson [79]	3 Nov.	1 Aug.	do	do	....	do	
41	1	1	Reynolds Palmer	17 Dec.	1 Oct.	do	do	....	do	
41	1	3	Richard Say Armstrong [80]	do	22 Mar. 09	do	do	....	do	
40	$1\frac{1}{12}$	10	Mark Evans [81]	4 April 08	1 May	do	do	....	do	
41	0	4	George [illegible]st Rowland	do	10 Sept.	31 Dec. 28	do	....	do	
38	$2\frac{7}{12}$	1	[illegible] James Nisbet Colquhoun [82]	1 June	8 Sept. 10	6 Nov. 27	2 Dec. 36	10 Nov. 40	do	
40	$1\frac{4}{12}$	4	[illegible] Anthony R. [illegible]rrison [83]	do	27 Oct.	do	23 Nov. 41	....	do	
41	0	5	[illegible] Henry [illegible]ird [illegible]right [85]	6 July	29 Dec.	11 July 29	1 Nov. 42	....	do	
41	0	11	[illegible] [illegible]m Henry Bent [86]	26 Nov.	11 Aug. 11	27 Oct. 29	....	....	do	
38	$2\frac{3}{12}$	11	Robert Clarke	do	12 Aug.	6 Nov. 27	23 Nov. 41	....	28 Nov.	
38	$2\frac{3}{12}$	11	[illegible] William Furneaux [87]	do	18 Nov.	do	do	....	19 Mar. 47	
40	0	12	[illegible] [illegible]ncis Warde [88]	4 Mar. 09	8 Mar. 12	3 July 30	9 Nov. 46	....	7 May	
40	0	12	[illegible] William Bates Ingilby [89]	1 April	9 April	22 July	do	....	do	
40	0	12	[illegible] Thomas Orlando Cater [90]	do	16 April	do	do	....	28 May	
40	0	2	[illegible] [illegible]nry Pester [91]	1 May 09	16 June 12	22 July 30	do	....	20 July 47	
40	0	1	[illegible] [illegible]ert William Story [93]	6 Nov.	18 Mar. 13	27 May 31	do	....	21 Dec.	
39	0	3	[illegible] [illegible]e James [94]	5 Mar. 10	25 Oct. 13	3 Sept. 31	9 Nov. 46	....	1 Nov. 48	
39	0	4	Charles Henry Nevett [94]	do	17 Dec.	26 Oct.	do	....	do	
39	0	5	[illegible] John [illegible]ld [95]	28 April	do	7 Feb. 32	do	....	do	
39	0	6	[illegible] Henry Palliser [96]	4 June	18 Feb. 14	27 Sept.	do	....	do	
39	0	7	[illegible] [illegible]ld Macbean [97]	13 Dec.	23 July	28 Dec.	23 Nov. 41	....	do	
37	$\frac{3}{12}$	8	Robert Longmore Garstin	12 Dec. 11	20 Dec.	1 Aug. 33	9 Nov. 46	....	do	
37	$\frac{4}{12}$	9	[illegible] John Alexander Wilson [98]	11 Sept. 12	do	17 Oct.	do	....	do	
36	$\frac{11}{12}$	10	Richard Tomkyns [98]	do	29 Dec.	21 Nov.	do	....	do	
36	1	11	Henry Williams [99]	17 Dec.	20 May 15	17 Dec.	do	....	do	
36	$\frac{7}{12}$	12	[illegible] R. Goodwin Bowen Wilson [100]	do	20 June	8 July 34	do	....	do	
			CAPTAINS.							
35	$1\frac{4}{12}$	9	[illegible] [illegible] [illegible]page [101] *Maj. of Bri.*	do	do	20 July	9 Nov. 46	....		
35	$1\frac{7}{12}$	3	Robert Burn, *s.*	do	do	14 Aug.	do	....		
35	$1\frac{11}{12}$	6	[illegible] [illegible]h. Beaumont Burnaby [102]	do	28 June	9 Sept.	do	....		
34	$2\frac{2}{12}$	8	John [illegible]ford Griffin [103]	5 July 13	28 Oct.	21 Nov.	do	....		
34	$2\frac{6}{12}$	5	[illegible]as Arscott [illegible]dge	do	17 Nov.	20 Dec.	do	....		
32	$3\frac{1}{12}$	2	[illegible] Wm. How Hennis [104]	13 Dec.	1 Aug. 16	5 June 35	20 Oct. 46	....		

	Captains.	2d Lieut.	1st. Lieut.	Captain.	Brev.-Major.
4	Daniel Thorndike	1 May 15	8 May 19	28 Dec. 35	9 Nov. 46
6	Harry Stow	do	26 Dec. 19	4 Feb. 36	do
4	William Fraser	do	5 Mar. 20	18 Mar.	do
5	Charles Gostling	do	22 April	19 April	do
8	Charles Henry Mee	do	11 May	27 April	do
3	Theophilus Desbrisay	do	12 May	25 May	do
9	Charles Bertie Symons	10 July	2 Dec. 21	1 July	do
2	Thomas Congreve Robe	11 Dec.	30 Dec. 22	10 Aug.	do
6	George Mark Glasgow	do	15 Nov. 24	10 Jan. 37	
1	William Wallace d'Arley	16 Dec. 16	10 Dec.	do	
3	Edmund Neal Wilford	do	3 Jan. 25	do	
9	John Tylden	do	13 Feb. 25	do	
3	Wm. Henry Pickering	do	9 April	do	
1	John Wheeler Collington	do	29 July	do	
4	Geo. Hooton Hyde	7 July 17	do	19 Jan.	
7	Thomas Peters Flude	do	do	29 Jan.	
1	John Morris Savage	do	do	27 Mar.	
5	Rich. James Dacres	15 Dec. 17	29 Aug. 25	18 Dec. 37	
R.T.	Chas. Wm. Wingfield	8 July 18	1 April 26	30 Dec.	
1	Alexander Tulloh	do	10 July	20 April 38	
2	Henry Poole	5 Oct.	1 Feb. 27	13 Nov.	
H.B.	Henry George Teesdale	8 Dec. 19	26 May	23 May 39	
H.B.	Noel Thomas Lake	5 July 20	5 July	10 Aug.	
3	Piercy Benn	3 Feb. 21	13 Oct.	14 Aug.	
8	Thomas Ackers Shone	11 July 22	6 Nov.	24 Nov.	
6	James Turner	15 Nov. 24	do	11 Apr. 40	
2	Ashton Ashton Shuttleworth	10 Dec.	8 Nov.	21 Apr.	
8	George William Bingham	26 Dec. 24	do	13 May	
H.B.	John Edward Dupuis	13 Feb. 25	do	15 June	8 Jan. 47
7	John Low	28 Feb. 25	do	19 June 40	
4	George Markland	9 April	12 Nov.	20 July	
8	John Hill	10 April	do	22 July	
7	Charles Herrick Burnaby	9 June	14 Nov.	12 Aug.	15 Sept. 48
5	Wm Fenwick Williams, *Lt.-Col.* 31 Mar. 48	14 July	16 Nov.	13 Aug.	22 May 46
5	John Geddes Walker	29 July	do	do	
2	Henry Joseph Morris	do	1 Jan. 28	27 Sept.	
5	John M'Coy	do	3 Jan.	25 Jan. 41	
H.B.	Edw. Fitzherbert Grant	do	30 April	19 Feb.	
10	John Wray Mitchell	18 Oct. 26	9 Dec.	1 Apr.	
10	George John Beresford	do	31 Dec.	do	
10	Rob. Fitzgerald Crawford	19 May 28	12 May 29	do	
10	John St. George	do	11 July	do	
10	William Robert Nedham	do	12 July	do	
H.B.	Edward Charles Warde	do	30 June 30	5 June	
7	Henry Coope Stace	6 Aug.	4 July	17 Aug.	
6	Robert Roe Fisher	do	22 July	2 Sept.	
6	John William Ormsby	do	do	16 Sept.	
9	Arthur Joseph Taylor	do	do	25 Sept.	
8	George Maclean	do	5 Aug.	1 Oct.	
7	William Baird Young	do	1 Oct.	23 Nov.	
5	Wm. Harrison Askwith, *Maj.* 28 Jan. 42	18 Dec. 29	6 Nov.	do	
7	Franklin Dunlop	do	25 Nov.	do	
1	Francis Dick,	do	26 Nov.	do	
3	Alfred Tylee	do	1 April 31	do	
1	Charles James Dalton	do	29 April	do	
9	William Henry Forbes	do	27 May	do	
H.B.	David Edward Wood	do	30 June	do	
4	Hugh Manley Tuite	6 Nov. 30	26 Aug.	do	
9	George Innes	do	4 Sept.	23 Dec.	
G.C.	Frederick Eardley Wilmot	do	27 Sept.	7 April 42	
3	James William Fitzmayer	do	26 Oct.	12 April	
7	George Robert Harry Kennedy	do	27 Oct.	13 April	
1	George Sandham	do	28 Oct.	do	
9	Chas. Vansittart Cockburn	do	2 Feb. 32	do	
10	Frederick Wodehouse	17 Dec.	29 May	do	
10	John Henry Francklyn	26 July 31	23 June	do	
10	Henry Thomas Fyers,	do	13 July	do	
2	Gloucester Gambier	do	31 July	do	
6	Francis Seymour Hamilton	do	17 Aug.	27 April	
7	Edward Walter Crofton	do	29 Aug.	2 Aug.	
4	Samuel Philip Townsend	do	16 Oct.	10 Aug.	
8	Powrie Ellis	do	28 Dec.	26 Nov.	

Years' Serv. Full Pay.	Half Pay.		Captains.	2nd Lieut.	1st Lieut.	Captain.
18	0	11	Nathaniel Evanson Harison	16 Dec. 31	7 May 33	4 April 43
18	0	11	Charles Cheetham	do	16 July	do
18	0	11	Gilbert John Lane Buchanan	do	1 Aug.	do
18	0	H.B.	Walter Raleigh Gilbert	do	17 Oct.	do
18	0	11	Alexander Fred. William Papillon	do	23 Oct.	do
18	0	11	Henry Aylmer	do	21 Nov.	do
18	0	11	George Charles Rawdon Levinge	do	25 Nov.	6 April
18	0	12	Alex. Graham Wilkinson Hamilton	do	17 Dec.	1 May
18	0	12	William Fulford	do	22 Jan. 34	3 May
18	0	12	Alexander Irving	do	10 Mar.	4 May
17	0	12	St. John Thos. Browne, *Major*, 15 Sept. 48	20 June 32	11 July	18 May
17	0	12	Charles Bingham	do	20 July	17 Aug.
17	0	12	Henry Sebastian Rowan, *s.*, *Maj.* 22 May 46	do	14 Aug.	18 Aug.
17	0	12	John Noble Arbuthnot Freese[108]	do	9 Sept.	22 Aug.
17	0	12	Frederick Darby Cleaveland	do	25 Sept.	1 Sept.
17	0	1	Henry Austin Turner	do	20 Nov.	14 Jan. 44
17	0	11	Thomas Beckett Fielding Marriott	20 Dec.	21 Nov.	30 Mar.
17	0	4	Thomas Elwyn	do	29 Dec.	1 April
17	0	2	Charles James Wright	do	30 Dec. 34	do
17	0	3	George Augustus Fred. Derinzy	do	28 Jan. 35	do
17	0	4	William Hamilton Elliot	do	4 April	do
17	0	11	Peter Maclean	do	6 May	14 April
17	0	9	Charles Robert Wynne	do	5 June	15 April
17	0	2	Anthony Benn	do	2 Sept.	do
16	0	5	Charles Lionel Fitzgerald	21 June 33	6 Jan. 36	15 May
16	0	6	George Drought Warburton[108]	do	17 March	28 May
16	0	6	Philip Reginald Cocks	do	18 Mar.	9 June
			Second Captains.			
16	0	1	Thomas de Winton	do	29 June	1 Feb. 45
16	0	1	William Thomas Crawford	do	1 July	5 April
16	0	H.B.	Pierrepont Henry Mundy	20 Dec.	2 July	do
16	0	8	George Edward Turner, *s. Maj.* 9 May 45	do	12 July	do
16	0	6	William Henderson	do	13 July	10 Apri
16	0	1	William James Smythe	do	10 Jan. 37	6 May
16	0	3	David William Paynter	do	do	9 May
15	0	3	George Robert Barker, *Adjutant*	21 June 34	do	21 May
15	0	7	Peter Pickmore Faddy	do	do	14 June
15	0	H.B.	Arthur Thomas Philipotts	do	do	3 Sept.
15	0	2	Hen. R. Eardly Wilmot, [109] *Maj.* 7 July 46	do	do	4 Sept.
15	0	8	William Bethell Gardner	do	do	29 Oct.
15	0	5	John Henry Lefroy	19 Dec.	do	30 Nov.
15	0	6	Chas. James Buchanan Riddell	do	do	12 Dec.
15	0	8	Arthur George Burrows	do	do	26 Feb. 46
15	0	5	Molyneux Chas. Marston	do	12 Jan.	1 April
15	0	1	Edward Price	do	28 do	do
15	0	6	Charles Colville Young,[110] *Maj.* 15 Sept. 48	do	29 Jan.	do
15	0	6	James William Domville	do	6 Feb.	do
15	0	2	Edwin Wodehouse, *Adjutant*	do	22 Feb.	do
15	0	H.B.	George Ashley Maude, *Adjutant*	do	27 Mar.	do
14	0	4	John Farnaby Cator, *Adjutant*	18 June 35	5 Apr.	do
14	0	7	Evan Maberly	do	24 June	do
14	0	10	John Russell Domvile, *Adjutant*	do	26 Sept.	do
14	0	10	Wm. Manley Hall Dixon	do	30 Oct.	do
14	0	10	Hen. Wm. Montresor	do	28 Nov.	do
14	0	10	Wm. Moffat Douglas Willan	do	do	do
14	0	H.B.	Collingwood Dickson, *Maj.* 22 May 46	18 Dec.	29 ditto	do
14	0	H.B.	*Hon.* R. Chas. Hen. Spencer[112] *do.*	do	30 Dec.	do
14	0	10	Henry John Thomas	do	1 Feb. 38	do
14	0	10	George Graydon	do	23 Mar.	do
14	0	10	Anthony Oldfield	do	20 April	do
14	0	8	Henry Paget Christie	do	11 June	do
13	0	9	Jas. Benjamin Dennis	18 June 36	28 June	do
13	0	8	Denis Wm. Pack	do	6 Aug.	do
13	0	4	John Travers	do	6 Oct.	6 April
13	0	7	*Hon.* George Talbot Devereux	do	13 Nov.	13 April
13	0	H.B.	Richard Blackwood Price	do	11 Dec.	13 April
13	0	9	Ralph Shuttleworth Allen	do	1 May 39	4 May
13	0	9	William Swinton	do	16 May	4 May
13	0	3	Edward William Rodwell	do	20 May	26 May
13	0	6	Spencer Delves Broughton	do	23 May	23 June
13	0	3	Allan Hamilton Graham	do	3 July	8 July

Years' Serv. Full Pay.	Half Pay.		Second Captains.	2nd Lieut.	1st Lieut.	Captain.
13	0	3	John Miller Adye	13 Dec. 36	7 July 39	29 July 46
13	0	9	Frederick Alex. Campbell, *Adjutant*	do	10 Aug.	14 Oct.
13	0	11	Henry Philip Goodenough	do	13 Aug.	9 Nov.
13	0	5	George Bucknall Shakespear	do	11 Sept.	do
12	0	5	Richard Henry Crofton	5 May 37	20 Nov.	do
12	0	11	Matthew Smith Dodsworth	do	24 Nov.	do
12	0	7	Murray Octavius Nixon	14 Dec.	25 Feb. 40	do
12	0	H.B.	Henry Lynedoch Gardiner	do	16 Mar.	do
12	0	2	Benjamin Bathurst	do	11 April	do
12	0	4	Henry Bourchier Osborne Savile	do	21 April	do
12	0	6	Robert Parker Radcliffe, *Adjutant*	do	13 May	do
12	0	10	Thomas Knox	do	15 June	do
12	0	8	Charles Wright Younghusband	do	19 June	28 Nov.
12	0	4	Thomas Cromie Lyle	do	20 July	1 Feb. 47
11	0	5	Robert Corcyra Romer	16 June 38	do	15 Mar.
11	0	H.B.	George Wilder	do	do	9 April
11	0	6	Charles Lawrence d'Aguilar	do	22 July	22 April
11	0	8	Hugh Archibald Beauchamp Campbell	do	31 July	7 May
11	0	1	Richard Bratton Adair	do	12 Aug.	7 May
11	0	G. C.	Robert Talbot	do	13 Aug.	28 May
11	0	9	Henry Lempriere	do	do	1 July
10	0	3	Arnold Thompson	19 Mar. 39	do	20 July
10	0	9	Henry Clerk	do	do	27 Sept.
10	0	7	Wm. Robert Gichard	do	27 Sept.	24 Nov.
10	0	12	Francis Beckford Ward	do	31 Dec.	21 Dec.
10	0	2	John James Brandling	do	25 Jan. 41	1 May 48
10	0	3	Alfred Romaine Wragge	do	18 Mar.	30 May
10	0	7	Frederick Wm. Haultain	do	1 Apr.	30 June
10	0	1	Tho. Wm. Lawrence	do	do	do
10	0	1	Frederick John Travers	do	do	do
10	0	6	Matthew Charles Dixon	do	11 Apr.	do
10	0	12	Henry Rogers	do	29 April	do
10	0	5	John Turner[114], *s.*	do	7 May	do
10	0	11	Augustus Charles Lennox Fitz-Roy	do	14 May	do
10	0	7	Edward Henry Fisher	do	5 June	do
10	0	6	Robert Frederick Mountain	do	17 Aug.	do
10	0	4	Samuel Cleaveland	do	16 Sept.	do
10	0	4	Augustus Chas. Stapleton Somerset	do	25 Sept.	do
10	0	12	Samuel Hood Stovin Inglefield	do	17 Nov.	do
10	0	4	Edward Mourrier Boxer	20 Dec.	23 Nov.	do
10	0	5	Charles Scudamore Longden	20 Dec.	do	do
10	0	1	Wm. Alex. Middleton	do	do	do
9	0	5	Rouquier John Cannon	20 June 40	do	do
9	0	11	James Robert Gibbon	18 Dec.	do	do
9	0	11	John Richard Anderson[116]	do	do	do
9	0	11	Percy Francis Gother Scott	do	do	do
9	0	11	Somerville M'Donald Calder	do	do	do
9	0	11	William Paul Pollock	do	20 Dec.	do
8	0	11	Henry Francis Strange	19 June 41	7 Apr. 42	do
8	0	12	John Saltren Willett	do	12 April	do
8	0	12	John Charles William Fortescue	do	13 April	do
8	0	12	William Hamilton Cox	do	do	do
8	0	7	Richard O'Connell	do	do	do
8	0	8	William Francis Smith Neill	do	do	do
8	0	12	Miller Clifford	do	do	do
8	0	12	Richard Wheatley Brettingham	do	do	do
8	0	12	Charles Taylor Du Plat	do	27 April	do
8	0	4	Mortimer Adye	do	28 April	9 Oct.
8	0	3	Thomas Richard M'Queen	do	24 May	do
7	0	5	Charles Trigance Franklin	1 Jan. 42	14 July	14 Oct.
7	0	4	Alexander Cæsar Hawkins, *s.*	do	2 Aug.	1 Nov.
7	0	9	James Morris Hill	do	10 Aug.	do
7	0	7	Barclay Lawson	do	4 Oct.	do
7	0	2	Algernon Peter	do	13 Oct.	do
7	0	2	Andrew Pellett Scrimshire Green	do	1 Nov.	do
7	0	3	Edward Arthur Williams	do	3 Nov.	do
7	0	8	Herbert Winsloe Patton	do	26 Nov.	do
7	0	2	Charles Henry Morris	do	29 Nov.	do
7	0	2	Neil M'Innes Mackay	do	7 Dec.	do
7	0	2	Wm. James Esten Grant	do	31 Dec.	do
7	0	1	Joseph Clark Childs	do	4 Apr. 43	do

Years' Serv. Full Pay.	Half Pay.		Second Captains.	2nd Lieut.	1st Lieut.	Captain.
7	0	9	Adolphus Frederick Connell	1 Jan. 42	4 April 43	16 Nov. 48
7	0	10	Robert Barlow M'Crea	18 June	do	26 Nov.
			First Lieutenants.			
7	0	1	John Lindredge Elgee	do	do	
7	0	7	John Desborough	do	6 April	
7	0	4	Disney Fred. Russell............	do	1 May	
7	0	9	George Shaw	do	3 May	
7	0	H.B.	Aug. Fred. Francis Lennox	do	4 May	
7	0	H.B.	Charles Stuart Henry	do	15 May	
7	0	5	Edmund Henry Rene Flint	do	18 May	
7	0	4	Wm. Ryves Nash Taylor	do	1 Aug.	
7	0	6	Edw. Swinton	do	17 Aug.	
7	0	5	Philip Gosset Pipon	do	18 Aug.	
7	0	8	Edw. Jas. Paterson	do	22 Aug.	
7	0	H.B.	John Davenport Shakespear	do	9 Sept.	
6	0	2	Edward Bruce Hamley..........	11 Jan. 43	15 Sept.	
6	0	5	George Thomas Field	do	30 Oct.	
6	0	4	Arthur Comyn Pigou	do	8 Nov.	
6	0	H.B.	David M'Dowall Fraser	do	14 Jan. 44	
6	0	G.C.	James Drummond Telfer	do	7 Mar.	
6	0	4	Charles John Strange	do	30 Mar.	
6	0	H.B.	Richard Gregory	do	1 Apr.	
6	0	H.B.	Horace Parker Newton	do	do	
6	0	10	Alexander Cameron Gleig	do	do	
6	0	H.B.	*Hon.* William Charles Yelverton..	do	14 Apr.	
6	0	8	George Henry Vesey............	do	15 Apr.	
6	0	2	Frederick Charles Standish	do	do	
6	0	2	Stapylton Robinson	17 June	do	
6	0	G.C.	Michael Shrapnel Biddulph	do	26 Apr.	
6	0	H.B.	Henry Arthur Vernon	do	28 Apr.	
6	0	1	Charles Manners Raynes	do	3 May	
6	0	H.B.	Gustavus Hamil. Lockwood Milman	do	15 May	
6	0	1	*Lord* William Kennedy	do	28 May	
6	0	11	Walter Ferguson Lock	do	9 June	
6	0	4	John Fraser Lodington Baddeley	do	17 Jan. 45	
6	0	8	George Lee Chandler	do	do	
6	0	5	Charles George Arbuthnot	do	1 Feb.	
6	0	9	Charles Richard Ogden Evans....	do	4 Feb.	
6	0	7	Guy Rotton	do	5 April	
6	0	7	Francis William Hastings	do	do	
6	0	1	Henry Augustus Smyth	20 Dec.	do	
6	0	6	Paul Winsloe Phillipps	do	10 April	
6	0	1	Edward Moubray	do	do	
6	0	3	Frederick Hugh Chancellor	do	17 April	
6	0	5	Charles Waller	do	9 May	
6	0	2	Richard King Freeth	do	21 May	
6	0	10	Charles William Grey	do	14 June	
6	0	2	Fran. Montague Maxwell Ommanney	do	3 Sept.	
6	0	3	Edmund Palmer	do	4 Sept.	
6	0	5	Francis Vansittart.............	do	7 Oct.	
6	0	H.B.	Leopold Grimston Paget	do	29 Oct.	
6	0	10	Richard Phelips	do	30 Nov.	
6	0	3	Henry Mercer	do	12 Dec.	
5	0	10	George Colclough	19 June 44	26 Feb. 46	
5	0	7	Thomas Walter Milward	do	1 April	
5	0	9	Henry Lowther Chermside	do	do	
5	0	6	Alex. Theophilus Blakely........	do	do	
5	0	9	Robert Emilius Fazakerley Craufurd	do	do	
5	0	H.B.	Frederick William Craven Ord ..	do	do	
5	0	H.B.	William Conyngham Lynch Blosse	do	do	
5	0	1	Matthew Bligh Forde	do	do	
5	0	3	William Townsend Barnett	do	do	
5	0	H.B.	Archibald Edward Harbord Anson	do	do	
5	0	2	Samuel Enderby Gordon	do	do	
5	0	H.B.	John George Boothby	do	do	
5	0	7	Charles Neville Lovell	do	do	
5	0	7	James Francis Eaton Travers	19 Dec.	do	
5	0	H.B.	*Hon.* Edward Thomas Gage	do	do	
5	0	H.B.	Neville Saltren Keats Bayly	do	do	
5	0	1	George Barstow	do	do	
5	0	4	George Leslie..................	do	do	

Years' Serv. Full Pay.	Half Pay.		First Lieutenants.	2nd Lieut.	1st Lieut.
5	0	9	Charles Wright	19 Dec. 44	1 April 46
5	0	10	John Everett Thring	do	do
5	0	10	William Magrath King	do	do
5	0	10	Henry Lambert Fulke Greville	do	do
5	0	8	Hugh Bent	do	do
5	0	H.B.	Francis Robert Glanville	do	do
5	0	6	Henry Jervis White Jervis	do	do
4	0	2	William Lovelace Dumaresq	18 June 45	do
4	0	10	Gaspard Le Marchant Tupper	do	do
4	0	10	Henry Heyman	do	do
4	0	10	Armine Dew	do	do
4	0	7	George Sidney Robertson	do	do
4	0	2	Edward Hinton East	do	do
4	0	H.B.	Dixon Edward Hoste	do	do
4	0	8	Edward Taswell	do	do
4	0	1	John Singleton	do	do
4	0	H.B.	Wm. Edmund Moyses Reilly	18 Dec.	3 April
4	0	H.B.	William Boyd Saunders	do	6 April
4	0	6	Charles Hodgkinson Smith	do	13 April
4	0	6	Henry Terrick Fitz Hugh	do	13 April
4	0	4	Wilmot Horton Moody	do	4 May
4	0	4	Whaley Nicoll Hardy	do	4 May
4	0	6	John Lawrance Bolton	do	26 May
4	0	7	James Rundle Lugg	do	4 June
4	0	6	George Henry John Alex. Fraser	do	23 June
4	0	6	Thomas Lambert	do	8 July
3	0	6	France James Soady	1 May 46	29 July
3	0	7	Edward Eldon Robert Dyneley[117]	do	4 Aug.
3	0	2	Frederic Harvey Bathurst Phillips	do	14 Oct.
3	0	2	Joseph Godby	do	20 Oct.
3	0	5	Dominick Sarsfield Greene	do	9 Nov.
3	0	1	Philip Francis Miller	do	do
3	0	6	William Wigram Barry	do	do
3	0	9	James Thomas Orme	do	do
3	0	4	George Hatton Colomb	do	do
3	0	8	George William Drummond Hay	do	do
3	0	2	Thomas Henry Harding	do	do
3	0	8	Philip Daves Margesson	do	do
3	0	9	Mervyn Stewart	do	do
3	0	9	James Frederick D'Arley Street	do	do
3	0	H.B.	Archibald Motteux Calvert	do	19 Nov.
3	0	5	O'Bryen Bellingham Woolsey	6 Aug.	26 Nov.
3	0	4	Alfred Wilkes Drayson	do	28 Nov.
3	0	2	Cadwallader William Elgee	do	1 Jan. 47
3	0	1	Edmund John Carthew	do	1 Feb.
3	0	8	George Harrison Aun Forbes	do	15 March
3	0	5	William Hunter Blair	do	22 March
3	0	3	Louis Martineau	do	9 April
3	0	7	Charles Hunter	do	22 April
3	0	3	Robert John Hay	do	7 May
3	0	3	Alexander John MacDougall	do	7 May
3	0	3	John Spurway	do	28 May
3	0	7	George Ramsay Craik Young	do	1 July
3	0	3	Henry Townsend Boultbee	do	20 July
3	0	6	John Edward Michell	16 Dec.	27 Sept.
3	0	7	George Cicil Henry	do	23 Oct.
3	0	4	Thomas Picton Warlow	do	23 Nov.
3	0	10	Philip Bedingfield	do	24 Nov.
3	0	4	Spencer Philip John Childers	do	21 Dec.
3	0	10	William Harper Mytton	do	8 Jan. 48
3	0	9	Richard Paget Campbell Jones	do	14 March
3	0	5	Henry Jermyn Montgomery Campbell	do	1 May
3	0	6	Reginald Onslow Farmer	do	30 May
3	0	4	Charles Maitland Govan	do	30 June
3	0	1	Charles Henry Ingilby	do	do
3	0	6	Robert Poole Gabbett	do	do
2	0	3	Henry Peel Yates	2 May 47	do
2	0	9	Murray Fraser Ferrers	do	do
2	0	5	Henry Andrew Thrupp	do	do

Years' Serv. Full Pay.	Half Pay.		First Lieutenants.	2nd Lieut.	1st Lieut.
2	0	9	Charles Edward Mainwaring	2 May 47	30 June 48
2	0	8	Alexander Gordon	do	do
2	0	1	William John Williams	do	do
2	0	2	Charles Frederick Young	do	do
2	0	11	Sanford Freeling	do	do
2	0	4	Oliver Robert Stokes	do	do
2	0	1	James Farrell Pennycuick	do	do
2	0	7	Walter John Grimston	do	do
2	0	10	William Dalgairns Guille	do	do
2	0	9	Charles Edward Oldershaw	do	do
2	0	9	Nathaniel Octavius Simson Turner	do	do
2	0	10	Samuel Digby Wright	1 Oct.	do
2	0	8	Augustus Young Earle	do	do
2	0	5	*Hon.* Leonard A. Addington	do	do
2	0	2	Arthur Vandeleur	do	do
2	0	8	Andrew Spotswood Orr	do	do
2	0	9	Charles Rowland Hill	do	do
2	0	5	Patrick John Campbell	do	do
2	0	3	Francis Cornwallis Maude	do	do
2	0	10	Arthur William Twiss	do	do
2	0	3	Reginald Curtis	do	do
2	0	8	Allen Sievwright	do	do
2	0	1	Frederic Southcote Seale	do	do
2	0	8	John Boulton	do	do
2	0	7	John De Luttrell Saunderson	do	do
2	0	6	Montray Anketell	do	do
2	0	11	Philip Dickson	do	do
2	0	11	Æneas Clarke	do	do
2	0	11	Francis Place	do	do
2	0	8	Edward Jackson Bruce	do	do
2	0	11	William Powell Richards	do	do
2	0	11	John Edward Hope	do	do
2	0	3	Henry Walpole J. Dashwood	do	do
2	0	11	Algernon Brendon	do	do
2	0	12	James de Havilland	do	do
2	0	12	Sidney Carden	do	do
2	0	12	George Allix Wilkinson	do	do
2	0	12	William Windham Augustus Lukin	do	do
2	0	12	William Walker	do	do
2	0	12	Charles Edmund Walcott	18 Dec.	do
2	0	10	Gilmore Burtchaell	do	do
2	0	12	Gronow Davis	do	do
2	0	11	Edgar Grantham Bredin	do	do
2	0	11	William John Bolton	do	do
2	0	11	George Bruce Traherne	do	do
2	0	11	Samuel George Batchellor	do	do
2	0	11	Herbert Taylor Middleton	do	do
2	0	11	Frederick Close	do	do
2	0	11	James Sinclair	do	do
2	0	11	Henry Lynch Talbot	do	do
2	0	8	Willoughby James Wilson	do	do
2	0	12	W. Hen. Randolph Simpson	do	do
2	0	12	Lewis William Penn	do	do
2	0	12	Henry Robe Saunders	do	do
2	0	12	Edward Geary Snow	do	do
2	0	12	John Duff Ramsay	do	do
2	0	12	William Morris	do	do
2	0	12	Henry Renny	do	do
2	0	4	John Thurlow Leathes	do	17 Aug.
2	0	9	Charles Paulett Rotton	do	do
2	0	3	John Morris Savage	do	9 Oct.
2	0	7	Dashwood Jones	do	do
2	0	8	Thomas Edmond Byrne	do	14 Oct.
1	0	8	Edward Taddy	27 June 48	1 Nov.
1	0	7	Henry Crofton Singer	do	do
1	0	6	Hill James Thomas Tomkinson	do	do
1	0	9	John Bawden Parkin	do	do
1	0	1	Charles Johnston	do	do
1	0	5	Thomas Samuel Poer Field	do	do
1	0	2	Lawrence Augustus Bradshaw	do	do

Years' Serv. Full Pay.	Half Pay.		First Lieutenants.	2d Lieut.	1st Lieut.
1	0	12	John M'Candie Campbell	27 June 48	1 Nov. 48
1	0	13	William French	do	do
1	0	13	*Sir* William George Johnson, *Bt.*	do	do
1	0	12	Edward Adolphus Seymour	do	do
1	0	10	Frederick Miller	19 Dec.	19 Dec.
1	0	6	Robert Wolseley Haig	do	do
1	0	12	Charles Henry Owen	do	do
1	0	5	George Alderson Milman	do	do
1	0	6	Robert Boyle	do	do
1	0	8	Claudius Buchanan Piers	do	do
1	0	6	Edward Luce	do	do
1	0	1	Lambert Henry Denne	do	do
1	0	3	George Malcolm Pasley	do	do
1	0	5	Walter L'Estrange	do	do
1	0	3	Charles Edward Burt	do	do
1	0	6	Guy Fitz Henry L'Estrange	do	do
1	0	3	Constantine Lemon H. McTernan	do	do
1	0	8	Hazlett Irvine	do	do
1	0	4	Claude George William Lacelles	do	do
1	0	4	Shadwell Morley Grylls	do	do
1	0	6	*Hon.* George Victor Agar Ellis	do	do
1	0	4	Reginald Henry Champion	do	do

Deputy Adjutant-General.

Maj.-Gen. [illegible] *Sir* Hew Dalrymple Ross, KCB. 23 April 40.

Assistant Adjutant-General.

Colonel.—J. R. Jones, 19th Jan. 18.

Adjutants.

H. B. 2nd *Capt.*—G. A. Maude, 7 April 46.
3 2nd *Capt.*—G. R. Barker, 22 July 46.
2 2nd *Capt.*—R. Wodehouse, 21 Nov. 46.
6 2nd *Capt.*—R. P. Radcliffe, do.
9 2nd *Capt.*—F. A. Campbell, do.
10 2nd *Capt.*—J. R. Domvile, 5 Feb. 47.
4 2nd *Capt.*—J. F. Cator, 7 Apr. 47.
I. A. 2nd *Lt.*—James Campbell, 1 July, 47.

Quarter-Masters.

8 William Porter,[120] 25 Sept. 32.
1 [illegible] William Perkin,[121] 1 Oct. 41.
5 James Nicoll, 1 Jan. 43.
7 Robert Eager, 1 April, 44.
2 Alexander Steele, 1 July, 44.
6 William Marvin, 10 Sept. 44.
9 James White, 1 Feb. 46.
H. B. George Oliphant, 1 July, 47.
10 James Freeburn, 1 April, 46.
4 Charles Dunbar, 2 May, 46.
G. C. William Elliott, 8 Feb. 47.
11 George Clarke, 1 Nov. 48.
12 William M'Kown, 1 Nov. 48.
3 Robert Moore, 1 Jan. 49.

Veterinary Surgeons.

Charles Percivall,[122] 26 April, 18.
James Burt, 1 June, 07.
William Stockley, 24 April, 05.

Chaplains.

Matthew R. Scott, 10 April, 37.
George Baily Tuson, B.D. 1 April, 39.

Company of Gentlemen Cadets.

Captain.—The Master-Gen. of the Ordnance.
2nd *Capt.*—F. Eardley Wilmot, 7 April, 42.
2nd *Capt.*—R. Talbot, 28 May 47.

1st *Lieutenants.*

J. D. Telfer, 7 March, 44.
M. S. Biddulph, 26 April, 44.

Riding Troop.

Captain.—C. W. Wingfield, 30 Dec. 37.
1st *Lieut.*—Henry Philips, 31 July, 26.
Cornet 7th Hussars, 25 March 23.
1st *Lieut.*—Alexander M'Pherson, 1 Jan. 26.

FIELD TRAIN DEPARTMENT.

Director General of Artillery.. *Maj.-Gen.* J. Webber Smith, *CB.* 1 Jan. 44.
Assistant Director-General.... *Lieut.-Colonel* J. A. Chalmer, 17 Jan. 43.
Commissary .... William Young, 28 Jan. 39.
Assistant-Commissary .... John Barr, 17 May, 41.

COMMANDING OFFICERS OF ARTILLERY AND ENGINEERS AT HOME AND ON FOREIGN STATIONS.

GREAT BRITAIN.

District	*Artillery.*	Station	*Engineers.*	Station
			Major Aldrich	*London*
Northern	Col. Whinyates, *CB.* & *KH.*	*Carlisle*	Major Lynn	*Newcastle*
Eastern	Capt. J. Turner	*Landguard Fort*	Major Wulff	*Harwich*
Kent	Lieut.-General *Sir* Thomas Downman, *CB. KCH.*	*Woolwich*	Lt.-Col. Slade	*Chatham*
			Lt.-Col. English	*Woolwich*
	Lieut.-Col. H. G. Jackson	*Dover*	Lt.-Col. Tylden	*Dover*
Medway	Lieut.-Col. Harrison	*Chatham*	Captain Forbes	*Exeter*
Wales	2nd Capt. M. O. Nixon	*Pembroke*	Lt.-Col. Tait	*Birmingham*
Inland	Capt. J. Hill	*Birmingham*	Major Foster	*Manchester*
			Captain Stace	*York*
Sussex				
South West	Lt.-Colonel Hanltain	*Portsmouth*	Colonel Lewis, *CB.*	
Western	Lt.-Colonel Rowland	*Devonport*	Colonel Oldfield, *KH.*	
Jersey	Major James	— —	Lt.-Colonel Streatfield	
Guernsey	Capt. Cockburn	— —	Lt.-Colonel Ward	
North Britain	Lt.-Colonel P. W. Walker	*Leith Fort*	Lt.-Colonel Yule	

IRELAND.

District	Artillery	Station	Engineers	Station
	Colonel Turner, *CB.*	*Dublin*	Col. Vavasour, *CB.*	*Dublin*
Limerick District	Lt.-Col. Louis	*Limerick*		
Dublin do.	Lt.-Col. T. Strangways	*Porto Bello*	Major Vicars	*Dublin District*
Belfast do.	Col. Crawford	*Charlemont*	Lt.-Col. Whinyates	*Belfast ditto*
Cork do.	Lt.-Col. F. R. Chesney	*Ballincollig*	Lt.-Col. Cole	*Cork ditto*
Athlone do.	Col. T. G. Browne	*Athlone*	Lt.-Col. Thomson	*Limerick ditto*
Pigeon-house Fort	Lieut-Colonel T. O. Cater	*Dublin*	Major Budgen	*Athlone ditto*

FOREIGN STATIONS.

Station	Artillery		Engineers	
Gibraltar	Colonel Cator		Colonel Harding, *CB.*	
Malta	Lieut.-Colonel Whitty	— —	Colonel Rice Jones, *KH.*	
Ionian Islands	Lieut.-Col. P. V. England	— —	Lt.-Col. Emmett.	
West Indies	Lieut.-Colonel C. Otway	— —	Lieut.-Col. Waters	
Jamaica	——— Armstrong	— —	Lt.-Col. Wright	
Canada	Col. T. Dyneley, *CB.*	— —	Colonel Holloway, *CB.*	
Quebec	Lieut.-Col. T. G. Higgins	— —	Lt.-Col. Ord	*Canada East*
Upper Canada	——— C. Dalton	— —	Lt.-Col. Fenwick	*Canada West*
Nova Scotia	——— B. Willis	— —	Colonel Calder	
Newfoundland	Capt. Kennedy	— —	Lt.-Col. Robe	
Bermuda	Lieut.-Colonel Andrews	— —	Lieut.-Colonel Barry	
St. Helena	Lieut.-Col. Fraser	— —	Major Luxmoore	
Cape of Good Hope	Lieut.-Colonel Wood	— —	Major Faris	
Ceylon	Lieut.-Colonel T. Grantham	— —	Lieut.-Colonel Brown	
Mauritius	Lieut.-Col. Sweeting	— —	Lieut.-Colonel Blanshard,	
Hong Kong	Lt.-Col. J. Eyre.	— —	Lt.-Col. Phillpotts	
Bahamas	Capt. H. J. Morris	— —	Lt.-Col. Alexander	
Van Diemen's Land		— —	Lt.-Col. Victor	
New South Wales		— —	Lieut.-Col. Gordon	
New Zealand	Capt. Henderson	— —	Lieut.-Col. Bolton	

Paymasters to the Ordnance Department, Messrs. Cox & Co.

War Services of the Officers of the Royal Artillery.

1 Lieut.-General Watson served in Flanders in 1793, 4, and 5, including battles of St. Amand, Famars, siege of Valenciennes, battle of Lincelles, attack of Dunkirk, actions of Lambric, Cateau, Lannoy, Roubaix, Mouveaux, Templeuve, Tournay, and capture of Fort St. Andrew. Present in the actions of the 20th Sept. 2nd and 6th Oct. 1799 at the Helder. Battle of the Blue Berg, and capture of Cape of Good Hope in 1806. Resigned an appointment and volunteered his services to South America; commanded the Artillery at the attack and capture of Maldonado, siege and capture of Monte Video, and attack and capture of Buenos Ayres: a senior officer arriving, he then acted as Aide-de-Camp to Major-Gen Sir Wm. Lumley until the Troops left the country, then returned to the Cape.

2 Sir Thomas Downman served in Flanders in 1793 and 4, including actions at Cateau, Lannoy, and Roubaix, at which last he was taken prisoner. Commanded a troop of horse artillery during the Corunna campaign. Served in the Peninsula from Sept. 1810 to May 1813, including siege of Ciudad Rodrigo, and battle of Salamanca. Medal for Salamanca.

3 Lieut.-General Evelegh served the Corunna Campaign.

4 Lieut.-General Hon. W. H. Gardner accompanied the expedition to Walcheren, and was present at the siege and capture of Flushing.

5 Lieut.-General Walker served on the Continent in 1794 and 5, and received three wounds in the retirement of the army across the Rhine near Arnheim, viz. one severely through the right arm below the elbow; the others above the elbow, and in the right hip.

6 Major-General Brough was at the capture of St. Lucia in 1796, and that of Guadaloupe in 1815.

7 Major-General Smith's services:—attack of Minorca in 1798; siege of Malta, 1800; defence of Porto Ferrajo, 1802; expedition to Walcheren, and siege of Flushing; Peninsular campaigns from January 1813, to May 1814, including the battle of Vittoria, passage of the Bidassoa and Nive, and siege of St. Sebastian. Campaign of 1815, including the battle of Waterloo. Medal and one clasp.

8 Major-General Munro served the Egyptian campaign of 1801, including the action of 21st March, and siege of Aboukir; expedition to Walcheren, and siege of Flushing; in action at New Orleans, 23rd Dec. 1814, 1st and 8th Jan. 1815. Medal for services in Egypt.

9 Sir Hew Ross served in the Peninsula and France from 9th June, 1809 to Feb. 1814, including the action of the Coa, battle of Busaco, actions of Pombal, Redinha (wounded in the shoulder), Casal Nova, Foz d'Arouce (wounded in the leg), and Sabugal; battle of Fuentes d'Onor, action of Aldea de Ponte, sieges of Ciudad Rodrigo and Badajoz, (dangerously wounded in the head); action at Castrajon, capture of forts at and battle of Salamanca, capture of Madrid and the Retiro, affairs of San Munoz and San Milan, battles of Vittoria, and the Pyrenees from 26th to 30th July, passage of the Bidassoa, Nivelle, and Nive; battle near Bayonne, 13 Dec. 1813. Served also the campaign of 1815, and was present at the battle of Waterloo. Cross and two clasps.

10 Major-General Birch served in Ireland during the Rebellion of 1798; expedition to Walcheren; in the Peninsula, at Cadiz, and Seville, under Lord Lynedoch and Sir George Cook in 1810, 11, 12, and 13.

11 Major-General Armstrong was at the capture of St. Lucia and Tobago in 1803; Surinam in 1804; and at St. Domingo in 1809.

12 Major-General Paterson served at the siege of Copenhagen in 1807; and at Walcheren in 1809.

13 Major-General Oliver served the Egyptian campaign of 1801, including the action on landing, 8th March, and battles of 13th and 21st March. Present at the siege of Flushing. Medal for services in Egypt.

14 Major-General Lacy served the campaign of 1799 in North Holland, and on the Eastern coast of Spain from November 1812 to the end of the war in 1814, including the battle of Castalla, and the two sieges of Tarragona.

15 Sir Robert Gardiner's services:—capture of Minorca in 1798; campaign in Portugal and Spain, including the battles of Roleia, Vimiera, and Corunna; expedition to Walcheren; Peninsular campaigns from early in 1810 to the end of the war in 1814, including the battle of Barrosa, capture of Badajoz, battle of Salamanca, siege of Burgos, affair of Morales, battles of Vittoria, Orthes, and Toulouse; campaign of 1815, including the battle of Waterloo. Cross and two clasps.

20 Colonel Campbell served the Egyptian campaign of 1801, including the actions of the 8th, 13th, and 21st March, capture of Rosetta, several affairs on the march to, and capture of Cairo, and afterwards at the capture of Alexandria. Medal for services in Egypt.

22 Colonel Turner was at the capture of the Cape of Good Hope in 1806. Served also in the Peninsula from Dec. 1813 to the end of the war, including the battles of Orthes and Toulouse, and the affairs of Vic Bigorre and Tarbes. Medal and one clasp for Orthes and Toulouse.

25 Colonel Cleaveland served the Kandian campaign in which the king and his territory were captured.

26 Colonel Wallace was on board the *Phœnix* Letter of Marque when she beat off a French Privateer near Barbadoes in Dec. 1800. Present at the siege of Flushing in 1809; and he commanded the Artillery at the attack of Sackets Harbour, United States, in 1813.

27 Colonel Richard Jones served in Holland in 1799, including the battles of Zuyp, Hoorn, Egmont, and Limmen. Present at the capture of Paris, and with the army of occupation until 2nd Dec. 1818.

28 Colonel John Edward Jones was employed afloat on board the bombs in 1801 and 02; commanded the artillery on board the *Volcano* bomb, and was present at the bombardment of Cronenburgh Castle, battle of Copenhagen, and bombardments of Boulogne under Lord Nelson.

29 Colonel Brandreth served at the blockade of Malta in 1800; at the bombardment of Havre-de-Grace, in 1803; the Corunna campaign; on the expedition to Walcheren, and siege of Flushing; Peninsular campaigns from Sept. 1812, to the end of the war in 1814, including the battles of the Pyrenees, Nivelle, and Toulouse. Medal and one clasp.

30 Colonel Hutchesson served in Holland in 1799; in the Peninsula and South of France from March 1813 to July 1814; Belgium and France from May 1815 to Nov. 1818.

31 Colonel Whinyates served in the expedition to the Helder and campaign in North Holland in 1799; expedition to Madeira in 1801, and to Copenhagen 1807; Peninsular campaigns from Feb. 1810 to July 1813, including the battles of Busaco and Albuhera; affairs at Usagre, Aldea de Ponte, and San Munos, attack and defeat of General Lalleman's cavalry at Ribera, and many other affairs. Served also the campaign of 1815, and was severely wounded in the left arm at Waterloo.

32 Colonel John Michell served the campaign in Holland in 1799; in the Peninsula and South of France from Aug. 1813 to May 1814, including siege of San Sebastian, passage of the Bidassoa, Nivelle, and Nive, battles of Orthes and Toulouse; in America from May 1814 to May 1815, including the attack of Washington, Baltimore, and New Orleans, and

other operations on the coast. Attached to the Prussian army in reducing the fortresses in the Netherlands. Medal and one clasp.

34 Colonel Hunt served in Ireland during the rebellion in 1798; at Cadiz from Feb. 1810 to Feb. 1812; in Belgium and France from 1814 to 1818, including the operations against the enemy in connection with the battle of Waterloo.

35 Colonel Cobbe served the campaign in the West Indies in 1801, under Lieut.-Gen. Sir Thos. Trigge.

36 Colonel Mercer served in South America in 1807 and 8. Also the campaign of 1815, including the battles of Quatre Bras and Waterloo.

37 Major-General W. G. Power served in Spain, Portugal, and France, from 14th Oct. 1808 to 4th June 1814, including the battle of Talavera, sieges of Ciudad Rodrigo (wounded), and Badajoz, capture of French works at Almaraz, reduction of forts at, and battle of Salamanca, siege of Burgos (wounded), siege of San Sebastian from 11th July to 8th Sept. 1813, passage of the Bidassoa, the Nive, and the Adour, and the investment of Bayonne. Col. Power led the reserve to the support of the assaulting party of Fort La Picurina during the last siege of Badajoz, and the Commandant surrendered to him personally.

38 Colonel Brown served at Walcheren in 1809. Also the campaign of 1815, including the battle of Waterloo and taking of Cambray.

39 Colonel Grant served in Hanover in 1805 under Lord Cathcart.

40 Colonel Scott served in the expedition to Walcheren, and was at the siege of Flushing.

41 Colonel Dyneley's services:—Campaign of 1805 in Italy under Sir James Craig; and that in Calabria in 1806 under Sir John Stuart, including the battle of Maida and siege of Scylla. Peninsular campaigns from July 1811, to November, 1813, including the siege of Ciudad Rodrigo (wounded in the head), siege of forts at Salamanca (wounded in the face), heights of St. Christovel, battle of Salamanca, defence of the Bridge of Simancas, affairs at Morales de Toro and San Munos, battles of Vittoria, and the Pyrenees. Campaign of 1815, including the battle of Waterloo. Taken prisoner at Malanahenda near Madrid, 11th Aug. 1812, when engaged with the rear-guard of Joseph Bonaparte's army; escaped from the enemy, and rejoined the army the 23rd of the same month.

43 Colonel Cator served the campaign of Walcheren and siege of Flushing. In the Peninsula and South of France, from the end of 1809 to the termination of the war in 1814, including the defence of Cadiz, lines at Torres Vedras and at Santarem, battle of Barrosa (wounded), affair at Osma, battle of Vittoria, affair at Tolosa, passage of the Bidassoa, and at the attack of Bidassoa by the French, battles of Nivelle and Nive, and four days' engagements in front of Bayonne.

44 Colonel Dansey was at the taking of Ischia in 1809, and Santa Maura in 1810. Served also the campaigns of 1812, 13, 14 and 15, in the Peninsula, France, and Flanders, including the last siege of Badajoz, battle of Salamanca, siege of Burgos (severely wounded), battle of Vittoria, siege of San Sebastian, battles of Nivelle, Nive, and Waterloo, (severely wounded), besides various minor actions and skirmishes.

45 Colonel Crawford served in a bomb vessel on the coast of France in 1804 and 5; in the lines in front of Sobral in Portugal, in 1809; with the army in Sicily in 1811, 12, and 13; at the capture of Genoa in 1814; and subsequently in the American War, including the battle of Bladensburg, and capture of Washington, and engagements before New Orleans, on 1st and 3rd Jan. 1815.

46 Colonel H. W. Gordon's services:—Expedition to Naples, Dec. 1805, and subsequent occupation of Sicily; battle of Maida, and attack and surrender of the Rock of Scylla, 1806.

47 Sir Wm. Colebrooke's services:—Campaigns of 1809 and 10, in India; expedition to Java in 1811, including the action of Weltyvreden, in batteries before Cornelis (until wounded in the groin 22d August), and the siege and capture of Jokjakarta. Expedition to Palembang, in Sumatra, 1813; campaign of 1817 and 18, in India, against the Pindarrees and Mahrattas; campaign of 1818 and 19 in Southern India. Present also at the sieges of Ras-el-Kyhma and Zaya, Arab fortresses.

48 Colonel W. D. Jones served with the Anglo-Russian expedition to Naples in 1805; present at the attack and capture of Reggio Castle, in Calabria, in 1806; expedition to Egypt in 1807; in charge of the division of Mortar-Boats forming part of the Anglo-Sicilian Flotilla prepared by Sir John Murray, and opposed in almost daily skirmishes with the batteries and Flotilla of Murât, King of Naples, in the Faro of Messina, the whole of the summer of 1810.

49 Colonel Dundas was at the siege of Flushing in 1809; at Cadiz in 1810 and 11; detached from Cadiz to Tarragona in 1811; wounded in right ankle at Ciudad Rodrigo, and most severely and dangerously at Badajoz,—left arm amputated, left thigh dislocated, and hip bone shattered.

50 Colonel Cruttenden was at the capture of Guadaloupe, in 1815; commanded the *Emma* troop ship when attacked by the *Nonsuch* American privateer, in the West Indies, which he beat off with great loss.

52 Colonel Wylde served in Holland in 1813 and 14, and commanded a battery before Antwerp and at the attack on Bergen-op-Zoom.

53 Lieut.-Colonel C. E. Gordon served in the Peninsula and France from May 1813 to the end of the war, including defence of Cadiz, siege of San Sebastian, passage of the

† N

Bidassoa, and Nivelle, actions in front of Bayonne (10th to 13th Dec.), battle of Orthes, occupation of Bourdeaux, subsequent affairs on the Dordogne, and investment of the fortress of Blaye.

54 Lieut.-Col. Walker was at the capture of Flushing in 1809. Served also part of the campaigns on the Frontier of Niagara in 1813 and 14.

55 Colonel Maclachlan served in Spain in 1813 and 14.

57 Major-General Macdonald was at the capture of the Cape of Good Hope in 1806, and proceeded from thence on the expedition to Buenos Ayres, where he was twice severely wounded and taken prisoner: served in the Peninsula and South of France, from June, 1809, to July, 1814, including the battles of the Coa and Busaco, affairs of Redinha, Pombal, Condeila, and Fox d'Arouce; battles of Fuentes d'Onor and Salamanca, affair of San Munos, battle of Vittoria, siege of San Sebastian, battles of the Pyrenees, affairs of the Gave d'Oleron and Aire, and battle of Toulouse. Served also the campaign of 1815, including the battle of Waterloo (severely wounded), and capture of Paris.

58 Lieut.-Colonel Jackson served in Canada from April, 1813, to Aug. 1815, including the actions of Chrystler's Farm, and Plattsburg: medal for the former.

59 Lieut. Col. Sabine served the campaign on the Niagara Frontier in 1814, and commanded the batteries at the siege of Fort Erie in August and September.

60 Lieut.-Col. Chalmer served on the expedition to Walcheren, and was present at the siege of Flushing.

62 Lieut.-Colonel Chesney was employed, from 1829 to 1832, in examining the principal parts of Western Asia; during which time, assisted only by a few Arabs, he descended the river Euphrates upon a Raft; and his reports to Government led to a Parliamentary vote to extend our commercial relations in that quarter, and open a communication with India through Arabia. His Majesty, through the Duke of Wellington, having conferred on him the rank of Colonel on a particular service, he sailed early in 1835 with a detachment of artillery, another of sappers, a proportion of seamen, and thirteen military and naval officers; with whose assistance Colonel Chesney accomplished the extraordinary achievement of transporting two iron steam vessels across Syria, and floating them in a perfect state on the Upper Euphrates, not very far from Aleppo. In the early part of the navigation thus commenced, a fearful hurricane carried the smaller vessel and twenty of her men to the bottom, Colonel Chesney and eight others being saved by swimming. The commander, however, persevered; and in the remaining vessel he not only completed the surveys of the river Euphrates, Tigris, and Kareen, but continued the undertaking until it was turned over in the following year to the East India Company. His late Majesty warmly approved of the intrepidity manifested in continuing the service after the calamitous loss of one-half of his force, and the brevet rank of Major was bestowed on him by the King, which was followed by that of Lieut.-Colonel by command of the Queen.

63 Lt.-Col. Bell's services:—Capture of the islands of St. Thomas and St. Croix in 1807; siege of fort Desaix, Martinique; capture of Les Saintes, near Guadaloupe, and bombardment and driving from the anchorage the French fleet in 1809; capture of Guadaloupe and adjacent islands in 1810. Served in the Peninsula and France from July 1813 to July 1814, including the passage of the Bidassoa, Nivelle, Nive, and four days' engagements near Bayonne; passage of the Adour, investment of Bayonne, affairs at Vic Bigorre, and Tarbes, passage of the Garonne, and subsequent operations to the battle of Toulouse where he was slightly wounded. Served also the campaign of 1815, including the battles of Quatre Bras and Waterloo, and capture of Paris.

64 Lieut.-Col. Louis served in the Peninsula and France from Jan. 1813 to June 1814, including the battle of Vittoria, siege of San Sebastian, passage of the Nivelle, and Nive, and investment of Bayonne. Served also the campaign of 1815, including the battle of Waterloo.

65 Lieut.-Colonel Grantham served at the defence of Cadiz.

66 Lieut.-Col. Brereton served in Spain, France, and the Netherlands, from December, 1809 to June, 1815, and was present at the defence of Cadiz and of Fort Matagorda (wounded), the Artillery of which last place he commanded. He served in the batteries at the siege of San Sebastian; was present in the battles of Barrosa (wounded), Vittoria, the Pyrenees, Orthes, Toulouse, Quatre Bras, and Waterloo (severely wounded), actions on the retreat from Burgos, at San Munos, near Salamanca, Helette, St. Palais, Sauveterre, Aire, and Tarbes. He commanded a Division, as second in command, of the expedition under Major-General D'Aguilar which assaulted and took the Forts of the Bocca Tigris in the Canton River, those of the Staked Barrier, and of the City of Canton, spiking 879 pieces of heavy ordnance.

67 Lt.-Col. England served the expedition to the Weser in 1805 and 6; to the Cape of Good Hope and South America in 1806 and 7; campaign of 1813 in the Peninsula, including the battle of Vittoria and siege of San Sebastian.

68 Lt.-Col. Whitty was present at the reduction of the Danish Islands in the West Indies in 1807; capture of Guadaloupe in 1810, and of Paris in 1815.

69 Lt.-Col. Sweeting served the whole of the Kandian campaign in Ceylon.

70 Lt.-Col. Wood served in the Peninsula and France, from Feb. 1813 to the end of the war, including the battle of Vittoria, blockade of Pampluna, battles of the Pyrenees, siege of San Sebastian, battle of the Nivelle, affairs of Vic Bigorre and Tarbes, battles of Orthes and Toulouse. Served the campaign in America, including the attack on Plattsburg.

71 Lt.-Col. Dalton served at Walcheren, and was present at the siege of Flushing.

72 Lt.-Col. Hardinge served in the Peninsula from Aug. 1812, to the end of the war in 1814, including the battle of Vittoria, siege of San Sebastian, battles of Orthes and Toulouse. Served also the campaign of 1815, and was present at Ligny, and Quatre Bras.

73 Lt.-Col. Lock served the campaign of 1808, in Portugal, and was present at the battles of Roleia and Vimiera.

75 Lt.-Colonel Gordon Higgins commanded the Royal Artillery in the Syrian campaign from August 1840 to the evacuation of that country in Dec. 1841, and was present at the bombardment and capture of Beyrout and of St. Jean d'Acre.

76 Lt.-Col. Strangways served the campaign of 1813 and 14 in Germany, including the battle of Goerde 16th Sept. and Leipsic 16th, 18th, and 19th Oct. 1813, for which the Swedish order of the sword was conferred on him, he having commanded the Rocket Troop after the death of Major Bogue killed in action. Served also the campaign of 1815, including the battles of Quatre Bras and Waterloo, at which last he was slightly wounded.

77 Lt.-Col. Eyre's services:—Expedition to Portugal and occupation of Lisbon, in 1808; advance upon Madrid and retreat to Corunna, in 1808-9; affair at Lugo and battle of Corunna. Eighteen years continued service in the West Indies, from Oct. 1810 to April, 1828.

79 Lt.-Colonel Anderson's services:—Siege and capture of Flushing, and the subsequent operations in 1809; Bombardment of Antwerp, also previous and subsequent operations, in 1813 and 1814; campaign of 1815, including the battle of Waterloo, and captures of Cambray and Paris.

80 Lt.-Colonel Armstrong served at Walcheren in 1809; and in Canada from May 1810 to July 1815, including the capture of a detachment on River Raisin, the cutting out of an enemy's vessel when in command of a gun-boat at Prescott, at Fort Erie during a cannonade of 17 hours; at the loss of Fort George, actions at Stoney Creek, and Black Rock, investment of Fort George, capture of Fort Niagara, Black Rock, and town of Buffalo, action at Streets Creek, and Chippawa, and at the siege of Fort Erie under an almost constant fire for about five weeks. Slightly wounded at Fort George, 27th May 1813.

81 Lt.-Colonel Evans served at Walcheren.

82 Lieut.-Colonel Colquhoun served in Spain from 1812 to the close of the war. He was employed under Lord John Hay during the late civil war in Spain; and he served also the Syrian campaign of 1840-41.

83 Lt.-Colonel Harrison served in the Peninsula from Jan. 1810 to Sept. 1814, and was present at Cadiz, Isla, and Tarifa.

85 Lt.-Colonel Wright served in Spain from 1st Jan. 1810, to the 31st Dec. 1812, including the defence of Cadiz, Fort Matagorda, and Tarifa.

86 Lt.-Colonel Bent's services:—Expedition to Walcheren, and bombardment of Flushing; Peninsular campaigns from Oct. 1810 to June 1813, including the first siege of Badajoz, battle of Albuhera, covering the second siege of Badajoz, capture of General Gerard's corps at Arroya de Molinos, covering the third siege of Badajoz, retreat from Madrid into Portugal, and the different affairs connected therewith. Severely wounded at San Munos.

87 Lt.-Colonel Furneaux served in the Peninsula from Oct. 1810 to April 1813, and was with the covering army at the siege of Badajoz.

88 Lt.-Col. Warde was present at the defence of Cadiz and at the battle of Waterloo.

89 Lt.-Col. Ingilby served in the Peninsula from July 1810 to Jan. 1813, including the sieges of Ciudad Rodrigo, Forts of Salamanca (wounded), and Burgos; and the battles of Busaco, Fuentes d'Onor, and Salamanca. Served also the campaign of 1815, and was present at the battle of Waterloo.

90 Lt.-Col. Cater served in the Peninsula from April 1810, to Jan. 1814, including the defence of Cadiz, battle of Barrosa, and siege of Tarragona. Served also the campaign of 1815, including the battle of Waterloo, and taking of Cambray and Paris.

91 Lieut.-Col. Pester was present at the defence of Cadiz, and at the battle of Barrosa, where he was severely wounded.

93 Lt.-Col. Story served in the Peninsula and France from Nov. 1812 to May 1814, including the siege of San Sebastian, and passages of the Bidassoa and Adour.

94 Lt.-Col. James served in the Peninsula and France, from October 1812 to April 1814, including the battles of Vittoria, the Pyrenees, Nivelle, and Orthes. Served subsequently in the American War.

94* Lt.-Col. Nevett served in Canada from 1812 to the end of the war.

95 Lt.-Col. Bloomfield served in the Peninsula and France, from March 1813 to June 1814, including the battle of Vittoria, siege of San Sebastian, crossing the Bidassoa, and battles of the Nivelle, Nive, Orthes, and Toulouse. Served also the campaign of 1815, including the battle of Waterloo.

96 Lt.-Col. Palliser served in the Peninsula and France, from November 1812 to May 1814, including the siege of San Sebastian, and battles of Vittoria, Orthes, and Toulouse. Served subsequently in the American War, including the battles of Bladensburg, and Baltimore, and operations before New Orleans.

97 Lt.-Col. Macbean served in the Peninsula and France, from July, 1812, to August, 1814, including the affair at Osma, battle of Vittoria, both sieges of San Sebastian and capture of it; passage of the Nivelle, 10th November, and actions of the Nive, 9th, 10th,

11th, and 12th December, 1813. Served also the campaign of 1815, including the capture of Paris. Served afterwards with the army of occupation until 1818.

97* Lt.-Col. J. A. Wilson served the campaign of 1815, including the battle of Waterloo and capture of Paris.

98 Lt.-Col. Tomkyns served the campaign of 1814 in Canada, including the actions near Fort George, and Lundy's Lane; blockade, attack, and final assault of Fort Erie, and attack by the American army on the British lines on the Chippawa River.

99 Lt.-Col. Williams was engaged in the actions before New Orleans, and at the capture of Fort Bowyer. Served also the campaign of 1815, and was present at the capture of Paris.

100 Lt.-Col. R. G. B. Wilson served in Holland, Belgium, and France, from December 1813 to January 1816, including the battles of Quatre Bras and Waterloo.

101 Major Cuppage served in the Peninsula and France, from February to August 1814, and was present at the repulse of the sortie from Bayonne. Served also the campaign of 1815, including the battle of Waterloo.

102 Major Burnaby served the campaign of 1815, including the battle of Waterloo.

103 Major Griffin served before Genoa in 1814.

104 Major Hennis served the campaign of 1815, and was present at the battle of Waterloo.

106 Capt. Freese served on the China Expedition, and was slightly wounded at Chin Kiang Foo.

108 Capt. Warburton served with the Royal Artillery on the north coast of Spain from Feb. 1837 to Oct. 1838, and was wounded on the 15th March 1837, near Hernani.

109 Major Wilmot volunteered for active service in New Zealand (being on the staff in Van Dieman's Land) in Jan. 1845, and commanded the Artillery at the attack of Kawiti's Pah at Ohiawai on the 1st July, and at the destruction of the same on the 11th July; also at the destruction of Arratua's Pah on the 16th July. He commanded the Artillery throughout the whole of the operations, and in the various affairs which took place before Ruapekapeka in Dec. 1845, and Jan. 1846, including the capture of that Stockade. He was also engaged in the occupation of the valley of Hutt in April 1846.

110 Major Young served on the north coast of Spain from January 1838 to August 1840, and was present in all the affairs and operations that took place from Jan. 1838 to the conclusion of the war in front of San Sebastian; and also at the camp of Paz y Fueros on the Bidassoa in Dec. 1838 and Jan. 1839. Also in the operations on the Yang-tse-Kiang in China, including the storm and capture of Chin Kiang Foo: he was also present at the demonstration before Nankin.

112 Major the Honourable R. C. H. Spencer served throughout the whole of the operations in China, and was present at the destruction of the batteries of Amoy, in H. M. S. *Blonde*, in 1840; at the capture of the forts of the Bocca Tigris, and subsequent operations in the Canton River; at the storm and capture of the heights of Canton; attack and captures of Amoy, Chusan (second operation), Chinhae, Chapoo, Woosung, Shanghae, and Chin Kiang Foo, and demonstration before Nankin.

114 Lieut. John Turner was present at the capture of Port Natal on the 26th June 1842.

116 Lieut. Anderson served in the operations in the Yiang-tse-Kiang in China, including the storm and capture of Chin Kiang Foo. He was also present at the demonstration before Nankin.

117 Lieut. Dyneley commanded the Royal Artillery in the action with and defeat of the rebel Boers at Bloem Plaats (South Africa) 29th Aug. 1848.

120 Quarter-Master Porter served on the expedition to Naples in 1805. In 1806 he was at the battle of Maida, and at the siege and reduction of Scylla in Calabria. He landed in Egypt, 17th March, 1807, and was present at the capture of Alexandria, and at the attack on Rosetta. In 1809 he was at the capture of Ischia and Procida; and in 1814 at the sieges and captures of Spezia, Genoa, and Savona. He served afterwards in America and was present at the battle of Bladensburg, capture of Washington, battle of Baltimore, operations before New Orleans, and capture of Fort Bowyer: he was wounded in the head before New Orleans on the 1st Jan. 1815.

121 Quarter-Master Perkin's services:—Campaign in Italy in 1805; occupation of Sicily in 1806 and 1807; battle of Maida; campaigns of 1813 and 1814 in the Peninsula, including the battle of Vittoria, siege of San Sebastian, passage of the Bidassoa, battles of the Nivelle and the Nive, passage of the Adour, operations against Bayonne, and repulse of the sortie. Expedition to America in 1814, including the attack on New Orleans in Dec. 1814, and the siege and capture of Fort Bowyer. Capture of Paris in 1815.

122 Quartermaster Powers served on the expedition to Denmark in 1807, and was present at the siege of Copenhagen and action at Kioge. Went with the army under Sir John Moore to Gottenburg, and afterwards to Portugal and Spain,—present on the retreat to and at the battle of Corunna. Served afterwards on the Walcheren expedition, and was several times engaged against the French Flotilla, in South Beveland. Accompanied the army under the Duke of Wellington to the Continent in 1815, and returned with the army of occupation.

123 Mr. Percivall served in the East Indies with the 11th Lt. Dragoons, and was present at the siege and capture of Bhurtpore in 1825-6.

Corps of Royal Engineers.

The Royal Arms and Supporters, with a Cannon, and the Motto, "*Ubique*" over the gun, and "*Quo Fas et Gloria ducunt*" below it.

Colonel-in-Chief.—P GM *Field Marshal The Marquis of* Anglesey, KG. GCB. GCH. Master-General of the Ordnance.

Years' Serv. Full Pay.	Years' Serv. Half Pay.	Colonels Commandant.	Second Lieut.	First Lieut.	Captain.	Brevet-Major.	Brevet Lt.-Col.	Reg.-Lt. Col.	Brevet-Col.	Regtl.-Colonel.	Colonel Comm.	Major-General.	Lieut.-General.
62	0	*Sir* Augustus De Butts, KCH.[1]	22 Aug. 87	21 Nov. 92	3 Mar. 97	....	....	1 July 06	4 June 14	30 Dec. 14	20 Mar. 27	19 July 21	10 Jan. 37
61	0	Henry Evatt[2]	11 July 88	16 Jan. 93	29 Aug. 98	....	....	24 June 09	....	11 Nov. 16	6 Apr. 32	27 May 25	28 June 38
56	0	Elias Walker Durnford[3]	24 Apr. 93	5 Feb. 96	11 Feb. 01	4 June 13	....	21 July 13	....	23 Mar. 25	29 Jan. 46	10 Jan. 37	9 Nov. 46
56	0	*Sir* George Whitmore, KCH.	18 Sept. 93	5 Feb. 96	28 Feb. 01	4 June 13	....	do	....	23 Mar. 25	1 Apr. 46	do	do
56	0	P Fred. Rennell Thackeray, CB.[4]	do	18 June 96	18 Apr. 01	19 May 10	....	do	....	2 June 25	29 Apr. 46	do	do
56	0	P John Francis Birch, CB.[5]	do	20 Nov. 96	do	6 Mar. 11	....	do	....	29 July 25	19 Oct. 47	do	do
		Removed from the Corps, having the Rank of *Major-General.*											
56	0	P *Sir* S. Rem. Chapman, CB. KCH.[6]	do	do	do	30 Sept. 10	26 Apr. 12	do	....	do		do	do
55	0	Gustavus Nicolls[7]	6 Nov. 94	3 Mar. 97	30 Mar. 02	4 June 13	....	1 Sept. 13	....	do		do	do
53	0	George Wright[8]	15 Aug. 96	29 Aug. 98	3 Apr. 04	4 June 14	....	20 Dec. 14	....	do		do	do
51	0	P *Sir* John Fox Burgoyne, KCB.[10] *Inspect.-Gen. of Fortifications*	29 Aug. 98	1 July 00	1 Mar. 05	6 Feb. 12	27 Apr. 12	do	22 July 30	10 Jan. 37		28 June 38	
52	0	P *Sir* Charles Wm. Pasley, KCB.[11]	1 Dec. 97	28 Aug. 99	1 Mar. 05	5 Feb. 12	27 May 13	20 Dec. 14	do	12 Nov. 31		23 Nov. 41	
47	0	P *Sir* Cha. Felix Smith, KCB.[17]	1 Oct. 02	9 Oct. 02	18 Nov. 07	31 Dec. 11	21 Sept. 13	29 July 25	do	10 Jan. 37		do	
51	0	P Henry Goldfinch, CB.[12]	1 Mar. 98	11 June 00	1 Mar. 05	17 Dec. 12	21 Sept. 13	20 Dec. 14	do	do		do	
51	0	Jas. Robertson Arnold, KH.[13]	do	do	do	....	....	do	do	do		do	
48	0	P Cha. Grene Ellicombe, CB.[15]	....	1 July 01	1 July 06	27 Apr. 12	21 Sept. 13	23 Mar. 25	do	do		do	
49	1 5/12	George Cardew	20 Dec. 98	18 Apr. 01	do	....	....	26 Nov. 16	....	do		9 Nov. 46	
48	0	Edward Fanshawe, CB.[16]	....	1 July 01	1 July 06	12 Aug. 19	....	23 Mar. 25	....	do		do	
48	0	Thomas Colby	21 Dec. 01	6 Aug. 02	1 July 07	19 July 21	....	29 July 25	....	do		do	
		Colonels.											
47	0	P George Judd Harding, CB.[18]	1 Oct. 02	1 Dec. 02	18 Nov. 07	do	....	do	28 June 38	23 Nov. 41			
46	0	John Ross Wright[19]	1 Mar. 03	1 April 03	do	19 July 21	....	do	do	do			
46	0	P Griffith George Lewis, CB.[20]	15 Mar. 03	2 July 03	do	21 Sept. 13	....	do	do	do			
45	0	P Wm. C. Elphinst. Holloway, CB.[21]	1 Jan. 04	1 Mar. 05	24 June 09	21 June 17	....	26 Feb. 28	....	do			
45	0	P Henry William Vavasour[22]	1 Feb. 04	do	24 June 09	....	....	28 Jan. 29	....	22 Apr. 45			
45	0	George Graydon, KH.[23]	1 June 04	1 Mar. 05	2 Dec. 09	do	....	22 May 29	....	1 Apr. 46			
45	0	P Robert Thomson[24]	1 Nov.	do	10 July 10	do	....	26 Dec.	....	do			
43	7/12	*Sir* John Mark Fred. Smith, KH.[25]	1 Dec. 05	1 Mar. 06	1 May 11	....	....	16 Mar. 30	....	9 Nov. 46			
41	2 3/12	P Rice Jones, KH.[26]	1 Feb. 06	1 July	do	do	....	8 June	....	do			
41	2 4/12	Thomas Moody[27]	1 April	1 July	do	23 May 16	....	2 Dec.	....	do			
38	5 6/12	GH John Oldfield, KH.[28]	2 do	do	do	22 July 30	....	12 Nov. 31	23 Nov. 41	do			
37	5 10/12	Matthew Charles Dixon[29]	2 do	do	do	do	....	25 June 35	....	do			

Years' Serv. Full Pay.	Half Pay.	Lieutenant-Colonels.	Second Lieut.	First Lieut.	Captain.	Brevet-Major.	Brevet-Lieut. Col.	Regiment. Lieut. Col.	Brevet-Colonel.
35	7 4/12	Patrick Doul Calder [30]	1 Aug. 06	1 Dec. 06	13 May 11	22 July 30	....	25 June 35	9 Nov. 46
43	0	William Henry Slade [31]	1 Nov.	1 May 07	4 March 12	do	....	10 Jan. 37	
43	0	William Burton Tylden [32]	19 Nov.	do	15 April	23 June 14	....	do	
42	0	Frederick English [33]	8 Sept. 07	1 April	21 July 13	....	....	do	
42	0	Thomas Blanshard, CB. [34]	28 ditto	do	do	29 Sept. 14	....	do	
41	0	Alexander Brown [35]	1 Feb. 08	1 Aug.	do	....	....	do	
41	0	Anthony Emmett [36]	16 Feb. 08	24 June 09	do	5 July 21	....	do	
41	0	William Cuthbert Ward [37]	10 May	do	do	10 Jan. 37	....	9 Dec.	
41	0	James Gordon [38]	11 July	do	1 Sept.	do	....	31 March 38	
41	0	*Harry David Jones* [40]	17 Sept.	do	12 Nov.	do	....	7 Sept. 40	
40	0	Philip Barry [44]	10 Feb. 09	1 March 10	1 Oct. 14	do	....	23 Nov. 41	
35	5 1/12	*William Reid*, CB. [45]	do	23 April	20 Dec.	20 March 17	10 Jan. 37	do	
34	6 2/12	William Redman Ord [46]	25 April	29 May	do	10 Jan. 37	....	18 Mar. 45	
32	8	Henry John Savage [47]	30 Sept.	1 May 11	1 Dec. 15	do	....	22 May	
32	8	Marcus Antonius Waters [48]	do	do	11 Nov. 16	do	....	12 July	
31	7 11/12	Pennel Cole	1 Feb. 10	do	7 Feb. 17	do	....	1 Apr. 46	
35	4	Edward Matson, [49] *Assistant Adjutant General*	7 May	do	9 Jan. 21	do	....	do	
36	3 4/12	James Conway Victor [50]	1 June	do	19 June	do	....	do	
39	1/12	Thomas Howard Fenwick	21 July 10	do	2 Dec. 24	28 June 38	....	do	
39	1/12	Lewis Alexander Hall	do	do	12 Jan. 25	do	....	do	
38	0	Patrick Yule [53]	1 May 11	11 do	23 March	do	....	do	
38	0	George Phillpotts [54]	1 May 11	7 June 11	23 Mar. 25	do	29 Mar. 39	20 Apr.	
38	0	Daniel Bolton [57]	do	1 July 12	7 June	do	....	9 Nov. 46	
38	0	Fred. William Whinyates [58]	do	do	29 July	do	....	do	
38	0	Alex. Watt Robe [59]	do	do	do	do	....	do	
38	0	*Ralph Carr Alderson* [60]	do	do	do	do	10 Nov. 40	26 Jan. 47	
37	0	Charles Wright [61]	1 July 12	1 Mar. 13	29 July 25	do	....	4 Feb.	
37	0	Francis Ringler Thomson [62]	do	21 July	do	do	....	1 Mar.	
37	0	*Hale Young Wortham* [63]	do	do	24 Sept.	28 June 38	....	16 Apr.	
37	0	*Joshua Jebb*, CB. [64]	do	do	26 Feb. 28	23 Nov. 41	....	do	
36	0	George Tait	20 Mar. 13	do	16 Feb. 30	9 Nov. 46	....	do	
36	0	Charles Ogle Streatfield	20 Mar. 13	21 July 13	21 June	do	....	1 Sept. 47	
36	0	Joseph Ellison Portlock [65]	20 July	15 Dec.	22 June	do	....	13 Dec.	
36	0	Charles Carson Alexander	do	do	7 Oct. 31	do	....	2 Feb. 48	
36	0	Henry Sandham	do	do	1 May 34	do	....	9 Aug.	

Years' Serv. Full Pay.	Half Pay.	Captains.	Second Lieut.	First Lieut.	Captain.	Brevet-Major.
35	0	Tho. Coryndon Luxmore	1 Jan. 14	1 Aug. 14	6 Nov. 34	9 Nov. 46
35	0	William Faris	do	do	1 Mar. 35	do
35	6/12	Fred. Henry Baddeley	do	do	25 June	do
32	2 11/12	*Geo. Gust. Cha. W. Du Plat*, KH. *Lieutenant-Colonel*, 10 *Nov.* 1840.	1 Aug.	1 July 15	8 Feb. 36	29 Mar. 39
30	4 11/12	Thomas Budgen	do	do	18 May	9 Nov. 46
31	4	Vincent Joseph Biscoe	do	do	11 June	do
29	5 10/12	Henry Powell Wulff	do	do	23 Sept.	do
27	7 2/12	*Montgomery Williams*	24 Mar. 15	1 May 16	10 Jan. 37	
27	7 1/12	John Hawkshaw	do	do	do	
30	4 7/12	Thomas Hore	do	7 Feb. 17	do	
29	5	Thomas Foster	1 Sept.	7 Sept. 19	do	29 Mar. 39
31	2 11/12	*John Isaac Hope*	do	1 July	do	
32	1 6/12	Wm. Cameron Forbes	do	25 Mar. 23	do	
33	7/12	Richard John Stotherd	do	13 Mar. 24	do	
34	0	Alexander Gordon[66]	do	2 Dec.	do	
34	0	Cowper Rose	do	12 Jan. 25	do	
34	0	Wm. Biddlecomb Marlow[67]	1 Sept.	23 Mar.	28 Mar.	7 July 46
33	0	*Robert Kearsley Dawson*	1 Mar. 16	do	18 Aug.	
33	0	Henry Tucker	do	9 April	25 Dec.	
33	0	Benjamin Spicer Stehelin	1 Aug.	2 June	31 Mar. 38	
33	0	Charles Oldershaw	do	29 July	13 June	
33	0	George St. Vincent Whitmore,	do	do	24 Jan. 39	
33	0	Henry Servaute	do	do	27 May	
33	0	Henry Owen Crawley	do	do	17 Aug.	
33	0	John Twiss	do	do	29 Sept.	
31	2	John Walpole,[68] *Major of Brigade to the Corps of R. Sappers and Miners*	do	24 Sept.	28 Nov.	15 Sept. 48
28	1 1/12	*Thomas Aiskew Larcom*	1 June 20	9 Feb. 26	19 Mar. 40	
26	11/12	Edward Vicars	28 Mar. 22	8 April	28 July	10 Nov. 40
25	0	St. Aubyn Molesworth	28 Aug. 24	19 Oct.	do	
24	0	*Edward Frome*	11 May 25	6 Dec.	7 Sept.	
24	0	Richard Howorth	6 Aug.	11 April 27	do	
24	0	Charles C. Wilkinson	do	26 Feb. 28	19 Feb. 41	
24	0	William Turnbull Renwick	do	7 Nov.	9 Mar.	
24	0	Thomas Hosmer Rimington	do	28 Jan. 29	1 Apr.	
24	0	*William E. Delves, Broughton*	do	24 Feb.	do	
23	0	Richard J. Nelson	7 Jan. 26	22 May	1 Sept.	
23	0	*George Burgmann*	15 March	27 Oct.	30 Sept.	
23	0	Edward Aldrich[69]	do	15 Feb.	do	31 Dec. 41
23	0	John Chaytor	do	16 Feb.	23 Nov.	
23	0	*Sir* William Thomas Denison, *Lt. Governor of Van Dieman's Land.*	do	22 June	do	
23	0	John Williams	22 Sept.	2 Dec.	do	
23	0	Edward William Durnford	do	5 Feb. 31	do	
23	0	Edward Thomas Lloyd	do	24 June	23 Feb. 42	
23	0	*Henry James*	do	22 July	28 June	
23	0	William Robinson	do	6 Oct.	24 Oct.	19 Feb. 47
23	0	*Thomas Rawlings Mould*	do	7 do	16 Mar. 43	
23	0	*George Wynne*	do	12 Nov.	4 Apr.	
23	0	James Lynn	do	13 do	1 May	28 July 43
22	0	William Stace	4 May 27	18 Mar. 32	27 May	
22	0	*Henry Drury Harness*	24 do	20 Sept.	30 June	
22	0	Edmund Twiss Ford	30 Aug.	5 Feb. 33	15 Nov.	
21	0	William Yolland	12 April 28	4 Sept.	19 Dec.	
20	0	Charles Erskine Ford	29 April 29	1 May 34	10 Jan. 44	
19	0	Richard Clement Moody	5 Nov. 30	25 June 35	6 Mar.	
18	0	Frederick Augustus Yorke	5 Oct. 31	12 Aug.	20 June	
18	0	Charles Francis Skyring[70]	do	19 Aug.	16 Aug.	
17	0	George Rowan Hutchinson	29 May 32	15 Sept.	30 Oct.	
17	0	Robert Gorges Hamilton	do	5 Dec.	18 Dec.	
17	0	Henry Williamson Lugard	do	6 Dec.	20 Dec.	
17	0	William Charles Hadden	do	8 Feb. 36	26 Dec.	

Years' Serv. Full Pay.	Years' Serv. Half Pay.	SECOND CAPTAINS.	2ND LIEUT.	1ST LIEUT.	CAPTAIN.
17	0	*Roger Stuart Beatson*	29 May 32	13 May 36	18 Mar. 45
17	0	Sampson Freeth	26 Sept.	do	do
16	0	John Graham M'Kerlie	27 Feb. 33	23 Sept.	1 April
15	0	Julian Fred. A. Symonds,[70] *Major* 22 May 46	1 Aug.	24 do	22 April
16	0	William George Hamley	5 Aug.	26 Sept.	1 May
16	0	Andrew Beatty	do	6 Nov.	22 May
16	0	John W. Gordon	1 Dec.	10 Jan. 37	12 July
16	0	Marcus Dill	do	do	1 Apr. 46
16	0	Philip J. Bainbrigge	do	do	do
16	0	Archibald P. G. Ross	do	do	do
15	0	John Claridge Burmester, *Major*, 2 Oct. 46	9 June 34	do	do
15	0	Edmund Ogle	do	do	do
15	0	Conolly M'Causland	do	do	do
15	0	John Cameron	12 Dec.	do	do
15	0	John S. Hawkins	do	do	do
15	0	James H. Freeth	do	do	do
15	0	Charles Duesbery Robertson	19 Dec.	31 Jan.	do
15	0	Charles Fanshawe, *Adjutant to the Corps of Royal Sappers and Miners.*	do	23 Feb.	do
14	0	Frederick E. Chapman	18 June 35	28 March	do
14	0	Thomas Fenwick	do	8 May	do
14	0	*Theodosius Webb*	do	18 Aug.	do
13	0	Gother Frederick Mann	18 June 36	31 March 38	do
13	0	Spencer Westmacott	do	25 May	do
13	0	Charles Acton Broke	do	13 June	do
13	0	Charles Edward Stanley	13 Dec.	14 June	do
12	0	William Collier Menzies	5 May 37	1 Aug.	do
12	0	*Robert Michael Laffan*	do	1 Apr. 39	1 May
12	0	Arthur Henry Freeling	14 Dec.	27 May	27 July
12	0	Harry St. George Ord	do	do	29 Oct.
12	0	David William Tylee	do	20 Sept.	9 Nov.
12	0	Hampden Clement Blamire Moody	do	22 Sept.	do
12	0	*John Linton Arabin Simmons*	do	15 Oct.	do
12	0	George Archibald Leach	do	28 Nov.	do
12	0	Richard Tylden	do	19 Mar. 40	do
12	0	Philip John Stapleton Barry	do	3 Apr.	17 Nov.
12	0	Henry Arthur White	do	28 July	26 Jan. 47
12	0	Paul Bernard Whittingham	do	28 July	4 Feb.
12	0	James William Gosset	do	7 Sept.	1 March
11	0	George Clement Baillie	16 June 38	19 Feb. 41	22 Mar.
11	0	Thomas Bernard Collinson	do	9 Mar.	16 Apr.
11	0	George Bent	do	1 Apr.	16 Apr.
11	0	Edmund Yeamans Walcott Henderson	do	do	22 Apr.
11	0	George Sorell	do	1 Sept.	19 Aug.
10	0	Augustus Frederick Hippolito Dacosta	19 March 39	14 Sept.	1 Sept.
10	0	John Bayly	do	16 Sept.	3 Sept.
10	0	Henry Charles Cunliffe Owen [71]	do	30 Sept.	28 Oct.
10	0	Wm. Francis Drummond Jervois[72]	do	8 Oct.	13 Dec.
10	0	Thomas Lionel John Gallwey	do	23 Nov.	2 Feb. 48
10	0	Charles Stuart Miller	do	do	12 Feb.
10	0	Anthony David Craigie	do	do	9 April
10	0	Richard Burnaby	do	7 Dec.	14 April
		FIRST LIEUTENANTS.			
10	0	Albert O'Donnel Grattan	do	23 Feb. 42	
10	0	Mervin Vavasour	do	do	
10	0	James Swayne Baker	do	23 Feb.	
10	0	*Hon.* Hussey Fane Keane	do	28 June	
10	0	William Cowper	20 Dec.	24 Oct.	
10	0	Charles John Gibb[73]	do	16 Mar. 43	
10	0	Charles Gordon Gray	20 Dec.	1 May	
9	0	William Driscoll Gossett	20 June 40	27 May	
9	0	Charles Sim	20 June	11 Sept.	
9	0	Fairfax Charles Hassard	do	23 Sept.	
9	0	*Douglas Galton*	18 Dec.	1 Oct.	
9	0	Henry William Barlow	do	15 Nov.	
9	0	Henry Young Darracott Scott	do	19 Dec.	
9	0	George Ross	do	10 Jan. 44	
9	0	William Mason Inglis	do	6 Mar.	

Years' Serv. Full Pay.	Half Pay.	First Lieutenants.	2nd Lieut.	1st Lieut.
9	0	James Robert Mann	18 Dec. 40	20 June 44
8	0	John Williamson Lovell	19 June 41	16 Aug.
8	0	Millington Henry Synge	do	30 Oct.
8	0	Edward Wolstenholme Ward	do	18 Dec.
8	0	William Howard Jesse	do	20 Dec.
7	0	Eustace Fane Bourchier	1 Jan. 42	26 Dec.
7	0	Henry Grain	do	22 Feb. 45
7	0	John Marshall Grant	do	18 Mar.
7	0	James Frankfort Manners Browne	do	1 April
7	0	FitzRoy Molyneux Henry Somerset	do	22 April
7	0	Horace William Montague	do	1 May
7	0	Valentine Thomas Mairis	do	22 May
7	0	Frederick William King	18 June	12 July
7	0	Francis Fowke	18 June	1 April 46
7	0	Charles Richard Binney	do	do
6	0	Frederick Henry Rich	11 Jan. 43	do
6	0	Francis Rawdon Chesney	do	do
6	0	Tho. Andrew Lumsden Murray	do	do
6	0	Herbert Newton Penrice	17 June	do
6	0	Wm. Lawtie Morrison	do	do
6	0	Anthony Charles Cooke	do	do
6	0	Thomas Inglis	do	do
6	0	Ben Hay Martindale	do	do
6	0	Charles Scrope Hutchinson	20 Dec.	do
6	0	Henry Wray	do	do
6	0	Charles Pasley	do	do
6	0	John Stokes	do	do
5	0	Andrew Clarke	19 June 44	do
5	0	Francis Du Cane	do	do
5	0	Robert Dundas Kerr	do	do
5	0	John Yerbury Moggridge	do	do
5	0	Francis Koe	do	do
5	0	John Gordon Jervis	19 Dec.	do
5	0	Henry Whatley Tyler	do	do
5	0	John Cromie Blackwood De Butts	do	do
5	0	Walter Samuel Stace	do	do
5	0	Gwavas Speedwell Tilly	do	do
5	0	Edward Stanton	do	do
4	0	Charles Cornwallis Chesney	18 June 45	do
4	0	Edward Charles De Molcyns	do	do
4	0	Louis John Amadée Armit	do	do
4	0	Charles Brisbane Ewart	do	do
4	0	Charles B. P. N. H. Nugent	18 Dec.	do
4	0	Edward Belfield	do	do
4	0	*Hon.* George Wrottesley	do	do
4	0	St. Andrew St. John	do	do
4	0	Edward C. A. Gordon	do	do
4	0	Whitworth Porter	do	do
4	0	John J. Wilson	do	do
4	0	George F. Dawson	do	do
4	0	Gustavus St. John Crofton	do	do
4	0	Henry Phillpotts	do	20 April
3	0	Joshua Henry Smith	1 May 46	1 May
3	0	Anthony Reynolds Vyvyan Crease	do	27 July
3	0	Frederic Charles Belson	do	5 Oct.
3	0	Charles Thomas Hutchinson	do	15 Oct.
3	0	Edward Metcalfe Grain	do	29 Oct.
3	0	Arthur Payne Smith	do	9 Nov.
3	0	Augattus Payne Lockner	do	do
3	0	Philip Ravenhill	do	do
3	0	Herbert Taylor Siborne	6 Aug.	do
3	0	Charles Style Akers	do	do
3	0	Berdoe Amherst Wilkinson	do	17 Nov.
3	0	Lothian Nicholson	do	26 Jan. 47
3	0	George Edmond Lushington Walker	do	4 Feb.
3	0	James Thomas Burke	do	20 Feb.
3	0	Francis Edward Cox	do	20 Feb.
3	0	Sidney Baynton Farrell	do	1 March
3	0	James Liddell	17 Dec.	29 March

Years' Serv. Full Pay.	Half Pay.	First Lieutenants.	2nd Lieut.	1st Lieut.
3	0	Charles William Barry	17 Dec. 46	16 Apr. 47
3	0	Charles Herbert Sedley	do	16 Apr.
3	0	William Francis Lambert	do	22 Apr.
3	0	Richard Warren	do	14 July
3	0	Hugh Williams	do	19 Aug.
3	0	*Hon.* John James Bury	do	1 Sept.
3	0	Alexander Mackenzie	do	3 Sept.
2	0	Richard Hugh Stotherd	2 May 47	28 Oct.
2	0	William Hatt Noble	do	13 Dec.
2	0	Henry Schaw	do	2 Feb. 48
2	0	Edward Nicholas Heygate	do	12 Feb.
2	0	George Hamilton Gordon	do	9 April
2	0	Augustus Jonathan Clerke	do	14 April
		Second Lieutenants.		
2	0	Charles Augustus Rice	do	
2	0	Charles John Fowler	do	
2	0	Alexander Ross Clarke	1 Oct.	
2	0	Edward Bainbrigge	do	
2	0	James Murray	do	
2	0	George Ranken	do	
2	0	Francis Horatio De Vere	do	
2	0	Henry Raymond Pelly	do	
2	0	Robert Mann Parsons	do	
2	0	Frederick Brine	do	
2	0	Arthur A'Court Fisher	do	
2	0	George Montague Stopford	do	
2	0	Edward Bridge	do	
2	0	Henry Reynolds Luard	do	
2	0	Montagu Stopford Whitmore	do	
2	0	Howard Craufurd Elphinstone	18 Dec.	
2	0	Charles Edward Cumberland	do	
2	0	Alexander Stephen Creyke	do	
2	0	William Coles Phillpotts	do	
2	0	Henry Sandeman	do	
2	0	Amelius Beauclerck Fyers	do	
2	0	Joseph Wallis O'Bryen Hoare	do	
2	0	Lionel Charles Barber	do	
2	0	James Grantham	do	
2	0	Glastonbury Neville	do	
2	0	James P. Cox	do	
2	0	Henry G. Savage	do	
2	0	George R. Lempriere	do	
1	0	Wilbraham Oates Lennox	27 June 48	
1	0	Arthur Leahy	do	
1	0	Edward Loftus Bland	do	
1	0	Charles Edward Stuart Baynes	do	
1	0	Charles Le Gallais	do	
1	0	Anthony William Durnford	do	
1	0	Donald Augustus Frazer	do	
1	0	Harry George Teesdale	do	
1	0	Thomas Molyneux Graves	do	
1	0	William Christian Anderson	do	

Assistant Adjutant General.—ℬ Lieut.-Colonel E. Matson, 15 June 46.
Scarlet.—*Facings*, Blue Velvet.
N.B. The officers in Italics are holding civil employment.

Corps of Royal Sappers and Miners.

(Officered by the Corps of Royal Engineers.)

Major of Brigade.—Major John Walpole, 1 June 48.
Adjutant.—Captain Charles Fanshawe, 26 Jan. 47.
Quarter-Master.—Jenkin Jones, 14 Jan. 48.

Establishment at Chatham for instructing the Corps in Military Field Works.

Director.—Colonel *Sir* J. M. Frederick Smith, KH.

War Services of the Officers of the Royal Engineers.

1 Sir Aug. De Butts was at the sieges of Toulon, Bastia, and Calvi, and was favourably mentioned by Lord Hood in his despatches on the surrender of Bastia.

2 Lieut.-Gen. Evatt was present at the attack of Fort Fleur d'Epée, Guadaloupe, June, 1794, and at the defence of Fort Matilda, from 10th Oct. to 10th Dec. following. In 1795 at Dominica at the attack and capture of the French force landed for the reduction of the island. In 1797 served at the attack of the island of Porto Rico. Wounded at the Helder in 1799.

3 Lieut.-General Durnford was present at the siege of Fort Bourbon, and capture of Martinique, St. Lucia, and Guadaloupe, in 1794.

4 Lieut.-General Thackeray was at the capture of Surinam in 1799; St. Martin's, and St. Bartholomew's, in 1801; directed the siege of Scylla Castle, in 1806; and that of the Fortress of Santa Maura in 1809. Served with the army in Spain, in 1812; at the battle of Castalla, and siege of Tarragona in 1813, and remained with the army until 1814.

5 Lieut.-General Birch served in Flanders, and Holland, in 1793, 94, and 95; the Egyptian campaign of 1801; taking of Copenhagen under Lord Cathcart; in the north of Spain, in 1808; at the taking of Flushing, in 1809; defence of Cadiz, in 1810 and 11. Medal for Barrosa. Shot through the thigh near Valmesada, 7 Nov. 1808.

6 Sir Stephen R. Chapman served in Holland, in 1799; at Copenhagen, in 1807; and in the Peninsula from March 1809 to Feb. 1811.

7 Lieut.-General Nicolls went out with a reinforcement of several Regts. to Gibraltar on the war breaking out with Spain in 1796, and remained blockaded in that fortress two and a half years; proceeded from thence to the West Indies in 1799. Went as Commanding Engineer with Lt.-Gen. Sir George Prevost to Nova Scotia in 1808, under expectations of hostilities with America. Remained there until the war broke out in 1812, and was actively employed in the protection of the frontiers of Nova Scotia and New Brunswick, and was present at the capture of Moose Island, Castine and Belfast. Commanding Engineer in Canada part of 1814 and 15.

8 Lieut.-General Wright served in the West Indies during the war with France, from 1800 to 1805 inclusive, including the capture of the islands of St. Lucia and Tobago from the French. Served in North America, Canada, Nova Scotia, and New Brunswick during the whole of the late war with the United States, under Sir George Prevost and Sir John Sherbrooke; and with the latter officer served as Deputy Quarter Master General of the Forces in the provinces of Nova Scotia and New Brunswick. Served in the island of Ceylon, having volunteered his services in that island during the rebellion of the Kandian provinces; and, on his return to England, visited the Court of Persia in an official capacity.

10 Sir John Burgoyne's services:—blockade of Malta, and surrender of Valetta, in 1800; campaign in Egypt, in 1807, including the capture of Alexandria, and attack of Rosetta, from 7th to 18th April, 1807. Campaigns in the Peninsula, including the retreat to Corunna, passage of the Douro, affair of Salamonde (blew up Fort Conception in presence of the enemy, 21st July); battle of Busaco, retreat to and occupation of the lines of Lisbon, siege of Badajoz, 2nd to 13th June, 1811; action of Elbodon, siege and storm of Ciudad Rodrigo, siege and storm of Badajoz, siege and capture of Forts at Salamanca, battle of Salamanca, advance to Madrid and capture of the Retiro, siege of Burgos, (wounded) 19th Sept. to 21st Oct. 1812; retreat from Burgos, advance of the army and crossing the Ebro, battle of Vittoria, siege and storming of San Sebastian, (wounded) 15th July to 13th Aug.; siege of Castle of San Sebastian, 31st Aug. to 9th Sept. 1813; passage of Bidassoa, battles of the Nivelle and Nive, passage of Adour, blockade of Bayonne and repulse of the sortie. Served afterwards in the Amerian war, at the attack on the lines before New Orleans, 8th Jan. 1815, and capture of Fort Bowyer. Sir John has received a cross and one clasp.

11 Sir Charles Pasley's services:—defence of Gaeta, in 1806; battle of Maida; siege of Copenhagen, in 1807; campaign of 1808-9, including several skirmishes, and battle of Corunna. Reconnoitered the enemy's coast under the fire of batteries, and was afterwards at the siege of Flushing. Received a bayonet-wound through the thigh, and a musket-wound, which injured the spine, in leading a storming party to attack an advanced work occupied by the French on the Dike in front of Flushing, 14th Aug. 1809.

12 Major-General Goldfinch's services:—expedition to Copenhagen, in 1807; campaigns of 1809, 10, 13, and 14, including the capture of Oporto, battles of Talavera, Busaco, Vittoria, Pyrenees, Nive, Orthes, and Toulouse. He has received a cross.

13 Major-General Arnold's services:—blockade and surrender of Malta, in 1800; the whole of the campaign in Egypt, in 1801, including the attack and surrender of Aboukir Fort and castle, battle of Alexandria, and afterwards accompanied the division of the army which expelled the French from Grand Cairo, and took possession of that city; also present at the surrender of Alexandria to the British troops. Served several years in the West Indies, and at the last attack and surrender of the colonies of Demerara, Essequibo, Berbice, and Surinam, at which latter he was severely wounded in successfully leading the storming party against the Redoubt Frederick and Fort Leyden. Was several times handsomely

mentioned in the public dispatches for his conduct at Surinam; and was on that occasion presented by the Committee of the Patriotic Fund with a sword of the value of one hundred pounds. He has since served several years in Bermuda and North America.

15 Major-General Ellicombe served in the Peninsula from Nov. 1811 to the end of the war, including the siege and storm of Ciudad Rodrigo, siege and storm of Badajoz, retreat from Burgos, advance of the army and crossing the Ebro, battle of Vittoria, as Brigade-Major; siege and storm of San Sebastian, 15th July to 9th Sept. 1813; passage of Bidassoa, battles of Nivelle and Nive (10th, 11th and 12th Dec. 1813); passage of the Adour, blockade of Bayonne and repulse of the sortie. Medal for San Sebastian.

16 Major-General Fanshawe's services:—capture of Cape of Good Hope, in 1806; expedition to South America, and siege and capture of Monte Video, in 1807; with the army in Portugal in 1808; expedition to the Scheldt, and siege of Flushing, in 1809.

17 Sir Charles Smith served at the capture of the Danish Islands of Santa Cruz, St. Thomas, and St. John, in 1807; at the siege of Fort Bourbon and capture of Martinique (wounded), in 1809. Senior engineer in charge of Cadiz and its environs in the operations connected with the battle of Barrosa, in 1811. Commanding engineer in the defence of Tarifa, and in the field operations which led to that event. Commanding engineer at Cadiz prior to and when the siege was raised in 1812. Subsequently present at the action of Osma, battle of Vittoria, actions of Villa Franca and Tolosa, siege of St. Sebastian,—commanding engineer in the early part of the siege. Capitulation of Paris, and with the army of occupation. Commanded the allied land forces, at the bombardment and surrender of Beyrout, and at the capture of St. Jean d'Acre in 1840, at which last he was severely wounded. Medal and one clasp for Vittoria and San Sebastian. Sir Charles has served 20 years in the West Indies.

18 Colonel Harding served with the army in Sicily, in 1812; on the eastern coast of Spain in 1813, including the battle of Castalla, attack of Denia, and siege of Tarragona. In 1815, he served as commanding engineer with the Prussian army under Prince Augustus of Prussia at the sieges of Maubeuge, Landrecy, Marienburg, Philippeville, and Rocroy; and continued with the army of occupation until 1818.

19 Col. Wright served in the expedition to the Helder.

20 Col. Lewis's services:—campaign in Naples and Calabria, in 1805 and 1806, including the battle of Maida and siege of Scylla Castle. Capture of Ischia and Procida, in the Bay of Naples, in Aug. 1809; and siege of the Castle of Ischia. Siege of the Fort at Santa Maura, in 1810. Campaign of 1813 in the Peninsula; wounded at the assault of the breach of St. Sebastian—lost the left leg above the knee.

21 Colonel Holloway served the campaigns of 1810, 11, and 12, in the Peninsula; wounded in the trenches before Badajoz, March 1812; shot through the body 26th March 1812, whilst storming the enemy's works.

22 Colonel Vavasour served at the defence of Cadiz.

23 Colonel Graydon was at the capture of Martinique, in 1809, and Guadaloupe, in 1810, on each of which occasions he was the senior officer of Royal Engineers serving with a Division of the Army.

24 Colonel Thomson served in Nova Scotia, in 1808, 9, 10, and 11; and at the capture of Martinique and siege of Fort Bourbon, with the division of the army under Sir George Prevost, in 1809. Commanding Engineer with the expedition on the north coast of Spain, at the blockade of Santona, under the orders of Sir Home Popham, in 1812. Served also in Holland and the Netherlands, in 1813, 14, and 15; was present at the operations against Antwerp, and as commanding Engineer with the separate expedition, in 1814, under Major-General Gibbs, for the reduction of Fort Baatz, in the island of South Beveland. Commanding Engineer at the Cape of Good Hope from 1830 to 1836, and in the campaign of 1835, in Kaffirland, consequent on the invasion of the colony by the Kaffirs Received the repeated thanks of Sir Benjamin D'Urban, the Commander-in-chief, in general orders.

25 Sir Frederick Smith served in Sicily from 1807 to June 1812.

26 Colonel Jones served in the Peninsula, and was present at the passage of the Douro and capture of Oporto, May, 1809; battles of Talavera and Busaco, siege of Badajoz, battle of Albuhera, siege and capture of Ciudad Rodrigo.

27 Colonel Moody has seen a great deal of active service in the West Indies, and has been twice wounded, for which he received the Brevet rank of Major, and the Cross of Knight of the Royal French Order of Military Merit.

28 Colonel Oldfield served in Holland, in 1814. From March to June 1815, he served as second in command under Sir Jas. Carmichael-Smyth in the Netherlands; as Brigade-Major with the Duke of Wellington's army at Waterloo, capitulation of Paris, and army of occupation.

29 Colonel Dixon served in Canada during the war, from 1812 to 1815, and was lightly wounded at the storming of Fort Sandusky. Medal for Detroit.

30 Colonel Calder served in the expedition to Walcheren, and siege of Flushing, in 1809.

31 Lieut.-Col. Slade was present at St. Sebastian in July and Aug. 1813; blockade of Bayonne and repulse of the sortie. He was one of the officers selected to accompany the boats from Socoa to the mouth of the river Adour, and to assist in laying the bridge across.

32 Lieut-Col. Tylden served at Gibraltar and in Sicily from 1807 to 1814. Commanding Engineer at the siege and capture of Fort Santa Maria, 29th March, 1814, and in the action before Genoa under Lord Wm. Bentinck; for which services he received brevet promotion. Commanded the Pontoon Train during the compaign in Belgium and France in 1815; was present at the capture of Paris, and with the army of Occupation.

33 Lieut.-Col. English's services:—campaign of 1808 and 9, from the period the British army landed in Portugal until the retreat to Corunna, including battles of Roleia, Vimiera, and Corunna; end of campaign of 1813, and campaign of 1814, including battles of Orthes and Toulouse; campaign of 1815, and with the army of occupation until August 1817.

34 Lieut-Col. Blanshard served at the blockade of Bayonne, and repulse of the sortie. Afterwards in the American war, and was present at the taking of Washington, the operations and engagement before Baltimore, field operations and engagement before New Orleans, taking by assault the lines on the right bank of the Mississippi, and capture of Fort Bowyer. Joined Sir James Kemp's division in France, 22d June 1815.

35 Lieut.-Col. Alex. Brown served at Walcheren.

36 Lieut.-Col. Emmett's services, &c.:—sieges of Badajoz in 1811 and 12; passage of the Nive, battles before Bayonne, Orthes, and Toulouse. Attack on the American lines at New Orleans, every affair on that expedition, and the siege of Fort Bowyer. Slightly wounded at Badajoz in 1811; again on the advance towards Orthes; and very severely wounded at the assault of Badajoz in 1812.

37 Lieut.-Col. Ward served with the army in Sicily in 1811 and 12; was present at the action of Castalla, attack of Denia, and siege of Tarragona in 1813; served with the army in the Netherlands in 1814.

38 Lieut.-Col. Gordon's services:—attack on the Castle of Scylla, June, 1809; siege and capture of Santa Maura, March, 1810.

40 Lieut.-Col. Jones served in the expedition to Walcheren, in 1809. Also the campaigns of 1810, 11, 12, 13, and 14, including the actions and sieges of Cadiz, Tarragona, (1811), Badajoz (1812), Vittoria, St. Sebastian, passage of the Bidassoa, Nivelle, Nive, Bayonne. Wounded leading the Forlorn Hope at the first assault of St. Sebastian. Appointed commanding engineer in charge of the fortifications on Montmâtre, after the entrance of the British troops into Paris, in 1815.

44 Lieut.-Colonel Barry served in the Peninsula from Aug. 1812, to Oct. 1813, and was severely wounded by a grape shot, 31st Aug. 1813, when leading a party to the breach at the storming of St. Sebastian.

45 Lt.-Col. Reid served in the Peninsula from April 1810 to the end of the war, including the three several sieges of Badajoz, siege of Ciudad Rodrigo, siege of the Forts at and battle of Salamanca, siege of Burgos, battle of Vittoria, siege of San Sebastian, and battles of Nivelle, Nive, and Toulouse. Present at the attack on Algiers, under Lord Exmouth, in 1816. Severely wounded in the knee, repulsing a sortie at Badajoz, 10th May, 1811; in the leg during the assault of Ciudad Rodrigo, 19th January 1812; in the neck during the assault of St. Sebastian, 28th July 1813.

46 Lieut.-Col. Ord served in Spain during 1810, 11, 12, 13, and one half of 1814, including the sieges of Cadiz and Tarragona.

47 Lieut.-Col. Savage served in the Peninsula from Nov. 1813 to the end of the war, including the investment of Bayonne and repulse of the sortie.

48 Lt.-Col. Waters served in the Peninsula from April 1812 to September 1814. Was at Cadiz when the siege was raised in the former year. In 1815 he was present in the actions of Quatre Bras and Waterloo. He led one of the columns to the assault of Peronne on the 20th June 1815, and was at the capture of Paris.

49 Lt.-Col. Matson served in the Peninsula from Nov. 1812 to the end of the war, including the battle of Vittoria, siege of San Sebastian, and battles of Nivelle and Nive. Served also at New Orleans in 1814.

50 Lt.-Col. Victor served in the Peninsula from Dec. 1812 to the end of the war, including the battles of the Nive, Orthes, and Toulouse.

53 Lt.-Col. Yule served in the American war in 1814, and was at Chippewa, 5th July, 1814, and Niagara, 25th July, 1814.

54 Lieut.-Col. Phillpotts was favourably noticed in Sir Gordon Drummond's despatch of the attack on Fort Erie, Sept. 1814. Served as Assistant Quarter-Master General with the army in Canada during the insurrection of 1837, 8, and 9, and was most actively employed with the local rank of Colonel.

57 Lieut.-Col. Bolton served in the Peninsula from Oct. 1813 to the end of the war.

58 Lieut.-Col. Whinyates was at the battle of Algiers, 27th Aug. 1816.

59 Lieut.-Col. Robe joined the 4th division of the army in the Peninsula in 1813. In 1814 he was employed in the operations of the passage of the Adour; blockade of Bayonne and repulse of the sortie. Afterwards in the expedition to New Orleans. In 1815, 16, 17, and 18, with the Army in France.

60 Lieut.-Colonel Alderson served in Spain during the Christino and Carlist war. Also the Syrian campaign of 1840-41 (Medal), including the advance against Gaza and the affair near Askelon.

61 Lt.-Col. Wright was wounded by a musket ball through the thigh, 12th Oct. 1821, at Zante, in an attack made by the Greeks upon a Turkish man-of-war.

62 Lt.-Col. Thomson was attached to the Prussian army in 1815, and served at Maubeuge, Landrecy, Phillipville, and Rocroi.

63 Lt.-Col. Wortham served the campaigns of 1813 and 14 in Spain and France, including the siege of St. Sebastian, from 20th August to 9th Sept. 1813; battles of Orthes and Toulouse. Served afterwards with the army in America, from 14th Sept. 1814, to 24th May 1815, including the attack on the American Lines before New Orleans, 8th Jan. 1815, and the siege and capture of Fort Bowyer from 8th to 11th Feb. 1815.

65 Lt.-Cols. Jebb and Portlock, served in the last American war.

66 Captain Gordon served, as senior officer, in Demerara, during the insurrection of the Negroes, in 1823 and 1824. He was mentioned in general orders, and received the thanks of the Court of Policy of the United Colony of Demerara and Essequibo.

67 Major Marlow was commanding Royal Engineer at the storming of Kawiti's Pah at Owrawai in New Zealand on the 1st July 1845, and the subsequent destruction of the same. Also at the burning of Aretua's Pah, and at the storming of Kawiti's Pah on the 11th Jan. 1846; for these services he received the Brevet rank of Major.

68 Major Walpole commanded the Royal Engineers on the eastern frontier of the Cape of Good Hope during the Kaffir war of 1846-7, was twice wounded on the 8th June 1846, and for his services received the rank of Major.

69 Major Aldrich was specially employed in command in Spain, Syria, and China. In Spain in 1839 obtaining the surrender of the Fortress of Melilla by the Carlists to the Queen of Spain. In Syria 1840-41 (Medal): commanding Royal Engineers from the first landing to the 12th Dec. 1840, including the operations at D'Jeane, Tyne, bombardment and assault of Sidon, bombardment and capture of Beyrout, and subsequent surrender to him, while in charge of detachments of Royal Marines and Turkish troops, of a division of the Egyptian Army (3000) with their encampment and 24 pieces of artillery: also bombardment and capture of Acre. From 13th Dec. employed on the Staff in the advance to Jaffa; and from the 30th Sept. 1841 as commanding Royal Engineers until the evacuation of Syria by the British troops. In China 1843 to 1847 as commanding Royal Engineer to the Field Forces until their withdrawal in 1846. In April 1847 he was employed in the combined Naval and Military expedition up the Canton River, charged in command with the assault and capture of seven Forts, viz., Napier's, Whampoa Creek, French Folly, Rouge, Zig-zag, Segment, and Shanneen Forts.

70 Capt. Skyring and Major Symonds served the Syrian campaign of 1840-41 (Medal).

71 Capt. Owen served at the Cape of Good Hope in the campaign against the insurgent Boers in 1845, and in the Kaffir War of 1846-7.

72 Capt. Jervois served at the Cape of Good Hope during the Kaffir War of 1846-7, made a military sketch of 2000 square miles of Kaffirland,—1,100 of which he surveyed during the war.

73 Lieut. Gibb served at the Cape of Good Hope from August 1841 to April 1848, accompanied the overland expedition to Port Natal, and commanded the Royal Engineers during the whole of the operations connected with the capture of that settlement in May and June 1842.

Years' Serv. Full Pay.	Years' Serv. Half Pay.				
		Director-General.			
55	$\frac{2}{12}$	Sir John Webb,[1] KCH. *Assist.-Surg.* 17 Mar. 94; *Surgeon*, 15 July, 95; *Deputy Inspector*, 30 June, 02; *Inspector*, 20 June, 09; *Director-General*, 1 Aug. 13.			
		Deputy Inspector-General.			
45	0	P Morgan Thomas,[2] *Assist.-Surgeon*, 14 July, 04; *Surgeon*, 11 Nov. 11; *Assist.-Inspector*, 14 July, 36; *Deputy Inspector-General*, 16 Jan. 41.			
		SENIOR SURGEONS.	ASSIST.-SURGEON.	SURGEON.	SENIOR SURGEON.
35	$8\frac{4}{12}$	PWS Thos. Macmillan Fogo,[4] M.D.	22 Jan. 06	26 Sept. 14	1 Jan. 43
42	0	H. B. James Stewart	1 Dec. 07	27 Jan. 27	do
41	0	John Wallon Halahan, M.D......	5 Dec. 08	5 June 27	do
38	1	James Verling, M.D............	25 Jan. 10	3 July 27	do
36	$1\frac{4}{12}$	Alexander Ogilvie, M.D.	11 June 11	10 Aug. 29	do
37	0	Thomas Haswell Quigley	3 Nov. 12	26 Aug. 30	24 Jan. 44
33	$4\frac{4}{12}$	Thomas Whitelaw	6 Jan. 13	14 June 36	1 June 46
28	$8\frac{1}{12}$	WS Stewart Chisholm[5]..........	30 Nov. 13	11 Sept. 38	do
		SURGEONS.			
22	0	William Richardson, M.D.	17 April 27	10 Apr. 41	
22	0	James B. Williams.............	11 May 27	23 July 41	
21	0	Wm. Kelly[7],..................	31 Jan. 28	1 Nov. 42	
21	0	Charles Dempsey	22 July 28	1 Jan. 43	
20	0	John Atkins Davis.............	10 Aug. 29	24 Jan. 44	
19	0	James Edw. Thomas Parratt[6]	11 Mar. 30	22 Feb. 44	
19	0	George Farr	1 June 30	1 June 46	
19	0	Chas. Fred. Staunton, M.B.......	13 Nov. 30	do	
19	0	Johnson Savage, M.D.	15 Dec. 30	do	
16	0	Robert Templeton, M.D.	6 May 33	5 Apr. 47	
13	0	Joseph Ambrose Lawson, M.D. ..	11 June 36	19 Apr. 47	
		ASSISTANT SURGEONS.			
13	0	Wm. Alston Dassauville, M.D. ..	14 June 36		
13	0	James Somerville Litle	2 Nov. 36		
13	0	John Mackintosh, M.D.	23 Nov. 36		
12	0	George Thomas Ferris	26 Sept. 37		
11	0	Melbourne Broke Gallwey	18 June 38		
11	0	John Bent	11 Sept. 38		
10	0	Rich. Coffin Elliot............	7 June 39		
9	0	Ross Hassard[7]	30 Apr. 40		
9	0	Charles Young	4 May 40		
8	0	Wm. Henry Mackintosh, M.D. ..	10 April 41		
7	0	Henry Briscoe, M.D.	27 May 42		
7	0	Orlando Sawle Donnall	1 Nov. 42		
6	0	Hugh Crawford Walshe, M.D....	6 May 43		
5	0	James Macmillan Scott Fogo	5 Mar. 44		
4	0	Edward Gilborne	1 May 45		
3	0	Edward Schaw Protheroe	18 Apr. 46		
3	0	Stanhope Hunter Fasson	1 July 46		
3	0	Robert Thornton...............	6 July 46		
3	0	Matthew Combe...............	20 July 46		
2	0	Frederick Howard	14 Apr. 47		
2	0	Edward Dawson Allinson........	31 May		
2	0	Henry Fisher	7 June		
2	0	William Pearson Ward	14 June		
1	0	Thomas Rhys.................	3 July 48		
1	0	Philip Splane Warren	10 Aug.		
1	0	David Field Rennie	19 Sept.		

5 Mr. Chisholm served in the campaign of 1815, including Waterloo, and the capture of Paris. Was engaged in both Rebellions of Upper Canada. Accompanied several naval expeditions against the brigands on Lake Ontario, & among "the Thousand Islands," and served in the gun-boats with the marines and Indians during the attack and surrender at Mill Point. Was the only medical officer of the regular force on the field, and a volunteer, during the sharp conflict with the rebels and Americans near Prescott, 13th Nov. 1838, where upwards of 80 of the small force were killed and wounded, including the two officers who landed with the expedition. Received high commendation in the official communications of the Commander of the Forces, "in admiration of his conduct," and for the "valuable services" he rendered on that occasion. The General commanding in chief directed "his congratulations" to be sent to Mr. Chisholm "with reference to his exertions in that affair;" and the Master-general expressed by 'minute' his gratification "at conduct so creditable and so honourable to him."

7 Surgeon Kelly and Assist.-Surg. Hassard served with the troops employed in Syria in 1841.

Paymasters to the Ordnance Department, Messrs. Cox & Co.

1 Sir John Webb served on the Continent in 1794 under the Duke of York, and was present at the action of Lannoi, 17th and 18th May. In 1796 he served at the siege of Morne Fortuné and capture of St. Lucia, also at the expulsion of the Caribs from St. Vincent; at the capture of Trinidad, and the descent on Porto Rico in 1797; reduction of the Helder, and capture of the Texel fleet in 1799; on the coast of Spain in 1800; the Egyptian campaign of 1801, including the action at the landing and those of the 13th and 21st March, the taking of Grand Cairo, and all the subsequent operations; siege of Copenhagen, and capture of the Danish fleet, in 1807; expedition to the Scheldt in 1809.

2 Mr. Thomas's services:—Campaign in Italy in 1805, including the occupation of Sicily. Descent on the coast of Calabria, battle of Maida, and siege of Scylla Castle in 1806. Expedition to Sweden, under Sir John Moore; and subsequently in Portugal and Spain, up to the retreat to Corunna, in 1808-9. Capture of Guadaloupe in 1815.

4 Doctor Fogo served the campaign of 1808-9, under Sir John Moore, including the battle of Corunna. Expedition to Walcheren. On a Secret Expedition in March, 1810, which landed at Cadiz in April, reinforcing the army under Lord Lynedoch. The Ordnance force being greater than an ordinary regiment (1150 men), and Doctor Fogo being senior medical officer, he was given the local rank of Surgeon: remained at Cadiz until July, 1811, when he returned to England for the benefit of his health. Went to Portugal in March, 1812, and from July was again Senior Ordnance Medical Officer at Cadiz. When the siege was raised in August, he accompanied the force which followed the retiring French army; but the pursuit being given up at Seville, he returned to Cadiz, and remained there until its final evacuation in Aug. 1814. Served also the campaign of 1815, including the battle of Waterloo, and advance to Paris.

6 Mr. Parratt served in the operations in the Yeang tse Kiang in China (Medal), including the storm and capture of Chin Kiang Foo. He was also present at the demonstration before Nankin.

"GIBRALTAR"—The *Globe*, with the motto "*Per Mare, per Terram.*" The *Crown*—The *Anchor & Laurel*—The *Cypher of George the Fourth*
(Post in the Line, between the 49th and 50th Regiments.)
Major-General.—Right Hon. Sir George Cockburn, GCB. *Admiral of the Red*........5 April, 1821.

Division	Years' Serv. Full Pay.	Years' Serv. Half Pay.		2nd Lieut.	First Lieut.	Captain.	Brev.-Maj.	Lieut.-Col.	Colonel.
			Colonels Commandant.						
Wo.	54	0	𝔅 Thomas Adams Parke, CB.[1]	19 May 95	23 Nov. 96	15 Aug. 05	12 Aug. 19	31 Dec. 32	26 Apr. 38
	53	0	ℭ John Owen, CB. KH.[2] *Deputy Adjutant General*	1 Mar. 96	22 Oct. 98	4 May 07	19 July 21	10 Jan. 37	26 Aug. 39
Cha.	53	1/12	John Wright, KH.[3]	21 Apr.	10 June 99	27 July 08	16 Sept. 16	10 Jan.	do
Ply.	43	8 7/12	ℭ John M'Callum[8]	29 Jan. 98	18 Oct. 00	12 May 12	22 July 30	10 July	12 Feb. 42
Por.	47	4 4/12	𝔅 Charles Menzies, KH.[9]	17 Feb.	21 Dec. 03	13 Apr. 13	10 Jan. 37	do	10 July 44
			Colonels and Second Commandants.						
Ply.	42	8 1/12	William Fergusson[10]	10 Sept.	29 Apr. 04	23 Feb. 14	do	do	9 Nov. 46
Por.	48	1	Walter Powell	31 Jan. 00	21 Sept.	14 Nov. 23	18 Mar. 37	7 Nov. 38	27 Dec. 47
Wo.	48	0	Abraham Henry Gordon	5 Jan. 01	18 July 05	18 Dec. 24	28 June 38	26 Aug. 39	4 Jan. 48
Cha.	48	4/12	John Montresor Pilcher[13]	15 Jan.	15 Aug.	11 Feb. 26	never	11 May 41	17 Aug.
			Lieutenant-Colonels.						
Cha	48	0	Thomas Stevens[14]	do	do	11 Mar.	do	14 May	
Ply.	47	1	Richard Edwards	10 Apr.	do	16 May	do	30 Oct.	
Por.	47	1	𝔅 David Anderson Gibsone,[15] *Commanding Artillery*	15 Apr.	do	31 July	23 Nov. 41	12 Feb. 42	
Por.	46	0	𝔅 David James Ballingall[16]	1 July 03	do	do	do	do	
Ply.	46	0	ℭ John Rawlins Coryton[18]	6 July	15 Aug.	do	do	6 May 44	
Ply.	46	0	Hugh Mitchell	9 July	do	do	do	10 July	
Ply.	46	0	𝔅 Robert Mercer[20]	11 July	18 Oct.	31 July	do	9 Nov. 46	
Por.	45	0	ℭ S. Burdon Ellis, CB.[21]	1 Nov. 04	29 Apr. 06	15 Nov.	6 May 41	26 May 41	
Cha.	42	3	James Whylock	25 Apr. 04	24 Mar. 07	31 Aug. 27	28 Sept. 40	7 Dec. 46	
Ply.	42	2 10/12	ℭ Thomas Wearing[22]	5 May	24 Apr.	20 Dec.	23 Nov. 41	18 Dec. 46	
Cha.	40	5	Stephen Giles	3 Oct.	13 Jan. 08	31 Aug.	do	27 July 47	
Wo.	40	5	George Butt Bury	10 Nov.	27 July 08	30 June 29	10 Nov. 40	27 Dec. 47	
Por.	38	7	James Irwin Willes,[24]	12 Nov.	do.	15 Oct.	6 May 42	4 Jan. 48	
Por.	38	6	Henry James Gillespie,	11 Jan. 05	do.	27 July 30	9 Nov. 46	17 May 48	
Wo.	37	6 2/12	David M'Adam[25]	19 Apr. 05	do.	7 Dec. 30	do	27 May	
Por.	39	4 8/12	Samuel Garmston,[26]	27 Sept.	24 Aug. 00	16 Apr. 32	do	17 Aug.	
Por.	44	0	𝔅 John Harvey Stevens,[27] *Artillery*	28 Sept.	2 Sept.	do.	do	17 Aug.	
			Captains.						
Cha.	38	6	William Taylor	30 Sept.	4 Sept.	do.	do		
Wo.	37	7	𝔅 Cha. Compton Pratt[28]	14 Oct. 05	14 May 09	12 Oct. 32	do		
Ply.	33	10 4/12	𝔅 Henry Ivatt Delacombe[29]	21 Oct.	30 June	do	do		
Por.	35	9	George Hunt Coryton	9 Nov.	22 Sept.	do	do		
Por.	35	9	John Ashmore	10 Nov.	19 Dec.	do	do		
Cha.	34	9 4/12	Charles Fegen,[31] *r.*	30 Nov.	26 Jan. 11	30 Sept. 38	do		
Ply.	34	0	Richard Lyde Hornbrook	8 Feb. 06	9 Jan. 12	19 Oct. 32	do		
Wo.	39	11	Charles Robinson[36]	1 Aug.	11 May	27 May 34	5 Nov. 40		
Por.	[illegible]	11	William Lewis Hawes,[37]	29 Aug.	14 July 13	do	9 Nov. 46		
[illegible]	[illegible]	[illegible]	ℭ 𝔅 John Alex. Phillips,[38]	29 Aug.	17 July	do	do		

Div.	Years' Serv. F. p.	Years' Serv. H. p.	CAPTAINS.	2ND LIEUT.	1ST LIEUT.	CAPTAIN.
Por.	34	8	William Jolliffe (*Major*, 9 Nov. 46)......	4 May 07	18 Apr. 14	27 May 34
Wo.	42	$\frac{4}{12}$	William Calamy[40] ....*do*........	18 June	14 June 20	24 Sept. 35
Ply.	37	$3\frac{8}{12}$	Richard William Pascoe	12 Sept. 08	10 May 23	23 May 37
Ply.	38	$1\frac{11}{12}$	James Clarke....................	19 Sept.	14 Nov.	19 July
Art.	40	1	John Buckley Castieau, (*Major*, 10 Nov. 40.)	22 Sept.	13 Apr. 24	do
Por.	40	1	John Tothill	8 Oct.	8 May	do
Por.	40	$\frac{11}{12}$	Robert Henry,[45] *Artillery*	1 Nov.	22 June	do
Ply.	40	1	𝔅 Fortescue Graham[46]	17 Nov.	6 May 25	do
Cha.	40	0	James Whitcomb,[47] (*Major*, 23 Dec. 42)..	13 Mar. 09	11 Mar. 26	do
Por.	39	$1\frac{4}{12}$	Peter John James Dusautoy,[48] *r.*	14 Mar.	16 May	do
Ply.	40	0	Edmond Hearle....................	4 Apr.	25 Sept. 27	do
Wo.	40	0	John M'Arthur	14 Apr.	do.	do
Ply.	40	0	Joseph Childs,[49] (*Major*, 9 May, 43)	21 Apr.	do.	do
Por.	40	0	Hugh Evans	14 June	24 Nov.	16 Nov.
	40	0	𝔅 S. Robert Wesley,[50] *Assist. Adj. Gen.*	26 June	do.	do
Cha.	40	0	Thomas Park,[51]......................	30 Aug.	28 Feb. 28	7 Dec.
Cha.	39	$\frac{4}{12}$	George Griffin	18 Sept.	6 Mar.	9 Dec.
Por.	31	$8\frac{4}{12}$	𝔅 James Dowman[53]...................	28 Nov	8 Mar.	1 Jan. 38
Ply.	38	$1\frac{7}{12}$	Charles Clarke, ...	8 Feb. 10	24 Mar.	26 Apr.
Por.	37	2	Edmund Nepean, *r.*	27 Nov. 10	2 Oct. 28	1 June
Cha.	36	$2\frac{1}{12}$	Wm. M'Kinnon	13 Mar. 09	18 Apr. 26	8 June
Cha.	33	5	Thomas Fynmore[57]	6 Apr. 11	23 Apr. 29	3 Oct.
Wo.	36	2	Francis Smith Hamilton, (*Maj.* 23 Dec. 42)	2 May	2 Oct.	7 Nov.
Cha.	33	$4\frac{11}{12}$	John Tatton Brown[60]	21 May	14 Nov.	28 Feb.
Cha.	33	$5\frac{8}{12}$	Charles Cartwright Williamson	23 May	18 Dec.	26 Aug.
Cha.	34	4	Edward Augustus Parker, *r.*	23 Sept.	23 Feb.	do
Wo.	37	$\frac{4}{12}$	Joshua Edleston	19 Nov.	22 July 30	10 Aug. 40
Por.	30	$7\frac{4}{12}$	Charles William Pearce	26 Mar. 12	3 Feb. 31	6 Nov.
Cha.	31	$6\frac{8}{12}$	Thomas Hurdle,[61] (*Major* 20 March 46) ..	24 Apr.	16 Apr.	13 Nov.
Wo.	37	0	Robert Wright (1st)	6 May	4 June	do
Cha.	30	7	William Gordon	13 July	10 Sept.	13 Jan. 41
Cha.	30	7	Edward Appleton[63]	26 Aug.	7 Oct.	5 Mar.
Por.	30	7	Thomas Peard Dwyer,[64] *Artillery*	19 Oct.	9 Nov.	26 Mar.
Cha.	30	7	William Clendon	9 Nov.	19 Jan. 32	11 May
Ply.	30	7	Caleb Barnes, *r.*....................	10 Nov	22 Feb.	do
Por.	28	8	John Colliss	26 Mar. 13	7 Mar.	11 May
Ply.	26	$10\frac{4}{12}$	Peter Martin M'Kellar, *r*	17 Apr.	4 Apr.	do
Ply.	27	$9\frac{4}{12}$	Thomas Stephens	18 Sept.	do	do
Ply.	24	$11\frac{4}{12}$	George Watson	20 Dec.	27 June	30 June
Ply.	26	$9\frac{4}{12}$	John Land	22 Dec.	11 July	30 Oct.
Wo.	24	11	James Buchanan	22 Feb. 14	24 Aug.	4 Nov.
Wo.	25	10	Henry George Mitford[65]	23 Feb.	29 Aug.	do
Wo.	25	10	Samuel Hawkins, *r.*[66]	28 Feb. 14	12 Oct.	21 Dec.
Cha.	28	0	William Lee	22 Aug. 21	do	12 Feb. 42
Por.	27	0	Henry William Parke,[66] *Artillery*	26 Nov. 22	do	do
Wo.	26	0	Anthony B. Stransham[69] *r.* (*Maj.* 15 Apr. 42)	1 Jan. 23	do	do
Ply.	26	0	Edward Rea	3 Feb. 23	do	19 Mar. 42
Cha.	26	0	Alexander Anderson[70]	13 May	do	5 May
Cha.	26	0	Robert Wright (2nd).................	7 Oct.	11 Apr. 38	18 July
Por.	25	0	John Fraser, *Artillery*..............	8 May 24	23 Apr.	29 Sept.
Ply.	24	0	Thomas Brown Gray,[71] *r.*............	31 Jan. 25	1 Oct. 33	5 Nov. 42
Por.	24	0	Thomas Holloway, *Artillery*	17 Mar.	9 Dec.	23 Nov.
Por.	24	0	John Charles Grey Courtis	30 May	28 Dec.	4 Jan. 43
Ply.	24	0	John Miller[73]........................	18 July	7 Jan. 34	12 April
Wo.	24	0	Richard Johns	1 Oct.	4 Mar.	7 Aug.
Por.	23	0	Peter Brames Nolloth	28 Jan. 26	19 Mar. 34	10 Aug. 44
Cha.	23	0	Fielding Alexander Campbell	23 Sept.	27 May	21 Sept.
Cha.	23	0	George Evans Hunt	16 Dec.	do.	3 May 44
Wo.	22	0	John Mitchell........................	5 Oct. 27	29 Nov.	6 May
Ply.	22	0	Thomas Lemon	8 Oct.	5 Feb. 35	10 July
Cha.	22	0	Peter Trant Murray Payne	22 Oct.	30 Mar.	12 July
Ply.	22	0	George Elliot[75]	1 Nov. 27	6 Apr. 35	16 Aug. 44
Wo.	22	0	Thomas Charles Cotton Moore	4 Dec.	26 Oct.	31 Oct.
Ply.	21	0	Augustus Flemyng	7 Jan. 28	28 Jan. 36	21 Jan. 45
Cha.	21	0	Wm. Bookley Langford[77] (*Major*, 7 July 46)	22 Jan.	22 Mar.	do
Por.	21	0	William Mackay Heriot, *r.*	28 Jan.	24 Mar.	16 June
Por.	21	0	Hamilton Fleming....................	10 Mar.	15 Apr.	16 Aug.
Wo.	21	0	Charles Miller	19 Mar.	20 July	7 Apr. 46
Ply	21	0	Arthur Sandys Stawell Walsh, ...	12 Apr.	6 Dec.	26 Aug.
Por.	21	0	John George Augustus Ayles, *r.*......	13 May	10 Jan. 37	10 Oct.
Cha.	21	0	John Hawkins Gascoigne	4 June	23 May	9 Nov.
Cha.	21	0	John Urquhart,[79]	14 July	26 May	9 Nov.
Por.	21	0	Thomas Fraser[80]	26 Nov.	10 July	26 Nov.
Ply.	20	0	John Hoskin Wright[81] *r.*	5 Feb. 29	do	7 Dec.

Div.	Years' Ser. F. p.	Years' Ser. H. p.	CAPTAINS.	2ND LIEUT.	1ST. LIEUT.	CAPTAIN.
Wo.	20	0	Robert John M'Killop, *r.*	4 Mar. 29	10 July 37	9 Dec. 46
Wo.	20	0	William Friend Hopkins	27 Apr.	do	20 Apr. 47
Por.	20	0	Henry Carr Tate, *Artillery*	30 June	do	4 May
Por.	20	0	George Colt Langley,[93] *Artillery*	do	do	4 May
Ply.	20	0	Joseph Francis Brittain,[94]	16 Nov.	do	27 July
Wo.	20	0	George Walkup Congdou	4 Dec.	do	do
Wo.	20	0	Richard William Meheux	26 Dec.	do	do
Ply.	19	0	Edward Hocker	30 Jan. 30	do	do
Por.	19	0	Francis Augustus Halliday, *Artillery*	23 Feb.	do	do
Wo.	19	0	Simon Fraser[95]	do	do	do
Wo.	19	0	John Wade	3 July	do	do
Por.	19	0	Hamnett Parke, *Artillery*	27 July	do	do
Cha.	19	0	Walter Cossar, *r.*	10 Aug.	do	do
Wo.	19	0	William Henry March	20 Nov.	do	11 Aug.
Cha.	18	0	Charles Allan Parker[96]	4 Feb. 31	do	25 Aug.
Ply	18	0	Edward Pownoll Snowe	17 Mar.	do	29 Oct.
Por	18	0	Gallway Byng Payne	17 May	do	4 Dec.
Por	18	0	Joseph Oates Travers,	10 Sept.	do	27 Dec.
Por	17	0	Robert Murray Curry, *r.*	22 Feb. 32	do	4 Jan. 48
Cha	17	0	Edward Stanley Browne	19 Mar.	28 Sept.	4 May
Por	17	0	Joseph Reid Jackson	4 Apr.	7 Nov.	17 May
Por	17	0	John Thompson Aslett	16 Apr.	16 Nov.	do
Wo.	17	0	Berney Varlo	16 Apr.	24 Nov.	do
Por.	17	0	Henry David Erskine	10 July	9 Dec.	do
Wo.	17	0	William Robert Maxwell,[97]	11 July	15 Dec.	do
Wo.	17	0	Thomas Dudley Fosbroke	30 Nov.	1 Jan. 38	do
Por.	16	0	Charles Joseph Hadfield	15 Feb. 33	26 Apr.	do
Ply.	16	0	John Philip Stevens	7 May	do	do
Ply.	16	0	Richard Carr Spalding[98]	do	4 May	do
Wo.	16	0	Edgar Walter	19 July	22 May	do
Cha.	16	0	Hayes Marriott,[99]	11 Oct.	16 June	do
Cha.	16	0	Walter Welsford Lillicrap	1 Nov.	do	do
Ply.	16	0	Thomas Baker Pleydell	do	3 Oct. 38	do
Por.	16	0	Samuel Netterville Lowder, *r.*	do	7 Nov.	do
Por.	16	0	Andrew Roger Savage, *Artillery*	11 Nov.	28 Feb. 39	27 May
Wo.	16	0	Pitcairn Onslow	13 Nov.	6 Apr.	14 July
Por.	15	0	Richard Searle Bunce	10 Jan. 34	10 May	17 Aug.
Por.	15	0	Edward Thornborough Parker Shewen[90]	28 Feb.	7 Feb. 40	31 Aug.
Por.	15	0	George Lambrick	14 Mar.	2 Mar.	1 Oct.
Por.	15	0	Hugh Kennedy	21 Mar.	10 Aug.	26 Oct.
			FIRST LIEUTENANTS.			
Por.	15	0	Robert Hockings	4 July	19 Sept.	
Por.	15	0	William Lawrence Sayer	14 Nov.	6 Nov.	
Por.	15	0	Richard George Connolly	26 Dec. 34	13 Nov. 40	
Por.	14	0	Augustus Dover Lyddon Farrant, *Adj.*	31 July 35	do.	
Ply.	13	0	Henry Timpson[92]	5 Jan. 36	do.	
Ply.	13	0	Nicholas Moore	15 July	do.	
Ply.	13	0	Henry Charles Moorhead Hawkey	27 Sept. 36	do.	
Ply.	13	0	Edw. Pellew Hamett Ussher, *Qr.-Mas.*	27 Dec.	13 Jan. 41	
Ply.	12	0	Charles Ogilvy Hamley[93]	27 Feb. 37	20 Jan.	
Wo.	12	0	Henry Varlo, *Qr.-Mast*	7 Apr. 37	28 Jan. 41	
Ply.	12	0	William Stratton Aslett, *Adjutaut*	26 July	5 March	
Wo.	12	0	William Francis Foote, *Adjutant*	1 Aug.	29 Mar.	
Ply.	12	0	Charles Penrose Coode	do	11 May	
Pro.	12	0	William Grigor Suther	do	do	
Wo.	12	0	Henry Edward Delacombe	do	do	
Wo.	12	0	Andrew John Buckingham Hambly[94]	1 Aug. 37	11 May 41	
Por.	12	0	William Ramsay Searle	17 Oct.	do	
Wo.	12	0	Henry Drury	19 Oct.	do	
Por.	12	0	Henry Atkins M'Callum	24 Oct.	11 May	
Por.	12	0	Charles Louis, *Qr.-Mast.*	21 Nov.	do	
Wo.	12	0	Richard King Clavell	do	13 May	
Wo.	12	0	John William Wearing, *Adjutant*	do	14 May	
Wo.	12	0	Richard Yates Stuart Moubray	5 Dec.	14 May	
Cha.	12	0	Alexander Ramsay	19 Dec.	14 May	
Wo.	12	0	Penrose Charles Penrose	do	3 July	
Cha.	12	0	George Brydges Rodney, *Adjutant*	do	14 Aug.	
Por.	12	0	Jermyn Charles Symonds	do	17 Aug.	
Por.	12	0	John Maurice Wemyss, *Artillery*	do	30 Oct.	
Cha.	11	0	John Henry Mercer	2 Jan. 38	4 Nov.	
Por.	11	0	Henry Hotham M'Carthy	30 Jan.	24 Nov.	
Cha.	11	0	Peregrine Henry Fellowes, *Adjutant*	31 Mar.	12 Feb. 42	
Cha.	11	0	Wm. Christopher Parkin Elliott	8 May	do	
Por.	11	0	Charles William Adair,[96] *Adjutant*	do	do	

Div.	Years' Serv. F.p.	Years' Serv. H.p.	First Lieutenants.	2nd Lieut.	1st Lieut
Ply.	11	0	Richard Farmar[97]	8 May 38	12 Feb. 4
Por.	11	0	William Jolliffe	12 June	19 Mar.
Cha.	11	0	Robert Seppings Harrison[98]	do	5 May
Por.	11	0	Wm. Jenny Pengelley	19 June	13 June
Por.	11	0	George Gardiner Alexander, *Artillery*	14 Aug.	17 June
Por.	11	0	Henry Wm. Brooker	15 Aug. 38	25 June
Cha.	11	0	Charles Frederick Menzies	21 Aug.	27 June
Cha.	11	0	John Huskisson, *Qr.-Master*	4 Dec.	18 July
Ply.	11	0	John Henry Stewart	18 Dec.	17 Aug.
Cha.	11	0	David Blyth	do	29 Sept.
Por.	11	0	Joseph Edward Wilson Lawrence,[99] *Adj. Art.*	27 Dec.	5 Nov.
Por.	10	0	James Ainslie Stewart[100]	11 May 39	21 Nov.
Por.	10	0	James Pickard[101]	do	23 Nov.
Wo.	10	0	Henry Charles Penrose Dyer[102]	do	do
Wo.	10	0	Wm. Barnham Thos. Rider	10 Sept.	4 Jan. 43
Wo.	10	0	Wm. Alfred Garner Wright	24 Sept.	12 April
Cha.	9	0	Gerard Montagu	15 Sept. 40	7 Aug.
Ply.	9	0	George Wentworth Forbes, *Adjutant*	17 Nov. 40	12 Aug.
Por.	8	0	George Augustus Schomberg, *Artillery*	16 Mar. 41	21 Sept.
Por.	8	0	Julius Roberts, *Artillery*	do	16 Mar. 4
Ply.	8	0	Fleetwood John Richards	do	3 May
Cha.	8	0	Hugh Hamilton Goold	do	6 May
Wo.	8	0	Arthur Butcher	do	10 July 4
Cha.	8	0	George Drury	do	12 July
Ply.	8	0	William Hutchinson	do	16 Aug.
Por.	8	0	Thomas Forrest	20 April	22 Nov.
Cha.	8	0	Edward Andrèe Wylde	18 May	21 Dec.
Por.	8	0	Ebenezer Tristram Thomas Jones	15 June	21 Jan.
Por.	8	0	Joseph Henry Jolliffe	do	do
Wo.	8	0	John William Alexander Kennedy[103]	do	do
Cha.	8	0	Robert Boyle	do	do
Ply.	8	0	Simon Ridley Little	do	17 April
Cha.	8	0	Tho. Alex. Masterson D'Veber Pennington	do	5 May
Por.	8	0	John Elliott	do	5 May
Por.	8	0	Samuel Lewin Wilson	do	16 June
Por.	8	0	Charles M'Arthur	6 July	9 Aug.
Wo.	8	0	Hamond Weston Gwyn	do	16 Aug.
Por.	8	0	Charles Loudon Barnard, *Artillery*	17 Aug. 41	18 Aug. 4
Cha.	8	0	Richard Franklin Tucker	do	4 Feb. 4
Por.	8	0	Henry Watson Hall, *Artillery*	do	do
Por.	8	0	Henry George Johnstone Davies	do	7 April
Cha.	8	0	Rodney Vansittart Allen	do	do
Ply.	8	0	Nevinson Willoughby de Courcy	do	11 Apr.
Ply.	8	0	Henry Bates Leonard	31 Aug.	21 May
Wo.	8	0	George Webb	do	25 June
Ply.	8	0	William Mansell Mansell[104]	do	26 Aug. 4
Wo.	8	0	Thomas Carstairs Gray	19 Oct.	9 Nov.
Cha.	7	0	Wm. Godfrey Rayson Masters	15 Feb. 42	9 Nov.
Por.	7	0	Richard Parke	do	26 Nov. 4
Cha.	7	0	John James Douglas Barclay	do	7 Dec.
Wo.	7	0	George Sheddan Dunbar	do	9 Dec.
Ply.	7	0	John Manger	do	18 Dec
Por.	7	0	Thomas Magin	19 April	24 Dec.
Ply.	7	0	Charles Slaughter	do	20 April 4
Wo.	7	0	James Splaine Dowman	do	6 May
Cha.	7	0	Fermor Bonnycastle Gritton	17 May	10 May
Por.	7	0	Henry John Tribe	14 June	27 July
Por.	7	0	John Wm. Collman Williams, *Artillery*	7 July	do
Por.	7	0	Hugh Stukely Buck, *Artillery*	do	do
Ply.	7	0	Thomas Valentine Cooke	do	do
Wo.	7	0	Lewis Scott Reeves	7 July 42	do
Por.	7	0	George Stephen Digby, *Artillery*	16 Aug.	do
Ply.	7	0	William Edward Farmar	18 Oct.	do
Por.	7	0	John Charles Downie Morrison	do	do
Wo.	7	0	Henry Thomas Swain	10 Nov.	do
Por.	7	0	Charles Reed Driver	do	do
Ply.	7	0	Alfred De Hochepied Nepean	15 Dec.	do
Wo.	7	0	Henry Spratt	27 Dec.	do
Wo.	7	0	George Edward Owen Jackson	do	do
Wo.	7	0	Frederick Augustus Percy Wood	do	do
Wo.	7	0	Edward Price Usher	do	do
Wo.	7	0	George Bruce Puddicombe	do	do
Wo.	7	0	Michael Spratt	do	do
Wo.	7	0	Charles Thomas Forest Onslow	do	do

Division.	Years' Serv. F. p.	Years' Serv. H. p.	FIRST LIEUTENANTS.	2ND. LIEUT.	1ST LIEUT.
Wo.	6	0	Julius Bunce	4 Jan. 43	27 July 47
Cha.	6	0	Thomas Page Casey	20 June	do
Por.	6	0	Henry Treffry Fox	15 Aug.	11 Aug.
Cha.	6	0	Edward Lawes Pym	21 Aug.	25 Aug.
Ply.	6	0	Henderson Ward	21 Aug.	29 Oct.
Cha.	6	0	Wm. Henry Whorwood Branch	18 Sept.	20 Nov.
Por.	6	0	John Crocket, *Artillery*	26 Dec.	20 Nov.
Cha.	6	0	Henry Nicholas Gell	do	4 Dec.
Por.	5	0	Charles John Ellis	16 Mar 44	21 Dec.
Por.	5	0	William Sandom Davis, *Artillery*	3 May	21 Dec.
Ply.	5	0	Edmund Charles Domville	6 May	27 Dec.
Cha.	5	0	Frederick Charles Knight	3 July	29 Dec.
Ply.	5	0	Frederick Edward Budd	17 July	4 Jan. 48
Por.	5	0	Thomas Quin Meade, *Artillery*	23 July	4 Jan.
Cha.	5	0	Benjamin Bousfield Herrick	27 Dec.	21 March
Por.	5	0	Wynder Kelly Ireland, *Artillery*	do	do
Ply.	5	0	Alexander Finlaison Sutherland	27 Dec.	3 May
Cha.	5	0	Edward Richards	do	4 May
Por.	5	0	Francis Harry Noott	do	27 May
Por.	4	0	William Pitt Draffen, *Artillery*	2 July 45	do
Por.	4	0	William James Kinsman	do	do
Por.	4	0	John Bastable, *Artillery*	do	do
Wo.	4	0	Thomas Burton Vandeleur FitzGerald	14 Oct.	do
Ply.	4	0	John Tunstall Haverfield	do	do
Ply.	4	0	John Sangster	do	do
Ply.	4	0	Ponsonby May Carew Croker	16 Dec.	do
Por.	4	0	John Cree Giles	do	do
Cha.	4	0	George Bayles Heastey	29 Dec.	do
Por.	4	0	Henry Adair, *Artillery*	do	do
Por.	4	0	Henry Way Mawbey, *Artillery*	do	do
Por.	3	0	Arthur Onslow Lake Lewis	9 Feb. 46	do
Por.	3	0	Frederick Llewellyn Alexander, *Artillery*	16 Feb.	do
Ply.	3	0	John Basset Prynn	5 May	do
Por.	3	0	Charles Osborn Baker	do	do
Cha.	3	0	Charles Wolrige	do	do
Cha.	3	0	Philip Harris	18 Aug.	do
Ply.	3	0	William James Dunn	do	do
Cha.	3	0	John Horndon Parry	do	do
Por.	3	0	Richard Kennett Willson	do	do
Ply.	3	0	Edmund Henry Cox	do	do
Wo.	3	0	Edmund Brighouse Snow	do	do
Cha.	3	0	James Taylor	do	do
Por.	3	0	John Barlow Butcher	28 Dec.	do
Ply.	3	0	John George Timpson	do	do
Por.	3	0	Arthur Charles Steele, *Artillery*	do	do
Por.	3	0	Edward Henderson Starr	do	do
Por.	2	0	Edward Joseph Ridgway Connolly	16 Feb. 47	do
Wo.	2	0	Edward Ralph Horsey	do	do
Cha.	2	0	Arthur Ellis	20 Apr.	do
Ply.	2	0	George Bazalgette	10 May	do
Wo.	2	0	Edward Gough M'Callum	do	do
Cha.	2	0	Richard Turberville Ansell	do	do
Ply.	2	0	George Henry Wriford	do	do
Wo.	2	0	John Poore	do	12 June
Wo.	2	0	Richard Goddard Hallilay	29 June	14 July
Por.	2	0	George Gregory	3 Aug.	8 Aug.
Ply.	2	0	Henry George Elliot	do	17 Aug.
Wo.	2	0	Jones Wright	3 Aug. 47	24 Aug.
Cha.	2	0	Henry Hewett	20 Sept.	28 Aug.
Wo.	2	0	Edward M'Arthur	do	31 Aug.
Por.	2	0	Henry Bradley Roberts	18 Oct.	1 Oct.
Ply.	2	0	James Shute	do	11 Oct.
Por.	2	0	John Burstead Seymour	9 Dec.	26 Oct.
			SECOND LIEUTENANTS.		
Cha.	2	0	Arthur John Stuart	14 Dec.	
Wo.	2	0	Charles Barker Parke	30 Dec.	
Por.	2	0	John Gate Holland	do	
Wo.	2	0	Nugent Macnamara	do	
Wo.	2	0	James Elphinstone Lock	do	
Por.	1	0	Archibald Alexander Douglas	12 Feb. 48	
Cha.	1	0	Charles Loftus Tottenham Usher	do	
Ply.	1	0	George Lascelles Blake	do	
Por.	1	0	Osborne Frederick Charles Fraser	14 March	

Division.	Years' Serv. F.p.	Years' Serv. H.p.	SECOND LIEUTENANTS.	2ND LIEUT.
Ply.	1	0	William Henry Worthy Bennett	14 Mar. 48
Por.	1	0	George Leslie....................	do
Wo.	1	0	Charles Roberts..................	do
Por.	1	0	William Penn Burton	16 May
Por.	1	0	Edward Octavius Pearse	do
Ply.	1	0	Nicholas Bennett Dalby	do
Por.	1	0	George Le Hardy Burlton	do
Cha.	1	0	Embule Dayah Thelwall	29 June
Ply.	1	0	William John Spencer Richards	do
Cha.	1	0	John Vaughan Carden Reed	do
Wo.	1	0	Richard Pentland Henry	do
Por.	1	0	Charles Louis Atterbury Farmar	do
Ply.	1	0	William Kelly	do
Por.	1	0	Charles Jolliffe	do
Por.	1	0	Henry Lindsay Searle	do
Por.	1	0	Henry Lewis Evans	do
Por.	1	0	Henry Nicholson Tinklar	do
Ply.	1	0	William Richard Jeffreys...........	25 July
Cha.	1	0	George Dare Dowell	do
Wo.	1	0	Harrisson John Jull	15 Aug.
Cha.	1	0	Theophilus Vaughton	do
Cha.	1	0	Augustus Tonyn Staines Cuttler........	do
Por.	1	0	William Taylor	do
Cha.	1	0	Edward Grant Stokes	do
Ply.	1	0	John Duff Pigou	do
Ply.	1	0	Dixon Whidbey Curry	do
Por.	1	0	Thomas Moore	do
Por.	1	0	William Cunningham Symonds	do
Ply.	1	0	Horatio Nelson Charles Blanckley	do
Por.	1	0	Archer Croft Critchell	19 Sept.
Wo.	1	0	Edward Fitzgerald Pritchard	do
Cha.	1	0	Charles William Carrington...........	do
Ply.	1	0	John James Douglas...............	do
Cha.	1	0	Robert William Bland Hunt	do
Wo.	1	0	Francis Robert Newton	do
Cha.	1	0	John Frederick Hawkey	do
Wo.	1	0	Edward Spry....................	do
Wo.	1	0	Frederick George Pym	do
Wo.	1	0	Henry Fallowfield Cooper	14 Nov.
Por.	1	0	Joseph Hamilton Maskery	do
Cha.	1	0	William Henry Hore West	do
Ply.	1	0	Henry Colton Mudge	do
Cha.	1	0	Francis Lloyd Dowse	19 Dec. 48
Cha.	1	0	Ambrose Wolrige	do
Ply.	3	0	Charles Pyne	2 July 45

ROYAL MARINE ARTILLERY.

Head-Quarters, Portsmouth.

Lieut.-Colonels.

David Anderson Gibsone, 10 July, 44.—ℬ John Harvey Stevens[27] 17 Aug. 48.

Captains.

J. B. Castieau (*Major*), 10 July, 37
Robert Henry,[44] 10 July, 37.
Thomas Peard Dwyer, 26 March, 41.
Henry William Parke,[66] 12 Feb. 42.
John Fraser, 29 Sept. 42.
Thomas Holloway, 23 Nov. 42.
Henry Carr Tate, 4 May 47.
George Colt Langley, 4 May 47.
F. A. Halliday, 27 July, 47.
Hamnet Parke, 27 July, 47.
Andrew Roger Savage, 26 Oct. 48.

First Lieutenants.

John Maurice Wemyss, 30 Oct. 41.
George Gardiner Alexander, 17 June 42
J. E. Wilson Lawrence, *Adj.* 5 Nov. 42.
George Aug. Scomberg, 21 Sept. 43.
Julius Roberts, 16 Mar. 44.
Charles Loudon Barnard, 18 Aug. 45.
Henry Watson Hall, 4 Feb. 46.
John William Colhman Williams, 27 July, 47.
Hugh Stukely Buck, 27 July, 47.
Geo. Stephen Digby, 27 July, 47.
John Crocket, 20 Nov. 47.
William Sandom Davis, 21 Dec. 47.
Thomas Quin Meade, 4 Jan. 48.
Wynder Kelly Ireland, 21 March 48.
William Pitt Draffen, 27 May 48.
John Bastable, 27 May 48.
Henry Adair, 27 May 48.
Henry Way Mawbey, 27 May 48.
Frederick Llewellyn Alexander, 27 May 48.
Arthur Charles Steele, 24 Aug. 48.

Second Lieutenants.

Adjutant.—J. E. W. Lawrence (*1st Lieut.*), 4 May 47.

STAFF OFFICERS OF THE ROYAL MARINES.

Deputy Adjutant-General.—𝕮 *Colonel* John Owen, CB. KH., 1 Jan. 38.

Assistant Adjutant-General.—𝕻 *Captain* Samuel Robert Wesley, 10 Nov. 46.

Office, 22, New Street, Spring Gardens.

Adjutants.

Por.	*1st Lieut.* A. D. L. Farrant, 10 Oct. 46.	*Cha.*	*1st Lieut.* Geo. Brydges Rodney, 27 July 47.
Ply.	——— W. S. Aslett, 22 May 48.	*Cha.*	——— P. H. Fellowes, 22 May 48.
Wo.	——— W. F. Foote, 22 May 48.	*Por.*	——— C. W. Adair, 22 May 48.
Wo.	——— John Wearing, 22 May 48.	*Ply.*	——— G. W. Forbes, 12 June 48.

Quarter-Masters.

Ch.	*1st Lieut.* John Huskisson, 25 Aug. 47.	*Ply.*	George Dibben, 7 July 46.
Ply.	——— E. P. H. Ussher, 22 May 48.	*Por.*	Thomas Cooper, 15 July 46.
Ch.	Norton Austin, 25 June 46.	*Wo.*	William Ruston, 23 June 46.
Wo.	*1st Lieut.* Henry Varlo, 14 July 48.	*Por.*	*1st Lieut.* Chas. Louis, 31 Aug. 48.

Paymasters.

Wo.	George Varlo, 23 Aug. 05; *2nd Lt.* 18 June, 93; *1st Lt.* 24 April, 95; *Capt.* 15 July, 03.
Por.	𝕻 John Lawrence,[116] 20 July, 30; *2nd Lt.* 6 July, 03; *Lt.* 15 Aug. 05; *Capt.* 31 July, 26.
Cha.	George Hookey,[107] 23 March, 36; *2nd Lt.* 27 Jan. 06; *1st Lt.* 8 Aug. 11; *Capt.* 12 Oct. 38.
Ply.	Robert Leonard,[114] 25 Aug. 47; *2nd Lt.* 27 Feb. 06; *1st Lt.* 3 Mar. 12; *Capt.* 28 Apr. 34; *Brevet-Major*, 4 Nov. 40.

Barrack-Masters.

Por.	Thomas Moore,[108] 16 Aug. 27; *2nd Lt.* 14 Jan. 01; *1st Lt.* 15 Aug. 05; *Capt.* 21 Nov. 10.
Wo.	Robert John Little,[109] 12 Sept. 29; *2nd Lt.* 4 July, 03; *1st Lt.* 15 Aug. 05; *Capt.* 31 July, 26.
Cha.	𝕻 Ambrose A. R. Wolrige,[110] 5 June, 32; *2d Lt.* 4 July, 03; *1st Lt.* 15 Aug. 05; *Capt.* 31 July, 26.
Ply.	Isaac Toby,[111] 21 March, 42; *2nd Lt.* 3 Apr. 10; *1st Lt.* 9 Sept. 28; *Capt.* 22 May, 38.

Deputy Inspectors of Hospitals.

Cha.	William Rae,[112] 22 Aug. 40.	*Wo.*	John Drummond, 7 July 47.

Surgeons.

Por.	Samuel Irvine,[113] 30 Nov. 41.	*Ply.*	Andrew Millar, M.D., 12 Aug. 48.

Assistant-Surgeons.

Por.	Arch. Elliott	*Cha.*	Alexander Leith Ehmslie, 8 April 46.
Ply.	Wm. Thompson Kay, 18 Jan. 47.	*Wo.*	J. Trail Urquhart Bremner, 16 Nov. 46.
Cha.	Albert Andrew Jack, 27 Nov. 45.	*Por.*	F. W. R. Sadler, 9 Mar. 48.
Wo.	Thomas William Nelson, 8 Apr. 46.		

Scarlet—Facings Blue. Artillery—*Blue*—Facings Red. *Agent*, Messrs. Cox & Son.

War Services of the Officers of the Royal Marines.

1 Colonel Parke was present in Duncan's victory near Camperdown, 11th Oct. 1797; commanded two companies of Marine Artillery in Spain in 1812, and three companies in America, from 1813 to 1816, including the attack and capture of the entrenched camp at Hampton; besides the above, he has been twelve times engaged with the enemy in boats and on shore.

2 Colonel Owen's services:—Battle of Camperdown; defence of the island of St. Marcou; bombardment of La Hogue; boarding and capture of India ship *Chanos* under the batteries at Mauritius; burning of French frigate *La Prenneuse;* boarding and capture of ship *Sea Nymph* in harbour of Port Louis; battle of Trafalgar; and, although wounded, was, nevertheless, the first person on board the Spanish 80 gun ship *Argonauta;* capture of Copenhagen; destruction of *Le Robuste* and *Lion*, French ships of the line, Cette; destruction of a French privateer brig in the port of Negaya; capture of a convoy at Languilia, the batteries being first carried by the Marines; destruction of the Forts of Alessis and Languilia by the Marines under his command, after having *charged with the bayonet and defeated a battalion of the French 52d of the line, of a very superior force.* Commanded a battalion on the North Coast of Spain, including the actions of Alza, 6th June; near Fontarabia, 11th July; and at Hernani, 16th March 1837, when the Royal Marines rendered such important services to the Queen of Spain and her Allies.

3 Colonel Wright's Services:—Engaged in most of Lord Nelson's attacks on Rota and Cadiz in 1797; battle of the Nile; campaign of Naples in 1799; surrender of Ovo and Novo, Fort St. Elmo, Capua, and Gaeta; cutting out of the *Guiep* at Vigo; Egypt in 1801; and battle of Algiers in 1816.

8 Colonel M'Callum was at the capture of the *Victorin* French privateer in boats under his command in 1800; battle of Trafalgar; forcing the Dardanelles and destroying a Turkish squadron in 1807. Employed on various occasions in cutting out and destroying enemy's vessels.

9 Colonel Menzies was attached to Lord Nelson's squadron off Boulogne, where he participated in all the desperate cutting-out affairs on the French coast against Buonaparte's flotilla. Commanded a detachment of Royal Marines landed at Port Jackson during an insurrection of convicts, in March, 1804; by his promptitude and exertions the town of Sydney and indeed the colony was in a great measure preserved and tranquillity restored. On the 22d June, 1806, he was in one of the boats of His Majesty's Ship *Minerva*, cutting out five vessels from under Fort Finisterre; and on the 11th July following he was in the barge which, when 50 miles from where the frigate lay at anchor, captured by boarding the *Buena Dicha* Spanish privateer, of three times the force of the boat, after a sharp conflict: this attack was planned by Colonel Menzies. Commanded and headed the marines at the storming of Fort Finisterre, being the first who entered the Fort. In boats cutting out the Spanish vessel of war, *St. Joseph*, from the Bay of Arosa, where he landed and made prisoner the Spanish Commodore who delivered to him his sword. Commanded the Marines at the capture of Fort Guardia. Slightly wounded cutting out the French corvette, *La Moselle*, from under a battery in Basque Roads. Taking of Fort Camarinus and gun-boats from under its protection. Repeatedly engaged in severe boat-actions, and against batteries. Right arm amputated. Received a sword of honour from the Patriotic Fund. Commanded the Royal Marine Artillery from 1837 to 1844.

10 Colonel Fergusson served at the capture of Rear Admiral Perrée's squadron from Egypt when in pursuit of the French and Spanish fleets in June, 1799. Blockade of Malta and capture of Admiral Perrée's squadron *Le Généreux* 74, *Ville de Marseilles*, &c. with a reinforcement and supplies for the relief of the garrison. Was wrecked and severely injured on board H.M.S. *Queen Charlotte* when *burnt* off Leghorn in 1800, only *four* saved out of a detachment of nearly 200 marines, including supernumeraries, in all upwards of 700 persons perished. Served at the siege of Genoa and Savona. Destruction of the fort of Port Espezie, and guns carried off by H. M. S. *Santa Dorothea* in 1800, to which ship he then belonged. Served in Egypt under the command of Sir Ralph Abercromby in 1801 (*medal*). In 1806 at Maida. Defence of Gaeta and surrender of Tropea; took possession of the latter town with his detachment. Served again in Egypt with the expedition under Major-General Fraser in 1807. He has been repeatedly engaged in severe boat actions, and against batteries, and debarked with detachments aiding in capturing and destroying ships and convoys on the enemy's coast.

13 Colonel Pilcher served with the boats of the British fleet, in 1801, in their occasional attack of the Spanish gun-boats and vessels off Cadiz. In 1803, served in His Majesty's Ship, *Raisonable*, in the North Sea; 1804, attack of the gun-boats and batteries at Boulogne; July 22, 1805, in the general action and defeat of the combined fleets of France and Spain. In August following, in action with *La Topaze*, French frigate. January 1806, landed with a battalion of Marines at the attack and capture of the Cape of Good Hope. In June following, with the same battalion, at the attack and defeat of the Spanish troops on the road to Buenos Ayres, and at the capture of that city: in August following, at the defence of that city against the Spanish forces, after three days' action, taken prisoner, with the rest of the British. 1811, served in the North Sea, in attacks with the Danish gun-boats. 1813 and 1814, off the coast of France and America. Appointed to the 2d batalion of Royal Marines, and was at the attack of the American army and its defeat on the road to Baltimore, when Maj.-Gen. Ross was killed. At the attack of the American troops at Farnham church: commanded upon this occasion the advance, consisting of small detachments of the 21st, 44th, and 85th regts. and marines. In 1815, was at the attack of the American Rifle force near Point à Petie, and the capture of that fort in West Florida. From 1819 to 1821, served in His Majesty's Ship, *Vigo*, at St. Helena, during the last nine months of Buonaparte's life, and assisted with the marines at his interment.

14 Lt.-Col. Thomas Stevens was present blockading Brest, the Helder, and Cadiz, and was engaged with batteries. In 1809 he was engaged with gun-boats in passing convoys through the Sound and Categat; in H. M. S. *Cerberus*, with convoy of armed transports and gun-boats in the Gulf of Friedland; in the boats of the squadron in the successful attack upon the Russian Flotilla of heavy armed gun-boats and armed Transports; and at the capture of a Russian schooner. From 1836 to 1840 he served in the Royal Marine Battalion on the north coast of Spain; was detached in command of a company for the defence of the Eastern Heights of Passages attacked by the Carlists, and in the Carlist attack of the Lines on the 6th June 1836; and he was also present at Fuentarabia, 11th July 1836.

15 Lieut.-Col. Gibsone was on board the *Safeguard* mortar brig in a severe action with a division of Danish gun-boats between Anholt and Jutland, on the 29th June 1811. The following year he was engaged at Cateria on the north coast of Spain, and was the officer who accompanied Capt. Parke with two 24-pounders intended for the British army before Burgos. In 1813 and 14 he served in the American war, and was present at the attack on Craney Island, taking of Hampton, defence of the Lines of Chippewa, and other affairs.

16 Lieut.-Col. Ballingall prior to entering the Royal Marines, served as a Midshipman at Copenhagen in 1801; landed at Vimiera, 21 Aug., 1808; was a volunteer in the boats of the *Resistance* at the boarding and carrying *La Mouche*, French man-of-war schooner, under a constant fire of grape and musquetry; the commander fell by the hand of Capt. B. 26 Feb. 1809. Served as a volunteer at the cutting out of four French luggers laden with supplies for the French army, from the harbour of Santa Clara, north coast of Spain, on the night of the 27th Feb. 1809, under a galling fire of musquetry, and defended by two batteries which commanded the entrance; landed at the head of the Marines from the *Resistance*, carried a battery of four guns; and assisted in the capture and blowing up of a French man-of-war schooner, and destroyed her convoy, laden with supplies for the French army, 10th March, 1809; was subsequently at the siege of Cadiz; and in 1832 in the castles of Naupoli de Romania, with an allied garrison during an attack on that city.

18 Lt.-Col. Coryton served at the battle of Trafalgar, and was subsequently engaged with the enemy on various occasions, in the course of which service he has been several times wounded.

20 Lieut.-Colonel Mercer assisted at the destruction of the French squadron in Basque Roads. He was repeatedly landed on the North Coast of Spain in 1810, co-operating with the Patriots. In 1812, while embarked on board H.M.S. *Java*, he was engaged with and captured by the United States frigate *Constitution*.

21 Lieut.-Col. Ellis's services:—The general action with the combined fleets of France and Spain, off Cape Finisterre, 22nd July 1805; battle of Trafalgar, 21st Oct. following; the Walcheren expedition in 1809, and in the *Lavinia*, the leading frigate of ten, forcing the passage of the Scheldt under a heavy fire from the batteries of Flushing and Cadsand. Capture of the island of Guadaloupe, in January 1810. Employed, in 1812 and 13, off the coasts of France, Spain, and Portugal. Taking of the American frigate *President*, Jan. 1814; various successful affairs of boats in North America. Bombardment and reduction of Fort Munora in Scinde in Feb. 1839; and, landing, the 25th of the following month, with the detachment of his corps at Bushire, under a smart fire from the Persians, for the protection of the East India Company's Political Resident, and in possession of the Residency until the 30th, when that agent was embarked in safety. China expedition, and as senior officer in command of the Royal Marines at the capture of Chusan on the 5th July 1840, battle of Chuen-pee, 7th Jan. 1841, wherein he commanded the advance (promoted Brevet-Major); bombardment of the Bogue Forts, assault and capture of the Island of North Wantung, 26th Feb.; the advance on Canton, March 8th; storming and taking the heights and forts before the walls of Canton, 26th May (promoted Lieut.-Colonel); capture of the strongly fortified Island of Colongso, near Amoy, 26th Aug.; 2nd capture of Chusan, 1st Oct.; assault and capture of citadel and city of Chinhae, 10th Oct.; advance on and entry into Ningpo, 13th Oct.; in garrison and command of Tay-woong-kaou fortress in the river and near to Canton, from 6th April to 24th May 1841; and on similar duties at Ningpo and Chusan, with battalion of Royal Marines, from 10th Oct. to 27th January 1842, following.

22 Lt.-Colonel Wearing was wounded at Trafalgar.

24 Lt.-Col. Willes's services: Sir Richard Strachan's action, 4 Nov 1805; West Indies, 1808 to 1812, including the capture of the city of St. Domingo in 1809; South Beveland, winter of 1813; Operations in the Chesapeake under Sir George Cockburn; Capture of Washington; Advance to Baltimore, in 1814; Capture of Cumberland Island on the coast of Georgia, and of the town of Saint Mary's, 1814; Coast of Africa, 1817; East Indies, 1833 to 1835. Various boat and other services.

25 Lt.-Col. M'Adam, during service in *L'Aigle* between Aug. 1805 and May 1809, was at the attack on the French Fleet by Admiral Cornwallis on the 21st Aug. 1805; gunboats in Vigo Bay 29th Oct. following; blockade of Fort Cygo, July and Aug. 1807; action with French frigates off L'Orient, 22d March 1808; Basque Roads, 11th and 12th April 1809; and various other affairs in the ship or her boats: above forty times under fire. During service in the *Thames*, between 7th Oct. 1809 and 27th Aug. 1812, he landed at Mount Cercilly, Amanthea, Citraco, in the Gulf of Policastro and near to Cape Palinuro, Porto del Infreschi, Palinuro, and many other places upon the coast of Calabria and on the Roman States in the ship, in her boats, or on shore: above twenty-five times under fire. During service in the *Forth*, between 31st July 1813 and 29th Sept. 1815, he landed on North Beveland, again on South Beveland on staff of Anglo-Russian Force forming siege of Bathz; and on the North American shores: above five times under fire. In all above seventy times under fire, and frequently mentioned in the dispatches.

26 Lt.-Colonel Garmston was at the taking of Fort Koupan, Isle of Timor, in 1811; capture of Java, in 1812; attack of Palembang, isle of Sumatra, and Sambass, isle of Borneo; Algiers in 1816. Present at the Sortie from Bilboa 15th May; the advance on the 28th May; and was wounded at the defence of the lines of San Sebastian 6th June, 1836.

27 Lt.-Colonel John Harvey Stevens served in the West Indies, &c. in 1806 and 1807, during the expedition to Walcheren in 1809, and was engaged in several flotilla affairs on the Scheldt. Served also at the successful defence of Cadiz and of Tarifa in 1810 and 1811; was engaged in several detached operations, particularly in one of a severe character on the river Guadalquiver. In 1813 was employed on the coast of America, where he was engaged

in an attack on Craney Island, and at the taking of Hampton and Ocracoke under Sir George Cockburn. Served in Canada at the taking of Oswego, on which occasion he was mentioned in Sir Gordon Drummond's despatches. Engaged during a six weeks' siege of Fort Erie, and was intrusted with the construction of a field-work for the defence of the right of the position on Chippewa Creek, which was menaced by a very superior force. In 1816 he was on board the *Queen Charlotte* at the attack on Algiers under Lord Exmouth, by whom he was detached to fire carcasses at the enemy's vessels within the Mole. He was also present at the demonstrations before Algiers under Admiral Sir H. B. Neale. Capt. Stevens is now superintendent of the Marine Artillery Laboratory, which establishment originated in his proposition, and was organized by him.

28 Major Pratt was at the taking of Capri in the Bay of Naples, under Sir Sidney Smith, 11th May, 1806. At the cutting out of six armed vessels from under the batteries of Lamica, in the island of Cyprus, in Jan. 1808. Belonged to the battalion of Royal Marines commanded by Sir James Malcolm, which served in Spain, the coast of America, and Canada, for four years, and was present at all the services performed by it, including the battle of Frampton in the Chesapeak, and the storming and taking of the enemy's fort and post of Oswego on Lake Ontario. Served also in the battalion of Royal Marines in Spain, and was present at the battles of the 16th June, 1836, and Ernani 16th March following, together with all the services performed there for nearly four years.

29 Major Delacombe served on board the *Tonnant* covering the embarkation of Sir John Moore's army at Corunna, and afterwards in various boat affairs in Basque Roads, in 1809, and at the defence of Cadiz the following year. In 1812 he was at the destruction of the batteries of Languelia, after charging with the bayonet and defeating a battalion of the French 52nd Regiment of the Line of a very superior force. In 1813 he was on board the *Imperieuse* at the attack on the batteries and tower of post D'Anzo, after which he was landed and the enemy driven from their posts, which were destroyed, and a convoy of 29 vessels laden with ship timber for Toulon brought out; he was afterwards at the attack on Leghorn under Sir Josias Rowley. Independent of the above, he has been employed on various and repeated boat service; partially engaged with the French fleet off Toulon; and several times with the Neapolitan squadron, gun-boats, and batteries in the Bay of Naples.

31 Major Fegen was at the taking of the fort and town of Guadia; capture of the enemy's convoy under batteries near Marseilles; destruction of French forts near Port Vendre; the taking of Zante, Cephalonia, and Cerigo; capture of enemy's forts and convoy at Pezzero, in the Adriatic; action in the Bay of Naples, 3rd May, 1810, when Sir Jahleel Brenton, in the *Spartan*, defeated the whole of the enemy's squadron, and captured a brig of war; at the capturing an enemy's convoy from under the batteries of Terracino, in 1810; and at the destruction of several American privateers in the Bay of Fundy, by the *Spartan*.

36 Major Robinson served at the siege of Copenhagen in 1807, and was engaged in the in-shore squadron with the Danish flotilla and crown batteries. In the action with and destruction of the French squadron in the inner roads of Aix, 12th April, 1809, in the *Valiant*, the senior officer's ship actually engaged. At the siege of Flushing, and the subsequent operations in the Scheldt in 1809. On the coast of France in 1810 and 1811 in boat affairs. In the 1st battalion of Royal Marines throughout the campaign of 1813 in the Chesapeak, commencing with the attack on Cranie Island. In the same battalion in the defence of Lower Canada in the winter of 1813 and in 1814 principally employed on the outposts of the army on the American frontier. In 1814 in command of a company of the 1st battalion Royal Marines in the capture of Cumberland Island, and the attack and capture of the fortified post and town of St. Mary's, Georgia. Served in Syria in 1840, and commanded the Royal Marines in the attack on Gebail, for which he received his promotion to the Brevet rank of Major.

37 Major Dawes was at the siege of Copenhagen in 1807.

38 Major Philips served as a Midshipman on board H. M. S. *Belleisle* at the battle of Trafalgar. As an officer of Royal Marines, he was present at the storming of three of the enemy's entrenched batteries and siege of Santa Maura, and frequently employed in boat affairs on the coasts of Italy and Dalmatia. In April 1812, he joined the first Battalion; served with it in Spain and in America, including the storming of the enemy's entrenched camp at Hampton in Virginia, and frequent affairs with the enemy there. Detached to Canada and served under Commodore Sir James Yeo, on the Lakes Ontario, Erie, and Champlain.

40 Major Calamy has served in every quarter of the globe, and in the actions of Nyburg, Flushing, Isle of France, Java, and several minor affairs with gun-boats, &c. He was Brigade Major to the British Forces landed in Syria in 1840.

45 Captain Henry was at the capture of Anholt, May, 1809; at Fort Mobile, 1815; the victory of Algiers, August 1816; and was frequently engaged with boats in the Baltic, and with the American troops in the Floridas.

46 Captain Graham served with the army in the battalion formed of the marines of the squadron at the taking of Walcheren in 1809. Also served in the 1st battalion in Portugal and in operations on the North Coast of Spain, at the taking and defence of Castro. Proceeded with the battalion to America, where it was brigaded under Sir Sidney Beckwith at

the attack upon Norfolk, and the taking of Hampton, and several small places. The brigade being broken up, he went with the battalion to Canada; whilst there, he was sent with a detachment in command of a division of gun boats to attack a battery at the head of Lake Champlain, with which they were engaged some hours. Returned with the battalion to the coast of America, and was at the attack and taking of Fort Point Petre and the town of St. Mary's, in Georgia; shortly after his promotion in 1837, he exchanged to join the battalion in Spain. He was afterwards at the demonstration before Nankin in China.

47 Major Whitcombe assisted in cutting out three Spanish gun-boats from under the fire of a battery, in the boats of H. M. S. *Edgar*. Commanded the detachment of marines in the flag ship of Sir P. Malcolm in the expedition to the Chesapeak and New Orleans: was present at the attack on the American Flotilla in the Potomac, at the capture of Washington, defeat of the American army before Baltimore, and the operations before New Orleans. Proceeded to China in H. M. S. *Blenheim;* landed with the marine battalion at the attack and capture of the forts and works at Chuenpee; assisted at the attack of the Anunghoy forts by the *Blenheim* and *Melville*, upon which occasion the seamen and marines were landed, and the three forts carried in succession. He was second in command of the marine battalion at the capture of the heights of Canton, the second capture of Chusan, and at the attack and capture of the fort and city of Chinhae. At the attack on Amoy by the *Blenheim* and *Wellesley* Major Whitcombe landed in command of the marines, when the enemy were driven from their guns and the fortifications, &c. captured.

48 Capt. Dusautoy served at Walcheren; was at the capture of Genoa; and in two partial actions with French fleets off Toulon and Marseilles.

49 Major Childs served in H. M. S. *Gibraltar*, blockading Cherbourg, L'Orient, and Basque Roads, and frequently in boats cutting out French coasters. Early in 1813 he volunteered to serve in the 1st battalion under Colonel Sir Richard Williams in the Chesapeake, and was at the attack of Craney Island, taking of the enemy's camp at Hampton, and capture of Kent Island, and in many minor engagements on the enemy's coast; after which he accompanied the battalion to Canada, and was actively employed on the Frontiers, and frequently in command of gun-boats on Lake Champlain. On the 11th Sept. 1814, he was engaged on board the *Confiance*, in one of the most severe actions fought during the war, in which Commodore Downie (the captain of the ship), Captain Anderson, R. M., and 41 men were killed, and upwards of 190 wounded, out of a complement of 260. He also served the Syrian campaign (Medal) of 1840, including the attack and capture of Sidon, capture of Beyrout, bombardment of Acre, and other desultory services.

50 Captain Wesley served in a battalion of Marines formed from the squadron under Sir Alex. Cochrane at the attack and capture of Guadaloupe, St. Martin's and St. Eustatia in 1810. In blockading squadrons off Brest, L'Orient, and Basque Roads, including several successful boat affairs under the Batteries of Rochelle and Isle d'Aix in 1811. In coast operations, North of Spain; and, with the first battalion of Marines, in Portugal, in 1812. At the attack on Norfolk, and the entrenched camp of Hampton, &c. in the Chesapeake. Served the campaigns of 1813 and 14 at the advanced posts in Lower Canada, and in command of a division of seven gun-boats employed blockading the enemy's flotilla at Plattsburg. At the defence of La Cole Mill. Adjutant to a Light Corps formed of the flank companies of the 2d West India Regiment and Marine Battalions at the attack and capture of Fort Peter, the fortified positions of St. Mary's and Cumberland Island (coast of Georgia). In command of a detachment of Artillery in H. M. S. *Phaeton* assisted in repelling an attack of Algerine gun-boats in 1821. Adjutant to a battalion under Colonel Owen serving in co-operation with the Spanish army in 1836-7, including the affair before Fuentarabia, 11 July 1836, the field actions of the 10th, 12th, and 14th March, and of Hernani, 16 March 1837. Served as Captain in the same battalion until the Force under Lord John Hay was withdrawn in 1840.

51 Captain Park was actively employed in the Baltic during 1810, 11, and 12. From 1813 until the peace, served on the coast of America, and the West Indies, including the attack on Cranie Island, and landed at the taking of Hampton, in the Chesapeake.

53 Captain James Dowman served at the defence of Cadiz in 1810, 11, and 12, during which period he was repeatedly engaged in action against the enemy both on land and in boats, cutting out, &c. At the blockading of the French fleet off Brest, in 1813. During the late campaign on the coast of Syria, in 1840 and 41, including the storming and capture of Sidon, surrender of Beyrout, bombardment and fall of St. Jean d'Acre. Served also with the Royal Marine Battalion at the camp at D'Jouni.

57 Captain Thomas Fynmore was at the capture of a French privateer schooner of 16 guns and 96 men, besides other boat service in 1811. In the partial action with the French fleet off Toulon in 1814. Was landed at Mahon in command of a guard to protect the person of the Spanish governor from the threatened violence of the Walloon guards. Sent to the city of Florence in 1815, to place himself under the directions of General Count Nugent, commander-in-chief of the Austrian army, as extra aide-de-camp, and was at the taking of the city of Naples. In 1823 he was sent up to the city of Lima to protect English merchants' property against the attacks of the Negro slaves during the civil war.

The 20th Oct. 1827, was at the battle of Navarino, for which service he was promoted by His Royal Highness the Duke of Clarence, but in consequence of belonging to a gradation corps the appointment was afterwards cancelled. Served with the French army at the reduction of the town and fortress of Patras and the Morea castle; served afterwards in the West Indies, North Sea, and off Oporto during the civil war between Don Pedro and Don Miguel. In 1833 joined the Royal Marine Battalion at Lisbon, commanded by Colonel Adair, C. B. In April, 1837, embarked on board H. M. S. *Castor* (36), on the 10th Oct. was landed in command of his detachment on the Albanian coast to attack Pirates. Served on the S. E. coast of Spain from 4th Jan. 38 to 30 Jan. 39.

59 Captain Brown's services:—attack on French forts at Ciota June 1812; attack and capture of the town of L'Escalia, in the Bay of Rosas, 1812; partial engagement with the French fleet, near Toulon, 1813; attack of Algiers; destruction of Greek pirates at Porto Bono, Isle of Candia, June, 1826.

61 Major Hurdle was at the attack on the forts and harbour of Courageaux in 1815; battle of Navarino in 1827; and engagement at Punta Obligada in the river Parana on the 20th Nov. 1845.

63 Captain Appleton served in the battalion of Marines in co-operation with the allied forces in Syria, and was present at the attack and surrender of the fortress of St. Jean D'Acre on the 3d November, 1840.

64 Captain Dwyer served in the blockading squadrons off Flushing, the Texel, and off Brest. Since the peace he has served in the East and West Indies, and the Mediterranean.

66 Captain Hawkins commanded the Royal Marines (about 200 strong) at the attack on and destruction of Malloodoo in Borneo.

67 Captain Mitford was employed on the coast of Syria during the whole of the operations against the Egyptians; he landed and served with the battalion at the Camp d'Jouni and was present at the bombardment of St. Jean d'Acre. He has been presented with a medal from the Sultan.

68 Captain Parke's services:—Co-operation with the Spanish forces and Legion near San Sebastian, and under Espartero in raising the siege of Bilboa.

69 Major Stransham served at the battle of Navarino, in 1827. Also on the China expedition, and was severely wounded at the attack on the defences of Canton, 18th March, 1841.

70 Captain Anderson served at the battle of Navarino, in 1827.

71 Captain T. B. Gray served at the battle of Navarino in 1827. Also in a battalion under Colonel Owen, on the north coast of Spain in 1836-7-8, in co-operation with the Spanish army, including the field actions of the 10th, 12th, and 14th March, and the action of Hernani, 16th March 1837: he was subsequently appointed Adjutant to that force under Colonel Parke. He served as Captain on the coast of Portugal and in the Tagus during the civil war in 1846-7, and was landed with his detachment from H. M. S. *Superb*, to guard the captured divisions of the rebel army under Count das Antas, prisoners in Fort St. Julian.

73 Captain John Miller served at the battle of Navarino, in 1827.

75 Capt. George Elliott served on the China expedition, and was wounded in the attack on the intrenched camps on the heights of Segoan, 15th March, 1842.

77 Major Langford served with the Battalion in Spain from June 1836 to Sept. 1840, and was present in the actions of Fuenterabia and Hernani, besides various minor affairs. While serving in H. M. S. *North Star*, from Sept. 1841 to Sept. 1846, he participated in the operations of the Expeditionary Force in China, including the blockade of the Woosung Rivers. On the termination of hostilities with China he proceeded in the *North Star* to New Zealand; and was landed with all the detachments of Royal Marines from H. M. ships present, and appointed to command that force, together with a detachment of the 96th Regt., with which he was actively employed in the field against the insurgent chiefs, whose strongly stockaded Pahs, or Villages, were successfully attacked and destroyed: for these services he obtained the Brevet rank of Major.

79 Captain Urquhart was at the reduction of the Fort of Munora in Scinde, in Feb. 1839. Debarked with a detachment of his Corps, under a brisk fire, at Bushier in the Persian Gulf, for the protection of the East India Company's Political Resident. He was present at nearly all the affairs in China, from the capture of Chusan up to the attack on the heights above Canton, under Sir Hugh Gough. His name was also favourably mentioned in the Dispatches of Sir Gordon Bremer.

80 Captain Fraser landed for the protection of British property at Lima, during the revolution in Dec. 1835, when in possession of the rebels. For his conduct on that occasion, he was presented with a piece of plate by the merchants.

81 Captain J. H. Wright served with the Battalion, in co-operation with the Spanish and Legion forces on the north coast of Spain, from 1836 to 1840, and was present at the actions of Fuenterabia and Hernani.

83 Capt. Langley served in the operations on the North Coast of Spain in command of the detachment of Royal Marines of H.M.S. *Castor*, during 1834 and two following years,

and was severely wounded on the 9th June 1836, defending the heights of Passages against a very superior force of Carlists.

84 Captain Brittain was presented with a sword by the merchants of Bombay, for services performed against pirates in the Straits of Malacca.

85 Capt. Simon Fraser served throughout the campaign in Syria, including the storm and capture of Sidon, the surrender of Beyrout, and the bombard. and capture of St. Jean d'Acre.

86 Capt. Parker was wounded through the arm at Prescott, in Upper Canada, 13th Nov. 1838.

87 Capt. Maxwell served on the China expedition, and was present at the battle of Chuenpee, attack of batteries of Anunghoy and North Wantung, advance on Canton, storming the heights and entrenched camp of Canton, bombardment of Colongso.

88 Capt. Spalding served in command of a Company throughout the operations in Syria, in 1840, and was slightly wounded at the attack on Gebail. He has received the Syrian Medal.

89 Capt. Marriott served two years with the expeditionary force in China, and was present at the first capture of Chusan; assisted at the demolition of the Bogue Forts in the Canton River; participated in the actions of the first and second Bars; was engaged in the destruction of all the enemy's sea and river defences, including the fortresses of French Folly and Hoqua's Fort; bombardment and taking of Macao Passage Fort; storming of the Bird's Nest Battery, and finally at the combined attack on the enemy's position and entrenched camp on the heights above Canton.

92 Lieut. Timpson served as Adjutant to the Royal Marine Battalion in 1842 at the capture of Tscke and heights of Segoan, attack on the hill defences and capture of Chapoo, capture of the batteries and city of Woosung, capture of the batteries of Le Shau, assault and capture of Chin Kiang Foo, and landing before Nankin.

93 Lieut. C. O. Hamley was present at the attack on and destruction of Malloodoo, in Borneo.

94 Lieut. A. J. B. Hambly served on the China expedition, and was severely wounded in the attack on the intrenched camps on the heights of Segoan, 15th March, 1842.

96 Lieut. Adair was slightly wounded in the assault upon Gebail, in Syria, 12th Sept. 1840.

97 Lieut. Farmar served on the China expedition, and was present at the battle of Chuenpee, attack of the Anunghoy batteries, advance on Canton, capture of the heights of Canton, capture of Colongso, second capture of Chusan, assault and capture of the citadel and city of Chinhae, entry into Ningpo.

98 Lieut. Harrison served in the operations on the Coast of Syria (Medal), including the attacks on the fortress of D'Jebail, and bombardment and capture of Acre. He served also in New Zealand, and was present at the taking of the fortified Pah at Ruapekapeka on the 11th Jan. 1846.

100 Lieut. J. A. Stewart served on the coast of Syria during the whole of the campaign, and was at the taking of Sidon, and at the siege of St. Jean d'Acre in H. M. S. *Edinburgh*. Served also on the coast of Africa for two years, during which time he assisted at the destruction of several Barracoons on the coast, when about 1200 slaves were liberated.

101 Lieut. Pickard served on the China expedition, and was present at the battle of Chuenpee, attack of batteries of Anunghoy and North Wantung, advance on Canton, storming the heights of Canton, bombardment of Colongso.

102 Lieuts. Dyer, J. W. A. Kennedy, and Mansell were present at the attack on and destruction of Malloodoo, in Borneo.

107 Capt. Hookey served as Volunteer 1st class, in His Majesty's ship *Prince of Wales*, from Jan. to Dec. 1805, and was in the general action of the 22nd Dec. 1805. Served in the West Indies, from 1806 until 1809, including the capture of Les Saints, and Martinique, and several actions in boats cutting out French vessels, and destroying batteries, &c. From 1809 to 1811 served on board H. M. S. *Theban*, blockading the French flotilla at Boulogne; several times in action with them. Assisted in the boats cutting out a large French lugger at Dieppe. From 1812 to 1814, served on board His Majesty's ship *Daphne*, in the Baltic, and was several times in action with Danish gun boats in the Belt.

108 Capt. Moore served in H. M. S. *Amphion*, from May, 1803 to July, 1811; was in the action with and capture of four Spanish frigates off Cape St. Mary's; action with flotilla of gunboats in Gibraltar Bay; cutting out a schooner in Corsica; a severe action with a French frigate, and driven on shore under the batteries in the Bay of Rivers in 1806. Served at the taking of Pecau, and capture of large convoys. Commanded the marines at the taking of Cootelazza in 1809, and taking six gunboats. Commanded the marines of the squadron at the taking of Grao and large convoys laden with military stores, after a most sanguinary action with a garrison of French troops at the point of the bayonet, when the whole of the garrison were killed, wounded, or made prisoners,—for this action and previous services he was made brevet-captain. Present also at the capture of several other towns on the coast of the Adriatic, and destruction of convoys. He was senior officer of marines in the action off Lissa, 13th March, 1810, and was twice very severely wounded and twice rewarded from Patriotic Fund. He has been in upwards of 30 successful contests with the enemy, and frequently officially mentioned for gallantry.

109 Capt. Little served in the channel fleet and at the blockade of Ferrol and Corunna in 1803-4. Appointed to the Royal Marine Artillery on the formation of that corps in 1804, and was employed in various bomb vessels on the enemy's coast co-operating with the land forces, or on detached service. In command of the mortars in the *Vesuvius* bomb at the attack of Boulogne. Defence of Cadiz in 1809; and subsequently at the blockade of Rochfort, where he commanded a storming party in a successful night attack on the coast, on which occasion he received the particular thanks of the Admiralty, and was rewarded by the Patriotic Fund:—at the commencement of this attack he was severely wounded by a musket-ball shattering the wrist which rendered amputation of the right hand necessary.

110 Captain Wolrige served in the year 1809 with Lord Cochrane in Basque Roads; and in the same year was engaged in action with gun-boats in the Baltic. From 1810 to 1812 defence of Cadiz and Tarifa. Severely wounded at South Beveland in 1814, and received a reward from the Patriotic Fund. Present at the battle of Algiers in 1816.

111 Captain Toby served from 1810 to 12 inclusive, on the Coast of France. From 1813 to 16, with the 1st battalion (Royal Marines) in America, and on the Lakes of Canada. Since the Peace, he has served in the Mediterranean, on the coasts of Africa, and South America. He has been frequently engaged in boat actions with batteries, &c. &c.

112 Doctor Rae has served in every quarter of the globe; eight years in the East Indies at one period, and was at the destruction of the Dutch squadron in Surabaya, in 1808. He has been in frequent engagements with batteries, and in the cutting out of numerous vessels, and in many boat-actions.

113 Doctor Irvine was actively employed on the coast of North America in 1814 and 15, as Assistant-Surgeon of H. M. S. *Spencer*, and Acting-Surgeon of H. M. sloop *Dispatch*, being in boat service, and frequently under the fire of the enemy. He was surgeon of the *Alligator* at Rangoon during the Burmese war, where he had also charge of the Hospital Ship established for the reception of the sick and wounded of the flotilla employed in the Irrawaddy. He was surgeon of the *Dartmouth* in the battle of Navarino, and of the flag ships *St. Vincent* and *Britannia* in the Mediterranean: whilst in the latter ship Dr. Irvine gained the gold medal of Sir Gilbert Blane for his Medical Journal.

114 Major Leonard served with the detachment of Royal Marines in the Fortress of Roses, in Catalonia, in 1808. In 1809, he was present at the reduction of Zante and Cephalonia; and in 1810 at that of Santa Maura, including the assault of the entrenched batteries and siege of the Fortress. He was afterwards present in several boat actions, during two years, off Corfu; and in H. M. S. *Perlen* in the action with the French squadron off Toulon, 22nd Nov. 1811. He served the Syrian campaign of 1840 (Medal), including the assault and capture of Sidon and bombardment of Acre; also at the camp D'Jonni, at Beyrout, and Jaffa: for the Syrian service he was promoted to the Brevet rank of Major. He was landed from H. M. S. *Alfred*, at Monte Video, with the Royal Marines of the squadron for the protection of British subjects and property, during the siege of the city by the Argentine Army under General Oribe, and commanded the brigade consisting of the Reserve Battalion 45th Regt. and Royal Marines for three months, and the Royal Marines from June 1843 to July 1847.

115 Lt. Lawrence acted as Aide-de-camp to Capt. Hotham, R. N. while taking and destroying the batteries, &c. at Punta Obligada, in the river Parana, on the 20th Nov. 1845.

116 Captain Lawrence served in bomb vessels in 1805 and 6 between Dunkirk and Boulogne, and was several times engaged with the French flotilla. In 1807 he was present at the passage of the Dardanelles, and destroying the Turkish squadron, and in Egypt. In 1808 he was at the defence of Roses. In 1809 he was in the Walcheren expedition, and engaged with the enemy's gun-boats at Batz. In 1811 he was serving with the Marine battalion in Lisbon, St. Julian, and Cascaes. In 1812 he was on the north coast of Spain, and was the officer who directed the guns from a rock at the entrance of the St. Andrew river against the castle of Vigo, and subsequently landed and blew it up: he was also at the taking of Castro, at all the attacks on that coast. In 1814 he was at the battle of Bladensburg, capture of Washington, action before Baltimore, and subsequently in all the attacks at New Orleans.

	Deputy Asst. Commis. Gen.	Assistant Commis. Gen.	Deputy Commis. Gen.	Commissary General	Station.
Commissaries-General.					
𝔓 William Filder		10 Aug. 11	22 Oct. 1	1 July 40	*Canada.*
Charles Palmer	Never	4 May 15	20 Jan. 37	26 Dec. 46	*Cape.*
Francis Edward Knowles	5 May 12	22 Oct. 16	20 Jan. 37	28 Dec. 47	*W. Ind.*
Deputy-Commissaries-General.					
𝔓 John Saumarez Dobree	6 Dec. 10	1 July 14	7 June 25		*Dublin.*
𝔓 Denzil Ibbettson	5 Oct. 10	25 Dec. 14	10 Sep. 30		
Henry James Wild		4 May 15	20 Jan. 37		*Malta.*
𝔓 William Miller	5 Aug. 11	22 Oct. 16	do.		*Cape of Good Hope.*
𝔓 John Laidley	11 Jan. 12	do.	do.		*Mauritius.*
𝔓 William Hayward, (*Accounts*)	2 Mar. 12	do.	do.		*Van Dieman's Land.*
𝔓 John Banner Price	25 Dec. 14	9 Feb. 27	5 June 38		*West Indies.*
Thomas Warton Ramsay	25 Nov. 13	7 June 25	28 June 38		*New South Wales.*
Lovell Pennell	23 May 12	7 June 25	26 Dec. 40		*Canada.*
Wm. Henry Robinson	2 Nov. 12	7 June 25	26 Dec. 40		*Nova Scotia.*
𝔓 George Maclean	22 Oct. 16	24 May 34	23 Dec. 42		*Van Dieman's Land.*
𝔓 Wm. Randolph Eppes	19 July 21	7 July 27	24 Dec. 44		*Jamaica.*
𝔓 Henry Bowers	25 Dec. 14	13 Dec. 33	do.		*Gibraltar.*
William Green	16 Mar. 13	10 Sep. 30	16 Dec. 45		*Cape of Good Hope.*
𝔓 John Edgcumbe Daniel	23 Aug. 12	23 Nov. 27	26 Dec. 46		
Assistant-Commissaries-General.					
𝔓 John Wood	9 Mar. 12	25 Apr. 15			*Montreal.*
Tannat H. Thomson	8 Dec. 12	10 Sep. 30			*Toronto, Upper Canada.*
George Yeoland	3 Feb. 13	10 Sept. 30			*Jamaica.*
𝔓 William Bishop	13 July 24	24 July 34			*Cork.*
Thos. C. Weir	15 July 26	11 Apr. 36			*Ionian Islands.*
𝔓 Edw. A. F. Cowan	5 Aug. 11	4 May 36			*Demerara.*
𝔓 Thomas Rayner	22 Apr. 13	20 Jan. 37			*Bermuda.*
𝔓 Alexander Trotter	27 Oct. 13	do.			*Dominica.*
William Bailey	10 Jan. 14	do.			*Canada.*
John Lane	31 Jan. 14	do.			*Montreal.*
George Elliot	2 May	do.			*Barbadoes.*
𝔓 William F. Bowman	4 May 14	do.			*Malta.*
𝔓 James D. Watt	do.	do.			*Belfast.*
Robert Lindsey	13 July 14	3 May 37			*Jamaica.*
Thomas Rae	25 Dec. 14	5 June 38			*Quebec.*
William Isaac Greig	13 May 14	28 June 38			*Nova Scotia.*
𝔓 Gilbert H. Dinwiddie		do.			*Gibraltar.*
Oliver Goldsmith	17 Dec. 14	do.			*Newfoundland.*
William Low	do.	do.			*St. Lucia.*
Fred. Thomas Mylrea	10 Sept. 30	6 Dec. 39			*Dublin.*
Charles Williams	25 Dec. 14	1 July 40			*Trinidad.*
Kenneth Cameron	4 May 15	do			*Dublin.*
Thomas Fraser	25 Apr. 15	1 July 40			*Jamaica.*
𝔓 Henry Charles Darling	12 Sept. 16	do.			*Western Australia.*
𝔓 James Wm. Reed	22 Oct. 16	do.			
𝔓 William Fletcher	do.	do.			*Van Dieman's Land.*
𝔓 William Milliken	do.	do.			*Athlone.*
Charles Bridgen, (*Accounts*)	19 July 21	24 Dec. 41			*Van Dieman's Land.*
George Adams	do.	do.			*Dublin.*
Charles Swain	do.	do.			*Barbadoes.*
Thomas Walker	13 July 24	do.			*New South Wales.*
Thomas Eggar Trew	7 June 25	do.			*Canada.*
Ferguson Thos. Coxworthy	7 June 25	24 Dec. 41			*Canada.*
Thos. Geo. S. Swan	do.	do.			*New South Wales.*
William Fisher Mends	1 July 37	15 June 43			*Barbadoes.*
Fulford Bastard Feilde	7 June 25	23 Dec.			*Canada.*
Henry Francis Oriel	7 June 25	do.			*Canada.*
William Looker, (*Accounts*)	15 July 26	do.			*Van Dieman's Land.*
John M'Farlan	do.	do.			*Canada.*
Thomas Graham	11 Dec. 34	15 June 44			*Grenada.*
𝔓 Joseph Wm. Wybault	23 Sept. 27	24 Dec.			*Malta.*
Richard Inglis	30 Oct. 27	do.			*Cape of Good Hope.*
John William Smith	1 Dec. 33	do.			*Hong Kong.*
Johannes de Smidt	29 Aug. 36	do.			*Cape of Good Hope.*
Thomas James Lempriere	20 Jan. 37	24 Dec. 44			*Van Dieman's Land.*
William Robinson	3 April 27	16 Dec. 45			*Cape of Good Hope.*

	Deputy Asst. Commis. Gen.	Assistant Commis. Gen.	Station.
Samuel Joseph Towesland	18 Sep. 27	16 Dec. 45	*Tobago.*
James Skyrme	28 Nov. 27	do	*Canada.*
Robert Ackroyd	14 May 29	do	*Mauritius.*
William Stanton	2 Jan. 31	do	*Canada.*
Wm. Robert Alex. Lamont	5 Oct. 32	do	*Nova Scotia.*
John Kent	do.	do	*Van Dieman's Land.*
Stephen Owen	do.	do	*New South Wales.*
Francis Bisset Archer	2 Jan. 34	do	
William Henry Drake	16 Apr. 35	do	*Van Dieman's Land.*
George Shepheard	20 Jan. 37	26 Dec. 46	*Ionian Islands.*
Robert Neill	do.	do	
William Hen. Maturin	do.	do	*South Australia.*
John William Bovell	do.	do	*St. Helena.*
Randolph Routh	do.	do	*Limerick.*
Maximilian Malassez	28 June 38	do	*Bermuda.*
Philip Turner	do.	do	*New Zealand.*

Deputy Assistant Commissaries-General.

	Deputy Asst. Commis. Gen.	Station.
Charles Thos. Malàssez	20 May 28	*Bahamas*
Wm. Hen. Dalrymple	20 Jan. 37	*Canada*
Alexander Edwards	do.	*Nova Scotia*
John Trimmer	28 June 38	*Kilkenny*
Edm. John M'Mahon	do.	*Barbadoes*
Wm. Spearman Archer	do.	*Ion. Islands*
John S. Davenport	do.	*Canada*
James Aug. Erskine	do.	*N. S. Wales*
Henry Clarke	27 Aug. 38	*Honduras*
Stanley Jones	1 July 40	*Canada*
Geo. Darley Lardner	do.	
James Lane	do.	*Nova Scotia*
Leonce Routh	do.	*Montreal*
Henry Browne Morse	do.	*Sierra Leone*
F. P. L. de Smidt	do.	*C. of G. Hope*
Peter Francis Paille	do.	*Mauritius*
George Horne	do.	*Norf. Island*
Henry Ashton	do.	*Van D. Land*
Henry Priaulx	do.	*Van D. Land*
Frederick Brathwaite	do.	*New Zealand*
Thomas W. Midwood, (*Accounts*)	do.	*Van D. Land*
Charles Anthony Horne	do.	*Dublin*
William Palmer	do.	*Mauritius*
Henry Wm. Woodforde Plant	26 Dec. 40	*Nova Scotia*
Wm. George Laidley	do.	*Van D. Land*
Montague Wm. Darling	do.	
Edward Strickland	do.	*Ion. Islands*
Thomas Wm. Goldie	do.	*Waterford*
Wm. Charles Cuming	13 July 41	*Bahamas*
John Tomes	24 Dec. 41	*Van D. Land*
Thomas M'Cann	24 Dec. 41	*Jamaica*
Fred. Stanley Carpenter	24 Dec. 41	*Hong Kong*
Kean Osborn	do.	*Dublin*
David Ross Lee	7 June 42	*Canada*
George Atkinson	23 Dec. 42	*Antigua*
Henry Green	do.	*C. of G. Hope*
William Le Mesurier	do.	*Gambia*
Henry Lambert Bayley	do.	*Barbadoes*
Fred. Henry Ibbetson	do.	*Ion. Islands*
Edward Barrington de Fonblanque	do.	*Canada*
James Douglas Willan	do.	
Robert Clement Major	19 Dec. 43	*West Indies*
Redmond Uniacke, (*Accounts*)	23 Dec. 43	*Van D. Land.*
James Knight Goold	do.	*Canada*
Francis Knowles	do.	*Barbadoes*
John Nicolson	do.	*Van D. Land*
Douglas Bennet Clarke	do.	*Demerara*
Robert May Gardiner	do.	*St. Vincent*
Fitzjames Edward Watt	do.	*N. S. Wales*
Henry Curll	17 Oct. 44	*Van D. Land*
Alfred Salwey	24 Dec. 44	*New Zealand*
John Thomas Comper	do.	*St. Vincent*
John Banner Price	do.	*Antigua*
James Charles R. Wood	do.	*New Zealand*
James Bell Lundy	do.	*Grenada*
Robert Baker	do.	*Demerara*
William Hewetson	do.	*Newfound.*
Charles H. Sheil	do.	*C. of G. Hope*

	Deputy Asst. Commis. Gen.	Station.		Deputy Asst. Commis. Gen.	Station.
Wm. Robertson Cooper	24 Dec. 44	*C. of G. Hope*	J. Ramsay M'Culloch	16 Dec. 45	
Hector J. Macaulay ..	do.	*Malta*	Fred. Saintbury Parker	26 Dec. 46	*Canada*
Henry Connell.......	do.	*W. Australia*	Thomas Browne	do.	*Van D. Land*
Wm. Jas. Tyrone Power	do.		Frederick Wm. Waldron	do.	*Van D. Land*
Patrick Nagle Telfer ..	16 Dec. 45	*Canada*	Conrad Potgièter ..	do.	*C. of G. Hope*
Wm. Henry Bernard Usher..........	do.	*Canada*	Henry Moore	do.	
Thomas Williams	do.	*Bermuda*	James Coxworthy	do.	*Honduras*
William Read Parrott	do.	*Van D. Land*	James H. Tubby	do.	*West Indies*
John Moira Maclean Sutherland	do.	*New Zealand*	Widdrington Tinling	do.	*West Indies*
Robert Cumming	do.	*C. of G. Hope*	Henry Bartlett	do.	*C. of G. Hope*
Charles William Eichbauen, (*Accounts*) ..	do.	*V. D. Land.*	Alexander Crowder Crookshank	do.	
Geo. Alexander Skinner	do.	*C. of G. Hope*	Henry Robinson	do.	*Athlone*
B. J. Montunaro	do.	*Malta*	John Hiram Allinson	28 Dec. 47	*Barbadoes*
James Mitchell, (*Accounts*)	do.	*V. D. Land*	Rupert B. B. Bower ..	do.	*Jamaica*
Villiers William Cæsar Hawkins..........	do.		Henry Maule........	do.	*Cork*
George Joseph Webb..	do.	*W. Australia*	John Francis Rogers..	do.	*Limerick*
Thomas Gem	do.		Hugh F. Durnford....	do.	*Mauritius*
Arthur Fulford Adams	do.	*Malta*	Thomas Strickland ..	do.	*C. of G. Hope*
			Charles Thomas Walcot	do.	*Canada*
			Jas. Wilkinson Woodley	do.	
			Robert Henry Smith..	do.	*Mauritius*
			Primrose G. Julyan ..	do.	

Blue.—*Facings*—Black Velvet.

DUTIES AND ORGANIZATION.

The Commissariat are charged with the following duties:—In the Field they have hitherto had the custody of the Military Chest, and provided and paid for everything necessary for the subsistence and transport of an army. At the present time, on stations abroad, they have the charge of the Military Chests, negotiation of Bills for their supply, and receipt of all surplus monies arising from various sources in the hands of public departments, as also monies for remittance to England. They make advances to Regimental Paymasters on account of the Pay of the Troops, and to the Heads of the Ordnance and Naval Departments, on account of their respective services. They pay in detail the Staff, all money allowances and contingencies; also the Half-Pay and retired allowances, Chelsea Pensions, Widows' Pensions, Compassionate allowances, and Naval Pensions, &c., to all persons resident at the several stations. They contract and pay for Provisions required on the spot for the supply of the Troops, and for land and water transport. In the West Indies they pay in detail the Assistant Commissioners and Stipendiary Magistrates under the Provisions of the Slave Compensation Act: at some stations they perform the duties of Naval Agents. In Canada, Nova Scotia, and Jamaica, they pay the Ecclesiastical Establishments, and at the former they have the custody and issue of Indian Presents, and charge of the Locks and Collection of the Tolls on the canals connected with the St. Lawrence. In New South Wales and Van Dieman's Land, they supply Provisions, Clothing, and Stores, of all descriptions for convict services. They enter into contracts for Ordnance Stores, Building Materials, &c., on the spot, and provide and pay for supplies for Army Hospitals, superintend the issue of provisions, forage, fuel, and light in kind made by Contractors, and issue such articles of Provision as are sent out for the use of the Troops from England. Their duties are blended with the Army, Ordnance, Navy, and many other branches of the public service. They are under the orders of and responsible for the execution of their duties to the General or Officers commanding at the various stations, and receive their instructions from the Board of Treasury, with whom they correspond through the Secretary on all points of service on which they are engaged.

See Report of Commissioners appointed to enquire into the expediency of Consolidating the Civil Departments of the Army, dated 21 July, 1837.

The following is the authority for its present organization:—

Commissary-in-Chief's Office, 19 March, 1810. His Majesty has been pleased to command that the following regulations should be established and acted upon in all future Promotions and Appointments in the Commissariat.

That the Gradation of Rank, be "Commissary-General," "Deputy Commissary-General, "Assistant Commissary-General," "Deputy Assistant Commissary-General," "Clerk." No person to enter but as Clerk,—to serve One year before eligible for Promotion.—Deputy Assistant to serve Four years, or Five from entrance as Clerk before eligible.—Assistant, Five years as Assistant, or Ten years from entrance as Clerk before eligible.—Deputy to be Three years in that rank before eligible.—Service to be counted as actual service on Full Pay. No person to be appointed Clerk previous to the age of 16.

The comparative ranks are Commissary-General as Brigadier-General.—Deputy as Major, after three years, Lieutenant-Colonel.—Assistant as Captain.—Deputy Assistant as Lieutenant.—Clerk as Ensign. See Army Regulations.

MEDICAL DEPARTMENT.

Years' Serv. Full Pay.	Half Pay.		HOSPITAL ASSIST.	ASSIST.-SURGEON.	REGTL. SURGEON.	STAFF SURGEON.	ASSIST.-INSPECT.	BREVET DEP. INSP.	DEPUTY INSP-GEN.	INSPEC.-GENERAL.	WHERE STATIONED.
		Directors General.									
55	$\frac{4}{12}$	P *Sir* James M'Grigor,[1] *Bart.* M.D. 13 June, 15	....	....	13 Sept. 93	....	....	....	27 June 05	25 Aug. 09	London.
		Inspectors General of Hospitals.									
40	1	P Henry Franklin[2]	13 Aug. 08	29 June 09	26 May 14	19 Nov. 30	....	....	14 Jan. 42	25 June 47	Bengal.
41	0	P Montagu Martin Mahony,[3] M.D. (*Local*)	....	29 Sept. 08	3 June 13	11 Aug. 35	30 Aug. 39	....	29 Oct. 41	16 Dec. 45	Canada.
33	$2\frac{1}{12}$	John Robertson, M.D. (*Local*)	14 Mar. 14	22 June 20	never	10 Sept. 29	....	....	13 Oct. 40	14 Apr. 46	Gibraltar.
51	$\frac{2}{12}$	*Sir* James Pitcairn,[4] M.D. (*Ireland only*)	19 June 98	....	....	Aug. 99	....	....	2 July 47	2 July 47	Dublin.
40	0	P Alexander Stewart,[8] M.D.	14 June 09	27 Dec. 10	13 May 24	24 Nov. 25	....	....	....	....	West Indies.
		Deputy Inspectors-General of Hospitals.									
26	$9\frac{1}{12}$	William Dawson, M.D.	18 Oct. 13	9 June 14	3 April 35	29 Dec. 37	....	....	13 Oct. 40		Sydney, Van Diemen's Land.
39	$9\frac{4}{12}$	William Hacket,[5] M.D.	....	12 June 01	25 Nov. 08	6 Jan. 14	....	....	6 Jan. 43		Ionian Islands.
38	$1\frac{1}{12}$	P Charles St. John,[6] M.D.	8 Aug. 11	3 Sept. 12	14 Feb. 22	9 Dec. 36	4 Jan. 39	....	20 Oct. 43		Madras.
38	0	P James French,[7] M.D.	....	8 Feb. 10	9 Dec. 24	1 Aug. 42	....	....	16 Dec. 45		
38	0	P Walter Henry,[9]	11 Apr. 11	19 Dec. 11	8 June 26	4 Jan. 39	....	....	do		Nova Scotia.
33	$3\frac{6}{12}$	John William Watson, M.D.	10 Dec. 12	4 Mar. 13	....	6 April 26	....	....	do		Jamaica.
33	0	Andrew Smith, M.D.	14 Mar. 16	27 Oct. 25	....	7 July 37	....	....	19 Dec.		London.
39	$1\frac{7}{12}$	P Samuel Crozier Roe,[10] M.D.	4 June 08	4 Aug. 08	26 May 14	17 Sept. 39	....	....	30 Dec. 45		Ceylon.
33	$1\frac{5}{12}$	John Hall, M.D.	24 June 15	12 Sept. 22	....	8 Nov. 27	....	....	25 Sept. 46		Cape of Good Hope.
34	0	John Kinnis, M.D.	16 June 15	14 Dec. 24	22 June 38	5 Feb. 41	....	....	25 June 47		Bombay.
36	0	Andrew Fergusson,[11] M.D. (*Local*)	21 June 13	20 July 15	28 Nov. 34	11 Jan. 39	....	....	25 June 47		Hong Kong.
36	$4\frac{11}{12}$	William Munro	6 Sept. 08	16 Feb. 09	22 June 15	5 Jan. 26	....	....	....		Nova Scotia.
		Staff Surgeons of the First Class.									
33	3	James Barry, M.D.	5 July 13	7 Dec. 15	....	22 Nov. 27	Malta.				
39	0	John Pickering, M.D.	24 April 10	29 April 13	....	29 June 32	Royal Military College.				
36	0	P Daniel Scott[12]	8 Feb. 13	18 Mar. 24	....	17 Oct. 34	Dublin.				
39	0	Alexander Melvin[13]	26 July 10	26 Sept. 11	10 Dec. 23	3 Aug. 26	Canada.				
33	$\frac{11}{12}$	Charles Whyte	19 Sept. 15	14 May 16	24 Aug. 26	30 Dec. 36	Portsmouth.				
23	0	Thomas Spence	3 Aug. 26	8 Feb. 27	....	12 July 39					
30	4	Alexander Sinclair, M.D.	20 July 15	9 May 16	28 Aug. 35	20 Sept. 39	Dublin.				
25	0	John Hawkey, M.D.	23 Dec. 24	16 June 25	....	20 Sept. 39	West Indies.				

Years' Serv. Full Pay.	Half Pay.		HOSPITAL-ASSISTANT.		ASSISTANT-SURGEON.		REGTL.-SURGEON, &c		STAFF SURGEON.		WHERE STATIONED.
		Staff Surgeons of the First Class.									
33	1 4/12	William Birrell, M.D.	3 June	15	12 April	21	7 April	37	6 Nov.	40	Newry.
25	10	John Collis Carter, M.D.	10 Jan.	14	2 June	25	19 Oct.	38	do.		West Indies.
36	4/12	Francis Sievwright [14]	7 June	13	13 Mar.	17	25 Sept.	35	2 Aug.	42	Mauritius.
40	0	℗ Charles Maclean,[15] M.D.	8 July	09	27 Dec.	10	14 July	25	5 Aug.	42	London.
34	4/12	Robert Sillery, M.D.	24 May	15	18 April	22	4 Jan.	39	1 Nov.	42	Yarmouth.
38	0	℗ ℭℌ James Moffitt,[16] M.D.	....		24 Oct.	11	17 Jan.	28	20 Jan.	43	Cork.
30	3 10/12	Thomas Hall	19 May	15	30 June	25	29 May	40	29 Sept.	43	Leeds.
23	0	William Michael Ford[17]	16 Feb.	26	1 June	26	2 July	41	16 Feb.	44	Corfu.
37	0	William Bell,[18] MD.	24 Aug.	12	4 Mar.	13	15 Mar.	31	7 June		Canada.
35	4/12	Archibald Shanks,[19] M.D	9 Nov.	13	17 Mar.	14	20 Mar.	35	17 Jan.	45	New South Wales.
29	0	George Russell Dartnell	30 Nov.	20	20 Oct.	25	4 Jan.	39	14 Mar.	45	Chatham.
23	0	Andrew Foulis	5 Dec.	26	4 June	29	2 July	41	11 July	45	Liverpool.
35	1 4/12	℗ John Millar,[20]	24 May	13	8 Feb.	21	5 Nov.	29	16 Dec.	45	
32	2	William Henry Burrell, M.D.	24 June	15	12 April	21	5 May	37	do		London.
36	0	Thomas Forrest Cotton [21]	4 Oct.	13	17 Aug.	15	13 March	35	30 Dec.	45	Edinburgh.
32	7 10/12	℗ John MacAndrew,[22] M.D.	27 June	09	15 Feb.	10	30 Apr.	22	7 July	46	Ceylon.
24	0	Stephenson Teevan, M.D.	16 June	25	23 Nov.	26	4 Sept.	40	25 Sept.	46	West Indies.
23	2/12	Thomas Atkinson, M.D.	22 Dec.	25	11 May	26	6 Nov.	40	25 Sept.	46	Cape of Good Hope.
34	11/12	Alexander Cumming[23]	7 March	14	23 Dec.	24	13 March	35	9 Oct.	46	Bristol.
14	0	Robert Lawson, M.D.	....		15 May	35	16 Dec.	45	27 Oct.	46	Sierra Leone.
44	0	℗ John Richardson[24]	9 July	05	18 Feb.	08	5 Jan.	26	20 Nov.	46	West Indies.
22	0	Robert Hope Alston Hunter,[25]	10 Jan.	27	15 June	30	2 July	41	30 July	47	West Indies.
22	1 4/12	David Dumbreck, M.D.	3 Nov.	25	12 Jan.	26	2 July	41	10 Sept.	47	
24	12	℗ John Miller,[26] M.D.	9 July	13	8 Feb.	16	4 Jan.	39	19 Nov.	47	Jamaica.
23	0	William Linton, M.D.	9 Dec.	26	18 Jan.	27	2 July	41	17 Mar.	48	Glasgow.
35	4/12	John Dempster,[27] M.D.	4 Oct.	18	1 Sept.	14	4 Mar.	36	27 Oct.	48	Glasgow.
32	1	William Bain, M.D.	24 June	15	30 June	25	29 Dec.	37			
		Staff Surgeons of the Second Class.									
28	7 11/12	Richard Dowse[29]	24 Jan.	14	25 Jan.	15	8 Jan.	36			Isle of Wight.
28	6 4/12	George Home	12 May	15	18 Aug.	25	23 Sept.	36			Canada.
28	0	John Mair, M.D.	8 Nov.	21	10 Nov.	25	30 Oct.	40			North America.
23	0	George Allman	8 Nov.	26	20 Sept.	27	26 Feb.	41			Jamaica.
24	0	James Connell	16 June	25	10 Nov.	25	2 July	41			
23	0	Wm. Charles Humfrey	10 Jan.	26	18 Jan.	27	do.				Corfu.
22	0	Thomas Fox, M.D.	15 Mar.	27	29 July	30	do.				Dublin.
22	0	Tho. Coke Gaulter, M.D.	22 Mar.	27	29 July	30	25 Feb.	42			Chelsea Hosp.
22	0	John Clark, M.D.	4 Oct.	27	20 July	30	17 June				London.
23	0	Samuel Maitland Hadaway	20 Nov.	26	20 July	30	2 Aug.	42			Cape of Good Hope.
22	0	Robert Allan	22 Nov.	27	20 July	30	1 Nov.				Mauritius.
[illegible]	[illegible]	[illegible]	....		11 Jan.	33	17 Feb.	43			Van Dieman's Land.
[illegible]	[illegible]	[illegible]	[illegible]	[illegible]	[illegible]	[illegible]	[illegible]	[illegible]			[illegible]

War Services of the Officers of the Medical Department.

1 Sir James M'Grigor entered the service in Sept. 1793, as Surgeon of the 88th Regt.; he served in [Hol-]land and Flanders in 1794 and 5; in the West Indies in 1796; in the East Indies in 1798; in Egypt, as [Su-]perintending Surgeon of the Anglo-Indian army in 1801; with the army at Walcheren in 1809; and [in the] Peninsula from 1811 to the end of the war.

2 Mr. Franklin served in the Peninsula from Sept. 1808 to the end of the war, including the ba[ttles of] Busaco, Vittoria, Pampeluna, Pyrenees, Nivelle, Orthes, and Toulouse; sieges of Olivença and Bad[ajoz;] served also in the American War, including the action at Plattsburgh.

3 Dr. Mahony served in the Peninsula from April 1809 to the end of the war, including the passage of the Douro, battle of Talavera,—taken prisoner and marched to Verdun; battle of Busaco, siege of Oli-vença, battle of Albuhera, affair of Aldea de Ponte, sieges of Ciudad Rodrigo and Badajoz, affair of [Aldea] de la Prima, battle of Salamanca, capture of Madrid, battle of Vittoria, affair of Roncesvalles, [battles] near Pampeluna, affair of Echalar, assault of San Sebastian, battles of Nivelle, Orthes, and Toulouse. Present also in the attack on New Orleans, 8th Jan. 1815; and subsequently at the capture of Paris.

4 Sir James Pitcairn served at the Helder in 1799, and the whole of the campaign in Egypt in 1801.

[For continuation of Notes, see page

Years' Serv. Full Pay.	Half Pay.	Surgeons of the Second Class.	HOSPITAL ASSISTANT.	ASSISTANT SURGEON.	SURGEON 2D. CLASS.	WHERE STATIONED.
22	0	James Clephane Minto ..	29 Mar. 27	29 July 30	30 June 43	Maidstone.
26	10	₱ George Hume Reade[30]	....	9 Sept. 13	21 July	Corfu.
21	0	John Stewart	13 Mar. 28	29 July 30	20 Oct. 43	Mauritius.
15	0	Thos. Ross Jameson, M.D.	....	10 Jan. 34	5 Dec.	C. of G. Hope.
17	0	Edward William Burton	....	21 Sept. 32	1 March 44	Malta.
16	0	Andrew Maclean, M.D...	....	4 Oct. 33	1 Mar. 44	Chatham.
14	0	JohnChas.Cameron,M.D.	....	27 March 35	15 April	Ceylon.
14	0	Richard James O'Flaherty	....	9 Jan. 35	23 May 45	Gibraltar.
15	0	James A. D. M'Bean....	....	12 Aug. 34	30 May	Jamaica.
14	0	John Garnett Courtenay.	....	10 April 35	8 Dec.	New Zealand.
15	0	Edward Hugh Blakeney.	....	17 Oct. 34	19 Dec.	Chatham.
14	0	Collis C. J. Delmege, M.D.	....	15 May 35	13 March 46	Limerick.
13	0	Henry Pilleau	....	22 Jan. 36	14 April 46	
14	0	John Thomson Telfer....	....	17 July 35	9 June 46	Nova Scotia.
14	0	John Duncan M'Diarmid	....	4 Dec. 35	7 Aug. 46	
13	0	T. Moore Fishbourne, M.D.	....	22 July 36	7 Aug. 46	Honduras.
13	0	William Carson, M.D. ..	....	7 Oct. 36	28 Aug. 46	Mauritius.
12	0	Alex. Douglas Taylor, M.D.	....	15 Sept. 37	do.	Jamaica.
11	0	G.S. Beatson, A.M., M.D.	....	13 July 38	do.	Ceylon.
11	1 4/12	Andrew Ferguson, M.D.	....	23 Dec. 36	25 Sept. 46	Cork.
12	0	Frederick Roberts	....	11 Aug. 37	25 Sept. 46	Canada.
21	0	John Loftus Hartwell ..	13 Mar. 28	1 Feb. 31	2 Oct. 46	New S. Wales.
11	0	William Home, M.D.....	....	12 Jan. 38	13 Nov. 46	London.
8	0	Adolphus Collings, M.D.	....	26 Feb. 41	20 Nov. 46	West Indies.
6	0	James Dickson	....	27 Jan. 43	5 March 47	Gambia.
8	0	George Williamson, M.D.	....	26 Mar. 41	13 July 47	Chatham.
10	0	Henry Mapleton,[32] M.D.	....	12 July 39	13 July 47	
10	0	Nicholas O'Connor, M.D.	....	5 April 39	12 Nov. 47	C. of G. Hope.
10	0	Edwin Adolphus, M.D...	....	20 Sept. 39	19 Nov. 47	
7	0	R. Winchester Fraser, M.D.	....	15 April 42	23 May 48	Gambia.
9	0	J. B. St. Croix Crosse ..	....	9 Oct. 40	16 June 48	West Indies.
10	0	John Donald	....	23 Aug. 39	18 July 48	West Indies
13	0	Tho. Graham Balfour, MD.	....	29 April 36	1 Aug. 48	R. M. Asylum.
3	0	Anthony John Dolce, M.D.	....	10 July 46	19 Sept. 48	Gold Coast.
10	0	John Stewart Smith, M.D.	....	22 Nov. 39	27 Oct. 48	Chatham.
10	0	G. Murray Webster, M.D.	....	6 Dec. 39	1 Dec. 48	West Indies.
8	0	Sandford M'Vittie Lloyd	....	5 Mar. 41	1 Dec. 48	West Indies.
10	0	James Alex. Fraser, M.D.	....	22 Dec. 39	22 Dec. 48	C. of G. Hope.

Full Pay.	Half Pay.	Apothecaries.	HOSPITAL ASSISTANT.	APOTHECARY, &c.	WHERE STATIONED.
24	18 7/12	₱ Joseph Schembri	17 Jan. 07	14 Oct. 13	Corfu.
26	12 1/12	James Woolley Simpson	24 June 11	18 May 15	
34	0	Francis Matthias Bassano....	Dispenser 4 April 15	18 Apr. 25	London.
		Assistant-Surgeons.		*Assist. Surg.*	
10	0	Geo. William Powell, A.M., M.D.		7 June 39	Ceylon.
10	0	Tho. Rose Dyce		7 June	Ceylon.
10	0	John Crespigny Millingen		20 Sept.	
10	0	Henry Downes, M.D.		1 Nov. 39	Canada.
10	0	James M'Gregor, M.D.		6 Dec.	C. of Good Hope.
9	0	Alexander Gibb, M.D.		10 Jan. 40	C. of Good Hope.
9	0	Robert Carew Anderson, M.D.		22 May 40	
9	0	James M'Grigor Grant		6 Nov.	Ceylon.
8	0	Richard Robert Dowse		15 Jan. 41	Chatham.
8	0	William Campbell Seaman, M.D.		16 Feb.	Canada.
8	0	Wm. Kilner Swettenham, M.D.		9 April	
8	0	Adam Alexander Prout		8 June	Chelsea.
8	0	Edward Booth		11 June	Portsmouth.
8	0	Thomas Joliffe Tufnell		11 June	Dublin.
8	0	William Rutherford[34]		2 July 41	Canada.
8	0	Edward Frederic Kelaart		16 July	Chatham.
8	0	Ethelbert Henry Blake, M.D		16 Nov.	Bermuda.
8	0	John Trench		3 Dec.	Jamaica.
7	0	Robert M'Wharrie, MD.		11 Mar. 42	Van Dieman's L.
7	0	Patrick Sinclair Laing[36]		8 April	Canada.
7	0	Thomas Dehane Lightbody, M.D.		8 April 42	
7	0	Charles Bush Hearn		15 April	Corfu.
7	0	Henry Lionel Cowen		17 June	Ceylon.
7	0	Francis Reid, M.D		2 Aug.	Mauritius.

Years' Serv. Full Pay.	Years' Serv. Half Pay.		Assistant Surgeon.	Where Stationed.
7	0	Alexander John Fraser, M.D.	1 Nov. 42	C. of Good Hope.
7	0	William Stuart, M.D.	2 Dec.	C. of Good Hope.
6	0	William Walter Weld..................	20 Jan. 43	Nova Scotia.
6	0	William Braybrooke	16 June	Ceylon.
6	0	Robert Cooper	21 July	Nova Scotia
6	0	William Barrett, M.B.................	20 Oct. 43	Chatham.
6	0	Edward William Bawtree, M.D.	24 Nov.	Canada.
6	0	Thomas Patrick Matthew..............	12 Dec.	Gibraltar.
5	0	Alfred Crocker	26 Jan. 44	Honduras.
5	0	John Macnamara, M.D.	15 March	Hong Kong.
5	0	Samuel Smith.........................	15 March	do.
5	0	Rowland Agar.........................	19 April 44	
5	0	John Thomas Watson Bacot.............	10 May 44	New Zealand.
4	0	Henry Huish, M.D.	31 Jan. 45	Van Dieman's L.
4	0	William George Swan, M.D.	28 Feb. 45	Chatham.
4	0	William Fred. Torcato Ivey	30 May	Jamaica.
4	0	Wellington Poole	1 Aug.	Jamaica.
4	0	Henry March Webb	23 Sept.	West Indies.
4	0	George Frederick Bone, M.D.	9 Dec.	Corfu.
4	0	Alexander George Montgomery	9 Dec.	New Zealand.
4	0	Henry Frederick Robertson	19 Dec.	do.
3	0	Thomas Kehoe, M.D.	16 Jan. 46	Gambia.
3	0	Richard Speir Peile	13 April	Gibraltar.
3	0	Richard Woodley, M.B.................	14 April	West Indies.
3	0	William Simpson, M.B.	1 May	Canada.
3	0	Michael Fenton Manifold..............	22 May	
3	0	Archibald Redfoord Ridgway, M.B.	12 June	
3	0	William Singleton, M.D.	10 July	West Indies.
3	0	William Lapsley	7 Aug.	West Indies.
3	0	Edward William Young, MD.	7 Aug.	Corfu.
3	0	Francis Reynolds	7 Aug.	Nova Scotia.
3	0	John M'Grigor Aug. Tho. Croft	28 Aug.	Ceylon.
3	0	William Donneland Marchant	8 Sept.	Gambia.
3	0	Dowell O'Reilly Clayton, M.D.	11 Sept.	China.
3	0	William Browne.......................	11 Sept. 46	
3	0	George Waterloo Pennington Sparrow ..	25 Sept.	C. of G. Hope.
3	0	Edward William Thomas Mandeville	do.	C. of G. Hope.
3	0	William Thomas Black	do.	do.
3	0	William Cameron, M.D.	do.	do.
3	0	Brinsley Nicholson, M.D.	do.	do.
3	0	Charles Lockhart Robertson, M.D.......	9 Oct. 46	Yarmouth.
3	0	Duncan M'Intyre, M.D.	27 Oct. 46	
2	0	Walter George Dickson................	8 Jan. 47	China.
2	0	Alfred Gosden........................	12 Feb.	China.
2	0	John Thomas Clarke, M.D.	27 Aug.	China.
2	0	Peter Henry Roe	3 Sept.	Gold Coast.
2	0	John Henry Smith, M.D.	24 Sept.	do.
2	0	William Freeman Daniell..............	26 Nov. 47	Gambia.
2	0	Frederick Augustus Kingdon	17 Dec.	do.
2	0	John Robertson, M.D.	24 Dec. 47	Dublin.
1	0	Ebenezer Alfred Jenkin...............	7 Jan. 48	Jamaica.
1	0	Nicholas John Watson	14 Jan.	Sierra Leone.
1	0	James Lewis Holloway	17 Mar. 48	Dublin.
1	0	David Charles Pitcairn...............	6 Oct. 48	Gambia.
1	0	Henry Neil Stewart, M.D.	1 Dec. 48	
1	0	Thomas Manners	do.	
1	0	Auchinleck Grahame, M.D.	do.	
1	0	Joseph F. Matthew	do.	
1	0	Nicolson Colin Mackenzie, M.D.	21 Dec. 48	

Full Pay	Half Pay	Deputy Purveyors.	Purveyor's Clerk.	Deputy Purveyor.	
		P Jonathan Croft	18 Aug. 03	16 April 12	Sydney, N.S.W.
		P Wm. Henry Clapp	1 July 09	15 Oct. 12	Cork.
38	14	P George Pratt [39]	25 Sept. 09	3 June 13	Chatham.
		P Matthew Wreford [41]	14 Oct. 12	3 Sept. 29	Portsmouth.

N.B.—Medical Officers who are entitled to have the letters M.D. affixed to their names, should make the same known.—*Uniform*, Scarlet.—Agents, *Sir* John Kirkland & Co.

CHAPLAIN DEPARTMENT.

Chaplain General to the Forces..P The Rev. George Robert Gleig, A.M., 2 July 46 .... *War Office.*

Chaplains to the Forces.

Rev. J. S. Pering, M.A. 20 April, 1821.... *Mauritius*
—— Robert Wm. Browne, A.M. 1 April, 44 *London.*

Rev. Charles Green, A.M., 26 June 46.
—— William Hare, A.M., 27 June 46.

5 Dr. Hacket served at Walcheren in 1809; in the American war, and was present at the different actions which took place there in 1813, and was wounded in the head. Served also the campaign of 1814 in Holland.

6 Dr. St. John served in the Peninsula from Sept. 1811 to the end of the war, and subsequently in the American war.

7 Doctor French served with the 4th Regt. in the Peninsula from May 1812 to the end of that war in 1814, including the battles of Salamanca and Vittoria, siege of the Castle of San Sebastian, passage of the Bidassoa and of the Nivelle, and actions of the Nive in Dec. 1813. He served in the American war at the battle of Bladensburg, and in all the operations before Baltimore and New Orleans. Served with the 49th (also as Superintending Surgeon from April, 1841, until towards the close of active operations), throughout the war in China (Medal), including the capture of Chusan, storming of the heights and forts above Canton, taking of Amoy, sortie and repulse of the night attack on Ningpo, and capture of Chapoo, Woosung, Shanghae, and Chin Kiang Foo, and investment of Nankin.

8 Dr. Alex. Stewart served in the Peninsula from 1802 to the end of that war in 1814, including the siege of the forts and battle of Salamanca, siege of Burgos, battles of the Pyrenees, the Nivelle, the Nive, Orthes, and Toulouse.

9 Mr. Henry served with the 66th Regiment in the Peninsula from May 1811 to the close of the War at Toulouse, including the last siege of Badajoz, battle of Vittoria, and actions in the Pyrenees; battles of the Nivelle and Nive, engagement at Garris, battle of Orthes and action at Aire. He served also with the same corps in the Nepaulese War in India in 1816-17, and in the two Canadian Rebellions of 1837-8. Mr. Henry was present with his Regiment in St. Helena during the last four years of the life of Napoleon; and after his death was charged with the duty of preparing the bulletin of the post mortem appearances of the body, which was published by the British Government.

10 Dr. Roe's services:—Campaign and battle of Corunna; expedition to Walcheren; Peninsula from May, 1811, to the end of the war, including the battle of Albuhera; sieges of Ciudad Rodrigo and Badajoz; battles of Salamanca, Vittoria, Pyrenees, Nivelle, Orthes and Toulouse.

11 Dr. Andrew Fergusson served in the American war.

12 Mr. Scott served in the Peninsula from March 1813 to the end of the war.

13 Mr. Melvin served at the capture of Guadaloupe in 1810.

14 Mr. Sievwright served with the 59th at the siege and capture of Bhurtpore in 1825-6.

15 Dr. Maclean served at Walcheren in 1809; and in the Peninsula from Feb. 1810 to the end of that war in 1814, including the battles of Busaco, Salamanca, Vittoria, and the Pyrenees, crossing the Bidassoa, and battles of Nivelle and Toulouse.

16 Dr. Moffitt served in the Peninsula from Aug. 1813 to the end of the war, including the battles of the Pyrenees, Orthes, and Toulouse. Present on the 16th, 17th and 18th June at Waterloo.

17 Mr. Ford served the campaign of 1835 in Caffreland. Served also in China, (Medal) and was present at the assault and capture of Chin Kiang Foo.

18 Dr. Bell served the campaign of 1814 in Holland, including both the attacks on Merxem and bombardment of Antwerp. Served also throughout the war in China with the 26th (medal), at Chusan, Canton, Ningpo, Tscke, Chapoo, Shanghai, Woosung, Chin Kiang Foo, and Nankin.

19 Doctor Shanks served the campaign of 1814 in Holland, including both the attacks on Merxem and the bombardment of Antwerp. Served also in China with the 55th, and was present at Amoy, Chusan, Chinhae, Chapoo, Woosung, Shanghai, and Chin Kiang Foo.

20 Mr. Millar served the campaigns of 1813 and 14, in the Peninsula, and the expedition to New Orleans.

21 Mr. Cotton served with the 14th at the siege and capture of Bhurtpore in 1825-6.

22 Dr. MacAndrew served on the Walcheren expedition, including the siege of Flushing and other operations. In 1811, 12, and 13, he served in the Peninsula, and was present at the siege of Badajoz, and retreat from Burgos. In 1839 he was at the capture of Fort Manora, and surrender of Kurrachee. In 1841 and 42 he served with Sir William Nott's army throughout the operations in Candahar and Affghanistan (medal), and was present in the various actions in which that army was engaged. He was afterwards present at the battle of Maharajpore (medal).

23 Mr. Cumming served at New Orleans in 1814-15; and in the Burmese war in 1826.

24 Mr. Richardson served at the capture of the Cape of Good Hope in 1806; reduction of Monte Video, and campaign of 1806 and 7 in South America; campaigns of 1808 and 9 in the Peninsula, including the battles of Roleia and Vimiera.

25 Mr. Hunter served in medical charge of the Belgaum field force in Canara, in 1837. Also in medical charge of the Queen's Royals during the campaign in Affghanistan and Beloochistan, including the capture of Ghuznee and Khelat. Medal for Ghuznee.

26 Dr. Miller served the campaigns of 1813 and 14 in Spain and the South of France; with the Expedition to New Orleans; and the campaign of 1815 under the Duke of Wellington.

27 Doctor Dempster served with 38th regiment throughout the Burmese war, including the capture of Rangoon, storm and capture of the stockades of Kincardine and Kamaroot, battles of Rangoon, Kokein, &c.

29 Mr. Dowse served at the surrender of Martinique and Guadaloupe in 1815.

30 Mr. Reade served in the Peninsula during the campaigns of 1812, 13 and 14; subsequently in the American War, including the affair at Plattsburg. Served also in Canada during the late insurrection.

32 Dr. Mapleton was present with the 40th in the action of Maharajpore (Medal).

34 Mr. Rutherford served with the 62nd in the campaign on the Sutlej, and was present at the battle of Sobraon (Medal).

36 Mr. Laing served the campaign under Sir Charles Napier against the Mountain and Desert Tribes situated on the right bank of the Indus, early in 1845.

39 Mr. Pratt joined the army in the Peninsula in Jan. 1810, and was present at the siege and capture of San Sebastian, and with the head-quarters during the operations in the Pyrenees.

41 Mr. Wreford served in the Peninsula from 1812 to the end of that war in 1814, and was present with head quarters during the operations in the Pyrenees in July, Aug., and Sept. 1813. He accompanied the expedition under the late Lord Keane to New Orleans, and was present with the troops in all the affairs before that city; after which he served in France, and recently in Turkey.

[*Notes continued from page 217.*]

16 Captain Berford (*Queen's Own*) served with the 5th in Portugal and Spain in 1808-9, and was present at the battles of Roleia and Vimiera, action at Lugo, retreat to and battle of Corunna. Subsequently on the expedition to Walcheren and at the siege of Flushing. Served afterwards in the Peninsula with the 2nd Queen's Royals, from 1812 to the end of that war in 1814, and was present at the battle of Vittoria, blockade of Pampeluna, actions in the Pyrenees from 25th to 31st July; with the covering army at San Sebastian and also at its capture; affair at the convent of St. Antonia, actions on the Nivelle and the Nive, and with the four companies of the Queen's which led the advance to the assault and capture of the principal redoubt in front of Sarre; and in all the affairs in the vicinity of St. Jean de Luz, Bayonne, and the Adour; also at the battles of Orthes and Toulouse, and the various affairs of posts and picquets in which the fourth Division were engaged.

17 Captain Graves's services (*2nd West York*):—Expedition to Copenhagen in 1807; campaign in Portugal and Spain, including the battles of Roleia and Vimiera, advance into Spain, retreat to, and battle of Corunna. Expedition to Walcheren, Siege of Flushing, and ascent of the Scheldt, 1809. Peninsular campaigns from June 1811 to Sept. 1813, including the siege of the Forts and battle of Salamanca (three wounds, two severe, one slight), siege of Burgos and retreat from thence, blockade of Pampeluna, battles of the Pyrenees, 28th, 29th, and 30th July (severely contused 28th), Maya Pass, advance into France, and various affairs of Posts and Piquets.

18 Captain Rawson (*3rd West York*) served at the siege and taking of La Valetta in Malta in 1800. Served with the British and Russian army in Naples in 1805, and the subsequent occupation of Sicily. The second Egyptian campaign in 1807, including the capture of Alexandria and the second attack on Rosetta. At Walcheren and at the siege and reduction of Flushing in 1809. The campaign of 1814 in Holland, including both attacks on Merxem and bombardment of Antwerp. Campaign of 1815, including the battle of Waterloo, taking of Cambray, and capture of Paris.

19 Captain Scott (*Fife*) served in the Peninsula from March 1813 to the end of that war in 1814, including the battle of Vittoria, siege of San Sebastian, passage of the Bidassoa, the Nive, and the Adour, investment of Bayonne, and repulse of the sortie, where he received a bayonet wound. Served also the campaign of 1815, and was present at the battles of Quatre Bras and Waterloo.

21 Captain Carrothers (*Antrim*) served in the Peninsula from June 1809 to Sept. 1811, and again from March 1813 to the end of the war in 1814, including the battle of Busaco, action at Campo Mayor, first siege of Badajoz, battles of Albuhera, Nivelle, and Nive, affair at St. Palais, battle of Orthes, affair at Lambeige, and battle of Toulouse. Served also the campaign of 1815, and was present at the battles of Quatre Bras and Waterloo, at which last he was severely wounded.

20 Colonel Fraser (*Ross*) lost a leg at the siege of Burgos, when serving in the Foot Guards.

22 Capt. Cox (*King's County*) served as Lieut. of the Royal Artillery in Sir John Moore's campaign in the north of Spain and battle of Corunna, from 1808 to 1809. Joined the Portuguese army in 1811, present at the siege and capture of Badajoz in 1812, battle of Castalla, both sieges of Tarragona in 1813, and blockade of Barcelona in 1814. Continued to serve with the Portuguese army till 1819.

23 Capt. Hon. J. de Blaquiere (*Limerick County*) served with the 41st throughout the campaign of 1842 in Affghanistan, and was present in the engagements of the 28th March and 28th April in the Pisheen Valley; also in the actions before Goaine and before Ghuznee; occupation and destruction of that fortress and of Cabool; expedition into Kohistan; storm, capture, and destruction of Istaliff; and the various minor affairs in and between the Bolan and the Khyber Passes. He has received the Medal inscribed "Candahar, Ghuznee, Cabul, 1842."

24 Captain Russell (*Dublin City*), was a Captain in the 98th with the expedition to the North of China (medal), in 1842, and was present at the storming of the city of Chin Kiang Foo, and also at the attack and capture of the Tartar entrenched camps on the heights outside the city; and he was also at the landing before Nankin.

25 Capt. Vere Webb (*Cardigan*), served with the Rifle Brigade during the campaigns of 1814 and 15 in Holland, the Netherlands, and France, including both the actions at Merxem, bombardment of Antwerp, and battle of Waterloo, at which last he was slightly wounded.

26 Capt. Cowell served the Kandian campaign of 1817 and 1818, and was engaged with the enemy on numerous occasions.

ROYAL ANGLESEA. (Light Infantry.) [61]
Beaumaris.
Maj. Com. Col. Wm. *Lord* Dinorben
Adjt. Capt. C. S. Jones

BEDFORD. [18]
Bedford.
Col. Rich. Tho. Gilpin
Adjt. Capt. T. J. Smith

ROYAL BERKS. [7]
Reading.
Col. John Blagrave
Adjt. Capt. Sherson

ROYAL BRECON. [31]
Brecon.
L. Col. Com. F. Chambre
Adjt. Lt. J. D. Dickinson 1

ROYAL BUCKS, (or KING'S OWN.) [35]
High Wycombe.
Col. R. J. *Lord* Carrington
Adjt. Capt. C. T. Grove

CAMBRIDGE. [68]
Ely.
Col. F. Pemberton
Adj. Capt. T. Sebborne

ROYAL CARDIGAN. (Rifle Corps.) [64]
Aberystwith.
Lt. Col. Com. Col. W. E. Powell
Adj. ☞ *Capt.* Vere Webb 25

R. CARMARTHEN. (Fusiliers.) [24]
Carmarthen.
Lt. Col. Com. Hon. G. R. Trevor
Adjt. Ca. E. J. Vaughan

ROY. CARNARVON. (Rifle Corps.) [56]
Carnarvon.
Maj. Com. O. J. E. Nanney
Ad. Cap.

ROY. CHESHIRE.
Chester. [6]
Col. Hon. Hugh Cholmondeley
Ad.

THE D. OF CORNWALL'S RANGERS. (Light Infantry.) [38]
Torpoint.
Colonel ☞ E. A. *Earl of* Mount Edgcumbe 2
Adj. Capt. Brockman

ROY. CORNWALL & DEVON MINERS. (Light Infantry.) [118]
Truro.
Lt. Col. Com. E. W. Wynne Pendarves
Adjt. Capt. Wm. Ward

ROYAL CUMBERLAND. [9]
Whitehaven.
Col. Hon. H. C. Lowther
Adjt. ☞ *Capt.* R. Pennington 3

ROYAL DENBIGH. (Rifle Corps.) [46]
Wrexham.
Col. R. Myddelton Biddulph
Adjt. Capt. E. Jones

DERBY. [69]
Derby.
Col. H. *Ld.* Waterpark
Adjt. ☞ *Capt.* F. Dixon 4

1st or EAST DEVON. [41]
Exeter.
Col. H. *Earl* Fortescue
Adjt. ☞ *Capt.* C. Holman 5

NORTH DEVON. [15]
Barnstaple.
Col. G. *Ld.* Poltimore
Adjt. ☞ *Capt.* J. A. Ridgway 6

SOUTH DEVON. [25]
Plymouth.
Col. Earl of Morley.
Adjt. Capt. W. H. Fisk 7

DORSET. [42]
Dorchester.
Col. J. J. Smith
Adjt. Capt. G. Wyatt

DURHAM. [3]
Barnard Castle.
Col. H. *Duke of* Cleveland
Adjt. Capt. R. H. S. Jackson

EAST ESSEX. [14]
Colchester.
Col. H. J. Conyers
Adj. ☞ *Cap.* J. Jones 8

WEST ESSEX. [19]
Chelmsford.
Col. Sir J. Tyrell, *Bt.*
Adjt. Capt. H. Pearson 9

ROYAL FLINT. (Rifle Corps.) [89]
Mold.
Lt. Col. Comm. Col. Sir Rich. Puleston, *Bt.*
Adjt. Capt. F. R. M'G. Dawson

ROY. GLAMORGAN. (Light Infantry.) [44]
Cardiff.
Col. J. *Marq. of* Bute
Ad. Capt. John Henry Armstrong

ROYAL (SOUTH) GLOUCESTER. (Light Infantry.) [23]
Gloucester.
Col. W. *Earl* Fitzharding.
Adj. Cap. Worthington

ROYAL (NORTH) GLOUCESTER. [69]
Cirencester.
Col. Tho. H. Kingscote
Adjt. Capt. John Tobin

NORTH HANTS. [13]
Winchester.
Col. Marq. of Winchester
Adj. Joseph Tomlinson

SOUTH HANTS. (Light Infantry.) [48]
Southampton.
Col. Sir J. W. Pollen, *Bt*
Adj. Capt. J. R. Norton

HANTS, Isle of Wight [63]
Newport.
Cap. Com. Percy Scott 10

HEREFORD. [59]
Hereford.
Col. J. S. *Earl* Somers
Adjt. Capt. J. E. Money Kyrle

HERTFORD. [30]
Hertford.
Col. J. *M. of* Salisbury
Adjt. Capt. E. S. James

HUNTINGDON. [2]
Huntingdon.
Maj. Com. Col. T. W. Vaughan
Adjt. Capt. Green

EAST KENT. [49]
Canterbury.
Col. S. E. Sawbridge
Adjt. Capt. C. Winter

WEST KENT. [37]
Maidstone.
Col. Sir J. K. Shaw, *Bt.*
Adjt. Capt. J. Eley

1st R. LANCASHIRE. (*The Duke of Lancaster's own.*) [45]
Lancaster.
Col. J. P. Tempest
Adjt. Capt. Henry Townshend

2d R. LANCASHIRE. (*The Duke of Lancaster's own.*) [118]
Liverpool.
Hon. C. J. F. Stanley
Adjt. Jas. Weir

3d R. LANCASHIRE. (*The Duke of Lancaster's own.*) [125]
Preston.
Col. J. W. Patten.
Adjt. Capt. J. Rooper

LEICESTER. [96]
Leicester.
Col. J. *Duke of* Rutland, *KG.*
Ad. Cap. H. F. Hawker.

NORTH LINCOLN. [8]
Lincoln.
Col. J. H. *Visc.* Alford
Adjt. ☞ *Capt.* F. Kennedy 11

SOUTH LINCOLN. [29]
New Sleaford.
Col. J. *Earl* Brownlow
Adjt. Capt. N. Campbell

ROYAL LONDON. [106]
Artillery Ground.
Col. Sir C. S. Hunter, *Bt*
Adj. Capt. W. T. Hall

ROY. MERIONETH. (Light Infantry.) [60]
Dolgelly.
Lt. Col. G. H. Vaughan.
Adjut. Capt. Anwyl.

ROYAL EAST MIDDLESEX. [65]
Hampstead.
Colonel T. Wood
Adjut. Capt. F. W. Hamilton

ROYAL WEST MIDDLESEX. [56]
Uxbridge.
Col. Visc. Enfield
Adj. Capt. J. Henry Evelegh

ROYAL WESTMINSTER, MIDDLESEX. [55]
Brentford.
Col. Rt. Hon. H. C. C. *Visc.* Chelsea
Adj. R. M'Ewen

ROY. MONMOUTH. [31]
Monmouth.
Colonel
Adj. Capt. J. Money Carter

R. MONTGOMERY. [57]
Welchpool.
Lt. Col. Com.
Adj. Capt. Edw. Dwen

WEST NORFOLK. [39]
Norwich.
Colonel H. *E. of* Orford
Adjut. James Powley

EAST NORFOLK. [40]
Yarmouth.
Colonel Hon. Berkeley Wodehouse
Adjut. Capt. W. P. K. Browne 12

NORTHAMPTON. [48]
Northampton.
Colonel. T. P. Maunsell
Adjut. Capt. T. Rose

NORTHUMBERLAND. (Light Infantry.) [27]
Alnwick.
Col. G. *E. of* Beverley
Adj. Cap. J. N. Frampton

NOTTINGHAM, (*or Royal Sherwood Foresters.*) [59]
Newark.
Col. Launc. Rolleston
Adjut. Capt. J. Barth

OXFORD. [31]
Oxford.
Colonel C. O. Bowles
Adjt. Capt. G. Cuming

ROYAL PEMBROKE (Rifle Corps) [28]
Haverfordwest.
Lt. Col. Com. H. Owen Owen
Adjut. Capt. J. Holland

ROYAL RADNOR (Light Infantry.) [50]
Presteigne.
Maj. Com. J. A. Whittaker
Adjut. Capt. F. P. Saunders

RUTLAND. (Light Infantry.) [4]
Oakham.
Captain Comm.
Hon. Wm. Middleton Noel

SHROPSHIRE. [54]
Shrewsbury.
Colonel F. Hill
Adj. ☞ *Capt.* J. G. Pardoy 13

1st SOMERSET. [16]
Taunton.
Col. J. *Earl* Poulett
Adjt. Capt. W. S. Cook

2d SOMERSET. [47]
Bath.
Col. Sir T. B. Lethbridge, *Bt.*
Adjt. Capt. A. J. Macpherson

THE (KING'S OWN) STAFFORD. [66]
Stafford.
Col. W. *Earl of* Dartmouth
Adj. Capt. Wm. Spring

WEST SUFFOLK. [10]
Bury St. Edmonds.
Col. F. W. *Earl* Jermyn
Adjut. J. M'Gregor

EAST SUFFOLK. (Light Infantry) [34]
Ipswich.
Col. ☞ H. Bence Bence
Adjut. Capt. Beckham

1st ROYAL SURREY. [20]
Richmond.
Colonel J. B. Delap
Adjut. Capt. H. E. Austen

2d ROYAL SURREY [11]
Guildford.
Col. Hon. T. C. Onslow
Adjut. Capt. F. Pyner

SUSSEX. (Light Infantry) [53]
Chichester.
Col. ☞ C. *Duke of* Richmond, *KG.* 14
Adj. Capt. ☞ Smith, 15

THE KING'S OWN LIGHT INFANTRY [97]
Stoke Newington Common.
Colonel The Earl of Dalhousie.
Adj. ☞ *Capt.* R. Berford 16

THE QUEEN'S OWN LIGHT INFANTRY. [83]
Bethnal Green.
Col T. *Earl of* Wilton
Adj. L. Cowell 96

WARWICK. [30]
Warwick.
Col. H. *Earl of* Warwick, *KT.*
Ad. Capt. Tho. Caman

ROYAL WESTMORELAND. [17]
Appleby.
Lt. Col. Com. W. *Earl of* Lonsdale
Adjut. Capt. E. H. Smith

R. WILTSHIRE. [33]
Marlborough.
Colonel Right Hon. Sir John Cam Hobhouse, *Bt.*
Adjut. Capt. Price

WORCESTER. [67]
Worcester.
Col. Tho. H. Bund
Adjut. Capt. E. Lavie

1st WEST YORK. [5]
Leeds.
Col. Lord Wharncliffe
Adj. Capt. C. A. Baines

2d WEST YORK. [21]
York.
Col. Wm. Markham
Ad. [illegible] *Cap.* A. Graves 17

3d WEST YORK. [1]
Doncaster.
Col. Geo. Cholmley
Ad. [illegible] *Cap.* Rawson 18

YORK (North Riding.) (Light Infantry) [22]
Richmond.
Col. F. *Duke of* Leeds
Adjut. Capt. J. Carter

YORK (East Riding.) [12]
Beverley.
Col. Chas. Grimston
Adj. Capt. Jas. Bell

ABERDEEN. [89]
Aberdeen.
Col. G. *M. of* Huntly, *KT.*
Adjut. Capt. J. Bland

ARGYLL & BUTE. [117]
Campbeltown.
Col. J. *Duke of* Argyll
Adjut. Brevet Major Colin Alex. Campbell

THE PRINCE REGENT'S ROYAL REGIMENT OF AYR. [115]
Ayr.
Col. Earl of Eglinton
Adj. James Miller

BERWICK, HADDINGTON, LINLITHGOW, and PEEBLES. [73]
Coldstream.
Col. Wm. Hay
Adjut. Capt. Jas. Cox

DUMFRIES, ROXBURGH & SELKIRK. [81]
Dumfries.
Col. M. of Queensberry
Adj. Capt. R. C. Noake

EDINBURGH (County and City of.) [126]
Dalkeith.
Col. F. W. *Duke of* Buccleugh
Adj. Capt. P. M'L. Petley

FIFE. [78]
Cupar.
Col. Jas. Lindsay
Adjt. [illegible] W. Scott 19

FORFAR and KINCARDINE. [105]
Montrose.
Col. Hon. D. Ogilvy
Adj. Capt. A. M'Neill

INVERNESS, BANFF, ELGIN, & NAIRN. [76]
Inverness.
Col. F. W. *Earl of* Seafield
Adj.

KIRKCUDBRIGHT and WIGTON. (Light Infantry.) [92]
Kirkcudbright.
Col. Sir D. Maxwell, *Bt.*
Adj.

ROY. LANARK. [74]
Hamilton.
Col. Marq. of Douglas and Clydesdale
Adj. Capt. Vaughan

ROYAL PERTH. [86]
Perth.
Col. T. R. H. *Earl of* Kinnoull.
Adj. Capt. G. D. Paterson

RENFREW. [129]
Paisley.
Col. Wm. Mure
Adj.

ROSS, CAITHNESS, SUTHERLAND, & CROMARTY. [96.]
Dingwall.
Col. [illegible] Chas. Fraser, 20
Ad. Cap. A. Mackenzie

STIRLING, DUMBARTON, CLACKMANNAN and KINROSS. [90]
Stirling.
C. J. Duke of Montrose
Adj. Capt. J. Fraser

ANTRIM. [79]
Randalstown.
Col. Geo. *Marq. of* Donegal
Adjut. [illegible] *Capt.* C. B. Carrothers 21
Agent, Sir E. Borough & Co.

ARMAGH. [75]
Market Hill.
Col. A. *Visc* Acheson
Adj. Cap. Barker
Agent, Sir E. Borough & Co.

CARLOW. [70]
Carlow.
Colonel H. Bruen
Adjut.
Ag. Cane & Co.

CAVAN. [101]
Cavan.
Col. A. Saunderson
Adj. Capt. N. Gosselin
Agent, Sir E. Borough & Co.

CLARE. [94]
Clare Castle, Ennis.
Col. O. M. Vandeleur
Adj. Capt. Wm. Gore
Ag. Cane & Co.

NORTH CORK. [116]
Fermoy.
Col. W. H. M. Hodder
Adjut. Lt. C. V. Foss
Agent, Sir E. Borough & Co.

SOUTH CORK. (Light Infantry. [87]
Rathcormac.
Col. Visc. Doneraile
Adjut. Capt. A. H. Lucas
Ag. Cane & Co.

CORK (CITY). [110]
Cork.
Col. Visc. Bernard
Adj. Cap. A. Warren
Ag. Cane & Co.

DONEGAL. [103]
Ballyshannon.
Col. N. *E of* Leitrim.
Adj. Capt. Searle
Ag. Cane & Co

ROYAL NORTH DOWN. [77]
Newtown Ards.
Col. Visc. Castlereagh
Adj. Capt. Howe
Agent, Sir E. Borough & Co.

ROYAL SOUTH DOWN. [112]
Hillsborough.
Col. Marq. of Downshire
Ad. Cap. J. A. Hodgson
Ag. Cane & Co.

DUBLIN (COUNTY.) [109]
Lucan.
Col. Lord Brabazon
Ad. Ca. H. J. V. Kemble
Ag. Cane & Co.

ROYAL DUBLIN (CITY). [100]
Dublin.
Col. Sir R. Shaw, *Bt.*
Adj. Capt. S. W. Russell 24
Agent, Sir E. Borough & Co.

FERMANAGH. [71]
Enniskillen.
Col. E. of Enniskillen
Adj. Wm. Corry
Agent, Sir E. Borough & Co.

GALWAY. [91]
Ballinasloe.
Colonel Ulic, *Marq. of* Clanricarde, *K.P.*
Adj. Capt. Eyre
Ag. Cane & Co.

KERRY. [107]
Tralee.
Col. V. *E. of* Kenmare
Adj. Capt. D. A. Curtayne
Agent, Sir E. Borough & Co.

KILDARE. [88]
Naas.
Col. J. *Earl of* Mayo
Adj. Lt. H. G. R. Robinson
Agent, Sir E. Borough & Co.

KILKENNY. [127]
Kilkenny.
Col. Marq. of Ormonde
Adj. Capt. J. M'Intyre
Ag. Cane & Co.

KING'S COUNTY. [98]
Parsonstown.
Col. W. *Earl of* Rosse
Adj. Capt. [illegible] T. Cox 22
Agent, Sir E. Borough & Co.

LEITRIM. [111]
Mohill.
Col. Visc. Clements
Adjut. Wm. Rose
Agent, Sir E. Borough & Co.

LIMERICK COUNTY [123]
St. Francis Abbey.
Col. Hon. R. Fitz Gibbon
Adj. Capt. R. Butler Low
Ag. Cane & Co.

LIMERICK CITY. [103]
Limerick City.
Col. Cha. *Visc.* Gort
Adj. Lt. Tho. Jervis
Agent, Sir E. Borough & Co.

LONDONDERRY. [95]
Londonderry.
Col. Sir R. A. Ferguson, *Bt.*
Ad. Capt. J. M'Clintock
Agent, Sir E. Borough & Co.

LONGFORD. [85]
Newtown Forbes.
Col. Henry White
Adjut. W. Walker
Ag. Mr. J. Atkinson.

LOUTH. [108]
Colton.
Col. Lord Bellew
Adj. Cap. Pendleton
Agent, Sir E. Borough & Co.

NORTH MAYO. [120]
Ballina.
Col. Cha. N. Knox
Adjut.
Agent, Sir E. Borough & Co.

SOUTH MAYO. [62]
Westport.
Col. G. *Marquis of* Sligo
Adj. Capt. Fitzgerald Higgins
Ag. Cane & Co.

ROY. MEATH. [119]
Kells.
Col. Mar. of Headfort, *K.P.*
Adj. Capt. Josh. Clare
Ag. Cane & Co.

MONAGHAN. [121]
Monaghan.
Col. Lord Rossmore
Adj. Capt. John Ross
Agent, Sir E. Borough & Co.

QUEEN'S COUNTY. [104]
Mountrath.
Col. Sir C. H. Coote, *Bt.*
Adj. H. Brereton
Agent, Sir E. Borough & Co.

ROSCOMMON. [88]
Boyle.
Col. .. *Gen.* R. *Visc.* Lorton
Adj. Capt. C. R. Dunnmin
Agent, Sir E. Borough & Co.

SLIGO. [124]
Sligo.
Col. A. Knox Gore
Adj. Capt. T. Ormsby
Ag. Cane & Co.

TIPPERARY. (*Or Duke of Clarence's Munster.*) [84]
Cahir.
Col. R. *E. of* Glengall
Adj. Capt. Daniell
Agent, Sir E. Borough & Co.

TYRONE. [60]
Caledon.
Col. E. of Caledon
Adj. Wm. Lundie
Ag. Cane & Co.

WATERFORD. (Light Infantry.) [128]
Waterford.
Col. H. *Lord* Stuart de Decies
Adj.
Ag. Cane & Co.

WESTMEATH. [114]
Mullingar.
Col. George, *Mar. of* Westmeath, K.P.
Adj. Lt. H. Robinson
Agent, Sir E. Borough & Co.

WEXFORD. [99]
Wexford.
Col. Lord Carew
Adj. Lt. D. Beatty
Agent, Sir E. Borough & Co.

WICKLOW. [80]
Arklow.
Colonel Sir Ralph Howard, *Bt.*
Adj. Lt. Gen. A. Bayly
Ag. Cane & Co.

1 Lt. Dickinson (*Brecon*) served with the Queen's Royals throughout the campaign in Affghanistan and Beloochistan, in 1838 and 39, and was present at the assault and capture of the fortresses of Ghuznée and Khelat, at which last he was severely wounded by a musket-shot,—leg broken. Medal for Ghuznée.

2 Lord Mount Edgcumbe (*Duke of Cornwall's Rangers*) served the campaign of 1815, and was present at the battle of Waterloo.

3 Captain Pennington (*Cumberland*) served in the Peninsula from June, 1809, and during the greatest part of the subsequent campaigns, including the battle of Busaco, where he commanded one of the advance picquets of the 3d division on the morning of the action, and was sharply engaged with the enemy; retreat to the lines of Torres Vedras, advance from thence, actions and affairs at Leria, Redinha, Pombal, Roblida, Condeixa, Foz d'Arouce, Guarda, and Sabugal; battles of Fuentes d'Onor, siege of Badajoz (wounded in the right thigh), actions at Campo Mayor, El Bodon, and Guinaldo; affairs and actions in the Pyrenees, St. Pé (contused wound), Hasparren, and Grassietta; battles of Nivelle, Nive, and Orthes (severely wounded), besides several other affairs of posts and picquets during the war.

4 Captain Dixon (*Derby*) served with the Grenadier Guards on the expedition to the North of Holland in 1799, and was in the actions of the 27th Aug., 10th and 19th Sept., 2nd and 6th Oct. In Sicily in 1806 and 7. In the Peninsula under Sir John Moore in 1808-9, including the action at Lugo and battle of Corunna. On the expedition to Walcheren in 1809. Went to Cadiz in April 1811, and was afterwards present at the capture of Seville, and on the retreat from Madrid and Salamanca; and remained with that army until June 1813. Served also the campaign of 1815, and was wounded through the leg at the battle of Quatre Bras.

5 Captain Holman (*East Devon*) served in the Peninsula from Nov. 1811 attached to the Portuguese service, and was present with Lord Hill's corps covering the siege of Badajoz, advance on Llerena, siege and storm of the three fortified convents of Salamanca,—led the storming party to the gate of San Vincente at its capture; battle of Salamanca,—slightly wounded by a musket shot in the leg; siege of Burgos and storming the works and the White Church; several skirmishes on the retreat from thence near Torrequemada, and blowing up the bridge of Duenas; battles of the Pyrenees on the 28th, 29th, and 30th July; night attack and defeat of a French battalion on the heights of Urdax, action near Zugarrimundi,—severe contused wound; battles of the Nivelle and the Nive, actions at Ustaritz and Villa Franque, battles of St. Pierre and Orthes, actions at Aire, Vic Bigorre, and Tarbes, and battle of Toulouse. Served the campaign of 1815, including the battle of Waterloo; also with the army of occupation in France.

6 Captain Ridgway (*North Devon*) served in the Peninsula with the Rifle Brigade, from May 1812 to the end of that war in 1814, including the battle of Vittoria, and various minor affairs. Served also the campaign of 1815, and was present at the battle of Waterloo. Severely wounded in the right shoulder by a musket-shot at the taking of Vera heights, and lost the fore-finger of the left hand by a musket-shot at Waterloo.

7 Captain Fisk (*South Devon*) served as Adjutant of the 17th Lt. Drs. during the campaign of 1820 in Kutch.

8 Captain Jones (*East Essex*) served with the Grenadier Guards at the defence of Cadiz and Isla de Leon from 1st April 1810 to May 1811, and in the battle of Barrosa. In 1813 and 14 he served in Holland, at the attack on Merxem and storming of Bergen-op-Zoom. At the battle of Waterloo the following year he was severely wounded through the body by a musket-ball.

9 Captain Pearson (*West Essex*) served in China (Medal) in the 49th—at Chusan and Canton (severely wounded).

10 Captain Percy Scott (*Hants*) served in the Peninsula with the 2nd Queen's.

11 Capt. Kennedy's services (*North Lincoln*):—Siege and capture of Flushing, 1809. Campaigns of 1811, 12, 13, 14, and 15, including the first siege of Badajoz, and covering the second siege, as also that of Ciudad Rodrigo, crossing the Esla, retreat from Burgos, actions of Val Moresco, Peyrehorade and Echalar, battles of Fuentes d'Onor, Salamanca, Vittoria, Pampeluna, Pyrenees, Nive, Orthes and Waterloo; and he led the column of attack at the storming of Cambray.

12 Capt. Browne (*East Norfolk*) served throughout the war with China (Medal) as Adj. of the 49th Regt., and latterly as a Brigade Major, and was present at Canton, Amoy, Chusan, Chinhae, Ningpo, Segoan, Chapoo (wounded), Woosung, Chin Kiang Foo, and Nankin.

13 Captain Pardey (*Salop*) served in the Peninsula from Feb. 1813 to the end of that war in 1814.

14 The Duke of Richmond (*Sussex*) joined the army in Portugal, on the 24th July 1810, as Aide-de-Camp and Assistant Military Secretary to the Duke of Wellington, with whom he remained until the close of the war in 1814, and was present in all the skirmishes, affairs, general actions, and sieges, which took place during that period, amongst which were the battles of Busaco and Fuentes d'Onor, storming of Ciudad Rodrigo, storming of Badajoz, battles of Salamanca, Vittoria, and the Pyrenees, the first storming of San Sebastian, action at Vera, and battle of Orthes. He was sent home with duplicate Dispatches of the battle of Salamanca, and the capture of Astorga by the Spaniards; and with the Dispatches of Vera and the entrance of the army into France. In Jan. 1814, being desirous of obtaining a practical knowledge of Regimental duty in the Field, he left the Duke of Wellington's Staff to join the first battalion of his Regt., the 52nd Light Infantry, and was present with it in the battle of Orthes, where he was severely wounded in the chest by a musket-ball, which has never been extracted. At the end of 1814, he was appointed Aide-de-Camp to the Prince of Orange, and was with him in the battles of Quatre Bras and Waterloo;—after the Prince of Orange was wounded the Duke of Richmond joined the Duke of Wellington as Aide-de-Camp, and remained with his Grace during the remaining part of that campaign.

15 Captain Smith (*Sussex*) served with the 1st Guards in Sicily in 1806 and 7; in the North of Spain in 1808-9, including the retreat to and battle of Corunna; defence of Cadiz in 1811 and

GARRISONS.

BELFAST.
Town Maj. *Lieut.* Peter Stuart.

BERWICK.
Gov. *Lt.-Gen. Sir* J. Bathurst, *KCB.*

CAPE BRETON.
Town Adj. *Lt.* Edw. Sutherland

CHARLES FORT AND KINSALE.
Fort Maj. *Lt.* John Black

DARTMOUTH.
Gov.... Ar. Howe Holdsworth
Fort Maj. *Lt. Col.* Robert Kelly

DUBLIN.
Town Maj. *Major* W. White

DUNCANNON FORT.
Fort Maj. *Lieut.* Thos. Austin

EDINBURGH CASTLE.
Governor, *Major-Gen.* J. H. Riddell, *KH.*
Lieut.-Gov.. Gen. F. T. Hammond, *GCH.*
Fort Maj. *Major.* Thos. Canch
Chaplain. *Rev.* W. B. Smith

GIBRALTAR.
Town Maj. *Maj.* T. E. Lacy, Unatt.
Town Adj. Qr. Mas. W. Hume, h. p. 72 F.

GRAVESEND & TILBURY FORT.
Fort Maj. *Lt.-Col.* Thos. Kelly.

GUERNSEY.
Fort Maj. & Adj. *Lt. Col.* J. H. Bainbrigge, Unatt.

HULL.
Lt.-Gov.. M. Gen. Sir C. W. Thornton, *KCH.*

JERSEY.
Gov.. *Gen.* W. C. *Visc.* Beresford, *GCB. & GCH.*
Fort Major & Adj. *Major* John Fraser.

INVERNESS, OR FORT GEORGE.
Fort Maj. *Col.* Alex. Findlay, *KH.*

LANDGUARD FORT.
Lieut.-Gov.. *Lt.-Col.* C. A. West

LONDONDERRY & CULMORE.
Gov. *Gen.* John *Earl of* Strafford, *GCB. & GCH*
Town Maj. J. Nicholson

MALTA.
Quart.-Mast. *Lt.* J. Colcroft

MILFORD HAVEN.
Gov.., Sir John Owen, *Bt.*

MONTREAL.
Town Maj. *Ens.* C. Macdonald, h. p. 60 F.

NEW BRUNSWICK.
Town Maj. *Lt.* J. Gallagher

NEW GENEVA.
Fort Maj. Anthony Wharton

PORTSMOUTH.
Town Maj. *Lieut.* Henry White
Physician *Sir* J. M'Grigor, *Bt. MD.*
Surgeon.... Isaac Chaldecott

ST. HELENA.
Town Maj. *Capt.* Geo. A. Barnes

ST. JOHN'S, NEWFOUNDLAND.
Fort Maj. *Lt.* Wm. Jenkins, Royal Newfoundland Company

ST. JOHN'S, OR PRINCE EDWARD'S ISLAND.
Town Maj. *Capt.* A. Lane

ST. MAWES.
Capt. or Keeper, Field Marshal Sir Geo. Nugent, *Bt. GCB.*

SCARBOROUGH CASTLE.
Gov.. *Maj. Gen.* Jas. Grant, *CB*

SHEERNESS.
Gov.... *Gen.* S. *Visc.* Combermere, *GCB. & GCH.*

STIRLING CASTLE.
Fort Major.. Lieut. Patrick Tytler
Chaplain.. Rev. Robt. Watson

TOWER OF LONDON.
Constable *Field Mar.* A. *D. of* Wellington, *KG. GCB. & GCH.*
Lieut... Gen. J. Sullivan Wood
Dep. Lieut... *Col. Hon.* George Cathcart
Major.. Capt. J. H. Elrington
Chaplain.. Rev. Henry Melville

ISLE OF WIGHT.
Capt. of Sandown Fort, *Capt. Sir* Wm. Wynn
——— *Carisb. Cast.* *Lt.-Gen. Sir* W. Paterson, *KCH.*
——— *Cowes Castle,* *Gen* H. W. *M. of* Anglesey, *KG. GCB. & GCH.*

FORT WILLIAM.
Lieut. Gov..... *Gen. Rt. Hon.* Sir Jas. Kempt, *GCB. & GCH.*

MILITARY ESTABLISHMENTS.

ROYAL HOSPITAL, CHELSEA.

Governor, *General Hon. Sir* Edward Paget, GCB.
Lieut.-Governor, *General Sir* George Anson, GCB.
Major, Lieut.-Colonel Henry Le Blanc,
Adjutant, *Colonel Sir* John Morillyon Wilson, CB. KH.
Secretary, Richard Neave, *Esq.*
Chaplain, Rev. George Mathias.
Physician & Surgeon, Daniel Maclachlan, MD.
Deputy Surgeon, Thomas Coke Gaulter, MD.
Assistant Surgeon, Adam Alex. Prout.
Storekeeper, Captain Edward Sutherland, h. p. Unatt.
Assist. Secretary, John Fasson, *Esq.*
Senior Clerk, F. B. Talman, *Esq.*

Captains of Invalids:

John Davern
George Peevor
Augustine Fitzgerald Evans
John Ford
W. Chadwick
Charles Edwards

Adjutant.— J. G. Hort, *Captain* late 12 R. Vet. Batt.
Physician and Surgeon.— Geo. Renny, *MD. Director General of Hospitals in Ireland.*
Assistant-Surgeon.— James Macauley, *MD.*
Chaplain.— Rev. J. T. Connel, *AM.*
Secretary, Registrar and Treasurer.— Chas. Banks, Esq.
Providore.— James Hay, Esq. (late Capt. 82nd regt.)
Chamberlain and Master of Works.— John George, Capt. h. p. Unatt.
Registrar's Clerk.— Mr. Charles Pengelly.
Solicitor.— Robert Disney, Esq.

ROYAL HOSPITAL, KILMAINHAM.

Master.— Lieut.-Gen. *Rt. Hon. Sir* Edw. Blakeney, *KCB & KCH. Comm. of the Forces in Ireland.*
Deputy Master. — Colonel Napier, *CB. Deputy Adjutant General in Ireland.*

Captains on the Establishment.

Edward D'Arcey
Purefoy Lockwood
Robert Cook
Edw. Gilborne
Thomas Gibbons

ROYAL MILITARY ASYLUM AT CHELSEA.
Commandant.— *Colonel* Peter Brown, h. p. Unatt.
Secretary & Adjutant. Capt. William Siborne, h. p. Unatt.
Quarter-Master. William Cousins
Surgeon.— Thomas Graham Balfour, *MD.*

ROYAL HIBERNIAN MILITARY SCHOOL, DUBLIN
Surgeon, James Goodall Elkington.

ROYAL MILITARY COLLEGE AT SANDHURST.
Governor, *Lt.-Gen. Sir* G. Scovell, *KCB.*
Lt. Gov. *Major-Gen.* Tho. W. Taylor, *CB.*
Major and Superintendent of Studies, Lieut.-Col. George Walter Prosser.

Captains of Companies of Gentlemen Cadets.

Capt. Robert Daly
Capt. James W. Dalgety

Chaplain, Librarian, &c. Rev. H. L. Chepmell.
Quarter Master, Lieut. J. W. Tipping
Surgeon, John Pickering, *MD.*
Assistant-Surg. Melville Neale, *MD.*

MILITARY KNIGHTS OF WINDSOR.

Major Charles Moore, formerly of 89 F. (*Governor*)
Lieut. Samuel Ragg, late 1 R. Vet. Bn.
Lieut. Cha. Hunt Lorimer, late 8 do.
Lieut. Hugh Fleming, late 7 R. Vet. Bn.
—— John Allen, h. p. 84 F, (formerly Captain Portuguese Service.)
Quarter-Master John Powell, h. p. 77 F.
Quarter-Master A. Heartley, h. p. R. Horse Gds.
Lieut. Tho. M'Dermott, late 7 R. Vet. Bn.
Major Geo. Wathen, formerly of 14 F.
Captain Robert Cochrane, late of Rifle Br.
Ensign John Lamb, late 2 R. Vet. Bn.
Major Thomas Cradock, late of 73 F.
Capt. A. W. Cassan, formerly of 68 F.
Lieut. Richard Nantes, h.p. 53 F.
Major John Clarke, late of 66 F.
Lieut. Henry Griffiths, h. p. R. Staff Corps.
Quarter-Master John Ledam, h. p. 7 F.
Lt.-Col. A. G. Campbell, formerly of 82 F.

N.B. *For Staff at the Horse Guards, see page* 117.

DISTRICTS.

Districts.	General and other Officers.	Aides-de-Camp.	Staff.
NORTHERN AND MIDLAND.—Head Quarters at Manchester.	P Lt.-Gen. *Sir* Tho. Arbuthnot, *KCB.*	Lieut. Fane, 54 F. Capt. *Ld.* Burghersh, 17 F.	*Assist. Adj.-Gen.* Col. H. W. Barnard, Gr. Gd. *Assist. Qr. Mas. Gen.* P [illegible] Colonel C. Yorke, Unatt.
North West Counties.—Head Qrs. Chester. Lancashire, Cheshire, Shropshire, Flintshire, Denbighshire, and Isle of Man.	P Major-General *Sir* Wm. Warre, *CB.*		*Major of Brigade.* Capt. Warr, 57 F.
North East Counties.—Head Qrs. York. Northumberland, Cumberland, Durham, Westmoreland, York, Derby, Nottingham, Leicester, and Rutland.	P Maj.-Gen. N. Thorn, *CB. KH.*	Lt. Kennedy, 86 F.	*Major of Brigade.* Capt. H. B. J. Wynyard, Unatt.
Midland Counties.—Head Qrs. Birmingham. Warwick, Stafford, Northampton, and Worcester.	Colonel Arbuthnot.		*Major of Brigade.* Capt. Mein, 13 F.
SOUTH WEST.—Head Qrs. Portsmouth. Wilts, Dorset, and Hants.	Major-Gen. *Lord* Fred. Fitz Clarence.	Major Harvey, 87 F.	*Major of Brigade.* Capt. J. H. Purves, Unatt.
WESTERN.—Head Quarters, Devonport. Devon, Cornwall, and Somerset, exclusive of Bristol and its vicinity.	P [illegible] Major-General *Hon.* H. Murray, *CB.*	Capt. Prothero, 14 F.	*Major of Brigade.* Capt. T. Nelson, 40 F.
Monmouth and South Wales.—Head Qrs. Carmarthen.	P [illegible] Col. Love, *CB. KH.* Unatt. *Col. on the Staff.*	Major Parkinson, Unatt.	Capt. Mann, 90 F.
JERSEY.	P Major-General *Sir* J. H. Reynett, *KCH. Lt.-Gov.*		
GUERNSEY AND ALDERNEY.	P Major-General John Bell, *CB. Lieut.-Gov.*		*Town Major of Alderney* P Lt.-Cl. W. A. Le Mesurier
INSPECTING GENERAL OF CAVALRY. Head Quarters, London.	P Maj.-Gen. T. W. Brotherton, *CB.*	Lt. Bourke, 75 F.	*Major of Brigade.* Col. William, *Lord* De Ros, h. p. Unatt.

The following Counties, &c. are not contained in any Military District, and the Troops stationed in those Countie report direct to Head Quarters, viz.:—

Bedford,	Buckingham,	Gloucester,	Kent,	Monmouth,	Surry,
Berkshire,	Cambridge,	Hereford,	Leicester,	Norfolk,	Sussex,
Brecon,	Essex,	Hertford,	Lincoln,	Oxford,	Wales, N. & S. (exc.
Bristol & vicinity,	Glamorgan,	Huntingdon,	Middlesex,	Suffolk,	Denbigh & Flint.)

The Troops in the Isle of Wight report to the General Officer Commanding the South West District.

RECRUITING DISTRICTS.

Leeds. Consisting of the counties of Northumberland, Durham, Cumberland, Westmoreland, and parts of Yorkshire and Lancashire.	*Insp. Fd. Off. Col.* Bush, *KH.* *Adj.—Lt.* P W. A. Courtenay, 22 Nov. 44 *Paymaster* . . C. H. Peirse *Surg. to the Forces*, Thomas Hall *Superintending Officers.* Lt. Keyt, 85 F. York — Poole, 1 F. Leeds — Wilson, 7 F. Durham — Martin, 18 F. . Sheffield
Liverpool. Consisting of the county of Cheshire, and parts of Yorkshire, Lancashire, Derby, & North Wales.	*Insp. F. Off.* Col. C. G. Falconar, *KH.* *Adj.* P *Lt.* B. H. Edwards, 7 May, 47 *Paymaster* . . P Capt. Woodgate *Sur. to the Forces*, A. Foulis. *Superintending Officers.* Lt. Byam, 59 F. . . . Liverpool — G. Macdonald, 16 F. Manchester Tongue, 30 F. . . Shrewsbury — Armstrong, 14 F. Newcastle-under-Lyne.
Coventry. Consisting of the counties of Lincoln, Stafford, Nottingham, Rutland, Leicester, Warwick, Salop, Hereford, & parts of Derby, Northampton, & South Wales.	*Ins. Fd. Off.* [illegible] *Col. J.* Campbell, *KH.* *Adj.* . . . . *Lt.* C. Pieters, 2 Apr. 47. *Paymaster* . P A. Thompson *Surg. to the Forces* . . P T. Lewis, *M.D.* *Superintending Officers.* Lt. Bourne, 17 F. . . Coventry — Lea, 9 F. . . . Leicester — Colvill, 29 F. . . Birmingham — Bowden, 22 F. . Nottingham — Straubenzee, 18 F. Lincoln
Bristol. Consisting of the counties of Cornwall, Devon, Dorset, Somerset, Wilts, Worcester, Gloucester, Hereford, and part of Hants, and South Wales.	*Insp. F. Off. Col.* Baumgardt, *CB.* *Adj.* P *Lt.* J. B. Hamilton, 6 Dec. 44. *Paymaster* . . . J. Sabine. *Surgeon to the Forces* } A. Cumming *Superintending Officers.* Lieut. Gould, 31 F. . . Bristol —— Stopford, 49 F. . . Gloucester —— Schaw, 55 F. . . Exeter —— Forrest, 5 F. . . Abergavenny
London. Consisting of the counties of Norfolk, Suffolk, Cambridge, Huntingdon, Bucks, Bedford, Hertford, Essex, Kent, Sussex, Surry, Oxford, Berks, and Middlesex, and parts of Northampton and Hants.	*Insp. Fd. Off. Col. Sir* R. Doherty *Adj. Lt.* Rob. M'Nair 14 July 37 *Paymaster* . P R. Jellicoe *Surgeon* . . M. H. Burrell W. Home, MD. *Superintending Officers.* Lt. Wedderburn, 9 Lanc. London Cav. Subdivision —— Montagu, 10 F. . . London 1st Inf. Subdivision —— Lecky, 86 F. 2nd Inf. Subdiv. —— *Hon.* J. L. Browne, 64 F. Reading —— Murray, 63 F. . Cambridge —— Bouverie, 78 F. . Southampton

CAVALRY DEPOT AT MAIDSTONE.

Commandant . . Col. C. Middleton, 3 Dragoons
Assist. Commandant, Lieut.-Col. F. C. Griffiths, Unatt.
Paymaster . . . Captain William Castle
Riding-Master . . * Major L. C. A. Meyer

Acting Adjutant . Lieut. Lee, 15 Hussars
Quarter-Master . John Swindley
Veterinary Surgeon Charles Brett, 8 March 33

GARRISON, INFANTRY, AND INVALID DEPOT AT CHATHAM.

Commandant Col. J. Simpson, Unatt.
Major of Brigade ....Capt. Wood, 18 F.
Staff Captain, Fort Pitt, Major Henry Anderson[1]

Adjutant ....Lieut. George Rand[2]
Paymaster ....Francis Edward Leech[3]
Paymaster of Indian Depots...James Macdonald, Esq.

Superintendent of Sword Exercise......Henry Angelo, Esq.

Principal Veterinary Surgeon...... Fred. Clifford Cherry,[4] Esq., *Clapham Common.*

ROYAL MILITARY COLLEGE AT SANDHURST.

For the Appointments of Officers held by *Commission*, see "*Military Establishments*," page 218.

Professors and Masters.

Mathematics and Arithmetic . . . . John Narrien, *FRAS.*; Wm. Scott, *AM. & FRAS.*; Cha. H. Barton, *BA.*; G. Hearn, *B.A.*
Fortification . . . . *Major* W. H. Adams, Unatt.; *Capt.* Garnet Man, Unatt.
Surveying . . . . . Geo. D. Burr
Drawing . . . . . . John Piercy; Thomas Costin.

Landscape Drawing . Edward de la Motte
History, Geography, and Classics . . Rev. George E. Cole, *M.A.*; Rev. Slater W. Heale, *M.A.*
French . . . . . G. Cambier; H. Marillier; G. Boully
German . . . . . F. Demmler
Riding Master . . . Lieut. John Gillies, h.p.

Students in the Senior Department.

Capt. Wetherall	1 F.	Lieut. Hammersley	14 F.	Capt. S. B. Lamb	Unatt.
Capt. Dickinson	59 F.	Lieut. Seton	49 F.	Lieut. Butler	36 F.
Capt. Grant	47 F.	Lieut. Rigaud	60 F.	Lieut. Rundle	40 F.
Capt. Stapylton	13 F.	Capt. Filder	70 F.		

EAST INDIA COMPANY'S DEPOT, RECRUITING OFFICERS, AND MILITARY SEMINARY.

DEPOT AT WARLEY, IN ESSEX.

Commandant ....Colonel Edward Hay.
(*2d in Command*) ......*Lt. Col.* John Thomas Leslie, *CB.*
Capt. and Paymaster .....Major William Elsey.
Adjutant ....Capt. W. Falconer Hay.
Lt. ....Geo. Bourchier, Bengal Art.
Surgeon ....A. R. Jackson, *MD.*

RECRUITING OFFICERS.

Lt. Col. Sir E.A. Campbell, *CB*, *Newry.*
Lt. Col. Henry Brown Smith ..*Bristol.*
Major Richard Axford ....*Liverpool.*
Major George Thomson, *CB*...*Cork.*
Major Henry Brown ....*London*, 28, *Soho-Square.*
Captains Rich. Geo. Grange...*Dublin.*
Henry Vibart Glegg..*Edinburgh.*

MILITARY SEMINARY AT ADDISCOMBE.

Public Examiner and Inspector ...... *Maj. Gen. Sir* Cha. W. Pasley, *KCB.* R.Eng. *FRS. FAS. FGS.*
Lieut.-Governor ...... Major General *Sir* Ephraim G. Stannus, *CB.*
Captain..................Major T. Ritherdon

Orderly Officers ......Lt. C. P. Taylor, Madr. Army; — R. J. Ferrers, Madr. Cav.
Public Examiner in the Oriental Department .. Horace H. Wilson

Professors and Masters.

Mathematics and Classics .... *Rev.* Jonathan Cape, *AM.*; *Rev.* Alfred Wrigley, *BA.*; *Rev.* W. H. Johnstone, *B.A.* (*Chaplain*); *Rev.* R. Inchbald, *B.A.*; Arthur Dusautoy
Fortifications ....Lieut. T. Cook, *RN. FRS.*; Major W. Jacob, Bombay Art.
Surveying...............Lt.Col. Basil Jackson, h.p. Royal Staff Corps
Drawing ....E. B. Metcalf

Landscape Drawing .... T. H. Fielding; J. C. Schetky.
Oriental Languages .... Rich. Haughton, *MRAS.*; Cha. Bowles
French ....Leon Contanseau
Geology and Mineralogy..D. T. Ansted, *A.M.*
Chemistry ....Edward Solly
Sword Exercise...........Hen. Angelo, *jun.*
Clerk for passing Cadets and Assist.-Surgeon T. R. Clarke, Cadet Depart. India House
Steward, R. J. Leeds—*Housekeeper*, Mrs. Leeds

STAFF, &c. OF SCOTLAND.

General Officer.	Station.	Aide de Camp.	Staff.
Maj.-Gen. H. J. Riddell, *KH.*	Edinburgh	Capt. Riddell, R. Art.	*Assist. Adj. Gen.*...Col. John Eden, *CB.*, Unatt. *Staff Adjut.*......Lieut. J. O'Neill

RECRUITING DISTRICT.

Paymaster .... Captain J. Middleton ....*Edinburgh.*
Surgeon to the Forces........... T. F. Cotton ....*Edinburgh.*

Glasgow. *Insp. F. Off.* Lt.-Col. C. Barnwell, *CB.*
Adj......... *Lt.* John Spence, 10 March, 48.
Paymaster.. George Hood
Surgeon to the Forces..W. Linton

Superintending Officers.
Lt. Faulkner, 2 F...Glasgow

Superintending Officers.
Lt. Park, 26 F...........Edinburgh
— Roney, 96 F. ....Perth
— Persse, 12 F. ....Aberdeen
— Forbes, 40 F. ... .Inverness

1 Major Anderson served the campaigns of 1814 and 15 in Holland and the Netherlands, including the action at Merxem, bombardment of Antwerp, storming of Bergen-op-Zoom, and actions at Quatre Bras and Waterloo. Severely wounded at Waterloo by a musket-ball, which broke the left shoulder, passed through the lungs, and made its exit at the back, breaking the scapula.

2 Lt. Rand served with the 49th throughout the operations in China.

3 Paymaster Leech served in the Peninsula from Jan. 1813 to the end of the war, including the Passage of the Bidassoa, the battle of Nivelle 10th Nov., and Nive 9th, 10th, 11th, and 12th Dec. 1813, and blockade of Bayonne. Served also at the escalade of Bouj Bouj in Cutch, March 1819, & at the siege of Rhas-el-Khyma, & of Zoa in the Persian Gulf in 1819 & 20. He was present also at Seinde (Turdo?)

4 Mr. Cherry served Sir John Moore's campaign in Spain, including the battle of Corunna; with the expedition to Walcheren, in 1809; the Peninsular campaigns from Jan. 1812 to the end of the war in 1814; also the campaign of 1815, including the battle of Waterloo.

Commanding the Troops.
₱ Lieut. Gen. *Rt. Hon. Sir* Edward Blakeney, *KCB. & GCH.* { Capt. *Hon.* St. G. G. Foley, Unatt. *Aide-de-Camp.* — *Lord* Cosmo G. Russell, 93 F. *do.* — *Hon.* C. H. Lindsay, Gr. Gds. *do.*

Military Secretary Lt. Col. Greaves, Unatt. | *Assist. Military Secretary*, Major *Hon.* C. R. W. Forester, Unatt.

ADJUTANT GENERAL'S DEPARTMENT. *(Head Quarters—Dublin.)*

Deputy Adjutant General.. ₱ *Col.* W. Cochrane, Unatt. | *Dep. Assist. Adjutant General*.... Major Draper, 64 F.
Assistant Adjutant General.. *Lt.-Col.* Wood, 80 F.

QUARTER-MASTER-GENERAL'S DEPARTMENT. *(Head Quarters—Dublin.)*

Dep. Quart. Mast-Gen. ₱ Colonel Mansel, *KH.* Unatt. | *Assist. Dep. Quar. Mast. Gen.* Capt. L. V. Smith h.p. R. Eng.

ORDNANCE DEPARTMENT. *(Head Quarters—Dublin.)*

Commanding R. Artillery .... ₱ Col. Turner, *CB.* | *Command. R. Eng.*, ₱ Col. Vavasour.
Assist. Adjutant General .. ₱ Lt. Col. C. E. Gordon. | *Major of Brigade*, Capt. Lugard, R. Eng.

DISTRICTS.

Districts.	General and other Officers.	Aides de Camp.	Staff.
Belfast.—Head Quarters, Belfast. The Province of Ulster, and County of Louth, with the exception of the Town of Drogheda.	₱ Major-Gen. Bainbrigge, *CB.* ₱ Col. St. John A. Clerke, *KH.*, Unatt. Lt. Col. E. Macarthur, Unatt., *Cavan.*	Capt. Duff, 74 F.	*As. Adj. Gen.* Lt.-Col. R. W. Brough, h. p. 2 F.
Dublin.—Head Quarters, Dublin. The Counties of Dublin, Kildare, Carlow, Kilkenny, Wexford, Wicklow, Meath, and the Towns of Drogheda and Waterford.	Major-Gen. *His Royal Highness Prince* George of Cambridge, *KG. GCMG.* ₱ Major-Gen. T. J. Wemyss, *CB.* Col. Pennefather, *C.B.* h. p. 28 F.	Capt. *Hon.* J. Macdonald, Unatt.	*Assist. Adj. Gen.* Lieut. Col. W. F. Forster, *KH.* Unatt. *As. Qua. M. Gen.* Major E. R. Scott, *Town Major.* ₱ Maj. W. White,
Athlone.—Head Quarters, Athlone. The Province of Connaught, with Counties of Longford, Westmeath, King's County, and Queen's County.	₱ WL Major-General *Sir* Guy Campbell, *Bart.*, *CB.*	Capt. George, 75 F.	*As. Adj. Gen.* ₱ Lt.-Col. W. F. Williams, *KH.* Unatt., *As. Qua. M. Gen.* Lt.-Col. C. C. Johnson, h. p.
Limerick.—Head Quarters, Limerick. The Counties of Clare, Limerick, Kerry, and Tipperary.	₱ Major-Gen. T. E. Napier, *CB.* *Sir* C. R. O'Donnell, Unatt. *Clonmel* ₱ Col. W. Cox, *KH.* Unatt. *Limerick* ₱ WL Col. Wm. Turner, *Ennis*	Capt. Kilvington, 64 F.	*As. Adj. Gen.* Lieut.-Col. C. H. Doyle, Unatt.
Cork.—Head Quarters, Cork. The Counties of Cork and Waterford, exclusive of the Town of Waterford.	Major-General Turner. Col. *Sir* M. Creagh, *KH.*	Lt. Turner, R. Art.	*As. Adj. Gen.* Col. M. Beresford, Unatt. *As. Qua. M. Gen.* Col. J. Spink, *KH.* Unatt. *Fort Major.* ₱ Lt. J. Black, *Charles Fort.*

RECRUITING DISTRICTS.

Northern. *Head Quarters, Newry.* Consisting of the counties of Antrim, Armagh, Donegal, Down, Fermanagh, Londonderry, Louth, Monaghan, and Tyrone.	*Insp. F. Off.* ₱ Col. N. Hamilton, *KH.* *Adj.* Tho. Shields, *Lt.* 3 Aug. 01 *Paymaster* . . . . Nich. Maunsel *Surg. to the Forces.* W. Birrell, *MD.* *Superintending Officers.* Lt. Mann, 92 F. . . *Armagh* —Thompson, 28 F. . *Belfast* —Goodwyn, 76 F. *Newry*	Leitrim, Longford, Mayo, Meath, Queen's, Roscommon, Sligo, Westmeath, Wicklow, and Carlow.	*Superintending Officers.* Lt. Hamilton, 39 F. . . . *Dublin* —Knipe, 89 F. . . . . *Cavan* — . . *Mullingar* —Evans, 69 F. . . . *Boyle* —Dorehill, 3 F. . . . *Birr*
Centre. *Head Quarters, Dublin.* Consisting of the counties of Cavan, Dublin, Galway, Kildare, King's,	*Insp. Field. Off.* Colonel J. W. Frith *Adj. Lt.* C. P. Hamilton 24 Feb. 43 *Paymaster* . . *Capt.* H. B. Adams. *Surgeon to the Forces.* . . . } A. Sinclair, M.D.	Southern. *Head Quarters, Cork.* Consisting of the counties of Clare, Cork, Kerry, Kilkenny, Limerick, Tipperary, Waterford, and Wexford.	*Insp. Fd. Off.* ₱ Col. F. Maunsell *Adj.* . *Lt.* Tho. Dagg, 31 Dec. 30 *Paymaster* . . J. H. Matthews. *Surg. to the Forces*, ₱ WL J. Moffitt, *M.D.* *Superintending Officers.* Lt. Bing, 21 F. . . . . *Limerick* —Spring, 83 F. . . . *Clonmel* —Hamilton, 47 F. . . *Cork*

AIDES-DE-CAMP TO HIS EXCELLENCY THE LORD LIEUTENANT.

Capt. Geo. Bagot	41 F.	Capt. S. Williams	2 Drs.
Capt. H. F. Ponsonby	Gr. Gds.	Capt. W. S. Sandes	11 Hussars.
Lieut. *Lord* Dunkellin	Coldst. Gds.	Lieut. F. C. Standish	R. Art.
Capt. Hervey	13 Drs.	Capt. H. F. Cust	8 Hussars.
Capt. *Sir* Wm. Russell, *Bt. Extra.*	7 Hussars.	Lt. *Lord* Otho A. FitzGerald . . .	R. Horse Gds.
Capt. T. Bernard	Unatt.	Lt. C. B. Molyneux	4 Drs.

JUDGE-ADVOCATE-GENERAL'S DEPARTMENT.

Deputy-Judge-Advocate . . . . . . D. Walker, *Esq. Dublin.*

29 Mr. Dowse served at the surrender of Martinique and Guadaloupe in 1815.

30 Mr. Reade served in the Peninsula during the campaigns of 1812, 13 and 14; subsequently in the American War, including the affair at Plattsburg. Served also in Canada during the late insurrection.

32 Dr. Mapleton was present with the 40th in the action of Maharajpore (Medal).

34 Mr. Rutherford served with the 62nd in the campaign on the Sutlej, and was present at the battle of Sobraon (Medal).

36 Mr. Laing served the campaign under Sir Charles Napier against the Mountain and Desert Tribes situated on the right bank of the Indus, early in 1845.

39 Mr. Pratt joined the army in the Peninsula in Jan. 1810, and was present at the siege and capture of San Sebastian, and with the head-quarters during the operations in the Pyrenees.

41 Mr. Wreford served in the Peninsula from 1812 to the end of that war in 1814, and was present with head quarters during the operations in the Pyrenees in July, Aug., and Sept. 1813. He accompanied the expedition under the late Lord Keane to New Orleans, and was present with the troops in all the affairs before that city; after which he served in France, and recently in Turkey.

[*Notes continued from page* 217.]

16 Captain Berford (*Queen's Own*) served with the 5th in Portugal and Spain in 1808-9, and was present at the battles of Roleia and Vimiera, action at Lugo, retreat to and battle of Corunna. Subsequently on the expedition to Walcheren and at the siege of Flushing. Served afterwards in the Peninsula with the 2nd Queen's Royals, from 1812 to the end of that war in 1814, and was present at the battle of Vittoria, blockade of Pampeluna, actions in the Pyrenees from 25th to 31st July; with the covering army at San Sebastian and also at its capture; affair at the convent of St. Antonia, actions on the Nivelle and the Nive, and with the four companies of the Queen's which led the advance to the assault and capture of the principal redoubt in front of Sarre; and in all the affairs in the vicinity of St. Jean de Luz, Bayonne, and the Adour; also at the battles of Orthes and Toulouse, and the various affairs of posts and picquets in which the fourth Division were engaged.

17 Captain Graves's services (*2nd West York*):—Expedition to Copenhagen in 1807; campaign in Portugal and Spain, including the battles of Roleia and Vimiera, advance into Spain, retreat to, and battle of Corunna. Expedition to Walcheren, Siege of Flushing, and ascent of the Scheldt, 1809. Peninsular campaigns from June 1811 to Sept. 1813, including the siege of the Forts and battle of Salamanca (three wounds, two severe, one slight), siege of Burgos and retreat from thence, blockade of Pampeluna, battles of the Pyrenees, 28th, 29th, and 30th July (severely contused 28th), Maya Pass, advance into France, and various affairs of Posts and Piquets.

18 Captain Rawson (*3rd West York*) served at the siege and taking of La Valetta in Malta in 1800. Served with the British and Russian army in Naples in 1805, and the subsequent occupation of Sicily. The second Egyptian campaign in 1807, including the capture of Alexandria and the second attack on Rosetta. At Walcheren and at the siege and reduction of Flushing in 1809. The campaign of 1814 in Holland, including both attacks on Merxem and bombardment of Antwerp. Campaign of 1815, including the battle of Waterloo, taking of Cambray, and capture of Paris.

19 Captain Scott (*Fife*) served in the Peninsula from March 1813 to the end of that war in 1814 including the battle of Vittoria, siege of San Sebastian, passage of the Bidassoa, the Nive, and the Adour, investment of Bayonne, and repulse of the sortie, where he received a bayonet wound. Served also the campaign of 1815, and was present at the battles of Quatre Bras and Waterloo.

21 Captain Carrothers (*Antrim*) served in the Peninsula from June 1809 to Sept. 1811, and again from March 1813 to the end of the war in 1814, including the battle of Busaco, action at Campo Mayor, first siege of Badajoz, battles of Albuhera, Nivelle, and Nive, affair at St. Palais, battle of Orthes, affair at Lambeige, and battle of Toulouse. Served also the campaign of 1815, and was present at the battles of Quatre Bras and Waterloo, at which last he was severely wounded.

20 Colonel Fraser (*Ross*) lost a leg at the siege of Burgos, when serving in the Foot Guards.

22 Capt. Cox (*King's County*) served as Lieut. of the Royal Artillery in Sir John Moore's campaign in the north of Spain and battle of Corunna, from 1808 to 1809. Joined the Portuguese army in 1811, present at the siege and capture of Badajoz in 1812, battle of Castalla, both sieges of Tarragona in 1813, and blockade of Barcelona in 1814. Continued to serve with the Portuguese army till 1819.

23 Capt. Hon. J. de Blaquiere (*Limerick County*) served with the 41st throughout the campaign of 1842 in Affghanistan, and was present in the engagements of the 28th March and 28th April in the Pisheen Valley; also in the actions before Goaine and before Ghuznee; occupation and destruction of that fortress and of Cabool; expedition into Kohistan; storm, capture, and destruction of Istaliff; and the various minor affairs in and between the Bolan and the Khyber Passes. He has received the Medal inscribed "Candahar, Ghuznee, Cabul, 1842."

24 Captain Russell (*Dublin City*), was a Captain in the 98th with the expedition to the North of China (medal), in 1842, and was present at the storming of the city of Chin Kiang Foo, to also at the attack and capture of the Tartar entrenched camps on the heights outside the city; and he was also at the landing before Nankin.

25 Capt. Vere Webb (*Cardigan*), served with the Rifle Brigade during the campaigns of 1814 and 15 in Holland, the Netherlands, and France, including both the actions at Merxem, bombardment of Antwerp, and battle of Waterloo, at which last he was slightly wounded.

26 Capt. Cowell served the Kandian campaign of 1817 and 1818, and was engaged with the enemy on numerous occasions.

ROYAL ANGLESEA. (Light Infantry.) [61] *Beaumaris.* *Maj. Com. Col.* Wm. *Lord* Dinorben *Adjt. Capt.* C. S. Jones

BEDFORD. [18] *Bedford.* *Col.* Rich. Tho. Gilpin *Adjt. Capt.* T. J. Smith

ROYAL BERKS. [7] *Reading.* *Col.* John Blagrave *Adjt.* Capt. Sherson

ROYAL BRECON. [31] *Brecon.* *L. Col. Com.* F. Chambre *Adjt. Lt.* J. D. Dickinson 1

ROYAL BUCKS, (or KING'S OWN.) [35] *High Wycombe.* *Col.* R. J. *Lord* Carrington *Adjt. Capt.* C. T. Grove

CAMBRIDGE. [68] *Ely.* *Col.* F. Pemberton *Adj. Capt.* T. Sebborne

ROYAL CARDIGAN. (Rifle Corps.) [64] *Aberystwith.* *Lt. Col. Com. Col.* W. E. Powell *Adj.* Capt. Vere Webb 25

R. CARMARTHEN. (Fusiliers.) [24] *Carmarthen.* *Lt. Col. Com. Hon.* G. R. Trevor *Adjt. Ca.* E. J. Vaughan

ROY. CARNARVON. (Rifle Corps.) [56] *Carnarvon.* *Maj. Com.* O. J. E. Nanney *Ad. Cap.*

ROY. CHESHIRE. *Chester.* [6] *Col. Hon.* Hugh Cholmondeley *Ad.*

THE D. OF CORNWALL'S RANGERS. (Light Infantry.) [38] *Torpoint.* *Colonel* E. A. *Earl of* Mount Edgcumbe 2 *Adj. Capt.* Brockman

ROY. CORNWALL & DEVON MINERS. (Light Infantry.) [118] *Truro.* *Lt. Col. Com.* E. W. Wynne Pendarves *Adjt. Capt.* Wm. Ward

ROYAL CUMBERLAND. [9] *Whitehaven.* *Col. Hon.* H. C. Lowther *Adjt. Capt.* R. Pennington 3

ROYAL DENBIGH. (Rifle Corps.) [46] *Wrexham.* *Col.* R. Myddelton Biddulph *Adjt. Capt.* E. Jones

DERBY. [69] *Derby.* *Col.* H. *Ld.* Waterpark *Adjt.* Capt. F. Dixon 4

1st or EAST DEVON. [41] *Exeter.* *Col.* H. *Earl* Fortescue *Adjt.* Capt. C. Holman 5

NORTH DEVON. [15] *Barnstaple.* *Col.* G. *Ld.* Poltimore *Adjt.* Capt. J. A. Ridgway 6

SOUTH DEVON. [25] *Plymouth.* *Col. Earl of* Morley. *Adjt. Capt.* W. H. Fisk 7

DORSET. [42] *Dorchester.* *Col.* J. J. Smith *Adjt. Capt.* G. Wyatt

DURHAM. [3] *Barnard Castle.* *Col.* H. *Duke of* Cleveland *Adjt. Capt.* R. H. S. Jackson

EAST ESSEX. [14] *Colchester.* *Col.* H. J. Conyers *Adj.* Cap. J. Jones 8

WEST ESSEX. [19] *Chelmsford.* *Col. Sir* J. Tyrell, *Bt.* *Adjt. Capt.* H. Pearson 9

ROYAL FLINT. (Rifle Corps.) [82] *Mold.* *Lt. Col. Comm. Col. Sir* Rich. Puleston, *Bt.* *Adjt. Capt.* F. R. M'G. Dawson

ROY. GLAMORGAN. (Light Infantry.) [44] *Cardiff.* *Col.* J. *Marq. of* Bute *Ad. Capt.* John Henry Armstrong

ROYAL (SOUTH) GLOUCESTER. (Light Infantry.) [23] *Gloucester.* *Col.* W. *Earl* Fitzharding. *Adj. Cap.* Worthington

ROYAL (NORTH) GLOUCESTER. [69] *Cirencester.* *Col.* Tho. H. Kingscote *Adjt. Capt* John Tobin

NORTH HANTS. [13] *Winchester.* *Col. Marq.* of Winchester *Adj.* Joseph Tomlinson

SOUTH HANTS. (Light Infantry.) [43] *Southampton.* *Col. Sir* J. W. Pollen, *Bt* *Adj. Capt.* J. R. Norton

HANTS, Isle of Wight [63] *Newport.* *Cap. Com.* Percy Scott 10

HEREFORD. [59] *Hereford.* *Col.* J. S. *Earl* Somers *Adjt. Capt* J. E. Money Kyrle

HERTFORD. [30] *Hertford.* *Col.* J. *M. of* Salisbury *Adjt. Capt.* E. S. James

HUNTINGDON. [2] *Huntingdon.* *Maj. Com. Col.* T. W. Vaughan *Adjt. Capt.* Green

EAST KENT. [49] *Canterbury.* *Col.* S. E. Sawbridge *Adjt. Capt.* C. Winter

WEST KENT. [37] *Maidstone.* *Col. Sir* J. K. Shaw, *Bt.* *Adjt. Capt.* J. Eley

1st R. LANCASHIRE. (*The Duke of Lancaster's own.*) [45] *Lancaster.* *Col.* J. P. Tempest *Adjt. Capt.* Henry Townshend

2d R. LANCASHIRE. (*The Duke of Lancaster's own.*) [113] *Liverpool.* *Hon.* C. J. F. Stanley *Adjt.* Jas. Weir

3d R. LANCASHIRE. (*The Duke of Lancaster's own.*) [125] *Preston.* *Col.* J. W. Patten. *Adjt. Capt.* J. Rooper

LEICESTER. [26] *Leicester.* *Col.* J. *Duke of* Rutland, *KG.* *Ad. Cap.* H. F. Hawker.

NORTH LINCOLN. [8] *Lincoln.* *Col.* J. H. *Visc.* Alford *Adjt.* Capt. F. Kennedy 11

SOUTH LINCOLN. [29] *New Sleaford.* *Col.* J. *Earl* Brownlow *Adjt. Capt.* N. Campbell

ROYAL LONDON. [106] *Artillery Ground.* *Col. Sir* C. S. Hunter, *Bt* *Adj Capt.* W. T. Hall

ROY. MERIONETH. (Light Infantry.) [60] *Dolgelly.* *Lt. Col.* G. H. Vaughan. *Adjut. Capt.* Anwyl.

ROYAL EAST MIDDLESEX. [65] *Hampstead.* *Colonel* T. Wood *Adjut. Capt.* F. W. Hamilton

ROYAL WEST MIDDLESEX. [58] *Uxbridge.* *Col. Visc.* Enfield *Adj. Capt.* J. Henry Evelegh

ROYAL WESTMINSTER, MIDDLESEX. [55] *Brentford.* *Col. Rt. Hon.* H. C. C. *Visc.* Chelsea *Adj.* R. M'Ewen

ROY. MONMOUTH. [81] *Monmouth.* *Colonel* *Adj. Capt.* J. Money Carter

R. MONTGOMERY. [57] *Welchpool.* *Lt. Col. Com.* *Adj. Capt.* Edw. Dwen

WEST NORFOLK. [39] *Norwich.* *Colonel* H. E. *of* Orford *Adjut.* James Powley

EAST NORFOLK. [40] *Yarmouth.* *Colonel Hon.* Berkeley Wodehouse *Adjut. Capt.* W. P. K. Browne 12

NORTHAMPTON. [48] *Northampton.* *Colonel.* T. P. Maunsell *Adjut. Capt.* T. Rose

NORTHUMBERLAND. (Light Infantry.) [27] *Alnwick.* *Col.* G. *E. of* Beverley *Adj. Cap.* J. N. Frampton

NOTTINGHAM, (*or Royal Sherwood Foresters.*) [59] *Newark.* *Col.* Launc. Rolleston *Adjut. Capt.* J. Barth

OXFORD. [51] *Oxford.* *Colonel* C. O. Bowles *Adjt. Capt.* G. Cuming

ROYAL PEMBROKE (Rifle Corps) [28] *Haverfordwest.* *Lt. Col. Com.* H. Owen Owen *Adjut. Capt.* J. Holland

ROYAL RADNOR (Light Infantry.) [50] *Presteigne.* *Maj. Com.* J. A. Whittaker *Adjut. Capt.* F. F. Saunders

RUTLAND. (Light Infantry.) [4] *Oakham.* *Captain Comm.* *Hon.* Wm. Middleton Noel

SHROPSHIRE. [54] *Shrewsbury.* *Colonel* F. Hill *Adj.* Capt. J. G. Pardey 13

1st SOMERSET. [16 *Taunton.* *Col.* J. *Earl* Poulett *Adjt. Capt.* W. S. Cook

2d SOMERSET. [47] *Bath.* *Col. Sir* T. B. Lethbridge, *Bt.* *Adjt. Capt.* A. J. Macpherson

THE (KING'S OWN) STAFFORD. [66] *Stafford.* *Col.* W. *Earl of* Dartmouth *Adj. Capt.* Wm. Spring

WEST SUFFOLK. [10] *Bury St. Edmonds.* *Col.* F. W. *Earl* Jermyn *Adjut.* J. M'Gregor

EAST SUFFOLK. (Light Infantry) [34] *Ipswich.* *Col.* H. Bence Bence *Adjut. Capt.* Beckham

1st ROYAL SURREY. [20] *Richmond.* *Colonel* J. B. Delap *Adjut. Capt.* H. E. Austen

2d ROYAL SURREY [11] *Guildford.* *Col. Hon.* T. C. Onslow *Adjut. Capt.* F. Pyner

SUSSEX. (Light Infantry) [53] *Chichester.* *Col.* C. *Duke of* Richmond, *KG.* 14 *Adj. Capt.* Smith, 15

THE KING'S OWN LIGHT INFANTRY [97] *Stoke Newington Common.* *Colonel The Earl of* Dalhousie. *Adj.* Capt. R. Berford 16

THE QUEEN'S OWN LIGHT INFANTRY. [83] *Bethnal Green.* *Col* T. *Earl of* Wilton *Adj.* L. Cowell 26

WARWICK. [30]
Warwick.
Col. H. *Earl of* Warwick, *KT.*
Ad. Capt. Tho. Gaman

ROYAL WESTMORELAND. [17]
Appleby.
Lt. Col. Com. W. *Earl of* Lonsdale
Adjut. Capt. E. H. Smith

R. WILTSHIRE. [33]
Marlborough.
Colonel Right Hon. Sir John Cam Hobhouse, *Bt.*
Adjut. Capt. Price

WORCESTER. [67]
Worcester.
Col. Tho. H. Bund
Adjut. Capt. E. Lavie

1st WEST YORK. [5]
Leeds.
Col. Lord Wharncliffe
Adj. Capt. C. A. Baines

2d WEST YORK. [21]
York.
Col. Wm. Markham
Ad. [illegible] *Cap.* A. Graves 17

3d WEST YORK. [1]
Doncaster.
Col. Geo. Cholmley
Ad. [illegible] *Cap.* Rawson 18

YORK (North Riding.) (Light Infantry) [22]
Richmond.
Col. F. *Duke of* Leeds
Adjut. Capt. J. Carter

YORK (East Riding.) [12]
Beverley.
Col. Chas. Grimston
Adj. Capt. Jas. Bell

ABERDEEN. [89]
Aberdeen.
Col. G. *M. of* Huntly, *KT.*
Adjut. Capt. J. Bland

ARGYLL & BUTE. [117]
Campbeltown.
Col. J. *Duke of* Argyll
Adjut. Brevet Major Colin Alex. Campbell

THE PRINCE REGENT'S ROYAL REGIMENT OF AYR. [115]
Ayr.
Col. Earl of Eglinton
Adj. James Miller

BERWICK, HADDINGTON, LINLITHGOW, and PEEBLES. [73]
Coldstream.
Col. Wm. Hay
Adjut. Capt. Jas. Cox

DUMFRIES, ROXBURGH & SELKIRK. [81]
Dumfries.
Col. M. of Queensberry
Adj. Capt. R. C. Noake

EDINBURGH (County and City of.) [126]
Dalkeith.
Col. F. W. *Duke of* Buccleugh
Adj. Capt. P. M'L. Petley

FIFE. [78]
Cupar.
Col. Jas. Lindsay
Adjt. [illegible] W. Scott 19

FORFAR and KINCARDINE. [105]
Montrose.
Col. Hon. D. Ogilvy
Adj. Capt. A. M'Neill

INVERNESS, BANFF, ELGIN, & NAIRN. [76]
Inverness.
Col. F. W. *Earl of* Seafield
Adj.

KIRKCUDBRIGHT and WIGTON. (Light Infantry.) [72]
Kirkcudbright.
Col. Sir D. Maxwell, *Bt.*
Adj.

ROY. LANARK. [74]
Hamilton.
Col. Marq. of Douglas and Clydesdale
Adj. Capt. Vaughan

ROYAL PERTH. [86]
Perth.
Col. T. R. H. *Earl of* Kinnoull.
Adj. Capt. G. D. Paterson

RENFREW. [129]
Paisley.
Col. Wm. Mure
Adj.

ROSS, CAITHNESS, SUTHERLAND, & CROMARTY. [96.]
Dingwall.
Col. [illegible] Chas. Fraser, 20
Ad. Cap. A. Mackenzie

STIRLING, DUMBARTON, CLACKMANNAN and KINROSS. [90]
Stirling.
C. J. Duke of Montrose
Adj. Capt. J. Fraser

ANTRIM. [79]
Randalstown.
Col. Geo. *Marq. of* Donegal
Adjut. [illegible] *Capt.* C. R. Carrothers 21
Agent, Sir E. Borough & Co.

ARMAGH. [75]
Market Hill.
Col. A. *Visc.* Acheson
Adj. Cap. Barker
Agent, Sir E. Borough & Co.

CARLOW. [70]
Carlow.
Colonel H. Bruen
Adjut.
Ag. Cane & Co.

CAVAN. [101]
Cavan.
Col. A. Saunderson
Adj. Capt. N. Gosselin
Agent, Sir E. Borough & Co.

CLARE. [94]
Clare Castle, Ennis.
Col. C. M. Vandeleur
Adj. Capt. Wm. Gore
Ag. Cane & Co.

NORTH CORK. [116]
Fermoy.
Col. W. H. M. Hodder
Adjut. Lt. C. V. Foss
Agent, Sir E. Borough & Co.

SOUTH CORK. (Light Infantry. [87]
Rathcormac.
Col. Visc. Doneraile
Adjut. Capt. A. H. Lucas
Ag. Cane & Co.

CORK (CITY). [110]
Cork.
Col. Visc. Bernard
Adj. Cap. A. Warren
Ag. Cane & Co.

DONEGAL. [102]
Ballyshannon.
Col. N. *E. of* Leitrim.
Adj. Capt. Searle
Ag. Cane & Co

ROYAL NORTH DOWN. [77]
Newtown Ards.
Col. Visc. Castlereagh
Adj. Capt. Howe
Agent, Sir E. Borough & Co.

ROYAL SOUTH DOWN. [112]
Hillsborough.
Col. Marq. of Downshire
Ad. Cap. J. A. Hodgson
Ag. Cane & Co.

DUBLIN (COUNTY.) [109]
Lucan.
Col. Lord Brabazon
Ad. Ca. H. J. V. Kemble
Ag. Cane & Co.

ROYAL DUBLIN (CITY). [100]
Dublin.
Col. Sir R. Shaw, *Bt.*
Adj. Capt. S. W. Russell 24
Agent, Sir E. Borough & Co.

FERMANAGH. [71]
Enniskillen.
Col. E. of Enniskillen
Adj. Wm. Corry
Agent, Sir E. Borough & Co.

GALWAY. [91]
Ballinasloe.
Colonel Ulic, *Marq. of* Clanricarde, K.P.
Adj. Capt. Eyre
Ag. Cane & Co.

KERRY. [107]
Tralee.
Col. V. *E. of* Kenmare
Adj. Capt. D. A. Curtayne
Agent, Sir E. Borough & Co.

KILDARE. [88]
Naas.
Col. J. *Earl of* Mayo
Adj. Lt. H. G. R. Robinson
Agent, Sir E. Borough & Co.

KILKENNY. [127]
Kilkenny.
Col. Marq. of Ormonde
Adj. Capt. J. M'Intyre
Ag. Cane & Co.

KING'S COUNTY. [98]
Parsonstown.
Col. W. *Earl of* Rosse
Adj. Capt. [illegible] T. Cox 22
Agent, Sir E. Borough & Co.

LEITRIM. [111]
Mohill.
Col. Visc. Clements
Adjut. Wm. Rose
Agent, Sir E. Borough & Co.

LIMERICK COUNTY [123]
St. Francis Abbey.
Col. Hon. R. Fitz Gibbon
Adj. Capt. R. Butler Low
Ag. Cane & Co.

LIMERICK CITY. [103]
Limerick City.
Col. Cha. *Visc.* Gort
Adj. Lt. Tho. Jervis
Agent, Sir E. Borough & Co.

LONDONDERRY. [95]
Londonderry.
Col. Sir R. A. Ferguson, *Bt.*
Ad. Capt. J. M'Clintock
Agent, Sir E. Borough & Co.

LONGFORD. [85]
Newtown Forbes.
Col. Henry White
Adjut. W. Walker
Ag. Mr. J. Atkinson.

LOUTH. [108]
Collon.
Col. Lord Bellew
Adj. Cap. Pendleton
Agent, Sir E. Borough & Co.

NORTH MAYO. [120]
Ballina.
Col. Cha. N. Knox
Adjut.
Agent, Sir E. Borough & Co.

SOUTH MAYO. [82]
Westport.
Col. G. *Marquis of* Sligo
Adj. Capt. Fitzgerald Higgins
Ag. Cane & Co.

ROY. MEATH. [119]
Kells.
Col. Mar. of Headfort, *K.P.*
Adj. Capt. Josh. Clare
Ag. Cane & Co.

MONAGHAN. [121]
Monaghan.
Col. Lord Rossmore
Adj. Capt. John Ross
Agent, Sir E. Borough & Co.

QUEEN'S COUNTY. [104]
Mountrath.
Col. Sir C. H. Coote, *Bt.*
Adj. H. Brereton
Agent, Sir E. Borough & Co.

ROSCOMMON. [96]
Boyle.
Col. .. Gen. R. *Visc.* Lorton
Adj. Capt. C. M'Cammon
Agent, Sir E. Borough & Co.

SLIGO. [126]
Sligo.
Col. A. Knox Gore
Adj. Capt. T. Ormsby
Ag. Cane & Co.

TIPPERARY. (Or Duke of Clarence's Munster.) [34]
Cahir.
Col. R. *E. of* Glengall
Adj. Capt. Daniell
Agent, Sir E. Borough & Co.

TYRONE. [80]
Caledon.
Col. E. of Caledon
Adj. Wm. Lamie
Ag. Cane & Co.

WATERFORD. (Light Infantry.) [136]
Waterford.
Col. H. *Lord* Stuart de Decies
Adj.
Ag. Cane & Co.

WESTMEATH. [114]
Mullingar.
Col. George, *Mar.* [illegible] Westmeath, [illegible]
Adj. Lt. H. Robinson
Agent, Sir E. Borough & Co.

WEXFORD. [illegible]
Wexford.
Col. Lord Carew
Adjt. Lt. D. Beatty
Agent, Sir E. Borough & Co.

WICKLOW. [illegible]
Arklow.
Colonel Sir Ralph Howard, *Bt.*
Adj. Lt. Geo. A. [illegible]
Ag. Cane & Co.

1 Lt. Dickinson (*Brecon*) served with the Queen's Royals throughout the campaign in Affghanistan and Beloochistan, in 1838 and 39, and was present at the assault and capture of the fortresses of Ghuznée and Khelat, at which last he was severely wounded by a musket-shot,—leg broken. Medal for Ghuznée.

2 Lord Mount Edgcumbe (*Duke of Cornwall's Rangers*) served the campaign of 1815, and was present at the battle of Waterloo.

3 Captain Pennington (*Cumberland*) served in the Peninsula from June, 1809, and during the greatest part of the subsequent campaigns, including the battle of Busaco, where he commanded one of the advance picquets of the 3d division on the morning of the action, and was sharply engaged with the enemy; retreat to the lines of Torres Vedras, advance from thence, actions and affairs at Leria, Redinha, Pombal, Roblida, Condeixa, Foz d'Arouce, Guarda, and Sabugal; battles of Fuentes d'Onor, siege of Badajoz (wounded in the right thigh), actions at Campo Mayor, El Bodon, and Guinaldo; affairs and actions in the Pyrenees, St. Pé (contused wound), Hasparren, and Grassietta; battles of Nivelle, Nive, and Orthes (severely wounded), besides several other affairs of posts and picquets during the war.

4 Captain Dixon (*Derby*) served with the Grenadier Guards on the expedition to the North of Holland in 1799, and was in the actions of the 27th Aug., 10th and 19th Sept., 2nd and 6th Oct. In Sicily in 1806 and 7. In the Peninsula under Sir John Moore in 1808-9, including the action at Lugo and battle of Corunna. On the expedition to Walcheren in 1809. Went to Cadiz in April 1811, and was afterwards present at the capture of Seville, and on the retreat from Madrid and Salamanca; and remained with that army until June 1813. Served also the campaign of 1815, and was wounded through the leg at the battle of Quatre Bras.

5 Captain Holman (*East Devon*) served in the Peninsula from Nov. 1811 attached to the Portuguese service, and was present with Lord Hill's corps covering the siege of Badajoz, advance on Llerena, siege and storm of the three fortified convents of Salamanca,—led the storming party to the gate of San Vincente at its capture; battle of Salamanca,—slightly wounded by a musket shot in the leg; siege of Burgos and storming the works and the White Church; several skirmishes on the retreat from thence near Torrequemada, and blowing up the bridge of Duenas; battles of the Pyrenees on the 28th, 29th, and 30th July; night attack and defeat of a French battalion on the heights of Urdax, action near Zugarrimundi,—severe contused wound; battles of the Nivelle and the Nive, actions at Ustaritz and Villa Franque, battles of St. Pierre and Orthes, actions at Aire, Vic Bigorre, and Tarbes, and battle of Toulouse. Served the campaign of 1815, including the battle of Waterloo; also with the army of occupation in France.

6 Captain Ridgway (*North Devon*) served in the Peninsula with the Rifle Brigade, from May 1812 to the end of that war in 1814, including the battle of Vittoria, and various minor affairs. Served also the campaign of 1815, and was present at the battle of Waterloo. Severely wounded in the right shoulder by a musket-shot at the taking of Vera heights, and lost the fore-finger of the left hand by a musket-shot at Waterloo.

7 Captain Fisk (*South Devon*) served as Adjutant of the 17th Lt. Drs. during the campaign of 1820 in Kutch.

8 Captain Jones (*East Essex*) served with the Grenadier Guards at the defence of Cadiz and Isla de Leon from 1st April 1810 to May 1811, and in the battle of Barrosa. In 1813 and 14 he served in Holland, at the attack on Merxem and storming of Bergen-op-Zoom. At the battle of Waterloo the following year he was severely wounded through the body by a musket-ball.

9 Captain Pearson (*West Essex*) served in China (Medal) in the 49th—at Chusan and Canton (severely wounded).

10 Captain Percy Scott (*Hants*) served in the Peninsula with the 2nd Queen's.

11 Capt. Kennedy's services (*North Lincoln*):—Siege and capture of Flushing, 1809. Campaigns of 1811, 12, 13, 14, and 15, including the first siege of Badajoz, and covering the second siege, as also that of Ciudad Rodrigo, crossing the Esla, retreat from Burgos, actions of Val Moresco, Peyrehorade and Echalar, battles of Fuentes d'Onor, Salamanca, Vittoria, Pampeluna, Pyrenees, Nive, Orthes and Waterloo; and he led the column of attack at the storming of Cambray.

12 Capt. Browne (*East Norfolk*) served throughout the war with China (Medal) as Adj. of the 18th Regt., and latterly as a Brigade Major, and was present at Canton, Amoy, Chusan, Chinhae, Ningpo, Segoan, Chapoo (wounded), Woosung, Chin Kiang Foo, and Nankin.

13 Captain Pardey (*Salop*) served in the Peninsula from Feb. 1813 to the end of that war 1814.

14 The Duke of Richmond (*Sussex*) joined the army in Portugal, on the 24th July 1810, as Aide-de-Camp and Assistant Military Secretary to the Duke of Wellington, with whom he remained until the close of the war in 1814, and was present in all the skirmishes, affairs, general actions, and sieges, which took place during that period, amongst which were the battles of Busaco and Fuentes d'Onor, storming of Ciudad Rodrigo, storming of Badajoz, battles of Salamanca, Vittoria, and the Pyrenees, the first storming of San Sebastian, action at Vera, and battle of Orthes. He was sent home with duplicate Dispatches of the battle of Salamanca, and the capture of Astorga by the Spaniards; and with the Dispatches of Vera and the entrance of the army into France. In Jan. 1814, being desirous of obtaining a practical knowledge of Regimental duty in the Field, he left the Duke of Wellington's Staff to join the first battalion of his Regt., the 52nd Light Infantry, and was present with it in the battle of Orthes, where he was severely wounded in the chest by a musket-ball, which has never been extracted. At the end of 1814, he was appointed Aide-de-Camp to the Prince of Orange, and was with him in the battles of Quatre Bras and Waterloo;—after the Prince of Orange was wounded the Duke of Richmond joined the Duke of Wellington as Aide-de-Camp, and remained with his Grace during the remaining part of that campaign.

15 Captain Smith (*Sussex*) served with the 1st Guards in Sicily in 1806 and 7; in the North of Spain in 1808-9, including the retreat to and battle of Corunna; defence of Cadiz in 1811 and

GARRISONS.

BELFAST.
Town Maj. *Lieut.* Peter Stuart.

BERWICK.
Gov. *Lt.-Gen. Sir* J. Bathurst, *KCB.*

CAPE BRETON.
Town Adj. *Lt.* Edw. Sutherland

CHARLES FORT AND KINSALE.
Fort Maj. *Lt.* John Black

DARTMOUTH.
Gov....Ar. Howe Holdsworth
Fort Maj. *Lt. Col.* Robert Kelly

DUBLIN.
Town Maj. *Major* W. White

DUNCANNON FORT.
Fort Maj. *Lieut.* Thos. Austin

EDINBURGH CASTLE.
Governor, *Major-Gen.* J. H. Riddell, *KH.*
Lieut.-Gov... *Gen.* F. T. Hammond, *GCH.*
Fort Maj. *Major.* Thos. Canch
Chaplain. *Rev.* W. B. Smith

GIBRALTAR.
Town Maj. *Maj.* T. E. Lacy, Unatt.
Town Adj. Qr. Mas. W. Hume, h. p. 78 F.

GRAVESEND & TILBURY FORT.
Fort Maj. *Lt.-Col.* Thos. Kelly.

GUERNSEY.
Fort Maj. & Adj. *Lt. Col.* J.H. Bainbrigge, Unatt.

HULL.
Lt.-Gov... *M. Gen. Sir* C. W. Thornton, *KCH.*

JERSEY.
Gov... *Gen.* W. C. *Visc.* Beresford, *GCB. & GCH.*
Fort Major & Adj. *Major* John Fraser.

INVERNESS, OR FORT GEORGE.
Fort Maj. *Col.* Alex. Findlay, *KH.*

LANDGUARD FORT.
Lieut.-Gov... *Lt.-Col.* C. A. West

LONDONDERRY & CULMORE.
Gov. *Gen.* John *Earl of* Strafford, *GCB. & GCH.*
Town Maj. J. Nicholson

MALTA.
Quart.-Mast. *Lt.* J. Colcroft

MILFORD HAVEN.
Gov... *Sir* John Owen, *Bt.*

MONTREAL.
Town Maj. *Ens.* C. Macdonald, h. p. 50 F.

NEW BRUNSWICK.
Town Maj. *Lt.* J. Gallagher

NEW GENEVA.
Fort Maj. Anthony Wharton

PORTSMOUTH.
Town Maj. *Lieut.* Henry White
Physician *Sir* J. M'Grigor, *Bt. MD.*
Surgeon....Isaac Chaldecott

ST. HELENA.
Town Maj. *Capt.* Geo. A. Barnes

ST. JOHN'S, NEWFOUNDLAND.
Fort Maj. Lt. Wm. Jenkins, Royal Newfoundland Company

ST. JOHN'S, OR PRINCE EDWARD'S ISLAND.
Town Maj. *Capt.* A. Lane

ST. MAWES.
Capt. or Keeper, *Field Marshal Sir* Geo. Nugent, *Bt. GCB.*

SCARBOROUGH CASTLE.
Gov... *Maj.-Gen.* Jas. Grant, *CB*

SHEERNESS.
Gov..... *Gen.* S. *Visc.* Combermere, *GCB. & GCH.*

STIRLING CASTLE.
Fort Major.. *Lieut.* Patrick Tytler
Chaplain.. *Rev.* Robt. Watson

TOWER OF LONDON.
Constable *Field Mar.* A. D. of Wellington, *KG. GCB. & GCH.*
Lieut... *Gen.* J. Sullivan Wood
Dep. Lieut... *Col.* Hon. George Cathcart
Major.. *Capt.* J. H. Elrington
Chaplain.. *Rev.* Henry Melville

ISLE OF WIGHT.
Capt. of Sandown Fort, *Capt.* Wm. Wynn
—— *Carisb. Cast.* *Lt.-Gen. Sir* W. Paterson, *KCH.*
—— *Cowes Castle,* Gen. H. W. M. *of* Anglesey, *KG. GCB. & GCH.*

FORT WILLIAM.
Lieut. Gov...... *Gen.* Rt. Hon. *Sir* Jas. Kempt, *GCB. & GCH*

MILITARY ESTABLISHMENTS.

ROYAL HOSPITAL, CHELSEA.

Governor, *General Hon. Sir* Edward Paget, GCB.
Lieut.-Governor, *General Sir* George Anson, GCB.
Major, Lieut.-Colonel Henry Le Blanc,
Adjutant, *Colonel Sir* John Morillyon Wilson, CB. KH.
Secretary, Richard Neave, *Esq.*
Chaplain, Rev. George Mathias.
Physician & Surgeon, Daniel Maclachlan, MD.
Deputy Surgeon, Thomas Coke Gaulter, MD.
Assistant Surgeon, Adam Alex. Prout.
Storekeeper, Captain Edward Sutherland, h. p. Unatt.
Assist. Secretary, John Passon, *Esq.*
Senior Clerk, F. B. Talman, *Esq.*

Captains of Invalids;
John Davern
George Peevor
Augustine Fitzgerald Evans
John Ford
W. Chadwick
Charles Edwards

Adjutant.— J. G. Hort, *Captain* late 12 R. Vet. Batt.
Physician and Surgeon.— Geo. Renny, *MD. Director General of Hospitals in Ireland.*
Assistant-Surgeon.— James Macauley, *MD.*
Chaplain.—Rev. J.T. Connel, *AM.*
Secretary, Registrar and Treasurer.—Chas. Banks, Esq.
Providore.—James Hay, Esq. (late Capt. 82nd regt.)
Chamberlain and Master of Works.—John George, Capt. h. p. Unatt.
Registrar's Clerk.—Mr. Charles Pengelly.
Solicitor.—Robert Dismey, Esq.

ROYAL HOSPITAL, KILMAINHAM.

Master.— Lieut.-Gen. *Rt. Hon. Sir* Edw. Blakeney, *KCB & KCH. Comm. of the Forces in Ireland.*
Deputy Master. — Colonel Napier, *CB. Deputy Adjutant General in Ireland.*

Captains on the Establishment.
Edward D'Arcey
Purefoy Lockwood
Robert Cook
Edw. Gilborne
Thomas Gibbons

ROYAL MILITARY ASYLUM AT CHELSEA
Commandant.— *Colonel* Peter Brown, h. p. Unatt.
Secretary & Adjutant. Capt. William Siborne, h. p. Unatt.
Quarter-Master. William Cousins
Surgeon.—Thomas Graham Balfour, *MD.*

ROYAL HIBERNIAN MILITARY SCHOOL, DUBLIN.
Surgeon, James Goodall Elkington.

ROYAL MILITARY COLLEGE AT SANDHURST
Governor, *Lt.-Gen. Sir* G. Scovell, *KCB.*
Lt. Gov. *Major-Gen.* Tho. W. Taylor, *CB.*
Major and Superintendent of Studies, Lieut.-Col. George Walter Prosser
Captains of Companies of Gentlemen Cadets.
Capt. Robert Daly
Capt. James W. Dalgety
Chaplain, Librarian, &c. *Rev.* H. L. Chepmell.
Quarter Master, Lieut. J. W. Tipping
Surgeon, John Pickering, *MD.*
Assistant-Surg. Melville Neale, *MD.*

MILITARY KNIGHTS OF WINDSOR.

Major Charles Moore, formerly of 82 F. (*Governor*)
Lieut. Samuel Ragg, late 1 R. Vet. Bn.
Lieut. Cha. Hunt Lorimer, late 8 do.
Lieut. Hugh Fleming, late 7 R. Vet. Bn.
—— John Allen, h. p. 84 F, (formerly Captain Portuguese Service.)
Quarter-Master John Powell, h. p. 77 F.
Quarter-Master A. Heartley, h. p. R. Horse Gds.
Lieut. Tho. M'Dermott, late 7 R. Vet. Bn.
Major Geo. Wathen, formerly of 14 F.
Captain Robert Cochrane, late of Rifle Br.
Ensign John Lamb, late 2 R. Vet. Bn.
Major Thomas Cradock, late of 73 F.
Capt. A. W. Cassan, formerly of 65 F.
Lieut. Richard Nantes, h.p. 53 F.
Major John Clarke, late of 66 F.
Lieut. Henry Griffiths, h. p. R. Staff Corps.
Quarter-Master John Ledgam, h. p. 1 F.
Lt.-Col. A. G. Campbell, formerly of 28 F.

N.B. *For Staff at the Horse Guards, see page* 117.

DISTRICTS.

Districts.	General and other Officers.	Aides-de-Camp.	Staff.
NORTHERN AND MIDLAND.—Head Quarters at Manchester.	Lt.-Gen. *Sir* Tho. Arbuthnot, *KCB.*	Lieut. Fane, 54 F. Capt. *Ld.* Burghersh, 17 F.	*Assist. Adj.-Gen.* Col. H. W. Barnard, Gr. Gd. *Assist. Qr. Mas. Gen.* Colonel C. Yorke, Unatt.
North West Counties.—Head Qrs. Chester. Lancashire, Cheshire, Shropshire, Flintshire, Denbighshire, and Isle of Man.	Major-General *Sir* Wm. Warre, *CB.*		*Major of Brigade.* Capt. Warr, 57 F.
North East Counties.—Head Qrs. York. Northumberland, Cumberland, Durham, Westmoreland, York, Derby, Nottingham, Leicester, and Rutland.	Maj.-Gen. N. Thorn, *CB. KH.*	Lt. Kennedy, 86 F.	*Major of Brigade.* Capt. H. B. J. Wynyard, Unatt.
Midland Counties.—Head Qrs. Birmingham. Warwick, Stafford, Northampton, and Worcester.	Colonel Arbuthnot.		*Major of Brigade.* Capt. Mein, 13 F.
SOUTH WEST.—Head Qrs. Portsmouth. Wilts, Dorset, and Hants.	Major-Gen. *Lord* Fred. Fitz Clarence.	Major Harvey, 87 F.	*Major of Brigade.* Capt. J. H. Purves, Unatt.
WESTERN.—Head Quarters, Devonport. Devon, Cornwall, and Somerset, exclusive of Bristol and its vicinity.	Major-General *Hon.* H. Murray, *CB.*	Capt. Prothero, 14 F.	*Major of Brigade.* Capt. T. Nelson, 40 F.
Monmouth and South Wales.—Head Qrs. Carmarthen.	Col. Love, *CB. KH.* Unatt. *Col. on the Staff.*	Major Parkinson, Unatt.	Capt. Mann, 90 F.
JERSEY.	Major-General *Sir* J. H. Reynett, *KCH. Lt.-Gov.*		
GUERNSEY AND ALDERNEY.	Major-General John Bell, *CB. Lieut.-Gov.*		*Town Major of Alderney* Lt.-Cl. W. A. LeMesurier
INSPECTING GENERAL OF CAVALRY. Head Quarters, London.	Maj.-Gen. T. W. Brotherton, *CB.*	Lt. Bourke, 75 F.	*Major of Brigade.* Col. William, *Lord* De Ros, h. p. Unatt.

The following Counties, &c. are not contained in any Military District, and the Troops stationed in those Countie report direct to Head Quarters, viz.:—

Bedford,	Buckingham,	Gloucester,	Kent,	Monmouth,	Surry,
Berkshire,	Cambridge,	Hereford,	Leicester,	Norfolk,	Sussex,
Brecon,	Essex,	Hertford,	Lincoln,	Oxford,	Wales, N. &S. (exc.
Bristol & vicinity,	Glamorgan,	Huntingdon,	Middlesex,	Suffolk,	Denbigh & Flint.)

The Troops in the Isle of Wight report to the General Officer Commanding the South West District.

RECRUITING DISTRICTS.

Leeds. Consisting of the counties of Northumberland, Durham, Cumberland, Westmoreland, and parts of Yorkshire and Lancashire.	*Insp. Fd. Off. Col.* Bush, *KH.* *Adj.—Lt.* W. A. Courtenay, 22 Nov. 44 *Paymaster* . . C. H. Peirse *Surg. to the Forces,* Thomas Hall *Superintending Officers.* Lt. Keyt, 85 F. York — Poole, 1 F. Leeds — Wilson, 7 F. Durham — Martin, 18 F. . Sheffield
Liverpool. Consisting of the county of Cheshire, and parts of Yorkshire, Lancashire, Derby, & North Wales.	*Insp. F. Off.* Col. C. G. Falconar, *KH.* *Adj.* *Lt.* B. H. Edwards, 7 May, 47 *Paymaster* . . Capt. Woodgate *Sur. to the Forces,* A. Foulis. *Superintending Officers.* Lt. Byam, 59 F. . . . Liverpool — G. Macdonald, 16 F. Manchester Tongue, 30 F. . . Shrewsbury — Armstrong, 14 F. Newcastle-under-Lyne.
Coventry. Consisting of the counties of Lincoln, Stafford, Nottingham, Rutland, Leicester, Warwick, Salop, Hereford, & parts of Derby, Northampton, & South Wales.	*Ins. Fd. Off.* *Col.* J. Campbell, *KH.* *Adj.* . . . *Lt.* C. Pieters, 2 Apr. 47. *Paymaster* . A. Thompson *Surg. to the Forces* . . T. Lewis, *M.D.* *Superintending Officers.* Lt. Bourne, 17 F. . . Coventry — Lea, 9 F. . . . Leicester — Colvill, 29 F. . . Birmingham — Bowden, 22 F. . Nottingham — Straubenzee, 18 F. Lincoln
Bristol. Consisting of the counties of Cornwall, Devon, Dorset, Somerset, Wilts, Worcester, Gloucester, Hereford, and part of Hants, and South Wales.	*Insp. F. Off. Col.* Baumgardt, *CB.* *Adj.* *Lt.* J. B. Hamilton, 6 Dec. 44. *Paymaster* . . . J. Sabine. *Surgeon to the Forces* } A. Cumming *Superintending Officers.* Lieut. Gould, 31 F. . . Bristol ——Stopford, 49 F. . . Gloucester ——Schaw, 55 F. . . Exeter ——Forrest, 5 F. . . Abergavenny
London. Consisting of the counties of Norfolk, Suffolk, Cambridge, Huntingdon, Bucks, Bedford, Hertford, Essex, Kent, Sussex, Surry, Oxford, Berks, and Middlesex, and parts of Northampton and Hants.	*Insp. Fd. Off. Col. Sir* R. Doherty *Adj. Lt.* Rob. M'Nair 14 July 37 *Paymaster* . R. Jellicoe *Surgeon* . . M. H. Burrell W. Home, MD. *Superintending Officers.* Lt. Wedderburn, 9 Lanc. London Cav. Subdivision —— Montagu, 10 F. . . London 1st Inf. Subdivision —— Lecky, 86 F. 2nd Inf. Subdiv. —— *Hon.* J. L. Browne, 64 F. Reading —— Murray, 63 F. . Cambridge —— Bouverie, 78 F. . Southampton

CAVALRY DEPOT AT MAIDSTONE.

Commandant . . Col. C. Middleton, 3 Dragoons
Assist. Commandant, Lieut.-Col. F. C. Griffiths, Unatt.
Paymaster . . . Captain William Castle
Riding-Master . . Major L. G. A. Meyer

Acting Adjutant . Lieut. Lee, 15 Hussars
Quarter-Master . John Swindley
Veterinary Surgeon Charles Brett, 8 March 33

GARRISON, INFANTRY, AND INVALID DEPOT AT CHATHAM.

Commandant Col. J. Simpson, Unatt.
Major of Brigade ....Capt. Wood, 18 F.
Staff Captain, FORT PITT, Major Henry Anderson[1]
Adjutant ....Lieut. George Rand[2]
Paymaster ....Francis Edward Leech[3]
Paymaster of Indian Depots....James Macdonald, Esq.

Superintendent of Sword Exercise......Henry Angelo, Esq.

Principal Veterinary Surgeon...... Fred. Clifford Cherry,[4] Esq., *Clapham Common.*

ROYAL MILITARY COLLEGE AT SANDHURST.

For the Appointments of Officers held by *Commission*, see "*Military Establishments*," page 218.

Professors and Masters.

Mathematics and Arithmetic . . . . John Narrien, *FRAS.*; Wm. Scott, *AM. & FRAS.*; Chs. H. Barton, *BA.*; G. Hearn, *B.A.*
Fortification . . . . *Major* W. H. Adams, Unatt.; *Capt.* Garnet Man, Unatt.
Surveying . . . . . Geo. D. Burr
Drawing . . . . . . John Piercy; Thomas Costin.
Landscape Drawing . Edward de la Motte
History, Geography, and Classics . . . Rev. George E. Cole, *M.A.*; *Rev.* Slater W. Heale, *M.A.*
French . . . . . G. Cambier; H. Marillier; G. Boully
German . . . . . F. Demmler
Riding Master . . . Lieut. John Gillies, h.p.

Students in the Senior Department.

Capt. Wetherall .... 1 F.	Lieut. Hammersley............14 F.	Capt. S. B. Lamb ....Unatt.
Capt. Dickinson ....89 F.	Lieut. Seton ....49 F.	Lieut. Butler ....86 F.
Capt. Grant ....47 F.	Lieut. Rigaud ....60 F.	Lieut. Rundle ....40 F.
Capt. Stapylton ....13 F.	Capt. Filder ....70 F.	

EAST INDIA COMPANY'S DEPOT, RECRUITING OFFICERS, AND MILITARY SEMINARY.

DEPOT AT WARLEY, IN ESSEX.

Commandant ....Colonel Edward Hay.
(*2d in Command*) ......*Lt.Col.* John Thomas Leslie, *CB.*
Capt. and Paymaster .....Major William Elsey.
Adjutant ....Capt. W. Falconer Hay.
Lt. ....Geo. Bourchier, Bengal Art.
Surgeon ....A. R. Jackson, *MD.*

RECRUITING OFFICERS.

Lt. Col. Sir R. A. Campbell, *CB. Newry.*
Lt. Col. Henry Brown Smith ..*Bristol.*
Major Richard Axford ....*Liverpool.*
Major George Thomson, *CB*...*Cork.*
Major Henry Brown ....*London*, 26, *Soho-Square.*
Captains Rich. Geo. Grange...*Dublin.*
Henry Vibart Glegg..*Edinburgh.*

MILITARY SEMINARY AT ADDISCOMBE.

Public Examiner and Inspector ...... Maj. Gen. *Sir* Cha. W. Pasley, *KCB.* R.Eng. *FRS. FAS. FGS.*
Lieut.-Governor ...... Major General *Sir* Ephraim G. Stannus, *CB.*
Captain..................Major T. Ritherdon
Orderly Officers ......Lt. C. P. Taylor, Madr. Army; — E. J. Ferrers, Madr. Cav.
Public Examiner in the Oriental Department .. Horace H. Wilson

Professors and Masters.

Mathematics and Classics .... *Rev.* Jonathan Cape, *AM.*; *Rev.* Alfred Wrigley, *BA.*; *Rev.* W. H. Johnstone, *B.A.* (*Chaplain*); *Rev.* R. Inchbald, *B.A.*; Arthur Dusautoy
Fortifications ....Lieut. T. Cook, *RN. FRS.*; Major W. Jacob, Bombay Art.
Surveying..............Lt.Col. Basil Jackson, h.p. Royal Staff Corps
Drawing ....E. B. Metcalf
Landscape Drawing .... T. H. Fielding; J. C. Schetky.
Oriental Languages .... Rich. Haughton, *MRAS.*; Chs. Bowles
French ....Leon Contanseau
Geology and Mineralogy..D. T. Ansted, *A.M.*
Chemistry ....Edward Solly
Sword Exercise..........Hen. Angelo, *jun.*
Clerk for passing Cadets and Assist.-Surgeon T. R. Clarke, Cadet Depart. India House
Steward, R. J. Leeds—*Housekeeper*, Mrs. Leeds

STAFF, &c. OF SCOTLAND.

General Officer.	Station.	Aide de Camp.	Staff.
Maj.-Gen. H. J. Riddell, *KH.*	Edinburgh	Capt. Riddell, R. Art.	*Assist. Adj. Gen*....Col. John Eden, *CB.*, Unatt. *Staff Adjut.*......Lieut. J. O'Neill

RECRUITING DISTRICT.

Paymaster .... Captain J. Middleton ....*Edinburgh.*
Surgeon to the Forces............ T. F. Cotton ....*Edinburgh.*

Glasgow. *Insp. F. Off.* Lt.-Col. C. Barnwell, *CB.*
Adj......... *Lt.* John Spence, 10 March, 46.
Paymaster.. George Hood
Surgeon to the Forces..W. Linton
Superintending Officers.
Lt. Faulkner, 2 F...Glasgow

Superintending Officers.
Lt. Park, 26 F.............Edinburgh
— Roney, 96 F. ....Perth
— Persse, 12 F. ....Aberdeen
— Forbes, 40 F. ....Inverness

1 Major Anderson served the campaigns of 1814 and 15 in Holland and the Netherlands, including the action at Merxem, bombardment of Antwerp, storming of Bergen-op-Zoom, and actions at Quatre Bras and Waterloo. Severely wounded at Waterloo by a musket ball, which broke the left shoulder, passed through the lungs, and made its exit at the back, breaking the scapula.

2 Lt. Rand served with the 49th throughout the operations in China.

3 Paymaster Leech served in the Peninsula from Jan. 1813 to the end of the war, including the Passage of the Bidassoa, the battles of Nivelle 10th Nov., and Nive 9th, 10th, 11th, and 12th Dec. 1813, and blockade of Bayonne. Served also at the escalade of Booj Booj in Cutch, March 1819, & at the siege of Rhas-el-Khyma, & of Zoa in the Persian Gulf in 1819 & 20. He was present also at [illegible].

4 Mr. Cherry served Sir John Moore's campaign in Spain, including the battle of Corunna; with the expedition to Walcheren, in 1809; the Peninsular campaigns from Jan. 1812 to the end of the war in 1814; also the campaign of 1815, including the battle of Waterloo.

Commanding the Troops.
Lieut. Gen. *Rt. Hon. Sir* Edward Blakeney, *KCB. & GCH.*
- Capt. *Hon.* St. G. G. Foley, Unatt. *Aide-de-Camp.*
- —— *Lord* Cosmo G. Russell, 93 F. *do.*
- —— *Hon.* C. H. Lindsay, Gr. Gds. *do.*

Military Secretary Lt. Col. Greaves, Unatt. | *Assist. Military Secretary*, Major *Hon.* C. R W. Forester, Unatt.

ADJUTANT GENERAL'S DEPARTMENT. *(Head Quarters—Dublin.)*

Deputy Adjutant General.. *Col.* W. Cochrane, Unatt. | *Dep. Assist. Adjutant General*....Major Draper, 64 F.
Assistant Adjutant General..*Lt.-Col.* Wood, 80 F.

QUARTER-MASTER-GENERAL'S DEPARTMENT. *(Head Quarters—Dublin.)*

Dep. Quart. Mast- Gen. Colonel Mansel, *KH.* Unatt. | *Assist. Dep. Quar. Mast. Gen.* Capt. L. V. Smith h.p. R. Eng.

ORDNANCE DEPARTMENT. *(Head Quarters—Dublin.)*

Commanding R. Artillery .... Col. Turner, *CB.* | *Command. R. Eng.*, Col. Vavasour.
Assist. Adjutant General .. Lt. Col. C. E. Gordon. | *Major of Brigade*, Capt. Lugard, R. Eng.

DISTRICTS.

Districts.	General and other Officers.	Aides de Camp.	Staff.
Belfast.—Head Quarters, Belfast. The Province of Ulster, and County of Louth, with the exception of the Town of Drogheda.	Major-Gen. Bainbrigge, *CB.* Col. St. John A. Clerke, *KH.*, Unatt. Lt. Col. E. Macarthur, Unatt., *Cavan.*	Capt. Duff, 74 F.	*As. Adj. Gen.* Lt.-Col. R. W. Brough, h. p. 2 F.
Dublin.—Head Quarters, Dublin. The Counties of Dublin, Kildare, Carlow, Kilkenny, Wexford, Wicklow, Meath, and the Towns of Drogheda and Waterford.	Major-Gen. *His Royal Highness Prince* George of Cambridge, *KG. GCMG.* Major-Gen. T. J. Wemyss, *CB.* Col. Pennefather, *C.B.* h. p. 28 F.	Capt. *Hon.* J. Macdonald, Unatt.	*Assist. Adj. Gen.* Lieut. Col. W. F. Forster, *KH.* Unatt. *As. Qua. M. Gen.* Major E. R. Scott, *Town Major.* Maj. W. White,
Athlone.—Head Quarters, Athlone. The Province of Connaught, with Counties of Longford, Westmeath, King's County, and Queen's County.	Major-General *Sir* Guy Campbell, *Bart., CB.*	Capt. George, 75 F.	*As. Adj. Gen.* Lt.-Col. W. F. Williams, *KH.* Unatt., *As. Qua. M. Gen.* Lt.-Col. C. C. Johnson, h. p.
Limerick.—Head Quarters, Limerick. The Counties of Clare, Limerick, Kerry, and Tipperary.	Major-Gen. T. E. Napier, *CB.* *Sir* C. R. O'Donnell, Unatt. *Clonmel* Col. W. Cox, *KH.* Unatt. *Limerick* Col. Wm. Turner, *Ennis*	Capt. Kilvington, 64 F.	*As. Adj. Gen.* Lieut.-Col. C. H. Doyle, Unatt.
Cork.—Head Quarters, Cork. The Counties of Cork and Waterford, exclusive of the Town of Waterford.	Major-General Turner. Col. *Sir* M. Creagh, *KH.*	Lt. Turner, R. Art.	*As. Adj. Gen.* Col. M. Beresford, Unatt. *As. Qua. M. Gen.* Col. J. Spink, *KH.* Unatt. *Fort Major.* Lt. J. Black, *Charles Fort.*

RECRUITING DISTRICTS.

Northern. *Head Quarters, Newry.* Consisting of the counties of Antrim, Armagh, Donegal, Down, Fermanagh, Londonderry, Louth, Monaghan, and Tyrone.	*Insp. F. Off.* Col. N. Hamilton, *KH.* *Adj.* Tho. Shields, *Lt.* 3 Aug. 01 *Paymaster* . . . . Nich. Maunsel *Surg. to the Forces.* W. Birrell, *MD.* *Superintending Officers.* Lt. Mann, 92 F. . . *Armagh* —Thompson, 28 F. . *Belfast* —Goodwyn, 75 F. *Newry*	Leitrim, Longford, Mayo, Meath, Queen's, Roscommon, Sligo, Westmeath, Wicklow, and Carlow.	*Superintending Officers.* Lt. Hamilton, 39 F. . . . *Dublin* —Knipe, 89 F. . . . . *Cavan* —— . . *Mullingar* —Evans, 69 F. . . . *Boyle* —Dorehill, 3 F. . . . *Birr*
Centre. *Head Quarters, Dublin.* Consisting of the counties of Cavan, Dublin, Galway, Kildare, King's,	*Insp. Field. Off.* Colonel J. W. Frith *Adj. Lt.* C. P. Hamilton 24 Feb. 43 *Paymaster* . . *Capt.* H. B. Adams. *Surgeon to the Forces.* . . A. Sinclair, M.D.	Southern. *Head Quarters, Cork.* Consisting of the counties of Clare, Cork, Kerry, Kilkenny, Limerick, Tipperary, Waterford, and Wexford.	*Insp. Fd. Off.* Col. F. Maunsell *Adj.* . *Lt.* Tho. Dagg, 31 Dec. 39 *Paymaster* . . J. H. Matthews. *Surg. to the Forces,* J. Moffitt, *M.D.* *Superintending Officers.* Lt. Ring, 21 F. . . . . *Limerick* —Spring, 83 F. . . . *Clonmel* —Hamilton, 47 F. . . *Cork*

AIDES-DE-CAMP TO HIS EXCELLENCY THE LORD LIEUTENANT.

Capt. Geo. Bagot	41 F.	Capt. S. Williams	2 Drs.
Capt. H. F. Ponsonby	Gr. Gds.	Capt. W. S. Sandes	11 Hussars.
Lieut. *Lord* Dunkellin	Coldst. Gds.	Lieut. F. C. Standish	R. Art.
Capt. Hervey	13 Drs.	Capt. H. F. Cust	8 Hussars.
Capt. *Sir* Wm. Russell, *Bt.*	7 Hussars.	Lt. *Lord* Otho A. FitzGerald	R. Horse Gds.
Extra.		Lt. C. B. Molyneux	4 Drs.
Capt. T. Bernard	Unatt.		

JUDGE-ADVOCATE-GENERAL'S DEPARTMENT.

Deputy-Judge-Advocate . . . . . D. Walker, *Esq. Dublin.*

IONIAN ISLANDS.

Comprising *Corfu, Vido, Paxo, Santa Maura, Cefalonia, Zante, Ithaca* and *Calamos,* and *Cerigo.*

Lord High Commissioner .... P W Lt.-Gen. *Lord* Seaton, *GCB. GCMG. GCH.*

Assist. Mil. Sec. . . . . Capt. *Hon.* F. Colborne, 15 F.
Aides-de-Camp . . { Capt. *Hon.* J. Colborne, 16 F.; Capt. Murray, Unatt.
Colonel on the Staff . P Major-Gen. C. E. Conyers, *CB.*
Aide-de-Camp . . . Lieut. C. E. Conyers, 2 Dr. Gds.
Dep.-Quarter.-Mast. Gen. Lieut. Col. Walpole, h. p. Rifle Br.
Major of Brigade . Major Finucane, h. p.

MALTA.

Governor and Commander-in-Chief . . . Richard More O'Ferrall
Commanding the Forces . . . . . . Lt.-Gen. Robert Ellice
Assistant Military Secretary . . . Major J. K. Pipon, h. p.
Aide-de-Camp . . . . . . Capt. C. H. Ellice, 24 F.
Town Major . . . . Capt. B. C. Mitford, Unatt.

GIBRALTAR.

Governor and Commander-in-Chief . . . P W Maj.-Gen. *Sir* Robt. Wm. Gardiner, *KCB.KCH.*
Assist. Mil. Sec. . . . .
Aide-de-Camp . . . . .
Commanding R. Artillery . . . . . P Col. Cator.
Commanding Royal Engineer . . . . P Colonel Harding, *CB.*
Town Major . Major Lacy, Unatt.
Town Adjutant . Qr.-Mast. Wm. Hume, h. p. 78 F. } *Garrison Quarter-Master* . Capt. Lane, 67 F.

NORTH AMERICA,

Comprising all Provinces within and adjacent thereto.

Captain-General & Governor-in-Chief . *The Earl of* Elgin, *K.T.*
Military Sec. to the Earl of Elgin Lt.-Col. *Hon.* R. Bruce. Gr. Gds.
Aides-de-Camp . . . . . { Capt. *Lord* Mark Kerr, 20 F.; Capt. *The Earl of* Erroll, Rifle Br.; Capt. *Hon.* E. Lascelles, Gr. Gds.; Lt. *Hon.* A. F. Egerton, Gr. Gds.; Ens. Grant, 79 F.

Commander of the Forces . . . . P Lieut.-Gen. *Sir* Benjamin D'Urban, *GCB. KCH.*
Military Secretary . . Capt. Kirkland, 20 F.
Aides-de-Camp . . . . . { Major Talbot, 43 F.; Major *Sir* James E. Alexander, 14 F.; Capt. V. Murray, h. p. (*Extra.*)

Lieut.-Governor of Nova Scotia . . Lieut. Gen. *Sir* John Harvey, *KCB. & KCH.* . *Halifax*
Aide-de-Camp . . . . Lieut. F. C. Harvey, 34 F.

Lieut.-Governor of New Brunswick . . *Sir* Edmund Walker Head, *Bart.* . . *Fredericton*

Lieut.-Gov. of Prince Edward's Island . *Sir* Donald Campbell, *Bart.*

Colonel on the Staff (Comm. R. Art.) P W Col. Dyneley, *C.B.* . . . . *Montreal.*
Major of Brigade . . . . Major R. Burn, R. Art. . . . . *ditto.*
Colonel on the Staff (Comm. R. Eng.) P Col. W. E. Holloway, *CB.* . . . . *ditto.*

General Officers.	Aides-de-Camp.	Majors of Brigade.
P W Maj.-Gen. *Hon.* C. Gore, *CB.* *Canada.*	Lt. Gore, 71 F.	
P W Major-General Wm. Rowan, *CB.* *Do.* *Nova Scotia.*	Capt. Wetherall, Rifle Br.	Major Tryon, Unatt.

Dep. Adj. Gen. Col. G. A. Wetherall, *CB.KH.* Unatt. *Montreal*
As. Adj. Gen. Lieut.-Col. P. Young, *KH.* *Kingston*
Do. P Lt.-Col. S. D. Pritchard, Unatt. *Quebec*
Dep. A. Ad. Gen. Capt. F. J. Griffin, Unatt. *Montreal*
Do. Capt. E. S. Claremont, Canadian Regt. *Quebec*
Dep. Qr. M. G. Lt.-Col. D'Urban, h. p. 26 F. Unatt. *Montreal*

As. Qr. M. Gen. .. Maj. de Rottenburgh, Unatt. *Kingst*
Dep. A. Q. M. G. .. Capt. Ingall, Unatt. *Queb*
— — Capt. Ready, 71 F. *Montr*
Town Major . W Ens. C. Macdonald, h. p. 50 F. *Montr*
— — Capt. Alfred Knight, Unatt. *Quebe*
— — Major Bourchier, h. p. *Kingst*
Fort Adjutant
— — Lt. J. Keating *Penetanguish*

Dep. Q. M. G. Lieut.-Col. Bazalgette, Unatt. *Halifax*
As. Mil. Sec. Lieut. Bourke, 34 F. *Do.*
Sub-Ins. & D. Adj of Mil. } *Capt. A. Lane *Prince Edw. Island*; * —— C. D. Rankin *Do.*

Town Major Lt. J. Gallagher, h. p. *New Brunsw*
*Capt. A. Lane, h. p. *Prince Edwar Island*
Town Adjutant Lt. Sutherland, h. p. *Cape Breton*

NEWFOUNDLAND.

Governor and Commander-in-Chief, Lieut.-Col. *Sir* J. Gaspard Le Marchant, Unatt.
Aide-de-Camp ....
Fort Major .. Lieut. Wm. Jenkins, R. Newf. Cos.

BERMUDA.

Governor .... Capt. C. Elliot, R. N.
Fort Adj. .... *Hon.* Lieut. Grant, 62 F.

WINDWARD AND LEEWARD ISLANDS.

Lieutenant General commanding the Troops ..Lt.-Gen. Sackville H. Berkeley ....*Barbadoes*
Military Secretary ..Capt. Carden, 60 F. .... *Do.*
Aides de Camp ... { Capt. Boyle, 72 F. / Lieut. Bancroft, 76 F.
Major of Brigade.. Capt. Maxwell, 88 F.
Governor and Commander-in-chief of Barbadoes, Grenada, St. Vincent, Tobago, and St. Lucia, and their Dependencies, } Col. *Sir* Wm. M. G. Colebrooke, *CB. KH.* R. Art.
Governor and Commander-in-Chief of Trinidad .. *Lord* Harris
Lieutenant Governors.......... { *Sir* John Campbell, *Bart.* ....*St. Vincent* / Major Lawrence Graeme, Unatt..........*Tobago* / Ker Baillie Hamilton, *Esq.* ....*Grenada* / Charles Henry Darling, *Esq*..............*St. Lucia*
Governor and Commander-in-Chief of the Leeward Islands .... } James Macaulay Higginson, *Esq.* ....*Antigua*
Lieutenant Governors .... { Robert Jas. Macintosh, *Esq.*, *St. Christophers and Anguilla* / 𝔓 𝔚 Lt.-Col. George Macdonald, h. p. 16 F...*Dominica*
Officer administering the Government { President of the Council.................*Montserrat* / Do. do. *Nevis* / Do. do. *Virgin Islands*
Governor and Commander-in-Chief of British Guiana.................................. } Henry Barkly, Esq....................................*Demerara*

Dep. Adj. Gen....Lt. Col. T. O'Brien, h. p. 87 F. *Barbadoes*	*Fort Adj*......Lieut. Caulfield, 66 F.......... *Tobago*
Dep. As. do....Capt. Maxwell, 66 F. .... *Do.*	Lieut. Cave, 54 F............*St. Lucia*
Dep. Q. M. G.....𝔓 Lt. Col. H. J. French, h. p. 85 F. *Do.*	Lieut. Macdonald, 3 W. I. R. ..*St. Kitt's*
D. A. Q. M. G...Capt. Stuart, 3 W. I. R..... *Do.*	Lieut. Birch, do..............*Antigua*
Act. Dep. Judge Adv. Capt. Wheeler, 54 F... *Do.*	—— Barstow, R. Art. ......*Dominica*
Fort Adj. ......Lt. J. Grant, R. Eng.......*St. Vincent*	—— Sankey, 1 W. I. R. ......*Trinidad*
Lt. Forman, 88 F............*Grenada*	—— Colman, 3 W. I. R. ....*Demerara*

JAMAICA, BAHAMAS, AND HONDURAS.

Captain-General and Governor-in-Chief..........*Rt. Hon. Sir* Charles Grey ....*Jamaica.*
Aide-de-Camp and Military Secretary ....Lt. C. W. Grey, R. Art.
Major General on the Staff ....Major-Gen. Bunbury, *K.H.* ....*Jamaica.*
Assistant Military Secretary ....Capt. Bunbury, 67 F.
Aide-de-Camp ....
Governor and Commander-in-chief of the Bahamas George Benvenuto Mathew, Esq.
Superintendent at Honduras ....Charles St. John Fancourt, Esq.

Dep. Adj. Gen.....Lt. Col. P. Farquharson, h. p.	*Fort Adj.*..Lt. Aggas, 1 W. I. R. .... *Bahamas*
Dep. Q. M. G.....	——— .. Capt. Glubb, 2 W. I. R. .... *Honduras*
Dep. Judge Adv. Capt. Minty, 1 W. I. R.	

EAST INDIES.

Captain-General and Governor-in-Chief....The *Earl of* Dalhousie
Military Secretary ....Colonel Mountain, *CB.*, 29 F.
Aides-de-Camp .... { Capt. Ramsay, 22 F. / *Hon.* Capt. Fane, 25 F.
Governor and Commander-in-Chief of Madras ....Major-Gen. *Rt. Hon.* Sir Henry Pottinger, *Bt. GCB.*
Military Secretary ....Major C. Colville Young, R. Art.
Aide-de-Camp............Capt. Fellowes, 77 F.
Governor of Bombay.........................Viscount Falkland
Military Secretary ......Colonel *Hon.* T. Ashburnham, h. p. 62 F.
Aides-de-Camp .... { Capt. Harrison, 10 Hussars. / Lieut. M'Mahon, 14 Lt. Drs.

Commander-in-Chief.........................𝔓 Gen. Hugh *Lord* Gough, *GCB.*
Military Secretary........Capt. F. P. Haines, 21 F.
Aides-de-Camp........... { Major Bates, 98 F.

Presidencies.	General Officers.	Aides de Camp.	Majors of Brigade.
Bengal.	𝔓 𝔚 Major-General *Sir* Joseph Thackwell, *KCB.* 𝔓 Major-Gen. *Sir* Dudley St. L. Hill, *K.C.B.*	Lt. Thackwell, 3 Drs. Lt. Hill, 75 F.	Capt. J. D. Young, 29 F.
Madras.	𝔓 𝔚 Lt.-Gen. *Sir* G. Berkeley, *KCB.* 𝔓 Major-General *Sir* Edm. K. Williams, *KCB.* 𝔓 Major-Gen. Aitchison.	Maj. Berkeley, Scots Fus. Gds. Lt. Vaughan, 94 F. Lt. Crawley, 15 Hussars.	Capt. Anderson, 86 F.
Bombay.	𝔓 Lieut.-Gen. *Sir* W. Cotton, *GCB.* 𝔓 Major-Gen. Auchmuty, *C.B.*	{ Lt. *Lord* A. Vane, S. F. Gds. / Lt. *Hon.* F. FitzClarence, 10 Hussars Capt. W. Auchmuty, 98 F.	Capt. Heally, 22 F.

Bengal.	*Madras.*	*Bombay.*
Adj. Gen. 𝔓 Col. C. R. Cureton, *CB.* h. p. 16 Drs. *As. Adj. Gen.*..Maj. R. Lugard, 29 F. *Q. M. Gen.* Lt.-Col. J. B. Gough, *CB.* 3 Drs.	*Dep. Ad. G.*..Lt.-Col. T. S. Pratt, *C.B.* h. p. 26 F. *D. Q. M. G.* 𝔚 Lieut.-Col. O. Felix, Unattached.	*Dep. Adj. Gen.* Lt.-Col. Havelock, *CB.* 53 F. *Military Sec.*..*Lt.-Col.* Brooke, 32 F.

CHINA.

Governor and Commander-in-Chief of Hong Kong . . . . Samuel George Bonham, *C.B.*
Major-General on the Staff . . . . 𝔓 𝔚 Major-General Staveley, *CB.*
Assistant Military Secretary . . . . Capt. Staveley, 44 F.
Aide-de-Camp . . . .
Major of Brigade . . . . Capt. R. Mylius, Ceylon R.
Acting Deputy Judge Advocate . . . . Capt. M'Leod, 42 Madras N.I.

CAPE OF GOOD HOPE.

Governor and Commander-in-Chief................Lt.-Gen. *Sir* H. G. W. Smith, *Bt. GCB.*
Military Secretary................Capt. Maydwell, 41 F.
Priv. Sec. and extra Aide de Camp..Lieut.-Col. Garvock, 31 F.
Aides de Camp................Lt. Holdich, 80 F.; Capt. Smith, 3 F.
Deputy Quarter-Master General...Lieut.-Col. Abraham Josias Cloete, *CB. KH.* Unatt.
Major of Brigade................Capt. C. H. Somerset, Cape M. Rifles.
Town Major................Capt. Carruthers, Unatt.
Lieutenant Governor of the Natal District..........Martin West, Esq.
Colonel Comm. of British Kaffaria................Colonel G. H. Mackinnon, *CB.* Unatt.
Major of Brigade, do.................Major Bissett, Cape M. Rifles.
Commandants................Capt. J. Brown, 91 F................*Port Elizabeth*; Col. Boys, 45 F. ....*Port Natal*

CEYLON.

Governor and Commander-in-Chief......*Visc.* Torrington.
Aide de Camp................Capt. Airey, 3 F.
Major-General on the Staff................Major-Gen. William Smelt, *CB.*
Assistant Military Secretary........Capt. Fanshawe, 13 F.
Aide de Camp................Lt. O'Callaghan, 39 F.
Dep. Adj. Gen.....Lt. Col. Charleton, *KH.* h. p. Unatt. | *Dep. Q. M. Gen.*..Col. John Fraser, h. p. 1 R. Vt. Bn.

WESTERN COAST OF AFRICA.

Captain General and Governor in Chief....Norman Wm. Macdonald, Esq.................... *Sierra Leone*
Governor and Commander-in-Chief of the Gambia......Richard Graves MacDonnell, Esq.
Lieut. Gov. of the Gold Coast................*Commander* Wm. Winniett, R. N.
Garrison Adjutants................Lieut. Webster, 3 West India Regt................ *Sierra Leone*; Lieut. Mockler, 3 West India Regt. .... *Gambia*

MAURITIUS.

Governor and Commander-in-Chief, Lieut.-General *Sir* Wm. M. Gomm, *KCB.*
Aide-de-Camp........................Major Fraser, 35 F.
Dep. Quarter-Master Gen. Lt.-Col. F. H. Robe, *CB.* h. p. | *Assist. Mil. Sec.* Lieut. E.R.W.W.Yates, 90 F.

AUSTRALIAN COLONIES.

NEW SOUTH WALES.

Captain General and Governor in Chief..............*Sir* Charles Augustus Fitz Roy, *KH.*
Major-Gen. on the Staff................Major-Gen. E. B. Wynyard, *CB.*
Assistant Military Secretary................Capt. Wynyard, Gr. Gds.
Aide-de-Camp................Capt. Battye, 23 F.
Deputy Adjutant General................Lieut.-Col. G. C. Mundy, Unatt., *Sydney.*
Major of Brigade................Capt. Jenner, 11 F., *Sydney.*

VAN DIEMEN'S LAND.

Lieutenant-Governor................Capt. *Sir* Wm.Thos. Denison, R. Eng. *Hobart Town.*
Aide-de-Camp................Captain Denison, 58 F.
Major of Brigade................Maj. Ainsworth, Unatt., *Van Diemen's Land.*

WESTERN AUSTRALIA.

Governor and Commander-in-Chief............ Commander Charles FitzGerald, R. N.
Commandant of the Troops................ Lt.-Col. Irwin, *KH.* Unatt.

SOUTH AUSTRALIA.

Governor................*Sir* Henry Edward Fox Young.
Private Secretary................Capt. Young, 65 F.

NEW ZEALAND.

Governor and Commander-in-Chief..........*Sir* George Grey, *KCB.*
Lieut.-Governor................Edward John Eyre, Esq.
Major-General................Major-Gen. G. D. Pitt. *KH.*
Aide-de-Camp................Lieut. G. D. Pitt, 80 F.
Deputy Quarter-Master General............Lieut.-Col. W. A. M'Cleverty, h. p. 48 F.
Majors of Brigade................Capt. Greenwood, 31 F. ....*Auckland*; Capt. O'Connell, 99 F..........*Wellington*

NORFOLK ISLAND.

Superintendent..........................

SAINT HELENA.

Governor................ Major Gen. *Sir* Patrick Ross, *GCMG. KCH.*
Aide-de-Camp................ Lieut. Ross, 85 F.
Town Major................ Capt. G. A. Barnes, St. Helena Regt.

HELIGOLAND.

Lieut.-Governor....................Capt. J. Hindmarsh, *RN.*

FALKLAND ISLANDS.

Governor and Commander-in-Chief......George Rennie, Esq.

ISLAND OF LABUAN.

Governor and Commander-in-Chief..............*Sir* James Brooke, *K.C.B.*
Aide-de-Camp................Capt. Brooke, 88 F.

MILITARY DEPARTMENTS, &c.

COLONIAL DEPARTMENT.

Prin. Sec. of State, Rt. Hon. Earl Grey.
Under Secretaries { Sir James Stephen, *KCB.* / Benjamin Hawes, Esq. *M.P.*
Office, Downing Street.

WAR-OFFICE.

Secretary at War, *Rt. Hon.* Fox Maule.
Deputy Secretary at War, Laurence Sulivan, *Esq.*
Chief Examiner of Army Accounts, Edw. Marshall, *Esq.*
First Clerk, John Borrow, *Esq.*
Private Sec. to Sec. at War, A. G. Carmichael, *Esq.*

Paymaster-General, *Rt. Hon. Earl* Granville

Judge Advocate General of the United Kingdom } Wm. Goodenough Hayter, *Esq.*
Deputy ditto Fra. Newman Rogers, Esq. *Q. C.*
Office, 35, Great George-street, Westminster.

BOARD OF GENERAL OFFICERS,

For the Inspection and Regulation of the Clothing of the Army, and for the Investigation of Claims for Losses, &c. &c.

Generals.

Hon. Sir E. Paget, *GCB.*
W. Eden
G. Gosselin
Sir J. W. Gordon, *Bt. GCB. & GCH.*
Sir R. Darling, *GCH.*
J. Orde
Sir C. B. Egerton, *GCMG. KCH.*
Sir C. Halkett, *GCB.*
Right Hon. Sir F. Adam, *KCB. & GCMG.*

Lieut.-Generals.

Sir Edward Kerrison, *Bt. KCB. GCH.*
Sir J. Nicolls, *KCB.*
Sir T. M'Mahon, *Bt. KCB.*
Sir A. Woodford, *KCB.*
Henry Shadforth

Major-Generals.

Henry D'Oyly
John Duffy, *CB.*
John Bell, *CB.*
Felix Calvert, *CB.*
Hon. H. F. C. Cavendish

Acting Committee.

President—Lt.-Gen. Sir Alex. Woodford, *KCB.*

Major-Generals.

Henry D'Oyly
John Duffy, *CB.*
Felix Calvert, *CB.*
Hon. H. F. C. Cavendish

Secretary—Henry Elliot, *Esq.*
Office, Whitehall Yard.

INSPECTOR OF REGIMENTAL COLOURS.

Albert Wm. Woods, Esq. Lancaster Herald.
Heralds' College, Doctors' Commons.

BOARD OF ORDNANCE.

Master General { Field Marshal *The Marquis of* Anglesey, *KG. GCB. GCH.*
Surveyor General, Major-General C. R. Fox.
Clerk of the Ordnance, Col. *Hon.* Geo. Anson.
Storekeeper, Capt. *Sir* Tho. Hastings, *RN.*
Secretary to the Master General, Capt. *Lord* Clarence E. Paget, R.N.
Secretary to the Board, Richard Byham, *Esq.*
Aide-de-Camp, Capt. P. L. C. Paget, Scots Fus. Gds.
Office, Pall Mall.

Inspector General of Fortifications { Major-General *Sir* John Fox Burgoyne, *KCB.*
Assistants do. { Major Gen. Edw. Fanshawe, *CB.*
Assistant Adjutant General, Lt.-Col. Matson.
Office, No. 84, Pall Mall.

COMMISSIONERS ROYAL MILITARY COLLEGE.

Field Marshal The *D. of* Wellington, *KG. GCB. & GCH.*
The Secretary at War.
Field Marshal *H.M. The King of Hanover*, *KG. GCB. GCH. & KP.*
Field Marshal *H. R. H. The Duke of* Cambridge, *KG.*
General *Hon. Sir* Edward Paget, *GCB.*
———*Viscount* Beresford, *GCB. & GCH.*
———*Right Hon. Sir* James Kempt, *GCB.*
———*Sir* T. Bradford, *GCB.*
———*Sir* J. W. Gordon, *Bt. GCB. GCH.—Quart. Mast. Gen.*
———*Sir* Ralph Darling, *GCH.*
Lt.-Gen. *Sir* Howard Douglas, *Bt. GCB. GCMG.*
———*Sir* John Macdonald, *GCB.—Adjutant General.*
———*Lord* FitzRoy Somerset, *GCB.*
———*Sir* J. Gardiner, *KCB.*
———Henry *Viscount* Hardinge, *GCB.*
———*Sir* G. Scovell, *KCB.—Gov. of Roy. Mil. College.*
Maj.-Gen. *Sir* Hew D. Ross, *KCB.* R. Art.
———Geo. Brown, *CB. KH.—Dep. Adj. Gen.*

COMMISSIONERS ROYAL MILITARY ASYLUM.

Field Marshal the *D. of* Wellington, *KG. GCB. & GCH.*
Field Marshal *H. M. The King of Hanover*, *KG. KP. GCB. GCH.*
Field Marshal *H. R. H. The Duke of* Cambridge, *KG.*
General *Hon. Sir* Edward Paget, *GCB.*
———*Viscount* Combermere, *GCB. GCH.*
———*Viscount* Beresford, *GCB. & GCH.*
———The *Marquis of* Londonderry, *GCB. GCH.*
———*Right Hon. Sir* James Kempt, *GCB.*
———*Sir* J. W. Gordon, *Bt. GCB.—Quart. Mast. Gen.*
———*Sir* Ralph Darling, *GCH.*
———*Sir* T. Bradford, *GCB.*
Lt.-Gen. *Sir* Howard Douglas, *Bt. GCB. GCMG.*
———*Sir* John Macdonald, *GCB.—Adjutant General.*
———*Sir* J. Gardiner, *KCB.*
———H. *Viscount* Hardinge, *GCB.*
———*Sir* G. Scovell, *KCB.—Gov. of Roy. Mil. College.*
Maj. Gen. *Sir* Hew D. Ross, *KCB.* R. Art.
———Geo Brown, *CB.—Deputy Adjt. General.*
The *Judge Advocate General.*
The *Paymaster General.*
Bishop of London.
Bishop of Winchester.
Laurence Sulivan, *Esq.—Deputy Secretary at War.*

BARRACK MASTERS.

1st Class,—with the relative rank of Major.

Baynton, *Capt.* Charles, *Brighton*
Mackenzie, *Capt.* Alex. *Woolwich*
Smith, Thomas 1 *Chatham*
Travers, Jos. O. *Portsmouth*

2d Class,—with the relative rank of Captain.

Barr, J. *Newport, Cardiff, &c.*
Baskeigh, S. F. *Stockport, &c.*
Berners, *Capt.* W. *Croydon*
Bosse, *Lt.* John 2 *Pendennis*
Burgoyne, J. J. H. *Dorchester and Weymouth*
• Custe, A. G. *Hull*
Chambers, *Lt.* S. *Coventry*
Chambre, *Capt.* A.
• Chawner, Edw. *Pembroke*
Child, A. *Leeds, &c.*
DeRenzy, *Major* G. W. 21 *Dundee and Perth*
• Downie, T. *Tynemouth and Sunderland*
Drummond, *Capt.* Geo. *Manchester*
Edmonds, *Capt.* H. *Hounslow and Hampton Court*
Edwards, *Maj.* R. Bidwell, *K.H.* 22 *Walmer*
• Farr, J. *Hyde Park & Kensington*
• Gange, John *Dover*
• Gibbs, Thomas *Stirling*
Gillmore, *Lt.* Joseph Albert *Glasgow*
Gleeson, *Capt.* T. *Sheffield, &c.*
Gore, *Hon.* W. J. P. *Gosport*
Halls, *Lt.* Thomas *Tower*
Hartley, *Maj.* W. 3 *Winchester and Southampton*
Hawkins, *Capt.* E. *Burnley*
Hay, John *Newcastle*
Hockings, *Lt.* Richard 4 *Norwich*
Jeffreys, *Capt.* Richard 20 *Exeter*
Kelly, R. S. *Hythe and Shorncliffe*
• Knight, J. T. *Tilbury Fort and Gravesend*
Lake, *Capt.* Charles 6 *Weedon and Northampton*
Lefroy, *Capt.* Anthony *York*
M'Dermott, *Capt.* J. *Hamilton*
MacDonald, R. D. *Brecon & Swansea*
Marshall, R. *Maidstone*
Murray, *Lt.* Fra. *Edinburgh, Leith Fort, and Piershill*
Murray, *Capt.* Jas. *Canterbury*
Nason, J. R. *Plymouth*
Nunn, *Capt.* John *Ipswich*
Phillips, E. W.
Philips, *Capt.* Jos. *Portman Street, Regent's Park, & St. John's Wood*
Raitt, G. R. *Aberdeen*
Raynes, *Major* W. A. *Isle of Man*
Renie, F. J. *Birmingham, &c.*
Romer, *Lt.-Col.* R. F. *Guernsey*
Ross, *Capt.* Robert *Devonport*
• St. George, James *Fort George*
• Sandes, G. *Alderney*
Servantes, *Capt.* W. T. 7 *Berwick-on-Tweed*
• Sharp, C. *Landguard Fort and Harwich*
Sinclair, *Hon.* John *Preston*
Townsend, T. *Liverpool*
Travers, *Capt.* N. C. 8 *Albany Barracks*
Treeve, *Capt.* R. *Jersey*
• Walker, J. *Chester*
Warren, S. R. *Windsor*
White, *Capt.* L. 25 *St. James's Park, Horse Gds. and St. George's*
Wright, J. G. *Nottingham*

3rd Class,—with the relative rank of Lieutenant.

Dusautoy, *Lt.* James *Taunton*
Graham, *Lt.* H. 19 *Chichester.*
Macdonald, *Capt.* D. *Paisley and Dumbarton*
Spalding, *Lt.* W. R. *Fort Augustus*
Stevens, P. *Sheerness*
Wilkie, *Major* P. 23 *Bristol*
• Wilkie, D. *Carlisle*

IN IRELAND.

Ashland, *Lt.* G.	*Templemore*
* Atkinson, T. J.	*Cork Harbour*
* Blackwell, W.	*Duncannon Fort*
Bowen, *Capt.* H.	*Belturbet and Cavan*
Browne, *Capt.* P.	*Carlow, Athy, and Baltinglass*
Buller, *Capt.* H. G. 18	
Campbell, *Capt.* J.	*Parsonstown, Banagher, Shannon Bridge, and Portumna*
	Wexford and Arklow
Daniel, *Ens.* R. A.	*Fermoy and Mitchelstown*
Doyle, *Lt. Col.* M. T. 24	*Ballincollig*
Eaton, *Capt.* G. H.	*Kilkenny and Castlecomer*
Lt.-Col. H. H. Farquharson	*Portobello, Beggar's Bush, and Pigeon House Fort*
Frizell, W. B.	*Caher, Clogheen, and New Inn*
Gaynor, *Capt.* B. 9	*Buttevant, Mallow and Millstreet*
Gillespie, Josh.	*Tullamore and Phillipstown*
Gore, *Maj.* H. Ross, *CB.*	*Cashel, Fethard and Tipperary*
Gossett, *Maj.* J. N. 10	*Cork*
Hewitt, *Lt.* R.	*Clonmel, Ballinamult and Carrick on Suir*
Hicks, *Capt.* J.	*Nenagh and Roscrea*
Hughes, *Lt.* J. 11	*Galway, Dunmore, Loughrea and Oughterarde*
Jephson, .	*Waterford and New Ross*
Kearney, Jas.	*Armagh and Monaghan*
Kirkman, 5 *Capt.* J.	*Richmond, Island Bridge, and Magazine Fort*
* Lamb, Samuel	*Athlone*
Lovelock, *Lt.* J. B. 13	*Castlebar, Foxford, Ballinrobe, and Westport*
Macintosh, R.	*Limerick*
MacQueen, J. D.	*Newry and Downpatrick*
Minchin, *Capt.* F. 14	*Boyle, Ballaghaderreen and Carrick on Shannon*
Munro, A. T.	*Sligo, Ballyshannon and Rutland*
Nisbett, *Capt.* F.	*Longford, Granard, Roscommon, &c.*
O'Brien, *Lt.* J.	*Drogheda*
O'Donnell, *Lt.* P.	*Yougal and Dungannon*
Oakes, *Lt. Sir* H. T. *Bt.*	*Derry, Lifford and Omagh*
Orr, *Lt.* J.	*Dublin Royal Barracks, Mountjoy and Royal Infirmary*
Phillips, *Lt.* R. J.[26]	*Dundalk*
* Pringle, R.	*Enniskillen*
Rowan, *Capt.* Rob.	*Belfast and Carrickfergus*
Roy, *Capt.* J. A.	*Gort and Clare Castle*
Rutherford, *Lt.* J. 20	*Kinsale, Charles Fort, Bandon, and Clonakilty*
* Thompson, Gordon	*Charlemont*
Vivian, *Capt.* R.	*Tralee*
Wall, J. T.	*Newbridge, Naas & Maryborough*
Warburton, W. B.	*Mullingar*
Zobel, *Capt.* S. 16	*Dublin, Linen Hall*

UPON FOREIGN STATIONS.

Antigua	P. P. Trotman
Bahamas	P. Druet
Barbadoes	J. Buckley
Berbice	* George Stokes
Bermuda	Wm. Tucker
Canada	
Amherstberg	Wm. Duff
Brockville	J. W. Luard
By Town	* S. Thomas
Carillon	* P. Monsell
Chambly	*Maj.* F. B. Eliot
Chatham	D. Hogg
Fort George	A. Garratt[29]
Isle aux Noix	* L. Woolls
Kingston	Fra. Raynes
London	T. Wilson
Montreal	W. H. Gray
Quebec	Tho. Trigge
St. John's	Thomas Bate
William Henry	T. H. A. Stephens[28]
Toronto	H. Cornwall
Cape of Good Hope	
Cape Town	*Lt.* J. R. K. Grogan
Graham's Town	*Capt.* N. Boyes
Simon's Town	* J. Pearson
Fort Beaufort	J. E. Turner
Algoa Bay	* H. W. Piers
Cephalonia	*Capt.* J. Huddlestone
Corfu	*Maj.* J. Daniell
Demerara	*Capt.* Mortimer
Dominica	* E. Black
Gibraltar	
South Dist.	*Capt.* F. W. Frankland 17
North Do.	*Lt.-Col.* E. Lascelles
Grenada	*Capt.* D. G. O'Meara
Honduras	* H. de R. Maxwell
Hong Kong	*Lt.-Col.* W. H. Thornton 15
Jamaica	
Newcastle	E. Harrison
Up Park and Kingston	
Stoney Hill and Port Royal	W. A. Stewart
Spanish Town	*Capt.* P. Campbell
Port Antonio	*Capt.* D. Gordon
Maroon Town	*Lt.* R. M'Goldrick
Montego Bay	Geo. Ford
Mauritius	*Lt.* J. S. Sedley; *Lt.* G. Hamilton
Malta	A. Lord Reay; *Col.* Fielding Browne, *CB*
Newfoundland	J. Tunbridge
New South Wales	
Sydney	
New Zealand	*Lt.* Robert Lynd
Nova Scotia & New Brunswick	
Annapolis	Joseph Norman
Prince Edw. Island	* L. Y. Nash
Fredericton	J. E. Woolford
Halifax	*Capt.* W. A. Chetwynd
St. John's, N. B.	Geo. Priestley
Sydney, Cape Breton	S. Rigby
St. Helena	* H. Topping
St. Kitts	*Capt.* W. Pennefather
St. Lucia	T. F. Sinclair
St. Vincent	R. J. Wickham
Santa Maura	* P. Deaton
Sierra Leone	* T. Ingleton
Tobago	* A. Pringle
Trinidad	F. N. Skinner
Van Diemen's Land	
Hobart Town	J. D. Mackay
Zante	* G. Wyat

N.B. The * distinguishes Ordnance Storekeepers acting as Barrack Masters.

War Services of the Barrack-Masters.

1 Major Smith served with the Rifle Brigade during the Peninsular war from 1808 to its termination in 1814, and was present at the actions of Calcavellas, Royales, Constantino, Betanzos, El Burgo, Corunna, Gallegos, Barquillo, and the Coa—dangerously wounded; siege and storm of Ciudad Rodrigo, siege and storm of Badajoz, battle of Salamanca, advance to and capture of Madrid, action of San Milan, battle of Vittoria, action at Echalar, both attacks of Vera, battle of the Nivelle, action of Arcangues, battle of Orthes, action of Tarbes, and battle of Toulouse. Served also the campaign of 1815, including the battle of Waterloo.

2 Lieut. Boase served in the Peninsula, France, and Flanders, with the 32nd, and was present at the battles of Roleia, Vimiera, and Corunna, siege of the forts and battle of Salamanca,—gun-shot wound in the left leg and another through the right shoulder; battles of the Pyrenees on the 28th and 30th July, 1813; battle of the Nivelle,—gun-shot wound in the forehead; battles of the Nive, Orthes, and Quatre Bras,—gun-shot through the left ankle joint.

3 Major Hartley served with the 23rd in the Egyptian campaign of 1801, including the storming of the heights of Aboukir,—wounded in the head; actions of the 13th and 21st March. Served with the 71st the campaign of 1808, including the battles of Roleia and Vimiera,—severely wounded in the leg. Served with the 62nd in the Peninsula from Oct. 1813 to the end of that war in 1814, including the passage of the Bidassoa, battle of the Nivelle, battles of the Nive on the 9th, 10th, 11th, 12th, and 13th Dec. 1813, and investment of Bayonne. Also the campaign of 1815, and was present at the capture of Paris. Medal for services in Egypt.

4 Lieut. Hockings served with the 25th in Holland in 1799, and was present at the battle of Egmont-op-zee. Also the Egyptian campaign of 1801, and lost his right leg in the action of the 22nd Aug. near Marabout. Medal for services in Egypt.

5 Captain Kirkman served with the Rifle Brigade during the campaigns of 1810, 11, 12, 13, and 14, in the Peninsula, including the actions and sieges of Cadiz, Tarragona, Barrosa, actions near Fuente Guinaldo and Aldea de Ponte, siege and capture of Ciudad Rodrigo

(volunteered the storming party), siege and capture of Badajoz (volunteered, and accompanied the forlorn hope, and was wounded in the head), battle of Salamanca, advance to and capture of Madrid, subsequent retreat through Spain, affairs of San Munoz and San Millan, battle of Vittoria, and three days' severe skirmishing in following the enemy to Pampeluna, which ended in the capture of their last gun; action at Echalar, passage of the Bidassoa, various actions in the Pyrenees, battle of Nivelle (gun-shot wound in the right arm), action of Arcangues, and passage of the Nive. Served also the campaign of 1815 in Belgium.

6 Captain Lake served in the Guards during the campaign of 1814 in Holland, including the action at Merxem, bombardment of Antwerp, and storming of Bergen-op-Zoom. Served also the campaign of 1815, and was present at the battles of Quatre Bras and Waterloo, at the latter of which he was severely wounded in the head whilst defending the advanced post of Hougomont.

7 Captain Servantes embarked for the Peninsula in Oct. 1810, as a volunteer, and served as such with the 48th and 66th regts. up to and at the battle of Albuhera, when he was gazetted to an Ensigncy in the 97th, which regt. being ordered to England, he got removed back to the 66th for the purpose of remaining on service, and continued to serve in the Peninsula until the end of that war in 1814, including the battles of Vittoria (wounded). Pyrenees, Nivelle, Nive, Orthes, Aire, and Toulouse, besides several minor engagements, Wounded in the face in 1811, when on escort duty.

8 Captain Travers, prior to entering the army, served as a Midshipman in the *Diana* frigate, under Captain Maling, for three years, on the West India Station, and was frequently engaged in boats cutting out vessels under the batteries at the islands of Curacoa and Cuba. In July 1806 he embarked with a detachment of the Rifle Brigade for South America, and was severely wounded in the shoulder at the attack on the suburbs of Buenos Ayres on the 3rd July 1807, but this did not prevent his entering the town on the 5th with General Crawfurd's Brigade. He served under Sir John Moore during the campaign and retreat to Corunna in 1808-9; and subsequently accompanied his Regt. to Walcheren. From 1811 to 1814 he served in the Peninsula, and was present at the battle of Salamanca,—where his horse was shot under him when acting as Adjutant; capture of the French rear guard on the following day, capture of Madrid and the Retiro, affair near Val Moresco, covering the siege of Burgos, and several skirmishes on the retreat to Portugal. Commanded the Advanced Guard of the Light Brigade at the battle of Vittoria, the Pyrenees, and various affairs of Out Posts. At Vera Bridge he commanded the advance Picquet. In 1814 he accompanied his Regt. to America, and was severely wounded in the attack on New Orleans.

9 Captain Gaynor served in the Peninsula with the Portuguese army during 1808, 9, and 10, when he was wounded and taken prisoner at Arroyo del Puerco.

10 Major Gossett served with the Rifle Brigade in the Peninsula from Oct. 1813 to July 1814, including the battle of the Nive on the 9th, 10th, 11th, 12th and 13th Dec., passage of the Gave d'Oleron, battle of Orthes, actions at Tarbes and Tournefeuille, and battle of Toulouse. Served afterwards in the American War, and was constantly engaged near New Orleans from 23d Dec. 1814, to the 7th Jan. 1815, and was also present at the attack on New Orleans on the 8th Jan.—wounded in the head.

11 Lieut. Hughes served in the Peninsula with the 57th from 1810 to the end of that war in 1814, and was present at the Battle of Busaco, first siege of Badajoz, battle of Albuhera,—severely wounded through the left thigh; retreat from Madrid, battles of Vittoria, the Pyrenees on the 28th and 30th July, and the Nivelle,—severely wounded in the right thigh, where the ball remained for nine years.

12 Capt. Hicks served in the Peninsula in 1812, 13, and 14, including the battle of Castalla, and siege of Tarragona. He was present with the Anglo-Sicilian army during the whole of the operations on the coast of the Faro against Murat, including the siege of Scylla Castle. He served as a Lieut.-Colonel with the Anglo-Spanish Legion in 1835, 36, and 37, including the action before Ernani, relief of Bilboa, storming the lines of San Sebastian (severely wounded in the side), operations on the 10th, 12th, 14th, and 15th March, general action on the 16th March, 1837, during which he was wounded, and had his horse killed under him. For his services in the British Legion he has received two medals.

13 Lieut. John B. Lovelock served with the 29th in the Peninsula, from 1809, and was present at the battle of Busaco, first seige of Badajoz, and battle of Albuhera, at which latter engagement he was severely wounded through both thighs and in the head. Served also in America in 1814, and was present at the operations in the Penobscot, Castine, and Macheas.

14 Captain Minchin served in the 51st the campaign and battle of Corunna. On the expedition to Walcheren, and at the siege of Flushing. Embarked with the regt. for Lisbon in Jan. 1811, and was present at the battle of Fuentes d'Onor, covering the siege of Ciudad Rodrigo, two sieges of San Christoval, covering the 2d siege of Badajos, affair near Val Moresco, battle of Salamanca, capture of Madrid and the Retiro, covering the siege of Burgos, actions of Monasterio and Quintana Pulla, and retreat into Portugal; battles of Vittoria and the Pyrenees, covering the siege of San Sebastian, action of Lesaca (severely wounded), and occupation of Bordeaux. Served also in the campaign of 1815, including the battle of Waterloo, capture of Cambray, and capitulation of Paris.

15 Lt.-Col. Thornton served in the Peninsula from the first landing of the army in 1808 until the final expulsion of the enemy beyond the Pyrenees in 1813; and was present with the 32nd at the battles of Roleia, Vimiera, and Corunna, together with the affairs of Lugo and Batonzas,—performing the duty of Adjutant from Vimiera. Appointed to the Portuguese service in May 1809, and was at the passage of the Coa, blockade of Almeida, battle of Fuentes d'Onor, retreat to Busaco, and subsequently to the lines of Lisbon. Commanded the Portuguese Picquets at the repulse of a large force of the enemy in their attack to carry the wind-mills in front of the lines of Alhandra. Followed the retreat of Massena's army from the lines, and was present at the Puente de Murcella, Guarda, and numerous minor affairs; also at the siege of Burgos, and on the retreat from thence when he commanded two companies at the destruction of the Bridge of Duanos on the Carrion, and subsequent defence of the same. Again served on the advance of the army to the Ebro, and at the battles

of Vittoria, Pampeluna, and the Pyrenees, where he succeeded to the temporary command in the action of the 28th July until dangerously wounded, having his thigh fractured.

16 Captain Zobel served with the 5th in the campaign of 1799 in Holland; and with the 26th during the campaign of 1805 in Hanover. Embarked with the 66th for the Peninsula in 1809, and was present at the taking of Oporto, and battle of Talavera; and returned with the Regt. in 1814.

17 Captain Frankland served in the Peninsula with the 2d Foot from Nov. 1812 to the end of that war, and was present at the blockade of Pampeluna, battles of the Pyrenees on the 28th and 30th July, passage of the Bidassoa, battles of the Nivelle, Nive, actions before Bayonne, and at Toulouse as acting aide-de-camp to General Sir Wm. Anson. In position at Halle during the battle of Waterloo, and at the assault of Cambray as aide-de-camp to General the Hon. Sir Charles Colville.

18 Captain Buller served with the 88th at Buenos Ayres, and was severely wounded in the head and thigh. He served afterwards in the Peninsula, and was present at the battle of Fuentes d'Onor, siege of Badajoz, battle of Vittoria (wounded), and various affairs of out-posts.

19 Lieut. H. Graham served in the West Indies, where he was engaged in several actions. He was also at the capture of Minorca; the expulsion of the French from Egypt; and in the Peninsula and France to the conclusion of the war,—at the capture of Badajoz was the first who entered that fortress. When on board the *Samuel* and *Jane* transport with 300 soldiers, captured a privateer which came alongside that vessel at night, when the fire of the troops annihilated her crew. Lieut. Graham has received four severe wounds during these services.

20 Lieut. Rutherford served in the Peninsula with the old 94th, was present at the defence of Cadiz in 1810, lines of Torres Vedras, pursuit of Massena, actions of Pombal, Redinha, Condeixa, and Sabugal, battle of Fuentes d'Onor, second siege of Badajoz, battle of Vittoria, blockade of Pampeluna, battles of the Pyrenees, Pampeluna, and the Nivelle, passage of the Gave d'Oleron, battle of Orthes, action of Vic Bigorre, and battle of Toulouse.

21 Major De Renzy served at Walcheren in 1809, and was present at the siege and capture of Flushing. Served afterwards in the Peninsula in the 82nd, and at the battle of Vittoria he was most severely wounded by a cannon-shot,—right arm amputated.

22 Major Edwards served with the 13th Dragoons through the Peninsular war.

23 Major Wilkie served with the 92nd the Egyptian campaign of 1801, including the action of the 13th March (wounded), capture of Cairo and of Alexandria. He served also in the Peninsula, France, and Flanders, and was present at Arroyo de Molino, Vittoria, the different affairs in the Pyrenees, Nivelle, Nive, Orthes, Toulouse, and Waterloo—where he was severely wounded.

24 Lt. Col. Doyle sailed in 1805 with Lord Cathcart's expedition to Hanover, and being shipwrecked became a prisoner of war to the Dutch. In 1808 he went with Sir Arthur Wellesley's expedition to Portugal, and was shot through the body at Roleia. In 1809 he was at the siege, sortie, and capture of Flushing, and storming of Fort Ramakins. In 1810, 11, and 12 he served in the Peninsula in Picton's Division,—in pursuit of Massena from Santarem, actions at Pombal, Redinha, Roblida, Condeixa, Sabugal, and Fuentes d'Onor; siege of Badajoz in 1811, cavalry affair at El Bodon, siege and storm of Ciudad Rodrigo, siege and storm of Badajoz (a ball lodged in the cavity of the chest, unextracted—a ball through the right arm, which was splintered—neck and head wounded); battle of Salamanca, capture of Madrid and the Retiro. In 1814 embarked for Canada in command of a detachment of the 5th—repelled two attacks on the Transport by Privateers. Present with the Army at Plattsburgh.

25 Captain White served on the expedition to the Elbe and Weser under Lord Cathcart; the principal campaigns in the Peninsula under the Duke of Wellington including the operations on the Coa during the siege and battle of Almeida, the siege of Ciudad Rodrigo, the siege and storming of Badajoz, the battle of Salamanca, capture of Madrid and the Retiro, the siege of Burgos and affair on retreat at Muriel. The campaigns in Flanders and France under Lord Lynedoch and the Duke of Wellington, including the attack on Merxem, bombardment of Antwerp, the affair of Fort Frederick Hendrick, and siege of Bergen-op-Zoom, the battle of Waterloo, storming of Cambray, and capitulation of Paris.

26 Lieut. R. J. Phillips served with the 27th Regt. in the Peninsula, and was present at the pursuit of Massena from Santarem, in various minor affairs, and at the siege and storming of Badajoz, at which last he was shot through the shoulder-joint of the right arm, and also through the left thigh.

27 Captain Jeffreys entered the corps of Royal Marines as 2nd Lieut. in 1808, and was appointed to the Marine Artillery in the following year. He served off Boulogne, and also in the action under Lord Cochrane at Basque Roads, as senior officer of Marine Artillery, on board the *Etna* bomb vessel. In 1811 he proceeded with the marine battalion, commanded by the late Sir Richard Williams, to Portugal, and returned to England in 1812. In 1813 he obtained a company in the Glamorgan Militia, and having volunteered the same year into the 53rd regt., he landed in Spain, and proceeded to join the army at Toulouse.

28 Captain Stephens served the campaign of 1815 with the 3rd battalion of the Royals, and carried the regimental colour at the battle of Quatre Bras, retreat on the following day, battle of Waterloo, and capture of Paris.

29 Mr. Garratt served with the 49th during the last American war, and was present at the battles of Queenstown, Stoney Creek, and Fort George, and in the expedition to Plattsburg, besides various skirmishes. On the outbreak of the Rebellion in 1837 he commanded a company of Volunteers at the attack on the Rebel position at Gallow's Hill, and served afterwards as an Adjutant of Militia until the suppression of the Rebellion in 1838.

STAFF OFFICERS OF PENSIONERS.

(*Employed in the Payment of Out-Pensioners, and Commanding the Local Companies.*)

MILITARY SUPERINTENDENT.

Lieutenant-Colonel Alexander Murray Tulloch, 31 May, 1844.

GREAT BRITAIN.

ABERDEEN	*Capt.* Geo. Munro, Unatt. 10 July 40
BATH	*Capt.* C. R. Shuckburgh, h.p. 70 F. 21 June 39
BIRMINGHAM	*Major* R. W. Bamford, Unatt. 9 Nov. 46
BOLTON	*Capt.* J. Richardson, Unatt. 2 April 41
BRIGHTON	*Lieut.* A. H. Hull, h.p. 50 F. 6 Nov. 27
BRISTOL	*Capt.* M. R. S. Whitmore, h.p. 19 Drs. 16 Feb. 38
CAMBRIDGE	*Lieut.* W. F. Webster, h.p. 2 Ceylon Regt. 12 July 33
CANTERBURY	—— J. O. Burridge, h.p. 10 Drs. 1 Sept. 36
CARDIFF	*Capt.* G. W. C. Jackson, 16th Lancers, 7 June 44
CARLISLE	*Lieut.* J. Taylor, h.p. 90 F. 14 July 14
CARMARTHEN	*Lieut.* J. P. Matthews, h.p. 10 F. 7 April 26
CHATHAM	*Capt.* R. Jenkins, Unatt. 16 June 37
CHESTER	—— J. D. De Wend, h.p. 52 F. 22 May 41
COVENTRY	*Major* S. J. Sutton, h.p. Port. Serv. 9 Nov. 46
DERBY	*Lieut.* V. Jones, h.p. 8 Gar. Bn. 12 Jan. 09
DUNDEE	*Capt.* H. Fenwick, h.p. 27 F. 17 Aug. 42
EDINBURGH	—— J. D. G. Tulloch, h.p. 84 F. 23 Aug. 41 *Lieut.* J. Hunter, h.p. 13 F. 27 Sept. 39
EXETER	*Capt.* H. B. H. Rogers, Unatt. 14 Oct. 36
FALMOUTH	*Lieut.* T. W. J. M'Dougall, h.p. R. Mar. 5 July 36
GLASGOW	*Capt.* J. Mullen, Unatt. 19 Aug. 41 *Lieut.* G. Sinclair, h.p. 92 F. 14 June 21
GLOUCESTER	*Capt.* H. C. C. Somerset, h.p. 27 F. 23 June 43
HALIFAX	*Major* J. E. Orange, h.p. 84 F. 9 Nov. 46
HULL	*Capt.* C. S. Teale, Unatt. 23 May 43
INVERNESS	*Major* A. Houston, h. p. 4 F. 23 Nov. 41
IPSWICH	*Capt.* C. Paget, h.p. R. Staff Corps, 9 Mar. 39
JERSEY, GUERNSEY, &c.	*Major* J. F. Du Vernet, h.p. R. African Corps, 9 Nov. 46
LEEDS	*Capt.* G. P. Pickard, h. p. 6 Dr. Gds. 17 Sept. 39
LEICESTER	*Major* H. F. Hawker, h.p. 9 Nov. 46
LINCOLN	*Lieut.* H. Rose, h.p. 24 F. 25 May 19
LIVERPOOL	*Capt.* J. J. Greig, Unatt. 16 June 43
LONDON DISTRICT.	
Northern Div.	*Capt.* W. Cartan, Unatt. 31 Aug. 38 —— W. Warde, Unatt. 25 Oct. 42
Eastern Div.	—— C. Holden, Unatt. 7 Oct. 37. 41 —— W. Wood, h.p. R. Mar. 11 May
Southern Div.	—— F. P. Nott, h.p. 1 Gar. Bn. 1 Nov. 40
Western Div.	*Major* M. Orr, Unatt. 9 Nov. 46. *Major* G. H. F. Campbell, h.p. R. Staff Corps, 9 Nov. 46
Woolwich Div.	*Major* J. Forbes, Unatt. 9 Nov. 46
MANCHESTER	*Capt.* A. F. Bond, h.p. R. Staff Corps, 12 Oct. 38 *Capt.* R. Pitcairn, h.p. 6 Gar. Bn. 6 Sept. 39
NEWCASTLE-UPON-TYNE	—— H. C. Powell, Unatt. 8 April 42
NORTHAMPTON	*Major* W. J. Crompton, Unatt. 9 Nov. 46
NORWICH	*Capt* J. Cockburn, Unatt. 8 June 38
NOTTINGHAM	*Major* W. Campbell, Unatt. 9 Nov. 46
OXFORD	*Lieut.* F. Smythe, h.p. 2 F. 10 July 40
PAISLEY	*Capt.* L. Macpherson, Unatt. 1 May 37
PERTH	*Major* A. Campbell, h.p. 2 Ceylon Regt. 9 Nov. 46
PLYMOUTH	*Maj.* E. Trevor, h.p. R. A. 9 Nov. 46 *Capt.* T. W. B. Mounsteven, h. p. 79 F. 8 May 35
PORTSMOUTH	*Capt.* P. L. Dore, Unatt. 29 Aug. 38 *Capt.* J. K. Willson, h.p. R. Mar. 7 Feb. 42
PRESTON	*Major* T. Beckham, Unatt. 9 Nov. 46
SALISBURY	*Capt.* D. Stewart, h.p. 84 F. 17 Sept. 39
SHEFFIELD	*Capt.* S. A. Capel, h.p. 51 F. 30 July 44
SHREWSBURY	*Lieut.* V. Browne, h.p. 18 F. 10 Aug. 15
SOUTHAMPTON	*Capt.* W. Lacy, Unatt. 6 Dec. 44.
STAFFORD North, BURSLEM	*Lieut.* M. F. Steele, h. p. 91 F. 10 Feb. 31
STIRLING	*Lieut.* W. Peddie, h.p. 21 F. 30 Jan. 12
STOCKPORT	*Major* E. S. Farmer, Unatt. 9 Nov. 46
TAUNTON	*Capt.* F. G. Christie, Unatt. 30 May 45
THURSO	*Qr. Master* Geo. Macdonald, h.p. 93 F 13 Dec. 39.
TROWBRIDGE	*Lt.* J. Lawson, Unatt. 17 Aug. 26
WOLVERHAMPTON	*Capt.* H. Russell, h. p. 60 F. 10 Sept. 41
WORCESTER	—— T. Knatchbull, h.p. R. Art. 28 Nov. 37

IRELAND.

ARMAGH	*Capt.* A. Donelan, h.p. York Chass. 6 May 42
ATHLONE	—— O. L. Ormsby, Unatt. 1 Nov. 39
BALLYMENA	*Lieut.* J. M. Tittle, h.p. R. African Corps, 1 Nov. 10
BELFAST	*Major* W. M'Pherson, Unatt. 9 Nov. 46
BIRR	*Major* W. H. Phibbs, Unatt. 9 Nov. 46
BOYLE	*Lieut.*
CARLOW	—— R. H. O'R. Hoey, h.p. 85 F. 17 Aug. 26
CASTLEBAR	*Lieut.* E. J. Taylor, h.p. 13 F. 28 Sept. 14
CAVAN	*Major* W. Beales, h.p. 9 Drs. 9 Nov. 46
CHARLEMONT	*Capt.* E. O. Broadley, Unatt. 28 Sept. 39
CLONMEL	*Lieut.* J. Inman, h.p. 63 F. 13 Oct. 39
CORK	*Major*
DROGHEDA	*Lieut.* T. Hodgetts, h.p. 49 F. 18 Mar. 35
DUBLIN	*Major* G. C. Swan, Unatt. 31 Dec. 41 *Capt.* R. R. Harris, h.p. 60 F. 31 Oct. 40
ENNIS	*Lieut.* R. A. M. Franklin, h.p. 55 F. 17 April 35
ENNISKILLEN	*Capt.* B. Beaufoy, Unatt. 14 Aug. 40
FERMOY	*Lieut.* B. Meredith, h.p. 16 F. 1 July 18
GALWAY	*Lieut.* R. N. Rogers, Unatt. 14 June 15
KILKENNY	*Lieut.* J. G. Rogers, Unatt. 5 Mar. 18
LIMERICK	*Major* W. Calder, Unatt. 9 Nov. 46
LONDONDERRY	*Major* J. Stuart, h. p. 84 F. 9 Nov. 46
LONGFORD	*Capt.* W. Mauleverer, h.p. 58 F. 28 July 42
MARYBOROUGH	*Lieut.* J. O. Lloyd, h.p. 74 F. 14 May 18
MONAGHAN	*Lieut.* W. J. Kirk, h.p. 46 F. 27 Oct. 37
NEWRY	*Capt.* J. Sampson, h.p. 8 Gar. Bn. 23 May 26
OMAGH	*Lieut.* F. B. Hingston, h.p. 84 F. Dec. 11
ROSCOMMON	*Lieut.* H. Hollinsworth, Unatt. 29 May 28
SLIGO	*Capt.* G. R. Pole, Unatt.
TRALEE	—— P. D. Stokes, h.p. 4 F. 8 Nov. 44
TULLAMORE	*Lieut.* W. Whitfield, h.p. 62 F. 13 April 14.
WATERFORD	*Capt.* Wm. Ready, Unatt. 24 Jan. 45.

NEW ZEALAND.

Major John Gray (*Commanding*), Unatt.	9 Nov. 46
Capt. W. H. Keany, h.p. 61 F.	12 Oct. 41
Capt. C. H. M. Smith, h.p. 60 F.	23 Aug. 44
Capt. Alexander Macdonald, Unatt.	11 Dec. 46
Lieut. J. A. Hickson, h.p. 31 F.	28 Nov. 45
Lieut. O. W. Gray, h. p. 30 F.	18 May 40

*** The date after the name refers to the Officer's Army-Rank.

Scale of Allowances in addition to Half-Pay.

1st Class.—Officers having the rank of Captains, and superintending Districts containing from 600 to 1000 Pensioners and upwards, ten shillings and sixpence per diem.

2nd Class.—Officers having the rank of Lieutenant, and superintending Districts containing from 400 to 600 Pensioners, eight shillings and sixpence per diem.

3rd Class.—Officers of whatever rank, in remote Districts where there are fewer than 400 Pensioners, a reduced allowance proportioned to the number of Pensioners, and the distance to be travelled in visiting them.

[For continuation see foot of next page.

OFFICERS OF THE LINE RETIRED ON FULL PAY,

Under the Royal Warrant of 1st October 1840,—and which, with the Officers of the late Royal Veteran Battalions, &c. complete an Establishment of 20 Lieutenant-Colonels, 20 Majors, and 115 Captains, of whom 45 may be Brevet Field Officers.

LIEUTENANT-COLONELS.

	Commission.	Retired.
Charles Hughes, 94 F.	10 Oct. 35	17 Aug. 41
P John Campbell, 97 F.	28 June 38	26 Oct. 41
W Joseph Mark Harty, *KH.* 33 F.	22 July 41	14 June 42
Edw. T. Tronson, 13 F.	23 July 30	2 Aug. 42
W Richard Westmore, 33 F.	14 June 42	14 Apr. 43
P W John Cross, *KH.* 68 F.	8 Feb. 31	21 April 43
James Lewis Basden, *CB.* 89 F.	22 July 30	16 June 43
P Patrick Grieve, 75 F.	9 Nov. 30	12 Dec. 43
Joseph Kelsall, 70 F.	28 June 38	23 Feb. 44
P Robert Hunt, 49 F.	29 Mar. 44	30 Mar. 44
Henry C. Streatfeild, 87 F.	4 Oct. 36	18 April 45
James W. Fairtlough, 63 F.	17 Sept. 33	16 Sept. 45
Richard Willington, 84 F.	8 April 42	16 Sept. 45
Henry Senior, 65 F.	19 Sept. 34	30 Dec. 45
P Edward James White, 70 F.	23 Feb. 44	30 Dec. 45
William Blois, 52 F.	11 May 30	16 Jan. 46
P Eyre John Crabbe, 74 F.	6 Nov. 41	1 May 46
P John Singleton, *KH.* 30 F.	17 July 40	10 July 46

MAJORS.

	Commission.	Retired.
W Thomas Reid, 33 F.	10 Jan. 37	30 Oct. 40
P Geo. Fitz Gerald Stack, *KH.* 24 F.	26 Oct. 35	8 Jan. 41
Alexander Sharrock, 29 F.	27 Sept. 39	26 Oct. 41
P Philip Aubin, 57 F.	12 April 31	11 Feb. 42
P Henry Clements, 16 F.	10 Jan. 37	27 Mar. 42
P Peter John Willats, 48 F.	10 Jan. 37	6 May 42
Samuel George Carter, 16 F.	8 Feb. 34	8 July 42
John M. Dalzell, 16 F.	28 June 38	19 Aug. 42
P William Cannon, 97 F.	28 June 38	27 Sept. 42
Gerald Rochfort, 3 F. *Lt.-Col.*	23 Nov. 41	14 Oct. 42
John Kitson, 62 F.	22 July 30	27 Dec. 42
J. C. Chads, 1 W. I. Regt. *Lt.-Col.*	1 July 42	3 Mar. 43
Robert Pattisson, 13 F. *Lt.-Col.*	4 Oct. 42	30 June 43
P W Wm. Burney, *KH.* Cape Mounted Riflemen, *Lt.-Col.*	23 Nov. 41	16 Feb. 44
Wm. Raban, 22 F.	18 Dec. 40	23 Feb. 44
Norman Maclean, *CB.* 55 F. *Lt.-Col.*	23 Dec. 42	11 Nov. 45
E. W. Bray, *CB.* 39 F. *Lt.-Col.*	30 Apr. 44	7 Aug. 46

CAPTAINS.

	Commission.	Retired.
P Isaac Richardson, 11 F. *Major*	28 June 38	30 Oct. 40
Aylmer Dowdall, 54 F.	2 May 29	do
Peter Eason, 61 F.	21 June 33	do
P John Clarke, 66 F. *Major*	28 June 38	do
W Brooke Pigot, 69 F.	29 Aug. 26	do
P John Doyle, 72 F. *Major*	10 Jan. 37	do
Peter Sutherland, 72 F. *Major*	do	do
P Richard Tatton, 77 F. *Major*	28 June 38	do
P James T. Moore, 87 F. *Major*	do	do
P John Marshall, 91 F. *Major*	do	do
P W Robert Cochrane, Rifle Br.	22 May 28	do
P John Bonamy, 6 F. *Major*	28 June 38	2 April 41
P W Rich. Handcock, 46 F. *Major*	10 Jan. 37	do
Wm. Henry Arthure, 56 F. *Major*	28 June 38	do
Richard Fry, 63 F.	5 June 30	do
James Mason, 77 F. *Major*	10 Jan. 37	do
P George Pinckney, 82 F. *Major*	22 July 30	do
R. B. F. Pasley, 82 F.	16 Mar. 32	do
Charles Gordon, 93 F.	28 Feb. 28	do
P Thomas Moore, 18 F.	18 Feb. 26	9 April 41
P Richard Manners, 59 F. *Major*	28 June 38	do
Dickens Mark Hastewood, 14 F.	10 July 31	1 June 41
John Kelly, 6 F.	27 May 36	25 June 41
P James Jackson, 57 F. *Major*	28 June 38	do
Adam Beverhoudt, 58 F.	29 April 36	do
Ambrose Spong, 60 F. *Major*	28 June 38	do
Robert Browne, 16 F. *Major*	28 June 38	1 July 41
Stephen Noel, 92 F. *Major*	22 July 30	5 Oct. 41
P Wm. Sall, *KH.* Newf. Cos. *Lt.-Col.*	do	26 Oct. 41
P G. H. E. Murphy, 22 F. *Major*	10 Jan. 37	25 Nov. 42
John M. Hewson, 89 F.	13 Mar. 35	14 April 43
Wm. White Warburton, 67 F. *Maj.*	23 Nov. 41	24 Nov. 43
P Charles Campbell, 61 F. *Major*	23 Nov. 41	12 Dec. 43
Tho. Hinton Hemmans, 78 F. *Major*	do	29 Dec. 43
Robert Terry, 31 F. *Lt.-Col.*	22 July 30	
P T. H. Shadwell Clerke, *KH. Maj.*	do	
P Alex. Campbell, 38 F. *Major*	23 Nov. 41	22 Mar. 44
James Johnston, 44 F. *Major*	22 July 30	29 Mar. 44
P John Adrian Lutman, 24 F.	13 Feb 35	10 May 44
P Henry Dixon, 81 F. *Major*	23 Nov. 41	do
John Blackall, 39 F.	1 June 38	27 Sept. 44
P James Poyntz, 30 F. *Major*	23 Nov. 41	30 Sept. 44
William Cox, 54 F. *Major*	10 Jan. 37	6 Dec. 44
P W John Griffith, 1 W. I. Regt.	29 July 36	do
P Robert Woodhouse, 38 F.	21 April 33	3 Jan. 45
Charles R. Wright, 43 F. *Major*	23 Nov. 41	9 May 45
Edw. Goate, 35 F. *Major*	22 July 30	8 May 46
P M. C. Lynch, 14 F. *Major*	23 Nov. 41	18 Sept. 46
William Dempster, 41 F. *Major*	23 Nov. 41	9 Oct. 46
W Charles Hill, 54 F. *Major*	do	do
John Harvey, 37 F.	9 Oct. 37	13 Nov. 46
Robert Alex. Andrews, 30 F. *Maj.*	9 Nov. 46	11 Dec. 46
George Mainwaring, 22 F.	5 June 40	29 Jan. 47
P R. W. Hooper, 69 F. *Major*	10 Jan. 37	do
Wm. John King, 21 F.	3 Oct. 40	14 May 47
John Campbell, 74 F.	15 Dec. 37	do
William Barnes, 17 F. *Major*	9 Nov. 46	17 Sept. 47
Wm. Donaldson Price	28 Aug. 38	8 Oct. 47
John Bolton, 75 F. *Major*	9 Nov. 46	28 Jan. 48
Daniel Riley, 24 F. *Major*	9 Nov. 46	7 Apr. 48
Robert Stuart Ridge, 36 F.	9 Sept. 37	12 May 48
P John Ovens, 57 F.	9 Sept. 37	do
David Dickson, 95 F.	26 Jan. 26	9 June 48
Richard Thompson, 51 F	28 Aug. 41	18 July 48
Hender Mountsteven, 48 F.	30 Nov. 38	13 Oct. 48
Charlton O'Neill, 97 F. *Major*	23 Nov. 41	20 Oct. 48
George Gardine Shaw, 63 F.	31 May 39	15 Dec. 48

The allowances to the two first classes have been calculated on the principle of placing each officer as nearly as possible in the same position, in respect of income, as if he were serving on full-pay, and is made up of the following items:—

	To a Capt. s. d.	To a Lieut. s. d.
Difference between half and full pay	4 7	3 0
Lodging and fuel allowance	2 0	1 8
Allowance for a horse, or for travelling	2 0	2 0
Allowance in lieu of a servant	1 0	1 0
Allowance in lieu of postage, stationery, and printing	0 5	0 5
	10 0	8 1

In the event of any of the Staff Officers of Pensioners being subject to additional expense in consequence of his employment in aid of the Civil Power at a distance from head-quarters, he will also receive a further allowance of five shillings a day while necessarily detained from home, together with the amount of travelling charges thus incurred by him.

Contingent Allowances.

For 50 enrolled men, one shilling a day.
" 100 and upwards, one shilling and sixpence a day.
" 200 " " two shillings a day.

ANNUAL PAY OF COLONELS.

CORPS.			If appointed on or before the 31st March, 1834.	If appointed after the 31st March, 1834.
Life Guards and Horse Guards, *without other emolument*			1,800*l.*	1,800*l.*
First Dragoon Guards, *and emoluments from Clothing*			1,100	1,000
Other Regiments of Cavalry	do.	do.	1,000	900
Grenadier Guards	do.	do.	1,200	1,200
Coldstream and Scots Fusilier Gds.	do.	do.	1,000	1,000
Regular Infantry	do.	do.	600	500
First West India Regiment	do.	do.	—	500
Second ditto	do.	do.	598 2 6	500

DAILY PAY OF OFFICERS.

RANKS.	Life Guards & Horse Guards.	Foot Guards.	Drg.Gds. and Dragns.	Foot.	Royal Artillery. Horse Brigade.	Royal Artillery. Foot.	Royal Enginrs.	Royal Marines
	l. s. d.	*l. s. d.*	*l. s. d.*	*l. s. d.*	*l. s. d.*	*l. s. d.*	*l. s. d.*	*l. s. d.*
Colonel Commandant	—	—	—	—	3 0 0	2 14 9½	2 14 9½	1 18 6
Colonel 2nd Commandant	—	—	—	—	—	—	—	1 0 0
Colonel	—	—	—	—	1 12 4	1 6 3	1 6 3	—
Lieut.-Colonel	1 9 2	1 6 9	1 3 0	0 17 0	1 7 1	0 18 1	{ 18 1 / 16 1 }	} 17 0
Major	1 4 5	1 3 0	0 19 3	0 16 0	—	—	—	0 16 0
Captain	0 15 1	0 15 6	0 14 7	0 11 7	0 16 1	0 11 1	0 11 1	0 10 6
Do. having higher Rank by Brevet	—	—	—	0 13 7	0 18 1	0 13 1	0 13 1	0 12 6
Lieutenant	0 10 4	0 7 4	0 9 0	0 6 6	0 9 10	0 6 10	0 6 10	0 6 6
Do. after 7 years' service	—	—	—	0 7 6	0 10 10	0 7 10	0 7 10	0 7 6
Cornet, Ensign, and 2d Lieutenant	0 8 0	0 5 6	0 8 0	0 5 3	—	0 5 7	0 5 7	0 5 3
Paymast. { On Appointment	—	—	0 12 6	0 12 6	—	—	—	}
Paymast. After 5 years' service	—	—	0 15 0	0 15 0	—	—	—	}
Paymast. 15 do.	—	—	0 17 6	0 17 6	—	—	—	} 16 6
Paymast. 20 do.	—	—	1 0 0	1 0 0	—	—	—	}
Paymast. 25 do.	—	—	1 2 6	1 2 6	—	—	—	}
Adjutant	0 13 0	0 10 0	0 10 0	§0 3 6	†0 10 8	0 ‡8 6	0 10 0	0 6 6
Quar. Mast. { On Appointment	0 9 6	0 6 6	0 8 6	0 6 6	}			
Quar. Mast. After 10 years' service	—	0 8 6	0 10 6	0 8 0	} 10 10	0 7 10	0 8 0	0 4 8
Quar. Mast. 15 do.	—	0 10 0	0 13 0	0 10 0	} 0			
Surgeon Major	—	0 18 9	—	—	— 0	—		—
Surgeon	0 13 0	0 13 0	0 13 0	0 13 0	— 0	0 13 0	—	1 0 0
After 10 years' service*	0 15 0	0 15 0	0 15 0	0 15 0	—	0 15 0	—	—
20 do.	0 19 0	0 19 0	0 19 0	0 19 0	—	0 19 0	—	—
25 do.	1 2 0	1 2 0	1 2 0	1 2 0	—	1 2 0	—	—
Assist. Surg.	0 8 6	0 7 6	0 8 6	0 7 6	—	0 7 6	—	0 8 0
After 10 years' service*	0 11 0	0 10 0	0 11 0	0 10 0	— 0	0 10 0	—	—
Veter. Surg.	0 8 0	—	0 8 0	—	01 0 0	—	—	—
After 3 years' serv.*	0 10 0	—	0 10 0	—	0 12 0	—	—	—
10 do.	0 12 0	—	0 12 0	—	0 15 0	—	—	—
20 do.	0 15 0	—	0 15 0	—	—	—	—	—

* In the Army in any capacity as a Medical Officer on Full Pay. † If 2d Capt. 17*s.* 9*d.* ‡ If 2d Capt. 12*s.* 9*d.*
§ In addition to the pay as a Subaltern.

STAFF COMMISSARIAT DEPARTMENT.

	£ s. d.		£ s. d.
Commissary General	4 14 11	Assistant Comm. Gen.	0 14 3
Deputy Comm. Gen.	1 8 6	Dep. Ass. Comm. Gen.	0 9 6

MEDICAL DEPARTMENT.

RANKS.	After 25 Years' actual Service.	After 20 but under 25 Years' actual Service.	After 10 but under 20 Years' actual Service.	Under 10 Years' actual Service.
	£ s. d.	£ s. d.	£ s. d.	£ s. d.
Inspector-General	2 0 0	1 18 0	1 16 0	....
Deputy Inspector-General	1 10 0	1 8 0	1 4 0	....
Staff Surgeon	1 4 0	1 2 0	0 19 0	....
Regimental Surgeon and Staff Surgeon, 2nd Class	1 2 0	0 19 0	0 15 0	0 13 0
Assistant Surgeon	0 10 0	0 10 0	0 10 0	0 7 6

N. B.—A Medical Officer hereafter promoted will be required to serve upon the minimum Pay of his new Rank *One Year*, if he was in the Medical Department prior to 29th July 1830; and *Two Years*, if he received his first Medical Commission subsequently to that date, unless he had higher Pay in his old Rank than such minimum, in which case he must serve the above period upon that *Rate of Pay* which may be next above his former Pay, before he can receive any Increase.

MEDICAL DEPARTMENT ON HALF PAY.

		Rates of Half Pay after a Service on Full Pay of 30 Years.	25 but under 30 Years.	20 but under 25 Years.	10 but under 20 Years.	Less than 10 Years.
	£ s. d.	£ s. d.	£ s. d.	£ s. d.	£ s. d.	£ s. d.
Inspector-General	..	*1 10 0	1 5 0	1 0 0	..	..
	..	†1 0 0	0 15 0	0 12 0	..	..
Deputy do.	..	*1 0 0	0 17 0	0 14 0	0 10 6	0 8 0
	..	†0 18 0	0 14 0	0 10 0	0 8 0	0 7 0
Staff Surgeon	..	*0 17 0	0 15 0	0 12 6	0 10 0	0 7 6
	..	†0 16 0	0 13 0	0 9 6	0 7 6	0 6 6
Regimental Surgeon and Staff Surgeon, 2nd Class	..	*0 15 0	0 13 0	0 11 0	0 8 6	0 6 0
	..	†0 15 0	0 11 6	0 8 0	0 6 0	0 5 6
Assistant Surgeon	..	*0 7 6	0 7 0	0 6 0	0 5 0	0 4 0
	..	†0 7 0	0 6 0	0 5 0	0 4 0	0 3 0
Apothecary	0 5 0	0 7 6	0 7 6	0 7 6	..	..
Purveyor	0 10 0	..	..	..	..	..
Deputy Purveyor	0 5 0	..	..	..	..	..
Hospital Assistant	0 2 0	..	..	..	..	..

* If placed on Half Pay on reduction. † If placed on Half Pay from any other cause.

REGIMENTAL RANK.	Old Rate Cavalry £	s.	d.	Old Rate Infant. £	s.	d.	New Rate Cavalry £	s.	d.	New Rate Infant. £	s.	d.
Colonel	0	13	0	0	12	0	0	15	[illegible]	0	14	6
Lieutenant-Colonel (20 *to receive £100 per annum in addition to Half Pay, but they must be Brevet Colonels, and have served thirty years on Full Pay*)	0	10	0	0	8	6	0	12	6	0	11	0
Major	0	8	0	0	7	6	0	10	[illegible]	0	9	6
Captain	0	5	6	0	5	0	0	7	6	0	7	0
Lieutenant	0	3	0	0	2	4	0	4	8	0	4	0
Do. above Seven Years standing	—			—			—			0	4	6
Do. of Five Years standing, and if at the Battle of Waterloo	—			—			0	5	2	—		
Cornet, 2d Lieutenant, or Ensign	0	2	6	0	1	10	0	3	[illegible]	0	3	0
Paymaster* above 5 and under 10 years actual service as Paymaster†	—			—			0	6	0	0	6	0
——10 —— 15	—			—			0	7	6	0	7	6
——15 —— 20	—			—			0	10	0	0	10	0
——20 years actual service as Paymaster	—			—			0	12	6	0	12	6
Adjutant,	—			—			0	4	0	0	4	0
Quarter Master‡ under 3 Years Service§	—			—			0	2	6	0	2	6
Above 3 and under 7	—			—			0	3	0	0	3	0
—— 7 —— 12	—			—			0	4	0	0	4	0
——12 Years as Quarter Master, after 20 Years total Service, but under 30 Years	—			—			0	5	0	0	5	0
Above 12 Years as Quarter Master, after 30 Years total Service	—			—			0	6	0	0	6	0
Veterinary Surgeon under 6 Years Service (*temporary*)	—			—			0	3	[illegible]	—		
Above 6 and under 10 Years	—			—			0	4	6	—		
——10 —— 20	—			—			0	5	6	—		
——20 —— 25	—			—			0	7	0	—		
——25 —— 30	—			—			0	8	0	—		
——30 Years Service	—			—			0	12	0	—		

N.B.—Lieutenants and Captains of the Foot Guards, 7s.—Ensigns and Lieutenants, 4s.

STAFF.—Commissary Gen. 29s. 8d. Dep. do. 14s. 8d. Assistant do. 7s. 4d. Dep. do. 4s. 11d. Chaplain under 6 Years Service (*temporary*), 5s. Ditto under 15 Years Service, 5s. Above 15 and under 20, 7s. 6d. Above 20 and under 30, 10s. Above 30 Years Service, 16s.

* If of less than 5 Years' actual service as Paymaster, the Half Pay of his former Commission.

† Or the Half Pay of his former Commission.

N.B.—Previous Service of 10 Years' duration or upwards, on Full Pay in other Ranks as a Commissioned Officer, after the Paymaster shall have completed 15 Years' actual Service as such, to reckon as equivalent to 5 Years' Service as Paymaster.

‡ If appointed from any other Commission in the Army, and retiring before having completed 7 Years' Service as Quarter-Master, the Half Pay of his former Commission.

§ If he shall have previously served 3 Years as a Non-commissioned Officer.

RATES OF HALF-PAY FOR THE ROYAL ARTILLERY AND ROYAL ENGINEERS.

Rank	s.	d.	Rank	s.	d.	Rank	s.	d.
Lieutenant Colonel	11	8	First Lieut. above seven years	4	8	Resident Surgeon	[illegible]	0
Major	10	1	Second Lieut	3	2½	Surgeon	7	[illegible]
Captain	7	4	Quarter-Master	4	8	First Assistant Surgeon	4	0
First Lieutenant	4	2	Surgeon-General	20	0	Second do.	3	[illegible]

PRICES OF COMMISSIONS.

RANK.	Full Price of Commissions. l.	s.	Difference in value between the several Commissions in succession. l.	s.	Difference in value between Full and Half-pay. l.	s.	d.
Life Guards.							
Lieutenant-Colonel	7250	0	1900	0			
Major	5350	0	1850	0			
Captain	3500	0	1715	0			
Lieutenant	1785	0	525	0			
Cornet	1260	0					
Royal Regiment of Horse Guards.							
Lieutenant-Colonel	7250	0	1900	0			
Major	5350	0	1850	0			
Captain	3500	0	1900	0			
Lieutenant	1600	0	400	0			
Cornet	1200	0					
Dragoon Guards and Dragoons.							
Lieutenant-Colonel	6175	0	1600	0	[illegible]	0	[illegible]
Major	4575	0	1350	0	[illegible]	[illegible]	[illegible]
Captain	3225	0	2035	0	1084	8	4
Lieutenant	1190	0	350	0	[illegible]	13	4
Cornet	840	0			[illegible]	0	[illegible]
Foot Guards.							
Lieutenant-Colonel	9000	0	700	0			
Major, with rank of Colonel	8300	0	3500	0			
Captain, with rank of Lieut-Colonel	4800	0	2750	0			
Lieutenant, with rank of Captain	2050	0	850	0			
Ensign, with rank of Lieutenant	1200	0					
Regiments of the Line.							
Lieutenant-Colonel	4500	0	1300	0	1214	0	0
Major	3200	0	1400	0	[illegible]	[illegible]	[illegible]
Captain	1800	0	1100	0	511	0	0
Lieutenant	700	0	250	0	[illegible]	0	0
Ensign	450	0			180	[illegible]	0
Fusilier Regiments and Rifle Corps.							
First Lieutenant	700	0	200	0	[illegible]	0	[illegible]
Second Lieutenant	500	0			[illegible]	[illegible]	[illegible]

OFFICERS

ON THE

RETIRED FULL PAY, AND HALF PAY,

INCLUDING

THE ROYAL REGIMENT OF ARTILLERY, CORPS OF ROYAL ENGINEERS, ROYAL MARINES, STAFF, AND MILITARY DEPARTMENTS.

N.B. *Officers whose names are in Italics are on retired full pay.*

Officers above the rank of CAPTAIN *will be found in the list of Field Officers, at the beginning of the book, according to the dates of their Rank in the Army.*

CAPTAINS.

	CORNET, 2d LIEUT. or ENSIGN.	LIEUT.	CAPTAIN.	WHEN PLACED ON HALF PAY.
Abbott, Christopher,[1] Royal Marines	11 Mar. 95	27 Jan. 96	18 July 05	26 Aug. 14
Adair, Johan Hein,[2] Unattached	19 Sept. 06	28 Sept. 09	6 Jan. 24	15 May 35
Adams, Edward, Unattached	9 April 25	31 Dec. 28	24 Feb. 38	8 Oct. 47
Adams, George, 21 Foot	4 Dec. 99	26 July 04	15 Feb. 10	18 Jan. 21
Adams, Michael Goold, Unattached	21 July 25	30 July 29	28 Dec. 38	31 Dec. 44
𝕻 *Agnew, Thos. Ramsden,*[3] 2 R. Vet. Bat. *Deputy Storekeeper at Tipner*	19 Dec. 07	12 Oct. 09	22 June 15	
*Ainsworth, John, 128 Foot............	never	never	7 Dec. 99	
𝕻 Alexander, Henry,[4] R. Staff Corps....	13 June 11	26 Aug. 13	13 Aug. 25	15 Jan. 29
Allen, Charles Davers, Unattached	17 Sept. 12	20 May 13	2 April 41	27 Dec. 42
𝕻 *Allen, John Penn, 1 Prov. Bn. of Mil.	never	never	25 Dec. 13	1814
*Allen, Robert, 5 Foot	never	never	25 Dec. 13	25 Sept. 14
𝕻 Alpe, Hamond, 18 Dragoons	11 Feb. 08	12 April 09	13 Jan. 20	15 Nov. 21
Andrews, Charles, Unattached..........	21 Mar. 11	23 June 14	27 Aug. 25	27 Aug. 25
Andros, William,[5] Unattached	24 Sept. 12	18 May 14	16 June 25	10 Aug. 32
Antill, Henry Colden, New Bruns. Fen...	31 Aug. 96	5 May 99	11 Jan. 09	5 April 21
Anton, Alexander, 8 West India Regt. ..	14 Sept. 04	25 Dec. 04	29 Feb. 16	25 Sept. 17
𝕻 *Appleton, William,*[6] 1 R. Vet. Batt.	30 June 01	12 Nov. 03	20 Sept. 10	
Arbuthnott, John, *Viscount*, Irish Brigade	27 Mar. 01	21 April 03	28 Aug. 04	
Arbuthnott, *Hon.* John, Unattached	23 June 25	8 April 26	25 June 30	25 June 30
𝕻 Archdall, Henry, 84 Foot	25 Sept. 04	14 Nov. 05	26 Aug. 13	23 April 18
Armstrong, John, 37 Foot	25 Mar. 05	28 April 06	10 Mar. 14	25 May 17
𝕻 Armstrong, John, 88 Foot	7 Aug. 03	26 Sept. 04	5 Jan. 15	25 Mar. 16
Armstrong, John, 12 R. Veteran Batt. ..	24 Mar. 95	1 June 97	15 Dec. 04	
𝕻 Armstrong, Robert,[7] 23 Dragoons	2 April 07	20 April 09	13 Feb. 27	20 Nov. 35
Askew, Thomas, Waller's Corps	Feb. 93	26 June 93	26 Feb. 94	
Atchison, Henry Alexander, Unattached..	7 April 25	7 Aug. 28	27 Feb. 35	12 July 44
Austen, Hen. Edmund, Sub. Insp. of Mil. *Adjutant, 1st R. Surrey Militia*....	10 June 26	27 Sept. 33	29 July 36	26 April 44
Aytoun, Marriot Chad. W., R. Artillery ..	3 Dec. 03	1 May 04	22 July 12	10 April 25
Baby, Anthony Duperon, Bourbon Regt.	April 01	14 May 01	27 Jan. 12	21 Aug. 16
Bace, Henry William, Unattached	15 Feb. 33	27 July 36	7 July 48	7 July 48
𝕻 Bace, William,[8] Unattached	9 Feb. 09	2 Oct. 11	10 Mar. 43	10 Mar. 43
𝕻 𝖂 Bacon, Cæsar, 23 Dragoons......	10 June 13	14 Oct. 13	10 July 17	25 Jan. 18
Bailey, Charles, Royal Engineers	25 April 26	21 June 30	23 Nov. 41	15 Nov. 43
Baillie, James, Unattached	28 Nov. 34	31 Dec. 39	3 Oct. 48	3 Oct. 48
Baines, Cuthbert A., Unattached, *Adj. 1st West York Militia*	12 June 28	8 Oct. 30	6 Mar. 40	21 April 46
Baker, George Granville, Unattached....	1 Aug. 34	23 July 38	18 Aug. 48	18 Aug. 48
Baker, Robert, 57 Foot................	31 Jan. 05	22 May 06	10 Aug. 15	4 May 20
𝕻 Baker, William, 60 Foot	3 Dec. 02	19 Nov. 03	11 Oct. 10	22 Dec. 25
Balck, George Philip, Unattached	29 Oct. 29	17 April 35	1 June 38	26 June 38
𝕻 Baldwin, Anthony, 7 Foot	never	27 Aug. 07	3 June 13	25 Feb. 16
Baldwin, John Henry, Unattached	20 Dec. 21	7 July 25	10 Feb. 29	12 Aug. 34
Barbor, Robert Douglas, Unattached	15 Mar. 27	9 April 29	28 April 37	6 June 45
Barclay, Edward, Unattached	12 July 27	14 Feb. 34	3 Dec. 47	3 Dec. 47
Barlow, B., Unattached	12 Dec. 16	13 May 19	23 Aug. 39	23 Aug. 39
Barnard, Henry Gee, 1 Dragoon Guards..	22 May 06	10 Dec. 07	15 July 13	2 Feb. 15
Barnes, Richard Knowles, Royal Marines	6 Mar. 10	4 June 28	26 April 38	13 Nov. 40
Barrett, Knox, Unattached	10 Mar. 08	3 Jan. 10	25 May 26	5 April 27
Barwell, Osborne, Unattached	12 Sept. 11	2 April 12	1 Aug. 26	24 Jan. 28
Basset, Richard,[9] Royal Artillery........	11 Dec. 15	26 Nov. 24	10 Jan. 37	31 Dec. 42
𝕻 *Bates, Robt. Montelieu, 1 Prov. Bn. of Mil.	never	never	25 Dec. 13	1814
Battersbee, Thomas, Royal Engineers ..	20 Mar. 13	21 July 13	22 May 29	

	CORNET, ETC.	LIEUT.	CAPTAIN.	WHEN PLACED ON HALF PAY.
Battley, William D'Oyley, 2 Garrison Batt.	2 Apr. 29	22 Aug. 34	17 Nov. 40	12 Nov. 47
P W Baynes, Geo. Macleod,[10] R. Art. ..	4 April 07	1 Feb. 08	1 Aug. 27	25 Sept. 34
Bayntun, Charles, Queen's Rangers, *Barrack-Master at Brighton*	Mar. 98	15 Oct. 98	1 Feb. 98	
Beadon, Richard, 92 Foot.............	11 May 96	never	25 Nov. 99	1811
Beadon, Valentine,[11] Royal Marines	14 Feb. 11	6 Feb. 29	8 June 38	
Bean, Isaac, 28 Foot	9 July 03	1 Nov. 04	7 Nov. 05	
Beare, Wm. Gabbett, Unattached	28 Jan. 26	26 Oct. 26	22 May 35	29 May 35
P Beaufoy, Benjamin,[12] Unattached, *Staff Officer of Pensioners*	8 Mar. 10	8 Oct. 12	14 Aug. 40	14 Aug. 40
P Beavan, John Griffiths,[13] 96 Foot	2 June 12	3 Feb. 14	7 Aug. 28	15 Mar. 33
*Beckham, Horatio, 43 Foot	never	never	25 Dec. 13	25 Sept. 14
*Bell, James, 3 Prov. Bn. of Militia	never	never	25 Dec. 13	1814
Belson, George, Royal Marines	6 May 78	6 July 80	28 April 95	28 April 95
P Belton, Samuel, Unattached	10 July 06	16 May 08	30 Dec. 24	29 Dec. 25
Bennett, James, Unattached............	9 April 09	2 Dec. 13	20 Feb. 23	31 May 27
Bennett, Wm. R. Lyon Bennett, Unatt...	12 April 31	24 Dec. 33	4 Feb. 48	4 Feb. 48
Bentley, Alex. C. Downing, 7 Foot......	9 Apr. 25	17 Aug. 32	18 June 41	8 Jan. 47
Bentley, Charles Thomas, Unattached ...	30 May 34	11 Mar. 37	27 Oct. 48	27 Oct. 48
Beresford, *Sir* Geo. de la Poer, *Bt.* Unatt.	8 Mar. 27	14 Feb. 28	19 Feb. 36	19 Feb. 36
Beretze, Francis, 1 R. Veteran Batt.	23 Dec. 02	10 Oct. 05	1 Aug. 13	25 June 26
Bernard, Peter, Unattached	29 Jan. 24	11 Feb. 26	5 Nov. 29	17 May 31
Bernard, Thomas, Unattached..........	24 Apr. 35	26 Apr. 39	26 Apr. 44	3 Sept. 47
Bernard, William, Unattached..........	17 Nov. 25	25 Jan. 28	26 Jan. 41	14 Feb. 45
Bernard, *Hon.* Wm. Smyth, 1 Dr. Gds...	9 Nov. 09	16 Aug. 10	10 Aug. 15	25 May 16
Berners, William, Royal Artillery, *Barrack-Master at Croydon*	16 Dec. 16	29 July 25	10 Jan. 37	
Berry, James Parsons,[15] York Chasseurs	8 Jan. 07	26 Jan. 08	7 July 43	8 Sept. 46
*Bettesworth, Henry, 4 Foot	never	never	25 Dec. 13	25 Sept. 14
Bevan, Howe Curtis, Royal Artillery	5 May 25	12 Nov. 27	31 July 40	21 July 41
Beverhoudt, Adam,[16] 58 Foot	21 Oct. 13	9 April 16	29 April 36	
W Biddulph, Theophilus, 6 Dragoons ..	22 Dec. 04	22 May 06	14 Sept. 14	25 Mar. 16
Bignell, Richard Roe, Royal Marines	3 Mar. 97	3 July 03	1 June 10	2 June 21
P Birch, James,[17] R. Engineers	12 July 09	1 May 11	20 Dec. 14	24 Sept. 25
*Bischhoffshausen, C. *Baron,* For. C. of Wag.	never	never	6 July 15	25 Sept. 16
P Bishop, James, 23 Foot	25 May 04	23 Dec. 04	27 June 11	2 May 23
P W Black, James,[18] Unattached......	16 May 11	22 July 13	12 Sept. 48	12 Sept. 48
W Black, Samuel, Unattached	5 April 10	8 July 13	28 July 25	8 April 26
Blackall, John, 98 Foot	6 July 09	8 July 13	14 Nov. 16	25 Nov. 16
Blackall, John, 39 Foot	14 Oct. 12	4 May 14	1 June 38	
W Blacklin, Richard,[19] Unattached ..	18 July 15	13 July 20	8 Aug. 33	6 Feb. 46
Blacknore, Henry, 2 R. Veteran Batt...	6 July 96	2 April 98	29 April 03	
Bland, James,[20] Unattached	4 Sept. 04	25 Aug. 09	12 Feb. 26	23 Dec. 31
Blane, Robert, Unattached	1 Nov. 31	25 Mar. 36	8 June 38	28 Jan. 48
W Blathwayt, Geo. Wm., Unattached ..	25 Nov. 13	4 May 15	9 June 25	9 June 25
W Blennerhasset, Aldworth,[21] Unatt. ..	23 Mar. 14	5 Oct. 15	26 Aug. 34	19 Jan. 38
Bloomfield, Edwin, 10 Foot............	13 Aug. 04	23 April 05	15 April 13	6 July 26
Blyth, Augustus Fred., 6 West India Regt.	19 Jan. 26	29 Aug. 26	5 April 33	20 June 34
Boldero, Henry Geo., Unattached	1 Aug. 14	1 July 15	31 Dec. 27	17 Dec. 30
Bolton, Philip, Unattached	6 July 09	25 July 11	10 Sept. 47	10 Sept. 47
**Bonavita, Vicenzo,* R. Malta Fenc. Regt.	24 Oct. 23	25 Jan. 25	2 Jan. 40	
Bond, Adolphus Fred., R. Staff Corps, *Staff Officer of Pensioners*	3 April 28	29 June 32	12 Oct. 38	28 July 43
Bonner, John, Ogle's Recruiting Corps ..	4 May 01	5 Jan. 04	18 July 09	
Boteler, Robert, R. Engineers	11 May 25	20 Oct. 26	15 Aug. 40	9 Mar. 41
Boulton, Richard, Coldstream Guards ..	11 April 94	never	13 July 97	25 Dec. 02
Bowen, John Watts, 56 Foot	19 Feb. 07	28 Jan. 08	12 May 14	1814
Bowles, Henry Oldfield, Unattached	4 Dec. 35	19 June 40	31 May 44	15 Jan. 47
Boyes, Robert Nairne,[22] 3 W. India Regt. *Barrack-Master at Grahamstown* ..	26 May 14	8 June 15	9 Aug. 31	2 Aug. 33
Boys, Henry, Unattached	8 April 26	13 Feb. 30	6 Sept. 33	26 Oct. 41
Brackenbury, John, 38 Foot	19 Nov. 03	28 Nov. 05	15 Oct. 18	10 June 23
Bradley, Wm. Brown, 104 Foot	9 July 03	27 July 04	16 April 12	25 July 17
W Brander, Tho. Coventry,[23] 59 Foot ..	27 June 11	30 Mar. 14	1 June 39	28 Feb. 40
Brannan, James, Unattached	6 June 16	25 Dec. 23	25 July 45	25 July 45
Bremer, Henry, Royal Marines	22 Mar. 28	7 Sept. 36	7 April 46	6 May 47
Brett, William, Unattached	11 April 94	23 Jan. 12	26 May 25	16 June 25

	CORNET, ETC.	LIEUT.	CAPTAIN.	WHEN PLACED ON HALF PAY.
Bridge, Robert Onslow, Royal Marines ..	2 April 22	12 Oct. 32	12 Feb. 42	16 Aug. 44
*Bridge, Samuel, 82 Foot..............	never	never	2 Dec. 99	1800
Briggs, Abraham, 5 Foot	26 Feb. 07	29 Feb. 08	8 April 25	26 May 25
Brinckman, John Richard, Unattached ..	8 July 19	24 Oct. 21	23 July 25	25 Oct. 27
Broadley, Edward Osborne, Unattached, *Staff Officer of Pensioners*	15 Aug. 26	29 Sept. 29	28 Sept. 39	25 Feb. 42
Brodie, Hugh,[24] 2 R. Veteran Batt.	11 Jan. 05	2 July 06	8 Sept. 14	
Brown, Hugh, Royal Marines..........	12 Feb. 06	16 Jan. 12	10 Feb. 34	
Brown, James Montagu, Unattached	17 Apr. 28	14 Oct. 36	1 Jan. 47	1 Jan. 47
Brown, Nathaniel, 62 Foot	30 June 04	27 Mar. 05	2 Jan. 17	25 June 17
P W Brown, Thomas,[25] 79 Foot	23 Oct. 06	15 Dec. 07	20 July 15	25 Feb. 16
Browne, Brotherton, Unattached........	1 Sept. 11	1 Sept. 13	8 April 26	8 April 26
Browne, David, 8 R. Veteran Battalion	May 99	11 Aug. 99	24 Nov. 07	
Browne, Lawrence, 4 Ceylon Regt.......	5 Oct. 04	1 Aug. 05	13 Mar. 10	18 Sept. 16
Browne, Peter Rutledge Montague, Unatt.	31 Oct. 11	24 Dec. 12	29 Aug. 26	28 June 31
P Browne, *Hon.* Thomas,[26] 16 Dragoons	6 Aug. 07	14 July 08	12 Aug. 12	25 Mar. 16
Browne, William, 24 Dragoons	16 Aug. 99	28 April 04	30 May 09	9 Dec. 19
Brutton, John, Royal Marines	15 Mar. 08	19 July 21	11 April 36	
Buchanan, John Grahame, Unattached ..	15 Feb. 16	9 April 25	2 Aug. 39	2 Aug. 39
Bulkeley, Charles, Unattached	14 April 19	19 April 22	31 May 25	24 Feb. 32
Bulkeley, Lempster, Unattached........	8 April 25	29 May 28	9 Jan. 35	28 May 36
Bull, Frederick G. 60 Foot	25 Oct. 27	8 Feb. 31	23 Nov. 38	18 Aug. 48
P W Burges, Som. Wald.,[27] 5 W. India R.	1 Oct. 12	never	20 Oct. 14	8 May 17
Burke, Alexander,[28] Unattached	8 Mar. 10	5 Nov. 12	20 Feb. 35	1 April 36
P Burke, Edmund, R. York Chasseurs ..	29 Oct. 12	21 Oct. 13	10 Nov. 15	3 Aug. 20
Burnaby, Edwin, Unattached	4 Nov. 19	12 June 23	8 April 26	12 Oct. 26
Burnett, Rich. Parry, Vet. Company....	10 July 99	5 May 00	13 June 05	1 Nov. 16
P Burton, John Curson,[29] Royal Artillery	4 April 07	1 Feb. 08	6 Nov. 27	25 Nov. 33
Burton, Joseph,[30] 37 Foot..............	5 Oct. 04	4 Nov. 05	21 April 14	19 Oct. 20
Busche, George, 26 Dragoons..........	never	never	13 Sept. 98	25 June 02
Butler, Richard Alexander, Unattached..	29 July 19	25 Sept. 23	10 Sept. 25	5 Nov. 29
P W Butler, Theobald, Unattached	8 Oct. 06	28 April 08	28 Nov. 34	28 Nov. 34
Butt, John Wells, Unattached..........	16 Jan. 16	2 Mar. 26	20 Nov. 40	28 July 43
Bygrave, Joseph, Unattached	never	never	25 Dec. 13	8 May 28
Caffin, Wm. Geo. Chart, Royal Artillery	16 Dec. 25	30 June 28	18 Mar. 41	14 April 41
P Cameron, John,[31] Unattached........	3 April 06	11 May 07	26 May 14	21 Aug. 35
Cameron, William, 18 Dragoons........	6 Aug. 03	14 Dec. 04	6 Nov. 11	6 Nov. 17
Campbell, Alexander, Royal Marines ..	4 July 03	15 Aug. 05	31 July 26	
Campbell, Duncan, Royal Marines......	21 May 96	4 Mar. 00	27 July 06	22 Oct. 19
Campbell, John, 74 Foot..............	16 Sept. 13	28 Sept. 20	15 Dec. 37	
Campbell, John,[35] 96 Foot	2 April 12	1 April 13	26 Dec. 25	10 Sept. 30
P Campbell, John, 91 Foot............	6 June 05	23 Aug. 07	19 May 14	25 Feb. 16
Campbell, Patrick Scott, Royal Artillery	19 May 28	19 Jan. 30	14 April 41	
P Campbell, William,[36] Unattached	28 Feb. 11	25 June 12	12 April 27	28 June 31
Capadose, Henry, Unattached..........	26 Feb. 28	17 May 34	29 Dec. 46	29 Dec. 46
Capel, Sydney Aug., 51 F. *Qr. M.* 11 Oct. 33, *Staff Officer of Pensioners*	7 July 37	25 May 39	30 July 44	1 May 46
Cardew, Christopher B. Unattached	27 Dec. 33	17 Mar. 38	21 April 46	1 Aug. 48
Carloss, John Baxter, 96 Foot..........	11 Sept. 06	29 Sept. 09	7 April 25	15 Mar. 33
P Carnegie, W. F. Lindsay,[38] Royal Art.	22 Dec. 03	20 July 04	1 July 13	1 Dec. 19
Carpenter, Digby Thomas, 61 Foot	23 Mar. 96	22 July 97	18 Aug. 08	6 July 15
Carr, Ralph,[39] Royal Marines	9 April 12	17 Mar. 31	13 Nov. 40	5 Mar. 41
P Carruthers, William,[40] Unattached, *Town Major, Cape of Good Hope..*	22 May 12	1 Dec. 13	1 Jan. 42	22 July 42
Cartan, William, Unattached, *Staff Officer of Pensioners*	17 July 15	12 Dec. 22	31 Aug. 38	31 Aug. 38
Carter, John Money, Unatt. *Adjutant Monmouth Militia*	18 May 32	7 Aug. 35	18 Sept. 39	21 April 46
Cary, William Lucius, Unattached	11 Jan. 15	*25 Dec 13 3 May 15	26 May 25	20 Jan. 32
Cassidy, Francis P. Unattached	25 Nov. 28	13 Dec. 31	10 Nov. 48	10 Nov. 48
Castieau, Thos. James, Unattached......	3 Mar. 14	7 April 25	23 Oct. 35	25 Aug. 37
Cater, Thomas Hicks,[41] Royal Marines..	12 Oct. 09	6 Mar. 28	27 Dec. 37	
Cathcart, *Hon.* Adolphus F., Unattached	7 Nov. 22	9 June 25	13 July 32	27 July 32
P Caulfield, Daniel,[42] 7 Foot	4 April 05	18 June 07	20 May 23	14 Sept. 32
P Chaloner, John, Independent Company	14 June 00	12 Nov. 03	11 Feb. 08	21 June 13

	Ensign, etc.	Lieut.	Captain.	When placed on half pay.
Chancellor, John, 61 Foot	30 Jan. 06	19 May 07	14 Sept. 09	10 July 23
Chapman, John James,[43] Royal Artillery	13 Sept. 05	1 June 06	21 April 20	2 June 29
P *Chapman, Joseph*, 1 R. Vet. Batt.	23 Jan. 00	6 June 04	9 Mar. 09	
Charlewood, John, Unattached	23 April 29	1 Aug. 34	6 Sept. 39	7 June 44
Charlton, Saint John, 14 Dragoons	10 Feb. 14	10 Nov. 14	12 Oct. 20	25 Oct. 21
Chatterton, Oliver Nicolls, Unattached	26 July 33	5 Aug. 36	15 Aug. 48	15 Aug. 48
Chawner, Edward Hoare, Unattached	9 June 25	10 June 26	7 Sept. 32	7 Sept. 32
Cheape, John, 95 Foot	17 June 77	28 Dec. 78	14 April 80	1783
*Cheape, John, 5 Garrison Battalion	never	never	9 July 03	1805
Chepmell, Charles, Unattached	May 04	23 Nov. 04	1 Oct. 12	25 April 26
Chesshire, Edward, 49 Foot	20 Oct. 96	11 May 97	15 Dec. 04	24 Sept. 12
Chichester, Arthur, Liverpool Regt.	27 Sept. 01	14 Jan. 02	12 Dec. 05	19 Mar. 07
Chichester, Arthur Charles, Unattached	12 Dec. 26	10 Nov. 29	3 April 35	8 Aug. 45
Chisholm, Andrew, Unattached	18 June 07	3 Aug. 09	14 May 29	30 June 34
P W *Chisholm, Donald*,[44] R. Vet. Batt.		10 Oct. 05	20 July 15	
Christie, Fred. Gordon, Unattached, *Staff Officer of Pensioners*	8 Apr. 34	20 July 38	30 May 45	9 Apr. 47
Christie, Napier Turner, Unattached	5 April 21	10 Sept. 25	1 Aug. 26	23 Oct. 35
Christie, Thomas, 99 Foot		14 Aug. 00	3 April 01	
Churchill, Edward William, Royal Marines	1 May 12	19 May 31	13 Nov. 40	30 June 41
Clare, Louis, Unattached	10 Sept. 12	26 Jan. 14	10 May 44	10 May 44
W Clark, Pryce,[45] Unattached	2 Mar. 15	27 June 22	16 July 23	8 April 46
Clayfield, Edward Ireland, Unattached	19 July 15	28 Mar. 22	17 Sept. 25	17 Sept. 25
Cleather, Edward John, R. Staff Corps	15 Oct. 12	22 Oct. 17	24 Aug. 32	24 Aug. 32
Clements, Wm. *Viscount*, Unattached, *Colonel of Leitrim Militia*	9 Dec. 24	31 Oct. 26	5 April 31	20 Mar. 35
P W Clerke, *Sir* Wm. H., *Bt.*,[46] 42 Foot	10 Jan. 11	25 July 11	25 April 22	2 May 23
Clinton, *Lord* Tho. Cha. Pelham, Unatt.	16 May 34	24 June 37	16 June 43	25 June 44
Clive, Edward, Unattached	27 April 15	21 Jan. 19	23 June 25	22 May 28
P Close, Charles,[47] Royal Artillery	28 April 04	13 Oct. 04	17 Dec. 13	23 April 24
P W *Cochrane, Robert*,[48] Rifle Brigade, *Military Knight of Windsor*	9 Nov. 09	8 May 12	22 May 28	
Cochrane, Robt. Mortimer,[49] Glengarry Fen.	17 Nov. 08	25 Dec. 10	6 Feb. 12	1 Nov. 36
Cockburn, James, Unat., *Staff Of. of Pen.*	12 April 27	23 Aug. 33	8 June 38	21 Feb. 40
P Cockburne, Wm. Horace,[50] Unattached	10 April 09	25 June 12	2 June 25	27 Dec. 27
Cocker, Barnard William, Unattached	23 May 16	27 April 20	8 April 26	24 May 28
Coddington, Joshua, Royal Engineers	25 April 26	8 June 29	23 Nov. 41	
Colby, Henry Augustus,[51] R. Engineers	12 July 08	24 June 09	2 Sept. 13	
Cole, *Hon.* Henry Arthur, Unattached	17 Jan. 28	12 Feb. 30	6 Mar. 35	3 July 41
Collis, Peter, Unattached	11 Mar. 12	14 June 15	3 Feb. 32	28 Aug. 38
Colman, Thomas, Unattached	28 May 07	26 July 08	26 Oct. 30	27 May 36
P W Colthurst, J. R.,[53] Sub. Insp. of Mil.	12 Nov. 07	13 Oct. 09	29 Sept. 25	25 June 30
P Colthurst, Nicholas, Unattached	27 Nov. 06	29 Mar. 08	25 Oct. 14	11 June 30
P Colvile, Frederick,[54] Scots Fusilier Gds.	22 Sept. 08	never	9 Dec. 13	25 Feb. 19
Colville, Charles John, Unattached	27 May 36	21 Feb. 41	31 May 44	13 July 47
Connop, Henry, Cape Regiment	2 Sept. 19	10 Feb. 25	22 April 26	26 April 27
Conolly, James, Unattached	17 June 36	28 Nov. 37	14 Mar. 45	30 Mar. 47
Conrady, Martinus,[55] Unattached	30 April 13	28 Sept. 18	26 Nov. 29	20 Nov. 38
Conroy, *Sir* John, *Bt.*, KCH., R. Artillery	8 Sept. 03	12 Sept. 03	13 Mar. 11	17 June 22
Cook, Jervis, Royal Marines	26 May 06	28 Oct. 12	27 May 34	
Cook, Wm. Surtees, Unatt., *Adjutant 1st Somerset Militia*	27 June 34	5 Jan. 39	30 Dec. 45	28 April 46
*Cooke, John, 56 Foot	never	never	25 Dec. 13	1814
*Cooper, Robert Henry, 2 Pr. Bn. of Mil.	never	never		1814
Coote, Chidley, Unattached	never	9 June 14	14 July 25	20 June 26
Cornelius, Richard Longfield, R. Artillery	5 July 13	4 July 16	4 April 35	30 Mar. 44
Corsy, Charles Juste de, 96 Foot	3 Mar. 03		6 Sept. 06	1811
P Costley, Theoph. Byers, 45 Foot	9 May 06	1 Jan. 07	7 Oct. 13	1814
Costobadie, James Palliser, Unattached	21 Sept. 32	28 June 36	23 Feb. 44	10 Mar. 48
Cotton, Edward Antonius,[56] R. Artillery	1 July 06	1 Feb. 08	29 July 25	29 July 25
Couche, Thomas, 103 Foot	9 Oct. 00	29 Nov. 01	17 Oct. 05	26 Dec. 17
Cowper, *Hon.* Wm. Francis, Unattached, *A Lord of the Admiralty*	31 Dec. 27	24 Feb. 32	25 Dec. 35	25 Dec. 35
P Cox, Charles, 41 Foot	17 Sept. 03	16 May 05	14 April 08	9 Nov. 15
Cox, Charles, 87 Foot	14 Feb. 05	9 Oct. 06	1 April 13	2 July 18

	2D LIEUT. ETC.	LIEUT.	CAPTAIN.	WHEN PLACED ON HALF PAY.
Cox, John George, 40 Foot	6 Aug. 03	25 Jan. 04	20 Feb. 11	8 July 19
Cox, John Hamilton, Unattached	10 Oct. 34	11 July 37	31 Mar. 48	31 Mar. 48
Cox, Joseph Lucas, Unattached	4 July 05	19 Mar. 07	20 Sept. 24	13 Jan. 25
Cracknell, James Thos., Royal Marines	17 Aug. 07	19 June 21	26 Oct. 35	
Cradock, Adam Williamson, 15 Foot	9 July 03	21 Mar. 05	7 Oct. 12	25 Nov. 14
Craigie, John, 47 Foot	3 Oct. 05	15 April 06	2 Dec. 13	1814
Cranfield, George Darley, Unattached ..	16 June 06	12 May 07	7 April 25	14 Sept. 26
Cremer, James Smith, Royal Artillery ..	7 July 17	29 July 25	2 June 37	4 May 40
Crichton, John, Hangers' Recruiting Corps	2 April 88	25 Jan. 92	26 April 98	
Crofton, Walter Fred., Royal Artillery ..	21 June 33	25 May 36	17 Jan. 45	1 Feb. 45
Crosbie, *Sir* William, *Bart.*, Unattached	4 Mar. 13	13 July 15	24 Feb. 17	1 June 26
Cross, William Jennings, Unattached....	1 April 19	1 Dec. 25	29 Aug. 26	29 Aug. 26
Crowther, Richard J. F., Royal Marines	2 Dec. 98	18 Aug. 04	19 July 21	
Cruice, Edmund John, Unattached......	9 April 25	13 June 30	5 April 44	3 Mar. 48
Cudbertson, John, 45 Foot	5 Oct. 04	8 Oct. 06	17 Mar. 14	21 Sept. 15
Cuddy, Alexander Daniel, Unattached ..	10 Oct. 22	18 May 26	13 Dec. 39	9 April 41
Cumberlege, Charles Lushington, Unatt.	12 Dec. 16	29 July 19	3 Oct. 34	17 June 42
Cumberland, Bentinck Harry, Meuron's R.	19 Aug. 19	13 Oct. 25	14 Nov. 26	9 Oct. 40
Cuppage, Alexander, Unattached	25 Aug. 09	29 Dec. 12	28 Mar. 16	11 June 30
Currie, George Alfred, Unattached	1 Sept. 25	16 Mar. 32	24 Nov. 43	23 Feb. 44
Curtis, Henry,[60] Royal Artillery	22 Dec. 03	20 July 04	25 Jan. 13	21 April 21
Cust, *Hon.* Peregrine Fra.,[61] 3 Dr. Gds.	31 Mar. 08	3 May 10	17 Oct. 11	25 Mar. 16
Custance, Neville, 1 R. Veteran Batt.....	2 July 12	9 Sept. 13	15 June 26	12 Oct. 26
Daintry, Michael, Unattached	22 June 20	9 June 25	10 Feb. 29	10 Feb. 29
D'Arcey, Edward, 6 Royal Veteran Battalion, *Captain of Invalids, Royal Hospital, Kilmainham*	13 April 09	22 Aug. 10	3 Aug. 15	
D'Arcy, John, Veteran Company........	3 Mar. 08	29 April 08	8 April 25	8 Oct. 31
D'Arcy, Judge Thos., 4 R. Vet. Batt. ..	31 Dec. 94	26 Sept. 95	11 May 08	
Darroch, Donald G. Angus,[63] Unattached	22 Mar. 33	26 Aug. 36	15 April 42	17 Mar. 48
Davern, John,[64] 27 Foot, *Captain of Invalids, Royal Hospital, Chelsea*..	27 Mar. 06	11 Nov. 07	31 Aug. 15	8 June 30
Davies, Arthur, Unattached	22 Nov. 21	17 Feb. 25	3 Oct. 26	3 Oct. 26
Davies, David,[65] Unattached	16 April 07	18 June 07	19 July 15	24 July 28
*Davies, John, 4 Foot	never	never	27 Nov. 99	25 Dec. 99
Davies, John, Royal Artillery	4 April 08	20 June 09	6 Nov. 27	9 Sept. 34
Davies, Joseph, Unattached...........	3 Dec. 25	14 Dec. 26	10 Mar. 42	3 June 42
Davis, Alfred,[66] Unattached............	21 Sept. 15	27 May 19	19 Jan. 26	13 Aug. 30
Davis, William,[67] Royal Marines	26 Feb. 07	23 Feb. 14	27 May 34	
Dawe, Charles, Unattached	28 Jan. 08	15 Feb. 10	1 Mar. 21	9 Jan. 29
Deacon, Charles Parke,[68] R. Artillery	1 April 02	12 Sept. 03	16 Dec. 08	1 Aug. 22
De Blaquiere, *Hon.* John,[66a] Unattached	30 Sept. 36	29 Jan. 39	20 Aug. 44	27 Oct. 46
De Burgh, Anth. Philip, Portuguese Ser.	7 Mar. 10	18 April 11	6 June 15	25 Dec. 16
De la Condamine, Thomas, Unattached ..	16 June 14	18 Mar. 25	15 June 32	15 June 32
Delancey, John, Unattached	27 Aug. 15	8 June 20	14 July 25	30 July 29
De Lisle, Hirzel Fred., Unattached......	23 Sept. 13	12 Feb. 24	22 April 26	14 Feb. 28
Delmont, Frederick, Royal Marines	8 June 96	11 Aug. 00	27 July 08	1 Jan. 16
D'Erp, Balthazar, *Baron*, 60 Foot	never	never	30 Dec. 07	
Despard, Philip Henry, Unattached	17 Mar. 25	22 Nov. 27	10 Feb. 43	10 Feb. 43
Des Vœux, *Sir* Charles, *Bart.*, 63 Foot..	5 Sept. 95	26 April 96	25 Dec. 02	21 April 04
Des Vœux, Henry, Unattached	8 April 25	9 Feb. 26	26 Nov. 29	22 Aug. 34
Devon, William Henry, Royal Marines	11 Feb. 06	15 Jan. 12	23 Dec. 33	
Dewell, Thomas,[69] Royal Artillery	14 Feb. 04	29 July 04	17 Dec. 14	1 Mar. 27
De Wend, James Douglas, 52 Foot, *Staff Officer of Pensioners*	29 April 24	17 Dec. 25	22 May 41	6 Dec. 44
Dick, John, 112 Foot	26 Sept. 95	24 June 96	19 Sept. 04	27 Oct. 08
Dickson, James Henry, Unattached	6 July 32	22 May 35	29 Dec. 43	30 Jan. 46
Dillon, Timothy,[70] 2 R. Vet. Battalion	25 Dec. 98	15 Dec. 00	12 May 13	
Dillon, William, Royal Staff Corps......	6 Aug. 12	18 April 16	19 April 31	24 July 31
Dixon, John, Unattached..............	10 Mar. 14	12 Feb. 18	5 Nov. 25	5 Nov. 25
*Dobbs, Francis, 12 Foot	never	never	25 Dec. 13	25 Sept. 14
*Dodsworth, Benja., 3 Prov. Bn. of Mil.	never	never	do	1814
Donelan, Anthony,[71] York Chasseurs, *Staff Officer of Pensioners*	9 April 25	7 Nov. 27	6 May 42	24 May 44
Donoughmore, J., *Earl of*, KP., Gr. Gds.	25 Sept. 07	never	19 Nov. 12	27 May 10

	CORNET, ETC.	LIEUT.	CAPTAIN.	WHEN PLACED ON HALF PAY.
Dore, Peter Luke,[72] Unattached, *Staff Officer of Pensioners*	8 April 13	21 Aug. 19	29 Aug. 38	13 Feb. 46
P Douglas, Arch. Murray, 52 Foot	20 Jan. 08	18 Feb. 09	28 April 14	25 Feb. 17
Douglas, Henry Hamilton, 78 Foot	12 Mar. 14	14 April 18	30 June 24	16 July 25
P Douglas, Joseph, Unattached	14 July 08	20 Dec. 10	8 April 26	14 Aug. 28
Dowdall, Aylmer,[73] 54 Foot	20 May 13	2 Mar. 17	2 May 29	
Dowland, John, 67 Foot	1 Nov. 04	28 Mar. 05	1 June 15	16 Nov. 18
Dowman, John,[74] Unattached	28 Sept. 30	21 Dec. 32	3 Sept. 47	3 Sept. 47
W Down, Richard, Unattached	7 Mar. 11	31 Mar. 14	29 Sept. 25	7 April 26
Downes, Wm. James, 11 Dragoons	10 Aug. 26	7 Sept. 32	22 Nov. 36	25 June 38
Drew, Richard Robinson, R. Artillery	4 June 10	10 Feb. 14	13 July 32	
P Drewry, Frederick George, 12 Foot	19 May 06	12 Oct. 09	10 Aug. 26	30 Sept. 36
W Dromgoole, N. Fleming, 35 Foot	1 Nov. 04	4 July 05	29 July 13	25 June 17
P W Drought, John Head, 93 Foot	3 Mar. 08	8 Sept. 08	10 Oct. 16	25 Mar. 17
Druitt, Edward, 37 Foot	18 Oct. 04	6 Mar. 06	3 Feb. 14	25 May 17
P Drummond, J. M'Gregor, 82 Foot	15 Dec. 08	23 May 11	4 Dec. 23	4 Dec. 23
P Drysdale, Alexander,[75] 27 Foot	1 July 04	10 Oct. 05	10 Feb. 14	27 Mar. 16
Du Bourdieu, John, 87 Foot	28 Feb. 28	8 July 34	20 Sept. 42	10 Nov. 48
Duncan, William,[76] Royal Artillery	10 May 05	1 June 06	11 Mar. 17	15 Mar. 25
Dunn, Thomas, 14 Foot	20 Jan. 03	11 Aug. 04	22 Sept. 08	18 Feb. 19
Dunne, Richard, Unattached	8 April 25	2 Mar. 26	16 May 34	23 Nov. 38
Dutton, Charles, Unattached	10 May 10	15 Oct. 12	30 Oct. 40	24 June 42
Dyer, John Edward,[77] Unattached	26 May 25	21 Dec. 26	24 Nov. 43	31 July 46
Dyson, John, Royal Artillery	11 Dec. 15	11 Aug. 23	10 Jan. 37	
Eason, Peter, 61 Foot	5 Oct. 09	8 Oct. 10	21 June 33	
P W Eaton, Charles, 10 Foot	4 Dec. 06	7 June 08	21 April 14	14 Aug. 23
Eckford, Alexander, Royal Marines	8 June 97	24 July 03	30 May 11	1 Sept. 14
P Edmonds, Hamilton,[78] 60 Foot, *Barrack-Master at Hounslow*	6 Feb. 08	23 Feb. 09	13 Feb. 27	18 Nov. 31
P W Edwardes, David John,[79] R. Artill.	1 Nov. 05	1 June 06	1 June 22	29 July 26
Edwards, George, 75 Foot	1 April 19	25 Oct. 27	11 Feb. 42	2 Mar. 47
Edwards, William Gamul, Unattached	14 Feb. 28	12 July 31	12 June 40	14 April 43
P W Elliott, Richard Chas., Unattached	5 June 09	23 June 11	28 Aug. 27	28 Aug. 27
P W Elliott, William,[79*] 11 Foot	4 Jan. 10	27 Nov. 12	14 April 18	22 Jan. 24
P Ellis, Hercules,[80] Unattached	5 Aug. 07	20 April 09	11 Aug. 25	4 Nov. 36
*Ellis, Thomas Davis, 81 Foot	never	never	25 Dec. 13	1814
Elrington, John Henry, 28 Dragoons, *Major of the Tower of London*	5 Nov. 94	10 Mar. 95	12 June 00	1 Dec. 08
Elton, Isaac, Unattached	2 Sept. 25	7 Nov. 26	5 July 31	29 Dec. 37
Emerson, John,[81] Unattached	30 July 07	12 April 09	13 Feb. 27	23 Sept. 36
Eminson, Thomas, 23 Dragoons	18 June 94	20 May 95	3 May 00	9 May 03
C Enderby, Samuel,[82] York Chasseurs	31 Oct. 11	16 April 12	27 May 19	17 Feb. 32
English, John Thomas Joseph, Unattached	7 Aug. 33	21 June 39	17 Nov. 48	17 Nov. 48
Enoch, James John, Unattached	16 Dec. 36	9 Feb. 39	17 Jan. 45	6 Oct. 48
P Evans, Aug. FitzGerald,[83] 37 Foot, *Capt. of Invalids, R. Hosp. Chelsea*	10 Mar. 08	9 Nov. 09	20 Mar. 27	11 Jan. 31
*Evans, Edward, 3 Prov. Batt. of Militia	never	never	25 Dec. 13	1814
Evans, James,[84] Royal Artillery	16 July 04	28 Jan. 05	20 Dec. 14	20 June 31
Evatt, Fra. (Adj. 23 May, 00) Vet. Comp.	25 June 02	28 Feb. 05	25 Mar. 13	
Evelegh, George Carter, Royal Artillery	20 Dec. 33	10 Jan. 37	17 April 45	9 May 45
Evelegh, John Henry, Unatt., *Adjt. West Middlesex Militia*	8 April 25	28 Jan. 26	20 Jan. 32	19 Dec. 40
P Falkiner, Samuel, Unattached	25 Sept. 06	11 June 07	5 Feb. 18	22 Feb. 27
Farmar, Richard, Royal Marines	1 July 03	15 Aug. 05	31 July 26	
Farrell, John Sidney, Royal Artillery	8 July 18	10 July 26	11 June 38	
Fayerman, Zaccheus,[85] Royal Marines	20 Feb. 96	1 June 98	24 Mar. 07	2 Feb. 10
Fenwick, Horatio, 27 Foot, *Staff Officer of Pensioners*	19 Dec. 24	13 June 30	17 Aug. 42	5 April 44
Fenwick, William Young, R. Artillery	15 Dec. 17	29 July 25	23 June 37	
P Ferguson, Adam, 101 Foot	1 Dec. 05	23 Oct. 06	4 Feb. 08	8 Oct. 16
Ficklin, Robert, Unattached	20 July 15	7 April 25	10 Aug. 26	26 Feb. 30
Fife, Adam, 69 Foot	28 April 06	15 Nov. 07	15 Oct. 12	25 Nov. 16
Findlater, Alexander Napier, 24 Foot	6 Mar. 06	15 Feb. 08	25 Aug. 23	25 Aug. 23
Finey, Alen George, Unattached	26 July 08	19 April 10	5 June 27	5 June 27
Fischer, John Nich., *Lieut.* R. Marines	6 July 03	15 Aug. 05	12 April 11	10 Sept. 14
Fisher, Seth Nuttall, Unattached	12 Feb. 24	13 May 26	3 April 35	23 June 43

	ENSIGN, ETC.	LIEUT.	CAPTAIN.	WHEN PLACED ON HALF PAY.
Fisk, William Hawley,[86] Unattached, *Adjutant, South Devon Militia*	27 April 15	25 Oct. 15	8 April 26	17 Feb. 37
*Fitzherbert, John, 80 Foot	never	never	25 Dec. 13	1814
Fleming, Arthur, Royal Artillery	17 Aug. 99	27 May 01	1 June 06	
Foley, *Hon.* St. George G. Unattached	29 June 32	27 May 36	3 Aug. 41	28 April 48
Follows, William,[86*] 18 Dragoons	13 Sept. 32	28 May 36	26 July 44	16 June 48
[illegible] Foot, George,[87] Royal Artillery	4 Oct. 06	1 Feb. 08	29 July 25	29 July 25
Ford, Charles,[88] Royal Artillery	1 July 06	1 Feb. 08	29 July 25	7 May 33
Ford, William,[89] Royal Marines	3 Oct. 05	2 Nov. 09	16 April 32	
Forde, William, Unattached	4 July 05	12 June 07	27 July 20	7 July 25
Foreman, George, Unattached	6 Aug. 07	22 Sept. 08	13 Mar. 27	24 Sept. 36
P [illegible] Forster, Henry,[90] Royal Artillery	1 July 06	16 Oct. 07	26 Dec. 24	7 Feb. 32
Fortescue, *Hon.* Geo. Matt., 25 Dragoons	12 Jan. 09	22 Mar. 10	24 Dec. 12	25 Oct. 16
Foskett, Joseph, Unattached	24 April 23	22 Oct. 25	7 Nov. 26	31 Aug. 30
Foss, Christopher, 6 Garrison Batt., *Sec. and Adjt., Royal Hibernian School*	26 June 01		28 July 07	14 Feb. 15
Foulston, John,[91] Unattached	1 Feb. 07	29 Sept. 08	31 Dec. 39	26 Jan. 44
P Fowden, Wm., 22 Dragoons	10 Oct. 05	6 April 07	4 Jan. 10	2 May 22
Fraser, Evan Baillie, Unattached	9 Jan. 23	15 Dec. 25	12 Dec. 26	14 June 33
P Fraser, Thomas,[91*] 83 Foot	16 Jan. 06	19 Feb. 06	2 July 12	25 June 17
*Frederick, *Sir* Richard, *Bart.*, 9 Foot	never	never	27 Nov. 99	25 May 02
Frederick, Roger, 7 R. Veteran Battalion	4 Oct. 06	18 Oct. 09	2 July 12	
Freeman, T. Inigo Wickham, Unattached	19 Dec. 16	9 Nov. 21	12 Nov. 25	12 Nov. 25
French, Acheson, Grenadier Guards	17 June 07	2 Feb. 07	7 April 25	9 Nov. 30
P French, Edward Francis, Unattached	3 May 10	10 Sept. 12	7 Jan. 19	8 April 26
Fry, John, 11 Foot	24 Oct. 99	25 June 03	2 May 11	25 May 16
Fry, Oliver, Royal Artillery	never	17 Oct. 94	14 Oct. 01	
Fry, Richard, 63 Foot	26 April 10	18 June 12	5 June 30	
P *Fullarton, Archibald*, 6 R. Vet. Batt.	19 Mar. 01	15 Oct. 03	2 April 12	
P Fuller, Fred. Hervey,[92] Unattached	21 Jan. 04	4 April 05	2 Aug. 15	22 May 28
Fuller, John Thomas,[93] Royal Artillery	1 July 06	1 Feb. 08	13 Feb. 25	13 Feb. 25
P Furnace, Norbury, 60 Foot	25 Dec. 06	16 Mar. 08	30 Dec. 19	3 April 23
P *Fyers, Edward*,[94] Royal Engineers	23 April 06	24 July 09	21 July 13	
P Fyfe, William,[95] 92 Foot	2 June 04	29 Aug. 05	16 Sept. 13	1814
*Fyler, Thomas, 5 Foot	never	never	25 Dec. 13	25 Sept. 14
Gale, Alexander Robinson, 26 Foot	15 July 05	14 Jan. 07	6 April 19	20 July 20
Galloway, David, Royal Marines	4 Mar. 06	10 April 12	21 May 34	
P Gapper, Edmund, 83 Foot	1 Aug. 04	5 May 05	3 June 12	25 June 17
Gardner, James, Unattached	27 July 15	8 May 19	15 June 26	5 Oct. 26
Gardner, *Hon.* Samuel Martin, 103 Foot	2 Mar. 05	1 May 05	17 Aug. 08	28 Dec. 17
P Garner, John Hutchinson,[95*] 40 Foot	25 June 12	21 April 14	1 Mar. 21	25 Oct. 21
Garth, Thomas, 15 Dragoons	23 Nov. 15	6 June 16	24 Aug. 20	25 Oct. 21
P Gascoyne, Thos. Bamber,[96] 3 Ceylon Reg.	5 Nov. 07	25 Mar. 09	7 Feb. 22	13 May 36
Geale, Marcus, Portuguese Service	29 Sept. 26	3 Feb. 32	11 April 40	16 June 48
P George, John,[96*] Unattached, *Chamberlain, R. Hospital, Kilmainham*	28 Feb. 10	7 Nov. 11	8 April 25	6 Dec. 27
Gerard, Robert Tolver, Unattached	3 July 28	16 Dec. 30	17 Mar. 37	22 Feb. 39
P Gibbons, Thomas,[97] Unattached, *Capt. of Invalids, R. Hosp. Kilmainham*	9 Sept. 12	7 April 25	7 Aug. 40	7 Aug. 40
Gibson, Charles Fred., Unattached	9 April 25	20 Sept. 33	15 July 43	8 Jan. 47
Gifford, George St. John, 11 R. Vet. Batt.	20 Feb. 96	25 April 97	3 Sept. 04	
P Gilbert, Francis Yarde,[98] R. Engineers	1 May 11	10 June 11	23 Mar. 25	6 June 25
Gilbert, James Anthony, Royal Artillery	16 Dec. 16	28 Feb. 25	10 Jan. 37	28 Nov. 37
Gilbert, Walter Raleigh, 123 Foot	26 Dec. 70	7 July 75	25 Aug. 94	
*Giles, Joseph, 9 Foot	never	never	25 Dec. 13	25 Sept. 14
Gilpin, Richard Thomas, Unattached, *Colonel of Bedford Militia*	29 Nov. 21	30 Dec. 24	24 Dec. 25	24 Dec. 25
Ginger, Joseph, 6 Foot	25 Sept. 03	6 Mar. 05	1 May 11	21 Dec. 26
P Girdlestone, James,[99] Unattached	20 Nov. 06	25 Dec. 07	20 Dec. 10	29 Dec. 25
P Glasse, Francis, 25 Foot	14 Aug. 01	9 Jan. 02	18 Sept. 06	8 Jan. 18
Glegg, Edward Holt, Unattached	3 Aug. 26	21 June 31	23 April 39	31 Jan. 45
Glenie, Isaac, Nova Scotia Fencibles	19 Sept. 05	17 July 06	14 Dec. 15	25 Sept. 16
Gloster, Richard, Unattached	17 Aug. 26	18 Feb. 30	31 Dec. 39	26 Jan. 44
Glumer, Weddo de, 4 Foot	never	never	30 Dec. 97	16 Mar. 02
Gold, Henry Yarburgh, Unattached	11 April 25	18 Sept. 28	5 April 31	25 Feb. 45
Goode, John,[100] Unattached	5 Sept. 11	12 Nov. 12	20 Feb. 35	20 Feb. 35

	2d Lieut. etc.	Lieut.	Captain.	When placed on half pay.
Goodwin, S. Osnaburgh, Unattached	25 Dec. 13	31 Oct. 22	22 Dec. 35	8 Feb. 39
Goold, James, Unattached	15 Sept. 25	21 May 28	24 May 44	20 Dec. 44
Gordon, Charles,[101] 93 Foot	22 June 09	15 Oct. 12	28 Feb. 28	
Gordon, David, 5 W. India Regt., *Barrackmaster, Port Antonio, Jamaica*	4 Aug. 00	30 May 03	10 Dec. 10	25 Nov. 18
Gordon, James, 3 West India Regt.	27 Nov. 23	26 May 25	12 Nov. 29	15 Mar. 31
Gordon, Thomas, Royal Waggon Train ..	1 June 20	9 June 25	1 May 28	10 May 33
Gore, John, Royal Artillery, *Professor, R. Military Academy at Woolwich*	8 Dec. 19	8 June 27	3 July 39	
Gossett, Arthur, Royal Artillery	5 Oct. 18	2 Mar. 27	1 May 30	
*Gould, Charles, 1 Foot	never	never	25 Dec. 13	25 Sept. 14
Gould, Francis Augustus, Unattached....	4 May 15	13 Mar. 23	10 Dec. 25	7 Sept. 32
Gouttebernard, J. M. de la, 8 W. I. Regt.		25 May 98	3 Mar. 06	1816
Graham, James John, Unattached	28 Oct. 24	8 April 26	25 Feb. 30	27 Sept. 42
Grant, James, Unattached	20 Dec. 21	30 June 25	6 Mar. 27	6 Mar. 27
Grant, James, Unattached	4 Nov. 12	6 Nov. 14	3 May 33	17 July 35
Grant, John, 24 Foot................	15 Feb. 10	5 Mar. 12	13 Aug. 30	14 Dec. 32
Grant, Robert, Unattached	8 May 17	18 July 26	11 Dec. 28	11 June 30
Grantt, John, 72 Foot	16 Dec. 95	23 June 96	27 Dec. 14	25 Dec. 17
Graves, William H., Unattached........	6 Jan. 08	26 Oct. 08	8 April 25	23 Nov. 26
Gray, Basil, Unattached	30 July 28	31 Jan. 34	29 Nov. 39	20 June 45
Gray, Charles, Royal Marines	10 Oct. 04	24 April 08	31 Aug. 27	
P *Gray, Robert*, 6 R. Veteran Battalion	2 May 00	9 July 03	10 Aug. 09	
P Gregor, Gordon Wm. Fra., 23 Foot ..	23 May 06	14 May 07	17 June 13	25 Dec. 14
Gregory, William, Royal Engineers	20 July 13	15 Dec. 13	6 Oct. 31	
Greig, John James, Unattached, *Staff Officer of Pensioners*	15 May 28	21 Mar. 34	16 June 43	4 Aug. 43
P W Grenfell, William, 21 Dragoons ..	11 April 11	11 Mar. 13	24 Dec. 18	26 Oct. 30
Grey, *Hon.* Henry Booth, Unattached ..	12 May 25	13 April 26	17 Dec. 30	9 Aug. 33
Grey, Matthew Robert, 6 W. India Regt.	7 Aug. 17	24 Oct. 21	12 Aug. 24	10 Sept. 30
Griffin, Francis John, Unatt., *Deputy Assist. Adjutant General at Montreal*	13 Oct. 25	12 June 28	29 Nov. 44	29 Nov. 44
P W *Griffith, John*,[102] 1 W. India Regt.	29 July 13	4 May 15	29 July 36	
Griffiths, Fred. Augustus, R. Artillery ..	13 Dec. 13	8 Oct. 16	19 Aug. 35	
P Grimes, John, 76 Foot	6 Oct. 08	1 Nov. 10	25 May 22	30 May 22
Guthrie, William, Unattached..........	22 April 26	20 Mar. 27	24 Feb. 37	13 Aug. 47
Gwynne, Henry Lewis Edward, 62 Foot	25 April 05	26 June 06	23 Aug. 10	25 Feb. 17
Hadley, William, 5 R. Veteran Batt. ..	21 April 04	6 May 05	2 Dec. 13	
Haig, William, Royal Marines..........	9 May 06	9 Oct. 12	27 May 34	17 Nov. 34
Halcott, Matthew Charles, Unattached ..	2 Feb. 15	10 April 23	7 Jan. 26	7 Jan. 26
Hamilton, George	16 June 30	22 July 36	6 Aug. 47	6 Aug. 47
Hamilton, Robert Charles[103]	3 Aug. 26	28 Apr. 31	23 Apr. 41	29 Jan. 47
Hammill, Thomas Cochrane,[104] Unattached	8 Oct. 07	5 April 10	26 June 27	26 June 27
Handcock, *Hon.* Robt. French, R. Artillery	26 July 31	23 Dec. 32	1 Nov. 42	9 Oct. 48
P W Harding, Robert,[105] R. Artillery ..	6 June 06	6 April 07	17 Oct. 23	17 Oct. 23
P Hardwick, William, 2 Foot	27 Aug. 04	12 Feb. 05	1 Mar. 10	26 Nov. 18
Hare, *Hon.* Richard, Unattached	10 Jan. 22	23 June 25	11 July 26	17 Mar. 37
Harris, Robert Russell, 60 Foot, *Staff Officer of Pensioners*	19 Oct. 20	18 Aug. 24	31 Oct. 40	25 April 45
W Harris, William, Unattached	16 April 12	21 Jan. 13	2 June 25	8 June 30
W Harrison, Hugh,[106] 5 Foot	21 Nov. 05	18 June 07	11 June 12	16 May 22
Harrison, John, Unattached	20 July 15	28 Oct. 24	3 Dec. 29	15 Mar. 39
P Harrison, John,[106*] 82 Foot, *Adjutant, Royal MidLothian Yeomanry Cav.*	25 June 24	13 Aug. 25	27 Oct. 35	25 Oct. 42
Harrison, Septimus,[107] Unattached	24 Dec. 08	1 May 12	26 Jan. 41	26 Jan. 41
Hart, Richard, 66 Foot................	27 Mar. 05	25 April 06	25 Mar. 25	19 May 25
Harvey, John, 37 Foot	14 April 14	10 April 25	9 Oct. 37	
Harvey, John, Royal Artillery..........	18 June 35	23 June 37	1 April 46	26 May 46
*Haselfoot, Charles, 3 Foot	never	never	25 Dec. 13	25 Aug. 14
*Haselfoot, William Henry, 3 Foot......	never	never	do	do
Haslewood, Dickens Mark,[108] 14 Foot ..	10 May 09	13 Dec. 10	10 July 31	
Hastings, *Sir* C. Abney, *Bt.*, 105 Foot ..	17 Jan. 08	15 Sept. 08	7 Mar. 11	17 Nov. 14
Haviland, Henry Hone, Royal Marines ..	8 May 95	11 April 96	15 Aug. 05	7 Mar. 10
Hawke, *Hon.* Stanhope, Unattached	17 July 23	12 May 25	26 Sept. 26	2 Dec. 31
Hawker, Peter Wm. Lance, Unatt.	9 Aug. 31	3 Oct. 34	6 May 42	15 Jan. 47
Hawkins, George Palme:, 'Unattached ..	30 Nov. 09	6 Jan. 11	15 May 27	15 May 27

	CORNET, ETC.	LIEUT.	CAPTAIN.	WHEN PLACED ON HALF PAY.
Hawkins, John, Unattached	25 Aug. 06	3 Nov. 08	1 July 20	7 Sept. 28
Hay, David Balfour, 26 Dragoons	25 Nov. 95	7 Dec. 96	7 Dec. 97	9 July 02
Hay, Francis, 34 Foot	24 May 04	1 Aug. 04	21 Sept. 09	21 Aug. 17
Hay, James, Unattached	16 Feb. 26	21 Dec. 32	9 May 45	3 Oct. 48
Hay, John, Royal Marines	8 July 03	15 Aug. 05	31 July 26	
Hayes, Robert, Royal Marines	20 Mar. 96	1 April 99	13 Jan. 07	22 Nov. 14
Hayne, Richard, Royal Staff Corps	7 July 17	9 April 25	24 Aug. 32	24 Aug. 32
P Healey, John, 39 Foot	4 June 08	8 Sept. 08	26 June 23	25 Jan. 24
Heath, Macclesfield William, R. Engineers	1 Aug. 14	1 July 15	13 May 36	25 May 38
*Heathcote, Cockshutt, 53 Foot	never	never	25 Dec. 13	1814
Heaton, John R., Unattached	19 Dec. 34	22 Aug. 37	24 Feb. 43	13 Aug. 47
P W Heaviside, Richard, Unattached	26 May 08	20 Sept. 09	15 June 15	14 Dec. 26
Hebden, Henry, Unattached	25 May 15	7 April 25	13 May 26	26 April 27
Henderson, David, 10 Foot	28 Nov. 06	23 Jan. 08	5 Jan. 15	25 Feb. 16
Heneage, Thomas, Independent Company	28 Mar. 92	21 Feb. 93	18 Mar. 94	
P Henry, Graham,[109] Unattached	6 Nov. 06	2 Mar. 08	25 Oct. 14	29 Nov. 27
Hepburn, Fra. J. Swayne, Unattached	2 April 18	12 May 25	28 June 38	30 Sept. 42
Hertford, R. S. C., *Marquis of*, KG., 22 Drs.	24 Feb. 20	24 Oct. 21	25 Mar. 23	17 April 28
Hewett, John, Royal Marines	12 Nov. 05	24 Sept. 10	12 Oct. 32	
Hewson, John Milliquet,[111] 89 Foot	2 Sept. 12	22 May 15	13 Mar. 35	
P *Hickie, Bartholomew*, 7 R. Vet. Batt.	2 June 04	18 April 05	31 Dec. 12	
Higgins, Hugh Brabazon, Unattached	1 Aug. 22	15 Dec. 25	28 Jan. 42	3 Feb. 43
Hill, George Staveley, Unattached	9 Sept. 19	6 June 22	25 Mar. 29	27 Dec. 33
P W Hill, Henry,[112] Unatt., *Adjutant Cheshire Yeomanry Cavalry*	19 Jan. 15	5 May 15	28 June 36	28 June 36
Hill, Nicholas Thomas, R. Staff Corps	20 Oct. 08	13 Sept. 10	23 Oct. 17	25 July 19
Hilliard, Edward Dav. Crosier, Unatt.	19 July 31	5 April 33	1 Dec. 37	22 July 42
Hinde, Henry Reynolds, 36 Foot	29 Jan. 00	13 Jan. 02	29 Nov. 05	25 Mar. 11
P Hobkirk, Samuel, 43 Foot	25 April 06	7 April 08	3 Dec. 12	25 Mar. 17
P W Hodges, George Lloyd,[113] Unatt.	28 Aug. 06	7 Jan. 08	31 Dec. 30	31 Dec. 30
Holcombe, Francis, Royal Artillery	1 May 15	9 Nov. 19	6 Jan. 36	
Holden, Charles, Unattached, *Staff Officer of Pensioners*	8 June 26	22 May 35	7 Oct. 37	9 June 43
Holland, William, 83 Foot	26 Mar. 07	28 Sept. 08	21 July 14	25 June 17
Holmes, Christ. Francis,[114] Unattached	25 June 12	14 Oct. 14	12 Feb. 29	9 June 37
Home, James Murray,[115] Unattached	24 Feb. 14	12 Dec. 16	11 Jan. 39	18 May 41
Home, Francis, 81 Foot	4 June 07	10 Aug. 08	24 Mar. 17	22 May 17
Hookey, George, Royal Marines, *Paymaster, Chatham Division*	27 Jan. 06	8 Aug. 11	12 Oct. 32	23 Mar. 36
Hopkins, Henry, 11 Garrison Battalion	7 Oct. 02	24 June 03	21 Aug. 06	2 Nov. 09
Hopkins, Henry, Unattached	15 July 12	2 Mar. 20	25 Sept. 35	25 Sept. 35
Hornbrook, Thomas Beckford, R. Marines	25 Aug. 99	1 Sept. 04	8 May 24	5 Jan. 26
Horsell, Bartholomew, R. Waggon Train	10 Sept. 03	12 Jan. 04	26 Nov. 12	1814
Horsford, George Fahie, Unattached	30 Jan. 23	20 April 36	14 June 42	2 Aug. 42
Horsley, Nicholas,[116] Unattached	18 Mar. 13	5 Oct. 15	16 Jan. 46	16 Jan. 46
P *Hort, Josiah George*,[117] 12 R. Vet. Batt. *Adjutant, Royal Hosp., Kilmainham*	19 Sept. 05	26 Feb. 07	23 Aug. 10	
Horton, James, Royal Staff Corps	11 July 11	2 July 12	31 Dec. 28	25 June 29
Hotham, Augustus, Unattached	20 Dec. 21	19 May 25	19 Dec. 26	28 Dec. 32
Hotham, George,[118] R. Engineers	24 Mar. 15	1 May 16	10 Jan. 37	17 Aug. 39
P *Sir* Houlton, George, 43 Foot, *Ensign of Yeomen of the Guard*	20 Nov. 06	6 Oct. 08	2 Nov. 15	25 Mar. 17
Howard de Walden, C.A., GCB., *Lord*, 8 F.	never	14 April 17	3 Oct. 22	3 Oct. 22
Howard, *Hon.* Henry, Unattached	21 July 25	14 May 26	9 Nov. 30	29 Nov. 33
Howell, James, Royal Artillery	2 April 10	17 Dec. 13	27 Oct. 41	
Hugo, Thomas, 91 Foot	1 July 05	2 July 05	22 July 13	25 Feb. 16
P *Hulme, John Lyon*,[119] R. Engineers	24 June 09	10 July 10	20 Dec. 14	
P W Humbley, William,[120] Rifle Brigade	15 April 07	13 Oct. 08	20 July 15	25 Dec. 18
Humby, John, Royal Marines	30 July 04	10 June 07	31 Aug. 27	
P Humfrey, Benjamin Geale,[121] 56 Foot	16 June 08	20 Oct. 08	31 Mar. 14	19 May 25
Humphreys, John Goullin,[122] Coldst. Gds.	14 May 07	14 July 08	8 April 25	18 Nov. 31
Hunt, John, Unattached	11 Dec. 12	9 April 15	10 Oct. 45	10 Oct. 45
Hunter, George James,[123] Royal Artillery	1 Oct. 08	13 Mar. 11	6 Nov. 27	23 Oct. 33
Hunter, James, 70 Foot	23 April 12	22 Aug. 15	14 Aug. 23	14 Aug. 23
Hunter, John, Unattached	27 Nov. 17	24 Oct. 21	4 Feb. 26	4 Feb. 26
Hurdle, Thomas, Royal Marines	15 Jan. 98	1 Dec. 03	18 Mar. 13	
Hussey, Thomas, Royal Marines	28 April 97	18 July 03	24 Sept. 10	1 Sept. 14

	2d Lieut. etc.	Lieut.	Captain.	When placed on half pay.
Hutchinson, Fred. James Taggart, Unatt.	18 Dec. 27	17 May 31	17 Mar. 30	27 May 42
Hutchinson, James,[124] 1 Garrison Batt. ..	8 Dec. 04	26 Sept. 06	25 May 10	18 Oct. 63
Ibbetson, Charles Parke, 89 Foot	24 Apr. 35	30 June 37	2 June 43	24 Sept. 47
Imlach, Alexander, Unattached	9 Nov. 15	7 Jan. 42	10 Sept. 47	10 Sept. 47
Ince, Ralph Piggott, Unattached	28 Sept. 15	8 April 25	25 June 37	20 Aug. 44
Ingall, Fred., Lenox, Unatt., *Deputy Assist. Qr.-Mast. Gen. at Quebec..*	8 April 13	14 Mar. 16	5 Feb. 41	5 Feb. 41
Inge, Charles, Unattached	7 Jan. 30	26 Feb. 36	27 Mar. 40	23 Jan. 46
Inge, William, Unattached	14 May 18	11 April 22	16 Sept. 24	12 July 27
Iremonger, Pennant Athelwold, Unatt. ..	27 April 38	8 April 42	27 Oct. 46	28 April 48
Irwin, Thomas, 6 Dragoons	26 Aug. 09	29 Oct. 12	8 Dec. 18	25 Oct. 21
Jackson, George Wm. Collins,[125] 16 Lancers, *Staff Officer of Pensioners*	29 Mar. 39	12 June 40	7 June 44	16 Mar. 47
Jackson, Henry Augustus, Unattached ..	27 Aug. 15	8 April 25	18 Dec. 35	30 June 48
𝔚𝔞𝔱 Jago, Darell,[126] Royal Artillery	5 July 13	26 Oct. 15	20 Nov. 34	6 Jan. 36
James, Demetrius Grevis, Royal Marines	19 April 96	8 June 99	29 June 08	25 Feb. 12
𝔓 *James, Henry,*[127] Royal Marines	7 Dec. 07	19 July 21	18 Mar. 36	
𝔚𝔞𝔱 James, William, Scots Fusilier Gds..	never	4 Mar. 13	8 May 17	25 Feb. 19
Jameson, James, 4 Foot	16 Aug. 01	17 Dec. 03	31 Oct. 10	25 Feb. 16
Jarvis, Samuel Raymond, 7 Dragoons ..	7 April 06	19 June 06	7 Sept. 15	25 Jan. 23
𝔓 *Jeffreys, Richard,[128] 58 Foot, *Barrack-master at Exeter...........*	never	never	25 Dec. 13	1814
Jenkins, Richard, Unatt., *Staff Of. of Pen.*	1 Feb. 27	4 June 28	16 June 37	19 May 46
Johnson, Yarrall, 63 Foot............	12 Aug. 03	22 Dec. 04	9 June 13	3 July 26
Johnston, William, Unattached	4 Mar. 01	27 July 02	1 Feb. 10	12 Dec. 25
𝔓 Johnstone, James, 7 Foot............	29 Dec. 08	30 Aug. 10	10 June 13	25 Feb. 16
Joliffe, *Sir* Wm. G. H., *Bt.*, Bourbon Regt.	10 April 17	26 Aug. 19	22 April 24	24 June 24
Jones, Ebenezer, Unattached	15 Dec. 17	10 April 25	9 Sept. 28	9 Sept. 28
*Jones, Edward, 29 Foot	never	never	25 Dec. 13	25 Aug. 14
Jones, John Evans, Royal Marines	21 Sept. 05	5 April 09	19 May 31	
Jones, Thomas, Irish Brigade	18 Nov. 99	20 May 00	31 Dec. 03	2 July 07
𝔓 Jones, William, 52 Foot	25 Feb. 08	5 Jan. 09	30 Sept. 19	5 June 26
𝔓* Jones, Wm., 1 Provisional Batt. of Mil.	never	never	25 Dec. 13	25 Oct. 44
Jones, William Prime, Unattached......	5 Oct. 26	5 Nov. 29	23 April 39	7 Feb. 45
Jordan, Jacob, Unattached	4 July 16	17 Jan. 22	7 Nov. 26	29 Mar. 27
Julius, Wm. Mayor, 13 Dragoons	9 July 29	18 April 34	4 Sept. 40	4 Sept. 40
Kaye, Wilkinson Lister, Royal Artillery..	11 Dec. 15	1 May 22	12 July 36	4 May 43
Keane, George Michael, Unattached	27 Mar. 23	27 Aug. 25	19 Dec. 26	17 Mar. 37
Keating, James Singer, Unattached	5 Feb. 18	24 Oct. 21	8 April 26	8 April 26
Keats, John Smith, Royal Waggon Train	16 Dec. 16	2 Mar. 25	5 July 29	31 May 33
Keens, John, Unattached............	2 Nov. 09	14 Nov. 11	5 June 27	5 June 27
𝔓 𝔚𝔞𝔱 Kelly, Townsend R.,[131] Unattached	8 June 09	25 Oct. 10	26 May 25	19 Jan. 26
Kellenbach, Frederick, 2 R. Veteran Batt.	never	30 Dec. 97	5 Dec. 05	
Kellet, John, Royal Marines	28 April 93	9 Oct. 94	3 Oct. 01	1 Feb. 04
Kelly, Edward Henry Moore, Unatt.	10 Sept. 30	31 July 35	22 July 42	10 Dec. 47
Kelly, John,[132] 6 Foot	8 Nov. 13	20 Dec. 24	27 May 36	
Kelly, John,[133] 25 Foot............	9 July 03	7 Sept. 04	4 June 13	25 April 16
Kelly, Thomas Daniel, Unattached......	12 April 33	10 Feb. 38	3 April 46	26 May 48
Kelly, William, 2 Royal Veteran Batt...	26 Oct. 99	23 July 04	15 Feb. 11	
Kennedy, Hugh Fergusson, Unattached..	31 July 23	16 June 25	27 Nov. 28	31 Dec. 31
Kenny, William Henry, 61 Foot, *Staff Officer of Pensioners in New Zealand*	3 April 28	15 Mar. 32	12 Oct. 41	5 April 44
𝔓 Kent, John, 53 Foot............	27 April 03	28 Aug. 04	10 May 09	12 Dec. 17
𝔓 Ker, Richard Hall,[134] Unattached	31 May 10	10 June 13	6 Feb. 35	6 Feb. 35
Kernmis, Thomas Arthur, Unattached ..	never	22 April 26	9 Dec. 30	4 July 34
Kerr, Samuel, Unattached	29 Oct. 09	14 Oct. 10	25 Nov. 28	25 Nov. 28
*Kettilby, James, 51 Foot............	never	never	25 Dec. 13	25 Aug. 15
𝔓 King, James,[135] 73 Foot	25 Sept. 06	10 Dec. 06	28 Feb. 11	1 Jan. 18
𝔓 King, John Duncan,[136] Unattached ..	28 Aug. 06	18 Feb. 08	16 Mar. 30	28 Dec. 30
King, John Lewis, 2 Foot............	3 Jan. 22	24 Jan. 25	15 Aug. 26	25 Dec. 28
King, *Sir* R. Duckworth, *Bt.*, Unattached	28 Feb. 22	29 May 25	22 April 26	5 Feb. 36
𝔓 King, Thomas Newton,[137] R. Artillery	4 Oct. 06	1 Feb. 08	29 July 25	30 June 30
King, William John,[138] 21 Foot	1 Mar. 17	29 Jan. 20	3 Oct. 40	
Kingsley, Charles, 9 R. Veteran Batt. ..	13 Nov. 04	17 July 06	13 June 11	
Kingsley, James Bell, Unattached	10 Nov. 13	9 Nov. 14	21 May 41	21 May 41
*Kinneir, Joseph Hall, 2 Prov. Bn. of Mil.	never	never	25 Dec. 13	1814
𝔓 Kirby, Michael, 65 Foot	25 June 12	29 Feb. 16	31 May 21	19 April 23

	ENSIGN, ETC.	LIEUT.	CAPTAIN.	WHEN PLACED ON HALF PAY.
Kirwan, Andrew Hyacinth, Unattached..	never	5 Aug. 13	29 Oct. 25	25 Nov. 28
Kirwan, Henry, 15 Foot	18 April 00	28 Nov. 00	22 May 04	25 July 12
P Kirwan, Richard, Unattached........	never	27 Oct. 07	16 Mar. 15	24 July 28
Knapman, *Wm. Stephens*, Royal Marines	1 Nov. 03	17 Jan. 06	31 July 26	
Knatchbull, Thomas, Royal Artillery, *Staff Officer of Pensioners*........	15 Dec. 17	29 July 25	28 Nov. 37	9 June 44
Knight, Alfred,[139] Unattached, *Town Major at Quebec*	18 June 12	14 Feb. 14	16 Sept. 45	16 Sept. 45
Knight, Brook John, Royal Staff Corps..	26 Oct. 26	8 June 30	26 June 35	2 Aug. 44
P Knipe, George Frederick,[140] 23 Foot ..	29 May 96	16 July 00	2 July 13	18 May 15
Knox, Charles, Unattached	8 April 26	9 Aug. 27	4 Mar. 36	10 Feb. 38
P Kyle, Alexander,[141] 94 Foot..........	13 May 05	7 Apr. 07	11 Oct. 10	25 Dec. 18
Kyrle, J. Ernle Money, R. Staff Corps, *Adjutant*, *Hereford Militia*	10 April 33	5 Oct. 38	22 July 42	29 Jan. 47
Lacy, William, Unattached, *Staff Officer of Pensioners*	20 April 26	30 Aug. 27	6 Dec. 44	6 Dec. 44
Lamb, Samuel Burges, Unattached......	14 Dec. 32	5 Feb. 36	7 July 48	7 July 48
Lambert, *Sir* Henry John, *Bt.*, 86 Foot..	6 April 09	never	27 May 13	12 Aug. 15
Lamotte, Chas. Wyndham, Unattached ..	6 Nov. 27	28 Oct. 31	22 July 36	10 Nov. 37
Lamphier, J. Philips Cosby, 25 Foot	27 Mar. 06	7 Sept. 09	19 April 18	6 Oct. 25
Lancey, *William*, Royal Engineers	1 Aug. 16	7 June 25	25 May 38	1 April 41
Lane, Charles,[142] Unattached	15 May 12	26 Oct. 13	9 July 33	7 Mar. 34
Langrishe, Hugh Henry, Unattached....	never	5 July 15	27 April 25	27 Oct. 25
Langdon, *Gilbert*, Royal Marines	3 May 95	27 Jan. 96	14 June 20	
Langford, Buller Rolle, Royal Marines ..	28 April 95	27 Jan. 96	15 Aug. 05	22 Nov. 09
Langley, George Richard, Unattached ..	24 Nov. 12	7 Jan. 14	26 April 44	26 April 44
P W Langton, Edward, 52 Foot	23 May 05	25 July 05	12 May 12	8 April 17
Latham, Matthew, Portuguese Service ..	15 Nov. 05	8 April 07	11 Feb. 13	20 April 13
La Touche, Robert, Unattached	28 Sept. 20	15 July 24	14 Jan. 26	12 Oct. 26
Law, James Horton, Unattached........	22 July 13	7 May 18	9 Sept. 25	11 Jan. 21
Law, *John*,[143] Royal Marines	14 Mar. 10	6 June 28	26 April 38	
Lawlor, Provo William,[144] R. Artillery ..	1 July 06	1 Feb. 08	8 April 25	20 April 30
P Lawrence, John, Royal Marines, *Paymaster*, *Portsmouth Division*	6 July 03	15 Aug. 05	31 July 26	20 July 30
P Lawrence, W. Hudson,[145] R. Artillery	28 April 10	17 Dec. 13	2 Feb. 32	8 Aug. 40
*Laxon, John, 7 Foot	never	never	25 Dec. 13	25 Sept. 14
Leahy, Henry, 95 Foot.................	25 April 06	28 Aug. 07	18 Oct. 10	7 Aug. 17
W Leatham, James, York Chasseurs....	26 Sept. 05	12 June 06	19 July 15	28 April 25
Le Couteur, John,[146] 104 Foot	15 Nov. 10	21 Nov. 11	15 May 17	25 Aug. 17
P *Leech*, *John*, 5 R. Veteran Batt.......	3 Sept. 03	7 Mar. 05	10 June 13	
Lefroy, Anthony, 4 Foot, *Barrackmaster at York*			22 May 94	17 Sept. 02
W *Lemoine*, *William*, Royal Artillery ..	3 Oct. 07	5 June 08	6 Nov. 27	
P Lempriere, Wm. Chas.,[147] R. Artillery	6 June 04	23 Oct. 04	17 Dec. 13	26 Nov. 27
Leslie, Lewis Xavier,[148] 14 Foot	25 Dec. 13	1 July 24	30 Oct. 40	15 Dec. 40
Lewis, Alexander, Unattached	15 June 97	27 May 01	18 June 11	22 Mar. 27
Lewis, *Geo. Cha. Degen*, R. Engineers..	1 Aug. 14	1 July 15	5 Dec. 35	
Lewis, Philip George, 5 West India Regt.	3 May 00	26 Aug. 01	29 Oct. 12	25 April 17
Lewis, Thomas Locke, Royal Engineers..	20 Mar. 13	21 July 13	8 June 30	5 Jan. 33
Lewis, Westenra Warner, 74 Foot	4 Jan. 05	26 Oct. 06	7 Dec. 20	16 Sept. 24
Lindsay, Wm. Chacon, Royal Artillery ..	11 Sept. 12	1 April 15	28 Oct. 38	3 July 39
P Litchfield, Richard,[150] Royal Artillery	26 Nov. 08	5 Sept. 11	6 Nov. 27	6 Nov. 27
Little, Robert John, R. Marines, *Barrack-master*, *Woolwich Division* ...	4 July 03	15 Aug. 05	31 July 26	12 Sept. 29
Lloyd, Kingston Dodd, Unattached	27 Nov. 11	21 April 14	31 May 27	31 May 27
Loftus, Frederick, Unattached..........	7 Oct. 19	9 June 25	8 April 26	8 April 26
Logan, George Home,[151] Royal Marines ..	1 July 23	20 Feb. 33	17 June 42	26 Oct. 48
*Long, John, 70 Foot	never	never	25 Dec. 13	25 Aug. 14
Louis, *Marcus*, 5 R. Veteran Batt.......	Jan. 95	8 Sept. 95	22 May 00	
Low, Richard Butler,[152] Unatt. *Adjutant Limerick Militia*	8 Nov. 33	1 Dec. 37	1 July 42	20 Oct. 48
Luard, Robert, Royal Artillery	8 Dec. 19	12 May 27	20 May 39	17 Jan. 45
P *Lutman*, *John Adrian*,[153] 24 Foot....	1 Feb. 09	13 May 13	13 Feb. 35	
P Lynch, Martin, 27 Foot	30 Aug. 04	8 Sept. 05	24 Dec. 12	25 July 17
Lyon, George, Unattached	8 Nov. 21	31 May 25	30 Dec. 26	30 Dec. 26

	ENSIGN, ETC.	LIEUT.	CAPTAIN.	WHEN PLACED ON HALF PAY.
P *M'Carthy, J. E. Connor,* 2 R. Vet. Bat.	9 July 03	2 April 05	4 Feb. 13	
M'Donald, Alexander, 56 Foot	25 Nov. 99	3 Sept. 02	15 April 07	1814
P M'Donald, Donald,[154] R. Engineers, *Barrackmaster at Paisley*	12 Sept. 08	24 June 09	20 Oct. 13	28 Sept. 24
M'Donald, Henry Thomas, 58 Foot	9 July 03	27 Mar. 05	31 Mar. 14	22 Dec. 17
M'Donell, Alexander, 6 R. Vet. Batt. ..	28 Sept. 04	7 Nov. 05	16 Mar. 15	
M'Dougall, Duncan, 21 Foot	30 June 01	8 Dec. 03	13 June 11	Mar. 17
M'Innes, Matthew, 8 Dragoons	9 July 09	5 Mar. 12	11 Oct. 32	15 Feb. 39
M'Intyre, Angus,[155] Unattached	26 Aug. 07	2 April 10	27 Aug. 24	9 July 29
M'Intyre, James, Unattached	22 July 19	7 April 25	1 Sept. 40	6 May 42
M'Kenzie, William, 6 Foot	2 Feb. 01	26 Jan. 03	24 Oct. 10	12 Aug. 19
M'Laine, Alexander, Unattached........	1 Mar. 06	19 Aug. 07	7 April 25	15 Sept. 25
M'Leod, John, Royal Marines	17 July 96	15 Jan. 01	5 Oct. 08	26 Sept. 14
M'Murdo, Alured Charles,[157] Unattached	1 Jan. 14	29 June 26	22 Mar. 31	22 Mar. 31
M'Neill, Alexander, 10 Foot	18 May 08	13 July 09	13 April 15	30 April 18
M'Pherson, Daniel,[158] 2 R. Veteran Batt.	26 June 06	18 Jan. 08	6 Feb. 12	
M'Queen, Simon,[159] Unattached	14 Aug. 13	23 Oct. 16	1 June 32	1 June 32
M'Vicar, John, Royal Waggon Train	27 Aug. 04	28 Oct. 08	20 July 15	25 Dec. 18
Macartney, James Nixon,[160] 16 Lancers, *Adjt. North Devon Yeomanry Cav.*	10 May 31	11 April 34	13 Nov. 42	20 July 47
Macdonald, Alexander, 62 Foot	18 Nov. 23	7 July 25	11 June 30	18 June 30
Macdonald, Alex., Unatt., *Staff Officer of Pensioners in New Zealand*	18 July 34	31 Oct. 38	11 Dec. 46	25 June 47
Macdonald, *Hon.* James Wm. Bosville, Unattached, *Aide-de-Camp to Prince George of Cambridge*	1 Oct. 29	24 Jan. 34	24 June 37	30 Dec. 42
Macdonald, John,[161] Unattached........	7 June 10	21 May 12	8 June 20	9 Aug. 31
Macdonald, Ranald, Unattached........	18 July 15	3 Dec. 18	19 Nov. 30	22 Mar. 33
Macdonald, Ronald, 12 Foot	5 Feb. 01	26 July 04	2 Jan. 12	20 April 29
Macdonald, William, York Light Infantry	14 Jan. 05	10 April 06	8 Sept. 14	20 May 17
P Mac Donnell, Ewen,[162] Unattached ..	20 Jan. 14	27 Mar. 23	6 May 35	28 Nov. 37
Macfarlane, Andrew, 91 Foot	20 Oct. 04	26 Oct. 04	10 Sept. 12	25 Feb. 16
Mac Gregor, John,[163] Unattached	19 Oct. 09	28 Nov. 11	29 Sept. 27	28 Mar. 34
Mackay, Henry Fowler, Unattached	9 June 25	12 Jan. 26	12 Feb. 30	26 Mar. 41
Mackay, William, 9 R. Veteran Batt. ..	8 Oct. 99	6 April 01	22 May 06	
Mackenzie, Alexander, Unattached......	30 Nov. 15	8 April 25	1 Aug. 26	7 Mar. 34
Mackenzie, Alex. Wedder, 3 Garrison Batt.	14 Jan. 07	11 Jan. 08	23 Jan. 12	6 Nov. 17
Mackenzie, Colin, Royal Engineers	20 July 13	15 Dec. 13	26 Oct. 34	
Mackenzie, Donald, 8 R. Vet. Batt.	11 July 00	17 Dec. 03	21 Mar. 11	
Mackey, John Alexander, 59 Foot	9 April 25	20 Nov. 27	3 Dec. 29	8 Oct. 30
Maclean, James,[164] 103 Foot	22 July 13	8 Nov. 14	22 Nov. 21	18 Sept. 23
Maclean, Lachlan H. G.[164a] Unattached..	26 Dec. 34	31 Aug. 38	25 Feb. 48	25 Feb. 48
Macneil, Archibald,[165] 3 R. Veteran Batt.	10 Feb. 96	26 July 97	13 Aug. 05	
Macpherson, Ewen, 14 Dragoons	8 April 25	20 Mar. 27	21 April 43	23 Jan. 46
P Macpherson, Lachlan,[166] Unattached, *Staff Officer of Pensioners*	31 Mar. 14	7 April 25	19 May 37	19 May 37
Maguire, John, Unattached	27 July 05	9 Oct. 06	10 Nov. 44	19 Nov. 44
Mainwaring, George,[167] 22 Foot........	3 May 15	17 Sept. 17	5 June 40	
Mair, William, Unattached	26 Nov. 30	22 April 36	17 Mar. 48	17 Mar. 48
Maitland, Fred. Thomas, R. Staff Corps	9 April 25	18 Feb. 26	12 April 33	25 Feb. 45
Man, Garnet, Unattached, *Professor Royal Military College*	13 Jan. 25	15 Mar. 27	5 July 44	4 July 45
P Mancor, Andrew, 59 Foot	26 Oct. 04	16 June 07	3 Sept. 12	1 Aug. 16
P *Manners, Charles,*[169] Royal Artillery..	3 Nov. 07	24 Sept. 08	6 Nov. 27	
Mansfield, John, 2 R. Veteran Battalion	15 Sept. 96	11 Jan. 00	26 Jan. 04	
March, C. H. G. L., *Earl of,* Unatt. *Aide-de-Camp to His Grace the Commander-in-Chief*	24 May 39	27 Sept. 42	27 Sept. 44	27 Sept. 44
W Marcon, Edward, 79 Foot..........	11 May 11	20 May 13	3 Jan. 22	6 Feb. 23
Marryatt, George, Unattached..........	19 Feb. 24	23 June 25	18 Dec. 27	31 Dec. 29
Martin, Henry Clinton,[171] Royal Artillery	20 Dec. 99	25 Dec. 01	13 Jan. 07	
Masboug, Ladislasde Villiers, 60 Foot....	never	never	30 Dec. 97	1799
Mascall, John Richard, Royal Marines..	7 Sept. 08	19 Dec. 22	10 Jan. 37	
Mason, John Monck,[172] Unattached	27 Sept. 15	25 Oct. 35	3 April 46	3 April 46
P Mason, William, Unattached[173]	23 Feb. 09	19 Mar. 12	5 Feb. 47	5 Feb. 47
Massy, John, Unattached[174]......	3 Dec. 29	16 Sept. 36	30 July 47	30 July 47
W Master, Richard Thomas,[175] Gr. Gds.	21 Jan. 13	never	1 July 15	25 Feb. 19

	CORNET, ETC.	LIEUT.	CAPTAIN.	WHEN PLACED ON HALF PAY.
Maule, John, Unattached	9 Apr. 25	30 Aug. 26	30 Oct. 40	25 Feb. 48
Mauleverer, William, 58 Foot, *Staff Officer of Pensioners*	31 Aug. 30	13 Jan. 37	22 July 42	23 Aug. 44
W Maunsell, John Edm.,[176] R. Artillery	14 June 05	1 June 06	24 Mar. 17	14 Nov. 26
Maxwell, Henry, Unattached	4 Mar. 13	13 Jan. 14	10 April 23	18 May 26
Mayne, William, Unattached	16 Dec. 16	26 Dec. 24	25 Oct. 27	25 Oct. 27
P Meech, Thomas Crosby,[177] 62 Foot	5 Sept. 05	26 Dec. 05	1 Oct. 12	3 May 21
Meek, Jacob,[178] Unattached	21 Mar. 10	22 Oct. 12	23 June 25	26 April 34
Meik, Francis Thomas,[179] 16 Lancers	1 Nov. 28	4 May 32	3 April 46	6 April 47
P *Melhuish, S. Camplin*,[180] R. Engineers	25 April 09	28 May 10	20 Dec. 14	
Mellis, John, Unattached	10 June 26	3 April 28	24 Jan. 40	24 Jan. 40
P Mends, Hugh Bowen, R. Staff Corps	13 Nov. 06	27 Nov. 06	12 Feb. 14	26 Feb. 29
Messiter, George Hughes, Unattached	15 June 30	29 Sept. 34	3 Sept. 47	3 Sept. 47
Metcalf, Thomas Levet, 6 R. Vet Batt.	5 Aug. 99	23 May 00	25 April 05	
Meynell, Edward Francis, 79 Foot	8 July 13	26 Aug. 13	19 June 17	30 May 22
Michell, Walter Taylor, Royal Marines	10 June 94	24 April 95	21 Dec. 03	5 Oct. 13
Mildmay, *Sir* Henry St. John, *Bart.* 60 F.	20 Nov. 28	8 June 30	7 Apr. 37	25 Apr. 48
Miller, Thomas,[182] Unattached	5 May 04	26 Sept. 04	17 Feb. 14	8 April 26
Millerd, Thomas, Unattached	29 Mar. 22	27 Feb. 24	8 April 26	8 April 26
P Minchin, John Paul,[183] 100 Foot	14 Aug. 04	8 Oct. 06	26 Nov. 12	6 April 20
Mitchell, Thomas Henry, Unattached	27 Feb. 35	29 Dec. 40	12 Nov. 47	12 Nov. 47
Mitchell, Thomas Peter, 69 Foot	1 June 00	5 April 01	11 April 11	3 June 13
Mitford, Bertram Charles, Unattached, *Town-Major at Malta*	27 April 27	3 May 31	26 Feb. 41	5 April 44
Mitford, John Philip,[185] Unattached	4 June 29	16 May 34	8 Feb. 41	20 Aug. 44
W Molesworth, A. Oliv.,[186] R. Artillery	17 Dec. 12	20 June 15	10 July 34	28 Dec. 35
Molesworth, Arthur, Royal Marines	6 Feb. 05	27 July 08	12 Oct. 30	9 Dec. 34
P W Molloy, John,[187] Unattached	17 Dec. 07	5 June 09	5 Aug. 24	28 May 29
Molyneux, John, 52 Foot	20 July 15	16 Sept. 19	21 July 25	18 Nov. 31
P Montgomery, Alex. Rich.,[188] 23 Foot	16 May 05	28 May 06	17 Sept. 12	16 Dec. 13
Moore, Frederick, 22 Dragoons	3 April 17	12 Sept. 22	23 June 25	16 Aug. 33
Moore, Henry, Unattached	6 July 15	17 Feb. 23	23 April 26	23 April 26
W Moore, James Stewart, 24 Dragoons	1 Aug. 11	7 April 13	15 April 19	25 Dec. 19
P *Moore, Thomas*,[189] 18 Foot	25 Oct. 07	8 Mar. 10	18 Feb. 26	
Moore, Thomas, Royal Marines, *Barrack Master, Portsmouth Division*	20 Jan. 98	23 Sept. 03	21 Nov. 10	16 Aug. 27
Moorhead, Alex. Gordon,[190] Unattached	26 May 22	3 Dec. 25	3 Mar. 48	3 Mar. 48
P Mordaunt, Lewis, 61 Foot	1 Sept. 04	20 Feb. 06	26 July 12	25 Dec. 14
Morgan, Charles, Royal Marines	11 Sept. 05	11 Nov. 08	17 Mar. 31	
P Morgan, Edward,[192] 75 Foot	never	4 Feb. 08	5 Mar. 12	22 Aug. 22
P *Morgan, Evan*,[193] Royal Artillery	17 Dec. 12	23 May 15	10 Feb. 34	
P *Morgan, Hugh*,[194] Royal Artillery	21 Dec. 08	7 Feb. 12	30 June 30	
P Morle, John,[195] 3 West India Regt.	18 Aug. 08	14 Sept. 09	2 Sept. 13	29 April 19
*Morris, Griffith Jeffrey, 22 Foot	never	never	25 Dec. 13	25 Sept. 14
P Morris, Samuel, 28 Foot	31 Jan. 05	2 April 06	25 Nov. 13	25 Dec. 14
P Morrison, Hans, 60 Foot	7 May 07	15 Feb. 08	13 Feb. 27	6 Dec. 27
Morshead, Pentyre Anderson, Royal Art.	19 Mar. 39	1 Oct. 41	30 June 48	9 Oct. 48
Mortimer, Edmund, Unattached	20 May 20	31 Dec. 27	18 July 34	18 July 34
Mottley, Thomas Martin, Royal Artillery	11 Dec. 15	15 Nov. 24	10 Jan. 37	30 Dec. 37
Mounsteven, Hender,[196] 48 Foot	30 Dec. 12	6 Jan. 14	30 Nov. 38	
W Mounsteven, Thos. Wm. Blewett,[197] 19 Foot, *Staff Officer of Pensioners*	25 Nov. 13	25 Oct. 20	8 May 35	1847
Mullen, John, Unattached, *Staff Officer of Pensioners*	13 July 20	3 Mar. 26	19 Aug. 41	13 July 43
Mundy, Charles Godfrey, Grenadier Gds.	13 April 96	never	23 Oct. 99	5 Dec. 02
Munro, George, Unattached, *Staff Officer of Pensioners*	20 Jan. 14	29 Mar. 21	10 July 40	10 July 40
Murray, Charles Robert, Unattached	1 Aug. 22	19 May 25	8 April 26	25 Nov. 28
Murray, George, Unattached	25 June 30	12 Aug. 34	30 Aug. 39	25 Feb. 48
Murray, Henry, Royal Artillery	20 June 32	24 Oct. 34	9 Sept. 43	15 May 44
Murray, John Digby, Unattached	never	5 Jan. 14	2 April 18	18 Aug. 25
Murray, Virginius, 86 Foot	22 May 35	4 Nov. 36	8 Aug. 45	2 July 47
Nelson, Alex. Abercromby,[198] Unattached	6 Mar. 35	15 Mar. 39	31 July 46	31 Dec. 47
Nesham, Thomas W., Unattached	14 April 25	29 Aug. 26	24 May 33	19 Mar. 41
Nestor, James, 19 Foot	16 Sept. 04	15 Nov. 05	24 Oct. 11	14 Mar. 22
Newbery, George, 44 Foot	31 Jan. 11	1 Oct. 12	24 Feb. 16	24 May 16
Newburg, Ar. R. Camac, Unattached	25 April 17	16 July 21	17 June 23	21 May 25

	2D LIEUT. ETC.	LIEUT.	CAPTAIN.	WHEN PLACED ON HALF PAY.
Newell, George, 4 R. Veteran Batt.	never	7 Oct. 94	15 Aug. 00	
Newhouse, William,[199] Unattached	14 Sept. 15	17 Sept. 18	13 Jan. 37	14 Dec. 38
P Newman, John, Portuguese Service ..	17 July 06	25 Nov. 07	25 Oct. 14	25 Dec. 16
Neynoe, Charles FitzRoy, Unattached....	25 May 20	9 Dec. 24	29 Sept. 29	21 May 33
Nicholas, James, Royal Marines........	21 Sept. 05	6 April 09	4 June 31	30 Sept. 33
Nicholls, John, Unattached	12 Feb. 18	7 Dec. 38	14 Jan. 48	14 Jan. 48
Nicholson, Chris. Hampden, Unattached	8 Mar. 25	14 Jan. 26	5 July 31	9 April 41
P Nicholson, Huntley,[201] Grenadier Gds.	10 Oct. 11	5 Aug. 18	24 Mar. 36	17 Sept. 39
P Nicolls, Augustus,[202] Unattached	5 Oct. 09	1 Sept. 13	17 Mar. 37	17 Mar. 37
P W Nisbet, Robert, 20 Dragoons	30 Nov. 09	26 Dec. 11	19 Nov. 18	19 Nov. 18
Nooth, Henry Stephen, 6 Dr. Guards....	never	14 May 12	29 Jan. 24	13 May 24
Norman, Robert,[203] Unattached	7 Sept. 26	2 Sept. 29	25 Aug. 42	31 July 46
Norris, John, Royal Marines	12 Sept. 05	20 Dec. 08	17 Mar. 31	20 July 36
North, Philip,[204] Unattached	5 Aug. 13	21 Sept. 20	16 Feb. 31	13 Nov. 32
Northey, Wm. Brook, Coldstream Guards	never	1 Aug. 22	20 April 26	25 May 29
Norton, James Roy, Unatt., *Adjutant South Hants Militia*	9 April 25	17 Dec. 30	29 Dec. 43	3 April 40
Nott, Francis Percy, 1 Garrison Batt. *Staff Officer of Pensioners*........	23 June 25	10 May 26	1 Nov. 40	29 Mar. 44.
Nunn, John, Unattached, *Barrack-Master at Ipswich*	4 June 12	7 Sept. 15	15 Nov. 39	15 Nov. 39
Oates, William Coape, Glengarry Fencibles	22 Aug. 11	7 Oct. 18	27 July 15	25 Aug. 16
O'Brien, Henry H. D., Royal Artillery	5 Oct. 18	2 Feb. 27	11 Dec. 36	
O'Connell, Daniel, Unattached	4 May 32	22 Aug. 37	14 April 40	23 May 45
P O'Hegerty, Charles, 60 Foot	21 Mar. 05	22 Feb. 09	16 Sept. 13	25 Mar. 16
P O'Neill, Charles,[205] 2 Foot	16 June 08	4 Jan. 10	5 June 27	30 Jan. 36
P O'Neill, William,[207] Unattached	12 Aug. 12	22 May 18	28 Dec. 41	28 Dec. 41
Onslow, *Sir* Henry, *Bart.*, Royal Artillery	20 Dec. 98	2 Dec. 00	1 June 06	9 June 19
W Ormsby, Arthur,[208] Unattached	2 June 14	27 Jan. 23	15 Jan. 36	25 Aug. 37
Ormsby, Augustus Howard,[209] Unattached	29 June 24	22 Mar. 26	3 Feb. 43	9 April 47
Ormsby, Owen Lloyd, Unattached, *Staff Officer of Pensioners*........	21 Dec. 32	2 Feb. 38	1 Nov. 39	29 Dec. 43
Osborne, William, Unattached..........	30 Jan. 23	13 Aug. 25	31 Oct. 26	7 Mar. 34
Ostheyden, Frederick, Unattached	27 Jan. 07	26 Jan. 11	11 Feb. 42	11 Feb. 42
Ouseley, William, Unattached..........	20 May 18	31 Jan. 22	9 June 25	9 Aug. 31
P *Ovens, John*,[210] 57 Foot	2 July 12	5 July 14	9 Sept. 37	
Owen, Robert, 12 Foot	4 April 98	3 July 00	29 May 07	2 July 18
W Packe, Geo. Hussey,[211] 21 Dragoons	24 June 13	6 Jan. 14	27 June 16	25 Mar. 17
*Page, Robert, 9 Foot	never	never	25 Dec. 13	25 Sept. 14
Paget, Catesby, R. Staff Corps, *Staff Officer of Pensioners*	8 Nov. 27	31 Aug. 30	9 Mar. 39	26 Jan. 44
W Pakenham, William, Royal Artillery	30 Aug. 04	10 April 05	20 Dec. 14	1 July 22
Paley, John Green, Unattached	26 June 27	29 Nov. 33	26 Feb. 41	29 Mar. 42
Palliser, Richard Bury, Unattached	2 Nov. 13	9 April 18	12 Aug. 24	6 April 26
Palmer, Edward Despard, 67 Foot......	Dec. 99	22 May 00	7 Sept. 09	18 Nov. 17
Palmer, John, Unattached	5 July 13	27 Oct. 16	5 April 31	5 April 31
Parker, Edward, Unattached	14 April 25	4 Dec. 28	16 Dec. 36	23 June 43
Parker, John, Unattached	29 Nov. 21	12 May 25	19 Sept. 26	19 Sept. 26
W Parker, Stephen,[213] Rifle Brigade....	9 Feb. 09	11 April 11	20 Mar. 27	9 Oct. 35
Parlby, George, Unattached............	1 Aug. 16	3 Oct. 19	30 Sept. 25	7 Dec. 26
Passley, Richard Brown Fuller, 82 Foot	8 Sept. 08	6 Nov. 09	16 Mar. 32	
Patriarche, Philip, Royal Marines	13 May 95	6 Oct. 96	15 Aug. 05	29 Nov. 14
*Patrick, James, 70 Foot..............	never	never	25 Dec. 13	25 Sept. 14
P Pattenson, Cooke Tylden, Rifle Brigade	19 Feb. 07	9 Mar. 09	18 Aug. 14	25 Dec. 18
Payne, Charles Wm. Meadows, Unatt. ..	1 Aug. 26	21 June 31	29 Dec. 35	24 Sept. 41
Payne, Wm. Aug. Townshend, Unatt.....	23 May 29	7 June 33	20 Sept. 39	14 Aug. 46
Payne, Wm. Staines, Royal Artillery	16 Dec. 31	19 Aug. 33	4 April 43	14 Oct. 46
Pattoun, George, Royal Marines........	28 Feb. 06	13 Mar. 12	15 May 34	
Peacocke, Stephen Ponsonby, Unattached	25 Oct. 33	15 Sept. 37	23 Aug. 39	23 Aug. 44
Pearson, Charles, Unattached	15 Dec. 17	18 May 25	22 April 26	6 Feb. 35
Peevor, George,[215] 3 Foot, *Captain of Invalids, Royal Hospital, Chelsea*..	1 Dec. 07	1 Jan. 10	2 Sept. 24	9 June 25
P Pemberton, G. Keating,[216] Royal Artil.	5 Mar. 10	17 Dec. 13	3 Oct. 31	8 July 34
Penruddocke, Thomas, Scots Fus. Gds. ..	15 Nov. 97	never	25 Nov. 99	25 Dec. 02
Pepyat, George Bownell, Royal Marines	31 Jan. 06	3 Sept. 11	12 Oct. 32	
Perry, Joseph, 34 Foot................	2 June 04	18 April 05	7 Dec. 18	24 Mar. 26

	Ensign, etc.	Lieut.	Captain.	When placed on half pay.
Petley, Patrick M'Leod, Unatt., *Adjutant Edinburgh Militia*	22 May 32	31 Aug. 36	24 June 42	3 Apr. 46
Petterson, Theophilus, Royal Marines ..	2 Dec. 96	4 Oct. 01	20 Feb. 09	5 May 28
Petre, John, 22 Dragoons..............			3 May 00	8 Dec. 02
Pettat, Thomas John, Unattached	4 May 26	14 April 29	18 Sept. 31	8 June 32
P * Pettingal, Francis, 1 Prov. Batt. Mil.	never	never	25 Dec. 13	1814
Pettingall, Francis William, R. Engineers	1 Mar. 16	23 Mar. 25	20 Nov. 37	
Phillippe, James Winsloe, Unattached ..	8 April 19	17 July 23	11 Feb. 26	19 Nov. 29
Phillippe, Henry, Unattached	30 May 22	22 Oct. 25	25 Nov. 28	18 Dec. 35
P *Phillips, Robt. Fryer*,[219] Royal Artillery	4 Oct. 06	1 Feb. 08	29 July 25	
Pickard, George Percy, 6 Dr. Gds. *Staff Officer of Pensioners*	20 April 24	11 Feb. 27	17 Sept. 39	13 July 47
W *Pigot, Brooke*,[220] 69 Foot..........	19 July 10	9 May 11	29 Aug. 26	
Pigott, Robert, 1 Garrison Battalion	16 June 04	18 Nov. 04	9 July 07	25 June 16
P Pigott, William, 11 Foot	19 Mar. 03	28 Aug. 04	5 Nov. 07	9 July 18
Pinkerton, Robert, Royal Marines	9 Mar. 96	15 Dec. 98	19 June 07	16 Oct. 15
Pitcairn, Robert, 6 Garrison Battalion, *Staff Officer of Pensioners*	19 Jan. 26	26 Oct. 30	6 Sept. 39	27 Sept. 44
P W Pitman, William,[223] Unattached ..	6 Aug. 12	27 Sept. 18	12 April 31	10 Jan. 34
Pitts, Francis, Unattached	25 Nov. 21	17 Feb. 25	15 April 36	15 April 36
Pocklington, Evelyn Henry Fred., Unatt.	10 Feb. 29	30 Aug. 33	24 May 39	13 July 47
Pode, William, 33 Foot................	8 June 09	12 Jan. 11	17 May 21	25 Oct. 21
Pole, George Robert, Unattached, *Staff Officer of Pensioners*	11 Aug. 25	24 April 28	27 Sept. 44	27 Sept. 44
W Poole, Wm. Halstead,[225] Royal Art.	11 Sept. 12	10 May 15	25 Nov. 33	22 Jan. 34
P Porteous, Alexander, 60 Foot	17 July 06	23 July 07	20 April 15	25 July 15
Porter, William, 3 R. Veteran Batt.....	28 Oct. 94	13 Jan. 95	9 July 08	
P Potter, Thomas, Portuguese Service ..	13 Nov. 06	2 Mar. 09	25 Oct. 14	25 Dec. 16
Poulden, Richard Mathews, R. Artillery	29 July 25	3 Jan. 28	22 Oct. 40	
Powell, Henry Caringbold, Unattached, *Staff Officer of Pensioners*........	9 April 25	17 July 26	8 April 42	7 April 43
Powell, Peter, 2 West India Regt.	26 Oct. 04	2 Mar. 06	4 Feb. 13	26 Feb. 30
Powys, Thomas, Unattached	never	30 April 12	2 Jan. 18	30 April 29
Pratt, James, 1 R. Veteran Battalion ..	26 May 81	22 Jan. 83	12 Feb. 07	
P Prendergast, James, Unattached......	28 Aug. 06	26 Nov. 07	7 April 25	1 Nov. 27
P Price, David, 36 Foot	25 Dec. 06	23 April 07	8 Oct. 12	25 Dec. 14
P Price, Rice,[226] 57 Foot	Mar. 08	21 July 08	27 April 20	25 Dec. 21
Price, Thomas Donaldson,[229] 62 Foot ..	8 Dec. 08	30 Apr. 12	28 Aug. 38	
* Prickett, William, Royal Waggon Train	never	never	25 Dec. 13	25 June 16
P W *Pringle, J. Watson*,[230] R. Engineers	23 Aug. 09	1 May 11	21 July 15	
P W Prior, Tho. Murray,[231] Unattached	6 Aug. 03	22 Feb. 06	28 Nov. 34	28 Nov. 34
Protheroe, W. Gar. Bridges,[232] 56 Foot ..	11 Mar. 01	12 Nov. 03	8 Oct. 07	18 Nov. 19
Purcell, Tobias, Unattached...........	28 Sept. 09	17 Sept. 12	30 Aug. 27	14 May 29
Purves, John Home, Unatt., *Brigade Major at Portsmouth*	never	29 Nov. 33	13 July 38	14 May 47
P Pyner, Francis, 58 Foot, *Adjutant 2nd R. Surrey Militia*............	25 Feb. 07	25 Mar. 08	4 April 13	25 Feb. 16
P Quentin, Geo. Edward, Portuguese Ser.	28 July 08	17 May 09	25 Oct. 14	25 Dec. 16
W Rainforth, William, Unattached	2 Dec. 12	23 Dec. 13	6 Feb. 35	9 June 38
Ralph, Joseph, Unattached	1 Jan. 26	11 June 30	16 Dec. 45	16 Dec. 45
Ramsay, Francis, Royal Artillery	20 Dec. 32	12 June 35	15 April 44	1 May 48
P W Ramsay, Thomas,[233] 14 Foot......	19 June 06	16 Feb. 08	17 May 10	25 Mar. 16
Rannie, William, Unattached	21 May 07	29 Jan. 08	5 Oct. 32	22 Feb. 39
W Rawson, William, 27 Foot, *Adjutant, 3rd West York Militia*	16 Aug. 99	29 Mar. 04	4 May 09	2 July 18
Read, Constantine, Royal Staff Corps....	7 Nov. 16	7 April 25	24 Aug. 32	24 Aug. 32
Ready, William,[234] Unattached, *Staff Officer of Pensioners*	19 May 25	28 June 27	24 Jan. 45	24 Jan. 45
Reeves, Thomas, 24 Foot	7 Sept. 94	9 Oct. 05	25 June 07	8 April 19
P Reynett, James Henry, 45 Foot	19 Sept. 04	4 June 06	28 July 12	1814
Reynolds, Edward, Royal Engineers	5 May 37	24 Jan. 39	20 Apr. 46	22 Apr. 47
Reynolds, Henry,[236] Unattached	8 Oct. 25	1 Mar. 33	27 Feb. 46	27 Feb. 46
Reynolds, John William, Unattached....	18 Sept. 35	2 Nov. 38	10 Jan. 40	26 Sept. 45
Rich, John Sampson,[237] Royal Artillery..	1 Mar. 08	30 April 09	9 Dec. 28	6 Nov. 30
Rich, Robert James Evelyn, 66 Foot	12 Aug. 24	29 June 26	1 Feb. 31	14 Feb. 31
Richards, George, Royal Marines	25 Jan. 98	18 Oct. 03	19 April 12	18 Mar. 13
Richardson, Frederick, 5 Foot..........	19 April 15	18 Dec. 24	17 Sept. 29	28 Dec. 32

	CORNET, ETC.	LIEUT.	CAPTAIN.	WHEN PLACED ON HALF PAY.
Richardson, James, Unat., *Staff Of. of Pen.*	7 April 20	3 Nov. 25	2 April 41	29 Dec. 43
Richardson, John George,[238] R. Marines	18 Sept. 05	14 Feb. 09	17 Mar. 31	
Richardson, Mervyn, Unattached	19 July 15	2 May 24	4 Feb. 26	4 Feb. 26
Richardson, Thomas, 7 Dragoons	3 Sept. 07	10 Mar. 08	22 May 16	4 Sept. 17
Rickards, Henry,[239] Unattached	29 Aug. 07	23 Sept. 08	3 Mar. 25	18 May 26
*Rickards, William, 64 Foot	never	never	25 Dec. 13	25 Aug. 16
Ridding, William, 59 Foot	21 Aug. 95	9 Oct. 97	3 Aug. 12	5 Mar. 18
*Riddlesden, Richard, 4 Foot	never	never	25 Dec. 13	25 Sept. 14
Ridge, Robert Stuart,[240] 36 Foot	8 Sept. 14	28 Dec. 21	29 Sept. 37	
P W Ridgway, John A.,[241] Unattached, *Adjutant, North Devon Militia*	25 Jan. 10	9 May 12	24 Dec. 29	19 July 31
*Ridgway, Samuel, 85 Foot............	never	never	25 Dec. 13	1814
Rivers, Jas. John Campbell, R. Marines	18 Mar. 06	17 April 12	27 May 34	
P W Roberts, John,[242] Unattached	21 April 08	12 Oct. 09	7 April 25	21 June 27
Roberts, John Cramer, Unattached......	18 Jan. 15	13 June 16	14 July 25	14 July 25
Robertson, Alexander, Unattached	16 Nov. 09	28 Nov. 10	6 Mar. 27	6 Mar. 27
Robertson, Archibald, Unattached	4 Dec. 23	31 Aug. 26	11 Dec. 28	12 Mar. 41
Robertson, Frederick, Royal Artillery....	22 Dec. 03	20 July 04	23 July 13	10 Oct. 21
Robertson, George Abercrombie,[243] Unatt.	26 April 28	13 May 31	12 April 46	1 Aug. 48
*Robertson, John, 14 Foot	never	never	25 Dec. 13	25 Sept. 14
Robertson, Patrick, Royal Marines......	10 Jan. 01	4 Aug. 05	13 Aug. 25	4 Feb. 35
Robinson, Beverley, Royal Artillery	10 May 05	1 June 06	20 Jan. 17	1 April 17
Roche, Joseph, 3 R. Veteran Battalion ..	15 Dec. 04	10 Feb. 07	16 May 11	
Roddy, Charles Hamilton, Unattached ..	15 Feb. 27	15 April 29	27 Oct. 37	31 Dec. 42
Rogers, Henry Blankley H., Unatt., *Staff Officer of Pensioners*	17 Jan. 28	12 April 33	14 Oct. 36	22 Nov. 42
Rollo, Robert A.,[244] Royal Artillery	17 Aug. 03	12 Sept. 03	29 Dec. 10	12 April 20
P Rose, Hugh Hay, Portuguese Service..	14 July 04	3 Oct. 05	25 Oct. 14	25 Dec. 16
Rose, William, 97 Foot...............	8 Feb. 94	3 Sept. 94	15 Nov. 94	
Rous, *Hon.* Wm. Rufus, Portuguese Serv.	never	17 Dec. 12	18 Nov. 19	24 April 23
Rowan, William, 84 Foot..............	27 May 02	6 April 09	9 June 20	1 Nov. 21
P Royds, William,[246] 52 Foot...........	16 Feb. 08	15 Feb. 09	9 June 14	25 Feb. 17
P Rudkin, Mark,[247] 47 Foot	12 July 05	29 Jan. 07	21 Jan. 13	15 May 28
Runnecles, Anthony, Royal Artillery	11 Dec. 15	22 Sept. 23	10 Jan. 37	27 Mar. 37
Rushout, George, Unattached	18 Jan. 33	10 Feb. 37	18 Mar. 42	4 June 47
Russell, Henshaw, 60 Foot, *Staff Officer of Pensioners*	16 May 34	24 Mar. 37	10 Sept. 41	25 June 44
Russell, John Ambrose, Unattached, *Staff Officer of Pensioners*	25 Dec. 23	28 Feb. 28	2 April 41	31 Mar. 48
Rutherford, James Hunter, R. Engineers	20 July 13	15 Dec. 13	12 Nov. 31	
Sampson, John,[248] 8 Garrison Batt. *Staff Officer of Pensioners*	29 Nov. 10	9 Dec. 13	23 May 38	29 Dec. 43
Sampson, W. H., Unattached	14 Oct. 13	15 April 19	3 Nov. 35	1 Feb. 39
Sanderson, Edward, Scotch Brigade	18 Mar. 95	6 Sept. 95	25 June 03	2 Feb. 08
P Sandwith, Fred. Browne, 38 Foot	8 Oct. 06	29 Aug. 07	31 Mar. 14	25 Dec. 14
P Saunderson, William Basset, 50 Foot..	6 Mar. 07	28 April 08	4 Mar. 13	9 May 22
Savage, Henry, Royal Marines	2 Dec. 11	22 July 30	26 Aug. 40	3 May 44
Savile, *Hon.* Frederick, Royal Artillery ..	18 June 35	8 Nov. 37	1 Apr. 46	9 Apr. 47
Sayer, Joshua Saffrey, Royal Marines ..	10 Aug. 99	1 Sept. 04	20 June 23	
Schalch, Andrew Archer Wm.[250] Roy. Art.	17 Dec. 07	10 Mar. 09	6 Nov. 27	
W Schreiber, George, 18 Dragoons	23 Dec. 13	11 July 16	9 Nov. 21	9 Nov. 21
Scott, Charles, Royal Marines..........	13 Feb. 06	16 Jan. 12	19 Mar. 34	11 April 36
Scott, Edward, 4 Dragoons	28 Dec. 26	8 June 30	31 Aug. 38	Mar. 42
Scott, Rich. Andrew, R. Staff Corps	28 Feb. 14	19 Mar. 25	24 Aug. 32	24 Aug. 32
Scriven, John, Royal Marines	28 Feb. 96	21 Oct. 98	4 May 07	9 Aug. 14
Sealy, Francis, 97 Foot...............	19 Nov. 30	21 Dec. 32	5 Oct. 38	16 July 41
Searle, Richard,[251] Royal Marines	30 Sept. 08	13 April 24	10 July 37	
P Seward, Elliot,[252] Royal Artillery	29 Sept. 04	3 July 05	10 May 15	16 Jan. 18
Shand, John Muller, 89 Foot	9 Feb. 01	28 Aug. 04	15 Jan. 12	25 Jan. 17
Shawe, Francis Manby, Unattached	never	6 May 13	5 Oct. 20	13 April 26
Shearman, John, 7 Foot	19 Feb. 06	27 Nov. 06	15 Feb. 16	20 Dec. 21
Sheppard, Walter Cope, Unattached	8 May 23	10 Nov. 25	9 April 29	25 June 31
P Sherran, William, 43 Foot	22 Aug. 99	10 July 01	8 Sept. 08	25 Sept. 16
Shoveller, William King, Royal Marines	2 Oct. 29	10 July 37	6 May 47	14 July 48
P Shuckburgh, Charles Robert,[254] 70 Foot, *Staff Officer of Pensioners* ..	25 July 11	5 Aug. 13	21 June 39	25 Sept. 40
P Shum, William, 3 Dragoon Guards ..	10 Dec. 07	21 Feb. 10	27 May 13	25 Mar. 10
Shute, James, Royal Marines..........	21 June 06	30 Jan. 13	27 May 34	

	2d Lieut. etc.	Lieut.	Captain.	When placed on half pay.
Shaw, George Gardine,[255] 63 Foot......	30 May 11	21 Dec. 13	31 May 39	
Siborne, William, Unatt. *Secretary and Adj. R. Mil. Asylum at Chelsea*....	9 Sept. 13	8 Nov. 15	31 Jan. 40	31 Jan. 40
Silver, Jacob, Unattached..............	11 Sept. 13	15 Oct. 18	11 Mar. 24	8 April 26
Sisson, Joseph, Unattached	18 Sept. 06	26 Aug. 08	7 April 25	14 Sept. 26
P *Skene, Alexander,* 4 R. Veteran Batt.	28 May 07	25 July 09	11 Nov. 13	
Skinner, Henry Bryant,[256] Royal Marines	10 Mar. 09	20 Jan. 26	10 July 37	
Skinner, Samuel James, Royal Artillery	23 Oct. 18	1 April 27	16 May 39	
Skirrow, James, 48 Foot	3 Dec. 03	28 Jan. 05	2 Sept. 13	25 Dec. 28
Slater, Henry Francis, Royal Artillery ..	1 May 15	6 Nov. 20	4 June 36	19 Aug. 39
Small, Robert, Unattached	4 Oct. 11	29 Sept. 14	29 Oct. 25	29 Oct. 25
Smith, Charles Henry Montressor, 60 F. *Staff Officer of Pens., New Zealand*	15 Mar. 39	6 Jan. 41	23 Aug. 44	22 June 47
Smith, Edm. Carrington, Unattached....	28 Dec. 19	10 Feb. 25	8 April 26	8 April 26
Smith, Henry, Royal Marines..........	18 Feb. 09	13 Aug. 25	10 July 37	
Smith, Henry Nelson, Royal Engineers ..	1 Mar. 10	1 May 11	26 Aug. 19	1 Feb. 20
Smith, John, Royal Artillery	17 Aug. 99	27 May 01	1 June 06	
Smith, Leicester Viney, R. Eng. *Assist.-Dep. Quar.-Master Gen. in Dublin*	1 Aug. 16	29 July 25	15 Oct. 39	4 Mar. 40
Smith, Thomas, Unattached............	13 Sept. 31	4 July 34	19 Nov. 47	19 Nov. 47
Smith, William,[257] Unattached..........	26 July 38	13 June 40	14 April 46	1 Aug. 48
Somerset, Henry Cha. Capel, 27 Foot, *Staff Officer of Pensioners*........	4 Oct. 33	14 July 37	23 June 43	27 Sept. 44
Somerville, John, Royal Artillery	5 July 13	9 Dec. 15	29 Dec. 34	
Southwell, Hon. *Chas.*, KH., 12 R. Vet. Batt.	never	3 July 95	17 Sept. 03	
Spearman, James Morton, Unattached ..	10 July 15	23 Jan. 21	25 Oct. 27	25 Oct. 27
P Spearman, John, 5 Foot	22 Mar. 98	9 Aug. 99	28 April 08	26 Nov. 18
Spedding, John, Irish Brigade..........	never	12 Aug. 95	25 May 98	23 Nov. 04
Spry, Henry, Royal Marines	6 Jan. 01	25 July 05	20 June 25	13 Aug. 25
Spurin, John, Royal Marines	7 Feb. 97	19 Nov. 01	22 July 09	15 Sept. 26
*Stanier, George, 82 Foot.............	never	never	3 Dec. 99	1800
P Stanley, Mark Anthony,[258] Unattached	15 June 09	16 Aug. 10	29 Dec. 24	10 Feb. 32
*Stapleton, William Philip, 51 Foot	never	never	25 Dec. 13	25 Aug. 15
Stapley, Thomas, Unattached	30 April 05	5 Aug. 06	26 July 21	17 Aug. 32
Staunton, William, 118 Foot	10 Jan. 95	8 June 96	20 Nov. 01	1806
P Steiger, Rodolphe,[259] Portuguese Serv.	11 May 06	9 July 07	25 Oct. 14	25 Dec. 16
P Stephens, Henry William, 6 Foot	31 Aug. 04	13 June 05	26 Feb. 07	25 Feb. 16
Stephens, John Morse, Royal Artillery ..	3 Oct. 07	5 June 08	6 Nov. 27	
Sterling, Anthony Coningham, Unattached	29 Jan. 26	14 April 29	11 Oct. 33	5 Dec. 43
W Steuart, John,[260] Unattached........	17 June 13	10 Nov. 14	12 Nov. 25	2 April 29
W Steuart, Robert, Unattached	12 Aug. 12	11 Aug. 14	3 Mar. 25	19 Jan. 26
Stevenson, Thomas, Royal Staff Corps ..	5 Oct. 15	6 Jan. 20	15 Oct. 25	28 Sept. 38
Steward, Thomas Carr, Royal Marines..	5 July 03	15 Aug. 05	31 July 26	
P Stewart, Daniel, 3 Foot	13 April 09	21 Nov. 10	19 Dec. 26	23 July 18
Stewart, Donald, 84 F., *Staff Off. of Pen.*	30 Sept. 30	7 Feb. 34	17 Sept. 39	8 Aug. 45
P W Stewart, Duncan,[262] Unattached ..	13 June 05	1 Jan. 07	3 Aug. 15	25 Dec. 26
Stewart, James, 87 Foot	16 May 05	15 Jan. 06	9 June 14	14 Mar. 21
Stewart, Joseph King, Unattached	11 Dec. 17	16 Dec. 19	8 April 26	8 April 26
Stewart, William, Royal Artillery	16 Dec. 16	29 July 25	10 Jan. 37	3 May 43
*Still, Nathaniel Tyron, 5 Foot	never	never	25 Dec. 13	25 Sept. 14
Stockenstrom, *Sir* And. *Bt.* R. Corsican Ran.	12 Sept. 11	7 June 14	25 May 20	20 July 20
Stocker, Ives, Royal Engineers	14 Dec. 11	1 July 12	29 July 25	
Stokes, Patrick Day, 4 F., *Staff Off. of Pen.*	22 Oct. 33	13 Jan. 38	8 Nov. 44	6 Dec. 44
Stokes, William John, Royal Artillery ..	10 July 15	2 April 21	29 June 36	
Story, George Walter, Unattached	7 Feb. 22	26 May 25	6 July 30	6 July 30
Strange, Charles, Unattached	6 May 19	25 Dec. 23	21 Nov. 28	21 Nov. 28
Strangwayes, Thomas, 12 Foot..........	17 Feb. 03	9 June 04	4 June 11	13 Jan. 20
Strangways, George Fox, Unattached....	5 Oct. 20	8 April 25	25 June 29	8 June 38
Straubenzee, Charles, 6 West India Regt.	28 Oct. 95	5 Sept. 96	14 Dec. 04	15 Oct. 07
Stuart, *Hon.* Arch. Geo., 6 West I. Regt.	30 April 29	30 Aug. 31	25 May 39	11 July 45
Stuart, Charles Augustus, Unattached ..	26 Nov. 06	18 Feb. 08	14 Oct. 24	16 April 29
Stuart, *Hon.* John, Unattached	12 July 15	14 Nov. 16	27 Aug. 25	27 Aug. 25
Suckling, Nelson Fleming, Unattached ..	16 Jan. 23	23 June 25	13 Mar. 27	13 Mar. 27
P *Sutherland, Andrew,* 5 R. Vet. Batt.	7 April 04	27 June 05	13 May 13	
Sutherland, Edward, Unatt., *Store-keeper, Royal Hospital, Chelsea*....	27 Nov. 16	14 April 25	25 Dec. 38	25 Dec. 38
P Sweeny, Charles Fred., Unattached ..	12 April 10	7 May 12	29 Dec. 37	20 Dec. 37
Sweny, Welbore Ellis, 9 Foot	1 May 13	6 Feb. 17	19 Nov. 25	21 Sept. 30

	ENSIGN, ETC.	LIEUT.	CAPTAIN.	WHEN PLACED ON HALF PAY.
Synnot, Walter, 89 Foot	7 June 93	3 Sept. 95	7 Dec. 97	1808
Tallan, Lawrence,[264] Unattached	1 Nov. 21	27 Aug. 24	22 Aug. 37	8 Aug. 45
Taylor, James, Unatt.	25 Aug. 14	4 Dec. 17	14 May 36	26 Oct. 41
Teale, Charles Shipley, Unattached, *Staff Officer of Pensioners*	7 April 25	10 Dec. 27	22 May 43	11 Oct. 44
P Tench, Henry, 10 Foot	9 July 03	15 Dec. 04	24 July 12	25 Feb. 16
* Terry, John, 74 Foot	never	never	25 Dec. 13	1814
* Terry, Stephen, 8 Foot	never	never	5 Dec. 99	3 Sept. 01
P Thatcher, Sackville Z.,[266] Unattached	1 Nov. 10	26 Aug. 13	8 Feb. 39	6 Dec. 39
Thomas, Thomas Rees, Royal Marines	19 April 06	4 July 12	27 May 34	
Thompson, Edward, Royal Staff Corps	9 Nov. 07	1 Mar. 10	13 June 16	10 Aug. 19
P Thompson, James, 89 Foot	19 June 06	15 Oct. 07	23 May 16	25 Jan. 17
Thompson, Pearson Scott, 7 Dragoon Gds.	5 Aug. 42	7 June 44	3 Sept. 47	9 Aug. 48
Thompson, Richard, 51 Foot	1 Jan. 19	8 Nov. 27	28 Aug. 41	
Tidy, Gordon Skelly,[267] Unattached	15 May 28	3 Dec. 29	5 July 44	28 Aug. 46
P *Tinling, Geo. Vaughan*,[268] R. Engineers	1 July 12	21 July 13	19 Oct. 26	
Tireman, Henry Stephen, Royal Artillery	6 Aug. 28	4 July 30	21 July 41	
Tobin, John, Unatt. *Adj. N. Glouces. Mil.*	28 Dec. 25	16 Aug. 27	30 Oct. 40	28 Aug. 46
Toby, Isaac, Royal Marines, *Barrack-Master, Plymouth Division*	3 April 10	9 Sept. 28	22 May 38	19 Mar. 42
W Tompkins, New. Rich., Unattached	21 Nov. 11	10 Dec. 13	19 Sept. 26	15 June 30
Tonge, John Henry, Unattached	29 April 36	1 June 38	30 April 41	25 Feb. 48
P Toole, William,[270] 40 Foot	5 Dec. 05	25 Aug. 07	9 Nov. 14	19 April 17
Torriano, C. Strangways,[271] Royal Artillery	25 April 06	22 Oct. 06	26 June 23	15 April 29
Townsend, Samuel Irwin, Grenadier Gds.	14 July 83	never	28 Aug. 99	16 July 08
W Trafford, Sigismund,[272] 1 Dragoons	7 June 10	25 July 11	9 Nov. 15	25 Mar. 16
Triscott, Joseph, Royal Marines	2 June 97	21 July 03	26 Oct. 10	1 Sept. 14
P Trotter, John,[273] Royal Artillery	26 Nov. 08	1 Nov. 11	19 Jan. 30	26 Aug. 31
Trotter, Robert Knox, Sub. Insp. of Mil.	12 May 25	6 July 26	9 Aug. 27	2 Dec. 36
Trower, Anthony, 4 Ceylon Regt.	1 Mar. 03	2 Dec. 04	15 July 13	15 June 15
Tucker, John Tudor,[274] Royal Marines	7 July 06	14 April 13	27 May 34	
Tulloch, James Dundas Gregory, 84 Foot, *Staff Officer of Pensioners*	18 July 30	14 Feb. 34	22 Aug. 41	16 Feb. 44
Turner, Richard, Royal Marines	12 Feb. 98	1 Dec. 03	9 Feb. 13	16 Feb. 14
Tweed, Augustus, Unattached	3 May 10	12 Sept. 11	5 June 27	5 June 27
P Tweedie, Michael,[275] Royal Artillery	1 May 09	17 June 12	22 July 30	17 Dec. 18
P W Tyndale, Charles W.,[276] Unatt.	9 May 11	3 June 13	5 Aug. 24	1 Sept. 37
Ussher, John,[277] Unattached	30 May 09	31 July 11	28 Dec. 32	13 Jan. 37
Vane, Charles Birch, Unattached	30 Dec. 26	17 Dec. 30	19 Jan. 39	25 June 47
Varlo, George, Royal Marines, *Barrack-Master, Woolwich Division*	18 June 93	24 April 95	15 July 03	23 Aug. 05
Vaughan, Eugene James, 57 Foot, *Adjutant Carmarthen Militia*	4 Nov. 25	9 Nov. 26	24 Oct. 41	6 June 45
P Vaughan, Herbert Henry,[278] Unatt.	29 June 09	16 Jan. 12	4 Sept. 23	25 Jan. 31
Veitch, Thomas George, Unattached	17 Aug. 26	10 July 28	26 June 35	1 July 42
P Ventry, T. T. Arem. *Lord*, 43 Foot	never	5 Feb. 07	8 Aug. 11	11 Dec. 17
Vereker, Charles, Unattached	9 April 25	27 Mar. 27	17 Aug. 38	21 Dec. 48
Vernon, Bowater Henry, Unattached	17 Oct. 16	8 July 24	28 Jan. 26	28 Jan. 26
P Vetch, James,[279] Royal Engineers	1 July 07	1 Mar. 08	21 July 13	11 Mar. 24
Vincent, Thomas, Royal York Rangers	20 Oct. 13	10 Aug. 15	28 June 27	12 Dec. 34
P Visme, Francis de, 60 Foot	22 Mar. 10	31 Dec. 12	19 Mar. 18	21 Feb. 22
Vyvyan, Thomas, 41 Foot	15 Aug. 04	28 Feb. 05	25 Dec. 07	13 July 15
Wake, Richard William, R. African Corps	10 April 25	22 April 26	16 July 30	25 May 38
P Walker, William, 24 Foot	6 July 09	13 June 11	22 Mar. 15	15 June 15
P Walker, William, 7 West India Regt.	Dec. 08	14 Sept. 08	30 Dec. 19	9 Aug. 20
Walsh, John, Royal Artillery	23 Nov. 04	1 Dec. 05	20 June 15	24 Feb. 23
Walsh, Lewis Edward, Royal Artillery	5 July 13	13 July 16	6 May 35	
Ward, John, 24 Foot	17 Sept. 03	20 Mar. 05	22 Oct. 12	26 Oct. 16
Ward, William, R. West India Rangers, *Adj. Cornwall and Devon Miners*	18 July 20	4 Dec. 32	9 May 43	29 Dec. 46
Ward, William, Unattached	18 Aug. 25	1 May 28	25 Oct. 44	25 Oct. 44
Warde, Walter, Unattached, *Staff Officer of Pensioners*	29 June 32	7 Aug. 35	25 Oct. 42	25 Oct. 42
* Warner, Richard, 5 Foot	never	never	25 Dec. 13	25 Sept. 14
Warrington, Thornhill, 76 Foot	13 Nov. 98	22 Nov. 98	23 Jan. 12	2 July 23
Waters, Thomas, Royal Marines	30 Nov. 04	27 July 08	22 July 30	
P Watkins, William Nowell, 48 Foot	16 June 03	2 June 04	8 Mar. 10	25 Oct. 21
Watson, William, 21 Dragoons	11 April 09	26 April 10	26 Nov. 18	7 Mar. 22
Webb, Daniel Peploe, Unattached	5 Oct. 15	11 July 22	12 Dec. 26	18 Dec. 28

	CORNET, ETC.	LIEUT.	CAPTAIN.	WHEN PLACED ON HALF PAY.*
Webb, John, Unattached	20 Dec. 04	18 July 05	3 July 29	3 July 29
Webb, John Wynne,[281] 7 R. Vet. Batt.	15 Mar. 08	20 July 10	23 Sept. 13	
Webb, Robert,[282] Royal Marines	24 Sept. 05	19 May 09	7 Mar. 32	
Webb, Vere,[283] Unat. *Adj. Cardigan Mil.*	12 May 12	9 Dec. 13	19 Aug. 31	6 Sept. 31
Webster, James C.,[284] Unattached	21 April 14	13 July 20	12 Nov. 25	1 Dec. 27
Weddenburn, J. K.[284a] Unattached	7 July 36	10 April 40	15 Dec. 48	15 Dec. 48
Welch, Stephen J. W. F., Cape Regt.	27 Aug. 25	19 Sept. 26	6 Sept. 27	6 Sept. 27
Welchman, Geo. Thomas, Royal Marines	31 Aug. 05	27 July 08	17 Mar. 31	
Weller, Francis, Royal Artillery	15 Dec. 17	29 July 25	12 Sept. 37	
Wellings, George, Unattached	14 Feb. 11	14 Nov. 11	23 Mar. 15	25 June 25
Wells, Fortescue,[285] Royal Artillery	4 Oct. 06	1 Feb. 08	29 July 25	29 July 25
Wemyss, James, Unattached	10 April 17	31 Jan. 21	22 Oct. 25	22 Oct. 25
Wetherall, Charles,[286] Unattached	15 Aug. 13	8 Aug. 16	29 June 24	27 June 34
Whalley, George Briscoe, Unattached	12 Dec. 26	12 Jan. 30	9 July 35	2 April 41
Wharton, William,[287] 43 Foot	4 Dec. 06	11 Dec. 06	13 Aug. 12	1 June 20
Whitle, Robert,[288] Unattached	25 Aug. 08	22 Feb. 10	22 Dec. 24	6 Dec. 27
Whitley, James, 9 Foot	22 Aug. 05	17 Dec. 06	17 June 13	25 Feb. 16
Whitmore, Mortimer R. S., 19 Dragoons, *Staff Officer of Pensioners*	26 June 27	5 Aug. 28	16 Feb. 38	23 June 43
Wightman, George, 48 Foot	5 July 00	30 May 09	17 Mar. 14	1814
Wilford, Ernest Christian, R. Staff Corps	2 Sept. 14	14 Mar. 23	19 April 31	19 April 31
Willard, Leonard Kilham, 11 R. Vet. Bat.	23 Aug. 99	3 April 01	1 Dec. 04	
Williams, James, 11 Foot	9 April 07	10 Aug. 08	14 Sept. 13	25 Feb. 16
Williams, Joseph, Royal Marines	2 July 97	28 July 03	8 Oct. 11	1 Sept. 14
Williams, Rowland Edward, 7 W. I. Regt.	12 Jan. 05	25 July 05	13 Oct. 08	25 June 16
Williamson, John, Unattached	30 Dec. 26	16 July 30	30 Oct. 40	15 Aug. 48
Wills, Thomas Lake, Royal Marines	12 Feb. 97	3 Dec. 01	9 Aug. 09	27 Nov. 15
Willson, James Kennett,[290] R. Marines, *Staff Officer of Pensioners*	15 Oct. 16	12 Oct. 32	7 Feb. 42	21 Sept. 43
Willson, Thomas, 20 Dragoons	12 Sept. 05	4 Feb. 06	7 Mar. 16	25 Mar. 16
Wilson, Edward, 57 Foot	5 June 06	9 Feb. 08	28 June 10	25 Feb. 16
Wilson, James, Coldstream Gds.	19 May 14	20 Dec. 24	7 April 37	5 May 37
Wilson, John, Royal Marines	22 June 04	10 June 07	31 Aug. 27	
Wilson, Joseph Fraser, Unattached	5 April 10	10 June 11	13 Feb. 27	13 Feb. 27
Wilson, Peter Theodore, Royal Marines	29 Mar. 95	27 Jan. 96	15 Aug. 05	24 Dec. 05
Windham, Joseph Smyth,[291] 17 Dragoons	22 Dec. 08	14 Dec. 09	5 Nov. 12	25 Dec. 14
*Winnington, Hen. Jeffreys, 39 Foot	never	never	25 Dec. 13	25 Sept. 14
Wise, William, 72 Foot	21 Feb. 27	17 May 31	23 Nov. 41	13 July 47
Wishart, Alexander, 15 Foot	14 Nov. 05	26 May 08	6 Sept. 21	6 Sept. 21
Witts, John, Royal Marines	12 May 96	1 Nov. 99	27 July 08	30 Sept. 13
Wolrige, Ambrose A. R., Royal Marines, *Barrackmaster, Chatham Division*	4 July 03	15 Aug. 05	31 July 26	5 June 32
Wood, James,[292] Royal Marines	25 April 12	14 May 31	13 Nov. 40	4 Aug. 43
Wood, William,[293] Royal Marines, *Staff Officer of Pensioners*	10 May 13	16 April 32	11 May 41	3 Nov. 41
Woodford, John, Unattached	30 Dec. 13	17 July 23	29 Oct. 25	12 July 33
Woodhouse, Robert,[294] 38 Foot	17 Aug. 09	5 June 12	21 April 33	
Woods, Richard,[295] 8 R. Veteran Batt.	2 Dec. 06	28 Dec. 09	13 Aug. 12	
Woolcombe, Robert,[296] Royal Artillery	1 July 06	18 June 07	18 June 24	18 June 24
Workman, Thomas, Unattached	3 Jan. 11	2 April 12	3 Aug. 30	8 Mar. 31
Worsley, James White, Sub. Insp. of Mil.	1 July 12	21 July 13	8 April 26	1 Jan. 33
Wright, George, Royal Marines	11 July 03	25 Oct. 05	31 July 26	30 Sept. 33
Wrixon, Nicholas,[297] Unattached	4 April 11	13 May 13	1 May 40	6 May 42
Wulff, Kenelm Chandler, Royal Artillery	29 Oct. 08	12 July 11	6 Nov. 27	6 Nov. 27
Wyatt, Alex. H. L., Unattached	17 Sept. 25	24 Feb. 29	29 June 32	31 Dec. 39
Wyatt, Samuel, Royal Artillery	28 Feb. 07	1 Feb. 08	1 Mar. 27	19 April 36
Wyndham, Alex. Wadham, Unattached	16 Mar. 20	25 Nov. 24	12 Dec. 26	26 July 27
Wynn, *Sir* William, Invalids, *Captain of Sandown Fort*	3 April 94	27 May 95	11 Jan. 00	
Wynne, John, Royal Artillery	16 Dec. 20	1 Aug. 27	13 Aug. 39	28 Sept. 39
Wynter, Robert, Royal Artillery	26 July 31	22 Jan. 33	31 Dec. 42	1 May 43
Wynyard, Henry Buckley Jenner, Unatt., *Brigade Major at York*	9 April 25	21 May 26	21 May 41	23 Jan. 46
Yonge, Gustavus Nigel K. Anker,[298] 9 Foot	22 Aug. 34	29 June 37	1 Jan. 47	11 Feb. 48
Young, Henry, Unattached	30 June 25	1 Aug. 26	3 Nov. 37	30 Dec. 45
Young, James, 88 Foot	11 Oct. 21	28 Jan. 26	31 July 28	19 Mar. 29
Young, William, Royal Marines	10 July 03	12 Sept. 05	31 July 26	

War Services of the Captains.

1 Captain Abbott served in Lord Bridport's action with the French fleet on the 23d June 1795. In the following year he was at the reduction of the French, Dutch, and Spanish Colonies in the West Indies. In 1797 he was at the capture of Trinidad, and in 1799 at the reduction of Surinam. In 1801 he served under Lord Nelson at the battle of Copenhagen. In 1806 he commanded the *Intrepid's* Marines in the attack upon Capri, and he was afterwards present at the defence of Gaeta. In 1809 he served at the reduction of Martinique and the Saintes; and in the following year he was wounded at the attack upon Guadaloupe. Subsequently he was engaged in various minor affairs with batteries and gunboats off Tarifa in the Straits of Gibraltar.

2 Captain J. H. Adair served with the 60th at the capture of Martinique and Les Saintes, in 1809; of Guadaloupe in 1810, and again in 1815.

3 Captain Agnew served with the 82nd during the Peninsular campaigns of 1808, 9, 12, and 13, and was present at the capture of Oporto, battle of Talavera, and subsequent affairs; also at the battle of Vittoria, where his leg was so severely fractured as to require three separate amputations of the thigh.

4 Captain Alexander served in the Peninsula and South of France from 1812 to the end of that war in 1814, including the battles of Vittoria (wounded), Maya Pass, the Pyrenees (28th, 29th, 30th, and 31st July 1813), Nivelle, St. Palais, Nive, Bayonne, Orthes, Aire, Tarbes, and Toulouse.

5 Captain Andros served with the 65th during the campaigns of 1814 and 15 in Guzerat and Kutch, and was present at the capture of the Forts of Joosin, Anjar Khuncoote, Dhingee, and Dwarka. Served also throughout the Mahratta campaigns of 1816, 17, and 18, including the battle before and subsequent capture of Poonah, and the affair of Ashtee.

6 Captain Appleton served in the Peninsula in 1809 and 10, and was present at the battle of Busaco.

7 Captain Robert Armstrong served in the Peninsula with the 61st, from July 1809 to Jan. 1810, and again from Oct. 1811 to Feb. 1814, including the battle of Talavera, storming the forts and battle of Salamanca, siege of Burgos, and blockade of Pampeluna.

8 Captain Bace crossed the desert in Egypt with the Indian army under Sir David Baird in 1801. He served also with the expedition to Italy under Sir James Craig in 1805-6; subsequently in Sicily and Calabria; and finally in the Peninsula, with the Duke of Wellington, and was present at the passage of the Huebra, blockade of Pampeluna, battles of Pyrenees (28th July to 2nd Aug.), Nivelle, Nive (9th to 13th Dec.), blockade of Bayonne, battles of Orthes and Toulouse (horse shot under him), and various minor affairs. He has received a medal for Toulouse, in which action he commanded the 61st for several hours and to its close. He subsequently served seventeen years as Assistant Deputy Quarter Master General in Dublin.

9 Captain Basset was employed in raising the siege of Bilboa, 25th December 1836. Present in the field actions on the 10th, 12th, 14th, 15th, and 16th March; attack and carrying by assault the town of Hernani, 12th May; and capitulation of the town of Fontarabia, 17th May, 1837.

10 Captain G. M'Leod Baynes served in the Peninsula, from Sept. 1812 to the end of the war in 1814, including the battles of the Pyrenees (30th July), Nivelle and Toulouse. Served also the campaign of 1815, and was present at the battles of Quatre Bras and Waterloo.

11 Captain Valentine Beadon served off the coast of France from 1811 to 1814, and was present in various boat actions. In 1815 he was at the capture of Naples and Gaeta; and in 1824 severely engaged with pirates in the West Indies.

12 Captain Beaufoy served with the 1st battalion 27th Regt. in Sicily in 1810; afterwards on the eastern coast of Spain from 1812 to 1814, and was present at the battle of Castalla (contused), taking of Alcoy, battle of Villa Franca, and siege of Tarragona. After the conclusion of the Peninsular War he embarked with the Army for N. America and was present at the battle of Platsburg. In 1819 he embarked for the East Indies and served afterwards as an acting engineer at Sholopore. He served also in Canada during the rebellion. Served also in the American war, in 1814.

13 Captain Beavan served in the Peninsula with the 37th from March 1813 to the end of that war in 1814, and was present at the investment of Bayonne.

15 Captain Berry served nearly five years with the army in Sicily, and was present at the taking of the islands of Ischia and Procida. Served on board the *Weazle* brig, cutting out gunboats on the coast of Calabria in 1811.

16 Captain Beverhoudt served at the capture of Guadalope, in 1815.

17 Captain Birch served at the defence of Cadiz.

18 Captain James Black served the campaigns of 1813, 14, and 15, in the Peninsula, France, and Flanders, with the 91st, including the battles of the Pyrenees, Nivelle, Nive, Orthes, Toulouse, and Waterloo; storming of Cambray (wounded) and capture of Paris.

19 Captain Blacklin served with the 3rd battalion Royals at Quatre Bras 16th June, the retreat on the 17th, at Waterloo on the 18th (at which last he was wounded), capture of Paris, and with the army of occupation in France in 1815 and 1816. Embarked to join the 2nd battalion in the East Indies, and served with the army in the Deccan the campaigns of 1817, 18, and 19; the pursuit of the Nagpore Rajah; battle of Nagpore, and other minor actions and skirmishes. Served with Sir John Doveton's force in pursuit of the Peishwa; the siege of Asseerghur in 1819, and commanded the leading company at the assault.

20 Captain Bland served in the Mahratta war with the Royals, and was present at the captures of Nagpore and Asseerghur. Commanded two companies of the Royals at the taking of the Hill Forts in Candeish. Received a contusion on the head from a matchlock ball at Nullyghaum, and was severely wounded in the leg at Asseerghur.

21 Captain Blennerhasset served with the 73d in the campaign of 1815, and was present at the battles of Quatre Bras and Waterloo. During the Kandian insurrection in Ceylon in 1818 and 19. Served with the 38th in Ava, in 1825.

22 Captain Boyes served in the American war with the 85th, and was present in the action at Bladensburg, capture of Washington, actions at Baltimore and New Orleans.

23 Captain Brander served the campaign of 1815 with the 1st Dragoon Guards, and was present at the battle of Waterloo.

24 Captain Brodie served with the Royals at the siege of Toulon in 1793, and was severely wounded in the right leg. In 1794 he served the campaign in Corsica, and was present at the storming of the Convention Redoubts and the capture of the Martello Towers with the garrison of St. Fiorenzo, capitulation of Bastia, storming the Mozelle Forts, and before Calvi during a siege of 52 days. In 1799 he served in Holland, and was at the battle on landing at the Helder, in the action of the 10th Sept., and was severely wounded in the right thigh in the action of the 2nd October. He served with Sir James Pulteney's expedition at Ferrol, Vigo, and Cadiz. In 1801 he served the Egyptian campaign, including the action at the landing, and those of the 13th and 21st March, battle of Rhamanah, capture of Bonaparte's Dromedary Corps in the Desert, and capture of Cairo. In 1803 he served with the expedition against St. Lucia, and landed at Anse de Clooc 21st June, when the outposts were driven in and the town of Castries taken; also at the storming of Morne Fortunee, and at the capitulation of Tobago. In 1809 he served in India with the Field Force in the Ceded districts; and in 1814 he joined the Field Force under General Doveton.

25 Captain Thomas Brown served with the 79th at the siege of Copenhagen, in 1807; and subsequently in the Peninsula from Jan. 1810 to the end of that war in 1814, including the defence of Cadiz, battle of Busaco (slightly wounded), lines of Torres Vedras, pursuit of Massena, action of Foz d'Arouce, battles of Fuentes d'Onor and Salamanca, siege of Burgos, battles of the Pyrenees, Nivelle, Nive, and Toulouse. Served also the campaign of 1815, and was severely wounded at Quatre Bras.

26 Captain the Honourable T. Browne landed with the first expedition to Portugal on the 3rd Aug. 1808, as a lieutenant in the 40th, and served during the campaigns of 1808, 9, 10, 11, and 12, including the battles of Roleia and Vimiera, capture of Lisbon, battles of Talavera and Busaco, the retreat to the lines of Torres Vedras, action of Redinha, capture of Campo Mayor, siege of Olivenca, first and third sieges of Badajoz, siege of Ciudad Rodrigo; and at the battle of Salamanca, capture of Madrid and subsequent retreat into Portugal, he commanded the light company of the 40th.

27 Captain Burges was severely wounded at Waterloo.

28 Captain Alexander Burke served in the American war with the 8th, and was present in the action at Plattsburg.

29 Captain J. C. Burton served on the eastern coast of Spain from March 1813 to the end of that war in 1814.

30 Captain Joseph Burton served the Egyptian campaign of 1807, and he was subsequently at the taking of the heights of Genoa.

31 Captain John Cameron served with the 79th during the campaign of 1808-9, including the battle of Corunna. Expedition to Walcheren and siege of Flushing in 1809. Subsequently in the Peninsula from Jan. 1810 to the end of that war in 1814, including the battles of Busaco, Fuentes d'Onor, Salamanca, Nivelle, Nive, and Toulouse.

35 Captain John Campbell (h. p. 26 F.) served at New Orleans with the 5th West India regt.

36 Captain William Campbell served in the Peninsula with the 30th from August 1811 to June 1813, including the storming of Badajos, battle of Salamanca, advance to Madrid, siege of Burgos, and affair of Villa Muriel on the retreat from Burgos.

38 Captain Carnegie served in Portugal from Nov. 1809 to 1811.

39 Captain Carr served in the North Sea, on the coast of France, and North and South America from 1812 to 1815.

40 Captain Carruthers served in the Peninsula with the 43d during the campaigns of 1813 and 14.

41 Captain Cater was engaged in several affairs with gun-boats in the Baltic, in 1810. In 1813 he was at the destruction of a French frigate under the batteries near Cherbourg, and at the counter-revolution in Holland, 21st Nov. 1813. From 1818 to 1821 at the capture of a num-

ber of slavers on the coast of Africa. Served in the north of Spain, including the sortie from Bilboa, 10th May; defence of the Lines of San Sebastian, 6th and 9th June; and attack of Lines 1st Oct. 1836.

42 Captain Caulfield served in the Mediterranean and the Peninsula with the 44th from April 1806 to the end of that war in 1814, including the captures of Santa Maura, and the Islands of Ischia and Procida; also the siege of Tarragona. Served also in the American war, including the actions of Bladensburg, Baltimore, and New Orleans, at which last he was slightly wounded.

43 Captain John J. Chapman served with the expedition to Walcheren, and was present at the siege of Flushing.

44 Captain Donald Chisholm was slightly wounded at Quatre Bras.

45 Captain Pryce Clark served with the 54th the campaign of 1815, including the battle of Waterloo and taking of Cambray. Served also in Caffraria in 1820 and 1821.

46 Sir William Clerke served with the 52d Light Infantry in the Peninsula, and was present at the battles of the Nivelle, Nive, (9th, 10th, and 11th Dec. 1813), Orthes, Tarbes, and Toulouse. Served also in the campaign of 1815, and was present at Waterloo, and subsequently with the Army of Occupation.

47 Captain Close joined the army under the Duke of Wellington at the close of the Peninsular war.

48 Captain Robert Cochrane served in the Peninsula with the Rifle Brigade from August 1811 to the end of that war in 1814, including the defence of Cadiz, actions of Aranjuez, San Munoz, and San Milan; battle of Vittoria, and action at the bridge of Vera. Served also the campaign of 1815, and was present at the battle of Waterloo and capture of Paris. Severely wounded in the left arm at Vera, and slightly in the left breast at Waterloo.

49 Captain R. Mortimer Cochrane served on the frontiers of the United States throughout the last war with America, including the operations at Fort George, Niagara, and Fort Erie.

50 Captain Wm. H. Cockburne was detached from Gibraltar for the defence of Tarifa in 1811 and 12, when the French were defeated, leaving their guns behind. Served subsequently in the Peninsula to the end of that war in 1814, and was present at the investment of Bayonne and repulse of the sortie. Embarked afterwards for America, where he served until the termination of the war with the United States.

51 Captain Colby served at Walcheren, in 1809.

53 Captain James R. Colthurst was slightly wounded at Waterloo.

54 Captain Colville embarked in 1810 with the Guards for Cadiz, then besieged, and was present at the battle of Barrosa. He served afterwards with the Peninsular army as Aide-de-Camp to Lord Lynedoch, and was present at the siege of Ciudad Rodrigo, the action of El Bodon, battle of Vittoria, the two sieges of San Sebastian, and passage of the Bidassoa; he then proceeded to Holland, and was present at the affair of Merxem, and the attack on Bergen-op-Zoom.

55 Captain Conrady served at the taking of Kandy and the Kandian provinces in Ceylon, in 1815. Also at the suppression of the rebellion in 1817 and 18.

56 Captain Cotton served at the capture of the islands of Ischia and Procida, in 1809; also at the siege of Genoa, in 1814.

60 Captain Curtis served at Walcheren in 1809, and was present at the attack of Ter Vere and siege of Flushing.

61 The Honourable Captain Cust served with the 3rd Dragoon Guards in the Peninsula from April 1809 to the end of that war in 1814, except the year 1812; and he was present at the battles of Talavera and Busaco, in all the affairs with his Regiment on the Retreat to the Lines of Lisbon, and lastly at the battle of Toulouse.

63 Captain Darroch served with the Royals in Canada during the rebellion of 1837-8. He served also with the 62d in the campaign on the Sutlej (medal) and was wounded at Ferozeshah.

64 Captain Davern served with the 88th at the attack on Buenos Ayres, 5th July 1807. At the defence of Cadiz in 1809 and 10; subsequent campaigns in the Peninsula, including the pursuit of the French from the Lines of Torres Vedras, action at Sabugal, battle of Fuentes d'Onor, second siege of Badajos, action at El Bodon, siege and capture of Ciudad Rodrigo, third siege and capture of Badajos (wounded at the assault), battles of Salamanca, Vittoria, Pampeluna, and the Pyrenees; passage of the Bidassoa, battles of Nivelle, Nive, and Orthes (wounded); actions at Vic Bigorre, Tarbes, and Hasparen, battle of Toulouse, and various other minor affairs. Served afterwards in the American war, and was present in the action in Plattsburg.

65 Captain David Davies served the campaign of 1815 with the 33rd, and was slightly wounded at Quatre Bras, and severely at Waterloo.

66 Captain Alfred Davis was present with a squadron of the 22nd Light Dragoons at the battle of Maheidpore, 21st Dec. 1817; and at the taking of Talneir in 1818

67 Captain William Davis was landed in 1809 at Mahon, in Minorca, in command of a detachment of Marines, to prevent the prisoners of war in the Lazaretto from rising and effecting their escape during a Mutiny of the Spanish Walloon Guards. At the capture and destruction of a fort on Isle Verte, near La Civitat, 1st June 1812, he received a severe wound by a rifle

ball, in the right thigh. On the 8th May, 1813, as a volunteer, at the cutting out of an armed Xybec from under the fort and tower of Orbitello. At the capture of the island of Ponza, under Sir Charles Napier, where, as a volunteer, with a detachment of Marines, he landed, and stormed and captured one of the batteries. On the 4th Oct. 1813, as a volunteer in the storming of the fort protecting the anchorage at Marinello, when one gunboat and thirteen of the enemy's vessels deeply laden were captured, and one gun-boat sunk. At the landing of the Italian Levy at Via Reggio, in 1813. At the landing near Leghorn, in Dec. 1813, when 270 Marines charged and defeated between 600 and 700 French Infantry, supported by 30 Cavalry, received a sabre wound from the charge of Cavalry. At the capture of a castle near Spizzia, 25th March 1814. Present at the siege and capture of fort Santa Maria, 29th March following. Also at the capture of Genoa, under Lord William Bentinck.

68 Captain C. P. Deacon served at Naples in 1804; in Sicily and Calabria in 1805 and 6, including the battle of Maida; in the Peninsula, including the siege of San Sebastian; subsequently in the American war, including the actions at Bladensburg, Baltimore, and New Orleans. On board the *Volcano* bomb in an engagement with the *Saucy Jack* American privateer.

68* Captain Hon. John De Blaquiere (*Limerick County*) served with the 41st throughout the campaign of 1842 in Affghanistan, and was present in the engagements of the 28th March and 28th April in the Pisheen Valley, also in the actions before Goaine and before Ghuznee; occupation and destruction of that fortress and of Cabool; expedition into Kohistan; storm, capture, and destruction of Istaliff; and the various minor affairs in and between the Bolan and the Khyber Passes. He has received the Medal inscribed "Candahar, Ghuznee, Cabul, 1842."

69 Captain Dewell served the campaign of 1814 in Holland, under Lord Lynedoch, and commanded the batteries in position against Fort Lillo. Continued with the army under the Prince of Orange; commanded the British and Dutch Artillery, under General Bergh, at Mons—in advance of the position of the allied army—during the battle of Waterloo; and was present with the Dutch Artillery, at the blockade and bombardment of Conde: and with the British Artillery, under Sir Alexander Dickson, when the Prussian army entered Maubeuge and Philipville; after which he advanced to Paris, and continued with the army of occupation until its return to England.

70 Captain Timothy Dillon, after serving in Ireland in the Rebellion in 1798, sailed with the 2nd (Queen's) on the expedition to the Helder in 1799, and was present in the battles of the 19th Sept., 2nd and 6th October. He next served the Egyptian campaign of 1801 (medal), including the action on the landing, blockade of Aboukir, actions of the 13th and 21st March, bombardment and surrender of Fort St. Julien, taking of Fort Rahmania together with about 860 French troops coming to its relief; surrender of Grand Cairo and of Alexandria. He served in the campaign under Sir John Moore and on the retreat to Corunna, in the 76th regt.

71 Captain Donelan served with the 48th in the operations against the Rajah of Coorg in April 1834.

72 Captain Dore served in the Nepaulese war in 1815 and 16; in the Deccan campaign in 1817 and 18; and in the action at Punniar, 29th Dec. 1843 (bronze star).

73 Captain Dowdall served the Mahratta campaigns of 1818 and 19, including the taking of Loghur, Isapoor, Kooaree, Rhygur, Raree, besides several other small forts, and he was severely wounded at the storming of Raree, having sustained the total loss of the right eye, and a portion of the nose and jaw-bone. Served also in the Burmese war under Sir Archibald Campbell, and was severely wounded in storming the Dalla stockades near Rangoon on the 9th Dec. 1824. Captain Dowdall commanded and led the Light Company of the 89th to five different storms.

74 Captain Dowmen served with the 40th throughout the operations in Candahar and in Affghanistan, in 1841 and 42; and he acted as Aide-de-camp to Major-General Dennis in the action at Maharajpore on the 29th Dec. 1843.

75 Captain Drysdale was present with the 27th at the taking of the islands of Ischia and Procida, in 1809. Served afterwards in Spain from 1812 to the end of that war in 1814, including the taking of Alcoy, battles of Biar and Castalla, siege of Tarragona, engagement at the Pass of Ordal, and blockade of Barcelona.

76 Captain Duncan served with the expedition to Bremen in Germany, in 1805. Also in the American war, including the capture of Moose Island.

77 Captain Dyer served the campaign of 1842 in Affghanistan (medal) with the 3d Light Dragoons.

78 Captain Edmonds served in the Peninsula with the 66th from March 1809 to the end of that war in 1814, and was slightly wounded at the battle of Talavera, 28th July 1809.

79 Captain Edwardes served in the Peninsula from Jan. 1813 to June 1814, and was present at the battle of Vittoria, siege of San Sebastian, passage of the Bidassoa and of the Adour, and investment of Bayonne. He served also the campaign of 1815, including the battle of Waterloo.

79* Captain William Elliott served with the 2nd Life Guards in the Peninsula, France, and Flanders, and was present at the battle of Vittoria, at Pampeluna, the Pyrenees, Toulouse, Waterloo, and capture of Paris.

80 Captain Hercules Ellis served in the Peninsula with the 88th, from March 1809 to the end

of that war in 1814, including the first siege of Badajos, and battles of Busaco, Fuentes d'Onor, Vittoria, and the Pyrenees.

81 Captain Emerson served with the 35th at the taking of Santa Maura, storming of the enemy's outposts, and at the taking of the Ionian Islands.

82 Captain Enderby served with the 22nd Light Dragoons at Belgaum and Sholapore, in 1818; and with the 16th Lancers at Bhurtpore in 1825-6. In addition to the above he served three years in the royal navy as midshipman, and was on board H. M. S. Defence at the battle of Trafalgar.

83 Captain A. FitzGerald Evans served in the Peninsula with the 5th battalion of the 60th from Sept. 1812 to the end of that war in 1814, including the action at Alba de Tormes, battles of Vittoria, the Pyrenees, Nivelle, and Nive, action of Garris, battle of Orthes, actions of Lambege, Vic Bigorre, and Tarbes, and battle of Toulouse.

84 Captain James Evans served at Walcheren, and was present at the siege of Flushing.

85 Captain Fayerman served in Egypt under Sir Ralph Abercromby, and has received the Egyptian medal.

86 Captain Fisk served as Adjutant of the 17th Lt. Dragoons during the campaign of 1820 in Kutch.

86* Captain Follows was present with the 43rd Light Infantry in the attack on New Orleans in Jan. 1815. He landed with his Regt. at Ostend on the 18th June following, and was present at the capture of Paris.

87 Captain Foot served the campaign of 1814 and 15 in Holland, Belgium, and France, including the attack on Merxem, bombardment of the shipping at Antwerp, attack on Bergen-op-Zoom, and battle of Waterloo.

88 Captain Charles Ford served at the siege of Flushing, in 1809; and at New Orleans, in 1814.

89 Captain William Ford served at the island of Anholt, and at Nyburg, in 1811; and he was at the capture of three Danish luggers from under the batteries.

90 Captain Forster served with the expedition to Copenhagen, in 1807; the campaign of 1808-9 under Sir John Moore, including the cavalry action at Sahagun, and battle of Corunna. Campaign of 1815, including the battle of Waterloo, where he was severely wounded in the foot by a grape shot.

91 Captain Foulston served during the Kandian war in Ceylon in 1803, 4, and 5, including the capture of Kandy:—wounded in the leg in repulsing an attack of the enemy on the 20th June, 1803. Served afterwards at the capture of Travancore in 1809; of Bourbon and the Isle of France in 1810; and of Java in 1811,—wounded on the 10th of August, when commanding the advanced piquet. At the capture of Kandy in Ceylon on the 3rd Feb. 1815, and on the 18th of the same month drove the King of Kandy into the hands of a force which took him prisoner. Served in the subsequent rebellion during 1817 and 18. Present also at the storming of Ghuznee on the 23rd July 1839. Was embarked with a detachment on board the Nereide frigate under Sir Nisbet Willoughby, destined for the reduction of Isle de la Passe, and was taken prisoner at the surrender of that ship after a most severe action with a French squadron on the 23rd Aug. 1810.

91* Captain Thomas Fraser was present at the operations before Ter Vere and Flushing in 1809. He served also in the Peninsula from Sept. 1813 until the end of that war, and afterwards at Genoa.

92 Captain F. H. Fuller proceeded to the Peninsula in 1808, and was present with the 53rd at the capture of Oporto, battles of Talavera, Busaco, and Fuentes d'Onor, besides various skirmishes.

93 Captain J. T. Fuller served at the siege of Copenhagen, in 1807; and at the bombardment of Algiers, 27th Aug. 1816.

94 Captain Fyers served in the Peninsula during the campaign of 1809.

95 Captain Fyfe served with the 92d with the expedition under Sir John Moore to Sweden in 1808, and afterwards in Portugal and Spain, including the battle of Corunna. He next served on the Walcheren expedition, after which he joined the army under the Duke of Wellington in the lines of Torres Vedras, and was present at the battle of Fuentes d'Onor, at Arroyo de Molino, Almarez, Alba de Tormes, Vittoria, Mayo Pass (twice wounded), and Pyrenees on 25th, 30th, and 31st July, at the Nive, Garris, Arriverette, Orthes, and Aire (severely wounded), besides various minor affairs and skirmishes.

95* Captain Garner joined the 1st battalion of the 40th in the Pyrenees in 1813, and he served in the campaign of that and the following year.

96 Captain Gascoyne served in the Peninsula with the 83rd from 1809 to 1813, and was severely wounded in the leg at the battle of Salamanca. Served also in Ceylon as Deputy-Assistant-Adjutant-General during the Kandian rebellion in 1818.

96* Captain George served with the second battalion of the 44th in the campaigns of 1810 and 11, including the defence of Cadiz, and of the Lines of Torres Vedras, also the retreat of Massena into Spain. In 1812, he was present with the 7th Fusiliers at the siege and storming of Badajos, on which last occasion he was wounded in four places by musket balls. In 1815 he was present with the Fusiliers during the operations before New Orleans; also at the capture of Paris, and with the Army of Occupation in France.

97 Captain Gibbons served in the rebellion in Ireland, and was at the taking of the French near Ballinamuck, 8th Sept. 1798. Served also in the Peninsula from Sept. 1811 to the end of that war in 1814, including the covering of the sieges of Ciudad Rodrigo and Badajoz, forcing the enemy out of Llerena on the night of the 25th March 1812, actions near Usagre (wounded in the right hand) and Llerena, affair with the enemy's cavalry 21st June, battle of Salamanca, and capture of the French rear-guard on the following day; captures of Madrid and Valladolid, investment and siege of Burgos, retreat from thence, blockade of Pampeluna, battles of the Pyrenees, 28th, 29th, and 30th July; Pass of Maya, battles of the Nivelle and Nive, blockade of Bayonne, from 12th Dec. 1813 to 22nd Feb. 1814; battle of Orthes, actions of Vic Bigorre and Tarbes.

98 Captain F. Y. Gilbert served in the Peninsula from Dec. 1812 to the end of that war in 1814.

99 Captain Girdlestone served with the 31st in the Peninsula, and was present at the battles of Talavera (wounded), Busaco, Albuhera, Vittoria, (wounded), Pyrenees (wounded), and the Nivelle (wounded—right arm severely fractured).

100 Captain Goode served in the American war, including the operations in the Chesapeake, battles of Bladensburg and capture of Washington and Alexandria, action near Baltimore, and destruction of the American flotilla. Served also at the attack and capture of Guadaloupe, in 1815.

101 Captain Charles Gordon served in the American war in 1814 and 15 with the 93rd, and was severely wounded in the left cheek at New Orleans, 8th Jan. 1815.

102 Captain John Griffith served in the 12th Dragoons the Egyptian campaign of 1801, and was wounded on the left thigh in the action of the 21st March. In 1809 he served at Walcheren; and in the Peninsula from July 1813 to the end of that war in 1814, and was present at the battle of Vittoria. He served also the campaign of 1815, including the battle of Waterloo.

103 Captain R. C. Hamilton served the campaign against the Rajah of Coorg in 1834 with the 48th regt.

104 Captain Hammill served the campaign of 1814 in Upper Canada.

105 Captain Harding served in the Peninsula from Aug. 1811 to the end of that war in 1814, including the battles of Salamanca and Vittoria, siege of San Sebastian, and battles of Orthes and Toulouse. Served also the campaign of 1815, and was present at the battle of Waterloo.

106 Captain Hugh Harrison served the campaign of 1815 with the 32nd, and was severely wounded at Waterloo.

106* Captain John Harrison (h. p. 82nd Foot) served in the Peninsula with the 18th Hussars from Jan. 1813 to the end of that war, and was present at the battles of Vittoria, the Pyrenees, Nivelle, Nive, Orthes, and Toulouse, as also in the minor actions of the Esla, at Morales de Toro, near Hillette, and at the bridge of Croix d'Orade (wounded in the hand).

107 Captain Septimus Harrison served with the 10th in the Nepaul campaigns of 1814 and 15, and commanded a company on the advanced guard in the action at Jeetghur, where he was wounded. Served also against the Mahrattas in 1816 and 17.

108 Captain Haslewood served with the 14th at the siege and capture of Flushing, in 1809. Also at the siege and capture of Bhurtpore, under Lord Combermere.

109 Captain Henry joined the Peninsular army in 1810, and was present at the sieges of Ciudad Rodrigo and Badajoz, defence of Alba de Tormes, attack on the Pass of Maya, battles of Vittoria, Nivelle, Nive, and St. Pierre, Orthes, and Toulouse, besides various minor affairs.

111 Captain Hewson, served in the American war, and was engaged at the battle of Niagara and siege of Fort Erie. Served also in the Burmese war.

112 Captain Henry Hill served in Peninsula with the 11th Light Dragoons from May 1811 to June 1813, and was present at the action near El Bodon, battle of Salamanca, with the advance and rear-guard to and on the retreat from Burgos. Served also the campaign of 1815, and was present at the battle of Waterloo.

113 Captain Hodges served in the Peninsula, from 1810 to 1814, including the battles of Vittoria and the Pyrenees, besides various minor actions and skirmishes. Served also the campaign of 1815, and was present at the battles of Quatre Bras and Waterloo. Commanded the Auxiliary land forces under the orders of his Imperial Majesty the Duke of Braganza, in Portugal, in 1832 and 1833. Was also present at the attack on the Egyptian Forces under Ibrahim Pasha, by the Turkish Army, commanded by Commodore Sir Charles Napier, on the heights above Beyrout in Syria, 10th Oct. 1840. He has been three times wounded in the course of his services.

114 Captain Holmes served with the 2nd Battalion of the 14th, on the expedition under Lord William Bentinck in the Genoese territory, in 1814; and also served in the South of France, in 1815. Served with the 20th, with the Madras and Bombay Force, against the Rajah of Kolapore, in 1827.

115 Captain J. M. Home served the campaign of 1814 in Upper Canada with the 104th.

116 Captain Horsley served the campaign of 1813 and 14 in Germany and Holland, and was severely wounded (three wounds) at the storming of Bergen-op-Zoom.

117 Captain Hort served with the 81st in Lower Calabria and Sicily, and accompanied the expedition under Major-General Ackland to the Bay of Naples, in 1806. Served also during the campaign under Sir John Moore, and lost his right leg at the battle of Corunna.

118 Captain George Hotham served at the bombardment of Algiers, under Lord Exmouth.

119 Captain Hulme served in the Peninsula from March 1810 to the end of that war in 1814, including the 2nd siege of Badajoz, battles of Nivelle and Nive (10th to 13th Dec.), passage of the Adour, investment of Bayonne and repulse of the sortie. In March 1815 he joined the army in the Netherlands, and assisted in the organization of the Pontoon train at Antwerp:— Early in May, in order to secure a shorter and more direct communication between Brussels and Antwerp, he was entrusted with the construction of a bridge of vessels at Boom, across the Rupel, a large navigable branch of the Scheldt, which having completed and maintained until the victory at Waterloo rendered it no longer requisite, he followed the army to Paris in command of a division of the Pontoon train, where he remained until 1816.

120 Captain Humbly served with the 95th (Rifle Brigade) at the siege of Copenhagen in 1807, and was present in some skirmishes near that city, and afterwards at the action of Kioge, the surrender of Copenhagen and the whole of the Danish Navy. In 1808 he landed with a detachment in Portugal, and was present at the battles of Roleia and Vimiera, the advance from Lisbon into Spain, the subsequent retreat from Salamanca, action at Calcavellas, and battle of Corunna. Served on the Walcheren expedition in 1809; commanded an advanced out-post before Flushing on the night of the 31st July, when he surprised and took prisoners an out-lying piquet of the enemy; the following day he was very severely wounded in the forehead, when under the fortifications of Flushing, by a musket-ball which lodged,—the ball extracted, and the head trepanned. Joined the Army in the Peninsula in March 1810, where he served until the end of the war in 1814, with the exception of four months in 1812;—present at the defence of Cadiz and Fort Matagorda, debarked at Tarifa, present at the battles of Barrosa, Salamanca, and Vittoria—severely wounded in the left arm; action at Vera bridge, storming the heights of Vera, battles of the Pyrenees—wounded near the left eye; crossing the Bidassoa, battles of the Nivelle, Nive, and Orthes—severely wounded in the right thigh; action at Tarbes, and battle of Toulouse, besides numerous minor actions, skirmishes, and affairs of out-posts. Served also the campaign of 1815, and was very severely wounded at Waterloo by a musket ball in each shoulder, the two balls having lodged, one of which was extracted two days afterwards,—the other still remains lodged under the scapula in the left shoulder. On the passage to Spain, 5th Dec. 1812, he was at the capture, after a running fight of several miles, of a large American merchant-ship well armed.

121 Captain Humfrey joined the 45th in the Peninsula in 1811, and served there until the end of that war in 1814, including the siege and storm of Ciudad Rodrigo—severely wounded, siege and storm of Badajoz,—in both of these attacks he served in the storming party composed of the flank companies; storm of Fort Picurina under General Kempt, battle of Salamanca, capture of Madrid, retreat therefrom into Portugal, battle of Vittoria, blockade of Pampeluna, battle of the Pyrenees—severely wounded, battles of the Nivelle, Orthes, and Toulouse, besides numerous minor affairs and skirmishes.

122 Captain Humphreys served with the 15th at the capture of Martinique and the Saintes, in 1809; and of Guadaloupe, in 1815.

123 Captain George James Hunter served during the campaign of 1814 on the Niagara frontier, including the action at Chippewa and attack on Fort Erie.

125 Captain Jackson served with the 16th Lancers in the campaign on the Sutlej, in 1846 (Medal); and was present in the actions of Buddiwal, Aliwal, and Sobraon.

126 Captain Jago served the campaign of 1815, and was present at the battles of Quatre Bras and Waterloo.

127 Captain Henry James was present at the capture of Fort San Philippe (Balaguer), and siege of Tarragona, in 1813. Also at the bombardment of Algiers, in 1816.

128 Captain Jeffreys; see Note 27, page 328.

131 Captain Keily was severely wounded at Waterloo.

132 Captain John Kelly (6 Foot) accompanied the effective men of the wing of the 6th Regt. stationed at Aden, which formed part of an expedition of 500 men under the command of Lt.-Col. Pennycuick, which destroyed the Arab posts of Sheik Medi and Sheik Othman, and skirmished between those places on the 6th Oct. 1841.

133 Captain John Kelly (h. p. 25 F.) served with the 25th at the taking of Madeira, in 1807, and also at the capture of Martinique, in 1809.

134 Captain Kerr served with the 37th at the investment of Bayonne, in 1814.

135 Captain James King served in the West Indies, and was present at the capture of the city of St. Domingo, in 1809. Served afterwards in the Peninsula in the 87th, from Jan. 1812 to June 1813, and was severely wounded at the battle of Vittoria.

136 Captain J. D. King served in Holland and the Peninsula, from July 1809 to the end of that war in 1814, including the capture of Walcheren and siege of Flushing; battle of Busaco, action at Fuente Guinaldo, affair at Alasa del Ponte, battle of Vittoria, and battles of the Pyrenees on the 25th, 26th, 27th, and 28th July, 1813,—severely wounded in the right shoulder on the 28th. Present also at the capture of Paris, in 1815.

137 Captain T. N. King served the Corunna campaign.

138 Captain W. J. King served the campaigns of 1818 and 19 in Concan, in India. Served in the Burmese war in 1824 and 5, and received a severe contusion when leading the attack on the White Pagoda, an out-work of the stockade of Donabew.

139 Captain Knipe was actively employed with the 22nd Dragoons in the North of Ireland, particularly at the battle of Antrim. Served a campaign in Egypt, and afterwards for about two years with the 11th Dragoons in the Peninsula: severely wounded in covering the retreat from Burgos in Oct. 1812, and then sent to Depot on account of his health.

140 Captain Alfred Knight served with the 62nd at the capture of Genoa in 1814, and subsequently at the taking of Castine and Hamiltown in the United States of N. America.

141 Captain Kyle served in the Peninsula with the old 94th, from Jan. 1810 to the end of that war in 1814, including the defence of Cadiz, lines at Torres Vedras, actions at Redinha, Casal Novo, Foz d'Arouce, and Sabugal; battle of Fuentes d'Onor, second siege of Badajoz, action at El Bodon, siege and storm of Ciudad Rodrigo (slightly wounded), third siege of Badajoz and storming of Fort Picurina, where he was severely wounded in leading the 94th party 3rd division to one of the most desperate assaults that took place during the war; retreat to Portugal, battles of Vittoria, the Pyrenees, Nivelle, and Orthes; action at Vic Bigorre, and battle of Toulouse. Medal for Vittoria, having succeeded to the command of the regiment.

142 Captain Lane served with the 41st in several skirmishes in the American war; and with the 47th at the taking of several islands in the Persian Gulf, in 1819 and 20.

143 Captain John Law was in the action with, and capture of, the *Chesapeake* by the *Shannon*, on the 1st June, 1813. He was also at the capture of Fort St. Elmo, and the batteries at Naples on the 21st May, 1815.

144 Captain Lawlor served in the American war, under Sir Gordon Drummond.

145 Captain W. H. Lawrence served in the Peninsula from April 1813 to the end of that war in 1814, including the siege of Tarragona.

146 Captain Le Couteur served during the whole of the last war in America. He was adjutant to Colonel De Harem, who commanded the Light Division and seven hundred Indians, under Generals Vincent and De Rottenburg on the Niagara frontier; was engaged at Sackett's Harbour the battle of Niagara, and was in the storming division at Fort Erie, where he was blown up by the springing of a mine; present also at the action of the Cross Roads and many skirmishes with the Light Division.

147 Captain Lempriere served the campaign in Spain under Sir John Moore, including the actions at Sahagun, and Benevente, and retreat to Corunna. In 1814, he served in the south of France, and was present at the battle of Toulouse; after which he served in the American war, and was present at the battle of Bladensburg, capture of Washington, and in all the operations with the army in the Chesapeake, and before New Orleans. In 1815 he served in the Netherlands, and was attached to the Prussian army in reducing the fortresses on that frontier.

148 Captain L. X. Leslie served the campaign of 1814 in Canada.

150 Captain Litchfield served at Walcheren in 1809; also the Peninsular campaigns of 1812, 13, and 14, including the action at Puerto del Almarez, and battles of Vittoria, Orthes, and Toulouse. Served afterwards in the American war, including the action at Plattsburg.

151 Captain Logan's services:—co-operation with the French Army in the Morea. Siege of Patras. Co-operation with the Spanish Forces and Legion near San Sebastian.

152 Captain Butler served with the 53rd in the campaign on the Sutlej in 1846 (Medal), including the battles of Aliwal and Sobraon.

153 Captain Lutman's services:—Campaign and battle of Corunna (wounded in the left thigh); expedition to Walcheren, and siege of Flushing; Sicily from May 1810 to June 1812; Peninsula from June 1812 until the end of the war, including the battle of Castalla, siege of Tarragona, July and Aug. 1813, and blockade of Barcelona, Feb. to May 1814; served also in the American war.

154 Captain Donald M'Donald served at Walcheren, in 1809; and at the defence of Cadiz.

155 Captain Angus M'Intyre served with the 41st in the American war.

157 Captain M'Murdo served with the 8th Hussars at the siege of Hattras, in 1817; and afterwards in the Pindaree war.

158 Captain Daniel M'Pherson served in the 8th on the expedition to Denmark, and was at the siege and capture of Copenhagen in 1807. In 1809 he served on the expedition against Martinique, and was at the storming of the heights of Surriere at the siege of Fort Bourbon, and capture of the Island. He served in the American war with the Glengarry Light Infantry until very severely wounded at the attack on Sackett's Harbour, the severity of which wounds compelled him to remove to a Veteran Battalion.

159 Captain M'Queen served in the American war with the 7th battalion of the 60th, and was present at the taking of Castile and Hampden, and the *John Adams* United States frigate.

160 Captain Macartney served with the 9th Lancers in the battle of Punniar on the 29th Dec. 1843 (Medal).

161 Captain John Macdonald served with the 93rd during the campaigns of 1811 and 12 against the Caffres on the frontier of the Cape of Good Hope. Also the campaign of 1814 in Louisiana, and battle before New Orleans on the 8th Jan. 1815,—severely wounded in the head and leg.

162 Captain Mac Donald served the campaign of 1814 with the 61st, including the affair of Tarbes, and battle of Toulouse.

163 Captain Mac Gregor served in the East Indies, with the Royals, and was severely wounded at the battle of Maheidore, 22nd Dec. 1817, and again at the assault on Fort Talneir, 27th Feb. 1818.

164 Captain Maclean embarked in Nov. 1813, for the western coast of Africa, where he served on several expeditions, and was present in almost every affair and skirmish that took place on the various parts of the coast at which he was stationed with the Royal African Corps and 2nd West India Regiment, from Jan. 1814 to May 1822, including the attack and capture of the town of Barra, River Gambia, in July 1817.

164* Captain L. G. H. Maclean served with the 49th throughout the War with China (Medal), and was present at the first taking of Chusan, storm and capture of the heights above Canton, attack and capture of Amoy, second capture of Chusan, attack and capture of the heights of Chinhae, occupation of Ningpo and repulse of the night attack, attack and capture of Chapoo, Woosung, and Chin Kiang Foo.

165 Captain Macneil served with the 75th in the East Indies; in 1800 and 1801 he was actively employed during the campaign in the district of Cotoite in Malabar, including the storm and capture of the fort of Pyche. In 1802 and 3 he was on service in Guzerat, and was present in the action at Kurrie, storm of the outworks and camp at Kurrie; siege and reduction of Brodera, and action of the 6th Feb. 1803, on the banks of the Mahe. Subsequently he served with the army under Sir John Murray, which advanced from Baroda to Doud, from which it retrograded in March and April 1804 after the peace with Scindia and the Rajah of Berar.

166 Captain Macpherson served in the Peninsula with the 74th from Jan. 1810 to the end of that war in 1814, including the battles of Busaco and Fuentes d'Onor, first siege of Badajoz, sieges and captures of Ciudad Rodrigo and Badajoz, battles of Vittoria Pyrenees, Nivelle, Orthes, and Toulouse. Severely wounded in the head at Vittoria, and in the left knee at Toulouse.

167 Captain George Mainwaring served with the 27th in the Burmese war, in 1825 and 26. He served with the 22nd throughout the operations in Scinde (Medal), under Sir Charles Napier, including the destruction of the Fort of Imaumghur, and the battles of Meeanee and Hyderabad.

169 Captain Manners served in the Peninsula from Feb. 1810 to Dec. 1813, and was present at the battle of Barrosa (wounded), and the defence of Tarifa and Cadiz.

171 Captain H. C. Martin served on the expedition against the Danish and Swedish West India Islands, in 1801; likewise on the expedition against the French Islands in 1803.

172 Captain J. M. Mason served in Canada, Flanders, and France, in 1814 and 15; also in Canada in 1838, and commanded a company of volunteers at the taking of Grand Brule.

173 Captain William Mason served in the Peninsula with the 82nd regt. from 1810 to the end of that war in 1814, including the final defence of Tarifa against Marshall Victor, retreat from Madrid, battles of the Pyrenees, Nivelle (severely wounded in the right hip), and Orthes. Served also in the American war, and was severely wounded at Niagara, in the right arm (where the ball still remains), in the neck, and seven buck shot wounds in the breast, and also one in the left arm. With a company of the 82nd under his command, he re-captured the guns, and No. 4 battery from the enemy, 17th September 1814.

174 Captain Massy served the campaign against the Rajah of Coorg, in 1834, with the 48th regiment.

175 Captain Master went with the expedition to the Hague in the 2d battalion of the Grenadier Guards, and served the campaign of 1813 and 14 in Holland, including the taking of Merxem, bombardment of Antwerp, and storming of Bergen-op-Zoom. Served also the campaign of 1815, and carried the King's Colour of the 3rd battalion Grenadier Guards at the battles of Quatre Bras and Waterloo. He was also present with the storming party at Peronne, and the subsequent capture of Paris.

176 Captain Maunsell served the campaign of 1815, and was present at the battle of Waterloo.

177 Captain Meech served two campaigns in the Peninsula with the 39th, in Lord Hill's Division.

178 Captain Meek served with the 2nd battalion of the 14th on the expedition under Lord William Bentinck, in the Genoese territory, in 1814; and with that under Sir Hudson Lowe in the South of France, in 1815.

179 Captain Meik served with the 16th Lancers throughout the campaign in Affghanistan, under Lord Keane, including the siege and capture of Ghuznee (Medal). He was also present in the battle of Maharajpore (Medal), on the 29th Dec. 1843; and in 1846 he served in the campaign on the Sutlej (Medal), including the actions at Buddiwal, Aliwal, and Sobraon.

180 Captain Melhuish served in the Peninsula from June 1811 to July 1814: was employed in the trenches during the whole of the siege of Badajos in 1812; was present at the sortie from that Fortress; and ultimately led the storming party under Sir George Walker, which succeeded in making a successful escalade at the Bastion of St. Vincent: twice wounded during the operations of this siege. He was afterwards employed in the trenches (wounded) during the whole of the operations against Bayonne, and made a correct plan of the citadel while under fire for the use of the Commanding Royal Engineer: at the repulse of the sortie he was again wounded. During the campaign of 1815 he was actively employed at Tournay.

182 Captain Miller served with the 46th at the defence of Dominica from an attack of the

French in 1805; the capture of Martinique in 1809; and of Gaudaloupe in 1810; and was present at the latter in the attack on the enemy's post, Belle Air, heights of St. Louis.

183 Captain Minchin served with the 38th at the capture of the Cape of Good Hope in 1806; at the storming and capture of Monte Video, in 1807; the campaign of 1808-9, including the battles of Rolsia, Vimiera, and Corunna; the Walcheren expedition; and subsequently in the Peninsula, including the battle of Salamanca, and retreat from Burgos.

185 Captain J. P. Mitford served on the Staff throughout the war in China (Medal), and was present at the operations before Canton, and at the investment of Nankin.

186 Captain A. O. Molesworth served the campaign of 1815, and was engaged at Cambray, 23rd and 24th June, and was present at the capture of Paris.

187 Captain Molloy served in the Peninsula with the Rifle Brigade. Also the campaign of 1815, and was severely wounded at Waterloo.

188 Captain Montgomery served at the siege of Copenhagen in 1807; and subsequently in the Peninsula, including the storming of Badajos, affairs previous to and battle of Salamanca, and retreat to Madrid.

189 Captain Moore (18 F.) served in the Peninsula with the 27th from 1808 to 1813, and was present at the siege of Ciudad Rodrigo, and both sieges of Badajoz. Severely wounded at the storming of Badajoz on the night of the 6th of April 1812.

190 Captain Moorhead served throughout the war in China as Sub-assistant Commissary-General, and was present at Chusan, the Bogue Forts, operations before Canton, at Amoy, Chusan, Ningpo—and sortie in defence, Chapoo, Woosung, Shanghae, Chin Kiang Foo and Nankin.

192 Captain Edward Morgan embarked with the 7th Fusiliers for Portugal, in March 1810, and was present at the battles of Talavera, Busaco, and Albuhera, where he was severely wounded in the knee, and disabled for nearly twelve months. In April 1813 he rejoined the regiment, in the Peninsula, and was present at the battles of Vittoria, the Pyrenees, Nivelle, Nive, Orthes, and Toulouse; after which he accompanied the Fusiliers to America, and was present at the attack on New Orleans, in January 1815.

193 Captain Evan Morgan served in the Peninsula and France from October, 1813, to June, 1814, including the passage of the Adour, and battle of Toulouse. Served also the campaign of 1814 in Canada, under Sir George Prevost.

194 Captain Hugh Morgan served on the expedition to Walcheren in 1809, and was present at the bombardment of Flushing; served afterwards in the Peninsula from 1812 to the end of the war in 1814, including the defence of Cadiz, battles of the Pyrenees, siege of San Sebastian (severely wounded), and battle of Toulouse.

195 Captain Morle served in the Queen's in Sir John Moore's retreat; at the siege of Flushing; and subsequently in the Peninsula, including the battles of Vittoria, Pampeluna, Nivelle, Nive, and Toulouse, besides several affairs of out-posts.

196 Captain Hender Mountsteven served at the attack of various posts, &c. on the Frontiers of Canada, and within the United States in 1813, 14, and 15. Served also with the 48th in the operations against the Rajah of Coorg, in April 1834.

197 Captain T. W. B. Mountsteven was severely wounded at Waterloo.

198 Captain A. A. Nelson served as Sub-Assistant Commissary-General Bombay Army, throughout the operations under Sir Wm. Nott in Candahar and in Affghanistan, during 1841 and 42; and as such under Sir Charles Napier at the battle of Hyderabad. He served as Aide-de-Camp to Sir Thomas Valient in the actions of Maharajpore, and had a horse shot under him. He has received a medal for Affghanistan, another for Scinde, and the Bronze Star to Maharajpore.

199 Captain Newhouse served in the Light Division of the Deccan Army in the Mahratta war of 1817 and 18, as extra Aide-de-Camp to Sir Lionel Smith, and commanded a Rassela of the Poona Auxiliary Cavalry, and was wounded at the action of the 31st Jan. 1818. Served also in two expeditions to Cutch, the first in 1819, under Sir William Kier Grant, in which he volunteered with the Grenadier Company of the 65th in the storming of the Hill Fort of Bhooj, which was taken by escalade: in the second in 1820 with the right wing of the 65th, with the force under Colonel the Honourable Lincoln Stanhope.

201 Captain Huntley Nicholson served in the Peninsula with the 42nd from July 1813 to the end of that war in 1814, including the battles of the Nivelle, Nive, Orthes, and Toulouse. Present at the quelling of the mutiny at Barrackpore, in Dec. 1824. Served also in the Burmese war, including the engagements near Prome on the 20th, 25th, and 26th Nov. 1825.

202 Captain Nicolls served in the Peninsula with the 66th from Feb. 1810 to the end of that war in 1814, including the battles of Busaco, Albuhera, Vittoria, Orthes, and Toulouse; and the actions of Arroyo de Molino, Garris, and Aire.

203 Captain Norman served with the 31st throughout the campaign of 1842 in Affghanistan, and was present in the actions of Mazeena, Tezeen, and Jugdulluck, the occupation of Cabool, and in the different engagements leading to it, and has received the medal. He was present with the 40th at Maharajpore, and has received the Bronze star.

204 Captain North served in Holland and France with the 44th from Nov. 1813 to Feb. 1816.

206 Captain Charles O'Neill served in the Peninsula with the 83rd from 1809 to the end of that war in 1814, including the following actions and sieges:—Talavera, Busaco, Oporto, Pombal, Leira, Condeixa, Fleur-de-lis, Guarda, Sabugal, Fuentes d'Onor, Badajos (2nd siege), Ciudad Rodrigo, Badajos (3rd siege, and severely wounded at the assault), Salamanca, Vittoria, Pyrenees, Nivelle, Nive, Sauveterre, Orthes, and Toulouse. Served also during the Kandian war in Ceylon.

207 Captain William O'Neill served as a volunteer with the 83rd from 1st Feb. 1812 to the 12th of August following, when he was appointed to an ensigncy in that regiment, present with it at the battle of Salamanca, capture of Madrid and the Retiro, retreat from Madrid and Salamanca, battle of Vittoria, blockade of Pampeluna, battles of the Pyrenees (from 27th to 30th July), Nivelle, Nive, and Orthes, actions of Sauveterre, Vic Bigorre, and Tarbes, and battle of Toulouse, besides several affairs and skirmishes. Served in Ceylon during the Kandian war in 1817, 18, and 19, and was the individual officer who made the two Kandian chiefs together with many of their followers prisoners, which at once put an end to that formidable rebellion, and for which he received the thanks, in general orders, of the Governor and Commander-in-Chief Sir Robert Brownrigg, as also of the Duke of York.

208 Captain Arthur Ormsby served the campaign of 1815 with the 14th, and was present at the battle of Waterloo and storming of Cambray, at which last he was slightly wounded. Served afterwards in the East Indies, and was present at the siege and capture of Hattras; also in the Deccan campaign of 1817 and 18; and the siege and capture of Bhurtpore under Lord Combermere.

209 Captain A. H. Ormsby served in the Burmese war from Sept. 1824 to Jan. 1826, and was present at the siege and capture of Aracan, and in the Talack expedition. Mentioned in Col. Wetherall's despatch for distinguished gallantry in action with the rebels at St. Eustache and St. Benoit, in Canada, 14th Dec. 1837.

210 Captain Ovens served in the Peninsula from Nov. 1812 to the end of the war, including the battles of Vittoria, Pampeluna (wounded), Nivelle, Orthes, and Toulouse. Served subsequently in the American war, including the action at Plattsburgh.

211 Captain Packe served the campaign of 1815, with the 13th Dragoons, and was slightly wounded at Waterloo.

213 Captain Stephen Parker served with the 69th in Holland, Flanders, and France, from Dec. 1813 to Dec. 1815, including the action at Merxem, bombardment of Antwerp, attack on Bergen-op-Zoom, battles of Quatre Bras and Waterloo, and three months on field service in India during the Pindaree war in 1818.

215 Captain Peevor served with the 17th in the Nepaul campaigns of 1815 and 16, and the Mahratta and Pindaree war of 1817 and 18, including the battle of Jubbulpore.

216 Captain Pemberton served in the Peninsula from Feb. 1814 to the end of that war.

219 Captain R. F. Phillips served with the expedition to Walcheren in 1809; also the Peninsular campaigns of 1812 and 13, including the siege of the forts of Salamanca, battles of Salamanca, Vittoria, and the Pyrenees; siege of San Sebastian, and battle of Nivelle.

220 Captain Brooke Pigot served in Holland, Belgium, and France, from Dec. 1812 to Jan. 1816, including both actions at Merxem, bombardment of the French fleet at Antwerp, and battle of Quatre Bras, at which last he was severely wounded in the head.

222 Captain Pitman served in the Peninsula with the 59th, from Sept. 1812 to the end of that war in 1814, including the battle of Vittoria, and capture of San Sebastian. Campaign of 1815, including the battle of Waterloo. Siege and capture of Bhurtpore.

226 Captain Poole served the campaigns of 1814 and 15, including the bombardment of the French fleet at Antwerp, and the battle of Waterloo, where he was wounded.

228 Captain Rice Price served in the Peninsula from Nov. 1811 to the end of the war. Was present at the battles of Vittoria, Pampeluna, 28th July (severely wounded in the left groin, where the ball still remains), and the Nive 9th and 13th Dec. 1813. Served subsequently in the American war.

229 Captain T. D. Price served in the American war, including the action and taking of Ogdensburg, actions of Messaguy, Fort George, Stony Creek, Lundy's Lane, Niagara, Chippewa, where he swam across the river to receive a flag of truce, which no other person would do at the time; storming of Snake Hill, and action of Fort Erie. Slightly wounded in the shoulder in a sortie made by the enemy in front of Fort Erie.

230 Captain Pringle served in the Peninsula from Jan. 1810 to the end of that war in 1814, including the battles of Nivelle and Nive (wounded), and investment of Bayonne. Served also the campaign of 1815, and was severely wounded at Waterloo.

231 Captain Prior served in the Peninsula with the 11th Dragoons, and was present at the battle of Salamanca, and various out-post affairs. Served also the campaign of 1815; commanded the skirmishes of the 18th Hussars on the 17th June, and received the first fire of the French army on that day; present also at the battle of Waterloo and capture of Paris.

232 Captain Protheroe served with the 46th at the defence of Dominica, in 1805; and commanded in Fort Young, which was cannonaded by five line-of-battle ships, and three frigates, &c., for nine hours, and was most honourably mentioned in the despatches for distinguished gallantry on that occasion.

233 Captain Ramsay served with the 52nd at the siege of Copenhagen and battle of Kioge in 1807; in the Peninsula in 1808-9, including the battle of Vimiera, and retreat through

Gallicia; and on the expedition to the Scheldt; served with the 47th at the defence of Cadiz, in 1810 and 11; and with the 14th at Genoa, and also at the battle of Waterloo, storming of Cambray, and capture of Paris.

234 Captain Ready served at the siege and capture of Bhurtpore in 1825-6, as Adjutant of the 11th Light Dragoons.

236 Captain Henry Reynolds served in the Queen's Royals throughout the campaign in Affghanistan and Beloochistan under Lord Keane, including the storm and capture of Ghuznee (Medal), and of Khelat.

237 Capt. J. S. Rich served at Walcheren in 1809; and in Holland from Dec. 1813 to May 1814.

238 Captain J. G. Richardson served in the Channel Fleet, under Lords Gardiner and St. Vincent; the Belleisle squadron, under Sir Richard Keates, when endeavouring to intercept Jerome Bonaparte; and at the capture of *La Rhin* by *Mars* 74. With Admiral Murray and Brigadier-General Crauford's expedition of 5000 men originally intended for Lima, but on arrival at the Cape of Good Hope ordered to join General Whitelocke's army in Rio Plata; landed with Marines at Monte Video, and brigaded with detachments under command of the Hon. Lieut.-Col. Deane, 38th Regiment. Served in the Baltic, and, while passing the Sound, partially engaged the castle of Cronenberg; joined the squadron under Sir James Saumarez, in pursuit of Russian fleet, to Rogerswick Bay. Severely wounded in several places on board *Africa* 64, in action with Danish flotilla consisting of 26 heavy gun and mortar boats, in Kioge Bay, near Copenhagen, 20 Oct. 1808—*Africa* seven killed, fifty-six wounded. Blockade of Texel, under Sir Samuel Hood; and Scheldt, under Sir Richard Strachan and Sir Edward Pellew. Served with the Walcheren expedition in the *Theseus* 74, and dismantled and brought away its last gun-boat. Toulon fleet. Landed in company with other detachments of marines and seamen, and some Spanish troops, on an island in the Bay of Rosas; dislodged French garrison and blew up the castle. Landed in company with other detachments of marines and seamen, 1812, at Sagona Bay, Island of Corsica,—destroyed and brought off great quantity of valuable ship timber. Affairs of coasts, &c. Served in the West Indies and North America; and has received a reward from the Patriotic Fund.

239 Captain Henry Rickards served at the capture of Guadaloupe, in 1815, as Aide-de-Camp to the late Major-General Sir Robert Douglas, and was wounded in the ankle by a musket-ball. On board the *Sinclair* (West Indiaman) troop ship, when she beat off an American brigantine of 14 guns, after an action of one hour and twenty minutes, on the 30th Jan. 1815.

240 Captain R. S. Ridge served the Mahratta and Pindarree campaigns of 1817 and 18, and afterwards with the expedition to the Persian Gulf, including the siege of Ras-el-Kyma.

241 Captain J. A. Ridgway (see page 317, note 6).

242 Captain John Roberts served with the 71st on the expedition to Walcheren in 1809, including the siege and surrender of Flushing. Subsequently he served in the campaigns in the Peninsula and Flanders, and was present at the battles of Vittoria, (wounded), Pyrenees, Mayo Pass (severely wounded in the head and body and taken prisoner), and Waterloo (wounded).

243 Captain George A. Robertson served with the 55th in the operations against the Rajah of Coorg in April 1834, and was wounded.

244 Captain Robert A. Rollo served in Egypt, in 1807.

246 Captain Royds accompanied the 52nd on Sir John Moore's expedition to Sweden, in 1808. He subsequently served with a battalion of detachments at the Passage of the Douro, and capture of Oporto, and was present with the 52nd in the action at Sabugal, battle of Fuentes d'Onor, siege and storming of Ciudad Rodrigo, siege and storming of Badajoz (wounded at the assault), battles of Salamanca, Vittoria, Heights of Vera, Nivelle, Nive, Orthes, Tarbes, and Toulouse, besides various minor affairs.

247 Captain Rudkin served with the 50th during the campaigns in the Peninsula, from 1808 to 1813 inclusive, and also on the Walcheren expedition; he was present at the battles of Vimiera and Corunna, occupying the lines at Torres Vedras, battles of Fuentes d'Onor (wounded), action of Arroyo de Molino, covering the siege of Badajoz, surprise of Almarez, and battles of Vittoria and the Pyrenees, at which last he was wounded and taken prisoner.

248 Captain John Sampson served the campaign in Tuscany, and was in the action before Genoa, and at the capture of that city in 1814. Served in the expedition to the Chesapeak, and was in the action of Bladensburg, and at the capture of Washington, 24th Aug. 1814. Present in the action before Baltimore, Sept. 1814. Served in Florida, and was in the action before New Orleans, 8th Jan. 1815; also at the capture of Fort Bowyer.

250 Captain Schalch served at the capture of Guadaloupe in 1815.

251 Captain Searle served at Walcheren in 1809. Also throughout the Syrian campaign (Medal).

252 Captain Seward served in the Peninsula from Oct. 1810 to Feb. 1813, including the siege of the forts and battle of Salamanca; also the siege of Burgos, from 19th Sept. to 21st October 1812.

254 Captain Shuckburgh served with the 40th in the Peninsula from 1811 to the end of that war in 1814, and was present at the battle of Vittoria, the blockade of Pampeluna from 3rd to 15th July; skirmishes from Roncesvalles to Pampeluna on the 25th and 26th July; attacks on the heights of Sorauren on the 28th and 30th July; action of Irun, action of Vera on the 7th Oct., battles of the Nivelle, Orthes, and Toulouse, besides various minor actions and skirmishes.

255 Captain Shaw served at the siege of Hattrass, and in the Mahratta campaigns of 1817 and 1818.

256 Captain H. B. Skinner served at the attack on New Orleans.

257 Captain William Smith served with the 45th in the Burmese war.

258 Captain M. A. Stanley served in the Peninsula with the 20th, from Oct. 1812 to the end of that war in 1814, including the battles of Vittoria, Roncesvalles, Pampeluna, and Orthes.

259 Colonel Steiger served with Watteville's Regt. in Sicily; at the taking of Santa Maura; near Messina on the landing of the enemy's troops on the 18th Sept. 1810; and at the defence of Cadiz in 1811. In Dec. 1812 he was appointed a captain in the 23rd Portuguese Regt., and was present at the battle of Vittoria (as a brigade-major), the blockade of Pampeluna, the actions of Roncesvalles and Suberi, battle of the Pyrenees on the 28th July 1813,—severely wounded in the head; battle of the Nivelle, the three days' fighting in front of Bayonne in Dec. 1813; and battles of Orthes and Toulouse. Appointed Lieut.-Colonel in his native country in 1822; and Colonel of the Swiss Confederation in 1828,—being the highest military rank in Switzerland, and corresponding with that of a general officer in other services.

260 Captain John Steuart served the campaign of 1815 with the 69th, and was severely wounded at Quatre Bras.

262 Captain Duncan Stewart served with the 42nd in the campaigns in the Peninsula, France, and Flanders, and was present at the battles of Salamanca, the Pyrenees (28th July to 2nd Aug.), Nivelle, Nive (9th to 13th Dec.), Orthes (shot through the left hand), and Quatre Bras (severely wounded in the left thigh, the ball remaining lodged).

264 Captain Tallan served with the 41st throughout the Burmese war, and was present at the capture of Rangoon, attack on Kemundine and on Pagoda Point, capture of Syriam, the several engagements in front of Rangoon from the 1st to the 15th Dec. 1824, capture of Tantabain, siege of Denobiu from 25th of March until its capture on the 2nd April 1825, engagements near Prome on the 1st, 2nd, and 5th Dec. following, capture of Meloom and of Pagahm Mew. Served also in Upper and Lower Scinde and in Beloochistan, in 1840 and 1841.

266 Captain Thatcher served in the Peninsula with the 48th, from Aug. 1811 to the end of that war in 1814, including the action at Fuente Guinaldo, sieges of Ciudad Rodrigo and Badajoz (wounded), battles of Salamanca (wounded), Vittoria, Pampeluna, Pyrenees, Nivelle, Nive, Orthes, and Toulouse. Wounded at Vera.

267 Captain Tidy served the campaign against the Rajah of Coorg in April 1834, with the 48th Regt.

268 Capt. G. V. Tinling served in the Peninsula from Nov. 1813 to the end of that war in 1814.

270 Captain Toole joined the 40th in the Peninsula early in Jan. 1810, and was present at the battle of Busaco, retreat to and occupation of the lines at Torres Vedras, pursuit of Massena, action of Redinha, capture of Campo Mayor, siege of Badajoz in May 1811 and repulse of the sortie from Fort San Christoval, siege and storming of Ciudad Rodrigo, siege and storming of Badajoz, in the breach of which fortress he was severely wounded. In October 1813 he rejoined the army at Vera, and was present at the battle of Nivelle, and in several minor affairs. Subsequently he served nearly one year and a half with the Army of Occupation in France.

271 Captain Torriano served at Walcheren, and was present at the siege of Flushing.

272 Captain Trafford served the campaign of 1815 with the 1st Royal Dragoons, and was slightly wounded at Waterloo.

273 Capt. John Trotter served at Walcheren; also at Cadiz during the latter part of the siege.

274 Captain Tucker served in the American war.

275 Captain Tweedie was present in the batteries of the Faro, under Sir James Stewart. Served also the campaign of 1814 in the south of France, including the battle of Toulouse.

276 Captain Tyndale served in the Peninsula with the 51st, from March 1812 to the end of that war in 1814, including the action of Val Moresco, battle of Salamanca, capture of the Retiro at Madrid, battles of Vittoria, the Pyrenees, Lesaca, Nivelle, and Orthes. Served also the campaign of 1815, including the battle of Waterloo (slightly wounded), taking of Cambray, and capitulation of Paris.

277 Captain Ussher served the Nepaul campaigns of 1816 and 1817, with the 66th.

278 Captain H. H. Vaughan served in the Peninsula with the 67th, from July 1810 to Jan. 1812, including the battle of Barrosa and defence of Cadiz. Served afterwards in the East Indies, including the Mahratta campaigns of 1817 and 18; and sieges of Rhygur, Amulneer, and Asseerghur.

279 Captain Vetch served at the defence of Cadiz.

281 Captain John Wynne Webb accompanied the 79th to Sweden with Sir John Moore; thence to Portugal, and was with it on landing at Mondego Bay, during Sir John's campaign, including the retreat to and battle of Corunna. Served afterwards at Walcheren, and during the siege of Flushing. Also at the defence of Cadiz and action of Sancti Petri, passage of the Coa, battle of Busaco, the Lines before Lisbon, actions of Zobral, Foz d'Arouce, and Sabugal; and battles of Fuentes d'Onor (severely wounded). Served in the 16th Portuguese Infantry at the successful siege of Badajoz, battle of Salamanca, and various minor affairs. In the attack of one of the Arapiles hills at the battle of Salamanca, his right thigh-bone was broken in two places by separate musket-shots, and he also received a severe contusion in the side from a third ball.

282 Captain Robert Webb served in H. M. S. *Superb* at the battle off St. Domingo, 6th Feb.

1806; at Copenhagen in 1807; at Walcheren in 1809. Wounded in an attack on an armed convoy in the Adriatic, 22nd May 1812.

283 Captain Vere Webb served with the Rifle Brigade during the compaigns of 1814 and 15 in Holland, the Netherlands, and France, including both the actions at Merxem, bombardment of Antwerp, and battle of Waterloo, at which last he was slightly wounded.

284 Captain James C. Webster served the campaign of 1815 with the 44th, and was severely wounded at Quatre Bras.

284* Captain Wedderburn served in the campaign on the Sutlej in 1846, and was present at the battle of Sobraon (medal).

285 Captain Wells served at Madeira, in 1807 and 8; at Walcheren in 1809; and the campaign of 1815, including the battles of Quatre Bras and Waterloo.

286 Captain Wetherall served in the Mahratta war in 1817, 18, and 19, with the 22nd Light Dragoons, and was engaged at Bodamy, Belgaum, Sholapore, and Capaul Droog.

287 Captain Wharton served with the 85th on the expedition to Walcheren, and at the siege and capture of Flushing in 1809; the campaigns of 1811 in Spain and Portugal, including the battle of Fuentes d'Onor and siege of Badajoz. Served with the 73rd during the campaigns of 1813, 14, and 15, in Swedish Pomerania, Hanover, and the Netherlands, including the battles of Goerde, Quatre Bras, and Waterloo, at which last he was severely wounded through both thighs by a musket-ball.

288 Captain Whitle accompanied Sir David Baird to Corunna in 1808, and was present in the subsequent retreat. In 1809 he was at the capture of Flushing; and in 1817 and 18 he served in the Mahratta campaigns under the Marquis of Hastings.

290 Captain Willson served as Adjutant to the Royal Marines of the Mediterranean fleet; in that capacity with the 1st battalion in the operations on the coast of Syria; at the attack and capture of Sidon; and on board the *Princess Charlotte* at the battle of St. Jean d'Acre. Served four years in the Royal Navy prior to his appointment as 2nd lieutenant.

291 Captain Windham was present at the battle of Toulouse.

292 Capt. James Wood served from 1812 to 1815 at the Texel, Flushing, Cherbourg, Basque Roads, north coast of Spain, and San Sebastian. During the war he served also in the West Indies, St. Helena, and Madeira.

293 Capt. Wm. Wood served in H. M. S. *Niger*, at the capture of the French frigate *La Ceres.*

294 Capt. Woodhouse served in the Peninsula in the 83rd from Jan. 1809 to Dec. 1811, and was present at the battles of Talavera, Busaco, and Fuentes d'Onor, and at the siege of Badajos in 1811.

295 Captain Woods served with the Buffs in the Peninsula in 1808, 9, 10, and 11, and was present at the passage of the Douro and capture of Oporto, battles of Talavera and Busaco, lines at Torres Vedras, action at Campo Mayor, and battle of Albuhera, where he was severely wounded, having lost his right leg.

296 Captain Woolcombe served in the Peninsula from the commencement of 1809 to the end of that war in 1814, including the battles of Fuentes d'Onor (slightly wounded) and Castalla, and the siege of Tarragona.

297 Captain Wrixon served in Spain from April 1812 to the end of the campaign, including the first siege of Tarragona, retreat therefrom, actions before Alcoy, battle of Castalla, second siege of Tarragona, action at Ordal. investment of Barcelona, besides various other affairs. Served also at the siege and capture of Genoa, and with the expedition to Naples.

298 Captain Yonge served with the Queen's Royals throughout Lord Keane's campaign in Affghanistan and Beloochistan, and was severely wounded at the storming ot Ghuznee (Medal). He served also the campaign in the Southern Mahratta country in 1844 (including the storm of the fortress of Punella), and that in the Concan in 1845.

	Cornet, 2d Lieut. or Ensign.	Lieut.	When placed on Half Pay.
Ackland, Graves, 61 Foot, *Barrackmaster at Templemore*	18 Nov. 13	23 April 18	7 June 19
Addison, John, 2 Dragoon Guards	1 Sept. 14	17 Oct. 16	6 June 22
Agar, Thomas, (Quarter-Master, 5 Oct. 09) 4 Royal Veteran Battalion	never	25 Mar. 13	
Alcock, Henry, 63 Foot	10 Mar. 08	22 Feb. 10	22 July 19
Alder, Walter K., Royal Marines	1 Nov. 03	1 Feb. 06	7 Oct. 14
Alexander, John, Royal Marines	27 April 11	18 Sept. 29	23 Feb. 30
Allan, William, 7 Foot	24 Feb. 13	3 Mar. 14	26 Nov. 18
*Allen, George, 88 Foot	never	25 Dec. 13	25 Mar. 16
W *Allen, John*,[1] Royal Artillery Drivers	10 Aug. 04	1 Dec. 05	1 Feb. 19
Allen, John, 38 Foot	10 Sept. 12	26 Sept. 13	25 Dec. 14
W Allen, John,[2] 84 Foot, *Military Knight of Windsor*	8 Mar. 10	28 May 12	6 May 16
Allen, Joseph, 52 Foot	Dec. 02	24 Dec. 02	11 May 16
Alley, Tottenham, Royal Corsican Rangers	23 Aug. 10	5 June 11	25 July 16
W [illegible] Alston, James,[3] 1 Foot	14 May 12	21 Oct. 13	9 May 17
Alt, Daniel, Royal Staff Corps	31 Mar. 14	26 July 15	6 Dec. 33
Altenstein, Henry, *Baron*, 6 West India Regt.	16 Jan. 09	10 Nov. 09	9 Dec. 24
W *Ames, John, 1 Prov. Bn. of Militia	never	25 Mar. 14	1814
Amyatt, Augustus, 26 Foot	24 June 12	22 Dec. 13	27 Feb. 23
Amyott, Richard Garret, Royal Marines	2 Aug. 99	21 Aug. 04	5 Dec. 14
Anderson, Thomas, 3 R. Veteran Battalion	23 Nov. 09	25 June 12	
Anderson, William, 5 R. Veteran Battalion	4 Oct. 04	3 Nov. 08	
Andrew, Charles, Royal Artillery	28 April 10	17 Dec. 13	19 Dec. 20
Arbuthnott, *Hon*. Mariott, 8 Foot	6 Mar. 18	14 Sept. 20	5 June 28
Archer, John, 6 Royal Veteran Battalion	Aug. 07	26 Feb. 08	
Archer, Thomas, 112 Foot	4 Feb. 08	11 Feb. 08	18 Feb. 08
*Arden, William, 4 Foot	never	25 Dec. 13	25 Sept. 14
Armstrong, Francis Wheeler, Coldst. Guards	1 Sept. 08	21 June 10	24 Oct. 22
Armstrong, John, Royal Irish Artillery		10 Mar. 95	
Armstrong, John, 40 Foot	19 Oct. 09	23 April 12	25 Feb. 16
W Armstrong, John Cooper,[4] R. Art. Drivers	1 Jan. 07	17 Dec. 08	1 July 16
Armstrong, Montgomery, R. York Rangers	10 June 13	25 May 15	25 Dec. 18
Armstrong, Richard, 70 Foot	16 May 07	7 Mar. 10	12 Mar. 18
Armstrong, Wm. Henry, 2 R. Vet. Battalion	27 Aug. 07	22 Sept. 08	
Arnold, Henry, Royal Marines	1 June 32	6 Dec. 37	4 Feb. 46
Arnott, Alexander, 26 Foot	27 April 09	28 Feb. 12	25 Mar. 17
Atkin, Christopher, 15 Foot	1 Mar. 98	21 Aug. 00	7 May 03
Atkin, John, 88 Foot	30 Jan. 12	19 Oct. 15	25 Feb. 16
Atkin, William, 88 Foot	12 May 14	11 Jan. 21	25 Aug. 21
*Atkinson, Charles, 14 Foot	never	25 Dec. 13	25 Sept. 14
Atkinson, John, 98 Foot	28 Feb. 05	12 Sept. 05	25 Nov. 18
W Austin, Edward Frederick, 47 Foot	11 July 11	30 Sept. 13	9 Jan. 14
Austin, Joseph, 42 Foot	6 April 09	22 Aug. 10	25 Dec. 15
Austin, Thomas, 5 Royal Vet. Batt., *Fort Major of Duncannon Fort*	17 May 10	6 Dec. 13	
Avarne, Thomas Jeffrey Jonah, 67 Foot	12 Aug. 13	6 Feb. 16	25 July 17
Avery, Thomas, Royal Marines	18 Nov. 95	1 Sept. 97	9 July 98
Aynge, George, Royal Artillery Drivers	6 Oct. 12	6 Jan. 13	1 Aug. 16
Ayshford, Aaron Moore, 12 Foot	17 Aug. 09	15 April 12	31 Mar. 14
Bailey, James Alderson, 60 Foot	5 May 14	21 Dec. 15	3 Jan. 22
W Baillie, Andrew, 30 Foot	29 June 09	27 June 11	3 July 17
Baily, John, Royal Marines	7 Feb. 06	24 Oct. 11	1 Sept. 14
Bain, John, 61 Foot	20 April 09	11 April 11	2 Dec. 14
Bainbrigge, Thomas Parker, 48 Foot	1 Oct. 07	3 May 10	20 Nov. 23
Baird, William Carpendale, 63 Foot	22 Dec. 43	9 April 47	15 Oct. 47
Baker, George, Royal Marines	16 Dec. 11	27 July 30	3 Feb. 31
Baker, Thomas, 15 Foot	2 Dec. 99	19 July 00	25 July 02
Baldock, Charles Robert, Royal Artillery	2 April 10	17 Dec. 13	8 Nov. 19
Bale, William, 3 Foot	3 July 06	28 Oct. 07	23 Oct. 16
Balinhard, John Allen Carnegy de, 13 Drags.	11 June 30	29 Mar. 33	1 June 40
Ball, Howell, Garrison Company	20 May 13	18 Mar. 15	
Ball, Robert, 59 Foot	27 Oct. 07	14 Nov. 09	22 Oct. 16
Ball, William, 23 Foot	25 Jan. 10	11 Mar. 13	9 Nov. 20

	CORNET, ETC.	LIEUT.	WHEN PLACED ON HALF PAY.
Bamford, Robert Carter, 59 Foot	5 Sept. 34	12 July 39	25 Jan. 45
*Banko, Christopher, 88 Foot	never	25 Dec. 13	25 Mar. 16
Barclay, Henry Ferguson, 21 Foot	9 May 45	14 April 46	
Baring, Frederick, 51 Foot	15 Nov. 11	8 Feb. 13	4 Aug. 37
Barlow, John Thomas, 98 Foot	8 Aug. 05	19 Mar. 07	20 Dec. 19
Barnetson, Alexander, 92 Foot............	1 Mar. 06	29 Sept. 07	28 Mar. 22
Barnewall, Bartholomew, 79 Foot	never	10 Oct. 95	
Baron, Jonathan, Royal Marines..........	8 Oct. 04	13 Feb. 08	27 Aug. 24
Barret, Thomas, 3 Foot.................	15 April 13	8 June 15	25 Feb. 16
Barry, St. George Ryder, 13 Dragoons	23 June 14	25 Oct. 15	14 Nov. 16
Bartlet, Frederick George, 7 Foot	20 Aug. 13	18 May 20	7 Oct. 24
Bate, Frederick, Royal Artillery Drivers....	1 Dec. 12	15 July 13	1 Nov. 14
P Battersby, James,[4*] 30 Foot	13 May 13	30 May 14	25 June 17
P Bayly, Frederick,[5] Royal Artillery	5 June 09	21 June 12	20 June 29
Bayly, Geo. Augustus, 57 Foot, *Adjutant, Wichlow Militia*	29 April 36	5 Jan. 41	22 Dec. 46
Bayly, Thomas, 1 Foot	25 Aug. 13	19 Oct. 14	25 Mar. 16
Bayntun, Edward, 2 Garrison Battalion....	31 Mar. 04	28 Mar. 05	24 Oct. 16
P Beamish, Bernard, 84 Foot.............	5 Feb. 08	11 Oct. 08	25 Oct. 21
Beauchamp, Charles Eustace, Royal Artillery	5 Oct. 18	15 Mar. 27	6 Feb. 37
Beauchant, Theophilus Samuel, R. Marines	9 Nov. 05	22 Sept. 10	3 May 17
P Bedell, Walter Death, 24 Foot	19 Mar. 07	11 Aug. 08	23 Nov. 15
Belford, William, 48 Foot................	18 Mar. 13	25 Jan. 25	25 Nov. 33
Bell, James,[6] 2 Ceylon Regt.	28 Mar. 06	25 Jan. 09	19 July 23
Bell, John Allan, 104 Foot	20 June 05	18 June 07	
Bell, Samuel, 90 Foot	15 Sept. 08	3 Jan. 11	25 Dec. 18
Bellot, Charles Joseph de, 60 Foot	never	30 Dec. 97	
Bennett, Bryan O'Donnell, 77 Foot	26 May 14	24 April 16	30 Mar. 26
Bennett, Francis Levett,[6*] 9 Foot	25 July 37	3 July 39	1 Sept. 48
P Bennett, James, 14 Dragoons	19 Nov. 12	21 Oct. 13	25 Mar. 16
Bennett, John, Royal Marines	22 Aug. 06	6 July 13	17 July 18
Bennett, John, (Quarter-Master, 3 Mar. 04) 5 R. Veteran Battalion	never	8 Mar. 10	
Benson, Wm. Welbore H., 30 Foot........	7 July 25	11 Dec. 28	7 Feb. 40
P Benwell, Thomas,[7] 4 Foot	21 Sept. 13	17 Mar. 15	25 Feb. 16
Berford, Richard, 2 Foot	25 Oct. 07	12 Sept. 09	30 Sept. 19
Berkeley, Aug. Fitzhardinge, R. Waggon Train	4 June 12	28 Jan. 13	15 May 16
Berry, Marlborough Parsons, 3 Foot	8 Dec. 96	26 Mar. 99	18 Mar. 13
Berry, Warton Pennyman, 97 Foot.........	2 Feb. 80	30 Sept. 87	
Bersma, Henry, 5 West India Regt.	20 April 09	22 Feb. 10	25 April 17
P W Best, Chas. Lewis, 1 Line Bn. Ger. Leg.	18 Jan. 08	12 May 12	24 Feb. 16
Bezant, John, Royal Marines............	3 Feb. 06	5 Sept. 11	6 Mar. 15
Birch, George, 64 Foot	15 Aug. 11	20 Aug. 12	15 Mar. 17
P *Black, John,*[8] 3 R. Veteran Batt. *Fort-Major of Charles Fort and Kinsale* ..	15 June 09	30 Dec. 10	
Blagg, James,[9] 25 Foot..................	25 Aug. 09	14 Mar. 11	25 Mar. 17
Blagrave, James, 89 Foot................	18 Dec. 06	8 May 11	24 Oct. 19
Blair, Thomas Newenham, 7 West India Regt.	23 Sept. 12	15 June 15	25 April 16
Blake, James Bunbury, 43 Foot	25 Jan. 25	5 Sept. 26	12 Mar. 29
Blake, John, Royal Artillery	5 July 13	4 July 15	22 Jan. 25
Blake, Isidore, 8 Dragoons	10 May 10	31 Aug. 13	30 Aug. 23
Blake, Maurice Lynch	11 Mar. 42	14 July 43	3 Nov. 46
Blake, Robert, 9 R. Veteran Battalion	30 April 12	23 Sept. 13	
Blanchard, William, Nova Scotia Fencibles	24 June 12	13 Oct. 14	25 Sept. 16
Bland, Robert John, 70 Foot	29 Aug. 11	12 June 15	8 Nov. 17
Blankeney, John Edward, Royal Marines ..		18 April 93	22 Aug. 96
P *Blood, Thomas,*[10] 8 R. Veteran Battalion	18 Nov. 13	8 Sept. 14	
Bloomfield, J. A. D., *Lord, CB.,* Coldstr. Gds.		9 April 18	25 Dec. 18
Blucke, Robert Stewart, Royal Marines....	8 Feb. 06	16 Dec. 11	1 Sept. 14
Blucke, William, Royal Marines	17 Sept. 05	21 Jan. 09	1 Sept. 14
P *Blyth, John Willis,*[11] R. Artillery Drivers	never	24 Oct. 03	1 Aug. 16
P W Bosse, John,[12] 94 Foot, *Barrack-Master, Pendennis*	Aug. 07	9 June 08	19 June 27
Boghurst, Edward, Royal Artillery	4 June 10	17 Feb. 14	1 Aug. 21
Boileau, John Peter, 90 Foot	18 Mar. 13	11 July 16	14 Aug. 17
W Boldero, Henry,[12*] 27 Foot	25 Jan. 13	16 Aug. 13	25 June 18

s 2

	2D LIEUT. ETC.	LIEUT.	WHEN PLACED ON HALF PAY.
Bolton, Samuel, 23 Foot	4 May 09	29 Mar. 10	27 April 15
Bond, William Spittle, Royal Marines	16 Mar. 01	15 Aug. 05	2 Feb. 15
Bonnor, Thomas, Corsican Regt.	Nov. 96	16 Mar. 97	
*Booth, William, 14 Foot	never	25 Dec. 13	25 Sept. 14
Bordes, Breon Charles, 13 Foot	10 June 26	3 April 27	2 Dec. 36
𝔚𝔐 Bott, Charles, Royal Waggon Train	19 June 11	22 April 13	25 Oct. 16
*Bourillion, Julius, 4 Foot	never	25 Dec. 13	25 Sept. 14
Bourne, William, Royal Marines	20 Nov. 78	11 Sept. 81	26 Mar. 90
Bovill, Edward, 29 Foot	3 Sept. 12	16 Sept. 13	2 May 17
Bowdler, George Andrew, 99 Foot	18 May 08	22 Sept. 08	30 Oct. 17
Bowles, Humphrey, 22 Dragoons	May 02	20 July 02	20 July 02
Boyd, Arthur, 2 Garrison Battalion	20 May 13	16 Feb. 14	24 Oct. 16
Boyd, *Sir* John, *Bt.*, 1 Garrison Battalion	8 July 08	2 May 11	25 June 16
Boyd, Robert, 7 R. Veteran Battalion	13 Oct. 08	15 Aug. 11	
Bradburne, Francis, 16 Dragoons	8 June 15	3 Sept. 16	3 Sept. 16
Bradshaw, Francis Green, 52 Foot	5 Jan. 05	5 Dec. 05	12 Mar. 18
Brady, Bernard, 97 Foot	13 April 09	18 May 13	25 Dec. 18
Brady, William, 60 Foot	4 Oct. 11	24 Dec. 12	25 Oct. 19
Braimer, James Louttit, Royal Marines	13 Mar. 38	21 Dec. 41	21 Dec. 44
𝔚𝔐 Bramwell, John,[13] 92 Foot	29 July 13	18 July 15	25 Feb. 17
ℭ Brattle, Thomas,[14] Royal Marines	8 July 03	15 Aug. 05	11 Aug. 14
𝔚𝔐 Brauns, Aug. Chris. Gottlieb, R. Staff Corps	15 Nov. 11	17 Feb. 14	22 April 19
𝔚𝔐 Brearey, Christ. Spencer,[14*] 27 Foot	21 July 08	2 Nov. 09	5 May 25
𝔚𝔐 Breton, John Frederick,[15] Royal Artillery	1 Oct. 08	15 Mar. 11	1 Oct. 23
Bretthauer, Christian William, 60 Foot	12 June 10	6 Oct. 11	25 April 16
𝔓 𝔚𝔐 Brice, Alexander Adair,[16] 66 Foot	8 Aug. 11	21 May 12	5 Oct. 20
𝔚𝔐 Bridge, George Dandrige,[17] 73 Foot	7 April 13	3 Oct. 15	25 June 17
Bridger, James, 16 Dragoons	25 Feb. 08	2 Jan. 09	25 Mar. 16
𝔓 *Bridger, John, 1 Prov. Batt. of Militia	never	30 Mar. 14	1814
Brierly, William, 77 Foot	9 May 11	2 Sept. 13	25 Mar. 17
Brock, James Loftus, 6 Foot	28 May 07	20 Sept. 08	2 Oct. 17
𝔓 Brohier, Cyrus,[18] York Chasseurs	25 Mar. 08	5 July 10	16 Jan. 23
𝔓 Brohier, John Boyle,[19] 61 Foot	21 Jan. 08	3 June 09	25 Dec. 18
Broomfield, Alex. Scott, 68 Foot	25 July 16	10 April 17	20 Nov. 22
Brown, Charles, 50 Foot	8 Mar. 10	7 Oct. 13	25 Dec. 14
𝔚𝔐 Brown, Eugene, 91 Foot	14 Sept. 09	9 July 12	25 April 17
Brown, Francis Carnac, 80 Foot	27 July 07	1 April 10	8 July 18
Brown, John, 82 Foot	16 April 07	26 Aug. 08	10 Dec. 12
Browne, Andrew, 53 Foot	3 Feb. 12	3 Nov. 14	17 Sept. 23
Browne, Courtney, 1 Garrison Battalion	27 April 09	3 Jan. 11	6 Dec. 14
Browne, Valentine, 13 Foot, *Staff Officer of Pensioners*	16 April 12	10 Aug. 15	25 Mar. 17
𝔚𝔐 Browne, *Hon.* William, 52 Foot	19 Sept. 11	26 Nov. 12	3 Jan. 22
Bruce, John, R. Artillery Drivers	6 June 04	12 April 05	1 Aug. 16
Brumby, Charles, Meuron's Regt.	29 Oct. 12	25 Feb. 14	25 Oct. 16
𝔓 Brydges, John Wm. Egerton, 14 Dragoons	15 Dec. 08	15 Feb. 10	25 Dec. 15
Bubb, Anthony, 61 Foot	20 Feb. 12	16 Dec. 13	1814
Buchanan, Drummond, 90 Foot	10 Aug. 09	28 Nov. 11	25 Dec. 18
𝔓 Buchanan, Wm. Theophilus,[19*] 13 Dragoons	10 Dec. 12	2 Sept. 13	25 July 16
Buckeridge, Francis Hotchkin, 30 Foot	6 April 20	7 April 25	13 April 26
Buckley, William Henry, Unattached	4 Oct. 21	28 July 25	2 Nov. 32
Budd, Samuel Hayward, Dillon's Regiment	23 Jan. 12	29 Oct. 12	1815
Budd, William Sidney, Royal Marines	27 Feb. 33	26 April 38	14 Aug. 41
Bulger, Andrew, Newfoundland Fenc. Corps	26 Oct. 04	30 July 06	25 June 16
Buller, John, 85 Foot	22 Aug. 05	19 Mar. 07	7 Oct. 19
Bunbury, Thomas Charles, 54 Foot	23 Jan. 28	28 Dec. 32	14 Dec. 41
Bunyon, Charles Spencer, Unattached	1 Aug. 26	16 July 29	16 Sept. 36
* Burchell, Frederick, 2 Prov. Batt. of Militia	never	25 Dec. 13	1814
Burdon, Charles, Royal Marines	17 Mar. 96	1 April 99	11 Nov. 01
Burge, Benjamin, 71 Foot	April 94	31 May 94	
Burgh, John Henry De, 21 Dragoons	17 Dec. 07	1 Mar. 10	13 Sept. 21
Burn, Henry Wilson, 1 Foot	25 Nov. 13	2 Mar. 16	21 Nov. 23
Burn, James, 72 Foot	13 Oct. 08	19 Feb. 11	1814
𝔚𝔐 Burnet, John, 52 Foot	27 May 13	8 May 15	25 Feb. 16
Burridge, John Osborne, 10 Dragoons, *Staff Officer of Pensioners*	9 Nov. 3[illegible]	1 Sept. 36	6 Dec. 44

	ENSIGN, ETC.	LIEUT.	WHEN PLACED ON HALF PAY.
Burroughes, Thomas D'Eye, 14 Dragoons ..	4 May 20	24 Oct. 21	24 Oct. 21
Burslem, James Godolphin,[20] R. Artillery	24 Sept. 96	1 June 98	1 Mar. 19
P Burton, Richard, 94 Foot..............	13 Nov. 09	5 Nov. 12	25 Nov. 19
Busteed, John, 16 Foot..................	2 April 12	29 Sept. 14	25 Mar. 17
Busteed, Michael, 57 Foot	30 Nov. 09	8 Aug. 11	1813
P Butler, Richard,[21] 91 Foot	16 July 12	9 June 14	25 Feb. 16
W Butler, Whitwell,[21a] Scots Fusilier Guards	never	12 Jan. 14	25 Feb. 19
P Butterworth, Henry, 35 Foot	25 Aug. 07	27 April 09	11 May 20
Byng, *Hon.* Gerald Frederick F., 53 Foot ..	Nov. 99	26 Jan. 01	
P Cahill, Nicholas, 36 Foot	10 Mar. 08	30 Aug. 10	11 May 15
Cameron, Alexander, 42 Foot	20 April 09	3 Oct. 11	9 Dec. 19
Cameron, Donald, 42 Foot	13 Dec. 04	7 Aug. 05	5 June 06
P Cameron, Donald,[22a] 60 Foot	never	7 May 11	23 Sept. 19
Cameron, Duncan, 1 Foot.................	22 April 13	21 April 14	27 June 16
Cameron, James, 27 Foot.................	14 Dec. 09	9 Dec. 19	7 Oct. 36
Cameron, James, 77 Foot.................	25 Aug. 08	21 Mar. 11	10 July 17
Cameron, John, 49 Foot	25 Dec. 13	7 July 37	9 June 43
Cameron, John,[144] 2 Garrison Battalion....	17 Aug. 06	13 Aug. 07	25 Dec. 15
P Cameron, Lachlan Maclean,[22] Unattached	13 Oct. 12	20 May 14	26 Feb. 29
Cameron, Peter Robert, 53 Foot	10 Dec. 12	1 Aug. 15	5 Feb. 24
Cameron, Thomas Cochrane, Unattached ..	26 Aug. 13	8 Feb. 21	1 Nov. 33
Campbell, Alexander, Royal Marines......	10 Sept. 05	10 Oct. 08	1 Sept. 14
*Campbell, Alexander, 93 Foot	never	25 Dec. 13	1814
Campbell, Alexander, 104 Foot	13 Dec. 10	5 Nov. 11	25 July 17
Campbell, Archibald, O'Connor's Recr. Corps			
Campbell, Charles, 99 Foot	24 June 13	29 Sept. 14	25 Sept. 18
P Campbell, Charles William, 39 Foot	21 May 09	2 May 11	17 April 17
Campbell, Dugald, 72 Foot	18 Feb. 11	8 July 13	31 Jan. 19
Campbell, Duncan, Royal Marines.........	1 May 95	27 Jan. 96	9 Dec. 01
Campbell, Duncan, Royal Marines	29 Oct. 05	25 July 10	1 Sept. 14
Campbell, George Andrew, Royal Marines..	5 Nov. 08	18 Dec. 24	28 Feb. 28
Campbell, James, Royal Marines	7 Feb. 05	27 July 08	30 Jan. 24
P Campbell, James, 50 Foot	14 Feb. 11	22 Oct. 13	25 Mar. 17
Campbell, James, Unattached	19 July 15	28 April 24	23 April 26
Campbell, James,[24] 41 Foot	24 Feb. 15	24 Oct. 34	5 Dec. 43
Campbell, Rupert,[23] 38 Foot..............	26 Sept. 31	7 July 37	27 July 38
W Campbell, Thomas, 40 Foot	24 Jan. 11	3 Sept. 12	25 Sept. 17
Campbell, William, 49 Foot..............	15 April 13	18 May 14	25 May 16
Canning, Edward Joseph, 33 Foot	8 April 13	12 Aug. 15	25 Mar. 17
Cannon, James, 3 Garrison Battalion......	4 Jan. 15	22 June 15	25 Nov. 16
Cardew, John Trevanion, Royal Marines ..	21 June 05	27 July 08	10 Sept. 24
Carew, John Hallowell, 16 Lancers........	11 June 41	7 July 43	30 Dec. 46
Carew, Robert, 41 Foot..................	20 July 15	8 April 25	11 Aug. 43
Carey, James, 101 Foot..................	7 Sept. 04	26 Mar. 05	19 Mar. 17
P Carey, Michael,[25] 40 Foot	27 Oct. 08	7 Mar. 11	7 Sept. 32
P W Carey, Thomas, KH.,[26] 1 Lt. Inf. Battalion German Legion............	1 July 11	25 Mar. 12	27 April 16
Carnaby, Alexander, 76 Foot	2 Nov. 09	24 Nov. 14	25 Mar. 17
Carr, Dawson, 60 Foot	12 July 10	1 Nov. 10	25 Dec. 22
P *Carrington, Walter Welland, 1 Prov. Battalion of Militia	never	25 Feb. 14	1814
Carrington, William, 2 Royal Veteran Batt.	22 Jan. 07	12 July 08	
Carrington, William Henry, Royal Marines	19 May 93	1 April 95	12 Sept. 99
Carroll, John, Scots Fusilier Guards	6 Mar. 06	26 Nov. 06	15 April 19
Carter, George, 6 Foot	7 May 07	28 Sept. 07	25 Feb. 16
Carteret, Hugh de, 12 Foot	24 Oct. 13	27 June 16	25 Mar. 17
Cary, Deering, 44 Foot..................	27 Feb. 10	14 May 12	25 Mar. 17
Cary, George Marcus, Rifle Brigade	2 Oct. 12	17 July 15	25 Dec. 18
Cassan, Edward Sheffield, West India Ran.	18 July 10	25 June 12	19 Dec. 22
Cassel, James, Royal Marines	5 July 03	15 Aug. 05	12 Nov. 14
Caulfield, John, 22 Foot	3 June 13	26 June 16	19 May 18
Chads, William Catherwood, Royal Marines	15 Oct. 05	5 June 10	1 Sept. 14
Chadwick, Wm., 5 R. Vet Batt., *Captain of Invalids, Royal Hospital, Chelsea*	18 Jan. 10	18 Jan. 12	
Challis, John Henry, 1 Royal Vet. Battalion	26 Feb. 06	1 Sept. 06	

	CORNET, ETC.	LIEUT.	WHEN PLACED ON HALF PAY.
Chamberlayne, J. Chamberlayne, Royal Art.	5 July 09	24 Oct. 12	1 April 26
Chambers, John, Royal Marines	17 Sept. 27	27 May 34	16 June 37
Chambers, Samuel, 54 Foot, *Barrack-Master at Coventry*	6 Mar. 10	10 Sept. 11	19 Dec. 19
Chambres, Wm. Chambres, R. Marines	8 Oct. 05	18 Nov. 09	1 Sept. 14
Champion, Edward Kendall, Unattached ..	7 July 14	12 Feb. 24	29 Dec. 25
Chapman, George,[27] 8 R. Veteran Battalion	29 April 18	29 June 15	
Chapman, William,[27*] Rifle Brigade	4 April 09	26 April 10	18 Mar. 19
Charsley, Charles, 56 Foot	2 May 11	7 Nov. 13	6 Sept. 17
Charteris, Charles, 28 Dragoons	16 June 95	12 April 96	25 June 02
Chatfield, Frederick, 20 Foot	24 Nov. 18	19 Nov. 21	19 Nov. 21
Chetham, Isaac, 40 Foot	6 Aug. 11	10 Dec. 12	25 Mar. 17
Chisholm, Alexander, Royal African Corps	1 Feb. 10	9 June 11	25 Mar. 17
Choiseul, Xavier, 27 Foot..................	20 Mar. 07	2 May 11	25 Feb. 15
Cinnamond, Joseph, Royal Marines	2 Nov. 08	22 Feb. 06	25 April 15
Clare, Benjamin, 60 Foot..................	21 Dec. 12	11 Dec. 14	25 Dec. 16
Clark, Edward Stevens, 44 Foot..........	30 Jan. 12	10 June 13	25 Mar. 17
Clark, Frederick, 14 Foot..................	11 June 12	16 Feb. 14	20 Sept. 31
Clark, John, 99 Foot....................	20 May 13	25 Aug. 14	25 Nov. 16
Clark, Robert, 68 Foot....................	12 April 09	26 Aug. 11	25 Mar. 19
Clark, Thomas, Royal Marines..............	8 June 93	24 April 95	8 Jan. 01
Clark, Thomas Noble, 24 Dragoons	25 Feb. 08	11 April 11	19 Feb. 25
Clark, William, 8 Garrison Battalion	7 May 12	9 Dec. 13	25 Nov. 16
Clarke, John Thorp, 3 Foot	5 Nov. 12	7 June 15	25 Feb. 16
Clarke, Marshal, 88 Foot..................	3 Feb. 14	12 Oct. 20	25 Aug. 21
Clarke, Thomas, 2 Royal Veteran Battalion	31 May 10	25 Jan. 13	
Clarke, Walter, 24 Dragoons	18 July 16	9 Nov. 18	1 Feb. 20
Clarke, William, Royal Marines	8 July 03	15 Aug. 05	1 Jan. 16
Clay, Wm. Waldegrave Pelham, 43 Foot ..	1 July 18	19 April 21	10 Oct. 22
Cleary, Richard Stanton, 76 Foot	2 June 08	23 Mar. 09	30 Sept. 19
Cleghorn, George, 52 Foot	5 Oct. 09	11 July 11	28 July 18
Clements, George Edward, 71 Foot........	28 Mar. 10	30 April 12	16 Mar. 20
Clendining, Andrew, 45 Foot	26 April 27	9 April 29	26 Dec. 37
Coates, Richard Aylmer, 47 Foot...........	22 Oct. 12	27 Jan. 14	29 Oct. 29
Cobbold, Frederick, Unattached	28 Aug. 10	15 Aug. 11	2 Feb. 30
*Cochrane, William, 32 Foot	never	25 Dec. 13	25 Sept. 14
Cockburn, Phineas Charles, 70 Foot	30 Dec. 13	28 Feb. 15	18 Sept. 23
Colclough, M'Carty, 62 Foot	25 April 11	23 Sept. 13	25 May 17
Colcroft, John, 74 Foot, *Garrison Quarter Master at Malta*	28 Feb. 12	27 May 13	9 Nov. 26
Cole, Charles, 16 Dragoons	21 Nov. 99	7 April 02	25 June 02
Cole, John William, 21 Foot	16 July 07	16 Nov. 09	13 Nov. 17
Collingwood, William Dixon,[28] 5 Royal Veteran Battalion	13 July 09	8 Oct. 12	
Collins, Benjamin Marshal, 6 West India Regt........................	27 April 09	1 Nov. 10	30 Dec. 16
Collins, Charles, 8 Royal Veteran Batt.	24 May 10	8 Oct. 13	
Collins, Joseph Ambrose, 3 West India Regt.	19 Sept. 13	14 Dec. 14	25 Dec. 16
Collins, George, 4 Foot..................	29 Mar. 44	27 Aug. 47	29 Nov. 48
Collis, William, Royal Marines	22 April 06	1 July 12	1 Sept. 14
Colls, William, York Light Infantry	1 Feb. 16	25 Sept. 17	26 Feb. 18
Condy, Nicholas, 43 Foot..................	9 May 11	24 Feb. 13	25 Dec. 18
Coningham, William, 63 Foot..............	24 Nov. 13	4 April 16	13 Mar. 17
Conway, Samuel, 10 Royal Veteran Batt...	1 May 14	24 Feb. 20	
Cooke, Adolphus, 76 Foot	30 Mar. 09	16 July 12	9 Aug. 21
Coombe, Joseph,[29] Royal Marines	1 Jan. 00	7 Sept. 04	25 Oct. 05
*Cooper, Charles Kelly, 52 Foot	never	25 Dec. 13	25 Oct. 14
Cooper, Samuel, 2 Foot	12 July 21	10 Sept. 25	25 Dec. 26
Coote, John,[30] 10 Royal Veteran Batt.	9 Nov. 09	27 May 12	
Coote, Richard Gethin Creagh,[31] 35 Foot ..	25 Sept. 13	10 May 15	1 Feb. 31
Coppinger, John Murray, Royal Marines ..	14 April 26	19 May 34	30 Mar. 35
Corham, William, Royal Marines	4 Mar. 96	13 Nov. 98	5 Dec. 01
Corry, Somerset, 18 Foot	26 Sept. 08	16 April 12	16 Sept. 13
Cosby, William, 5 West India Regt.	18 Sept. 04	8 May 06	2 April 18

	2d Lieut. etc.	Lieut.	When placed on half pay.
𝔚 𝔓 Cottingham, Thomas,[31*] 52 Foot....	11 May 12	5 Aug. 13	25 Dec. 18
Couche, John, Royal Marines	1 Jan. 04	26 April 06	13 Jan. 16
Coulthard, Robert, 1 Dragoon Guards	27 July 09	23 Nov. 09	7 May 18
Courtenay, George Henry, 6 Foot	9 Mar. 32	8 April 36	4 Mar. 42
Covenay, James, 60 Foot	never	20 Feb. 16	23 Oct. 17
Coventry, Richard,[31] 4 Royal Veteran Batt.	11 Jan. 10	20 Aug. 12	
𝔓 Cowcher, John, 3 Foot	14 Jan. 07	23 May 09	25 Aug. 14
𝔓 Cowley, Charles, 39 Foot	24 May 09	10 Sept. 12	18 July 16
𝔓 𝔚 Cox, Charles Thomas,[33] 71 Foot	29 June 09	29 May 11	25 Oct. 21
Cox, Samuel, Royal Marines	22 Dec. 09	19 Mar. 28	6 Feb. 29
Cozens, George, 101 Foot................	27 June 09	5 Dec. 11	27 Mar. 17
𝔓 Crabtree, George Longbottom, 5 Dr. Gds.	11 Mar. 12	29 Oct. 12	10 April 23
Craig, Aylmer Strangford,[33*] 28 Foot......	31 Mar. 43	10 Oct. 45	20 Oct. 48
Crampton, Josiah, 97 Foot	6 Sept. 04	22 May 04	25 Dec. 18
Cranford, William, 70 Foot	22 May 12	24 Aug. 15	25 Mar. 17
Crause, Charles, Royal Marines	3 Aug. 00	12 Dec. 04	31 Oct. 14
𝔚 Crawford, Alex. Spiers,[34] 67 Foot	18 May 14	27 July 15	3 Feb. 25
Crawford, John Charles, 52 Foot..........	11 July 11	27 Dec. 15	29 Sept. 19
Crawford, Joseph, 2 Garrison Battalion	4 July 11	23 July 12	24 Oct. 16
𝔓 Crawley, William, 27 Foot	7 Nov. 11	31 Dec. 12	25 Mar. 17
Creagh, Arthur Gethen, 17 Foot	6 June 05	10 April 06	3 Dec. 07
Cree, John, R. York Rangers		24 July 02	1805
Crespin, Henry, Royal Marines	3 June 31	10 July 37	5 May 45
Crispo, Sidney Smith, Royal Marines......	11 Mar. 28	18 July 36	7 Nov. 37
Crookshank, Richard, 4 Dragoon Guards ..	23 July 12	4 Feb. 13	25 Sept. 14
Cross, Richard, 20 Foot	16 Mar. 30	22 June 32	21 April 37
Croudace, William, 2 Ceylon Regt.........	19 April 10	4 Feb. 14	25 Aug. 22
Crow, William, 9 Foot	Sept. 99	18 Nov. 99	25 Nov. 02
𝔓 Crowe, Charles, 27 Foot	14 Aug. 11	24 Dec. 12	25 Mar. 17
Crowe, Joseph, 60 Foot..................	26 Oct. 10	29 Mar. 12	28 June 19
Crowther, Jeremiah, Royal Waggon Train ..	15 Jan. 04	27 Aug. 04	1806
Crozier, Acheson, Royal Marines..........	2 July 03	15 Aug. 05	1 May 17
𝔓 Cubitt, Edward George, 4 Dragoons	31 Oct. 11	23 Jan. 12	8 Jan. 24
Cull, George,[35] Royal Marines	5 Aug. 99	1 Sept. 04	10 Jan. 16
Cumming, Alexander, 26 Foot............	27 Jan. 14	6 Oct. 14	25 Dec. 14
Curling, Henry, 52 Foot	22 Oct. 25	20 Aug. 29	30 Dec. 34
Curzon, *Hon.* John Henry Roper, 37 Foot..	14 Oct. 24	15 Nov. 27	30 Dec. 31
Cusine, John, Unattached................	22 Mar. 10	4 Mar. 13	13 Dec. 26
Cutting, Thomas, 3 Line Batt. German Legion	9 Jan. 13	13 Sept. 14	24 Feb. 16
𝔓 Dalgairns, William,[36] 55 Foot	7 Sept. 09	5 July 10	24 July 17
Dalgety, Alexander, 89 Foot	19 June 06	28 July 08	25 Sept. 16
Dalgleish, Robert, 73 Foot	1 April 12	1 July 13	25 June 17
Dalrymple, Alexander, 46 Foot	May 95	1 Sept. 95	
D'Alton, Edward Richard, Chass. Britanniques	3 June 12	7 Sept. 13	1814
Dalton, Philip Tuite, 9 Dragoons	3 Oct. 11	1 April 13	25 July 14
Daly, Edward Nugent, 63 Foot	19 April 44	16 Sept. 45	29 Aug. 47
Daly, George, 99 Foot	17 Mar. 14	4 Oct. 15	30 Oct. 17
Dalzell, William John, Royal Artillery	1 May 15	29 July 20	17 Jan. 24
Dames, Mansell, 6 Dragoons	6 Feb. 12	25 May 15	25 Mar. 16
Daniel, Peter Fane Edge, Royal Marines ..	4 April 34	26 Aug. 40	11 Oct. 48
𝔚 Daniell, Robert,[37] 59 Foot	21 Sept. 09	15 July 11	9 Dec. 19
Darcy, Isaac Roboteau, 8 R. Veteran Batt.	15 April 07	2 Oct. 09	
Daubuz, James Barill, Unattached	3 Aug. 20	24 Oct. 21	22 Mar. 27
Davidson, James Batchelor, 2 W. India Regt.	25 May 32	13 Aug. 35	25 Feb. 42
Davies, David, Royal Marines............	21 Nov. 06	1 Oct. 13	8 May 27
Davis, Charles Winter, 30 Foot	3 Sept. 12	24 Feb. 14	17 Sept. 29
Davis, John, 2 Royal Veteran Battalion ..	7 Aug. 06	19 Nov. 07	
Davis, William Henry, 8 West India Regt.	21 Jan. 13	25 May 15	18 April 17
Davison, James, 99 Foot	18 Aug. 14	5 Oct. 15	7 Nov. 17
Davys, Edmund Soden, 90 Foot	11 Nov. 08	16 May 11	25 Dec. 18
Dawson, Wm., 2 Line Batt. German Legion	6 May 12	6 May 13	25 April 16
Day, Alexander, Royal Marines	14 May 90	18 Aug. 04	1 Oct. 14
Dean, Robert, 16 Dragoons	1 Jan. 13	5 June 15	20 Oct. 16
𝔓 Delamain, Edward Smith,[38] 60 Foot	20 Feb. 11	28 July 14	2 July 29
𝔓 Delme, Henry Peter,[39] 88 Foot	7 Mar. 11	3 Sept. 12	25 Feb. 16

	ENSIGN, ETC.	LIEUT.	WHEN PLACED ON HALF PAY.
*Denford, Charles, 95 Foot	never	25 Dec. 13	1814
Denison, George, 19 Foot	18 June 12	29 Jan. 18	20 July 20
Dent, Robert, Unattached	21 Dec. 20	16 Dec. 24	29 Sept. 25
Desbarres, Henry Windham, Unattached	26 May 14	8 Dec. 14	2 Feb. 26
Dickinson, Douglas John, 2 Foot, *Adjutant Brecon Militia*	30 June 37	30 Jan. 39	27 Feb. 46
W Dickson, Charles Lennox, Unattached	11 June 12	21 April 14	7 Sept. 26
Dickson, David, 42 Foot	8 Dec. 15	23 Dec. 24	3 July 28
Diddep, John, 41 Foot	27 July 15	18 Oct. 36	13 Sept. 43
Digges, Charles, West India Rangers	4 Mar. 13	11 May 15	3 Oct. 18
P Dighton, Robert,[40] Unattached	27 April 09	7 Sept. 12	7 Nov. 34
Dillon, Anthony, Unattached	9 April 10	17 Nov. 25	2 Oct. 35
Dillon, Edward Walter Percy,[40*] 63 Foot	21 April 08	5 Oct. 09	23 Dec. 19
Dillon, Thomas, 8 R. Veteran Battalion	3 July 06	2 Feb. 09	
Disney, James Robert, York Chasseurs	10 Nov. 14	20 July 15	25 Aug. 19
Dixon, John William, 48 Foot	2 Nov. 09	14 Aug. 11	1814
Dobyns, Robert William, 7 W. India Regt.	19 July 09	27 Mar. 11	2 Sept. 16
P W Dodwell, George, 23 Dragoons	6 July 04	25 April 05	30 May 16
Dolmage, Julius, 4 Foot	14 Aug. 00	28 Aug. 01	12 Sept. 05
Donnelly, John, 2 R. Veteran Battalion	21 Nov. 13	18 July 15	
Dormer, Charles, Unattached	28 Nov. 16	2 Dec. 19	16 May 34
Doswell, Henry, Royal Marines	18 Sept. 05	1 Feb. 09	1 April 17
W Dowbiggin, William Henry,[41] 16 Foot	22 Mar. 10	8 Aug. 11	25 Aug. 21
P Dowker, Thomas, 38 Foot	20 April 09	15 Mar. 10	24 Nov. 14
Downer, Geo. P. Maxwell, York Lt. Inf. Vol.	3 Feb. 14	19 Jan. 15	25 Mar. 17
Downie, Alexander, 6 Foot	10 June 13	18 May 21	25 Nov. 22
Doyne, Robert Stephen, 7 Dragoons	22 Sept. 25	28 Sept. 26	17 Sept. 29
W Drake, Edward, 28 Foot	25 Nov. 13	15 June 15	25 April 16
Drawbridge, Charles,[42] Royal Artillery	21 Dec. 08	3 Dec. 11	24 Aug. 20
Dreghorn, Allan Hamilton, 7 R. Vet. Batt.	26 Mar. 12	6 May 13	
Drew, Matthew, R. Waggon Train	28 Jan. 07	25 May 08	25 Dec. 18
P W Drummond, Geo. Duncan, 3 R. Vet. Bn.	30 May 11	28 Jan. 13	25 June 26
Dunlevie, George Gerald, 11 Foot	26 Mar. 29	18 Oct. 33	24 Aug. 44
Dunlop, Archibald, Royal Marines	18 Nov. 03	1 April 06	17 Aug. 18
W Dunnicliffe, Henry,[43] Royal Artillery	12 Dec. 11	20 Dec. 14	1 April 19
Dusautoy, James, Royal Marines, *Barrackmaster at Taunton*	5 Feb. 77	21 Jan. 79	
Dyer, Robert Turtliff, Royal Marines	16 Feb. 05	27 July 08	14 Dec. 14
Eagar, Alexander, 57 Foot	31 Mar. 14	14 Dec. 15	25 Feb. 16
Eagar, James, 7 R. Veteran Battalion	10 Nov. 08	21 June 11	
Eagles, Edward, Bampfield, Royal Marines	29 Sept. 04	28 Mar. 07	1 Sept. 14
Earle, Alexander Hamilton, Royal Artillery	4 Dec. 00	28 Aug. 13	10 Aug. 21
P Easter, Jeremiah,[44] 23 Dragoons	31 Mar. 08	26 July 09	25 July 14
P Eaton, John, 20 Dragoons	22 June 09	17 Jan. 11	25 Mar. 16
P Eccles, Cuthbert,[45] 83 Foot	19 Nov. 12	20 May 14	25 Mar. 17
Ede, Denzil, Royal Marines	7 June 99	18 Aug. 04	1 Jan. 16
Ede, John, Royal Marines	14 Mar. 96	1 Jan. 99	
Edgworth, Thomas Bridgman, Royal Marines	17 Feb. 95	30 Dec. 95	19 Mar. 96
P Edington, John, 81 Foot	7 Feb. 11	23 Jan. 12	3 April 16
Edmonds, Robert, 27 Foot	6 July 09	4 Jan. 10	25 Mar. 17
P Edwards, Charles,[46] 71 Foot, *Capt. of Invalids, Royal Hospital, Chelsea*	27 Sept. 13	24 Dec. 18	3 Mar. 25
Edwards, John, 27 Foot	2 Sept. 07	16 Dec. 07	28 Jan. 13
Edwards, Richard, Royal Marines	24 May 06	20 Oct. 12	1 Sept. 14
Edwards, Thomas, 66 Foot	11 April 09	8 Oct. 12	8 July 19
Edwards, Wright, 58 Foot	2 Sept. 12	10 Nov. 13	11 July 22
Edyvean, Robert Bradlick, 103 Foot	31 May 10	4 Mar. 13	28 Dec. 17
Eliot, Charles, 43 Foot	14 Oct. 13	11 Jan. 21	15 Jan. 24
Elliot, Henry, Royal Marines	11 July 03	5 Nov. 05	11 Dec. 16
Elliott, George Henry, 44 Foot	15 June 09	8 Feb. 10	2 April 18
Ellis, William, 89 Foot	1 Feb. 10	9 June 12	25 Jan. 17
Elrington, Thomas Gerard, 62 Foot	5 Mar. 12	12 Feb. 14	25 May 17
Elton, William, 19 Dragoons	31 Dec. 18	10 Feb. 20	21 Mar. 22
* Emery, John, 3 Prov. Bn. of Militia	never	25 Mar. 14	1814
Erskine, Robert, Royal African Corps	2 April 22	25 June 24	5 July 31

	CORNET, ETC.	LIEUT.	WHEN PLACED ON HALF PAY.
Eustace, James, Irish Brigade	24 Dec. 83	23 May 86	30 April 92
Evans, George, 1 Garrison Battalion	30 Aug. 07	19 Nov. 07	25 Sept. 17
Evans, John, 28 Foot	1 Mar. 10	13 April 13	25 Dec. 14
Evans, John, 83 Foot	26 Oct. 08	21 June 10	23 July 20
P W *Evans, Matthew,*[47] R. Artillery Drivers	1 Dec. 05	1 Jan. 07	
Evans, Ralph, 62 Foot	24 Sept. 12	16 Feb. 14	25 May 17
P Evans, Thomas,[48] 38 Foot	26 Nov. 12	19 Jan. 14	25 Feb. 17
Eyma, John Adrian, Royal Waggon Train	11 Sept. 11	15 Oct. 12	1814
Fairtlough, Henry Blackler, Royal Marines	26 Dec. 04	27 July 08	1 April 17
Farmer, Richard, 36 Foot	28 Nov. 99	11 Aug. 01	25 Sept. 02
P Farmer, Wm. John George, 9 Foot	31 Oct. 11	6 Dec. 13	10 April 17
Fenton, William, 69 Foot	15 Aug. 05	31 July 06	8 Mar. 21
P Ferguson, Donald, Rifle Brigade	14 May 12	10 Dec. 13	25 Dec. 18
Fergusson, James, 57 Foot	23 June 13	21 April 14	25 Feb. 16
Fergusson, Thomas, 8 Foot	13 April 09	5 Aug. 13	14 May 29
Ferrier, Walter, Independent Company	30 April 95	23 Mar. 96	
Ffennell, Richard, 98 Foot	25 April 06	26 Oct. 06	10 Dec. 18
Fitchett, John, 7 Garrison Battalion	23 Dec. 00	8 Oct. 02	
Fitz Gerald, James, 77 Foot	21 Nov. 11	21 April 14	25 Mar. 17
Fitz Gerald, Richard Henry, Unattached	1 Oct. 12	23 Mar. 15	26 May 25
Fitz Gibbon, William, 83 Foot	29 May 11	16 Sept. 13	25 Sept. 17
Fitzherbert, George, 14 Foot	5 Oct. 09	31 July 11	25 Jan. 18
P Fleetwood, James,[49] 25 Dragoons	4 Oct. 10	30 April 12	9 Oct. 23
P *Fleming, Hugh,*[50] 7 R. Veteran Battalion *Military Knight of Windsor*	11 Jan. 10	26 Mar. 13	
Flynn, Patrick,[51] 39 Foot	9 Jan. 40	17 June 41	29 Oct. 47
Fonblanque, John Samuel, Mar. de Grenier, 21 Foot	3 Jan. 10	18 June 12	25 Mar. 17
Foot, Randall, 14 Foot	11 July 26	6 Aug. 29	3 Feb. 32
Foote, John Hollis Rolle, 9 Foot	18 April 11	29 April 13	25 Feb. 16
Forbes, Nathaniel, 102 Foot	31 Jan. 82	15 May 84	
Forbes, Peter, 95 Foot	18 Mar. 13	21 Aug. 17	25 Jan. 19
Ford, Arthur White, 2 R. Veteran Battalion	27 April 09	3 Oct. 11	
P Ford, John,[52] 3 West India Regt., *Captain of Invalids, Royal Hospital, Chelsea*	25 May 09	30 May 11	15 Nov. 21
*Forster, John Augustus, 2 Prov. Bn. of Militia	never	25 Dec. 13	1814
*Fortescue, George, 3 Prov. Batt. of Militia	never	25 Mar. 14	1814
*Fortescue, John Mill, 103 Foot	19 Aug. 13	7 Mar. 16	1 Oct. 17
Forward, Samuel, 21 Dragoons	7 June 15	8 June 20	8 June 20
Fowler, William, Royal Marines	11 May 96	1 Nov. 99	1 July 02
Franklin, Richard A. M., 55 Foot, *Staff Officer of Pensioners*	28 Sept. 30	17 April 35	25 Oct. 44
P Franklin, Robert Deane, 36 Foot	3 Aug. 09	25 Aug. 13	8 June 15
W Fraser, Andrew Simon,[53] Unattached	16 Sept. 13	20 July 15	18 Jan. 27
Fraser, Arthur John, 2 Garrison Battalion	14 Sept. 04	12 Jan. 05	6 Dec. 14
P Fraser, David, 82 Foot	9 May 11	2 Dec. 13	25 Mar. 17
Fraser, Donald, 1 Foot	11 Mar. 11	3 July 13	25 Mar. 16
Fraser, Hugh, 4 Royal Veteran Battalion	6 Sept. 10	6 June 14	
Freame, Wm. Horwood, 58 Foot	8 Dec. 13	14 Dec. 25	2 Feb. 26
Freeman, Alfred P. Isidore Walsh, 15 Foot	1 Oct. 96	14 May 12	22 Feb. 16
Freeman, Richard Francis, 30 Foot	5 April 99	11 Nov. 99	2 July 03
French, Hyacinth, 97 Foot	27 July 09	17 May 13	25 Dec. 18
French, Lucius, 67 Foot	3 Sept. 12	4 May 16	25 July 17
French, William, 36 Foot	8 May 06	11 Nov. 07	3 Aug. 20
French, William Lasinby, Royal Marines	8 June 95	19 Jan. 97	10 Aug. 02
Froger, Leopold de, 63 Foot	15 Jan. 08	30 Aug. 09	24 July 22
Fullarton, John, 71 Foot	22 July 13	7 Dec. 14	7 April 16
Fyers, Robert Morse, Royal Artillery	21 June 33	19 April 36	
P Gaggi[illegible], Pierce, 6 Foot	15 Aug. 11	9 Feb. 14	18 April 17
W Gairdner, Patrick, 2 Line Batt. Ger. Leg.	27 July 12	30 Jan. 14	25 April 16
Gale, William, 1 Dragoons	12 April 15	26 June 17	22 Sept. 20
Gallagher, John, 98 Foot, *Town Major, New Brunswick*	10 June 04	22 May 04	25 Sept. 18

	2D LIEUT. ETC.	LIEUT.	WHEN PLACED ON HALF PAY.
*Gamlen, Charles Arthur, 3 Prov. Batt. of Mil.	never	16 Mar. 14	1814
Garden, John Campbell, Newfoundland Fenc.	16 Dec. 07	4 Oct. 10	25 June 16
Gardiner, Arthur, 2 Garrison Battalion	25 Mar. 08	11 July 11	7 Dec. 14
Gardiner, Wm. Gregory, Rifle Brigade	21 Mar. 11	12 Aug. 12	24 May 21
P W Gardner, Andrew, 27 Foot	14 Nov. 11	30 Sept. 13	25 Mar. 17
Garstin, James, 15 Foot	26 Oct. 07	12 Nov. 09	10 Nov. 17
Gatty, Joseph, 60 Foot	10 Dec. 11	26 Oct. 12	13 Nov. 17
Geddes, Alexander, 5 West India Regt.	16 May 11	14 Jan. 13	29 Dec. 17
Geddes, James, 42 Foot	17 Mar. 13	9 June 14	25 Dec. 14
W Gerard, Arthur, 4 Foot	29 April 13	16 Mar. 15	25 Feb. 16
Gibb, Harry Wm. Scott, Royal Artillery ..	11 July 14	27 Sept. 18	1 Dec. 22
Gibbins, Thomas, 81 Foot	20 Dec. 10	4 Feb. 14	25 Mar. 17
Gibbon, Stephen, 29 Foot	20 May 12	10 Nov. 14	1 May 17
Gibbons, Thomas, Royal Artillery	8 June 04	1 Dec. 05	1 Jan. 26
Gibson, William, 1 Royal Veteran Batt. ..	11 Feb. 08	13 Sept. 10	
P *Gibson, Wm. Joseph,* 8 R. Veteran Batt.	27 Sept. 04	11 Mar. 06	
P Gichard, Edward,[54] 4 Foot	21 Aug. 06	28 July 08	25 April 16
Giffard, Thomas Frederick, 18 Foot	9 July 12	5 May 14	20 May 24
P W Gilborne, Edward,[55] 71 Foot, *Capt. of Invalids, Royal Hospital, Kilmainham*	4 Oct. 08	18 Oct. 09	25 Dec. 16
Gilchrist, James, 30 Foot	23 Nov. 20	31 Oct. 34	23 April 41
P Gilder, Matthew William, 6 Foot	19 July 10	26 Aug. 13	16 April 17
Gill, George, Royal Marines	29 Jan. 06	26 Aug. 11	1 Sept. 14
Gillies, John, Unattached, *Riding Master, Royal Military College*	12 May 25	8 Oct. 30	10 May 39
Gillman, Wm. Howard, R. Artillery Drivers	18 Dec. 12	16 July 13	1 July 16
Gillmore, Joseph Albert, 27 Foot, *Barrack-master at Glasgow*	12 Nov. 12	1 Sept. 14	7 Aug. 17
Gilse, Frederick de, Royal Waggon Train ..	6 Feb. 06	26 Sept. 09	7 Mar. 15
Glasson, Caldwell, Royal Marines	4 May 10	11 Sept. 28	29 Aug. 29
Glendinning, Adam, 9 Royal Veteran Batt.	16 Dec. 05	26 June 06	
W Glendinning, Thomas, 60 Foot	9 Dec. 13	20 July 15	27 Sept. 17
W Glynn, Henry, 40 Foot	25 Nov. 13	20 Sept. 15	25 Feb. 16
Goddard, George Anthony, 50 Foot	14 Dec. 09	21 Jan. 13	7 Sept. 15
Godfrey, Whiteside, 5 Royal Veteran Batt.	16 July 06	3 July 08	
* Goodair, William, Independent Company	18 Aug. 78	5 Mar. 82	
P Goodall, William,[56] 52 Foot	30 Mar. 09	21 Dec. 09	6 June 16
Gordon, Alexander, 92 Foot	22 May 06	3 Mar. 08	25 Oct. 10
P Gordon, George, 85 Foot	20 Feb. 12	6 Jan. 14	30 Dec. 19
Gordon, *Sir* John, *Bt.*, 4 Foot	23 May 97	24 April 98	26 May 03
Gordon, John Ponsonby, Unattached	17 Jan. 22	15 Aug. 26	15 Aug. 26
Gordon, Lewis, 35 Foot	Feb. 02	27 May 02	25 Oct. 02
Gordon, *Sir* Orford Gordon, *Bt.*, 3 Gar. Batt.	10 Mar. 14	27 July 15	25 Nov. 16
Gordon, Wm., York Lt. Infantry Volunteers	27 May 12	16 Sept. 13	20 May 17
Goudie, John, 72 Foot	23 May 11	1 Dec. 14	28 May 19
P W Græme, G. Drummond,[57] *KH.*, 2 Light Infantry Batt. German Legion	14 May 12	30 Aug. 12	25 April 16
P Graham, Hector,[58] 60 Foot, *Barrack-master at Chichester*	26 Oct. 09	8 June 11	18 Nov. 19
Graham, Walter, 6 Royal Veteran Batt. ..	24 Mar. 10	4 June 12	
Grant, Alexander, Canadian Fencible Infantry	20 Oct. 08	24 Dec. 10	11 Oct. 16
Grant, Charles, 81 Foot		5 Jan. 78	13 May 83
Grant, George Colquhoun, 2 Ceylon Regt...	15 June 09	2 Jan. 11	19 Dec. 22
*Grant, James, Royal Waggon Train	never	25 Dec. 13	25 June 16
*Grant, James, Royal Waggon Train	never	25 Dec. 13	1814
P Grant, John,[59] Royal Artillery	1 Oct. 08	8 May 11	21 Oct. 25
P Grant, John,[60] Unattached	5 Oct. 09	15 April 13	31 Aug. 38
Grant, Robert, 19 Dragoons	28 Sept. 15	31 May 21	13 Sept. 21
Grant, William, 7 Garrison Battalion	16 Aug. 04	17 April 05	15 Mar. 10
Grant, William, 7 Garrison Battalion	21 Oct. 08	19 April 10	17 Sept. 12
Grape, Henry, Royal Marines	3 Oct. 00	9 April 05	22 Oct. 14
P Grattan, James, 9 Dragoons	9 Aug. 10	4 July 11	18 Aug. 14
Graves, William, Royal Marines	23 Sept. 05	12 May 09	2 Sept. 09
Gray, Owen Wynne,[60a] 39 Foot, *Staff Officer of Pensioners in New Zealand*	9 Nov. 38	18 May 40	1 July 47

	ENSIGN, ETC.	LIEUT.	WHEN PLACED ON HALF PAY.
Greatrex, Charles Butler, Royal Marines ..	15 Oct. 05	1 June 10	1 Sept. 14
Greaves, Charles, Unattached	25 Oct. 27	8 June 30	9 May 34
Greaves, Spencer, 14 Foot	7 Nov. 26	8 June 28	1 Aug. 31
Green, Samuel, 78 Foot	31 Oct. 10	10 Sept. 12	23 Dec. 24
Greene, Edward,[61] Royal Artillery	13 Dec. 13	1 Aug. 16	1 Feb. 19
Greer, Alexander, 6 Foot		8 Jan. 01	17 Sept. 02
Greer, William, 11 Foot	6 July 09	9 July 12	25 May 17
Greetham, John Henry, Unattached	2 April 22	25 June 24	23 Mar. 32
W Grier, Robert,[62] 44 Foot	26 Feb. 10	13 May 12	27 Mar. 17
Grierson, Charles, 1 Dragoon Guards	25 May 15	2 Mar. 20	25 Oct. 21
Griffin, John, 67 Foot	8 May 11	23 Sept. 13	25 May 17
Griffith, Charles, Royal Marines	2 July 03	15 Aug. 05	
P Griffiths, Edwin,[63] Royal Artillery Drivers	6 Jan. 13	12 Nov. 13	1 July 16
W Griffiths, Henry, Royal Staff Corps, *Military Knight of Windsor*	4 Aug. 14	24 May 15	12 Mar. 29
P Griffiths, John George,[64] Royal Art. Drivers	10 Feb. 11	1 Nov. 12	1 Nov. 14
Griffiths, William Stuart, 23 Foot	8 Oct. 12	21 Jan. 14	5 Oct. 15
P *Grimes, Robert*,[65] Royal Artillery	4 Mar. 09	16 Mar. 12	
Grove, Charles Thomas, 14 Foot	4 June 12	13 Oct. 14	24 Feb. 16
P * Grove, James, 1 Prov. Batt. of Militia..	never	25 Feb. 14	1814
P Grueber, Daniel, 39 Foot.............	24 Dec. 12	21 April 14	25 Mar. 17
Guest, Edward, 2 Royal Veteran Battalion	25 Aug. 07	10 Sept. 12	
Gümoëns, Nich. Theo. de, Dillon's Regiment	22 Nov. 09	27 April 11	1815
Gun, John, 15 Foot	11 Jan. 10	15 Oct. 12	13 Nov. 17
Gunn, George, Royal Marines	4 Mar. 06	1 April 12	1 Sept. 14
Gunning, Alexander, 61 Foot	29 Oct. 07	2 Jan. 10	1815
P W Gunning, George,[66] 1 Dragoon Guards	19 July 04	2 Sept. 07	10 Jan. 22
W *Hackett, William*, 1 Royal Veteran Batt.	never	19 Dec. 11	
Hadwen, Thomas, 80 Foot	21 May 18	18 Mar. 24	13 Feb. 35
P W Haggup, William, Unattached......	30 Aug. 10	13 May 12	14 Feb. 28
Haire, John, 1 Garrison Battalion	12 Nov. 06	18 Feb. 08	1815
Halaban, Richard Newton Chr., 25 Foot ..	12 Mar. 12	24 May 15	25 April 16
*Hall, Chambers, 14 Foot	never	25 Dec. 13	25 Sept. 14
Halls, Thomas, Royal Marines, *Barrack-master, Tower of London*	5 July 93	24 April 95	
P Hamel, Michael Greatheed, 5 Foot......	6 April 09	23 April 12	2 April 18
P Hamilton, George, Unattached	3 Oct. 05	23 April 07	25 Oct. 27
P Hamilton, George, Unattached	29 April 13	4 Aug. 15	22 Sept. 37
W Hamilton, John, 2 Line Bn. German Leg.	26 July 12	17 Aug. 13	25 Mar. 16
Hamilton, William Henry, 14 Foot........	27 Oct. 08	18 Jan. 10	1 Jan. 18
Hammersley, William, 3 Garrison Battalion	4 July 15	28 Feb. 16	12 Aug. 17
Hardcastle, William Augustus, 75 Foot	7 Mar. 11	29 April 19	14 Mar. 22
Harden, William, 2 Garrison Battalion	22 Feb. 10	22 Oct. 13	25 Feb. 16
Hardman, Henry Anthony, 7 West India Regt.	16 June 06	15 Jan. 07	25 April 16
W Hardman, Samuel, 10 Dragoons	19 May 13	9 Dec. 13	6 June 16
Hargrove, John Langford, 10 R. Vet. Batt.	18 Oct. 10	28 Mar. 12	
P *Harland, John, 1 Prov. Batt. of Militia..	never	25 Feb. 14	1814
Harrington, Henry, Royal Marines........	20 May 06	12 Oct. 12	1 Sept. 14
Harris, Charles, 60 Foot	11 Aug. 13	12 June 16	25 Oct. 17
Harris, William, 8 Royal Veteran Battalion	31 July 12	25 Jan. 13	
Hart, John, 2 Foot..................	26 June 11	12 Aug. 13	25 Dec. 18
Hasleham, William Gale, 6 R. Vet. Batt...	11 Feb. 08	25 Aug. 09	
Hassard, Richard, Royal Irish Artillery ..		20 Oct. 94	
Haswell, John Stepney, Royal Marines	10 Dec. 98	18 Aug. 04	30 Aug. 14
Hatheway, Charles, New Brunswick Fencibles	25 Mar. 13	25 Aug. 14	25 April 16
Hawkins, George Drew, Royal Marines....	17 Oct. 04	24 Mar. 08	1 Sept. 14
P Hawkins, John,[67] 62 Foot.............	5 Nov. 12	1 Dec. 14	25 Mar. 17
Hawley, Trevor, 9 Foot................	2 July 41	20 Sept. 44	15 Oct. 47
Hay, Alexander Murray, Unattached	10 Nov. 14	22 July 24	12 April 33
Hayes, George James, Royal Marines......	26 Sept. 25	12 Feb. 34	25 June 42
Hazen, John, 49 Foot	24 April 13	23 June 14	25 Mar. 17
Hearn, John Heming, 60 Foot...........	5 May 08	18 Feb. 10	25 Oct. 22
W Hearn, William Marcus,[68] 44 Foot	10 June 12	7 July 14	25 Mar. 16
W Hearne, George Henry, 4 Foot........	16 Mar. 09	29 Oct. 10	29 Aug. 16
Heath, Phillip, Royal Artillery	16 Dec. 16	29 July 25	3 Dec. 30

	CORNET, ETC.	LIEUT.	WHEN PLACED ON HALF PAY.
*Heath, Thomas, 38 Foot	never	25 Dec. 13	25 Sept. 14
P Heathcote, Josh. Chappell, Cape Corps	13 Sept. 10	10 Dec. 12	27 Mar. 28
Heddle, Alexander, Royal African Corps	4 May 09	20 Mar. 10	25 Dec. 21
WL Hemsley, Henry, 28 Foot	25 April 13	18 July 15	5 Dec. 22
Henderson, James Allen, 10 Foot	28 Mar. 10	26 Feb. 12	25 Sept. 18
P Henderson, William, 5 Foot	4 July 11	17 Oct. 14	25 May 17
Hendley, Henry Earbery, 3 Ceylon Regiment	4 Jan. 10	20 Mar. 12	29 Dec. 17
*Herbert, John James, 41 Foot	never	25 Dec. 13	25 Sept. 14
Herbert, Isaac, 8 Royal Veteran Battalion	8 Dec. 99	31 Mar. 08	
Herrick, Edward Henry, 15 Foot	8 Oct. 12	22 June 15	25 Mar. 16
P Herron, Samuel, 24 Foot	7 Sept. 09	30 May 11	6 Nov. 28
Hewat, William, 62 Foot	19 Sept. 11	22 Oct. 13	25 May 17
Hewetson, Henry, 101 Foot	30 Nov. 09	10 Dec. 12	25 Mar. 26
Hewett, James Waller, 1 Foot	9 May 11	7 July 13	24 Jan. 18
Hewett, William, 7 Royal Veteran Battalion	14 June 10	23 Jan. 12	
Hickman, Richard, Royal Marines	7 Jan. 08	19 July 21	1 Mar. 27
Hickson, John Annesley,[69] 31 Foot, *Staff Officer of Pensioners in New Zealand*	25 Dec. 13	28 Nov. 45	7 Dec. 46
Higgin, Robert, 12 Foot	11 Aug. 13	4 May 15	25 Mar. 17
Higginbotham, Henry, 22 Dragoons	18 May 13	2 April 18	25 Sept. 20
*Hilder, Jesse, 15 Foot	never	25 Dec. 13	25 Sept. 14
Hilditch, Charles, 3 Foot	2 July 07	15 Sept. 08	11 Oct. 10
P Hilliard, Christopher, 5 Foot	7 July 08	22 Feb. 10	25 Nov. 18
Hilton, William Legh, 98 Foot	21 May 12	1 Dec. 14	22 Feb. 22
*Hinde, Edward, Rifle Brigade	never	25 Dec. 13	1814
P Hine, John,[70] Unattached	1 Aug. 27	30 April 32	8 May 40
Hingston, Francis Bernard, 84 Foot, *Staff Officer of Pensioners*	13 Oct. 08	5 Dec. 11	17 Feb. 20
Hockings, Richard, 92 Foot, *Barrack-master at Norwich*		7 Sept. 94	6 July 04
WL Hodder, Edward,[71] 69 Foot	29 July 13	10 Aug. 15	25 Nov. 16
Hodgetts, Thomas, 49 Foot, *Staff Officer of Pensioners*	4 Sept. 30	13 Mar. 35	23 Aug. 44
P Hodgson, Alderson,[72] 2 Foot	25 Jan. 10	22 Aug. 11	22 June 20
Hoey, Richard Hudson O'Reilly, 85 Foot, *Staff Officer of Pensioners*	11 Nov. 13	17 Aug. 26	30 Oct. 35
Hojel, James, Caithness Fencible Infantry			
P Holborn, Charles, 10 Dragoons	9 June 07	6 Feb. 12	2 Oct. 17
Hole, William, 43 Foot	10 Dec. 12	7 Feb. 14	25 Mar. 17
Holgate, Edward Milton, 82 Foot	8 May 11	23 Sept. 13	25 Jan. 16
Holland, Rupert Charles, Royal Marines	27 Sept. 05	11 Aug. 09	1 April 17
Holland, John, Royal Marines, *Adjutant Pembroke Militia*	26 Mar. 28	15 Nov. 36	11 April 46
P Hollinsworth, Henry,[73] Unattached, *Staff Officer of Pensioners*	3 Dec. 25	29 May 28	8 Jan. 41
P Hollis, William Henry, 57 Foot	26 Aug. 07	5 May 08	24 July 17
P WL Holman, Charles,[74] 52 Foot, *Adj., East Devon Militia*	10 Sept. 12	11 Nov. 13	25 Dec. 18
P Holmes, Benjamin Hayes, 36 Foot	2 Nov. 09	13 Aug. 12	25 Mar. 17
Holmes, Charles Wm. Scott D., 3 Dragoons	21 April 14	7 Sept. 15	13 April 17
P Holmes, David, 9 Foot	21 Oct. 12	20 Jan. 14	14 April 17
Holmes, James, Royal Marines	23 Feb. 96	17 Sept. 98	12 Dec. 04
*Holt, George Francis, 2 Prov. Bn. of Militia	never	25 Dec. 13	1814
Holyoake, Henry, 84 Foot	22 Oct. 13	24 Feb. 15	1816
P Home, John, 3 Foot	11 Oct. 10	26 Nov. 12	3 July 17
Home, William, York Light Infantry	24 Nov. 04	7 Jan. 06	15 Jan. 24
P WL *Hood, James*,[75] 9 Royal Veteran Batt.	28 Aug. 07	3 Aug. 09	
P Hopkins, William Randolph, 5 Foot	14 Sept. 08	5 Oct. 13	25 July 16
Houghton, William, 15 Foot	6 Feb. 12	4 May 15	1 Oct. 48
How, Johnson, Royal Marines	26 July 09	14 Jan. 28	9 Sept. 28
How, Thomas, Royal Marines	16 Oct. 05	8 June 10	1 Sept. 14
Hubbard, James, Royal Marines	1 Nov. 05	20 Aug. 10	1 Sept. 14
Hudson, Henry, 60 Foot	16 Oct. 10	27 Mar. 12	25 Oct. 19
Hughes, Edward, 19 Foot	12 Nov. 12	9 Sept. 13	25 Dec. 18
WL Hughes, George, 73 Foot	29 April 13	4 Oct. 15	3 Aug. 22
Hughes, Henry Francis, Glengarry Fencibles	8 June 09	6 Feb. 12	25 Aug. 16

	2d Lieut. etc.	Lieut.	When placed on half pay.
Hull, Arthur Hill, 50 Foot, *Staff Officer of Pensioners*	24 Aug. 25	6 Nov. 27	28 June 31
Humphreys, Chas. Gardiner, 14 Dragoons	9 May 11	11 Mar. 13	4 Sept. 17
Humphreys, John, 72 Foot	3 Aug. 09	12 Mar. 12	1816
Hunt, Michael, 61 Foot	13 April 09	8 Aug. 11	2 Mar. 15
Hunt, William, Royal Staff Corps	14 Jan. 14	29 June 15	5 Feb. 29
Hunter, James, 13 Foot, *Staff Officer of Pensioners*	17 Nov. 37	27 Sept. 39	2 Sept. 45
Hunter, Thomas, 18 Dragoons	25 Feb. 16	27 Nov. 18	10 Nov. 21
Hunter, William Dodsworth, 64 Foot	23 April 05	17 April 06	25 Nov. 16
Hart, Francis, 15 Dragoons	Nov. 00	16 June 01	25 June 02
Hutchinson, John, 60 Foot	12 Nov. 12	6 Nov. 15	24 April 23
Hutton, William, Royal Marines	26 Nov. 24	14 May 33	28 Sept. 37
Huyghue, Samuel, 60 Foot	30 Aug. 10	26 Jan. 15	25 Oct. 17
Ibbotson, Henry, 103 Foot	1 April 12	12 June 15	5 Oct. 17
Ince, Charles, 1 Royal Veteran Battalion	22 May 06	17 Jan. 08	
Inglis, Edward, 3 Dragoon Guards	1 Oct. 12	17 June 13	25 Mar. 16
Inman, John, 63 Foot, *Staff Officer of Pensioners*	15 Dec. 37	13 Oct. 39	13 Dec. 44
Inman, Thomas Withy, 45 Foot	4 Jan. 10	7 Oct. 13	16 Mar. 15
Innes, Alexander, Unattached	19 July 10	15 Oct. 12	24 Nov. 28
Innes, Robert, 48 Foot	2 Dec. 13	4 April 15	25 Dec. 28
Irvine, Robert, 7 West India Regiment	22 July 13	4 May 15	11 July 16
Irving, Jacob Æmilius,[77] 13 Dragoons	24 Mar. 14	18 May 15	5 Nov. 18
Irving, Robert, 32 Foot	16 May 11	7 July 14	26 Oct. 15
Irwin, Alexander,[78] 3 Foot	4 Mar. 13	24 Nov. 14	13 Jan. 37
Irwin, Charles, Unattached	22 April 13	9 Oct. 18	5 Aug. 29
Irwin, John Robert, 54 Foot	25 Feb. 08	28 Dec. 09	1814
Isaacson, Egert. Cha. H.,[79] Gar. Comp.	30 Dec. 12	14 July 14	25 Sept. 23
Jackson, Frederick, 27 Foot, *Adjutant, Leicester Yeomanry Cavalry*	24 Aug. 26	8 Sept. 32	29 Aug. 34
Jackson, James, Royal Marines	2 May 04	15 April 07	26 June 12
Jackson, John, 4 Foot	19 May 14	24 May 20	25 Oct. 21
Jackson, William, 64 Foot	3 Oct. 11	29 June 15	15 Mar. 17
Jago, Charles,[80] 16 Foot	4 May 09	23 Jan. 12	25 June 41
James, Robert, 56 Foot	18 May 11	5 Dec. 13	13 April 15
James, Robert Unwin Donnithorne, R. Mar.	28 May 07	27 July 14	1 Sept. 14
Jameson, Thomas, 3 West India Regiment	15 Dec. 08	15 Oct. 10	25 Dec. 18
Jameson, William, 37 Foot	21 May 12	2 Feb. 14	7 Aug. 17
Jappie, William, 14 Foot	14 May 11	29 April 13	25 Mar. 17
Jeffreyson, George, 2 Royal Vet. Battalion	28 July 95	12 Jan. 96	
Jeffries, Joseph, 1 Foot	8 May 11	5 July 13	14 May 18
Jennings, George, 1 Garrison Battalion	18 July 05	19 Mar. 07	25 Aug. 16
Jervis, Thomas, 24 Foot	30 July 18	25 Sept. 23	6 May 24
Johns, James, Royal Marines	6 Dec. 05	29 Jan. 11	1 Sept. 14
Johnson, J., (Qr.-Mast. 14 Sept. 26) 40 F. *Adjt., R. Wiltshire Yeomanry Cavalry*	8 May 34	11 Mar. 37	26 July 39
Johnson, William Proude, 103 Foot	21 May 12	4 Nov. 13	22 Sept. 17
*Johnston, Galbraith, 2 Prov. Batt. of Militia	never	25 Dec. 13	1814
Johnston, John Rollo, Unattached	22 Sept. 25	19 Sept. 26	7 July 38
Johnstone, William, 86 Foot	28 Oct. 78	25 Mar. 83	1783
Jones, Edward, 10 Royal Veteran Battalion	31 Mar. 08	2 Dec. 13	
Jones, Jeremy, 60 Foot	9 May 11	10 Feb. 13	9 April 19
Jones, Richard, 40 Foot	28 Mar. 11	8 Oct. 12	21 April 17
Jones, Vaughan, 8 Garrison Battalion, *Staff Officer of Pensioners*	12 Nov. 07	12 Jan. 09	25 May 10
Jones, William, 44 Foot	25 Mar. 12	21 May 13	25 Mar. 17
Jones, William John Williams, 101 Foot	14 Mar. 15	27 Nov. 16	22 May 17
Jordan, Edward, 26 Foot	25 Aug. 07	10 Aug. 08	16 Oct. 17
Kane, John Joseph, 4 Foot	21 Oct. 13	4 May 15	25 Mar. 17
Kayes, William, 73 Foot	14 May 12	10 Aug. 14	1815
Kearnes, John, 68 Foot	5 Jan. 14	26 Feb. 18	25 July 19
Keep, William Thornton, 28 Foot	29 Aug. 11	8 Sept. 13	25 Dec. 14
Keir, John, 5 Foot	28 April 06	21 Aug. 06	29 Sept. 08
Kelly, William, Royal Irish Artillery	never	17 Dec. 94	

	ENSIGN, ETC.	LIEUT.	WHEN PLACED ON HALF PAY.
P W Kennedy, Francis,[81] 51 Foot, *Adj., North Lincoln Militia*	13 April 09	21 Feb. 11	26 Feb. 24
Kennedy, John, 4 Ceylon Regiment	19 Dec. 05	5 Feb. 06	2 Jan. 17
*Kennedy, P. Henry, 2 Prov. Batt. of Militia	never	25 Dec. 13	1814
Kentish, Edward, Royal Marines	30 Mar. 79	16 Oct. 82	1 Sept. 83
Kenworthy, William, 48 Foot	17 June 13	1 Oct. 18	25 Sept. 22
Ker, John, 90 Foot	31 Dec. 12	25 June 18	25 Dec. 18
Kerr, Charles, 72 Foot	23 Feb. 09	7 Mar. 11	11 April 16
W Kerr, John Henry, 104 Foot	21 Jan. 13	23 Nov. 20	15 Mar. 21
W Kerr, Robert, 60 Foot	11 Feb. 11	25 May 15	25 Mar. 17
Kersteman, Harry Gobins, Royal Artillery	12 Dec. 11	20 Sept. 14	2 Sept. 22
Kettlewell, Evans, 96 Foot	3 June 07	21 April 08	25 Dec. 18
Kierulf, William Duntzfelt, 22 Dragoons	1 Jan. 19	2 Jan. 20	11 April 20
King, William, Royal Artillery	19 June 41	13 April 42	3 Nov. 47
Kingsley, Jeffries, 3 Dragoons	24 June 13	25 Nov. 13	19 Feb. 18
Kingsmill, William, 10 Royal Veteran Batt.	15 Sept. 08	30 May 11	
Kingston, Robert, *Earl of*, Unattached	6 July 14	24 Dec. 18	12 June 26
Kirk, William John, 46 Foot, *Staff Officer of Pensioners*	27 Sept. 31	27 Oct. 37	18 April 45
Knight, Richard Lott, 22 Foot	16 May 11	15 July 19	25 Dec. 23
Knight, William, 28 Foot	14 Feb. 05	28 May 07	3 Dec. 18
P Knox, Francis,[82] 31 Foot	23 Mar. 08	23 May 10	14 Aug. 17
La Berthodierre, P. Marie, 8 West India Regt.	15 Aug. 10	12 Nov. 12	20 June 16
P Lacy, Samuel Walter, 10 Foot	4 Oct. 10	16 Sept. 13	24 June 24
La Grange, Jas. Warrington, 3 Dragoon Gds.	10 Mar. 14	5 Oct. 15	25 Mar. 16
*Lambert, John, 3 Prov. Battalion of Militia	never	25 Mar. 14	1814
P Lane, Ambrose, 83 Foot	28 May 11	28 July 13	25 June 17
Lane, Ambrose, 98 Foot	13 Aug. 07	7 Mar. 11	25 Sept. 18
Lane, John, Unattached	22 June 15	30 Dec. 26	24 April 28
Lang, John, 23 Foot	23 Aug. 10	10 Dec. 12	1 June 20
P Langdon, Colwell, 60 Foot	6 April 09	21 Dec. 09	30 Sept. 19
*Langdon, John, 2 Prov. Battalion of Militia	never	25 Dec. 13	1814
Laplain, John, 56 Foot	10 Oct. 11	6 Dec. 13	6 Sept. 17
Latham, John, 92 Foot	1 July 13	14 July 14	1814
Laurie, James, Royal Marines	15 Mar. 04	24 Sept. 06	7 April 17
Lawson, John, Unattached, *Staff Officer of Pensioners*	10 Oct. 22	17 Aug. 26	5 Sept. 35
Lawson, William, Garrison Company	20 June 99	14 Nov. 06	
Laye, George, 24 Foot	14 July 14	29 April 19	24 Mar. 25
Leach, Henry, Scots Fusilier Guards	never	5 July 15	25 Dec. 18
Leathes, Edward, 8 Dragoons	14 Nov. 10	25 Sept. 23	6 May 24
Leavach, John, 3 West India Regiment	17 Aug. 09	3 July 11	17 Feb. 20
Lee, Edward, 85 Foot	26 Aug. 07	2 Feb. 09	24 Feb. 20
Lee, George, 21 Foot	30 April 12	5 Aug. 13	19 Mar. 18
P Leggett, John, 3 Dragoon Guards	28 Feb. 08	15 Sept. 08	16 Oct. 16
Leslie, Angus, 93 Foot	12 Mar. 12	10 Feb. 14	25 Mar. 17
P L'Estrange, George, Scots Fusilier Guards	16 Jan. 12	17 June 13	11 July 22
L'Estrange, Torranio Francis, Coldstream Guards	20 Oct. 14	16 Oct. 17	16 Nov. 20
Lewis, Henry, Royal Marines	1 Sept. 06	4 Aug. 13	1 Sept. 14
Lewis, Thomas, 3 Garrison Battalion	12 May 14	10 Oct. 15	25 Nov. 16
Lewis, William, 19 Foot	12 Mar. 10	10 May 14	20 July 20
Lind, Robert, 1 R. Vet. Batt., *Barrack-master at Auckland, New Zealand*	11 Feb. 08	10 Oct. 09	
P Lindsey, Henry John, Unattached	5 Dec. 11	11 Jan. 16	31 Jan. 26
Lisle, Benjamin de, Canadian Fencibles	6 Dec. 10	2 Sept. 12	11 Oct. 16
C Lister, John,[83] Royal Marines	23 Feb. 05	27 July 08	26 Nov. 25
Little, John, 27 Foot	27 April 09	9 Sept. 12	25 July 17
Little, John William, Unattached	1 Jan. 19	11 Mar. 24	11 July 29
Lloyd, Charles, Royal Marines	5 June 06	28 Oct. 12	14 Nov. 26
W Lloyd, Edward Bell, 16 Dragoons	30 May 11	12 Mar. 12	25 Aug. 19
P Lloyd, John Ormsby,[84] 74 Foot, *Staff Officer of Pensioners*	25 Nov. 13	14 May 18	15 Oct. 19
Locke, William, 5 Dragoon Guards	9 June 14	3 July 17	20 Mar. 23

	CORNET, ETC.	LIEUT.	WHEN PLACED ON HALF PAY.
P W Lockwood, Purefoy,[95] 30 Foot, *Capt. of Invalids, R. Hospital, Kilmainham*	18 April 11	22 April 13	25 Aug. 16
Long, Edmund Slingsby, 23 Foot	3 Aug. 04	8 Aug. 05	5 Aug. 13
Long, William, Unattached	17 Mar. 14	7 April 25	21 Nov. 28
Lonsdale, Alured, 84 Foot..................	20 May 26	3 Aug. 30	8 April 36
P W Lonsdale, William, 4 Foot	1 Feb. 10	15 May 12	25 Mar. 17
P *Lorimer, Charles Hunt,*[96] 8 Royal Vet. Batt., *Military Knight of Windsor* ..	12 Jan. 05	28 April 06	
P Love, James,[97] Royal Artillery..........	6 Nov. 09	19 Mar. 13	1 April 19
Lovelace, Henry Philip, Unattached	25 Aug. 09	24 May 11	23 Aug. 27
P Lovelock, John Birmingham,[98] 29 Foot, *Barrackmaster at Castlebar*	3 Aug. 09	4 July 11	25 Oct. 21
*Lovett, Joseph Venables, 3 Provisional Battalion of Militia	never	25 Feb. 14	1814
Lovett, Thomas, Royal Artillery..........	1 April 09	17 April 12	1 Mar. 22
P Lowry, Armar, 45 Foot..................	31 Dec. 12	28 July 14	1814
P Lowry, John,[99] 95 Foot..................	7 June 10	24 Dec. 12	13 July 20
W Lucas, Jasper, 32 Foot	6 Jan. 13	19 July 15	25 Mar. 17
*Luckhurst, Thomas, 3 Prov. Batt. of Militia	never	25 Jan. 14	1814
Lupton, William, 60 Foot..................	28 Nov. 11	9 Feb. 13	25 June 17
Lynam, Charles, 15 Foot	25 June 12	16 Nov. 15	25 Mar. 16
Lynch, Edward Crean, 22 Foot	11 Dec. 23	21 Jan. 26	8 April 34
Lynd, Robert, 65 Foot, *Barrackmaster at Sydney, New South Wales*	14 Feb. 16	31 Oct. 18	4 April 23
Lyon, George, 99 Foot	4 Sept. 06	10 Feb. 08	25 Nov. 18
Lyster, Arthur O'Neil, 46 Foot	2 Sept. 24	13 June 30	7 Sept. 33
Lyster, Henry, 7 Dragoons	29 May 17	7 Sept. 20	25 Oct. 21
Lyster, William John, 8 Garrison Battalion		12 Mar. 83	25 June 10
M'Annally, Charles, 84 Foot...............	26 Nov. 06	31 Dec. 07	5 Oct. 20
M'Arthur, James Earle, 14 Foot..........	17 May 11	4 Dec. 13	12 Oct. 19
M'Bean, Alexander, 2 Light Infantry Battalion, German Legion	25 April 13	27 Nov. 13	25 Mar. 16
M'Carthy, Justin Thadeus Courtney, Royal Marines	17 Jan. 33	13 Jan. 38	10 May 39
M'Carthy, William, 16 Foot...............	7 Oct. 13	18 July 16	25 Mar. 17
M'Clure, Arthur, 1 Foot	15 Jan. 07	26 April 09	5 Feb. 18
P M'Cormick, James, 94 Foot............	25 May 09	17 Mar. 14	25 Dec. 18
P *M'Crohan, Denis Eugene,* 3 R. Vet. Batt.	16 May 12	21 Oct. 13	
M'Cullock, James Murray, Royal Marines..	2 Nov. 98	17 July 04	11 June 16
M'Dermott, James, 20 Dragoons...........	15 Oct. 12	31 Mar. 14	25 Mar. 16
M'Dermott, Thomas, 7 Royal Veteran Batt., *Military Knight of Windsor* ..	1 Nov. 94	25 Feb. 05	
M'Donald, Alexander,[91] 26 Foot	13 Mar. 29	12 Oct. 32	4 Sept. 43
M'Donald, Charles Alexander, 32 Foot	2 July 12	3 Oct. 16	25 June 18
M'Donald, Colin, 72 Foot..................	25 Nov. 08	21 Feb. 11	25 Feb. 16
P W M'Donald, Donald, 40 Foot........	22 Oct. 12	7 June 15	25 Feb. 16
W M'Donough, Thomas, 34 Foot	31 Aug. 07	30 Oct. 09	21 June 27
M'Dougall, Thomas Wm. John, R. Marines, *Staff Officer of Pensioners*	10 Mar. 28	5 July 36	6 Dec. 37
Macduff, Alex., 100 Foot	23 Feb. 09	9 July 12	15 May 18
M'Farlane, William, 17 Dragoons	11 July 11	1 April 14	28 Aug. 23
M'Goldrick, *Æneas,* 62 Foot, *Barrack-master at Maroon Town, Jamaica* ..	11 Nov. 13	15 Jan. 18	25 Feb. 22
M'Gregor, John, 46 Foot	12 May 20	22 Dec. 24	25 Dec. 28
M'Gregor, John, 3 West India Regt.	11 Dec. 06	6 Feb. 08	23 June 25
M'Intosh, Andrew, (Q. M. 12 Apr. 10) Royal Veteran Batt.	never	25 Dec. 14	
M'Intyre, Peter, Royal Marines	21 Sept. 05	16 May 09	1 Sept. 14
M'Iver, Donald, 77 Foot	22 Feb. 10	9 April 12	17 May 21
M'Kenzie, John, Canadian Fencibles	31 Dec. 12	8 Sept. 14	11 Oct. 16
M'Kenzie, William Fleming, R. Staff Corps	18 April 11	10 Feb. 14	5 Feb. 29
M'Kinnon, John, 104 Foot	18 Dec. 06	15 Mar. 10	25 July 17
M'Lachlan, Lachlan, 3 West India Regt. ..	21 Sept. 96	11 Dec. 97	24 July 00
P M'Laren, Alexander Donald, 91 Foot....	3 June 12	31 Mar. 14	25 Feb. 16

	2d Lieut. etc.	Lieut.	When placed on half pay.
M'Leod, James, 2 Royal Veteran Batt.…	21 Jan. 08	11 June 08	
M'Leroth, Thomas, Royal Marines……	17 June 13	16 April 32	22 April 33
M'Manus, Henry, 62 Foot ……		23 June 04	25 Mar. 17
M'Millan, John, 82 Foot ……	17 Sept. 13	31 Aug. 15	10 Mar. 16
M'Namara, Henry, 62 Foot……	1 Jan. 01	27 Nov. 01	25 June 02
M'Namara, Michael, 60 Foot ……	2 Nov. 09	18 Oct. 10	28 June 19
M'Nicol, Duncan, Royal Marines ……	16 Oct. 04	29 Feb. 08	15 Oct. 22
𝔓 M'Nicol, Nicol, 27 Foot ……	14 May 12	10 Feb. 14	16 April 17
M'Niel, Donald, Cape Regt.……	23 Aug. 10	4 June 14	17 July 18
M'Phee, John, 79 Foot……	25 Feb. 13	17 July 15	25 Mar. 17
𝔓 M'Pherson, Æneas, 59 Foot……	25 June 12	26 Sept. 13	25 April 16
𝔚 M'Pherson, Alexander,[92] 92 Foot……	15 Dec. 08	22 Oct. 12	25 Mar. 17
M'Rae, Farquhar, 66 Foot ……	24 June 05	21 Jan. 08	7 Feb. 22
M'Rae, Theodore, Royal African Corps ….	26 July 15	14 May 18	25 Dec. 18
Macalpine, James, 8 Dragoons……	5 Mar. 12	15 Aug. 13	25 July 20
Macartney, Charles, 11 Dragoons ……	11 Dec. 28	13 Nov. 34	1 Nov. 38
Macdonald, James, 76 Foot ……	29 Dec. 77	9 Sept. 80	1783
𝔓 𝔚 Macdonald, John,[93] 91 Foot……	18 May 09	30 April 12	9 May 17
Macdonald, John, 4 West India Regt.……	6 Feb. 14	26 June 19	12 June 23
Macdonald, Stephen, 1 Lt. Inf. Batt. Ger. Leg.	22 Dec. 12	5 April 14	25 April 16
Macdonell, Duncan, Elford's Corps……	26 Sept. 94	15 July 95	
𝔓 Macdougall, Colin, 91 Foot……	12 Oct. 09	19 July 13	1815
Mac Gachen, John, 72 Foot……	5 Dec. 11	28 Dec. 14	20 Feb. 19
Mac Gregor, John,[94] 4 Royal Veteran Batt.	9 May 11	26 Jan. 14	
𝔚 Machell, John Thomas, 18 Dragoons ..	12 Aug. 13	24 Feb. 14	10 Nov. 21
Macintire, Andrew, Royal York Rangers ..	27 Feb. 23	9 Oct. 27	28 Sept. 30
Mackay, Hugh, Queen's American Rangers	30 Dec. 81	25 Dec. 82	
𝔓 Mac Kay, Lachlan,[95] 42 Foot ……	31 Oct. 11	23 Sept. 13	18 Jan. 31
Mackay, Hugh Donald, 5 West India Regt.	1 April 13	31 Mar. 14	1 Oct. 17
Mackay, Neil, 76 Foot ……	9 May 05	27 Feb. 06	25 Oct. 19
Mackenzie, William, 3 Dragoons……	20 July 15	7 Sept. 20	25 Oct. 21
𝔓 *Mackie, John*, 7 Royal Veteran Batt.…	1 June 09	25 Jan. 13	
Maclauchlan, James Augustus, 104 Foot ..	5 Mar. 12	24 Feb. 14	25 July 17
Maclean, George, Royal African Corps ….	18 Jan. 15	15 Aug. 26	25 Jan. 30
Macnab, John, 94 Foot……	4 July 11	16 Feb. 15	25 Dec. 18
𝔓 *Macnamara, Michael, 1 Prov. Bn. of Mil.	never	25 Feb. 14	1814
Macpherson, Duncan, 52 Foot……	26 Mar. 08	2 Jan. 12	13 Dec. 16
Macpherson, Lachlan, 52 Foot……	21 Aug. 99	20 Mar. 00	
Madden, Henry, 7 Royal Irish Artillery ..	25 July 95	22 Feb. 99	
Magin, William, Royal Marines ……	2 July 03	15 Aug. 05	25 Sept. 09
Maher, Martin, Royal Veteran Battalion..	6 April 09	17 Jan. 11	
Mahon, Edmond, 70 Foot……	12 Mar. 12	15 June 15	4 Nov. 17
Mahon, James, 26 Foot……	2 Jan. 12	2 Feb. 14	25 Dec. 14
Major, Stephen, 13 Foot ……	3 Oct. 09	26 July 10	25 Mar. 17
Manners, John, Royal Marines ……	24 Feb. 96	26 Sept. 98	29 Nov. 98
Marcer, Richard Harvey, Royal Marines ..	1 Aug. 99	18 Aug. 04	9 Jan. 16
March, Leopold George Fred., Royal Marines	5 Feb. 33	26 April 38	3 July 41
Marder, Henry, 71 Foot ……	22 Nov. 98	1 June 99	24 Jan. 03
Marklove, John, 56 Foot ……	8 April 13	20 June 16	28 Dec. 17
Marsh, Henry, Independent Company ….		8 July 95	
Marshall, Ralph, 89 Foot……	3 Feb. 08	12 April 10	12 June 23
Marshall, Thomas, Royal Marines ……	2 Sept. 98	1 April 04	14 Aug. 07
𝔓 𝔚 Martin, Benjamin, 85 Foot ……	26 Dec. 98	3 June 02	11 Nov. 18
Martin, Edward, Royal Artillery ……		3 Dec. 00	
Martin, Johnston, Bourbon Regt. ……	25 Jan. 12	29 Oct. 12	24 April 16
Martin, Richard Bartholomew, Unattached	12 April 21	9 April 26	15 June 30
Martin, William Neufville, 64 Foot……	15 April 12	3 Mar. 14	15 Mar. 17
Mason, Francis, 8 Garrison Battalion……	25 June 05	9 Oct. 06	22 Mar. 10
Mason, James, 11 Foot……	5 Jan. 09	9 May 11	25 Mar. 17
Masters, Stephen, 30 Foot ……	13 Nov. 05	15 Jan. 07	2 July 17
Matheson, Roderick, Glengarry Fencibles ..	6 Feb. 12	5 Aug. 13	4 Dec. 16
𝔓 Mathews, Joseph,[96] 83 Foot ……	6 April 09	13 June 11	25 June 17
𝔓 Mathison, John Augustus, 77 Foot……	8 May 11	12 Aug. 13	25 Mar. 17
𝔚 Matthews, John Powell, 10 Foot, *Staff Officer of Pensioners* ……	3 Nov. 14	7 April 25	31 Dec. 30
𝔚 Matthews, Wm. M'Donald,[97] 62 Foot..	25 Dec. 13	7 Jan. 19	26 Jan. 26

	ENSIGN, ETC.	LIEUT.	WHEN PLACED ON HALF PAY.
*Mawby, Joseph, 3 Prov. Bn. of Militia....	never	9 Mar. 14	1814
Maxwell, John, 8 West India Regt.........	18 July 11	24 Dec. 12	1816
Mayhew, Henry, 1 Garrison Battalion	7 Mar. 00	23 May 04	7 Dec. 14
Meade, Thomas Harold, 13 Foot..........	4 Oct. 10	27 July 12	10 July 17
Meares, John, Royal Marines	20 Mar. 09	18 Sept. 27	2 Oct. 28
Mellish, William, Royal Waggon Train	29 Nov. 05	17 Nov. 08	16 Mar. 15
Mence, Haffez,[98] 32 Foot	13 Aug. 12	27 April 15	25 Mar. 17
Menzies, Alexander, 5 Royal Veteran Batt.	25 Aug. 08	11 May 09	
Mercer, Alexander, 42 Foot	15 April 13	1 June 15	25 Mar. 17
Meredith, Boyle, 16 Foot, *Staff Officer of Pensioners*....................	29 Mar. 10	1 July 13	24 Oct. 22
Meredith, George, Royal Marines	9 Aug. 96	1 Oct. 01	
Meuron, John Frederick de, 2 Lt. Inf. Batt. Ger. Leg.	15 April 12	19 Aug. 12	24 Feb. 16
Middleton, Thos. Falkner, 1 Drag. Gds.	28 Oct. 13	4 May 15	25 July 16
Miles, George,[100] 7 Foot	25 May 09	16 May 11	14 Mar. 22
Miller, David, Royal Marines	19 April 05	27 July 08	4 Jan. 25
Miller, Donald, 33 Foot	30 May 11	6 April 14	25 Oct. 21
*Miller, Gavin, 19 Foot.................	never	25 Dec. 13	26 Sept. 14
Miller, Henry, Royal Marines	14 Mar. 04	15 Sept. 06	1 Sept. 14
Miller, William, Royal Artillery	10 July 15	7 April 21	25 Jan. 25
Miller, Zaccheus,[101] Royal Marines........	20 May 97	19 July 03	
Mills, James, 30 Foot	3 Dec. 25	12 Dec. 26	3 Sept. 29
Milne, James Miles, 5 Royal Vet. Batt.	2 Mar. 08	31 Mar. 10	
Milnes, Alfred Shore, Royal Artillery......	5 July 13	15 Jan. 16	5 Sept. 22
Milnes, Thomas Milnes Smith, 28 Foot	28 Nov. 11	9 Feb. 15	25 Mar. 17
Minchin, Charles Humphrey, R. Engineers	1 Jan. 14	1 Aug. 14	24 June 19
Minchin, George, New Brunswick Fencibles	25 Mar. 13	25 Dec. 14	25 May 16
Mitchell, Robert,[102] 28 Foot...........	15 Feb. 10	11 Feb. 13	25 Mar. 17
Moffatt, Abraham, 71 Foot	5 Aug. 13	22 June 15	25 Feb. 16
Mogridge, James Edward, 34 Foot......	11 April 09	28 June 10	2 Oct. 17
Molesworth, Arthur John, Royal Marines ..	20 Mar. 30	10 July 37	2 Mar. 40
Moller, Charles Champion, 18 Dragoons	16 June 14	19 April 15	23 April 17
Monck, Charles Stanley, 44 Foot..........	10 Oct. 11	31 Dec. 12	25 Mar. 17
Money, George, 12 Foot	1 Jan. 12	15 July 13	25 Mar. 17
Monro, Frederick, Royal Artillery	20 Dec. 09	3 Sept. 13	23 June 24
Moore, Frederick George, 28 Foot	4 Nov. 42	20 Nov. 45	
Moore, James Adolphus,[103] Royal Marines..	14 Oct. 05	14 May 10	8 Sept. 20
*Moore, Joshua John, 14 Foot............	never	25 Dec. 13	25 Sept. 14
Moore, Samuel, 7 Foot..................	27 May 13	7 Mar. 16	4 June 18
*Moore, Samuel, 38 Foot..............	never	25 Dec. 13	25 Sept. 14
Moorhead, Charles, 71 Foot........	23 Aug. 10	3 Sept. 12	25 Dec. 18
Moreton, Moses, 54 Foot	26 Nov. 07	28 April 08	4 Sept. 17
Morgan, Edward, Royal Marines..........	9 July 03	15 Aug. 05	25 Jan. 16
Morgan, Thomas, Royal Marines..........	2 Oct. 00	30 Mar. 05	17 Oct. 14
Moriaty, James Robert, Royal Marines	11 Sept. 05	10 Nov. 08	1 Sept. 14
Morley, Edward Lacy, Royal York Rangers	16 Aug. 10	13 Jan. 13	25 Mar. 17
Morphy, Richard, 3 Foot..............	2 April 12	26 Aug. 13	25 Mar. 17
Morrison, J. Whiteford,[104] 9 R. Vet. Batt.	26 Aug. 07	17 Aug. 09	
Morton, William, 66 Foot................	10 Nov. 13	1 Sept. 16	25 Nov. 17
Morton, William, French's Recruiting Corps	9 Aug. 99	21 Feb. 00	
Moss, George, 8 West India Regiment	23 Dec. 13	16 Nov. 15	18 Aug. 16
Mosse, Henry Alexander, 94 Foot	31 Dec. 07	4 Jan. 10	25 Mar. 19
Mosse, Peter Benjamin, 80 Foot..........	20 May 10	3 May 12	25 Sept. 17
Mostyn, Robert, 81 Foot	28 Aug. 08	26 Sept. 11	18 April 17
Moulin, Andrew du, 9 Foot.............	10 Aug. 96	16 Mar. 97	23 July 02
*Mount, Edward, Royal Waggon Train	never	25 Dec. 13	1814
Mount Edgcumbe, E. A., *Earl of*, Gr. Gds., *Colonel of the Duke of Cornwall's Rangers, Aide-de-Camp to the Queen*	never	12 Jan. 14	25 Feb. 19
Mountford, Joseph, Royal Marines........	12 April 06	2 June 12	1 Sept. 14
Muckleston, Edward, 25 Foot	14 Dec. 08	27 June 11	13 Oct. 17
Munro, Frederick,[105] Royal Artillery	20 Dec. 09	3 Sept. 13	23 June 24
Murchison, Kenneth, 3 Royal Veteran Batt.	23 July 07	21 June 10	
Mure, George, Grenadier Guards......	never	14 April 14	15 June 20
Murray, Alexander, Royal Marines........	18 Mar. 97	12 July 03	15 Nov. 08

	CORNET, ETC.	LIEUT.	WHEN PLACED ON HALF PAY.!
Murray, Edward, Unattached	28 April 13	11 Aug. 14	9 June 25
P Murray, Francis,[109] 94 Foot, *Barrack-master at Edinburgh*	29 June 09	7 July 14	25 Dec. 18
P Muskett, Thomas Willis,[110] R. Art. Drivers	17 May 07	11 Mar. 09	1 July 16
*Myers, William, 2 Prov. Bn. of Militia	never	25 Dec. 13	1814
Nangle, George, 76 Foot	29 Jan. 06	30 June 08	4 Sept. 17
Nankivell, James, 98 Foot	16 Dec. 99	16 Nov. 00	
P Nantes, Richard,[111] 55 Foot, *Military Knight of Windsor*	never	19 Oct. 09	1814
Napier, Duncan Campbell, Meuron's Regt.	24 Feb. 14	4 May 15	5 Aug. 16
W Nash, John,[112] 79 Foot	18 Nov. 13	19 July 15	11 May 17
Nason, Henry, 8 West India Regt.	19 Sept. 11	29 Feb. 16	25 Dec. 16
Nayler, Charles, 63 Foot	24 June 13	2 June 14	25 May 15
Naylor, Edward,[113] Royal Marines	6 May 99	18 Aug. 04	16 Dec. 15
Neligan, Thomas, 83 Foot	28 Nov. 10	11 Nov. 13	25 Sept. 17
P Nelson, John Clarke, 28 Foot	16 May 11	25 Aug. 13	18 May 15
Nesfield, William Andrews, 48 Foot	26 June 12	30 Mar. 14	25 Dec. 18
*Newbolt, Francis, Royal Waggon Train	never	25 Dec. 13	1814
Newcomen, Arthur, Royal Artillery	16 Dec. 31	10 Feb. 34	4 Oct. 42
Newton, Beauch. Bartholomew, 34 Foot	28 Mar. 16	28 June 21	4 Dec. 23
Newton, Hibbert, 32 Foot	27 July 09	13 April 13	25 Mar. 17
Newton, John, 15 Dragoons	16 Sept. 95	2 Dec. 95	23 Aug. 02
Newton, Thomas Charles, R. Waggon Train	23 April 13	7 Sept. 15	25 Aug. 16
Newton, Walter, 21 Dragoons	6 Aug. 09	2 Nov. 10	2 Aug. 20
Neynoe, Joseph, 5 Royal Veteran Battalion	17 July 00	25 June 03	
W Nicholson, John, 14 Foot	25 Dec. 13	5 April 15	25 Mar. 16
Nicholson, Ralph, 101 Foot	29 May 10	31 Dec. 12	27 July 20
P Nicholson, Richard, 5 Foot	27 Dec. 10	7 Oct. 13	25 July 16
P Nicholson, Robert Dring,[114] 58 Foot	29 Nov. 10	21 April 14	25 Feb. 16
C Nicolas, Paule Harris,[115] Royal Marines	6 July 05	27 July 08	1 Sept. 14
Nisbett, Henry, 24 Dragoons	20 Mar. 06	16 Feb. 09	25 Dec. 18
P W Nixon, Wm. Richmond, 52 Foot	26 July 10	11 May 12	25 Nov. 19
Norman, William, 69 Foot	7 Mar. 10	14 May 12	25 April 26
Norris, Robert, 20 Dragoons	9 May 16	18 Mar. 18	31 Dec. 18
Nowlan, Thomas, West India Rangers	12 Aug. 13	18 May 15	26 Oct. 30
P Nowlan, William, 91 Foot	3 Jan. 06	12 Jan. 09	22 June 20
Nugent, Walter, 26 Foot	8 June 09	9 Nov. 09	25 Mar. 11
W Oakes, *Sir* Henry Tho., *Bt.*, 95 Foot, *Barrack Master at Derry*	22 Oct. 12	11 Feb. 14	25 Mar. 17
O'Brien, James, 6 R. Vet. Batt. *Barrack-Master at Drogheda*	6 Dec. 10	28 July 12	
*O'Brien, John, 16 Foot	never	25 Dec. 13	25 Sept. 14
O'Conner, Bernard Richard, 44 Foot	18 May 09	22 Nov. 10	18 July 16
P O'Conner, James, 27 Foot	22 Oct. 12	19 Jan. 15	2 April 16
P O'Conner, Maurice, 97 Foot	10 Aug. 08	25 Oct. 10	20 Jan. 20
O'Dell, Edm. Westropp, 98 Foot	12 Sept. 05	13 Aug. 07	25 Sept. 18
O'Flyn, Andrew, 87 Foot	3 Feb. 08	27 Oct. 08	19 Aug. 19
P Ogilvy, David,[116] 94 Foot	18 May 09	17 Feb. 14	25 Dec. 18
P W O'Hara, Patterson, 59 Foot	8 Nov. 10	2 Sept. 12	25 Mar. 16
O'Kelly, James, 4 Foot	8 Mar. 10	16 Nov. 12	20 Mar. 23
*Oliver, John, 33 Foot	never	25 Dec. 13	25 Sept. 14
Olpherts, Robert, Unattached	18 June 18	13 April 20	20 Sept. 26
O'Neill, Henry, Unattached	30 June 25	29 Aug. 26	11 July 37
W Onslow, Phipps Vansittart,[117] R. Artillery	17 Dec. 07	16 Dec. 08	9 Dec. 24
P O'Reilly, John, 11 Foot	25 April 11	16 Sept. 13	25 May 16
Ormsby, Henry Michael, 36 Foot	2 Jan. 12	1 Oct. 12	25 Mar. 17
P Ormsby, James, 25 Dragoons	10 Oct. 06	14 Mar. 08	10 Feb. 20
P Ormsby, Sewell, 6 Foot	7 Mar. 05	8 Jan. 07	11 Dec. 17
Orr, James, Royal Marines	26 Nov. 04	27 July 08	1 April 17
P W *Orr, John*,[118] 8 Royal Veteran Batt.	3 Oct. 11	29 April 13	
P Orrell, Andrew, 34 Foot	30 May 11	21 April 14	25 June 17
O'Sullivan, Eugene, 98 Foot	3 June 08	20 Feb. 12	18 Sept. 17
Ottley, Benjamin Robert, 61 Foot	14 Mar. 11	16 July 12	25 April 22
Oughton, James, 61 Foot	20 Feb. 12	20 Oct. 16	25 Mar. 19
P Owens, John Walker, 31 Foot	29 Sept. 08	7 Feb. 11	25 Sept. 17
W Pagan, Samuel Alex.,[119] 55 Foot	31 Oct. 11	7 April 14	14 Feb. 22

	2D LIEUT. ETC.	LIEUT.	WHEN PLACED ON HALF PAY.
Paget, Robert, 7 Royal Veteran Battalion..	4 June 12	17 Feb. 14	
Palling, John Graveley, 24 Dragoons	21 Dec. 13	21 Nov. 17	25 July 19
Pannell, Robert, 60 Foot	30 Mar. 12	2 Aug. 13	25 June 19
Parke, Samuel, 2 Garrison Battalion	9 Feb. 09	4 Mar. 11	7 Sept. 15
Parker, Frederick, Royal Marines	4 Mar. 09	7 Jan. 26	6 Mar. 28
Parker, John Frederick, 105 Foot	31 Mar. 82	29 May 83	31 Jan. 84
Parker, Kenyon Stevens, Royal Marines ..	26 Nov. 05	15 Jan. 11	1 Sept. 14
*Parker, Michael, 3 Prov. Bn. of Militia ..	never	25 Jan. 14	1814
Parker, Thomas Robert, 6 R. Veteran Batt.	6 Aug. 07	28 Sept. 08	
W Parkinson, Robert, Royal Waggon Train	22 April 13	4 May 15	30 Oct. 17
P Parratt, Hillebrant Mered.,[120] R. Artillery	29 Oct. 08	11 July 11	12 Sept. 22
P W Parry, James, 28 Foot	10 Sept. 12	27 Jan. 14	25 Mar. 17
*Parry, Thomas, 3 Prov. Bn. of Militia....	never	25 Feb. 14	1814
Parsons, Richard Tapper, Royal Marines ..	18 May 99	18 Aug. 04	5 May 08
Paterson, Alexander, 2 Line Bn. German Leg.	25 July 12	4 June 13	25 April 16
Paton, George, 22 Dragoons..............	12 July 10	1 July 12	25 Sept. 16
Patterson, Edward, 31 Foot..............	1 Sept. 08	20 Sept. 10	25 Sept. 17
Patterson, John Williams, 60 Foot	18 April 11	3 Sept. 12	11 Oct. 19
P Pattison, Joseph, 5 Dragoon Guards	21 Feb. 11	2 Jan. 12	3 Nov. 14
Pawley, George, Murray's Recruiting Corps	21 Mar. 05	9 Oct. 06	14 April 08
P Paxton, Archibald Frederick, 11 Dragoons	26 June 11	19 Dec. 11	23 July 17
Peach, John Carroll, Royal African Corps..	3 Sept. 12	25 Aug. 14	25 Feb. 19
Peacocke, Warren William Richard, 17 Foot	18 Jan. 39	1 April 42	13 Aug. 47
Pearson, Matthew, 95 Foot	April 94	19 July 94	
Pearson, William Rex, Royal Marines......	11 Mar. 09	11 Feb. 26	3 Mar. 29
Peddie, William,[122] 21 Foot, *Staff Officer of Pensioners*....................	2 Jan. 10	30 Jan. 12	20 April 17
Peel, Edmund, 25 Foot..................	15 Mar. 15	13 Mar. 17	2 May 22
Peers, Henry de Linné, 53 Foot	29 Jan. 12	22 July 13	17 Aug. 20
P Pell, Edwin, 36 Foot..................	27 July 09	25 Mar. 13	25 Mar. 17
P Penfold, Edward, 14 Dragoons	29 Aug. 11	25 Mar. 12	25 Mar. 17
Pengelley, Edward, Royal Marines........	5 July 03	15 Aug. 05	21 Jan. 23
P Pennefather, Richard, 87 Foot..........	14 June 10	26 Sept. 11	31 July 17
P *Pennington, Rowland*,[123] 5 R. Vet. Batt.	8 Sept. 08	23 May 11	
Pepper, Theobald, 3 Dragoon Guards......	14 Sept. 08	27 June 11	25 Mar. 16
Perceval, Charles, 68 Foot	13 June 11	4 Mar. 13	19 Oct. 20
Percy, Francis, 51 Foot..................	22 July 13	16 Oct. 17	25 Dec. 18
Perham, John, Royal Marines............	26 June 06	9 Feb. 13	9 Sept. 26
Perham, William, Royal Marines	20 Sept. 05	20 Feb. 09	1 Sept. 14
Perry, Henry, Royal Waggon Train	5 Jan. 05	18 Aug. 14	31 Jan. 15
Perry, Richard Lavite, 44 Foot	20 Dec. 10	3 Sept. 12	25 Mar. 17
Petley, Robert, 24 Dragoons, *Professor of Drawing, Royal Military College*	24 Dec. 29	12 Aug. 34	27 Mar. 46
W Petre, Henry William, 18 Dragoons ..	14 May 07	26 Jan. 09	18 Feb. 19
Phair, William Barry, 104 Foot	9 July 07	7 Dec. 09	25 July 17
Phillips, John (*Cornet*), Royal Waggon Train	17 Nov. 96		25 Nov. 02
P Phillips, Robert Jocelyn, 27 Foot, *Barrack-master at Dundalk*	20 July 09	6 Oct. 12	25 Mar. 15
W Philpot, Edward,[124] R. Artillery Drivers	16 Aug. 06	1 Sept. 08	1 Aug. 16
Pickard, Henry William,[125] Royal Artillery	17 Dec. 12	21 May 15	29 April 31
Pickering, Joseph, 4 Foot................	8 Oct. 12	16 Nov. 13	25 Feb. 16
Pictet, Armand Jacques,[126] Unattached	9 Feb. 15	6 April 26	21 Feb. 28
Pictet, Frederick, 60 Foot................	25 June 12	22 Jan. 14	24 Sept. 19
Pigott, Henry, 49 Foot..................	9 July 29	14 June 33	3 Nov. 43
Pigou, Lawrence, 2 Dragoon Guards	17 Nov. 14	8 Aug. 16	25 Mar. 17
Pigou, William George, 83 Foot	3 Oct. 16	8 Feb. 21	1 May 23
Pike, John, 6 Royal Veteran Battalion	20 Oct. 08	25 June 12	
Pinhey, William Towley, Royal Marines ..	1 Oct. 05	25 Sept. 09	1 April 17
Pinniger, Broome, 6 West India Regiment	2 April 12	1 Dec. 13	28 Dec. 17
Piper, Thomas, Royal Marines............	14 Jan. 01	15 Aug. 05	11 Nov. 08
Playfair, Andrew William, 104 Foot	26 April 10	7 Nov. 11	25 July 17
*Plowman, Thomas, Royal Waggon Train..	never	25 Dec. 13	1814
Plunkett, Thomas Richard, 18 Dragoons ..	6 Mar. 11	1 July 13	6 Oct. 25
P Poe, Purefoy, 39 Foot	13 June 09	1 July 13	17 April 17

	ENSIGN, ETC.	LIEUT.	WHEN PLACED ON HALF PAY.
W Polhill, William, 23 Dragoons	1 July 13	13 Dec. 15	10 Jan. 19
Pontcarré, E. L. E. C. De, R. Foreign Artillery	12 Mar. 06	26 July 10	17 Jan. 15
P Poole, Walter Croker, 88 Foot	21 Dec. 09	26 Mar. 12	1815
Porter, Henry, Royal Marines	7 July 03	15 Aug. 05	9 Sept. 14
Porter, Robert, 7 Foot	7 Dec. 09	3 Mar. 12	11 April 16
Powel, James Bruce, 12 Foot	22 June 09	26 Feb. 12	16 April 18
Pratt, Richard, 50 Foot	1 Dec. 04	10 Sept. 07	25 June 18
Price, Stephen, 60 Foot	10 Oct. 09	10 Oct. 10	25 Dec. 18
Pridham, William,[128] Royal Marines	13 July 99	18 Aug. 04	23 Oct. 16
P *Priest, John*,[129] R. Artillery Drivers	13 July 05	1 Jan. 06	
Pringle, James, 81 Foot	3 Aug. 09	5 Aug. 13	18 April 17
Probyn, John, 20 Foot	4 June 01	14 April 04	16 June 08
Puddicombe, Robert Bruce, Royal Marines	20 Feb. 34	10 May 39	22 Nov. 44
Purdon, Philip, 41 Foot	10 Sept. 12	27 Dec. 15	25 Mar. 17
*Pycroft, Charles, 14 Foot	never	25 Dec. 13	25 Sept. 14
W *Quill, Henry*,[130] 9 R. Veteran Battalion	16 Mar. 09	17 Dec. 12	
Ragg, Samuel,[131] 1 Royal Veteran Batt. *Military Knight of Windsor*	1 Feb. 10	5 Mar. 12	
Rainsforth, Charles, 67 Foot	2 Sept. 12	5 Feb. 16	28 Feb. 20
Rainsforth, Charles, Unattached	2 Feb. 15	8 April 25	19 May 25
Ramsden, George, Royal Artillery	10 July 15	7 Nov. 21	30 Mar. 25
Rankin, Coun Douly, 8 Foot	21 June 10	2 Nov. 11	4 April 16
Rankine, David, Rifle Brigade	25 Feb. 13	17 Nov. 14	25 Dec. 18
Ratcliff, William, 1 Garrison Battalion	25 Aug. 07	13 April 09	6 Dec. 14
Rawlins, John Hart, 13 Foot	18 Feb. 13	20 Nov. 17	3 Dec. 18
Rea, Andrew Charles, Royal Marines	27 Sept. 04	21 Nov. 07	1 April 17
P Read, Robert, Unattached	21 Mar. 11	23 April 13	26 May 25
Reed, Thomas Borrett, Royal Marines	24 April 12	17 Mar. 31	7 Oct. 31
Reeves, Lewis Buckle, Royal Marines	23 April 04	12 Mar. 07	1 April 17
Reeves, Thomas, Royal Marines	2 Nov. 04	27 July 08	do
P W Reid, Thomas,[132] R. Artillery Drivers	8 Feb. 08	1 May 09	1 July 16
Renny, Henry Laws, Royal Engineers	20 July 13	15 Dec. 13	
Reveley, George Williamson, 30 Foot	15 May 11	6 July 14	20 June 19
P Reynett, William France, 73 Foot	20 July 09	28 Feb. 11	24 Dec. 18
W Reynolds, Thos. Matthew,[133] 12 Foot	20 Feb. 12	10 Mar. 14	8 April 24
P Ribton, *Sir* John, *Bt.*, 23 Foot	6 Feb. 11	25 June 12	5 Feb. 18
Rich, Henry, 4 West India Regiment	21 Jan. 12	4 Feb. 13	30 Nov. 20
Richardes, William Eardley,[134] R. Artillery	11 July 14	25 Jan. 19	12 May 24
P Richardson, George Henry, 38 Foot	27 Aug. 07	23 Nov. 09	15 May 17
*Richardson, James, 3 Prov. Batt. of Militia	never	25 Dec. 13	1814
P *Richardson, Thomas Lothian*, R. Art. Drivers	never	10 Sept. 03	
Richmond, James, 24 Dragoons	26 Nov. 07	1 May 12	25 July 19
Richmond, Sylvester, 48 Foot	9 Aug. 11	24 April 13	3 Oct. 22
Ricketts, Alfred, 9 Foot	8 July 13	22 Dec. 14	25 Feb. 16
P Riddock, William, 4 Foot	8 April 13	15 Mar. 15	25 Feb. 16
Rideout, Henry Wood, 19 Foot	21 Sept. 15	19 April 18	20 July 20
Riet, William Van der, Cape Regiment	6 June 14	13 April 15	25 Dec. 16
Rigby, Samuel, New Brunswick Fencibles	28 June 10	3 Nov. 11	27 June 16
P W Ripley, William, 52 Foot	15 Mar. 10	2 May 11	1 Aug. 16
Ritchie, James, 1 Foot	20 Feb. 17	21 Feb. 27	25 Sept. 27
Robb, David, 25 Dragoons	14 July 08	16 Oct. 09	6 Jan. 20
P W Roberts, John,[136] R. Artillery Drivers	1 Sept. 08	1 Dec. 09	1 July 16
Roberts, John, Unattached	28 Dec. 15	8 April 25	22 April 26
Robertson, Donald, 45 Foot	24 Nov. 14	13 Dec. 35	15 May 40
Robertson, Donald, 82 Foot	8 June 09	7 Jan. 13	25 Mar. 17
Robertson, George Duncan, 21 Foot	4 Aug. 40	9 Nov. 43	20 Oct. 48
W Robertson, James,[137] 79 Foot	6 Jan. 14	20 July 15	25 Feb. 16
Robinson, Anthony, 3 R. Veteran Battalion	24 Nov. 02	17 Dec. 06	
Robinson, Daniel, Royal Marines	18 May 07	27 July 14	1 Sept. 14
Robinson, Fenton, Royal Artillery	13 Dec. 13	1 Aug. 16	20 June 22
Robinson, George, 60 Foot	15 Sept. 08	7 Nov. 09	25 April 19
P W Robinson, James,[138] 50 Foot	10 Dec. 07	17 May 10	20 Mar. 23
Robinson, John, 85 Foot	14 Mar. 05	8 Jan. 07	30 Sept. 19
Robinson, Isaac Byrne, 92 Foot	17 Dec. 18	3 Nov. 25	8 Feb. 48
P Robinson, William Henry, 45 Foot	28 Nov. 11	27 Aug. 13	11 Feb. 15
Roch, George, 98 Foot	11 May 14	9 July 18	25 Dec. 18

	CORNET, ETC.	LIEUT.	WHEN PLACED ON HALF PAY.
*Rochfort, John, 100 Foot	never	25 Dec. 13	1814
Rogers, Adam, 6 Garrison Battalion	25 Oct. 07	15 Mar. 09	4 Feb. 15
Rogers, Jacob Glynn, Unattached, *Staff Officer of Pensioners*	6 Oct. 14	5 Mar. 18	28 Dec. 38
Rogers, John, Royal Marines	10 April 11	30 June 29	14 May 31
Rogers, Robert Naylor,[139] Unattached, *Staff Officer of Pensioners*	29 July 13	14 June 15	12 Nov. 36
Rolfe, Joseph,[140] 53 Foot	3 July 01	14 Sept. 04	25 Mar. 17
Rollo, James, 59 Foot	27 Mar. 12	5 Aug. 13	25 May 16
Rooke, Lewis, Royal Marines	6 Oct. 04	16 Jan. 08	1 Sept. 14
Rooney, Bernard, 2 Garrison Battalion	4 Nov. 13	24 May 15	24 Oct. 15
Rose, Hugh, 24 Foot, *Staff Officer of Pensioners*	31 Dec. 12	25 May 19	19 Aug. 24
Rose, John, Irish Brigade	12 Feb. 94	13 Feb. 94	11 Oct. 98
Roseingrave, Matthew, 10 Foot	2 April 07	11 Feb. 08	25 Sept. 17
Ross, Emilius, Unattached	10 Aug. 15	26 June 27	28 June 39
Ross, Ewen,[141] 92 Foot	13 April 09	26 Nov. 12	25 Mar. 17
Ross, Hamilton, 81 Foot	30 July 94	15 July 95	1803
Ross, John, 7 Garrison Battalion		21 Sept. 05	8 Mar. 10
Ross-Lewin, Thomas,[142] 32 Foot	27 Nov. 06	15 Dec. 08	26 Sept. 22
Rotely, Lewis, Royal Marines	27 July 05	27 July 08	
Rothwell, William, Unattached	10 July 11	25 Nov. 13	12 Oct. 26
Rouse, Richard, Royal Marines	3 Nov. 98	18 Aug. 04	13 Dec. 05
Rowan, John Hill, Unattached	15 Nov. 27	8 July 32	31 Aug. 39
Royse, Abraham Foord, 87 Foot	20 May 13	15 June 15	2 April 17
Rudland, Jones, 10 Foot	9 May 11	20 May 13	25 May 18
Ruel, John Godfrey, Royal Marines	2 Sept. 05	29 July 08	1 Sept. 14
Russell, Henry James, 60 Foot	4 Aug. 08	10 Aug. 13	25 Aug. 19
Russell, James, 3 Royal Veteran Battalion	never	27 July 15	
Russell, William, 5 Royal Veteran Battalion	10 Sept. 07	10 Dec. 12	
Rutherford, James,[143] 23 Foot	15 Feb. 10	27 Oct. 14	15 June 15
Ryan, John Dennis, 22 Dragoons	29 Aug. 15	10 Oct. 16	25 Sept. 20
Ryan, Richard, 96 Foot	1 July 13	7 Sept. 15	25 Dec. 18
Ryan, William, 63 Foot	10 July 10	21 April 14	25 Dec. 18
Ryneweld, William Van, 93 Foot	29 Nov. 06	14 July 08	23 May 16
St. John, John, 12 Foot	15 July 13	9 Aug. 15	25 Mar. 17
St. John, Richard Fleming, Royal Artillery	16 Dec. 16	8 April 25	1 Oct. 30
Sanders, David Morison, Unattached	12 May 13	9 Mar. 20	25 May 26
Sandwith, Geo. Aug. Elliott, Royal Marines	14 Oct. 05	25 April 10	1 Sept. 14
Sandys, Myles, 40 Foot	1 Dec. 08	5 April 10	2 April 18
Sargent, Samuel, 1 Royal Veteran Battalion	1 Nov. 09	17 Oct. 10	20 Feb. 23
Sarsfield, Bingham, Unattached	1 Aug. 11	30 Dec. 14	27 July 26
Saunders, Andrew Childers, 1 Dragoons	19 Aug. 13	31 Mar. 14	25 Mar. 16
Saunders, Joseph, 1 Garrison Battalion	12 Oct. 09	28 Dec. 12	25 Sept. 17
Saunders, Robert Francis, 68 Foot	16 Mar. 09	7 Dec. 09	8 Jan. 20
Saunders, Robert John,[144] Royal Artillery	26 Nov. 08	11 Aug. 11	1 April 21
Sawkins, William, 3 Garrison Battalion	26 Dec. 11	6 Jan. 14	25 July 17
Sawyers, John, Royal Marines	24 Dec. 04	27 July 08	14 June 18
Saxby, Robert, Royal Marines	25 Sept. 05	15 June 09	1 Sept. 14
Sayer, George, 55 Foot	11 July 11	27 Aug. 13	25 Mar. 17
Sayers, Arthur, 27 Foot	6 Sept. 05	9 Oct. 06	26 Aug. 13
Sayers, William, Unattached	22 Aug. 11	15 July 13	7 Sept. 26
Schaw, John Sauchie, Royal Artillery	11 Dec. 15	1 June 22	1 June 22
Schneider, Robert Wilmot, Unattached	10 April 25	8 April 26	29 Nov. 27
Scobell, John, Royal Marines	27 Jan. 96	20 Oct. 97	27 Nov. 02
Scott, David, 7 Royal Veteran Battalion	28 Nov. 11	25 Jan. 13	
Scott, Edward, 7 Foot	never	10 Dec. 99	25 June 02
Scott, Henry, 5 Foot	22 Aug. 10	11 May 12	15 Jan. 18
Scott, Percy, 98 Foot, *Captain, commanding Isle of Wight Militia*	22 June 12	28 Nov. 15	20 Aug. 17
Scott, Thomas,[145] 94 Foot	25 Aug. 08	28 Feb. 12	25 Dec. 18
Scott, William Fitzgerald, 6 West India Regt.	30 Dec. 12	14 Dec. 14	20 Sept. 38
Searanke, John, 4 Dragoon Guards	27 Aug. 12	18 Feb. 13	11 May 15
*Sebborne, Thomas Hall, 3 Foot	never	25 Dec. 13	25 Sept. 14

	2D LIEUT. ETC.	LIEUT.	WHEN PLACED ON HALF PAY.
PW Sedley, John Somner, Roy. Staff Corps, *Bar.-Mast. at Mahebourgh, Mauritius*	6 May 13	23 Oct. 17	25 Dec. 18
Segrave, O'Neil, Unattached	23 June 25	13 May 26	26 Mar. 30
Serjeant, John, Royal Marines	10 Oct. 05	22 Jan. 10	1 Sept. 14
PW Seward, Charles, 69 Foot	24 Feb. 14	13 Aug. 15	25 Nov. 16
P Seymour, Charles Marlborough, 82 Foot	11 Aug. 08	29 June 09	11 May 15
Shadforth, Henry,[147] Unattached	14 Oct. 19	4 Dec. 23	21 Mar. 29
Shadwell, Henry Eugene, 35 Foot	24 June 05	22 Jan. 07	17 Dec. 18
Shafto, William Henry, 16 Foot	5 Aug. 13	28 Sept. 15	25 Mar. 17
Sharpe, John, 54 Foot	14 April 08	19 April 09	10 Sept. 12
Sharpin, Henry, 53 Foot	4 Feb. 13	7 Nov. 15	10 Feb. 32
PW Sharpin, William,[148] Royal Artillery	12 Dec. 11	20 Dec. 14	1 July 23
Shaw, George, Unattached	17 May 14	4 Sept. 23	13 July 26
Shaw, James Peter, 33 Foot	29 Feb. 04	8 Jan. 07	29 June 15
Shaw, Samuel, 4 Foot	17 Oct. 05	29 Sept. 08	30 Sept. 19
Shiel, Theobald, 60 Foot	never	1 April 26	13 July 26
Simmons, James F., Royal Artillery	5 July 13	23 Dec. 15	1 April 19
Simpson, James, 89 Foot	23 May 11	23 Sept. 13	28 Nov. 16
Simpson, John, Royal Marines	1 Nov. 03	1 Jan. 06	6 Oct. 14
Sinclair, George,[149] 92 Foot, *Staff Officer of Pensioners*	17 Feb. 14	14 June 21	24 Nov. 25
Sinclair, John, 8 Royal Veteran Battalion	30 May 05	10 Dec. 07	
*Singleton, Jonathan Felix, 2 Prov. Bn. of Mil.	never	25 Dec. 13	1814
Singleton, Michael Creagh,[150] 50 Foot	6 May 42	29 Dec. 43	
Skene, William, Independent Company	25 July 94	21 Feb. 95	
Slaney, Moreton, 25 Dragoons	21 Nov. 05	24 Aug. 07	1 Dec. 20
P Slattery, Bartholomew, 27 Foot	14 April 13	23 Mar. 15	26 Mar. 16
Sleator, John, 5 Royal Veteran Battalion	25 June 10	20 April 14	
Smith, Alexander, Royal Marines	12 Sept. 99	1 Sept. 04	15 Dec. 06
PW Smith, Alexander, 42 Foot	4 Aug. 08	22 Feb. 10	30 Sept. 19
Smith, Edward, 58 Foot	22 Feb. 10	20 Jan. 14	25 Feb. 16
Smith, Edward Atkins, 31 Foot	25 July 09	2 May 11	11 April 22
Smith, George Charles, 63 Foot	23 June 04	4 Aug. 05	24 Jan. 22
Smith, Henry,[151] 6 West India Regiment	12 Nov. 12	16 Nov. 15	28 Dec. 27
*Smith, Henry Pasco, 12 Foot	never	25 Dec. 13	25 Sept. 14
Smith, Henry Porter, Rifle Brigade	16 June 14	24 June 19	24 May 21
Smith, Hugh William, 67 Foot	28 Mar. 10	29 Oct. 11	13 Aug. 12
Smith, James Berridge, 21 Dragoons	1 Oct. 12	26 Aug. 13	30 Oct. 23
PW Smith, James Ramsay, 38 Foot	13 Oct. 14	20 Mar. 24	6 July 26
P Smith, John,[152] 14 Foot	10 April 09	7 Oct. 12	9 Mar. 20
P Smith, John, 27 Foot	12 May 12	8 Feb. 14	19 April 17
*Smith, John, 2 Prov. Battalion of Militia	never	25 Feb. 14	1814
Smith, Joseph, (Qr.-Mast. 28 Ap. 08) 3 Royal Veteran Battalion	never	7 Sept. 15	
Smith, Leonard Fleming, 26 Foot	5 June 12	19 May 14	14 May 15
P Smith, Michael, 40 Foot	29 Aug. 11	23 Aug. 13	20 April 17
Smith, Peter, Royal Artillery Drivers	never	30 April 04	
Smith, Peter, Royal Artillery Drivers	1 Dec. 12	15 July 13	1 Nov. 14
P Smith, Ralph, 53 Foot	22 Sept. 08	22 Mar. 10	8 May 23
Smith, Robert, 1 Foot	4 April 05	20 Feb. 06	11 July 16
Smith, Thomas Flynn, 7 Foot	26 Feb. 06	26 Mar. 07	
Smith, Thomas Francis, 24 Foot	4 June 12	25 June 18	20 Oct. 23
Smith, William,[153] Royal Artillery Drivers	14 Jan. 07	3 Mar. 09	1 July 16
P Smith, William, 31 Foot	11 Oct. 10	26 Oct. 15	25 Sept. 17
P PW Smith, William, 71 Foot	1 Sept. 13	19 July 15	25 Feb. 16
Smyth, James Ryan, 15 Foot	3 Sept. 12	21 June 15	25 Mar. 16
Smyth, Thomas, 34 Foot	29 June 09	28 Aug. 11	25 Jan. 17
Smyth, William, Scots Fusilier Guards	16 May 11	3 June 19	30 Dec. 19
Smythe, Frederick, 2 Foot, *Staff Officer of Pensioners*	24 Feb. 37	10 July 40	27 Mar. 46
Sneyd, William, 88 Foot	17 Feb. 83	14 April 83	1783
Spaight, Henry, 2 Dragoon Guards	3 Mar. 14	11 Oct. 21	23 June 25
Spalding, Warner Reeve, 8 R. Vet. Batt., *Barrack-master at Fort Augustus*	26 Mar. 07	13 Nov. 10	
Spencer, Thomas,[154] Royal Artillery Drivers	never	2 Aug. 03	1 June 04
PW Sperling, John,[155] Royal Engineers	14 Dec. 11	1 July 12	24 Jan. 24

	ENSIGN, ETC.	LIEUT.	WHEN PLACED ON HALF PAY.
𝔓 Spong, Francis Mallett,[157] R. Art. Drivers	1 Dec. 09	5 June 11	1 Nov. 14
Spooner, Henry, 15 Dragoons	21 Nov. 99	12 June 01	25 June 02
Spotiswood, Andrew, 21 Foot	4 July 11	3 Feb. 14	25 Mar. 17
Sproule, Edward, 69 Foot	26 Jan. 08	1 Feb. 10	5 Nov. 18
𝔓 Stacey, Edwin, 12 Dragoons	30 May 11	26 Mar. 12	25 Aug. 14
𝔚 Stainforth, George, 23 Foot	29 July 13	19 July 15	25 Mar. 17
Stanley, Edward, Royal Artillery Drivers	2 Sept. 04	1 Jan. 06	
Stansfield, Robert, 20 Foot	19 Sept. 26	2 Nov. 32	4 Aug. 37
Stapleton, Richard, Unattached	19 April 14	7 April 25	24 May 27
Stapleton, William Bull, Staff Corps of Cav.	26 Nov. 12	25 Feb. 13	9 Nov. 15
𝔓 Stavely, John, 4 Foot	25 Dec. 06	9 Mar. 09	12 Nov. 18
𝔓 Stawell, William, 98 Foot	19 Sept. 11	9 Nov. 15	25 Dec. 17
Steade, Charles, 60 Foot	never	22 Feb. 16	23 Oct. 17
Steed, Edward Henry, 25 Dragoons	29 Sept. 14	26 April 17	25 Dec. 18
𝔓 Steel, William Robert, 48 Foot	7 May 06	16 June 08	2 Mar. 15
Steele, Matthew Frederick,[158] 91 Foot, *Staff Officer of Pensioners*	9 April 25	16 Feb. 31	30 Dec. 34
𝔓 𝔚 Steele, Robert,[159] 10 Foot	23 Mar. 26	26 Sept. 33	18 Nov. 42
*Steggall, William Charles, 43 Foot	never	25 Dec. 13	25 Sept. 14
Stewart, Charles, 4 Foot	25 July 09	17 Oct. 11	24 Jan. 21
𝔓 Stewart, Duncan, 104 Foot	9 Mar. 09	22 Feb. 10	30 Oct. 17
Stewart, Edward Hobbs, Royal Marines	3 Dec. 96	4 Oct. 01	1 Feb. 17
Stewart, Mervyn, 21 Dragoons	12 Jan. 15	25 Jan. 16	10 July 20
Stobart, Henry,[160] Royal Artillery	12 Dec. 11	29 Aug. 14	10 July 26
Stobie, John, 4 Royal Veteran Battalion	April 08	14 June 08	
Stock, Frederick, Royal Irish Artillery	23 June 04	16 May 05	5 Nov. 07
Stowards, Robert,[161] 10 R. Veteran Battalion	7 Mar. 11	2 July 18	
Stretch, Bolton Edward, 7 Foot	21 Oct. 13	4 May 15	9 Aug. 33
Stritch, William Luke, 95 Foot	24 Dec. 12	4 Aug. 14	25 Mar. 17
𝔓 Strode, George, 20 Foot	30 Mar. 09	5 April 10	25 Feb. 17
Stronach, William, Royal Engineers	24 Mar. 15	11 Nov. 16	31 Dec. 24
Stuart, Charles George, 88 Foot	9 May 11	20 April 14	25 Mar. 16
Stuart, George, 86 Foot	10 Nov. 13	2 Jan. 17	11 Jan. 20
𝔓 Stuart, George Evans, 61 Foot	28 Feb. 12	20 Jan. 14	25 Dec. 14
Stuart, James, 3 Royal Veteran Battalion	9 July 03	14 April 04	
Stuart, Peter, 1 Royal Veteran Battalion *Town Major of Belfast*	never	14 Oct. 06	
𝔚 Stuart, Robert Thomson, 28 Foot	5 Aug: 13	18 July 15	25 Mar. 17
Stuart, William,[162] Royal Marines	24 April 04	24 Mar. 07	25 June 16
*Suberkrub, John Jacob, 3 Prov. Bn. of Mil.	never	25 Dec. 13	1814
Sullivan, Bartholomew, Royal Marines	26 Nov. 06	6 Oct. 13	2 Sept. 26
𝔓 Sullivan, James, 19 Foot	18 May 09	20 June 11	24 June 24
*Sullivan, John, 49 Foot	never	25 Dec. 13	15 Aug. 14
Sunbolf, George, 33 Foot	18 Feb. 08	28 Feb. 11	18 June 18
Supple, Kerry, 60 Foot	4 Aug. 13	14 Feb. 16	28 May 17
Sutherland, Edward, Unattached, *Town Major of Cape Breton*	9 Sept. 12	26 Aug. 13	12 July 33
Sutherland, Sutherland Hall, 65 Foot	22 June 15	15 Feb. 16	4 April 23
Suttie, George Grant, Scots Fusilier Guards	never	17 April 17	25 Dec. 18
Swanson, Thomas, 42 Foot	25 May 08	25 Oct. 10	17 Mar. 13
Sweeting, George, 7 Foot	never	4 Aug. 14	16 Dec. 19
Swiny, Shapland William, 39 Foot	16 May 11	29 April 13	11 July 16
Symonds, William, 60 Foot	27 Jan. 07	2 July 07	25 Mar. 17
𝔓 Syret, James, 9 Foot	23 Jan. 12	26 Aug. 13	25 Mar. 17
𝔓 Tasker, James, 57 Foot	30 Nov. 04	16 Oct. 06	24 April 17
𝔓 Tatlock, Thomas, 62 Foot	8 Mar. 09	15 Aug. 11	2 Oct. 17
Tayloe, John, 77 Foot	12 Mar. 12	27 April 15	25 Mar. 17
𝔓 Taylor, Edward James,[164] 13 Foot, *Staff Officer of Pensioners*	31 Dec. 12	28 Sept. 14	22 July 45
Taylor, Ingram Pank, Royal Marines	14 Jan. 06	14 June 11	1 Sept. 14
Taylor, John, 74 Foot	25 Dec. 13	1 June 20	25 Nov. 21
Taylor, John, 90 Foot, *Staff Officer of Pensioners*	30 July 12	14 July 14	25 Dec. 18
Taylor, Joseph Henry, Unattached	16 Dec. 19	26 July 26	2 Feb. 30
Taylor, Nathaniel, 90 Foot	21 May 12	13 July 15	25 Dec. 18
Taylor, William, Royal Marines	25 Dec. 78	2 Dec. 81	22 Jan. 83

	CORNET, ETC.	LIEUT.	WHEN PLACED ON HALF PAY.
* Thackeray, Joseph, 51 Foot	never	25 Dec. 13	25 Sept. 14
Thiballier, Hubert, 3 Foot	8 July 06	26 Dec. 06	11 June 18
𝕻 Thomas, James, 50 Foot	7 April 08	4 May 09	2 Feb. 15
𝕻 *Thompson, Benjamin*, 1 R. Vet. Battalion	11 July 11	29 Aug. 16	
𝖂𝕷 Thompson, Henry Walker, 74 Foot	16 Sept. 13	20 July 15	25 Mar. 17
Thompson, John, Unattached	15 May 28	15 Aug. 34	26 May 38
𝕻 Thompson, Ralph Keddey, 26 Foot	26 Mar. 12	21 Oct. 13	2 April 18
𝕻 Thompson, Tho. James, Unattached	10 Nov. 08	24 May 10	28 Dec. 26
Thomson, David, 3 Royal Veteran Battalion	Dec. 07	3 Mar. 08	
𝕻 *Thomson, James*, 10 R. Veteran Battalion	17 Aug. 08	19 April 10	
Thomson, Jeremiah, 17 Foot	7 Aug. 99	25 Oct. 99	25 Sept. 02
Thomson, Joseph, 15 Foot	29 April 13	7 Sept. 15	25 Mar. 16
Thornley, Thomas, 43 Foot	21 Oct. 13	28 Sept. 15	3 April 17
𝕻 Thornton, John,[165] 42 Foot	27 Aug. 07	2 Aug. 10	17 July 17
Thorold, Frederick, Unattached	3 Oct. 26	16 Jan. 29	18 May 32
𝖂𝕷 Tighe, Daniel, Grenadier Guards	never	26 Nov. 14	15 Feb. 21
Timbrell, Sidney James,[165] 31 Foot	27 May 42	10 Nov. 43	17 Nov. 48
Tinling, Charles Stubbs, Unattached	5 April 15	3 July 23	24 Nov. 25
Tipping, John Whitacre, Staff Corps of Cav. *Quar.-Master, Royal Military College*	17 June 13	7 Mar. 16	25 Feb. 19
Tisdall, James, 10 Foot	3 Jan. 11	14 April 13	25 Jan. 16
𝕻 Tittle, John Moore,[165*] R. African Corps, *Staff Officer of Pensioners*	7 July 08	1 Nov. 10	12 April 21
Tolcher, Christopher, 2 Foot	20 July 15	9 July 18	25 Dec. 18
Toole, Francis Norris, 43 Foot	11 Nov. 24	17 Aug. 26	12 June 30
Torkington, Henry Theodore, 16 Foot	14 Aug. 35	26 June 38	29 Mar. 42
Torrance, David, 15 Foot	14 Sept. 09	8 Oct. 12	4 Jan. 17
Tour, Augustus de la, R. Foreign Artillery	26 July 10	1 Mar. 15	1 Feb. 17
Towers, William Riley, 6 Garrison Battalion	10 Feb. 00	5 April 01	
𝕻 Town, Edward, Dillon's Regiment	26 Nov. 12	17 Mar. 14	9 Nov. 15
Townly, James, Royal Marines	11 April 06	20 May 12	6 July 27
𝕻 Townsend, John, Royal Artillery	21 Dec. 08	1 Dec. 11	6 Feb. 26
Townsend, Joseph, Royal Engineers	1 Sept. 15	20 Dec. 22	21 April 23
Townsend, Richard, 54 Foot	29 Oct. 94	22 Feb. 96	
Townsend, Robert Lawrence, 18 Dragoons	2 Dec. 13	13 Jan. 20	30 Aug. 21
Townshend, William, 83 Foot	18 Oct. 04	29 Oct. 06	15 Jan. 18
Trant, William, 80 Foot	23 April 07	25 May 08	11 Dec. 17
Travers, Joseph, 60 Foot, *Barrack-Master at Portsmouth*		29 Aug. 22	7 Sept. 22
Trebeck, Thomas, Royal Artillery	11 Dec. 15	18 June 24	18 June 24
Trench, Thomas,[166] Royal Artillery	21 Dec. 08	2 Dec. 11	25 Aug. 29
Trevenen, James, 2 West India Regiment	28 Nov. 11	1 July 13	30 Nov. 20
Tristram, Barrington, Royal Artillery	11 Sept. 12	11 May 15	1 Feb. 19
Trollope, *Sir* John, *Bart.*, 10 Dragoons	10 July 17	24 Oct. 22	25 Sept. 23
Tucker, J. Owen Edwards, 20 Foot	16 July 29	18 Oct. 33	14 April 37
Tucker, Thomas Elliot, 84 Foot	23 June 08	13 Dec. 10	25 Oct. 21
𝕻 𝖂𝕷 Tudor, Charles, 23 Dragoons	6 April 04	26 Oct. 08	25 Jan. 18
Tudor, Henry, 37 Foot	1 June 14	5 May 16	5 April 21
Tunstall, Gabriel, Unattached	13 Jan. 14	25 July 16	8 Nov. 27
𝕻 Tunstall, William, 36 Foot	11 May 09	21 Jan. 12	22 April 19
𝕻 Turner, Thomas, 23 Foot	25 Aug. 07	16 Mar. 09	25 Dec. 14
Turner, Young, Sicilian Regiment	19 April 10	1 May 11	25 June 16
Twyford, John, Royal Marines	10 Oct. 05	15 Mar. 10	1 Sept. 14
Tytler, Patrick, 4 R. Vet. Batt., *Fort Major of Stirling Castle*	never	5 May 04	
Uniacke, Thomas Fane, Rifle Brigade	15 Dec. 08	11 June 11	28 Mar. 22
Upton, William, 15 Foot	3 Oct. 08	20 Oct. 08	25 May 14
Urquhart, Donald, 60 Foot	27 Oct. 10	30 Mar. 12	25 Dec. 17
Ussher, John Theophilus, 28 Foot	30 May 43	14 April 46	
𝕻 Vallencey, Richard, 1 Foot	1 Sept. 07	20 July 09	23 July 18
Vanderbrouck, Francis, 60 Foot	never	30 Dec. 97	
Vaughan, Travers Hartley, New Bruns. Fenc.	5 Mar. 12	25 Mar. 14	25 Aug. 16
Vavasour, Thomas Hippon, 73 Foot	3 Mar. 14	15 Feb. 16	25 June 17
Veitch, Charles, 6 Garrison Battalion	Jan. 06	22 July 06	4 Feb. 15
Vereker, Henry, 18 Foot	25 Sept. 11	11 Feb. 13	11 Feb. 17

	2d Lieut. etc.	Lieut.	When placed on half pay.
P Vereker, Henry Thomas, 62 Foot	23 April 07	29 Sept. 08	7 Mar. 22
Vernon, John Russell, 1 Foot	30 June 25	7 Aug. 27	28 Sept. 30
P Vesey, John, 76 Foot	21 Sept. 09	2 Aug. 10	21 Oct. 17
Victor, George, Royal Marines	18 April 09	25 Sept. 27	6 June 28
Vieth, Frederick William, Unattached	14 Mar. 11	3 Aug. 13	29 Dec. 25
Wade, George, 18 Foot	9 May 11	14 Jan. 13	25 Mar. 17
Walbridge, Henry William, York Chasseurs	3 Nov. 08	2 Jan. 12	30 Dec. 19
Walford, John Thomas, 72 Foot	5 May 08	22 June 09	21 Aug. 23
Walker, Alexander, 96 Foot..............	27 Oct. 07	26 Feb. 11	25 Dec. 18
Walker, James, Royal Marines	11 May 05	27 July 08	15 Oct. 22
Walker, James, 96 Foot	14 Oct. 13	23 May 16	25 Dec. 18
Walker, James, Royal African Corps	12 Nov. 12	16 Feb. 14	25 Dec. 18
Walker, John Allen, 34 Foot	5 Oct. 20	7 April 25	15 Feb. 27
Walker, Roger Boyce, 43 Foot	15 Nov. 10	10 June 13	9 July 18
Wall, Henry, Royal Marines	17 Feb. 06	25 Feb. 12	24 April 13
Wall, Richard, 7 Royal Veteran Battalion	7 Nov. 05	1 May 09	
P Wallace, Hugh Ritchie, 7 Foot	14 July 09	16 Nov. 09	9 July 18
Wallace, Robert Grenville, York Chasseurs	17 Dec. 13	4 May 16	7 Dec. 20
P Waller, Kilner, 57 Foot	20 Sept. 10	25 Feb. 13	3 April 16
P Walsh, Lawrence De Courcy, 34 Foot....	14 May 07	8 June 09	25 Aug. 23
Walsh, Patrick, Newfoundland Fencibles ..	31 July 06	2 Nov. 09	25 June 16
Walsh, William, 51 Foot	9 June 08	24 Jan. 10	26 Nov. 18
Ward, Henry, Royal Marines	30 Jan. 07	11 Dec. 13	23 Feb. 30
*Ward, John, 15 Foot	never	25 Dec. 13	25 Sept. 14
Wardell, John, 19 Foot..................	17 Mar. 11	1 Aug. 18	20 July 20
Waring, Edward, Royal African Corps	8 Dec. 25	15 Mar. 27	25 Feb. 29
Warren, Edward Townsend, 90 Foot	8 Aug. 11	13 Oct. 14	25 Dec. 16
W Watson, Andrew, 24 Foot	10 June 13	16 Aug. 15	25 Sept. 23
P Watson, Feltham, 57 Foot	25 April 06	8 Feb. 08	23 June 13
P Watson, George,[167] Unattached	28 Feb. 12	22 Oct. 12	14 Sept. 32
Watson, Henry Vincent, 3 Foot	3 April 40	11 Aug. 43	1 Aug. 45
Watson, Thomas Brereton, 8 Foot	23 Nov. 09	21 Nov. 11	18 April 16
P Watson, William Henry,[168] 6 Dragoons..	11 Nov. 11	7 May 12	25 Mar. 16
Watton, Edward John, 20 Foot	27 Aug. 99	9 June 04	15 May 05
Watts, Henry, Unattached	24 Jan. 15	25 Feb. 18	11 Nov. 29
Wauch, David, 6 Dragoon Guards	8 Nov. 10	19 May 14	25 July 14
Weaver, William Henry, Royal Artillery ..	12 Dec. 11	1 Oct. 14	1 Jan. 23
Webb, George, 21 Foot..................	24 Sept. 41	7 Dec. 42	
Webster, William Francis, 2 Ceylon Regt. *Staff Officer of Pensioners.........*	6 Feb. 23	12 July 33	18 Oct. 39
Weight, Edward, 8 Dragoons	10 Aug. 15	28 Feb. 22	10 Mar. 25
P Weir, Thomas, 1 Foot	19 Sept. 11	22 Aug. 13	25 June 17
P Weir, William, 27 Foot	31 Mar. 08	17 Oct. 11	25 July 17
P Welch, John West,[169] 11 Foot..........	3 Oct. 08	19 Oct. 09	25 Sept. 14
Welstead, William, 8 West India Regt.	12 Sept. 11	12 Aug. 13	10 Oct. 16
West, Henry, Royal Marines	10 July 77	1 July 79	29 Oct. 92
Westcott, John Hancock,[170] 7 Foot........	20 July 09	12 Aug. 12	23 April 17
Whaley, Robert, 14 Dragoons	8 Oct. 12	22 April 13	2 Jan. 17
P Wheatley, William, 39 Foot	19 Feb. 06	19 May 09	18 Mar. 19
Whimster, James, Sicilian Regt...........	27 Nov. 10	5 Aug. 13	25 June 16
*Whitby, William, 1 Prov. Batt. of Militia	never	25 Feb. 14	1814
White, Frederick John,[171] Royal Marines ..	19 Oct. 36	18 Dec. 40	17 April 45
White, George, 36 Foot..................	28 Feb. 12	13 May 13	25 Mar. 17
White, Henry, 63 Foot..................	20 Sept. 44	31 July 46	
P *White, Henry,*[172] 7 Royal Vet. Batt. *Town Major of Portsmouth ....*	5 April 10	29 April 12	
White, William, Royal Marines	13 Sept. 08	10 May 23	27 Jan. 36
Whiteford, John, 13 Foot................	12 Sept. 11	8 Aug. 15	25 Mar. 17
P Whitfield, William,[173] 62 Foot, *Staff Officer of Pensioners ....*	23 April 12	13 April 14	25 Mar. 17
Whiting, George William,[174] Royal Marines	2 Jan. 38	4 Nov. 41	25 June 46
Wigley, George James, 63 Foot	13 July 08	25 Mar. 10	20 May 19
P Wigton, James, 9 Foot	25 Mar. 08	2 Sept. 08	25 Mar. 15
P *Wilford, John,*[174*] Royal Art. Drivers ..	1 Dec. 05	1 Sept. 06	
W Wilkinson, Henry, 40 Foot	8 May 10	12 May 12	14 May 16
Wilkinson, John Alexander, 24 Foot	6 Oct. 08	3 Oct. 11	11 Sept. 23

	ENSIGN, ETC.	LIEUT.	WHEN PLACED ON HALF PAY.
W Willett, Augustus Saltren, 22 Dragoons	5 June 06	27 Aug. 07	7 Feb. 22
Willey, Edward, 19 Dragoons	22 Oct. 18	23 May 22	19 June 23
P Williams, Charles, 53 Foot	24 June 13	29 May 17	24 Dec. 19
Williams, Robert, 53 Foot................	26 Sept. 05	28 Jan. 08	25 Sept. 26
P Willis, George Brander,[176] Royal Artillery	2 May 08	17 Nov. 09	3 April 23
Wilson, Alexander Lockhart, 83 Foot......	11 Feb. 13	6 April 20	28 June 21
Wilson, Henry, 89 Foot..................	21 July 25	29 Nov. 27	11 Oct. 31
Wilson, Robert, Royal Marines............	14 April 06	20 June 12	1 Sept. 14
Wilson, W. Henry Bowen Jordan, Gar. Comp.	10 Sept. 25	12 Oct. 26	1 Feb. 31
Winckworth, John, 75 Foot	14 Nov. 10	22 Feb. 16	16 July 17
P Windle, John Shepard,[177] 53 Foot	11 Dec. 06	25 Jan. 08	16 May 22
Winton, James, 17 Foot	10 Aug. 99	27 Oct. 99	25 Sept. 02
Wisdom, John, 17 Foot...................	25 Dec. 06	10 Dec. 07	20 July 09
P W Wood, Frederick,[178] 11 Dragoons....	28 April 04	14 June 05	25 Mar. 17
Wood, George, 95 Foot..................	28 Feb. 12	2 Dec. 13	20 Mar. 19
Wood, George Horsley, 67 Foot	25 Nov. 13	12 April 21	20 Jan. 27
P Wood, Henry,[179] 23 Foot	25 Mar. 13	13 Aug. 18	11 Nov. 24
Wood, William Sumpter, 30 Foot	22 July 19	26 Dec. 21	24 July 28
P Woods, Wm.,[180] 6 Dragoons, *Adjutant, Northumberland Yeomanry Cavalry*..	7 April 08	28 Dec. 09	15 Feb. 16
Worsley, George, 39 Foot................	8 Dec. 03	21 Mar. 05	10 Sept. 12
Wraxall, Charles Edward, Royal Artillery..	11 Sept. 12	1 April 15	1 Aug. 19
W Wray, Hugh Boyd, 40 Foot	23 Jan. 11	10 Sept. 12	19 April 17
Wright, Alexander, 11 Royal Vet. Batt. ..	1 Oct. 95	27 Mar. 96	
Wright, Edward, 35 Foot................	Dec. 01	13 Aug. 02	25 Oct. 02
Wright, John, 27 Foot	8 June 09	10 Sept. 12	25 July 17
P Wright, John, Unattached	14 June 11	5 Feb. 12	22 Mar. 27
W Wright, William,[181] Rifle Brigade	11 Mar. 13	20 July 15	25 Dec. 18
Wrighte, William, 3 Foot................	20 May 12	26 May 14	19 April 17
*Wynter, John Jonathan, 63 Foot	never	25 Dec. 13	25 Feb. 16
Yarnold, Benjamin, Royal Marines.........	23 July 12	17 Sept. 31	29 Nov. 34
Yelverton, *Hon.* Barry Charles, 79 Foot....	5 Oct. 32	13 Sept. 33	11 Aug. 37
Yonge, Weston, 84 Foot	24 Oct. 13	19 Oct. 15	1817
P W Yonge, Wm. Grawley, 17 Foot......	14 May 12	29 April 13	13 Feb. 23
Young, Henry Harman, 31 Foot...........	3 April 06	25 Nov. 08	22 Jan. 18
Young, Henry, 6 Royal Veteran Battalion	31 May 09	1 Aug. 11	
Young, John George, 90 Foot	20 Jan. 14	12 Aug. 24	14 May 29
Young, Robert, 1 Royal Veteran Battalion	3 Oct. 11	6 Sept. 14	

War Services of the Lieutenants on retired Full Pay and Half Pay.

1 Lieut. John Allen (R. Artillery Drivers) served in the Peninsula from 1809 to 1814, and was present at the battle of Talavera.

2 Lieut. John Allen (h. p. 84 F.) served the Peninsular campaigns of 1811 and 1812, and was present at the siege and capture of Ciudad Rodrigo.

3 Lieut. Alston served in the Peninsula, France, and Flanders, with the 3rd battalion of the Royals, and was slightly wounded at Quatre Bras.

4 Lieut. J. Cooper Armstrong served at Copenhagen, in 1807; and in the Peninsula from 1812 to 1814.

4* Lieut. Battersby joined the 20th in the summer of 1813, then serving near Pampeluna, and was with the Regt. all the remainder of the campaign of that year, and until the return of the Army in 1814—in which years he was present at the battles of Orthes and Toulouse.

5 Lieut. Frederick Bayly served in the Peninsula from June 1810 to the end of that war in 1814, including the battles of Busaco and Castalla. In the American war in 1814 and 15, including the attacks on Baltimore and New Orleans, at which last he was slightly wounded. With the Prussian army in 1815, at the taking of the fortresses of Maubeuge, Landrecies, Philippeville, and Rocroy.

6 Lieut. James Bell served the arduous campaign of 1794 and 95, in Flanders and Holland. In 1796 he was present at the reduction of Granada and St. Vincent, and in subduing the Caribs in the latter island. In 1800 he was present at the capture of the Islands of St. Martin, St. Bartholomew, St. Thomas, St. John, Santa Cruz, and ultimately St. Eustatia. In 1805 he accompanied the expedition to Hanover, under Lord Cathcart. In 1809 he served in India, with the southern division, in the Travancore war. In 1815 he served at the capture of the Kandian Provinces in Ceylon; and afterwards, for nearly a year and a half, in the suppression of a rebellion throughout the interior of that island.

6* Lieut. F. L. Bennett served the campaign on the Sutlej in 1845-6 (Medal) with the 9th, and was present at the battles of Moodkee, Ferozeshah, and Sobraon.

7 Lieut. Benwell joined the 4th in the Peninsula, as a volunteer, and was present at the action of Osma, battle of Vittoria, the several stormings and capture of San Sebastian, passage of the Bidassoa and attack on the Heights, battles of Nivelle and Nive, investment of Bayonne, and repulse of the sortie. Served afterwards in the American war, at Bladensburg, Washington, Baltimore, and New Orleans, at which last he was several times wounded, and severely by grape-shot.

8 Fort-Major Black served in the Peninsula with the 74th, and was present in the actions of Aldea de Ponte and Fuentes Guinaldo, capture of Madrid and the Retiro, retreat from Madrid into Portugal, passage of the Ebro, battle of Vittoria, action at the Maya Pass, battles of the Pyrenees on the 27th July and 2nd Aug., passage of the Bidassoa, blockade of Pampeluna, battles of Nivelle and Nive (9th to 13th Dec.), actions of Vic Bigorre, Tarbes, and Sauveterre, battle of Orthes, action at Aire, and battle of Toulouse, besides various minor affairs.

9 Lieut. Blagg served the whole of the campaign of 1813 and 1814 in Germany and Holland, and was engaged with the light company of his regiment (the 25th), in conjunction with the Rifle Brigade, in driving in the French out-posts, and in both the attacks on Merxem, the bombardment of Antwerp and the French fleet in the Scheldt. On picquet near Fort Lillo in a stockade on the banks of the Scheldt, when attacked by a French line-of-battle ship of 80 guns, which was beaten off. Also in the operations in Flanders in connection with the battle of Waterloo.

10 Lieut. Blood served in the Peninsula from June 1811 to the close of that war in 1814, including the siege and storm of Ciudad Rodrigo and Badajoz, battle of Salamanca, retreat from Madrid to Portugal, passage of the Huebra, battle of Vittoria, various actions in the Pyrenees, the successful storming of San Sebastian (with the stormers of the Light Division), battle of Nivelle, action at Arcangues, battle of the Nive on the 9th, 10th, 11th, 12th, and 13th Dec.—The above services with the 43rd. Carried the Regimental Colour of the 6th, at the battle of Orthes, where he was severely wounded by a ball which entered his right knee; he was also severely wounded at the top of the breach at San Sebastian, by a musket ball which struck him in the face and passed through his nose.

11 Lieut. Blyth served in the Peninsula, and was present at the first siege of Badajoz, and battle of Albuhera, at which latter he was wounded.

12 Lieut. Boase (*see note* 2, *page* 326).

12* Lieut. Henry Boldero served in Holland, in 1814, as Aide-de-camp to Lieut.-General Sir Ronald Ferguson; was present at the capitulation of Antwerp; was also present at the battle of Waterloo, and led the storming party of the 14th regiment at the capture of Cambray. After the surrender of Paris, was placed in the Head Quarters Staff as a Deputy-assistant Adjutant-General.

13 Lieut. Bramwell served the campaign of 1815 with the 92nd, and was severely wounded at Quatre Bras,—right leg amputated.

14 Lieut. Brattle served in the battle of Trafalgar, on board H. M. S. *Africa*, 64. Joined the force under General Whitelock at Monte Video, in 1807. In action with Danish gun-boats near Copenhagen, 20th Oct. 1808 (severely wounded). Served afterwards with the Channel Fleet off Brest, Basque Roads, and Belleisle.

14* Lieut. Brearey served on the Walcheren expedition in 1809, and was present at the siege and reduction of Flushing. He served also the campaigns of 1814 and 1815 in Holland and the Netherlands, including the action at Merxem, bombardment of Antwerp, storming of Bergen-op-Zoom, battle of Waterloo, storming of Cambray, and capture of Paris.

15 Lieut. Breton served the campaign of 1815, and was present at the battle of Waterloo.

16 Lieut. Brice served in the Peninsula with the 23rd, from May 1812 to the end of that war in 1814, and was present at the battles of Salamanca, Vittoria, and the Pyrenees (wounded). Served also the campaign of 1815, including the battle of Waterloo, storming of Cambray, and capture of Paris.

17 Lieut. Bridge served the campaign of 1815 with the 73rd, and was severely wounded at Waterloo.

18 Lieut. Cyrus Brohier served in the Peninsula with the 2nd battalion of the 58th, from July 1809 to 1813, including the battle of Salamanca, capture of Madrid, driving the enemy from Valladolid to Burgos, siege of Burgos, and retreat therefrom. Embarked for America in 1814, and was present at the battle of Plattsburg (wounded), and at the crossing of the Saranac.

19 Lieut. J. B. Brohier served with the 59th at Walcheren, in 1809; at the capture of the Isle of France in 1810; and of Java in 1811. In 1813, joined the 2nd battalion in the Peninsula, and was present at the battle of the Nive (severely wounded), and the repulse of the sortie from Bayonne.

19* Lieut. Wm. T. Buchanan landed at Passages in Spain, and was engaged almost daily during the march of Lord Hill's division across the Pyrenees, as also frequently on the banks of the Bidassoa. He was afterwards present at the battles of Bayonne, Orthes, and Toulouse.

20 Lieut. Burslem served at the siege of Houat, and commanded a detachment of Artillery in a night attack on the batteries of Morbihan. Landed at Ferrol with the army under the command of Sir James Pulteney, and was attached to the reserve on the heights. Served the campaign of 1801 in Egypt, including the siege of Aboukir and battle of Alexandria, at which latter he lost his right leg by a cannon-shot. Medal for services in Egypt.

21 Lieut R. Butler served the campaigns of 1813 and 14, in the Peninsula, including the battles of the Pyrenees, Nivelle, Nive, Orthes, and Toulouse.

21* Lieut. W. Butler served the campaign of 1815 with the 3rd Guards, and was present at the battle of Waterloo.

22 Lieut. L. M. Cameron served the campaigns of 1813 and 14 in the Peninsula, and was present at the battle of the Pyrenees on the 28th, 29th, and 30th July, the blockade of Pampeluna, battle of the Nivelle, battle of the Nive from 9th to 13th Dec., investment of Bayonne, and battle of Toulouse. Served also during the late Canadian Rebellion, and commanded a party of Volunteers on the Niagara frontier.

22* Lieut. Donald Cameron (h. p. 60 Foot) served in the Peninsula with the 7th Fusiliers from Aug. 1811 to the end of that war in 1814, including the actions at Fuentes Guinaldo and Aldea de Ponte, battles of Salamanca, Vittoria, the Pyrenees, St. Marcial near St. Sebastian 31st Aug., Nivelle, Nive, and Orthes (wounded). He was afterwards present at the assault on New Orleans, and at the capture of Paris.

23 Lieut. Rupert Campbell served the campaign of 1806, in Sicily and Italy, including the skirmish at Eufemia, battle of Maida, attack on and taking of the Castle of Scylla, also the capture of Catrone. Campaign of 1807, in Egypt, including the attack on the forts and heights of Alexandria, and capture of that city on the 19th, 20th, and 21st March; also the attacks in the Desert, and siege of Rosetta. Campaign in Holland and the Netherlands in 1814 and 15, including both the actions of Merxem, and bombardment of Antwerp, where he rendered important personal service to his late Majesty King William IV., then present with the army as Duke of Clarence.

24 Lieut. James Campbell (h. p. 41st), served the campaign in Affghanistan with the 41st and was present at the action of Hykulzie on the 28th March, 1842.

25 Lieut. Michael Carey served in the Peninsula with the 83rd, from March 1809 to the end of that war in 1814, including the passage of the Douro, battles of Talavera (severely wounded in the head) and Busaco, first siege of Badajoz, battle of Fuentes d'Onor, siege of Ciudad Rodrigo, siege and storming of Badajoz, battles of Salamanca, Orthes, and Toulouse.

26 Lieut. Thomas Carey was slightly wounded at Waterloo.

27 Lieut. George Chapman served the campaign of 1814 in Holland, with the 37th, including the investment of Bergen-op-Zoom, action at Merxem, and bombardment of Antwerp, at which last he was severely wounded, and lost his right leg.

27* Lieut. William Chapman served in the Peninsula and at Waterloo with the Rifle Brigade.

28 Lieut. Collingwood embarked with the 2nd Queen's Royals, for Walcheren, in 1809, and

was present at the siege of Flushing and all the operations of the island; was made prisoner, but escaped with the whole of his working party from a French picquet. He served afterwards in the Peninsula, and was present during the pursuit of Massena from Santarem; at the passage of the Mondego, investment and blockade of Almeida, affair at Barba del Puerco, siege of Ciudad Rodrigo till the raising of it by Marshal Marmont; at Badajoz with the covering army; affairs of Llerena and Usagre, in Spanish Estramadura under Sir Thomas Graham; battle of Salamanca and capitulation of its forts, investment of Burgos and retreat therefrom, together with minor details connected with the 6th division.

29 Lieut. Coombe served in Egypt in 1801, and has received the Egyptian medal.

30 Lieut. John Coote served the campaign of 1815, and was slightly wounded at Waterloo.

31 Lieut. R. G. C. Coote served in the Burmese war.

31* Lieut. Cottingham served in the Peninsula with the 52d in the campaigns of 1812, 13, and 14, and was present at the storming and capture of Badajos (as a volunteer), battles of Salamanca, Vittoria, Nivelle, Nive, Orthes, and Toulouse. He served also the campaign of 1815, including the battle of Waterloo.

32 Lieut. Coventry served in the East Indies from March 1783 to Aug. 1798, including the siege of Cannanore (medal), relief of Mangalore, siege of Paulgautcherry, affair of Kisnaporam, siege and assault of Bangalore, battle near Seringapatam, siege of Savandroog (severely wounded in the right hip when with the forlorn hope), actions of the 6th and 7th Feb. 1792, siege of Pondicherry, siege of Trincomalee and capture of Ceylon. Served also at the capture of the Cape of Good Hope in 1806, and of the Isle of France in 1810.

33 Lieut. Charles Thomas Cox served with the 71st during the campaigns of 1810, 11, 12, 13, 14, and 15, in the Peninsula, France, and Flanders, including the retreat to and occupation of the lines of Torres Vedras, the subsequent pursuit of Massena through Portugal, action of Sobral, battles of Fuentes d'Onor (wounded), actions of Arroyo de Molino, Almaras, and Alba de Tormes, covering the sieges of Badajos, the advance to and retreat from Madrid, battle of Vittoria,—severely wounded and taken prisoner, a musket ball having passed through the lungs and lodged in his body; being unable to keep up with the enemy, they left him on the field when they were hard pressed and under a cannonade from the British artillery. Present at the invasion of France from the Pyrenees, and subsequent actions of the Nivelle, Nive, Cambo, Garris, St. Palais, Arriverete, Hellette, Orthes, Aire, Tarbes, Urt, Toulouse, and many affairs of picquets, &c. At the battle of Waterloo he received a contusion on the hip from the fragment of a shell, but was present at the capture of Paris, and served three years with the Army of Occupation. In 1821, the change of position of the ball received at Vittoria compelled him to relinquish the active duties of his profession and retire on half-pay.

33* Lieut. Craig served with the 62nd in the campaign on the Sutlej (Medal), and received a severe wound at the battle of Ferozeshah, causing amputation of the right fore-arm.

34 Lieut. A. S. Crawford served the campaign of 1815 with the 79th, and was slightly wounded at Waterloo.

35 Lieut. Cull served in Egypt in 1801, and has received the Egyptian Medal.

36 Lieut. Dalgairns served in the Peninsula with the 7th Fusiliers, and was present at the battle of Busaco, occupation of the lines of Torres Vedras, advance after Massena, taking of Olivença, 1st siege of Badajos, battles of Albuhera and Vittoria, investment of Pampeluna and battles of the Pyrenees; after which he went to Holland with Sir James Graham's Army as Adjutant of the 55th Regt, and was wounded at the storming of Bergen-op-Zoom, and taken prisoner.

37 Lieut. Daniell served the campaign of 1815 with the 30th, and was slightly wounded at Waterloo.

38 Lieut. Delamain served with the 2nd battalion of the 67th in Spain from the latter part of 1811 to the close of that war, including the sieges of Cadiz, Tarragona, and Barcelona, the affair of Villa Franca, and others connected with the army on the Eastern coast of Spain. He was also present at the siege and capture of Asseerghur in the East Indies, in 1819.

39 Lieut. Delmé served in the Peninsula with the 88th, and was present at the battle of Vittoria, sortie from Pampeluna, battles of the Pyrenees, the Nivelle, the Nive, and Orthes, actions of Vic Bigorre and Tarbes, and battle of Toulouse; served afterwards in the American war, and was present in the action of Plattsburg, and the passage of the Sarinac.

40 Lieut. Dighton served in Spain and Portugal, from April 1810 to July 1812, including Massena's retreat. Served also in the South of France in 1814, and was present at the investment of Bayonne and repulse of the sortie,—slightly wounded.

40* Lieut. E. W. P. Dillon accompanied the expedition to Walcheren in 1809, and was present at the siege and capture of Flushing. Served also at the reduction of Guadaloupe in 1815.

41 Lieut. Dowbiggin served the campaign of 1815 with the 12th Light Dragoons, and was slightly wounded at Waterloo.

42 Lieut. Drawbridge served at Walcheren, and was present at the siege of Flushing.

43 Lieut. Dunnicliffe served the campaign of 1815, and was present at the battles of Quatre Bras and Waterloo.

44 Lieut. Easter served in the Peninsula with the 2nd battalion of the 24th, and was present at the battles of Talavera, Busaco, Fuz d'Aronce, and Fuentes d'Onor.

45 Lieut. Eccles served in the Peninsula with the 61st, and was present at the battles of the Nivelle, Nive (9th to 13th Dec.), Orthes, and Toulouse, besides various minor affairs.

46 Captain Charles Edwards served in the Peninsula with the 47th, from July 1813 to the end of that war in 1814, including the second assault and capture of San Sebastian, passage of the Bidassoa, battle of the Nivelle, battles of the Nive on the 9th, 10th, 11th, 12th, and 13th Dec. 1813, and blockade of Bayonne. Served also the campaigns of 1817 and 18 in Malwa against the Mahrattas.

47 Lieut. Matthew Evans served at Copenhagen in 1807; at Flushing in 1809; and subsequently in the Peninsula, including the sieges of Ciudad Rodrigo and Badajos, and battle of Salamanca. Served also the campaign of 1845, including the battle of Waterloo.

48 Lieut. Thomas Evans served the campaigns of 1813 and 14 with the 38th Regt., including the battles of the Nivelle and the Nive, the investment of Bayonne, and repulse of the sortie.

49 Lieut. Fleetwood served in the Peninsula with the 74th, and was present at the siege of Badajos in 1811, siege and capture of Ciudad Rodrigo and of Badajos in 1812, storm and capture of Fort Picurina, action at El Bodon, battles of Salamanca, Nivelle, Vic Bigorre, Orthes, Sauveterre, and Toulouse.

50 Lieut. Hugh Fleming served in the campaigns in Flanders, in 1793, 94, and 95; in Holland, in 1799; in Germany, in 1805; at Copenhagen, in 1807; in the Peninsula from 1809 to 1814. He was present in the actions of St. Amand, Famars, Lincelles, Dunkirk, Lannoi, Vaux, Cateau, Robaix, Moveaux, Tournay, Fort St. André, Helder, Zuyp, Walmenhuysen, Bergen (wounded), Oporto, Busaco, Espinhal, Foz d'Arouce, Fuentes d'Onor, Salamanca, Vittoria, Pyrenees, Echalar (wounded), Nivelle, and Orthes; and sieges of Valenciennes (wounded), Copenhagen, Ciudad Rodrigo, and Burgos. He was taken prisoner at Placentia, 2d Aug. 1809; escaped ten days afterwards, and rejoined the army.

51 Lieut. Flynn served the campaign against the Rajah of Coorg in 1834, with the 39th Regt.

52 Captain Ford served the campaigns of 1809, 10, 11, 13, and 14, and was present at the siege of Flushing, defence of Cadiz, and battles of Fuentes d'Onor, Nivelle, Nive, and Toulouse besides other actions of less importance. Served as an assistant engineer during four of the campaigns.

53 Lieut. A. S. Fraser served the campaign of 1815, and was slightly wounded at Quatre Bras

54 Lieut. Gichard served with the 4th at the capture of Copenhagen, in 1807; on the expedition to Sweden, in 1808, and subsequently to Portugal, under Sir John Moore, including the advance into Spain, retreat to and battle of Corunna. Expedition to Walcheren, 1809; Peninsular campaigns of 1812, 13, and 14, including the reduction of the Forts at Salamanca, battle of Salamanca, capture of Madrid, siege of Burgos, action at Villa Muriel (slightly wounded), battle of Vittoria, siege and capture of San Sebastian, attack upon the Heights after crossing the Bidassoa, battles of Nivelle and Nive, in which latter he was severely wounded in the left thigh by a musket shot.

55 Captain Gilborne served with the 11th at the siege of Flushing in 1809. Subsequently in the Peninsula with the 71st, including the battles of the Pyrenees and the Nive, actions at Aire and at Bayonne, and battles of Orthes and Toulouse. Served also the campaign of 1815, including the battle of Waterloo and capture of Paris.

56 Lieut. Goodall served with the Queen's Royals on the Walcheren expedition in 1809; and subsequently in the Peninsula, from Feb. 1811 to June 1813, including the operations before Ciudad Rodrigo and Badajoz, storming the Forts and battle of Salamanca, siege of Burgos, and retreat from thence.

57 Lieut. Græme joined the 2nd Light Battalion of the King's German Legion in Portugal in 1812, and served with it until embarkation at Bordeaux in 1814, having been present in action at Osma, Vittoria, Villa Franca, Tolosa, San Sebastian (both attacks), affairs on the Bidassoa and passage of that river; passages of the Nivelle, the Nive, and the Adour investment of Bayonne and repulse of the sortie. He served also the campaign of 1815, including the actions of the 16th, 17th, and 18th June—severely wounded at Waterloo. He has received William the Fourth's Gold Cross for 25 years' service, and the King of Hanover's Peninsular Medal.

58 Lieut. Hector Graham (*see Note* 19, *page* 328).

59 Lieut. John Grant (R. Artillery) served with the expedition to Walcheren, and was present at the siege of Flushing. Served afterwards in the Peninsula, from Oct. 1813 to Feb. 1814.

60 Lieut. John Grant (Unattached) served in the Peninsula from Aug. 1811 to Dec. 1813, including the action at Alba de Tormes, retreat from Madrid, and battles of Vittoria and the Pyrenees. Wounded in the side at the Maya Pass.

60* Lieut. Gray served with the 39th at the affair of Gorapore, near Kurnool, on the 18th Oct. 1839; and also at the battle of Maharajpore, 29th Dec., 1843 (Medal).

61 Lieut. Edward Greene served with the battering train attached to the Prussian besieging army, and was employed in taking several fortresses on the French frontier in July and Aug 1815.

62 Lieut. Grier served in the campaign of 1815 with the 44th, and was severely wounded at Quatre Bras.

63 Lieut. Edwin Griffiths (*see Note* 7, 96*th Regt.*).

64 Lieut. J. G. Griffiths served in the Peninsula, and was present at the battle of Vittoria, siege of San Sebastian, and battles of the Pyrenees, Orthes, and Toulouse.

65 Lieut. Grimes served in the Peninsula from March 1811 to Sept. 1812, and was present

at the siege of Ciudad Rodrigo, and the successful siege of Badajos, at which latter he was severely wounded in the right thigh by a cannon-shot.

66 Lieut. George Gunning was slightly wounded at Waterloo.

67 Lieut. John Hawkins served in the Peninsula from Oct. 1813 to the end of that war in 1814, including the battles of the Nivelle 10th Nov., and Nive on the 9th, 10th, 11th, and 12th Dec. 1813.

68 Lieut. Wm. M. Hearn served the campaign of 1815 with the 44th, and was severely wounded at Quatre Bras.

69 Lieut. Hickson served the campaign of 1814 in Canada, and that of 1815 in the Netherlands and France.

70 Lieut. Hine served in the Peninsula with the 48th from April 1809 to the end of that war in 1814, including the battles of Oporto, Talavera, and Albuhera (twice wounded); assault and capture of Ciudad Rodrigo and Badajos, battles of Salamanca (wounded), Vittoria, Pyrenees, Nivelle, Nive, Orthes, and Toulouse.

71 Lieut. Hodder served with the 2nd battalion of the 69th during the campaigns of 1814 and 15, in Holland and Flanders, and was present at the attack on Merxem, the bombardment of Antwerp, assault on Bergen-op-Zoom, and battles of Quatre Bras and Waterloo, at which last he was severely wounded.

72 Lieut. Hodgson served in the Peninsula with the 4th Dragoon Guards during the campaigns of 1811, 12, and 13.

73 Lieut. Hollinsworth served the campaign of 1799, in Holland, including the actions of the 10th Sept., 2nd and 6th October. The Egyptian campaign of 1801, including the actions of the 17th and 25th August. At the battle of Maida, 1806. Campaign of 1808-9, including the battles of Vimiera and Corunna. Expedition to Walcheren, 1809. Peninsular campaigns from Oct. 1812 to the end of that war in 1814, including the battle of Vittoria, actions at Roncesvalles, in the Pyrenees (28th July, 1st and 2nd Aug.); affairs on entering France, and battle of Orthes, at which last he was severely wounded in the right thigh.

74 Captain Holman (*see Note* 5, *at page* 317).

75 Lieut. Hood served with the 91st in South and North Beveland, and at Walcheren in 1809. Joined the army in the Peninsula on its retreat from Burgos in 1812, and served with it until the end of that war in 1814, including the battles of Vittoria, the various actions in the Pyrenees, battle of the Nivelle, battles of the Nive on the 9th, 10th, 11th, 12th, and 13th Dec., battle of Orthes, actions at Aire and Tarbes, battle of Toulouse (severely wounded), besides a great many minor actions and skirmishes. Served also the campaign of 1815, and was engaged with the enemy on the 16th, 17th, 18th, and 19th June, at and near Waterloo; the storming of Cambray, and capture of Paris.

77 Lieut. J. Æ. Irving served the campaign of 1815 with the 13th Dragoons, and was slightly wounded at Waterloo.

78 Lieut. Alexander Irwin served at the siege and capture of Hattras in 1816-17; the Mahratta campaign of 1817 and 18; in the Burmese war in 1825 and 26.

79 Lieut. Isaacson served in the Peninsula and at Waterloo with the 52nd Light Infantry.

80 Lieut. Charles Jago served in the Peninsula with the 24th, and was present at the battles of Busaco, Vittoria, and Echalar.

81 Capt. Francis Kennedy (*see Note* 11, *page* 317).

82 Lieut. Knox served the Peninsular campaigns of 1808, 9, 10, 11, and 12 with the 2nd battalion of the 31st, including the battles of Talavera (severely contused on the head by a musket ball), Busaco, Albuhera, and Arroyo de Molino, retreat to Portugal, occupation of the Lines of Torres Vedras, and pursuit of Massena, besides several minor affairs.

83 Lieut. Lister served at the battle of Trafalgar.

84 Lieut. J. O. Lloyd served in the Peninsula with the 27th and 74th regts.

85 Captain Lockwood served in the Peninsula with the 30th during the campaigns of 1811, 12, and 13, including the assault and capture of Badajos, battle of Salamanca, and action at Villa Muriel on the retreat from Burgos. Campaign of 1814 in Holland, including Fort Frederick Henry. Campaign of 1815, including the battle of Quatre Bras, where he was severely wounded by a musket-ball, which passed through the frontal bone, and lodged on the brain, to extract which the operation of the trepan was resorted to.

86 Lieut. Lorimer served in the 3rd Battalion of the Royals with Sir David Baird's army in the north of Spain: on the retreat, when closely pursued by the enemy's mounted Riflemen, he saved a convoy of provisions with which he was entrusted; and at the battle of Corunna he was severely wounded. He served afterwards at Walcheren, and at the siege of Flushing he was wounded in both legs by the bursting of a shell from the enemy's battery.

87 Lieut. Love served in the Peninsula from July 1810 to Dec. 1812, including the sieges of Ciudad Rodrigo and Badajos (wounded), storming the Forts at Almaraz, siege of the Forts at Salamanca (wounded), battle of Salamanca, and siege of Burgos. Served afterwards in the American war, and was present in the action at Plattsburg.

88 Lieut. Lovelock (*see Note* 13, *page* 327).

89 Lieut. John Lowry served with the 8th in the American war of 1812, 13, and 14, and was present in the actions of Prescot, Sackett's Harbour (severely wounded), Chippewa, Lundy's Lane (contused), assault on Fort Erie, and sortie (severely wounded) in Sept. 1814, and was severely wounded through the body in action at Sackett's Harbour.

91 Lieut. Alexander M'Donald served with the 26th at the first capture of Chusan, and at the attack on Canton.

92 Lieut. Alex. M'Pherson served the campaign of 1815, with the 92nd, and was severely wounded at Quatre Bras.

93 Lieut. John MacDonald (h. p. 91st) served the campaign of 1808-9, including the battles of Roleia and Vimiera, advance into Spain and retreat through Gallicia under Sir John Moore, action at Lugo, and battle of Corunna. Expedition to Swedish Pomerania in 1813, and campaign of 1814 in Holland, including the attack on Bergen-op-Zoom (wounded). Served also the campaign of 1815, and was present at the battle of Waterloo, storming of Cambray, and capture of Paris.

94 Lieut. MacGregor served with the 24th during the Nepaul campaigns of 1814, 15, and 16, and was present at the taking of Harriapore.

95 Lieut. Lachlan MacKay served in the Peninsula with the 42nd from 1812 to the end of that war in 1814, including the battles of the Pyrenees, Nivelle, Nive, Orthes, and Toulouse.

96 Lieut. Joseph Mathews served in the Peninsula with the 83rd, and in the action at Santarem, and various skirmishes prior to the siege and storming of Ciudad Rodrigo, where he lost his left hand.

97 Lieut. Wm. M'Donald Matthews served the campaign of 1815 with the 4th, and was slightly wounded at Waterloo.

98 Lieut. Mence served with the 44th at the taking of Tarragona; also at the battle of Bladensburg, capture of Washington, actions before Baltimore, attack on the American Lines before New Orleans, and capture of Fort Bowyer.

100 Lieut. George Miles served in the Peninsula with the 5th Dr. Guards from 1811 to the end of that war in 1814, including the action at Llerena, battle of Salamanca, capture of the French rear-guard on the following day, capture of Madrid, siege of Burgos, and retreat into Portugal, battle of Vittoria, investment of and action on the heights before Pampeluna, and battle of Toulouse.

101 Lieut. Zaccheus Miller served in Egypt in 1801, and has received the Egyptian medal.

102 Lieut. Mitchell served in the Peninsula with the 28th from 1810 to 1813 inclusive, and was present at the battle of Barrosa, storming of Badajoz, and battle of Vittoria (severely wounded), besides various minor affairs.

103 Lieut. J. A. Moore served in the American war.

104 Lieut. Morrison served at Gottenburg, in 1808; at the battle of Corunna, and siege of Flushing, in 1809; also at the siege of Burgos, and battle of Salamanca.

108 Lieut. Frederick Munro served in the Peninsula from March 1812 to the end of that war in 1814, including the sieges of the forts at Salamanca, Burgos, and San Sebastian, and the battles of Salamanca, Vittoria, the Bidassoa, and St. Jean de Luz.

109 Lieut. Francis Murray served in the Peninsula with the old 94th, from Jan. 1810 to the end of that war in 1814, including the defence of Cadiz from Jan. to Sept. 1810, lines of Torres Vedras, the pursuit of Massena, actions at Redinha, Condeixa, and Sabugal; battle of Fuentes d'Onor, second siege of Badajoz, action of El Bodon, siege and storm of Ciudad Rodrigo, siege and storm of Badajoz, battle of Salamanca, capture of Madrid, battles of Vittoria, the Pyrenees, Nivelle, and Orthes; action of Vic Bigorre, and battle of Toulouse.

110 Lieut. Muskett served at Walcheren in 1809; and afterwards in the Peninsula, including the sieges of Ciudad Rodrigo and Badajoz. Served also in Holland in 1814, including the action at Merxem, and attack on Bergen-op-Zoom.

111 Lieut. Nantes served with the 7th Fusiliers in the Peninsula and South of France in 1811, 12, 13, and 14, and was present at the siege of Ciudad Rodrigo, and commanded a company in the action of the Guarena, and at the battles of Salamanca and Toulouse. He was slightly wounded at the Guarena; most severely at Salamanca, his right arm having been broken in two places; and again slightly wounded at the battle of Orthes. He was also accidentally hurt by one of his own men, and carried off the field in the operations at the Nive.

112 Lieut. John Nash served the campaign of 1815 with the 79th, and was slightly wounded at Waterloo.

113 Lieut. Naylor served in Egypt in 1801, and has received the Egyptian medal.

114 Lieut. R. D. Nicholson joined the 2nd Battalion of the 58th in the Peninsula in 1811, and was present at the battle of Salamanca, siege of Burgos, battles of Vittoria, the Pyrenees, Nivelle, Nive, and Orthes, besides other minor affairs, and entered Bourdeaux with the 7th Division.

115 Lieut. Nicolas served at the battle of Trafalgar.

116 Lieut. Ogilvy served in the Peninsula with the old 94th from Jan. 1810 to the end of that war in 1814, including the defence of Cadiz, lines of Torres Vedras, advance in pursuit of Massena, actions of Redinha, Condeixa, and Sabugal, battle of Fuentes d'Onor, second siege of Badajoz, battle of Salamanca, capture of Madrid, battles of Vittoria, the Pyrenees, Nivelle, and Orthes, action of Vic Bigorre, and battle of Toulouse.

117 Lieut. Onslow served at the siege of Flushing in 1809; the campaign of 1814 in Holland, including the bombardment of the French fleet at Antwerp. Campaign of 1815, including the battle of Waterloo.

118 Lieut. John Orr (6 R. Vet. Bn.) accompanied the 1st battalion of the 42nd to the Penin-

suls in April 1812, and joined the army at Salamanca, during the siege of the forts in that city; present at the battle of Salamanca, siege of Burgos, and storming of San Michael; retreat to Portugal, advance in 1813, and all the actions in the Pyrenees. Served also the campaign of 1815, including the battles of Quatre Bras and Waterloo. Slightly wounded at Burgos, and severely at Waterloo.

119 Lieut. Pagan served the campaign of 1815 with the 33rd, and was severely wounded at Waterloo.

120 Lieut. Parratt served at Walcheren in 1809; and in the Peninsula from 1811 to the end of that war in 1814, including the defence of Cadiz, siege of San Sebastian, battle of Nivelle, actions at Vic Bigorre and Tarbes, and battles of Orthes and Toulouse.

122 Lieut. Peddie served in Holland with the 21st in 1813 and 14, and was present at the attack on Merxem, bombardment of the French fleet at Antwerp, and assault on Bergen-op-Zoom.

123 Captain Pennington (*see Note* 3, *page* 317).

124 Lieut. Philpot served the campaign of 1815, and was present at the battle of Waterloo.

125 Lieut. Pickard served the campaign of 1814 in Lower Canada, under Sir George Prevost, and was present at the attack on Plattsburg. Served also the campaign of 1815 in Upper Canada under Sir Gordon Drummond.

126 Lieut. A. J. Pictet served in the Burmese war with the Royals, and was present at the taking of Donabew.

128 Lieut. Pridham served in Egypt in 1801, and has received the Egyptian medal.

129 Lieut. Priest served in Portugal and Spain in 1808 and 9, and was present at the battle of Corunna.

130 Lieut. Quill served the campaign of 1815 with the 32nd, and was severely wounded at Quatre Bras.

131 Lieut. Ragg served the campaigns of 1793, 94, and 95 in Flanders, and that of 1799, in Holland; present at the following actions and sieges, viz. St. Amand, Famars, Valenciennes, Lincelles, Dunkirk, Lannoy, Vaux, Cateau, Robaix, Moveaux, Tournay, Helder, Zuyp, Walmenhuysen, and Bergen.

132 Lieut. Reid served at Corunna, and also at Walcheren, in 1809; in the Peninsula in 1813 and 14; also the campaign of 1815, including the battle of Waterloo where he was wounded.

133 Lieut. Reynolds served the campaigns of 1813, 14, and 15, in Germany, Holland, and the Netherlands, including the action of Goerde, attack upon Merxem, defence of Fort Frederick Henry against the French Fleet, battle of Quatre Bras, retreat on the following day, and battle of Waterloo (severely wounded by a cannon shot in the left thigh. In 1818 he served the campaign in the interior of Ceylon, and commanded a small Division, a detachment of which captured Madugall's one of the three Chiefs.

134 Lieut. Richardes served the campaign of 1815, and was present at the sieges of Maubeuge, Philippeville and Landrecies.

136 Lieut. John Roberts (Royal Artillery Drivers) served at Corunna, in 1809; in Holland in 1814, including the action at Merxem, and bombardment of Antwerp. Served also the campaign of 1815, and was present at the battles of Quatre Bras and Waterloo.

137 Lieut. James Robertson served the campaign of 1815 with the 79th, and was severely wounded at Quatre Bras.

138 Lieut. James Robinson was severely wounded at Quatre Bras.

139 Lieut. R. N. Rogers served in the Peninsula from August 1813 to the end of that war in 1814. Served also the campaign of 1815 and carried the colours of the 2nd battalion of the 30th at the battles of Quatre Bras and Waterloo; he was also present at the capture of Paris

140 Lieut. Rolfe served at Walcheren in 1809 with the 9th Light Dragoons, and was present at the siege of Flushing. Accompanied that regiment to the Peninsula in 1811, and was present in the action near Las Nava, covering the siege of Badajoz in 1812, affair near Rebeira, action of San Munos, retreat from Madrid to Portugal, defence of Alba de Tormes.

141 Lieut. Ewen Ross served in the Peninsula with the 92nd, and was present at the battle of Fuentes d'Onor, siege of Badajoz, actions at Arroyo de Molino (severely wounded), Almaraz, and Alba de Tormes. Also the campaign of 1815, and was severely wounded at Quatre Bras.

142 Lieut. Ross-Lewin served with the 32nd in the Peninsula, France, and Flanders; he was severely wounded at Pampeluna, and again at Waterloo.

143 Lieut. Rutherford served in the Peninsula with the old 94th, and was present at the defence of Cadiz in 1810, lines of Torres Vedras, pursuit of Massena, actions at Pombal, Redinha, Condeixa, and Sabugal; battle of Fuentes d'Onor, second siege of Badajoz, battles of Vittoria, Pyrenees, and Nivelle; passage of the Gave d'Oleron, battle of Orthes, action of Vic Bigorre, and battle of Toulouse.

145 Lieut. R. J. Saunders served the campaign of 1815 and was present at the battle of Waterloo.

146 Lieut. Thomas Scott served in the Peninsula with the old 94th from Jan. 1810 to the end of that war in 1814, including the defence of Cadiz and Fort Matagorda,—three times wounded; lines of Torres Vedras, pursuit of Massena, actions of Pombal, Redinha, Condeixa, Ponte de Murilla, Guarda, and Sabugal; battle of Fuentes d'Onor, second siege of Badajoz, actions at Campo Mayor and El Bodon, siege and storm of Ciudad Rodrigo—wounded at the assault; third siege and storm of the castle of Badajoz, action of San

Christoval heights, covering the parties attacking the forts of Salamanca, battle of Salamanca, capture of Madrid and the Retiro, retreat from Madrid into Portugal with the rear-guard, subsequent advance, battle of Vittoria, blockade of Pampeluna, battles of the Pyrenees, Pampeluna, and Nivelle; actions of Vic Bigorre and Tarbes, and battle of Toulouse.

147 Lieut. Seymour's services :—Campaign of 1808-9 under Sir John Moore, including actions at Lugo, Benevente, and Corunna. Expedition to Walcheren, including siege and capture of Flushing (wounded). Subsequent campaigns in the Peninsula from Nov. 1812 to the end of that war in 1814, including the siege of Ciudad Rodrigo, covering siege of Badajos, battle of Salamanca, capture of Madrid, siege of Burgos, battle of Vittoria, siege of San Sebastian, passage of the Bidassoa, the Nive, and the Adour, and investment of Bayonne.

148 Lieut. William Sharpin served the campaigns of 1814 and 15, in Holland, the Netherlands, and France, and was present at the battle of Waterloo.

149 Lieut. George Sinclair served the campaign of 1814 in Holland as a volunteer, and was severely wounded at the attack on the fortified village of Merxem on the 2nd Feb. 1814.

151 Lieut. Henry Smith served the campaign of 1799 in Holland, including the battles of the 19th Sept., 2nd and 6th October. Campaign of 1800, on the coast of France and Spain; expedition to Quiberon Bay; attack on Ferrol; expedition to Vigo and Cadiz; Egyptian campaign of 1807, including the surrender of Alexandria, attack and storming of Rosetta, in which he took a Turkish colour. Capture of Guadaloupe, in 1815.

152 Lieut. John Smith (h. p. 14 Foot) served on the Walcheren expedition in 1809, and was present at the capture of Flushing. Served also in the North of Spain and South of France in 1814.

153 Lieut. W. Smith (Royal Artillery Drivers) served at Walcheren, in 1809; and the campaigns of 1813, 14, 15, in Holland, Belgium, and France, and was wounded at Merxem.

155 Lieut. Spencer served with the expedition to the Helder, in 1799.

156 Lieut. Sperling served the campaigns of 1814 and 15 in Holland and Flanders; led the right column at the assault of Bergen-op-Zoom.

157 Lieut. Spong served in the Peninsula, in 1811 and 12.

158 Lieut. M. F. Steele served at the Capture of Java in 1811, as an officer of Royal Marines.

159 Lieut. Robert Steele served the campaign and battle of Corunna, where he was slightly wounded in the neck. Expedition to Walcheren. Peninsula, from April 1810 to 1814, including the defence of Cadiz, and blockade of Bayonne.

160 Lieut. Stobart served in the American war under Sir Gordon Drummond.

161 Lieut. Stowards served the campaign of 1814 in Holland, with the 37th, including the investment of Bergen-op-Zoom, action at Merxem, and bombardment of Antwerp, at which last he was severely wounded—left leg amputated.

162 Lieut. William Stuart served under Sir Samuel Hood in the West Indies. At Copenhagen. In the Mediterranean on board the *Cyane* 28 guns under Sir Thomas Staines, when that officer lost his arm in action with the *Cérès* 40 gun Neapolitan frigate. Gun-boats and batteries in the bay of Naples, on the 27th June 1809. Served also at the reduction of Trieste, in 1814.

164 Lieut. E. J. Taylor prior to entering the army served as a midshipman on board H. M. S. *Belvidere*, and was present in an engagement in 1809. Served in the south of France from Sept. 1813 to the end of that war in 1814, including the passage of the Bidassoa, battles of the Nivelle and St. Pé, and Orthes.

165 Lieut. Thornton served in the Peninsula with the old 94th from Feb. 1810 to Feb. 1814, including the defence of Cadiz from April to Sept. 1810, Lines of Torres Vedras, actions of Redinha, Condeixa, and Sabugal; battle of Fuentes d'Onor, second siege of Badajos, action of El Bodon, siege of Ciudad Rodrigo, siege and assault of Badajos, battle of Salamanca, capture of Madrid, battles of Vittoria, the Pyrenees, and Nivelle, at which last he was dangerously wounded through the neck by a musket-ball, which carried away the lower part of the ear.

165* Lieut. Tittle served in the 38th, on the Walcheren expedition in 1809; also the Peninsular campaigns, from April, 1811, to the end of that war in 1814, including the storming of Badajos, battle of Salamanca, various skirmishes on the retreat from Burgos, action at Osma, battle of Vittoria, siege of San Sebastian, and investment of Bayonne. In 1818 he served on Commando through Cafferland. At the siege of San Sebastian he acted as an engineer, and was severely wounded on the 31st August, whilst showing a ford to Col. Fernes of the Portuguese service.

166 Lieut. Trench served at Walcheren, in 1809.

167 Lieut. George Watson served in the Peninsula with the 3rd Dragoons from June 1813 to the end of that war in 1814, and was present at the battle of Toulouse.

168 Lieut. Wm. Henry Watson served the campaigns of 1813 and 14 in Spain and France with the Royal Dragoons.

169 Lieut. Welsh served in the Peninsula, and was present at the battles of Nivelle, Nive, Orthes, and Toulouse.

170 Lieut. Westcott served with the 7th Fusiliers in the American war, and was present in the attack on New Orleans, on the 8th January 1815. Served afterwards with the Army of Occupation in France, until 1817.

171 Lieut. Fred. J. White served in the north of Spain with the Royal Marine Battalion against the Carlists from March 1837 until April 1839. He was present at the capture of

Hernani, Fuentarabia, and Irun; and was eleven months a prisoner of war in the hands of the Carlists, closely confined, and several times sentenced to be shot. Served also on the China expedition, from Feb. 1840, during the whole of the operations, and was in the following actions, chiefly employed on shore, viz., assault and capture of the forts and batteries of Chuen-Pee (wounded), attack on the Anunghoy forts (Bocca Tigris), when three strong forts were carried in succession; first advance on Canton, including the destruction of Hoqua's Fort and other river defences; capture of the Heights of Canton, attack on Amoy,—commanded a streng detachment of the Royal Marines, when the enemy were driven from their guns, and the fortifications, &c., captured; second capture of Chusan, capture of the citadel and walled city of Chinhae; capture of the city of Sykee, and of the Heights of Segoan; attack on the Hill defences and capture of the city of Chapoo, capture of the batteries and city of Woosung, capture of the batteries of Le-Shan, assault and capture of the city of Chin Kiang Foo, and operations against Nankin.

172 Town-Major Henry White served in Holland and Flanders, under the Duke of York, and was present in the following actions, sieges, &c., viz., St. Amand, Famars, Valenciennes, Lincelles, Dunkirk, Cateau and Vaux, Roubaix and Lannoi, Mouveaux, Malines, Boxtel, Nimeguen, Tiel, Fort St. Andre, landing and capture of the Helder in 1799, Zyp Dyke, Bergen, and Callants Ogg (severely wounded in the neck), and Alkmaar. In Spain with Sir John Moore, at Benevente, Lugo, and Corunna. Subsequently in the Peninsula with the Duke of Wellington, including the battle of Busaco, actions at Pombal, Redinha, Foz d'Arouce, and Guarda; different affairs on the retreat to and advance from Torres Vedras, action at Sabugal, battle of Fuentes d'Onor (severely wounded in the right hand and left wrist), actions at Aldea de Ponte and Fuente Guinaldo, first siege of Badajoz, action at El Boden, different affairs during the investment of Ciudad Rodrigo, also siege and storm of that fortress, battle of Salamanca (severely wounded in the throat), capture of Madrid and the Retiro, affairs on the retreat from Madrid and Salamanca, battle of Vittoria, where he was severely wounded in the shoulder joint and back.

173 Lieut. Whitfield, when an ensign in the 7th West India Regt., volunteered and served with the 1st Battalion of Royal Marines at the operations on the North Coast of Spain, and at the taking and defence of Castro. He served in the Peninsula in 1812, 13, and 14, on the staff of Sir Parker Carroll; and with the 62nd at the capture of Paris in 1815.

174 Lieut. Whiting served on the Chinese expedition, and was present at the battle of Chuenpee, attack of the Anunghoy batteries, advance on Canton, capture of the heights of Canton, capture of Colongso, second capture of Chusan, assault and capture of the citadel and city of Chinhae.

174* Lieut. Wilford served in the Peninsula, and was present at the siege of Burgos, and battles of Vittoria and Toulouse.

175 Lieut. Willis served at Walcheren, and was present at the siege of Flushing. Served also the Peninsular campaigns of 1811, 12, and 14, including the 2nd and 3rd sieges of Badajoz, investment of Bayonne, and repulse of the sortie.

177 Lieut. Windle served with the 10th at the siege of Scylla Castle, in 1808. Present with the Anglo-Sicilian army during the whole of its operations on the coast of the Faro, against Murat. With the army on the eastern coast of Spain, in 1812 and 13.

178 Lieut. Frederick Wood was severely wounded at Waterloo.

179 Lieut. Henry Wood served in the Peninsula with the 76th, from June 1813 to the end of that war in 1814, including the siege of San Sebastian, passage of the Bidassoa, battles of Nivelle and Nive, and investment of Bayonne. Served afterwards in the American war, and was present in the action of Plattsburg.

180 Lieut. Woods served in the Peninsula with the 48th in 1810 and 1811, and with the 4th Dragoon Guards in 1812, including the Lines of Torres Vedras, pursuit of Massena, and the operatiens in the Alemtejo; action of Campo Mayor, siege of Olivença, and first siege of Badajoz; with Colonel Colborne's Brigade, when, by a rapid advance, several convoys were intercepted, and the country cleared to Guadalcanal and the fortified post of Benalcazar; battle of Albuhera, where he received two wounds and some severe contusions, and was taken prisoner in the charge of the Polish Lancers, but subsequently escaped and rejoined the army on its advance.

181 Lieut. Wm. Wright (h. p. Rifle Brigade) served in the campaign of 1815, and was severely wounded at Waterloo.

182 Lieut. Farmar served with the 50th in the campaign on the Sutlej, and was present at Buddiwal and Aliwal (Medal), at which last he was severely wounded in the right thigh by a grape-shot while carrying the colors.

183 Lieut. Singleton served with the 10th in the campaign on the Sutlej, and was present at the battle of Sobraon.

184 Lieut. John Cameron (h. p. 2nd Garrison Battalion) served at Copenhagen in 1807.

185 Lieut. Timbrell served the campaign of 1845-6 on the Sutlej (Medal), and was present in the battles of Moodkee, Ferozeshah, Buddiwal, Aliwal, and Sobraon, in which last he had both his thigh bones broken by grape-shot.

2nd LIEUTENANTS, SUB-LIEUTENANTS, CORNETS, AND ENSIGNS.

	CORNET, 2d LIEUT. or ENSIGN.	WHEN PLACED ON HALF PAY.
Agassis, Lewis, Royal Marines	21 Aug. 09	14 May 17
Aickin, Francis, 14 Dragoons	25 May 15	5 Dec. 19
Ainslie, Robert, 77 Foot	14 Mar. 88	
Allen, William, Royal Marines	10 Mar. 06	31 May 23
Anderson, William, Royal Marines..........	12 July 09	1 Jan. 16
Ashe, William, Kingston's Recruiting Corps..	27 Nov. 97	
Atkinson, Charles, Royal Marines	11 Nov. 11	11 Aug. 14
Backhouse, John Iggulden, Royal Marines....	17 Mar. 31	26 Feb. 36
Backhouse, Peter, 8 Dragoons	5 Aug. 15	2 Oct. 23
Bakewell, Robert, 27 Foot..................	17 Jan. 15	25 July 17
Barker, Anthony, New Brunswick Fencibles ..	1 Mar. 15	25 April 16
Barrett, William Newman, 60 Foot	6 May 13	30 Sept. 19
Barry, James, Royal Marines	21 Feb. 11	1 Jan. 16
Barry, James, Royal Marines	30 July 11	
Baugh, James, Royal Marines................	7 Dec. 12	1 Sept. 14
Bayley, John, 13 Dragoons	3 Mar. 13	30 July 18
* Bell, John, 3 Provisional Battalion of Militia		1814
Bellon, Achilles, 130 Foot	24 Dec. 94	
Berkeley, *Hon.* G.C.Grantley Fitzhardinge, 82 F.	7 Nov. 16	28 Aug. 23
Bernard, Walter, 60 Foot	20 Oct. 14	27 Nov. 17
Bevan, Michael, Royal Marines	19 Nov. 04	8 Oct. 24
Biddulph, Walter, Royal Marines	7 Sept 08	24 April 15
Bignell, Charles Philips, Royal Artillery	18 Oct. 26	7 Sept. 29
Black, James, Royal Waggon Train..........	8 July 15	25 June 16
Black, Thomas, 19 Foot.....................	24 Feb. 14	22 May 23
Blake, Edward John, Royal Marines	26 Mar. 12	1 Jan. 16
Blois, Sir Charles, Bart., Horse Grenadier Gds.	14 July 90	
Bolomey, Louis William James, 2 Light Infantry Battalion German Legion	26 Sept. 13	24 Feb. 16
Bonavia, Calcedonia, Maltese Military Artificers	25 Oct. 15	
Bond, Thomas, Royal Marines...............	25 May 10	1 Jan. 16
Boulton, William, 4 Royal Veteran Battalion	11 June 12	
Bowden, George, Royal Marines.............	30 July 10	1 Jan. 16
Boyce, Thomas, Royal Artillery Drivers......	16 July 13	1 Aug. 16
Bradley, Edward Sands, 99 Foot	13 Oct. 14	25 Sept. 18
Branch, George Ferguson, Royal Marines	16 April 32	14 July 37
[illegible] * Brew, Charles,[1] 2 Prov. Battalion of Militia	Dec. 13	1814
[illegible] * Brew, William,[1] do. do.	Dec. 13	1814
Brisac, Douglas Pettiward, Royal Marines....	12 June 12	1 Jan. 16
Brokenshire, Joseph, 11 Royal Veteran Batt..	7 May 07	
Bruyeres, Henry Pringle, Royal Engineers....	1 Sept. 15	21 Feb. 23
Burton, Emanuel, Unattached	17 Aug. 15	14 Sept. 26
Bush, Thomas, 5 Royal Veteran Battalion....	26 May 14	
Butcher, John Lewis, 8 West India Regiment	18 Oct. 09	1816
* Cameron, James, 3 Provisional Batt. of Militia		1814
Campbell, Alexander Brodie, 49 Foot.........	24 June 02	24 June 02
Campbell, Colin, Royal Marines	28 Oct. 09	26 Oct. 14
Campbell, George, 58 Foot	20 Mar. 17	7 Feb. 22
Campbell, James, Royal Marines.............	2 Sept. 08	17 June 13
Campbell, James, 92 Foot...................	11 Nov. 13	1814
Carden, Paul Kyffin, Royal Marines	22 Jan. 11	3 Aug. 20
Carey, John Westropp, 30 Foot	23 June 14	30 Dec. 19
Cary, John, Royal Marines, *Adjutant, Portsmouth Dock-yard Battalion*............	15 April 47	15 April 47
Carroll, Thomas, 53 Foot	20 Nov. 17	26 Oct. 20
Chambers, Montague, 71 Foot	9 Nov. 15	1 Oct. 18
Charles, Deskford, Royal Sappers and Miners	1 July 11	
Child, George Richard, Royal Marines	24 July 09	14 Nov. 17
Chittem, John, 4 Royal Veteran Battalion....	14 Nov. 11	
Church, Boneval, Royal Waggon Train	20 Jan. 14	25 Oct. 19
Christie, John, Royal Marines, *Adjutant, Woolwich Dock-yard Battalion*........	15 April 47	15 April 47
Clark, William Richard, Royal Marines......	3 Sept. 08	18 Aug. 14
Clarke, George Dacres, Royal Marines	5 July 80	21 April 89

	CORNET, ETC.	WHEN PLACED ON HALF PAY.
Clarke, James R.,[3] Royal Artillery	1 Nov. 06	
Coleman, Charles, Royal Marines	13 Feb. 98	1 Jan. 03
Collier, James, Royal Marines	26 July 08	24 Oct. 11
Collings, William Moore, 85 Foot	3 Mar. 14	23 Oct. 23
Collins, Stephen Edward, Royal Marines	14 Dec. 12	1 Sept. 14
Collyer, George Samuel, 87 Foot	24 Jan. 83	24 Jan. 83
Cosnard, John, 88 Foot	11 May 91	
Couche, Richard, Royal Marines	28 April 08	15 Sept. 17
Cranage, John, Independent Company	26 Aug. 94	
Crespin, George Henry Legassick, R. Marines	11 Jan. 00	25 May 02
Crombie, James,[3] 2 Royal Veteran Battalion	31 Aug. 20	
Crossgrove, James, 104 Foot	29 July 13	4 Feb. 19
Crown, George Frederick, Royal Marines	17 Feb. 13	1 Sept. 14
Crozier, Henderson, 22 Foot	12 May 14	25 Dec. 14
Cumming, Alexander, 42 Foot	17 Feb. 14	26 Aug. 19
Curzon, George Henry Roper, Royal Artillery	16 Dec. 16	2 Jan. 21
Daly, Lawrence, 75 Foot	3 Jan. 11	
D'Anfossy, *Le Chevalier*, Royal Artillery	29 June 15	1 Aug. 15
Dardis, John, 14 Foot	29 Oct. 12	26 Dec. 16
Davis, John Henry, Royal Marines	21 May 08	
Davis, William, Royal Marines	12 Aug. 09	
Day, John, 60 Foot	10 Dec. 14	25 Aug. 23
Deaman, Thomas, Bradshaw's Recruiting Corps	28 April 14	11 July 22
Deane, Thomas, 96 Foot	26 Mar. 83	1783
Deans, Robert, 6 Royal Veteran Battalion	25 April 11	
De Beauvoir, *Sir* John Edmund, 104 Foot	3 Mar. 14	14 May 18
De Fauche, Charles, 60 Foot	15 June 15	25 Mar. 17
Devereux, George Alfred, Royal Marines	2 Oct. 09	12 Aug. 14
Dillon, John, 3 Dragoon Guards	5 Mar. 18	1 April 24
Dillon, Theobald Augustus, 58 Foot	21 April 14	25 Feb. 16
Dixon, John Smart, 94 Foot	20 July 15	4 Jan. 21
Dixon, Richard, York Hussars	27 June 00	24 Aug. 02
Dobree, Harry Hankey, 7 Dragoons	24 June 02	24 June 02
Dodd, Chas. Wm. Macarmick, Newfoundland Fencibles	6 Aug. 13	25 June 16
Donovan, Henry Douglas, 9 Foot	25 Aug. 13	13 Feb. 17
Downer, George, Royal Marines, *Adjutant, Chatham Dock-yard Battalion*	15 April 47	15 April 47
Drinkwater, Thomas, Royal Marines	4 April 09	1 Jan. 16
Duckers, Charles, 82 Foot	24 Dec. 12	21 Mar. 16
Dufresne, Louis Flavien, Canadian Fencibles	13 Nov. 13	11 Oct. 16
Durnford, Andrew Mont. Isaacson, 2 Royal Veteran Battalion	18 May 20	
Eaves, John, Royal Sappers and Miners	2 Dec. 06	
Edgelow, George, 8 Royal Veteran Battalion	14 July 14	
Elliott, John Furzer, Royal Marines	4 June 09	23 April 19
Ensor, James, Royal Marines	19 Mar. 97	31 May 02
Evans, Daniel, Royal Marines	16 Dec. 12	1 Sept. 14
Evans, John, 1 Garrison Battalion	9 May 11	6 Dec. 14
Evans, William, Royal Marines	11 Oct. 81	1 Sept. 83
Eyre, Thomas Dowling, Royal Marines	11 Nov. 11	28 Dec. 14
Field, John Stroud, Royal Marines	7 April 09	6 June 15
Fitz Gerald, John, 22 Dragoons	9 Dec. 99	2 Feb. 03
Fletcher, James, 100 Foot	11 Feb. 85	
Flexman, James, Royal Marines	27 Jan. 08	11 Jan. 16
Flint, William Richard, Royal Marines	3 Sept. 10	1 Jan. 16
Forbes, John, 107 Foot	1 June 96	
Ford, William, Royal Marines	29 April 09	6 Jan. 19
Forsey, John, Staff Corps of Cavalry	29 April 13	25 Oct. 14
Forster, George, 8 West India Regiment	25 July 01	1802
Forsyth, Robert, 7 Royal Veteran Battalion	23 July 12	
Fosbery, Henry William, 12 Foot	17 Feb. 14	25 Oct. 21
Francis, Henry (*Ensign*), Rifle Brigade	6 Aug. 13	13 Jan. 20
Frazer, William (Lieut. 27 Jan. 37), 60 Foot	1 April 13	27 July 38
Fraser, John, 72 Foot	29 Dec. 14	
Frett, John, Royal Marines	21 Feb. 14	1 Sept. 14

	2D LIEUT. ETC.	WHEN PLACED ON HALF PAY.
Gage, John Ogle, 9 Dragoons	25 Dec. 13	8 May 23
Garden, Alexander, 104 Foot	3 Mar. 14	25 July 17
Gardner, Charles, 4 Ceylon Regiment	15 Dec. 14	31 Dec. 18
Gardner, John, 7 Royal Veteran Battalion	28 Sept. 15	
Geffrard, John, Independent Company	24 Jan. 91	
Gillbee, James, Sicilian Regiment	13 April 13	25 Mar. 16
Gillies, Walter, Royal Marines, *Adjutant, Pembroke Dock-yard Battalion*	29 April 47	29 April 47
Glanville, Francis (*Lieut.*), 19 Dragoons	20 April 15	11 April 22
Gordon, Francis, 16 Foot	6 Oct. 84	23 Mar. 85
Gould, Matthew, 4 Royal Veteran Battalion	25 Dec. 06	
Graham, Humphrey, Hanger's Recruiting Corps	19 July 98	
Grant, John, Bradshaw's Recruiting Corps	4 July 98	
Grattan, Charles, Royal Sappers and Miners	1 Dec. 12	
*Gray, John, 3 Provisional Battalion of Militia		1814
Griffith, Richard, Royal Irish Artillery	15 Aug. 00	
Gritton, Henry, Royal Marines	8 Sept. 08	20 Feb. 17
Gunn, William, Bourbon Regiment	23 Aug. 15	24 April 16
Gunthorpe, Joshua Rowley, Royal Marines	4 June 95	16 Oct. 95
Hailes, Augustus, Royal Marines	28 June 11	1 Jan. 16
Hallum, James, Royal Marines	31 Mar. 08	30 Mar. 20
Hamilton, John, 1 Foot	24 Mar. 00	25 Mar. 02
Hammond, William, Royal Marines	17 Oct. 14	1 Jan. 16
Hamond, William, 71 Foot	26 Sept. 87	
W Handcock, Tobias, 27 Foot	4 May 15	26 Mar. 16
Hannay, James, Royal Marines	26 Aug. 82	21 Feb. 91
Harrison, William, 38 Foot	26 Dec. 16	26 Dec. 16
Harvey, John, Royal Marines	29 Dec. 13	8 Nov. 28
Harvey, John, Royal Corsican Rangers	24 Dec. 12	25 April 16
Harwood, Edward, 32 Foot	12 Oct. 13	25 Dec. 14
Haydon, Joseph, Royal Marines	27 Mar. 97	27 May 00
Haydon, Robert Luckcombe, 20 Foot	24 Feb. 14	1 April 19
Hayes, Henry Horace, 81 Foot	5 Jan. 15	25 June 18
Haymard, Joseph Peter, 5 West India Regt.	29 Sept. 14	25 April 17
Hayter, George, Royal Waggon Train	10 June 13	1814
Hemmings, John Exham, Invalids	1 June 97	
Hewett, Frederick, Royal Marines	9 Sept. 12	1 Jan. 16
Hewson, George, 24 Foot	2 April 12	25 Dec. 14
Hinton, John Thomas, Royal Marines	25 May 12	1 Jan. 16
Hoare, Charles Vyvyan, Royal Marines	12 Mar. 11	3 Aug. 15
P*Hobro, Edward, 1 Provisional Batt. of Militia		1814
Hodgson, Frederick Æmilius, R. Waggon Train	10 Feb. 14	1814
W Holland, Thomas Edward, 83 Foot	25 Dec. 13	14 Jan. 19
Holmes, Richard, Royal Marines	20 Nov. 80	6 April 90
Horne, John, 15 Foot	14 Mar. 01	13 Aug. 02
Hoyland, John, Royal Sappers and Miners	1 April 15	1 Mar. 17
Hugoe, Samuel, Royal Marines	1 Oct. 11	1 Jan. 23
Huthnance, John, Royal Artillery Drivers	12 Nov. 13	1 Nov. 14
Jack, Thomas,[6] Royal Artillery Drivers	23 Feb. 13	
Jackson, John, Royal Marines	22 Feb. 09	1 Jan. 16
P W Jagger, Joseph,[7] Royal Artillery Drivers	16 July 13	1 Aug. 16
Jenkins, John, Royal Marines	19 Jan. 10	1 Jan. 16
Innes, Robert, 94 Foot	14 May 13	8 Mar. 21
Johnstone, Hamilton Trail, Royal Marines	25 Aug. 10	1 Jan. 16
Jones, Stopford Thomas, 61 Foot	15 Nov. 10	25 Mar. 16
Jop, Robert, 25 Foot	11 May 15	25 April 16
Karr, Peter, 4 Royal Veteran Battalion	29 July 13	
Kennett, Charles Leighton, 4 West India Regt.	21 Sept. 15	20 April 20
Kruger, Carl Wevell von, 2 Ceylon Regiment	22 Jan. 14	23 Sept. 24
Kyles, James, 2 Royal Veteran Battalion	19 Oct. 15	
Lamb, John, 2 Royal Veteran Battalion, *Military Knight of Windsor*	9 Nov. 15	
Lamborn, John Sherrard, Royal Marines	24 Aug. 32	24 July 35
Lane, George Dawkins, Royal Marines	15 Feb. 12	1 Jan. 16
Lane, James Reece, Royal Marines	15 April 07	7 Nov. 12
Lanfranchi, Ruggero, Queen's Germans	3 Sept. 01	

	ENSIGN, ETC.	WHEN PLACED ON HALF PAY.
Langdale, Marmaduke Robert, 9 Foot	17 June 02	25 July 02
Leatham, Francis, 62 Foot	4 Nov. 13	25 April 17
Lee, Frederick Richard, 96 Foot	6 Dec. 13	21 Dec. 15
Lee, John, 78 Foot	8 Sept. 14	25 April 16
Lee, Robert Newton, 2 Ceylon Regiment	29 June 15	13 Nov. 23
Lennan, Edward, 7 West India Regiment	3 Aug. 15	16 April 18
Lewis, Stephen, 73 Foot	19 May 14	6 July 20
Lidderdale, Thomas Robertson, 6 West India Regt.	14 Aug. 00	
Lloyd, Henry Vereker, 86 Foot	31 Jan. 16	26 Oct. 21
Lloyd, Samuel, Royal Marines	24 Feb. 09	10 April 16
Loft, John Henry, 15 Dragoons	30 Dec. 13	12 Mar. 18
Losack, Augustus, 84 Foot	18 May 15	5 Aug. 19
Lum, William Purefoy, 35 Foot	25 Dec. 13	27 July 20
Lyons, Anthony Munton, Royal Marines	3 Nov. 12	1 Sept. 14
Lyte, Thomas, Royal Marines	22 July 80	19 Sept. 88
M'Connechy, James, Royal Marines	10 Mar. 12	1 Jan. 16
M'Dermott, George Augustus, Rifle Brigade	2 Dec. 13	10 Aug. 20
M'Donell, Alexander, Glengarry Fencibles	6 Feb. 12	25 Aug. 16
M'Kinnon, John, 64 Foot	24 June 83	1783
M'Lachlan, Neil, 64 Foot	7 Sept. 04	
M'Leod, Norman, 6 Foot	11 Aug. 14	8 Mar. 21
P CB Macdonald, Colin,[8] 50 Foot, *Town Major at Montreal*	*30 Jan. 35 28 Jan. 48	28 Jan. 48
Maclachlan, Colin, 72 Foot	9 July 00	25 June 15
Maclean, Alexander, Newfoundland Fencibles	24 June 13	25 June 16
Maclean, Samuel, Royal Sappers and Miners	22 April 15	1 Mar. 17
MacWilliam, John, 100 Foot	14 Sept. 15	15 May 18
Manico, Edward, Royal Marines	2 Feb. 11	1 Jan. 16
Margitson, Joseph, 27 Foot	6 Sept. 15	25 Feb. 16
Mason, Richardson, 94 Foot	14 April 13	25 Dec. 18
P *Mead, Charles,*[9] Royal Artillery Drivers	1 May 13	
Meredith, James Henry, Royal Marines	2 May 11	1 Jan. 16
Milliken, John, 63 Foot	1 June 01	
Monk, John, Royal Marines	30 May 12	14 Sept. 14
Montgomery, Robert, 95 Foot	2 Dec. 13	25 Jan. 19
Mooney, John, Royal Marines	25 April 98	26 April 98
Moore, Charles William, Royal Marines	31 May 09	22 Sept. 17
P * Moore, John, 1 Provisional Batt. of Militia		1814
Morehouse, George, New Brunswick Fencibles	25 Oct. 13	25 April 16
Morgan, James Hungerford, Royal Marines	8 Sept. 08	2 Jan. 21
Morris, John, 4 Foot	27 July 15	15 May 17
Mortashed, John, 35 Foot	27 Jan. 14	25 Oct. 21
Moss, Henry, Royal Marines	31 Aug. 13	1 Sept. 14
Murray, Adam, 84 Foot	18 Jan. 16	13 Feb. 18
Nason, George, 68 Foot	9 Oct. 15	25 June 22
Nelson, Richard, 3 Foot	27 Jan. 14	18 July 16
Nixon, John Isaac, 4 Foot	7 Dec. 15	1 Jan. 18
North, Roger, Royal Marines	9 Mar. 13	11 Nov. 24
Nugent, Christopher Edm. John, 17 Dragoons	24 June 02	24 June 02
O'Shea, Thomas, 3 Garrison Battalion	5 July 15	25 Nov. 16
Orme, Lewis, Royal Marines, *Adjutant, Sheerness Dock-yard Battalion*	15 April 47	15 April 47
Owen, Robert Hassall, Royal Marines	22 Feb. 11	1 Jan. 16
Palling, Henry, 95 Foot	8 July 13	Jan. 19
Parsons, Guy, Royal Marines	16 May 09	
Pasheller, Charles, Royal Marines	16 Nov. 80	1 Sept. 83
Patterson, Thomas, Royal Marines	6 April 13	1 Sept. 14
Pawsey, George, Royal Marines	20 Nov. 81	8 Mar. 91
Pegg, William, 28 Dragoons	17 June 02	31 Mar. 03
Philipps, George, Royal Marines	15 April 12	1 Jan. 16
Pitt, Henry, Royal Marines	2 Sept. 12	1 Jan. 16
Pleuderleath, David, 4 Foot	6 May 02	25 May 02
Porter, John Hall, Royal Marines	4 Feb. 11	1 Jan. 16
Potts, Thomas, Royal Marines, *Adjutant, Devonport Dock-yard Battalion*	15 April 47	15 April 47
Poussin, Balthazard, Corsican Rangers	23 Dec. 13	25 Mar. 16

	2d Lieut. etc.	When placed on half pay.
Powell, Wm. Edward (*Ensign*), 18 Dragoons *Colonel of the Cardigan Militia*	21 Mar. 11	12 Sept. 22
Prendergast, Maurice, 2 Hussars German Legion	22 Feb. 13	25 April 16
Pulliblank, Edward Cooper, Royal Marines ..	18 July 09	16 Jan. 16
Radcliffe, Thomas, Royal Marines	1 Sept. 09	1 Sept. 14
Raye, Henry Robert, Royal Marines	14 Dec. 12	1 Sept. 14
Read, Thomas, Royal Marines..............	1 Feb. 06	7 May 10
Reid, Thomas, 22 Dragoons................	3 May 00	9 Feb. 03
Resius, Frederick, 60 Foot	1 June 15	4 Oct. 19
Rickard, Martin, Royal Waggon Train	25 Dec. 13	25 Dec. 18
Ridge, James Stuart, 6 West India Regiment	22 Feb. 14	29 June 20
Robertson, William, Royal Sappers and Miners	1 July 12	
Rogers, Thomas, 40 Foot	17 Oct. 99	25 Aug. 02
Rose, Philip, 56 Foot.....................	17 Nov. 13	1814
Ross, Henry Paget Bayly, Royal Marines	16 Dec. 12	1 Sept. 14
Ross, John, 6 Garrison Battalion...........	20 Oct. 10	4 Feb. 15
Ross, William, 10 Foot	20 June 83	1783
Sallery, William Ogle, 7 Garrison Battalion ..	19 Feb. 07	23 Aug. 10
Samson, Richard, Royal Marines, *Adjutant, Deptford Dock-yard Battalion*	29 April 47	29 April 47
Saunders, Edward, Royal Sappers and Miners	14 Jan. 14	1 April 17
Sargent Richard, Royal Marines	15 Dec. 13	1 Sept. 14
Savage Rowland, 1 Foot....................	2 Dec. 14	12 Mar. 18
Scott, William, 61 Foot....................	16 June 14	1814
Scully, William, 13 Dragoons	24 June 02	24 June 02
Serjeant, George, Royal Marines............	11 April 12	1 Jan. 16
Shackel, William, Royal Waggon Train	21 Sept. 15	25 June 16
Shepherd, William, Royal Waggon Train	18 Nov. 13	14 Nov. 16
P Shore, John,[11] Royal Artillery Drivers	19 May 13	15 Nov. 14
Simpson, John Bridgman, (*Cornet*,) 48 Foot..	17 Oct. 16	5 Aug. 24
Simpson, John W., Royal Marines	2 Aug. 10	1 Jan. 16
Sired, William, 2 Royal Veteran Battalion ..	24 Aug. 20	
Skinner, William Dunstan, Royal Marines	25 July 12	23 Sept. 24
Skues, George, Royal Marines..............	25 Oct. 13	1 Sept. 14
Smith, John, Royal Sappers and Miners	1 June 11	
Smith, Michael Cusac, 11 Dragoons	19 Aug. 13	10 June 19
CA Smith, Wm. Slaytor, (Lt. 17 Oct. 08,) 72 F.	25 Dec. 06	8 Nov. 19
Smithwick, Robert, Royal Marines..........	8 Oct. 10	1 Jan. 16
Spark, John, Royal Sappers and Miners	8 April 12	
Sparkes, Thomas, 56 Foot..................	7 April 13	1814
Spearman, Ralph William, 21 Foot	30 Jan. 21	25 Aug. 21
Standish, Richard, Royal Marines	28 June 11	1 Jan. 16
Stevens, William, Royal Sappers and Miners..	1 Nov. 15	1 April 17
Stewart, Robert, 7 Royal Veteran Battalion..	25 May 15	
Strattan, William, Royal Sappers and Miners	1 April 13	
Sunderland, Henry, 52 Foot	26 July 21	7 Mar. 22
Sweeney, Francis Bernard, 62 Foot..........	20 Jan. 14	25 April 17
Sympson, Robert, 60 Foot	25 Feb. 83	
CA Talbot, James, (*Lieut.*,) 2 Dragoon Gds.	16 Feb. 15	23 May 22
Talmash, *Hon.* Arthur Cæsar, (*Lieut.*,) 6 Dragoons	24 Aug. 15	13 Oct. 20
Taylor, Robert,[12] Royal Artillery	22 Jan. 08	
Taylor, William, 7 West India Regiment	16 May 16	5 Sept. 16
Temple, Gustavus Hancock, Royal Marines ..	15 May 09	18 Mar. 13
Thierry, Lewis de, Royal Marines	8 Feb. 14	1 Sept. 14
Thomas, Mark, 98 Foot....................	9 Nov. 15	25 Nov. 18
Thomson, George, 12 Foot	5 May 14	25 Jan. 18
Thornton, Robert Innes, 78 Foot...........	1 Aug. 16	1 Aug. 16
Tickell, John Arscott, Royal Marines	8 Sept. 08	7 Oct. 19
Todd, William, Royal Marines..............	2 Feb. 10	1 Jan. 16
Tracey, Henry, Royal Artillery Drivers	23 May 13	
Trewhitt, Henry, 34 Foot..................	30 Dec. 13	8 Jan. 18
Turnbull, William George, 73 Foot..........	12 Aug. 13	25 June 18
Turner, William, Sicilian Regiment	6 Feb. 12	25 June 16
Tweedie, David, Royal Marines	28 Aug. 12	1 Jan. 16
Veitch, William, 58 Foot	30 Jan. 12	30 May 16

	ENSIGN, ETC.	WHEN PLACED ON HALF PAY.
Vincent, John Tunnadine, Royal Marines	18 Nov. 80	1 Sept. 83
Wade, Thomas, Royal Marines	5 Dec. 08	1 Jan. 16
Walker, William Hislop, 3 West India Regt. ..	16 Nov. 15	25 Feb. 25
Wallace, Alexander, Royal Sappers and Miners	1 July 11	
Wallace, James, (*Ensign*,) 22 Dragoons......	14 April 14	22 June 23
Walsh, George, 45 Foot..................	14 April 14	25 June 20
Walter, George, Royal Marines	17 Jan. 11	1 Jan. 16
Walter, Rawlins George, Royal Marines......	1 April 09	1 Jan. 16
Walters, Henry, Royal Marines	13 Dec. 13	1 Sept. 14
Watson, Atherton, 91 Foot	31 May 91	12 April 93
Watts, David John, Royal Marines	20 May 08	1 Jan. 16
Watts, William, 2 Dragoon Guards..........	8 Oct. 03	24 May 04
Weir, Hector John, Royal Marines	10 Dec. 82	1 April 92
Weir, Henry, Royal Marines	18 Feb. 14	1 Sept. 14
Weiss, Frederick, 60 Foot	24 Jan. 14	25 July 18
Whaley, George, 17 Foot..................	24 Sept. 02	25 Sept. 02
Wilcocks, John Lodge, 1 Dragoon Guards....	3 May 00	25 June 02
Wilde, Joshua John, Royal Marines	18 Nov. 81	1 Sept. 83
Wilkins, Samuel Martin, 86 Foot............	7 Jan. 06	
Wills, John, Kingston's Recruiting Corps	23 May 00	
Wilson, Edward Lumley, Homspech's Mounted Riflemen	24 Oct. 02	24 Oct. 02
Wolff, Alexander Joseph, 11 Foot	25 Dec. 21	11 Nov. 24
Woodcock, Frederick, Royal Marines	3 Aug. 12	20 Feb. 15
Woolhouse, Andrew Mackason, Unattached ..	13 Aug. 25	17 July 28

War Services of Second Lieutenants, Cornets, and Ensigns.

1 Ensigns C. and W. Brew accompanied the 2nd Provisional Battalion of Militia to the South of France, in 1814.

2 Second Lieut. James R. Clarke served on the Continent in 1794 and 95, and was present in several skirmishes, and at the siege of Nimeguen, where he was wounded.

3 Ensign Crombie was at the capture of the Cape of Good Hope in 1806. Served also the campaigns before new Orleans in 1814 and 15, and was severely wounded.

6 Second Lieut. Jack served in Holland in 1799, and was three times wounded. Served also in the American war, including the actions of Le Bleuf, Chippewa (wounded), and Lundy's Lane.

7 Second Lieut. Jagger served in the Peninsula, and was present at the battle of Talavera. Served also the campaign of 1815, including the battle of Waterloo.

8 Ensign Macdonald served the campaigns of 1811, 12, 13, 14, and 15, with the 79th, including the siege of Ciudad Rodrigo, covering last siege of Badajoz, battle of Salamanca, capture of Madrid, sieges of Burgos, subsequent retreat through Spain, battles of the Pyrenees (28th and 30th July), Nivelle, Nive, Toulouse, and Waterloo, besides various minor affairs, and was four times severely wounded, viz., in the right thigh at the battle of the Pyrenees, in the right groin at the Nive, in the right leg and right cheek at Waterloo.

9 Second Lieut. Mead served in the campaigns of 1814 and 15 in the Peninsula, France, and Flanders, and was present at the capture of Paris.

11 Second Lieut. Shore served in the Peninsula from Sept. 1813 to the end of that war in 1814.

12 Second Lieut. Robert Taylor served at the siege of Fort Bourbon, and captures of Martinique, St. Lucia, and Guadaloupe, in 1794. In 1795, when the Caribs rose to take the Island of St. Vincent, he commanded the Artillery in the field for ten months, during which period he was in eleven different engagements.

	CORNET, 2d LIEUT. or ENSIGN.	LIEUT.	PAY-MASTER.	WHEN PLACED ON HALF PAY.
Acton, Edward, 2 Garrison Battalion	.. ..	.. ..	9 Mar. 12	6 Dec. 14
Aitken, Alexander, 42 Foot	.. ..	.. ..	26 Aug. 13	17 Feb. 21
Armstrong, James, 67 Foot	.. ..	.. ..	6 Jan. 14	25 Aug. 17
Bell, William,[1] (*Capt.* 25 Nov. 24) 89 Foot	3 Mar. 08	9 May 11	9 May 34	26 Mar. 41
Bell, William, 56 Foot	.. ..	.. ..	12 Dec. 11	19 Aug. 19
Bews, John, 73 Foot	.. ..	.. ..	28 Nov. 11	1 July 36
Boustead, John, Ceylon Rifle Regiment..	.. ..	.. ..	21 June 10	1 May 36
P Bowden, Wm. Carey, 21 Dragoons ..	.. ..	.. ..	12 May 08	4 Nov. 24
P Boyle, William,[2] 21 Foot............	21 July 08	6 Feb. 12	3 Nov. 25	1 May 32
Brenan, Patrick, 97 Foot	.. ..	.. ..	11 Nov. 13	23 May 22
P W Brown, Evan Mered. (*Cap.* 20 July 15) 23 F.	23 Aug. 07	20 April 09	23 Oct. 17	16 Oct. 2[illegible]
P Burnet, John,[3] 16 Dragoons..........	.. ..	.. ..	25 June 02	11 April 11
Cahill, David, 88 Foot	10 Nov. 25	31 Dec. 32	11 Nov. 42	1 Sept. 48
P Call, George Isaac,[4] 18 F. (*Capt.* 26 Dec. 11)	4 Mar. 02	1 July 04	7 Dec. 36	29 Oct. 47
Chapman, Benjamin, 5 Line Bn. Ger. Leg.	.. ..	.. ..	27 Aug. 03	23 Dec. 19
Chase, John Woodford, Malta Regiment..	.. ..	.. ..	24 Oct. 05	1811
Christie, George, 8 West India Regiment	.. ..	.. ..	25 Dec. 06	25 July 17
Collins, Michael, 76 Foot.............	8 Aug. 16	never	21 Mar. 27	June 39
P Cowper, Henry,[5] 7 Line Bn. Ger. Leg.	.. ..	.. ..	1 Mar. 06	25 Sept. 16
Cox, Charles, 75 Foot	.. ..	.. ..	29 Jan. 06	7 May 29
Cox, Douglas Leith, 47 Foot	30 Nov. 09	29 Oct. 12	25 Sept. 40	1 Sept. 48
Creser, Richard, 27 Foot	10 Jan. 11	3 June 13	14 Jan. 19	17 Nov. 25
Cross, Anthony, 24 Dragoons	.. ..	.. ..	6 Nov. 01	11 Sept. [illegible]
Crowe, George William, 27 Foot........	.. ..	.. ..	7 Mar. 11	25 Dec. 24
Dana, Wm. Pulteney, 6 Garrison Batt. ..	.. ..	.. ..	25 April 07	25 Dec. 16
P Davies, Richard,[8] 74 Foot	6 June 11	31 Dec. 12	1 Dec. 25	20 Aug. 41
Dawe, Andrew Moore, 53 Foot	.. ..	.. ..	8 Oct. 07	5 April 33
P W Dean, William,[9] 25 Foot	9 Feb. 09	14 Aug. 11	10 Dec. 29	30 Sept. 42
P W *Deane, William*, 18 Dragoons ..	.. ..	.. ..	13 Aug. 02	1822
De Carteret, George, 5 R. Veteran Batt.	.. ..	.. ..	15 Feb. 98	
Dive, Hugh, 10 Foot..................	.. ..	.. ..	31 Mar. 08	21 Aug. 23
Doughty, Edward, 4 West India Regt. ..	.. ..	.. ..	2 April 12	8 Sept. 19
P Drawwater, Augustus Charles,[10] 4 Dr. Gds. (*Capt.* 15 Aug. 11)	1 May 05	20 Mar. 06	11 Nov. 19	1847
Edmonds, Edward, Recruiting District ..	.. ..	.. ..	5 Sept. 03	16 July 41
Fisher, James, Recruiting District	.. ..	.. ..	23 July 03	25 Mar. 17
Furlong, Charles John,[12] Unattached	29 Sept. 08	3 Jan. 10	22 April 24	26 July 3[illegible]
Gapper, Peter, 104 Foot	20 June 05	25 Dec. 06	14 Nov. 16	11 Nov. 1[illegible]
Geddes, Adam Gordon, 10 R. Vet. Batt.	.. ..	.. ..	31 Mar. 14	25 June 21
Goddard, John, 15 Foot	.. ..	.. ..	29 Aug. 11	27 Feb. 21
P W Gordon, James, 92 Foot	.. ..	.. ..	4 April 05	2 Mar. 2[illegible]
Grant, Peter, 55 Foot	.. ..	.. ..	20 Aug. 98	15 May [illegible]
Grimes, Charles,[13] Invalid Depot........	.. ..	.. ..	16 April 12	18 July 48
P Halfhide, James, 37 Foot............	.. ..	.. ..	29 June 09	22 July 4[illegible]
P Hall, Henry William, 39 Foot........	.. ..	.. ..	4 April 05	29 July 19
Hall, John, Recruiting District	.. ..	.. ..	2 Oct. 12	25 Sept. 2[illegible]
Halpin, William, 1 Lt. Dr. Germ. Leg. ..	.. ..	.. ..	6 Jan. 07	25 June 16
Hanbury, Capel S., 1 Dragoons	26 May 14	23 Nov. 15	26 Dec. 21	27 Mar. 2[illegible]
Harman, Robert, 17 Dragoons..........	.. ..	.. ..	26 May 08	19 Oct. 2[illegible]
Harvey, Geo. Frederick, Recruiting Dist.	.. ..	.. ..	3 Nov. 13	1814
Heath, Edwin, 88 Foot................	.. ..	*1814	28 June 27	30 Aug. 39
P W Hilliard, Henry,[14] 68 Foot	25 Feb. 08	16 Nov. 09	22 Mar. 21	10 May 39
Holden, Wm.,[15] Rifle Br. (*Capt.* 12 July 21)	15 Dec. 04	31 Dec. 06	26 Feb. 24	1 Sept. 47
P Holdsworth, Samuel,[16] 82 Foot	31 Dec. 07	1 Nov. 09	22 Sept. 25	27 Aug. 41
Home, David, 35 Foot	.. ..	.. ..	20 June 98	2 April 1[illegible]
Hunter, Thomas, 7 Dragoon Guards	12 May 14	1 Oct. 25	3 Nov. 25	1 Oct. 3[illegible]
Jefferson, Richard, Ceylon Regt.........	23 Oct. 23	1 Sept. 26	6 May 36	8 Sept. 4[illegible]
Johnson, Ralph Boetler, 45 Foot.......	.. ..	.. ..	27 Oct. 10	25 June 15
P Jones, Michael, 80 Foot	.. ..	.. ..	21 April 98	25 Aug. 1[illegible]
Irvin, Martin, 61 Foot	5 May 04	16 Jan. 06	17 May 04	25 Dec. 14
Irvine, John Christ. Caulfield, 80 Foot ..	.. ..	.. ..	27 Sept. 10	13 Oct. 2[illegible]
Ker, Thomas, 103 Foot...............	27 April 09	12 July 10	14 May 17	30 June 2[illegible]
King, Thomas, 98 Foot...............	.. ..	.. ..	5 Sept. 11	25 Dec. 1[illegible]
W Knight, John, 2 Lt. Inf. Bn. Ger. Leg.	.. ..	.. ..	20 Jan. 14	25 May 16
P Ledlard, Thomas, 66 Foot	.. ..	.. ..	4 April 11	25 Dec. 77

	CORNET, ETC.	LIEUT.	PAY-MASTER.	WHEN PLACED ON HALF PAY.
Ledingham, George, 34 Foot	1 Aug. 05	17 July 06	16 Sept. 19	30 Nov. 38
Lukis, John,[18] 3 Foot..................	22 Feb. 10	6 Aug. 12	24 Dec. 29	25 June 47
𝔓 M'Leod, Martin, 25 Foot............	8 Oct. 12	18 Jan. 15	15 Jan. 24	15 Jan. 30
Mackay, James Duff, 50 Foot	.. ..	.. ..	26 Nov. 12	1814
𝔚 Mackenzie, Hugh, 71 Foot	.. ..	.. ..	8 Nov. 98	16 Aug. 24
𝔓 Maclaurin, David Scott Kin.,[19] 1 Dr. Gds., *Dep. Assist. Commissary Gen.*	.. ..	.. ..	18 Sept. 23	30 July 41
Malassez, Nicholas, Hompesch's Mount. Riflemen	.. ..	.. ..	30 Dec. 97	29 Oct. 02
Meiklejohn, J. Hope Johnstone, 92 Foot..	7 May 12	10 Dec. 13	2 Mar. 20	23 July 44
Mockler, John, 82 Foot................	25 May 32	12 Sept. 34	27 Aug. 41	1 Oct. 48
𝔓 Moss, William, York Light Infantry ..	.. ..	.. ..	3 Mar. 04	25 Aug. 16
𝔓 Nicholson, Joseph,[20] 75 F. (*Capt.* 15 Mar. 31.)	11 Aug. 08	9 Aug. 10	7 Sept. 26	13 Aug. 47
O'Keefe, James, 48 Foot	.. ..	.. ..	16 Jan. 12	1 April 37
O'Meara, Daniel,[21] 45 Foot	25 Aug. 14	11 Jan. 16	20 Oct. 25	3 Nov. 43
𝔓 Pardey, J. Quin,[22] 53 F. (*Capt.* 31 Dec. 28) *Adjutant, Shropshire Militia*......	18 July 11	17 Dec. 12	12 Feb. 36	28 June 44
Pillon, John, 54 Foot..................	.. ..	.. ..	26 Nov. 18	29 July 25
Prior, Lodge Morres Murray, 12 Lancers	12 Sept. 11	9 Dec. 13	6 July 20	3 Oct. 48
Read, George, 5 Foot	.. ..	.. ..	6 May 13	11 Nov. 24
𝔚 Robinson, P. Vyvyan, 88 Foot......	.. ..	.. ..	28 Jan. 13	28 June 27
𝔓 Rodgers, James,[24] 26 Foot	17 May 27	.. ..	7 Oct. 36	1 June 37
Rose, Hickman Leland, 30 Foot	.. ..	.. ..	26 Jan. 15	16 Aug. 21
Sherwood, Henry, Brunswick Cavalry....	.. ..	.. ..	1 May 04	23 July 18
Strong, Richard Henry,[25] 26 Foot	7 Aug. 27	9 Dec. 31	1 June 37	18 Aug. 43
𝔓 Teighe, Thomas, 1 Line Bn. Ger. Leg.	.. ..	.. ..	8 Sept. 04	25 June 16
Terry, Henry, 99 Foot	13 Sept. 10	19 May 14	27 Dec. 27	1 June 35
𝔓 𝔚 Thomson, J. Crooke, 1 Foot......	.. ..	.. ..	31 Jan. 11	22 Oct. 16
Tiddeman, Henry, 75 Foot	.. ..	.. ..	28 May 07	26 Mar. 18
𝔓 Tovey, Alexander, 24 Foot	22 Oct. 13	11 June 18	4 Feb. 19	29 Mar. 42
Trattle, John Kerr, 88 Foot	.. ..	.. ..	26 July 10	11 Aug. 25
Trick, Thomas, 1 R. Veteran Battalion ..	.. ..	.. ..	14 Sept. 09	12 July 14
Wainwright, David,[26] 11 R. Vet. Batt...	.. ..	.. ..	7 Sept. 08	
Wardell, Charles, 42 Foot..............	1 Sept. 10	20 Dec. 13	7 Feb. 21	25 Jan. 28
Ware, Robert,[27] 49 Foot	25 Oct. 12	25 Sept. 13	28 June 31	9 Apr. 47
Webster, William,[28] 76 Foot............	20 May 08	1 Feb. 09	7 Sept. 26	1 Jan. 44
Wemys, Francis, Recruiting District	.. ..	.. ..	25 May 11	12 July 44
Wetherall, William, 87 Foot	.. ..	.. ..	17 Aug. 99	
Whitaker, John Gibson, 8 Hussars	Jan. 05	31 Oct. 05	9 Jan. 17	3 Nov. 40
𝔓 White, John Lewis, 81 Foot	.. ..	.. ..	25 Feb. 13	8 Oct. 18
𝔓 White, Warren Hastings, 2 Light Dr. German Legion	.. ..	.. ..	17 Sept. 12	21 Sept. 15
𝔓 𝔚 Williams, James, 44 Foot........	.. ..	.. ..	4 Oct. 10	25 April 16
𝔓 Wright, James,[29] 94 Foot............	.. ..	.. ..	25 Mar. 10	25 Dec. 18

War Services of the Paymasters.

1 Captain Bell served at the capture of the Isle of France in 1810. Also at the taking of the following Forts in the Concan, East Indies, viz., Seedghur, Bagwuntghur, Ryghur, in 1818; Newtee and Raree, in 1819; at the first and last places led the storming parties, as also at the taking of a stockade commanding a ford near Bugwuntghur.

2 Paymaster Boyle served in the Peninsula from May 1809 to the end of that war in 1814, including the battle of Busaco, retreat to Torres Vedras, pursuit of Massena, actions of Foz d'Arouce and Campo Mayor, siege and capture of Olivença, assault and capture of Badajoz, capture of Madrid and the Retiro, battles of Vittoria and the Pyrenees. Slightly wounded in the ear at Fort St. Christoval, 10th May 1813, and again in the face in the Pyrenees, 28th July 1813.

3 Paymaster Burnet accompanied the 16th Light Dragoons to Flanders in 1793, and returned home with them in 1795. Proceeded with the regiment to the Peninsula, in the spring of 1809, and remained with them until August 1810.

4 Captain Call served with the 24th Light Dragoons at Agra, Deig, Bhurtpore, Allyghur, Delhi, Laswarrie, Futteghur, and also in several skirmishes in Lord Lake's campaigns of 1803, 4, 5, and 6. He served afterwards in the Peninsula on the staff of Major-General MacKinnon, and was present at the storming of Ciudad Rodrigo. He served also throughout the China war with the 18th, including the first capture of Chusan, Chinhae, Ningpo, Chapoo, Woosung, and Chin Kiang Foo.

5 Paymaster Cowper served on the expedition to Stralsund and Copenhagen in 1807; to Sweden with Sir John Moore, in 1808; thence the same year to Portugal, where he served until July 1811; thence to Malta, Sicily, and Genoa, until the peace. He has received the war medal bestowed by the King of Hanover to every officer, non-commissioned officer, and soldier of the German Legion, in commemoration of the services of the corps.

8 Paymaster Davies served in the Peninsula from Sept. 1811 to the end of that war in 1814, including the capture of Fort Picurina and Badajoz, battles of Salamanca, Vittoria, Pyrenees, Nivelle, Tarbes, Orthes, and Toulouse.

9 Paymaster Dean (h. p. 25 Foot) served in the Peninsula from April 1809 to the end of that war in 1814. Also the campaign of 1815, including the battle of Waterloo.

10 Captain Drawwater served in the expedition to Copenhagen in 1807; the capture of Martinique; and subsequently in the Peninsula, including the battle of Busaco.

12 Paymaster Furlong was in the action before Genoa, and the taking of that city, 7th April 1814. Served afterwards in the American war, including the operations in the Chesapeak, battle of Bladensburg and capture of Washington, action before Baltimore, and the subsequent service in the Chesapeak; operations of the army before New Orleans, the actions of the 2nd Dec. 1814, and 1st Jan. 1815, and storm of the American lines before New Orleans, taking of Fort Bowyer. On board the *Golden Fleece* transport when attacked by an American privateer, off the island of St. Domingo, 28th Nov. 1814.

13 Paymaster Grimes served the campaigns of 1813, 14, and 15 in Lower Canada, under Sir George Prevost. He served also in the Burmese War with the 38th Regt.

14 Paymaster Hilliard served in the Peninsula from June 1809 to the end of that war in 1814, including the battle of Busaco, action of Campo Mayor, first siege of Badajoz, battle of Albuhera, affairs at Arroyo de Molino and Almaraz. Served also the campaign of 1815, including the battles of Quatre Bras and Waterloo, at which latter he was severely wounded.

15 Captain Holden served at the siege of Scylla Castle, in Calabria, in 1810; embarked on board the *Spartan* frigate in 1812, forming a part of an expedition against Gallipoli at the entrance of the Adriatic, where he was employed in the gun-boats; on coasting back to Messina, he assisted to destroy several towers and forts, and to take many boats laden with stores and provisions. At the attack and capture of the island of Ponza, on the coast of Naples, in 1813, he was landed in command of a company, under a heavy fire of grape-shot, to silence the battery Frontini, commanding the entrance of the harbour, which surrendered to him, as well as another on the opposite side of the island.

16 Paymaster Holdsworth served on the expedition against Belle Isle, in June 1800; at the siege and capture of Flushing, in 1809; in the Peninsula from June 1812 to the end of that war in 1814, including the battles of Vittoria, Maya Pass, Heights of Pampeluna 30th (wounded in the wrist by a musket-ball and contused on the shoulder), and 31st July, Heights of Lesaca 31st Aug., battles of Nivelle and Orthes.

18 Paymaster Lukis was present with the Buffs at the battle of Punniar (Medal).

19 Paymaster Maclaurin served in the Peninsula during the campaign of 1813, and that in Holland in 1814, and subsequently at Waterloo, and with the army of occupation, as Deputy Assistant Commissary General.

20 Capt. Nicholson served in the Peninsula from April 1809 to the end of the war, including the battles of Talavera, Busaco, and Salamanca, where he was severely wounded.

21 Paymaster O'Meara served in Senegal, west coast of Africa, as a Lieut. under Col. Brereton; in Sierra Leone under Governor M'Carthy; in Caffraria, in the campaigns of 1819 and 20, under the present Sir Thomas Willshire; in the Birman Empire under Sir Archibald Campbell; and in India with the 45th regiment.

22 Captain Pardey served in the Peninsula from Feb. 1813 to the end of that war in 1814.

23 Paymaster Prior served the campaign of 1817 in the East Indies against the Pindarrees.

24 Paymaster Rodgers served in the Peninsula from May 1813 to the end of that war in 1814, including the siege of Tarragona. Served afterwards in the East Indies, and was present at Amulnier, Malligaum, and Asseerghur.

25 Paymaster Strong served with the 26th on the China expedition, and was present at the first taking of Chusan.

26 Paymaster Wainwright served with the Queen's Royals on board the *Russell* 74, in Lord Howe's actions of the 28th and 29th May, and 1st June 1794: the *Russell* took possession of the *Impetueux*, one of the seven French line-of-battle ships taken. Engaged with the French brigands at Vaughlin, Martinique, in 1795; at the capture of Trinidad, in 1797; in the Irish rebellion, in 1798, including the action at Fowk's Mill, liberation of Lord Kingsborough and other Protestants at Wexford, and taking of the French at Ballinamuck. Embarked for the Helder in 1799, and was present at the first landing on the 27th Aug. and battles of the 19th Sept., 2nd and 6th Oct. and retreat from Egmont-op-Zee. Served also the Egyptian campaign of 1801, including the action at the landing, siege and capture of Fort Aboukir, battle of Alexandria, reduction of Rosetta and Fort St. Julian, action at Rahmania, surrender of Cairo and Alexandria. Slightly wounded in Lord Howe's action, and again at the Helder. Medal for services in Egypt.

27 Paymaster Ware served with the 38th in the Burmese war, and was present at the capture of Rangoon and subsequent operations before that place. Served with the 49th throughout the operations in China, except Segoan.

28 Paymaster Webster served at the capture of Martinique in 1809; of Guadaloupe in 1810; and also in the American war in 1814.

29 Paymaster Wright served in the Peninsula with the late 94th, from April 1810 to the end of that war in 1814, including the defence of Cadiz, lines of Torres Vedras, pursuit of Massena, actions of Redinha, Condeixa, Foz d'Arouce, and Sabugal; battle of Fuentes d'Onor, siege and storm of Ciudad Rodrigo, siege and storm of Badajoz, battle of Salamanca, retreat from Madrid to Portugal, battles of Vittoria, Pyrenees, Nivelle, and Orthes; action at Vic Bigorre, and battle of Toulouse.

ADJUTANTS.

	CORNET, 2d LIEUT. or ENSIGN.	LIEUT.	ADJUTANT	WHEN PLACED ON HALF PAY.
Bangs, Wm. Rickett, 47 Foot	3 Feb. 12	10 June 14	3 Aug. 13	25 Mar. 16
P Brown, John Tho., 1 Prov. Bn. of Mil.		26 Oct. 99		25 June 14
Bruce, Thomas, Windsor Foresters	never	never	18 July 99	
Bury, Wm. Aug., 22 Foot	10 Mar. 14	never	10 Mar. 14	25 Dec. 14
Cooke, Robt., Newfoundland Fencibles, *Captain of Invalids, Royal Hospital, Kilmainham*	2 Dec. 03	19 Nov. 05	2 Dec. 03	10 Nov. 16
Crause, John, Recruiting District	29 Dec. 08	25 April 11	6 April 15	25 May 17
Crawford, James, 8 Royal Veteran Batt.	17 April 06	5 May 07	17 April 06	
Ellis, Richard, 97 Foot	29 Jan. 07	17 July 12	2 Feb. 09	25 Dec. 18
Farnan, John, 8 Foot..............	7 April 13	10 Aug. 14	7 April 13	25 Feb. 16
FitzGerald, Dennis, 41 Foot............	15 July 13	never	15 July 13	25 June 16
Fletcher, Richard, Recruiting District....	28 Oct. 08	7 Mar. 11	4 Mar. 13	25 May 17
Fraser, Alexander,[1] New Brunswick Fenc.	25 Mar. 13	24 June 15	25 Mar. 13	25 Feb. 16
Halden, John, 7 Foot..................	18 July 16	never	18 July 16	25 Sept. 17
Henry, John, 91 Foot	9 June 14	never	9 June 14	25 Feb. 16
Holmes, John, Durham Fencible Infantry	never	never	11 May 97	
P W Hope, James,[2] Recruiting District	1 Nov. 09	7 Jan. 13	29 Jan. 36	30 Dec. 43
Ingram, James, Breadalbane Fenc. Inf. ..	10 Mar. 97	never	10 Mar. 97	
Leith, John Kenneth, 12 Foot	12 June 17	never	12 June 17	17 Sept. 18
Lowrie, James, 2 Royal Veteran Batt. ..	24 Feb. 20	never	26 Sept. 22	
Mackenzie, Thomas, 77 Foot...........	never	never	19 Feb. 83	
Muller, William, 85 Foot	never	never	30 Mar. 83	1783
Osborne, Francis, 62 Foot..............	9 Dec. 10	never	9 Dec. 19	15 Mar. 21
Packett, John, Greek Light Infantry	23 May 14	never	23 May 14	1815
Parlour, William, 6 West India Regiment	5 Aug. 13	5 Mar. 16	5 Aug. 13	28 Dec. 17
Peacocke, George, 88 Foot	never	never	31 Mar. 83	1783
Peckett, Sampson, 34 Foot	25 Feb. 13	20 Nov. 16	14 Oct. 13	25 June 17
Reed, Lancelot, 75 Foot	never	never	24 Jan. 83	1783
Stewart, James, 2 Royal Veteran Batt. ..	1 July 95	22 Aug. 96	16 Oct. 06	
Tassie, George, 7 Royal Veteran Batt. ..	13 Dec. 10	never	13 Dec. 10	
Thompson, Tho., Ross & Cromarty Fen. Inf.	never	never	6 June 99	
P Trotter, Thomas, 27 Foot............	27 Oct. 14	never	27 Oct. 14	25 Oct. 16
Turner, Alexander, 3 West India Regt. ..	29 Dec. 14	2 April 18	1 Oct. 18	23 June 25
Young, Robert, 1 Royal Veteran Batt. ..	30 Mar. 20	never	30 Mar. 20	

1 Colonel Fraser served in the American war with the 49th, and highly distinguished himself in the night attack upon the American army at Stoney Creek, where he bayoneted seven of the enemy and took the American General Winder prisoner. He is now a Colonel of Militia in Upper Canada.

2 Lieut. Hope served in the Peninsula from Sept. 1811 to Dec. 1813, including the storming of the enemy's works at Almaraz, action at Arroyo de Molino, battles of Vittoria, the Pyrenees (25th, 30th, and 31st July), and Nivelle. Served also the campaign of 1815, including the battles of Quatre Bras and Waterloo.

	QUARTER-MASTER.	WHEN PLACED ON HALF PAY.
Alexander, John, Royal Artillery	26 Aug. 36	
Allen, Thomas, 1 Garrison Battalion	21 Oct. 13	6 Dec. 14
Amaron, Charles, 23 Dragoons		25 Sept. 07
Anderson, John, 6 West India Regiment	11 Oct. 05	25 June 16
𝔚 Anderton, William, 1 Life Guards	13 Nov. 27	1 Jan. 39
𝔓 Andrews, John, 4 Dragoon Guards	20 June 34	3 Oct. 48
Armstrong, Charles, 12 Lancers	7 July 37	18 July 48
Armstrong, John, 58 Foot	25 April 05	16 Dec. 19
Austin, Nathaniel, 3 Ceylon Regiment	1 May 14	25 June 17
𝔚 Bagshaw, Isaac, 84 Foot	13 Oct. 14	19 Sept. 22
Barker, Alexander, Royal Artillery	27 April 26	31 Dec. 42
Barnes, Samuel, Royal Artillery	1 Feb. 08	
𝔓 Bathurst, William, 1 Life Guards	1 June 28	1 Jan. 31
Bell, Robert, 5 West India Regiment	25 Sept. 12	29 Dec. 17
Benton, William, 72 Foot	1 Nov. 04	
Betson, William,[7] 15 Hussars	1 Nov. 35	1 Sept. 48
𝔓 𝔚 *Bishop, William*, 1 Life Guards	19 June 15	
Black, James,[1] Ceylon Regiment	10 Aug. 26	30 May 43
Blay, Samuel Sutton, 72 Foot	5 Mar. 12	25 June 16
𝔓 Blenkinsop, William,[2] 10 Foot	13 Aug. 29	21 Sept. 41
Blythman, William, 69 Foot	28 Sept. 15	25 Nov. 16
𝔓 Booth, Jonathan,[3] 60 Foot	4 May 26	27 July 38
𝔓 Brand, James,[4] 5 Dragoon Guards	17 July 35	18 June 41
𝔓 𝔚 Brannan, John,[5] 60 Foot (*Ens.* 5 Sept. 35)	18 Sept. 35	28 May 47
𝔚 Brown, John,[6] 1 Dragoon Guards	15 June 15	30 Mar. 38
Browning, Henry, Cambridge Fencible Cavalry		
Buchanan, William, (Ens. 24 Feb. 20), 1 R. Vet. Batt.	6 Feb. 12	
Burns, Cormick, 96 Foot	11 Mar. 13	1814
Burrough, Thomas, 60 Foot	26 Aug. 13	10 July 17
Calder, James, 92 Foot	8 Feb. 35	6 Sept. 39
Calueve, Pierre de, Royal Waggon Train		
Cambidge, Robert, 21 Dragoons		25 Aug. 02
Campbell, Jeremiah, 12 Foot	28 July 14	11 Nov. 24
Campbell, William, 80 Foot	31 Jan. 22	10 Feb. 37
Carden, James, 30 Dragoons		1 Mar. 98
Carroll, James, 18 Foot	4 June 29	23 July 44
𝔓 𝔚 Carter, John Henry, 1 Life Guards	25 Oct. 26	1 Jan. 31
Carter, William, Rutland Fencible Cavalry		
Chalmers, William, 94 Foot	27 July 05	
Cherriman, John, 11 Dragoons	4 Jan. 10	25 Sept. 18
Clark, Alexander, Royal Artillery	16 Jan. 07	
Clarke, William, Royal Staff Corps	24 April 28	25 Aug. 29
Clayton, Thomas, Hants Fencible Cavalry		
Cockburn, James, 8 Dragoons	13 July 15	24 June 24
𝔓 Collins, Francis,[9] 11 Hussars	6 Feb. 34	5 Mar. 47
𝔚 Collins, John, 18 Dragoons	12 June 17	10 Nov. 21
Conolly, Patrick, 20 Foot	19 Aug. 27	17 Sept. 41
Costello, Pierce, 32 Dragoons		1 Mar. 98
Crooks, William Smedley, 2 Life Guards	7 Jan. 28	1 Jan. 31
Crymble, William, 64 Foot	27 May 13	
Daines, Charles, 26 Foot	24 Sept. 41	2 April 47
Dallas, Alexander, Bourbon Regiment	3 Aug. 20	18 Nov. 24
Dandy, John, 90 Foot	7 Mar. 22	7 Sept. 26
𝔚 Davidson, James,[11] 41 Foot	14 Feb. 28	22 July 36
Debenham, Thomas, 56 Foot	17 Feb. 35	3 May 44
Dixon, James (*Cor.* 13 Oct. 19), 104 Foot	25 June 24	8 Jan. 29
𝔓 𝔚 *Dobson, William*, 1 Life Guards	8 Sept. 12	
Duncan, James, Perth Fencible Cavalry		
𝔓 Dwelly, Thomas,[12] Coldstream Guards	15 Oct. 12	25 July 37
Ebdon, Richard, 3 Dragoons		25 Mar. 10
Edwards, George, 85 Foot	25 Oct. 27	30 April 41
Edwards, Peter, 10 Dragoons		8 Jan. 03
Edwards, Thomas Willock,[13] 84 Foot	3 Dec. 12	17 Feb. 32
Ellary, William,[14] 59 Foot	10 June 21	21 May 41
𝔚 Ellington, John,[15] 2 Life Guards	19 June 15	11 Mar. 22
Elliott, James, 65 Foot	23 Nov. 04	26 April 39

	QUARTER-MASTER.	WHEN PLACED ON HALF PAY
Ellis, John, 22 Dragoons		25 June 03
P W Emmott, William,[16] Royal Horse Guards, *Adjutant, Worcestershire Yeomanry Cavalry*	25 Sept. 28	1 Jan. 31
P Fair, William,[17] (*Ens.* 14 Dec. 20), 53 Foot	15 April 13	25 June 41
P W Fairbrother, Carter,[18] Royal Horse Guards	7 Nov. 29	1 Jan. 31
W Falconer, Robert, 1 Life Guards	2 Sept. 36	29 Jan. 47
Farrants, James, 103 Foot	9 May 11	29 Mar. 18
Farrell, James, 84 Foot	12 May 37	23 May 48
Fife, James, Royal Artillery	10 Sept. 32	
Fitzgerald, Thomas, 71 Foot	17 Oct. 45	10 Mar. 48
Forbes, John, 91 Foot	6 Sep. 39	1 Aug. 48
Fortune, Alexander, Royal Artillery	26 July 27	
Fox, Samuel, 96 Foot	19 July 39	25 Feb. 48
Frith, Joseph, Royal Horse Guards, *Adjutant, Dorset Yeomanry Cavalry*	25 Dec. 28	1 Jan. 31
Fraser, Alexander, Canadian Fencibles	28 Sept. 09	11 Oct. 16
Fraser, Donald, 74 Foot	25 Nov. 05	
P W Frost, John,[19] Royal Horse Guards	31 May 28	1 Jan. 31
Gates, William, Royal Artillery	15 Nov. 09	24 Mar. 41
Gillan, James, 41 Foot	20 Sept. 44	9 April 47
Gillie, John, 12 Dragoons		25 Dec. 22
Godwin, John, Hants Fencible Cavalry		
Goodfellow, Joseph,[20] 10 Foot	21 Feb. 28	3 Mar. 48
W Grant, Bernard,[21] 82 Foot	28 Aug. 35	11 Feb. 48
Greig, George, 2 Life Guards	26 Jan. 24	1 Jan. 31
Grimwood, Thomas, 56 Foot	25 Nov. 11	25 July 14
Grove, Joseph, 3 Dragoon Guards		25 June 16
Guest, Charles, Pembroke Fencible Cavalry		
P Guy, Wm.[22] 62 F. (*Ens.* 2 May 34; *Lt.* 27 May 36.)	8 Apr. 35	10 Sept. 47
Haddon, Richard, 10 Dragoons		25 Mar. 10
Hadley, Wm. H.S.,[23] (*Ens.* 10 Apr. 25; *Lt.* 24 Sept. 31) 2 Foot	12 Aug. 36	27 Oct. 46
W Hall, John, 6 West India Regiment	29 Sept. 14	14 Jan. 19
P W Hanna, William,[24] 4 Foot	8 Jan. 29	27 May 36
Harding, John, 3 Foot	31 Oct. 03	8 May 17
W Hardy, Luke, New Brunswick Fencibles	13 Jan. 25	3 Aug. 26
W Hardy, Thomas, Royal Horse Guards	13 Feb. 12	25 Aug. 22
Harker, Robert,[25] 41 Foot	6 Jan. 32	20 Sept. 44
Harrison, Alexander, 1 Garrison Battalion	22 Jan. 13	25 Sept. 17
Harrison, Daniel Charles Rogers, 11 Foot	8 Sept. 08	15 July 16
Haslam, Richard, 5 Dragoon Guards	25 Aug. 09	17 June 13
P W Healey, Thomas,[26] 32 Foot	29 Nov. 27	28 June 44
P W Heartley, Andrew,[27] Royal Horse Guards, *Adjutant, East Kent Yeomanry Cavalry, Military Knight of Windsor*	12 Dec. 22	1 Jan. 31
Hendley, Thomas, Royal Artillery	23 Jan. 34	1846
Henstock, Henry, 5 Foot	1 Feb. 16	25 July 16
Hewetson, Hamilton, 4 Dragoon Guards		25 June 02
P Higgins, Henry,[28] 7 Dragoon Guards	14 April 25	10 Mar. 43
W Hill, William, Rifle Brigade	25 Dec. 26	29 Mar. 39
Hilliard, John, Cornwall Fencible Cavalry		
Hilton, James, Royal Sappers and Miners	9 Nov. 35	14 Jan. 48
Hodder, John, 1 Regiment Fencible Cavalry		
Hornby, William, 66 Foot	1 Feb. 27	27 Sept. 42
Horne, Robert, 2 Dragoon Guards	5 April 08	25 Aug. 18
Horner, Isaac, 33 Dragoons	21 Oct. 95	1 Mar. 98
P Hudson, Edward,[29] 23 Foot	28 Sept. 09	25 Dec. 14
Hume, Wm., 72 F., *Town Adjutant at Gibraltar*	24 April 38	23 July 47
Jackson, Henry, Royal Horse Guards	28 April 27	1 Jan. 31
Jackson, John, 3 Dragoons		25 Jan. 13
Jennings, John, Essex Fencible Cavalry		
Innes, William, Nugent's Recruiting Corps	22 Dec. 09	
Johnston, Alexander, 60 Foot	24 Sept. 12	28 Sept. 20
Julyan, Thomas, Cornwall Fencible Cavalry		
Kelly, Richard Seymour, Royal Staff Corps	26 Jan. 26	July 38
Kenny, William,[31] 51 Foot	10 June 13	20 Aug. 44
Kenyon, Henry, (*Ens.* 29 Oct. 12), 2 R. Veteran Batt.	15 June 20	

	QUARTER-MASTER.	WHEN PLACED ON HALF PAY.
𝔚 Kerr, William, 28 Foot (*Ens.* 7 *July* 37)	1 June 38	23 July 44
Kewin, Miles, 5 Royal Veteran Battalion	2 July 12	
𝔓 𝔚 Kinkee, Frederick,[33] 19 Dragoons	1 July 24	18 Aug. 25
Ledger, Thomas, 15 Dragoons		25 April 11
𝔓 Ledsam, John,[34] 7 Foot, *Military Knight of Windsor*	20 Apr. 26	1 Oct. 47
Lord, Robert, Royal Horse Guards	16 Oct. 12	
M'Clellan, James Creighton,[36] 10 Dragoons	28 Jan. 19	19 May 46
M'Clenahan, Thomas, 2 Garrison Battalion	4 Nov. 13	25 Dec. 16
M'Curdy, Daniel, 74 Foot	28 Aug. 31	26 April 44
M'Pherson, John,[38] 72 Foot	9 Sept. 13	2 Mar. 38
Macdonald, Geo.,[39] 93 Foot, *Staff Offi. of Pensioners*	13 Dec. 39	22 Mar. 44
Macdonald, William, 104 Foot	14 April 14	25 July 17
Mackay, Donald, 42 Foot	12 Oct. 04	18 Mar. 13
Mackenzie, John, 7 Foot	16 Mar. 20	2 Jan. 23
Maitland, John, 37 Foot	22 July 13	25 May 17
Maitland, Peter, 90 Foot	9 Feb. 09	15 Sept. 37
Manley, John, 36 Foot	22 Oct. 12	25 Dec. 14
Mansfield, William,[40] 22 Foot	21 April 11	
Matthews, William, Royal Artillery	25 July 31	4 Aug. 43
Maudsley, John,[35] 8 Hussars	29 Sept. 25	29 Nov. 39
Merrie, William, 2 Dragoons		25 Aug. 10
Mew, William, 67 Foot	16 Feb. 26	25 Oct. 39
Midwinter, Thomas, 1 Life Guards	19 June 15	
Miller, George, 2 Life Guards	21 Sept. 21	1 Jan. 31
Mingay, John, 92 Foot	12 May 83	
𝔓 𝔚 Moore, Garrett,[41] 23 Foot	8 Nov. 27	5 July 44
Moore, George, 57 Foot	18 Dec. 06	
Moore, John, 3 Garrison Battalion	26 Oct. 15	25 Nov. 16
𝔓 Morgan, John,[42] 52 Foot	1 Jan. 24	29 Dec. 37
Morris, William, 19 Foot	15 Oct. 14	
Mulholland, Andrew, 18 Foot	28 May 12	25 Dec. 14
Murray, James,[43] 24 Foot	4 Dec. 17	16 Aug. 42
Newland, William, 90 Foot	15 Sept. 37	18 April 4
North, William, 2 Life Guards	11 July 15	
𝔓 O'Brien, Bartholomew,[44] 5 Dragoon Guards	1 Feb. 27	17 July 35
𝔓 *O'Grady, William*,[44]* 12 Foot	1 Oct. 07	
O'Reilly, John, 13 Dragoons	25 Dec. 28	2 April 47
Palmer, Samuel, 31 Foot	8 May 26	13 July 41
Paterson, Charles, Princess Royal's Own Fenc. Cav.		
Pegley, Robert, 4 Royal Veteran Battalion	24 Feb. 20	
Pittard, Thomas, Oxford Fencible Cavalry		
𝔓 Powell, John,[45] 77 Foot, *Military Knight of Windsor*	21 June 10	7 April 37
𝔓 Pratt, David,[46] (*Cornet*, 5 *Sept.* 11; *Lieut.* 26 *Oct.* 12), 16 Dragoons	25 Jan. 16	23 Sept. 36
Proudfoot, William, Perth Fencible Cavalry		
Quaile, Robert Orr, 17 Dragoons		25 Feb. 27
Rafferty, George William, 6 Foot	4 Mar. 42	28 June 44
𝔓 Rand, Samuel,[47] 43 Foot	8 Oct. 30	15 Aug. 48
Rendell, John Gill, 40 Foot	14 Mar. 11	25 Feb. 16
Rice, Thomas, Cinque Ports Fencible Cavalry		
Roberts, James, 16 Dragoons		25 Feb. 14
𝔓 *Roberts, John*,[48] 81 Foot	28 April 08	
Rogers, Thomas, 25 Dragoons		25 Dec. 18
Russell, Richard, 25 Dragoons		25 Jan. 20
Ryall, John, Dumfries Fencible Cavalry		
Salter, Robert, Fife Fencible Cavalry	20 Nov. 94	
Sanderson, Joseph Prossor, 47 Foot	28 May 07	28 May 18
Sewell, William, Staff Corps of Cavalry	20 Jan. 14	25 Feb. 19
Sheridan, Mark,[49] 13 Foot	18 Feb. 13	16 Apr. 47
𝔓 Shirley, John,[50] Royal Horse Guards, *Adjutant, North Salopian Yeomanry Cavalry*	14 Sept. 26	1 Jan. 31
𝔚 *Sidley, George*, 23 Foot	14 April 08	
Simpson, Edward, 2 Life Guards	25 Mar. 22	1 Jan. 31
𝔓 Sleator, Joseph,[51] 97 Foot	24 Feb. 25	12 June 46

	Quarter-Master.	When placed on Half Pay.
Smart, Robert, 6 Foot	2 April 07	
P Smedley, Thomas,[52] 77 Foot	7 April 37	23 June 48
P W Steel, Joseph, 1 Life Guards	10 Oct. 26	1 Jan. 31
Stephens, John,[53] Royal African Corps	14 Sept. 15	9 Dec. 31
Stevens, George, 5 West India Regiment	13 Aug. 18	28 July 25
P Stubbs, Joshua,[54] 48 Foot	5 May 08	26 June 35
W Thompson, William, Scots Fusilier Guards....	6 May 19	7 April 37
Thomson, Joseph, 4 Royal Veteran Battalion	11 May 15	
Thomson, William, 22 Foot	17 Mar. 14	25 Dec. 14
P Tiller, William,[55] 5 Foot	5 May 25	23 July 47
P W ***Troy, Thomas,***[56] Royal Horse Guards	5 Aug. 13	
W ***Waddall, William,*** 1 Dragoons	8 July 13	
Wagstaff, William, 1 Dragoon Guards	24 Oct. 05	25 Mar. 16
Wakefield, William, 3 W. Ind. Regt. (*Ens.* 1 Feb. 28.)	13 Dec. 30	16 Apr. 47
Wales, John, 6 Dragoons		25 April 15
Wallis, Samuel,[57] 69 Foot	1 Feb. 23	3 Nov. 37
Walsh, William, 21 Foot	16 June 08	
P Ward, John,[58] 30 Foot	21 Oct. 24	28 May 47
Watson, John Thomas, 5 Foot	10 Oct. 11	26 Mar. 18
Webster, William, 2 Life Guards	11 Mar. 22	1 Jan. 31
P Weston, Charles,[59] Scots Fusilier Guards	28 Dec. 15	9 Aug. 33
Williams, Harry,[60] 3 Foot (*Ens.* 12 Aug. 18)	14 Dec. 32	16 Sept. 45
Williamson, David, Breadalbane Fencible Infantry	25 April 96	
W Willox, James, 54 Foot	27 Sept. 27	11 Sept. 46
Wilton, Samuel, 2 Dragoon Guards		25 June 02
Winkworth, William, Cambridge Fencible Cavalry		
Wright, Thomas,[61] 9 Dragoons	11 Aug. 25	17 Aug. 38
* Wynne, Richard Miles, 3 Prov. Batt. of Militia..	25 Dec. 13	1814

War Services of the Quarter-Masters.

1 Quarter-Master Black served the campaigns of 1813 and 14, in Germany and Holland, and as present at the attack upon Bergen-op-Zoom.

2 Quarter-Master Bleakinsop was present in the action before Alcoy, in Spain.

3 Quarter-Master Booth served the campaign in Spain from Oct. 1808 to Jan. 1809.

4 Quarter-Master Brand served in the Peninsula with the 1st Life Guards.

5 Quarter-Master Brannan served in the Peninsula, France, and Flanders, from July 1809, the end of the war, including the battle of Busaco; 1st siege of Badajoz; battle of Albuhera everely wounded); actions of Arroyo del Molinos and Castle Murrenito; battles of Vittoria lightly wounded), the Pyrenees, 7th, 10th, 25th, and 31st July, Nivelle, Nive, 9th Dec., and efore Bayonne 13th Dec. (slightly wounded), St. Palais, Orthes, Lambeige, Toulouse, Quatre ras, and Waterloo.

6 Quar.-Master Brown served the campaign of 1815, and was present at the battle of Waterloo.

7 Quarter-Master Betson served at the siege and capture of Bhurtpore in 1825-6.

9 Quarter-Master Francis Collins served in the Peninsula from Oct. 1809 to the end of that ar in 1814, including the Battle of Busaco, retreat to the lines of Torres Vedras and subsequent advance, battle of Fuentes d'Onor, siege of Ciudad Rodrigo, battle of Salamanca, capture Madrid, siege of Burgos and retreat to the frontiers of Portugal, battle of Vittoria, siege of an Sebastian, crossing of the Bidassoa, battle of the Nive, passage of the Adour, investment of ayonne and repulse of the sortie, on which occasion he was wounded through the left arm.

11 Quarter-Master Davidson served the campaigns of 1814 and 15 in Holland, Flanders, and rance, including the action at Merxem, bombardment of Antwerp (wounded), storming of ergen-op-Zoom, battles of Quatre Bras and Waterloo (twice wounded), and capture of Paris.

12 Quarter-Master Dwelly served with the 1st battalion of Coldstream Guards, in Holland, 1799; in Egypt in 1801; at Bremen, in 1805; at Copenhagen, in 1807; and in the Peninsula om the beginning of 1809 to early in 1813.

13 Quarter-Master T. W. Edwards served in the East Indies from Nov. 1796 to 1830, during hich long period he was actively employed in nearly all the campaigns and engagements hich took place, commencing with the battle of Malavelly, and terminating with the Burmese ar. Medal for the capture of Seringapatam.

14 Quarter-Master Ellary served at the capture of the Cape of Good Hope in 1806; in the ravancore war, in the East Indies, in 1809; capture of the Isle of France in 1810; storming of ort Cornelius and capture of Java in 1811; Balli and Macassar in 1814; Kandian campaign 1818; siege and assault at Bhurtpore in 1825-6.

15 Quarter-Master Ellington served the campaign of 1815, and was present at the battle of aterloo.

16 Quarter-Master Emmott served in the Peninsula from Oct. 1812 to the end of that war in 14, and was present at the battle of Vittoria. Served also the campaign of 1815, including battle of Waterloo.

17 Quarter-Master Fair served in the expedition to South America in 1807, including the rming and capture of Monte Video (wounded), attack and reduction of the enemy's camp at lonia, advance and attack on Buenos Ayres, attack and reduction of the convent of St. mingo, at which he was taken prisoner. In the Peninsula, under Sir John Moore, including retreat to Corunna. Expedition to Walcheren in 1809.

18 Quarter-Master Fairbrother served in the Peninsula from Oct. 1812, to the end of that r in 1814, and was present at the battle of Vittoria. Served also the campaign of 1815, luding the battle of Waterloo.

19 Quarter-Master Frost served in the Peninsula from Oct. 1812 to the end of that war in 14, and was present at the battle of Vittoria. Served also the campaign of 1815, including battle of Waterloo.

20 Quarter-Master Goodfellow served with the 14th in the Nepaul war in 1814-15; at siege and capture of Hattras in 1817; in the Pindarree and Mahratta campaigns of 1817 1 18; and at the siege and storming of Bhurtpore in 1826. He served with the 26th oughout the war in China (medal), and was present at the capture of Chusan, operations ore Canton, repulse of the night attack on Ningpo, attack and capture of the enemy's renched camp on the heights of Segoan, attack and capture of Chapoo, taking of Shanghae l Woosung, assault and capture of Chin Kiang Foo, and investment of Nankin.

21 Quarter-Master Grant served the campaign of 1815, including the battle of Waterloo and ture of Paris.

2 Lieut. Guy served in the Peninsula, from Sept. 1813 to the conclusion of the war, and was he battles of the Nivelle and the Nive, and in the action at the Mayor's House; also at the estment of Bayonne in 1814.

3 Lieut. Hadley served with the Queen's Royals throughout the campaign in Affghanistan Beloochistan, under Lord Keane, and was present at the storm and capture of Ghuznee unded), and of Khelat. He served also the campaign in the Southern Mahratta country in 4 (including the storm of the Fortress of Punella), and that in the Concan in 1845. Medal Ghuznee.

4 Quarter-Master Hanna was present at the assault and capture of Badajos, battles of amanca and Vittoria, and siege of San Sebastian. Served in the American war in 1814

and 15, and was present at Washington, Baltimore, and New Orleans. Also the campaign of 1815, including the battle of Waterloo.

25 Quarter-Master Harker served with the 22nd throughout the campaign of 1843 in Scinde, under Sir Charles Napier, and was present at the battles of Meeanee and Hyderabad.

26 Quarter-Master Healey served with the 32nd at Copenhagen in 1807; in the Peninsula in 1808-9, including the battles of Roleia, Vimiera, and Corunna; at the siege of Flushing; in the Peninsula from 1811 to the end of that war in 1814, including the battles of Salamanca, the Pyrenees, the Nivelle, the Nive, and Orthes. He served also the campaign of 1815, and was present at the battles of Quatre Bras and Waterloo.

27 Quarter-Master Heartley served in the Peninsula from Oct. 1812 to the end of that war in 1814, and was present at the battle of Vittoria. Served also the campaign of 1815, including the battle of Waterloo.

28 Quarter-Master Higgins served at Walcheren in 1809, and in the Peninsula from July 1811 to the end of that war, including the battles of Salamanca, Vittoria, and Toulouse, and other minor actions in which the 3rd Light Dragoons were engaged.

29 Quarter-Master Hudson joined the 23rd in 1796, and was on the expedition with the flank companies to Ostend in 1798, and taken prisoner. The following year he served the campaign in Holland, including the landing at the Helder, and the actions of the 10th and 19th Sept., 2nd and 6th October. In 1801 he served the Egyptian campaign, including the action on the landing, and those of the 12th, 13th, and 21st March (severely wounded). In 1805 he served in Hanover; and in 1807 on the expedition to Denmark, and was present in the actions of the 17th and 24th August in front of Copenhagen. From 1810 to 1814 he served in the Peninsula, and was present at the battle of Albuhera, the siege and storming of Badajoz, and other actions during the above period.

31 Quarter-Master Kenny served at the taking of Castine in North America, in 1814.

33 Quarter-Master Kinkee served in the Peninsula, France, and Flanders, from Jan. 1811 to the end of the war in 1815, including the action at Morales de Toro, and battles of Vittoria, Pyrenees, Orthes, and Waterloo.

34 Quarter-Master Ledsam's services:—Expedition to Copenhagen in 1807; Peninsula from July 1810 to the end of the war, including the battles of Busaco, and Albuhera; siege and capture of Ciudad Rodrigo, and Badajoz; battles of Salamanca, Vittoria, Pampeluna, Orthes, and Toulouse. Present at the attack on New Orleans in 1815.

35 Quarter-Master Mandsley served under Sir Thomas Trowbridge in an engagement with three French ships in 1810. Served also at Callinger in the East Indies in 1810 and 11; Husscinabad, Ramnaghur, and Kalunga; Hattrass, and in the Deccan in 1817 and 18. Wounded in the right arm, left shoulder, and slightly in the abdomen at the attack of Fort Kalunga.

36 Quarter-Master M'Clellan served throughout the campaigns of 1813 and 14 on the Niagara Frontiers, including the action before Fort George, Blackrock, Buffalo, Chippewa, Lundy's Lane, Niagara, before Fort Erie, Cook's mills, and pass of Grand River. Received a contusion in the head by a musket shot at the moment of passing through the enemy's line in the charge at Chippewa 4th July 1814.

38 Quarter-Master M'Pherson served in Ireland during the rebellion in 1798, including the battle of Ballinamuck. Served also at the capture of the Cape of Good Hope in 1806, and was present at the battle of Blueberg.

39 Quarter-Master Macdonald was actively employed with his Regt. in suppressing the insurrection in Canada in 1838, and was present at the attack and capture of the American brigands at the Windmill, near Prescote.

40 Quarter-Master Mansfield served during twenty years in the East Indies, including the storming of Fort Barabatty in 1803, where he was wounded; and the Mahratta campaigns of 1804, 5, and 6, under Lord Lake. Served also at the capture of the Isle of France, in 1810.

41 Quarter-Master Garrett Moore's services:—Campaign of 1799 in Holland, including the actions on the landing near the Helder, Zyp Dyke, Sand Hills, and Egmont-op-Zee, and taking of Hoorn by surprise. Egyptian campaign of 1801, including the action on landing, 8th March, and the actions of the 12th, 13th, and 21st March; siege and capture of Alexandria. Expedition to, and actions of the 17th and 24th Aug. 1807, in front of Copenhagen. Sieges of Forts Royal and Bourbon, and action in front of Fort Bourbon, Martinique. Peninsula from 1810, to the end of the war, including the following; viz., actions near Redulia, Condeixa, Aldea de Ponte; battles of Salamanca, Vittoria, Nivelle, Nive, Orthes, and Toulouse; sieges of Olivença, Badajoz, Ciudad Rodrigo, Badajoz taken by storm, and forts near Salamanca. Present at Waterloo and the storming of Cambray.

42 Quarter-Master Morgan served throughout the whole of the Peninsular war, with the exception of a few months, including the following battles, sieges, &c., viz., Corunna, Almeida, Busaco, Pombal, Redinha, Miranda de Corvo, Condeixa, Foz d'Arouce, Sabugal, Fuentes d'Onor, Ciudad Rodrigo (a volunteer on the storming party, and wounded in the left leg), and Badajoz (again a volunteer on the storming party, and severely contused on the head).

43 Quarter-Master Murray's services:—Egyptian campaign of 1801; capture of the Cape of Good Hope in 1806; Nepaul campaigns of 1814, 15, and 16; Mahratta war, in 1817 and 18.

44 Quarter-Master O'Brien served in the Peninsula from Aug. 1811 to the end of that war in 1814, including the action at Llerena (wounded) and battles of Vittoria, Orthes, and Toulouse.

44* Quarter-Master O'Grady embarked with Lord Moira's expedition to Ostend in 17[illegible] received a sabre wound in the head at Alost, was subsequently wounded on Picquet by a musket-ball in the left ankle, and taken prisoner when Bergen-op-Zoom was given up. In 1797 he embarked for the West Indies, and was afterwards present with the expedition to Martinique, capture of Surinam and Curaçoa. He next served on the expedition to South America; was one of the forlorn hope at the storming of Monte Video, and also present at the taking of Buenos Ayres. In 1809 he accompanied his Regt. (the 87th) to Spain, and was present at the defence of Cadiz and Tarifa (wounded in the hand), and at the battles of Talavera, Barrosa, Vittoria, Nivelle, Orthes, and Toulouse.

45 Quarter-Master Powell served in the East Indies from May 1788 to Sept. 1807, including the reduction of Cannanore, campaign against Tippoo, terminating at Seringapatam 14th Feb. 1792; capture of Cochin, 20th Oct. 1795; capitulation of Colombo and its dependencies, 16th Feb. 1796; campaign against Tippoo in 1799, including the affair of Seedasseer, and the reduction of Seringapatam; assault and capture of Jamalabad, Sept. 1799; campaign against Doondia Waugh; campaign in Wynaad (severely wounded through the left wrist by a musket-shot on a reconnoitring party, 22nd Jan. 1801); assault of Pangalamoourchy; assault and capture of Anakenny. Served also in the Peninsula from June 1811 to the end of that war in 1814.

46 Lieut. Pratt served in the Peninsula from April 1809 to the end of that war in 1814, including the passage of the Douro, and battles of Talavera, Busaco, Fuentes d'Onor, Salamanca, Vittoria, and investment of Bayonne. Served also at Bhurtpore, under Lord Combermere.

47 Quarter-Master Rand's services:—battles of Vimiera and Corunna. Expedition to Walcheren 1809. Peninsular campaigns from 1811 to the end of the war, including the siege and storming of Badajoz (severely wounded at the assault); battles of Salamanca and Vittoria; attack on the heights of Vera; battles of Nivelle, Nive, and Toulouse. Battle in front of New Orleans, 8th Jan. 1815.

48 Quarter-Master John Roberts served on Lord Moira's expedition and with the Duke of York, in 1794 and 1795, and was present at the siege of Nimeguen and other affairs of imporance. From 1795 to 1801 he served in Hanover, Madeira, and the West Indies, and was present at the taking of the Danish and Swedish Islands, and he served also against the Brigands in Grenada, and against the Caribs in St. Vincent. From 1808 to 1810 he served in the Peninsular Campaigns, including the passage of the Douro, battle of Talavera, and several affairs of outposts.

49 Quarter-Master Sheridan served at the Ferrol; throughout the campaign of 1801 in Egypt; at the capture of Martinique in 1809; throughout the Burmese war.

50 Quarter-Master Shirley served in the Peninsula from Oct. 1812 to May 1813, and again from Jan. 1814 to the end of that war.

51 Quarter-Master Sleator served in Sicily and in the Peninsula from 1805 to the end of that war in 1814.

52 Quarter-Master Smedley served in the Peninsula with the 77th, from July 1811 to Feb. 1813, and again from Oct. 1813 to the end of that war in 1814.

53 Quarter-Master John Stephens served in the Nepaul war in the East Indies.

54 Quarter-Master Stubbs served at the blockade of Malta, in 1800; and in the Peninsula from June 1809 to the end of that war in 1814; including the battles of Talavera and Busaco, siege and capture of Badajoz, and battles of Vittoria, Pampeluna, Orthes, and Toulouse.

55 Quarter-Master Tiller served with the 5th at Walcheren, and was severely wounded in the head, and slightly in the left hand at the siege of Flushing on the 7th Aug. 1809. In the Peninsula from 1812 to May 1814, including the battles of Vittoria, the Nivelle, Orthes, and Toulouse.

56 Quarter-Master Troy served in the campaigns in the Peninsula, France, and Flanders with the Royal Horse Guards, and was present at every action in which that Regt. was engaged, including the battle of Waterloo.

57 Quarter-Master Wallis served in the Burmese war.

58 Quarter-Master Ward served in the Peninsula with the 30th from March 1809 to June 1813, including the defence of Cadiz from 4th June to 25th Sept. 1810; occupation of the Lines of Torres Vedras, pursuit of Massena, actions of Sabagul, Almeida, and Barba del Puerco, battle of Fuentes d'Onor, siege of Badajos, and action of Villa Muriel. Served the campaign of 1814 in Holland, under Sir Thomas Graham; and that of 1815, under the Duke of Wellington.

59 Quarter-Master Weston served with the expedition to Hanover in 1805; and with that to Copenhagen in 1807. Served also in the Peninsula from 30th Dec. 1808 to the end of that war in 1814, including the passage of the Douro and capture of Oporto, battles of Busaco and Fuentes d'Onor, siege of Ciudad Rodrigo, covering the siege of Badajoz, battle of Salamanca, capture of Madrid, siege of Burgos, battle of Vittoria, siege of San Sebastian, passage of the Bidassoa, battle of the Nive (9th to 13th Dec.), passage of the Adour, investment of Bayonne and repulse of the sortie.

60 Quarter-Master Williams was present with the Buffs at the battle of Punniar on the 29th Dec. 1843, and has received the Bronze Star.

61 Quarter-Master Willox served with the 54th in Stralsund under General Gibbs in 1813, and the subsequent campaign in Holland under Lord Lynedoch, including the attack on Mexem and bombardment of Antwerp. He served also the campaign of 1815, including the storming and capture of Paris; and finally in the Burmese war, including the attack and capture of Mahatee, and the assault and capture of Arracan.

62 Quarter-Master Thomas Wright served in South America in 1807, under General Whitelock; also at Walcheren in 1809, including the siege of Flushing.

COMMISSARIAT DEPARTMENT.

COMMISSARIES-GENERAL.

𝔓 Adams, Joseph Hollingworth 20 Jan. 37
𝔓 Bisset, *Sir* John, KCH. ....31 July 11
𝔓 Carey, Tupper ....24 Dec. 44
Cocksedge, Henry ....20 Jan. 37
𝔓 Coffin, Edward Pine .... 1 July 40
𝔓 Dalrymple, *Sir* Charles ....29 Jan. 12
𝔓 Dickens, James............19 July 21
𝔓 Drake, John ....30 Aug. 33
𝔓 Dunmore, Thomas ....25 Dec. 14
Granet, Augustus ....25 Dec. 14
𝔓 Haines, Gregory ....30 Aug. 33
Hewetson, William ....23 Dec. 43
Luscombe, Tho. Popham ......15 Aug. 26
𝔓 Routh, *Sir* Randolph Isham, KCB.15 Aug. 26

DEPUTY-COMMISSARIES-GENERAL.

Allan, David ....13 June 13
𝔓 Auther, William ....20 Jan. 37
𝔓 Barney, Richard............19 July 21
Bent, Thomas Hamlyn ....19 Mar. 07
Bland, John ....26 Dec. 46
𝔓 Booth, William ....18 Dec. 18
Brown, Richard..............29 May 93
Clarke, Charles A............16 Dec. 45
Couche, Edward..............12 Aug. 06
𝔓 Cumming, William ....10 Sept. 30
Forbes, Charles John..........25 July 15
𝔓 Grieve, William............ 3 Feb. 13
Hagenau, John Frederick ......25 Dec. 14
𝔓 Hill, Hugh ....20 Jan. 37
Hopkins, Samuel..............25 Dec. 14
𝔓 Kearney, Daniel ....13 Dec. 33
Low, Isaac ....25 May 97
𝔓 Lukin, William .... 2 Sept. 14
𝔓 Major, Francis Wm. A. C. ..16 Dec. 45
Malassez, Nicholas............20 Jan. 37
Miles, George................ 8 Sept. 10
𝔓 Moore, George ....10 Sept. 30
𝔓 Nugent, Geo. Steph. N. Hodges22 Oct. 16
𝔓 Ogilvie, James ....22 Mar. 12
Osborn, Thomas..............28 June 38
𝔓 Robinson, Edward Cooke....22 Oct. 16
𝔓 St. Remy, P. C. Lelievre de 19 July 21
Schmidchen, Augustus ....27 July 12
Singer, Paulus Æmilius (*Ireland*) 1 April 00
Somerville, Alexander ....19 July 21
𝔓 Spurrier, John ....10 Sept. 30
Sweetland, John..............16 Nov. 02
Tochell, John (Musters) ......19 Nov. 05
Telfer, Buchan Fraser ....25 Dec. 14
Tench, John ....16 Dec. 45
Thompson, James ....16 Dec. 45
Thomson, William ....26 Dec. 46
𝔓 Wemyss, William ....25 Dec. 14
Wethered, Thomas............21 Mar. 07
𝔓 White, George ....20 Nov. 15
Woodhouse, James, CMG. .... 7 June 25

ASSISTANT-COMMISSARIES-GENERAL.

Allsopp, Robert ....10 Sept. 30
Bailey, Michael ....20 Jan. 37
𝔓 Bayley, Henry A. .... 1 July 40
Beech, William ....24 Feb. 10
Birney, George (*Ireland*)......25 June 08
Campbell, James ....26 Dec. 46
Carr, Samuel ....24 Dec. 41
𝔓 Carruthers, David..........24 Feb. 10
𝔓 Chalmers, Andrew..........20 Jan. 37
Charters, Robert.............. 1 July 40
𝔓 Chiaranda, Francis Leonard ..10 Sept. 30
Child, George................ 4 May 15
Clark, Thomas .... 1 July 40
Colvill, Robert (*Ireland*)......23 Feb. 09
Courtenay, George Townsend ..26 Sept. 06
Cramer, Henry John .... 4 May 15
Crookshank, George .... 3 Aug. 14
Davidson, John ....20 Jan. 37
Davidson, Peter Fraser ....19 July 21
Dillon, William (*Ireland*) ....25 June 03
Engelbach, Thomas Lewis .... 1 May 01
Gelston, Thomas (*Ireland*) ....25 June 03
Goldriak, James (*Ireland*) .... 1 Jan. 99
Grellier, George.............. 3 Feb. 07
Grindlay, Robert ....30 July 25
𝔓 Head, *Sir* George ....25 Dec. 14
Heydinger, William Charles....26 May 12
Hoffay, Ernest Albert .... 1 July 40
Howard, Charles..............26 Dec. 43
𝔓 Jennings, William.......... 7 June 25
𝔓 Kearney, Thomas ....10 Aug. 11
Ledwith, William (*Ireland*)....25 Mar. 14
Lee, Robert .... 1 July 40
Lithgow, William ....22 Oct. 15
Low, William ....28 June 38
𝔓 M'Leod, Donald ....25 Dec. 14
𝔓 M'Nab, Duncan............10 Sept. 30
Mason, James .... 1 July 40
Matthey, Alphonso............ 9 Nov. 13
Palmer, Constantine John ...... 4 Feb. 06
Pryce, Josiah ....26 Oct. 27
Ragland, William ....20 Jan. 37
Raguenean, Charles ....10 Sept. 30
𝔓 Riddell, Archibald.......... do
Roberts, Peter .... 1 July 40

Rogerson, Ralph .... 31 Mar. 14
P Scobell, Thomas .... 5 June 38
Skelton, Thomas Lourey .... 22 Oct. 16
Stevens, William .... 1 July 40
Swainson, William .... 29 Mar. 13
Swinney, George .... 20 Jan. 37
P Wemyss, Charles .... 1 July 40
P Wilkinson, John Walter .... 10 Aug. 11
Williams, Charles .... 1 July 40
P Wilson, James .... 1 July 40
Woolrabe, John .... 20 Jan. 37
P Wybault, Patrick Robert .... 25 Dec. 14

DEPUTY-ASSISTANT-COMMISSARIES-GENERAL.

Anderson, John David .... 11 Oct. 14
P Archdeacon, E. M. .... 5 Oct. 32
P Bain, George .... 20 May 28
Bayley, Thomas .... 10 Aug. 11
Baynes, *Sir* E. Stuart, KCMG. 16 Dec. 13
Belts, Samuel .... 31 Mar. 14
Billings, Francis Thomas .... 9 Sept. 14
P Boyes, Geo. Thos. Wm. Blaney 3 Feb. 13
Brackenbury, Langley .... 7 June 25
Brathwait, Frederick .... 1 July 40
Browne, Joseph Steere .... 19 July 21
Byndloss, Edward .... 31 Dec. 13
Calder, Patrick .... 2 Jan. 13
Camm, John Philip .... 28 June 38
Castle, Slodden .... 13 Jan. 29
P Charlier, Joseph .... 25 Dec. 14
Coates, William .... 1 Oct. 13
Curran, Boaventura Romero .... 25 Dec. 14
David, John .... 11 Oct. 11
Davies, Peter .... 15 Jan. 14
Davis, Lionel .... 4 Jan. 14
P Dilke, William .... 22 Oct. 16
P Eyl, John George .... 25 Dec. 14
Faxardo, Aug. Maria Guazardo 25 Dec. 14
Fitzgerald, James David .... 22 Oct. 16
Freeborn, John .... 25 Dec. 14
Graham, Frederick .... 22 Oct. 16
Greig, William .... 25 April 15
Grist, James Bond .... 19 July 21
Hansord, S. E. .... 20 May 28
Harper, Charles .... 22 Oct. 16
Harris, Anthony Charles .... 25 Dec. 14
Hodson, James .... do
Horne, James .... do
Le Mesurier, Henry .... 4 May 14
Macpherson, James .... 10 Sept. 30
Marter, Thomas Peter .... 4 May 15
Montgomerie, Frederick .... 22 Oct. 16
P O'Meara, William .... 9 Mar. 12
Petrie, Samuel .... 25 Dec. 14
Richardson, Fran. Mosely .... do
Robinson, Augustus Facey .... 25 April 15
Rodney, *Hon.* Mortimer .... 27 Aug. 12
Ross, Robert William .... 22 Feb. 42
P Schmitter, John Solomon .... 3 Feb. 13
Sedgwick, Thomas .... 12 July 14
Simpson, Geo. Aug. Fred. .... 24 Dec. 41
P Sisson, Marcus Jacob .... 22 Oct. 16
Smith, Tho. Tringham .... 9 Nov. 13
Stanton, William .... 19 July 21
Stayner, Thomas Allen .... 11 May 13
Streatfield, Wm. Sandeforth .... 4 May 15
Thomson, Edmund .... 3 Dec. 42
Thornton, Charles .... 13 July 14
Turner, Thomas .... 22 Oct. 16
Whitehead, Hen. Lowe .... 25 Dec. 14
Wilson, Thomas .... 10 Sept. 30

MEDICAL DEPARTMENT.

	HOSPITAL ASSISTANT	ASSISTANT SURGEON.	REGI-MENTAL SURGEON.	STAFF SURGEON.	ASSIST.-INSPEC., or PHYSICIAN.	BREVET-DEP.-INSP.	DEPUTY INSP.-GEN.	BREVET.-INSP.-GEN.	INSPECTOR GENERAL.	PRINCIPAL INSP.-GEN.
PRINCIPAL INSPECTOR-GENERAL.										
Somerville, William, *MD.*	25 Mar. 95	.. ..	Mar. 05	.. ..	.. ..	.. ..	25 Mar. 05	.. ..	never	28 Dec. 15
INSPECTORS-GENERAL.										
P Bone, Hugh,[1] *MD.*	8 Sept. 03	17 Sept. 03	13 July 09	26 Mar. 12	7 Sept. 15	27 Sept. 25	1 Nov. 27	.. ..	2 Oct. 43	
Borland, James, *MD.*	20 Dec. 90	never	2 April 94	Sept. 95	never	never	5 Dec. 99	never	22 Jan. 07	
Davy, John, *MD.*	19 May 15	9 Nov. 15	1 Feb. 21	29 Mar. 21	8 Nov. 27	.. ..	.. ..	.. ..	30 May 45	
P Draper, Thomas[2]	25 April 95	April 99	17 April 04	1 Sept. 08	never	never	18 Jan. 16	never	24 Feb. 40	
Farrell, Charles, *MD.*	never	16 Nov. 99	never	1 Jan. 06	1 Aug. 11	never	9 Oct. 17	27 May 25	22 July 30	
P Fellowes, *Sir* James, *MD.*	June 94	never	never	never	28 Oct. 95	never	11 Mar. 13	never	29 April 13	
P Gillkrest, James,[3] *MD.*	10 Oct. 00	19 Aug. 01	15 Dec. 04				5 Nov. 29		16 Dec. 45	
CB Grant, *Sir* James Robert,[4] *MD.*	never	22 Jan. 92	24 Feb. 94	never	never	never	16 April 07	never	14 July 14	
P CB Gunning, John[5]	Oct. 93	never	never	30 July 94	never	never	17 Sept. 12	never	1 Feb. 16	
Gunning, Thomas[6]	never	23 Mar. 97	11 April 00	never	never	never	11 July 11	17 July 17	1 Jan. 28	
P CB Hume, John Robert,[7] *MD.*	28 Oct. 98	9 May 00	9 July 03	17 Aug. 09	never	never	26 May 14	never	3 Dec. 18	
Keate, Robert	Aug. 94	never	never	10 May 98	5 Sept. 99				21 Jan. 07	
P Kidd, Thomas,[8] *MD.*	17 June 96	6 April 97	25 July 99	27 Aug. 03			27 Jan. 37		16 Dec. 45	
P Nixon, Thos. (*Surg.-Maj.* 9 June 14)	never	26 Dec. 96	20 Mar. 99	never	never	never	never	never	10 Nov. 24	
Pym, *Sir* William, *MD. KCH.*							20 Dec. 10		25 Sept. 16	
Roberts, Rich. Worthington (*Ordnance*)	28 May 97	20 Sept. 97	1 Jan. 04	never	16 Feb. 14	never	22 July 15	never	17 Nov. 24	
Skey, Joseph, *MD.*	.. ..	.. ..	.. ..	.. ..	18 July 05	11 Dec. 23	26 Oct. 26	.. ..	15 Feb. 39	
P CB Stewart, Arthur,[9] *MD.*	5 Nov. 05	10 April 06	3 Sept. 12	9 Nov. 26	27 Sept. 27	26 Nov. 18	9 Dec. 36		16 Dec. 45	
P Thomson, Thomas,[10] *MD.*	June 96		4 April 00			10 Mar. 10	21 Jan. 13	27 May 25	22 July 30	
P Warren, John[12]	Feb. 92	never	Sept. 95	Nov. 95	never		22 Aug. 05	never	18 Jan. 16	
P CB Woolriche, Stephen[13]	never	never	30 May 94	18 June 07	never	never	26 May 14	9 Dec. 23	22 July 30	
DEPUTY-INSPECTORS-GENERAL.										
Albert, George Frederick,[19] *MD.*	never	never	never	30 Aug. 99	never	never	4 Nov. 13			
P Arthur, James,[20] *MD.*	never	1 June 01	18 Aug. 08	15 Oct. 12	29 Mar. 21	never	22 July 30			
P Arthur, John, *MD.*	never	14 Sept. 04	5 Sept. 11	never	3 Aug. 15	27 May 25	do			
P CB Barry, William,[21] *MD.*	15 April 08	4 Jan. 10	never	19 Nov. 21	never	never	10 Nov. 25			
Buckle, Dickens[22]	never	never	never	30 July 94	never	never	18 Jan. 10			
Calvert, Robert, *MD.*	never	never	never	never	23 Oct. 07	25 Nov. 18				
P Collier, Charles,[23] *MD.*	Sept. 06	4 Oct. 06	Aug. 09	4 June 12	never	3 Feb. 25	22 July 30			

	HOSPITAL ASSISTANT	ASSIST.-SURGEON.	REGI-MENTAL SURGEON.	STAFF SURGEON.	ASSIST.-INSPEC., or PHYSICIAN.	BREVET-DEP.-INSP.	DEPUTY INSP.-GEN.
[illegible] Daun, Robert,[27] *MD.*	22 Oct. 03	17 Dec. 03	4 Aug. 14	19 Jan. 32	never	never	20 Jan. 32
Duncan, [illegible][28]	4 Feb. 94	1 Feb. 97	9 July 03	8 Aug. 11	never	17 July 17	
[illegible] Forbes, *Sir* Charles Fergusson,[29] *MD. KCH. KC.*	May 98	9 Jan. 99	22 Dec. 04	1808	31 Jan. 11	never	18 Feb. 13
[illegible] Guthrie, [illegible] [illegible]	23 June 00	5 Mar. 01	20 Mar. 06	4 Jan. 10	never	never	16 Sept. 13
Hartle, Robert[32]	1 Dec. 96	22 Nov. 01	25 Feb. 04	28 Jan. 13	never	6 Mar. 23	22 July 30
[illegible] Howell, John,[33] *MD.*	11 June 01	28 Aug. 04	17 Mar. 08	16 April 12	never	never	do
[illegible] Knipe, John Augustus[34]	1 April 97	1 May 97	3 Oct. 05	28 May 12	never	17 July 17	26 Oct. 26
[illegible] [illegible]y, Owen,[36] *MD.*	never	31 Dec. 03	2 Nov. 09	5 Nov. 12	never	never	22 July 30
M'Mullin, John, *MD.*	never	never	never	never	19 Oct. 09	25 Nov. 18	22 July 30
Marshall, Henry[38]	24 Feb. 06	17 April 06	15 April 13	21 Dec. 13	never	never	22 July 30
[illegible] [illegible]n, Brinsley, *MD.*		29 April 13	5 Nov. 29	19 June 35	1 June 38		26 Jan. 41
[illegible] Shortt, John,[39] *MD.*	June 04	19 Oct. 04	25 Mar. 24	never	1 June 08	never	10 Nov. 43
[illegible] [illegible]st, *Sir* Augustus,[40] *MD.*	26 May 04	7 Nov. 05	never	25 Mar. 13	never	29 April 18	18 Nov. 24
[illegible] White, Andrew,[41] *MD.*	9 Sept. 99	16 Sept. 03	30 May 05	23 May 11	never	never	25 Sept. 17
[illegible] White, William Ramsay[42]	4 Nov. 05	21 Nov. 05	24 Feb. 14	14 Jan. 42	never	never	16 June 48
ASSISTANT INSPECTORS AND PHYSICIANS.							
[illegible]e, William, *KH.* (*Ordnance*)	never	20 Nov. 97	18 Nov. 05	never	26 Sept. 14		
[illegible] Evans, Lewis,[45] *MD.*	7 April 06	26 Nov. 07	never	never	26 May 14		
Greaves, William[47]	never	never	9 April 94	April 95	30 Aug. 99		
[illegible] Hume, Thomas, *MD.*	never	never	never	never	16 June 08		
[illegible] Jones, Griffith[48]		15 Oct. 00	28 Mar. 11	19 Nov. 30	9 Dec. 36		
Knight, Edward,[49] *MD.*	never	never	never	never	1809		
[illegible] L'Affan, *Sir* J. de Courcy, *Bt. MD.*	never	never	never	never	13 June 11		
[illegible] [illegible]lugan, David,[50] *MD.*	never	10 Sept. 07	never	never	26 May 14		
[illegible] Morewood [illegible] Geo. Alexander,[51] *MD.*	never	never	never	never	7 Sept. 07		
[illegible] Morison, [illegible]es, *MD.*		10 Sept. 03	20 June 11	never	29 June 15		
[illegible] Robson, William,[52] *MD.*	never	7 Mar. 05	never	never	30 Sept. 13		
[illegible] Sibbald, William,[53] *MD.*	Aug. 10	13 Dec. 10	never	7 Sept. 15	22 Nov. 27		
[illegible] Walker, Thomas,[54] *MD.*	20 May 05	20 June 05	3 Sept. 12	never	18 Feb. 13		
Wright, James, *MD.*		23 June 04	8 Sept. 08	never	26 May 14		

SURGEONS.	HOSPITAL-ASSIST., &c.	ASSISTANT SURGEON.	SURGEON.
𝔓 Abell, Joseph,[55] 60 Foot	4 Nov. 05	10 April 06	15 July 13
Abercrombie, John, 60 Foot	9 June 98	6 Mar. 99	19 July 00
Allan, Colin, *MD.*, Staff	never	25 June 03	8 May 06
𝔓 Allardyce, James, 5 Garrison Battalion	never	4 Aug. 01	30 May 09
𝔓 Anderson, Andrew,[57] *MD.* Staff	1 Mar. 05	4 Feb. 08	25 June 12
Anderson, Charles, Scotch Brigade			5 July 89
𝔓 Anderson, Thomas, 3 Foot	25 June 95	27 June 98	4 April 00
Annesley, Charles,[58] *MD.* 2 Dragoons	22 Jan. 05	5 May 08	21 Jan. 13
𝔓 𝔚 Armstrong, Abraham,[59] Staff	April 09	18 May 09	7 Mar. 16
𝔓 Armstrong, Arch. Nicolls, 5 Royal Vet. Batt.	never	14 May 04	21 July 14
Arnott, Archibald, *MD.*, 20 Foot	never	25 Dec. 96	23 Aug. 99
Ayton, Robinson, 34 Foot	23 Sept. 05	1 May 06	10 Sept. 10
Bacot, John, 21 Dragoons	never	2 July 03	9 June 14
Baird, John, *MD.*, Staff	8 July 11	21 Jan. 13	12 Dec. 26
Beckett, Thomas (*Savoy*), Staff			8 July 95
𝔓 Berry, Titus, Staff	never	never	24 June 03
Bett, James,[61] 2 Life Guards	6 Nov. 13	9 Nov. 15	1 Sept. 37
Black, Ebenezer, 18 Dragoons	19 May 06	2 Mar. 09	21 Jan. 13
𝔓 Boggie, John, *MD.*, Staff	17 Oct. 99	8 Jan. 01	15 Oct. 07
𝔚 Bolton, John, 7 West India Regiment	never	never	14 Sept. 91
𝔓 Bolton, Robert Henry, *MD.*, 78 Foot	26 Nov. 07	9 Feb. 09	7 Oct. 13
𝔓 Boyle, Alexander,[62] *MD.*, Staff	21 Sept. 99	11 Dec. 99	12 Nov. 03
Brady, James Patricius, *MD.* (*Dist.*), Staff	Jan. 01	25 Dec. 02	3 Mar. 06
Brandes, Christian Louis, Staff			2 July 07
Bromet, William, *MD.*, 1 Life Guards	4 Oct. 13	3 Nov. 14	6 Nov. 35
𝔓 Brown, Frederick, *MD.*, 73 Foot	19 May 08	4 Jan. 10	8 Sept. 25
𝔓 Brown, Joseph, Staff Corps of Cavalry	19 Jan. 08	25 Feb. 08	28 Oct. 13
Brown, Robert, Staff	8 July 99	11 Jan. 00	11 Dec. 06
Burton, Edward, Staff	9 May 11	21 Jan. 13	1 June 26
Byrne, William Gibson, Staff	8 Dec. 25	19 Oct. 26	2 July 41
Cahill, Alexander, 25 Foot	20 Aug. 03	15 Oct. 07	25 Aug. 09
𝔓 𝔚 Callander, John, Royal Waggon Train	1805	7 May 07	25 Mar. 13
Campbell, James, 28 Foot	24 Feb. 20	25 Oct. 25	19 June 35
Carnegie, John, *MD.*, 62 Foot	Feb. 04	25 Feb. 04	5 Sept. 11
Carter, John, 60 Foot	never	25 Sept. 03	2 Mar. 09
Carver, Walter, 4 Royal Veteran Battalion		25 June 01	6 April 09
Cathcart, Martin,[63] 7 Dragoon Guards	5 Jan. 08	23 Mar. 09	27 April 15
𝔚 Chenevix, Geo. (*Surgeon-Major*, 4 Sept. 86), Coldstream Guards	never	17 Dec. 12	24 Feb. 25
Clark, Thomas, 19 Foot			16 Sept. 95
Clark, Thomas, Staff	24 July 12	3 June 13	15 Jan. 24
𝔓 Coates, Edw. Fred. (*Local*), Staff	never	20 Aug. 07	10 Oct. 11
Coates, William Henry, Staff	8 April 94	never	16 June 96
Coghlan, John, 86 Foot	9 Nov. 12	19 Sept. 22	5 Sept. 34
Colchester, Thomas, Ordnance	never	27 Jan. 27	16 Jan. 41
Colclough, Anthony Cæsar,[64] 9 Dragoons	never	11 Nov. 02	14 April 13
Coombe, Charles, Coldstream Guards	never	April 01	14 Nov. 06
Cooper, Samuel, Staff	7 Jan. 13		26 May 14
Corfield, Charles, 38 Foot	13 Sept. 90	25 Dec. 96	25 Feb. 99
𝔓 Coulson, Alexander, 48 Foot	April 00	11 Sept. 02	31 Jan. 11
𝔓 Cross, James, 83 Foot	7 Jan. 11	11 Mar. 13	19 Nov. 30
Cuddy, Stephen, Ordnance	never	1 Aug. 06	1 Nov. 14
Cunningham, Alexander,[67] 86 Foot	13 July 04	26 Oct. 04	6 Feb. 12
Daunt, William,[68] *MD.*, 6 Dragoons	12 Sept. 07	3 Mar. 08	12 May 14
Davidson, James,[66] 50 Foot	24 June 15	30 Oct. 25	28 July 40
𝔓 Davies, Daniel Owen,[69] 18 Foot	20 April 10	25 Mar. 13	26 Oct. 30
Davies, Henry, *MD.*, 100 Foot	3 Aug. 08	20 Oct. 08	5 Sept. 11
𝔓 Dealey, Charles,[70] 81 Foot	Feb. 11	4 Mar. 13	19 Oct. 32
Desailly, Joseph, 4 Foot	July 99	8 May 01	3 Sept. 12
Dickinson, Nodes, Staff	17 Oct. 95	never	25 June 98
Docker, Thomas, Staff	never	never	3 Aug. 15
Drysdale, James Murray, 33 Foot	19 Feb. 24	10 Nov. 25	26 Feb. 41
𝔓 Este, Michael Lambton,[72] 1 Life Guards	never	4 Sept. 00	3 Oct. 12
Ewing, Joseph, 95 Foot	7 Sept. 09	4 Dec. 35	12 Sept. 48
Ferguson, John,[73] 45 Foot	7 Mar. 13	3 Mar. 14	8 Mar. 38
Ferris, Henry, Ordnance	28 May 97	June 97	1 Jan. 04

	HOSPITAL-ASSIST., &c.	ASSISTANT SURGEON.	SURGEON.
Fitzpatrick, Nicholas, Ordnance	25 April 03	1 Jan. 04	11 Nov. 11
Fletcher, Joseph, Ordnance	17 July 99	4 April 00	2 May 07
Forster, Thomas, 3 Foot	never	8 Dec. 03	26 July 10
Forster, John, *MD.*,[75] 73 Foot	22 Nov. 13	9 Nov. 15	1 April 36
Fraser, Arch. Campbell, Staff	never	Dec. 08	20 July 15
Fraser, Hugh, 60 Foot	10 May 13	26 Jan. 15	30 Dec. 34
Fraser, Peter,[76] 8 Foot	16 July 12	10 Dec. 12	6 Dec. 36
Freer, John, *MD.*, 97 Foot	21 Jan. 09	16 Nov. 09	24 Feb. 25
Galeani, Michael,[78] *MD.*, 46 Foot	12 Nov. 12	16 June 25	7 Nov. 34
Galliers, William, Staff	2 May 03	25 Mar. 04	10 Sept. 07
Gardiner, William, 4 Dr. Guards, *Medical Officer, Military Prison at Greenlaw*	never	7 Feb. 11	5 May 37
Garrett, George, *MD.*, 70 Foot	1 May 97	4 Sept. 06	18 June 12
Gibson, John Bushby,[79] (*Reg.*) Staff	8 Aug. 08	17 Sept. 08	7 Dec. 09
Gilder, Frederick, Coldstream Guards	never	9 June 14	16 June 38
Glasco, John, (*Reg.*), Staff	never	21 April 06	8 Feb. 16
Good, Samuel,[80] (*Surgeon-Major*, 24 Feb. 37), Scots Fusilier Guards	never	20 Feb. 06	25 Dec. 13
Grant, John, Staff	never	11 April 00	15 Oct. 03
Grant, Robert, Staff	never	15 June 97	27 Aug. 03
Grattan, Copeland, *MD*	never	14 June 10	11 Sept. 28
Griffin, George, 85 Foot	11 June 11	28 April 14	26 Sept. 34
Griffith, John, Staff	6 April 06	7 May 07	17 Sept. 12
Griffith, Moses,[82] 20 Foot	4 Nov. 09	24 Oct. 11	8 Feb. 27
Hair, Archibald,[83] *MD.*, R. Horse Guards	never	12 Nov. 12	12 Jan. 26
Hamilton, Henry, 18 Foot	never	26 Oct. 04	10 Aug. 09
Harrison, John,[84] (*Surgeon-Major*, 17 Mar. 1837,) Grenadier Guards	never	29 June 09	29 April 24
Harthill, Robert,[85] 69 Foot	never	29 Dec. 37	27 Oct. 46
Heir, Matthew, 60 Foot	1797	27 Nov. 02	2 Nov. 04
Henderson, Duncan,[86] *MD.*, 5 Foot	24 Oct. 11	16 Apr. 12	23 Mar. 26
Henley, John, Staff	never	4 Aug. 08	13 June 16
Hichens, Richard, Ordnance	never	1 Sept. 06	22 July 15
Hodson, John,[87] *MD.*, (*Reg.*), Staff	23 May 01	Sept. 12	29 Oct. 12
Hogg, Thomas, 76 Foot	8 Sept. 94	30 Nov. 97	22 Jan. 07
Hunter, William,[88] *MD.*, (*Surgeon-Major*, 16 Mar. 38), Coldstream Guards	never	10 Feb. 14	4 Sept. 36
Hutchesson, Francis Pery, Ordnance	1 Aug. 05	1 Aug. 06	20 Nov. 13
Ingham, Charles Thomas,[89] *MD.*, 54 Foot	24 May 10	16 Aug. 10	25 June 26
Jameson, David, *MD.*, 1 Dragoons	10 June 06	15 Oct. 07	6 Mar. 17
Jeyes, Samuel, *MD.*,[90] Staff	14 Nov. 11	28 Nov. 11	2 May 22
Johnson, Edward, *MD.*, 39 Foot	April 07	19 Nov. 07	15 July 13
Jones, William,[91] *MD.*, 1 Dragoon Guards	never	12 May 08	9 Mar. 09
Jones, Wm., *MD.*, (*Reg.*) Staff	12 Nov. 05	21 Nov. 05	3 Sept. 12
Kettle, William, 49 Foot	Aug. 05	10 April 06	26 Aug. 13
Kindell, Alexander, Staff	15 Oct. 03	3 Dec. 03	25 Sept. 14
Knox, George, 6 Foot	19 June 15	23 June 25	11 July 40
Leath, John, *MD.*, Staff		1 Jan. 05	12 April 10
Leonard, Daniel,[93] 11 Foot	12 Mar. 11	11 May 15	2 Aug. 33
Lewis, John,[94] York Chasseurs	25 Sept. 99	24 Mar. 03	28 Mar. 16
Lewis, Thomas,[326] *MD.*	8 July 11	9 Sept. 13	19 Nov. 30
Lightbody, John,[95] Staff	20 Aug. 04	20 June 05	15 Oct. 12
Lloyd, William,[96] *MD.*, 36 Foot	12 May 15	9 Nov. 15	18 Sept. 35
Lorimer, William,[92] 49 Foot	10 June 11	22 June 15	3 Nov. 27
M'Arthur, James,[97] *MD.* (*Reg.*), Staff	24 Jan. 14	27 April 15	14 April 25
M'Donald, Alexander, *MD.*, Ordnance	never	2 Sept. 07	30 Sept. 26
M'Kechnie, Andrew, Staff Corps	never	9 July 04	30 July 12
M'Munn, Robert Andrew,[97*] *MD.*, Staff	22 Nov. 13	1 Sept. 14	1 Nov. 33
Macarthur, Peter,[98] 1 Royal Veteran Batt.	24 May 95	8 Dec. 04	5 Sept. 05
Macnish, William,[99] *MD.*, 23 Foot	10 Aug. 03	4 Aug. 04	6 June 09
Macredie, Thomas, 71 Foot		3 Mar. 08	24 Jan. 11
Magrath, Denis Jos., *MD.*, Staff (*2nd Class*)	1 Feb. 27	29 June 30	2 July 41
Marsdin, William, (*Reg.*) Staff	never	25 Mar. 97	24 Aug. 79
Mein, Pulteney, 73 Foot	never	25 Dec. 96	3 May 00
Melville, Alexander, *MD.*, Staff	24 Mar. 04	10 Sept. 07	26 Sept. 11

	HOSPITAL-ASSIST., &c.	ASSISTANT SURGEON.	SURGEON.
Millar, Archibald, (*Reg.*) Staff	7 Nov. 04	15 Dec. 04	12 April 21
Millar, James, *MD.*, Staff	......	7 June 33	14 Feb. 45
Milligan, William, *MD.*, 6 Dragoons	19 July 13	10 Feb. 14	1 Mar. 39
Morgan, Alex. Braithwaite, 57 Foot	21 Dec. 15	27 Oct. 25	22 Nov. 39
Morgan, John, Ordnance	11 Dec. 05	2 Oct. 06	16 Feb. 14
Morison, James, 20 Foot	never	14 Oct. 36	25 Sept. 46
Murray, Adam Walker, Staff (*2nd Class*)	6 July 26	8 Feb. 27	2 July 41
Murray, Peter Daly, Staff (*2nd Class*)	4 Aug. 28	29 July 30	9 June 43
𝕻 Neill, Matthew,[101] 56 Foot	10 Jan. 14	6 Nov. 23	29 Dec. 37
Nelson, Wm. Fred., Ordnance		12 Feb. 13	26 Oct. 36
Nicolson, Patrick, *MD.*, 75 Foot	......	31 Dec. 33	28 Mar. 45
Nivison, James Finlayson, Staff	24 June 15	30 June 25	20 Sept. 39
O'Brien, Francis, 69 Foot	12 July 15	27 Oct. 25	11 Jan. 39
O'Brien, John Terence, 94 Foot			28 May 94
O'Connor, James, *MD.*, 22 Dragoons	1 June 91	never	16 Sept. 95
Palmer, Charles Quartley, Staff	18 Oct. 13	17 April 17	30 Dec. 34
Parrott, William, Cape Mounted Riflemen	15 Oct. 03	10 Mar. 04	20 Oct. 25
Parry, William, 4 Foot	20 Dec. 13	7 Mar. 22	17 April 38
𝕻 Paterson, James,[103] *MD.*, 42 Foot	7 June 10	22 Aug. 11	25 May 26
Peach, George, (*Reg.*) Staff	11 Mar. 00	4 April 00	15 Aug. 05
𝖂 Pearson, Richard Arthur, *MD.*, 87 Foot	30 Apr. 11	13 May 13	19 Nov. 30
𝕻 𝖂 Perston, David, *MD.*,[104] 13 Dragoons	19 Oct. 08	1 Feb. 10	17 Feb. 25
Pilkington, Edward, Staff		16 May 11	30 Aug. 27
Piper, Samuel Ayrault, M.D.,[105]	never	27 Dec. 06	20 Feb. 23
Pollok, William,[106] *MD.*, 53 Foot	8 Sept. 03	24 Oct. 03	8 Oct. 18
𝕻 Pooler, John,[107] Staff	10 Oct. 94	16 June 98	9 July 03
Preston, John, Staff			30 July 98
𝕻 Prichard, Octavius, New Brunswick Fenc.	21 Jan. 07	25 Feb. 08	13 May 13
Pyper, Robert, *MD.*, 4 Dragoon Guards	2 Dec. 95	25 June 97	30 Jan. 00
𝕻 Ranken, Robert,[108] Rifle Brigade	13 June 11	16 April 12	11 June 30
Reynolds, Michael, (*Reg.*) Staff	1 May 94	26 July 97	1 Dec. 02
𝕻 Rhys, Thomas,[109] 3 West India Regt.	25 Mar. 13	25 May 15	2 Oct. 40
𝖂 Riach, John,[110] *MD*	18 May 12	2 July 12	19 Nov. 30
Roberts, William, 1 Foot	never	7 Nov. 05	29 Oct. 12
𝕻 Robertson, Henry, *MD.*, Staff	Sept. 09		25 Feb. 13
Robertson, William, *MD.*	8 May 28	29 July 30	14 July 43
𝕻 𝖂 Robinson, Benjamin, 12 Dragoons	22 Oct. 94	never	2 Feb. 95
𝕻 Rogers, Wm. Reynolds,[111] 10 Dragoons	22 Aug. 11	7 Nov. 11	3 Aug. 26
𝕻 Salmon, Edw.,[112] (*S.-Maj.* 4 Dec. 23,) S.F.Gds.	never	16 Aug. 97	25 May 09
Savery, John Robert, 1 West India Regiment	17 Feb. 09	1 June 09	28 Dec. 20
𝕻 𝖂 Scott, Francis,[113] *MD.*, Rifle Brigade	never	14 May 03	25 Jan. 10
𝕻 𝖂 Scott, Robert, *MD.*, Staff	24 June 10	5 Nov. 12	8 Nov. 27
Scratchley, James, Ordnance	30 June 04	1 Aug. 06	11 Nov. 11
Seaton, Thomas, Ordnance	never	23 Oct. 12	25 Aug. 30
𝕻 Shean, Robert,[115] *MD.*, 7 Foot	never	28 Jan. 13	26 Oct. 30
𝕻 Shekleton, Robert, 51 Foot	never	5 Nov. 07	9 Sept. 13
Shelley, John Nichols, 1 Greek Light Inf.	13 July 05	22 Aug. 05	25 Feb. 11
𝕻 Shorland, James,[116] 96 Foot	7 Oct. 07	29 June 09	14 July 14
Silcock, Isaac, 12 Foot	11 May 01	10 Mar. 04	16 Feb. 09
𝖂 Simpson, Edward,[117] Ordnance (*Senior Surgeon*, 16 Jan. 41)	never	25 April 05	5 Aug. 13
𝕻 𝖂 Smith, Thomas,[118] *MD.*, Staff	29 Mar. 12	2 July 12	13 July 26
𝕻 Smyth, William, 45 Foot	never	7 April 04	22 Aug. 11
𝕻 Spence, William, Staff	3 Oct. 04	20 Nov. 04	4 Feb. 13
Spencer, Richard, York Rangers	7 April 00	5 June 00	9 July 03
Squair, John, *MD.*, 8 Dragoons	16 June 15	30 June 25	3 Mar. 37
𝕻 Stanford, Joseph Arthur,[119] *MD.*, Cape Regt.	22 Oct. 03	25 Oct. 03	4 Jan. 10
𝕻 𝖂 Steed, George, *MD.*, 1 Dragoons	4 Mar. 05	15 Aug. 05	17 Jan. 11
Stuart, Hugh Lindsay, 38 Foot	28 Dec. 20	15 Dec. 25	17 Sept. 39
Stewart, Charles, 25 Foot	never	12 Sept. 03	26 Nov. 07
Stewart, William, 58 Foot	11 Dec. 25	28 Sept. 26	5 Mar. 41
𝕻 Stratton, Robert, Staff	25 Sept. 99	21 Mar. 00	3 Oct. 05
𝕻 Taberger, John, *MD.*, Staff		3 Nov. 04	22 July 09
𝕻 Taylor, John, Staff	4 Sept. 94	never	30 April 99
Thomas, Thomas, 93 Foot			7 Feb. 80
Tighe, James Lowry, 12 Lancers	24 June 15	20 Oct. 25	10 Jan. 40

	HOSPITAL-ASSIST., &c.	ASSISTANT SURGEON.	SURGEON.
Trevor, Andrew,[120] 33 Foot	never	23 Sept. 93	9 May 94
P Trigance, Joseph,[121] 30 Foot	25 Oct. 12	9 Nov. 20	5 Dec. 34
Tucker, John, Staff	Sept. 94	never	18 Mar. 95
Turner, William, 7 Royal Veteran Batt.	9 June 98	15 May 02	9 Aug. 10
P Vallange, William, *M.D.*, 69 Foot	8 July 06	7 Dec. 09	19 Jan. 15
P W Van Millingen, J. G., *M.D.*, Staff	16 May 01	26 Jan. 02	16 Nov. 09
Ward, John Richard, Scots Fusilier Guards		21 Aug. 06	4 Dec. 23
Waring, Charles, 5 Foot	25 Feb. 08	6 July 09	6 Jan. 14
Warren, James Low, *M.D.*, 7 Dragoons, *Medical Officer, Military Prison at Devonport*	14 July 15	19 Feb. 24	17 April 38
W Watson, Sam. Wm., (*Surg.-Major*, 11 Nov. 24,) Grenadier Guards		20 Mar. 99	14 July 09
West, Henry, 10 Dragoons	4 Oct. 99	25 June 01	27 Nov. 06
White, Moses, *M.D.* Staff	4 April 14	5 May 25	29 July 36
White, Peter, 72 Foot	21 Dec. 07	15 Nov. 10	7 Oct. 13
Whitfield, Charles Tomlins, Ordnance	never	20 May 12	1 June 30
P W Whymper, *Sir* Wm.,[124] *M.D.*, (*Surgeon-Major*, 24 Feb. 25,) Coldstream Guards		14 Nov. 05	25 Dec. 13
P Widmer, Christopher, Staff	June 04	15 Aug. 05	24 Oct. 11
P Williams, William,[125] 99 Foot	9 July 09	19 Dec. 11	21 Sept. 30
Wilson, James, *M.D.*, Staff	3 June 15	30 June 25	20 Sept. 39
P W Winterscale, John,[126] 2 Dragoons	17 Sept. 09	8 Feb. 10	12 June 28
Wright, Robert, 2 Prov. Bn. of Militia	never	never	
Wybrow, William, 17 Dragoons	never	26 Dec. 96	3 July 99
Wyer, John, 19 Foot		9 Sept. 13	13 April 32
P Wylde, John Fewtrell, 7 Royal Vet. Batt.	10 April 98	14 Mar. 05	12 Feb. 07
Young, Colin, *M.D.*, 6 Royal Veteran Batt.	never	1 Mar. 98	15 Oct. 07
P Young, Thomas,[127] 16 Foot	10 Dec. 10	9 Sept. 13	4 May 26

APOTHECARIES.	HOSPITAL-ASSIST., &c.	APOTHECARY.
Cowan, John		14 Nov. 97
P Graham, John	19 April 08	31 Aug. 09
P Jones, Samuel	Aug. 09	31 Aug. 09
Middleton, George	never	7 Sept. 15
O'Brien, Edward		20 June 98
White, Henry		14 April 04

ASSISTANT-SURGEONS.		ASSISTANT SURGEON.
Apreece, Thomas, Ordnance	never	21 June 10
Barker, John Cricklow, Staff	24 Oct. 96	24 Nov. 25
Bartlett, Thomas, 44 Foot	never	4 Aug. 37
Benza, Pasquale Maria, Staff	8 Aug. 15	26 Jan. 26
P Bremner, Alexander, 3 Foot	6 July 10	3 Sept. 12
P W Brisbane, Thomas, *M.D.*, 58 Foot	19 June 12	3 June 13
Browne, Francis, 26 Foot	12 Oct. 26	24 July 28
Burke, Thomas, 27 Foot	never	4 Aug. 08
Butler, George, Staff	......	7 Oct. 42
P Campbell, Alexander, 3 Dragoon Guards	24 Feb. 14	13 July 15
Cannon, Æneas, *M.D.*, Ordnance	11 June 11	23 July 11
Chislette, Henry, 81 Foot		15 Dec. 04
Clarke, Charles Edward, Grenadier Guards		4 June 01
Coleman, John, 7 Dragoon Guards	never	31 Aug. 97
Cooper, Bransby, Ordnance	20 May 12	2 Dec. 12
Cumin, William, 3 Royal Veteran Battalion	never	21 Mar. 16
Cupples, Charles, Ordnance	18 July 12	4 Dec. 12
P Develin, Henry William, 49 Foot	20 July 09	20 May 13
Douglas, John, 8 Foot	Aug. 10	26 Sept. 11
Dyason, William, 4 Garrison Battalion		

	HOSPITAL-ASSISTANT	ASSISTANT SURGEON.
Dyce, Robert, *MD.*, Staff	8 Feb. 21	23 Sept. 25
Eddowes, James, Ordnance	never	25 Aug. 10
Evers, George, 14 Foot	3 June 15	23 Dec. 24
Fisher, Henry, *MD.*, Staff	never	28 Nov. 11
Fitzmaurice, George Lionel, Ordnance	6 July 29	1 July 31
Furnival, John James, *MD.*, Ordnance	never	1 Dec. 09
Gatty, Henry, Ordnance	26 April 13	20 Nov. 13
Gibb, William Richardson, *MD.*, 88 Foot	6 July 11	25 July 12
Hardy, Simeon Henry, *MD.*, Staff	never	2 Nov. 26
Hendrick, John, *MD.*, 34 Foot		3 July 17
Hewat, Richard, 65 Foot	4 Jan. 11	15 June 15
Holden, Horatio Nelson, 21 Foot	1 Feb. 27	9 Aug. 31
Hollier, Edward, 37 Foot		7 Oct. 13
Hollmann, Joseph, 60 Foot		30 Dec. 97
Huggins, John, 58 Foot	10 Jan. 14	28 Dec. 15
Ince, Henry Robert, 10 Royal Veteran Battalion		26 June 00
Inglis, Charles, Ordnance	never	4 April 10
Jarvis, James, 65 Foot		3 Oct. 00
Johnston, Arthur, *MD.*, 60 Foot	July 11	28 May 12
Jones, John, 1 Royal Veteran Battalion		6 July 04
Kehoe, Patrick, 52 Foot	June 10	25 June 19
Kenny, Matthias, *MD.*, Ordnance	never	1 Dec. 10
Knott, William, 6 Dragoons	16 June 15	5 May 25
La Cloche, Thomas, 7 Royal Veteran Battalion	7 Nov. 97	24 Dec. 02
Lawder, James, 66 Foot	never	12 Nov. 12
Ligertwood, Andrew, 3 Royal Veteran Battalion	8 April 05	11 July 05
Lukis, Thomas, 50 Foot	never	9 April 12
M'Crae, Farquhar, *MD.*, 6 Dragoons	never	28 Sept. 32
M'Culloch, Samuel, Ordnance	18 Aug. 12	1 Jan. 13
M'Lean, George Gordon, 35 Foot	7 Feb. 14	1 Sept. 14
Mac Bain, Giles, 62 Foot	15 Feb. 10	19 Mar. 12
Maclachlan, Daniel, *MD.*, 79 Foot	14 Aug. 27	21 Feb. 28
Martin, George, 67 Foot	Feb. 09	28 Feb. 11
Martin, James, 9 Foot	29 Dec. 14	10 Oct. 16
Miller, John, *MD.*, Ordnance	never	7 Mar. 07
Millet, Edward, *MD.*, 4 Foot	June 05	25 June 19
Morgan, Evan, 35 Foot		1 Nov. 99
Morice, David, *MD.*, 60 Foot	never	29 May 35
Mullarky, Daniel, 27 Foot	22 Nov. 13	6 Oct. 25
Neale, Melville, Staff	......	18 Sept. 35
Nixon, James, Ordnance	29 June 15	8 Jan. 16
Nugent, Morgan, Ordnance	8 Dec. 12	20 Nov. 13
O'Beirne, James, *MD.*, Ordnance	never	11 Oct. 10
O'Donnell, John, 77 Foot	7 Mar. 14	25 Jan. 25
Poett, Joseph, 4 Royal Veteran Battalion	Dec. 09	14 Dec. 09
Reilly, William, Staff		
Robins, Jacob William, Corsican Rangers		27 June 03
Rolland, James Henderson, Staff	29 May 28	29 July 30
Ross, William Baillie, *MD.*, 5 Roy. Veteran Batt.	7 April 25	16 June 25
Rudge, Edward, Ordnance	20 May 12	3 Dec. 12
Sprague, John Hanmer, 8 Royal Veteran Batt.	5 May 10	14 June 10
Swift, Richard, 60 Foot	never	19 Aug. 13
Thompson, John, Ordnance	never	1 Dec. 09
Tobin, John, 9 Dragoons	7 Dec. 09	19 Dec. 11
Venables, Robert, *MD.*, Ordnance	28 Aug. 11	11 Nov. 11
Verner, Edw. Donovan, Ordnance	9 June 13	29 Nov. 13
Vowell, Christ. Maxwell, 73 Foot	29 Mar. 27	18 Dec. 28
Webb, Boloyne Gordon, Staff	28 Dec. 26	29 July 30
Wilkinson, John William, Royal Marines		28 Sept. 91
Williams, David, 67 Foot	20 Dec. 13	12 Aug. 19
Woodroff, John, *MD.*, Staff	Dec. 03	25 June 19

Lancers..

PURVEYORS.	DEPUTY PURVEYOR	PURVEYOR
P Hodges, Edward[128]	29 June 09	9 Sept. 13
P James, William	19 Mar. 00	29 June 09
P Usher, William	13 Nov. 00	2 June 14

DEPUTY PURVEYORS.

P Bacon, Harry	21 Dec. 09
Bonnin, Henry Gousse	28 Sept. 09
Cleave, Richard	29 June 09
P Dunn, John	9 Sept. 13
P Findley, Thomas	10 Mar. 14
Gibbons, Samuel	14 Mar. 00
P Harrington, Joseph	9 Sept. 13
P M'Pherson, Lachlan	19 Aug. 13
Moore, John	25 Sept. 14
Newcombe, Joseph	26 May 15
P O'Reilly, Henry William	5 Jan. 09
Pierce, Thomas Estwick	17 Jan. 22
Power, Hugh	12 June 06
W Robinson, George	7 Sept. 15
P Smyth, Thomas	3 Sept. 12
P Soare, Charles	15 Oct. 12
Tucker, Richard	5 Nov. 29
P Wallington, James	9 Sept. 13
P Winnicki, Christopher	24 June 02
P Winter, George	15 Oct. 12
P Winter, John	21 Dec. 09

HOSPITAL ASSISTANTS.

Blackwood, John	25 April 14
Brereton, Charles	9 Nov. 13
Bruce, Alexander	4 July 15
Carter, Henry Collis	11 Jan. 10
Ker, James	9 Nov. 15
Randazzo, Francis	12 Oct. 15
Robertson, Patrick, *MD.*	24 June 15

VETERINARY SURGEONS.

Berington, James, Depôt	16 Dec. 13
W Constant, John,[1] 5 Dr. Gds.	3 Mar. 14
Goodwin, Joseph, R. Art.	24 April 05
Grellier, James, R. Waggon Train	21 Feb. 00
P W Hogreve, Henry,[2] 15 Drs.	12 July 06
Home, James, 2 Life Guards	31 May 39
Lythe, John, R. Art.	1 June 09
O'Connor, Charles, R. Art.	7 Mar. 08
Percivall, Wm., R. Art.	30 Nov. 12
Price, Edmund, 17 Drs.	13 June 16
Schroeder, John, 7 Dr. Gds.	25 June 12
Steed, Edward Henry, Depôt	15 Mar. 98
Timm, Isaac, 3 Dr. Gds.	17 Feb. 25
Woodman, Wm., 2 Dr. Gds.	25 Feb. 13

1 Mr. Constant served the campaign of 1815 with the 13 Dragoons, and was present at Quatre Bras, the retreat on the following day, and battle of Waterloo.

2 Mr. Hogreve served in the Peninsula, France, and Flanders, from Dec. 1811 to the end of that war in 1814, including the third siege of Badajoz, and battles of Vittoria, Toulouse, and Waterloo.

War Services of the Medical Officers.

1 Dr. Bone's services:—Expedition to South America in 1807; campaign of 1808 and 9, including the battles of Roleia, Vimiera, and Corunna; Expedition to Walcheren; Peninsula from May 1812 to the end of the war.

2 Mr. Draper served in Sicily in 1806; in Egypt in 1807; the Corunna campaign; in Portugal in 1811; in Holland in 1814.

3 Dr. Gillkrest was present with the expedition in the West Indies in 1801 under Sir Thomas Trigge, including the capture of the islands of St. Martin, St. John, St. Bartholomew, St. Thomas, and Santa Cruz. Served as Surgeon of a regiment in the Light Division throughout the war in the Peninsula, including the battle of Vimiera; retreat to, and battle of Corunna; retreat from Burgos, actions of the Coa (near Almeida), Busaco, Sabugal, Fuentes d'Onor, Salamanca, Vittoria, the Pyrenees, Nivelle, Nive, and Toulouse; and the sieges of Ciudad Rodrigo and San Sebastian, at which latter he accompanied the storming party. Served also at New Orleans in 1815.

4 Sir James Grant served as Hospital-Assistant in the campaign of 1793 with the army under the Duke of York. In 1795 he was senior Staff Surgeon to the expedition for the capture of the Cape of Good Hope. In 1809 he served throughout the Walcheren campaign, in which he was appointed Inspector to the Forces in the Field, having the charge at the bombardment of Flushing, and in South Beveland. He served the campaigns of 1813 and 14 in Holland and Belgium as chief of the department. In 1815 he served the campaign of Waterloo as chief of the medical department of the Duke of Wellington's army; and he continued as medical chief of that army during the three years' occupation of France.

5 Mr. John Gunning served in Flanders under the Duke of York, in 1793 and 94. In 1808 he accompanied the army to Portugal as surgeon to the Duke of Wellington; served with it throughout the whole of the Peninsular war, without being absent from his duty for a single day, and was in every action and siege in which the Duke was present. In 1811 his name was inserted in General Orders as surgeon-in-chief to the army; this, as a temporary appointment, ceased with the war, in 1814; but when the Duke assumed the command of the army at Brussels in 1815, his Grace again put him in General Orders as Deputy Inspector of Hospitals and Surgeon-in-chief to the army, in which capacity he was present on the field of the battle of Waterloo.

6 Mr. Thomas Gunning served in Holland in 1799. Embarked for the Mediterranean with Sir James Craig's expedition in April 1805, and was employed on active service at Naples, Sicily, Maida, the taking of the islands in the Bay of Naples, and the Ionian Islands. Wounded at the taking of Santa Maura.

7 Doctor Hume served in Egypt in 1801. Also in the Peninsular war.

8 Doctor Kidd served in Ireland during the rebellion in 1798; on the Expedition to North Holland in 1799; at the Ferrol in 1800; on the expedition to South America in 1806; in the Peninsula from 1807 to March 1813; campaign of 1813 and 14 in Germany and Holland.

9 Doctor Stewart served on the expedition to South America in 1807; in the Peninsula from March 1809 to Sept. 1812; the campaign of 1815; including the battle of Waterloo.

10 Doctor Thomson served in Egypt; also at the capture of Martinique, the Saintes, and Guadaloupe. Served also in the Peninsula from 1813 to the end of that war in 1814, and afterwards with the expedition against New Orleans.

12 Mr. Warren volunteered to accompany the expedition from Jamaica to St. Domingo, in 1793, and served in that Island until evacuated by the British forces in 1798, having been present in most of the actions that took place; viz., Tiburon, L'Acul, Bizotton, &c. In 1808 he joined the Army in the Peninsula under the Duke of Wellington, a few days prior to the action of Vimiera; was ordered with 500 wounded to Oporto, and established an hospital there; and, in some weeks following, he joined Sir John Moore's forces in Lisbon, and accompanied the Army to Sahagun, and in the retreat to Corunna.

13 Mr. Woolriche served in Holland under Sir Ralph Abercromby and the Duke of York; with the expedition to Copenhagen in 1807; and, with the rank of staff-surgeon, was principal medical officer with the reserve, commanded by Sir Arthur Wellesley at the battle of Kioge; after four years of colonial service, he joined the Peninsular army, with which he served from the battle of Salamanca until the end of the war; and was present in charge of the 7th division of the army, commanded by Lord Dalhousie, at the battles of Vittoria and the Pyrenees. At the renewal of the war in 1815 he joined the army at Brussels, under the command of the Duke of Wellington, and was appointed to take charge of the field-duties in the event of a general action; in this responsible situation he was present at the battles of Quatre Bras and Waterloo, where he was occupied several days and nights before the field was cleared of the numerous wounded, including British, Belgians, French, &c. &c. In 1827 he embarked for Portugal with the army, under Sir William Clinton, as chief of the medical department on that service.

19 Doctor Albert served at the Helder, in 1799; also the campaign of 1814, in Holland, under Lord Lynedoch.

20 Doctor James Arthur was present and professionally employed at the assault of Buenos Ayres, the defence of Cadiz, action at Sabugal, battle of Fuentes d'Onor, action at El Bodon, siege and assault of Ciudad Rodrigo, two sieges and assault of Badajos, battles of Salamanca, Vittoria, Pyrenees, Nivelle, and Orthes, action at Vic Bigorre, and battle of Toulouse.

21 Doctor Barry served in the Peninsula from Aug. 1808 to Aug. 1811, and again from Aug. 1813 to the end of that war in 1814. Also the campaign of 1815, including the battle of Waterloo.

23 Mr. Buckle served with the expedition to Ostend under Sir Eyre Coote, in 1798.

25 Doctor Collier served at the capture of Martinique, in 1809; and in the Peninsula from the latter part of 1812 to the end of that war in 1814.

27 Doctor Daun served at the capture of the Cape of Good Hope in 1806. Also the campaign of 1815, including the battle of Waterloo.

28 Mr. Duncan has seen a great deal of active service in the East Indies.

29 Sir Charles Forbes joined the Medical Staff in Portugal in 1798, and was appointed Assistant-Surgeon to the 2nd Battalion of the Royals in Jan. 1799. He landed with the Battalion at the Helder in the ensuing August, and went through the campaign in Holland under Sir Ralph Abercromby and the Duke of York. In 1800, after the expedition to Ferrol, he served with the army in Egypt, and subsequently at Malta and Gibraltar. Embarked with the Royals in May 1803 for the West Indies, and was present at the capture of St. Lucia and Tobago. Accompanied Sir David Baird's expedition to the Peninsula in 1808; and in June 1809 he sailed with the Light Brigade for Portugal, continuing to serve under the Duke of Wellington during the whole of the war until the peace of 1814.

32 Mr. Hartle served on the expedition to St. Lucia in 1803, and accompanied the storming party of Morne Fortunée. Present at Dominica when the French attacked the island in 1805; served also at the capture of the islands of St. Thomas and St. Croix in 1807; and Martinique in 1809, including the actions of the 1st and 2nd Feb. Also at the capture of Guadaloupe in 1815.

32* Doctor Lewis served in the Peninsula from July 1811 to June 1813.

33 Doctor Howell served in Egypt on the first expedition, and accompanied Sir David Baird's army to Grand Cairo on its return to India. Appointed Surgeon to the Grenadier Battalion, on Sir James Craig's expedition to Naples, and served with it in Sicily and Calabria in 1806, and was present at the battle of Maida. In 1807 he accompanied the Royal Sicilian Regiment, on the second expedition to Egypt, and was appointed Surgeon to it in May 1808; transferred to the 61st in May 1809, and served in the Peninsula from April 1810 to Oct. 1812. Slightly wounded on the left shoulder by the Bedouin Arabs on the first expedition to Egypt, while employed on a mission to the Mamelukes and Mahomet Ali; and severely wounded in the loins in Portugal.

34 Mr. Knipe served in Ireland during the rebellion in 1798, and was present in the action of Vinegar Hill; at the siege of Copenhagen, and battle of Kioge, in 1807; campaign in Portugal and Spain in 1808 and 1809; and in Belgium in 1814 and 1815.

35 Mr. Lamert served in St. Domingo in 1796 and 97; in Egypt in 1801 (wounded in the action of the 13th March); at Copenhagen in 1807; campaign in Portugal and Spain under Sir John Moore, including the battles of Roleia and Vimiera, retreat to and battle of Corunna. Served also with the expedition to Walcheren in 1809; and subsequently in the Peninsula until 1811.

36 Doctor Lindsey served in the Peninsula from Jan. 1810 to the end of that war in 1814.

38 Mr. Marshall served in South America, in 1807.

39 Doctor Shortt served in the Peninsula from Sept. 1810 to the end of that war in 1814, and subsequently in the American war.

40 Sir Augustus West served in Hanover in 1805; at Copenhagen and Sweden in 1807; in Portugal and Spain in 1808; at Walcheren in 1809; and in the Peninsula from 1809 to the end of that war in 1814.

41 Doctor Andrew White served in Egypt with the Indian army in 1801. He was afterwards present with the 88th at the battles of Talavera and Busaco, and in the Lines of Torres Vedras. He next served in Sicily, and on the eastern coast of Spain, and was present at the battle of Castalla; after which he served on the coast of Italy, and at the surrender of Genoa and of Naples.

42 Mr. William Ramsay White served with the expedition to Naples in 1809, and was present at the capture of Ischia and Procida, and at the siege and capture of Ischia Castle. Served with the army in Sicily in 1810 and 11; and in the Peninsula during the campaigns of 1813 and 14, and was present at the repulse of the sortie from Bayonne. Served eighteen years in India, and accompanied the army of the Indus in 1838, 39, and 40, and was present at the storm and capture of Ghuznee.

45 Doctor Evans served in the Peninsula with the 29th regiment, and on the staff.

47 Mr. Greaves served on the Continent in 1794 and 95; and at the Helder in 1799.

48 Mr. Jones served at the capture of the Islands of Ischia and Procida in 1809. Employed n the gun-boats in the Faro of Messina, under Sir John Stewart. Present at the capture of he Ionian Islands, and siege of Santa Maura, under Sir John Oswald. Served also the cam-paign in Catalonia under Lord William Bentinck; afterwards in the American war, including he actions at Bladensburg and Baltimore, capture of Washington, and operations against New Orleans.

49 Doctor Knight served at Walcheren in 1809.

50 Doctor Maclagan served at Walcheren in 1809. Also in the Peninsula from Dec. 1811 to he end of that war in 1814.

51 Doctor Morewood served with General Beresford's Expedition to Madeira and occupation f that Island; the campaign in Spain and at Corunna under Sir John Moore; the Walcheren xpedition; with army of Sir John Stewart in Sicily; with Lord Wellington in the Peninsula, icluding the siege of Badajoz; and during the last year of the war in N. America; at Walheren in 1809; in the Peninsula in 1812; and in the American war in 1813.

52 Doctor Robson served in the Peninsula from Dec. 1811 to the end of that war in 1814.

53 Doctor Sibbald served in the Peninsula during the campaigns of 1813 and 14, including ie battles of Orthes and Toulouse. Served subsequently at New Orleans.

54 Doctor Walker served at Copenhagen in the expedition under Lord Cathcart in 1807. He rved also in the Peninsula from the battle of Vimiera—at which he was present with the 2nd attalion of the 52nd Light Infantry—to the termination of that war in 1814, with the exception a few months, he having been made prisoner in the hospital at Talavera and carried to Verdun.

55 Mr. Abell served in Hanover in 1805 with the 95th (Rifle Brigade); at the siege of Copen-agen and battle of Kioge, in 1807; with the army under Sir John Moore on the retreat to and ttle of Corunna; in the Peninsula from 1810 until promoted to a Surgeoncy in the 7th battalion the 60th, in 1813, with which he served in America from 1814 to 1818.

57 Doctor Andrew Anderson served in Naples and Calabria, and was present at the battle of aida and siege of Scylla Castle. Expedition to Walcheren and siege of Flushing in 1809. eninsula, from Dec. 1809 to Nov. 1813, including the defence of Cadiz, battles of Busaco, uentes d'Onor, and Salamanca; siege of Burgos Castle, and actions in the Pyrenees.

58 Doctor Annesley served at the siege and capture of Santa Maura in March 1810; siege id capture of Trieste, Oct. 1813. Also against the Viceroy of Italy, under General Nugent id Colonel Robertson, in 1813, and was at the taking of Comachio, Ferrara, Ravenna, Bogna, and Genoa.

59 Mr. Abraham Armstrong served in the Peninsula from March 1810 to the end of the war, including the battles of Albuhera, Vittoria, Orthes, Pyrenees, and Toulouse. Present also at Waterloo.

61 Mr. Bett was at the capture of Genoa, and also at the capture of Castine in America in 1814.

62 Doctor Boyle was actively employed in Ireland during the rebellion of 1798, and afterwards at the Helder in 1799; also in Sicily and Egypt from Dec. 1806 till June 1812, as Surgeon of the 62nd regt. He was employed on the eastern coast of Spain on the Medical Staff in 1812, 13, and 14, and was at the affair of Biar, battle of Castalla, at Tarragona in June and Aug. 1813, and at the retreat from Ordal and Villa Franca. He had charge of the General Hospitals at Alicant, Castalla, and Valencia; was senior medical officer with the Head Quarters of the Army under Sir Wm. Clinton during the blockade of Barcelona; was at Genoa and Corsica, and accompanied the army from the Mediterranean to Bermuda under General Gosselin, as principal medical officer, and was at the Penobscot.

63 Mr. Cathcart served at the capture of Martinique in 1809, and Guadaloupe in 1810. Also throughout the Burmese war, and was present in almost every action and storming party during the war.

65 Mr. Colclough served in the Mahratta war from Aug. 1812 to Dec. 1813; the Kandian campaign of 1815, including the capture of Kandy in the island of Ceylon. Deccan campaign of 1818 and 19, including the storm and capture of Capaul Droog.

66 Mr. Davidson served with the 50th in the battle of Punniar (Medal). Also the campaign on the Sutlej (Medal), including the battles of Moodkee and Ferozeshah.

67 Mr. Cunningham served the campaigns of 1813 and 14 in Upper Canada, under Sir Gordon Drummond.

68 Doctor Daunt served at the capture of Madeira in 1807; of Martinique in 1809; and of Arracan in 1825.

69 Mr. D. O. Davies served in the Peninsula from June 1810 to the end of that war in 1814, including the defence of Cadiz and Tarifa; battles of Barrosa, Victoria, Pyrenees, Nivelle, and Nive; actions at St. Palais, Aire, and Tarbes; battles of Orthes and Toulouse. Served also at the attack on New Orleans.

70 Mr. Dealey served in the Peninsula in 1811 and 1812, and was present at the battle of Albuhera and first siege of Badajos.

72 Mr. Este served the Egyptian campaign of 1801, including the actions of the 8th (slightly wounded), 13th, and 21st March, and siege of Alexandria. Served also in the Peninsula from Oct. 1812 to the end of that war in 1814, including the battles of Vittoria, Pampeluna, Orthes, and Toulouse. Medal for services in Egypt.

73 Mr. John Ferguson served the campaigns of 1813 and 14 in Canada; was engaged in an action on Lake Ontario and Lake Huron; also in the action of Michilinachnar.

75 Doctor Foster served the campaign of 1814 in Holland.

76 Mr. Peter Fraser served in the American war, and was present at the capture of Oswego.

78 Doctor Galeani joined the army in Sicily, in 1812, and was employed in the field until landed at Leghorn, 14th March 1814. Present in the campaign of Italy with the advanced army, including the taking of the Castle of St. Maria, in Spezia, action at Seshi, siege and surrender of Genoa, and taking of the castle of Savona and Novi.

79 Mr. J. B. Gibson was present in 1807 at the capture of Alexandria, siege of Rosetta, and affair of El Hamet (made prisoner). In 1809 he was at the capture of Ischia and Procida after which he served in the Peninsula, and was present at Sabugal, Fuentes d'Onor, Marcalva, siege of Ciudad Rodrigo, San Milan, Vittoria, Lesaca and Bidassoa, Vera, Nivelle, Arbonne, Nive (9th, 10th, and 11th Dec. 1813), Orthes, Tarbes, and Toulouse. Finally, he served the campaign of 1815, including the battle of Waterloo.

80 Mr. Good served with the expedition to Copenhagen in 1807; proceeded with the army to the Peninsula in 1808, and served there until the end of the war, including the passage of the Douro, taking of Oporto, battles of Busaco and Fuentes d'Onor, sieges of Ciudad Rodrigo and Badajos, battle of Salamanca, capture of Madrid, siege of Burgos, battle of Vittoria, siege of San Sebastian, passage of the Bidassoa, the Nive, and the Adour, and investment of Bayonne. Present at Quatre Bras and Waterloo.

82 Mr. M. Griffith served in the Peninsula from Jan. 1810 to the end of that war in 1814, including the battles of Busaco and Fuentes d'Onor, siege and assault of Ciudad Rodrigo, siege and assault of Badajos, battles of Salamanca, Vittoria, Pyrenees, Nivelle, Nive, and Orthes, action at Vic Bigorre (wounded), and battle of Toulouse. Served also in India, Arabia, and the Burmese empire, from May 1818, including sieges of Asseerghur, Ras-el-Kyma, and Zea, siege and assault of Dwarka, affair of Beni-Boo-Ali, assault of a fortress on the banks of the Pegu river, assault of Syrian Pagoda, siege of Donabew, and battle near Prome.

83 Doctor Hair's services:—Peninsular campaigns from Nov. 1812 to the end of that war in 1814, including the battle of Vittoria, siege of San Sebastian in August and Sept. 1813, battles of the Nivelle, Nive, and Orthes, and the affairs of Vera. Subsequently in the action in front of New Orleans, and, finally, at the capture of Paris.

84 Mr. Harrison served in the Walcheren expedition, 1809; at Cadiz and in the Peninsula in 1811, 12, and 13; expedition to Holland, 1814; Netherlands and France from 1814 till 1818

Present at the assault of Seville, bombardment of Antwerp, storming of Bergen-op-Zoom, battles of Quatre Bras and Waterloo, and taking of Peronne.

85 Mr. Hartle served with the 9th throughout the campaign of 1842 in Affghanistan (Medal) under General Pollock.

86 Doctor Henderson served in the Peninsula, and was present at the siege of Badajos, and both the actions of Salamanca, 18th and 22nd July 1812.

87 Doctor Hodson served in Egypt in 1801.

88 Doctor Hunter served with the Coldstream Guards at the blockade of Bayonne in 1814; also the campaign of 1815, including the battle of Waterloo.

89 Doctor Ingham served in the American war, and was present at the battles of Fort George, Chippewa, and at the Falls of Niagara.

90 Doctor Jeyes served in the Peninsula from Jan. 1813 to the end of the war, including the affair at Morales, battles of Vittoria, Pyrenees, Orthes, and Toulouse. Present at Waterloo.

91 Doctor Jones (h. p. 1st Dr. Gds.) served at Copenhagen in 1807; in the Peninsula under Sir John Moore; and subsequently at Walcheren.

92 Mr. Lorimer served in the Peninsula from June 1810 to end of that war in 1814.

93 Mr. Leonard served in the Peninsula from May 1811 to Sept. 1814.

94 Mr. Lewis served with the expedition to Ostend under Sir Eyre Coote in 1798; at the Helder in 1799; with the expedition to Madeira in 1807; at Corunna under Sir John Moore; and in Portugal from May 1809 to Dec. 1812.

95 Mr. Lightbody served at Gibraltar during the epidemic in 1804; with the army in Sicily in 1807 and 8; in the Peninsula from March 1812 to April 1813; and again from April 1814 to the end of the war, including the defence of Alba de Tormes and retreat from Salamanca.

96 Doctor Lloyd served the campaign in Flanders in 1815; also in the interior of Ceylon during the Kandian rebellion in 1817.

97 Doctor M'Arthur served at the capture of Guadaloupe in 1815.

97* Doctor M'Munn served the campaigns of 1813, 14, and 15 in Holland and Flanders, including the action at Merxem and bombardment of Antwerp.

98 Mr. Macarthur was severely wounded at the storming of Seringapatam.

99 Doctor Macnish served with the expedition to Hanover in 1805; expedition to South America under General Whitelock, in 1806 and 7; campaign of 1808 and 9, in the Peninsula, including the battles of Roleia and Vimiera. Expedition to Walcheren, including the siege of Flushing.

101 Mr. Neill served the Peninsular campaign of 1814.

102 Mr. Nivison served in Upper and Lower Canada during the Rebellion in 1837 and 38.

103 Doctor Paterson served in the Peninsula from Sept. 1810 to Dec. 1811. Served also in the Burmese war.

104 Doctor Perston served in the Peninsula from Jan. 1809 to April 1813, including the combat of Foz d'Arouce, battle of Salamanca, capture of Madrid, siege of Burgos, and retreat therefrom. Served also the campaign of 1815, and was present at the battles of Quatre Bras and Waterloo, and capture of Paris.

105 Doctor Piper served twenty years in the East Indies, and was present at the destruction of the Dutch Squadron in Sourabaya in 1809. Accompanied the expedition under Admiral Drury to Macoa, in China, as auxiliaries to the Portuguese, in 1809. Served also with the Army of Reserve during the Pindaree war from 1816 to 1821.

106 Doctor Pollok served in the East Indies from 1805 to 1823. He was in the action at sea with the French squadron under Admiral Linois, in the *Marengo*, 84, on the voyage to Madras, in Aug. 1805; he was at the siege and capture of the fortress of Adjighur in Bundlecund, in 1809; and he served throughout the Nepaul war in 1814 and 1815, including the sieges of Kalunga, of Nahn, and of Jeytuck.

107 Mr. Pooler served in the West Indies, at Barbadoes, St. Domingo, and Jamaica, in 1796, 97, and 98; on the expedition to the Helder in 1799; at the capture of the Cape of Good Hope in 1806; the subsequent campaign in Spanish South America in 1806 and 7; on the expedition to Walcheren in 1809; in the Peninsula from Aug. 1811 to Dec. 1813; at Brussels and Antwerp immediately after the battle of Waterloo.

108 Mr. Ranken served in the Peninsula from June 1811 to the end of that war in 1814, including the battles of Vittoria and the Pyrenees, blockade of Pampeluna and repulse of the sortie, battles of Nivelle, Nive, and Orthes; actions of Vic Bigorre and Tarbes, and battle of Toulouse.

109 Mr. Rhys served in the Peninsula from April 1813 to March 1814; from that period, on the coast of America and at New Orleans, until the conclusion of the war with America.

110 Doctor Riach served the campaigns of 1813 and 14, in Germany and Holland, including the action of Goerde in Hanover, 16th Sept. 1813; affair near Antwerp in Jan. 1814; attack on Merxem, and subsequent operations against the French fleet at Antwerp. Present in the actions at and near Waterloo on 16th, 17th, and 18th June.

111 Mr. Rogers served in the Peninsula from January 1813 to the end of that war in 1814, including the action at Morales, battles of Vittoria, Pyrenees, Orthes, and Toulouse.

112 Mr. Salmon served in Holland in 1799, including the actions of the 27th Aug., 10th and 19th Sept., 2nd and 6th October. Served also in the Peninsula from Jan. 1809 to June 1810, from March 1811 to March 1813, and from March 1814 to the end of that war, including the

passage of the Douro and capture of Oporto, affair at Salamanca, battle of Fuentes d'Onor, sieges of Ciudad Rodrigo and Badajoz, battle of Salamanca, capture of Madrid, siege of Burgos, investment of Bayonne, and repulse of the sortie.

113 Doctor Francis Scott's services:—Capture of the Cape of Good Hope in 1806; expedition to Walcheren in 1809; Peninsular campaigns from April 1813 to the end of that war in 1814, including the following battles and affairs, viz., Vera, and Vera Heights, Nivelle, Orthes, Tarbes, and Toulouse. Also the campaign of 1815, including the battle of Waterloo.

115 Doctor Shean served in the Peninsula from March 1813 to the end of the war, and was present at the battles of Vittoria, the Pyrenees, and the Nive.

116 Mr. Shorland served the campaign of 1808-9, including the battle of Corunna. Campaign of 1810 and 11 in Portugal, including the battle of Busaco. Served also during the whole of the war with the United States of North America.

117 Mr. Simpson's services:—Siege and capture of Pigeon Island, siege and capture of Fort Bourbon, and capture of Martinique in 1809. Capture of Guadaloupe and dependencies, in 1810. Two attacks of Merxem, bombardment of Antwerp, and night attack of Bergen-op-Zoom in 1814. Campaign of 1815, including the battle of Waterloo and capture of Paris.

118 Doctor Smith served the campaigns of 1813, 14, and 15, including the battles of Vittoria, the Pyrenees, Nivelle, Orthes, Toulouse, and Waterloo.

119 Doctor Stanford served with the expedition to Hanover in 1805; at the capture of Madeira in 1807; and subsequently in the Peninsula with the Buffs and the 29th, and was present in Sir John Moore's retreat, at the battles of Talavera, Busaco and Albuhera, retreat to and defence of the lines of Torres Vedras, pursuit of Massena, actions of Pombal, Redinha, and Campo Mayor, first siege of Badajoz. In 1814 he accompanied the expedition to America and was present at the attack and capture of the Forts of Castine and Machias. He served also in the campaign of 1815, including the capture of Paris. Doctor Stanford was professionally employed at Cadiz during the Epidemic Fever in 1813.

120 Mr. Trevor served the campaign in Flanders, in 1794, and was present with his regt. (the 33rd) in all the operations in that country, and in the retreat of the army through Holland. Served subsequently in the East Indies, from 1796 to 1808, and was present at the battle of Malavelly, and at the storming and capture of Seringapatam.

121 Mr. Trigance served in the Peninsula from Dec. 1812 to the end of the war. Served also during the whole of the Kandian war in Ceylon, and was wounded in the leg by an arrow.

124 Sir William Whymper served with the 1st Battalion of the Coldstream Guards the campaigns of 1809 and 10 in Portugal; at Barrosa in 1811; again in Spain, Portugal, and France, in 1813 and 14; in Flanders in 1814 and 15; and with the Army of Occupation from 1815 to 1818. Was present in the battles of Oporto, Talavera (taken prisoner), Busaco, Vittoria, passage of the Bidassoa, battle of the Nive, siege of San Sebastian, and lastly at Waterloo.

125 Mr. Williams served at Walcheren in 1809, and in the Peninsula from 1810 to 1812.

126 Mr. Winterscale served at Walcheren, in 1809, and in the Peninsula, from Sept. 1810, to Dec. 1812, including the battle of Fuentes d'Onor. Present at Waterloo.

127 Mr. Young served in the Peninsula from May 1811 to the end of that war in 1814, including the capture of Badajoz, and battles of Vittoria, the Pyrenees, Nivelle, Nive, Orthes (taken prisoner), and Toulouse.

128 Mr. Hodges joined the army in Egypt in April 1801, and remained there till after the French had been driven out. In 1809 he joined the army in the Peninsula, where he remained until the end of that war in 1814, having had the formation of the great hospital at Elvas after the storming of Badajoz, and also of the one at Salamanca after that battle; and he was attached to the Head Quarters in all the movements to Vittoria, the Pyrenees, and South of France, until the close of the war after the battle of Toulouse.

CHAPLAIN'S DEPARTMENT.

Principal Chaplain to the Forces.

Reverend William Whitfield Dakins, *D.D.*, 16 March 1810.

Chaplains.

Name	Date	Name	Date
Rev. Carey, Nicholas	19 Feb. 95	*Rev.* James, Maurice	25 Nov.
— Cautley, Wm. Grainger	25 Dec. 09	— Jepson, George	8 Apr.
— Crigan, Claudius	15 July 95	— Irwin, Henry	
— Curtois, R. C.	11 Sept. 12	*The Venerable Archdeacon*, le Mesuriah, J. T. H., *AM.*	16 Apr.
— Denius, Nathaniel Robert	29 June 16	*Rev.* Lyon, Charles Jobson, *BA.*	9 Apr.
— Dobbs, John	24 Sept. 94	— Rose, John	11 July
— Frith, Edward Cockayne	4 May 11	— Stonestreet, George Griffin	4 Apr.
— Goff, Thomas	28 July 98	— Symonds, Henry John	12 Apr.
— Hill, Samuel	20 Sept. 10	— Timbrell, John	30 June
— Hudson, Joseph, *MA.*	25 Nov. 25		

OFFICERS

ON THE

FOREIGN HALF-PAY.

GERMAN LEGION.

	1st LIGHT DRAGOONS.	Rank in the Army.	When placed on half-pay.
Captains	W Hans von Hattorf, *KCH.*	8 June 07	24 Feb. 16
	W Bernard von Bothmer	28 Aug. 10	do
	W Henry George von Hattof	25 Feb. 12	do
	W Charles Elderhost	10 Mar. 13	do
	Hartwig von Witzendorff	13 June	do
	W Morris de Cloudt	17 Sept.	do
	W Benedix, *Baron* Decken	18 Sept.	do
Lieutenants	W Augustus Fischer	13 Mar. 12	do
	Frederick Nattermann	do	do
	W Otto von Hammerstein	13 May 15	do
	W Conrad Poten	6 July	do
	W Lewis Kirchner	8 July	do
Cornets	W Frederick Breymann	15 Mar. 14	25 Feb
	Charles von der Decken	18 April	do
	W Ludewig von Müller	22 April	do
	W Hannach Boguslaw Leschen	27 May	do
	George von Uslar Gleichen	13 May 15	do
	W Edward Trittau	14 May	24 Feb.
	Hen. Anth. Fred. Cleve	7 July	do
	Christian von Bülow	25 Oct.	do
Veter.-Surg.	W Ludolph Heuer	26 May 05	do
	2nd LIGHT DRAGOONS.		
Captains	W Charles, *Baron* Marschalck	24 Nov. 09	24 Feb. 16
	W George Braun	3 July 15	do
	W Augustus Poten	15 Oct.	do
Lieutenants	W Ludolph de Hugo	24 Mar. 12	do
	W Johannes Justinis von Fumetti	do	do
	Augustus Kuhls	28 May	do
	W Carl Schaeffer	2 Oct.	do
	W Herman Hen. Con. Ritter	18 Sept. 13	do
	W Ern. Theo. Chr. Meier	15 Mar. 14	do
	W Ferdinand Küster	21 Nov. 15	do
Cornets	Fred. Carl. Edmund Kuhls	10 April	do
	Ernest von Voss	4 July	do
	Ferdinand von Stolzenberg	21 Nov.	do
	Christian Schanmann	23 Nov.	do
Surgeon	W Frederick Detmer	13 July 13	do
Veter.-Surg.	Conrad Dallwig	29 April 13	21 Aug.

1st HUSSARS.

		Rank in the Army.	*When placed on half-pay.*
Captains	W George, *Count* von der Decken ..	11 July 11	24 Feb. 16
	W Louis Krauchenberg	13 Jan. 13	do
	W Gustavus Schaumann	10 Oct.	do
	W Hieronimus von der Wisch	6 April 14	do
Lieutenants	W Conrad Poten	14 July 11	do
	W Leopold Sigismond Schultze	19 Nov.	do
	W Henry Christoph. Behrens......	19 Nov. 13	do
Cornets	W Franz Geo. von Oldershausen ..	27 Jan. 14	do
	W William Theodore Gebser	14 Feb.	do
	W Frederick Jacob Rahlwes	26 April	do
	W William de Hassell	13 Sept.	do

2nd HUSSARS.

Captains	Urban Cleve	10 July 11	do
	Theodor von Stolzenberg	14 Nov. 12	do
Lieutenants	Dav. Cha. Corn. Wieboldt..........	29 Aug. 12	do
	Michael Löning	16 Nov.	do
Cornets	Frederick Herman Meyer	16 Dec.	do
	Ernest Soest......................	27 Nov. 13	do
	Herman Westfield	23 Mar. 14	do
	Victor von Aiten..................	27 April	do
	Theodor von Marschalck	28 July 15	do
Adjutant	Henry Gotze ....*Lieut.*	28 Mar. 12	do

3rd HUSSARS.

Captains	W Quintus, *Baron* Goeben	2 May 11	do
	W William von Schnehen	20 Sept.	do
	W August. de Harling............	8 Oct.	do
	W George Meyer................	27 Dec.	do
	W Diede Wm. von der Hellen	17 Feb. 14	do
	Gustavus Meyer..................	5 July 15	do
Lieutenants	W John Christ. Fred. Nanne	13 Nov. 12	do
	W John Henry D'Homboldt	14 Nov.	do
	W Charles Augustus Reinecke	15 Nov.	do
	W Christian Oehlkers	9 Oct. 13	do
	W Eberhard Gerstlacher	17 Feb. 14	do
	W Anthony Frederick Hoyer	5 July 15	do
	W Frederick de Fresnoy..........	29 July	do
Cornets	W Alex. *Baron* Hammerstein......	9 Oct. 13	do
	W Rudolph. Fredrichs............	10 Oct.	do
	W Conrad von Dassel	22 Oct.	do
	W Hans. *Baron* Holdenberg	1 Dec.	do
	George Julius Meyer	5 May 14	do
	Carl. Fred. Deichmann	23 Oct. 15	do
Assist.-Surg.	W Geo. Lewis Bauermeister	7 Sept. 13	do
Veter.-Surg.	Frederick Eidmann................	12 July 06	do

1st LIGHT INFANTRY.

		Rank in the Army.	*When placed on half-pay.*
Captains	W Frederick de Gilsa	16 April 11	24 Feb. 16
	W Gustavus, *Baron* Marschalck	26 Jan. 14	do
	W Augustus Wahrendorff	4 July 15	do
Lieutenants	W William de Heugel............	20 Mar. 12	do
	W Adolphus Koester	22 Oct. 13	do
	W Nicholas de Miniussir..........	29 Jan. 14	do
	W Harry Leonhart	25 Mar.	do
Ensigns	W Gustavus George Best	26 Nov. 13	do
	W Adolph. von Gentzkow	27 Nov.	do
	W Otto de Marschalck	16 May 14	do
	Cha. Martin A. Heckscher	20 Aug. 15	do
Adjutant	W John Fred. Wm. Bushe ....*Ens.*	29 May 15	do

2nd LIGHT INFANTRY.

Captains	William Stolte	24 April 11	do
	W Charles Meyer	1 July 15	do
Lieutenants	W James Oliver Lindham	8 July 11	do
	W William Doring	10 April 14	do
Ensigns	W George Frank	5 Jan. 14	do
	W Henry Augustus Knop	14 Jan.	do
	W Lewis Charles Baring..........	11 April	do
	Chr. Aug. Jacob Behne............	26 June 15	do
Assist.-Surg.	Joseph Tholon	6 Oct.	do

1st BATTALION OF THE LINE.

Major	W Frederick Robertson, *CB. KCH.* *Lt.-Col.*	18 June 15	do
Captains	W George, *Baron* Goeben	18 Mar. 12	do
	W Leopold von Rettberg..........	18 Aug. 13	do
	Ernest, *Baron* Hodenberg	22 Sept.	do
	W Frederick von Rössing	2 Sept. 15	do
Lieutenants	W Christian Hen. von Düring	17 Aug. 09	do
	W Ludolph Kumme............	18 Aug.	do
	W Diederich de Einem	18 Mar. 12	do
	W George Wichmann	30 Oct.	do
	W Charles von Weyhe	24 Nov.	do
	W Adolph. von Arentsschildt	18 Aug. 13	do
	Fred. Augustus Muller	22 Sept.	do
	W William Best	26 Nov.	do
Ensigns	W Augustus, *Baron* Le Fort	9 Sept.	do
	W Augustus von Brandis	6 Jan. 14	do
	W Arnold William Heise	7 Jan.	do
	Adolphus de Beaulieu..............	21 Mar.	do
	W Cha. Aug. von der Hellen	7 May	do
Assist.-Surgs.	Frederick Harzig..................	7 Dec. 05	do
	W Philip Langeheineken..........	31 Jan. 11	do

	2ND BATTALION OF THE LINE.	*Rank in the Army.*	*When placed on half-pay.*
Captains	𝔚 Wm. *Baron* Decken, *KH. Major*	18 June 15	24 Feb. 16
	𝔚 Aug. Chas. Fred. Hartmann	3 Jan. 09	do
	Ferd. Adolphus *Baron* Holle	28 May 15	do
Lieutenants	𝔚 Godfrey Tiensch	17 Mar. 12	do
	Augustus Frederick Schmidt	do	do
	𝔚 Chas. Augustus Lewis Billeb	do	do
	𝔚 Francis La Roche	27 Mar. 14	do
	George Fabricius..................	29 April	do
	𝔚 Augustus Ferdinand Ziel	17 June	do
	𝔚 Lewis Henry de Sichart	28 May 15	do
Ensigns	𝔚 Charles Lewis de Sichart	16 Feb. 14	do
	𝔚 Gust. Fred. Wm. Hartmann	8 May	do
	𝔚 Thilo von Uslar Gleichen	29 May	do
	𝔚 Augustus Luning	17 June	do
Adjutant	𝔚 Adolphus Hesse..........*Lieut.*	17 Mar. 12	do

	3RD BATTALION OF THE LINE.		
Captains	𝔚 Albert Cordemann	8 Sept. 14	24 Feb. 16
	Frederick Erdmann	19 June 15	do
	𝔚 George Appuhn	25 July	do
Lieutenants	George W. F. von Weyhe	30 Oct. 07	do
	𝔚 Charles Brauns	14 Sept. 10	do
	𝔚 Christian de Soden	18 Mar. 12	do
	𝔚 Augustus Kuckuck	do	do
	𝔚 Julius Brinkmann	11 May	do
	𝔚 Henry Dehnel	20 Mar. 13	do
	𝔚 Lewis de Bachellé, *Baron* von dem Brinck	20 Sept.	do
	𝔚 Henry Edward Kuckuck........	8 Dec.	do
Ensigns	Frederick de Storren	18 Feb.	do
	𝔚 Frederick von Schlutter	6 May	do
	𝔚 Augustus William Kuckuck	8 Jan. 14	do
	𝔚 Richard Hupeden	9 Jan.	do
Adjutant	𝔚 Fred. Bern. Schneider ....*Lieut.*	18 Mar. 12	do

	4TH BATTALION OF THE LINE.		
Captains	𝔚 George Ludewig	13 Dec. 08	do
	Frederick Ludewig	29 Oct. 12	25 May 15
	𝔚 Justus Formin	9 June 15	24 Feb. 16
	Christian Bacmeister	7 July	do
Lieutenants	𝔚 Caspar von Both	13 Dec. 08	do
	𝔚 Adolphus Ludewig	19 Mar. 12	do
	𝔚 Hen. Fred. Theo. de Witte......	31 Oct.	do
	𝔚 Ernest Brinckmann............	4 Mar. 13	do
Ensigns	𝔚 William Lüning	7 May	do
	Augustus Schulze	15 June	do
	𝔚 Frederick von Brandis	26 July	do
	𝔚 Ferd. von Uslar Gleichen	30 May 14	do
	𝔚 Arnold Appuhn	6 June 13	do
	𝔚 Lewis von Soden..............	25 May 15	do
Quar.-Master	Augustus Becker..................	25 Sept. 04	do
Assist.-Surg.	John Henry Wicke	28 Feb. 12	do

5th BATTALION OF THE LINE

		Rank in the Army.		*When placed on half-pay.*	
Major	W Philip Henry Fred. Mejer	4 June	14	24 Feb.	16
Captains	Julius Bacmeister	26 Sept.	11	25 July	15
	John George Hagemann............	16 Dec.	12	do	
	Charles, *Baron* Linsingen	16 April	13	24 Feb.	16
	Henry, *Baron* Dachenhausen........	8 Dec.		do	
	W Charles Berger	21 Aug.		do	
Lieutenants	W Geo. Aug. Hen. Buhse	27 Sept.	11	do	
	W Augustus Winckler	20 Mar.	12	do	
	W Charles Schlaeger	do		do	
	Joseph Korschann	25 Sept.	12	25 July	15
	W George Klingsöhr	16 Dec.		do	
	W Lewis de Geissmann	16 April	13	24 Feb.	16
	W George Wischmann	10 April	15	do	
Ensigns	W Ferdinand Scharnhorst	27 Mar.	13	do	
	W Charles Winckler..............	10 Jan.	14	do	
	W Lewis Klingsöhr	22 Mar.		do	
	W Ernest Baring	25 May		do	
	W Adolphus Scharnhorst..........	7 June		do	
	Geo. Cha. Aug. von Loesecke	15 April	15	do	
	Carl Peter Arnold Meier	16 April		do	
	W Rudolph Carstens	15 May		do	
Adjutant	W William Walther ....*Ensign*	22 Nov.	13	do	

6th BATTALION OF THE LINE.

Captains	Charles von Brandis	14 Mar.	12	24 May	16
	Ernest, *Baron* Magius	25 Jan.	14	do	
Lieutenants	Joseph Kersting	16 Jan.	08	do	
	Ernest, *Baron* Heimburg	16 Mar.	09	do	
	Otto Schaumann..................	20 Sept.	10	do	
	Christ. Arnold Volger	25 Jan.	11	do	
	Frederick Hurtzig	21 Mar.	12	do	
	Ernest Mensing	do		do	
	Francis, *Baron* Acton	4 April	14	do	
	W Christ. Lewis von Ompteda	26 May		do	
Ensigns	Alexander Autran	2 April	14	do	
	W Lew. Albrecht von Ompteda	15 April		do	
	Herman Schwencke................	8 June		do	
	Edward von Brandis	9 June		do	
Adjutant	Fra. Matthias Debs................	25 Feb.	12	do	
Assist.-Surg.	Solomon Jurdan Einthoven..........	29 Feb.		do	

7th BATTALION OF THE LINE.

Captains	Frederick Munter	21 Sept.	10	24 May	16
	Arnold Backmeister	21 Mar.	12	do	
Lieutenants	Frederick von Diebitsch	23 July	11	do	
	Theodore von Sebisch..............	23 Mar.	12	do	
	Christian Frederick Eichhorn........	3 April	14	do	
	Augustus Steffen..................	27 May		do	

	7th BATTALION OF THE LINE—(*cont.*)	*Rank in the Army.*	*When placed on half-pay.*
Ensigns	Arnold Erich Backhaus	18 July 14	24 May 16
	Charles Ernest F. Neuschäffer ..	19 April	do
	Franz Frederick Backhaus	29 April	do
	Augustus von Hodenberg	2 June	do
Adjutant	John Ernest Stutzer ....*Lieut.*	28 Oct. 09	do
Assist.-Surg.	Henry Schuchardt	16 Jan. 14	do

	8TH BATTALION OF THE LINE.		
Captains	Frederick Marburg	27 Mar. 12	24 Feb. 16
	George Delius................	11 Sept. 14	do
	Frederick Luderitz	24 June	do
	Charles Poten	8 Sept.	do
Lieutenants	Frederick Ziermann............	27 Mar. 12	do
	Augustus Helmich	12 Sept. 14	do
Ensigns	Frederick Dorndorf...............	12 July 12	do
	Godlove Künoth	13 July	do
	William de Moreau	11 Oct.	do
	Frederick Henry Müller........	13 April 14	do
	Henry Seffers	3 June	do
	Geo. Fred. Godfrey Lunde......	12 Sept.	do
Adjutant	Frederick Brinckmann ....*Lieut.*	10 April 11	do
Assist.-Surg.	Ernest Sander................	4 July 06	do

	ARTILLERY.		
Major	*Sir* Geo. Julius Hartmann, *KCB. GCH. Lt.-Col.*	17 Aug. 12	do
Captains	Lewis Daniel[1]	26 Nov. 08	do
2nd Captains	George Wiering	23 Nov. 09	do
	Lewis Jasper	25 Nov. 13	do
	Frederick Erythropel	16 May 15	do
1st Lieuts.	Victor Preussner	5 June 07	do
	Ferdinand de Brandis	28 Sept.	do
	William Rummel................	14 Dec. 12	do
	William de Goeben	25 Nov. 13	do
	William de Scharnhorst	26 Nov.	do
	Frederick Drechsler	27 Nov.	do
	Augustus Pfannkuche..........	28 Nov.	do
	Henry Hartmann	26 Mar. 14	do
	Henry Bostlemann	16 May 15	do
2nd Lieuts.	Lewis Haardt	14 Dec. 12	do
	Lewis Heise.................	15 Dec.	do
	Lewis Scharnhorst	15 Nov. 13	do
	Lewis de Wissell............	30 Nov. 13	do
	Charles Herman Ludowieg	16 Feb. 14	do
	Augustus Capelle...............	19 May	do

1 Capt. Daniel has received a medal and a clasp for the battles of Orthes and Toulouse.

	ARTILLERY—(*continued*)	*Rank in the Army.*	*When placed on half-pay.*
2nd Lieuts.	John Fred. Schlichthorst	20 May 14	24 Feb. 16
	Frans Rottiger......................	26 Nov.	do
	Adolphus Rechtern	24 July 15	do
	Lewis Hagemann....................	25 July	do
Paymaster	John Blundstone	9 April 05	do
Veter.-Surg.	John Frederick Hilmer	22 Aug. 06	do

	ENGINEERS.		
Captain	Victor Prott, *KCH*................	23 Mar. 05	do
1st Lieuts.	William Unger......................	14 Aug. 11	do
	John Luttermann	21 Nov. 12	do

	STAFF.		
Brig.-Majors	Ern. de Kronenfeldt ....*Capt.*	20 Feb. 13	do
	[illegible] J. Godf. de Einem ....*Capt.*	28 April 14	do
	Fr. Chr. *Baron* Heimburg ......*Capt.*	26 July 15	do
	[illegible] George Baring...........*Capt.*	20 Nov.	do

MISCELLANEOUS CORPS.

	BRUNSWICK CAVALRY.		
Captains	* William de Wulffen..............	28 Sept. 09	14 June 16
	* Alexander von Erichsen	7 Mar. 11	do
	* Gustavus Conrad Alex. von Girsewald	4 Nov. 13	do
Lieutenant	William von Lubeck	1 Nov.	24 Feb.
Cornet	Frederick Moeller	10 Mar. 14	24 June
Adjutant	William Butze ....*Lieut.*	26 Sept. 09	do
Quar.-Master	Ferdinand de Bothmer	21 June 10	do

	BRUNSWICK INFANTRY.		
Captains	* Frederick von Wolffradt	16 Aug. 10	1814
	* Henry von Brandenstein	20 Feb. 11	do
Lieutenants	Ernest von Patzinsky	27 Sept. 09	do
	* Fred. John Adrian von der Heyde	do	do
	* Carl. Ernest Berner	do	do
	J. D. W. L. von Schwarzenberg......	21 Feb. 11	do
	Frederick Hausler	27 June	do
	Albert von Greisheim	27 Aug.	24 June 15
	Augustus Grutteman	10 Dec. 12	1814
	Charles Haberland	1 April 14	do
Ensigns	Johannes Cornelius Schot	1 April 13	do
	Michael Charles Edwards..........	28 Oct.	do
	E. A. William de Bernewitz	1 Dec.	do
Surgeon	Charles Wehsarg..................	12 Aug.	do
Assist.-Surg.	Lewis Aug. T. Heimburgh..........	28 Oct.	do

	CHASSEURS BRITANNIQUES.	Rank in the Army.	When placed on half-pay.
Captains	Nich. Philibert de Brem....... *Major*	4 June 14	24 June 14
	Fridolin de Freuller..................	2 Sept. 06	1814
	Francois Jos. Spitz.................	22 Aug. 08	do
Lieutenants	Etienne de Planta	3 Dec. 07	2 Nov. 15
	J— N— de Pouchalon	24 May 10	1814
	Jean Nepomacene Stoeber..........	28 June	do
	Armand Casimir G. Dufief..........	18 Oct.	do
	Pietro Santa Columba..............	8 Aug. 11	do
	Silvain de Precorbin	4 June 12	do
	Jos. Ignace Goussencourt	22 July 13	do
	Frederick Wolf	21 April 14	do
Chaplain	Francois Nicolle	4 May 09	do
Adjutant	Pierre F. Louis Boussingault .. *Lieut.*	3 Apr. 10	do
Assist.-Surg.	Ignation Stumpa	12 Apr. 10	do

	ROYAL CORSICAN RANGERS.		
Captains	Joseph Panattieri	6 Jan. 07	1817
	Jacques Guanter....................	27 May 13	do
Lieutenants	Peter Francis Ciavaldini............	6 Jan. 07	do
	Antonio Astuto	2 June 08	do
	Jean Baptiste Zerbi................	13 Sept. 10	do
	Louis de Kamptz....................	31 May 11	do
	Antonio D'Odiardi	10 Feb. 12	do
	Dominico Antonio Peretti	25 June	do
	Francois Salvatelli	21 Jan. 13	do
	Giovanni Ant. Vincenti	19 May 14	do
Ensigns	Joseph Susini	19 May 14	do

	DILLON'S REGIMENT.		
Captains	Charles de Boylesve	3 Sept. 06	1814
	Pierre du Sage.....................	8 Feb. 10	do
	Jean de Chesse	20 Mar. 11	do

	GREEK LIGHT INFANTRY.		
Captain	Joseph Coppon.....................	7 Jan. 13	do
Lieutenants	Pietro Antonio Salvatorio	2 July 13	do
	Pierre Astuto	25 June 14	do

	ROYAL MALTA REGIMENT.		
Lieutenant	Ern. Fer. Cha. Bern. Richter	20 Mar. 05	1811

MEURON'S REGIMENT.

		Rank in the Army.	When placed on half-pay.
Major	Cha. Emanuel May	17 June 18	25 Sept. 16
Captains	Nich. Julien de Bergeon	23 May 00	1810
	George Alexander Dardel	24 Sept. 04	1808
	Frederick Matthey	25 April 08	25 Sept. 16
Lieutenants	Laurent Boyer	25 Sept. 08	
	Frederick *Baron* Bibra	1 Sept. 06	25 July 16
	Charles Jos. Zehupfenning	9 Mar. 09	do
	Francois de Graffenried	1 Mar. 10	do
	Charles de Gumoens	28 April 11	25 Sept.
	Antoine Fred. de Graffenried	30 April	do
	August. de Loriol	28 Sept. 14	do
	Charles Cæsar de Meuron	do	do
	Jules Cæsar Saum	15 Jan. 16	do
Assist.-Surg.	Ludwig Aug. Winter	1 Sept. 03	25 July

ROLL'S REGIMENT.

Captains	Nicholas Muller ....*Major*	4 June 14	1816
	Ferd. *Compte* de la Ville	21 Oct. 04	25 Dec. 17
	Antoine Courant	5 April 10	1816
	Frederick Rusillion	21 April 14	do
Lieutenants	Joseph Tugginer	30 Oct. 06	do
	Jost Muller	5 Nov. 07	do
	Amans Glutz	23 May 08	do
	Pierre P. Auguste de Courten	15 Dec.	do
	John Peter Sorgenfrey	21 Dec.	do
	Hector de Salis	22 Dec.	do
	Charles Pannach	25 Jan. 10	do
	Jean Juliani	18 Feb. 11	do
	Edmund de Tugginer	26 Feb.	do
	Otto Henry Salinger	28 Feb.	do
	Henry d'Holbreuse	16 Oct. 12	do
	Joseph Gurtler	9 Dec.	do
	Edward de Tugginer	29 Sept. 13	do
	Nicholas Stutzer	30 Sept.	do
	Jean Baptiste Phil. Stutzer	27 Oct. 14	do
Ensigns	Patricio Schmid	11 Dec. 12	do
	Charles de Bronner	22 June 15	do
Chaplains	John Becker	9 Dec. 94	1810
	William Peter Macdonald	1 July 12	1816
Assist.-Surg.	Charles Gemmellaro	25 Nov. 13	do

SICILIAN REGIMENT.

Captain	Francesco Stuart	19 Oct. 15	20 Mar. 16
Lieutenants	Henry Stuart	12 June 08	25 Mar.
	Thomas de Fossi	6 April 09	do
	Marino Zugiani	8 Feb. 10	do
	Gustave de Roquefeuil	23 Aug.	do
	Andrieu Vieusseux	11 April 11	do
Ensign	Charles Hegler	28 Feb. 12	do
Quar.-Master	John Nurg	3 Nov. 08	do

	WATTEVILLE'S REGIMENT.	*Rank in the Army.*		*When placed on half-pay.*	
Lieut.-Col.	Rudolphe May	21 May	12	24 Oct.	16
Captains	Amand de Courten ....*Major*	4 June	18	1815	
	Pancrace Ledergerw	9 July	06	26 Oct.	16
	Chs. Zahender De Thiel	25 Mar.	11	do	
	Jean Christian Weyssen............	25 Aug.	13	25 Mar.	
Lieutenants	Albert Steiger....................	6 May	07	24 Oct.	16
	Cæsar Augus. Champeaux..........	7 May		do	
	Albert Manuel	5 Sept.	10	do	
	Charles Louis Sturler..............	6 Sept.		25 July	
	Francis Dicenta	28 Aug.	11	24 Oct.	
	Rodolph de Watteville	22 Feb.	14	do	
	Charles May	23 Feb.		do	
Ensigns	Fra. Louis Con. Fischer............	25 Jan.	14	do	
	Jean Albert Fischer................	27 Jan.		do	
Chaplain	Peter James de la Mothe	23 April	12	do	
Adjutant	Joseph Mermet..............*Lieut.*	27 Jan.	08	do	
Assist.-Surg.	Jean Baptiste Boidin	1 May	01	25 July	16

	YORK LIGHT INFANTRY VOLUNTEERS.				
Captain	Arthur Leon de Tinseau............	15 June	15	25 July	16
Lieutenants	Antoine Louis de Mendibus	8 July	11	19 Mar.	17
	John Ordon	10 July		do	
	Alexander Schmitt................	13 Sept.	13	24 May	16
Ensign	Louis Tholon	14 Sept.		25 July	16

	FOREIGN VETERAN BATTALION.				
Captains	Frederick Wyneken	8 July	11	24 Feb.	16
	Christian *Baron* Goeben............	27 Feb.	15	do	
Lieutenants	George de Witte..................	20 Aug.	11	do	
	[illegible] Frederick von Finke	20 Mar.	12	do	
Ensigns	George Augustus Rumann..........	25 June		do	
	Henry Brackmeyer................	31 Jan.	14	do	
	John Henry Wegener..............	18 Aug.	15	do	
	Frederick Schultze	20 Aug.		do	
Assist.-Surg.	John Christ. Fred. Fischer..........	17 Feb.	14	do	

	FOREIGN CORPS OF WAGGONERS.				
Lieutenants	Andrew Philip Cramer	21 June	10	25 Sept.	16
	*David Crusius	14 May	15	25 April	
	Philip Aug. von Harlessem	18 May		25 June	
Cornets	John Albert Kropp................	1 June	15	25 July	

GARRISONS.

		Per Ann. £	s.	d.	Date of Appointment.
	BELFAST.				
Town-Major	.. *Lieut.* Peter Stuart, late 1 R. Vet. Bn.	63	13	8	24 Dec. 18
	BERWICK.				
Governor	*Lieut.-Gen. Sir* James Bathurst, *KCB.*	568	15	10	1 Feb. 33
	CAPE BRETON.				
Town-Adjutant	*Lieut.* Edw. Sutherland, Unattached	86	13	9	12 July 38
	CHARLESFORT AND KINSALE.				
Fort-Major	*Lieut.* John Black, late 3 R. Vet. Bn.	63	13	8	5 Dec. 22
	DARTMOUTH.				
Governor	Arthur Howe Holdsworth				10 Sept. 07
Fort-Major	*Lt.-Col.* Robert Kelly, Unattached	69	19	2	11 Dec. 28
	DUBLIN.				
Town-Major	.. *Major* Walter White, Unattached	173	7	6	25 July 25
	DUNCANNON FORT.				
Fort-Major	*Lieut.* Thomas Austin, late 5 R. Vet. Bn.	63	13	8	27 July 20
	EDINBURGH CASTLE.				
Governor	Major-Gen. Henry James Riddell, *KH.*				1 Jan. 47
Lieut.-Governor	*Gen.* F. Tho. Hammond, *GCH.*	173	7	6	20 July 31
Fort-Major	*Major* Thomas Cauch, Unattached	86	13	9	21 Feb. 40
Chaplain	*Rev.* William Beattie Smith				24 April 38
	GIBRALTAR.				
Town-Major	.. *Major* Thomas E. Lacy, Unattached	182	10	0	13 Aug. 47
Town-Adjutant	*Quarter-Master* William Hume, h. p. 72 F.	91	5	0	23 July 47
	GRAVESEND AND TILBURY FORT.				
Fort-Major	*Lt.-Col.* Thomas Kelly, h. p. Cheshire Fenc.	86	13	9	13 Jan. 14
	GUERNSEY.				
Fort-Maj. & Adj.	*Lt.-Col.* John Hankey Bainbrigge, Unatt.	82	2	6	22 Nov. 39
	HULL.				
Lieut.-Gov.	*Lieut.-Gen. Sir* Chs. Wade Thornton, *KCH.*	173	7	6	25 Sept. 16
	INVERNESS, or FORT GEORGE.				
Fort-Major	*Colonel* Alex. Findlay, *KH.* h. p. R. African Corps	86	13	9	12 Feb. 47
	ISLE OF WIGHT.				
Capt. of Sandown Fort,	*Capt. Sir* Wm. Wynn, late Invalids	173	7	6	29 Mar. 10
——— Carisbrooke Castle,	*Lieut.-Gen. Sir* W. Paterson, *KCH.*	173	7	6	20 Feb. 17
——— Cowes Castle,	*Field Marshal The Marquis of* Anglesey, *KG. GCB. GCH.*	173	7	6	25 Mar. 26
	JERSEY.				
Governor	*Gen.* W. C. *Visc.* Beresford, *GCH. KCH.*	no pay			29 Jan. 29
Fort-Maj. & Adj.	*Major* John Fraser, Unattached	82	2	6	19 Mar. 47
	LANGUARD FORT.				
Lieut.-Gov.	*Lt.-Col.* Charles Aug. West, late 1 R. Vet. Bn.	173	7	6	20 June 11

		Per Ann. £	s.	d.	*Date of Appointment.*
	LONDONDERRY AND CULMORE.				
Governor	*Gen.* John *Earl of* Strafford, *GCB. GCH.*	no pay			15 June 22
Town-Major	John Nicholson	63	13	8	26 May 00
	MALTA.				
Quarter-Master	*Lieut.* John Colcroft, h. p. 74 Foot	136	17	6	26 Oct. 26
	MILFORD HAVEN.				
Governor	*Sir* John Owen, *Bart.*				14 June 21
	MONTREAL.				
Town-Major	*Ensign* Colin Macdonald, h. p. 50 Foot	86	13	9	30 Jan. 35
	NEW BRUNSWICK.				
Town-Major	*Lieut.* John Gallagher, h. p. 98 Foot	86	13	9	25 Feb. 19
	NEW GENEVA.				
Fort-Major	Anthony Wharton	159	4	0	26 Dec. 16
	PORTSMOUTH.				
Town-Major	*Lieut.* Henry White, late 7 R. Vet. Bn.	136	17	6	2 Oct. 23
Physician	*Director-Gen.* *Sir* James M'Grigor, *Bart., MD.*	173	7	6	13 June 11
Surgeon	Isaac Chaldecott	44	2	1	3 Nov. 90
	ST. HELENA.				
Town-Major	*Captain* George Adams Barnes, St. Helena Regt.	173	7	6	6 Nov. 35
	ST. JOHN'S, NEWFOUNDLAND.				
Fort-Major	*Lieut.* William Jenkins, R. Newf. Companies	86	13	9	5 Nov. 47
	ST. JOHN'S, or PRINCE EDWARD'S ISLAND.				
Town-Major	**Captain* Ambrose Lane	86	13	9	1 Jan. 19
	ST. MAWES.				
Capt. or Keeper	*Field Marshal Sir* Geo. Nugent, *Bt. GCB.*	104	18	9	2 Nov. 96
	SCARBOROUGH CASTLE.				
Governor	*Major-Gen.* James Grant, *CB.*	15	4	2	30 Jan. 32
	SHEERNESS.				
Governor	*Gen.* S. *Visc.* Combermere, *GCB. GCH.*	284	7	11	25 Jan. 21
	STIRLING CASTLE.				
Major	*Lieut.* Patrick Tytler	86	13	9	5 Aug. 95
Chaplain	*Rev.* Robert Watson	76	0	10	26 April 38
	TOWER OF LONDON.				
Constable	*Field Marshal* Arthur *Duke of* Wellington, *KG. GCB. GCH.*	947	9	7	29 Dec. 26
Lieutenant	*General* John Sulivan Wood	663	1	8	26 Feb. 33
Deputy-Lieut.	*Colonel Hon.* George Cathcart, Unattached	346	15	0	13 Feb. 46
Major	*Captain* John Henry Elrington, 28 Dragoons	173	7	6	4 July 16
Chaplain	*Rev.* Henry Melville	115	11	8	6 April 40
	FORT WILLIAM.				
Lieut.-Gov.	*General Rt. Hon. Sir* James Kempt, *GCB. GCH.*	173	7	6	10 Oct. 12

MILITARY ESTABLISHMENTS.

CHELSEA HOSPITAL.

		Per Ann. £	s.	d.	Date of Appointment.
Governor	𝔓 *Gen. Hon. Sir* Edward Paget, *GCB.*	500	0	0	10 Jan. 37
Lieut.-Gov.	𝔓 *Gen. Sir* George Anson, *GCB.*	400	0	0	23 Feb. 46
Major	*Lieut.-Col.* Henry Le Blanc	300	0	0	22 Sept. 14
Adjutant	𝔓 *Col. Sir* John Morillyon Wilson, *CB. KH.*	100	0	0	16 Nov. 22
Chaplain	*Rev.* G. Mathias, *MA.*	300	0	0	1847
Phys. and Surg.	Daniel Maclachlan, *MD.*	500	0	0	8 May 40

ROYAL MILITARY COLLEGE.

		£	s.	d.	Date of Appointment.
Governor	𝔓 𝔚 *Lieut.-Gen. Sir* Geo. Scovell, *KCB.*	1000	0	0	3 Feb. 37
Lieut.-Gov.	𝔚 *Major-Gen.* Thomas William Taylor, *CB.*	383	5	0	3 Feb. 37
Major and Superintendent of Studies,	𝔓 *Lt.-Col.* G. W. Prosser				13 May 42
Captains of Companies of Gentlemen Cadets	*Captain* Robert Daly[1]	129	5	5	23 June 43
	Captain James W. Dalgety	129	5	5	28 June 44
Chaplain, &c.	*Rev.* H. L. Chepmell	300	0	0	25 Mar. 04
Quarter-Master	*Lieut.* John Whitacre Tipping	97	6	8	10 Sept. 30
Surgeon	John Pickering, *MD.*	255	10	0	29 June 32
Assist.-Surg.	Melville Neale, *MD.*	136	17	6	5 Dec. 43

ROYAL MILITARY ASYLUM AT CHELSEA.

		£	s.	d.	Date of Appointment.
Commandant	𝔓 *Colonel* Peter Brown	400	0	0	15 Dec. 43
Sec. and Adjt.	*Captain* William Siborne	182	10	0	10 Nov. 43
Quarter-Master	William Cousins	180	0	0	1 July 47
Surgeon	Thomas Graham Balfour, *MD.*	273	15	0	1 Aug. 48

ROYAL HIBERNIAN SCHOOL IN DUBLIN.

		£	s.	d.	Date of Appointment.
Surgeon	𝔓 𝔚 James Goodall Elkington[2]	431	3	6	5 Mar. 41

1 Captain Daly served with the 14th at the siege and capture of Bhurtpore in 1825-6, and was severely wounded at the assault,—left leg amputated.

2 Mr. Elkington served at the capture of Madeira in 1807, and in the Peninsula from April 1809 to Nov. 1812; present at the battle of Talavera; left prisoner with the wounded at that city, and marched into France; released in 1810, and rejoined the army in Portugal, on its retreat from Busaco; present with it in the lines of Torres Vedras; battle of Fuentes d'Onor; sieges of Ciudad Rodrigo and Badajoz; battle of Salamanca; capture of Madrid; and during the whole siege of Burgos in charge of the Hospital for receiving the wounded; on the retreat of the army he was left in charge of the English and French wounded, and again made prisoner. He served the campaign of 1814 in Holland, and was present with the 30th in Fort Frederick Henry on the Scheldt, when it was commanded by a line-of-battle ship and gun brigs. He served also the campaign of 1815, including the battles of Quatre Bras and Waterloo, and the capture of Paris. *Hospital-Assistant* 8 Aug. 07; *Assist.-Surg.* 7 July 08; *Surgeon* 11 Mar. 43.

OFFICERS

TO WHOM

HONORARY DISTINCTIONS

HAVE BEEN GRANTED

IN COMMEMORATION OF THEIR SERVICES IN THE FOLLOWING BATTLES OR ACTIONS.

Maida		4 July	1806
Roleia		17 Aug.	08
Vimiera		21 Aug.	
Sahagun, Benevente, &c.	(actions of Cavalry)	Dec. 1808 & Jan.	09
Corunna		16 Jan.	
Martinique	(attack and capture)	Feb.	
Talavera		27 & 28 July	
Guadaloupe	(attack and capture)	Jan. & Feb.	10
Busaco		27 Sept.	
Barrosa		5 Mar.	11
Fuentes d'Onor		5 May	
Albuhera		16 May	
Java	(attack and capture)	Aug. & Sept.	
Ciudad Rodrigo	(assault and capture)	Jan.	12
Badajos	(do. do.)	17 March & 6 April	
Salamanca		22 July	
Fort Detroit, America	(capture of)	Aug.	
Vittoria		21 June	13
Pyrenees		28 July to 2 Aug.	
St. Sebastian	(assault and capture)	Aug. & Sept.	
Chateauguay, America		26 Oct.	
Nivelle		10 Nov.	
Chrystler's Farm, America		11 Nov.	
Nive		9 to 13 Dec.	
Orthes		27 Feb.	14
Toulouse		10 April	

On the 7th October, 1813, a General Order, of which the following is an abstract, was issued by the Commander-in-Chief:—

Whereas considerable inconvenience has arisen from the number of Medals which have been issued in commemoration of the brilliant and distinguished events in which the success of His Majesty's arms has received the Royal approbation, the Prince Regent has been pleased to command that the following Regulations shall be adopted in the grant and circulation of such marks of distinction: viz.—

1st. That one Medal only shall be borne by each Officer recommended for such distinction.

2nd. That for the second and third events, which may be subsequently commemorated in like manner, each individual recommended to bear the distinction shall carry a gold Clasp attached to the ribbon to which the Medal is suspended, and inscribed with the name of the Battle or Siege to which it relates.

3rd. That upon a claim being admitted to a fourth mark of distinction, a Cross shall be borne by each officer, with the names of the four Battles or Sieges respectively inscribed thereupon; and to be worn in substitution of the distinctions previously granted to such individuals.

4th. Upon each occasion of a similar nature that may occur subsequently to the grant of a Cross, the Clasp shall again be issued to those who have a claim to the additional distinction, to be borne on the ribbon to which the Cross is suspended, in the same manner as described in No. 2 of these Regulations.

His Royal Highness was further pleased to command that the distribution of Medals or Badges for Military services of distinguished merit shall be regulated as follows: viz.—

1st. That no General or other Officer shall be considered entitled to receive them, unless he has been personally and particularly engaged upon those occasions of great importance and peculiar brilliancy, in commemoration of which such marks of distinction are to be bestowed.

2nd. That no Officer shall be considered a candidate for the Medal, or Badge, except upon the special selection and report of the Commander of the Forces upon the spot, as having merited the distinction by conspicuous services.

3rd. That the Commander of the Forces shall transmit to the Commander-in-Chief, Returns, signed by himself, specifying the names and ranks of those Officers whom he shall have selected as particularly deserving.

4th. The Commander of the Forces in making the selection will restrict his choice to the under-mentioned ranks: viz.—

General Officers.
Commanding Officers of Brigades.
Commanding Officers of Artillery, or Engineers.
Adjutant-General, and Quarter-Master-General.
Deputies of ditto, and ditto, having the rank of Field Officers.
Assistants, Adjutant and Quarter-Master-Generals, having the rank of Field-Officers, and being at the head of the Staff, with a detached Corps, or distinct division of the Army.
Military Secretary, having the rank of Field Officer.
Commanding Officers of Battalions, or Corps equivalent thereto; and Officers who may have succeeded to the actual command during the engagement, in consequence of the death or removal of the original Commanding Officer.

The Crosses, Medals, and Clasps, are to be worn by the General Officers, suspended by a Ribbon of the colour of the sash, with a blue edge, round the neck; and by the Commanding Officers of Battalions, or Corps equivalent thereto; and Officers who may have succeeded to the actual command during the engagement; the Chiefs of Military Departments, and their Deputies and Assistants (having the rank of Field Officers); and such other Officers as may be specially recommended, attached by a Ribbon of the same description to the button-hole of their uniform.

Those Badges which would have been conferred upon the Officers who have fallen at or died since the Battles and Sieges, shall, as a token of respect for their memories, be transmitted to their respective families.—*Vide the London Gazette, 9th October*, 1813.

NAMES AND PRESENT RANK.	DISTINCTIONS.	SIEGES, BATTLES, ETC.	RANK OR COMMAND AT THE TIME.
Abercromby, Col. *Hon. Alex., CB.*, late of Colds. Gds.	Cross	*Albuhera, Vittoria, Pyrenees, Orthes	*Lt.-Col. 28 F. comm. a Brigade Assistant Quar.-Mas.-Gen.
Allan, Major-Gen. James, *CB.* ....from 57 F.	do	Toulouse	Major 94 Foot.
Anderson, Lieut.-Gen. Paul, *CB.* ....78 F.	do	Corunna	Acting Dep.-Adj.-General
Anglesey, Field Marshal *The Marq. of, KG. GCB. GCH.* Royal Horse Guards	do	Sahagun, &c.	Commanding the Cavalry
Anson, Gen. *Sir* George, *GCB.*........4 Dr. Gds.	Medal and 2 Clasps	Talavera, Salamanca, Vittoria	A Brigade of Cavalry
Arbuthnot, Lieut.-Gen. *Sir* Thomas, *KCB.*.....71 F.	Cross and 1 Clasp	Roleia and Vimiera, Corunna, Pyrenees, Nivelle, Orthes	Assistant-Adjutant-General Assistant Quar.-Mas.-Gen.
Arbuthnot, Lieut.-Gen. *Sir* Robert, *KCB.* ....76 F.	Cross and 3 Clasps	Busaco, Albuhera, Badajoz, Nivelle, Nive, Orthes, Toulouse	Military Secretary to Lord Beresford.
Arbuthnott, Lieut-Gen. *Hon.* Hugh, *CB.* ......38 F.	Medal	Busaco	Major 52 Foot
Armstrong, Major-Gen. *Sir* Richard, *CB.* ....95 F.	Medal and 2 Clasps	Busaco, Vittoria, Pyrenees	16 Portuguese 10 Caçadores
Auchmuty, Major-Gen. Samuel Benj., *CB.*	Medal and 1 Clasp	Orthes, Toulouse	Light Companies
Aylmer, General *Lord, GCB.*..................18 F.	Cross and 1 Clasp	Talavera, Busaco, Fuentes d'Onor, Vittoria, Nive	Assistant-Adjutant-Gen. Deputy-Adjutant-Gen. A Brigade
Bace, Captain William ....Unattached	Medal	Toulouse	1 Battalion 61 Foot
Balvaird, Col. *William, CB.* ....late of 37 F.	Medal and 1 Clasp	Nivelle, Nive	Capt. 3d Battalion 95 Foot
Barnard, Lieut.-Gen. *Sir* Andrew F., *GCB. GCH.* Rifle Brig.	Cross and 4 Clasps	Barrosa, Ciudad Rodrigo, *Badajoz, Salamanca, Vittoria, Nivelle, Orthes, Toulouse	A Battalion 95 Foot *A Division
Barns, Lieut.-Gen. *Sir* J. Stevenson, *KCB.* ....20 F.	Cross	Busaco, Salamanca, St. Sebastian, Nive	Lieut.-Col. 3d Battalion 1 Foot
Bathurst, Lieut.-Gen. *Sir* James, *KCB.*............	do	Roleia and Vimiera, Corunna, Talavera, Busaco	Military Secretary
Beckwith, Major-Gen. Charles, *CB.*	Medal	Toulouse	Assistant-Quar.-Mas.-Gen.
Bell, Major-Gen. John, *CB.*....................	Cross	Pyrenees, Nivelle, Orthes, Toulouse	Assistant-Quar.-Mas.-Gen.
Bell, Lieut.-Col. *Thomas, CB.* ....late of 48 F.	do	Pyrenees, Nivelle, Salamanca, Orthes	Major 48 Foot
Beresford, General *Viscount, GCB. GCH.* ....16 F.	Cross and 7 Clasps	Corunna Busaco, Albuhera, Badajoz, Salamanca, Vittoria, Pyrenees, Nivelle, Nive, Orthes, Toulouse	Major-General Lieut.-General and Marshal commanding Portuguese
Berkeley, Lieut-Gen. *Sir* Geo. H. F., *KCB.* 35 F.	Cross and 3 Clasps	Busaco, Fuentes d'Onor, Badajoz, Salamanca, Vittoria, St. Sebastian, Nive	Assistant-Adjutant-General
Blake, Col. *Wm. Williams, CB.* ......late of 11 Dr.	Medal	Roleia and Vimiera	
Blakeney, Lt.-Gen. *Rt. Hon. Sir* E., *KCB. GCH.* 7 F.	Cross and 1 Clasp	Martinique, Albuhera, Badajoz, Vittoria, Pyrenees	Lieut.-Col. 7 Foot
Bouverie, Lieut.-Gen. *Sir* H. F., *KCB.*........97 F.	do	Salamanca, Vittoria, St. Sebastian, Nive, Orthes	Assistant-Adjutant-General

P Bradford, General *Sir* Thomas, *GCB. GCH.*.....4 F.	Cross and 1 clasp.	Corunna, Salamanca, Vittoria, St. Sebastian, Nive	Portuguese Brigade
P Brandreth, Colonel Thomas Alston, *CB.*......R. Art.	Medal and 1 Clasp	Pyrenees, Toulouse	
P Brisbane, Gen. *Sir* Thos. M., *Bt.*, *GCB. GCH.* 34 F.	Cross and 1 Clasp	Vittoria, Pyrenees, Nivelle, Orthes, Toulouse	A Brigade
P *Browne*, Lieut.-Col. *Gustavus*, *CB.* ....late of 95 F.	Cross	Salamanca, Pyrenees, Nivelle, Nive	9 Portuguese Caçadores
P WL *Browne*, Col. *Fielding*, *CB.*..................	Medal	Badajoz	Capt. 40 Foot
P Buchan, Lieut.-Gen. *Sir* John, *KCB.* ....32 F.	Cross and 1 Clasp	Guadaloupe, *Vittoria, *Pyrenees, *Nivelle, *Nive	*Col. 7 Portuguese
Bunbury, Lieut.-Gen. *Sir Henry Edward*, *Bt. KCB*..	Medal	Maida	Deputy-Quar.-Mas.-Gen.
Bunce, Lieut.-Col. Richard ....h. p. R. Marine.	do	Java	Capt. Royal Marines
P Burgoyne, Major-Gen. *Sir* John F. *KCB.* from R. Eng.	Cross and 1 Clasp	Badajoz, Salamanca, Vittoria, *St. Sebastian, *Nive	*Comm. Royal Engineers
Burslem, Col. *Nathaniel*, *KH.* ....late of 67 F.	Medal	Java..	Deputy-Quar.-Mas.-Gen.
P WL Cameron, Major-Gen. *Sir* Alexander, *KCB.* 74 F.	Medal and 2 Clasps	Ciudad Rodrigo, Badajoz, Salamanca...........	Rifle Brigade
P Campbell, Gen. *Sir* Henry Frederick, *KCB.GCH.*25 F.	Medal and 1 Clasp	Talavera, Salamanca............................	{ Brigadier-Gen. and Major-General comm. a Brigade of Guards
P WL Campbell, Maj.-Gen. *Sir* Guy, *Bart.*, *CB.* 3 W. I. R.	Medal	Pyrenees..	Major 6 Foot
P pbell, Lieut-Col. Patrick, *CB.* ....Unatt.	Medal and 1 Clasp	Nivelle, Nive	52 Foot
P pbell, Colonel Charles Stuart, *CB.* ....h. p. 1 F.	do	Vittoria, St. Sebastian	3 Portuguese
P WL Cathcart, Lieut.-Gen. *Earl*, *KCB.* ..3 Dr. Gds.	Medal and 2 Clasps	Barrosa, Salamanca, Vittoria	Assistant-Quarter-Master-General
P Chapman, Lt.-Gen. *Sir* S. R., *CB. KCH.* from R. Eng.	Medal	Busaco	
P Charleton, Lieut.-Col. Edward, *KH.* ....Unatt.	do	Toulouse	
P WL Clifton, Lieut.-Gen. *Sir* Arthur B. *KCB. KCH.* 1 Dr.	Medal and 1 Clasp	Fuentes d'Onor, Vittoria	1 Dragoons
P Combermere, General Stapleton, *Lord Viscount*, *KCB. GCH* .... 1 Life Gds. }	Medal and 1 Clasp }	Talavera, Fuentes d'Onor, Salamanca, Orthes, Toulouse	{ Maj.-Gen. comm. Brig. Cavalry { Lieut.-Gen. comm. Cavalry
P Conyers, Maj.-Gen. Charles E., *CB.*	Medal	Orthes	82 Foot
P WL *Cooke*, Lieut.-Col. *R. H.*, *CB.*, late of Gren. Gds.	do	St. Sebastian	Detachment of Guards
P *Cother*, Lt.-Col. *Charles*, *CB.* ....late of 83 F.	do	Vittoria	71 Foot
P Cumming, General *Sir* Henry John, *KCH.*....12 Dr.	do	Salamanca	Colonel comm. 11 Dragoons
P WL Dalmer, Major-Gen. Thomas, *CB.* ....47 F.	Medal and 1 Clasp	Salamanca, Vittoria	A Light Battalion
P Daniel, Captain Lewis......h. p. late German Legion	do	Orthes, Toulouse	Artillery German Legion
P Darling, General *Sir* Ralph, *GCH*............69 F.	Medal	Corunna	Lieut.-Col. 51 Foot
P Davy, Lieut.-Gen. *Sir* Wm. Gabriel, *CB. KCH.* 60 F.	Medal and 1 Clasp	Roleia and Vimiera, Talavera	Major 5th Battalion 60 Foot
P Derinzy, Lieut.-Col. Barth. Vigors, *KH.* ......86 F.	Medal	Toulouse..	7 Caçadores
Dixon, Colonel Matthew Charles .....Royal Engineers	Medal	Detroit	Commanding Royal Engineers
P Douglas, Lieut.-Gen. *Sir* James, *KCB.*........93 F.	Cross and 3 Clasps }	Busaco, Salamanca, Pyrenees, Nivelle, Nive, Orthes, Toulouse	{ Colonel 8 Portuguese, { A Brigade
P WL Douglas, Lieut.-Gen. *Sir* Neil, *KCB. KCH.* 72 F.	Cross	Pyrenees, Nivelle, Nive, Toulouse	
P Douglas, Colonel Robert, *CB.* ....late of R. Art.	do	Salamanca, Vittoria, Pyrenees, Nivelle,	
P Downes, Lieut.-Gen. Ulysses, *Lord*, *KCB.* ....54 F.	Cross and 1 Clasp	Vittoria, Pyrenees, Nivelle, Nive, Toulouse	A. D. C. to the Duke of Wellington

NAMES AND PRESENT RANK.	DISTINCTIONS.	SIEGES, BATTLES, ETC.	RANK OR COMMAND AT THE TIME.
Dowman, Lieut.-Gen. *Sir* Thos., *CB. KCH.*...R. Art.	Medal	Salamanca	
Doyle, Col. *Sir John Milley*, *KCB.* late of 12 Garr. Bn.	Cross and 1 Clasp	Fuentes d'Onor, Ciudad Rodrigo, Vittoria, Pyrenees, Orthes	Colonel 19 Portuguese
Duffy, Major-Gen. John, *CB.*	Medal	Badajoz	Brevet-Major 43 Foot
D'Urban, Lieut.-Gen. *Sir* B., *GCB. KCH.*....51 F.	Cross and 5 Clasps	Busaco, Albuhera, Badajoz, Salamanca, Vittoria, Pyrenees, Nivelle, Nive, Toulouse	Brigadier-General Portuguese
Eden, General William	Medal	Java	Quarter-Master-General
Ellicombe, Maj.-Gen. C. Grene, *CB.*....from R. Eng.	Medal	St. Sebastian	
Eustace, Lieut.-Gen. Wm. C., *CB. KCH.*......60 F.	Medal and 1 Clasp	Fuentes d'Onor, Salamanca	Chasseurs Britanniques
Fannce, Major-Gen. Alured Dodsworth, *CB.*	Medal	Salamanca	4 Foot
Fergusson, Major-Gen. James, *CB.*	do	Badajoz	Captain 43 Foot
FitzGerald, Lieut.-Gen. *Sir* John Foster, *KCB.* 62 F.	Cross	Badajoz, Salamanca, Vittoria, Pyrenees	A Light Battalion A Brigade
Forbes, Major-Gen. David, *CB.*	Medal	Java	Flank Battalion
Fuller, Lieut.-Col. *Francis*, *CB.* ..late of 59 F.	do	St. Sebastian	
Gardiner, Lieut.-Gen. *Sir* John, *KCB.* ....50 F.	Medal and 1 Clasp	Nivelle, Orthes	A Brigade
Gardiner, Maj.-Gen. *Sir* Robert, *KCB. KCH.* from R. Art.	Cross and 2 Clasps	Barrosa, Badajoz, Salamanca, Vittoria, Orthes, Toulouse	
Goldfinch, Major-Gen. Henry, *CB.* .... from R. Eng.	Cross	Vittoria, Nive, Orthes, Toulouse	
Goldie, Major-Gen. George Leigh, *CB.*	Medal	Albuhera	Major 66 Foot
Gomm, Lieut.-Gen. *Sir* W. M. *KCB.* ....13 F.	Cross and 1 Clasp	Badajoz, Salamanca, Vittoria, St. Sebastian, Nive	Assistant-Quarter-Master-General
Gordon, Lieut.-Gen. Gabriel..................91 F.	Medal and 1 Clasp	Martinique, Guadaloupe	Deputy-Quarter-Master-General
Gordon, Major-General William A., *CB.*	Medal	Nive	A Light Battalion
Gough, Lieut.-Gen. Hugh, *Lord*, *GCB.*........87 F.	Cross	Talavera, Barrosa, Vittoria, Nivelle	87 Foot
Griffiths, Lieut.-Col. Hugh....East India Comp. Service	Medal	Java	Captain 5 Bengal Volunteer Battalion
Guise, Lieut.-Gen. *Sir* John Wright, *Bt.*, *KCB.* 85 F.	Cross	Fuentes d'Onor, Salamanca, Vittoria, Nive	Col. comm. 3 Foot Guards
Halkett, General *Sir* Colin, *GCB. GCH.* ..45 F.	Cross	Albuhera, Salamanca, Vittoria, Nive	Col. comm. a Brig. Ger. Leg.
Halkett, Lt.-Col. *Hugh*, *CB. KCH.* late Ger. Leg.	Medal and 1 Clasp	Albuhera, Salamanca	2 Light Infantry German Legion
Hardinge, Lt.-Gen. Henry, *Visc. GCB.*....57 F.	Cross and 5 Clasps	Busaco, Albuhera, Badajoz, Salamanca, Vittoria, Pyrenees, Nivelle, Nive, Orthes	Deputy-Quarter-Master-General, Portuguese
Hare-Clarges, Maj.-Gen. Richard Goddard, *CB.*	Medal and 1 Clasp	Nivelle, Nive	Assist.-Adjutant-General
Harrison, Lt.-Col. *John Bacon*, *CB.*....late of 50 F.	Medal and 2 Clasps	Pyrenees, Nive, Orthes	50 Foot
Hartmann, Lieut.-Col. *Sir* Julius, *KCB. GCH.* late Ger. Leg.	Cross and 2 Clasps	Talavera, Albuhera, Salamanca, Vittoria, St. Sebastian, Nive	Artillery German Legion

Name	Decoration	Actions	Command
Harvey, Lieut-Gen. *Sir* John, *KCB. KCH.* ......59 F.	Medal	Chrystler's Farm	Deputy-Adjutant-General
Harvey, Maj.-Gen. *Sir* Robert John, *CB.* ..2 W. I. R.	do	Orthes	Assist.-Quarter-Master-Gen. Port.
Hawkins, Lieut.-Col. *John P., CB.* ....late of 68 F.	Medal and 2 Clasps	Vittoria, Pyrenees, Nivelle	68 Foot
Hay, Maj.-Gen. James, *CB.*	Medal and 1 Clasp	Vittoria, Nive	16 Light Dragoons
Hill, Col. *Sir Robert C., CB.* late of R. H. Gds.	Medal	Vittoria	A Brigade of Cavalry
Hill, Maj.-Gen. *Sir* Dudley St. Leger, *KCB.*	Cross and 1 Clasp	Fuentes d'Onor, Badajoz, Salamanca, Vittoria, St. Sebastian	8 Caçadores
Hope, Maj.-Gen. *Sir* James Archibald, *KCB.* ..9 F.	Cross and 1 Clasp	Vittoria, Nivelle, Nive, Orthes, Toulouse	Assist.-Adjutant-General
Hunt, Lieut.-Col. *John Philip, CB.* ..late of 11 F.	Medal & 2 Clasps	Badajoz, Salamanca St. Sebastian	1st Battalion 52 Foot Colonel of Light Division
Jackson, Lieut.-Col. Henry George ....R.Art.	Medal	Chrystler's Farm	
Kempt, General, *Right Hon. Sir* James, *GCB. GCH.* ..1 F.	Cross and 3 Clasps	Maida Badajoz, Vittoria, Nivelle, Nive, Orthes, Toulouse	Lieut.-Col. Light Infantry A Brigade
Kerrison, Lt.-Gen. *Sir* Ed. *Bt. KCB.GCH.* 14 Dr.	Medal	Orthes	Lieut.-Col. 7 Hussars
King, Lieut.-Gen. *Sir* Henry, *CB. KCH.* ......3 F.	Medal	Vittoria	82 Foot
Kyle, Captain Alexander..............h. p. 94 F.	do	do.	Captain 94 Foot
Langlands, Major George........late 13 R. Vet. Bat.	Medal and 1 Clasp	Ciudad Rodrigo, Badajoz	Captain 74 Foot
Leith, Lieut.-Gen. *Sir* Alexander, *KCB.* ......90 F.	Cross and 1 Clasp	Vittoria, Pyrenees, Nivelle, Nive, Orthes	31 Foot
Lightfoot, Maj.-Gen. Thomas, *CB.*	Medal and 2 Clasps	Vittoria, Pyrenees, Toulouse	Major 45 Foot
Lillie, Lieut.-Col. *Sir* John Scott, *CB.*........Unatt.	Cross	Pyrenees, Nivelle, Orthes, Toulouse	Lieut.-Col. 7 Caçadores
Londonderry, Gen. Charles Wm. *Marq. of, GCB. GCH.*..........2 Life Gds.	Cross and 1 Clasp	Sahagun and Benevente Talavera, Busaco, Fuentes d'Onor, Badajoz	A Brigade of Cavalry Adjutant-General
Lumley, Gen. *Hon. Sir* Wm. *GCB.*......1 Dr. Gds.	Medal	Albuhera	Major-General comm. Cavalry
M'Donald, Major-Gen. John, *CB.*........from 92 F.	Medal and 1 Clasp	Vittoria, Pyrenees	A Portuguese Brigade
Macbean, Lieut.-Gen. *Sir* William, *KCB.*......92 F.	Cross	Busaco, Salamanca, St. Sebastian, Nive	19 Portuguese 24 do
Macdonald, Lieut.-Gen. *Sir* John, *GCB.* ......42 F.	Medal and 1 Clasp	Barrosa Nive	Deputy-Adjutant-General Assistant-Adjutant-General
Macdonald, Lieut.-Col. *Robert, CB.*..late of R. Art.	Medal	Salamanca	
Macdonell, Lieut.-Col. *George, CB.*........late of 79 F.	Medal	Chateauguay	Glengarry Light Infantry
Macdonell, Lt.-Gen. *Sir* James, *KCB. KCH.* 79 F.	do	Maida	Major 2nd Batt. 78 Regiment
Macpherson, Maj.-Gen. Robert Barclay, *CB.KH.*	Medal and 1 Clasp	Vittoria, Orthes	Major 88 F.
Maitland, General *Sir* Peregrine, *KCB.*....17 F.	Medal	Nive	Colonel comm. 1 Brig. of Guards
Manners, Maj.-Gen. *Lord* Charles S., *KCB.*....3 Dr.	Medal and 2 Clasps	Salamanca, Toulouse	3 Dragoons
Manners, Lieut.-Col. *Russell, CB.*......late of 74 F.	Cross	Fuentes d'Onor, Ciudad Rodrigo, Badajoz, Orthes	74 F.
Mansel, Lieut.-Col. *John, CB.* ....late of 53 F.	Medal and 1 Clasp	Salamanca, Toulouse	A Provisional Battalion

NAMES AND PRESENT RANK.	DISTINCTIONS.	SIEGES, BATTLES, ETC.	RANK OR COMMAND AT THE TIME.
Meade, Lieut.-Gen. *Hon.* John, *CB.*	Medal	Busaco	Lieut.-Colonel 45 F.
Michell, Colonel John, *CB.* ... R. Art.	Medal and 1 Clasp	Orthes, Toulouse	
Michell, Lieut.-Col. Chas. C., *KH.* ... h. p. Port. Serv.	Medal and 1 Clasp	Vittoria, Toulouse	Captain Portuguese Artillery
Middlemore, Lieut.-Gen. George, *CB.* ... 48 F.	Medal	Talavera	Major 48 F. succeeded to the comm.
Murphy, Major George H. E. ... late of 22 F.	Medal	Toulouse	Major 23 Portuguese
Napier, Lieut.-Gen. *Sir* Charles James, *GCB.* .. 22 F.	Medal	Corunna	Major commanding 50 Foot
Napier, Lieut.-Gen. *Sir* Geo. T., *KCB.* ... 1 W. I. R.	Medal and 1 Clasp	Martinique Ciudad Rodrigo	 Major 52 F. comm. the Advance
Napier, Major-Gen. *Sir* William F. P., *KCB.* .. 27 F.	Medal and 2 Clasps	Salamanca, Nivelle, Nive	Major 43 Foot
NETHERLANDS, Field Marshal *His Majesty the King of the, GCB.*	Cross and 2 Clasps	Ciudad Rodrigo, Badajoz, Salamanca, Vittoria, Pyrenees, Nivelle	Aide-de-Camp to the Duke of Wellington.
Nickle, Col. *Sir* Robert, *KH.* ... Unatt.	Medal	Nivelle	Capt. 88 Foot
Nicol, Lieut.-Gen. Charles, *CB.* ... 68 F.	do	Nive	
Nicolls, Lieut.-Gen. *Sir* Jasper, *KCB.* ... 5 F.	do	Corunna	Lieut.-Col. 2nd Battalion 14 Foot
Paget, Gen. *Hon. Sir* Edward, *GCB.* ... 28 F.	do	do	Major-General
Pakenham, Lieut.-Gen. *Hon. Sir* H. R. *KCB.* .. 43 F.	Cross	Busaco, Fuentes d'Onor, Ciudad Rodrigo, Badajoz	Assistant-Adjutant-General
Parker, Major-Gen. John Boteler, *CB.* late of R. Art.	Medal	Vittoria	
Patrickson, Col. *C. C., CB* ... late of 43 F.	Medal	Toulouse	43 Foot
Plenderleath, Lieut.-Col. *Charles, CB.* ... late of 49 F.	Medal	Chrystler's Farm	49 Foot
Purvis, Lieut.-Col. Charles ... h. p. Canad. Fencibles	Medal	Vittoria	Major 1 Dragoons
Pynn, Lieut.-Col. *Sir Henry, CB.* .. late of Port. Serv.	Medal and 2 Clasps	Fuentes d'Onor, Pyrenees, Orthes	18 Portuguese
Quentin, Lt.-Gen. *Sir* George A., *CB. KCH.*	Medal and 1 Clasp	Orthes, Toulouse	10 Hussars
Rainey, Major John ... late of 82 F.	Medal	Roleia and Vimiera	Assistant-Quarter-Master-General
Riall, General *Sir* Phineas, *KCH.* ... 15 F.	Medal and 1 Clasp	Martinique, Guadaloupe	Lieut.-Col. commanding a Brigade
Roberts, Colonel William ... late of R. Art.	Medal	Barrosa	
Robinson, General *Sir* Fred. Philipse, *GCB.* ... 39 F.	Medal and 2 Clasps	Vittoria, St. Sebastian, Nive	A Brigade
Rolt, Major-Gen. *Sir* John, *KCB.*	Cross and 1 Clasp	Vittoria, Nivelle, Nive, Orthes, Toulouse	Lieut.-Col. 17 Portuguese
Ross, Maj.-Gen. *Sir* Hew Dalrymple, *KCB.* R. Art.	Cross and 2 Clasps	Busaco, Badajoz, Salamanca, Vittoria, Nivelle, Nive	
Rowan, Lieut.-Col. *Charles, CB.* ... late of 52 F.	Medal and 2 Clasps	Ciudad Rodrigo, Badajoz, Salamanca	Assist. Adjutant-General
Schoedde, Colonel *Sir* James Holmes, *KCB.* .. Unatt.	Medal	Nivelle	
Scovell, Lieut.-Gen. *Sir* Geo., *KCB.* .. 7 Dr. Gds.	Cross and 1 Clasp	Vittoria, Pyrenees, Nivelle, Nive, Toulouse	Staff Corps of Cavalry
Seaton, Lieut.-Gen. John, *Lord, GCB. GCMG. GCH.* ... 26 F.	Cross and 3 Clasps	Corunna Albuhera Ciudad Rodrigo,* Nivelle,* Nive, Orthes, Toulouse	Military Secretary 66 Foot, commanding a Brigade 52 Foot, *a Brigade
Slade, General *Sir* John, *Bt., GCH.* ... 5 Dr. Gds.	Medal and 1 Clasp	Corunna, *Fuentes d'Onor	Brigadier-Gen., *Major-Gen.

𝔓 𝔚 Smith, Major-Gen. James Webber, *CB.* ..... R. Art.	Medal and 1 clasp	Vittoria, St. Sebastian	
𝔓 Smith, Major-Gen. *Sir* Charles Felix, *KCB.* from R. Eng.	do	do	
𝔓 *Snodgrass*, Colonel *Kenneth*, *CB.* .... late Unatt.	Cross	*St. Sebastian, Nivelle, Nive, Orthes	*13th Portuguese, 1 Caçadores
𝔓 𝔚 Somerset, Lieut.-Gen. *Lord* FitzRoy James Hen. *GCB.* .... 53 F.	Cross and 5 Clasps	Fuentes d'Onor, Badajoz, Salamanca, Vittoria, Pyrenees, Nivelle, Nive, Orthes, Toulouse	A.-de-C. and Military Secretary to the Duke of Wellington
𝔓 *Stewart*, Maj.-Gen. *William* .... late of 3 F.	Medal	Albuhera	
𝔓 Stovin, Major-Gen. *Sir* Frederick, *KCB. KCMG.* 83 F.	Cross and 2 Clasps	Salamanca, Vittoria, Pyrenees, Nivelle, Orthes, Toulouse	Assistant-Adjutant-General
𝔓 𝔚 Strafford, Gen. John, *Earl of*, *GCB. GCH.* 29 F.	Cross and 1 Clasp	Vittoria, Pyrenees, Nivelle, Nive, Orthes	A Brigade
𝔓 Thomas, Major-Gen. Henry, *CB.*	Medal and 2 Clasps	Nivelle, Orthes, Toulouse	A Light Battalion
𝔓 Thomson, Major-Gen. Alexander, *CB.*	Medal	St. Sebastian	Assistant Engineer
𝔓 *Thornton*, Colonel *Henry*, *CB.* .... late of 82 F.	Cross	Talavera, Nivelle, Orthes, Toulouse	Lieut.-Col. 40 Foot
𝔓 Tonson, Major-Gen. Jacob, *CB.*	Medal	Nive	Major 84 Foot
𝔓 Trevor, Lieut.-Gen. *Hon.* Henry Otway, *CB.* .... 31 F.	do	Salamanca	Commanding Coldstream Gds.
𝔓 Turner, Colonel George, *CB.* .... R. Art.	Medal and 1 Clasp	Orthes, Toulouse	
𝔓 Tweeddale, Lieut.-Gen. G., *Marq. of*, *KT. CB.* 30 F.	Medal	Vittoria	Assist.-Quarter-Master-General.
𝔓 Upton, Lieut.-Gen. *Hon.* Arthur Percy, *CB.*	Medal and 1 Clasp	Vittoria, Nive	do
𝔓 𝔚 Vandeleur, Gen. *Sir* John, *GCB* .... 16 Dr.	Cross	Ciudad Rodrigo, Salamanca, Vittoria, Nive	A Brigade
𝔓 Vernon, Major-Gen. Henry Chas. Edw., *CB.*	Medal	Salamanca	Staff
𝔓 Wallace, Lieut.-Gen. *Sir* John A., *Bt.*, *KCB.* .. 88 F.	Medal and 2 Clasps	Busaco, Fuentes d'Onor, *Salamanca	Commanding 88 Foot, *a Brigade
𝔓 *Ward*, Col. *John Richard*, *CB.* .... late of 2 Dr.	do	Badajoz, Salamanca, Pyrenees	2nd Batt. 27 F. Light Inf. 4 Div. 1 Battalion 36 Foot
Watson, Lieut.-Gen. *Sir* James, *KCB.* .... 14 F.	Medal	Java	Lieut.-Col. 14 Foot
𝔓 Watson, Major-Gen. *Sir* Henry, *CB.* .... 63 F.	do	Salamanca	1 Portuguese Cavalry.
𝔓 𝔚 Wellington, Field Marshal Arthur, *Duke of*, *KG. GCB. GCH.* Gren. Gds. Rifle Brig., Constable of the Tower of London, and Lord Warden of the Cinque Ports	Cross and 9 Clasps	Roleia and Vimiera, Talavera, Busaco, Fuentes d'Onor, Ciudad Rodrigo, Badajoz, Salamanca, Vittoria, Pyrenees, Nivelle, Nive, Orthes, Toulouse	COMMANDER OF THE FORCES
𝔓 𝔚 *Wilkins*, Lt.-Col. *Geo.*, *CB. KH.* late of Rifle Brig.	Medal	Salamanca	A Battalion of the Rifle Brigade
𝔓 Williams, Major-Gen. *Sir* Edm. Keynton, *KCB.* .. 80 F.	Cross and 1 Clasp	Busaco, Salamanca, Vittoria, St. Sebastian, Nive ..	4 Caçadores
𝔓 𝔚 *Wilson*, Lieut.-Col. *Geo. Davis*, *CB.* .. late of 4 F.	Medal	Badajoz	
𝔓 Wilson, Lieut.-Gen. *Sir* John, *KCB.* .... 11 F.	do	St. Sebastian	Brigadier-General Portuguese
𝔓 𝔚 Woodford, Lieut.-Gen. *Sir* Alex. *KCB. GCMG.* 40 F.	Medal and 2 Clasps	Salamanca, Vittoria, Nive	
𝔓 𝔚 *Woodford*, Major-Gen. *Sir John Geo.* *KCB. KCH.*	Cross	Nivelle, Nive, Orthes, Toulouse	Assist.-Quarter-Master-General
𝔓 *Woodgate*, Col. *Williams*, *CB.* .... late of 60 F.	Medal	Fuentes d'Onor	5 Battalion 60 Foot

OFFICERS

NOW HOLDING RANK IN THE ARMY

OF THE

MOST NOBLE ORDER OF THE GARTER.

(*According to their Stalls.*)

KNIGHTS, (KG.)

Field Marshal *His Royal Highness Prince* Albert, *KT. KP. GCB. GCMG.*, Scots Fus. Guards
Field Marshal *His Majesty the King of* Hanover, *KP. GCB.*
Field Marshal *His Royal Highness* A. F. *Duke of* Cambridge, *GCB. GCMG. GCH.* Coldst. Gds.
Major-General *His Royal Highness Prince* George W. F. C. of Cambridge, *GCMG.* 17 Lancers
Field Marshal *His Majesty the King of the* Belgians, *GCB. GCH.*
P W Field Marshal Arthur, *Duke of* Wellington, *GCB. GCH.* Gren. Gds.
P W Field Marshal H. W. *Marq. of* Anglesey, *GCB. GCH.* Royal Horse Guards.
P W Colonel Charles, *Duke of* Richmond, Aide-de-Camp to the Queen. Sussex Militia.
Colonel W. F. *Duke of* Buccleuch, Edinburgh Militia.
Colonel Henry, *Duke of* Cleveland, Unatt.
Colonel Thomas *Earl* de Grey, York Hussars, Yeomanry Cavalry.

OFFICERS

NOW HOLDING RANK IN THE ARMY

OF THE

MOST ANCIENT AND MOST NOBLE ORDER OF THE THISTLE.

KNIGHTS, (KT.)

Field Marshal *His Royal Highness Prince* Albert, *KG. KP. GCB. GCMG.* Scots Fus. Gds.
Lieut.-General George, *Marq. of* Tweeddale, CB. 30F.
Colonel George, *Marq. of* Huntly, Aide-de-Camp to the Queen Aberdeen Militia.
General, John, *Earl of* Stair, 46 F.

OFFICERS

NOW HOLDING RANK IN THE ARMY

OF THE

MOST ILLUSTRIOUS ORDER OF ST. PATRICK.

KNIGHTS, (KP.)

Field Marshal *His Royal Highness Prince* Albert, *KG. KT. GCB. GCMG.* Scots Fus. Gds.
Field Marshal *His Majesty the King of* Hanover, *KG. GCB.*
General Edmund, *Earl of* Cork.
Lt.-Col. Francis N. *Marq. of* Conyngham, GCH. Unatt.
Captain John, *Earl of* Donoughmore, h. p. Gr. Gds.

OFFICERS

NOW HOLDING RANK IN THE ARMY

OF THE

MOST HONOURABLE ORDER OF THE BATH.

KNIGHTS, GRAND CROSS. (GCB.)

Field Marshal *His Royal Highness Prince* Albert, *KG. KT. KP. GCMG.* Scots Fusilier Guards. (*Great Master of the Order.*)
Field Marshal *His Majesty the King of* Hanover, *KG. KP.*
Field Marshal *His Royal Highness the Duke of* Cambridge, *KG. GCMG. GCH.* Coldstream Guards. 60 F.
Field Marshal *His Majesty the King of the Belgians, KG.* and *GCH.*
P Wa Field Marshal *His Majesty the King of the* Netherlands.

P Wa Adam, Gen. *Rt. Hon. Sir* Fred., *GCMG.* 21 F.
P Wa Anglesey, Field Marshal H. W. *Marquis of, KG. GCH.* Royal Horse Guards.
P Anson, General *Sir* George ....4 Dr. Gds.
P Aylmer, Gen. Matthew, *Lord* ....18 F.
P Wa Barnard, Lt.-Gen. *Sir* A. F. *GCH.* Rif. Br.
P Beresford, Gen. W. Carr, *Visc. GCH.*... 16 F.
P Bradford, Gen. *Sir* Thomas, *GCH.* ......4 F.
P Brisbane, Gen. *Sir* Thomas M. *Bt. GCH.* 34 F.
Caldwell, Lt.-Gen. *Sir* James L... Madras Engineers
P Combermere, Gen. S., *Visc. GCH.*..1 Life Gds.
P Cotton, Lt.-Gen. *Sir* Willoughby, *KCH.* 98 F.
P D'Urban, Lt.-Gen. *Sir* Benjamin, *KCH.*.51 F.
P Douglas, Lt.-Gen. *Sir* H. *Bt. GCMG.* (*Civil*) 99 F.
Drummond, General *Sir* Gordon ....8 F.
P Gordon, Gen. *Sir* J. Willoughby, *Bt. GCH.* 23 F.
P Gough, Lt.-Gen. Hugh, *Lord* ....87 F.
P Wa Halkett, Gen. *Sir* Colin, *GCH.* ....45 F.
P Wa Hardinge, Lt.-Gen. Henry, *Viscount* (*Civil*) 57 F.
P Wa Kempt, Gen. *Rt. Hon. Sir* Jas. *GCH.* 1 F.
Littler, Major-Gen. *Sir* John Hunter, Bengal Infantry
P Londonderry, Gen. C. W. *Marq. of, GCH.* 2 L.G.
P Lumley, Gen. *Hon. Sir* William.... 1 Dr. Gds.
Lushington, Lieut.-Gen. *Sir* J. L... Madras Cavalry
P Macdonald, Lt.-Gen. *Sir* John *Adj.-Gen.* 42 F.
P Napier, Lt.-Gen. *Sir* Charles J. ....22 F.
Nugent, Field Marshal, *Rt. Hon. Sir* Geo. *Bart.* 6 F.
P Paget, Gen. *Hon. Sir* Edward ....28 F.
Pollock, Maj.-Gen. *Sir* George .. Bengal Artillery
Pottinger, Maj.-Gen. *Right Hon. Sir* Henry, *Bart.* (*Civil*) Bombay Infantry
P Robinson, Gen. *Sir* Fred. Philipse ......39 F.
P Wa Seaton, Lt.-Gen. John *Lord, GCMG. GCH.* 26 F.
P Wa Smith, Major-General *Sir* Henry George Wakelyn, *Bart.*, Rifle Brigade
P Wa Somerset, Lt.-Gen. *Lord* Fitz Roy....53 F.
P Wa Strafford, Gen. John, *Earl of, GCH.* 29 F.
P Wa Vandeleur, Gen. *Sir* John Ormsby..16 Dr.
P Wa Wellington, Field Marshal Arthur, *Duke of, KG. GCH.* Gren. Gds. Rifle Brig., Constable of the Tower of London, and Lord Warden of the Cinque Ports: Commander-in-Chief.
P Westmorland, Lt.-Gen. John, *Earl of, GCH.* (*Civil*) 56 F.

KNIGHTS COMMANDERS. (KCB.)

P Arbuthnot, Lt.-Gen. *Sir* Thomas ....71 F.
P Arbuthnot, Lt.-Gen. *Sir* Robert ....76 F.
P Barns, Lt.-Gen. *Sir* James Stevenson ....20 F.
P Bathurst, Lt.-Gen. *Sir* James... *Gov. of Berwick*
P Wa Berkeley, Lt.-Gen. *Sir* G. H. F. ....35 F.
P Blakeney, Lt.-Gen. *Rt. Hon. Sir* E. *GCH.* 7 F.
P Bourke, Lt.-Gen. *Sir* Richard ....64 F.
P Bouverie, Lt.-Gen. *Sir* H. F. *GCMG.*...97 F.
P Buchan, Lt.-Gen. *Sir* John ....32 F.
Bunbury, Lt.-Gen. *Sir Henry Edw. Bart.*
P Burgoyne, Maj.-Gen. *Sir* John F. from Roy. Eng.
P Wa Cameron, Maj.-Gen. *Sir* Alex.......74 F.
P Campbell, Gen. *Sir* Henry F. *GCH.*.....25 F.
P Wa Cathcart, Lt.-Gen. Chas. M. *Earl*, 3 Dragoon Guards
P Wa Clifton, Lt.-Gen. *Sir* A. B. *KCH.* ..1 Dr.
Dennis, Col. *Sir* James ....3 F.
P Douglas, Lt.-Gen. *Sir* James ....93 F.
P Douglas Lt.-Gen. *Sir* Neil, *KCH.* ......72 F.
Doveton, Lt.-Gen. *Sir* John...... Madras Cavalry
P Downes, Lt.-Gen. Ulysses, *Lord* ....54 F.
P *Doyle*, Col. *Sir John Milley*
P England, Col. *Sir* Richard, *KH.* ......Unatt.
P Wa Evans, Maj.-Gen. *Sir* De Lacy
P Fitz Gerald, Lt.-Gen. *Sir* John Forster ..62 F.
Fraser, Lt.-Gen. *Sir* Hugh ......Madras Infantry
Galloway, Maj.-Gen. Arch. ....Bengal Infantry
P Gardiner, Lt.-Gen. *Sir* John ....50 F.
P Gardiner, Maj.-Gen. *Sir* R. *KCH.* from R. Art.
Gilbert, Maj.-Gen. *Sir* Walter Raleigh, Bengal Infantry
P Wa Gomm, Lt.-Gen. *Sir* W. Maynard ..13 F.
Grant, Gen. *Sir* Wm. Kier, *GCH.*........ 2 Dr.
P Grey, Maj.-Gen. *Sir* John ....73 F.
P Guise, Lt.-Gen. *Sir* John Wright, *Bt.*....85 F.
P Wa Hartmann, Lt.-Col. *Sir* Julius, *GCH.* h.p. late Germ. Legion
Harvey, Lt.-Gen. *Sir* John, *KCH.* ....59 F.
P Hill, Maj.-Gen. *Sir* Dudley St. Leger
P Hope, Maj.-Gen. *Sir* James A. ....9 F.
Houstoun, Lt.-Gen. *Sir* Rob. ....Bengal Cavalry
P Wa Kerrison, Lt.-Gen. *Sir* E. *Bt. GCH.* 14 Dr.
Lawrence, Lt.-Col. *Sir* H. M. (*Civil*) Beng. Artillery
Leighton, Lt.-Gen. *Sir* David .. Bombay Infantry
P Leith, Lt.-Gen. *Sir* Alexander..........90 F.
P Macbean, Lt.-Gen. *Sir* Wm. ....92 F.
P M'Mahon, Lt.-Gen. *Sir* Thomas, *Bt.*... 10 F.
P Wa Macdonell, Lt.-Gen. *Sir* Jas. *KCH.* 79 F.
P Wa Maitland, Gen. *Sir* Peregrine ......17 F.
Malcolm Lt.-Col. *Sir James* ......late of R. Mar.
P Manners, Lt.-Gen. *Lord* Charles S......3 Dr.
Morison, Maj.-Gen. *Sir* Wm., (*Civil*) Madras Art.
P Napier, Lt.-Gen. *Sir* Geo. T. ......1 W. I. R.
P Napier, Maj.-Gen. *Sir* William F. P.....27 F.
P Nicolls, Lt.-Gen. *Sir* Jasper ....5 F.
P Pakenham, Lt.-Gen. *Hon. Sir* H. R. ....43 F.
P Pasley, Maj.-Gen. *Sir* Chas. Wm. from R. Eng.
P Pilkington, Lt.-Gen. *Sir* Andrew........82 F.

KNIGHTS COMMANDERS—*continued.*

Richards, Lt.-Gen. *Sir* Wm. ....Bengal Infantry
𝔓 Rolt, Maj.-Gen. *Sir* John
Rose, Lt.-Gen. *Sir* John ....Bengal Infantry
𝔓 𝔚 Ross, Maj.-Gen. Sir Hew D. *Dep. Adj.-Gen.* to the Royal Artillery
Russell, Lt.-Gen. *Sir* James ....Madras Cavalry
𝔓 𝔚 Saltoun, Lt.-Gen. A. *Lord*, *GCH*.....2 F.
𝔓 Schoedde, Col. *Sir* James H. ....Unatt.
Scott, Lt.-Gen. *Sir* Hopeton S. ...Madras Infantry
𝔓 𝔚 Scovell, Lt.-Gen. *Sir* George, 7 Dr. Gds. *Governor of the Royal Military College*
𝔓 Smith, Maj.-Gen. *Sir* Chs. F. Smith ..R. Eng.
𝔓 Stovin, Maj.-Gen. *Sir* Frederick, *KCMG*. 83 F.
𝔓 𝔚 Thackwell, Maj.-Gen. *Sir* J. *KH*. from 3 Dr.
𝔓 Wallace, Lt.-Gen. *Sir* John Alex. *Bt*.....88 F.
Watson, Lt.-Gen. *Sir* James ....14 F.
Whitehead, Lt.-Gen. *Sir* Thomas .. Bengal Infantry
𝔓 Williams, Maj.-Gen. *Sir* Edm. K. ....80 F.
𝔓 Willshire, Maj.-Gen. *Sir* Thomas, *Bt.*
𝔓 𝔚 Wilson, Lt.-Gen. *Sir* John ....11 F.
𝔓 𝔚 Woodford, Lt.-Gen. *Sir* Alex. *GCMG*. 40 F.
𝔓 𝔚 *Woodford*, Maj.-Gen. *Sir J. G. KCH.*

COMPANIONS. (CB.)

Abbot, Lt.Col. Augustus ......Bengal Artillery
Abbott, Lieut.-Col. Frederick ..Bengal Engineers
𝔓 𝔚 *Abercromby*, Col. *Hon. Alex.*
𝔓 A'Court, Maj.-Gen. Charles Ashe, *KH*...41 F.
𝔓 Adair, Maj.-Gen. Thomas ..late of R. Marines
Adams, Lt.-Col. Henry Wm. ....49 F.
Alexander, Lt.-Col. James......Bengal Artillery
𝔓 Allan, Maj.-Gen. James ....from 57 F.
𝔓 *Anderson*, Lt.-Col. *Joseph*, *KH*. .. late of 50 F.
𝔓 Anderson, Lt.-Gen. Paul ....78 F.
Anderson, Major William........Bengal Artillery
Andrews, Maj.-Gen. Augustus ..Madras Infantry
Anstruther, Major Philip ......Madras Artillery
𝔓 Arbuthnott, Lt.-Gen. *Hon.* Hugh........38 F.
𝔓 𝔚 Arguimbau, Maj.-Gen. Lawrence
𝔓 Armstrong, Maj.-Gen. *Sir* Richard......95 F.
Ashburnham, Col. *Hon.* Thomas ......h.p. 62 F.
𝔓 Auchmuty, Maj.-Gen. Sam. B.
Backhouse, Major Julius Brackman, late Bengal Art.
𝔓 Bainbrigge, Maj.Gen. Philip.
Balders, Lt.-Col. Charles Wm. Morley, 5 Dr. Gds.
𝔓 *Balvaird*, Col. *William*
𝔓 Barnwell, Lt.-Col. Charles..Insp. Field Officer
Basden, Lt.-Col. James Lewis ......late of 89 F.
Battine, Maj.-Gen. William ....Bengal Artillery
Baumgardt, Col. John Gregory, *Inspecting Field-officer*
𝔓 𝔚 Beckwith, Maj-Gen. Charles
𝔓 Bell, Maj.-Gen. John
𝔓 *Bell*, Lt.-Col. *Thomas*............late of 48 F.
Benson, Lt.-Col. Richard ......Bengal Infantry
Biddulph, Lt.-Col. Edward ......Bengal Artillery
𝔓 Birch, Lt.-Gen. John Francis ....from R. Eng.
𝔓 Bisshopp, Col. Cecil ....Unatt.
𝔓 Blair, Maj.-Gen. Thomas Hunter
Blair, Major Charles Devaynes ..Bengal Cavalry
𝔓 *Blake*, Col. *William Williams* ..late of 11 Dr.
𝔓 Blanshard, Lt.-Col. Thomas ....R. Engineers
Blenkins, Maj. William B. G. ..Bombay Infantry
Blundell, Lt.-Col. Frederick....Madras Artillery
Bowen, Maj.-Gen. Herbert ......Bengal Infantry
Bowyer, Lt.-Col. Cornelius .. late of Bengal Army
𝔓 Brandreth, Col. Thomas Alston ....R. Artillery
Bray, Lt.-Col. Edward Wm. ....late of 39 F.
𝔓 𝔚 Brereton, Lt.-Col. Wm. *KH*.... Royal Art.
Brooke, Lt.-Col. George ......Bengal Artillery
𝔓 Brotherton, Maj.-Gen. Tho. Wm...from 16 Dr.
𝔓 Brown, Maj.-Gen. George, *KH. Deputy-Adjut.-General* ....from Rifle Brigade
𝔓 *Brown*, Lt.-Colonel *Gustavus*......late of 95 F.
𝔓 𝔚 *Browne*, Col. *Fielding*
Browne, Lt.-Col. Gore ....41 F.
Browne, Lt.-Col. Walter John ......Bombay Inf.
𝔓 Bunbury, Lt.-Col. Thomas ....80 F.
Burlton, Lt.-Col. William ......Bengal Cavalry
Burrell, Maj.-Gen. George ....from 18 F.
Butterworth, Lt.-Col. Wm. John, late Madras Inf.
Byrne, Lt.-Col. John ....53 F.
𝔓 𝔚 Calvert, Maj.-Gen. Felix
Cameron, Lt.-Col. Geo. Poulett ..Madras Infantry
Campbell, Col. Alex. *KH*. ....9 Drs.
𝔓 Campbell, Col. Charles Stewart......h.p. 1 F.
𝔓 Campbell, Col. Colin..................98 F.
Campbell, Lt.-Col. Sir Edward Alex., late Bengal Cav.
Campbell, Lt.-Col. John ....Madras Infantry
𝔓 𝔚 Campbell, Maj.-Gen. *Sir* Guy, *Bt*. 3 W. I. R.
𝔓 𝔚 Campbell, Lt.-Col. Patrick ....Unatt.
𝔓 𝔚 Campbell, Maj.-Gen. William
Carmichael, Lt.-Col. Charles M. ..Bengal Cavalry
Carruthers, Lieut.-Col. Richard ....2 F.
Caulfield, Major-Gen. James ....Bengal Cavalry
𝔓 𝔚 Chalmers, Maj.-Gen. *Sir* Wm. *KCH*.
𝔓 Chapman, Lt.-Gen. *Sir* S. R. *KCH*. ..R. Eng.
Cheape, Col. John ....Bengal Engineers
𝔓 𝔚 *Childers*, Col. *Michael* ......late of 6 Dr.
Church, Lt.-Col. *Sir R. GCH*. late of Gr. Lt. In.
Clarke, Lt.-Col. *Isaac B.*
Cloete, Lt.-Col. A. J. *KH*................Unatt.
Clunie, Lt.-Col. *Jas. Oliphant* ......late of 44 F.
Cock, Col. Henry ....Bengal Infantry
Colebrooke, Col. *Sir* Wm. M.G. *KH*. (*Civil*) R. Art.
Colvin, Lieut.-Col. John ....late of Bengal Army
Congreve, Lt.-Col. Geo. ....29 F.
Conway, Maj. Thomas S....................22 F.
𝔓 Conyers, Maj.-Gen. Chas. Edw.
𝔓 𝔚 *Cooke*, Lt.-Col. *R. Harvey*, late of Gr. Gds.
𝔓 *Cother*, Lt.-Col. *Charles* ....late of 83 F.
𝔓 *Couper*, Col. *Sir Geo. Bart. KH.*
Craigie, Col. P. Edmonstone ....h. p. 55 F.
Craigie, Major John Halkett.......Bengal Infantry
Croker, Col. *William* ....late of 17 F.
Crosdill, Lieut.-Col. John....late of Madras Army
Cunliffe, Maj.-Gen. *Sir* R. H. *Bt*., Bengal Infantry
𝔓 Cureton, Col. Cha. Robert.........h.p. 16 Dr.
𝔓 D'Aguilar, Maj.-Gen. Geo. C. ....58 F.
𝔓 𝔚 Dalmer, Maj.-Gen. Thomas......... 47 F.
𝔚 *Damer*, Lt.-Col. *Hon. Geo. L. D.* late of 89 F.
𝔓 𝔚 Dansey, Col. Chas. Cornw. ....R. Art.
Daubeney, Major Henry C. Barnston ....55 F.
𝔓 Davis, Lt.-Col. George Lenox .... 9 F.
𝔓 Davy, Lt.-Gen. *Sir* W. Gabriel, *KCH*.. 69 F.
Delamain, Maj. Charles Henry ..Bombay Cavalry
De la Motte, Maj.-Gen. Peter ..Bombay Cavalry
Denniss, Lt.-Col. George Gladwin Bengal Artillery
Despard, Col. Henry.......................99 F.
𝔓 Douglas, Col. Robert ......late of R. Artillery
𝔓 Downman, Lt.-Gen. *Sir* Tho., *KCH* ....R. A.
Drummond, Lt.-Col. John Gavin..Bengal Infantry
𝔓 Duffy, Maj.-Gen. John
Dundas, Col. *Hon*. Henry ....60 F.
𝔓 Dundas, Col. Wm. Bolden ....R. Artillery
𝔓 𝔚 Dyneley, Col. Tho. ....R. Artillery

COMPANIONS—*continued.*

Eden, Col. John, Unatt. *Assist. Adj.-General in Scotland.*
Edwardes, Major Herbert Benj...Bengal Infantry
Egerton, Maj.-Gen. Richard
Ellicombe, Maj.-Gen. C. Grene, from R. Eng.
Ellis, Lt.-Col. Samuel Burdon........R. Marines
Eustace, Lt.-Gen. Wm. C., *KCH.* ......60 F.
Evans, Maj.-Gen. Thomas ....81 F.
Everard, Col. Mathias, *KH.* .... 14 F.
Ewart, Maj.-Gen. John Frederick
Fair, Lt.-Gen. Alex............Madras Infantry
Fanshawe, Maj.-Gen. Edward, fm. Royal Engineers
Faunce, Maj.-Gen. Alured Dodsworth
Fearon, Maj.-Gen. Robert Bryce
Fergusson, Maj.-Gen. James
Ferris, Major Joseph ....Bengal Infantry
Finch, Col. *Hon.* John .... Unatt.
Fisher, Major George ....Bombay Infantry
Fitzgerald, Lt.-Col. Charles ..late of Bengal Army
Fleming, Maj.-Gen. Edw.
Forbes, Maj.-Gen. David
Forster, Major Henry ....Bombay Artillery
Franks, Lt.-Col. Thomas Harte ....10 F.
Fraser, Lt.-Gen. Hastings................61 F.
Fraser, Major James ....Bengal Cavalry
Frederick, Maj.-Gen. Edward ..Bombay Infantry
Fuller, Lt.-Col. *Francis*..... late of 59 F.
Gabriel, Maj.-Gen. Robert Burd, *KH.*
Gairdner, Lt.-Col. William......Bengal Infantry
Garden, Lt.-Col. William ......Bengal Infantry
Geddes, Lt.-Col. William ......Bengal Artillery
George, Major, Frederick Darley..........22 F.
Godby, Lt.-Col. Christopher ....Bengal Infantry
Godwin, Maj.-Gen. Henry
Goldfinch, Maj.-Gen. Henry ....from R. Eng.
Goldie, Maj.-Gen. Geo. Leigh
Gordon, Maj.-Gen. William Alex.
Gore, Maj.-Gen. *Hon.* Charles, *KH.*
Gore, Maj. Henry Ross ....h. p. 3 F.
Gough, Lt.-Col. J. Bloomfield............3 Drs.
Gowan, Col. Geo. Edw. ....Bengal Artillery
Graham, Lt.-Col. Charles ......Bengal Artillery
Grant, Lt.-Col. Patrick ....Bengal Infantry
Grant, Major J. Hope ....9 Drs.
Grant, Maj.-Gen. Jas. *Gov. of Scarboro' Castle.*
Grattan, Lt.-Col. John ....18 F.
Green, Major Edward...........Bombay Infantry
Greenwood, Major Wm. ..late of Royal Artillery
Halkett, Lt.-Col. *Hugh*, *KCH.* late of Ger. Legion.
Hall, Col. Henry ....Bengal Infantry
Hamerton, Lt.-Gen. John Millet ....55 F.
Hamilton, Lt.-Col. Charles ......Bengal Artillery
Harding, Col. Geo. Judd ....Royal Engineers
Hare-Clarges, Maj.-Gen. Richard Goddard
Harriott, Col. David............Bengal Cavalry
Harrison, Lt.-Col. *John Bacon* ....late of 50 F.
Harvey, Maj.-Gen. *Sir* Robert John 2 W. I. R.
Havelock, Lt.-Col. Henry ....39 F.
Hawkins, Lt.-Col. *John P.* ......late of 68 F.
Hawkins, Lt.-Col. Francis Spencer, Bengal Infantry
Hay, Maj.-Gen. James
Henderson, Major Robert ....Madras Engineers
Herbert, Col. Charles ....Madras Infantry
Herries, Maj.-Gen. *Sir* Wm. L., *KCH.*
Hicks, Lt.-Col. George ....Bengal Infantry
Hill, Col. *Sir Robert C.* late of R. Horse Gds.
Hogarth, Major Geo. ....26 F.
Holloway, Col. W. C. E. ....Royal Engineers
Hopkinson, Col. *Sir* Cha. ....late of Madras Army
Hughes, Col. Samuel ....Bombay Infantry
Huish, Lt.-Col. Geo. ....Bengal Infantry
Hunt, Lt.-Col. *John Philip*.......late of 11 F.
Hunter, Maj.-Gen. George ......Bengal Infantry
Huthwaite, Lt.-Col. Edward....Bengal Artillery
Hutt, Major George..........Bombay Artillery
Innes, Maj.-Gen. William ......Bengal Infantry
Irvine, Lt.-Col. Arch...........Bengal Engineers
Jackson, Major John ....Bombay Infantry
Jebb, Lt.-Col. Joshua (*Civil*) ....Royal Engineers
Kenah, Maj.-Gen. Thomas
Kennedy, Col. Alex. Kennedy Clark, *KH.* Unatt.
Kennedy, Maj.-Gen. James ......Bengal Cavalry
Kennedy, Maj-Gen. Jas. Shaw
King, Lt.-Gen. *Sir* Henry, *KCH.* ....3 F.
Lane, Lieut.-Col. C. R. W.......Bengal Infantry
Lane, Lt.-Col. John Theophilus..BengalArtillery
Latour, Maj.-Gen. P. A., *KH.*
Lawrence, Maj.-Gen. Elias ....late of R. Marines
Lawrenson, Lt.-Col. George Simson BengalArtillery
Leach, Lt.-Col. *Jonathan*, late of Rifle Br.
Leslie, Lt.-Col. John Thomas, late Bombay Artillery
Lewis, Maj.-Gen. George......late of R. Marines
Lewis, Col. Geo. Griffith ....R. Engineers
Lightfoot, Maj.-Gen. Thomas
Lillie, Lt.-Col. *Sir* John Scott ....Unatt.
Lindsay, Maj.-Gen. Alex. ......Bengal Artillery
Lloyd, Lt.-Col. John ....Bombay Artillery
Lloyd, Col. Geo. Wm. Aylmer ....Bengal Infantry
Lluellyn, Maj.-Gen. Richard
Lockwood, Lieut.-Col. Geo. Henry........3 Drs.
Love, Col. Jas. Fred., *KH.* ....Unatt.
Low, Lt.-Col. John............Madras Infantry
Luard, Lt.-Col. John Kynaston ..Madras Infantry
Lumsden, Lt.-Col. Thomas....late of Bengal Army
Lushington, Major Franklin ....37 F.
Lygon, Lt.-Gen. *Hon.* E. P.......13 Drs.
M'Donald, Maj.-Gen. John ....from 92 F.
M'Dowell, Lt.-Col. G. J. M. ......late of 16 Drs.
M'Gregor, Major George Hall....Bengal Artillery
M'Leod, Maj.-Gen. Charles ....Madras Infantry
M'Pherson, Lt.-Col. Philip ....17 F.
Macdonald, Maj.-Gen. Alex...R. Artillery
Macdonald, Lt.-Col. *Robert* ..late of 35 F.
Macdonald, Lt.-Col. *Robert* ..late of Royal Art.
Macdonell, Lt.-Col. *George* ....late of 79 F.
Mackeson, Major Fred...........Bengal Infantry
Mackinnon, Lt.-Col. Geo. Henry ....Unatt.
Maclaine, Maj.-Gen. *Sir* Archibald
Maclean, Lt.-Col. Norman ....late of 55 F.
Macleod, Lt.-Gen. *Sir* John, *KCH.* ....77 F.
Macleod, Lt.-Col. *Geo. Francis*, late of R. Eng.
Macpherson, Maj.-Gen. R. Barclay, *KH.*
Mactier, Lt.-Col. William ......Bengal Cavalry
Malcolm, Lt.-Col. Geo. Alex. ....Unatt.
Manners, Lt.-Col. *Russell* ....late of 74 F.
Mansel, Lt.-Col. *John*............late of 53 F.
Manson, Col. Alex. ....Bombay Artillery
Meade, Lt.-Gen. *Hon.* John ......from 45 F.
Mercer, Maj.-Gen. Douglas
Michell, Col. John ....Royal Artillery
Middlemore, Lt.-Gen. George ....48 F.
Miller, Lt.-Col. *F. Sanderson*....late of 6 Dr.
Milnes, Lt.-Col. *Colin J.*............late of 65 F.

COMPANIONS—*continued.*

𝔓 𝔚 Money, Maj.-Gen. Archibald
Monteath, Col. Thomas ....Bengal Infantry
Montgomerie, Col. Patrick ......Madras Artillery
Moore, Major Henry............Bengal Infantry
Moore, Major R. Cornwallis ....Madras Artillery
Morgan, Col. John ....Madras Infantry
Morris, Col. Edmund ....Unatt.
Moseley, Lieut.-Col, Geo. W.....Bengal Infantry
Mountain, Col. Armine S. H. ....29 F.
𝔓 𝔚 Murray, Maj.-Gen. *Hon.* Henry
𝔚 *Muttlebury*, Lt.-Col. *George* ....late of 69 F.
𝔓 Napier, Maj.-Gen. Thomas Erskine
Nash, Lt.-Col. Joseph ....Bengal Infantry
𝔓 Nicol, Lt.-Gen. Charles................68 F.
𝔓 *O'Donoghue*, Lt.-Col. *John Wm.* ....late Unatt.
Oldfield, Lt.-Col. C. E. T. ......Bengal Cavalry
𝔓 Otway, Lt.-Gen. *Sir* Loftus Wm. ......84 F.
Outram, Lt.-Col. James ....Bombay Infantry
Owen, Col. John, *KH. Dep. Adj.-Gen. R. Mar.*
𝔓 Parke, Col. Thomas Adams ......R. Marines
𝔓 𝔚 Parker, Maj.-Gen. John Boteler, late of R. Art.
𝔚 Parkinson, Maj.-Gen. Edward
Parlby, Maj.-Gen. B. Brydges ..Madras Infantry
Parsons, Lt.-Col. James........Bengal Infantry
𝔓 *Patrickson*, Col. *C. Clarges* ....late of 43 F.
Pattle, Col. William ....Bengal Cavalry
𝔓 Paty, Maj.-Gen. Geo. Wm. *KH.*
Pears, Major Tho. Townsend ..Madras Engineers
Pennefather, Col. John Lysaght ......h. p. 28 F.
Penny, Lt.-Col. Nicholas ......Bengal Infantry
Pennycuick, Lt.-Col. J., *KH.*............24 F.
𝔓 *Persse*, Col. *William* ....late of 16 Dr.
Petit, Lt.-Col. Peter John ....50 F.
Phillips, Lt.-Col. Harry Shakespear ......Unatt.
Plenderleath, Lt.-Col. *Charles*........late of 49 F.
Poole, Lt.-Col. John ....22 F.
Pope, Lt.-Col. Alexander ....Bengal Cavalry
𝔓 Power, Maj.-Gen. W. G....from Royal Artillery
Pratt, Lt.-Col. Thos. Simson............h. p. 26 F.
𝔓 Proctor, Maj.-Gen. Henry Adolphus
Purton, Major John ....late of Madras Army
𝔓 *Pynn*, Lt.-Col. *Sir Henry*..late of Portuguese Ser.
𝔓 𝔚 Quentin, Lt.-Gen. *Sir* Geo. Aug., *KCH.*
𝔓 Rainey, Maj.-Gen. Henry, *KH.*
Rawlinson, Maj. H. Creswicke ..Bombay Infantry
𝔓 Reade, Col. *Sir* Thomas............h. p. 24 F.
𝔚 Reed, Colonel Thomas ....62 F.
Reid, Lt.-Col. Geo. Alex. T.....Bombay Infantry
Reid, Major Fra. Archibald ......Madras Infantry
𝔓 Reid, Lt.-Col. William ......Royal Engineers
Reignolds, Lt.-Col. Tho. Scott ....18 F.
Richards, Maj.-Gen. Alfred ......Bengal Infantry
Richmond, Lieut.-Col. Arch. F. ..Bengal Infantry
Robe, Lt.-Col. Fred. Holt (*Civil*) ....h. p. 87 F.
Roberts, Col. Abraham..........Bengal Infantry
Roberts, Maj.-Gen. Henry T......Bengal Cavalry
𝔓 𝔚 Robertson, Lt.-Col. F. *KCH.*, h. p. Ger. L.
𝔚 *Rooke*, Maj.-Gen. *Sir Henry W.*, *KCH.*
Rose, Lt.-Col. Hugh H. ....Unatt.
𝔓 𝔚 *Rowan*, Lt.-Col. *Charles*......late of 52 F.
𝔓 𝔚 Rowan, Maj.-Gen. William
Russell, Maj.-Gen. Lechmere Coore Graves, Bombay Artillery
Salter, Maj.-Gen. James F......Bombay Infantry
Salusbery, *Lt.-Col. Charles*
Sandwith, Maj.-Gen. Wm.......Bombay Infantry
Sandwith, Lt.-Col. Bentham ....Bombay Cavalry
Scott, Col. John........................9 Dr.
Scott, Major Thomas Hare ......Bengal Infantry
Seaton, Major Thomas ....Bengal Infantry
𝔓 Sewell, Maj.-Gen. Wm. Henry
Sheil, Lt.-Col. Justin (*Civil*) ....Bengal Infantry
𝔓 *Simmons*, Lt.-Col. *Joseph* ....late of 41 F.
Simpson, Major Wm. Henry, late Madras Infantry
𝔓 𝔚 Sleigh, Lt.-Gen. James Wallace ....9 Dr.
Smelt, Maj.-Gen. William
𝔓 𝔚 Smith, Maj.-Gen. J. W. ....R. Art.
Smith, Lt.-Col. Robert ......late of Bengal Army
Smyth, Lt.-Col. Rowland ....16 Lancers
𝔓 *Snodgrass*, Col. *Kenneth* ....late Unatt.
𝔓 𝔚 Somerset, Col. Henry, *KH.* ..Cape M. R.
Sotheby, Major Fred. Samuel..late of Bengal Army
Spence, Lt.-Col. James..................31 F.
Stack, Lt.-Col. Maurice ....Bombay Cavalry
Stalker, Lt.-Col. Foster ....Bombay Infantry
Stanhope, Col. *Hon.* Leicester ....Unatt.
Stannus, Maj.-Gen. *Sir* Ephraim G. Bombay Infantry
𝔓 𝔚 Staveley, Maj.-Gen. William
Stedman, Lt.-Col. Robert Adrian ..Bengal Cavalry
Steel, Lt.-Col. S. Winde ....Madras Infantry
Stevens, Major Stephen James ..Bombay Infantry
Stopford, Lt.-Col. James ....40 F.
Story, Lt.-Col. Philip Francis ....Bengal Cavalry
Stuart, Col. James ....Bengal Infantry
Tait, Major Joshua ....Bombay Infantry
Tait, Major Tho. Forsyth ......Bengal Infantry
Taylor, Maj.-Gen. Henry Geo. A...Madras Infantry
𝔚 Taylor, Maj.-Gen. T. W. *Lt.-Gov. R. Mil. C* [illegible]
𝔓 Thackeray, Lt.-Gen. Fred. Rennell, fm. R. Eng.
𝔓 Thomas, Maj.-Gen. Henry
Thompson, Lt.-Col. John Armstrong Bengal Infantry
Thompson, Lt.-Col. Wm. John ..Bengal Infantry
𝔓 Thomson, Maj.-Gen. Alexander
Thomson, Major George ....late of Bengal Army
𝔓 Thorn, Major-Gen. Nath. *KH.*
𝔓 *Thornton*, Col. *Henry*............late of 82 F.
Tickell, Maj.-Gen. Richard ....Bengal Engineers
Timbrell, Maj. Thos. ....late of Bengal Army
𝔓 Tonson, Maj.-Gen. Jacob
𝔓 Trevor, Lt.-G. *Hon.* H. Otway..........31 F.
Tucker, Major Auchmuty ....Bengal Cavalry
Tulloch, Col. Alex. ....Madras Infantry
Tulloch, Col. John..............Bengal Infantry
𝔓 Turner, Col. George ....Royal Artillery
𝔓 Tweeddale, Lt.-Gen. Geo. *Marq. of, KT.*..30 F.
Upton, Lt.-Gen. *Hon.* A. P.
𝔓 Vernon, Maj.-Gen. Henry C. E.
Waddington, Lt.-Col. Charles..Bombay Engineers
Wade, Lt.-Col. *Sir* C. Martine..late Bengal Infantry
Wade, Major Hamlet Coote .... h. p. 1 Dr. Gds.
𝔓 *Ward*, Col. *John Richard* ....late of 2 Dr.
𝔓 Warre, Maj.-Gen. *Sir* William ....94 F.
Warren, Lt.-Col. Charles ....55 F.
Waters, Maj.-Gen. Edmund Fred. Bengal Infantry
𝔓 Watson, Maj.-Gen. *Sir* Henry ....63 F.
Watson, Lt.-Col. Wm. L.....late of Bengal Army
𝔓 Wells, Lt.-Col. John Neave...... R. Engineers
𝔓 Wemyss, Maj.-Gen. Thomas James
Weston, Lt.-Col. John S. Henry..Bengal Infantry
Wetherall, Col. Geo. Aug. *KH.* ....Unatt.
Wheatley, Maj.-Gen. Sir Henry, *Bt.* (*Civil*)
Wheeler, Col. Hugh Massey ....Bengal Infantry
𝔓 Whinyates, Col. Edward C., *KH.* ..R. Artillery
Whish, Maj.-Gen. William S. ....Bengal Artillery
White, Col. Michael......................3 Dr.
White, Major Ferdinand ....8 F.

COMPANIONS—*continued.*

Whittingham, Major Ferdinand............26 F.
Whitlie, Major Wm. Thomas ....Bombay Artillery
Wilkinson,Lt.-Col.Christ.Dixon..BengalInfantry
Willoughby, Major M. Franklin..Bombay Artillery
𝔓 𝔚 *Wilkins*, Lt.-Col. *Geo. KH.* late of Rif. Br.
Wilkinson, Major A. P. S.................13 F.
𝔓 Wilson, Col. *Sir* J. M., *KH. Adj. of Chelsea Hos.*
Wilson, Maj.-Gen. Thomas......Bengal Infantry
Wilson, Maj.-Gen. Francis W. ..Madras Infantry
𝔓 *Wilson*, Lt.-Col. *Geo. Davis*........late of 4 F.
Wilson, Lt.-Col. Roger Wm. ....Bengal Infantry
Wood, Lt.-Col. Henry John ....Bengal Artillery
Wood, Lt.-Col. Robert Blucher ....80 F
𝔓 Wood, Maj.-Gen. William, *KH.*
Woodburn, Lt.-Col. Alexander ..Bombay Infantry
𝔓 *Woodgate*, Col. *William* ....late of 60 F.
Wright, Lt.-Col. Thomas..................39 F.
Wylde, Col. William ....Royal Artillery
Wyllie, Lt.-Col. William ......Bombay Infantry
Wymer, Colonel Geo. Petre ....Bengal Infantry
Wynyard, Maj.-Gen. Edward
Wynyard,Lt.-Col.RobertHenry ....58 F.
Yates, Col. Walter Alex.........Bengal Infantry
Young, Lt.-Col. Cha. Wallace ...Madras Infantry

OFFICERS OF THE ORDER.

Dean—William Buckland, *DD.*
Genealogist—Walter Aston Blount, Esq., *Chester Herald.*
Bath King of Arms—Algernon Greville, Esq.
Registrar and Secretary—Captain Michael Seymour, R. N.
Deputy—Albert Wm. Woods, Esq., *Lancaster Herald, Herald's College.*
Gentleman Usher—Albert Wm. Woods, Esq., *Lancaster Herald.*
Messenger—W. H. Stephenson, Esq.

OFFICERS

NOW HOLDING RANK IN THE ARMY OF THE MOST DISTINGUISHED ORDER OF

SAINT MICHAEL AND SAINT GEORGE.

GRAND MASTER.

Field Marshal *His Royal Highness* Adolphus F. *Duke of Cambridge, KG. GCB. GCH.*

KNIGHTS, GRAND CROSS. (GCMG.)

Field Marshal *H.R.H. The Duke of* Cambridge. *KG. GCB. GCH.* Coldst. Guards, and 60 Foot.
𝔓 𝔚 Lt.-Gen. *Lord* Seaton, *GCB. GCH.* ..26 F.
𝔓 𝔚 Gen. *Rt. Hon. Sir* Fred. Adam, *GCB.* 21 F.
𝔓 𝔚 Lt.-Gen. *Sir* Alex. Woodford, *KCB.*..40 F.
Colonel *Sir Frederick Hankey* ......late of 15 F.
𝔓 Lt.-Gen. *Sir* Howard Douglas, *Bt. GCB.* 99 F.
𝔓 Lt.-Gen. *Sir* Hen. Frederick Bouverie, *KCB.* 97 F.
𝔓 Gen. *Sir* C. Bulkeley Egerton, *KCH.* ....89 F.
𝔓 Maj.-Gen. *Sir Patrick Ross, KCH.* late of 75 F.
Field Marshal *His Royal Highness Prince* Albert, *KG. KT. KP. GCB.*
Lt.-Gen. *Hon. Sir* Patrick Stuart ....44 F.
Maj.-Gen. *H. R. H. Prince* George W. F. C. *of* Cambridge, *KG.* 17 Lancers.

KNIGHTS COMMANDERS. (KCMG.)

𝔓 Major-Gen. *Sir* Frederick Stovin, *KCB.* ..83 F.
Dep.-Assistant Com. Gen. *Sir* Edward Stuart Baynes, h. p.
Lt.-Gen. Francis *Count* Rivarola, *KCH.* late of R. Malta Fencible Regt.

COMPANIONS. (CMG.)

𝔓 Col. Thomas Drake, Unatt.
𝔓 Lt.-Col. Charles Andrews Bayley, Unatt.
Lt.-Col. *Marq.* Guiseppe de Piro. R. Malta Fencible Regt.
𝔓 Maj.-Gen. Henry Balneavis, *KH.*
Dep.-Com. Gen. James Woodhouse, h. p.

OFFICERS OF THE ORDER.

Chancellor............
King of Arms ....*Sir* Charles Douglas, *CMG.*
Chancery of the Order..The Colonial Department, Downing Street.

OFFICERS

NOW HOLDING RANK IN THE ARMY

WHO ARE PERMITTED TO WEAR

FOREIGN ORDERS.

The Orders mentioned in this List belong to the following Countries, and the Dates are those of the Institution of the Order:—

Affghanistan—Dooranée Empire (3 Classes) 1839.
Austria—Maria Theresa (3 Classes) 18 June, 1757.
Leopold (3 Classes) 14 July, 1806.
Bavaria—Maximilian Joseph (3Classes) 1 Jan. 1806.
Belgium—Leopold (3 Classes) 11 July, 1832.
France—Military Merit (3 Classes) Mar. 1759.
Legion of Honour (5 Classes) 13 May, 1802.
Greece—Saviour (5 Classes) 1 June, 1833.
Hanover—Guelphs (3 Classes) 18 June, 1815.
Naples—St. Januarius (1 Class) July, 1738.
St. Ferdinand and Merit, (3 Classes) 1 April, 1800.
St. George and Reunion (3 Classes) 1 Jan. 1819.
Netherlands—Wilhelm (4 Classes) 30 April, 1815.
Persia—Lion and Sun (3 Classes) 1801.
Portugal—Tower and Sword (3 Clas.) 17 Apr. 1748.
St. Bento d'Avis (2 Classes) 1789.
Conception (3 Classes) 6 Feb. 1818.
Prussia—Black Eagle—18 Jan. 1701.
Military Merit—1740.
Red Eagle (3 Classes) 12 June, 1792.
Russia—St. Andrew—30 Nov. 1698.
St. Alexander Newski—1722.
St. Ann (2 Classes) 3 Feb. 1735.
St. George (4 Classes) 26 Nov. 1769.
St. Wladimir (5 Classes) 4 Oct. 1782.
Sardinia—St. Maurice and St. Lazarus (2 Clas.) 13 Nov. 1572.
Saxony—St. Henry (3 Classes) 7 Oct. 1736.
Ernestine (4 Classes) 25 Dec. 1833.
Spain—Charles the Third (3 Clas.) 19 Sept. 1771.
San Fernando (5 Classes) 31 Aug. 1811.
St. Hermenigilde (2 Classes) 10 July, 1815.
St. Isabella the Catholic (3 Classes) 1815.
Sweden—Sword (3 Classes) 17 April, 1748.
Turkey—Crescent (2 Classes) 6 July, 1804.
Tuscany—St. Joseph (3 Classes) 1807.
Wirtemburg—Military Merit (3 Classes) 1759.

ROYAL HANOVERIAN GUELPHIC ORDER.

KNIGHTS, GRAND CROSS. (GCH.)

Field Marshal *His R. H.* Aug. Frederick, *Duke of* Cambridge, *KG. GCB. GCMG.*
Field Marshal His Majesty, *The King of the* Belgians, *KG. GCB.*

𝔓 𝔚 Anglesey, Field Marshal H. W. *Marq. of, KG. GCB.* Royal Horse Guards.
𝔓 𝔚 Barnard, Lt.-Gen. *Sir* A. F. *GCB.* Rifle Br.
𝔓 Beresford, Gen. Wm. Carr. *Visct. GCB.*...16 F.
𝔓 Blakeney, Lt-Gen. *Rt. Hon. Sir* Edw. *KCB.* 7 F.
𝔓 Bradford, Gen. *Sir* Thomas, *GCB.*.........4 F.
𝔓 Brisbane, Gen. *Sir* T. M. *Bt. GCB.* ....34 F.
𝔓 Campbell, Gen. *Sir* Hen. Fred. *KCB.* ....25 F.
Church, Lt.-Col. *Sir R. CB.* late Greek Lt. Inf.
Cockburn, Maj.-Gen. *Sir* James, *Bt.*
𝔓 Combermere, Gen. S. *Visc. GCB.* ..1 Life Gds.
Conyngham, Lt.-Col. F. N. *Marq. of, KP*..Unatt.
𝔓 Darling, Gen. *Sir* Ralph ....69 F.
Duff, Gen. *Hon. Sir* Alex....................37 F.
Fitz Clarence, Maj.-Gen. *Lord* Frederick
𝔓 Gordon, Gen. *Sir* J. Willoughby, *Bt. GCB. Quarter-Master-General*.....................23 F.
Grant, Gen. *Sir* Wm. Keir, *KCB.* ....2 Dr.
𝔓 𝔚 Halkett, Gen. *Sir* Colin, *GCB.*.......45 F.
𝔓 𝔚 Halkett, Lt.-Col. Hugh, *CB.* h. p. Ger. L.
Hammond, Gen. Fra. Thos.
𝔓 𝔚 Hartmann, Lt.-Col. *Sir* J. *KCB.* h. p. G. L.
𝔓 𝔚 Kempt, Gen. *Rt. Hon. Sir* Jas. *GCB.* 1 F.
𝔓 𝔚 Kerrison, Lt.-Gen. *Sir* Edw. *Bt. KCB.* 14 Dr.
𝔓 Londonderry, Gen. C. W. *Marq. of, GCB.* 2 Life Guards
Mackenzie, Gen. *Sir* Alex. *Bt*..........from 36 F.
𝔓 𝔚 Saltoun, Lieut.-Gen. A. *Lord, KCB.*..2 F.
𝔓 𝔚 Seaton, Lt.-Gen. John, *Lord, GCB. GCMG.* 26 F.
𝔓 Slade, Gen. *Sir* John, *Bt*.............5 Dr. Gds.
𝔓 𝔚 Strafford, Gen. J. *Earl of, GCB.* .....29 F.
𝔓 𝔚 Wellington, Field Marshal, *Duke of, KG. GCB.* Gren. Gds. and Rifle Brigade. *Commander-in-Chief.*
𝔓 Westmorland, Lt.-Gen. J. *Earl of, GCB.* 56 F.
Wheatley, Maj.-Gen. *Sir* Henry, *Bart., CB.*

KNIGHTS COMMANDERS. (KCH.)

Adams, Lt.-Gen. *Sir* Geo. Pownall ....6 Dr.
Arthur, Maj.-Gen. *Sir* Geo. *Bart.*
𝔓 Barton, Lt.-Gen. *Sir* Robert
𝔓 Bisset, Commissary-General *Sir* John ....h. p.
𝔓 𝔚 Bowater, Lt.-Gen. *Sir* Edw. ....49 F.
𝔓 Browne, Lieut.-Gen. *Sir* John ....8 Hussars
𝔓 Browne, Maj.-Gen. *Sir* Thomas H.
𝔓 *Chabot*, Maj.-Gen. *Louis W. Visc.* late of 50 F.
𝔓 𝔚 Chalmers, Maj.-Gen. *Sir* Wm. *CB.*
𝔓 Chapman, Lt.-Gen. *Sir* S. R. *CB.* from R. Eng.
𝔓 𝔚 Clifton, Lt.-Gen. *Sir* A. B. *KCB.*.....1 Dr.
Conroy, Capt. *Sir* John, *Bt*.......h. p. Royal Art.
𝔓 Cotton, Lt.-Gen. *Sir* Willoughby, *GCB.*..98 F.
𝔓 Cumming, Gen. *Sir* H. J..............12 Dr.
𝔓 Cust, Col. *Hon. Sir* Edward ....Unatt.
𝔓 Davy, Lt.-Gen. *Sir* Wm. Gabriel, *CB.* ..60 F.
De Butts, Lt.-Gen. *Sir* Augustus.........R. Eng.
D'Este, Col. *Sir Aug. Fred.* ....late of 60 F.

KNIGHTS COMMANDERS—*continued.*
Douglas, Maj.-Gen. *Sir* Neil, *KCB.* 72 F.
Downman, Lt.-Gen. *Sir* Thomas, *CB.* .. R. Art.
D'Urban, Lt.-Gen. *Sir* Benj. *GCB*.......51 F.
Egerton, Gen. *Sir* Chas. Bulkeley, *GCMG.* 89 F.
Eustace, Lt.-Gen. Wm. Cornwallis, *CB.* ..60 F.
Forbes, Dep.-Insp.-Gen. *Sir* Chas. F. *MD.KC.*
Gardiner, Maj.-Gen. *Sir* Robert, *KCB.* fr. R. Art.
ant, Lt.-Gen. *Sir* Lewis ....96 F.
lkett, Gen. *Sir* Alex. ....from late 104 F.
nbury, Lieut.-Gen. *Sir* John....from Gr. Gds.
rvey, Lt.-Gen. *Sir* John, *KCB*..........59 F.
Hawker, Lt.-Gen. *Sir* Thomas......6 Dr. Gds.
Herries, Maj.-Gen. *Sir* Wm. Lewis, *CB.*
King, Lieut.-Gen. *Sir* Henry, *CB.* ....3 F.
Macdonell, Lt.-Gen. *Sir* Jas. *KCB.*..79 F.
acleod, Lt.-Gen. *Sir* John, *CB.* ....77 F.
atresor, Gen. *Sir* T. Gage ....2 Dr. Gds.
Paterson, Lt.-Gen. *Sir* Wm. *Capt. of Carisbrooke Castle.*
Peacocke, Gen. *Sir* W. M. *KC.* ....19 F.
Prott, Capt. Victor ....h. p. late Ger. Leg.
Pym, *Sir* Wm., Insp. Gen. of Hospitals ......h. p.
Quentin, Lt.-Gen. *Sir* Geo. Aug. *CB.*
Reynett, Maj.-Gen. *Sir* J. H.
Riall, Gen. *Sir* Phineas..................15 F.
Rivarola, Lt.-Gen. Fra. *Count KCMG.* R. Malta Fenc.
Robertson, Lt.-Col. Fred. *CB.* h. p. late Ger. Leg.
Rooke, Maj.-Gen. *Sir H. W. CB.*
Ross, Maj.-Gen. *Sir Patrick, GCMG.*
Thornton, Lt.-Gen. *Sir* C. Wade, late of R. Art.
Trench, Lt.-Gen. *Sir* Fred. Wm.
Tuyll, Lt.-Gen. *Sir* William ....7 Lt. Dr.
Webb, *Sir* John, *MD.* Director-General Ordnance Medical Department.
Whitmore, Lt.-Gen. *Sir* George, ... from R. Eng.
Woodford, Maj.-Gen. *Sir J. G. KCB.*

KNIGHTS. (KH.)

A'Court, Maj.-Gen. C. Ashe, *CB.* ....41 F.
Anderson, Lt.-Col. *Joseph, CB.* ....late of 50 F.
Angelo, Col. *E. A.*
Arnaud, Lt.-Col. John .... Unatt.
nold, Maj.-Gen. Jas. Robertson, from R. Eng.
sten, Lt.-Col. John.................. Unatt.
Balneavis, Maj.-Gen. Henry, *CMG.*
Beckwith, Col. Wm. .... Unatt.
Bradshaw, Col. Geo. Paris ....Unatt.
Brereton, Lt.-Col. Wm. *CB.* .... R. Art.
Briggs, Lt.-Col. John F.................h. p.
Brock, Col. Saumarez .... do.
Brown, Maj.-Gen. Geo. *CB.* from Rifle Brig. *Deputy-Adjutant-General.*
Bruce, Lt.-Col. Wm...............48 F.
nbury, Maj.-Gen. Thomas ....from 67 F.
nes, Surgeon James ....E. I. C. Service
Burney, Lt.-Col. W. late of Cape M. Riflemen
rrowes, Lt.-Col. Robert Edward........Unatt.
rlem, Col. *Nathaniel* ....late of 67 F.
h, Col. William .... *Insp. Field Officer.*
npbell, Col. Alexander, *CB.* .... 9 Dr.
Campbell, Col. James ....95 F.
Campbell, Col. James, *Insp. Field Officer.*
Carey, Lieut. Thos. ...... h. p. Ger. Leg.
Charlton, Lt.-Col. Edward ....Unatt. *Deputy-Adjutant-General at Ceylon*
Chatterton, Col. Jas. Chas. ....Unatt.
Clark, Lt.-Col. John ....54 F.
Clerke, Maj. Thomas Henry Shadwell, Retired full pay.
Clerke, Col. St. John Aug. ....Unatt.
ste, Lt.-Col. A. J. *CB.* Unatt. *Deputy-Quarter-Master-General, Cape of Good Hope*
nbrooke, Col. *Sir* Wm. M. G., *CB.*....R. Art.
ouper, Col. *Sir George, Bart. CB.*
Cox, Lt.-Col. John ....Unatt.
ox, Col. William ....Unatt.
gh, Col. *Sir* Michael................Unatt.
Cross, Lt.-Col. John ....late of 68 F.
Crowe, Lt.-Col. John ....Unatt.
beney, Major-Gen. Henry
son, Lt.-Col. *Sir* William ....h. p.
ne, Lt.-Col. Charles .... 1 F.
Decken, Maj. Wm. *Baron* ....late Ger. Leg.
erinzy, Lt.-Col. B. Vigors ....86 F.
Diggle, Lt.-Col. Charles ....R. Mil. Coll.
Du Plat, Lt.-Col. Geo. Gust. Chas. Wm. R. Eng.
Durie, Assist.-Insp. Wm.....h. p. Ord. Med. Dep.
Elliott, Lt.-Col. Wm. Hen. ....51 F.
England, Col. *Sir* Rich. *KCB.* ....Unatt.
Eustace, Col. *Sir* J. R. ....Unatt.
Everard, Col. Matthias, *CB.* ....14 F.
Falconar, Col. C. Grant, *Insp. Fd. Off. Rec. Dist.*
Findlay, Col. Alex. ....h. p.
Fitz Maurice, Lt.-Col. John.........Unatt.
Forlong, Lt.-Col. James................43 F.
Forster, Lt.-Col. W. F. ....Unatt.
Freeth, Colonel Jas... *Assist.-Quar.-Mast.-Gen.*
Fulton, Lt.-Col. Jas. Forrest ....late of 92 F.
Gabriel, Maj.-Gen. Robert Burd, *CB.*
Garland, Lt.-Col. J................Unatt.
Garrett, Lt.-Col. Robert ....46 F.
Gawler, Col. George ....Unatt.
Geddes, Col. John .... do.
Gore, Maj.-Gen. *Hon.* Charles, *CB.*
Grant, Insp.-Gen. *Sir* Jas. Robt. *MD.* ..h. p.
Graydon, Col. George ....R. Eng
Græme, Lt. G. D. ....h. p. Ger. Leg.
Green, Lt.-Col. William ....Unatt.
Hamilton, Col. *J. Potter* ..late of Sco. Fus. Gds.
Hamilton, Col. Nicholas *Ins. F. O. Rec. Dist.*
Hardinge, Lt.-Col. Richard ....R. Art.
Harris, Col. *H. Bulteel* ....late of 93 F.
Harty, Lt.-Col. Jos. Mark ......late of 33 F.
Harvey, Lt.-Col. Bissell ....*Insp. F. O. Rec. Dist.*
Harvey, Lt.-Col. James ....h. p.
Hastings, Lt.-Col. *Sir* Charles Holland
Havelock, Lt.-Col. William ....4 Dr.
Hely, Lt.-Col. Jas. Price...............Unatt.
Henderson, Maj.-Gen. Geo. Aug.
Henderson, Lt.-Col. James ....Unatt.
Henderson, Lt.-Col. John Wm. ....h. p.
Higgins, Col. *Warner Westenra*
Hogge, Col. *John*
Howden, Col. J. H. *Lord*................Unatt.
Irwin, Lt.-Col. F. C. Unatt. *Commandant of the Troops in Western Australia.*
Jackson, Col. James ....6 Dr. Gds.
Jervois, Maj.-Gen. William
Jones, Col. George E. .... h. p. 31 F.
Jones, Col. James .... Unatt.
Jones, Col. Rice .... R. Eng.

KNIGHTS—*continued.*

Kennedy, Col. Alex. Kennedy Clark, *CB.* Unatt.
Latour, Maj.-Gen. P. A. *CB.*
Law, Lt.-Col. Robert R. Newf. Companies
Leslie, Col. *Charles*
Leslie, Col. John ....4 F.
Lockyer, Lt.-Col. Henry Fred..........97 F.
Love, Col. James Fred. *CB.* ......Unatt.
Lovell, Col. L. B.................15 Hussars
Macadam, Col. *William*
Macintosh, Col. A. F. ....Unatt.
Mackworth, Lt.-Col. *Sir* Digby, *Bt.* ..do.
Macpherson, Maj.-Gen. R. B. *CB.*
Madox, Col. *Henry*
Mansel, Col. Robert Christopher ....do.
Marten, Col. Thomas .... 1 Dr.
Meade, Maj. Roche, Unatt. ..*Deputy-Assistant-Adjutant-General.*
Menzies, Colonel Charles ....R. Marines
Michell, Lt.-Col. Chas. Cornwallis ......h. p.
Miller, Lt.-Col. William ....h. p. R. Art.
Morice, Maj. T. H. ....late of R. Mar.
Munro, Maj.-Gen. Alex. ....from R. Art.
Newton, Lt.-Col. Wm. Hen. .. R. Can. Rifle Regt.
Nickle, Col. *Sir* Robert ....h. p.
Norcliffe, Lt.-Col. Norcliffe ....h. p.
Oates, Lt.-Col. Jas. Poole............... do.
Oldfield, Col. John.................R. Eng.
Owen, Col. John, *CB.* ..*Dep.-Adj.-Gen. R. Mar.*
Parry, Lt.-Gen. *Sir* Love Parry Jones
Paty, Maj.-Gen. Geo. Wm. *CB.*
Pennycuick, Lt.-Col. John, *CB.*........... 24 F.
Pitt, Maj.-Gen. G. Dean
Power, Maj.-Gen. Wm. G. *CB.* ...... R. Art.
Rainey, Maj.-Gen. Henry, *CB.*
Riddall, Maj.-Gen. Wm.
Riddell, Major-Gen. Henry Jas.
Roberts, Col. Rich.................... Unatt.
Robyns, Lt.-Col. John ....late of R. Mr.
Ross, Lt.-Col. Jas. Kerr ....Unatt.
Sall, Lt.-Col. William....late of R. Newf. Co.
Singleton, Lt.-Col. John ....90 F.
Smith, Col. *Sir* J. M. F. ....R. Eng.
Smith, Lt.-Col. C. Hamilton ....h. p.
Somerset, Col. Henry, *CB.*..Cape Mounted Rif.
Southwell, Capt. *Hon.* Cha.........late 12 R. V. B.
Spink, Col. John ....Unatt.
Stack, Maj. Geo. Fitz Gerald.......late of 24 F.
Stephens, Maj. Hen. Sykes ....Unatt.
Taylor, Lt.-Col. Pringle ....Unatt.
Thackwell, Maj.-Gen. *Sir* J., *KCB.* from 3 Dn.
Thorn, Maj.-Gen. Nathaniel, *CB.*
Thorn, Lt.-Col. William ....late of 25 Dr
Thorpe, Maj. Samuel ....Unatt.
Tremenheere, Maj.-Gen. Walter, ..late of R. Mar.
Trevor, Lieut.-Col. A. H. ....59 F.
Wallace, Col. *Sir* J. Maxwell...............h. p.
Wallace, Col. Robert ....do.
Weare, Col. Thomas.............Prov. Bat.
Wetherall, Col. Geo. Aug. *CB.* ....Unatt.
Whinyates, Col. E. C. *CB.*.........R. Art.
Wilkins, Lt.-Col. *Geo. CB.* ..late of Rif. B.
Williams, Lt.-Col. Thos. Molyneux......Unatt.
Williams, Lt.-Col. W. F.................h. p.
Wilson, Col. *Sir* J. M. *CB.* *Adj.* to Chel. Hosp.
Wilson, Lieut.-Col. Nicholas.............77 F.
Wood, Major-Gen. William, *CB.*
Wood, Lt.-Col. Wm. Leighton ....h. p.
Wright, Lt.-Col. Charles ..late of R. Mil. College
Wright, Col. John.........................R. Mar.
Young, Lt.-Col. Plomer ....Unatt.

OTHER FOREIGN ORDERS.

Abercromby, Col. *Hon. Alex. CB.* late of Coldstream Gds. — Knight of Tower and Sword; Knight Maria Theresa; Fourth Class St. George
A'Court, Major-Gen. Chas. A. *CB. KH*.........41 F. — Commander St. Ferdinand and Merit; Knight St. Maurice and Lazare
Adam, Gen. *Right Hon. Sir* Fred. *GCB. GCMG.* 21 F. — Knight Maria Theresa; First Class St. Anne
Alderson, Lt.-Col. Ralph Carr ....Royal Engineers — First Class St. Fernando; Commander Isabella the Catholic; Knight Charles the Third
Alexander, Major *Sir* James Edward .... 14 F. — Second Class Lion and Sun
Anglesey, Field Marshal H. W. *Marq. of, KG. GCB. & GCH.*..........................R. H. Gds. — Commander Maria Theresa; Second Class St. George
Ansley, Col. *Benj.*...............late of Scots Fus. Gds. — Second Class of Crescent
Anson, Gen. *Sir* Geo. *GCB.* .... 4 Dr. Gds. — Commander of Tower and Sword
Arbuthnot, Lieut.-Gen. *Sir* R. *KCB.* ....76 F. — do do
Armstrong, Maj.-Gen. *Sir* Rich. *CB.* ....95 F. — Knight do do
Arnold, Major-Gen. J. R. *KH.* ....from R. Eng. — Second Class of Crescent
Askwith, Major W. H.................Royal Artillery — First Class St. Fernando; Commander Isabella the Catholic; Knight Charles the Third
Barnard, Lt.-Gen. *Sir* A. F. *GCB. GCH.* Rifle Brigade — Knight Maria Theresa; Fourth Class St. George
Barns, Lt.-Gen. *Sir* James S. *KCB.* ....20 F. — Knight Tower and Sword; Crescent
Bassett, Capt. Rich. ....h. p. Royal Artillery — First Class St. Fernando; Knight Isabella the Catholic
Baumgardt, Col. J. G. *CB.* ....Insp. Field Officer — Second Class Dooranée Empire
Beckham, Capt. Horatio ....h. p. 43 F. — First Class San Fernando
Beckwith, Maj.-Gen. Charles, *CB.* .... — Second Class St. Anne

Beresford, Gen. W. C. *Viscount*, *GCB. GCH.* ..16 F.	Grand Cross Tower and Sword ———— St. Ferdinand and Merit ———— of St. Hermenigilde ———— Charles the Third ———— San Fernando
Berkeley, Lt.-Gen. *Sir* G. H. F. *KCB.* ....35 F.	Knight Tower and Sword Fourth Class of St. Wladimir ———— Wilhelm
irrell, Lieut.-Colonel David ....Bengal Inf.	Third Class Dooranée Empire
Blakeney, Lt.-Gen. *Rt. Hon. Sir.* E. *KCB. GCH.* 7 F.	Knight Tower and Sword
Blunt, Lt.-Gen. Richard .... 66 F.	Commander Tower and Sword
Bradford, Gen. *Sir* T. *GCB. GCH.* ....4 F.	Commander Tower and Sword
radshaw, Maj.-Gen. *Lawrence* ...... late of 1 Life Gds.	Second Class of Crescent
Browne, Lt.-Gen. *Sir* John, *KCH.* ....8 Hussars	Knight Tower and Sword ———— Charles the Third
Buchan, Lt.-Gen. *Sir* John, *KCB.* ....32 F.	Commander Tower and Sword
Bunbury, Lt.-Col. Thomas, *CB.* ....80 F.	Knight Tower and Sword
Burgoyne, Maj.-Gen. *Sir* J. F. *KCB.* .. from R. Eng.	do do
Cameron, Maj.-Gen. *Sir* A. *KCB.* ....74 F.	Second Class St. Anne
ameron, Lt.-Col. George Poulett, *CB.* ....Madras Inf.	Knight Tower and Sword Knight of the Conception
ampbell, Lt.-Col. Neil, *Dep.-Qr.-Mas.-Gen. Bombay Army*	Second Class Dooranée Empire
Campbell, Lt.-Col. Patrick, *CB.* ....Unatt.	Knight Charles the Third
Campbell, Maj.-Gen. Wm. *CB.*	Second Class St. Anne
armichael, Lt.-Col. Chas. M. *CB.*.......Bengal Cavalry	Third Class Dooranée Empire
arruthers, Lt.-Col. Richard, *CB.* ....2 F.	do do
Cathcart, Lt.-Gen. C. M. *Earl*, *KCB.* 11 Hussars	Fourth Class of St. Wladimir ———— of Wilhelm
athcart, Col. *Hon.* Fred..................b. p. 92 F.	Second Class St. Anne
Cathcart, Col. *Hon.* George................Unatt.	Fourth Class St. Wladimir
hurch, Lt.-Col. *Sir Richard*, *CB. GCH.* late of Greek Lt. Inf.	Grand Cross St. George and Reunion of Naples Commander St. Ferdinand and Merit
Clifton, Lt.-Gen. *Sir* A. B. *KCB.* ....1 Dr.	Fourth Class Wilhelm Second Class St. Anne
Colquhoun, Lt.-Col. J. N. ....Royal Artillery	Second Class St. Fernando Commander Isabella the Catholic
Combermere, Gen. S. *Visc.* *GCB. GCH.* .. 1 Life Gds.	Grand Cross Tower and Sword ———— Charles the Third ———— St. Fernando
Cooke, Lt.-Col. *R. Harvey*, *CB.* late of Gren. Gds.	Fourth Class St. Wladimir
onroy, Capt. *Sir* John, *Bart. KCH.* ..h. p. R. Artillery	Grand Cross Ernestine ———— St. Bento d'Avis Commander Tower and Sword
Cotton, Lt.-Gen. *Sir* Willoughby, *GCB. KCH.*..98 F.	First Class Dooranée Empire
Cox, Col. *Sir William* ....late of Port. Serv.	Knight Tower and Sword
rofton, Captain Edward Walter........Royal Artillery	First Class St. Fernando
Cureton, Col. Charles Robert, *CB.* ....h. p. 16 Dr.	Third Class Dooranée Empire
ickson, Major Collingwood ....Royal Artillery	Knight Charles the Third First Class San Fernando Knight of Isabella the Catholic
Douglas, Lt.-Gen. *Sir* Howard, *Bt. GCB. GCMG.* 99 F.	Knight Charles the Third
Douglas, Lt.-Gen. *Sir* N. *KCB. KCH.* ....72 F.	Knight Maria Theresa Fourth Class St. Wladimir
Downes, Lt.-Gen. U. *Lord*, *KCB.* ....54 F.	Commander Tower and Sword
Doyle, Col. *Sir J. M. KCB.* ...... late of 12 Gar. Bn.	Knight Tower and Sword
Duffy, Maj.-Gen. John, *CB.*	Second Class of Crescent
u Plat, Lt.-Col. G. G. C. W. *KH.*...Royal Engineers	Second Class Charles the Third First Class San Fernando Commander Isabella the Catholic
D'Urban, Lt.-Gen. *Sir* B. *GCB. KCH.* ....51 F.	Commander Tower and Sword
Evans, Maj.-Gen. *Sir* De Lacy, *KCB.*	Grand Cross St. Fernando Third Class do Fifth Class do Grand Cross Charles the Third
arrant, Lieut.-Col. Francis ....Bombay Cavalry	First Class Lion and Sun
Forbes, *Sir* Chas. F. *MD. KCH.* .... Dep. Insp. Gen.	Second Class of Crescent
raser, Major James, *CB.* ....Bengal Cavalry	Third Class Dooranée Empire
arden, Lt.-Col. Wm. *CB.*.............Bengal Infantry	Second Class Dooranée Empire

Gardiner, Maj.-Gen. *Sir* Robert, *KCB. KCH.*...R. Art.	Second Class St. Anne
Giles, Lt.-Col. Stephen ....Royal Marines	Knight Tower and Sword
Gomm, Lt.-Gen. *Sir* W. M. *KCB.*.........13 F.	Second Class St. Anne
Gough, Lt.-Gen. Hugh, *Lord GCB.* ....87 F.	Knight Charles the Third
Grant, Gen. *Sir* Wm. Keir, *KCB. GCH.*..........2 Dr.	First Class Lion and Sun Knight Maria Theresa
Grant, *Sir* James Rob. *MD. KH*........Med. Dep.	Second Class St. Anne
Grey, Maj.-Gen. *Sir* John, *KCB.* ....73 F.	Knight Tower and Sword Commander St. Bento d'Avis
Haggart, Major Crawford ....E. I. C. Serv.	Third Class Dooranée Empire
Halkett, Gen. *Sir* Colin, *GCB. GCH.*.......45 F.	Commander Maximilian Joseph Third Class Wilhelm Knight Tower and Sword
Harvey, Maj.-Gen. *Sir* Robert J. *CB.* 2 W. I. Regt.	Commander St. Bento d'Avis Knight Tower and Sword
Henderson, Maj.-Gen. G. A. *KH.*	Second Class of Crescent,
Hill, Col. *Sir R. C. CB.*....late of R. Horse Gds.	Knight Maria Theresa Fourth Class St. George
Hill, Maj.-Gen. *Sir* Dudley St. L., *KCB.*	Commander St. Bento d'Avis Knight Tower and Sword
Hockings, Lt. Robert ....R. Marines	First Class San Fernando
Hodges, Capt. G. L. ....h. p.	Knight Tower and Sword Commander St. Bento d'Avis
Howden, Col. J. H. *Lord, KH.*................Unatt.	Second Class St. Anne Commander Legion of Honour Knight Charles the Third Third Class Leopold Commander Saviour
Imhoff, Gen. *Sir* Charles	Grand Commander St. Joachim
Johnson, Lt.-Col. Chas. C.................h. p. 10 F.	Second Class Lion and Sun
Johnson, Surg. *Sir* Edward, *MD.* ......h. p. 39 F.	Knight Charles the Third
Jones, Col. James, *KH.* ....Unatt.	do do
Jones, Lt.-Col. B. O. ....Unatt.	Knight Tower and Sword
Kempt, Gen. *Right Hon. Sir* James, *GCB. GCH.* 1 F.	Knight Maria Theresa Third Class St. George ——— Wilhelm
Lacy, Maj.-Gen. R. J. J.........from Royal Artillery	Knight Charles the Third First Class San Fernando Commander Isabella the Catholic
Langley, Lt. George Colt ....Royal Marines	First Class San Fernando
Laughton, Major John ....Bengal Engineers	First Class Lion and Sun
Le Marchant, Lt.-Col. *Sir* John Gaspard ....Unatt.	Third Class San Fernando Knight Charles the Third
Logan, Capt. George...............h. p. Royal Marines	Knight Legion of Honour Cross of the Redeemer
Londonderry, Gen. C. W. *Marq. of*, *GCB. GCH.* 2 Life Guards	Commander Tower and Sword Fourth Class St. George Black Eagle Grand Cross Red Eagle ——— Sword Russian Medal in Commemoration of the Capture of Paris
Lygon, Lt.-Gen. *Hon.* E. P. *CB.* ....13 Gds.	Fourth Class St. Wladimir
Lynn, Major James ....Royal Engineers	Knight Charles the Third First Class San Fernando Commander Isabella the Catholic
M'Dowell, Lt.-Col *Gen. Jas. CB.* ......late of 16 Dr.	Third Class Dooranée Empire
M'Grigor, *Sir J. Bt. MD. Dir.-Gen. of Med. Dep.*	Commander Tower and Sword
Macbean, Lt.-Gen. *Sir* Wm. *KCB.*............92 F.	Commander Tower and Sword
Macdonald, Maj.-Gen. Alex. *CB.* from R. Artillery	Second Class St. Anne
Macdonald, Lt.-Col. *Robt. CB.*......late of 35 F.	Second Class St. Anne
Macdonell, Lt.-Gen. *Sir* James, *KCB. KCH.* 79 F.	Knight Maria Theresa Fourth Class St. Wladimir
Mackenzie, Gen. *Sir* Alex. *Bt. GCH.*.........from 36 F.	St. Januarius
Maclachlan, Lt.-Col. Alexander ....R. Artillery	Knight St. Maurice and St. Lazare
Maclaine, Major-Gen. *Sir* Arch. *CB.* ....52 F.	Knight Charles the Third
Maitland, Gen. *Sir* P. *KCB.* ....17 F.	Third Class St. Wladimir ——— Wilhelm
Meade, Major Roche, *KH.*....................Unatt.	Knight of the Sword

Menzies, Colonel Charles, *KH.* .... Royal Marines	Knight Charles the Third
Michell, Lt.-Col. Charles Cornwallis, *RH.* h.p.	Knight of St. Bento d'Avis
Money, Maj.-Gen. Arch. *CB.*	Second Class of Crescent
Montagu, Major Willoughby ...... h. p. R. Artillery	Fourth Class St. Wladimir
Monteath, Col. Tho. *CB.* .... Bengal Infantry	Third Class Dooranée Empire
Montresor, Gen. *Sir* T. Gage, *KCH.* .... 2 Dr. Gds.	Second Class of Crescent
Moody, Colonel Thomas .... Royal Engineers	Knight Military Merit of France
Muttlebury, Lt.-Col. G., *CB.* .... late of 69 F.	Fourth Class Wilhelm
Otway, Lt.-Gen. *Sir* Loftus W. *CB.* .... 84 F.	Knight Charles the Third
Outram, Lt.-Col. James, *CB.* .... Bombay Infantry	Second Class Dooranée Empire
Owen, Col. John, *CB. KH.* .. *Dep.-Adj.-Gen.* R. Marines	Second Class San Fernando
Paget, Gen. *Hon. Sir* Edw. *GCB* .... 28 F.	Grand Cross Tower and Sword
Parker, Capt. Edw. Aug. .... Royal Marines	Knight Tower and Sword
Parsons, Lt.-Col. Jas. *CB.* .... Bengal Infantry	Second Class Dooranée Empire
Paty, Maj.-Gen. Geo. Wm. *CB. KH.*	Commander St. Bento d'Avis Knight Tower and Sword
Peacocke, Gen. *Sir* W. M. *KCH.* .... 19 F.	Commander Tower and Sword Second Class of Crescent
Peacocke, Lt.-Col. Thomas .... h. p. Port. Ser.	Knight Tower and Sword
Powell, Lt.-Col. Walter .... Royal Marines	Second Class San Fernando
Pynn, Lt.-Col. *Sir Henry,* *CB.* ...... late of Por. Ser.	Commander Tower and Sword Knight St. Fernando ——— Charles the Third
Rawlinson, Major Henry Creswicke, *CB.* Bombay Infantry	First Class Lion and Sun Third Class Dooranée Empire
Reade, Col. *Sir* Thomas, *CB.* .... h. p. 24 F.	Knight St. Ferdinand and Merit
Rivarola, Lt.-Gen. *F. Count,* *KCMG. KCH.* R. Malta F.	Commander St. Maurice and St. Lazare
Roberts, Col. Abraham, *CB.* .... Bengal Infantry	Second Class Dooranée Empire
Rolt, Maj.-Gen. *Sir* John, *KCB.*	Knight Tower and Sword
Ross, Maj.-Gen. *Sir* Hew Dalrymple, *KCB.* *Deputy-Adjutant-General,* R. Art.	Knight Tower and Sword Second Class St. Anne
Salter, Lt.-Col. H. F. .... Bengal Cavalry	Third Class Dooranée Empire
Saltoun, Lt.-Gen. Alex. *Lord,* *KCB. GCH.* .. 2 F.	Knight Maria Theresa Fourth Class St. George
Sandwith, Lt.-Col. Bentham, *CB.* ...... Bombay Cavalry	Third Class Dooranée Empire
Scott, Col. John, *CB.* .... 9 Dr.	Second Class Dooranée Empire
Scovell, Maj.-Gen. *Sir* G. *KCB.* *Gov. R. Mil. College,* 4 Drs.	Fourth Class St. Wladimir
Seaton, Lt.-Gen. John, *Lord,* *GCB. GCMG. GCH.* 26 F.	Knight Maria Theresa Fourth Class St. George
Shearman, Capt. John .... h. p. 7 F.	Knight St. Maurice and St. Lazare
Sheil, Lt.-Col. Justin, *CB.* .... Bengal Infantry	First Class Lion and Sun
Sleigh, Lt.-Gen. J. W., *CB.* .... 9 Drs.	Knight of Maximilian Joseph
Smith, Maj.-Gen. *Sir* Chas. F. *KCB.* from R. Engineers	Knight Charles the Third
Smith, Lt.-Col. Chas. Hamilton, *KH.* .... h. p. 15 F.	Fourth Class Wilhelm
Somerset, Lt.-Gen. *Lord* Fitz Roy J. H. *GCB.* 53 F. *Military Secretary to His Grace the Comm.-in-Chief*	Knight Maria Theresa Fourth Class St. George Knight Maximilian Joseph Commander Tower and Sword
Stalker, Lt.-Col. Foster, *CB.* .... Bombay Infantry	Third Class Dooranée Empire
Stanhope, Col. *Hon.* Leicester, *CB.* .... Unatt.	Commander of Saviour
Strafford, Gen. John, *Earl of,* *GCB. GCH.* 29 F.	Knight Maria Theresa Second Class St. Wladimir
Swan, Maj. Graves C. .... h. p.	Second Class St. Fernando
Thackwell, Maj.-Gen. *Sir* J., *KCB. KH.* from 3 Dr.	Second Class Dooranée Empire
Thompson, Lt. Chas. Wm. .... 14 Dr.	First Class St. Fernando
Thomson, Maj. Geo. *CB.* .... late of Bengal Army	Second Class Dooranee Empire
Turner, Major Geo. Edward .... Royal Artillery	First Class St. Ferdinand Knight Charles the Third Commander Isabella the Catholic
Upton, Lt.-Gen. *Hon.* A. P. *CB.* .... from Gren. Gds.	Knight Maximilian Joseph
Vandeleur, Gen. *Sir* J. O. *GCB.* .... 16 Dr.	Second Class St. Wladimir Commander Maximilian Joseph
Vicars, Maj. Edward .... Royal Engineers	First Class San Fernando Knight Isabella the Catholic
Wade, Lt.-Col. *Sir* C. M. *CB.* .... late Bengal Infantry	First Class Dooranée Empire Auspicious Star of the Punjaub
Wade, Maj. Hamlet Coote, *CB.* .... h.p.	Third Class Dooranée Empire
Warburton, Captain G. D. .... Royal Artillery	First Class St. Fernando

Warre, Maj.-Gen. Sir William, *CB*. ....94 F.	Knight Tower and Sword Commander St. Bento d'Avis
Watson, Maj.-Gen. *Sir* Henry, *CB*. ....63 F.	Commander Tower and Sword
Wellington, Field Marshal Arthur, *Duke of*, *KG*. *GCB*. *GCH*. Col. of Gren. Gds. and of the Rifle Brigade, Constable of the Tower of London, and Lord Warden of the Cinque Ports. *Commander-in-Chief*.	*First and highest Class of nearly every Order in Europe*
West, *Sir* Aug. *MD*. ....h. p. Dep. Ins. Gen.	Commander Tower and Sword
Westmorland, Lt.-Gen. J. *Earl of*, *GCB*. *GCH*. 56 F.	Knight Maria Theresa Grand Cross St. Ferdinand and Merit ——— St. Joseph First Class of Henry the Lion
Wheeler, Col. Hugh M. *CB*. ....Bengal Infantry	Second Class Dooranée Empire
Williams, Maj.-Gen. *Sir* E. K. *KCB*. ....80 F.	Knight Tower and Sword
Willshire, Maj.-Gen. *Sir* Thomas, *Bart*. *KCB*.	First Class Dooranée Empire
Wilson, Lt.-Gen. *Sir* John, *KCB*. ....11 F.	St. Bento d'Avis Commander Tower and Sword
Wilson, Gen. *Sir* Robert T. ....15 Hussars	Commander Tower and Sword Commander Maria Theresa St. Anne of Russia Grand Order of the Red Eagle of Prussia Third Class St. George of Russia Second Class of Crescent
Woodford, Lt.-Gen. *Sir* A. *KCB*. *GCMG*. .40 F.	Knight Maria Theresa Fourth Class of St. George
Wylde, Col. William, *CB*. ....Royal Artillery	Knight Charles the Third Second Class San Fernando Commander Isabella the Catholic
Wymer, Colonel George Petre, *CB*. ..Bengal Infantry	Third Class Dooranée Empire

---

ERRATA, AND ALTERATIONS WHILE PRINTING.

Page 36, *insert* Francis John Davies, *Lt.-Col.* Unattached; *Cornet*, 3 Feb. 08; *Lieut.* 26 Ja. 09; *Capt.* 12 Aug. 13; *Lt.-Col.* 30 April 27; *Col.* 23 Nov. 41.
— 36, *insert* Col. Jeremiah Taylor, *instead* of p. 42.
— 332, *erase Lord* T. C. Clinton.
— 341, *for* Mellis, John, *read* Nairne, John Mellis.
— 341, *insert* Capt. Allen Menzies, Unattached; *Cornet*, 18 Oct. 31; *Lieut.* 16 Aug. 35; C-. 15 Dec. 48; *half-pay*, 15 Dec. 48.
— 344, *erase* Capt. John Ambrose Russell.

Lieut.-Col. G. Buller to be *CB*.
Lieut.-Col. Charles Rowan, *CB*. to be *KCB*.
Col. Duncan M'Gregor to be *KCB*.

INDEX.

CASUALTIES SINCE THE LAST PUBLICATION.

RETIREMENTS BY SALE OF COMMISSIONS.

Colonels.

Sir Aug. F. d'Este, 69 F.
J. Linton, Coldst. Gds.
Wm. Fraser, Gr. Gds.
Sir R. Burdett, *Bt.* 68 F.
Sir C. F. Maclean, 13 Drs.
P. Dundas, 6 F.
J. M. Robertson, 4 Dr. Gds.
F. V. Harcourt, Coldst. Gds.
Sir J. M. Burgoyne, *Bt.* Gr. Gds.
Geo. Baker, 16 Drs.
G. Teulon, 16 F.

Lieutenant-Colonels.

R. S. Webb, 1 Drs.
W. F. Tinling, 68 F.
J. Luard, 30 F.
G. Smith, R. H. Gds.
G. Deare, 21 F.
S. R. Warren, 14 Drs.
J. Anderson, 50 F.
Sir H. Bayly, 77 F.
G. Brown, 78 F.
W. Harding, 2 F.
T. W. C. M'Niven, 70 F.
M. G. T. Lindsay, 91 F.
R. Hort, 81 F.
H. Bathurst, Scots Fus. Gds.
G. Whannell, 33 F.
J. C. Clunie, 44 F.
J. H. Hudson, Gr. Gds.
F. Brandreth, Scots Fus. Gds.
A. A. O'Reilly, Unatt.
R. H. Willcocks, 81 F.
J. Allen, 2 W. I. Regt.
R. Vansittart, Coldst. Gds.
F. Romilly, Scots Fus. Gds.
J. L. Elrington, Coldst. Gds.
J. J. Slater, 82 F.
T. Hutton, 32 F.
J. Mill, 50 F.
H. A. Fraser, 45 F.
Lord C. J. F. Russell, 60 F.
G. C. Page, h. p. R. Eng.
E. Von Schrader, h. p. Brunswick Cavalry

Majors.

H. Cooper, 35 F.
J. G. S. Gilland, 2 F.
G. Deedes, 35 F.
R. Fawkes, 27 F.
W. Amsink, 53 F.
C. A. Young, 33 F.
T. Lt. L. Alcock, 81 F.
R. Campbell, 46 F.
J. B. Thomas, 9 F.
T. Bulkeley, 31 F.
G. Tennant, 85 F.
Hon. D. H. Murray, Scots Fus. Gds.
J. H. Mathews, 34 F.
H. D. Warden, Cape M. R.
F. Brown, 52 F.
J. Browne, 2 W. I. Regt.
E. S. N. Campbell, 90 F.
Lord H. F. Chichester, 2 F.
G. Cressewell, 92 F.
J. S. Dodsworth, 2 Life Gds.
A. G. Fullerton, do.
J. N. Hibbert, 97 F.
E. Kingsley, 3 F.
T. St. G. Lister, 6 Dr. Gds.
W. Milligan, 38 F.
M. Pole, 46 F.
W. H. Sitwell, 35 F.
T. Wright, 45 F.
W. Arkwright, 6 Drs.
Hon. R. Needham, 12 Drs.
E. Foy, 71 F.

Captains.

Power, 1 Dr. Gds.
Newland, do.
Crofts, do.
Ley, 2 Dr. Gds.
Garratt, 3 Dr. Gds.
Jacob, 4 Dr. Gds.
Campbell, 7 Dr. Gds.
T. Smales, h. p. 1 W. I. Regt.
Morris, 1 Drs.
Grant, 2 Drs.
Martin, 3 Drs.
Fraser, 4 Drs.
May, 6 Drs.
Carrol, do.
Peel, 7 Drs.
Maunsell, 12 Drs.
Bromwich, 14 Drs.
Perrott, 15 Drs.
Powell, 16 Drs.
Lyon, 17 Drs.
Oswald, Gr. Gds.
G. J. Johnson, 11 Drs.
Melville, Gr. Gds.
Pryce, 2 F.
Cookson, 9 F.
Duff, 12 F.
Marcon, do.
Longfield, 14 Drs.
Rattray, 13 F.
Sir M. A. H. Tuite, *Bt.* 19 F.
Frith, 20 F.
Andrews, 21 F.
Souter, 22 F.
Coultman, 24 F.
Cole, 27 F.
Steele, 30 F.
Wilkinson, do.
Robyns, 32 F.
Maude, 33 F.
Talbot, 34 F.
Halkett, 40 F.
Douglas, 42 F.
Rooke, 47 F.
Collins, do.
Emmett, 48 F.
J. Grant, 49 F.
Brownrigg, 52 F.
Fountaine, do.
Mansel, 60 F.
Graves, 62 F.
Jauncey, do.
Norris, 64 F.
Parker, do.
Yelverton, do.
Canavan, do.
Taylor, 66 F.
Blount, do.
Kennedy, 68 F.
Browne, do.
Ricard, 73 F.
Wardlaw, do.
De Butts, 74 F.
Elrington, 78 F.
Aynsely, 79 F.
Boyd, 87 F.
Turner, do.
Isacke, 89 F.
Griffis, do.
D'Arcy, do.
Webb, 90 F.
Chester, do.
Woodgate, do.
Stewart, 92 F.
Fisher, 94 F.
Rowse, 95 F.
Bull, 99 F.

Keane, Rifle Br.
Dickson, 1 W. I. Regt.
Ogilby, 3 do.
M. Archdall, 50 F.
A. Blair, 52 F.
A. L. Bourke, 95 F.
G. Brown, 16 Drs.
L. Cowell, 15 F.
G. F. Duckett, 69 F.
R. Dyott, 36 F.
R. J. Hanley, 1 Dr. Gds.
H. J. V. Kemble, 40 F.
A. Mainwaring, 56 F.
J. B. Parkinson, 70 F.
E. H. Poyntz, 62 F.
R. Rose, 74 F.
W. Lt. L. Alcock Stawell, 44 F.
J. White, 93 F.
C. W. Miles, 17 Lancers
Lord S. C. Pelham Clinton, 27 F.
C. M. Creagh, 80 F.
W. R. Ramsay, Rifle Brigade

Lieutenants.

Visc. Seaham, 1 Life Gds.
King, 2 Life Gds.
Hesketh, do.
Ridley, 2 Dr. Gds.
Oakes, 3 Dr. Gds.
Buchanan, 6 Dr. Gds.
Casement, 3 Drs.
J. D. White, do.
Maycock, 36 F.
Colmore, 7 Drs.
Saltmarshe, 8 Drs.
Robarts, 9 Drs.
Kortright, do.
Parker, 10 Drs.
Alexander, 11 Drs.
Morant, do.
Fullerton, 12 Drs.
Wilson, 13 Drs.
Holder, 14 Drs.
Bennett, do.
Jennyns, 15 Drs.
Bill, 6 Drs.
Colston, 15 Drs.
Miles, 17 Drs.
Codrington, do.
Sir E. Poore, *Bt.* Scots Fus. Gds.
Pennefather, 6 F.
Fardell, 9 F.
Dashwood, 10 F.
Bewes, 11 F.
Montgomery, 15 F.
Codd, 17 F.
Jones, 18 F.
Daly, 20 F.
E. S. Smith, 22 F.
Frere, 24 F.
Scudamore, 29 F.
Broome, 30 F.
Bennett, 33 F.
Fyfe, 34 F.
Parker, do.
Ellis, 36 F.
Smith, 39 F.
Burrowes, 42 F.
Spilling, 46 F.
Menzies, do.
Wemyss, 48 F.
O'Sullivan, do.
Riley, 52 F.
Redmond, 54 F.
Denny, 55 F.
Saunders, 56 F.
Johnson, 60 F.
Maycock, 61 F.
Egan, do.
Singleton, 64 F.
Peel, 67 F.
Aitchison, 69 F.
Hussey, do.
Hall, 73 F.
Capel, 75 F.
Mahony, do.
Sleigh, 77 F.
Gordon, 78 F.
Murray, 79 F.
Leader, do.
Kingsley, 80 F.
Gordon, do.
T. H. Kingscote, 1 Life Gds.
W. L. Wrey, Newf. Col.
Lord A. Churchill, 83 F.
Mildmay, 86 F.
O'Donel, 88 F.
Conyngham, do.
Stein, 91 F.
Shuter, 93 F.
Campbell, 94 F.
Campbell, 96 F.
Raitt, do.
Knox, 98 F.
Williams, 2 W. I. Regt.
Bertles, 3 do.
Forster, do.
Anquetil, do.
Werge, Ceylon Regt.
Bradley, do.
Hill, do.
Wm. Harvey, Cape M. R.
Phillpotts, do.
Gahan, do.
Young, Canadian Regt.
W. B. Burne, 1 Life Gds.
W. R. Bustin, 98 F.
G. Damerum, 58 F.
J. Eagar, Ceylon Regt.
F. Hankey, 75 F.
R. Hewitt, 60 F.
L. Heyland, 73 F.
R. Hill, 90 F.

Cornets, Ensigns, &c.

Burke, 1 Dr. Gds.
Errington, do.
Saunders, 2 Dr. Gds.
Burton, 4 Drs.
Hoghton, 9 Drs.
Dury, 10 Drs.
Hollinshead, 12 Drs.
Lalor, 12 F.
Walmsley, 15 F.
Blencowe, do.
Lloyd, do.
Taylor, 19 F.
Kelley, 20 F.
Blakeney, 23 F.
Stead, 37 F.
Willson, 41 F.
Barry, 50 F.
Lloyd, 51 F.
Lloyd, 52 F.
Wyse, 57 F.
Coghill, 59 F.
Armstrong, 64 F.
Toll, 74 F.
Becher, 77 F.
Lamont, 91 F.
Hay, 93 F.
Pemberton, 94 F.
Wright, 99 F.
Fottrell, 1 W. I. Regt.
G. H. Marsack, 16 F.
T. Traill, 31 F.

Received a Commuted Allowance.

Captain E. de Brandis, h. p. German Legion
Captain L. Benne, do.

RESIGNATIONS.

Captain.

E. F. Thorndike, R. Art.

Lieutenants.

F. W. Davis, R. Marines
J. A. Fynmore, do.
J. Grieve, do.
G. J. Power, R. Art.

Cornet and Ensigns.

Hoghton, 9 Drs.
Fead, 22 F.
Lennox, 28 F.
Quill, 35 F.
Browne, 45 F.
Barry, 50 F.
Davy, 67 F.
Fraser, 99 F.
Knapman, 2 W. I. Regt.
Le Mesurier, 66 F.

Surgeon.

Dr. Johnston, 26 F.

Assistant Surgeons.

Macintosh, 42 F.
Dr. Purdon, 64 F.
Dr. Hodgson, 73 F.
Dr. Johnstone

Dep. Assist. Com. Gen.

P. H. St. J. Mildmay

SUPERSEDED.

Ens. Byrne, 3 W. I. Regt.
Qr. Master Hanrahan, 13 F.

DISMISSED.

Assist.-Surg. Viret, 98 F.
Lt. J. J. Winne, R. Marines

CASHIERED.

2d Lt. H. H. Vaughton, 60 F.
Lt. J. A. Macdonald, 98 F.

DEATHS.

Generals.

F. Maitland, 58 F.
P. Heron
L. B. Wallis
A. J. Goldie
J. Vincent, 69 F.
J. Walker
G. B. Mundy

Lieutenant-Generals.

W. Thomas
Sir Tho. Reynell, *Bt.* 71 F.
M. Burrowes
G. Salmon, R. Art.
Hon. G. Murray
Sir J. Maclean, 27 F.
Sir M. O'Connell, 80 F.
A. Bethune
J. Lomax
Sir C. M. Maxwell, 3 W. I. Regt.
J. Wardlaw, 55 F.
E. Lindsay, 2 W. I. Regt.
G. G. C. L'Estrange, 61 F.
Sir D. Ximenes
D. Colquhoun
Sir J. Dickson, 61 F.

Major-Generals.

W. G. Strutt
E. Walker
R. M'Donall
S. Lambert
T. Steele
C. J. Doyle
Sir W. Gossett
T. T. Woolridge
R. Dalyell

Colonels.

F. Sherlock, late of 4 Dr. Gds.
H. Freke, late of 51 F.
E. H. Cheney, late of 7 Dr. Gds.
G. Rochfort, late of 12 F.
P. Dumas, h. p. 4 W. I. Regt.
H. Stapleton, h. p. 50 F.
E. S. Mercer, R. Mar.
Visc. Guillamore, Unatt.
C. Chambers, 25 F.
H. Capadose, 1 W. I. Regt.
T. Peebles, R. Mar.

Lieutenant-Colonels.

R. Oswald, late of Greek Lt. Inf.
J. Califfe. late of 60 F.
P. Dorville. Unatt.
G. *Baron* Von Baring, h. p. Ger. Leg.
S. South, h. p. 8 F.
H. Obins, h. p. 53 F.
W. Moore, h. p. 14 F.
T. Maling, late of 2 W. I. Regt.
J. Johnson, Unatt.
W. Ross, do.
F. A. M. Frazer, do. *Assist.-Qr.-Master-Gen. in Canada*
J. W. Parsons, Unatt.
Hon. J. Massey, do.
L. Dowse, R. Art.
O. Phibbs, 88 F.
R. T. R. Pattoun, 32 F. *Killed in action at Mooltan*
C. L. Strickland, 10 F.
A Erskine, 45 F.
C. J. Selwyn, R. Eng.
H. Deedes, 34 F.
H. R. Brandreth, R. Eng.
R. Ford, R. Mar.

Majors.

G. Wolfe, late of R. Mar.
J. Staunton, late 1 Vet. Bn.
F. Hawker, late 8 do.
F. Wemyss, late of R. Mar.
G. Luard, Unatt.
T. Seward, late of R. Mar.
W. Smith, Unatt.
W. E. Maling, h. p. R. Art.
C. Wallett, late of Cey. Regt.
G. Duff, h. p. 90 F.
J. Hutchinson, h. p. 5 F.
T. Nickoll, Unatt.
E. N. Macready, do.
C. O'C. Higgins, 56 F.
W. Egerton, 43 F.
W. O'Connor, 25 F.
G. S. Montizambert, 10 F. *Killed in action at Mooltan*
H. G. Ross, R. Art.
P. Brown, h. p. 62 F.
R. Carr, 38 F.
H. Grimes, 98 F.
H. J. Pogson, h. p. 2 Ceylon Regt.
E. C. Ansell, 74 F.
W. L. Y. Baker, 73 F.
H. G. Boyce, Unatt.

Captains.

Sir C. W. Kent, *Bt.* 1 Life Gds.
Holder, 8 F.
Hollinsworth, 10 F. *of wounds received in action at Mooltan*
Granet, 12 F.
A. D. A. Stewart, 61 F.
Routh, 23 F.
Gardiner, 32 F.
Creighton, 36 F.
Hill, 57 F.
Bligh, 61 F.
Herbert, do.
Herbert, 62 F.
Smith, 64 F.
Jopp, do.
Carmichael, 68 F.
J. A. Russell Unatt.
Murray, Rifle Br. *of wounds received in action at the Cape*
Losack, 1 W. I. Regt.
Charles Murray, do.
Gray, Ceylon Regt.
P. J. Hornby, R. Eng.
J. G. Amos, h. p. 40 F.
T. M. Bagnold, h. p. R. Mar.
Sir J. Bateman, h. p. R. Art. Driver
J. T. Bayly, Unatt.
T. Berington, h. p. R. Art. Driver
H. Bertles, Unatt.
W. Blathwayt, h. p. 3 Drs.

J. B. Bown, 60 F.
E. M. Bray, h. p. York Lt. Inf.
J. Breynton, h. p. Indep. Comp.
G. Buchan, h. p. 83 F.
A. Cameron, h. p. Indep. Comp.
D. Campbell, late 2 Vet. Bn.
J. Campbell, late of R. Mar.
C. Clark, h. p. York Rang.
J. Clark, h. p. 38 F.
W. B. Cock, late of R. Mar.
J. Cox, h. p. 77 F.
G. Croasdaile, h. p. Colds. Gds.
H. F. Cubitt, h. p. R. Art.
F. Dayrell, Unatt.
J. Dennis, do.
A. Disney, York Hussars
J. Fellowes, h. p. 1 Prov. Bn.
J. G. Fitzgerald, late 7 Vet. Bn.
R. Folkes, h. p. Indep. Comp.
A. H. Frazer, h. p. R. Art.
T. W. French, h. p. 71 F.
J. Grant, h. p. Indep. Comp.
J. W. Groombridge, h. p. 91 F.
R. Hackett, h. p. 14 F.
T. R. Hemsworth, h. p. 31 F.
H. L. Herbert, Unatt.
T. A. Heriot, do.
W. Hore, h. p. 103 F.
E. H. Hunt, Unatt.
J. Hutchinson, h. p. 1 Gar. Bn.
M. Jenour, Unatt.
E. B. Law, h. p. R. Wag. Tr.
J. Macdermid, h. p. 100 F.
J. Marlow, h. p. R. Art.
F. *Earl of* Moray, h. p. Indep. Comp.
G. G. Morgan, h. p. Coldst. Gds.
N. O Donnell, late 4 Vet. Bn.
R. Phelan, Unatt.
J. Place, h. p. 2 Gar. Bn.
M. Pointon, late of 26 F.
H. W. Roberts, h. p. R. Eng.
J. P. Rose, h. p. 66 F.
J. Ryves, h. p. 58 F.
J. F. Schultz, h. p. Port. Serv.
J. Smith, Unatt.
A. Stampa, do.
H. J. Swyny, do.
F. J. Weeks, h. p. Glen. Fenc.
W. Wilkinson, late 3 Vet. Bn.
W. H. Wrench, h. p. African Corps
F. von U. Gleichen, h. p. German Legion
L. Bacmeister, do.
J. A. C. Anthony, do.
B. G. Von Housledt, do.
A. Schweitzer, do.
J. de Susini, h. p. Corsican Rangers
E. Merckhel, h. p. Meuron's Regt.
F. Bothe, late Foreign Vet. Bn.
R. A. de May (d'Ugistort) h. p. Meuron's Regt.

Lieutenants.

Greville, 2 Dr. Gds.
H. W. White, 3 Drs.
Bennett, 15 Drs.
Parker, (*Adj.*) 1 F.
Chalmers, 11 F.
Stainforth, 24 F.
Whitty, 25 F.
F. Nelson, 41 F.
De Montmorency, 50 F.
Boughton, 57 F.
Master, 58 F.
Stirling, 60 F.
Holmes, 66 F.
Pyne, do.
Faunt, 73 F.
Nash, do.
Fellowes, 74 F.
Machen, 75 F.
Reed, 78 F.
Lane, 83 F.
Jennings, 91 F.
Pilfold, 96 F.
Gernon, 1 W. I. Regt.
Dick, do.
M'Donagh, 2 do.
Kelson, Ceylon Regt.
Drake, do.
Kingsmill, do.
Parson, R. Art.
Norie, do.
Swiany, do.
Polkinghorne, (*Adj.*) R. Mar.
Haberfield, R. Mar.
C. C. Bailey, late 5 Vet. Bn.
E. Bailey, h. p. R. Mar.
C. Bellock, h. p. York Hussars
R. Blakeney, h. p. R. Mar.
C. W. Bowsar, h. p. 84 F.
W. Bradford, h. p. 8 F.
T. Brereton, h. p. Rifle Br.
T. Bridgewater, h. p. 36 F.
F. Bristow, h. p. 3 F.
T. Browning, h. p. 68 F.
P. Bryson, h. p. R. Mar.
J. Campbell, late 8 Vet. Bn.
W. Cary, Unatt.
W. Cliffe, h. p. 42 F.
A. Connor, h. p. 38 F.
C. Coote, Unatt.
G. Dardis, h. p. 1 Prov. Bn.
H. Disney, h. p. 37 F.
S. Dudley, h. p. 11 Drs.
S. Edwards, h. p. 7 Gar. Bn.
W. Edwards, h. p. 89 F.
J. Every, h. p. 15 Drs.
T. Gould, h. p. 11 Drs.
J. Hewetson, h. p. 35 F.
J. G. James, h. p. 69 F.
J. Kent, h. p. W. I. Rangers
J. Leslie, h. p. 18 Drs.
V. Loson, h. p. 63 F.
S. S. Lynch, h. p. 77 F.
R. W. M'Ilree, h. p. 96 F.
R. MacGibbon, h. p. 45 F.
J. Marrie, h. p. R. Mar.
J. Maxwell, h. p. 99 F.
G. Menzies, h. p. 93 F.
J. M. Miles, h. p. 43 F.
R. Moore, h. p. 27 F.
J. Morgan, h. p. 12 F.
J. Morrish, h. p. R. Mar.
T. S. Perkins, h. p. do.
A. N. Purefoy, h. p. 21 F.
C. Rea, late of R. Mar.
J. Rhodes, h. p. 19 F.
J. Richardson, h. p. Canadian Fenc.
J. W. Shelton, h. p. 28 F.
G. Sicker, h. p. 23 F.
D. Stapleton, h. p. 41 F.
J. Stewart, h. p. 53 F.
J. S. Stokes, h. p. 80 F.
K. Sutherland, late 2 Vet. Bn
T. J. W. Fane, R. Eng.
R. Trotter, late 9 Vet. Bn.
F. M. Turner, h. p. 7 F.
G. G. Watkins, h. p. 9 F.
W. W. Williams, h. p. 87 F.
S. S. Fisher (*Adj.*) h. p. 88 F.
L. Krause, h. p. German Legion
L. Heise, h. p. do.
G. F. C. Von Schauroth, h. p. do.
B. Croon, h. p. do.
W. Kirch, h. p. do.

Cornets, Ensigns, &c.

Rodwell, 1 Life Gds.
Gray, 3 F.
Taylor, 20 F.
Gardiner, 22 F.
Bull, 24 F.
Cheetham, 56 F.
Paterson, 63 F.
Burnop, (*Adj.*) 73 F.
Lloyd, 76 F.
Gray, do.
Darley, 77 F.
Macbean, 84 F.
Maddock, 98 F.
Dixon, Ceylon Regt.
Baynes, R. Mar. Art.
J. Atkinson, late 3 Vet. Bn.
W. Blackiston, h. p. 36 F.
J. Boyd, h. p. 80 F.
A. Dewell, h. p. R. Mar.
R. J. Dobree, h. p. 22 F.
J. Douglas, late 4 Vet. Bn.

J. Evans, h. p. Irish Br.
J. Fullom, late 4 Vet. Bn.
W. Hart, h. p. R. Wag. M.
J. Henderson, h. p. 1 Gar. Bn.
J. Hill, h. p. R. Mar.
G. Loftin, h. p. do.
J. M'Kay, h. p. 1 F.
R. Middleton, late 10 Vet. Bn.
E. W. Pearce, h. p. 18 F.
J. Pellett, h. p. 38 F.
J. Toy, late 5 Vet. Bn.
J. Tyndale, h. p. 4 Drs.
W. Williams, h. p. Gar. Comp.
C. D. Cleve, h. p. Ger. Leg.
W. Rubens, h. p. do.
A. Heise, h. p. do.
H. Garvens, h. p. do.
L. Crocicchia, h. p. Corsican Rangers
W. Riddle, late Foreign Vet. Bn.
H. Van Sande, h. p. For. Wag.

Paymasters.

Greene, 1 Dr. Gds.
Capt. Cormick, 3 Drs.
Mitchell, 1 F.
Capt. Watker, 15 F.
Macdonald, 92 F.
Blake, 93 F.
Forster, Recr. Dist.
H. B. B. Adams, h. p. do.
W. Fraser, h. p. 36 F.
W. Mackie, h. p. 27 F.
A. Tod, h. p. 38 F.

Quartermasters.

Collins, 16 F.
Taylor, 32 F.
Richardson, 48 F.
Moore, 50 F.
Dukes, 89 F.
S. Carkeek, h. p. Cornwall Fenc. Cavalry
L. Castray, h. p. 98 F.
J. Connoir, h. p. 35 F.
H. Cooper, h. p. 1 Life Gds.
H. Flaherty, h. p. 100 F.
W. Hurst, h. p. 32 Drs.
J. Masters, h. p. 1 Prov. Bn.
H. Mitchell, h. p. 8 Drs.
J. Newell, h. p. 1 Dr. Gds.
W. Page, h. p. 12 F.
S. Palmer, h. p. C. P. Fenc. Cav.
J. Patterson, h. p. 81 F.
R. Reynolds, h. p. 1 W. I. Regt.
W. Wilkinson, h. p. 2 Life Gds.

Commissariat Department.

Deputy Commissary General.

C. Lutyens, h. p.

Assist.-Comm.-Generals.

H. Lawrie
A. Lister
J. Jennings, h. p.
T. White, h. p.

Deputy-Assist. Com.-Gen.

R. Low
E. M. Jennings
T. M. Gilbert, h. p.

Medical Department.

Director-General.

Dr. G. Renny, h. p.

Inspector-General.

Dr. J. F. Clarke, h. p.

Deputy Inspector-Generals.

A. Browne, h. p.
M. Lamert, h. p.
S. Macleod, h. p.
J. Robinson, h. p.

Surgeons.

Dr. Campbell, 1 Life Gds.
Macolm, 9 F.
Dyce, 48 F.
Dr. Campbell, 73 F.
Dr. C. Grant, Staff
Dr. A. Smith, do.
Dr. Robinson, do.
T. H. Wheeler, do.
T. Batt, h. p. 7 F.
J. Dick, h. p. 5 F.
R. Gibson, h. p. Gr. Gds.
Dr. E. S. Graham, h. p. 4 Drs.
Dr. S. M'Mullen, h. p. Staff
Dr. H. T. Mostyn, h. p. 47 F.
J Paddock, h. p. Staff
G. Purdon, h. p. 32 F.
J. H. Radford, h. p. Staff
B. Sandham, h. p. do.
G. Vermeulen, h. p. 60 F.
G. B. Volmar, h. p. Staff
Dr. J. H. Walker, h. p. 92 F.
Dr. R. Williams, h. p. 68 F.
J. H. Brummell, Staff

Assistant-Surgeons.

Dr. Lock, 7 Dr. Gds.
Dr. Hart, 41 F.
Dr. Barlow, 50 F.
Belcher, 51 F.
Dr. O'Brien, 60 F.
Dr. Irwin, 72 F.
Dr. Concannon, 3 W. I. Regt.
Staunton, Ordnance
English, Staff
Matthew, do.
Waller, do.
Dr. J. Bartlett, h. p. 9 Vet. Bn.
G. Galland, h. p. Staff
J. M'Laine, h p. 60 F.
M. A. Ranclaud, h. p. Ordnance
Dr. W. T. Rankin, h. p. 84 F.
B. de St. Croix, h. p. Staff
J. A. Sproule, h. p. 2 Vet. Bn.

Apothecary.

J. H. Newton, h. p.

Deputy Purveyor.

Wm. Ivey

Veterinary Surgeons.

Miniken, 7 Dr. Gds.
Browne, 3 Dr. Gds.
R. S. Cumming, h. p. R. Art.
J. Field, h. p. 2 Life Gds.
J. Mellowes, h. p. 1 Dr. Gds.
R. Thomson, h. p. 14 Drs.
F. Eicke, h. p. German Leg.

Chaplains.

Rev. E. C. Frith, h. p.
Rev. S. Leggatt, h. p.

Lightning Source UK Ltd.
Milton Keynes UK
UKHW052349031218
333390UK00027B/1059/P